A Topical Approach to
The Developing Person Through the Life Span

 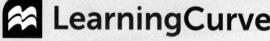

LaunchPad
macmillan learning

LearningCurve

for *A Topical Approach to the Developing Person Through the Life Span*

Available at launchpadworks.com

Each chapter in LaunchPad for *A Topical Approach to the Developing Person Through the Life Span* features a collection of activities carefully chosen to help master the major concepts. The site serves students as a comprehensive online study guide, available any time, with opportunities for self-quizzing with instant feedback, exam preparation, and further explorations of topics from the textbook. For instructors, all units and activities can be instantly assigned and students' results and analytics are collected in the Gradebook.

For Students

- Full e-book of *A Topical Approach to the Developing Person Through the Life Span*
- *Developing Lives* interactive simulation
- Data Connections activities
- LearningCurve Quizzing
- Student Video Activities

For Instructors

- Gradebook
- Worth Video Collection for Human Development
- Presentation Slides
- Instructor's Resource Guide
- Test Bank
- Electronic Figures, Photos, and Tables
- Correlation of *A Topical Approach to the Developing Person Through the Life Span* to NCLEX-RN Test and NAEYC Standards

LearningCurve

What Is LearningCurve? LearningCurve is a cutting-edge study tool designed to increase your understanding and memory of the core concepts in every chapter. Based on insights from the latest learning and memory research, the LearningCurve system pairs multiple-choice and fill-in-the-blank questions with instantaneous feedback and a rich array of study tools including videos, animations, and lab simulations. The LearningCurve system is adaptive, so the quiz you take is customized to your level of understanding. The more questions you answer correctly, the more challenging the questions become. Best of all, the e-book of *A Topical Approach to the Developing Person Through the Life Span* is fully integrated, so you can easily review the text as you study and answer questions. LearningCurve is a smart and fun way to study each chapter.

LearningCurve is available as part of **LaunchPad** for *A Topical Approach to the Developing Person Through the Life Span.* To find out more or purchase access, go to **launchpadworks.com.**

A Topical Approach to
The Developing Person Through the Life Span

Kathleen Stassen Berger
Bronx Community College of the
City University of New York

worth publishers
Macmillan Learning
New York

Senior Vice President, Content Strategy: Charles Linsmeier
Program Director, Social Sciences: Shani Fisher
Senior Executive Program Manager: Christine Cardone
Senior Development Editor: Andrea Musick Page
Assistant Editor: Dorothy Tomasini
Executive Marketing Manager: Katherine Nurre
Marketing Assistant: Steven Huang
Executive Media Editor: Laura Burden
Director of Media Editorial, Social Sciences: Noel Hohnstine
Assistant Media Editor: Conner White
Director, Content Management Enhancement: Tracey Kuehn
Senior Managing Editor: Lisa Kinne
Senior Content Project Manager: Peter Jacoby
Lead Media Project Manager: Joseph Tomasso
Senior Workflow Supervisors: Susan Wein, Paul Rohloff
Photo Editors: Sheena Goldstein, Robin Fadool, Alexis Gargin
Photo Researcher: Donna Ranieri, Lumina Datamatics, Inc.
Director of Design, Content Management: Diana Blume
Design Services Manager: Natasha Wolfe
Cover Design Manager: John Callahan
Interior Design: Studio Montage and Lumina Datamatics, Inc.
Art Manager: Matthew McAdams
Illustrations: Lumina Datamatics, Inc., Charles Yuen, Matthew McAdams
Composition: Lumina Datamatics, Inc.
Printing and Binding: LSC Communications
Cover Photograph: Alphotographic/iStock Unreleased/Getty Images

Library of Congress Control Number: 2020922548
ISBN-13: 978-1-4641-8086-6
ISBN-10: 1-4641-8086-5

Printed in the United States of America

1   2   3   4   5   6   26   25   24   23   22   21

Worth Publishers
One New York Plaza
Suite 4600
New York, NY 10004-1562
www.macmillanlearning.com

ABOUT THE AUTHOR

Kathleen Stassen Berger received her undergraduate education at Stanford University and Radcliffe College, and then she earned an M.A.T. from Harvard University and an M.S. and a Ph.D. from Yeshiva University. Her broad experience as an educator includes directing a preschool, serving as chair of philosophy at the United Nations International School, and teaching Child and Adolescent Development to graduate students at Fordham University, and to undergraduates at Montclair State University and Quinnipiac University. She also taught Social Psychology to inmates at Sing Sing Prison who were earning paralegal degrees.

Currently, Berger is a professor at Bronx Community College of the City University of New York, as she has been for most of her professional career. She began as an adjunct in English, and for the past decades she has been a full professor in the Social Sciences Department, which includes sociology, economics, anthropology, political science, human services, and psychology. She has taught Introduction to Psychology, Social Psychology, Abnormal Psychology, Human Motivation, and all four developmental courses—child, adolescent, adulthood, and life span. Her students—who come from many ethnic, economic, and educational backgrounds, with many ages, interests, and ambitions—consistently honor her with the highest teaching evaluations.

Berger is also the author of *The Developing Person Through the Life Span* (Chronological Approach), *Invitation to the Life Span*, and *The Developing Person Through Childhood and Adolescence*. Her developmental texts are currently being used at more than 700 colleges and universities worldwide and are available in Spanish, French, Italian, and Portuguese, as well as English. She is among the top 100 female authors (living or dead—Jane Austen is on the list) assigned in colleges in the United States and the United Kingdom. Her research interests include adolescent identity, immigration, bullying, and grandparents, and she has published articles on human development in the *Wiley Encyclopedia of Psychology* and in publications of the American Association for Higher Education and the National Education Association for Higher Education. She has recently published a trade book, *Grandmothering: Building Strong Ties with Every Generation* (Rowman & Littlefield Publishers, 2019). Kathleen continues teaching and learning from her students as well as from her four daughters and three grandsons.

BRIEF CONTENTS

CONTENTS

5 Brain Development and Neuroscience 118

Plan Shoot/Multi-bits/ImaZinS/Getty Images

6 Sensation, Perception, and Movement 148

Hero Images/Getty Images

7 Memory and Information Processing 181

Albert Shakirov/Alamy

8 Language: Communication from Birth to Death   212

9 Intelligence and Cognition   239

10 Personality, Identity, and Self   271

11 Sex and Gender   300

Westend61/Getty Images

Copyright Crezalyn Nerona Uratsuji/Getty Images

Image Source/DigitalVision/Getty Images

Peathegee Inc/Blend Images/Getty Images

PREFACE

Many instructors have asked me over the years to write a textbook that presents the excitement of human development topically. In doing so, I realized that they are right: A topical organization offers strengths and continuity that are beyond those in my chronological texts.

My texts are personal to me and to everyone else (we are all developing persons), and they all highlight many controversies—about conception, breast-feeding, ethnic identity, immigration, family dynamics, addictive drugs, marriage, love, punishment, health, and more. That is what makes human development intriguing as well as important for all of us, as apparent in the many editions of my chronological texts.

Beyond my wish to provide a book for my colleagues who teach topically, I now understand the merits of this approach. Although the basics of human development are the same no matter how they are presented, a topical organization has two advantages: continuity and depth.

First, consider continuity. Language development (Chapter 8), for example, builds lifelong on earlier vocabulary, grammar, and theory. A baby's babbling is a direct precursor to the increasing sentence length (MLU) of the preschooler, which leads to the logic of the 8-year-old, and then the addition of new vocabulary lifelong, including some words (*email, fracking, coronavirus*) that most 80-year-olds now use but none of them knew at age 18.

Continuity is especially evident to researchers. Scientists know that the brain, or the emotions, or morbidity, or any other topic do not stop or start developing at age 2, or 12, or 50. Even phenomena that seem transformative, such as puberty, can be understood as a way station on the path from conception to death. That understanding is what I hope to convey in this text, which considers each topic in a developmental frame.

Now consider the second advantage of a topical approach, depth. Many times I have been able to dig deeper into the research because the sweep of the topic demanded it. The most obvious example is with sex and gender (Chapter 11). The limitations of the gender binary and the complexity of gender identity are best understood via the changing interplay of nature and nurture lifelong. Professors and students can dive deep into these issues, when all the terms (e.g., *sexual orientation, transgender, sexism*) and examples are in a single chapter.

That is why I wrote this book, which presents both enduring and current findings from the science of human development using a topical approach. Of course, some material can be understood chronologically *or* topically, as our science includes well-accepted facts and themes, as well as new issues and controversies, that every student of human development should know—no matter in what sequence they learn them.

All my textbooks emphasize the need for evidence, alternatives, and ethics. I hope we all become more critical thinkers with insights and knowledge we did not have before. That is what I found in considering development topically: I hope everyone who reads it will do so as well.

A Fresh and Engaging Approach

My topical text is far more than a rearrangement of the concepts. As you might imagine, arranging the material topically allows more detail and an altered perspective, without the repetition required in a chronological account. One example of this new arrangement is in the discussion of the brain, featured in a separate chapter. The brain is mentioned in every chapter of my chronological texts, but now I am better able to explain neurological maturation while continuing to stress plasticity and epigenetics.

I have tried to maintain what instructors and students have told me they appreciate about my other books:

- a warm, accessible voice that tells a compelling story of the life span;
- clear and comprehensive coverage of contemporary science;
- appreciation for the diversity of human experience; and
- consistent emphasis on developing critical-thinking skills.

Writing That Communicates the Excitement and Applications of the Field

This course is about our lives and our experiences as well as about science. An overview of the science of human development should be lively, just as real people are. Each sentence conveys tone as well as content. Each chapter begins with an anecdote, usually about my life as a mother, wife, daughter, teacher, and grandmother—real situations (not hypothetical) to illustrate the immediacy of development. My understanding of human development informs every day of my life.

I know you have stories like mine, and I hope my examples bring yours to mind. Examples and explanations abound, helping every student to connect theory, research, and their own experiences.

Up-to-Date Research

Every year, scientists discover and explain new concepts and research. The best of these are integrated into the text, including hundreds of references on many topics such as epigenetics, prenatal nutrition, the microbiome, early-childhood education, autism spectrum disorders, vaping, high-stakes testing, opioid addiction, cohabitation, gender identity, the grandmother hypothesis, living wills, COVID-19, continuing bonds, and diversity of all kinds—ethnic, economic, and cultural.

Cognizant that the science of human development is interdisciplinary, I include recent research in biology, sociology, neuroscience, education, anthropology, political science, and more—as well as my home discipline, psychology.

Appreciation for the Diversity of Human Experience

Cross-cultural, international, racial, intersectional, multiethnic, sexual orientation, multilingual, socioeconomic status, age, gender identity—all of these words and ideas are vital to appreciating how people develop. We have much in common, yet each human is unique. Each chapter examines research, topics, and examples that illustrate human diversity.

Respect for culture and diversity is evident throughout. New research on family structures, immigrants, bilingualism, and ethnic differences are among the many topics that illustrate human diversity.

Coverage of Neuroscience

This text has a separate chapter on neuroscience and development that tells a cohesive story about brain development across the life span. In addition, in some chapters contain *Inside the Brain* features, offering cutting-edge research on the brain. This material is accompanied by numerous charts, illustrations, and photos, helping students fully grasp the science.

Emphasis on Critical Thinking

Critical thinking is an essential skill for all of us, lifelong. Virtually every page of this book presents not only facts but also questions, often revealing my own need to reconsider my assumptions. **Think Critically** questions encourage students to examine the implications of what they read; **Especially For** questions prompt students to apply concepts to their own family and vocational life.

Every chapter is organized around **learning objectives**. Much of what I hope students will always remember from this course is a matter of attitude, approach, and perspective—all hard to quantify. The **What Will You Know?** questions at the beginning of each chapter indicate important ideas or provocative concepts—one for each major section of the chapter.

In addition, after every major section, **What Have You Learned?** questions help students review what they have just read. Some questions on these lists are straightforward, requiring only close attention to the chapter. Others are more complex, seeking comparisons, implications, or evaluations. Cognitive psychology and research on pedagogy show that vocabulary, specific knowledge, and critical thinking are all part of learning. These features are designed to foster all three; I hope students and professors will add their own questions and answers, following this scaffolding.

Unique Features That Dig Deeper and Engage Students

- **Opposing Perspectives** focuses on controversial topics—from prenatal sex selection to "death with dignity" legislation. I have tried to present information and opinions on both sides of each topic so that students will weigh evidence, assess arguments, and recognize their biases while reaching their own conclusions.

- **A View from Science** provides more in-depth discussion of the research related to key topics of interest to students, such as children's eyewitness testimony, the impact of music instruction on brain development, and stereotype threat.

- Data are often best understood visually and graphically. **Visualizing Development** infographics extend the book's multicultural coverage, linking together graphics, text, and photographs to tell a visual story about an important concept in life-span development, from age structure and development to the impact of adult obesity around the globe.

VISUALIZING DEVELOPMENT Childhood Obesity Around the World

Obesity now causes more deaths worldwide than malnutrition. Reductions are possible. A multifaceted prevention effort—including parents, preschools, pediatricians, and grocery stores—has reduced obesity among U.S. 2- to 5-year-olds:

Overall, the prevalence of obesity among adolescents (20.6%) and school-aged children (18.4%) is higher than among pre-school-aged children (13.9%) (Hales et al., 2017). However, obesity rates from age 6 to 60 remain high everywhere.

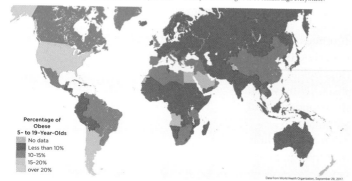

Percentage of Obese
5- to 19-Year-Olds
No data
Less than 10%
10–15%
15–20%
over 20%

Data from World Health Organization, September 29, 2017.

FACTORS CONTRIBUTING TO CHILDHOOD OBESITY, BY THE NUMBERS

Children's exposure to ads for unhealthy food continues to correlate with childhood obesity (e.g., Hewer, 2014), but nations differ. For instance, the United Kingdom has banned television advertising of foods high in fat, sugar, and salt to children under age 16. The map above shows data from the World Health Organization; other groups' data may differ. However, the overall fact is clear: Childhood obesity is far too common.

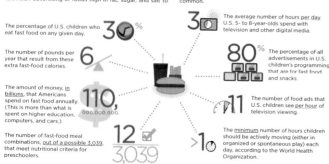

The percentage of U.S. children who eat fast food on any given day. **30**%

The number of pounds per year that result from these extra fast-food calories. **6**

The amount of money, in billions, that Americans spend on fast food annually. (This is more than what is spent on higher education, computers, and cars.) **110,000,000,000**

The number of fast-food meal combinations, out of a possible 3,039, that meet nutritional criteria for preschoolers. **12** of **3,039**

The average number of hours per day U.S. 5- to 8-year-olds spend with television and other digital media. **3**

The percentage of all advertisements in U.S. children's programming that are for fast food and snacks. **80**%

The number of food ads that U.S. children see per hour of television viewing. **11**

The minimum number of hours children should be actively moving (either in organized or spontaneous play) each day, according to the World Health Organization. **>1**

Data from Council on Communications and Media, 2011, p. 202; Rideout, 2017.

- **A Case to Study** focuses on particular individuals (myself included), helping students to identify the personal implications of what they learn about development.
- **Career Alerts** present career options in various applied settings, such as in medicine and education.

Photographs, Tables, and Graphs That Are Integral to the Text

Students learn a great deal from this book's illustrations because Worth Publishers encourages authors to choose the photographs, tables, and graphs and to write captions that extend the content. The photos for this text have been carefully selected so that they reflect the content, research, and diversity of development. Some visuals are accompanied by **Observation Quizzes**, which challenge students to think more deeply about a particular figure or photo.

Ariel Skelley/DigitalVision/Getty Images

LaunchPad: Technology That Supports Active Learning and Engagement

Macmillan Learning provides an online learning system that supports students and instructors at every step, from the first point of contact with new content to demonstrating mastery of concepts and skills. The technology for *A Topical Approach to the Developing Person Through the Life Span* has been developed to spark student engagement and improve outcomes while offering instructors flexible, high-quality, research-based tools for teaching this course. Powerful multimedia resources with an integrated e-book, robust adaptive quizzing, videos, and a wealth of interactives create an extraordinary learning resource for students. Our technology includes:

- An **interactive e-book**, which integrates the text and all student media, including Data Connections activities, videos, and much more.
- *Developing Lives*, the robust interactive experience in which students "raise" their own virtual child. This simulation integrates more than 200 videos and animations, with quizzes and questions to assign and assess.

- *Data Connections* **activities**, requiring interpretation of data on important topics. Evidence is crucial for scientists, and I hope students will understand that experientially as they contend with topics from rates of breast-feeding to prevalence of risk-taking. These interactive activities engage students in active learning, promoting a deeper understanding of the science of development. Instructors can assign these activities and accompanying assessment in the online courseware that accompanies this book.
- **LearningCurve adaptive quizzing**, based on current research on learning and memory. It combines individualized question selection, immediate and valuable feedback, and a gamelike interface to engage students. Each LearningCurve quiz is fully integrated with other resources through the Personalized Study Plan, so students can review using Worth's extensive library of videos and activities. *Question analysis reports* allow instructors to track the progress of individuals and the entire class.
- Worth's **Video Collection for Human Development in LaunchPad**, an extensive collection of video clips that covers the full range of the course, from classic experiments (like Ainsworth's Strange Situation and Piaget's conservation) to illustrations of many topics. Instructors can assign these videos to students or choose some of 50 activities that combine videos with short-answer and multiple-choice questions.
- *Visualizing Development* infographics, which tell a visual story about important concepts in development and are assignable with quiz questions.
- *i-Clicker questions*, which encourage active learning and interactive class participation.
- *Lecture Slides* feature customizable, comprehensive chapter lecture material and chapter art and illustrations.
- The **Gradebook** gives a clear window on performance for the whole class, for individual students, and for individual assignments.

Also Available:

Achieve Read & Practice combines LearningCurve adaptive quizzing and our mobile, accessible e-book in one easy-to-use and affordable product. Among the advantages of Achieve Read & Practice:

- It is easy to get started.
- Students are better prepared: They can read and study in advance.
- Instructors can use analytics to help their students.
- Students learn more.

Robust Support for Instructors

Instructor's Resource Guide

Our collection has been hailed as the richest collection of instructor's resources in developmental psychology. Included are learning objectives, chapter guides, topics for discussion and debate, handouts for student projects, course-planning suggestions, ideas for term projects, and a guide to audiovisual and online materials.

Macmillan Learning Test Bank (MLTB)

The test bank includes for every chapter at least 100 multiple-choice and 70 fill-in-the-blank, true-false, and essay questions. Good test questions are crucial; each has been carefully crafted. Challenging questions and basic ones are included, allowing instructors to tailor their tests to their students. All questions are keyed to the textbook by topic, page number, and level of difficulty. Questions are also organized by NCLEX, NAEYC, and APA goals and Bloom's taxonomy. Rubrics for grading short-answer and essay questions are also suggested.

The MTLB is accessible online, only to verified instructors. With this system, instructors can:

- Create paper or online tests that can be exported to the relevant LMS using a web browser;
- Drag and drop questions to create tests; and
- Create and edit their own questions and edit publisher-created question sets.

Learn more here: https://macmillan.force.com/macmillanlearning/s/article/Getting-Started-with-the-Macmillan-Learning-Test-Bank.

Intuitive and useful analytics, along with a **gradebook**, let you track how students in the class are performing individually and as a whole.

LMS Integration means that online homework is easily integrated into a school's learning management system and that an instructor's gradebook and roster are always in sync.

FRANCK FIFE/AFP/Getty Images

THANKS

I want to thank the many academic reviewers and focus group participants who have provided invaluable feedback on this text. They have made this book better with their insights, suggestions, and disciplinary expertise.

Tsippa Ackerman, *Queens College*
Katherine Bailey, *Okanagan College*
Catherine Barnard, *Kalamazoo Valley Community College*
Rebecca Bigler, *University of Texas at Austin*
Anne Blanchard, *Western Washington University*
Janet Boseovski, *Univserity of North Carolina–Greensboro*
Erin Briggs, *Augusta University*
Amy Buckingham, *Red Rocks Community College*
Janinne Chadwick, *California State University, Monterey Bay*
Isabelle Chang, *Temple University*
Jason Chen, *University of South Florida*
Jessamy E. Comer, *Rochester Institute of Technology*
Alecia Dager, *Yale University*
Lisa Daniel, *East Texas Baptist University*
Kimberly D.R. DuVall, *James Madison University*
R. Cole Eidson, *Northeastern University*
Marla Elliott, *Paris Junior College*
Marion Eppler, *East Carolina University*
Jay Green, *Tarrant County Community College NW*
Jessica Greenlee, *Virginia Commonwealth University*
Maria Guarneri-White, *University of Texas–Austin*
James P. Guinee, *University of Central Kansas*
Lynn Haller, *Morehead State University*

Julie Hanauer, *Suffolk County Community College*
Rachel Hayes, *Nebraska Wesleyan University*
Jennifer Headrick, *Augusta University*
Lauren Holleb, *Husson University–Bangor*
Krisztina Jakobsen, *James Madison University*
Leona Johnson, *Florida A and M University*
Stefanie M. Keen, *University of South Carolina–Upstate*
Sue Kelley, *Lycoming College*
Elizabeth J. Kiel, *Miami University*
Marina Klimenko, *University of Florida–Gainesville*
Jennifer Knack, *Clarkson University*
Dawn K. Kriebel, *Immaculata University*
Shenan Kroupa, *Indiana University–Purdue University, Indianapolis*
Tru Kwong, *Mount Royal University*
Geri M. Lotze, *Virginia Commonwealth University*
Karin Machluf, *Pennsylvania State University–Worthing-Scranton*
Meredith McGinely, *University of Wisconsin-Parkside*
Julia Mendez-Smith, *University of North Carolina–Greensboro*
Jane Mendle, *Cornell University*
Ronnie Naramore, *Angelina College*
Jessica Niedermayer, *Carroll University*
Carmen Ochoa-Galindo, *University of Illinois at Chicago*
Allison P. O'Leary, *Brevard College*
Amy Osmon, *Daytona State College*
Rob Palkovitz, *University of Delaware*
Eirini Papafratzeskakou, *Mercer County Community College*
Elise Pepin, *Southern New Hampshire University*
Lakshmi Raman, *Oakland University*
Miranda Richmond, *Vanderbilt University*
Sabrina Rieder, *SUNY Rockland Community College*
Rachael Robnett, *University of Nevada-Las Vegas*
Kelly Schuller, *Florida Gulf Coast University*
Rick Shifley, *Massachusetts College of Pharmacy and Health Sciences*
Rachelle M. Smith, *Husson University*
Christopher Stanzione, *Georgia Institute of Technology*
Jovana Vukovic, *Broward College North*
Christine Weinkauff, *California State University–San Bernardino*
Marcia Winter, *Virginia Commonwealth University*

The editorial, marketing, and production teams at Worth Publishers are dedicated to high standards. They devote time, effort and talent to every aspect of publishing, a model for the industry. I am particularly grateful to my senior executive program manager, Christine Cardone; my senior development editor, Andrea Musick Page; my assistant editor, Dorothy Tomasini; and Macmillan's senior vice president, Charles Linsmeier. I also thank other members of my Macmillan team: Diana Blume, Laura Burden, Matthew Christensen, Shani Fisher, Sheena Goldstein, Noel Hohnstine, Steven Huang, Peter Jacoby, Lisa Kinne, Tracey Kuehn, Jennifer MacMillan, Matthew McAdams, Michael McCarty, Hilary Newman, Katherine Nurre, Susan Wein, and Charles Yuen.

New York, December 2020

CHAPTER 1

Understanding Human Development

In midsummer, I was surrounded by over a hundred sealed boxes in my new home. I could not find some things I needed—scissors, clean sheets, an alarm clock, a dog dish—and was frustrated to open boxes and see what I did not want—cords to electronic devices that were long gone, light bulbs for fixtures I no longer own, three heating pads, more than a thousand paper clips, and about 200 dried-out markers.

The worst part was not boxes, but memories. I thought about the life span, not in generalities, but very personally. I found my parents' marriage photo, read old letters from people who apparently loved me but whose names I do not recognize, and came across hundreds of photos and school reports of my children, now grown. I unpacked dozens of books published decades ago that I never read and found sympathy cards sent when my husband died.

Scientists are trained to be objective, collecting data, making plans, and drawing conclusions. So, I made a list: I had 36 boxes in the children's room, 44 boxes in the guest bedroom, 16 boxes in my home office. I needed to find a nearby vet, plumber, grocery store, post office, and compost collector. The list helped: I set a goal, five boxes a day, and I found all those people.

Developmentalists know that people need other people, so next I reached out to my neighbors. A friendly family down the hall has a 6-month-old baby; I offered emergency child care. An elderly couple lives across from them; the wife walks back and forth with her walker in the hall. She smiled when I encouraged her daily exercise. Another elderly couple lives next door. They were unreceptive when I said hello, and their huge Doberman barks behind their double-locked door when my much smaller mutt and I walk by. No matter; developmentalists also know that some people have some private pain.

Stockbyte/Getty Images

Now, in the middle of fall, all the boxes are empty, and my thoughts return to the present. I see the sunrise and the river from my windows; I greet people of many colors, sizes, and backgrounds on the street; I feel at home, where I should be, as a scientist, a developmentalist, and an author.

Finally, I recognize that my personal transition benefits from a life-span perspective: People of all ages move on with their lives, experiencing frustration and joy, with unique circumstances and universal patterns. I hope this chapter, and the book as a whole, helps you appreciate that everyone has significant memories of their past and boxes to open in their future. We may all, eventually, find what we need.

What Will You Know?

1. Is growth over the life span the same for everyone?
2. Is the study of people a science, like the other sciences?
3. Do scientists need special methods to understand how people change as they grow older?
4. What are the most important questions about human development?

The Life-Span Perspective

life-span perspective An approach to the study of human development that takes into account all phases of life, not just childhood or adulthood.

The **life-span perspective** takes into account all phases of life, every aspect of family and culture, and many forces of biology. By including the entirety of life, it leads to recognition that human development is *multidirectional*, *multicontextual*, *multicultural*, *multidisciplinary*, and *plastic*, each now explained.

Development Is Multidirectional

Multiple changes, in all directions, characterize every age and topic. Some traits appear and disappear; others increase, decrease, or zigzag (see **Figure 1.1**). The traditional idea—that development advances step-by-step until about age 18, steadies, and then declines—is refuted by life-span research. Not only is growth multidirectional, each age has gains and losses.

Sometimes *discontinuity* is evident: Change can occur rapidly and dramatically, as when caterpillars become butterflies. Puberty is such a time: Young adolescents gain the ability to reproduce, losing some loyalty to their parents.

Sometimes *continuity* is found: Growth can be gradual, as when redwoods grow taller over hundreds of years. If you had a best friend at age 20 and then didn't see them for a decade, would you still recognize them? Of course!

Likewise, adults looking in the mirror think they see the same person every day and are surprised when a gray hair or other signs of aging occurs. Often that first gray hair is plucked or dyed, as if that could stop time. It never can; that is why we study development.

Finally, some characteristics seem stable, unchanging. The chromosomes of almost every person are XY or XX, male or female, at the moment of conception. (Exceptions are explained in Chapter 3.) The chromosomes of the tiny zygote continue even centuries after death, when a fragment of a bone reveals male or female.

Of course, culture shapes gender. Although XX and XY do not change, continuity and discontinuity are evident in traits that begin

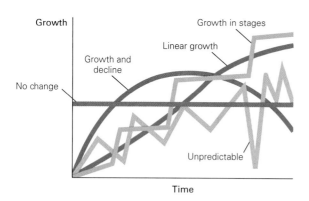

FIGURE 1.1

Patterns of Developmental Growth Many patterns of developmental growth have been discovered by careful research. Although linear (or nonlinear) progress seems most common, scientists now find that almost no aspect of human change follows the linear pattern exactly.

with those chromosomes. For instance, menopause reduces female (XX) hormones quite dramatically, and age slowly reduces male (XY) hormones.

Both of those changes increase rates of heart disease and major neurocognitive disorder (formerly known as *dementia*), a marked increase in women and a more gradual increase in men. Discontinuity and continuity are also evident in transgender people: They do not think, or act, in accord with their XX or XY, although their chromosomes themselves do not change.

Overall, multidirectional growth is evident in sudden transformations, steady improvement, and unexpected decline, as well as in stability, stages, and continuity—day to day, year to year, and generation to generation. This is apparent in every topic in this book. For example, adult intellectual abilities are multidirectional: Some peak early (e.g., reaction time), and others improve decade by decade (e.g., vocabulary). Time brings losses and gains.

Critical Periods

The speed and timing of impairments or improvements vary. Some changes are sudden and profound because of a **critical period**, either a time when something *must* occur to ensure normal development or the *only* time when an abnormality might occur. For instance, the human embryo grows arms and legs, hands and feet, fingers and toes, each over a critical period between 28 and 54 days after conception. After that, it is too late: Unlike some insects, humans never grow replacement limbs.

We know this because of a tragedy. Between 1957 and 1961, thousands of newly pregnant women in 30 nations took *thalidomide,* an anti-nausea drug. This change in nurture (via the mother's bloodstream) disrupted nature (the embryo's genetic program). If an expectant mother ingested thalidomide during the 26 days of that critical period, her newborn's limbs were malformed or absent.

Specifics (e.g., whether arms and legs, or just arms, or only hands were affected) depended on when she swallowed the pills. Surprisingly, if an expectant woman took thalidomide before day 28 or after day 54, but not during the critical period, no harm was evident.

Sensitive Periods

Life has few critical periods. Often, however, a particular development occurs more easily—but not exclusively—at a certain time. Such a time is called a **sensitive period**.

For example, if children do not learn their first language before age 2, they might do so later (hence, the first years are not *critical*), but their grammar is usually impaired (hence, these years are *sensitive*). Similarly, childhood is a sensitive period for learning to pronounce a language with a native accent.

As is often the case with development, generalizations (like those in the preceding sentence) do not apply in every case. Accent-free speech *usually* must be learned before puberty, but some teenagers or adults with exceptional nature and nurture (naturally adept at hearing, and then immersed in a new language) master new languages with no detectable accent—although multilingual speakers may still have lingering evidence of their first language (Birdsong, 2018).

The easiest time to learn many things is early childhood: Those sensitive years are recognized in every nation as the best time to learn to read and write. But some things are better learned in adulthood. For example, when 15-year-olds become parents, many have trouble mastering the necessary emotional regulation. Such learning is easier at age 30.

critical period A crucial time when a particular type of developmental growth (in body or behavior) *must* happen for normal development to occur, or when harm (such as from a toxic substance or destructive event) can occur.

sensitive period A time when a certain type of development is most likely, although it may still happen later with more difficulty. For example, early childhood is considered a sensitive period for language learning.

I Love You, Mommy We do not know what words, in what language, her son is using, but we do know that Sobia Akbar speaks English well, a requirement for naturalized U.S. citizens. Here she obtains citizenship for her two children born in Pakistan. Chances are they will speak unaccented American English, unlike Sobia, whose accent might indicate that she learned British English as a second language.

John Moore/Getty Images

Indeed, a team who studied resilience in late adulthood contended that:

> Very late life is characterised by a unique balance between losses, associated with vulnerability and resource restrictions, and potential gains based upon wisdom, experience, autonomy and accumulated systems of support, providing a specific context for the expression of resilience.
>
> *[Hayman et al., 2017, p. 577]*

All these examples illustrate the life-span perspective: People change as they grow older, and the direction of those changes varies. One reason for those changes, as just reviewed, is time. Another reason is context.

Development Is Multicontextual

The second insight from the life-span perspective is that development is multi-contextual. It takes place within many contexts, including physical surroundings (climate, noise, population density, etc.), family configurations (married couple, single parent, cohabiting couple, extended family, etc.), and larger contexts such as nations and cultures (explained soon). Developmentalists who study the life span take all these contexts into account, as well as dozens more.

ecological-systems approach

A perspective on human development that considers all of the influences from the various contexts of development. (Later renamed *bioecological theory.*)

Ecological Systems

A leading developmentalist, Urie Bronfenbrenner (1917–2005), led the way to considering contexts. Just as a naturalist studying an organism examines *ecology* (the multifaceted relationship between the organism and its environment), Bronfenbrenner believed that each person is affected by many social contexts and interpersonal interactions. Therefore, he recommended that developmentalists take an **ecological-systems approach** (Bronfenbrenner & Morris, 2006).

The ecological-systems approach recognizes three nested levels that surround individuals and affect them (see **Figure 1.2**). The most direct are *microsystems*: each person's immediate surroundings, such as family and peer group. The two other systems are *exosystems* (local institutions such as school or college, church or temple) and *macrosystems* (the larger social forces, including cultural values, economic policies, and political processes). Throughout his life, Bronfenbrenner studied people in natural settings, as they actually lived their lives, taking their contexts into account.

Bronfenbrenner also stressed historical conditions, and therefore he included the *chronosystem* (literally, "time system"). He also included a fifth system, the *mesosystem, which* consists of the connections between systems. A smooth mesosystem means an easy connection, such as between parents

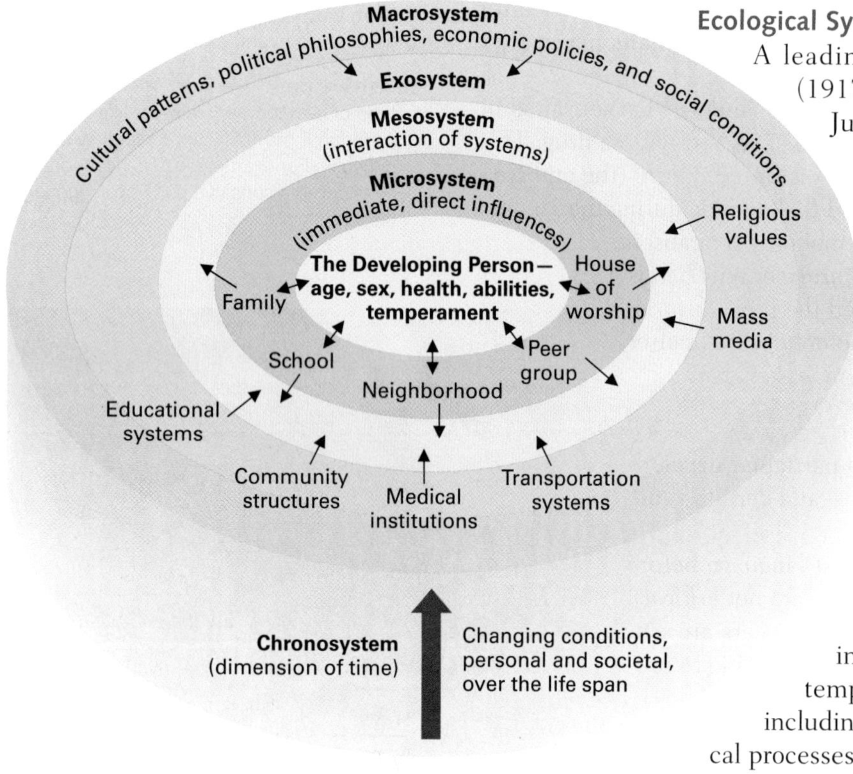

FIGURE 1.2

The Ecological Model According to Bronfenbrenner, each person is significantly affected by interactions among a number of overlapping systems, which provide the context of development. Microsystems—family, peer group, classroom, neighborhood, house of worship—intimately and immediately shape human development. Surrounding and supporting the microsystems are the exosystems, which include all the external networks (such as community structures and local educational, medical, employment, and communications systems) that affect the microsystems. Influencing both of these systems is the macrosystem, which includes cultural patterns, political philosophies, economic policies, and social conditions. Mesosystems refer to interactions among systems, as when parents and teachers coordinate to educate a child. Bronfenbrenner added a fifth system, the chronosystem, to emphasize the importance of historical time.

(microsystem) and primary school (exosystem) via conferences, notes home, parent involvement with homework, and so on. As Bronfenbrenner noted, the mesosystem is not always smooth. For example, if a child is disruptive, parents and teachers may blame each other, both influenced by their cultural biases and values, and then the mesosystem impedes development of the child.

Before he died, Bronfenbrenner renamed his approach *bioecological theory* to highlight biology. He recognized that systems within the body (e.g., the cardiovascular system) affect all the other systems (Bronfenbrenner & Morris, 2006).

A parent with a heart condition, for instance, is not only personally affected by that internal biological system, but they might not play outside with their children (microsystem) and might have surgery in an excellent hospital (exosystem), which might be paid by national insurance (macrosystem). The hospital might encourage children to visit or exclude them (mesosystem). Thus, to understand that parent, or their children, every system needs to be considered.

Dynamic Systems

The idea of dynamic systems is that human development is an ongoing, ever-changing interaction of all the systems (body, brain, and environment), of past, present, and future, and of each individual with all their surrounding contexts.

The **dynamic-systems approach** began with observations of the natural world:

[S]easons change in ordered measure, clouds assemble and disperse, trees grow to a certain shape and size, snowflakes form and melt, minute plants and animals pass through elaborate life cycles that are invisible to us, and social groups come together and disband.

[Thelen & Smith, 2006, p. 271]

Thus, our entire world is *dynamic*. Physical and emotional influences, time, personality, and every aspect of the environment are always interacting, always in flux, always in motion. This is especially apparent now that we know that body, mind, and emotions interact lifelong. No longer is development focused only on childhood and physical development (such as tooth eruption or running speed). Each type of development, from vision to schooling, changes dynamically and systemically over the life span.

As you can see, a contextual approach to development is complex; many contexts need to be considered. In this first chapter we focus only on two that affect every topic, at every point in the life span.

The Historical Context

All persons born within a few years of one another are called a **cohort**, a group defined by their shared age. Cohorts travel through life together, affected by the interaction of their chronological years with the values, events, technologies, and culture of the times.

If you know someone named Emma, she is probably young: Emma is the most common name for girls born between 2014 and 2018 but was not in the top 100 until 1996, nor in the top 1,000 in 1990 (see **Table 1.1**). If you know someone named Mary, she is probably old: Mary was the first or second most popular name from 1900 to 1965; now only 1 baby in 800 is named Mary. Variation is evident by nation, by culture, and by region—within the United States and elsewhere.

For example, emerging adulthood (ages 18–25) is a sensitive period for consolidation of social values: Historical conditions when a person was about age 20 affect young adults more than they affect older or younger cohorts. Thus, people who were in college during what is called the Great

dynamic-systems approach A view of human development as an ongoing, ever-changing interaction between the physical, cognitive, and psychosocial influences. The crucial understanding is that development is never static but is always affected by, and affects, many systems of development.

cohort People born within the same historical period who therefore move through life together, experiencing events, technologies, and cultural shifts at the same ages. For example, the effect of the internet varies depending on what cohort a person belongs to.

TABLE 1.1

Most Popular First Names by Cohort

Girls Born in...

2018: Emma, Olivia, Ava, Isabella, Sophia

1998: Emily, Hannah, Sarah, Samantha, Ashley

1978: Jennifer, Melissa, Jessica, Amy, Heather

1958: Mary, Susan, Linda, Karen, Patricia

1938: Mary, Barbara, Patricia, Betty, Shirley

Boys Born in...

2018: Liam, Noah, William, James, Oliver

1998: Michael, Jacob, Matthew, Joshua, Christopher

1978: Michael, Jason, Christopher, David, James

1958: Michael, David, James, Robert, John

1938: Robert, James, John, William, Richard

Information from U.S. Social Security Administration.

Recession (2007–2009) developed attitudes about job security and home owner-ship unlike those of their 50-year-old parents, who were college students in the 1980s, when jobs and houses were readily available. One leading team of scholars suggests that "in the aftermath of the Great Recession" young adults will suffer "economic scarring" for decades (Schoon & Mortimer, 2017, p. 1).

Medical innovations also affect each cohort differently. Childhood vaccinations to prevent polio, measles, mumps, and rubella became widespread by about 1970, so the current cohort of parents never knew the harm those diseases could cause. That is thought to be one reason some people in this cohort are suspicious of vac-cines, unlike older cohorts who welcomed them.

Cohorts are affected by how many people are within their group. For exam-ple, the U.S. birth rate exploded from 1946 and 1964, producing a "baby boom" that was in marked contrast to the "baby bust" years of the Great Depression and World War II (1929–1944).

Partly because of their numbers, boomers changed the macrosystem, making laws regarding drugs, sex, and women's rights more responsive to the needs of young adults. Now, as they enter old age, that cohort is transforming life after age 65. One reason the U.S. Congress protects Social Security and Medicare is that there are so many voters in that cohort.

Clashing needs of different cohorts are reconciled by families and govern-ments, tilting toward one generation or another. For example, should taxes support $100,000 for dialysis for someone who is 80, or for intensive care for someone born weighing 1 pound? Vigorous debates erupt about Medicare, CHIP (Chil-dren's Health Insurance Program), and federally subsidized health insurance for adults. This is a U.S. example, but every nation responds more readily to the needs of some cohorts than others, in part because of how many people are in that cohort, and because of the particular historical experience has been for the people who make the laws. That leads to socioeconomic status, the second context that is evident throughout life.

The Socioeconomic Context

Another influential developmental context is **socioeconomic status**, abbreviated **SES**. (Sometimes SES is called *social class* as in *middle class* or *working class*.) SES reflects income and much more, including occupation, education, and neighbor-hood. These affect the context of development for everyone, whether their neigh-borhood is wealthy or disadvantaged.

Income alone does not determine SES. Suppose a U.S. family is composed of an infant, an unemployed mother, and a father who earns $20,000 a year. Their SES would be low if the wage earner is an illiterate dishwasher living in an under-served urban neighborhood, but it would be much higher if the wage earner is a postdoctoral student living on campus and teaching part time.

SES brings advantages and disadvantages, opportunities and limitations—all affecting housing, health, nutrition, knowledge, and habits. Although poverty obvi-ously limits a person, education is also pivotal. Every scientist studying human development now takes SES—ideally measured with education and occupation as well as with financial assets—into account.

In the United States, the gap between rich and poor has been increasing over the past decades, as shown in **Figure 1.3**. As the gap gets wider, those on the low-est rungs experience poorer physical health and psychological well-being (Odgers & Adler, 2018), and that affects every aspect of their development.

This suggests that growing up without new clothes and expensive food is much less problematic if every child you knew had hand-me-downs. But low SES might

---

THINK CRITICALLY: How has the recent coronavirus pandemic affected each cohort?

---

socioeconomic status (SES) A person's position in society as determined by income, occupation, education, and place of residence. (Sometimes called *social class*.)

be much worse if you were the only child in your class who brought peanut-butter-and-jelly sandwiches for lunch and couldn't afford the class trip. As an adult, you might worry about material possessions, unlike adults who never were concerned about basic needs in childhood.

This is particularly interesting to developmental psychologists, for it suggests that physical comforts — food in the belly, an indoor toilet, and a bed of your own — are nice, but that thoughts about your status in life may be more influential. When income inequality is high, social trust and cohesion are low — neighbors do not ask each other to borrow a cup of sugar, to keep a spare house key, to receive a package, to watch a child.

Low SES harms everyone, but not equally at all ages. For example, neighborhood conditions (e.g., litter, broken windows, violence, empty buildings, drug dealing) affect 6- to 12-year-olds more than people of other ages. Their parents do, or do not, let them go to local parks, play on empty lots, walk to school — all of which make the neighborhood more influential for them than it is for infants or adults. On the other hand, parents may be more affected by other aspects of SES, such as the labor market and neighborhood cohesion than older adults are.

The socioeconomic context is influenced by the national and historical contexts. If everyone shares in community activities, and income seems to be rising overall, citizens may be quite happy, even if everyone is poor compared to people in richer nations. This seems true, for example, in the Philippines (Peterson, 2016). That leads to the next aspect of the life-span perspective: community culture matters.

Income Inequality in the United States

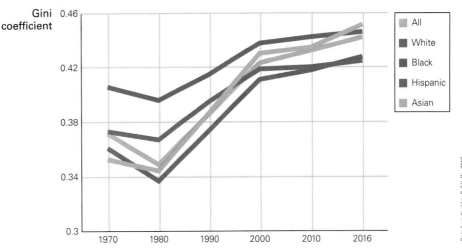

Data from Kochhar & Cilluffo, 2018.

FIGURE 1.3
The Rich Get Richer The Gini index does not measure wealth; it measures inequality. Thus, if everyone is equally poor or equally rich, the Gini would be zero, and if every person had all the money and the others had none, it would be 1.0. As you see, inequality was once highest for African Americans, but now it has increased for every group.

⬤ **Observation Quiz** Which ethnic group has the most very wealthy people and very poor people? (see answer, page 31) ⬆

🔎 **DATA CONNECTIONS: Economic Equality and Human Development** explores various nations' Gini indices, which measure economic equality in a particular society. 📖 **LaunchPad**

Development Is Multicultural

For social scientists, **culture** is "the system of shared beliefs, conventions, norms, behaviors, expectations and symbolic representations that persist over time and prescribe social rules of conduct" (Bornstein et al., 2011, p. 30). Thus, culture is far more than food or clothes; it is a set of ideas, beliefs, customs, and patterns.

Every social scientist agrees that culture matters, but they disagree about how much it matters. Some stress the similarities of all humans everywhere, and others highlight cultural differences. For example, many argue that all humans of every age (even infants) want to help rather than harm other people (Kagan, 2018). Others contend that cultures differ in whether national loyalty requires hurting — even killing — outsiders, and that the development of humans within those cultures is profoundly affected by that.

Social Constructions

Culture is a powerful **social construction**, that is, a concept created, or constructed, by a society. Social constructions affect how people think and act — what they value, ignore, and punish. Should the very old be revered or

culture A system of shared beliefs, norms, behaviors, and expectations that persist over time and prescribe social behavior and assumptions.

Watch **VIDEO: Interview with Barbara Rogoff** to learn more about the role of culture in the development of Mayan children in Guatemala.

social construction An idea that is built on shared perceptions, not on objective reality. Many age-related terms (such as *childhood, adolescence, yuppie,* and *senior citizen*) are social constructions, connected to biological traits but strongly influenced by social assumptions.

excluded? Should dogs be pets who sleep on their owner's beds, enjoy day care with other dogs, experience daily exercise, tooth-brushing, grooming? Or should they run wild until they are captured, killed, and eaten? Both of these scenarios are a dog's life in some places, reflecting social constructions of what a dog is.

If you are heartsick that any culture would allow eating dogs, consider that some people have a social construction about cows, others about pigs. Thus, some people would be horrified that your local fast food restaurant sells hamburgers and bacon.

Each group of people creates social constructions as part of their culture; there are ethnic cultures, national cultures, family cultures, college cultures, and so on. Thus, everyone is multicultural, and everyone sometimes experiences a clash between their cultures. One of my students wrote:

> My mom was outside on the porch talking to my aunt. I decided to go outside; I guess I was being nosey. While they were talking I jumped into their conversation which was very rude. When I realized what I did it was too late. My mother slapped me in my face so hard that it took a couple of seconds to feel my face again.
>
> *[C., personal communication]*

Notice that my student reflects her family culture; she labels her own behavior "nosey" and "very rude." She later wrote that she expects children to be seen but not heard and that her own son makes her "very angry" when he interrupts.

However, her "rude" behavior may have been encouraged by her school culture, as she attended a New York public school, far from her mother's native land. In the United States, many teachers want children to speak up, so children's talking is welcomed. Do you think my student was nosey or, on the contrary, that her mother should not have slapped her? Your answer reflects your culture.

Deficit or Just Difference?

As with my student's mother, everyone is inclined to believe that their culture is better than others. This tendency has benefits: Generally, people who appreciate their own culture are happier, prouder, and more willing to help strangers, especially strangers who want to blend in with the values and language of the new group. However, that belief becomes destructive if it reduces respect for people from other cultures. Too quickly and without thought, differences are assumed to be problems (Akhtar & Jaswal, 2013).

Developmentalists recognize the **difference-equals-deficit error**, which is the belief that people unlike us (different) are inferior (deficit). Sadly, when humans realize that their ways of thinking and acting are not universal, they may believe that people who think or act differently are to be pitied, feared, and encouraged to change.

Developmental scientists are not immune to this error. Indeed, one anthropologist argues that scientists who consider evolution the obvious explanation for the development of all living things may consider creationists severely deficient "ignoramuses" (Laats, 2015). It would be much better, when someone's view is contrary to what we believe, to listen and respond with respect to their underlying reasons.

The difference-equals-deficit error is one reason that a careful multicultural approach is necessary. Never assume that another culture is wrong and inferior—or the opposite, right and superior. Assumptions can be harmful.

Difference, But Not Deficit This woman is a Syrian refugee living in a refugee camp in Greece. The infant, with a pacifier in her mouth and a mother who tries to protect her, illustrates why developmentalists focus on similarities rather than on differences.

Myrto Papadopoulos/The WashingtonPost/Getty Images

🔴 **Observation Quiz** What signs do you see that this woman and the aid workers differ in culture? (see answer, page 31) ⬆

difference-equals-deficit error The mistaken belief that a deviation from some norm is necessarily inferior to behavior or characteristics that meet the standard.

macmillan learning

VIDEO: Research of Geoffrey Saxe further explores how difference does not equal deficit.

VISUALIZING DEVELOPMENT Diverse Complexities

It is often repeated that "the United States is becoming more diverse," a phrase that usually refers only to ethnic diversity and not to economic and religious diversity (which are also increasing and merit attention). From a developmental perspective, two other diversities are also important—age and region, as shown below. What are the implications for schools, colleges, employment, health care, and nursing homes in the notable differences in the ages of people of various groups? And are attitudes about immigration, or segregation, or multiracial identity affected by the ethnicity of one's neighbors?

THE CHANGING ETHNIC AND RACIAL MAKEUP OF THE UNITED STATES

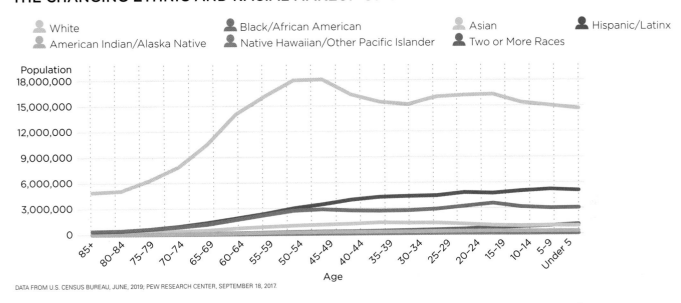

DATA FROM U.S. CENSUS BUREAU, JUNE, 2019; PEW RESEARCH CENTER, SEPTEMBER 18, 2017.

Regional Differences in Ethnicity Across the United States

In the United States, there are both regional and age differences in ethnicity. This map shows which counties have an ethnic population greater than the national average. Counties where more than one ethnicity or race is greater than the national average are shown as multiethnic. Areas for which data are unavailable are left unshaded.

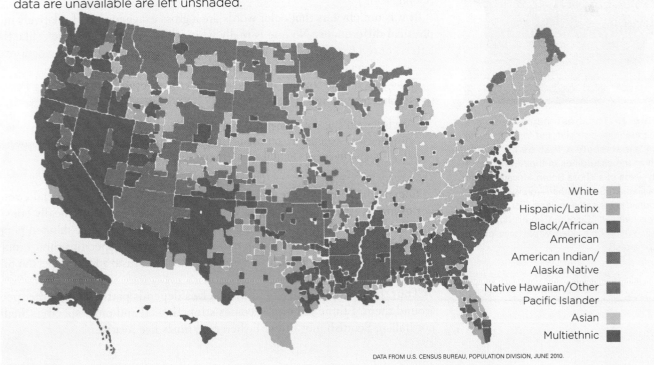

DATA FROM U.S. CENSUS BUREAU, POPULATION DIVISION, JUNE 2010.

For example, one immigrant child, on her first day in a U.S. school, was teased about the food she brought for lunch. The next day, she dumped the contents of her lunchbox in the garbage soon after she arrived at school, choosing hunger over being different.

This illustrates the problem with judging another culture: A lunch from another culture might, or might not, be more nutritious than a sandwich. In this example, the children did not consider culture or nutrition; the mother thought the lunch she packed was best; the student wanted to be accepted. The difference was misjudged as a deficit, and then it harmed that girl (hungry children learn less.) She was not seriously harmed: The girl learned how to adapt without going hungry. But adaptation is not always simple, as is now explained.

Ethnic and Racial Groups

Cultural clashes fuel wars and violence when differences are seen as deficits. A step toward preventing that is to understand the terms *ethnicity* and *race*. Members of an **ethnic group** almost always share ancestral heritage and often have the same national origins, religion, and language. Ethnicity is a social construction, a product of the social context, not biology.

Ethnic groups often share a culture, but they may not. There are "multiple intersecting and interacting dimensions" to ethnic identity (Sanchez & Vargas, 2016, p. 161). Cultural differences are apparent, for instance, among people of Irish descent in Ireland, Australia, and North America, or among those who are Roman Catholic, Protestant, or not religiously affiliated. It is also true that people may share a culture but come from several ethnic groups (consider British culture).

Historically, most North Americans believed that **race** was an inborn biological characteristic that differentiated members of one large ethnic group from another, each distinct. A person could not be multiracial. This belief sometimes led people to extremes, such that a U.S.-born person with one Black great-grandparent and seven White ones was considered Black. As in this example, races were categorized by skin color: white, black, red, and yellow (Coon, 1962).

It was not obvious that color words are a gross exaggeration of relatively minor physical differences. No one is really white (like this page) or black (like these letters) or red or yellow (both terms offensive). Genetic diversity is evident within groups, and genes are shared by people with quite different appearance.

Biologists now recognize race as a social construction (see Opposing Perspectives). One team wrote:

> We believe the use of biological concepts of race in human genetic research—so disputed and so mired in confusion—is problematic at best and harmful at worst. It is time for biologists to find a better way.
>
> *[Yudell et al., 2016, p. 564]*

Social constructions are fluid, depending on the immediate social context. For example, African-born people who live in North America typically consider themselves African, distinct from Caribbean or U.S.-born dark-skinned people. But African-born people in African nations identify with a specific ethnic group. A Nigerian person might identify as Yoruba, or Ibo, or Hausa; a Kenyan person might be Kikuyo, or Luhya, or Luo.

Thus, how people understand themselves depends partly on the other people around them. Ethnic identity becomes strengthened and more specific (Sicilian, not Italian; Scottish, not British) when co-ethnics live nearby.

ethnic group People whose ancestors were born in the same region and who often share a language, culture, and religion.

race A group of people who are regarded by themselves, or by others, as distinct from other groups on the basis of physical appearance, typically skin color. Social scientists think race is a misleading concept, as biological differences are not signified by outward appearance.

Mike Coppola/Getty Images

Fitting In The best comedians are simultaneously outsider and insider, giving them a perspective that helps people laugh at the absurdities in their lives. Trevor Noah—son of a Xhosa South African mother and a German Swiss father—grew up within, yet outside, his native culture. For instance, he was seen as "Coloured" in his homeland but as "White" on a video, which once let him escape arrest!

OPPOSING PERSPECTIVES

Using the Word *Race*

Although race is a social construction, overlapping with culture and ethnicity, it was once considered a biological characteristic, as when color was used to designate race. Historically, this led to odd conclusions. For instance, in nineteenth-century United States, people of Greek descent were considered non-White; now they are counted as White. In the twentieth century, although most Westerners considered Chinese, Japanese, and Koreans to be of the same race, according to South African apartheid laws, people of Chinese descent were not allowed in "White-only" places, but people of Japanese descent were.

Genetic analysis confirms that the biological concept of race is inaccurate. A study of the genes for skin tones found marked diversity among people from Africa. The lead scientist explained, "there is so much diversity in Africans that there is no such thing as an African race" (Tishkoff, quoted in Gibbons, 2017, p. 158). Indeed, dark-skinned people from many parts of the world share neither culture nor ethnicity with Africans. Likewise, a study of East Asians found 20 genetic variants that affect their skin color (Hider et al., 2013).

Race is not just a flawed concept; it is a destructive one. Slavery, lynching, and segregation in the United States were directly connected to the belief that race was inborn; genocide in Nazi Germany, Rwanda, Cambodia, and elsewhere in the world began with the notion that one group is biologically distinctive from another.

Since race is a social construction that leads to racism, most nations no longer refer to racial groups. Only 15 percent of nations use the word *race* on their census forms (Morning, 2008). The United States is the only nation whose census distinguishes race and ethnicity, stating that Hispanics "may be of any race." Such distinctions are not always clear or consistent: Between the 2000 and 2010 U.S. Census, 6 percent of individuals changed their racial or ethnic identification (Liebler et al., 2017).

Because words that categorize people tend to encourage people to think of themselves as belonging to one category or another, which can lead to harmful stereotyping, should the word "race" not be used?

Now the opposite perspective. In a society with a history of racial discrimination, reversing that culture may *require* recognizing race. Although race is a social construction, not a biological distinction, it is powerful nonetheless. Many medical, educational, and economic conditions—from low birthweight to college graduation, from family income to health insurance—reflect racial disparities.

In the United States, people who insisted that "Black lives matter" were offended by the counter phase "All lives matter." Why? Because that ignored the racism that the original slogan attempted to expose.

Many social scientists agree that pretending that race does not exist allows racism to thrive. Two political scientists studying criminal justice found that people who claim to be color-blind display "an extraordinary level of naiveté" (Peffley & Hurwitz, 2010, p. 113). A sociologist writes about people in the United States, "we are all baptized in the waters" of racism. This is true for everyone, whether they consider themselves White, Black, any other color, or post-racial. He also contends that to call someone racist is a distraction: It ignores the pervasiveness of racism (Bonilla-Silva, 2018).

A person's concept of race depends partly on their culture, cohort, and—particularly relevant to a life-span view—their age. Racial awareness may be crucial for adolescents: Pride in racial identity may help teenagers achieve academically, resist drug addiction, and feel better about themselves (Crosnoe & Johnson, 2011; Wittrup et al., 2016; Zimmerman et al., 2013). To see differences as assets, not deficits, "race" may still be relevant.

In this book, we refer to ethnicity more often than to race, but we use race or color when the original data are reported that way. Racial categories may crumble someday, but not here, not yet.

Intersectionality

Intersectionality begins with the idea that we each are pushed and pulled—sometimes strongly, sometimes weakly, sometimes by ourselves, sometimes by authorities—by our gender, religion, generation, nation, age, and ethnic group. Our many identities interact with and influence each other (see **Figure 1.4**). Intersectionality then recognizes that those identities can be used to discriminate by dividing people—White women versus Black women, Asian men versus Latino men, immigrant women versus immigrant men, and so on, instead of uniting us.

Intersectionality focuses attention on power differences between groups, bringing special attention to the needs of people who are simultaneously in several marginalized groups. They are most harmed when their intersectional identities are ignored.

intersectionality The idea that the various identities need to be combined. This is especially important in determining if discrimination occurs.

THINK CRITICALLY: How does the difference-equals-deficit error apply to attitudes of native-born citizens about immigrants, and vice versa?

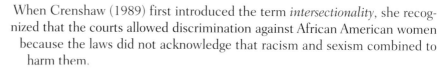

FIGURE 1.4

Identities Interacting We all are in the middle, with many identities. Our total selves are affected by them all, with variation by culture and context as to which are more salient.

When Crenshaw (1989) first introduced the term *intersectionality*, she recognized that the courts allowed discrimination against African American women because the laws did not acknowledge that racism and sexism combined to harm them.

Intersectionality highlights discrimination in many institutions. For example, do judges give African Americans harsher prison sentences than European Americans for the same crimes? The data say yes. That is unfair, but unfairness may be deeper than that.

A careful study of all sentences meted out to incarcerated individuals in Pennsylvania found more age and gender disparities than ethnic ones. For the same crime, young adults were sentenced more harshly than older ones, and men more harshly than women (Steffensmeier et al., 2017). Thus, young Black men may be particularly misjudged; older White women may be particularly protected. Note that this was in Pennsylvania. Would this be better or worse in North Dakota, or Arizona, or another nation? We need more data to know.

More generally, like interlocking gears (see **Figure 1.4**), systems of social categorization and group power intersect to influence everyone, every day. How would your life be different if you were of another gender, ethnicity, family background, sexual orientation, health status, ability, and so on? Cultures matter for everyone.

Development Is Multidisciplinary

Scientists specialize, studying one phenomenon in one species at one age. For example, some investigate the rhythms of crying in 3-month-olds, others the effects of alcohol on adolescent mice, and still others the brain waves that signify brain death. (Results from each of these specialists inform later conclusions in this book.)

To understand human development, we need insights and information from many scientists, past and present, specializing in particular topics in many disciplines, from many cultures. Together, they broaden our perspective.

Genetics

The need for multidisciplinary research has become obvious with genetic analysis. The final decades of the twentieth century led to a momentous accomplishment at the turn of the twenty-first century: The Human Genome Project mapped all the genes that comprise a human being. To the surprise of many, it became apparent that every trait—psychological as well as physical—is influenced by genes (see Chapter 3).

At first it seemed that genes might determine everything, that humans become whatever their genes destine them to be—heroes, killers, or ordinary people. However, that idea was quickly modified as research from other disciplines took genes into account.

Criminology and Medicine Punishment of criminals and the health of newborns are central concerns of the disciplines of criminology and medicine, not psychology or political science. However, here you see 100 psychologists about to inform the U.S. Congress about the hazards of using restraints (e.g., handcuffs) on women giving birth, which is the practice in many prisons. As in this example, many human problems require a multidisciplinary approach.

Multidisciplinary research confirms that genes affect everything but determine almost nothing. For instance, one team of scientists found that an infant with a fearful temperament (presumably genetic) can become an unusually difficult toddler or a much happier one. The difference depended on the parents' interactions, with the child and with each other (Hentges et al., 2015). The citations for that study include psychology, neuroscience, sociology, forensics, as well as biology.

Bio-Psycho-Social Perspectives

To understand life-span development, several disciplines provide insight. The combination of biology, psychology, and sociology is known as a *biopsychosocial* perspective. Using this view, and research from these three areas, a child's recovery from injury (biological) is affected by their appraisal (psychological) of the injury, and the social support (sociology) they receive (Marsac et al., 2017).

Other disciplines — history, medicine, anthropology, political science, and more — aid development at every age. In an adult example, stroke victims vary in how much they walk, from 377 to 14,433 steps daily. Why? Their actual physical condition is only one factor. For most, their personal feelings of competence and their therapist's skill determine whether or not they walk thousands of steps per day (Danks et al., 2016). And that, of course, depends partly on national politics, cultural attitudes, and higher education, for both the stroke victim and the therapist.

Teenage Rebellion

To understand how the multidisciplinary perspective works in detail, consider a study of 246 adolescents (average age 16) that was multimethod, multi-informant, and multimeasure (Tu et al., 2017). Before beginning, the researchers consulted research in physiology, education, family relations, statistics, and abnormal psychology.

In the study design, the scientists used biological measures (e.g., skin conductance to measure autonomic arousal via sweat when the participants traced the outline of a star seen only in a mirror), psychological measures (e.g., participants' answers on a confidential questionnaire about law-breaking and peer-rejection), and social measures (e.g., parental involvement).

For example, parents disagreed or agreed with several items, such as:

- I influence my child's selection of friends.
- I talk with my child about the pros and cons of hanging out with certain people.
- If my child's friends do things that I don't approve of, then my child stops being friends with them.

After they collected all the data, their analysis and conclusions showed the benefits of multidisciplinary research. *If* an adolescent was low on physiological arousal, *and* his parents tried to direct his friendship, he was less likely to become a delinquent. However, *if* the teen's arousal systems (both the sympathetic and parasympathetic nervous systems) were naturally at high alert, parental meddling in friendship increased law-breaking.

Two caveats for these results. First, this is a correlational study not yet replicated (correlation and replication are explained later in this chapter) and second, we used masculine pronouns in reporting these results because the published results were found for boys but not for girls (Tu et al., 2017). Why? Hypotheses can be suggested from many disciplines — more multidisciplinary research needed.

Development Is Plastic

The fifth characteristic of the life-span perspective confirms the importance of the previous four: Development is dynamic (multidirectional), affected by a myriad of influences from contexts and cultures (multicontextual and multicultural), measured by many disciplines (multidisciplinary). Humans, perhaps more than any other creature, adjust to their circumstances. Our genetic diversity is only the beginning; our social diversity is the rest.

plasticity The idea that abilities, personality, and other human characteristics can change over time. Plasticity is particularly evident during childhood, but even older adults are not always "set in their ways."

nature In development, nature refers to the traits, capacities, and limitations that each individual inherits genetically from his or her parents at the moment of conception.

nurture In development, nurture includes all of the environmental influences that affect the individual after conception. This includes everything from the mother's nutrition while pregnant to the cultural influences in the nation.

This is reflected in the fifth characteristic, **plasticity**, which denotes two complementary facts: (1) Human traits can be molded (as plastic can be), and (2) people maintain a certain durability of identity (as plastic does). The concept of plasticity provides both hope and realism—hope because change is possible, and realism because development builds on what has come before, as A Case to Study explains.

The Nature–Nurture Controversy

The concept of plasticity is helpful in understanding a historic debate: nature versus nurture. **Nature** refers to the genes that people inherit. **Nurture** refers to environmental influences, beginning with the health and diet of the embryo's mother and continuing lifelong, including family, school, community, culture, and society.

The nature–nurture debate has many other names, among them *heredity versus environment* and *maturation versus learning*. Under whatever name, the question is: Which characteristics, behaviors, or emotions are the result of genes and which the result of parents, education, or society? Some people believe that most traits are inborn, that children are innately good ("an innocent child") or bad ("beat the devil out of him"); other people credit or blame families, or schools, or neighborhoods.

A CASE TO STUDY

Plasticity and Interacting Systems

My sister-in-law contracted rubella (also called German measles) early in her third pregnancy, a fact not recognized until David was born, blind and dying. Heart surgery two days after birth saved his life, but surgery at 6 months to remove a cataract destroyed that eye. Malformations of his thumbs, ankles, teeth, feet, spine, and brain became evident. David did not walk or talk or even chew for years; he tested as severely disabled, intellectually and socially as well as physically. Some people wondered why his parents did not place him in an institution.

Yet dire early predictions—from me as well as many others—were wrong. Plasticity is, thankfully, apparent. David is a productive and happy adult. When I questioned him about his life he said, "I try to stay in a positive mood" (personal communication).

Remember that difference is not always deficit. When his father died, most of us were sad. (I still miss my big brother.) But David seemed amazingly upbeat: "I miss him, but I know that he is in a better place," he said. Does that indicate brain damage or a better understanding of life?

Plasticity cannot erase a person's genes, childhood experiences, or permanent damage. David's disabilities are always with him (he still lives with his mother). For David, rubella impaired part of his body, but genes and childhood gave him lifelong strengths.

I have noticed many specifics. His parents loved and nurtured him (consulting the Kentucky School for the Blind when he was a few months old). Educators taught him: He was a student in several preschools, each with a different schedule and specialty (for children with cerebral palsy, intellectual disability, and blindness), and then in public kindergarten at age 6.

By age 10, David had skipped a year of school and, as a fifth-grader, could read at an eleventh-grade level. He learned a second and a third language and joined the church choir. In young

My Brother's Children Michael, Bill, and David (left to right) are adults now, with quite different personalities, abilities, numbers of offspring (4, 2, and none), and contexts (in Massachusetts, Pennsylvania, and California). Yet despite genes, prenatal life, and contexts, I see the shared influence of Glen and Dot, my brother and sister-in-law — evident here in their similar, friendly smiles.

adulthood, after one failing semester (requiring family assistance again), he earned several As and graduated from college.

David now works as a translator of German texts, which he enjoys because, "I like providing a service to scholars, giving them access to something they would otherwise not have" (personal communication). As his aunt, I have seen him repeatedly defy predictions. All five of the characteristics of the life-span perspective are evident in David's life, as summarized in **Table 1.2**.

TABLE 1.2

Five Characteristics of Development

Characteristic	Application in David's Story
Multidirectional. Change occurs in every direction, not always in a straight line. Gains and losses, predictable growth, and unexpected transformations are evident.	David's development seemed static (or even regressive, as when early surgery destroyed one eye), but then it accelerated each time he entered a new school or college.
Multidisciplinary. Numerous academic fields—especially psychology, biology, education, and sociology, but also neuroscience, economics, religion, anthropology, history, medicine, genetics, and many more—contribute insights.	Two disciplines were particularly critical: medicine (David would have died without advances in surgery on newborns) and education (special educators guided him and his parents many times).
Multicontextual. Human lives are embedded in many contexts, including historical conditions, economic constraints, and family patterns.	The high SES of David's family made it possible for him to receive daily medical and educational care. His two older brothers protected him.
Multicultural. Many cultures—not just between nations but also within them—affect how people develop.	Appalachia, where David lived, is more accepting of people with disabilities.
Plasticity. Every individual, and every trait within each individual, can be altered at any point in the life span. Change is ongoing, although it is neither random nor easy.	David's measured IQ changed from about 40 (severely intellectually disabled) to about 130 (far above average), and his physical disabilities became less crippling as he matured.

Extensive research from thousands of scientists finds that neither extreme is accurate. "How much?" is a better question than "Which?," because genes and experience both affect every characteristic. Some traits are mostly nature (height, skin color), and some are mostly nurture (vocabulary, hair style), but nature always affects nurture, and then nurture affects nature.

The concept of plasticity suggests that even "how much" is misleading: It implies that nature and nurture each contribute a fixed amount, when really their dynamic interaction is crucial (Daw et al., 2015; Lock, 2013; Sasaki & Kim, 2017). When any specific trait is concerned, the specific outcome reflects both genes and the environment, their interaction is more crucial than either alone.

A further complication is that the impact of any bad or good experience—a beating, or a beer, or a blessing—is magnified or inconsequential because of the individual's particular genes and past experiences. Thus, every aspect of nature and nurture depends on other aspects of nature and nurture in ways that vary for each person. That is plasticity!

THINK CRITICALLY: Why not assign a percent to nature and a percent to nurture so that they add up to 100 percent?

Dandelions and Orchids

There is increasing evidence of **differential susceptibility**. The idea is that sensitivity to any particular experience differs because of each individual's genes and because of events experienced years earlier. In other words, some individuals are sensitive because of their nature or nurture, while other individuals are unaffected. Susceptibility makes people open to influence, either positive or negative.

Developmentalists have an apt botanical metaphor for this variation.

Some people are like *dandelions*—hardy, growing and thriving in good soil or bad, with or without ample sun and rain. They are naturally protected from the destructive influences of their neighborhood, their family, or anything else. Other people are like *orchids*—exquisite, but only in ideal growing conditions (Ellis & Boyce, 2008; Laurent, 2014). Orchids are differentially susceptible.

For example, in one study, depression in pregnant women was assessed, and then the genes and emotional maturity of their children was measured later.

differential susceptibility The idea that people vary in how sensitive they are to particular experiences. Often such differences are genetic, which makes some people affected "for better or for worse" by life events. (Also called *differential sensitivity.*)

Those children who had a particular version of the serotonin transporter gene (5-HTTLPR) were likely to be emotionally immature *if* their mothers were depressed, but *more* mature than average *if* their mothers were not depressed (Babineau et al., 2015). The gene made them susceptible (an orchid) and then their mother's emotions affected them.

Do you have friends who expect you to smile when you see them? If you do not notice them, do they ask, "What's wrong?" or wonder if they have offended you? Do you have other friends who do not notice if you greet them or not? That's differential susceptibility!

WHAT HAVE YOU LEARNED?

1. What aspects of development show continuity?

2. What is the difference between a critical period and a sensitive period?

3. Why is it useful to know when sensitive periods occur?

4. What did Bronfenbrenner emphasize in his ecological-systems approach?

5. How does cohort differ from age group?

6. What factors comprise a person's SES?

7. How are culture, race, and ethnicity distinct from each other?

8. Why is it important to have an intersectional perspective on development?

9. What does it mean to say that human development is plastic?

Development and Science

science of human development The science that seeks to understand how and why people of all ages and circumstances change or remain the same over time.

The **science of human development** *seeks to understand how and why people—all kinds of people, everywhere, of every age—change over time.* It describes what is universal and what is unique about each developing person and predicts each person's development, from conception to death.

History of the Science

Humans have always had opinions about how their children develop. Children should talk a lot or be "seen and not heard"; they were innocent until adults corrupted them or headed for hell unless they were baptized (or circumcised, or named); they needed no education because they had to start work at age 10 or younger, or they needed college.

Adults, too, could expect a difficult life, because life was "solitary, poore, nasty, brutish, and short" (Hobbes, 2010, p. 78), or the goal of life was happiness. Opinions about human development were shared by most people in a particular culture, unaware that people elsewhere held opposite ideas.

Then the scientific revolution began, first in physics and biology, spreading to psychology in the nineteenth century. By the twentieth century, thousands of scientists turned their attention to development.

At first, researchers emphasized physical growth, especially for children. Height and weight were measured, with charts that indicated expected growth each year. Motor skills were listed and measured. The emphasis was on physical health, especially exercise and nutrition. Norms were based on middle-class, White children in the United States, and those norms were thought to apply to all children, as in dozens of books from the Gesell Institute at Yale (e.g., Ilg & Ames, 1959).

Now, as the previous description of the life-span perspective makes clear, developmentalists study the entire life span, including cognitive and psychosocial development, with appreciation for people in other cultures and contexts.

As evident in Chapter 4, body growth is still important, but so is intellectual and social growth (Chapters 5–15). Bronfenbrenner's stress on all the systems was revolutionary when he first proposed it; now it is assumed.

Ages and Stages
It may seem as if early childhood, middle childhood, adolescence, and so on are fixed demarcations, stages that all humans recognize. That is far from true. Even adolescence was not considered a stage until G. Stanley Hall (president of the American Psychological Association) wrote *Adolescence*, a two-volume, 1,419-page account of the period from puberty until about age 16 (Hall, 1904). He described puberty, calling adolescence as a time of "storm and stress."

Hall's perspective prevailed: Adolescence became a stage, and late childhood disappeared. By contrast, in many traditional cultures, unaware of the expected turbulence, late childhood moved rather quickly into adulthood.

Both brain and behavior are affected by the social construction (Hall's ideas) of adolescence. In one U.S. study, the more 13- to 15-year-olds believed in Hall's depiction of adolescence, the more they disobeyed their parents and took risks, and the more their brains were affected, especially the neurological structures that foster cognitive control (Qu et al., 2018).

This is one small example. But the general finding seems valid: What cultures expect of a particular age affects human behavior at that age, including how brains and bodies grow. Life's stages are themselves plastic — moldable by culture, a social construction.

A dramatic illustration comes from seventeenth-century Europe (Ariès, 1965). Children were dressed like adults and worked like adults; "fairy tales" were originally produced for people of all ages — which may explain why many are gruesome. Childhood, as we know it and as children live it, may be a new invention.

Topics and Terms
Just as the boundaries of the stages are variable, so are the terms and topics of human development. The underlying problem is that each human life unfolds simultaneously in every dimension. Yet to study it, we must segment it, considering one age at a time, or one topic at a time, as if each is a discrete entity.

For instance, an early chapter (Chapter 3) is about genes, but genes affect everything. Another chapter (Chapter 7) is about memory, but memory also relates to perception (Chapter 6), language (Chapter 8), cognition (Chapter 9), and so on. Further, each topic can be segmented by age or category, but norms, standards, ages, and categories are much more variable than they once appeared.

The problem is easy to see in physical development. If we study mobility (one aspect of physical development) should we consider creeping, crawling, walking, running, jogging, and strolling to be distinct or all part of the same topic? Babies who walk before age 1 are usually those who crawl early, because the leg muscles that crawling strengthens are used to walk. Even at age 100, those people who ran marathons are less likely to need a wheelchair. The same patterns are evident in education, family structures, sensations, and so on; that is why a life-span perspective makes sense.

No one can comprehend the entirety of development simultaneously. However, as you approach the science of development, remember dynamic systems, and ask how each phenomenon affects all the others lifelong. The scientific method is especially needed in multidisciplinary studies such as this one.

The Need for Science
Always, whether the emphasis is chronological or topical, this study is a *science*. Everyone has opinions regarding human growth, but scientists depend on theories, data, analysis, critical thinking, and sound methodology.

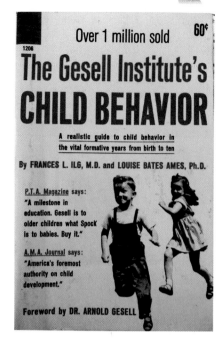

Blond Boy Running Gesell norms, as in this 1959 book, were thought to be universal. The ideas that not all children were like these two, that child development was much more than norms for motor skills, and that girls did not always follow along wearing skirts were not part of this book by the "foremost authority on child development."

All scientists begin with curiosity. They wonder "How?" and "Why?" For example, biologists seek to understand how cells function, chemists to describe the interactions of the elements around us, physicists to explain the force of black holes, astronomers to know what is beyond our galaxy. All these scientists ask much more about cells, or elements, or the universe, just as all developmentalists wonder about everything people do and think lifelong.

Science is essential when we study "all kinds of people, everywhere, at every age." Individuals have strong opinions about human development, about brain cells, genes, language, diet, morals, marriage, work, love, hate . . . about everything that humans do, or think, or value. We need science to move us from opinion to truth, from subjective to objective, from prejudice to evidence.

The Scientific Method

scientific method A way to answer questions using empirical research and data-based conclusions.

hypothesis A specific prediction that can be tested.

empirical evidence Evidence that is based on observation, experience, or experiment; not theoretical.

As you surely realize, facts may be twisted, opinions may lead people astray, and false assumptions may overwhelm data. To counter our many prejudices, scientists follow the five steps of the **scientific method** (see **Figure 1.5**):

1. *Begin with curiosity.* Ask questions: Consider theory, study research, and gather observations, all of which suggest topics or issues to be studied.
2. *Develop a hypothesis.* Form a **hypothesis**, a prediction that can be verified. Theories are comprehensive ideas, hypotheses are more specific.
3. *Test the hypothesis.* Design a study and conduct research to gather **empirical evidence** (data) to test the hypothesis. Pay special attention to the selection of participants and the measurement of variables. (More on this soon.)
4. *Draw conclusions.* Use the evidence (Step 3) to support or refute the hypothesis (Step 2). Consider alternate interpretations, unexpected results, and possible biases; raise new questions (Step 1). The hypothesis can be verified or not. (Disproving a hypothesis is as enlightening as supporting it.)
5. *Report the results.* Share data, conclusions, and limitations. Suggest further research to explore unanswered questions and to corroborate conclusions. Ideally, the results are published in sufficient detail so that other scientists can understand exactly how the conclusions were reached.

Thus, developmental scientists begin with curiosity and then collect data, drawing conclusions after analyzing the evidence. The process arises not only from observations and personal experience, but also from careful study of the reports (Step 5) of other scientists. Each researcher builds on the past, considers the present, and predicts the future—always using critical thinking.

replication Repeating a study, usually using different participants, perhaps of another age, SES, or culture.

Replication

Repeating the procedures and methods of a study with different participants is called **replication**. This is often a sixth step of the scientific method. Scientists study the reports of other scientists (Step 5) and build on what has gone before (back to Step 1). Sometimes they try to duplicate a study exactly; often they follow

FIGURE 1.5
Process, Not Proof Built into the scientific method—in questions, hypotheses, tests, and replication—is a passion for possibilities, especially unexpected ones.

A VIEW FROM SCIENCE

Music and the Brain

An illustration of the scientific method at work arose from research on music and the mind. Does music make people smarter? That question arose from the results of one study 25 years ago, in which 36 college students who listened to Mozart for ten minutes had higher scores on tests of spatial intelligence (Rauscher et al., 1993).

That study did <u>not</u> replicate or generalize, but the popular press did not wait. Nor did some politicians. The governor of Georgia in the mid-1990s proposed a budget item of $105,000 to give every Georgia newborn a free CD of classical music. (The legislature voted it down.) Some popular manuals for parents advocated playing classical music for children to help their minds.

Although the original study was flawed in many ways, the topic intrigued scientists, who asked new questions (Step 1). Dozens of studies have investigated the relationship between music and cognition (Perlovsky et al., 2013).

Sometimes the researchers investigate tiny details. For example, one study of brain scans compared what happens when someone listens to Mozart versus listening to Bach (Verrusio et al., 2015). Another group of researchers examined how rats react to hearing Mozart (Sampaio et al., 2017). Studying rats may seem odd.

However, the reactions of rodents, dogs, and other primates suggest hypotheses regarding people.

Particularly interesting to developmentalists is how the effects of music vary as people grow older. Some research finds that the brains of fragile newborns in hospitals develop better if they hear music (Lordier et al., 2019). At the other end of the life span, one review of music and major neurocognitive disorder (formerly called dementia) concluded:

> Although promising effects are reported on a small scale, general effects on cognition are not commonly reported, and music therapy appears to be more effective at improving mood and emotion than at enhancing cognition.
>
> *[de Bruin & Schaefe, 2017, p. 273]*

The impact of music on learning is a thriving area of research within psychology. For most children and adults, merely listening to music in childhood is unlikely to benefit cognition, but learning to play a musical instrument may advance intelligence and academic achievement (Rose et al., 2019).

This shows how one study — even one that failed to replicate — can raise new questions regarding human development. Questions, data, and replication are the basics of science.

up with related research (Stroebe & Strack, 2014). Conclusions are revised, refined, rejected, or confirmed after replication.

Obviously, the scientific method is not foolproof. Scientists sometimes draw conclusions too hastily, misinterpret data, or ignore alternative perspectives, or, very rarely, report what is not true. About 1 published article in 5,000 is withdrawn because of falsified data (Brainard, 2018).

As in several examples in this chapter, scientists do not accept conclusions until several studies agree. Ideally, results are replicated, not only by other researchers performing the same study again (Step 3), but also by designing other studies that can verify and extend the same hypothesis (Larzelere et al., 2015).

Of course, the fact that we study humans of all ages, in diverse contexts and cultures, means that no study can exactly mirror another (De Boeck & Jeon, 2018). Perfect replication is impossible; that is why new research is inspired by what has gone before. Any single study might be flawed in unsuspected ways (see A View from Science).

WHAT HAVE YOU LEARNED?

1. How is the science of human development similar to the other sciences?

2. Which stages of human development are universal?

3. What benefits occur if a hypothesis is not confirmed?

4. Why is replication crucial?

5. What benefits result from relying on the scientific method?

Using the Scientific Method

There are hundreds of ways to design scientific studies and analyze results. Often statistical measures help scientists discover relationships between various aspects of the data. (Some statistical perspectives are presented in **Table 1.3**.)

Studying People

Every research design, method, and statistic has strengths as well as weaknesses. The basic methods are similar for all scientists, but when we study people, ethics precludes some strategies. As you will see, the first step is to observe carefully, and then to use experiments and surveys.

Observation

scientific observation A method of testing a hypothesis by unobtrusively watching and recording participants' behavior in a systematic and objective manner—in a natural setting, in a laboratory, or in searches of archival data.

Scientific observation requires researchers to record behavior systematically and objectively. Observation often occurs in a naturalistic setting (such as a home, school, or public park), where people behave as they usually do and where the observer is ignored or even unnoticed. Observation can also occur in a laboratory, where scientists record human reactions in various situations, often with wall-mounted video cameras or with the scientist unseen behind a one-way mirror.

Observation develops hypotheses. For example, researchers noticed that some preschool children were more outgoing than others. Why? What are the consequences? One hypothesis is that some parents were hesitant to leave their children, and then their children noticed that anxiety and were less outgoing as a result. Then those children might make fewer friends, and not join in the education that was offered.

To test that hypothesis, the researchers began with careful observation at a preschool (J. Grady et al., 2012). Several weeks after the beginning of the year, they sat in a corner of the room and used their stopwatches to record how long each parent stayed to hug and kiss their children before saying goodbye. The researchers compared parents who left within three minutes of arriving and those who took longer. They also tallied how much each child interacted with other children.

TABLE 1.3

Statistical Measures Often Used to Analyze Search Results

Measure	Use
Effect size	There are many kinds, but the most useful in reporting studies of development is called *Cohen's d*, which can indicate the power of an intervention. An effect size of 0.2 is called small, 0.5 moderate, and 0.8 large.
Significance	Indicates whether the results might have occurred by chance. If chance would produce the results only 5 times in 100, that is significant at the .05 level; once in 100 times is .01; once in 1,000 is .001.
Cost-benefit analysis	Calculates how much a particular independent variable costs versus how much it saves. This is useful for analyzing public spending, such as finding that preschool education programs or preventative health measures save money over the long term.
Odds ratio	Indicates how a particular variable compares to a standard, set at 1. For example, one study found that although less than 1 percent of all child homicides occurred at school, the odds were similar for public and private schools. The odds of it in high schools, however, were 18.47 times that of elementary or middle schools (set at 1.0) (MMWR, January 18, 2008).
Factor analysis	Hundreds of variables could affect any given behavior. In addition, many variables (such as family income and parental education) overlap. To take this into account, analysis reveals variables that can be clustered together to form a factor, which is a composite of many variables. For example, SES might become one factor, child personality another.
Meta-analysis	A "study of studies." Researchers use statistical tools to synthesize the results of previous, separate studies. Then they analyze the accumulated results, using criteria that weigh each study fairly. This approach improves data analysis by combining studies that were too small, or too narrow, to lead to solid conclusions.

When parents lingered three minutes or more, their "children spent less time involved in the preschool peer social environment," playing less with their classmates. The authors suggested that this "has implications for not only children's later peer interactions and peer status, but also for children's engagement in school and, ultimately, academic achievement" (J. Grady et al., 2012, p. 1690).

The thought was that, by staying, the parents made the children anxious about school. But note: Those implications are not proven. Observation found a correlation (to be defined later) and then suggested a possible cause.

There are alternate explanations. Perhaps some children were naturally shy, so their parents stayed a little longer to help them become more comfortable with school. If that was the case, then the children's diminished engagement with other children could be the result not of the parents' lingering, but of the children's shyness.

The outcome might differ as well. Perhaps children who socialized less might become better students later on, because they are less distracted by peers.

Thus, these observational data led to at least two alternative hypotheses: (1) Parental anxiety impairs child social engagement, or (2) shy children are given parental support. One sign of a good scientist is that every observation can lead to several possible explanations. To further the process of discovery, observation often leads to hypotheses that require an experiment.

What Can You Learn? Scientists first establish what is, and then they try to change it. In one recent experiment, Deb Kelemen (shown here) established that few children under age 12 understand a central concept of evolution (natural selection). Then she showed an experimental group a picture book illustrating the idea. Success! The independent variable (the book) affected the dependent variable (the children's ideas), which confirmed Kelemen's hypothesis: Children can understand natural selection if instruction is tailored to their ability.

Experiments

An **experiment** tests a hypothesis. In the social sciences, experimenters typically impose a particular treatment on a group of participants (formerly called *subjects*), or expose them to a specific condition and then note whether their behavior changes.

In technical terms, the experimenters manipulate an **independent variable**, the imposed treatment or special condition (also called the *experimental variable*). (A *variable* is anything that can vary.) They note whether this independent variable affects whatever they are studying, called the **dependent variable**, which *depends* on the independent variable.

Thus, the independent variable is the new, special treatment; any change in the dependent variable is the result. The purpose of an experiment is to find out whether an independent variable affects the dependent variable.

In a typical experiment (as diagrammed in **Figure 1.6**), two equal groups of participants are studied. One group, the *experimental group*, gets a particular treatment (the independent variable). The other group, the *control group* (also called the *comparison group*), does not.

To follow up on the observation study above, researchers could experiment. For example, they could assess the social skills (dependent variable) of hundreds of children in the first week of school and then require parents of 100 children to stay longer than three minutes, another 100 to leave quickly, and in the final 100 to do whatever they normally would do.

This experiment would have two experimental groups and one comparison group. The independent variable is the timing of parental departure; the dependent variable is how much the children play with each other.

The same rules would be needed for all the parents in each class, so the children would encounter the same treatment as their peers. This experiment would require several classes in each group, randomly selected, to balance out any

experiment A research method in which the researcher tries to determine the cause-and-effect relationship between two variables by manipulating one (called the *independent variable*) and then observing and recording the ensuing changes in the other (called the *dependent variable*).

independent variable In an experiment, the variable that is introduced to see what effect it has on the dependent variable. (Also called *experimental variable*.)

dependent variable In an experiment, the variable that may change as a result of whatever new condition or situation the experimenter adds. In other words, the dependent variable *depends* on the independent variable.

The Experiment

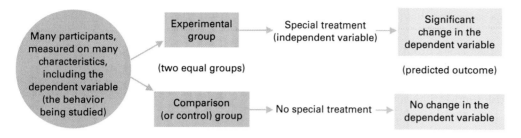

Procedure:

1. Divide participants into two groups that are matched on important characteristics, especially the behavior that is the dependent variable on which this study is focused.

2. Give special treatment, or intervention (the independent variable), to one group (the experimental group).

3. Compare the groups on the dependent variable. If they now differ, the cause of the difference was probably the independent variable.

4. Publish the results.

FIGURE 1.6

How to Conduct an Experiment The basic sequence diagrammed here applies to all experiments. Many additional features, especially the statistical measures listed in Table 1.3 and various ways of reducing experimenter bias, affect whether publication occurs. (Scientific journals reject reports of experiments that were not rigorous in method and analysis.)

ESPECIALLY FOR Nurses In the field of medicine, why are experiments conducted to test new drugs and treatments? (see response, page 31)

survey A research method in which information is collected from a large number of people by interviews, written questionnaires, or some other means.

effects of having a particular teacher, and to ensure that the children in each group were similar on other variables.

For example, the 200 or so children in the experimental groups would be of the same average age and gender as the 100 or so in the control classes. This is a safeguard: Perhaps age and gender make no difference, but if they do, having the same proportion of boys and girls in each group would compensate for any gender differences that might occur. Probably this experiment would need to be done in several schools, partly to find 300 children, and partly as a way to control for any differences in neighborhoods or other factors.

Months later, the children's social skills (dependent variable) could be measured again. A few years later, their school achievement (another dependent variable) could be recorded. Suppose the children whose parents lingered eventually had higher reading scores than the other group, contrary to the researchers' original hypothesis. Would this experiment *prove* that lingering at drop-off *caused* later academic success?

Not exactly. Critical thinking is needed. For instance, lingering might have instigated more parental involvement. Or, these two groups might have differed in ways that were not balanced out, because the experimenter didn't realize that something other than age or gender made a difference. Replication is needed. But at least an experiment is a step closer to scientific discovery than the speculation of the original researchers.

Surveys

A third research method is the **survey**, when information is collected from many people, often by asking them directly. This is a quick way to obtain data. It is better than assuming that the experiences and attitudes of people we know are valid for everyone.

For example, suppose you know a 16-year-old who is pregnant, or a 40-year-old who hates his job, or an 80-year-old who watches television all day. Are those people typical? Surveys have already answered those questions. Surprisingly, teenage pregnancy is uncommon, many people enjoy their jobs, and older adults watch less television than children do. As you see, surveys are useful: Assumptions based on personal observation may be wrong.

Unfortunately, surveys are not always accurate. One of the most interesting questions for developmentalists is how satisfied people are with their lives, a variable that correlates with marriage, religion, nationality, and more. However, surveys report conflicting results, depending on how the questions are worded (Stundziene, 2019).

There is another problem: People do not want to admit whatever they are ashamed of, and some want to say what they think the researcher wants to hear.

This is a major problem in political polling: Most adults say they will vote, even if they will not. For example, most polls wrongly predicted that Clinton would win the U.S. presidency in 2016, because about 3 percent of people who said they would vote actually stayed home.

Inaccurate surveys harm development. For example, developmentalists want to know how many families are *food insecure*, because hungry people do not learn as much as others (Seligman & Berkowitz, 2019). Accordingly, the U.S. Department of Agriculture developed, tested, and revised the Food Security Scale, with 18 questions. When answered honestly, that survey is quite accurate, but it is cumbersome to administer and score. Pediatricians created a briefer survey: As they examine infants, they ask parents to say YES or NO to two questions:

1. Within the past 12 months, we worried whether the food we bought would run out before we got money to buy more.

2. Within the past 12 months, the food we bought just didn't last and we didn't have money to get more.

[*Council on Community Pediatrics, 2015, p. e1435*]

One study compared answers on the short and long version. If a parent answered "yes" on the short survey, then almost all of them (97 percent) were also rated food insecure on the longer survey. So far, so good.

But many (about 25 percent) who say "no" on the short version were food insecure on the longer version, which asks "often true?," "sometimes true?," or "never true?" instead of merely YES or NO (Cutts & Cook, 2017; Makelarski et al., 2017). On that long set, they say that they have sometimes gone hungry and skipped meals because there was not enough food.

Apparently, many people who say "sometimes" are ashamed to say "yes," perhaps because it implies poor budgeting. So even if the people who say "sometimes" have no money for food and go hungry, they do not say "yes." Food insecurity is "a highly stigmatized condition that is not commonly disclosed" (Makelarski et al., 2017, p. 1812). To help all hungry children, a better survey than the one created by pediatricians is needed.

Don't blame the pediatricians; every survey is sometimes flawed. Accuracy depends on wording, circumstances, and on who asks and who answers. This is a warning to every scientist: A survey may not be accurate. Indeed, this is true with friends as well, as you know if your friend says "fine" when you ask, "How are you?"

cross-sectional research A research design that compares groups of people who differ in age but are similar in other important characteristics.

Studying Development over the Life Span

In addition to conducting observations, experiments, and surveys, developmentalists must measure how people *change or remain the same over time,* as the definition of developmental science stresses. Remember that systems are dynamic, ever-changing. To capture that dynamism, developmental researchers design cross-sectional, longitudinal, or cross-sequential studies.

Cross-Sectional versus Longitudinal Research

The quickest way to study development over time is with **cross-sectional research**. People of different ages are compared, and, differences are considered an effect of age.

For example, cross-sectional research finds that people get heavier with age, and then, with later adulthood, they get thinner again. A cross-section of U.S. residents aged 20–40 found that 36 percent were obese, and then among 40- to 60-year-olds, 43 percent were obese. Then, rates fall a little: 41 percent of those over 60 were obese (Hayes et al., 2017).

"It's a one-year timer. It gives an added sense of urgency to my research grant."

Not Long Enough For understanding the human life span, scientists wish for grants that are renewed for decades.

Cross-sectional design seems simple. However, it is difficult to ensure that the various groups being compared are similar in every way except age. For example, we do not know if those age differences in obesity are because those over 60 eat healthier, or because middle-age obese adults are more likely to die before 60 so fewer of them were surveyed in old age.

Predictions are particularly suspect. Cross-sectional research finds that the average adult gains a pound each year from age 30 to 60. Does that mean that contemporary 30-year-olds who weigh 140 will be 170 pounds at age 60? Not necessarily. That prediction assumes that this current cohort of young adults will eat and exercise in the same way that adults did decades ago. That may not be the case. The data suggest that they drink less beer and more water than their parents did. They may not follow the nutritional path of early cohorts, and thus cross-sectional research may be accurate for the present but not the future.

> **longitudinal research** A research design in which the same individuals are followed over time, as their development is repeatedly assessed.

To help discover whether growing older or the historical context causes a developmental change, **longitudinal research** is needed, collecting data repeatedly on the same individuals as they age. That may produce a more accurate prediction. For example, in the example of the parents' lingering at drop-off with preschoolers, we will not know the academic consequences until those same children are several years older.

However, longitudinal research is not perfect, either. Over time, participants may withdraw, move to an unknown address, or die. Those who stay are not a representative group. Also, if they are tested and questioned repeatedly, that itself may change a person, making the results inaccurate for people as a whole.

The biggest problem with longitudinal research is the changing, and unpredictable, historical context. Science, popular culture, and politics alter life experiences, which limits the relevance of data collected on people born decades ago.

For example, thousands of new chemicals are in the air, water, and food. What is their effect on human health? Some people think *phthalates* and *bisphenol A* (BPA) (chemicals used in manufacturing), *hydrofracking* (used to get gas for fuel from rocks), *e-waste* (from old computers and cell phones) and *glyphosate* (a pesticide used in the herbicide RoundUp) are beneficial for humankind, while others think they are destroying our health. Some nations and states ban or regulate each of these. Others do not. We cannot prove whether the former are overcautious or, instead, prescient, because verified, longitudinal data on the effects of long-term use are not yet available.

A current longitudinal conundrum is climate change. Some predict global civil wars, agriculture failure, disaster, deaths—and that life on our planet itself may be snuffed out within a century—because of warming in the atmosphere now. Others call that view alarmist, suggesting that mitigation can protect humanity (Murphy et al., 2018). Longitudinal research cannot tell us: We will not know until it is too late.

Cross-Sequential Research

> **cross-sequential research** A hybrid research design in which researchers first study several groups of people of different ages (a cross-sectional approach) and then follow those groups over the years (a longitudinal approach). (Also called *cohort-sequential research* or *time-sequential research*.)

Scientists have discovered a third strategy, combining cross-sectional and longitudinal research. This combination is called **cross-sequential research** (also referred to as *cohort-sequential* or *time-sequential research*). With this design, researchers study several groups of people of different ages (a cross-sectional approach), follow them over the years (a longitudinal approach), and then combine the results.

A cross-sequential design lets researchers compare findings for, say, 16-year-olds with findings for the same individuals at age 1, as well as with data for people who were 16 long ago, who are now ages 31, 46, and 61 (see **Figure 1.7**). Cross-sequential research is complicated in recruitment and analysis, but it lets scientists disentangle age from history.

CROSS-SECTIONAL
Total time: A few days, plus analysis

age 1	age 16	age 31	age 46	age 61
Time 1	Time 1	Time 1	Time 1	Time 1

Collect data once. Compare groups. Any differences, presumably, are the result of age.

LONGITUDINAL
Total time: 61 years, plus analysis

age 1	age 16	age 31	age 46	age 61
	[15 years later]	[15 years later]	[15 years later]	[15 years later]
Time 1	Time 1 + 15 years	Time 1 + 30 years	Time 1 + 45 years	Time 1 + 60 years

Collect data five times, at 15-year intervals. Any differences for these individuals are definitely the result of passage of time (but might be due to events or historical changes as well as age).

CROSS-SEQUENTIAL
Total time: 61 years, plus double and triple analysis

age 1	age 16	age 31	age 46	age 61

[15 years later] [15 years later] [15 years later] [15 years later]

	age 1	age 16	age 31	age 46

For cohort effects, compare groups on the diagonals (same age, different years).

[15 years later] [15 years later] [15 years later]

		age 1	age 16	age 31

[15 years later] [15 years later]

Time 1	Time 1 + 15 years	Time 1 + 30 years	Time 1 + 45 years	Time 1 + 60 years

Collect data five times, following the original group but also adding a new group each time. Analyze data two ways, comparing groups of the same ages studied at different times and the same group as they grow older.

FIGURE 1.7
Which Approach Is Best? Cross-sequential research is the most time-consuming and complex, but it yields the best information. One reason that hundreds of scientists conduct research on the same topics, replicating one another's work, is to gain some advantages of cohort-sequential research without waiting for decades.

The first well-known cross-sequential study (the *Seattle Longitudinal Study*) found that some intellectual abilities (vocabulary) increase even after age 60, whereas others (speed) start to decline at age 30 (Schaie, 2005/2013), confirming that development is multidirectional. This study also discovered that declines in adult math ability are more closely related to education than to age, something neither cross-sectional nor longitudinal research could reveal.

Cross-sequential research is useful for young adults as well. For example, drug addiction (called *substance use disorder,* or *SUD*) is most common in the early 20s and decreases by the late 20s. But one cross-sequential study found that the origins of SUD are much earlier, in adolescent behaviors and in genetic predispositions (McGue et al., 2014). Other research finds that heroin deaths are more common after age 30, but the best time to intervene seems to be in emerging adulthood (Carlson et al., 2016).

ESPECIALLY FOR Future Researchers
What is the best method for collecting data?
(see response, page 31)

WHAT HAVE YOU LEARNED?

1. Why do careful observations not prove what causes what?

2. Why do experimenters use a control (or comparison) group?

3. What are the advantages and disadvantages of cross-sectional research?

4. What are the advantages and disadvantages of longitudinal research?

5. Why isn't every study of human development cross-sequential?

Cautions and Challenges from Science

The scientific method illuminates and illustrates human development as nothing else does. Facts, consequences, and possibilities have emerged that would not be known without science—and people of all ages are healthier, happier, and more capable because of it.

For example, thanks to science, infectious diseases in children, illiteracy in adults, depression in late adulthood, and sexism and racism at every age, are much less prevalent today than a century ago. Young adults, aware of the Black Lives Matter and Me Too movements, might doubt that progress is evident; they need to ask someone over age 70 to learn what life was like for women and for African Americans decades ago. Early death—from violence, war, or disease—is also less likely, with scientific discoveries and education as likely reasons (Pinker, 2018).

Developmentalists have also discovered unexpected sources of harm. Video games, cigarettes, television, shift work, lead, asbestos, and even artificial respiration are all less benign than people first thought.

The benefits of science are many, in improving lives and discovering hazards. However, science also entails complications that can lead us all astray. We now discuss three of them: misinterpreting correlation, depending on numbers, and ignoring ethics.

Correlation and Causation

Probably the most common mistake in interpreting research is confusing correlation with causation. A **correlation** exists between two variables if one variable is more (or less) likely to occur when the other does. A correlation is *positive* if both variables tend to increase together or decrease together, *negative* if one variable tends to increase while the other decreases, and *zero* if no connection is evident. (Try the quiz in **Table 1.4**.)

Expressed in numerical terms, correlations vary from +1.0 (the most positive) to −1.0 (the most negative). Correlations are almost never that extreme; a correlation of +.3 or −.3 is noteworthy; a correlation of +.8 or −.8 is astonishing.

Many correlations are unexpected. For instance: First-born children are more likely to develop asthma than are later-born children; teenage girls have higher rates of mental health problems than do teenage boys; U.S. counties with more dentists have fewer obese residents. That last study controlled for the number of medical doctors and the poverty of the community. The authors suggest that dentists provide information about nutrition that improves health (Holzer et al., 2014).

That dentist explanation may be wrong. Every scientist knows the mantra: *Correlation is not causation.* Just because two variables are correlated does not mean that one causes the other—even if it seems logical that it does. It proves only that the variables are connected somehow. Either one could cause the other (might dentists prefer to work where fewer people are obese?) or a third variable may cause the correlation. Unless people

VIDEO ACTIVITY: What's Wrong with This Study? explores some of the major pitfalls of the process of designing a research study.

correlation A number between +1.0 and −1.0 that indicates the degree of relationship between two variables, expressed in terms of the likelihood that one variable will (or will not) occur when the other variable does (or does not). A correlation indicates only that two variables are somehow related, not that one variable causes the other to occur.

TABLE 1.4

Quiz on Correlation

Two Variables	Positive, Negative, or Zero Correlation?	Why? (Third variable)
1. Ice cream sales and murder rate	_____	_____
2. Reading ability and number of baby teeth	_____	_____
3. Adult's sex assigned at birth and average number of offspring	_____	_____

For each of these three pairs of variables, indicate whether the correlation between them is positive, negative, or nonexistent. Then try to think of a third variable that might determine the direction of the correlation. The correct answers appear on the next page.

remember that correlation is not causation, they may draw mistaken and even dangerous conclusions.

Quantity and Quality

A second caution concerns whether scientists should rely on data produced by **quantitative research** (from the word *quantity*). Quantitative research data can be ranked or numbered, allowing easy translation across cultures. One example of quantitative research is using children's achievement scores to assess education within a school or a nation.

A Pesky Third Variable Correlation is often misleading. In this case, a third variable (the supply of fossil fuels) may be relevant.

Since quantities can be easily summarized, compared, charted, and replicated, many scientists prefer quantitative research. Statistics require numbers. Quantitative data are easier to replicate and less open to bias.

However, when data are presented in categories and numbers, some nuances and individual distinctions are lost. Many developmental researchers thus turn to **qualitative research** (from the word *quality*) — asking open-ended questions, reporting answers in narrative (not numerical) form.

Qualitative researchers are "interested in understanding how people interpret their experiences, how they construct their worlds . . ." (Merriam, 2009, p. 5). Qualitative research reflects cultural and contextual diversity, but it is also more vulnerable to bias and harder to replicate. Both types of research are needed (Morgan, 2018).

For that reason, some studies now use both methods, which provides richer, but also more verifiable, details. For example, one study compared the very old (over age 90) and their children (age 51–75) (Scelzo et al., 2018). Research compared scores on various measures of psychological and physical health and reported the numbers. Generally, the very old were in poorer physical shape but better psychological health than the merely old.

This study also reported qualitative data. For example, one man over age 90 said:

> I lost my beloved wife only a month ago and I am very sad for this. We were married for 70 years. I was close to her during all her illness and I have felt very empty after her loss. But thanks to my sons I am now recovering and feeling much better. I have 4 children, 10 grandchildren, and 9 great-grandchildren. I have fought all my life and I am always ready for changes. I think changes bring life and give chances to grow. I have had a heart condition for which I have undergone surgery but I am now okay. I have also had two very serious car accidents and I have risked losing my life. But I am still here!! I am always thinking for the best. There is always a solution in life. This is what my father had taught me: to always face difficulties and hope for the best. I am always active. I do not know what stress is. Life is what it is and must be faced. . . . I feel younger now than when I was young!
>
> [Scelzo et al., 2018, p. 33]

Ideally, qualitative research illustrates quantitative research, as was true in this study. This man is in poor physical health (heart condition) but good psychological health (much hope, no stress). As you see, any one study, with any one method, benefits from other studies and methods.

Ethics

The most important challenge for all scientists is to follow ethical standards. Each professional society involved in research of human development has a *code of ethics* (a set of moral principles). Most colleges and hospitals have an *Institutional Review Board* (IRB), a group that permits only research that follows certain guidelines set by the federal government.

quantitative research Research that provides data that can be expressed with numbers, such as ranks or scales.

qualitative research Research that considers qualities instead of quantities. Descriptions of particular conditions and participants' expressed ideas are often part of qualitative studies.

Answers:

1. Positive; third variable: heat

2. Negative; third variable: age

3. Zero. Each child must begin with a sperm from a male and an ovum from a female. No third variable.

Although IRBs often slow down scientific study, some research conducted before they were established was clearly unethical, especially when the participants were children, members of minority groups, prisoners, or animals. Even with IRBs, serious ethical dilemmas remain, particularly when research occurs in developing nations (Leiter & Herman, 2015).

Ebola and Coronavirus

Many ethical dilemmas arose in the 2014–2015 West African Ebola epidemic (Gillon, 2015; Rothstein, 2015; Sabeti & Salahi, 2018). Those problems have reemerged in the more recent Ebola crisis (Gostin et al., 2019) and the coronavirus pandemic (Wang et al., 2020). Among them:

- Should vaccines be given before their safety is demonstrated with large control and experimental groups?
- What kind of informed consent is needed to avoid both false hope and false fears?
- Should children with Ebola or coronavirus be isolated from family, even though social isolation is harmful?
- Is it fair for public health care systems to be inadequate in some countries and high-tech in others?
- When should each nation be responsible for the health of their own people, and when and how should other nations or the United Nations intervene?
- Should quarantine restrict the travel of healthy people?

Medicine tends to focus on individuals, ignoring the customs and systems that make some people more vulnerable. One observer noted:

> When people from the United States and Europe working in West Africa have developed Ebola, time and again the first thing they wanted to take was not an experimental drug. It was an airplane that would cart them home.
>
> *[Cohen, 2014, p. 911]*

A systemic understanding of the Ebola crisis has led to an effort to establish secure biocontainment laboratories in many nations, in order to quickly recognize deadly diseases (Le Duc & Yuan, 2018). Public health doctors note that the political and economic cooperation necessary for world health tends to respond only when a crisis is immediate: A life-span perspective is needed. Developmental scientists need to bring their expertise to international research, with a longitudinal, multicultural, multidirectional perspective — and faith in plasticity.

But before coasting on that optimism, remember that everyone has strong opinions that they expect research to confirm. Scientists might try (sometimes without noticing it) to achieve the results they want while maintaining national and cultural values. As one team explains:

> Our job as scientists is to discover truths about the world. We generate hypotheses, collect data, and examine whether or not the data are consistent with those hypotheses . . . [but we] often lose sight of this goal, yielding to pressure to do whatever is justifiable to compile a set of studies we can publish. This is not driven by a willingness to deceive but by the self-serving interpretation of ambiguity.
>
> *[Simmons et al., 2011, pp. 1359, 1365]*

macmillan learning

VIDEO ACTIVITY: Eugenics and the "Feebleminded": A Shameful History illustrates what can happen when scientists fail to follow a code of ethics.

John Bompengo/AP Images

Risky Shot? Most vaccines undergo years of testing before they are used on people, but vaccines protecting against Ebola were not ready until the 2014 West African epidemic finally waned after 11,000 deaths. Thus, the effectiveness of Ebola vaccines is unknown. However, when deadly Ebola surfaced again in the Democratic Republic of Congo in 2018, public health doctors did not wait for longitudinal data. Here Dr. Mwamba, a representative of Congo's Expanded Program on Immunization, receives the vaccine. He hopes that it will protect him and thousands of other Congolese. We will know by 2021 if the vaccine halted a new epidemic.

Obviously, collaboration, replication, and transparency are essential ethical safeguards. Answers to hundreds of questions regarding human development might benefit everyone, but researchers have yet to find them. For instance:

- Do we know enough about prenatal drugs to protect every fetus?
- Do we know enough about world poverty to enable everyone to be healthy?
- Do we know enough about transgender children to ensure their healthy development?
- Do we know enough about family structures to advise about single parenthood, or divorce, or same-sex marriages?
- Do we know enough about dying to enable everyone to die with dignity?

The answer to these questions is *NO, NO, NO, NO, NO.*

Consider research on guns, the leading cause of child death from age 2 to 20. In 1996, the U.S. Congress, in allocating funds for the Centers for Disease Control and Prevention, passed a law stating that "None of the funds made available for injury prevention and control at the Centers for Disease Control and Prevention may be used to advocate or promote gun control." The National Rifle Association (NRA) interpreted this as a reason to stop research on the most common means of suicide in the United States, or the most used weapons of homicide, because it might — or might not — be used to advocate gun control.

Two highly respected scientists summarize recent research on gun deaths:

> There is only very sparse scientific evidence [regarding] . . . which policies will be effective . . . Even the seemingly popular view that violent crime would be reduced by laws prohibiting the purchase or possession of guns by people with mental illness was deemed to have only moderate supporting evidence.
>
> *[Leshner & Dzau, 2018, p. 1195]*

It is unfair to blame Congress, or to focus on guns. Indeed, there are unanswered questions about almost every aspect of human development, and opinions precede or distort research. Human thinking is limited by culture and context.

Awareness of bias is only the first step for the next cohort of developmental scientists. They will build on what is known, mindful of what needs to be explored, raising questions that earlier cohorts have not asked. The goal of our study remains the same, to help everyone fulfill their potential. The next 14 chapters are a beginning.

ESPECIALLY FOR Future Researchers and Science Writers Do any ethical guidelines apply when an author writes about the experiences of family members, friends, or research participants? (see response, page 31)

THINK CRITICALLY: Can you think of an additional question that researchers should answer?

WHAT HAVE YOU LEARNED?

1. Why does correlation not prove causation?
2. What are the advantages and disadvantages of quantitative research?
3. What are the advantages and disadvantages of qualitative research?
4. What is the role of the IRB?
5. Why might a political leader avoid funding developmental research?
6. What questions about human development remain to be answered?

SUMMARY

The Life-Span Perspective

1. The assumption that growth is linear has been replaced by the realization that both continuity and discontinuity are part of every life. Developmental gains and losses are apparent lifelong.

2. Time is a crucial variable. Everyone changes with age. Critical periods are times when something must occur for normal development; sensitive periods are times when a particular kind of development occurs most easily.

3. Development occurs within many contexts and cultures, as Urie Bronfenbrenner's ecological-systems approach emphasizes. Each person is situated within larger systems of family, school, community, and culture.

4. Each cohort is influenced by the innovations and events of their historical period, and each person is affected by their socioeconomic status (SES), with effects of both cohort and SES varying depending on the age and circumstances of the person.

5. Culture, ethnicity, and race are social constructions, concepts created by society. Culture includes beliefs and patterns; ethnicity refers to ancestral heritage. Race is also a social construction, sometimes mistakenly thought to be biological.

6. Humans have many ways to think or act, influenced by age, gender, and culture. Developmentalists try to avoid the difference-equals-deficit error. A multidisciplinary, dynamic-systems approach is needed because each person develops in many ways — biosocially, cognitively, and psychosocially — simultaneously.

7. Throughout life, human development is plastic. Brains and behaviors are molded by experiences. Cultures also adjust to social needs.

Development and Science

8. The universality of human development and the uniqueness of each individual's development are evident in both nature (the genes) and nurture (the environment); no person is quite like another. Nature and nurture always interact, and each human characteristic is affected by that interaction.

9. Differential susceptibility is evident when we study nature and nurture. Each person's genes and experiences affect their vulnerability to developmental change, for better or worse.

Using the Scientific Method

10. Commonly used research methods are observation, experiments, and surveys. Each can provide insight, yet each is limited. Replication, or using other methods to examine the same topic, is needed.

11. Developmentalists study change over time, often with cross-sectional and longitudinal research. Cross-sequential research, which combines the other two methods, attempts to avoid the pitfalls of cross-sectional and longitudinal studies.

Cautions and Challenges from Science

12. A correlation is a statistic that indicates that two variables are connected, both increasing in tandem or changing in opposite directions. Correlation does not prove cause.

13. Quantitative research provides numerical data. This makes it best for comparing contexts and cultures via verified statistics. By contrast, more nuanced data come from qualitative research, which reports on individual lives. Both are useful.

14. Ethical behavior is crucial in all of the sciences. Results must be fairly gathered, reported, and interpreted. Participants must be informed and protected.

15. The most important ethical question is whether scientists are designing, conducting, analyzing, publishing, and applying the research that is most critically needed. This does not always occur: The next cohort of developmental scholars will add to our scientific knowledge.

KEY TERMS

life-span perspective (p. 2)
critical period (p. 3)
sensitive period (p. 3)
ecological-systems approach (p. 4)
dynamic-systems approach (p. 5)
cohort (p. 5)
socioeconomic status (SES) (p. 6)

culture (p. 7)
social construction (p. 7)
difference-equals-deficit error (p. 8)
ethnic group (p. 10)
race (p. 10)
intersectionality (p. 11)
plasticity (p. 14)
nature (p. 14)
nurture (p. 14)

differential susceptibility (p. 15)
science of human development (p. 16)
scientific method (p. 18)
hypothesis (p. 18)
empirical evidence (p. 18)
replication (p. 18)
scientific observation (p. 20)
experiment (p. 21)

independent variable (p. 21)
dependent variable (p. 21)
survey (p. 22)
cross-sectional research (p. 23)
longitudinal research (p. 24)
cross-sequential research (p. 24)
correlation (p. 26)
quantitative research (p. 27)
qualitative research (p. 27)

APPLICATIONS

1. It is said that culture is pervasive, but that people are unaware of it. List 30 things you did *today* that you might have done differently in another culture. Begin with how and where you woke up.

2. How would your life be different if your parents were much higher or lower in SES than they are? Consider all three domains.

3. A longitudinal case study can be insightful but is also limited in generality. Interview one of your older relatives and explain what aspects of their childhood are unique and what might be relevant for everyone.

ESPECIALLY FOR ANSWERS

Response for Nurses (from p. 22) Experiments are the only way to determine cause-and-effect relationships. If we want to be sure that a new drug or treatment is safe and effective, an experiment must be conducted to establish that the drug or treatment improves health.

Response for Future Researchers (from p. 25) There is no best method for collecting data. The method used depends on many factors, such as the age of participants (infants can't complete questionnaires), the question being researched, and the time frame.

Response for Future Researchers and Science Writers (from p. 29) Yes. Anyone you write about must give consent and be fully informed about your intentions. They can be identified by name only if they give permission. For example, family members gave permission before anecdotes about them were included in this text. My nephew David read the first draft of his story (see pp.14–15) and is proud to have his experiences used to teach others.

OBSERVATION QUIZ ANSWERS

Answer to Observation Quiz (from p. 7) Asian Americans. This partly because those from East Asia (Japan, China, South Korea) tend to be relatively high in SES, while some from South Asia (Bangladesh, Pakistan) are quite poor.

Answer to Observation Quiz (from p. 8) Note the hijab and the cross. Often people who are Muslim and Christian differ culturally.

Tetra Images-Jessica Peterson/Brand X Pictures/Getty Images

CHAPTER 2

Theories

On a frigid November night, Larry DePrimo, a 25-year-old police officer on duty in Times Square, saw a man with "blisters the size of his palm" on his bare feet. He asked the man his shoe size (12) and bought him boots. As DePrimo bent down to help the man don his gift, a tourist from Arizona snapped his photo. Days later, the tourist wrote to the New York Police Department, who put the image on their Web site. It went viral.

Then came theories, in half a million comments on Facebook.

Commentators asked: Was this real or a hoax? Was DePrimo's act typical ("most cops are honorable, decent people"), atypical ("truly exceptional"), or in between ("not all NYC cops are short-tempered, profiling, or xenophobic")? Is the officer young and naive? Are his parents proud? Was his assignment (anti-terrorism patrol) neglected?

One year later, DePrimo was promoted. His proud father, wanting people to understand the totality of his son, said that his service record was the reason, not the boots. DePrimo himself was pleasantly surprised, commenting on the new detective badge on his shirt: "I look down and it's still unreal to me" (DePrimo, quoted in Antenucci, 2013). For him and for all of us, a badge is a symbol, infused with decades of theories about honor and country.

In this chapter, we explain six insightful theories of human development. Three of them—psychoanalytic, behaviorist, and cognitive—have been touchstones for developmentalists for decades and are called "grand theories." Each has evolved over the years, with twenty-first-century versions of the originals set out by Freud, Pavlov, and Piaget, and extended by Erikson, Skinner, and many others. The other three theories—sociocultural, evolutionary, selectivity—are more recent. All provide insight on life-span development.

What Will You Know?

1. What is practical about a theory?
2. Do childhood experiences affect adults?
3. Would you be a different person if you grew up in another place or century?
4. Why do we need so many theories?

Theories of Development

Theories organize scattered facts and confusing observations into patterns, weaving the details into a meaningful whole. A **developmental theory** is a comprehensive statement of general principles that provides a framework for understanding how and why people change as they grow older. This is much more than a hunch or speculation: Developmental theories emerge from data, survive analysis, lead to experiments, and raise new questions.

developmental theory A group of ideas, assumptions, and generalizations that interpret and illuminate the thousands of observations that have been made about human growth. A developmental theory provides a framework for explaining the patterns and problems of development.

Theory and Practice

Sometimes people think of theories as impractical. Not at all. As Kurt Lewin (1945) once quipped, "Nothing is as practical as a good theory." In this, he disputes the idea that theory and practice are opposites. Like many other scientists, Lewin found that theories not only organize thoughts and experiences so people can grasp generalities and conclusions, but also that theories inform daily life.

For example, what if a child tells their mother, "I hate you"? A theory can guide the mother's reaction. Punishment? Love? Laughter? Or maybe no response.

Imagine trying to build a house without a design. You might have willing workers and all the raw materials: the bricks, the wood, the nails. But without tools and a plan you could not proceed. Science provides the tools; theories provide the plan; scientists are the workers who follow the plan.

Sometimes, over the years, the house needs more work—another bedroom, a new roof, an additional door. Likewise, theories are revised over time. But without theories, we would be lost with a jumble of observations, confused as to how they fit together to make a life.

- Theories produce *hypotheses*.
- Theories generate *discoveries*.
- Theories offer *practical guidance*.

Remember from Chapter 1 that testing a hypothesis is the third step of science, the middle of the five steps. To get to that pivot, scientists need a question and a hypothesis. That is one reason that theories are needed, to stimulate Steps 1 and 2. Once the question is framed as a hypothesis, the actual research begins, which then leads to analysis and conclusions to be shared with other scientists, to confirm, extend, revise, or refute the theory.

Theories and Facts

Sometimes people say dismissively, "that's just a theory," as if theories were disconnected from facts. In truth, facts are essential: A good theory begins with facts and discovers more of them. As one scientist explains, imagine a world without facts, "a world of ignorance where many possibilities seem equally likely. . . . [with] unreliable conclusions. . . . [and] shoddy evidence," (Berg, 2018, p. 379). Theories and facts work together. Facts lead to theories, and then theories lead to discovery of previously unrecognized facts.

"I'm going to refer to an educational theory which was first published in February and is still applicable today."

The Test of Time Grand theories have endured for decades and still guide contemporary scientists.

We are born with the desire to understand the world, and that desire is evident at every age. Adolescents have theories about what needs changing in society, young adults have theories about who would make a good mate, parents have theories about the best way to discipline their children, older adults have theories about when and how to retire. In each case, those theories begin with facts and questions and proceed from there.

It is a fact, not a theory, that everywhere and for all time, part of being a person is to be "perpetually driven to look for deeper explanations of our experience, and broader and more reliable predictions about it" (Gopnik, 2001, p. 66). The perpetual need to understand is evident throughout history.

All six theories echo ideas written by ancient sages in Greece, China, India, and elsewhere, and all are considered relevant by some contemporary scientists. Insights from these theories might apply to all humans, past, present, and future.

Therefore, consider these six theories a touchstone, useful for understanding human development. None is the final word. As explained in Chapter 1, human growth is dynamic, always affected by cohort and culture. Theories are a springboard. Get ready to leap forward.

WHAT HAVE YOU LEARNED?

1. What is the focus of a developmental theory?
2. What three things do theories do?
3. How are facts and theories connected?
4. Who develops theories—everyone or just scientists?

psychoanalytic theory A theory of human development that contends that irrational, unconscious drives and motives underlie human behavior.

Freud at Work In addition to being the world's first psychoanalyst, Sigmund Freud was a prolific writer. His many papers and case histories, primarily descriptions of his patients' symptoms and sexual urges, helped make the psychoanalytic perspective a dominant force for much of the twentieth century.

AKG/Science Source

The Grand Theories

Some theories are called "grand theories" because they are comprehensive and have endured for decades. These three, originating with Freud, Pavlov, and Piaget, have inspired thousands of scientists to revise, refute, and then restructure them, and each has led to newer, better theories (Erikson, Skinner, information processing). That ongoing process is evidence that these grand theories are still useful, which is why we begin with them.

Psychoanalytic Theory: Freud and Erikson

Inner drives, deep motives, and unconscious needs rooted in childhood—especially the first six years—are the focus of the first grand theory, called **psychoanalytic theory**. These unconscious forces are thought to influence every aspect of thinking and behavior, from the smallest details of daily life to the crucial choices of a lifetime.

Freud's Ideas

Sigmund Freud (1856–1939) was an Austrian physician who treated patients with mental illness. He listened to their remembered dreams and to their uncensored streams of thought, and he read widely in classic Greek literature. From that, he constructed an elaborate, multifaceted theory.

According to Freud, development in the first six years of life occurs in three stages. His theory is sometimes called *psychosexual*, because each stage is characterized by sexual interest and pleasure arising from a particular part of the body.

In infancy, the erotic body part is the mouth (the *oral stage*); in early childhood, it is the anus (the *anal stage*); in the preschool years, it is the penis (the *phallic stage*), a source of pride and fear among boys and a reason for sorrow and envy among girls. [One neo-Freudian, Karen Horney (1967), was particularly critical of this aspect of Freud's theory, suggesting that boys had "womb envy" because they could not give birth.] According to Freud, children of every gender have a quiet, nonsexual period (*latency*), and then the *genital stage* arrives at puberty, lasting throughout adulthood. (**Table 2.1** describes stages in Freud's theory.)

Freud maintained that early sensual satisfaction (from stimulation of the lips, anus, or penis) is linked to major developmental conflicts, needs, and challenges. During the oral stage, for example, sucking provides the infant not only nourishment but also erotic joy and attachment to the mother. Next, during the anal stage, pleasures arise from self-control, initially with toileting, but later with wanting everything to be clean, neat, and regular (an "anal personality"). (Freud's ideas about personality in adulthood are noted later in the book.)

TABLE 2.1

Comparison of Freud's Psychosexual and Erikson's Psychosocial Stages

Approximate Age	Freud (Psychosexual)	Erikson (Psychosocial)
Birth to 1 year	*Oral Stage* The lips, tongue, and gums are the focus of pleasurable sensations in the baby's body, and sucking and feeding are the most stimulating activities.	*Trust vs. Mistrust* Babies either trust that others will satisfy their basic needs, including nourishment, warmth, cleanliness, and physical contact, **or** develop mistrust about the care of others.
1–3 years	*Anal Stage* The anus is the focus of pleasurable sensations in the baby's body, and toilet training is the most important activity.	*Autonomy vs. Shame and Doubt* Children either become self-sufficient in many activities, including toileting, feeding, walking, exploring, and talking, **or** doubt their own abilities.
3–6 years	*Phallic Stage* The phallus, or penis, is the most important body part, and pleasure is derived from genital stimulation. Boys are proud of their penises; girls wonder why they don't have them.	*Initiative vs. Guilt* Children either try to undertake many adultlike activities **or** internalize the limits and prohibitions set by parents. They feel either adventurous **or** guilty.
6–11 years	*Latency* Not really a stage, latency is an interlude. Sexual needs are quiet; psychic energy flows into sports, schoolwork, and friendship.	*Industry vs. Inferiority* Children busily practice and then master new skills **or** feel inferior, unable to do anything well.
Adolescence	*Genital Stage* The genitals are the focus of pleasurable sensations, and the young person seeks sexual stimulation and satisfaction in heterosexual relationships.	*Identity vs. Role Confusion* Adolescents ask themselves "Who am I?" They establish sexual, political, religious, and vocational identities **or** are confused about their roles.
Adulthood	Freud believed that the genital stage lasts throughout adulthood. He also said that the goal of a healthy life is "to love and to work."	*Intimacy vs. Isolation* Young adults seek companionship and love **or** become isolated from others, fearing rejection. *Generativity vs. Stagnation* Middle-aged adults contribute to future generations through work, creative activities, and parenthood **or** they stagnate. *Integrity vs. Despair* Older adults try to make sense of their lives, either seeing life as a meaningful whole **or** despairing at goals never reached.

A Legendary Couple In his first 30 years, Erikson never fit into a particular local community, since he frequently changed nations, schools, and professions. Then he met Joan. In their six decades of marriage, they raised a family and wrote several books. If Erikson had published his theory at age 73 (when this photograph was taken) instead of in his 40s, would he still have described life as a series of crises?

ESPECIALLY FOR Teachers Your kindergartners are talkative and always moving. They almost never sit quietly and listen to you. What would Erik Erikson recommend? (see response, page 56)

behaviorism A grand theory of human development that studies observable behavior. Behaviorism is also called *learning theory* because it describes the laws and processes by which behavior is learned.

Erikson's Ideas

Many of Freud's followers became famous theorists themselves—Carl Jung, Alfred Adler, and Karen Horney among them. They agreed with Freud that early-childhood emotions affect everyone, often unconsciously, but they also expanded and modified Freud's ideas.

For scholars in human development, another neo-Freudian, Erik Erikson (1902–1994), is particularly insightful. He proposed a theory of the entire life span, with eight stages, each characterized by a particular challenge, or *developmental crisis* (Erikson, 1993a) (summarized in Table 2.1).

Erikson emphasized the social contexts of development; his theory is called *psychosocial*. He understood that the people—family, friends, and larger community—who nurture each person are crucial for their development. Those people follow the norms of their culture, and that makes some stages easier or more difficult.

For example, in the United States, the fifth stage, *identity versus role confusion*, is particularly difficult: Erikson (1994) wrote an entire book about the lifelong implications of the identity crisis. (Erikson's stages are mentioned where relevant throughout this book.)

Typically, development at each stage leads to neither extreme but to something in between. For example, in the sixth stage, *intimacy versus isolation*, young adults seek closeness with another person, usually in a socially recognized commitment such as marriage that involves emotional, practical, and sexual intimacy. The opposite would be an isolated person who always keeps to themselves, trusting no one, unable to commit to anyone.

In actuality, people have moments of close intimacy and moments of aloneness. It is rare for a marriage to be intimate in every way lifelong, or for a person to be a loner all the time. What Erikson recognized by describing that sixth stage was that the dominant emotional need for young adults is social connection, because the drive for intimacy is strongest at this stage.

In sum, Erikson's psychoanalytic theory diverges in two crucial ways from Freud's:

1. It is psychosocial, not psychosexual. Erikson's stages emphasized family and culture.
2. It is lifelong, with three stages after adolescence.

Behaviorism

Psychology in the United States for most of the twentieth century was dominated by the second grand theory, **behaviorism**, which describes how a particular response (behavior) is learned (conditioned). This theory began in Russia, with Ivan Pavlov (1849–1936), a medical doctor who had already won a Nobel Prize for his medical research.

Classical Conditioning

Pavlov decided to study salivation, because he noticed that dogs "lick their wounds" to heal themselves. Is something in saliva beneficial? Pavlov decided to collect saliva and analyze its chemistry. Consequently, he attached a test tube to a hole in the cheeks of some dogs, who were led to a bowl of food. As they smelled the food and then ate, their saliva was collected.

He noticed that his research dogs soon drooled not only at the smell of food but also at the sound of the footsteps of the people who would bring them to the food. This observation led him to perform a famous experiment: He conditioned dogs to salivate (response) when hearing a particular noise (stimulus). That learning process is called **classical conditioning**.

In the next decade, Pavlov performed hundreds of experiments to examine the link between something (such as a sight, a sound, a touch) that affected a living creature and the reaction of that creature. Technically, he was interested in how a *stimulus* affects a *response*.

In one series of studies, Pavlov sounded a tone just before presenting food. After a number of repetitions of the tone-then-food sequence, the dogs began salivating at the sound even when there was no food. This simple experiment demonstrated classical conditioning (also called *respondent conditioning*).

In classical conditioning, a person or animal learns to associate a neutral stimulus with a meaningful one, gradually responding to the neutral stimulus in the same way as to the meaningful one. In Pavlov's original experiment, the dog associated the tone (the neutral stimulus) with food (the meaningful stimulus), becoming conditioned to respond to the tone as if it were the food itself. The tone was no longer neutral but became a conditioned stimulus, and the conditioned response was evidence that learning had occurred.

Behaviorists describe dozens of instances of classical conditioning in humans. Infants learn to smile at their parents because they associate them with food and play; toddlers become afraid of busy streets if the noise of traffic repeatedly frightens them; students enjoy — or fear — school, depending on what happened in kindergarten.

Think of how some people react to a wasp, or a final exam, or a police car in the rearview mirror. Such reactions are learned; an announcement about a future exam triggers sweat or chills in some students — as would not happen to a child with no exam experience. Many students find that the stress hormones triggered by seeing the exam paper makes them forget what they know — an unwelcome conditioned response.

Behaviorism in the United States

The first of three famous Americans who championed behaviorism was John B. Watson (1878–1958). He argued that if psychology was to be a true science, psychologists should examine only what they could see and measure, not invisible impulses. In his words:

> Why don't we make what we can *observe* the real field of psychology? Let us limit ourselves to things that can be observed, and formulate laws concerning only those things. . . . We can observe *behavior — what the organism does or says.*
> [*Watson, 1924/1998, p. 6*]

According to Watson, everything is learned. He wrote:

> Give me a dozen healthy infants, well-formed, and my own specified world to bring them up in and I'll guarantee to take any one at random and train him to become any type of specialist I might select — doctor, lawyer, artist, merchant-chief, and yes, even beggar-man and thief, regardless of his talents, penchants, tendencies, abilities, vocations, and race of his ancestors.
> [*Watson, 1924/1998, p. 82*]

Other North American psychologists developed behaviorism to study observable behavior, objectively and scientifically. They undertook hundreds of thousands of experiments with mice and pigeons, as well as with people, seeking the laws that govern behavior of every living creature at every age.

According to this theory, all learning follows the same laws: Everything that people do and feel is learned, step-by-step, via conditioning. For example, newborns need to *learn* to suck on a nipple; infants *learn* to smile at a caregiver; preschoolers

classical conditioning The learning process in which a meaningful stimulus (such as the smell of food to a hungry animal) is connected with a neutral stimulus (such as the sound of a tone) that had no special meaning before conditioning. (Also called *respondent conditioning*.)

Hulton Deutsch/Getty Images

A Contemporary of Freud Ivan Pavlov was a physiologist who received the Nobel Prize in 1904 for his research on digestive processes. It was this line of study that led to his discovery of classical conditioning, when his research on dog saliva led to insight about learning.

● **Observation Quiz** How is Pavlov similar to Freud in appearance, and how do both look different from the other theorists pictured? (see answer, page 56) ↑

AP Images

Rats, Pigeons, and People B. F. Skinner is best known for his experiments with rats and pigeons, but he also applied his knowledge to human behavior. For his daughter, he designed a glass-enclosed crib in which temperature, humidity, and perceptual stimulation could be controlled to make her time in the crib enjoyable and educational. He encouraged her first attempts to talk by smiling and responding with words, affection, or other positive reinforcement.

operant conditioning The learning process by which a particular action is followed by something desired (which makes the person or animal more likely to repeat the action) or by something unwanted (which makes the action less likely to be repeated). (Also called *instrumental conditioning*.)

CHAPTER APP 2

 My Token Board

iOS:
https://tinyurl.com/yy6hmbuq

RELEVANT TOPIC:
Behaviorism and positive reinforcement for children

My Token Board is a visual reward system that helps motivate children of all ages and abilities to learn and complete tasks. The app's use of reinforcers is based on the principles of operant conditioning and effective with children who are on the autism spectrum.

---

learn to hold hands when crossing the street. Once conditioned learning occurs, it generalizes to other situations and stimuli. Babies are conditioned to suck on nipples for nourishment, which is why children suck lollipops and adults suck on cigars. Adults are friendly because they learned that behavior, because caregivers encouraged smiling in infancy. I still grab my adult children's hands when crossing the street.

Operant Conditioning

The most influential North American behaviorist was B. F. Skinner (1904–1990). He agreed with Pavlov that classical conditioning occurs, and with Watson that psychology should focus on observable behavior. But, as a good scientist, he extended their conclusions.

Skinner's most famous contribution was to recognize another type of conditioning — **operant conditioning** (also called *instrumental conditioning*) — in which animals (including people) act, and then something follows that action.

Thus, Skinner went beyond learning by association (classical conditioning, with one stimulus linked to another) and focused on consequences, on what happens *after* the response. If the consequence is enjoyable, the creature (any living thing — a bird, a mouse, a person) tends to repeat the behavior; if the consequence is unpleasant, the creature is unlikely to perform that action again.

According to Skinner (1953), almost all of our daily behavior, from saying "Good morning" to earning a paycheck, is the result of operant conditioning. Pleasant consequences are *reinforcers*. Behaviorists do not call them rewards, because what some people consider a reward may actually be a *punishment*, an unpleasant consequence.

For instance, a teacher might reward good behavior by giving the class extra recess time, but some children hate recess. Then recess is not a reinforcer.

The opposite is true as well: Something thought to be a punishment may actually be a reinforcer. For example, parents "punish" their children by withholding dessert. But if a child dislikes the dessert, being deprived of it is no punishment. The crucial question is, "what works to reinforce or punish a particular person?"

The answer varies by age, and also by differential susceptibility. For instance, adolescents find the excitement of risk-taking reinforcing. That was one conclusion of a study of violent teenagers: For them, the thrill of breaking the law was a powerful reinforcer, outweighing the pain of possible arrest and prison (Shulman et al., 2017).

Evident in the example is that immediate consequences are more potent than long-term ones, a phenomenon called *delay discounting*. A life-span perspective notes that, with maturation, immediacy does not always outweigh the future.

Behaviorism stresses the importance of the social context of past learning. For example, you may be puzzled that some abusive relationships continue for decades. Why would someone beat a romantic partner, and, if that happens, why doesn't the partner leave?

Behaviorists contend that they both learned destructive patterns in childhood. The abuser may have learned that people hit when they are angry and may have succeeded in school by being a bully. And the victim may have learned that being hit was an expression of love, perhaps because a spanking parent said, "I am doing this because I love you."

Remember, behaviorists focus on the *effect* a consequence has on future behavior, not whether it is intended to be a reward or a punishment. Children who misbehave again and again have been reinforced, not punished, for their actions, perhaps by their parents or teachers, perhaps by their friends, perhaps by themselves.

TABLE 2.2

Three Types of Learning

Behaviorism is also called *learning theory* because it emphasizes the learning process, as shown here.

Type of Learning	Learning Process	Result
Classical conditioning	Learning occurs through association.	Neutral stimulus becomes conditioned response.
Operant conditioning	Learning occurs through reinforcement and punishment.	Weak or rare responses become strong and frequent—or, with punishment, unwanted responses become extinct.
Social learning	Learning occurs through modeling what others do.	Observed behaviors become copied behaviors.

Social Learning

At first, behaviorists thought all behavior arose from a chain of learned responses, the result of (1) the association between one stimulus and another (classical conditioning) or (2) past reinforcement (operant conditioning). Hundreds of thousands of experiments inspired by learning theory demonstrated that both classical conditioning and operant conditioning occur in everyday life.

A crucial extension began with the third famous American behaviorist, Albert Bandura. He noticed that people at every age are social and observant. They do not merely react to their own personal conditioning. Instead, "people act on the environment. They create it, preserve it, transform it, and even destroy it. . . . [in] a socially embedded interplay" (Bandura, 2006, p. 167).

That social interplay is the foundation of **social learning theory** (see **Table 2.2**), which holds that humans sometimes learn without personal reinforcement. This learning often occurs through **modeling**, when people copy what they see others do (also called *observational learning*) (Bandura, 1986, 1997).

Modeling is not simple imitation: People copy only some actions, of some individuals, in some contexts. Sometimes they do the opposite of what they observed. That is also social learning.

Generally, modeling is most likely when the observer is uncertain or inexperienced (modeling is especially powerful in childhood) and when the model is admired, powerful, nurturing, or similar to the observer. Social learning occurs not only for behavior (haircuts? Shoes?) but also for morals (Bandura, 2016).

social learning theory An extension of behaviorism that emphasizes the influence that other people have over a person's behavior. Even without specific reinforcement, every individual learns many things through observation and imitation of other people. (Also called *observational learning.*)

modeling The central process of social learning, by which a person observes the actions of others and then copies them.

THINK CRITICALLY: Is your speech, hairstyle, or choice of shoes similar to those of your peers, or of an entertainer, or of a sports hero? Why?

Cognitive Theory

According to **cognitive theory**, thoughts and expectations profoundly affect attitudes, values, emotions, and actions. This may seem obvious now, but it was not always so. Social scientists describe a "cognitive revolution" that began around 1960, when *how* and *what* people think became important to understanding how and what people do.

Cognitive theory diverged from psychoanalytic theory (which emphasized hidden impulses) and behaviorism (which emphasized observed actions) to stress that thoughts are the crucial link between those impulses and actions.

The cognitive revolution continues: Contemporary researchers use new tools to study cognition, with neuroscience, large quantities of data, and body–mind

cognitive theory A grand theory of human development that focuses on changes in how people think over time. According to this theory, our thoughts shape our attitudes, beliefs, and behaviors.

Would You Talk to This Man? Children loved talking to Jean Piaget, and he learned by listening carefully—especially to their incorrect explanations, which no one had paid much attention to before. All his life, Piaget was absorbed with studying the way children think. He called himself a "genetic epistemologist"—one who studies how children gain knowledge about the world as they grow.

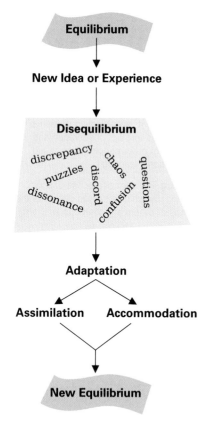

FIGURE 2.1

Challenge Me Most of us, most of the time, prefer the comfort of our conventional conclusions. According to Piaget, however, when new ideas disturb our thinking, we have an opportunity to expand our cognition with a broader and deeper understanding.

connections (e.g., Glenberg et al., 2013; Griffiths, 2015). This is further described in three chapters of this book: Chapters 5 (Neuroscience), 7 (Memory), and 9 (Cognition). To understand the impact of cognitive theory on development, we begin with Piaget.

Piaget's Stages of Development

Jean Piaget's (1896–1980) academic training was in biology, with a focus on shellfish—a background that taught him to observe small things, beginning with his own children. Piaget tested them as infants every day, taking detailed notes. His work over the next decades eventually led to the cognitive revolution.

Before Piaget, most scientists believed that babies could not yet think. But Piaget used scientific observation with his own three infants. Later he studied hundreds of schoolchildren. From this work emerged the central thesis of cognitive theory: *How* children think changes with time and experience, and those thought processes affect behavior. According to cognitive theory, to understand humans of any age, try to understand what they are thinking.

Piaget maintained that cognitive development occurs in four age-related periods, or stages: *sensorimotor*, *preoperational*, *concrete operational*, and *formal operational*. Each period is characterized by certain cognitive processes: Infants think via their senses; preschoolers have language but not logic; school-age children have simple logic; adolescents and adults can use formal, abstract logic (Inhelder & Piaget, 1958/2013b; Piaget, 1952/2011).

Piaget's ideas are presented in greater detail in Chapter 9. For now, what you need to understand is that at every age, Piaget found that intellectual advancement occurs because humans seek *cognitive equilibrium*—a state of mental balance. The easiest way to achieve this balance is to interpret new experiences through the lens of preexisting ideas.

Prejudices of all kinds occur because it is easier to think in simple terms, but our thoughts become deeper with cognitive disequilibrium. Ignorance is challenged when we live in another culture, or learn facts that contradict a familiar thought, or become friends with someone who challenges a stereotype. Those experiences cause cognitive development, according to Piaget.

As **Figure 2.1** illustrates, disequilibrium advances cognition if it leads to adaptive thinking. Piaget describes two types of adaptation:

- *Assimilation*: New experiences are reinterpreted to fit, or *assimilate*, into old ideas.
- *Accommodation*: Old ideas are restructured to include, or *accommodate*, new experiences.

Accommodation is more difficult than assimilation, but it advances thought. New concepts are developed when old ones fail. In Piagetian terms, people *construct* ideas based on their experiences; the idea of constructed knowledge is that knowledge is built in the mind, an inner process not an external one. For example, infants first assimilate everything using their senses—they taste and touch everything they can. But experience requires accommodation: They learn what should *not* be put in their mouths.

You probably are in the midst of your own cognitive revolution. One purpose of college, and of this book, is to challenge students, to help them expand their minds.

Information Processing

Piaget is credited with discovering that mental constructs affect behavior, an idea now accepted by most social scientists. However, many think Piaget's theories were limited. *Neuroscience* (the science that studies the brain) and cross-cultural studies (within nations as well as between them) have extended our understanding of cognitive development.

This is most evident in **information-processing theory**, an expression of cognitive theory inspired by the input, programming, memory, and output of the computer. When conceptualized in that way, thinking is affected by the synapses and neurons of the brain. (Chapter 5 is entirely devoted to neuroscience, and Chapter 7 begins with information processing. Here we focus on the theory about cognition that undergirds this approach.)

Instead of interpreting *responses* by infants and children, as Piaget did, this cognitive theory focuses on the *processes* of thought—that is, when, why, and how neurons fire before a response. Brain activity is traced back to what activated those neurons. Information-processing theorists examine stimuli and responses from the senses, body movements, hormones, and organs, all of which affect thinking (Glenberg et al., 2013). These scientists believe that details of cognitive processes shed light on what people think and know, and that by understanding those details we can better understand cognition.

For example, our emotions affect our thinking, and then our thinking affects our behavior. When we are happy, for example, we are less critical of other people and therefore we act more kindly toward them. Information processing looks at the biochemical origins of emotions, at the underlying neurotransmitters, hormones, digestive processes, and so on that affect our happiness and hence our actions.

Until we consider the gut and brain connections that lead to emotions, we cannot fully understand why people act as they do (Damasio, 2018). Hundreds of scientists now focus on *biomarkers* (signs in the body), such as blood pressure, brain waves, or hormones, to reveal how bodies affect thoughts, and thoughts affect actions (Buss et al., 2018).

This theory has led to many practical applications, when one person seeks to expand the thinking of another. For example, in teaching counselors how best to advise other people to change their behavior, an information-processing perspective begins by uncovering each client's underlying cognitive approach (Tangen & Borders, 2017).

More broadly, with the aid of sensitive technology, information-processing research has overturned some of Piaget's findings, especially his description of what children understand at what age. However, the basic tenet of cognitive theory is equally true for Piaget, neuroscience, and information processing: *Ideas matter*.

Thus, how children interpret a hypothetical social situation, such as whether they anticipate welcome or rejection, affects the quality of their actual friendships; how teenagers think about heaven and hell influences their sexual activity; how adults view the proper role of women affects whether or not they have sex, marry, become parents, divorce. For everyone, ideas frame situations and affect actions.

information-processing theory
A perspective that compares human thinking processes, by analogy, to computer analysis of data, including sensory input, connections, stored memories, and output.

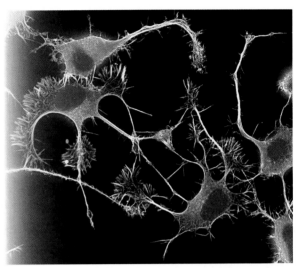

Brain Cells in Action Neurons reach out to other neurons, shown here in an expansion microscopy photo that was impossible even a decade ago. No wonder Piaget's description of the four stages of cognition needs revision from the information-processing perspective.

WHAT HAVE YOU LEARNED?

1. What is the basic emphasis of psychoanalytic theory?
2. What similarities and differences are found between Freud's and Erikson's theories of adulthood?
3. How does the central focus of behaviorism differ from psychoanalytic theory?
4. When is social learning most powerful?
5. What did Piaget discover that earlier psychologists did not realize?
6. How does information processing contribute to the cognitive revolution?
7. What does neuroscience make possible that was impossible for Freud, Skinner, or Piaget?

Newer Theories

The three theories just explained are comprehensive and enduring, which is why they are called *grand*. But they all share a major limitation: They began with men in Europe a century ago. Of course, background factors limit women and non-Europeans as well, but at least newer theories benefit from another perspective. Developmental scientists today are as often women as men, benefiting from extensive global, historical, and multidisciplinary research.

This is evident in each of the next trio of theories. Sociocultural theorists benefit from anthropologists who report on cultures in every part of the globe; evolutionary psychologists use data from archeologists who examine the bones of humans who died 100,000 years ago; selection theories began with medical studies that found the many ways the human body compensates for disabilities.

As newer theories, none has been refined by decades of later application and clarification. Nonetheless, each provides what theories do best: a practical way to organize the many thoughts, observations, and sensations of the life span.

Sociocultural Theory: Vygotsky and Beyond

sociocultural theory A newer theory that holds that development results from the dynamic interaction of each person with the surrounding social and cultural forces.

The central thesis of **sociocultural theory** is that human development results from the dynamic interaction between developing persons and their surrounding society. Culture is not something external that impinges on developing persons but is internalized, integral to everyday attitudes and actions. This idea is so central to understanding the life span that it was first explained in the multicultural perspective of Chapter 1. Now it is further noted as a theory of development.

Teaching and Guidance

The pioneer of the sociocultural perspective was Lev Vygotsky (1896–1934). Like the three original grand theorists, he was born at the end of the nineteenth century, but unlike them, he studied Asian and European groups of many faiths, languages, and social contexts. He noted that people everywhere were taught whatever beliefs and habits were valued within their community and studied those variations.

Dr. James Wertsch

Affection for Children Vygotsky lived in Russia from 1896 to 1934, when war, starvation, and revolution led to the deaths of millions. Throughout this turmoil, Vygotsky focused on learning. His love of children is suggested by this portrait: He and his daughter have their arms around each other.

He was both celebrated and marginalized during his lifetime, as the turbulent politics of Russia lurched from one government to another. After his death from tuberculosis at age 38, his work was admired and then banned. Partly because of international politics, his writing was not translated and widely read in the United States until the end of the twentieth century (e.g., Vygotsky, 2012).

Among his many ideas, one that has been increasingly influential in developmental psychology is that people develop not in isolation but rather in relationship to the culture of their community, as transmitted by the words and actions of other people. In Vygotsky's view, everyone, schooled or not, is guided by mentors in an **apprenticeship in thinking** (Vygotsky, 2012).

apprenticeship in thinking Vygotsky's term for how cognition is stimulated and developed in people by more skilled members of society.

guided participation The process by which people learn from others who guide their experiences and explorations.

The word *apprentice* once had a specific meaning, often spelled out in a legal contract that detailed what a novice would learn from a master, and what that learner must do. For example, in earlier centuries, a boy wanting to repair shoes would be apprenticed to a cobbler, learning the trade while assisting his teacher.

Vygotsky believed that children become apprentices as they learn, guided by knowledgeable parents, teachers, and other people. Mentors teach children how to think within their culture by explaining ideas, asking questions, demonstrating actions.

To describe this process, Vygotsky developed the concept of **guided participation**, the method used by parents, teachers, and entire societies to teach novices expected skills, values, and habits. Tutors engage learners (*apprentices*) in joint activities, offering "mutual involvement in several widespread cultural practices with great importance for learning: narratives, routines, and play" (Rogoff, 2003, p. 285).

Active apprenticeship and sensitive guidance are central to sociocultural theory because we all depend on the knowledge of others. Sociocultural theorists contend that most human beliefs are social constructions, not natural laws, and thus societies need to teach them.

For example, Vygotsky thought that children with disabilities should be educated (Vygotsky, 1994b). This belief was not part of U.S. culture until about 1970, when a sociocultural shift occurred, propelled mostly by parents of such children. Many other social constructions—about the role of women, about professional sports, about family—have been revised in the past half century.

Sociocultural theory stresses that customs are shaped by people, as well as vice versa. The culture provides tools, or *artifacts*, that aid a particular kind of learning. In contemporary North America, smartphones are such an artifact, teaching children patterns of thought, behavior, and skills that the current culture values.

The Zone of Proximal Development

According to sociocultural theory, all learning is social, whether people are learning a manual skill, a social custom, or a language. As part of the apprenticeship of thinking, a mentor (parent, peer, or professional) finds the learner's *zone of proximal development* (ZPD), an imaginary area surrounding the learner that contains the skills, knowledge, and concepts that are close (proximal) to being grasped but not yet reached. (Vygotsky's ideas, including the ZPD, are further explained in Chapter 9.)

Through sensitive assessment of each learner, mentors engage mentees within their zone. Together, in a "process of joint construction," new knowledge is attained (Valsiner, 2006). The mentor must avoid two opposite dangers: boredom and failure. Some frustration is permitted, but the learner must be actively engaged, never passive or overwhelmed (see **Figure 2.2**).

A mentor must sense whether support or freedom is needed and how peers can help (they may be the best mentors). Skilled teachers know when a person's zone of proximal development expands and shifts. The shared language of both mentor and mentee is an integral part of the sociocultural process of education. Words are the tools of thought.

Excursions into and through the zone of proximal development are everywhere. At the thousand or so science museums in the United States, exhibits are designed to guide children's scientific learning (Haden, 2010). Fifty years ago, there were few science museums: Now almost every city has one—a sociocultural shift as the culture recognizes the significance of STEM (science, technology, engineering, math).

Consider another example. Within the past decade, biking to work has become an accepted, even admired, behavior. Children are expected to know how to ride a bicycle. How do they learn that? There are many possibilities, but to illustrate the sociocultural understanding of apprenticeship, consider how a father might teach a daughter.

Dad begins by rolling his child along on a small bike, supporting her weight while telling her to keep her hands on the handlebars, to push the right and left pedals in rhythm, and to look straight ahead. As she becomes more comfortable and confident, he jogs beside the bike, still holding it upright himself, praising her for steadily pedaling.

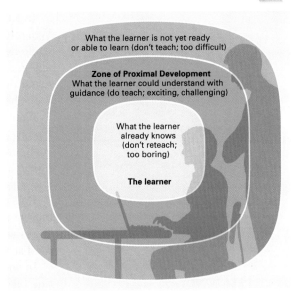

FIGURE 2.2
The Magic Middle Somewhere between the boring and the impossible is the zone of proximal development, where interaction between teacher and learner results in knowledge never before grasped or skills not already mastered. The intellectual excitement of that zone is the origin of the joy that both instruction and study can bring.

In later days or weeks, he runs beside her, lightly holding only the handlebars. When he senses that she can maintain her balance, he urges her to pedal faster while he loosens his grip. Perhaps without realizing it, she rides on her own, ideally in a wide place without cars or hard pavement. If she falls, he picks her up, reassuring her that she is not seriously hurt and that she is getting better. Someday soon she waves goodbye and bikes around the block.

Note that this is not instruction by preset rules. Sociocultural learning is active: No one learns bike-riding by reading and memorizing written instructions, and no good teacher merely repeats a memorized script. Guided practice in the zone of proximal development is essential: The mentor must know exactly what, when, and how support is needed.

Role models and cultural tools also teach, according to sociocultural theory. The bicycle-riding child wants to learn because she has seen other children biking, and stores sell tricycles, training wheels, and small bikes without pedals. Thus, cultural artifacts guide learning.

In another culture, everything might be different. In some nations, no females ride bikes, and no fathers teach their daughters, or even allow them outside the house without a female companion. Recognizing such cultural differences is crucial for understanding development, according to this theory. Children in every culture are taught to walk, dress, and behave in ways that their culture believes are proper.

I experience reactions every day that show the power of sociocultural learning. On crowded subways, often some younger man sees my white hair and gives me his seat. I take it, thanking him. This is the result of our apprenticeship: I may in fact be more able to stand than he is, but we are responding to cultural norms. Some of these come from childhood (one man said, in response to my thank you, "my mother would kill me if I didn't give you a seat"), and some are broadcast by loudspeaker announcements: "Offer your seat to someone who is pregnant or elderly."

Universals and Specifics

By emphasizing the impact of each culture, sociocultural theory aims to be sensitive to everyone, everywhere. Thus, mentors, attuned to ever-shifting abilities and motivation, continually urge new competence—the next level, not the moon.

For their part, learners ask questions, show interest, and demonstrate progress, which informs and inspires the mentors. When education goes well, both mentor and learner are fully engaged and productive within the zone. Particular skills and lessons vary enormously, but the overall process is the same.

One of the most important insights from sociocultural theory regards family. Universally, children thrive best when they grow up within families. However, the specifics of family type and family relationships vary a great deal, a topic discussed later. A View from Science presents a small example—children's family drawings (Rübeling et al., 2011).

Evolutionary Theory

You are likely familiar with Charles Darwin and his ideas, first published 150 years ago, regarding the evolution of plants, insects, and birds over billions of years (Darwin, 1859). But you may not realize that serious research on human development inspired by **evolutionary theory** is quite recent (Simpson & Kenrick, 2013). As a proponent of this theory recently wrote:

> Evolutionary psychology . . . is a revolutionary new science, a true synthesis of modern principles of psychology and evolutionary biology.
>
> *[Buss, 2015, p. xv]*

The basic idea of evolutionary psychology is that in order to understand the emotions, impulses, and habits of humans over the life span, we must appreciate

evolutionary theory When used in human development, the idea that many current human emotions and impulses are a legacy from thousands of years ago.

A VIEW FROM SCIENCE

Children's Drawings

Children's drawings may reflect their emotions. In the United States and Western Europe, well-adjusted children are expected to draw their families with smiling people, holding on to each other or with their arms raised. By contrast, if a child draws a family with small people, neutral facial expressions, and arms downward, that suggests that the child is not securely attached to the family (Fury et al., 1997).

This interpretation is increasingly challenged by drawings produced by children in Africa (Gernhardt et al., 2013). A study compared the family drawings of 32 middle-class 6-year-olds from Berlin, Germany, with the family drawings of 31 children from rural areas of Cameroon (Gernhardt et al., 2016). (Note that this study compared contrasting economic and urban cultures, as well as contrasting nations.) The Cameroonian children were no less happy and loved by their caregivers, but they drew small people (see **Figure 2.3**).

The drawings of all 63 children were rated on 20 features used to describe the attachment of children to their caregivers

FIGURE 2.3

Standing Firm When children draw their families, many child therapists look for signs of trouble—such as small, frowning people with hands down floating in space. But cross-cultural research shows that such depictions reflect local norms. The Cameroonian 6-year-olds were as well adjusted in their local community as were the German children.

(Kaplan & Main, 1986). Attachment is considered a universal indicator of the relationship between caregivers and children, and thus measuring it has become crucial for many researchers.

The drawings of children from the two cultures were quite different. Yet, research on attachment finds, overall, that children in Africa are at least as often securely attached as children elsewhere. This research is among many studies that suggest that, before Westerners intervene with families elsewhere to make them more responsive to their children, they need to understand the goals within each culture (Morelli et al., 2018).

This research is evidence for the need for sociocultural theory: The cultural context needs to be considered in order to understand people of any age, from newborns to centenarians. The authors "substantiated children's family drawings as an important cultural document for learning more about children's representation of their social world. However, the interpretation of drawing signs has to be derived from local cultural models of relationships" (Gernhardt et al., 2016).

A Sacred River? This is the Ganges river at Allahabad in 2013, which the Indian government is working to clean — a monumental task. No nation is working to rid the Pacific Ocean of a much bigger garbage site. What would evolutionary theory recommend?

● **Observation Quiz** Beyond the pollution of the Ganges by humans' garbage, what characteristics of the river, visible here, contribute to the pollution? (see answer, page 56) ↑

how those same emotions, impulses, and habits developed within *Homo sapiens* over the past 100,000 years.

Why We Fear Snakes More than Cars

Evolutionary theory has intriguing explanations for many issues in human development, including 1-year-olds' attachment to their parents, pregnant women's nausea, and adult attraction to major sports contests. These may have evolved to help human survival.

Another specific example comes from phobias, which are hard to understand without considering human life in prehistoric times. You know that fear of snakes makes some people scream and sweat upon seeing one. However, snakes currently cause less than one death in a million, whereas the death rate from cars is a thousand times higher (OECD, 2014). Why is no one terrified of automobiles?

The answer from evolutionary theory is that human fears began when snakes were common killers. Thus,

> ancient dangers such as snakes, spiders, heights, and strangers appear on lists of common phobias far more often than do evolutionarily modern dangers such as cars and guns, even though cars and guns are more dangerous to survival in the modern environment.
>
> *[Confer et al., 2010, p. 111]*

Since our fears have not caught up to automobiles, evolutionary theory explains that our instincts will not protect us. Instead, we must legislate infant seats, child-safety restraints, seat belts, red lights, and speed limits. Thankfully, such measures are succeeding: The 2018 U.S. motor-vehicle death rate was 11 per 100,000, half the rate of 40 years earlier.

Other modern killers — climate change, drug addiction, obesity, pollution — also require social management, because instincts are contrary to what we know about these dangers. Evolutionary theory contends that we must recognize the origins of destructive urges — such as the desire to eat calorie-dense cake — in order to control them (King, 2013).

Why We Protect Babies

According to evolutionary theory, every species has two long-standing, biologically based drives: (1) survival and (2) reproduction. Understanding these provides insight into protective parenthood, the death of newborns, infant dependency, child immaturity, the onset of puberty, the formation of families, and much more (Konner, 2010).

Here is one example. Adults see babies as cute, even though babies have little hair, no chins, stubby legs, and round stomachs — none of which is considered attractive in adults. The reason, evolutionary theory contends, is that adults are instinctually attuned to protect and cherish infants. That was essential when survival of the species was in doubt.

But humans do not protect every baby. Indeed, another evolutionary instinct is that all creatures seek to perpetuate their own descendants more than those who are unrelated. That might lead to murdering of infants who are not one's own. Some primates do exactly that: Chimpanzee males who take over a troop kill babies of the deposed male. This occurred among ancient humans as well. The Christian Bible chronicles at least three examples, two in the story of Moses and one in the birth of Jesus. Modern humans, of course, have created laws against infanticide — a necessity because evolutionary instincts might be murderous (Hrdy, 2009).

Critics point out that people do not always act as evolutionary theory predicts: Parents sometimes abandon newborns, adults sometimes handle snakes, and so on. However, evolutionary theorists contend that ancient impulses within our species need to be understood in order to protect the lives of people today.

Selectivity Theories

We now consider theories that focus on the human need to choose what to do with one's life. Selectivity is increasingly necessary as people grow older, and thus these theories apply particularly to human development over the life span.

Babies are not selective. They are born with wide-ranging curiosity and a readiness to bond with anyone — woman or man, biological or adoptive parent, caregiver of the same skin color or not. They eat what they are fed, sleep where they are put, speak whichever of the 6,000 languages they hear. By age 1, infants may insist on a particular person, a special blanket, a favorite food — but they could have had quite different preferences if their caregivers had decided that.

Gradually, as children grow, they have a few more choices, but selection is still quite limited. They do not choose where to live, what religion to practice, which family is theirs. Adolescents begin to have some say about their lives, but their parents' decisions still shape their lives. Teenage rebellion may be our species' way of preparing people for independent adulthood.

Currently in North America, adults decide whether and where to seek education or work; who and when to marry; what to do about contraception, vocation, residence, retirement; and much more. To describe this process, developmentalists have developed theories about how selection processes change with age.

A Hierarchy of Needs

Current selectivity theories were foreshadowed by Abraham Maslow (1908–1970). He proposed that human needs can be arranged in a hierarchy (see **Figure 2.4**), from basic requirements for survival (food, water) to the highest level, *self-actualization*, when people can become whomever they were destined to be, fully themselves — creative, spiritual, curious, appreciative of nature, able to respect everyone else (Maslow, 1954).

His hierarchy is like a ladder: Once a person stands firmly on a higher rung, the lower rungs are less urgent, although they are still there as a backup. Thus, someone who seeks love (level three) is not as concerned about getting basic needs met, because those needs are already satisfied. Indeed, such a person could readily decide to skip a meal: Many people striving for success and esteem do not take a lunch break.

This pyramid caught on almost immediately; it was one of the most "contagious ideas of behavioral science" since it seemed insightful about human psychology (Kenrick et al., 2010, p. 292.)

As with all the selectivity theories, Maslow recognized that infants and young children do not have much power of selection. Ideally, the microsystem and

ESPECIALLY FOR Teachers and Counselors of Teenagers Teen pregnancy is destructive of adolescent education, family life, and sometimes even health. According to evolutionary theory, what can be done about this? (see response, page 56)

FIGURE 2.4

Moving Up, Not Looking Back Maslow's hierarchy is like a ladder: Once a person stands firmly on a higher rung, the lower rungs are no longer needed. Thus, someone who has arrived at level four might devalue safety (level two) and be willing to risk personal safety to gain respect.

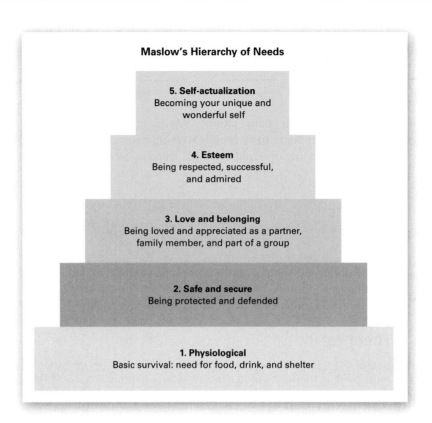

Maslow's Hierarchy of Needs

5. Self-actualization
Becoming your unique and wonderful self

4. Esteem
Being respected, successful, and admired

3. Love and belonging
Being loved and appreciated as a partner, family member, and part of a group

2. Safe and secure
Being protected and defended

1. Physiological
Basic survival: need for food, drink, and shelter

macrosystem (family and community) within the exosystem (a national culture that values life) ensures care and safety (levels one and two) for each child. Level three also begins in childhood, continuing through early adulthood, as families provide love and communities affirm belonging.

That frees adults to be selective in levels four and five, finding their own path toward success, esteem, and self-actualization. Maslow believed that when people are not consumed by unmet lower needs they can focus on higher needs. That is suggested by current research on Maslow's hierarchy. Adults who are able to meet their higher needs are those whose lower needs are satisfied (Taormina & Gao, 2013).

As to the specifics of this process, Maslow was less clear. He was among those who advocated a theory called **humanism**, which suggested that therapists be empathetic listeners who respect the power of the individual to select their goals and destiny. Each of us must decide what our actions might be. Selectivity!

humanism A theory that stresses the potential of all humans, who have the same basic needs regardless of culture, gender, or basic background.

Selective Optimization with Compensation

One review explains how "It could be argued that we are in the midst of a golden age of life course studies" (Ferraro & Schafer, 2017). Although many famous people have described the life span (including Shakespeare, Erikson, and G. Stanley Hall), the person most associated with starting this new golden age is Paul Baltes (1987). With his wife, Margret, he developed the theory of **selective optimization with compensation** (Baltes & Baltes, 1990).

As you remember from Chapter 1, every stage of development has gains and losses, part of the multidirectional nature of life. Extensive longitudinal research led by the Baltes suggested that, as people grow older, losses may outweigh gains. Consequently, adults need to focus on some aspects of life, compensating with increased strengths for any losses.

This is comprehensive: It describes a "general process of systematic functioning" (Baltes, 2003, p. 25), including physical, cognitive, and social domains. Adults seek to maximize gains and minimize losses, a process of selection and optimization made necessary because abilities can be enhanced or diminished, depending on how, when, and why a person uses them.

selective optimization with compensation The theory, developed by Paul and Margaret Baltes, that people try to maintain a balance in their lives by looking for the best way to compensate for physical and cognitive losses and to become more proficient in activities they can already do well.

According to this theory, when adults are motivated and practice whatever abilities they select to optimize, few age-related deficits are apparent. The brain is plastic, developing new dendrites and activation sequences, adjusting to whatever the person chooses to learn.

This theory is easier to understand with examples. Baltes cites typists (1987). Typists must see a letter and transmit that image to the visual cortex, which must activate the motor cortex, and send an impulse to the muscle of the proper finger (left hand from right cortex, right hand from left). For all that, younger typists are quicker.

However, Baltes cited research that older typists type faster than younger ones, because practice has accelerated brain connections and strategy has improved. They have compensated for a systemic slowdown. In this particular example, older typists scan more of the text at a time, so they are better at anticipating what their fingers must do next.

Other examples of selective optimization with compensation abound. This theory has been applied to figuring out how to perform on the job (Moghimi et al., 2017), to play music (Glen, 2018), to succeed in sports, and to balance work and family (Baltes et al., 2011). That evokes what is probably the best compensation of all—enjoying one's close family and friends. That leads to the other selectivity theory.

Socioemotional Selectivity Theory

In an intriguing series of studies (Carstensen, 2011), people were presented with the following scenario:

> Imagine that in carrying out the activities of everyday life, you find that you have half an hour of free time, with no pressing commitments. You have decided that you'd like to spend this time with another person. Assuming that the following three persons are available to you, whom would you want to spend that time with?
>
> - A member of your immediate family
> - The author of a book you have just read
> - An acquaintance with whom you seem to have much in common

Older adults, more than younger ones, choose the family member. This is part of a general trend, which Laura Carstensen described with a theory called **socioemotional selectivity**. With age, adults become more selective in their social interactions. As a result, as time goes on, fewer people are in a person's social network.

The loss of quantity is offset by an increase in quality: People optimize the friends they have, choosing to invest in the people closest to them—who often are immediate relatives. The peripheral and the disagreeable people are jettisoned, while close friends and family remain (English & Carstensen, 2014).

In many ways, older adults seem to optimize their emotional life, developing what is called a *positivity effect*, or a *late-life paradox* (Carstensen & DeLiema, 2018). Socioemotional selectivity leads people to pay more attention to positive sights, memories, and people than negative ones. Walking down the street, a person might remember the sweet smell of a rose and forget the sudden appearance of a rat. Age itself seems to lead to such positivity, because people realize that their life is not forever. Indeed, some research finds that people have a similar socioemotional selectivity when they have been diagnosed with a serious illness (Pressman et al., 2019).

One intriguing research direction is to compare emotional selectivity and brain functioning. Although the brain slows down somewhat with age, the more positive emotional life of the elderly seems to result from active choices, not passive acceptance of neurological change. As one review explains,

> [The] brain regions involved in both positive and negative emotional processing in young adulthood appear to be selectively responsive to positive

socioemotional selectivity theory The theory that older people prioritize regulation of their own emotions and seek familiar social contacts who reinforce generativity, pride, and joy.

⬤ **Observation Quiz** Beyond conversation, what do you see that predicts cognition? (see answer, page 56) ↓

Keeping Alert These three men on a park bench in Malta are doing more than engaging in conversation; they are keeping their minds active through socialization and the discussion of current events and politics.

Doug McKinlay/Lonely Planet Images/Getty Images

material in older adults. The evidence to date suggests that older adults are effectively regulating emotional responses. … cortical activity is compensating for faulty age-related functioning in other regions.

[Samanez-Larkin & Carstensen, 2011, pp. 513–514]

WHAT HAVE YOU LEARNED?

1. Why is the sociocultural perspective particularly relevant within the United States?
2. How do mentors and mentees interact within the zone of proximal development?
3. How do the customs and manufactured items in a society affect human development?
4. Why would behaviors and emotions that benefited ancient humans be apparent today?
5. How does an understanding of ancient people help protect modern humans?
6. Why are selectivity theories especially relevant for life-span understanding?
7. How do older adults compensate for loss, according to selectivity theories?

VIDEO ACTIVITY: Modeling: Learning by Observation features the original footage of Albert Bandura's famous experiment.

What Theories Contribute

Each major theory discussed in this chapter has contributed to our understanding of human development (see **Table 2.3**):

- *Psychoanalytic theories* make us aware of the impact of early-childhood experiences, remembered or not, on subsequent development.
- *Behaviorism* shows the effect that immediate responses, associations, and examples have on learning, moment by moment and over time.
- *Cognitive theories* bring an understanding of intellectual processes, including the fact that thoughts and beliefs affect every aspect of our development.
- *Sociocultural theories* remind us that development is embedded in a rich and multifaceted cultural context, evident in every social interaction.
- *Evolutionary theories* suggest that ancient human impulses and instincts need to be recognized so they can be guided.
- *Selectivity theories* alert us that setting priorities is increasingly crucial with age.

Remember that each theory is designed to be practical. This is evident with a very practical issue for many parents: how to toilet-train their children (see Opposing Perspectives).

TABLE 2.3

Six Perspectives on Human Development

Theory	Area of Focus	Fundamental Depiction of What People Do	Relative Emphasis on Nature or Nurture?
Psychoanalytic theory	Psychosexual (Freud) or psychosocial (Erikson) stages	Battle unconscious impulses and overcome major crises.	More nature (biological, sexual impulses, and parent–child bonds)
Behaviorism	Conditioning through stimulus and response	Respond to stimuli, reinforcement, and models.	More nurture (direct environment produces various behaviors)
Cognitive theory	Thinking, remembering, analyzing	Seek to understand experiences while forming concepts.	More nature (mental activity and motivation are key)
Sociocultural theory	Social control, expressed through people, language, customs	Learn the tools, skills, and values of society through apprenticeships.	More nurture (interaction of mentor and learner, within cultures)
Evolutionary theory	Needs and impulses that originated thousands of years ago	Develop impulses, interests, and patterns to survive and reproduce.	More nature (needs and impulses apply to all humans)
Selectivity Theories	Alternative Priorities	Adults select what to value most, such as family, money, mobility.	More nature, but with nurture evident in adulthood.

OPPOSING PERSPECTIVES

Toilet Training—How and When?

Parents hear conflicting advice about almost everything regarding infant care, including feeding, responding to cries, bathing, and exercise. Often a particular parental response springs from one of the theories explained in this chapter—no wonder advice is sometimes contradictory.

One practical example is toilet training. In the nineteenth century, many parents believed that bodily functions should be controlled as soon as possible in order to distinguish humans from lower animals. Consequently, they began toilet training in the first months of life (Accardo, 2006). Then, psychoanalytic theory pegged the first year as the oral stage (Freud) or the time when trust was crucial (Erikson).

Consequently, psychoanalytic theory led to postponing toilet training to avoid serious personality problems later on. This was soon part of many manuals on child rearing. For example, a leading pediatrician, Barry Brazelton, wrote a popular book for parents advising that toilet training should not begin until the child is cognitively, emotionally, and biologically ready—around age 2 for daytime training and age 3 for nighttime dryness.

> As a society, we are far too concerned about pushing children to be toilet trained early. I don't even like the phrase "toilet training." It really should be toilet learning.
>
> [Brazelton & Sparrow, 2006, p. 193]

Toward the end of the twentieth century, many U.S. psychologists had rejected psychoanalytic theory and become behaviorists. Since they believed that learning depends primarily on conditioning, some suggested that toilet training occur whenever the parent wished, not at a particular age.

In one application of behaviorism, children drank quantities of their favorite juice, sat on the potty with a parent nearby to keep them entertained, and then, when the inevitable occurred, the parent praised and rewarded them—a powerful reinforcement.

Children were conditioned (in one day, according to some behaviorists) to head for the potty whenever the need arose (Azrin & Foxx, 1974). The power of early conditioning is thought to be why the urge to urinate wakes adults up from a sound sleep. People no longer can do what they did so naturally when they were newborns; instead people endure pain rather than pee in their pants.

Cognitive theorists would consider such a concerted effort, with immediate reinforcement, unnecessary, and they might wonder why any parent would think toilet training should occur before the child understands what is happening. Instead, cognitive theory suggests that parents wait until the child can understand reasons to urinate and defecate in the toilet.

Sociocultural theory might reject all of these theories. Instead, the cultural context is crucial, which is why the advent of disposable diapers in the United States has pushed the age of toilet training about a year later than it was a century ago.

Context is also the explanation for some African cultures in which children toilet train themselves by following slightly older children to the surrounding trees and bushes. This is easier, of course, if toddlers wear no diapers—possible only in some climates. Sociocultural theory explains that practices differ because of the ecological context, and infants adjust.

Meanwhile, some Western parents prefer to start potty training very early. One U.S. mother began training her baby just 33 days after birth. She noticed when her son was about to defecate, held him above the toilet, and had trained him by 6 months (Sun & Rugolotto, 2004).

Such early training is criticized by all four theories in this box, each in their own way:

- Psychoanalysts would wonder what made her such an anal person, valuing cleanliness and order without considering the child's needs.
- Behaviorists would say that the mother was trained, not the son. She taught herself to be sensitive to his body; she was reinforced when she read his clues correctly.
- Cognitive theory would question the mother's thinking. For instance, did she have an odd fear of normal body functions?
- Sociocultural theorists would be aghast that the U.S. drive for personal control took such a bizarre turn.

What is best? Some parents are reluctant to train, and according to one book, the result is that many children are still in diapers at age 5 (Barone, 2015). Dueling theories and diverse practices led to an article for pediatricians that concluded "despite families and physicians having addressed this issue for generations, there still is no consensus regarding the best method or even a standard definition of toilet training" (Howell et al., 2010, p. 262).

Many sources explain that because each child is different, there is no "right" way: "the best strategy for implementing training is still unknown" (Colaco et al., 2013, p. 49).

That may suggest sociocultural theory, which notes vast differences from one community to another. A study of parents' opinions in Belgium found that single mothers with low socioeconomic status were more likely to wait too long, until age 3 or so (van Nunen et al., 2015). Of course, "too long" is a matter of opinion.

What values are embedded in each practice? Psychoanalytic theory focuses on later personality, behaviorism stresses conditioning of body impulses, cognitive theory considers variation in the child's intellectual capacity, and sociocultural theory allows vast diversity.

There is no easy answer, but many parents firmly believe in one approach or another. That confirms the statement at the beginning of this chapter. We all have theories, sometimes strongly held, whether we know it or not.

VISUALIZING DEVELOPMENT Historical Highlights of Developmental Science

As evident throughout this textbook, much more research and appreciation of the brain, social context, and the non-Western world has expanded our understanding of human development in the twenty-first century. This timeline lists a few highlights of the past.

200,000–50,000 BCE
With their large brains, long period of child development, and extensive social and family support, early humans were able to sustain life and raise children more effectively than other primates.

c. 400 BCE In ancient Greece, ideas about children from philosophers like Plato (c. 428–348 BCE) and Aristotle (384–322 BCE) influenced further thoughts about children. Plato believed children were born with knowledge. Aristotle believed children learn from experience.

1650–1800
European philosophers like John Locke (1632–1704) and Jean Jacques Rousseau (1712–1778) debate whether children are born as "blank slates" and how much control parents should take in raising them.

1797 First European vaccination: Edward Jenner (1749–1823) publicizes smallpox inoculation, building on vaccination against smallpox in Asia, the Middle East, and Africa.

1750–1850 Beginning of Western laws regulating child labor and protecting the rights of children.

1879 First experimental psychology laboratory established in Leipzig, Germany.

1885 Sigmund Freud (1856–1939) publishes *Studies on Hysteria*, one of the first works establishing the importance of the subconscious and marking the beginning of psychoanalytic theory.

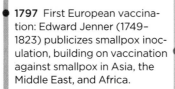

1895 Ivan Pavlov (1849–1936) begins research on dogs' salivation response.

1905 Max Weber (1864–1920), the founder of sociology, writes *The Protestant Work Ethic*, about human values and adult work.

1905 Alfred Binet's (1857–1911) intelligence test published.

1907 Maria Montessori (1870–1952) opens her first school in Rome.

1913 John B. Watson (1878–1958) publishes *Psychology As the Behaviorist Views It*.

50,000 BCE — 400 BCE — 0 — 500 — 1000 — 1500 — 1650 — 1700 — 1750

140 BCE In China, imperial examinations are one of the first times cognitive testing is used on young people.

500–1500 During the Middle Ages in Europe, many adults believed that children were miniature adults.

1100–1200 First universities founded in Europe. Young people pay to be educated together.

1837 First kindergarten opens in Germany, part of a movement to teach young children before they entered the primary school system.

1859 Charles Darwin (1809–1882) publishes *On the Origin of Species*, sparking debates about what is genetic and what is environmental.

1900 Compulsory schooling for children is established for most children in the United States and Europe.

1903 The term "gerontology," the branch of developmental science devoted to studying aging, first coined.

1920 Lev Vygotsky (1896–1934) develops sociocultural theory in the former Soviet Union.

1923 Jean Piaget (1896–1980) publishes *The Language and Thought of the Child*.

1933 Society for Research on Child Development, the preeminent organization for research on child development, founded.

1939 Mamie (1917–1983) and Kenneth Clark (1914–2005) receive their research grants to study race in early childhood.

1943 Abraham Maslow (1908–1970) publishes *A Theory of Motivation*, establishing the hierarchy of needs.

1950 Erik Erikson (1902–1994) expands on Freud's theory to include social aspects of personality development with the publication of *Childhood and Society*.

1951 John Bowlby (1907–1990) publishes *Maternal Care and Mental Health*, one of his first works on the importance of parent–child attachment.

1953 Publication of the first papers describing DNA, our genetic blueprint.

1957 Harry Harlow (1905–1981) publishes *Love in Infant Monkeys*, describing his research on attachment in rhesus monkeys.

1961 The morning sickness drug thalidomide is banned after children are born with serious birth defects, calling attention to the problem of teratogens during pregnancy.

1961 Albert Bandura (b. 1925) conducts the Bobo Doll experiments, leading to the development of social learning theory.

1979 Urie Bronfenbrenner (1917–2005) publishes his work on ecological systems theory.

1986 John Gottman (b. 1942) founded the "Love Lab" at the University of Washington to study what makes relationships work.

1987 Carolyn Rovee-Collier (1942–2014) shows that even young infants can remember in her classic mobile experiments.

1990–Present New brain imaging technology allows pinpointing of brain areas involved in everything from executive function to Alzheimer's disease.

1994 Steven Pinker (b. 1954) publishes *The Language Instinct*, focusing attention on the interaction between neuroscience and behavior.

1996 Giacomo Rizzolatti publishes his discovery of mirror neurons.

2000 Jeffrey Arnett conceptualizes emerging adulthood.

2003 Mapping of the human genome is completed.

2013 DSM-5, which emphasizes the role of context in understanding mental health problems, is published.

| 1800 | 1850 | 1900 | 1950 | 2000 |

1953 B. F. Skinner (1904–1990) conducts experiments on rats and establishes operant conditioning.

1955 Emmy Werner (1929–2017) begins her Kauai study, which focuses on the power of resilence.

1956 K. Warner Schaie's (b. 1928) Seattle Longitudinal Study of Adult Intelligence begins.

1965 Head Start, an early childhood education program, launched in the United States.

1965 Mary Ainsworth (1913–1999) starts using the "Strange Situation" to measure attachment.

1966 Diana Baumrind (1927–2018) publishes her first work on parenting styles.

1972 Beginning of the Dunedin, New Zealand, study—one of the first longitudinal studies to include genetic markers.

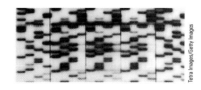

1990 Barbara Rogoff (b. 1950) publishes *Apprenticeship in Thinking*, making developmentalists more aware of the significance of culture and context. Rogoff provided new insights and appreciation of child-rearing in Latin America.

1993 Howard Gardner (b. 1943) publishes *Multiple Intelligences*, a major new understanding of the diversity of human intellectual abilities. Gardner has since revised and expanded his ideas in many ways.

2013 U.S. President Barack Obama announces his administration's Brain Research through Advancing Innovative Neurotechnologies (BRAIN) Initiative.

2017 Several U.S. cities expand public funding for early-childhood education (universal pre-k).

2020 and beyond Onward. Many more discoveries are chronicled in this book, as researchers continue to test and explore.

eclectic perspective The approach taken by most developmentalists, in which they apply aspects of each of the various theories of development rather than adhering exclusively to one theory.

No comprehensive view of development can ignore any of these theories, yet each has encountered severe criticism: *psychoanalytic theory* for being too subjective; *behaviorism* for being too mechanistic; *cognitive theory* for undervaluing emotions; *sociocultural theory* for neglecting individual choice; *evolutionary theory* for ignoring the power of current morals; and *selectivity theory* for downplaying the regrets and losses of life.

Most developmentalists prefer an **eclectic perspective**, choosing what they consider to be the best aspects of each theory. Rather than adopt any one of these theories exclusively, they make selective use of all of them.

Obviously, all theories reflect the personal background of the theorist, as do all critiques. Being eclectic, not tied to any one theory, is beneficial because everyone, scientist as well as layperson, is biased. But even being eclectic may be criticized: Choosing the best from each theory may be too picky or the opposite, too tolerant. One or more of these theories might be destructive, not merely misleading, in some details.

Nonetheless, for most developmentalists, all six theories merit respect. It is easy to dismiss any one of them, but using several perspectives opens our eyes and minds to aspects of development that we might otherwise ignore. As one overview of developmental theories concludes, "Because no one theory satisfactorily explains development, it is critical that developmentalists be able to draw on the content, methods, and theoretical concepts of many theories" (Miller, 2011, p. 437).

As you will see in many later chapters, theories provide a fresh look at behavior. Imagine a mother, father, teacher, coach, grandmother, and grandfather discussing the problems of a particular child. Each of the six people might be influenced by a different one of these theories, and each might suggest a possible explanation that makes someone else say, "I never thought of that." If they listen to each other, together they might find the best strategy to help the child.

Using six theories is like having six perceptive observers. All six are not always on target, but it is better to use theory to consider alternate possibilities than to stay in one narrow groove. To understand the complexities and nuances of human development, many perspectives are needed.

WHAT HAVE YOU LEARNED?

1. What are the criticisms of each of the six theories?
2. Why are most developmentalists eclectic in regard to theories?
3. Why is it useful to know more than one theory to explain human behavior?
4. What might be a disadvantage of being eclectic?

SUMMARY

Theories of Development

1. A theory provides general principles to guide research and to explain observations. Each of the six major developmental theories—psychoanalytic, behaviorist, cognitive, sociocultural, evolutionary, and selectivity—interprets human development from a distinct perspective, providing a framework for understanding human emotions, experiences, and actions.

2. Theories are neither true nor false. They are not facts; they suggest hypotheses to be tested and interpretations of the myriad human behaviors. Good theories are practical: They aid inquiry, interpretation, and daily life.

3. A developmental theory focuses on changes that occur over time, uncovering the links between past, present, and future. Developmental theories attempt to answer the crucial questions of the life span.

Grand Theories

4. Psychoanalytic theory emphasizes that adult actions and thoughts originate from unconscious impulses and childhood conflicts. Freud theorized that sexual urges arise during three stages of childhood—oral, anal, and phallic—and continue, after latency, in the genital stage.

5. Erikson described eight successive stages of development, each involving a crisis to be resolved. The early stages are crucial, with lifelong effects, but the emphasis is not only on the body and sexual needs. Instead, Erikson stressed that societies, cultures, and family shape each person's development.

6. Behaviorists, or learning theorists, believe that scientists should study observable and measurable behavior. Behaviorism emphasizes conditioning—lifelong learning processes in which an association between one stimulus and another (classical conditioning) or the consequences of reinforcement and punishment (operant conditioning) guide behavior.

7. Social learning theory recognizes that people learn by observing others, even if they themselves have not been reinforced or punished. Children are particularly susceptible to social learning, but all humans are affected by what they notice in other people.

8. Cognitive theorists believe that thoughts and beliefs powerfully affect attitudes, actions, and perceptions, which in turn affect behavior. Piaget proposed four age-related periods of cognition, each propelled by an active search for cognitive equilibrium.

9. Information processing focuses on each aspect of cognition— input, processing, and output. This perspective has benefited from technology, first from understanding computer functioning and more recently by the many ways scientists monitor the brain.

Newer Theories

10. Sociocultural theory explains human development in terms of the guidance, support, and structure provided by each social group through culture and mentoring. Vygotsky described how learning occurs through social interactions in which mentors guide learners through their zone of proximal development.

11. Evolutionary theory contends that contemporary humans inherit genetic tendencies that have fostered survival and reproduction of the human species for tens of thousands of years. Through selective adaptation, the fears, impulses, and reactions that were useful 100,000 years ago for *Homo sapiens* continue to this day.

12. Evolutionary theory provides explanations for many human traits, from lactose intolerance to the love of babies. Selective adaptation is the process by which genes enhance human development over thousands of years. Societies use laws and customs to protect people from some genetic impulses.

13. Selectivity theories emphasize that people make choices throughout their lives, and that setting priorities becomes increasingly necessary for a happy late adulthood. Selective optimization with compensation stresses the need for both choice and compensating, and socioemotional selectivity explains why older adults are happier than younger ones.

What Theories Contribute

14. Psychoanalytic, behavioral, cognitive, sociocultural, evolutionary, and selectivity theories have aided our understanding of human development. However, no single theory describes the full complexity and diversity of human experience. Most developmentalists are eclectic, drawing on many theories.

KEY TERMS

developmental theory (p. 33)
psychoanalytic theory (p. 34)
behaviorism (p. 36)
classical conditioning (p. 37)
operant conditioning (p. 38)
social learning theory (p. 39)

modeling (p. 39)
cognitive theory (p. 39)
information-processing theory (p. 41)
sociocultural theory (p. 42)

apprenticeship in thinking (p. 42)
guided participation (p. 42)
evolutionary theory (p. 44)
humanism (p. 48)

selective optimization with compensation (p. 48)
socioemotional selectivity theory (p. 49)
eclectic perspective (p. 54)

APPLICATIONS

1. Developmentalists sometimes talk about "folk theories," which are theories developed by ordinary people, who are unaware that they are theorizing. Choose three sayings that are commonly used in your culture, such as (from the dominant U.S. culture) "A penny saved is a penny earned" or "As the twig is bent, so grows the tree." Explain the underlying assumptions, or folk theory, that each saying reflects.

2. Cognitive theory suggests the power of thoughts, and sociocultural theory emphasizes the power of context. Find someone who disagrees with you about some basic issue (e.g., abortion, immigration, socialism) and listen carefully to their ideas and reasons. Then analyze how cognition and experience shaped their ideas *and your own.*

3. Ask three people to tell you their theories about male–female differences in mating and sexual behaviors. Which of the theories described in this chapter is closest to each explanation, and which theory is not mentioned?

ESPECIALLY FOR ANSWERS

Response for Teachers (from p. 36) Erikson would note that the behavior of 5-year-olds is affected by their developmental stage and by their culture. Therefore, you might design your curriculum to accommodate active, noisy children.

Response for Teachers and Counselors of Teenagers (from p. 47) Evolutionary theory stresses the basic human drive for reproduction, which gives teenagers a powerful sex drive. Thus, merely informing teenagers of the difficulty of caring for a newborn (some high school sex-education programs simply give teenagers a chicken egg to nurture) is not likely to work. A better method would be to structure teenagers' lives so that pregnancy is impossible—for instance, with careful supervision or readily available contraception.

OBSERVATION QUIZ ANSWERS

Answer to Observation Quiz (from p. 37) Both are balding, with white beards. Note also that none of the other theorists in this chapter have beards—a cohort difference, not an ideological one.

Answer to Observation Quiz (from p. 46) The river is slow-moving (see the boat) and shallow (see the man standing). A fast-moving, deep river is able to flush out contaminants more quickly.

Answer to Observation Quiz (from p. 49) Friendship is protective at every age. In addition, being outside in daylight, wearing appropriate clothing (note the hats and shoes), and simply experiencing fresh air and greenery are all correlates of a healthy mind and body.

CHAPTER 3

Genes and Generations

"**S**he needs a special school. She cannot come back next year," Elissa's middle school principal told us.

Martin and I were stunned. Apparently, the school staff thought that our wonderful seventh-grade daughter was severely learning disabled.

We had noticed that she misplaced homework, mislaid her bus pass, got lost coming home, left needed textbooks at school, forgot where each class met on which day—but that seemed insignificant compared to her strengths in reading, analyzing, and friendship. Disorganization has a good side: She was creative, innovative, adventurous.

I knew the first lesson from genetics: Genes affect everything, not just appearance, diseases, and intellect. That made me wonder: Had Elissa inherited this disability from us? I thought about our disorganized home: If we needed masking tape, or working scissors, or silver candlesticks, we had to search in several places. Could that be why we were oblivious to Elissa's failings?

Genes are passed down over the generations. All eight of her great-grandparents boarded crowded ships to cross the Atlantic. They were brave immigrants—did this also mean that they were untethered to routines, uncomfortable with rules and regulations?

Elissa resisted regulations. For example, she convinced her math teacher to make homework optional for students like her who scored high on tests. His mistake; her charisma. Did our admiration of her persuasive power keep us from recognizing her difficulty with the expectations of middle school?

Science had taught me the second lesson from genetics: Nurture matters as much as nature. Spatial disorganization could be inherited, or it could be learned—probably both. In any case, my husband and I had overcome it. For example, since he often got lost, Martin did not hesitate to ask strangers for directions; since I mislaid things, I kept my students' papers in clearly marked folders at my office.

We needed to help our daughter gain the skills that she did not have. Martin attached her bus pass to her backpack; we got a second copy of her textbooks so she could leave one set at school and have another at home; I found a tutor who taught Elissa to list her assignments, check them off when done, put them neatly in her backpack, and then take it to school. I made sure she did those four steps, and I wrote an impassioned, persuasive letter to the principal. Elissa herself began to study diligently, even doing the optional math homework.

Success! Elissa aced her final exams, and the principal allowed her to return. Now, as an adult, she still misplaces keys, gives wrong directions, and relies on shopping lists. But she is an accomplished, creative lawyer, a conscientious and careful mother of two boys who have her wonderful traits. She helps them stay organized.

This chapter is about genes and generations. Our genes come directly from ancestors who lived thousands of years ago. Expressing those genes depends on many factors, including our parents, our culture, and ourselves. Genes can be harmful, but they need not be. Elissa inherited our genes and learned our habits (nature and nurture again), and we admired her for it. But scattered, independent, disorganized 12-year-olds are not admired by middle school principals. We needed to give her necessary skills.

The plasticity highlighted in Chapter 1 is evident in genetic interactions, in epigenetics, and in differential susceptibility, all soon explained. This chapter also describes some serious problems and ethical dilemmas that arise from genes. I hope you recognize the implications long before you have a seventh-grade daughter.

What Will You Know?

1. Genetically, are males and females opposites, or are they almost the same?
2. What are the practical implications of knowing that a problem is inherited?
3. When does it matter if a person carries a recessive gene for a serious disorder?

The Genetic Code

zygote The single cell formed from the union of two gametes, a sperm and an ovum.

Every person starts life as a **zygote**, a single cell unlike any other cell ever created. Yet the genes in the zygote are not new at all; they have been passed down for hundreds of thousands of years. This chapter is about that paradox: Each human is unique, and yet all living people share many traits with all other members of our species that has existed for the past 200,000 years.

What Genes Are

deoxyribonucleic acid (DNA) The chemical composition of the molecules that contain the genes, which are the chemical instructions for cells to manufacture various proteins.

chromosome One of the 46 molecules of DNA (in 23 pairs) that virtually every cell of the human body contains and that, together, contain all the genes. Other species have more or fewer chromosomes.

gene A small section of a chromosome; the basic unit for the transmission of heredity. A gene consists of a string of chemicals that provide instructions for the cell to manufacture certain proteins.

First, some basic biology. All living things are composed of cells. The work of cells is done by *proteins*. Each cell manufactures certain proteins according to a code of instructions stored by molecules of **deoxyribonucleic acid (DNA)** at the center of the cell. These coding DNA molecules are located on a **chromosome**.

Humans have 23 pairs of chromosomes, 46 in all (with rare exceptions explained later). Those chromosomes contain the genes, and those genes carry instructions for making the proteins necessary for life and growth (see **Figure 3.1**). Each **gene** is located at a particular spot on a chromosome. Humans have about 21,000 genes, each on a specific chromosome.

Every cell (with one important exception) of every person contains a copy of that individual's original 46 chromosomes, arranged in 23 pairs. After the zygote is formed, that original cell, with 21,000 paired genes and 46 chromosomes, duplicates itself millions of times. Each new cell is a copy of the original. With the help of other genetic material (to be described soon), each new cell follows a subset of those genetic instructions, becoming a specific part of the body and brain.

The genetic instructions to make proteins are further broken down into instructions to make 20 amino acids, which combine to produce those proteins. And those amino acids are themselves the result of instructions from a strings of four chemicals—thymine (T), adenine (A), guanine (G), and cytosine (C), connected in four possible base pairs (AT, TA, GC, CG), arranged in precise order to make the genetic code, the genome. There are more than 3 billion base pairs.

Most of those pairs are identical for every human, even for every mammal, and most are positioned in a particular place on a particular chromosome. But some genes vary, with deletions, doublings, transpositions of a string of base pairs. When a particular gene varies in base pairs, each variation is called an **allele** of that gene.

Most alleles cause small differences (such as the shape of an eyebrow), but some are crucial. Another way to state this is that some genes are *polymorphic* (literally, "many forms"). Many have *single-nucleotide polymorphisms* (abbreviated SNPs, pronounced "snips"), which is a variation in only one part of the code, causing an allele of that gene.

In addition, some genes and chromosomes are added or absent, which is one reason each species differs. Occasionally, major variations occur in people as well, with an extra chromosome or an aberrant gene, explained later in this chapter. All told, variations create some major differences (such as between a man and a mouse) and billions of minor ones, such as between a pale, blond woman and her darker sister.

We humans care a lot about alleles, those minor differences. It bothers me if someone mistakes me for another person. I am especially annoyed if that person adds "she could be your twin." No, she couldn't! How wrong can you be? Like everyone else, I am unique. [Actual twins are discussed soon.]

This is fortunate, because genetic diversity helps the species: Creativity, prosperity, and survival increase when one person is unlike another. Genetic diversity also benefits public health, in that any particular genetic disease or condition is less likely to be widespread in the community.

Too much diversity may not be good, however, because diversity makes people less trusting and less cooperative. There is an optimal balance between diversity and universality for each species: Humans are close to optimal (Ashraf & Galor, 2013).

This idea of the costs and benefits of diversity has been applied most often to economics, in that nations are wealthier when they are not too *homogeneous* ("similar genes") or too *heterogeneous* ("different genes"). Apparently, the costs occur quickly when a new population arrives, and the benefits appear over time (Spolaore & Wacziarg, 2018). Communities try to reap the benefits and avoid the costs of diversity.

Common traits shared by an entire species are also beneficial. That is certainly evident among humans. We all use elaborate language, develop within families, express love, fear, and curiosity. Genetic similarities define each species: Any

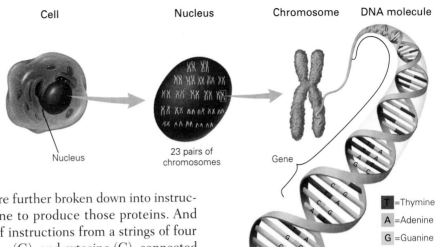

Cell   Nucleus   Chromosome   DNA molecule

Nucleus

23 pairs of chromosomes

Gene

T = Thymine
A = Adenine
G = Guanine
C = Cytosine

FIGURE 3.1

How Proteins Are Made The genes on the chromosomes in the nucleus of each cell instruct the cell to manufacture the proteins needed to sustain life and development. The code for a protein is the particular combination of four bases, T-A-G-C (thymine, adenine, guanine, and cytosine).

allele A variation that makes a gene different in some way from other genes for the same characteristics. Many genes never vary; others have several possible alleles.

THE WORLD'S FIRST GENETICALLY ENGINEERED HUMAN HITS ADOLESCENCE

We buy you the best genes in the world – FOR THIS?

So, I got my nose pierced. So what, man.

I remember checking "genius" on the order form – AND NOW LOOK!

Roz Chast/The New Yorker Collection/The Cartoon Bank

Not All Genetic Every child becomes their own person—not what their parents fantasize.

copy number variations Genes with various repeats or deletions of base pairs.

microbiome All the microbes (bacteria, viruses, and so on) with all their genes in a community; here, the millions of microbes of the human body.

fertile man can mate with any fertile woman to create a new person, and all human children have similar patterns of growth.

In terms of physical traits, although we notice differences, similarities are far more common: Each of us is like every other person, indeed with every mammal! (Two eyes, two ears, a brain, and all the other organs.) Modern medicine depends on these similarities. If someone develops a blockage in their cardiovascular system, surgeons can repair it because they have learned from thousands of scientists who have studied a million other hearts, each almost identical to the others.

Copy Number Variations

When the human genome was first mapped almost two decades ago, worldwide headlines trumpeted that accomplishment. Some anticipated finding a gene for each genetic disorder, hoping that a genetic cure would soon follow.

That "one gene/one trait" hope proved to be fantasy, as did the idea that all genes are perfectly coded with identical base pairs. Instead, everyone has some genetic variations that are unlike most other people. Seemingly minor alleles, with small deletions, repetitions, or transposition in any of the 3 billion base pairs, may be inconsequential, lethal, or something in between.

Some variations, such as a particular allele interacting with another allele, can have notable impact. Many forms of cancer, and many psychological disorders, including schizophrenia and autism spectrum disorder, correlate with **copy number variations** (Rees & Kirov, 2018; Shao et al., 2019). On the other hand, an estimated 100 genes can be deleted completely (no copy at all) with no evident ill effects (Zarrei et al., 2015).

One example is particularly relevant for child development. Children who are slow to develop are more likely to have copy number variations than other children (Park et al., 2019), and when researchers analyzed the genes of 420,000 British adults with no known impairment, those with certain copy variations were likely to have cognitive difficulties (Kendall et al., 2019).

The Microbiome

Another factor that profoundly affects each person is the **microbiome**, which refers to all of the microbes (bacteria, viruses, fungi, archaea, yeasts) that live within every part of the body. The microbiome includes "germs," the target of disinfectants and antibiotics. Nonetheless, most microbes are helpful, enhancing life, not harming it.

Microbes have their own DNA, reproducing every day. The newborn inherits microbiota from the mother, but from then on, the microbiome continually changes, depending primarily on diet. There are thousands of varieties of microbes, and together they have an estimated 3 million different genes—influencing immunity, weight, diseases, moods, and much more (Dugas et al., 2016; Gilbert et al., 2018). Particularly crucial is the effect of the microbiome on nutrition, since bacteria in the gut break down food for nourishment.

Experiments find that obese or thin mice change body size when the microbiota from another mouse with the opposite problem are added (Dugas et al., 2016). Thus, when a child weighs too little or too much, the microbiome may be more to blame than the parents.

The microbiome is now recognized as crucial in causing, as well as halting, childhood malnutrition (Kane et al., 2015; H. Smith et al., 2014). In one telling study, researchers in Malawi studied twins when one was malnourished and the other was not, even though both lived together and were fed the same. Did a greedy twin grab food from his brother? No! When scientists analyzed each twin's microbiome, they found crucial differences. That is why only one suffered.

One innovation of modern medicine is to implant feces (which are rich in microbes) from one person into another to cure illnesses. This has cured certain infections (especially *Clostridium difficile*) and gastrointestinal diseases (Vaughn et al., 2019).

ESPECIALLY FOR Medical Doctors
Can you look at a person and then write a prescription that will personalize medicine to their particular genetic susceptibility? (see response, page 85)

In the Beginning

The numbers cited previously may be hard to grasp: 3 billion base pairs, with 4 chemicals creating 20 amino acids that direct the formation of proteins on about 21,000 genes, many with several versions and copy number variations, on 46 chromosomes. To add to the complexity of numbers, almost 8 billion genetically unique humans are alive, each the direct descendant of perhaps 7,000 generations of great, great, great . . . grandparents.

But now we must explain another difficult equation: 1 + 1 = 1. How can the genes of one man added to the genes of one woman create only one child? To understand that, we begin again.

Gamete Plus Gamete

A reproductive cell is called a **gamete**. A gamete from one man combines with a gamete from one woman to create one child, who begins life as one cell, the zygote.

If a person is male, his gametes are *sperm* (Latin for "seed"); if a person is female, her gametes are *ova* (singular *ovum*, Latin for "egg"). Sperm and ova are made in a complex process (meiosis and mitosis) that prepares them to start a new life. But how does 1 sperm cell + 1 egg cell = only 1 new cell (the zygote)?

The answer is that each gamete has only 23 chromosomes, half as many as on the other body cells. Since there is a pair of chromosomes at each of 23 sites, a given gamete has either one or the other from each of the 23 pairs. At each of the 23 sites, it seems random which of the two possible chromosomes each gamete has. Thus, each man or woman can produce 2^{23} different sperm or ova—more than 8 million versions of their chromosomes (actually 8,388,608).

Usually a woman ovulates one ovum a month, and usually a man ejaculates between 200 million and a billion sperm, all of which are aided by the others as they are propelled toward that ovum. When one enters the ovum, the ovum shell hardens so no other sperm can enter, and fertilization occurs.

About 2 percent of all pregnancies in the United States in 2018 happen via *in vitro fertilization (IVF)* (Sunderam et al., 2019). IVF conceptions occur in a medical laboratory, where ripe ova are surgically removed from the ovaries, put in a laboratory dish (in vitro means "in glass"), and one sperm is inserted into each. Ideally, fertilization results in several zygotes, which begin to grow. Then, the most viable one (or several) is inserted into the uterus.

Either way, when a sperm and an ovum combine, the new cell combines the 23 chromosomes of one of those 8 million possible sperm with the 23 chromosomes of one of the 8 million possible ova to have 23 pairs of chromosomes, 46 in total. You could have an astronomical number of full siblings, none exactly like you.

Genetic Identity

Stop for a moment to think how useful it is that every tiny cell of a person is stamped with a unique code. By the time a baby is born, that first single-celled zygote has become about 26 billion cells. By adulthood, those cells become about 37 trillion. (These numbers are approximate: Adults lose several trillion cells over time.)

But no matter how old a person is or how large the total number of cells, DNA testing of any body cell, even from a drop of blood, can identify "the real father,"

gamete A reproductive cell. These sperm (for males) and ova (for females) each contain 23 chromosomes, so the zygote will contain 46 chromosomes, in 23 pairs.

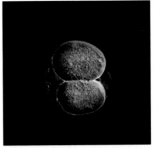
(a)

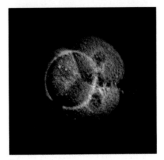
(b)

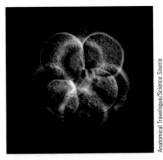
(c)

Anatomical Travelogue/Science Source

First Stages of the Germinal Period The original zygote as it divides into (a) two cells, (b) four cells, and (c) eight cells. Occasionally at this early stage, the cells separate completely, forming the beginning of monozygotic twins, quadruplets, or octuplets.

"the guilty criminal," "the long-lost brother." Many for-profit companies have analyzed drops of saliva from millions of curious people who want to know what characteristics, diseases, and traits they might carry, or where their ancestors lived.

Complete accuracy from commercial genetic testing or police labs is not yet reached. An imperfect sample of cells, or simplistic faith in test results, may lead to needless worry, false reassurance, and even mistaken criminal convictions (Starr, 2016; Tandy-Connor et al., 2018).

However, current technology can verify who is <u>not</u> a match. In 1966, when he was 30, a Japanese man was convicted of murder and sentenced to death. He pled not guilty. He continued to appeal, which postponed execution. Finally, advanced genetic analysis found him innocent. He was released from prison at age 78 (Honda, 2015).

Genes can be identified long after death. Indeed, genetic testing suggests that thousands of living East Asians are descendants of Genghis Khan, a famous (or infamous) general who lived in the twelfth century (Stoneking & Delfin, 2010). Another surprising discovery is that 1 to 4 percent of the genes of many living people came from Neanderthals or Denisovans—human species that predated *homo sapiens* (Gokhman et al., 2014).

Match and Mismatch

Each of the father's first 22 chromosomes, from number 1 to number 22, contains hundreds of genes in the same locations and sequence as each of the mother's chromosomes, from 1 to 22. Usually the match is exact; the gene pair is *homozygous* (literally, "same zygote").

Sometimes, however, one parent has a different allele for a particular gene than the other parent has. If one gene's code differs from that of its counterpart, the two genes still pair up, but they are *heterozygous* ("different zygote"). Usually this is no problem. Indeed, it often is better to be heterozygous than homozygous. (That is why marriages between siblings are ill-advised.)

The 23rd Pair

Now you know the "one important exception" to the general rule that every cell of a person contains a copy of all of that person's original 46 chromosomes. That

FIGURE 3.2

Determining a Zygote's Sex Any given couple can produce four possible combinations of sex chromosomes; two lead to female children and two to male children. In terms of the future person's sex, it does not matter which of the mother's Xs the zygote inherited. All that matters is whether the father's Y sperm or X sperm fertilized the ovum. However, for X-linked conditions it matters a great deal because typically one, but not both, of the mother's Xs carries the trait.

Possible Combinations of Sex Chromosomes

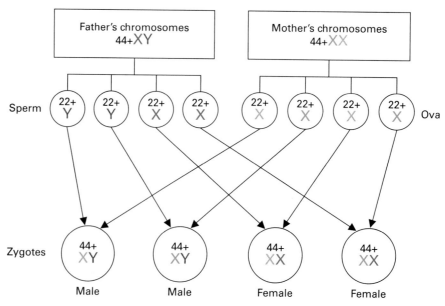

exception is the gamete itself. As you see, gametes usually have only half of the person's chromosomes. Usually, for 22 chromosomes, it does not matter much if a zygote happens to inherit one half of the pair at that site or the other. However, for the 23rd pair, it matters tremendously.

In females, the 23rd pair is two X-shaped chromosomes. Accordingly, it is called **XX**. In males, the 23rd pair has one X-shaped chromosome and one smaller chromosome, shaped like a Y. His 23rd pair is **XY**. (See **Figure 3.2**.)

Because a female's 23rd pair is XX, when her 46 chromosomes split to make ova, every ovum contains either one X or the other—but always an X. And because a male's 23rd pair is XY, half of his sperm carry an X chromosome and half a Y. The Y has fewer genes, but one crucial gene (called *SRY*) directs the embryo to make male hormones and organs. Thus, the sex of a zygote depends on which sperm penetrates the ovum—a Y sperm with the SRY gene, creating a boy (XY), or an X sperm, creating a girl (XX).

For humans, sex is assigned at conception. Curiously, in many reptiles and fish, prenatal temperature affects embryo sex, turning embryos into females when it is too hot or too cold. Biologists worry that climate change might produce an abundance of female lizards (Holleley et al., 2015)!

The Y chromosome directs the embryo to grow a penis, and much more. Typically, the SRY gene causes hormone production that affects the brain, skeleton, body fat, and muscles, beginning in the first weeks of prenatal development and continuing to the last breath in old age. As you have surely noticed, sex differences vary among individual men and women, influenced by the genes, hormones, and culture.

One review suggests that "gender identity is a multifactorial complex trait with a heritable polygenic component" (Polderman et al., 2018, p. 95). Many traits are affected by the XX or XY chromosomes, although even for biological traits, overlap between males and females is substantial and context dependent.

For example, some people who are transgender are convinced that they are not the gender that they seemed to have been at birth. (Sex and gender differences are discussed in Chapter 13.)

At conception, about 120 male zygotes are conceived for every 100 females, probably because the lighter sperm (fewer genes) have a slight advantage in the race to the ovum. From that moment on, male life is more fragile: More male embryos die.

At birth, the male/female ratio is 105:100 in developed nations and 103:100 in the poorest ones. That ratio not only reveals that male embryos die at higher rates but also the importance of context: In nations where many pregnant women are malnourished, male embryos are particularly vulnerable.

Currently, female embryos are vulnerable in another way, a cultural difference, not a biological one, as Opposing Perspectives explains.

Gene–Gene Interaction

Now we consider the specific genetic interactions that begin life. We focus first on interactions within the **genotype**, which are all the genes a person inherits. Those genes affect the **phenotype**, which are a person's appearance and other evident characteristics. As detailed later in this chapter, the phenotype is affected by many influences beyond the genotype; in many instances, nurture is more significant than nature. Nonetheless, genetic interactions matter, so we begin with them.

XX A 23rd chromosome pair that consists of two X-shaped chromosomes, one each from the mother and the father. XX zygotes become females.

XY A 23rd chromosome pair that consists of an X-shaped chromosome from the mother and a Y-shaped chromosome from the father. XY zygotes become males.

genotype An organism's entire genetic inheritance, or genetic potential.

phenotype The observable characteristics of a person, including appearance, personality, intelligence, and all other traits.

Twelve of 3 Billion Pairs This is a computer illustration of a small segment of one gene. Even a small difference in one gene can cause major changes in a person's phenotype.

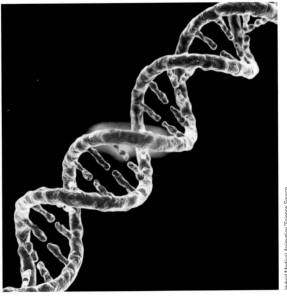

Hybrid Medical Animation/Science Source

OPPOSING PERSPECTIVES

Liberty Versus Legislation

In past centuries, millions of newborns were killed because they were the wrong sex, a practice that would be considered murder today. Now advances in science are enabling the same goal long before birth in various ways, such as inactivating X or Y sperm before conception.

Should it be legal for couples to choose their newborn's sex? It is against the law in at least 36 nations. It is legal in the United States (Murray, 2014).

One nation that recently tried to forbid prenatal sex selection is China. In about 1979, China began a "one-child" policy, urging, and sometimes forcing, couples to have only one child. That achieved the intended goal: fewer children to feed . . . or starve. Severe poverty was almost eliminated.

But the policy makers did not anticipate innovations in prenatal testing, which allowed prospective parents to know if a fetus is male or female. Chinese tradition is that sons care for aging parents, so couples wanted their only child to be male.

In 1993, the Chinese government forbade prenatal testing for sex selection. In 2007, China restricted international adoption (7,905 Chinese children were adopted in the United States in 2005, but only 2,231 were adopted in 2016). In 2013, China rescinded the one-child policy. Too late! Many couples now prefer to have only one child, and for that child to be a boy. The 2018 infant boy/girl ratio in China was about 117:100.

Some people believe prenatal sex selection is a reproductive right. The argument in its favor is freedom from government interference. Some fertility doctors and many individuals believe that couples should decide the timing, number, and gender of their children (Murray, 2014).

There is another argument in favor of sex selection, that parents will take better care of their daughters. Before prenatal sex selection, many nations had "excess mortality" among young girls. The data on boy/girl death ratios in nations with strong male preference suggested that parents did not nourish and protect their daughters as much as their sons.

Might prenatal sex selection protect girls, since they would have been chosen? Not necessarily. Some nations (e.g., South Korea) with an unbalanced birth ratio (evidence of prenatal sex selection) no longer have excess infant girl deaths, but other nations (e.g., India) still do (Kashyap, 2019).

The one-child policy in China suggests that prenatal sex selection may be harmful to society. Among the unanticipated results:

- Since 1980, an estimated 9 million abortions of female fetuses.
- Between 1980 and 2006, international adoption of about 200,000 Chinese girls.
- Beginning in 2000, far more unmarried young men than women.
- In 2020, many elders and not enough caregiving daughters-in-law. (Reduction of poverty allowed longer life: The average life span in China was 45 in 1965, but now it is 77.)

Many more young Chinese men than women die prematurely: For 2015–2020, the United Nations estimates 228,000 deaths of 15- to 24-year-old men and 136,000 15- to 24-year-old women (United Nations, 2019). A developmental explanation: Unmarried young men are more often depressed and take risks. Without wives, they have higher rates of suicide, substance abuse, and poor health practices (Srinivasan & Li, 2018).

The rate of HIV infection among Chinese college students has increased by 30 percent or more every year since 2015 (Li et al., 2019). Explanations are many, but one is that the unbalanced gender ratio leads to unprotected sex with more partners.

Problems with an unbalanced gender ratio include far more than death or HIV rates. Worldwide, more males than females are learning disabled, criminal, or violent; older men start wars and suffer heart attacks more often than women do. If many more boys than girls are born, the entire society will later suffer.

But wait! Is that sexist? Every male–female difference in the previous paragraph is a product of culture. Even traits that originate with genes, such as the propensity to heart attacks, are affected more by environment (in this case, diet and cigarettes) than by chromosomes.

Already, medical measures and smoking reductions have reduced heart attacks in men. In the United States in 1950, among people under age 65, four times as many men as women died of heart disease. By 2010, the rate for people under age 65 was lower for both sexes, but especially for men. The sex ratio in adulthood for heart deaths is 2:1 (two male deaths for every one female death), not 4:1. For the oldest adults, the male–female ratio of cardiovascular mortality is almost 1:1.

My Strength, My Daughter That's the slogan these girls in New Delhi are shouting at a demonstration against abortion of female fetuses in India. The current sex ratio of children in India suggests that this campaign has not convinced every couple.

From this it is evident that genes and gender are not destiny. Might nurture change? If national policy, scientific research, and cultural values create a gender imbalance, as they did in China, all three might mitigate the consequences. Learning disabilities could be remediated and then overcome, diplomacy could reduce wars, and so on.

If . . . might . . . could . . . those words explain why this is an Opposing Perspective. Is sex selection a parental right or a social wrong?

THINK CRITICALLY: Might laws prohibiting prenatal sex selection be unnecessary if culture shifted?

Additive Heredity

Some genes are *additive* because their effects *add up*. When genes interact additively, the outcome reflects the contributions of every gene that is involved. Height, hair curliness, and skin color, for instance, are affected by many additive genes: No single gene makes a person tall or short. Instead, height can be affected by more than a thousand genes, each contributing a very tiny amount (Zimmer, 2019).

How any additive trait turns out depends partly on all the genes a child happens to inherit (half from each parent, thus one-fourth from each grandparent). Most people have ancestors of varied height, hair curliness, skin color, and so on, and each of these traits ranges on a continuum, rather than either tall or short, curly or straight, dark or light. Consequently, no one's phenotype exactly mirrors the parents' phenotypes (although it always reflects their genotypes).

I see this in my family: Our daughter Rachel is of average height, shorter than her sisters or parents but taller than either of her grandmothers. Why? Although height is highly heritable (as you will learn later in this chapter), nurture matters, too. Rachel may have been undernourished, before she was born or during early childhood. For obvious reasons, I prefer a genetic explanation. Unlike her sisters, Rachel may have chanced to inherit her grandmothers' height genes from our genotypes.

Skin color is also additive, apparent in my family as well. None of my four daughters have exactly my skin color. This is not simply shades of light or dark, but instead subtle tints of pink, yellow, and brown. Strangers might not notice the differences, but when we try on each other's clothes, some colors are attractive on one but ugly on another.

Dominant–Recessive Heredity

Remember that, for every trait, the gene from the father matches up with the gene from the mother. If they are homozygous (identical in every base pair), the code is straightforward. If they are heterozygous and additive, each gene contributes to the trait.

But the most interesting—and sometimes unexpected—interaction occurs if the pair is heterozygous, *and* the alleles interact in a **dominant–recessive pattern**. In that case, one allele is so influential that it dominates the other. Accordingly, the influential gene is called the *dominant gene*, and the other, the *recessive gene*.

The recessive gene is still on the genotype, of course. When someone inherits a recessive gene that is not apparent in their phenotype, that person is said to be a **carrier** of that gene because the recessive gene is *carried* on the genotype.

Most recessive genes are harmless, so it does not matter if it is paired with a dominant or recessive gene from the other parent. Some recessive genes are destructive: examples are cited later in the chapter. Now, however, we explain dominant–recessive interaction with a harmless example, eye color.

Blue eyes result from a recessive allele and brown eyes result from a dominant one. If both parents have blue eyes, all their gametes will have a blue-eye allele; their children will inherit a blue-eye gene from each parent. Then the children's phenotype will be blue eyes, because no dominant brown-eye gene is in their genotype.

The same is true if both parents have brown eyes, and if neither is a carrier for blue eyes. In that case, when the eye color genes split so that one or the other of the

---

ESPECIALLY FOR Future Parents
Suppose you wanted your daughters to be short and your sons to be tall. Could you achieve that? (see response, page 85)

dominant–recessive pattern The interaction of a heterozygous pair of alleles in such a way that the phenotype reflects one allele (the dominant gene) more than the other (the recessive gene).

carrier A person whose genotype includes a gene that is not expressed in the phenotype. The carried gene occurs in half of the carrier's gametes and thus is passed on to half of the carrier's children. If such a gene is inherited from both parents, the characteristic appears in the phenotype.

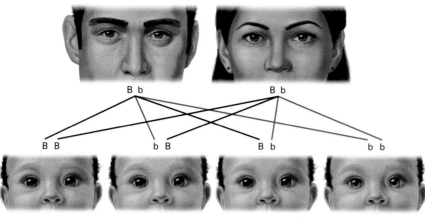

B = Gene for brown eyes   b = Gene for blue eyes

FIGURE 3.3

Changeling? No. If two brown-eyed parents both carry the blue-eye gene, they have one chance in four of having a blue-eyed child. Other recessive genes include the genes for red hair, Rh-negative blood, and many genetic diseases.

🔵 **Observation Quiz** Why do these four offspring look identical except for eye color? (see answer, page 85) ↑

X-linked A gene carried on the X chromosome. If a male inherits an X-linked recessive trait from his mother, he expresses that trait because the Y from his father has no counteracting gene. Females are more likely to be carriers of X-linked traits but are less likely to express them.

pair is on each gamete, every zygote will have two brown-eye genes, and every baby will have brown eyes, like the parents.

Complications arise with a blue-eye/brown-eye couple. If both eye-color genes of the brown-eyed parent are for brown eyes, all their children will have one blue-eye gene and one brown-eye gene. The blue-eyed parent will have a blue-eye gene on every gamete, so each child will be a carrier of that gene, but that will not affect the child's phenotype. Since brown is dominant, every child will have brown eyes.

But what if that brown-eyed parent (with a blue-eyed partner) is a carrier for blue eyes? When the 46 chromosomes of the carrier parent split to make gametes, half will have the blue-eye recessive gene and half the brown-eye dominant gene. Consequently, half of the children will inherit not only one blue-eye gene from the blue-eyed parent but also a blue-eye gene from their brown-eye parent. That's two recessive blue-eye genes, and that means blue eyes. The other half will have one brown-eye gene and one blue-eye gene (from their blue-eyed parent). They will have brown eyes because the brown-eye gene is dominant.

Finally, the most surprising possibility. Two brown-eyed parents may *both* carry the blue-eye recessive gene. Then they could have a blue-eyed child (one chance in four). A word to the wise here—when a child does not look like either parent, do not assume adoption, stepparenthood, or extramarital sex! It could be two carried recessive genes (see **Figure 3.3**).

More Complications

If you understand all possible pairings of brown-eye and blue-eye genes, each with different odds for the eye color and carrier status of their children, congratulations. But reality is even more complicated.

Remember that almost never does a single gene determine a trait; almost always other genes have some influence. Thus, the blue-eye/brown-eye example above is not quite accurate, because more than two genes affect eye color, sometimes additively. Hazel eyes, greenish eyes, and many shades of brown and blue are evidence.

Another complication is a special case of the dominant–recessive pattern. Some genes are **X-linked** (located on the X chromosome). If an X-linked gene is recessive—as are the genes for most forms of color blindness, many allergies, several diseases, and some learning disabilities—the fact that it is on the X chromosome is critical in determining whether it will be expressed in the phenotype (see **Table 3.1**).

If the zygote is female, she has two Xs, and thus a recessive gene on one of her Xs will not usually affect the phenotype. However, for a boy, an X-linked recessive gene almost never has a counterpart on the Y chromosome (because the Y chromosome has far fewer genes than the X). Therefore, recessive traits carried on the X affect the phenotypes of sons (XY) more often than those of daughters (XX).

This explains why males with X-linked disorders inherit it from their mothers, not their fathers. Females may be carriers, but their phenotype is rarely affected. Because of that, many more boys than girls are color-blind.

A study of color-blind children from six ethnic groups in northern India found a sex ratio of nine boys to one girl. The fact that people tend to marry within their group demonstrated that color blindness is genetic. The incidence of color blindness was 7 percent in one group but only 3 percent in another (Fareed et al., 2015).

TABLE 3.1

The 23rd Pair and X-Linked Color Blindness

23rd Pair	Phenotype	Genotype	Next Generation
1. XX	Typical woman	Not a carrier	No color blindness
2. XY	Typical man	Typical X from mother	No color blindness
3. ⊗X	Typical woman	Carrier from father	Half her children will inherit her ⊗. The girls with her ⊗ will be carriers; the boys with her ⊗ will have color blindness.
4. X⊗	Typical woman	Carrier from mother	Half her children will inherit her ⊗. The girls with her ⊗ will be carriers; the boys with her ⊗ will have color blindness.
5. ⊗Y	Color-blind man	Inherited from mother	All his daughters will have his ⊗. None of his sons will have his ⊗. All his children will have typical vision, unless their mother also had an ⊗ for color blindness.
6. ⊗⊗	Color-blind woman (rare)	Inherited from both parents	Every child will have one ⊗ from her. Therefore, every son will have color blindness. Daughters will be only carriers, unless they also inherit an ⊗ from the father, as their mother did.

⊗ = x that carries recessive gene for color blindness

Worldwide, ethnic groups vary in incidence of every disorder—some nations are high in stomach cancer, others in breast cancer, others in lung cancer, and so on (Torre et al., 2015). Part of the reason is genetic frequency, although diet and pollution also matter.

One final complication relates, again, to the sex of the parent. Some genes have a different effect depending on which parent they came from. This is called **parental imprinting**. Imprinting causes a problem if an active gene has a deleterious variation.

The best-known example occurs when a child inherits a small deletion or malfunction of the UBE3A gene on chromosome 15. If that deletion came from the father's chromosome 15, the child may have Prader–Willi syndrome. Such children have fewer biological curbs on their appetite, so they are often overweight. Temperamentally, they resist authority (including their parents). If that deletion is from the mother, the child will have Angelman syndrome and be thin, hyperactive, and too happy—laughing when no one else does. In both cases, children with that aberrant UBE3A gene are intellectually impaired.

Parental imprinting is common. Early in prenatal development (day 15), an estimated 553 genes act differently depending on which parent they came from, although usually the consequences are not harmful. It is thought that imprinted genes are crucial for growth, especially of the placenta (Cassidy & Charalambous, 2018).

Genetics Plus

Everything is genetic, in that genes affect everything. However, sometimes when people say that something is genetic, they mean that a particular trait is fixed, destined, inevitable. If people use that meaning of *genetic*, then nothing is genetic. Instead, everything is *genetics plus*.

Epigenetics

At conception, the "plus" includes RNA (ribonucleic acid, another molecule), mitochondria (the so-called powerhouse of the genes), and the microbiome, which was discussed earlier. Each affects how the genes function, from conception until death.

parental imprinting Some genes, or absence of needed genes, reflect whether that genetic condition came from the father or the mother. The concept is that the influence of the XX or XY chromosomes extends past the 23rd pair, as if the parent tattoos (imprints) a particular signature on them.

She Laughs Too Much No, not the smiling sister, but the 10-year-old on the right, who has Angelman syndrome. She inherited it from her mother's chromosome 15, and her two siblings inherited the mother's other chromosome 15. If she had inherited the identical deletion on her father's chromosome 15, she would have developed Prader–Willi syndrome, which would cause her to be overweight, always hungry, and often angry. With Angelman syndrome, however, laughing, even at someone's pain, is a symptom.

Maria Platt-Evans/Science Source

Indeed, as already mentioned, "a sea of microorganisms" in every person affects many basic functions, including immunity, metabolism, digestion, mood, and energy (Ash & Mueller, 2016). The numbers and kinds of these influences vary from one person to another, affecting the expression of the genes themselves (Douglas, 2018).

Thus, genes alone have no effect. Instead, all important human characteristics are *epigenetic*, which means that dozens of factors influence the expression of the genes, sometimes multiplying the effect, sometime halting it completely. Nothing is solely genetic; everything is epigenetic, including good qualities such as intelligence or compassion, mental illnesses such as schizophrenia and autism, and deadly diseases such as diabetes and strokes.

Diabetes has been studied in detail. Type 1 diabetes begins in childhood, but it is possible that a drug (*teplizumab*) can slow down the progression (Couzin-Frankel, 2019; Greenbaum, 2019). The more common form is type 2, which usually does not begin until middle or late adulthood. Many people inherit genes that put them at risk for diabetes but never develop the disease. The reason: epigenetics. For type 2 diabetes, the person's diet matters.

The relationship between genes and genetic traits is an example of *differential susceptibility*, first mentioned in Chapter 1. Most of the research on epigenesis has focused on biological factors in the first hours of prenatal life, but many later factors also affect genetic expression, some beneficial (e.g., nourishing food, loving care, and play) and some harmful (temperature extremes, drug abuse, and crowding).

Epigenetic factors can be psychosocial more than biological: If a person feels lonely and rejected, that is a social stress that allows genetic potential for heart disease or social anxiety to be expressed (Denhardt, 2018). Substance use disorder is also epigenetic. Some people inherit a particular reaction to alcohol, or nicotine, or heroin, but repeated use connects genes and craving, turning an experimenter into an addict (Hamilton & Nestler, 2019). Indeed, no trait—even one with strong, proven, genetic origins, such as high blood pressure or severe depression—is determined by genes alone because "development is an epigenetic process that entails cascades of interactions across multiple levels of causation, from genes to environments" (Spencer et al., 2009, p. 80).

Because epigenetic influences occur lifelong, latent genes can become activated at any point. Time itself is an epigenetic influence, as repeated copying of genetic instructions allows errors to accumulate (Veitia et al., 2017). Repeated environmental stresses—such as death of one parent, then another, then death of other loved ones—can become overwhelming, triggering a genetic tendency for depression or other psychological problems.

To reiterate, every trait, action, and attitude has a genetic component: Without genes, no development could occur. Yet every trait, action, and attitude has an environmental component; without context, genes have no power.

WHAT HAVE YOU LEARNED?

1. What is the relationship between genes and chromosomes?

2. What are copy number variations?

3. Why do siblings from the same two parents differ genetically?

4. How many chromosomes determine sex?

5. Which cells carry a person's entire genetic code?

6. How do genotype and phenotype connect?

7. Why do humans vary so much in skin color and height?

8. What is the difference between additive and dominant–recessive inheritance?

9. Why are sons more likely to inherit recessive conditions from their mothers than their fathers?

Nature and Nurture

Developmentalists had long hoped to pinpoint which genes are responsible for which traits. That hope was dashed by evidence that almost every important trait is **polygenic** (affected by many genes) and **multifactorial** (influenced by many factors, both nature and nurture).

A new question arose: Since genes have at least some influence on everything, how much is any particular trait determined by genes, and how much by environment? You remember from Chapter 1 that even "how much" is a simplification. However, it is true that some traits are more strongly influenced by genes (e.g., height) than others (e.g., religion). Scientists have some answers regarding the power of genes by studying twins.

Twins

All twins develop together prenatally, sharing a uterus and a birthday—that's what makes them twins. Most have only half their genes in common, just like any other siblings from the same two parents. However, some (about 25 percent of all twins) have exactly the same genes. How does that happen?

One Zygote or Two?

As you know, every zygote is genetically unique, copying itself as it multiplies to become two identical cells, then four, then eight, and so on, to become trillions of cells at birth, each with the same DNA. However, about once in every 250 human conceptions the zygote does something odd after it copies itself; it splits completely, creating two, or four, or even eight separate yet identical cells. That separation rate (0.4 percent) is for natural conceptions; IVF conceptions split to become twins about five times more often (2 percent) (Kanter et al., 2015). (See Visualizing Development on page 70.)

Those separate cells are *stem cells*, capable of becoming an entire person. If a stem cell duplicates, implants, and survives embryonic and fetal life, multiple births occur. One separation results in **monozygotic (MZ)** twins, from one (*mono-*) zygote (also called *identical twins*). Two or three separations create monozygotic quadruplets or octuplets.

Because they are genetically identical, MZ multiples can befuddle their parents and teachers, who may be unable to tell them apart. If necessary, an MZ twin can donate an organ (such as a kidney) for surgical implantation into their ailing twin, and the recipient will not experience organ rejection. MZ twins often have similar diseases, personalities, and life spans, although postconception events (nutrition, disease, accidents, the social context) may cause notable differences.

By contrast, most twins are **dizygotic (DZ)** (also called *fraternal twins*). They began life as two separate zygotes created by two ova fertilized by two sperm at the same time. (Usually, women release only one ovum per month, but not always.) Rates of dizygotic twinning vary by genes and culture: Rates are higher in West African women, lower in East Asian woman, higher in women aged 35 and older, and lower in woman under age 20.

Since they have only half of their genes in common, DZ twins can differ markedly in appearance, or they can look so much alike that only genetic analysis reveals that they are dizygotic. When a woman ovulates two ova, chance determines which sperm fertilizes each ovum, so about half the DZ twins are boy–girl pairs.

Research on Twins

The history of developmental science is peppered with studies of twins. Half a century ago, one study began by summarizing the previous 100 years:

> Since 1875, when Galton published an article entitled "The History of Twins as a Criterion of the Relative Power of Nature and Nurture" the study of twins has

polygenic Referring to a trait that is influenced by many genes.

multifactorial Referring to a trait that is affected by many factors, both genetic and environmental, that enhance, halt, shape, or alter the expression of genes, resulting in a phenotype that may differ markedly from the genotype.

monozygotic (MZ) twins Twins who originate from one zygote that splits apart very early in development. (Also called *identical twins*.) Other monozygotic multiple births (such as triplets and quadruplets) can occur as well.

dizygotic (DZ) twins Twins who are formed when two separate ova are fertilized by two separate sperm at roughly the same time. (Also called *fraternal* twins.)

Not Exactly Alike These two 4-year-old boys in South Carolina are identical twins, which means they originated from one zygote. But one was born first and heavier, and, as you see here, one appears to be more affectionate to his brother.

sarahwolfephotography/Moment/Getty Images

VISUALIZING DEVELOPMENT   One Baby or More?

Humans usually have one baby at a time, but sometimes twins are born. Most often they are from two ova fertilized by two sperm (*left*), resulting in dizygotic twins. Sometimes, however, one zygote splits in two (*right*), resulting in monozygotic twins; if each of these zygotes splits again, the result is monozygotic quadruplets.

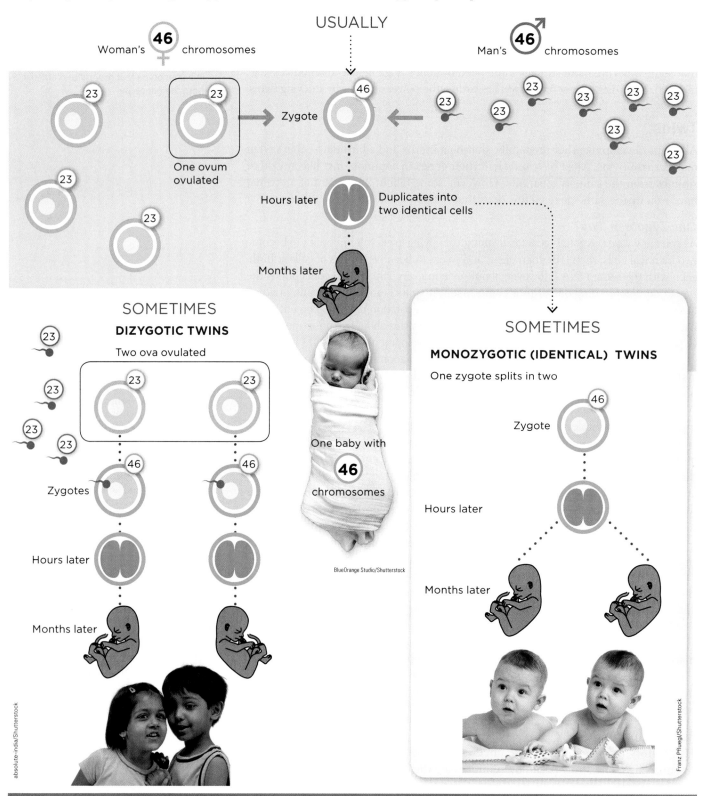

USUALLY

Woman's **46** chromosomes

Man's **46** chromosomes

23

23 — One ovum ovulated

46 — Zygote

23   23   23   23   23   23   23

Hours later — Duplicates into two identical cells

Months later

One baby with **46** chromosomes

BlueOrange Studio/Shutterstock

SOMETIMES
DIZYGOTIC TWINS

Two ova ovulated

23

23

23   23

Zygotes — 46   46

Hours later

Months later

absolute-india/Shutterstock

SOMETIMES
MONOZYGOTIC (IDENTICAL) TWINS

One zygote splits in two

46 — Zygote

Hours later

Months later

Franz Pfluegl/Shutterstock

been actively pursued by psychologists and biologists seeking to learn how heredity and environment influence the development of the biological and psychological characteristic of individuals.

[Loehlin & Nichols, 1976]

Those authors proudly proclaimed that they studied 800 sets of twins, unlike earlier studies that were smaller. Later studies critiqued this study, not for the size but for the cultural narrowness—all 800 were from the United States, all college-bound. We now have studies from many nations, and many types of families.

It seems logical that if pairs of MZ twins are more similar in some trait than DZ pairs, the reason must be genes. But even with the best current research, conclusions from twins are not as straightforward as they first seem. As scientists learn more about the interaction between heredity and the environment, and about the history of genetic research, some have been far more impressed with the power of genes than others.

In the first half of the twentieth century, when genes were thought to be much more powerful than the environment, a "eugenics" movement was used to justify deaths in Nazi Germany and forced sterilization in the United States. By mid-century, scientists were horrified by that outcome. Many downplayed genes and stressed the power of parents and of social conditions, especially family income.

Those scientists found nongenetic explanations for the similarities in monozygotic twins. For example, prenatal life (nongenetic) might make MZ twins more similar than dizygotic twins, in part because MZ twins usually share one placenta and DZ twins do not. After birth, since MZ twins look alike, parents might treat them as more alike than DZ twins. Thus, the shared traits of MZ twins may arise from nurture, not nature.

The Minnesota Study of Twins Reared Apart

The realization that parents treat look-alike twins the same, and thus their childhood experiences are identical, led researchers to find twins raised in separate homes in an attempt to distinguish the effects of genes from rearing. The first large-scale and well-funded effort to study such pairs occurred in the Minnesota Study of Twins Reared Apart (Bouchard et al., 1990).

They studied over 100 such twins, among them Oskar and Jack, monozygotic brothers born in the 1930s in Trinidad. Their parents separated when the boys were 6 months old. Their Catholic mother took Oskar to Nazi Germany and their Jewish father kept Jack. For obvious political reasons, the boys did not know their brother.

As an adolescent, Jack proudly joined the Israeli navy; as an adult he moved to California, where he started a business. Meanwhile, Oskar stayed in Germany. He was too young to fight in Hitler's army, but he became a patriotic German and a strong member of his labor union. Jack was also patriotic: He loved the United States, hated Germany, and thought labor unions demanded too much.

As part of the Minnesota Study, scientists flew Oskar and Jack to Minneapolis, where they disagreed vehemently on politics and worker's rights. Both were the same height, weight, and shape: Everyone expected those differences and similarities.

Other aspects of appearance required creative explanations. Both men had small moustaches, wire-rimmed glasses, and arrived wearing light blue shirts. Could a biological reason be found? Yes! Perhaps both discovered that their particular facial structure was enhanced with a moustache, perhaps both were nearsighted and wire-rimmed glasses were fashionable; perhaps their skin tone looked good with light blue.

But a genetic, biological explanation was hard to find for odd habits. Both Oskar and Jack washed their hands before and after they went to the bathroom;

VIDEO ACTIVITY: Identical Twins: Growing Up Apart gives a real-life example of how genes play a significant role in people's physical, social, and cognitive development.

both carried rubber bands on their wrists; both sneezed on elevators as a joke. They had almost identical scores on every test of intelligence, temperament, and personality.

Other sets of separated monozygotic twins in the Minnesota study also had striking similarities in hobbies, romances, vocations, and habits (Segal, 2012). From this and hundreds of other studies of twins, siblings, and adopted children in dozens of nations, scientists are convinced that genes affect every human trait. Genes influence marriage and divorce, college graduation and travel, employment and unemployment, and even dog or cat ownership. Instead of believing that genes affect only physical traits, developmentalists now think genes influence everything.

Three Identical Strangers

Another famous set of monozygotic adoptees were the triplets David, Bobby, and Eddy, featured in a documentary entitled *Three Identical Strangers*. Each was adopted, one by a wealthy family, one by a middle-class family, and one by a low-SES family. In each family, the boys had an older sister.

The researchers wanted to find out the power of wealth, siblings, and genes. The boys and their parents were unaware of each other (one adoptive father said he would have taken all three) until they discovered each other at age 19.

They were thrilled by their similarities and started a business together. But, in middle age, one became severely depressed and died by suicide. The other two wished they had known; they would have tried to stop him. Obviously, genes are not everything. Scientists now are very critical of this study: The families should have been told, and the boys should have met much earlier than they did.

Other ethical questions abound. Probably the most important is that genes should be appreciated, but not overemphasized. Too much stress on genes might undercut efforts to provide good health care, excellent schools, and a living wage for everyone; too little might downplay the inherent diversity of humankind.

Heritability

heritability A statistic that indicates what percentage of the variation in a particular trait within a particular population, in a particular context and era, can be traced to genes.

The twin research raises an important distinction between two words that sound similar: *heredity* and **heritability**. Heredity is something inherited that is passed down from one generation to the next. Inherited wealth is money bequeathed from the parents or grandparents to the next generation, as in a trust fund.

When referring to genetics, heredity refers to genes that are passed down from the parents. As you remember, each child inherits half of each parent's genes, which means, of course, one-fourth of each grandparent's genes, one-eighth of each great-grandparent's genes, and so on for millennia. We all have inherited traits that came from our genetic ancestors who lived 200,000 years ago.

However, heritability refers to populations, not individuals. Heritability indicates how much of the variation *in a particular trait, within a particular population, context,* and *era* can be traced to genes.

Heritability is high for some traits (e.g., eye color) and low for others (e.g., political party affiliation). Heritability is affected by the social context as well as by genes. For example, the heritability of height is very high (about 90 percent) when children receive good medical care and nutrition, but low (about 20 percent) when children are malnourished.

Nature and Nurture Interactions

Now we consider four complex nature/nurture issues: addiction, visual acuity, allergies, and life expectancy, each distinct in both inheritance and heritability. As you read about specific manifestations (alcohol use disorder, nearsightedness, asthma, and longevity), you will better understand the practical implications of genetic research.

Alcohol Use Disorder

Abuse of any drug, legal or not, is now called a *substance use disorder (SUD)*. We focus here on alcohol, as the most prevalent and most studied SUD; similar forces are found for other drugs.

Alcohol abuse has been evident for millennia. People have blamed addicts, or their parents, or cultures, or laws. Alcohol has been declared illegal (in the United States from 1919 to 1933) or considered sacred (in many religious rituals). People with SUD have been jailed, jeered, and even burned at the stake.

That was before an understanding of heritability and inheritance. We now know that genes create an addictive pull that can be overpowering, extremely weak, or somewhere in between. Each person's biochemistry reacts to alcohol in different ways, causing sleep, nausea, aggression, joy, relaxation, forgetfulness, depression, tears, or lust. And then, each society encourages or punishes addiction.

The genetic pull is polygenic: There is no "alcoholic gene." Alleles that affect substance abuse are widespread in the genome, some on every chromosome except the Y. Addiction is polygenic and multifactorial, with environmental factors interacting with genetic ones.

For example, one study assessed four genes that predisposed to addiction and found that, even when those genes were inherited, coping measures learned in childhood modified the risk of addiction (Trucco et al., 2018). Many studies find that parents affect their children's alcoholism, but differential susceptibility and family diversity makes it impossible to prescribe simple rules for parents (Mynttinen et al., 2017).

Punishing those with the genes does not stop addiction, although both nurture and nature are crucial. Indeed, some genes are protective. One gene, common in East Asia, makes people sweat and become red-faced after just a few sips. In Japan, personal embarrassment and social criticism discourage drinking in people with that inherited "flushing" response. That is beneficial: It avoids alcohol use disorder as well as a particular cancer that is likely in a flusher who keeps drinking (Newman et al., 2017).

Ethnicity matters for everyone: In the United States, adults of European origin are more likely to abuse alcohol than those of African origin, with variations by nation (Ireland high, Senegal low). Hispanic people born in the United States are more likely to abuse alcohol than those born in Latin America (Grant et al., 2012). Is this genetic or cultural? Both, of course.

Age also matters. Many teenagers start drinking because they think it makes them grown-up; some abuse alcohol only with friends; others soon begin drinking alone. Teenagers also brag about being drunk, seeing the room spin, even blacking out.

That contrasts with adults, who deny such effects. Generally, as people grow older, they drink less alcohol. Those who are addicted try to hide their drinking, and they are more likely to stop (Grant et al., 2012). Of course, those adults had the same genes when they were teenagers, but maturation has affected their reactions.

The 23rd pair of chromosomes is another genetic factor that affects risk. For biological reasons (body size, fat composition, metabolism), women become drunk on less alcohol than men, and female heavy drinkers double their risk of mortality compared to males (Wang et al., 2014). More men than women develop SUD, but women with SUD tend to begin drinking, and quit drinking, at later ages than men.

Hero Images Inc./Alamy Stock Photo

Welcome Home For many women in the United States, white wine is part of the celebration and joy of a house party, as shown here. Most people can drink alcohol harmlessly; there is no sign that these women are problem drinkers. However, danger lurks. Women get drunk on less alcohol than men, and females with alcohol use disorder tend to drink more privately and secretly, often at home, feeling more shame than bravado. All that makes their addiction more difficult to recognize.

Many cultures are more tolerant of male drinking (Chartier et al., 2014). As a result, in Japan, for example, both sexes inherit the same genes for metabolizing alcohol, yet women drink only about one-tenth as much as men. That disparity is cultural: When women of Japanese ancestry live in the United States, their alcohol consumption increases.

As you see from all these examples, both nature and nurture affect drinking. Genes are powerful; the social context is crucial. The final outcome: Those recovering from addiction are vulnerable to both nature and nurture. Once latent genes are activated, one drink awakens them. Then, nurture becomes crucial; psychosocial forces can push away from SUD or toward it.

Nearsightedness

Age, genes, and culture affect vision as well. The effects of age are straightforward, part of the genetic heritage shared by everyone in our species.

- Newborns focus only on things within 1 to 3 feet of their eyes, the rest is blurry.
- From age 3 months to 10 years, vision improves steadily.
- At puberty, the eyeball changes shape, increasing nearsightedness (*myopia*).
- In middle age, the eyeball shape reverses, decreasing myopia but increasing farsightedness.
- In late adulthood, vision often is less sharp, as cataracts cloud vision.

The effect of genes is more complex. Is eyesight inherited? For this you need to remember the discussion above regarding heritability.

A study of British twins found that the PAX6 gene, which governs eye formation, has many alleles that make people somewhat nearsighted (Hammond et al., 2004). Those alleles are inherited, which made heritability within this population almost 90 percent: If one monozygotic British twin was nearsighted, the other twin almost always was too. But remember the difference between inherited and heritability. The 90-percent heritability of nearsightedness among the British does not apply elsewhere, where circumstances differ.

Indeed, in some African nations, vision heritability is close to zero because severe vitamin A deficiency is common. Children with no vitamin A may become blind, even if their genotype is programmed for great vision. Scientists are adding a gene to maize (the local staple) to increase the vitamin A in it. If they succeed, and if people eat it, heritability will increase as vision improves (Fiedler et al., 2014).

What about children who are well nourished? Is their vision entirely genetic? Cross-cultural research suggests that, even with good nutrition, it is not. Indeed, as a review of the research explains, there are "widely divergent prevalences of myopia among genetically similar populations in different environments, suggesting that development of myopia is controlled by both environmental and genetic factors" (Coviltir et al., 2019).

"We are going down the path of having a myopia epidemic," according to the head of a vision program in Australia (Sankaridurg, quoted in Dolgin, 2015, p. 276). The problem was first recognized in Singapore and now is acute in China, where 90 percent of the teenagers and young adults are nearsighted, compared to 10 to 20 percent 60 years ago (Dolgin, 2015).

Myopia increased rapidly everywhere since 1980. Estimates are that half of the world's population will be nearsighted by 2050 (Holden et al., 2016).

This trend is apparent in the United States. Between the early 1970s and the early twenty-first century, nearsightedness increased from 25 to 42 percent (Vitale et al., 2009). Ophthalmologists agree that genes affect myopia, but "any genetic differences may be small" in explaining this increase (I. Morgan et al., 2012, p. 1739). Thus, something in the environment must have changed.

Observation Quiz Name three visible attributes of these young men that differ from a typical group of freshmen in North America. (see answer, page 85) ↓

Applauding Success These eager young men are freshmen at the opening convocation of Shanghai Jiao Tong University. They have studied hard in high school, scoring high on the national college entrance exam. Now their education is heavily subsidized by the government. Although China has more college students than the United States, the proportions are far lower, since the population of China is more than four times that of the United States.

Lai xinlin/AP Images

What could it be? One suggested culprit is academic work. Contemporary East Asian children study for long hours. That may be a reason for their excellent scores on international measures of math and science. As their developing eyes focus on their books, they may lose acuity for objects far away—which is exactly what nearsightedness means.

Another suggested culprit is screen time; U.S. children watch television and other screens more than they once did, again focusing on near vision.

Some ophthalmologists believe that myopia is increasing because children are kept inside, and therefore spend too little time in natural light. "We're kind of a dim indoors people nowadays" says one expert (Mutti quoted in Holden, 2010, p. 17). Might adjusting to images near and far (necessary when playing outside) counteract a genetic tendency for myopia (Dolgin, 2015)?

A fourth possibility is that sunlight provides natural vitamin D, and a deficiency of vitamin D causes nearsightedness in those who are genetically vulnerable (Tang et al., 2019). Differential susceptibility again!

No matter what the explanation, all these hypotheses begin with the fact that vision is not simply genetic. Nature interacts with nurture; heritability varies dramatically among nations.

Asthma

All allergies have a strong genetic component. However, the particular triggers for an allergic reaction vary. Some children inherit the tendency to be allergic, but one child might be allergic to cat hair, another to bee stings.

Their body's reaction varies as well. One person might get hives, another might develop **asthma**, a chronic inflammatory disorder of the airways that makes breathing difficult. We focus here on asthma, not only because it is common but also because it can be deadly.

Asthma is increasing worldwide, with rates tripling in the United States since 1980. (See **Figure 3.4** for current rates among those younger than 18 years old.) Parents report that 14 percent of U.S. 5- to 17-year-olds have been diagnosed with asthma at some time, and 9.5 percent have had an attack in the past year (National Center for Health Statistics, 2018). If we understood exactly which genes, in what way, trigger attacks, that would help with treatment and even cure.

However, this is complicated because asthma is polygenic. One region of chromosome 17 seems particularly implicated, but hundreds of genes, some on virtually every chromosome are involved. One group of 22 scientists counted only those genetic variants that increased the risk of asthma by at least 5 percent. They found 48 such genes (Ferreira et al., 2017).

The environment affects those genes. Several aspects of modern life—carpets, pollution, house pets, airtight windows, cigarette smoke, cockroaches, dust mites, stale air—correlate with asthma attacks, but no single factor is the sole trigger. Indeed, some research finds that infants exposed to cats, dogs, and cockroaches before age 3 are *less* likely to develop asthma (O'Connor et al., 2018).

asthma A chronic disease of the respiratory system in which inflammation narrows the airways from the nose and mouth to the lungs, causing difficulty in breathing. Signs and symptoms include wheezing, shortness of breath, chest tightness, and coughing.

FIGURE 3.4

Look For the Good News These data from the United States come from parents' answers to two questions: "Has your child ever had asthma?" and "Has your child had an asthma episode in the past year?" It is easy to spot the bad news: One child in every eight has had asthma. But can you see the good news? As children grow older, more of them have had asthma attacks but no longer do.

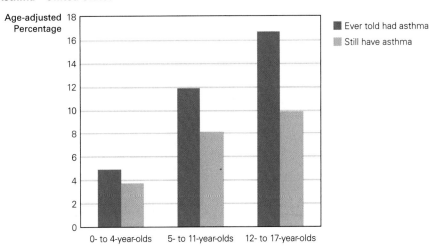

Children Who Have Ever Had Asthma versus Children Who Still Have Asthma—United States

Data from National Center for Health Statistics, 2018.

Age also matters. Many young children have an episode of strained breathing, but only some episodes are sufficiently intense to be diagnosed as asthma. Often asthma is outgrown as the lungs mature.

After puberty, asthma is half as common but twice as dangerous. In 2018, the U.S. Centers for Disease Control and Prevention reported 3,441 asthma deaths. Half of them were adults under age 65. To be specific, children under age 18 accounted for 6 percent of those deaths; adults aged 18–64 were 50 percent; and older adults (who comprise about 14 percent of the overall population) accounted for 44 percent. Thus, as with nearsightedness and substance abuse, genetic susceptibility combines with age and environment.

The search for culprit genes is becoming even more complicated because each aspect of asthma (the shortness of breath, the fear, the need for oxygen) is influenced by distinct genes. A combination of sensitivity, respiratory infections, obesity, and compromised lung functioning increases wheezing and shortness of breath (Mackenzie et al., 2014).

Some experts suggest a *hygiene hypothesis*: that "the immune system needs to tangle with microbes when we are young" (Leslie, 2012, p. 1428). This raises the possibility that modern babies may be overprotected from viruses and bacteria and consequently are more vulnerable.

In their concern about germs, parents limit exposure to infections and family pets that would strengthen immunity. Remember that immunity itself is affected by the microbiome as well as by genes.

The hygiene hypothesis is suggested by several facts: (1) First-born children develop asthma more often than later-born ones; (2) children born by cesarean delivery (very sterile) are more likely to develop asthma; and (3) children who grow up on farms, especially when they have direct contact with animals because their parents farm the traditional, nonindustrial way, have lower rates of asthma (Ober et al., 2017).

Some experts blame modern chemicals for most of the current increase in asthma; others consider that alarmist and anti-progress. What is known is that people differ regarding the genetic and environmental causes, but the consequences (frequency and severity of attacks) depend on medical treatment, which correlates with family SES (Beck et al., 2015). Thus, nature begins sensitivity, but nurture is crucial from conception on.

Longevity

How long you will live depends on what genes you inherit from your parents, right? No. One of the topics for which the term "genetic" is often misunderstood is determining the life span.

There are two aspects of the life span, each influenced by genes. The **maximum life span** is the longest time that a member of a particular species can live. The **average life span** is the length of life for an average member of a species.

maximum life span The oldest possible age to which members of a species can live under ideal circumstances. For humans, that age is approximately 122 years.

average life span The number of years the average newborn in a particular population group is likely to live.

The maximum life span is primarily genetic, and therefore varies dramatically from one species to another. For mice the maximum is 4 years; for humans, 122; for the bowhead whale, about 200 (Austad, 2010). If you were a mouse, genes would not let you reach your fifth birthday, but since you are human your genes might allow you to live a century.

The maximum human life span is thought to be 122, an age reached by Jeanne Calment, a French woman who died in 1997. No one has come close since then, and some people question whether Jeanne herself actually did (Zak, 2019). But no one before or after Calment has lived past 120.

Certain alleles (FOXO, APOE2, IGF1, DR1) are known to promote longevity—allowing their bearers to reach 90 or 100. Calment had DR1. She also avoided addiction, used lots of olive oil, and exercised (hiking, fencing) daily until she broke her leg at age 110.

Time and Place

With longevity, genes matter for average as well as maximum, but nurture matters more (van den Berg et al., 2019). That is true for every one of the nature–nurture interactions we just described. Let us look at maximum life span in detail.

You may have read about remote areas of the world (the Andes, an area in Russia, Northern Pakistan) where people live to 150 or so—but don't believe it. After about age 80, people brag about their age, adding years more quickly than the usual 365 days. They themselves may not know what year they were born. For them, human genes still stop life long before 122.

Although the maximum life span is set, genetically, one careful estimate puts the direct *genetic* contribution to longevity at 25 percent. The other 75 percent includes lifestyle (such as exercising more and eating less, with ample fruits, nuts, fish, and vegetables) and medical care (Passarino et al., 2016).

This may clash with what you know about the average life span in ancient times, sometimes said to be about 20 or 30. From that, some people imagine that human genes have changed. Time to remember how to calculate "average."

Before good nutrition, clean water, and immunization, life was especially fragile for babies and young children. Since the mean is calculated by adding up numbers and dividing by how many numbers are being summed, think about what the early deaths do to the average life span.

For example, suppose a given couple in the eighteenth century had eight children. Typically, one underweight newborn would die soon after birth, two would die of smallpox, measles, or other childhood diseases before age 5, one would be a risk-taking teenager who died at 17 because no hospitals existed to save him after a serious injury, one would die in childbirth at age 20, and three would live to have many children of their own, dying at ages 45, 55, and 80). For those eight, the mean would be about 25, and the median and mode (two other ways to calculate "average") would be less than 25. However, note that one would live to 80, as did a few fortunate people in every previous century.

Even among the wealthy, the average life span in ancient Greece was about 30 years (Finch, 2010). Yet long life was possible: Socrates lived to 71, when he was forced to drink hemlock. If he were not poisoned, he might have lived another decade or more.

Similarly, in U.S. history, Benjamin Franklin lived to 84, Thomas Jefferson, 83. George Washington died prematurely at age 67, probably because a sore throat led doctors to remove 6 pints of blood.

Place and time are crucial. In 2020, the United Nations reported average life expectancy for newborns in Japan to be 85, but for newborns in Chad the average life expectancy is only 54. This is primarily nurture, not nature, evident in that people in Japan live a few years longer than people of Japanese descent in other nations, and Chadians who emigrate to the United States live decades longer than those who stay in Chad. Within the United States, life span depends on region: The average Minnesotan lives six years longer than the average Mississippian.

Most of the differences in longevity between one person and another are related to diet, lifestyle, and medical care, more than to genes. That is likewise true for every nature–nurture example: A child who has no vitamin A can become blind no matter what their genes; a person vulnerable to alcohol use disorder (that is nature) will not develop alcoholism unless they drink alcohol (that is nurture); the genes for asthma have many "triggers" in the environment.

Some scientists emphasize the power of genes and believe that we can, and should, figure out how to change our genes. Other scientists think that is impossible and immoral. But one conclusion held by all developmentalists is that genes are not destiny.

Still Together At age 104 in 2016, the Lamolie twins are twice fortunate to be alive. The first time was at birth, when Paulette *(left)* weighed 3 pounds and Simone *(right)* weighed 2 pounds. The second is genetic—their shared genes must include some for longevity.

ESPECIALLY FOR Drug Counselors Is the wish for excitement likely to lead to addiction? (see response, page 85)

Practical Applications

No one should be blamed or punished for inherited problems. However, knowing that genes never act in isolation makes it easier to prevent, or at lease modify, genetic vulnerability.

For instance, if a family predisposition to substance abuse is evident, parents can keep drugs and alcohol out of their home and engage their teenagers in other activities, hoping their children become cognitively and socially mature before experimenting. If nearsightedness runs in the family, parents can play outdoors with their children every day. Outdoor play may also help those susceptible to asthma; exercise may promote longevity.

Of course, limiting alcohol and increasing exercise are recommended for everyone, as are dozens of other behaviors, such as flossing, saying "please," getting enough sleep, appreciating the sunrise, and writing thank-you notes. But no one can do everything. Awareness of genetic risks can guide priorities. Awareness of the interaction of nature and nurture promote both acceptance and action.

WHAT HAVE YOU LEARNED?

1. What is the difference between monozygotic and dizygotic twins?
2. How have twins been used to understand the influence of nature and nurture?
3. What is the difference between inheritance and heritability?
4. What in nature affects alcohol use disorder, and what in nurture does?
5. What suggests that nearsightedness is affected by nurture?
6. What can be done to help a child who is genetically vulnerable to asthma?
7. How much of longevity is genetic?
8. What indicates the power of nurture on longevity?

Chromosomal and Genetic Problems

Our discussion of this topic would not be complete without a review of problems that arise from genes and chromosomes. These are particularly relevant to life-span development for four reasons:

1. They provide insight into the complexities of genetics.
2. Knowing their origins helps limit their effects.
3. They are developmental—a person's age affects the impact.
4. Information combats prejudice: Difference is not always deficit.

Not Exactly 46

As you know, most gametes have 23 chromosomes, which gives most zygotes 46 chromosomes. However, sometimes gametes are formed with only 45, or with more than 46, chromosomes. That may occur in as many as half of all conceptions, but usually those zygotes do not implant (Kim & Kim, 2017). If implantation does occur, *spontaneous abortion* (known as *miscarriage*) is common: About half of all spontaneous abortions have an odd number of chromosomes (Milunsky & Milunsky, 2016).

Sometimes, however, if the extra chromosome is at the 11th, 19th, 21st, or 23rd site, a live birth is possible. Usually such conceptions are not inherited. Age increases the risk. Since ova begin to form before a girl is born, older mothers

VIDEO: Genetic Disorders offers an overview of various genetic disorders.

have older ova, which may have lost or gained a chromosome. Age also increases the rate of sperm with an extra chromosome, but usually only those sperm with 23 chromosomes manage to fertilize an ovum.

Trisomies

A person born with 47 chromosomes has a recognizable *syndrome*, a cluster of distinct characteristics that tend to occur together. This is called a *trisomy*, for three (*tri-*) chromosomes (*-somy*).

For all trisomies, it is possible for a person to have some cells with 47 chromosomes and some with 46, or for a chromosome to have only part of that third chromosome. Such conditions are called *mosaicism*, which one analyst calls "the rule rather than the exception," in that precise duplication of all the trillions of cells of a person is unusual (Lupski, 2013, p. 358).

Once in about 5,000 births a newborn has an extra chromosome at site 18, called *Edwards syndrome*. Even rarer is *Patau syndrome*, or *trisomy 13*. In both cases, multiple malformations in body and brain lead to early death.

By contrast, decades of happy life are now possible for newborns with *trisomy 21*, called **Down syndrome**, which occurs in about 1 in 200 newborns. Most people with Down syndrome have thick tongues, round faces, and slanted eyes, as well as distinctive hands, feet, and fingerprints, and heart abnormalities—which once meant death before age 5. No longer.

It is still true that people with Down syndrome have a distinctive appearance and physical problems, including with hearing, muscles, height, and the heart. Many are slow to develop intellectually, especially in language.

Regarding genes, about 300 distinct characteristics can result from that third chromosome 21; no one has them all. Regarding environment, historically, such children were considered uneducable (they were called "Mongolian idiots") until a British physician, John Down, opened a home for them, and showed that many could function well. Currently, most children with Down syndrome live at home, go to school, and learn to read and socialize (Laws et al., 2015).

Predicting Aging

Beyond slower learning in childhood, there are other developmental consequences of Down syndrome. One is that the aging process is accelerated: Many middle-aged Down syndrome individuals have wrinkled skin, gray hair, heart disease, and Alzheimer's disease. But remember variability: Their age-related problems can begin at any age from 30 to 60.

Research on people with Down syndrome has helped to develop an *epigenetic clock*, a process of analyzing the cells of a person (particularly the cells of the blood and skin) to indicate the rate of *methylation* (a process that begins at conception and continues lifelong). More methylation means faster aging, a better indicator than sheer chronological age.

The epigenetic clock is an example of a scientific application pioneered in the study of Down syndrome. In this way, chromosomal anomalies can lead to benefits for everyone (Horvath et el., 2015). The hope is that if adults know how fast their own bodies are aging, not only will they personally benefit but also scientists will better understand what diet, exercise, and so on to recommend. A team of scientists calls the epigenetic clock a "crystal ball" that can predict future illness, disability, and death (Ecker & Beck, 2019).

Problems of the 23rd Pair

Beyond trisomy 21, the only other common chromosomal miscount that allows a person to live a long life occurs with the 23rd pair of chromosomes. About 1 in

Claudia Daut/REUTERS

Universal Happiness All young children delight in painting brightly colored pictures on a big canvas, but this scene is unusual for two reasons: Daniel has trisomy-21, and this photograph was taken at the only school in Chile where typical and special-needs children share classrooms.

Down syndrome A condition in which a person has 47 chromosomes instead of the usual 46, with 3 rather than 2 chromosomes at the 21st site. People with Down syndrome typically have distinctive characteristics, including unusual facial features, heart abnormalities, and language difficulties. (Also called *trisomy-21*.)

ESPECIALLY FOR Teachers Suppose you know that one of your students has a sibling who has Down syndrome. What special actions should you take? (see response, page 85)

TABLE 3.2

Common Abnormalities Involving the Sex Chromosomes

Chromosomal Pattern	Physical Appearance	Psychological Characteristics	Incidence*
XXY (Klinefelter syndrome)	Males. Usual male characteristics at puberty do not develop—penis does not grow, voice does not deepen. Usually sterile. Breasts may develop.	Can have some learning disabilities, especially in language skills.	1 in 700 males
XYY (Jacob's syndrome)	Males. Typically tall.	Risk of intellectual impairment, especially in language skills.	1 in 1,000 males
XXX (Triple X syndrome)	Females. Normal appearance.	Impaired in most intellectual skills.	1 in 1,000 females
XO (only one sex chromosome) (Turner syndrome)	Females. Short, often "webbed" neck. Secondary sex characteristics (breasts, menstruation) do not develop.	Some learning disabilities, especially related to math and spatial understanding; difficulty recognizing facial expressions of emotion.	1 in 6,000 females

*Incidence is approximate at birth.
Information from Aksglaede et al., 2013; Benn, 2016; Hamerton & Evans, 2005; Powell, 2013; Stochholm et al., 2012.

every 500 infants is born with only one sex chromosome (no Y) or with three or more (not just two) sex chromosomes. Each causes a particular syndrome, impairing cognition and sexual maturation (see **Table 3.2**). Specifics depend on epigenetics (Hong & Reiss, 2014), which means, of course, that nurture matters.

One example is *Turner syndrome*, with only one chromosome, an X, at the 23rd site. Since there is no Y, the person is always a girl. She is typically short, with a webbed neck. Treatment involves hormones—some to increase growth and others to promote sexual characteristics at puberty (Lucaccioni et al., 2015).

Another pattern is *Jacob's syndrome*, in which a boy has two Y chromosomes (XYY). Boys with Jacob's syndrome are tall. Once it was thought that they were unusually aggressive, likely to become violent criminals. Later research, however, found some XYY men who were upstanding citizens (Re & Birkhoff, 2015).

This illustrates a common problem: Genetic anomalies are misinterpreted and misunderstood, leading to prejudice against those who are different when actually nurture matters for them as for all of us. The link between chromosomal problems, including Jacob's syndrome, and crime is no longer significant when SES is considered (Beckwith & Pierce, 2018).

Gene Disorders

Everyone carries genes for serious disabilities, and all of us have some unwanted genetic traits, sometimes minor (oddly shaped ears, hair in a cowlick) and sometimes major (vulnerability to diabetes or severe depression). Most such conditions are polygenic and multifactorial; nurture always matters. Here we focus on serious problems that are caused by a single gene.

Dominant Disorders

Most of the thousands of *known* single-gene disorders are dominant. Severe dominant disorders are uncommon because children who inherit them usually die before they reproduce. Since they have no children, the gene dies with them.

Severe dominant disorders occur in only three situations:

1. A spontaneous mutation. Sometimes neither parent has the dominant gene, but the gene appears when the gametes are formed.

2. Varied penetrance. Some dominant disorders can "penetrate" the genome slightly or more intensely. In such cases, adults might have a mild version, but their child is severely affected.

3. Adult onset. A few dominant disorders do not appear until mid-adulthood, including one form of Alzheimer's disease and all manifestations of *Huntington's disease* (a severe disorder of the central nervous system). They begin years after puberty, so adults could unknowingly transmit the dominant gene to half of their children.

Recessive Disorders

Recessive diseases are far more numerous, because only when two carriers mate might they have a child with the disease, and even then only one child in four has the double recessive. (Two of four are carriers, and one of four is not even a carrier—as explained on pages 65–66 regarding brown and blue eyes.)

Genetic analysis finds that everyone carries several recessive conditions, most of them exceedingly rare. Only about one in a million children is afflicted with one of those rare conditions because both parents happened to carry the same recessive gene. Odds of that happenstance increase when the parents are close relatives, or are members of a small group that, for generations, marries only people within that group.

Some recessive conditions are X-linked, including hemophilia, Duchenne muscular dystrophy, and many allergies. Interestingly, hemophilia—also known as the Royal Disease—became common among the royal families of Europe in the early nineteenth century because they tended to intermarry.

The most famous carrier was Queen Victoria of England. Half of her daughters and granddaughters were carriers. They bore rulers in Spain, Germany, and Russia, with hemophilia affecting many of their male descendants. Some historians believe that the Russian revolution of 1917 would not have occurred if Alexei, the only son of the Tsar, did not inherit the recessive gene from his mother, who was Queen Victoria's granddaughter.

Another X-linked disease is **fragile X syndrome**, caused by more than 200 repetitions of one base pair (Plomin et al., 2013). (Some repetitions are common, but not this many.) Fragile X is the most common form of *inherited* intellectual disability (many other forms, such as trisomy-21, are not usually inherited). Boys are more impaired by fragile X than are girls, since girls have a second X without the disorder.

Sometimes a genetic problem is caused not by genes, but by their absence. That is the case for *Williams syndrome*, caused by a deleted stretch of 26 to 28 genes on chromosome 7. People with the syndrome are quite verbal and friendly, sometimes too friendly and talkative to strangers. They have some unusual facial characteristics, sensitivity to sounds, and problems with spatial understanding, which makes math much harder for them than reading.

Many syndromes raise questions about what is typical and what is unusual. For instance, the "problem" of children with Williams syndrome is that they are too friendly and happy. But why is that a problem? Apparently, learning to be appropriately wary of strangers is expected for children. The danger is the difference-equals-deficit error, that people tend to consider those who are unlike themselves as deficient.

When Carriers Benefit

A few recessive diseases are quite common, because carriers benefit. About 1 in 12 North American men and women is a carrier for cystic fibrosis, thalassemia, or

Who Has the Fatal Dominant Disease? The mother, but not the children. Unless a cure is found, Amanda Kalinsky will grow weak and experience significant cognitive decline, dying before age 60. She and her husband, Bradley, wanted children without Amanda's dominant gene for a rare disorder, Gerstmann-Straussler-Scheinker disease. Accordingly, they used IVF and preimplantation testing. Only zygotes without the dominant gene were implanted. This photo shows the happy result.

fragile X syndrome A genetic disorder in which part of the X chromosome seems to be attached to the rest of it by a very thin string of molecules. The cause is a single gene that has more than 200 repetitions of one triplet.

sickle-cell disease, all devastating if a person inherits the gene from both parents. Nonetheless, it is thought that whenever a recessive condition becomes common, the gene must provide some benefits for carriers, even as it harms those who inherit the recessive gene from both parents. Cystic fibrosis carriers, for instance, may have some protection against cholera; Tay-Sachs carriers may have some protection against tuberculosis (Withrock et al., 2015).

 DATA CONNECTIONS: Common Genetic Diseases and Conditions provides more details about several different gene disorders. 🐾 **LaunchPad**

The carrier protection most apparent in the United States is the protection from malaria bestowed by the recessive gene for sickle-cell anemia. Indeed, four distinct alleles, each of which originated in a malaria-prone region, cause sickle-cell anemia.

Remember the blue eye/brown eye example to see how the recessive gene can become widespread. People who carry one copy of the sickle-cell gene also have one copy of the dominant gene for normal blood cells, so they are not much harmed by their recessive gene. If both parents are carriers, half of their gametes will have the sickle-cell genes and half will not.

Odds are, if such a couple had four children, one would have the normal genes from both parents and be vulnerable to malaria, one would have the sickle-cell gene from both parents and would die of sickle cell, and two would be carriers (one because of their father and one because of their mother). Those two would be likely to survive to have children of their own. Thus, the sickle-cell gene would become more common with each generation.

That explains why about 11 percent of Americans with African ancestors are carriers of the sickle-cell gene. Similar prevalence within a particular ethnic group is apparent for many genetic diseases. Carriers of the cystic fibrosis gene had some protection against cholera, so Americans with ancestors from northern Europe are the most common carriers. Carriers of Tay-Sachs had some protection from tuberculosis, so carriers often had ancestors from Central Europe.

Dark skin is protective against skin cancer, and light skin allows more vitamin D to be absorbed from the sun. The former is beneficial in very sunny climes, and the latter if a person lives where sunlight is scarce. Genetic analysis finds that the genes for light skin became common relatively late in the history of homo sapiens, when people began moving north from Africa.

Genetic protection may occur with current diseases as well. Some people in West Africa seem genetically protected against Ebola. Most other species of mammals also have some genetic protection against Ebola, a fact the provides clues for researchers trying to develop a vaccine (McElroy et al., 2018). A rare allele provides protection against HIV, the cause of AIDS. That allele is not yet common because, unlike malaria and cholera, the AIDS epidemic is recent.

A hundred years ago, after the birth of a child with a severe disorder, couples blamed witches or each other, not genes or chromosomes. That has changed. Many adults wonder what hidden health risks they have. Virtually everyone has a relative with a serious condition, or, if they query older family members, learns of infertility, miscarriages, or infant deaths that were never mentioned. Only when my cousin researched old U.S. Census documents did I learn that four of my grandmother's first six children died young, of causes then unknown.

Family history raises concerns, but discovering latent genes requires laboratory analysis, and interpreting those results requires expertise. Misinterpreting the results may lead to needless depression, abortion, or even sterilization when risk

CHAPTER APP 3

📱 Gene Screen

iOS:
https://tinyurl.com/yxvxbzun

RELEVANT TOPIC:
Genetic disorders, counseling, and testing

The Gene Screen app provides information about the inheritance and prevalence of recessive genetic diseases in different cultures and ethnicities.

CAREER ALERT   The Genetic Counselor

An understanding of life-span development is useful for every career. As students contemplate their future work, they should consult career counselors and check the Occupational Handbook of the Department of Labor, which lists prospects, salary, and qualifications.

Beyond those basics, however, these Career Alerts raise questions and issues that arise from a developmental perspective, issues that might not be found in a standard description of the career. You will see some of these issues in this discussion of genetic counseling.

There is far greater demand for genetic counselors than there are people trained in this area, so job prospects are good. Salary is good, too: The median in 2017 was $77,500. Training requires a Master's degree and then passing an exam to be certified (not required in every state). That all seems simple, but the reality is much more challenging.

The first challenge is to understand and communicate complex biological and statistical material, so that clients understand the implications of whatever genes they have. This is difficult: Not only are new discoveries made every day, but every disorder is polygenic and multifactorial, and mosaicism, methylation, and the microbiome are all relevant.

One reason this is a rapidly growing career is that many people are curious about their ancestry and pay for commercial tests (such as 23 and Me) to identify where their ancestors lived. In the process, they may discover confusing implications for their health, making genetic counseling essential (Smart et al., 2017). Further, since is it now apparent that almost every disease is partly genetic, many people are concerned about their own health, the health of their family members, or the health of their prospective children, and they want answers.

This is complex regarding the genes of an adult, but it is doubly difficult when discussing a prospective child, who will inherit only half of the genes from each parent.

Facts, medical treatments, and quality of life for a future, not-yet-conceived child are difficult to explain, but genetic counselors must consider much more than that. Each adult has emotions, assumptions, and values that differ between a husband and wife, and those values are not identical to the counselor. Not only does each person have a particular attitude about risk, religion, and abortion, but also communication is complex. People misunderstand results; counselors must draw charts, rephrase results, and repeat basic facts.

Thus, counselors must not only know facts, recent discoveries, and explain odds and consequences, but they must also be sensitive to complex social dynamics, respecting everyone—especially when a couple decides to terminate or continue a pregnancy when the counselor would have made the opposite choice.

Theoretical decisions often conflict with reality. If a woman knows that her embryo has trisomy-21, should she terminate the pregnancy? About two-thirds of prospective parents say no, but about two-thirds of pregnant women at high risk (e.g., over age 35) say yes, as do almost all (87 to 96 percent) women who know they are carrying a Down syndrome embryo (Choi et al., 2012).

Similarly, variation was evident when 152 pregnant women in Wisconsin learned that their embryo had trisomy-13 or trisomy-18. Slightly more than half of the women decided to abort; most of the rest decided to give birth but provide only comfort care for the newborn; and three chose full intervention to preserve life (their three babies lived for a few days but died within the first weeks) (Winn et al., 2018).

Many factors—including childhood memories, prior children, religion, opinions of others—make a difference (Choi et al., 2012). Unfortunately, no matter what the decision, outsiders sometimes tell parents they made the wrong choice—something genetic counselors never do.

Before deciding on this profession, ask yourself what you would do in the following situations, each of which has occurred:

- Parents of a child with a disease caused by a recessive gene from both parents ask whether another baby will suffer the same condition. Tests reveal that the husband does not carry that gene. Should the counselor tell the parents that their next child won't have this disease because the husband is not the father of the first child?

- A woman learns that she is at high risk for breast cancer because she carries the BRAC1 gene. She wants to have her breasts removed, but she refuses to inform her four sisters, half of whom probably carry BRAC1.

- A pregnant couple are both "little people," with genes for short stature. They want to know whether their embryo will have typical height. They plan to abort such a fetus.

- A person is tested for a genetic disease that runs in the family. The results are good (not a carrier) and bad (the person carries another serious condition). Should the counselor reveal a risk that the client did not ask about?

This fourth issue is new: Even a few years ago, the cost of testing precluded learning about unrequested results. But now GWAS (genome-wide association study) is routine, capturing the entire genome, so counselors learn about thousands of unsuspected conditions.

Even with careful counseling, people with identical genetic conditions often make opposite choices. For instance, 108 women who had one child with fragile X syndrome were told that another pregnancy would have a 50/50 chance of fragile X. Most decided to avoid pregnancy, but some (20 percent) deliberately conceived another child (Raspberry & Skinner, 2011).

In another study, pregnant women learned that their fetus had an extra sex chromosome. Half the women aborted; half did not (Suzumori et al., 2015). These decisions highlight why this career is not for everyone. Professionals explain facts and probabilities; people decide. Can you live with that?

---

is actually small, or the opposite—the birth of one impaired child after another. Genetic counselors are needed (see Career Alert).

As you have read many times in this chapter, genes are part of the human story. They influence every page, but they do not determine the plot or the final paragraph. The remaining chapters of this book describe the rest of the story. Each reader provides the conclusion.

WHAT HAVE YOU LEARNED?

1. How common is it for a zygote to have 46 chromosomes?

2. What is the cause and consequence of Down syndrome?

3. What are the consequences of too few or too many chromosomes at the 23rd pair?

4. How likely is it that you would conceive a zygote with too many or too few chromosomes?

5. How likely are you to be a carrier of serious genetic conditions?

6. Why are serious dominant diseases uncommon?

7. Why are some recessive conditions much more common than others?

8. What genetic conditions might you have inherited that also have benefits?

SUMMARY

The Genetic Code

1. Genes are the foundation for all development, first instructing the developing creature to form the body and brain, and then affecting thought, behavior, and health lifelong. Human conception occurs when two gametes (a sperm with 23 chromosomes and an ovum with 23 chromosomes) combine to form a single cell called a zygote.

2. A zygote usually has 46 chromosomes (half from each parent), which carry a total of about 21,000 genes. Genes and chromosomes from each parent match up to make the zygote, but the match is not always letter-perfect because of genetic variations called alleles, or polymorphisms.

3. People have about 3 billion base pairs, which are pairs of chemicals that code for the proteins that make up each gene. Variation in the number of base pairs are called copy number variations, which are sometimes harmless and sometimes devastating.

4. The microbiome also affects each developing person, usually aiding development (as with digestion) but sometimes harming it (as with some viruses).

5. Twenty-two pairs of chromosomes are autosomes, equally likely to be inherited by a boy or a girl. The 23rd pair of chromosomes determines inborn sex, XX in females and XY in males. The sex of the embryo depends on the sperm, since only men have a Y chromosome and thus can make Y gametes.

6. Genes interact in many ways, sometimes additively with each gene contributing to development and sometimes in a dominant–recessive pattern. If a recessive trait is X-linked, it is passed from mother to son.

7. Epigenetics refers to the effects on the genes of nongenetic material. This begins at conception, and continues lifelong, including social circumstances such as loneliness or more direct influences such as pollution.

Nature and Nurture

8. Twins are either monozygotic (identical, from one zygote) or dizygotic (called fraternal, from two zygotes). Since monozygotic twins share 100 percent of their genes, and dizygotic only 50 percent, comparing twins has been helpful in research on nature and nurture.

9. Genetic makeup can make a person susceptible to many conditions. Examples include substance use disorder (especially alcohol use disorder), poor vision (especially nearsightedness), allergies (especially asthma), and relatively early death.

10. Culture and family affect these conditions dramatically. Notable are cohort effects, as evident in early deaths caused by nurture in earlier centuries and in many nations today.

Chromosomal and Genetic Problems

11. Often a gamete has fewer or more than 23 chromosomes, which may create a zygote with 45, 47, or 48 chromosomes. Usually such zygotes do not duplicate, implant, or grow.

12. Infants may survive if they have three chromosomes at the 21st site (Down syndrome). These individuals may have fulfilling lives, although they are vulnerable to heart and lung problems, and, in midlife, to Alzheimer's disease.

13. Another possible problem is a missing or extra sex chromosome. Such people have intellectual disabilities or other problems, but they may also lead a fulfilling life.

14. Everyone is a carrier for genetic abnormalities. Usually these conditions are recessive, not apparent unless the mother and the father both carry the gene. Serious dominant disorders, such as Huntington's, usually do not appear until midlife.

15. Serious recessive diseases can become common if carriers have a health advantage. This is true for sickle-cell disease, which protected carriers against malaria, for cystic fibrosis, and for many other conditions.

KEY TERMS

zygote (p. 58)
deoxyribonucleic acid (DNA) (p. 58)
chromosome (p. 58)
gene (p. 58)
allele (p. 59)
copy number variations (p. 60)

microbiome (p. 60)
gamete (p. 61)
XX (p. 63)
XY (p. 63)
genotype (p. 63)
phenotype (p. 63)
dominant–recessive pattern (p. 65)

carrier (p. 65)
X-linked (p. 66)
parental imprinting (p. 67)
polygenic (p. 69)
multifactorial (p. 69)
monozygotic (MZ) twins (p. 69)

dizygotic (DZ) twins (p. 69)
heritability (p. 72)
asthma (p. 75)
maximum life span (p. 76)
average life span (p. 76)
Down syndrome (p. 79)
fragile X syndrome (p. 81)

APPLICATIONS

1. Pick one of your traits and explain the influences that both nature *and* nurture have on it. For example, if you have a short temper, explain its origins in your genetics, your culture, and your childhood experiences.

2. Many adults have a preference for having a son or a daughter. Interview adults of several ages and backgrounds about their preferences. If they give the socially preferable answer ("It does not matter"), ask how they think the two sexes differ. Listen and take notes—don't debate. Analyze the implications of the responses you get.

3. Draw a genetic chart of your biological relatives, going back as many generations as you can and listing all serious illnesses and causes of death. Include ancestors who died in infancy. Do you see any genetic susceptibility? If so, how can you overcome it?

4. List a dozen people you know who need glasses (or other corrective lenses) and a dozen who do not. Are there any patterns? Is this correlation or causation?

ESPECIALLY FOR ANSWERS

Response for Medical Doctors (from p. 61) No. Personalized medicine is the hope of many physicians, but appearance (the phenotype) does not indicate alleles, recessive genes, copy number variations, and other genetic factors that affect drug reactions. Many medical researchers seek to personalize chemotherapy for cancer, but although this is urgently needed, success is still experimental, even when the genotype is known.

Response for Future Parents (from p. 65) Possibly, but you wouldn't want to. You would have to choose one mate for your sons and another for your daughters, and you would have to use sex-selection methods. Even so, it might not work, given all the genes on your genotype. More important, the effort would be unethical, unnatural, and possibly illegal.

Response for Drug Counselors (from p. 78) Maybe. Some people who love risk become addicts; others develop a healthy lifestyle that includes adventure, new people, and exotic places. Any trait can lead in various directions. You need to be aware of the connections so that you can steer your clients toward healthy adventures.

Response for Teachers (from p. 79) As the text says, "information combats prejudice." Your first step would be to make sure you know about Down syndrome by reading material about it. You would learn, among other things, that it is not usually inherited (your student need not worry about his or her progeny) and that some children with Down syndrome need extra medical and educational attention. This might mean you need to pay special attention to your student, whose parents might focus on the sibling.

OBSERVATION QUIZ ANSWERS

Answer to Observation Quiz (from p. 66) This is a figure drawn to illustrate the recessive inheritance of blue eyes, and thus eyes are the only difference shown. If this were a real family, each child would have a distinct appearance.

Answer to Observation Quiz (from p. 74) Not nearsightedness! Rates of corrective lenses (estimated at 85 percent) might be as high among university students in the United States, but more Americans

would have contacts. Two other visible differences: uniforms and gender. Except for in the military, no U.S. university issues uniforms, and the majority of North American students are women. A fourth difference may be inferred from their attentiveness: The graduation rate of incoming college students in China is about 90 percent, compared to about 50 percent in the United States.

Growth Over the Life Span

"Never draw on the walls," parents tell their children. Yet Daniel's father, my nephew Bill, drew pencil lines on the kitchen wall every year to indicate how tall his son had become. Those marks are still there, despite major renovations.

Daniel is now 19, one inch shorter than Bill, and much taller than 5-foot, 4-inch Anne, his mother. I remember when Anne was thrilled to be "showing," because that bump meant that Daniel was developing, unlike her previous pregnancy that had ended in miscarriage.

Every day—from zygote to late adulthood—bodies develop. My nephew and his family illustrate this well. Bill is now 6 feet, 1 inch tall, an inch shorter than his height decades ago. He says he is shrinking with age, which I don't want to hear. If he is getting old, I am getting older; if he has shrunk, I have shrunk more.

But why do we celebrate that babies and children grow and yet wish that adults did not age? Isn't development good at every age? Why urge children to eat more and adults to eat less?

Growth means not just getting bigger; it also means getting better, appreciating life as bodies change, seeking a new balance. The life-span perspective (Chapter 1) emphasizes multidirectional growth, with gains and losses at every age.

To reflect this view, this chapter appreciates old age as well as embryonic growth, celebrating the good and preventing the bad—at every age. The focus is on physical growth and the nourishment that supports it (other chapters detail other aspects of growth, such as emotional, intellectual, neurological, and so on). Physical growth is stunningly quick, then fast, then slower, then rapid again, then stable, and finally reversed. Throughout, balancing gains and losses is crucial.

What Will You Know?

1. How many weeks of growth are needed after conception for a fetus born early to survive?
2. Are more of the world's children too thin or too fat?
3. Why are eating disorders particularly likely to begin during adolescence?
4. What is the effect on the body if adults restrict their food intake?

From One Cell to a Newborn

"Stunningly quick" growth occurs before birth, when the *zygote*, that single cell smaller than the period at the end of this sentence, becomes a baby. Between zygote and newborn, prenatal development is often divided into three main periods. The first two weeks are the **germinal period**; the third through the eighth week is the **embryonic period**; the ninth week until birth is the **fetal period** (see **Table 4.1** for alternative terms).

The Zygote

Within hours after conception, the zygote begins *duplication* and *division*. First, the 23 pairs of chromosomes duplicate, forming two complete sets of the genotype. These two sets move toward opposite sides of the zygote, and the single cell divides neatly down the middle into two cells, each containing the original genetic code. These two duplicate and divide, becoming four, which duplicate and divide, becoming eight, and so on.

Stem Cells

The first eight cells are **stem cells**, able to produce any other type of cell and thus to become a complete person (or monozygotic twins, quadruplets, or octuplets).

germinal period The first two weeks of prenatal development after conception, characterized by rapid cell division and the beginning of cell differentiation.

embryonic period The stage of prenatal development from approximately the third week through the eighth week after conception, during which the basic forms of all body structures, including internal organs, develop.

fetal period The stage of prenatal development from the ninth week after conception until birth, during which the fetus gains about 7 pounds (more than 3,000 grams) and organs become more mature, gradually able to function on their own.

stem cells Cells from which any other specialized type of cell can form.

TABLE 4.1

Timing and Terminology

Popular and professional books use various phrases to segment the stages of pregnancy. The following comments may help to clarify the phrases used.

- *Beginning of pregnancy:* Pregnancy begins at conception, which is also the starting point of *gestational age*. However, the organism does not become an *embryo* until about two weeks later, and pregnancy does not affect the woman (and is not confirmed by blood or urine testing) until implantation. Perhaps because the exact date of conception is usually unknown, some obstetricians and publications count from the woman's last menstrual period (LMP), usually about 14 days *before* conception.

- *Length of pregnancy:* Full-term pregnancies last 266 days, or 38 weeks, or 9 months. If the LMP is used as the starting time, pregnancy lasts 40 weeks, sometimes expressed as 10 lunar months. (A lunar month is 28 days long.)

- *Trimesters:* Instead of *germinal period*, *embryonic period*, and *fetal period*, as used in this text, some writers divide pregnancy into three-month periods called *trimesters*. Months 1, 2, and 3 are called the *first trimester*; months 4, 5, and 6, the *second trimester*; and months 7, 8, and 9, the *third trimester*.

- *Due date:* Although a specific due date based on the LMP is calculated, only 5 percent of babies are born on that exact day. Babies born between two weeks before and one week after that date are considered *full term*. [This is recent; until 2012, three weeks before and two weeks after were considered full term.] Because of increased risks for postmature babies, labor is often induced if the baby has not arrived within 7 days after the due date, although many midwives and doctors prefer to wait to see whether labor begins spontaneously.

If conception happens via *in vitro fertilization (IVF)*, explained in Chapter 3, technicians can remove one stem cell to analyze it for a lethal gene or extra chromosome. Even without that cell, if the remaining cells continue to multiply, are inserted, and implant, they can become an embryo, a fetus, and then a complete baby nine months later.

After about the eight-cell stage, a third process, *differentiation*, begins. With that, although every cell has the same genetic code as the original zygote, cells specialize, taking different forms and reproducing at various rates. Some become part of an eye, others a foot, others a brain. The rapidly duplicating and dividing cells are no longer omnipotent stem cells.

Implantation

About a week after conception, the multiplying cells (now numbering more than 100) separate into two distinct masses. The outer cells will become the *placenta* (the organ that surrounds and protects the developing creature). It grows first, so it can nourish the future embryo and then the fetus for the entire prenatal period. The first task of those outer cells, about 10 days after conception, is *implantation*—that is, to embed themselves in the lining of the uterus (see **Figure 4.1**).

Implantation allows the cell mass to tap into nutrition from the mother's uterine wall, beginning the interdependence of mother and child. Pregnancy is not diagnosed until the developing embryo implants and produces hormones.

Implantation is far from automatic; most conceptions do not implant. The cause of any specific failure is usually unknown. However, the rate of implantation is reduced if something is amiss in the zygote, in the lining of the uterus, or in the uterus itself. For example, scar tissue from an earlier infection may interfere with implantation.

How often natural conceptions do not implant is unknown (how could it be?). When viable zygotes are inserted in the uterus as part of IVF, only about a third implant (Somigliana, 2018).

Note that this occurs a few days before the woman's next menstrual period: Ideally the new embryo is nourished by ample nutrients in the mother's blood. When that occurs, hormones halt the next menstrual period, and a pregnancy test reveals that an embryo is about to develop.

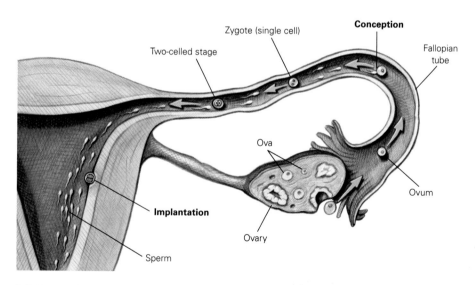

FIGURE 4.1

The Most Dangerous Journey In the first 10 days after conception, the organism does not increase in size because it is not yet nourished by the mother. However, the number of cells increases rapidly as the organism prepares for implantation, which occurs successfully not quite half of the time.

The Embryo

After implantation, the *embryonic period* begins. The formless mass of cells is not yet recognizably human but worthy of a new name, **embryo**. (The word *embryo* is often used loosely, but for scientists, embryo refers to the developing human from day 14 to day 56.)

At about day 14, a thin line called the *primitive streak* appears down the middle of the cell mass; it forms the neural tube 22 days after conception. The neural tube develops into the central nervous system, that is, the brain and spinal column. Soon the head appears. Eyes, ears, and mouth start to form; a minuscule blood vessel that will be the heart begins to pulsate.

By the fifth week, buds that will become arms and legs emerge. The upper arms and then forearms, palms, and webbed fingers grow. Thighs, knees, lower legs, feet, and webbed toes, in that order, appear a few days later, each with the beginning of a skeleton. Then, 52 and 54 days after conception, respectively, the fingers and toes separate.

Teratogens

Particularly in this early period, the health and habits of the mother are critical, as mentioned in Chapter 1. Women need to avoid every **teratogen**, which is something that can harm the body and brain before birth.

Among the most common teratogens are many viruses that seem mild to women. For instance, many young adults do not get a flu shot because they are willing to risk an episode of influenza that will trouble them for a few days. However, pregnant women need that vaccination, because flu is much worse for an embryo.

A newly recognized teratogen is Zika, caused by the bite of a virus-carrying mosquito. If that bite occurs in a newly pregnant woman, the brain of the embryo may not develop, and the newborn will have *microcephaly* (literally, "small head"). Zika was first identified in Brazil in 2015 and now is found in 86 other countries (Pielnaa et al., 2020). Vaccine trials are underway: 2021 is the likely date.

It is very difficult to avoid all teratogens. Some are chemicals in typical household products, particularly in pesticides and cosmetics, and some are drugs that many women take. Fortunately, most of them only sometimes cause damage, with dose, timing, frequency, and genes all affecting risk.

Research has focused on alcohol, which was once thought to be harmless. In about 1960, scientists linked maternal alcohol abuse during pregnancy to facial deformities, brain damage, and intellectual disabilities.

Fetal alcohol syndrome (FAS) occurs when alcohol consumed early in pregnancy distorts the eyes, ears, and upper lip as well as the brain. Later in pregnancy, alcohol use can cause *fetal alcohol effects (FAE)* that include emotional disorders, hyperactivity, and poor academic achievement (Nulman et al., 2018).

DATA CONNECTIONS: Teratogens examines both the effects of various teratogens and the preventive measures that mitigate their risk to a developing fetus. **LaunchPad**

From Embryo to Fetus

At the end of the eighth week after conception (56 days), the embryo weighs just one-thirtieth of an ounce (1 gram) and is about 1 inch (2½ centimeters) long. It moves frequently, about 150 times per hour, imperceptible to the woman. The developing person has the beginning of all the organs and body parts, except the sex organs.

Since the basic form of the future person emerges during the embryonic period, weeks 2–8 of prenatal life are sometimes called *the critical period*. Teratogens during

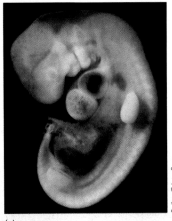

(a)

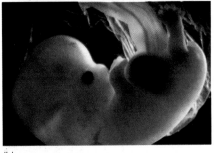

(b)

The Embryonic Period *(a)* At 4 weeks past conception, the embryo is only about 1/8 inch (3 millimeters) long, but already the head has taken shape. *(b)* By 7 weeks, the organism is somewhat less than an inch (2 centimeters) long. Eyes, nose, the digestive system, and even the first stage of toe formation can be seen.

embryo The name for a developing human organism from about the third week through the eighth week after conception.

teratogen An agent or condition, including viruses, drugs, and chemicals, that can impair prenatal development and result in birth defects or even death.

fetal alcohol syndrome (FAS) A cluster of birth defects, including abnormal facial characteristics, slow physical growth, and reduced intellectual ability, that may occur in the fetus of a woman who drinks alcohol while pregnant.

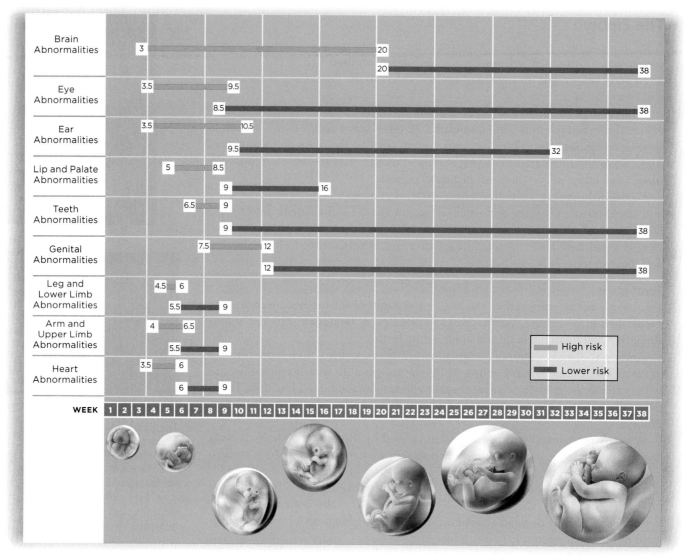

FIGURE 4.2

One More Reason to Plan a Pregnancy The embryonic period, before a woman knows she is pregnant, is the most sensitive time for structural birth defects. However, at no time during pregnancy is the fetus completely safe. Individual differences in susceptibility to teratogens may be caused by a fetus's genetic makeup or peculiarities of the mother, including the effectiveness of her placenta or her overall health. The dose and timing of the exposure are also important.

● ● **Observation Quiz** What part of the embryo and fetus has the longest period of vulnerability? What has the shortest? (see answer, page 117) ↑

this time can disrupt organ and skeletal formation, causing heart defects or misshapen limbs, for instance (see **Figure 4.2**). But do not assume all is well from then on. When the critical period ends, the fetus remains vulnerable, because the entire pregnancy is *a sensitive period*, especially for the brain, the eyes, and the sex organs.

Gender differentiation, in hormones as well as organs, begins at about 8 weeks after conception. It was once thought that female was the default sex, that the embryo would become male if the SRY gene on the Y chromosome caused primitive sex organs to move from inside the body to outside it. Otherwise, the embryo stayed female.

But we now know that becoming female is an active process as well. The early embryo has both male (via *Wolffian ducts*) and female (via *Müllerian ducts*) potential, in a tiny intersex gonad. At the end of the embryonic period, hormonal and genetic influences from the XX or XY typically cause one or the other to shrink, and then ovaries or testes, a vagina or penis, grow (Zhao et al., 2017). That early inter-sex period may explain why everyone has male and female hormones (testosterone and estrogen); the ducts cause most of us to have much more of one than the other.

fetus The name for a developing human organism from the start of the ninth week after conception until birth.

The Fetus

The organism is called a **fetus** from the ninth week after conception until birth. The fetal period encompasses dramatic changes. During these seven months, a tiny creature smaller than the final joint of your thumb, with no brain waves or capacity to live, becomes a newborn about 20 inches (51 centimeters) long with dozens of reflexes and instincts that allow entry into the human family. Newborns have many reflexes that aid survival. They react to faces, speech, a loving touch.

At every point in fetal growth, an *ultrasound* (sound waves that detect shape, also called *sonogram*) reveals growth and position, brain development, and sex organs. At 3 months, the fetus is about 3 inches (7.5 centimeters) long and weighs about 3 ounces (87 grams). Those numbers (3 months, 3 ounces, 3 inches) are rounded off for easy recollection, but growth rates vary: Some 3-month-olds are not quite 3 ounces and others already weigh 4. (On the metric system, 100 days, 100 grams, 100 millimeters, are similarly memorable and imprecise.)

By mid-pregnancy, the fetus weighs about 2 pounds or 1,000 grams, and the brain starts to regulate basic activity such as breathing and sucking. Not only do organs begin to function, but the fetus also has eyelashes, fingernails, and all the parts of the brain. This is also the point when many women feel *quickening*, the movement of the growing fetus.

Advances in neurological functioning at about 22 weeks past conception allow *viability*, when a fetus born far too early can become a baby who survives. At that point the surface of the brain is relatively smooth, but soon so many neurological connections form that the cerebral cortex folds into the bumpy surface of a func-tioning human brain.

Survival of babies born before 30 weeks was impossible 50 years ago, but now tiny respirators, intravenous feeding tubes, and heart monitors allow survival. However, the human womb is best: Fetuses born before 22 weeks do not live, because technology cannot produce essential brain maturation.

Currently, about 80 percent of babies born at 22 weeks past conception are via-ble, although often they have serious disabilities (Grisaru-Granovsky et al., 2019; Park et al., 2019). Much better, of course, is for prenatal growth to continue for another 16 weeks or so; every week *in utero* increases organ maturity, brain func-tion, and overall health.

A fetus typically gains more than 4½ pounds (2.1 kilograms) in the final three months, increasing, on average, to almost 7½ pounds (about 3.4 kilograms) at birth. Notice that weight more than doubles—think how much you would have to eat to weigh twice as much three months from now! A full-term baby is born at 38 weeks, although any time from 36 to 39 weeks past conception, and any weight from 5½ pounds (2,500 grams) to 9 pounds is considered good.

With modern medical care, underweight newborns usually survive, although even in advanced nations, low birthweight risks neonatal death (Zylbersztejn et al., 2018). Beyond survival, everyone—mother, father, baby, and society—would benefit if all newborns weighed 5½ pounds (2,500 grams) or more.

Prenatal Nutrition

Prenatal growth is not guaranteed. Teratogens affect growth, as do genes. Now we focus on another crucial influence, maternal nutrition. The fetus is harmed by anything that impairs appetite or digestion: drugs, exhaustion, anxiety, stress.

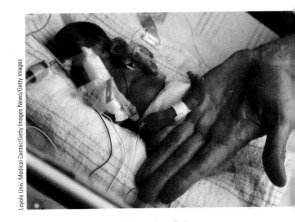

One of the Tiniest Rumaisa Rahman was born in 2004 after 26 weeks and 6 days, weighing only 8.6 ounces (244 grams). Rumaisa gained 5 pounds (2,270 grams) in the hospital and then, six months after her birth, went home. Her twin sister, Hiba, who weighed 1.3 pounds (590 grams) at birth, had gone home two months earlier. At their one-year birthday, the twins seemed typical, with Rumaisa weighing 15 pounds (6,800 grams) and Hiba 17 pounds (7,711 grams) (Nanji, 2005). Now, at age 15, Rumaisa is living a full, normal life.

body mass index (BMI) The ratio of a person's weight in kilograms divided by height in meters squared.

low birthweight (LBW) A body weight at birth of less than 2,500 grams (5½ pounds).

very low birthweight (VLBW) A body weight at birth of less than 1,500 grams (3 pounds, 5 ounces).

extremely low birthweight (ELBW) A body weight at birth of less than 1,000 grams (2 pounds, 3 ounces).

preterm A birth that occurs two or more weeks before the full 38 weeks of the typical pregnancy—that is, at 36 or fewer weeks after conception.

small-for-gestational age (SGA) A term for a baby whose birthweight is significantly lower than expected, given the time since conception. For example, a 5-pound (2,265-gram) newborn is considered SGA if born on time but not SGA if born two months early. (Also called *small-for-dates*.)

Poor prenatal nourishment stunts growth and shortens life, not only immediately but lifelong. Indeed, for many reasons, underweight newborns are likely to develop heart disease in middle age (Bavineni et al., 2019).

The Mother's Diet

Ideally, women begin pregnancy with a store of iron, calcium, and folic acid, and their **body mass index (BMI)** is between 20 and 25. [The formula for BMI is: weight in kilograms divided by height in meters, squared, or weight in pounds divided by height in inches, squared, multiplied by 703.]

Some obstetricians advise against a vegan diet, and most recommend prenatal vitamins to ensure sufficient folic acid and iron. If a woman begins pregnancy at a healthy BMI, she is expected to gain about 20 pounds without raising her blood pressure. Heavy women should gain less; thin women should gain more.

Women who begin pregnancy underweight, who then eat poorly, and who gain less than 3 pounds (1.3 kilograms) per month in the last six months often have newborns who are too small. If the mother is under age 16, still growing herself, her fetus is especially likely to be born early and underweight.

In poor nations, maternal hunger is the most common cause of slow fetal growth, preterm birth, and newborn death. For example, one study in rural Ethiopia compared pregnant women with and without adequate diets. In the latter, rates of low birthweight and preterm births (16 and 23 percent) were notably higher. Eight percent of their newborns were stillborn (Zerfu et al., 2016).

In nations with the best maternal nutrition, such as Sweden, only 3 percent of all newborns weigh less than 2,500 grams, and only 1 in 500 newborns dies soon after birth. That is one-fortieth the rate for those hungry Ethiopian women.

Low Birthweight

The World Health Organization defines **low birthweight (LBW)** as less than 2,500 grams. LBW babies are further grouped into **very low birthweight (VLBW)**, under 1,500 grams (3 pounds, 5 ounces), and **extremely low birthweight (ELBW)**, under 1,000 grams (2 pounds, 3 ounces). Some ELBW newborns weigh as little as 500 grams.

In the United States, poor health, drug use, and twin pregnancies are common reasons for LBW. Since multiples gain weight more slowly and are born several weeks earlier than singletons, some nations allow only one zygote to be implanted via IVF. However, in the United States, more than one viable zygote is inserted in about 75 percent of all IVF procedures (Sunderam et al., April 26, 2019). One consequence: Far more LBW twins and triplets than before IVF. The rate has fallen slightly since 2015, but it is still high (Martin & Osterman, 2019).

Preterm (no longer called *premature*) babies are usually LBW, because fetal weight doubles in the last trimester of pregnancy, with 900 grams (about 2 pounds) of that gain occurring in the final three weeks.

Not every LBW newborn is preterm. When weight gain is slow throughout pregnancy, babies are *small-for-dates*, or **small-for-gestational age (SGA)**. A full-term baby who weighs only 2,600 grams and a 30-week-old fetus weighing only 1,000 grams are both SGA, even though the first is not technically low birthweight.

Ranking worse than developed nations—and similar to Uruguay, Tanzania, Romania, and Spain—is LBW in the United States (see **Figure 4.3**). In addition to IVF, drug use is a major reason: Every psychoactive drug slows fetal growth, with tobacco the most common. Some pregnant women switch from tobacco to electronic cigarettes. That alarms scientists who deplore the lack of research on prenatal effects of vaping (Greene & Pisano, 2019).

Unfortunately, many risk factors — underweight, undereating, underage, drinking, and smoking — tend to occur together. To make it worse, many LBW infants are born to women who live in city neighborhoods where pollution is high — another risk factor (Erickson et al., 2016). Babies born in rural areas have risk factors as well — distance from advanced prenatal and newborn care, unwanted pregnancies, and exposure to pesticides (American College of Obstetricians and Gynecologists, 2011).

Many public health doctors and developmental scientists consider the prenatal period the most crucial of the entire life span. Unfortunately, that message is not reflected in many cultural practices and norms. For example, some nations provide free prenatal care for everyone: The United States is not one of them.

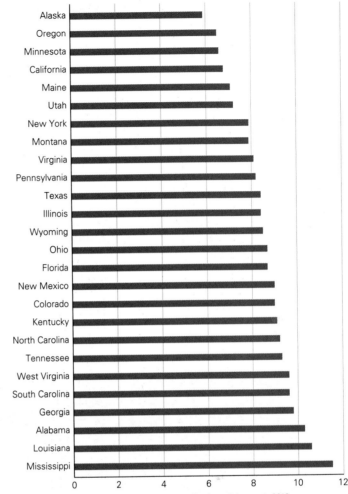

Percentage of LBW Babies — Selected U.S. States

Data from U.S. Department of Health and Human Services, February 1, 2018.

WHAT HAVE YOU LEARNED?

1. Why are the first days of life the most hazardous?

2. When do sex organs appear?

3. What is needed for a fetus to become viable?

4. What are the causes of low birthweight?

5. What occurs in the final three months of pregnancy?

FIGURE 4.3
Where Were You Born? Rates of low birthweight vary by nation, from about 4 to 20 percent, and, as you see here, within nations. Why? Poverty is a correlate — is it also a cause?

From Birth to Puberty

Human genes propel growth, from about 7½ pounds at birth to about 60 pounds before puberty. Nutrition, exercise, and medical care all help genes do their work.

Growth in Infancy

Newborns lose about 10 percent of their body weight in the first three days and then gain an ounce a day. Birthweight typically doubles by 4 months and triples by a year. If a newborn weighs 7 pounds, that child is expected to be 21 pounds at 12 months (9,525 grams, up from 3,175 grams at birth). Height increases, too, though less dramatically: Infants grow from about 20 inches at birth to 30 inches at their first birthday.

Variations

The numbers above are averages. As explained in Chapter 3, genes destine some people to be tall or short, light or heavy, and then nutrition allows that genotype to manifest itself in the phenotype. For healthy growth, it does not matter whether children are genetically short, tall, or middling. What matters is steady growth: Well-nourished, short 1-year-olds become healthy, short 9-year-olds.

Often measurements are expressed as a **percentile**, from 0 to 100; percentile rankings compare a person to others the same age (see **Figure 4.4**).

percentile A point on a ranking scale of 0 to 100. The 50th percentile is the midpoint; half of the people in the population being studied rank higher and half rank lower.

Weight of Girls and Boys, Birth to 24 Months

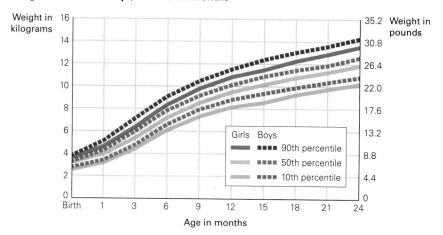

FIGURE 4.4

Averages and Individuals Norms and percentiles are useful—most 1-month-old girls who weigh 10 pounds should be at least 25 pounds by age 2. Individuals do not always follow the norms, which is not necessarily a problem.

For example, weight at the 30th percentile means that 29 percent of peers weigh less and 70 percent weigh more. Height and weight correlate: A taller-than-average child should also weigh more than average, perhaps being at the 80th percentile in both height and weight at every medical check-up.

An early sign of trouble occurs when:

- The height percentile is far from the weight percentile; or
- ranking changes markedly, either up or down; or
- a child is at the low extremes, for example, at the 2nd percentile.

For example, if weight is at the 80th percentile but height is at the 20th, that child is probably overweight. Or if weight decreases from the 50th to the 20th percentile, that could signify *failure to thrive*, a symptom of several serious conditions. The cause must be discovered and remedied; no longer are parental practices blamed (Jaffe, 2011).

Infant Nutrition

The best nutrition in infancy is breast milk. The World Health Organization recommends *exclusive* (no juice, cereal, or water) breast-feeding for the first months of life, an endorsement based on extensive research from all nations of the world. The specific fats and sugars in breast milk make it more digestible and better for the brain than any substitute (Wambach & Spencer, 2019). Especially for low-birthweight babies, breast milk from the mother is best, and donor milk is second best, although some nutrients may be added (Shakeel et al., 2019).

Ideally, infant nutrition starts with *colostrum*, a thick, high-calorie, high-protein fluid secreted by the mother's breasts at birth. However, in some cultures, mothers are forbidden to breast-feed until their milk "comes in" two or three days after birth. Instead, other women nurse the newborn or herbal tea is given. This illustrates that cultures do not always benefit development: Colostrum saves infant lives, especially if the infant is preterm (Moles et al., 2015; Andreas et al., 2015).

Breast-feeding mothers should be well nourished and hydrated; then their bodies will make the perfect baby food. Formula is preferable only in unusual cases, such as when the mother is HIV-positive or uses toxic or addictive drugs. Even then, however, exclusive breast-feeding may be best. In some nations, the infants' risk of catching HIV from their infected mothers is lower than the risk of dying from infections, diarrhea, or malnutrition as a result of bottle-feeding (A. Williams et al., 2016).

In China, a large study (more than a thousand babies in eight cities) compared babies in three conditions: (1) exclusively breast-fed (by their own mothers or wet nurses), (2) fed a combination of foods, formula, and breast milk, and (3) fed no breast milk. Based on the data, the researchers wrote that the WHO recommendation for exclusive breast-feeding for the first six months "should be reinforced in China" (Ma et al., 2014, p. 290).

Same Situation, Far Apart: Breast-Feeding
Breast-feeding is universal. None of us would exist if our foremothers had not successfully breast-fed their babies for millennia. Currently, breast-feeding is practiced worldwide, but it is no longer the only way to feed infants, and each culture has particular practices.

That same study also notes that most formula-fed babies develop well. This is an important finding: If some mothers find breast-feeding impossible, alternatives can result in quite healthy children. The idea that "breast is best" sometimes leads to *lactivism*, the extreme view that breast milk is the only way infants should be fed (Jung, 2015).

Nonetheless, the advantages of breast milk are many. Its composition adjusts to the age of the baby, with milk for premature babies distinct from that for older infants, and with the nutrients in breast milk adjusting to the needs of the growing infant (Lönnerdal et al., 2017). Quantity also increases to meet the demand: Twins and even triplets can thrive exclusively on breast milk for months. In terms of lifelong nutrition, breast-fed babies are less likely to become overweight children and are more likely to become healthy adults.

Each generation of scientists, pediatricians, and mothers knows more about breast milk. This is evident in four generations of my own family (see A Case to Study).

VIDEO: Nutritional Needs of Infants and Children: Breast-Feeding Promotion shows UNICEF's efforts to educate women on the benefits of breast-feeding.

Growth in Childhood

From ages 1 to 9, growth slows down. On average, children gain almost 3 inches and between 4 and 5 pounds each year. The brain grows as well, reaching almost full size (but not maturation) by age 5. That makes early education, nutrition, and activity vital.

Body Proportions

Maturation is evident in the sequence of growth, which is *proximo-distal* (near to far), from the spine to the extremities, and *cephalo-caudal* (from the head down). As a result, children sit before walking, chew food before kicking a ball, and read small print before writing legibly.

Proportions change following the same timetable, with the top-heavy toddler becoming the cartwheeling school-aged child. By age 10, the head is about one-sixth and the legs almost half a child's height. Older children can do somersaults and catch balls, because maturation of the body allows it.

This may be easier to grasp if you can visualize an unsteady 24-month-old and a 10-year-old doing the latest dance move. Increased weight and height are obvious, but also the relation between weight and height changes markedly. By age 10, the toddler's protruding belly, round face, short limbs, and large head are distant memories; feats of balance and coordination occur.

From Grandmother to Granddaughter

A hundred years ago, my grandmother, an immigrant who spoke accented English, breast-fed her 16 children. That's what all women of her cohort did. If they could not (for instance, if they were seriously ill), they found alternatives (milk from another mother, from a cow, or from a goat), all of which increased the risk of death.

That risk was much reduced by the middle of the twentieth century, when scientists created *formula* that was designed to be superior to cow's milk and better in some ways to breast milk. For example, formula solved some problems with breast-feeding, such as insufficient milk and the exhaustion that some breast-feeding mothers experienced. Bottle-fed babies gained more weight than breast-fed ones, which seemed to confirm that formula was best.

In the United States, in 1950, only poor, uneducated, or immigrant women breast-fed. That is why I was formula-fed. My mother told me that she wanted the best that modern medicine could provide.

When I became a mother, American companies were hiring local women in African and Latin American nations to dress as nurses and give new mothers a small supply of formula. When the free formula was used up, breast milk had dried up, so those mothers used what little money they had to buy more formula, diluting it to make it last, supplementing it with herbal tea.

The data on infant mortality were collected. Public health workers reported more deaths in formula-fed babies. They successfully convinced the World Health Organization (WHO) to recommend a return to breast-feeding.

They also convinced me. I breast-fed my babies and joined thousands of Americans who boycotted products from offending companies. However, my babies seemed hungry and I was stressed. Breast pumps were ineffective at the time, and my employer did not provide private places to pump. I gave my 2-month-olds occasional bottles of formula (carefully sterilized), juice, water, and, soon, baby cereal, mashed bananas, and applesauce in tiny jars.

Today, breast pumps are effective and employers are more accommodating. Currently most (about 80 percent) U.S. mothers breast-feed in the beginning (unlike my mother) and 19 percent breast-feed exclusively until 6 months (unlike me). My grandchildren were nourished solely on breast milk for six months.

About 25 percent of all babies in the United States are born in "Baby-Friendly" hospitals, a UNICEF designation that includes breast-feeding every newborn within half an hour of birth, frequent nursing, and no other foods or liquids until 6 months (Patterson et al., 2019). The result is higher breast-feeding rates throughout early infancy.

Four generations of my own family, each nourished differently, have led to three thriving grandchildren. Will norms change again when they have newborns?

Nutrition

Many factors influence physical health and growth, including exercise, clean water, exposure to pollution, and medical care. All are detailed in later chapters.

Here we focus on nutrition, which needs to be adequate but not excessive. As proximo-distal growth proceeds, the ideal BMI is lower at ages 5 and 6 than at any other age, making children seem thin. Don't worry: Energy and agility, not weight, are the best indicators of health. For most contemporary children, overfeeding is more common than underfeeding.

Malnutrition in Childhood

stunting The failure of children to grow to a normal height for their age due to severe and chronic malnutrition.

In the poorest nations, some children are **stunted** (short for their age), because chronic malnutrition prevents growth. Severe stunting is 3 standard deviations from typical height of North American children. Less than 1 percent of children are genetically that short, but in some nations, 35 percent are stunted because they are chronically underfed (see **Figure 4.5**).

wasting The tendency for children to be severely underweight for their age as a result of malnutrition.

Even worse, some children are **wasted**, severely underweight (3 or more standard deviations below average). Adults who were wasted in infancy are not only short but also have lower IQs later on, even if they are well fed in adulthood (Waber et al., 2014). This may be directly related to reduced brain growth, but in addition, severely malnourished infants are less active. A child with no energy is a child who is not learning.

In many nations, especially those in East Asia, Latin America, and central Europe, child nutrition has improved. Fewer children are stunted. This is evident with a glance: Teenagers are notably taller than elders (see photo).

India is one such nation (Dasgupta et al., 2016). More than half of all Indian children were stunted in 1980, but in 2014, stunting was at 17 percent and wasting at 5 percent (UNICEF, 2015). China and Chile have almost eliminated stunting.

Improvement is not universal. In some African nations, wasting is increasing for three reasons: (1) Climate change is causing drought that reduces crops, (2) civil wars prevent transport of food, and (3) AIDS has sickened and killed the parents, who, worldwide, are the adults most devoted to the welfare of young children. International aid and grandmothers have helped millions of motherless children, but many more millions are hungry. Stunting is at 18 percent in Niger and at 13 percent in Mali and Chad (Akombi et al., 2017).

Prevention, more than treatment, is needed. Ideally, prenatal nutrition, breast-feeding from well-fed mothers, and then iron and vitamin A with adequate local food, stops malnutrition before it starts. If that fails, highly nutritious formula (usually fortified peanut butter) may restore weight, and antibiotics control infection.

Such medical help is not always available. Many rural families in sub-Saharan Africa are hours away from a doctor. Some children die before they reach treatment, and some severely underweight children die even with good medical care, because long-term starvation causes failure of the digestive system (Freerks et al., 2019; Gough et al., 2014).

Too Much Body Fat

In a dramatic reversal, in most nations the most common nutritional problem is now overeating of unhealthy food. This leads to **overweight**, which is defined as a BMI above the 85th percentile, and **obesity**, defined as a BMI above the 95th percentile. Both are increasing worldwide.

In the United States in 2016, 35 percent of 6- to 11-year-olds were overweight and 19 percent were obese. Childhood overweight correlates with asthma, high blood pressure, and elevated cholesterol (especially LDL, the "lousy" cholesterol), as well as cognitive and social problems. School achievement decreases, self-esteem falls, loneliness rises, and victimization increases (Nabors et al., 2019; Ryabov, 2018).

Severe obesity increases throughout childhood. In the United States, it is three times higher in middle childhood than in early childhood, and it doubles again in adolescence (Ogden et al., 2017). It may be worse in nations that once were poor. As food becomes more plentiful, cultural practices have not caught up. Adults encourage children to eat, causing later illness rather than, as once was true, preventing early death.

For instance, in China, in only two decades (from 1991 to 2011), overweight among 6- to 12-year-olds more than doubled (from 11 percent to 26 percent) (Jia et al., 2017) (see Visualizing Development, page 99). Many Chinese elders remember when children died of malnutrition, but they ignore the dangers of obesity.

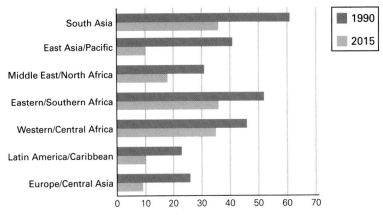

Stunting Prevalence (in Percent) by World Region—1990 and 2015

Data from UNICEF, January 13, 2017.

FIGURE 4.5
Evidence Matters Genes were thought to explain height differences among Asians and Scandinavians, until data on hunger and malnutrition proved otherwise. The result: starvation down and height up almost everywhere—especially in Asia. Despite increased world population, far fewer young children are stunted (255 million in 1970; 156 million in 2015). Evidence now finds additional problems: Civil war, climate change, and limited access to contraception have increased stunting in East and Central Africa, from 20 to 28 million in the past 50 years.

Observation Quiz Which regions have the most and least improvement since 1990? (see answer, page 117) ↑

overweight Weighing as much or more than the top 15 percent of U.S. children of the same age in about 1990 as indicated by the 2000 CDC growth charts. Far more than 15 percent of U.S. children now exceed the earlier norms.

obesity Weighing as much or more than U.S. children of the same age in about 1990 who were in the top 5 percent as indicated by the 2000 CDC growth charts. Far more than 5 percent of U.S. children are now obese.

ESPECIALLY FOR Medical Professionals You notice that a child is overweight but hesitate to say anything to the parents, who are also overweight, because you do not want to offend them. What should you do? (see response, page 117)

One Chinese father complained:

> I told my boy his diet needs some improvement . . . my mum said she is happy with his diet . . . [that he] eats enough meat and enough oil is used in cooking. . . . In their time, meat and oil were treasures so now they feel the more the better. . . . I decided to move out with my wife and son . . . his grandparents were a big problem . . . we couldn't change anything when we lived together.
>
> *[Li et al., 2015]*

This helps explain why children of recent immigrants to North America are more likely to be overweight than their parents. A Canadian review of 49 studies on immigrants found that when they switch to a North American diet, obesity increases (Sanou et al., 2014). (See Opposing Perspectives.)

OPPOSING PERSPECTIVES

Who Is to Blame?

Obesity increases if: (1) Newborns are born too early; (2) infants are formula-fed and eat solid foods before 4 months; (3) young children have televisions in their bedrooms and drink large quantities of soda; (4) older children sleep too little but have several hours of screen time each day; and (5) children of any age rarely play outside.

All five are under parental control, but parents themselves often blame genes for their children's weight, in part because heavy adults tend to have heavy children. However, although both parental practices and genes contribute to obesity, culture may be crucial. Look at the figure on obesity among 6- to 19-year-olds in the United States (see **Figure 4.6**). Are the large ethnic gaps (such as only 11 percent of Asian Americans but 26 percent of Hispanic Americans) genetic?

Note that African American *girls* are more often obese than boys, while Asian and Hispanic American *boys* are more often obese than girls, even though children of the same ethnicity inherit the same 45 chromosomes, with only one different chromosome. The fact that gender influences the ethnic groups differently suggests that the social context is crucial.

Obesity increases as family income falls, which is the opposite of a century ago. That is also evident in the data: In developed nations, ethnic differences in rates of childhood obesity closely track ethnic differences in SES. Some analysts point to the cost of food: Cheaper foods are calorie dense and nutrition poor.

However, detailed data in California find that childhood obesity increases as income falls among children of European and Latinx backgrounds, but not in African American children (Fradkin et al., 2015). Could genes or parenting practices be the cause?

Explanations vary, because some people are more likely to blame social factors and others to blame personal ones. That is the reason for opposing perspectives. Blaming individuals suggests that the solution is to enlighten parents and children. One U.S. study educated parents *and* children together. Childhood weight declined

Prevalence of Obesity among 2– to 19-Year-Olds—United States

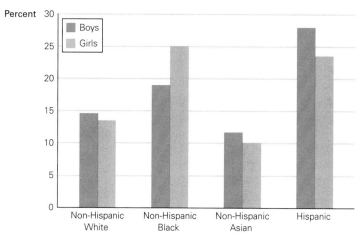

Data from Hales et al., 2017.

FIGURE 4.6

Ethnic or Economic? Obesity increases as income decreases. Is that obvious from this figure?

and health improved, not just during the intervention, but also over the long term (Yackobovitch-Gavan et al., 2018).

Blaming societies suggest that nations should restrict advertising of fast foods, salty and fatty snacks, and candy. Thirty-four nations and one U.S. city (in California) now tax sugary soda, a known cause of obesity, and those taxes generally lead to fewer purchases of soda and better nutrition overall. That results in lower rates of obesity, but also anger and resentment among some U.S. manufacturers and individuals who oppose any government restriction of personal choice (Niederdeppe et al., 2014).

Although perspectives vary, one thing is clear: Obesity is a major health problem, beginning in childhood and continuing throughout life. Something should be done about it.

VISUALIZING DEVELOPMENT   Childhood Obesity Around the World

Obesity now causes more deaths worldwide than malnutrition. Reductions are possible. A multifaceted prevention effort—including parents, preschools, pediatricians, and grocery stores—has reduced obesity among U.S. 2- to 5-year-olds:

Overall, the prevalence of obesity among adolescents (20.6%) and school-aged children (18.4%) is higher than among pre-school-aged children (13.9%) (Hales et al., 2017). However, obesity rates from age 6 to 60 remain high everywhere.

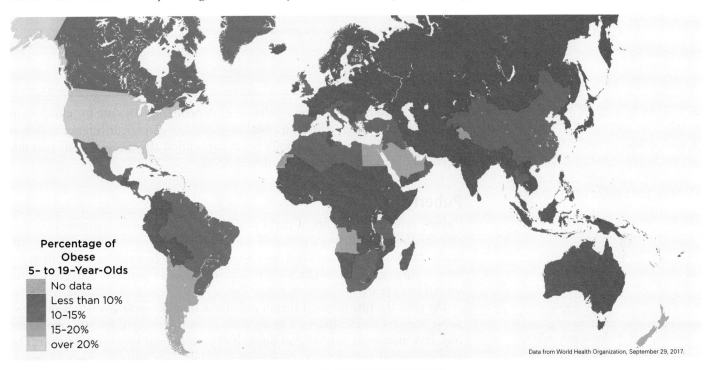

Percentage of Obese 5- to 19-Year-Olds
- No data
- Less than 10%
- 10–15%
- 15–20%
- over 20%

Data from World Health Organization, September 29, 2017.

FACTORS CONTRIBUTING TO CHILDHOOD OBESITY, BY THE NUMBERS

Children's exposure to ads for unhealthy food continues to correlate with childhood obesity (e.g., Hewer, 2014), but nations differ. For instance, the United Kingdom has banned television advertising of foods high in fat, sugar, and salt to children under age 16. The map above shows data from the World Health Organization; other groups' data may differ. However, the overall fact is clear: Childhood obesity is far too common.

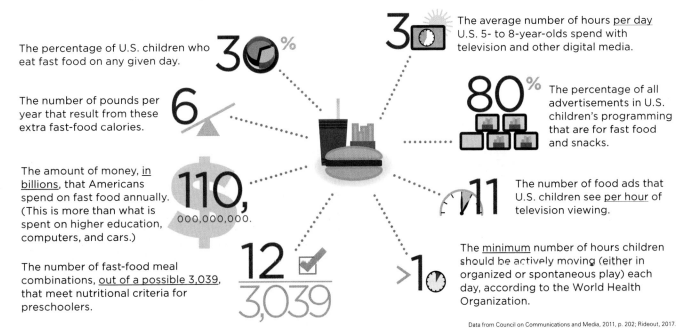

The percentage of U.S. children who eat fast food on any given day. **30%**

The number of pounds per year that result from these extra fast-food calories. **6**

The amount of money, in billions, that Americans spend on fast food annually. (This is more than what is spent on higher education, computers, and cars.) **$110,000,000,000.**

The number of fast-food meal combinations, out of a possible 3,039, that meet nutritional criteria for preschoolers. **12/3,039**

The average number of hours per day U.S. 5- to 8-year-olds spend with television and other digital media. **3**

The percentage of all advertisements in U.S. children's programming that are for fast food and snacks. **80%**

The number of food ads that U.S. children see per hour of television viewing. **11**

The minimum number of hours children should be actively moving (either in organized or spontaneous play) each day, according to the World Health Organization. **>1**

Data from Council on Communications and Media, 2011, p. 202; Rideout, 2017.

Adolescence

As you just read, growth slows down in childhood, equally true for children of every gender because children's bodies show few gender differences. But at puberty growth explodes, and one's sex at conception affects every body part differentially, from top to bottom (hairline to feet).

Puberty

Puberty refers to the years of rapid physical growth and sexual maturation that end childhood, producing a person of adult size, shape, and sexuality. Puberty typically starts sometime between ages 8 and 14 and is complete about four years later—although some height, weight, and reproductive potential are affected for several more years.

For girls, the first outward sign of puberty is usually nipple growth. Soon a few pubic hairs are visible, followed by a growth spurt, widening of the hips, **menarche** (the first menstrual period), full pubic-hair pattern, and breast maturation. The average age of menarche among normal-weight U.S. girls is about 12 years, 4 months (Biro et al., 2013).

For boys, the usual sequence is growth of the testes, initial pubic-hair growth, growth of the penis, **spermarche** (first ejaculation of seminal fluid), first facial hair, peak growth, deepening of the voice, and final pubic-hair and beard pattern (Herman-Giddens et al., 2012; Susman et al., 2010). The typical age of spermarche is just under 13 years. Age varies markedly, from about age 8 to about age 14.

These changes are observable, but the most dramatic growth is unobserved, in hormones and the brain, discussed in more detail in Chapter 5. Although

menarche A girl's first menstrual period, signaling that she has begun ovulation. Pregnancy is biologically possible, but ovulation and menstruation are often irregular for years after menarche.

spermarche A boy's first ejaculation of sperm. Erections can occur as early as infancy, but ejaculation signals sperm production. Spermarche may occur during sleep (in a "wet dream") or via direct stimulation.

Do They See Beauty? Both young women—the Mexican 15-year-old preparing for her Quinceañara and the Malaysian teen applying a rice facial mask—look wistful, perhaps even worried. They are typical of teenage girls everywhere, who do not realize how lovely they are.

children's level of sex hormones is low, and although all children increase in estradiol and testosterone at puberty, sex differences are dramatic. Compared to prepubertal boys, by early adulthood, testosterone is 45 times higher; compared to prepubertal girls, by late adolescence estradiol is 8 times higher (Herting & Sowell, 2017).

Ethnic and Gender Differences

In the United States, African Americans reach puberty, on average, seven months earlier than European or Hispanic Americans; Asian Americans average several months later (Dvornyk & Waqar-ul-Haq, 2012; Biro et al., 2013). This is probably more nurture than nature, because families vary more than ethnic groups: Siblings from one home may begin puberty years before their same-ethnicity friends.

XX or XY chromosomes have marked impact. In height, the average girl is two years ahead of the average boy, but she stops growing sooner. The female height spurt occurs *before* menarche, whereas for boys the increase in height is relatively late, *after* spermarche.

By late adolescence, the boys are taller than the girls: Adult men in the United States are 5 feet, 10 inches, on average; adult women, 5 feet, 5 inches. Thus, a sixth-grade boy with sexual fantasies about the taller girls in his class is neither perverted nor precocious; his hormones are ahead of his height. Soon he will be taller than most of his female peers.

The Growth Spurt

Growth during puberty has two thrusts: overall increase in size and sexual maturation. First, we describe the growth spurt.

As the word "spurt" implies, growth during adolescence increases quickly. Imagine that you have a nephew whom you see only at Thanksgiving. Get ready for a surprise at puberty. Not only is he suddenly bigger (some boys gain 6 inches and 20 pounds in a year) but also his proportions have changed.

At puberty, growth proceeds from the extremities to the core (the opposite of the earlier proximo-distal growth). Thus, fingers and toes lengthen before hands and feet, hands and feet before arms and legs, arms and legs before the torso, facial features (ears, nose, and lips) before the head, which is not only bigger but more oval and less round.

Because the torso grows last, many pubescent children are temporarily big-footed, long-legged, and short-waisted. If they complain that their jeans don't fit, they are probably right—even if those jeans fit perfectly a month earlier. If they are clumsy, knocking over a lamp or a glass of water, forgive them: They are not yet adjusted to their new reach.

With that pubescent nephew at Thanksgiving, you may also be astonished at how much he eats. To fuel the growth spurt, appetites increase before height shoots up. Exactly when, where, and how much weight is gained depends on heredity, hormones, diet, stress, exercise, and gender, but many pubescent youth seem gangly and pudgy.

The normal body changes of puberty horrify some adolescents. Indeed, puberty can precipitate unhealthy eating and exercise (Klump, 2013). A related problem is drug use. Girls may smoke cigarettes to curb their appetite; boys may take steroids to increase their muscles; adolescents of any sex use diet pills to change their size and drugs to quell their anxiety. All these disrupt growth and nutrition. Although drug abuse is harmful at any age, it is particularly disruptive when a person is not yet fully grown.

A height spurt follows the weight spurt; a year or two later a muscle spurt occurs. Thus, the pudginess and clumsiness of early puberty are usually

VIDEO: The Timing of Puberty depicts the usual sequence of physical development for adolescents.

Ancient Rivals or New Friends? One of the best qualities of adolescents is that they identify more with their generation than their ethnic group, here Turk and German. Do the expressions of these 13-year-olds convey respect or hostility? Impossible to be sure, but given that they are both about mid-puberty (face shape, height, shoulder size), and are both in the same school, they may become friends.

Running Speed of Girls and Boys, Ages 5 to 18

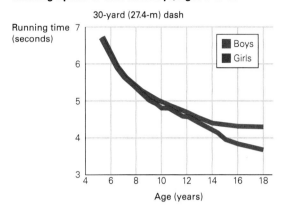

Data from Malina et al., 2004, p. 222.

FIGURE 4.7
Little Difference Both sexes develop longer and stronger legs during puberty.

primary sex characteristics The parts of the body that are directly involved in reproduction, including the vagina, uterus, ovaries, testicles, and penis.

secondary sex characteristics Physical traits that are not directly involved in reproduction but that indicate sexual maturity, such as a man's beard and a woman's breasts.

body image A person's idea of how their body looks.

gone by late adolescence. Inner organs grow as well, but coaches especially need to remember that the torso—which houses the vital organs—grows last.

By the end of puberty, lungs have tripled in weight, allowing adolescents to breathe more deeply and slowly. The heart doubles in size, the heartbeat slows, pulse decreases, and blood pressure rises. Red blood cells increase, dramatically so in boys. Consequently, endurance improves: Some older teenagers can run for miles, dance for hours, stay up all night, and still seem alert (see **Figure 4.7**). The crash comes later than it would for children or older adults.

One organ system, the lymphoid system (including tonsils and adenoids), *decreases* in size: Compared to children, teenagers are less susceptible to respiratory ailments. As a result, mild asthma often switches off at puberty—half as many teenagers as children have asthma (MMWR, June 8, 2012), and teenagers have fewer colds and allergies than they did.

When the larynx grows, the voice lowers, especially noticeable in boys. Another organ system, the skin, becomes oilier, sweatier, and more prone to acne, an unwelcome sign of maturation. Hair becomes coarser and darker, and grows under arms, on faces, and over sex organs. Specifics depend on genes as well as on hormones.

Sexual Characteristics

The body changes that turn boys and girls into men and women are the other aspect of pubescent growth. Those characteristics that are directly involved in conception and pregnancy are called **primary sex characteristics**. During puberty, every primary sex organ (the ovaries and uterus, the penis and testes) increases dramatically in size and matures in function. By the end of the process, reproduction is possible.

At the same time, development occurs in **secondary sex characteristics**, not needed for reproduction (hence secondary), but triggering delight and/or distress because they indicate sexuality. One such characteristic is shape. At puberty males widen at the shoulders and grow about 5 inches taller than females, while girls widen at the hips and develop breasts. Female curves are considered signs of womanhood, but neither breasts nor hips are required for conception; they are secondary, not primary, sex characteristics.

Although primary characteristics are crucial biologically, secondary sex characteristics are important psychologically, and few teenagers are happy with them. Breasts are an obvious example. Many adolescent girls buy "minimizer," "maximizer," "training," or "shaping" bras, hoping that their breasts will conform to an idealized body image.

That explains why, during the same years, many boys are horrified to notice a swelling around their nipples—a temporary result of the erratic hormones of early puberty. If a boy's breast growth is very disturbing, drugs can reduce the swelling, although many doctors prefer to let time deal with the problem (Sansone et al., 2017).

If you can think back to your body during middle school, you can remember why growth may be upsetting. Few teenagers welcome every change; many have a distorted **body image**—that is, their idea (often inaccurate) of how their body looks. As one book on body image begins, each person's body "feels, conceives, imagines, represents, evaluates, loves, hates, and manipulates itself" (Cuzzolaro & Fassino, 2018, p. v).

Almost two-thirds of U.S. high school girls try to lose weight, even though less than one-third are actually overweight (MMWR, June 15, 2018) (see **Figure 4.8**). No one looks like the bodies portrayed online and in magazines, movies, and television programs that are marketed to teenagers. Unhappiness with appearance—especially with weight for girls—is common among teenagers in every nation, especially if they seek to display their bodies on social media (Salomon & Brown, 2019).

Eating Disorders

All the hormonal, appetite, and size increases of puberty make adolescents susceptible to disordered eating. Adolescents go to extremes, overeating, undereating, binging, following very restrictive diets. Obesity rises to 21 percent of U.S. 12- to 19-year-olds, with the highest rates among Hispanic boys and African American girls (Skinner et al., 2018). This problem is getting worse: In 2003, only three U.S. states (Kentucky, Mississippi, and Tennessee) had high school obesity rates at 15 percent or more; in 2017, 42 states did (MMWR, June 15, 2018).

Simultaneously, harmful diets and poor nutrition both increase. Serious eating disorders are not usually diagnosed before age 18, and death from anorexia almost never occurs until adulthood, but problems become apparent in adolescence.

When distorted body image and excessive dieting result in severe weight loss, that indicates **anorexia nervosa**. Few adolescent girls warrant a diagnosis of anorexia (estimates are about 1 percent), but those who do dramatically restrict their calorie intake, obsessively avoiding food. Their BMI may fall below 17 in cases of mild anorexia or below 15 in extreme cases, with any sudden weight loss or weight that is "less than that minimally expected" a cause for concern (American Psychiatric Association, 2013).

About three times as common as anorexia is **bulimia nervosa**. Sufferers overeat compulsively, consuming thousands of calories within an hour or two, and then purge through vomiting or laxatives. Most are close to normal in weight. However, they risk serious health problems, including damage to their gastrointestinal system and cardiac arrest from electrolyte imbalance (Mehler, 2018).

The DSM-5 also recognizes **binge eating disorder**, when a person periodically and compulsively overeats, quickly consuming large amounts of ice cream, cake, or snacks. Their stomach hurts and they feel shame, binging in private. Such behavior is common in adolescence, although a clinical diagnosis of binge eating disorder requires that a person binges at least weekly for several months.

From a life-span perspective, eating disorders are not limited to adolescence. The origins begin in family eating patterns. Children need to learn to eat sensibly—when they are hungry, without food being used as a punishment or a reward. The problem may begin even earlier, at conception, since some genes make eating disorders more likely, and may continue in adulthood.

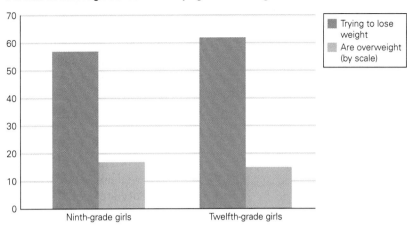

Percent of U.S. High School Girls Trying to Lose Weight

Legend: Trying to lose weight / Are overweight (by scale)

Data from MMWR, June 15, 2018.

FIGURE 4.8

Satisfied with Your Body? Probably not, if you are a teenager. As this graph shows, this is particularly true for girls. Fortunately, some learn that no matter what their body type, good nutrition and adequate exercise make a person feel more attractive, energetic, and happy.

anorexia nervosa An eating disorder characterized by distorted body image, severe calorie restriction, and intense fear of weight gain. Affected individuals voluntarily undereat or binge and purge, depriving their vital organs of nutrition. Anorexia can be fatal.

bulimia nervosa An eating disorder characterized by binge eating and subsequent purging, usually by induced vomiting and/or use of laxatives.

binge eating disorder An eating disorder common in adolescence, which involves compulsive overeating.

WHAT HAVE YOU LEARNED?

1. What is the sequence of puberty for girls?
2. What is the sequence of puberty for boys?
3. What is the difference between primary and secondary sexual characteristics?
4. What is the difference between anorexia and bulimia?
5. Why are eating disorders a life-span issue, not merely an adolescent one?

Adulthood

Peak health and physical strength begin when external body growth ends. Maximum height is usually reached by age 16 for girls and age 18 for boys, with final touches in size and shape evident in emerging adulthood. Bodies begin aging, called **senescence**, as soon as growth stops, at age 20 or so. Thus, a life-span look at physical development needs to include a description of what happens in adulthood.

senescence The process of aging, whereby the body becomes less strong and efficient.

Appearance

Partly because of their overall health, strength, and activity, most young adults look vital and attractive. The oily hair, pimpled faces, and awkward limbs of adolescence are gone.

The organ that protects people from the elements, the skin, becomes clear and taut (Whitbourne & Whitbourne, 2014). The attractiveness of young skin is one reason that newly prominent fashion models, pop singers, and movie stars tend to be in their early 20s, looking fresh and glamorous.

Most emerging adults value appearance more than older adults do. Before criticizing this as superficial, remember that appearance attracts sexual interest. Since society functions best if young adults find partners, it benefits the community if young adults care about how they look.

However, society benefits if external appearance becomes less important over the decades of adulthood, because people begin to look older long before their brains and other organs show senescence. The skin becomes rougher and dryer, with "looseness, withering, and wrinkling" particularly notable at about age 50 for women, as a result of lower estrogen during menopause (Piérard et al., 2015, p. 98). Body shape also changes. The bones in the spine become closer together, causing an overall loss of height (about an inch before age 60), a wider waist, and more fat on the abdomen, the upper arms, the buttocks, and the chin.

Muscles weaken; joints lose flexibility; stiffness is more evident; bending is harder; agility is reduced. Rising from sitting on the floor, twisting in a dance, or even walking "with a spring in your step" is more difficult. A strained back, neck, or knee may occur. Lower back pain occurs at least once to more than a third of all adults worldwide. The age incidence is curvilinear, with higher prevalence in middle age (Hoy et al., 2012).

Internal Body Systems

As has been true for thousands of years, every body system—digestive, respiratory, circulatory, musculoskeletal, and sexual-reproductive—functions optimally in early adulthood and gradually becomes less efficient.

A study of senescence, including many measures of biological aging and appearance, found that some people age three times faster than others, with about half of the difference between fast and slow aging evident by age 26 (Belsky et al., 2015). As a result of poor health habits, by the mid-30s, some people have faces and bodies like those in their 20s and some like those in their 40s.

Experience matters. Already by age 40, athletes who stress one part of their body, such as their knees, shoulders, or elbows, are likely to experience strains in that part; office workers who strain their wrists day after day may develop carpel tunnel syndrome; women find that pregnancy tires out their body more than it did in their early 20s.

On average, manual laborers grow old more rapidly than managers. One detailed study found that ongoing physical labor—specifically heavy lifting, crouching, or

See the Sweat This is "hot yoga," a 90-minute class in London with 26 positions and 2 breathing exercises, in 105°F (40.5°C) heat. Homeostasis allows young adults to stretch their muscles more easily in an overly heated room.

● Observation Quiz Who is less likely to choose hot yoga? (see answer, page 117) ↑

Matt Cardy/Getty Images News/Getty Images

standing for hours each day—speeds up aging, as measured medically, not just by appearance (Ravesteijn et al., 2017). Giving birth to many children takes a toll on the female body, so a mother of a dozen children looks and feels older at age 40 than a woman who had only one child. To understand this, we must explain organ reserve, homeostasis, and allostatic load.

Organ Reserve

Organ reserve is the extra power that each organ can employ when needed. This reserve capacity shrinks each year of adulthood so that by old age, a strain—shoveling snow, catching the flu, minor surgery—can be overwhelming because no more reserve is available.

Organ reserve is evident overall (capacity of the heart, lungs, and so on) but also in the cells' metabolic reserve—the "functional resilience of a biochemical network" that protects the organs (Atamna et al., 2018). This is crucial when adults undergo surgery or radiation for serious health problems, or when a person drinks too much alcohol, or overexerts, or otherwise abuses their body. For all these circumstances, younger adult bodies and brains recover much more quickly than older ones, because more reserves are available.

Homeostasis

Closely related to organ reserve is **homeostasis**—a balance among body reactions that keeps every physical function in sync with every other. For example, if the air temperature rises, people sweat, move slowly, and thirst for cold drinks—three physiological reactions that cool the body.

The next time you read about a rash of heat-wave deaths, note the age of the victims. Aging slows homeostasis, so the body dissipates heat and protects against cold less efficiently. The physical demands to maintain temperature may temporarily overwhelm the heart, kidneys, or other organs, causing death before recovery occurs. Even by age 40, adults are less protected from temperature changes—or any other stress on the body—than younger adults (Larose et al., 2013).

Heat-wave deaths are increasing in recent years, in part because of climate change, in part because more people are living in cities (which radiate the heat), and in part because more people live to be very old, when homeostasis is slower (Guo et al., 2017). At every age, external efforts to aid homeostasis, such as extra oxygen when breathing is strained, or finding a chair when standing makes a person feel faint, may help. In one specific example, some runners in a long, hot race collapsed with abnormally high body temperatures. Organ failure was averted if they were immersed immediately in ice water (Demartini et al., 2015).

The most recent confirmation comes from data on Covid-19. Age pushed some people over the edge from life to death, even as many other factors (testing capacity, political leadership, comorbidity) were part of the cascade (Zhao et al., 2020).

Allostasis

Also related to organ reserve is **allostasis**, a dynamic body adjustment that gradually changes physiology. The main difference between homeostasis and allostasis is time: Homeostasis requires an immediate response from body systems, whereas allostasis refers to long-term adjustment. Both draw on organ reserve.

Allostasis depends on the biological circumstances of every earlier time, beginning at conception. The process continues over the decades, with poor health habits gradually increasing *allostatic load*. Although organ reserve usually protects young adults, the effects of lack of sleep, drug use, inactivity, unhealthy eating, and so on accumulate, loading down health. Eventually, adults experience *metabolic syndrome*, a collection of factors that, together, make several illnesses more likely, including heart disease, diabetes, and stroke.

organ reserve The capacity of organs to allow the body to cope with stress, via extra, unused functioning ability.

homeostasis The adjustment of all of the body's systems to keep physiological functions in a state of equilibrium. As the body ages, it takes longer for these homeostatic adjustments to occur, so it becomes harder for older bodies to adapt to stress.

allostasis A dynamic body adjustment, related to homeostasis, that affects overall physiology over time. The main difference is that homeostasis requires an immediate response, whereas allostasis requires longer-term adjustment.

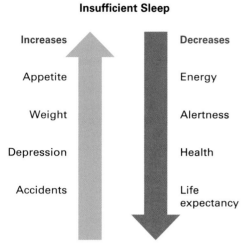

Insufficient Sleep

Increases | Decreases
Appetite | Energy
Weight | Alertness
Depression | Health
Accidents | Life expectancy

FIGURE 4.9
Don't Set the Alarm? Every emerging adult sometimes sleeps too little and is tired the next day—that is homeostasis. But years of poor sleep habits reduce years of life—a bad bargain. That is allostatic load.

A Good Night's Sleep

All three (organ reserve, homeostasis, and allostatic load) are illustrated by sleep. One night of poor sleep makes a person tired the next day—that is homeostasis, the body's way of maintaining equilibrium (see **Figure 4.9**). Organ reserve allows quick recovery of digestion, brain functioning, and so on that are affected by temporary sleep deprivation.

But if poor sleep is typical every day, then appetite, mood, and activity adjust (more, down, less) to achieve homeostasis, while allostatic load rises and organ reserve declines. By mid- and late adulthood, years of inadequate sleep load down overall health (McEwen & Karatsoreos, 2015; Itani et al., 2017).

Sleep is directly biological, but the quality of sleep is affected by many social and psychological factors. Among the habits of adults that impair sleep are drug use, especially alcohol, and bedtime media use (computer games, smartphones, TV). Further, ongoing experiences of ethnic or racial discrimination often lead to impaired sleep, and that affects health (Hope et al., 2015). Indeed, many aspects of physical growth and maintenance over the years of adulthood are affected by social and psychological factors as well as biological ones, a phenomenon called *weathering* (Simons et al., 2018).

Exercise

Exercise is another example of the relationship between organ reserve and homeostasis. Judicious exercise reduces allostatic load and helps maintain health, even if someone smokes and overeats.

Exercise lowers blood pressure, strengthens the heart and lungs, and makes depression, osteoporosis, diabetes, arthritis, dementia (now called *major neurocognitive disorder*) and some cancers less likely. Health benefits are substantial for men and women, old and young, former sports stars and those who never joined an athletic team (see **Table 4.2** for U.S. exercise guidelines).

Every movement—gardening, light housework, walking up the stairs or to the bus—helps. Walking briskly for 30 minutes a day, five days a week, is good; more intense exercise (swimming, jogging, bicycling, and the like) is better; and adding muscle-strengthening exercise is best.

Even a few minutes of exertion increase heartbeat and breathing—that is homeostasis. Because of organ reserve, such temporary stresses on the body are usually no problem and may even be protective. Over time, allostasis allows longer and more intense exercise. That decreases allostatic load by reducing the health risks that otherwise increase, as evident in blood analysis and body fat. Metabolic syndrome does not appear in middle age for those who developed healthy movement patterns decades earlier.

The CARDIA Study

We know the long-term effects of exercise because of a multifaceted longitudinal study, CARDIA (Coronary Artery Risk Development in Adulthood), that began

TABLE 4.2

Federal Guidelines for Physical Activity

The U.S. guidelines for physical activity, first issued in 2008 and updated in May 2016, are:

1. Aerobic exercise, several days a week, with the weekly total 150 minutes of moderate exercise (brisk walking, swimming, bicycling slowly) or 75 minutes of intense exercise (jogging, racing, bicycling fast), at least 10 minutes at a time.

2. Muscle-strengthening, including all of the major muscle groups (legs, hips, back, abdomen, chest, shoulders, and arms) at least twice a week. Resistance training and the like should reach the level that another set would be almost impossible.

Information from U.S. Department of Health and Human Services, 2018.

with thousands of healthy 18- to 30-year-olds. They were queried about their exercise habits; their strength, endurance, and many blood and body fat markers were measured.

Many (3,154) were reexamined decades later. Compared to those who were most fit in emerging adulthood, those who were the least fit at the first assessment (more than 400 of them) were four times more likely to have diabetes and high blood pressure. Repeated demands on organ reserve and allostatic load led to long-term effects (Camhi et al., 2013). By age 65, a disproportionate number of the least fit had died.

Another finding from CARDIA was that brain size is affected by drug use. Those young adults who smoked cigarettes and drank alcohol had, by age 50, less gray matter in several crucial parts of their cerebral cortex compared to their drug-free peers (Elbejjani et al., 2019). Overall, body and brain health were as much affected by attitude and social context as by biological factors (Meyer et al., 2019).

Nutrition in Adulthood

As you have already seen, food is crucial for growth, but not just any food. Selection, attitude, and cognition are all pivotal.

Natural Diets

What and how much a person eats are affected by dozens of physiological and psychological factors. An empty stomach triggers hormones, stomach pains, low blood sugar, and so on, signaling hunger. Then the person decides what to do, influenced by culture and availability.

If an empty stomach is occasional, this cascade of homeostatic reactions makes people suddenly realize at 6 P.M. that they haven't eaten since breakfast. Dinner becomes a priority; most people eat enough but not too much.

Scientists are impressed with the many physiological measures that keep mammals functioning well. Blood chemistry, hormones, stomach grumbling, mental alertness, and circadian rhythm are all part of this homeostatic system. Our ancestors had no scales or medical check-ups, wore loose clothing, and knew nothing about calories and vitamins, yet almost all naturally maintained a healthy weight (Augustine et al., 2018).

Currently, however, selectivity is required (remember from Chapter 2), because processed food is designed to be tempting. Many adults ignore body signals, eating too much or too little. Allostatic load increases; eating disorders may become fatal. Many aspects of a healthy diet are debated, but generally adults consume too much sugar, salt, and saturated fat.

Attitudes and Nutrition

Poor nutrition is more common in adults whose parents are immigrants to the United States. They may seek to prove that they are upstanding citizens by striving to "eat American," avoiding curry, hot peppers, or wasabi—each of which has health benefits. Instead, they tend to choose fast foods, which are not designed to be nutritious. That may explain why older immigrants born in other nations are healthier than the average native-born American, but the children of immigrants have higher rates of obesity and diabetes than their parents (Oza-Frank & Narayan, 2010).

No matter what their ancestry, today's emerging adults are heavier than past cohorts. As they age, they gain weight—about a pound a year, according to the CARDIA study. Specifics of diet matter: CARDIA found that high-fat diets, soda, and fast food each had independent effects, with the cumulative allostatic load causing poor health (Duffey et al., 2012). Few CARDIA young adults were obese, but those participants who dieted because they thought

Having Fun? Here are some of the 98,247 aspiring marathoners running on the Verrazano-Narrows Bridge from Staten Island to Brooklyn, New York, as part of a 26.2-mile race. Everyone should exercise and should figure out how to make that enjoyable to them. Some choose this.

Fastest Increase Obesity rates are rising faster in China than in any other nation as new American restaurants open every day. McDonald's and Starbucks each have about 5,000 outlets in China, with students particularly likely customers.

THINK CRITICALLY: Does SES protect health because of personal habits or social conditions?

that their eating was sometimes out of control, were, 25 years later, more often obese (Yoon et al., 2018).

One surprising influence is neighborhood: Some places are walking-friendly; some not. In the latter, people stay home or drive wherever they need to go—getting heavier by the mile. Longitudinal evidence finds that this is not simply correlation, it is causal (Christian et al., 2017). In other words, it is not merely that heavier people tend to choose, or be stuck in, locations where walking is less pleasant. Instead, people who move to a place that encourages exercise improve their body mass and strength.

Surgery to Lose Weight

People whose BMI is 40 or above are considered *morbidly obese*, more common in middle age than earlier or later. For them, health risks (especially diabetes and heart disease) increase with every gram or pound. Many opt for *bariatric surgery* to reduce their weight.

Serious complications from bariatric surgery are not rare, especially if allostatic load is high. In Norway (where medical care is excellent) a six-year follow-up study of 932 adults who had bariatric surgery found that about 25 percent required another operation to alleviate complications (Jakobsen et al., 2018). This and every other study find that, for the morbidly obese, surgery reduces later deaths from almost every cause, with diabetes and heart disease dramatically reduced. The problem now is that many morbidly obese people—especially if they are low SES—avoid doctors and surgery (Moussa et al., 2019).

Sexual Systems in Adulthood

One more set of changes needs to be discussed. Many adults worry about decline of their sexual and reproductive systems as they age.

Sexual Responsiveness

Sexual arousal occurs more slowly, and orgasm takes longer with senescence. However, some say that sexual satisfaction improves. Could that be? Might familiarity with one's own body and with that of one's partner make slower response a pleasure?

A U.S. study of women aged 40 or older found that sexual activity decreased each decade but that sexual satisfaction did not (Trompeter et al., 2012). A British study of more than 2,000 adults in their 50s found that almost all of them were sexually active (94 percent of the men and 76 percent of the women) and, again, that most were quite satisfied with their sex lives (D. Lee et al., 2016).

Long-Lasting Joy In every nation and culture, many couples who have been together for decades continue to delight in their relationship. Talk shows and headline stories tend to focus on bitter divorces, ignoring couples like these who are happy together.

Variability is evident. A study of 38,207 adults in the United States who had been in a committed relationship for more than three years found that about half (55 percent of the women and 43 percent of the men) were highly satisfied with their sex lives, but about one-third (27 percent of the women and 41 percent of the men) were not (Frederick et al., 2017).

Interestingly, age was not a major factor, but variety of sex acts (including oral sex) and quality of communication were. Although sexual satisfaction tends to be highest early on, some long-married couples report that their happiness with their sex lives is as strong as it was early on (Frederick et al., 2017).

Every large study finds a vast range of sexuality. Some people are strongly heterosexual or homosexual, and others less so; some people are pansexual and others bisexual. Some are asexual, not interested or aroused by sex, while others think about sex almost all the time.

Biology and age do not seem to be the most important factor. Sexual arousal, orgasm, and, as we will soon see, fertility and menopause are all connected to senescence, but the effects, and even the occurrence, are strongly influenced by the mind (Pfaus et al., 2014). As many say: "The most important human sexual organ is between the . . . ears."

Seeking Pregnancy

Rates of **infertility** (failure to conceive after one year of trying) vary from nation to nation, primarily because the rate increases when medical care is scarce. Infertility is usually kept secret from friends, as are the results of various tests. Some women do not even discuss it with their partners, although most do (Sormunen et al., 2018). In general, keeping such concerns to oneself adds to the problem for both partners and for their friends and family.

Age matters. In the United States, about 12 percent of all adult couples do not conceive after one year of trying, partly because many postpone childbearing. Peak fertility is at about age 18. Most babies born in the United States have mothers aged 23 to 33, and only about 3 percent are born to women over 40.

If couples in their 40s try to conceive, about half fail (a 50-percent infertility rate), and the other half risk various complications. Of course, risk is not reality: In 2018 in the United States, 126,911 babies were born to women age 40 or older (Hamilton et al., 2019). Most of those babies become healthy, well-loved children.

Fertility of both men and women declines in adulthood. Depending on the man's age, each day about 100 million sperm reach maturity after a developmental process that lasts about 75 days. Anything that impairs body functioning over those 75 days (e.g., fever, radiation, drugs, time in a sauna, stress, environmental toxins, alcohol, cigarettes) reduces sperm number, shape, and motility (activity), making conception less likely. Sedentary behavior, perhaps particularly watching television, also correlates with lower sperm count (Gaskins et al., 2013).

As with men, women's fertility is affected by anything that impairs physical functioning—including disease, smoking, extreme dieting, and obesity. Many infertile women do not realize that they have contracted one specific disease that impairs conception—*pelvic inflammatory disease (PID)*. PID creates scar tissue that may block the fallopian tubes, preventing sperm from reaching an ovum (Brunham et al., 2015).

Fertility Treatments

In the past 50 years, medical advances have solved about half of all fertility problems. Surgery can repair some problems directly, and *assisted reproductive technology (ART)* overcomes obstacles such as a low sperm count and blocked fallopian tubes. In vitro fertilization (IVF) is the most common ART procedure.

infertility The inability to conceive a child after trying for at least a year.

Choosing Motherhood In 2018, U.S. Senator Tammy Duckworth, age 50, had her second baby via IVF and won the right to bring her infant daughter to the Senate floor. Next: Will the United States continue to be the only nation (except for New Guinea) without mandated paid family leave?

What was not discussed was the impact on the parents, who may be depressed if they are unable to have a baby. Infertility and subsequent fertility measures affect the psyche, not just the body. People may question their own morality (is parenthood selfish?) and their partner's wishes. Remember that communication is crucial for a satisfying adult sex life; this is especially true when ART is involved.

Fifty years ago, many religious leaders condemned ART, but now ART is morally acceptable to virtually everyone, especially when couples anticipate disease-related infertility. For example, many cancer patients freeze their ova. When the treatment is over, if they want a baby, their IVF success rate (about one-third of attempts) is similar to that for young women who freeze their ova because they do not want a baby until they are age 35 or older (Cardozo et al., 2015). Otherwise, when women over 40 have babies via IVF, most use donor ova (Hamilton et al., 2015).

ART has helped millions who thought they could never have a baby. The most dramatic example is with HIV-positive adults. Three decades ago, doctors recommended sterilization and predicted early death for them. Now, they can live happily for decades, using condoms for sex and taking antiviral drugs.

If an HIV-positive woman wants a child, drugs and cesarean delivery almost always protect the fetus. If an HIV-positive man wants a child, his sperm can be collected, washed, and used in IVF to achieve conception (Sauer et al., 2009). Indeed, conception for HIV-positive men can occur naturally with virus-suppressing drugs, but IVF is safer (Wu & Ho, 2015).

The Sexual-Reproductive System in Middle Age

During adulthood, the level of sex hormones circulating in the bloodstream declines—suddenly in women, gradually in men. Both sexes are affected by those changes, with some taking hormones to replace the hormones that are lost. That may be ill-advised—as you will see.

Menopause

menopause The time in middle age, usually around age 50, when a woman's menstrual periods cease and the production of estrogen, progesterone, and testosterone drops. Strictly speaking, menopause is dated one year after a woman's last menstrual period, although many months before and after that date are menopausal.

For women, sometime between ages 42 and 58 (51 is average), ovulation and menstruation stop because of a marked drop in production of several hormones. This is **menopause**. The age of natural menopause is affected primarily by genes (17 have been identified) (D. Morris et al., 2011; Stolk et al., 2012) and normal aging but also by smoking (earlier menopause), exercise (later), and moderate alcohol consumption (later) (Taneri et al., 2016).

Menopause is connected to many physical reactions beyond the cessation of menstruation and ovulation. The symptoms include vaginal dryness and body temperature disturbances, including *hot flashes* (feeling hot), *hot flushes* (looking hot), and *cold sweats* (feeling chilled). Those physical responses can be hardly noticeable, or they can be dramatic—interfering with sleep, which can make a woman tired and irritable.

The psychological effects of menopause vary a great deal, with some women sad that they can no longer become pregnant and other women happy for the same reason. Anthropologist Margaret Mead famously said, "There is no more creative force in the world than the menopausal woman with zest." Some menopausal women are depressed, some are moody, and others are more energetic.

In the United States, about one in five women has a *hysterectomy* (surgical removal of the uterus), which may include removal of her ovaries (Morgan et al., 2018). If she was pre-menopausal, removal of the ovaries suddenly reduces estrogen and therefore causes menopausal symptoms.

Early menopause, surgical or not, correlates with various health problems later on, including heart disease, sleep difficulties, and frailty (Verschoor & Tamim, 2019). Female hormones protect health, which is one reason why hysterectomies

are less common than they were 40 years ago. Many current hysterectomies are done laparoscopically, without major surgery, and keep the ovaries intact.

Hormone Replacement

Toward the end of the twentieth century, millions of post-menopausal women used **hormone replacement therapy (HRT)**. Some did so to alleviate symptoms of menopause, others to prevent *osteoporosis* (fragile bones), heart disease, strokes, or cognitive loss. Correlational studies found that these diseases occurred less often among women taking HRT.

However, that correlation was misleading. In a multiyear study of thousands of women, half (the experimental group) took HRT and half (the control group) did not. The results were a shock: Taking estrogen and progesterone *increased* the risk of heart disease, stroke, and some types of cancer (U.S. Preventive Services Task Force, 2002).

The most dramatic difference was an increase in breast cancer, at the rate of 6 per year for 1,000 women taking HRT compared to 4 per 1,000 for women who did not take the hormone (Chlebowski et al., 2013). The women had been randomly assigned to the experimental or control group, which meant that the results were solid. The study was halted before its scheduled end because the researchers were convinced that the experimental group was at risk.

How could the previous research have been mistaken? In retrospect, scientists realized that simply comparing women who chose HRT with women who did not resulted in women with higher SES being compared with women of lower SES (who could not afford HRT). Benefits were the result of some women's education and health care, not of HRT.

HRT is sometimes beneficial. It relieves the symptoms of menopause, which some women find very troubling, psychologically as well as physically. It strengthens bones and may improve hearing. But HRT also has risks, as that longitudinal study discovered.

Overall, experts now recognize the need for "individualized decision." For example, the risk of heart disease depends on genes, diet, age, and exercise, as well as the timing and specifics of HRT (Keck & Taylor, 2018). That is true for many aspects of growth and health in adulthood: Bodies vary, each person makes choices about drugs, diet, and so on, guided by the research but not ruled by it.

One study emphasizing the need for individualized decision included 872 women in 17 nations whose ovaries were surgically removed because they carried the BRAC1 gene, which increases the risk of ovarian cancer. If they were under age 45 when they took estrogen (but not progesterone) for symptoms of menopause, they did *not* have higher rates of breast cancer than similar women who did not take hormones (Kotsopoulos et al., 2018).

Pausing, Not Stopping During the years of menopause, these two women experienced more than physiological changes: Jane Goodall (*left*) was widowed and Ellen Johnson-Sirleaf (*right*) was imprisoned. Both, however, are proof that post-menopausal women can be productive. After age 50, Goodall (shown visiting a German zoo at age 70) founded and led several organizations that educate children and protect animals, and Johnson-Sirleaf (shown speaking to the International Labor Organization at age 68) became the president of Liberia.

hormone replacement therapy (HRT)
Taking hormones (in pills, patches, or injections) to compensate for hormone reduction. HRT is most common in women at menopause or after removal of the ovaries, but it is also used by men as their testosterone decreases. HRT has some medical uses but also carries health risks.

andropause A term coined to signify a drop in testosterone levels in older men, which typically results in reduced sexual desire, erections, and muscle mass. (Also called *male menopause*.)

Andropause?

Do men undergo anything like menopause? Some say yes, suggesting that the word **andropause** should be used to signify an age-related lower testosterone level, which reduces sexual desire, erections, and muscle mass (Samaras et al., 2012). Even with erection-inducing drugs such as Viagra and Levitra, sexual desire and speed of orgasm decline with age, as do many other physiological and cognitive functions.

But most experts think that the term *andropause* (or *male menopause*) is misleading because it implies a sudden drop in reproductive ability or hormones. That does not occur; some men produce viable sperm at age 80 and older. Sexual inactivity and anxiety reduce testosterone—superficially similar to menopause but with a psychological, not physiological, cause. Sometimes treatment for diseases requires reduction of testosterone.

To combat hormonal decline, some men take HRT. Of course, their H is the hormone testosterone, not estrogen. The result seems to be less depression, more sexual desire, and leaner bodies. (Some women also take smaller amounts of testosterone to increase their sexual desire.)

One recent study found that men who took testosterone for years had lower rates of cardiovascular disease and fewer deaths, but in the short term more deaths occurred than usual (Wallis et al., 2016). Another study found the testosterone reduced the harm from chronic respiratory disease (Baillargeon et al., 2019).

One team found that older men were most likely to seek more testosterone when they were troubled by declining sexual desire and function, but the added hormones did not necessarily help (Rastrelli et al., 2019). Many scientists call for more longitudinal randomized studies, a wise suggestion given the results from women's HRT.

Late Adulthood

Do not be surprised to see a section on late adulthood in a chapter on physical development. Maintaining biological systems is crucial lifelong, and there is much that older people can do to make that happen. As already stated, *senescence* begins when the growth process stops. Some losses and slowdowns occur every decade of adulthood, with slightly less lung function, blood circulation, organ reserve, and so on.

However, remember that body systems are plastic, dependent on experience. Muscles, for instance, grow stronger with exercise, or weaker if they are not used. Even in early adulthood, bedrest weakens the legs. By late adulthood, *sarcopenia* (muscle loss), occurs even if a person is as active as they were at age 20, but the rate is affected by exercise (see **Figure 4.10**).

Height and weight also decrease in late adulthood. The average person loses 2 inches or more between age 65 and death, as distance between the discs of the spine is reduced. People lose, on average, 10 pounds or so, because muscles (the heaviest part of the body) shrink.

Variability—already emphasized in the discussion of percentiles at the beginning of this chapter—is even more evident among elders, as decades of habits and allostatic load combine: Some people are decrepit at age 60 while others seem youthful at age 90. Nutrition, exercise, medical care, pollution, climate, personality, and cognition influence how long, how strong, and how full each adult life is.

THINK CRITICALLY: How do you compare to other people your age?

U.S. Adults Who Met 2008 Federal Physical Activity Guidelines

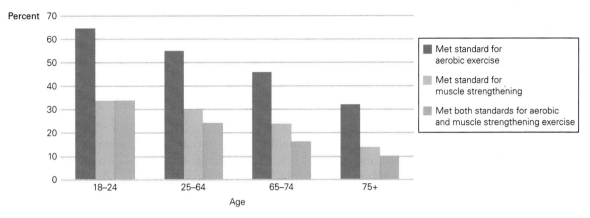

Data from National Center for Health Statistics, October 30, 2019.

FIGURE 4.10

Worse and Worse As people grow older, they should exercise more, because exercise is the best defense against all ailments of age. Unfortunately, the opposite is true: Twice as many of the oldest do not exercise compared to the youngest. These data are from the United States, where the standards for aerobic exercise and weight-bearing exercise are defined by minutes spent per week. Elders could meet the standards even if they move more slowly, but most of them simply stop.

A surprising study of 55- to 79-year-olds who bicycled over 100 miles per week (they enjoyed the exercise and the scenery!) found very little age-based deterioration of the muscles. Indeed, on most measures those older bikers had much stronger legs than the average 30-year-old (Pollock et al., 2018).

Selectivity is the main reason one individual lives twice as long, with more vitality, than another. Variation in aging among humans, currently and over the centuries, is vast, *not* primarily because of genes (Robert & Labat-Robert, 2015).

The goal is to keep all the body systems in balance, so that no one organ — the heart, the brain, the liver, and so on — fails before the others, and so that cells renew themselves as they should, and they do not succumb to abnormal growth (cancer).

Exactly when all the systems fail is hard to predict. In one study, researchers studied almost 2 million recipients of Medicare (the U.S. insurance system that covers everyone over 65) and estimated how likely death was to occur. They gathered data on many factors, including gender, age, and ethnicity, as well as recent diagnosis, severity, and number of illnesses.

Considering all the predictors, the likelihood of death in the next year ranged from 95 percent (true for about 5 percent of the Medicare beneficiaries) to less than 5 percent (true for most people). But after a year, half of those 95 percent were still alive, and some of those 5 percent had died. The conclusion: "death is highly unpredictable" (Einav et al., 2018, p. 1462).

Doctors have been asked, "Would you be surprised if this patient died in the next 12 months?" That seems sensible, since doctors know all the indicators of health. However, the accuracy of doctors ranges from modest to poor (Downar et al., 2017).

Thus, we know what impairs health (allostatic load), and that analysis of blood and urine, echocardiograms, mammograms, and more can diagnose life-threatening cancer, heart disease, respiratory ailments, and so on. However, many people survive deadly illnesses, with cognitive factors sometimes more influential than biological one. On average, every measure of growth shows a year-by-year decline, beginning by age 30, but individuals can maintain abilities, improve, or suddenly fall. The multidirectional life-span perspective is especially apparent in late adulthood.

Regarding ongoing physical development, the hope is that all the body systems continue to function, with selective compensation as needed. Then morbidity will

compression of morbidity A shortening of the time a person spends ill or infirm, accomplished by postponing illness.

Touch Your Toes? This woman could even put both feet behind her neck. Although everyone loses some flexibility with age, daily practice is crucial. Tao Porchon-Lynch has taught yoga for a half-century. At age 99, shown here, she could balance on one leg in tree pose, stretch her hamstrings in downward dog, and then relieve any remaining stress in cobra pose. She died at age 101 in February 2020, peacefully and without pain.

occur only for a short time until final collapse. This is **compression of morbidity**, the idea that deadly illness (morbidity) is brief (compressed), when the entire body weakens, and all the organs fail. The person dies rather quickly, without years of frailty and dependence. The goal is to add life to years, not years to life. How can this be achieved?

The answer is the same in late adulthood as in all the early years: good health habits, ample exercise, and life-sustaining nutrition.

The Life Span

In many ways, health in late adulthood is a continuation of earlier years. Habits of a lifetime continue; averages may be misleading. For example, you have read that obesity is harmful for health. In fact, the average life span in the United States has slipped from 79 to 78, for several reasons, not only midlife suicide and opioid addiction but also rising obesity and alcohol abuse.

Older people are less often obese than adults under age 65, but two of the reasons for that decline are not good ones: (1) A disproportionate number of the morbidly obese die before old age, and (2) the weightier parts of the body—bones and muscles—have shrunk.

Many nutritionists criticize American eating habits: too much sugar, salt, and saturated or trans fat, and too few fruits and vegetables (Christ & Latz, 2019; Ludwig, 2016). For many older adults, those harmful eating habits began in childhood, depleting organ reserve and increasing allostatic load lifelong. In late adulthood, they reach the point that vital organs are impaired. For example, of U.S. older residents (age 65+), 26 percent have type 2 diabetes, and 29 percent have heart disease—both diseases strongly affected by diet (National Center for Health Statistics, 2018).

At every age, physical growth and health affect cognition and emotion. You already read that malnutrition in infancy reduces IQ lifelong, that depression and anxiety are one cause of eating disorders. The same connections are apparent in late adulthood. A study in China found that elders who had experienced famine earlier in life were twice as likely to be depressed as their peers the same age (Li et al., 2018). This is part of a vicious cycle: Depression is a major cause of poor eating habits in late adulthood, as well as of social isolation. Those two factors increase disease and shorten life.

For several reasons, it may be difficult for the elderly to ensure they are getting good nutrition. For one thing, their favorite foods may not have the best nutrients, and yet many elders—especially if they eat alone—consume the same things day after day. A varied diet might be crucial to optimal functioning, so a limited diet, even of nutritious foods, will omit some micronutrients.

What is the harm? In truth, research is ongoing, and experts dispute specifics. They agree, however, that an inadequate diet, with insufficient water and vitamin B_{12}, may precipitate a neurocognitive disorder.

It is known that metabolism and digestion slow down with age, so an older person needs to eat less to avoid gaining weight and yet consume more to get the same amount of nutrition. Medical needs may make some healthy foods off limits, including high-fiber foods for someone with diverticulitis, or cheese for someone with high cholesterol. Blood pressure is too high for 64 percent of U.S. adults over age 65: They especially need to avoid salt (high in canned soups, cheese, pickles, salted nuts), and keep body weight down and exercise up—good advice at any age, but for them the difference between life and death.

Many other aspects of aging make a good diet more difficult. Taste buds become less acute: A person may use too much salt or sugar without realizing it. If oral health has not been good, and especially if dentures rather than natural teeth are in the mouth, chewing may be difficult, and that may impair swallowing and digestion (Altenhoevel et al., 2012).

One scholarly tome, recently reissued, includes this warning: "if a particular food is said to slow aging, improve energy, or protect against disease or conditions that are common in late adulthood," then the elderly are particularly vulnerable. They consume fad diets, supplements, boosters, strange liquids, pills, and so on—spending money with no real benefits (Gibbs & Turner, 2017).

Anti-Aging?

As you might imagine, scientists hesitate to select a certain food as the antidote for aging. Many foods have been suggested—blueberries, avocados, Greek yogurt, oat milk, and red grapes are among the more recent—but controlled studies have not confirmed that any of them holds the magic that older adults hope for. Nutritionists continue to wish that everyone would eat a balanced diet lifelong, and yet humans continue to search for some new substance that adds years and energy.

A particular fear in old age is losing the ability to think clearly and remember well, and with that fear comes the hope that some food or vitamin will prevent loss of cognitive ability. No particular food has been found, but obesity, diabetes, and allostatic load increase the risk of cognitive decline, and thus a lifetime of healthy eating is a good preventive strategy.

One intriguing measure related to growth and nutrition may make a difference. If people reduce the load on their digestion, metabolism, and so on by eating 1,800 calories a day instead of the usual 3,000, would that slow all aging processes? That question has led to thousands of studies. The answer seems to be yes, especially for preventing diabetes and heart disease.

Calorie restriction—a drastic reduction in calories consumed—increases the life span in many species, from fruit flies to monkeys. Extensive research on mice finds that specifics of genes and diet matter but also that many creatures live twice as long as average if their diet is restricted (Rizza et al., 2014).

Regarding humans, thousands of members of the Calorie Restriction Society voluntarily undereat (Roth & Polotsky, 2012). They give up some things that many people cherish, not just cake and hot dogs but also a strong sex drive and high energy. As a result, they have lower blood pressure, fewer strokes, less cancer, and almost no diabetes. Thus, they maintain their bodies much longer and healthier than most people.

In several places (e.g., Okinawa, Denmark, and Norway), wartime occupation forced severe calorie reduction for almost everyone. People ate local vegetables and not much else, and disease deaths were markedly lower (Fontana et al., 2011).

Similar results were reported from Cuba. Because the United States led an embargo, Cuba experienced food and gas shortages from 1991 to 1995. People walked more, ate homegrown fruits and vegetables, and lost weight. They had much less heart disease and diabetes, and they lived longer (Franco et al., 2013).

But in all of these nations, once more food was available, people ate more, gained weight, and died earlier. Consequently, many researchers seek a drug with the benefits of calorie restriction without the diet. No success.

However, one strategy may work: **intermittent fasting**, in which people periodically fast but eat normally most of the time. Several versions have been tried: Fasting for two of the seven days per week, or every other day, or not eating at all for 14 to 20 hours each day. Intermittent fasting results in lower blood pressure, less obesity, and better metabolism, not only because the digestive system is less active but also because some other physiological responses increase to protect against temporary starvation (Mani et al., 2018).

The benefits of intermittent fasting are similar to the benefits of calorie restriction, but this strategy is more palatable to most people. For example, one study entailed four comparison groups, about 35 healthy but overweight women in each group (Schübel et al., 2018). One group reduced daily calories by 20 percent (the

calorie restriction The practice of limiting dietary energy intake (while consuming sufficient quantities of vitamins, minerals, and other important nutrients) for the purpose of improving health and slowing down the aging process.

intermittent fasting A pattern of eating that includes periods of restricted eating interspersed with usual consumption. The most popular pattern is two days per week eating less than 750 calories and five days of normal eating, all while drinking plenty of water.

"If you give up alcohol, cigarettes, sex, red meat, cakes and chocolate, and don't get too excited, you can enjoy life for a few more years yet."

Find the Joy Most elders are happier than when they were younger. They appreciate nature, other people, and life itself, and are less often dependent on food, drugs, or possessions.

classic calorie reduction), one reduced weekly calories by 20 percent but could eat more on some days and less on others, one group fasted (75 percent fewer calories) two days a week and then ate without restriction on the other five days. The fourth group was the experimental control—no special diets.

The results: Weight loss was about the same for all three groups with restricted calories. However, the women preferred the two-day fasting version.

Fasting is not recommended for children, pregnant or breast-feeding women, or elders with certain health problems, including diabetes. But with careful medical supervision, even those with diabetes may be helped by intermittent fasting (Grajower & Horne, 2019).

This returns us to the beginning of this chapter. It is apparent that growth is not always benign, and that every period of life builds on the previous one. Many studies of late adolescence refer back to prenatal development as laying the foundation for physical development lifelong. Some practices—avoiding drugs and chemicals in prenatal life, restricting some tasty foods in adulthood, eating mostly fruits and vegetables in adulthood, being hungry occasionally in middle age—produce optimal development over a long life.

As you have seen, the specifics of growth vary from age to age, from explosive growth to universal decline, but the overall conclusion is the same. The experience of a developing person of any age affects all the later ages. For that, cognition and the social context are crucial: The next 11 chapters explain specifics!

WHAT HAVE YOU LEARNED?

1. When do the major body systems begin to weaken?
2. Why is it important to maintain organ reserve?
3. How do homeostasis and allostasis compare?
4. How is hormone replacement therapy beneficial and how is it harmful?
5. Why is compression of morbidity a goal for late adulthood?
6. What are some variations of calorie restriction?

SUMMARY

From One Cell to a Newborn

1. In the days after conception, the single-cell zygote duplicates again and again, becoming eight stem cells before it begins to differentiate into the various parts of the placenta and body.

2. After passing through the fallopian tube to implant in the uterus, some cells form the placenta, which implants in the uterus to obtain nourishment, and other cells form the embryo. The central nervous system is the first to form, followed quickly by the face and other organs.

3. By eight weeks after conception, the embryo has virtually all the body parts, and is worthy of a new name, the fetus. Sex organs form at that point, and hormones affect brain development.

4. The fetus rapidly gains weight, weighing about 2 pounds and becoming viable at 22 weeks. For the future life and health of the future baby, it is best for all the organs to develop within the uterus for another three months; the fetus becomes a well-functioning baby after 38 weeks of prenatal growth.

5. Low birth weight, defined at less than 2,500 grams or 5 ½ pounds, occurs when a fetus is born preterm or when prenatal growth is slow.

Such babies are vulnerable to many health risks, especially when teratogens have impaired growth.

From Birth to Puberty

6. Infant growth is measured in percentiles, since steady growth of both weight and height is needed. Breast milk is the ideal infant food, with other nourishment added to prevent stunting and wasting.

7. As growth occurs, the body changes proportions, from the top-heavy toddler to the more agile child. During childhood, children need to be well nourished, but not overfed.

Adolescence

8. Although much variation occurs, the hormones that begin the process of puberty increase at about age 10, causing a spurt of body growth, as well as many aspects, both physical and psychological, of sexual maturation. Much individual, family, and cultural variation is apparent.

9. The growth spurt begins with the extremities and moves to the torso. Often weight and appetite increase before height and muscles do.

10. Sexual growth includes primary sexual characteristics (those that are involved in reproduction) and secondary ones (those that indicate gender). Many male/female differences in body growth and shape appear. Reproduction becomes possible.

Adulthood

11. The body systems (heart, lung, muscle, etc.) function most strongly in early adulthood and then decline, as senescence gradually occurs. Each organ has a reserve that protects against sudden strain.

12. Homeostasis keeps the body in daily balance, and allostasis works over a longer term. Sleep, exercise, and nutrition protect the adult body.

13. Sexual responsiveness is most rapid in early adulthood, when conception, pregnancy, and birth are easiest. Many adults are more satisfied with sexuality as they age, and many turn to IVF and other measures to remedy infertility.

14. In many ways, late adulthood is the result, and continuation, of health habits earlier in life. Variability is increasingly evident.

15. The goal is compression of morbidity, which is to add healthy, active years to life, not merely to add years. Exercise seems crucial for that. With lower animals, eating fewer calories adds health and life. Many adults hope for the same results by periodic fasting.

KEY TERMS

germinal period (p. 87)
embryonic period (p. 87)
fetal period (p. 87)
stem cells (p. 87)
embryo (p. 89)
teratogen (p. 89)
fetal alcohol syndrome (FAS)
  (p. 89)
fetus (p. 91)
body mass index (BMI)
  (p. 92)
low birthweight (LBW) (p. 92)

very low birthweight (VLBW)
  (p. 92)
extremely low birthweight
  (ELBW) (p. 92)
preterm (p. 92)
small-for-gestational age (SGA)
  (p. 92)
percentile (p. 93)
stunting (p. 96)
wasting (p. 96)
overweight (p. 97)
obesity (p. 97)

menarche (p. 100)
spermarche (p. 100)
primary sex characteristics
  (p. 102)
secondary sex characteristics
  (p. 102)
body image (p. 102)
anorexia nervosa (p. 103)
bulimia nervosa (p. 103)
binge eating disorder
  (p. 103)
senescence (p. 104)

organ reserve (p. 105)
homeostasis (p. 105)
allostasis (p. 105)
infertility (p. 109)
menopause (p. 110)
hormone replacement therapy
  (HRT) (p. 111)
andropause (p. 112)
compression of morbidity
  (p. 114)
calorie restriction (p. 115)
intermittent fasting (p. 115)

APPLICATIONS

1. Interview three mothers of varied backgrounds about their birth experiences. Make your interviews open-ended—let the mothers choose what to tell you, as long as they give at least a 10-minute description. Then compare and contrast the three accounts, noting especially any influences of culture, personality, circumstances, and cohort.

2. Go to a playground or another place where young children play. Note the motor skills that the children demonstrate, including abilities and inabilities, and keep track of age and sex. What differences do you see among the children?

3. Interview two to four of your friends who are in their late teens or early 20s about their memories of menarche or spermarche, including their memories of others' reactions. Do their comments indicate that these events are or are not emotionally troubling for young people?

4. Guess the age of five adults you know, ideally of different ages. Then ask them how old they are. Analyze the clues you used for your guesses and the reactions to your question.

ESPECIALLY FOR ANSWER

Response for Medical Professionals (from p. 97) You need to speak to the parents, not accusingly (because you know that genes and culture have a major influence on body weight) but helpfully. Alert them to the potential social and health problems that their child's weight poses. Most parents are very concerned about their child's well-being and will work with you to improve the child's snacks and exercise levels.

OBSERVATION QUIZ ANSWERS

Answer to Observation Quiz (from p. 90) Brain. Legs.

Answer to Observation Quiz (from p. 97) Most is East Asia, primarily because China has prioritized public health. Least is western and central Africa, primarily because of civil wars. In some nations, high birth rates have dramatically increased the numbers of stunted children, even though rates in the region are lower.

Answer to Observation Quiz (from p. 104) Fewer men, non-Whites, and people over age 30, choose this, as evident in this photo. London is now very diverse, as are most U.S. cities.

CHAPTER 5

Plan Shoot/Multi-bits/ImaZinS/Getty Images

Brain Development and Neuroscience

"**U**se your BRAIN!" the instructor told our class of pregnant women and their birth partners. "Always ask the <u>B</u>enefits, <u>R</u>isks, and <u>A</u>lternatives and then use your <u>I</u>ntuition and your ability to say <u>N</u>o or <u>N</u>ot yet. She added that, after B-R-A-I, if we concluded that we didn't need N, we could say *Yes*. Brainy?

We nodded. Some wrote down details of procedures we should evaluate — epidural, c-section, induction. My daughter, not I, was the pregnant one, so my thoughts were more general: I was grateful that human brains can weigh benefits and risks, consider alternatives, plumb the unconscious (via intuition), and then respond.

Emotions, ideas, and even life itself depend on brains. We choose *Not yet*, *No*, or *Yes* many times each day. To approach the goal of this text—for everyone to reach their full potential—this chapter provides the basics of neuroscience.

Included are highlights from every developmental period, since brain activity is the first, and the last, sign of life. The final section discusses conditions and diseases that impede analysis, memory, and thought, and how to prevent them.

That instructor was right: We use our brains to protect our brains.

What Will You Know?

1. Do left-handed people have stronger left brains?
2. Do psychoactive drugs increase or decrease the brain's neurotransmitters?
3. Why is it easier for a preschooler to learn a new language than for a college student?
4. Does everyone become forgetful and confused if they live long enough?

Naming the Parts of the Brain

To know how to "use our brains," it helps to refer to specific areas, each of which contributes to overall function (Horien et al., 2019). We think, sense, and act because each part of the brain coordinates with other parts. Now we explain three distinct ways to describe those parts: (1) back to front, (2) four lobes, or (3) two sides.

From Brainstem to Cerebrum

Remember that the developing human becomes an embryo about two weeks after conception, an event marked by the *neural streak*, then *neural groove*, then *neural tube*, then *spine* (called the *backbone*, the defining feature of a vertebrate). That tube grows a bulb at the top—the beginning of the brain.

Throughout prenatal development, the brain expands forward from that tube, growing faster than any other organ (see **Figure 5.1**). To hold the brain, the newborn head can barely squeeze through the birth canal. That is why birth is so difficult for humans, unlike for other mammals. At birth the human brain already weighs 25 percent of what it will eventually weigh, a marked contrast to the rest of the newborn body, about 4 percent of adult weight.

Together, the spine and the brain make up the **central nervous system**, the first of the systems that sustain life. (The cardiovascular system is next; the sexual-reproductive system is last.) All vertebrates have a brain within their heads; they all have a central nervous system to support development. Mammal brains have three parts that develop in sequence: **hindbrain** (*behind*, at the lower back of the head), **midbrain** (*middle*), and **forebrain** (*front*).

The Hindbrain

The hindbrain begins with the first structure to arise from that bulb at the top of the neural tube. This is the beginning of the **brainstem**, which includes all the structures that allow basic body functions, such as breathing and heartbeat. Every vertebrate has a brainstem to connect the backbone to the brain.

central nervous system The brain and the spinal cord, crucial for our senses, thoughts, and emotions. The central nervous system is often distinguished from the peripheral nervous system, the noncentral parts such as the arms and legs.

hindbrain The very back of the brain, part of the brainstem.

midbrain In humans, a relatively small cluster of brain regions that aid in movement and the senses, although the primary site for these functions is in the cerebral cortex.

forebrain Another name for the cerebrum.

brainstem The part of the brain in the very back of the head, which connects to the spinal cord (the backbone). The hindbrain and the midbrain are considered part of the brainstem.

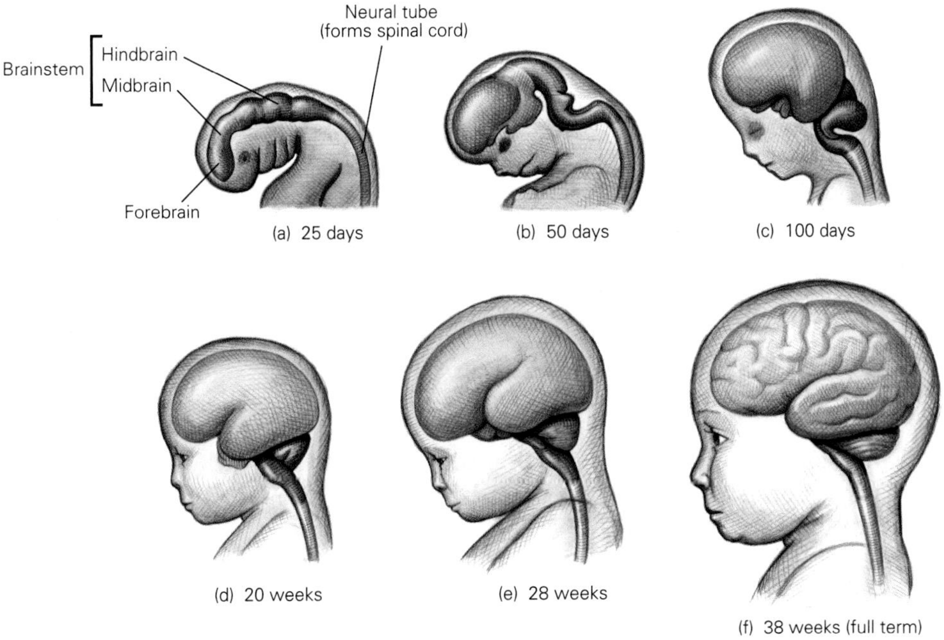

Neural tube
(forms spinal cord)

Brainstem [Hindbrain
Midbrain

Forebrain

(a) 25 days

(b) 50 days

(c) 100 days

(d) 20 weeks

(e) 28 weeks

(f) 38 weeks (full term)

FIGURE 5.1
Prenatal Growth of the Brain Just 25 days after conception *(a)*, the central nervous system is already evident. The brain looks distinctly human by day 100 *(c)*. By the 28th week of gestation *(e)*, at the very time brain activity begins, the various sections of the brain are recognizable. When the fetus is full term *(f)*, all parts of the brain, including the cortex (the outer layers), are formed, folding over one another and becoming more convoluted, or wrinkled, as the number of brain cells increases.

In the hindbrain are the *pons, medulla*, and the *cerebellum*. Together those parts sustain life. Hearts beat and lungs breathe, animals move without any conscious awareness, because the pons and medulla activate those muscles.

Have you wondered why some living things—trees and grass, for instance—are alive but cannot move? No brainstem! The medulla and the pons have primitive sensory receptors for basic movement and urges, including for sex and sleep. Trees do not mate or sleep; all living creatures do.

In former centuries, stopped breath or absent heartbeat meant death. Now respirators and defibrillators can replace automatic lung and heart activity from the hindbrain. Currently, to determine death, doctors touch the cornea of the open eye to see if that touch is felt. A blink or a flinch means that the hindbrain still functions: The person is alive (Mahanes & Greer, 2018).

The Cerebellum

cerebellum A structure of the hindbrain that is particularly crucial for movement.

In a separate area of the hindbrain is the **cerebellum**, a structure that refines basic movement. The cerebellum allows coordination: People dance and draw, not just walk and scribble.

The role of the cerebellum is obvious when it is impaired: Alcohol is toxic to the central nervous system, especially to this part of the brain. This can be temporary, as when a drunk person cannot walk a straight line, or permanent, as in fetal alcohol syndrome, when a pregnant woman's drinking damages the cerebellum of her fetus. Excessive drinking can even be fatal, when death occurs because the cerebellum shuts down and breathing stops.

The Midbrain

Next to the hindbrain is the *midbrain*, which processes inputs from the hindbrain. Often considered part of the midbrain is the *diencephalon* (literally, "between brain"), which includes the *pituitary*, the *hypothalamus* (described later as part of the *limbic system*), and the *thalamus*. Those structures relay information back and forth, to and from the *forebrain*.

The term *midbrain* suggests a large middle structure. The midbrain is indeed relatively large in some creatures and in the human embryo. During prenatal development, however, the midbrain is soon overwhelmed by the forebrain, which grows and matures for decades.

The Forebrain

cerebrum The forebrain, small in some animals but huge in humans. The cerebrum is the location of emotions as well as sensations. It grows rapidly in prenatal life, infancy, and childhood, and is not fully grown and connected until early adulthood.

The forebrain, also called the **cerebrum**, is by far the biggest part of the human brain. The forebrain begins with the *thalamus*, which connects the more primitive, unconscious brain with the conscious parts. For humans, 90 percent of the brain is cerebrum. Because of the size of the forebrain, human brains are big, eventually weighing about 3 pounds.

By contrast, adult chimpanzees (our closest primate relatives) weigh half as much as a person, but their brains are much smaller, only a fourth of the human size. A few mammals (elephants, whales) have brains that weigh more, but their bodies are about 100 times as heavy as a person: Proportionally, human brains are by far the largest among all the mammals.

The Cerebral Cortex

cerebral cortex The outer layers of the brain, which are the location of most human sensations and thoughts.

The forebrain includes the **cerebral cortex**, which covers the cerebrum with six layers of cells. The cortex is large: Most of the human brain is cortex (see **Figure 5.2**).

The cerebral cortex is sometimes called the *neocortex*, to distinguish it from an older, three-layered structure called the *limbic cortex*. The word *cortex* comes from the Latin word for "bark," because the cortex covers the brain like bark covers a

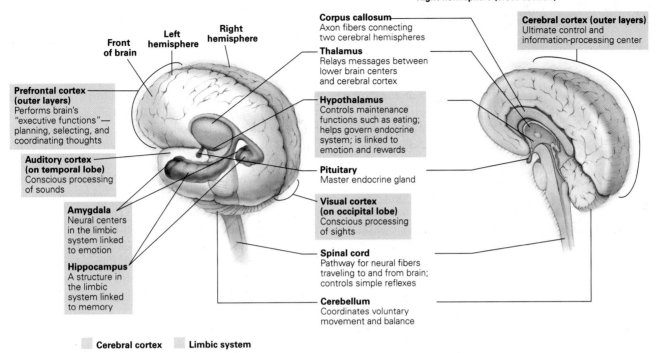

Right hemisphere (cross section)

Corpus callosum
Axon fibers connecting
two cerebral hemispheres

Thalamus
Relays messages between
lower brain centers
and cerebral cortex

Hypothalamus
Controls maintenance
functions such as eating;
helps govern endocrine
system; is linked to
emotion and rewards

Pituitary
Master endocrine gland

**Visual cortex
(on occipital lobe)**
Conscious processing
of sights

Spinal cord
Pathway for neural fibers
traveling to and from brain;
controls simple reflexes

Cerebellum
Coordinates voluntary
movement and balance

Cerebral cortex (outer layers)
Ultimate control and
information-processing center

**Front
of brain**

**Left
hemisphere**

**Right
hemisphere**

**Prefrontal cortex
(outer layers)**
Performs brain's
"executive functions"—
planning, selecting, and
coordinating thoughts

**Auditory cortex
(on temporal lobe)**
Conscious processing
of sounds

Amygdala
Neural centers
in the limbic
system linked
to emotion

Hippocampus
A structure in
the limbic
system linked
to memory

Cerebral cortex   Limbic system

FIGURE 5.2
Connections A few of the hundreds of named parts of the brain are shown here. Although each area has particular functions, the entire brain is interconnected. The processing of emotions, for example, occurs primarily in the limbic system, where many brain areas are involved, including the amygdala, hippocampus, and hypothalamus.

tree. That name was given before advanced technology allowed observation of the brain. We now see that the cortex is much more than a bark-like covering; it is the location of most of our conscious thought.

The surface of the cortex in the first prenatal months is smooth, covering the brain. But toward the end of prenatal development, the human cortex develops hills and valleys (called *gyri* and *sulci*), allowing an extensive cortex to fit into the fetal skull. Imagine a drawing on a smooth piece of paper. If that paper were then crumpled up, the drawing would be still there, but the paper would have less surface. That is why depictions of the brain show lumps and wrinkles: Space is needed for the elaborate cortex.

Each part of the cerebral cortex specializes in particular functions. The *visual cortex* contains about 20 distinct areas that allow recognition of colors, shapes, motion, and so on; the *auditory cortex* interprets many discrete sounds; the *motor cortex* has areas for each body part, from the right pinky finger to the left big toe.

Four Lobes

The second way to describe the brain is to note that the cerebral cortex has four lobes, which are large areas of cortical substance. The four lobes are:

- the *occipital lobe* at the back of the forebrain, which includes vision;
- the *temporal lobes* at the sides, which include hearing;
- the *parietal lobe* at the top, which specializes in touch, sequence, and processing;
- the *frontal lobe* at the front, which specializes in reasoning.

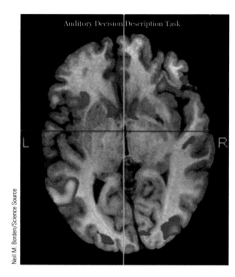

Auditory Decision Description Task

Neil M. Borden/Science Source

Listen, Imagine, Think, and Tap A person has just heard "banana" and "round, red fruit," and is told to tap if the two do not match. An MRI reveals that 14 areas of the brain are activated. As you see, this simple matching task requires hearing (the large region on the temporal lobe), imagined seeing (the visual cortex in the occipital lobe at the bottom), motor action (the parietal lobe), and analysis (the prefrontal cortex at the top). Imagine how much more brain activation is required for the challenges of daily life.

prefrontal cortex The area of the cortex at the very front of the brain that specializes in anticipation, planning, and impulse control.

ESPECIALLY FOR Early-Childhood Teachers You know you should be patient, but frustration rises when your young charges dawdle on the walk to the playground a block away. What should you do? (see response, page 147)

Especially in infancy, the boundaries between these four lobes are somewhat fluid. Lack of visual stimulation in blind infants, for instance, leads to fewer neurons within the occipital lobe and more in the temporal lobes, since hearing compensates for sight. For all of us, the senses and abilities that garner extensive neuronal networks are those that we use most. More information about the senses is in Chapter 6.

With maturation, the brain grows, reaching 75 percent of adult size by age 6. The four lobes become larger and more specialized, while connections between them strengthen. One example is in learning to read, an ability that does not have a particular location, unlike for talking or gesturing (Sousa, 2014). There is no brain region dedicated to reading because no written languages existed until about 10,000 years ago. For millennia after that, almost no one aside from scribes and scholars could read, and thus, human brains did not evolve to support reading.

Now literacy is useful for everyone, so all four lobes do their part: temporal for sounds, occipital for recognizing letters, parietal for sequencing, and finally the frontal cortex for comprehension and analysis. Earlier educators thought that children with dyslexia had difficulty seeing letters (with small differences such as between *b*, *d*, and *p* particularly hard). But research finds that most people with dyslexia can see normally but have problems with hearing, timing, or comprehension (Lachman, 2018).

Beyond helping with specific neurological skills, extensive practice with reading is needed, enabling the child's brain to develop links between various parts (Huettig et al., 2018). Likewise, all the lobes are needed for many other skills; young brains need practice to develop connections for whatever skills are valued in their community.

The Prefrontal Cortex

At the front of the frontal lobe is the **prefrontal cortex**, which contains the brain centers for long-term anticipation, planning, and reflection—all virtually absent in other animals. (Dogs don't worry or fantasize about the future, plan for a rainy day, fear climate change, or hope that their puppies will marry well and have a better life than they did.) The prefrontal cortex is inactive in early infancy, gradually becoming more efficient over the years.

Long-term planning—where to live, whom to marry, when to have a baby, how to raise that child, whether and when to retire—requires the prefrontal cortex. Thus, that part of the human brain "opens the brain to the future" (Fuster, 2015). It is not fully developed until the mid-20s, which may explain why younger adults often change jobs, partners, and college majors. That is their strength: Emerging adults are creative and innovative (Dougherty & Clarke, 2018). They are not ready, neurologically, to settle down.

The lengthy maturation of the prefrontal cortex is a uniquely human phenomenon. Consequently, human children—unlike the young of other species—require adult care for decades. Traditionally, when teenagers were expected to marry and have babies, older relatives (usually grandparents) helped. Everyone knew that young parents were not yet able to be solely responsible for another human life.

Data on child maltreatment still point in this direction. The younger parents are, the more likely they are to mistreat their children. Official statistics find that parents under age 35 are twice as likely than those over age 35 to be neglectful or abusive, although they are only about one-third of all the parents and grandparents (U.S. Department of Health and Human Services, January 19, 2017).

When children are officially removed from parental care, about a third of the time their grandparents are designated as caregivers—the same grandparents who raised the abusive parent. One reason for this is that older adults tend to be more patient, responsive caregivers than they were at a younger age (Sampson & Hertlein, 2015). Credit brain maturation!

Impulsive and Perseverative

Immaturity of the prefrontal cortex makes young children impulsive, flitting from one activity to another. Poor **impulse control** may signify a personality disorder in adulthood but not in early childhood; many 3-year-olds suddenly run, yell, laugh, cry, or grab.

Or, a young child might have the opposite problem, **perseveration**, the tendency to persevere in, or stick to, one thought or action, unable to inhibit action after it occurs. A young child might repeat one question again and again or have a tantrum when told to end an activity. (Wise teachers give a warning—"Clean-up in 5 minutes"—which may help.) The tantrum itself may perseverate. Crying may become uncontrollable because the child is stuck in the emotion that triggered the tantrum (see Career Alert).

As the prefrontal cortex matures, children, adolescents, and young adults gradually become better able to regulate their emotions and focus their attention. For example, compare incoming first-year college students, age 18 or so, with graduating seniors. Of course, some of the past experiences of those 18-year-olds have already sculpted their brains, but sheer neurological maturation matters. Many young students impulsively quit college, returning years later with more conscientious work habits.

In adulthood, procrastination and impulsiveness are correlates, not opposites. Both are controlled by the prefrontal cortex (Gustavson et al., 2015; Rebetez et al., 2018). In some of the oldest adults, the prefrontal cortex shrinks and, once again,

"I would share, but I'm not there developmentally."

Good Excuse It is true that emotional control of selfish instincts is difficult for young children, because the prefrontal cortex is not yet mature enough to regulate some emotions. However, family practices can advance some understanding.

impulse control The ability to postpone or deny the immediate response to an idea or behavior.

perseverate To stay stuck, or persevere, in one thought or action for a long time. The ability to be flexible, switching from one task to another, is beyond most young children.

CAREER ALERT   The Preschool Teacher

As you see, brain development is lifelong, beginning in the first years of life. Social skills, eating habits, exercise practices, and so on are learned before age 5, when brains are especially plastic. Early childhood teachers, who understand the brains of the very young, are increasingly in demand.

This realization has not yet led to high pay—quite the opposite. The U.S. Bureau of Labor Statistics reports that, compared to teachers overall, early-childhood educators are most in demand and least paid: The average annual salary is below $30,000 a year. There is marked variation in state-by-state certification requirements and in neighborhood-by-neighborhood salary levels.

Wise preschool teachers need brain research to understand what young children can and cannot learn. For example, since myelination is particularly rapid in the auditory, visual, and motor cortex, young children need to connect both hemispheres of brain and body by running, climbing, balancing. But the immature motor cortex is not yet ready for writing, or tying shoelaces, or sitting quietly in one place.

Since the developing brain is primed to learn language, the curriculum should be rich in language—talking, listening, singing, hearing stories, making rhymes, engaging in verbal play, ideally in more than one language. Children should not be pushed to read; their brains are not ready. They can recognize and name letters just as they learn to distinguish a baseball from a soccer ball, but the immature visual cortex does not yet allow following a line of small print.

Fostering control of gross motor skills may be particularly important for children who are at risk for *attention-deficit/hyperactivity*

disorder (ADHD), the label given to overactive children who find it especially hard to concentrate, quietly, on one activity. Such children need to exercise their bodies, which helps their brains mature (Halperin & Healey, 2011; Hillman, 2014).

Hyperactive 3-year-olds have active and immature brains; if neurological maturation is allowed to proceed, by age 8 they are likely to develop normal activity patterns (Rajendran et al., 2013). That is another reason for early education—children develop their brains by playing with other children. By contrast, watching television or a video alone (a common activity for those not in preschool) does not foster the brain regulation that children need.

Ideally, preschool teachers know exactly what aspects of brain development to encourage and what aspects need to wait, lest they frustrate everyone, including themselves. Of course, brains differ and readiness varies, so it is not necessarily worrisome if one child reads and writes by age 6 and another does not. For neurons to connect, practice is needed. Teachers encourage drawing as well as dancing since early scribbles help children to someday write their names.

If you are interested in this career, more details are available from the professional group National Association for the Education of Young Children (NAEYC). Don't be discouraged by the working conditions or starting salaries. Some nations (the Netherlands, Denmark) already fund early-childhood education at the rates of teachers for older children, since young brains need as much professional attention as the brains of older children, teenagers, or adults. That may become true in the United States, as the research in this book is better understood.

an older adult might be impulsive or perseverate in "off-target verbosity," saying more than they intend to say (impulsive) or repeating themselves (perseverative) (Kemper, 2015).

Hemispheres

The third major way to describe the brain is as composed of a left and right hemisphere. The entire body of every mammal, bird, or insect has two sides. Humans have a left and right eye, ear, nostril, arm, hand, leg, foot, kidney, lung, and ovary or testicle. There are a few exceptions (such as the heart, stomach, and mouth), but the brain is not among them. Brains have a **left hemisphere** and a **right hemisphere**, each with complementary functions.

In general, the left hemisphere controls the right side of the body and the right hemisphere controls the left. That explains why survivors of a *cerebral hemorrhage* (a *stroke*) in their right brain have a limp left leg, a dysfunctional left arm, and/or a blind left eye. The opposite is true if a stroke occurs on the left hemisphere.

Cognitive abilities also become specialized. Usually logic, math, and language abilities are on the left hemisphere, while creativity, the arts, and emotions are on the right. (This is reversed in some left-handed people.) The divide is less pronounced early in life. If surgery or massive injury destroys half of a young child's brain, the other hemisphere may take over: A child with a destroyed left hemisphere may develop language on the right. Recovery of destroyed brain functions is more difficult, sometimes impossible, if severe brain damage occurs in adulthood.

Understanding brain specialization may be useful. Since language areas are usually in the left hemisphere, a stroke on the left side might impair comprehension or production of speech. The right hemisphere may compensate via music (located on the right). Thus, a stroke victim who cannot talk might be able to communicate with song (Birkett, 2008)!

Prediction of cognitive loss, and efforts to reprogram deficiencies, are particularly crucial when neurosurgery is considered to cure severe epilepsy by silencing parts of the brain. Even in children, the specific functions in each half of the brain are much more varied than a simple left brain/right brain analysis suggests (Benjamin et al., 2018).

Connecting the Hemispheres

The two halves of the brain, and thus the two sides of the body, are connected by a long thick band of 200 million axons in the **corpus callosum** (Gooijers & Swinnen, 2014). When small children finally (at about age 5) can skip, balance a two-wheel bicycle, or hop on one foot, that signifies that their corpus callosum has matured enough to make that possible. Dancing, athletic prowess, and many academic skills require coordination of both hemispheres, and thus older children can be more skilled than younger ones. It is a myth that we use only 10 percent of our brains (Jarrett, 2014). In fact, all the parts are active in turn.

Think of a huge orchestra: Instruments in various sections play while other instruments are temporarily silent. If, instead, every part were active simultaneously, the overload would make reflection impossible, the orchestral equivalent of a deafening cacophony. The corpus callosum coordinates the sides, the thalamus coordinates the senses, the prefrontal cortex calls forth the memories, and the result is a symphony.

Experience matters. To extend that metaphor, some music includes extensive use of violins, others the drums, but a score might call forth dozens of instruments, each playing in turn. In the same way, each of us develops some areas of our brains more than others, although, ideally, every part can be activated when needed. Practice strengthens connections.

For example, some children practice balance first on a balance beam and eventually on a tightrope. By adulthood, their brains have mastered balance so well

left hemisphere The left half of the brain. This half controls the right side of the body.

right hemisphere The right half of the brain, which controls the left side of the body.

corpus callosum A long, thick band of nerve fibers that connects the left and right hemispheres of the brain and allows communication between them.

A CASE TO STUDY

Lefties

I thought left-handed people were odd until my eldest daughter, Bethany, wrote her name YANHTEB, with the N, E, and B facing the other way.

Thanks to Bethany, I now notice many cultural biases favoring right-handed people. Some are in language: No one wants to have "two left feet" or to be "out in left field." In Latin, *dexter* (as in *dexterity*) means "right," and *sinister* means "left." In French, left is "gauche," which means "socially inept" in English. Letters and words are, in most languages, written from left to right.

Many objects (doorknobs, books, faucets, and scissors among them) are designed for me, not Bethany, and many customs assume that no one is left-handed. Why shake hands with the right hand? Because knights in medieval England could not quickly pull out their swords while shaking hands. Why do some cultures expect the left hand to be used *only* for wiping after defecation, making it an insult to give someone food with that "dirty" hand. That taboo originated because it reduced transmission of disease. As often happens, customs that begin for good reason continue when the reason is gone.

Historically, adults forced left-handed children to write with their right hand. Most still used their left to brush their teeth, throw a ball, or wield a hammer, as my husband did. (Until Bethany, I did *not* notice that he was left-handed, because he wrote with his right hand.)

Educators now understand that handedness originates in the brain; children should be allowed to follow their neurological preferences. Consequently, the rate of left-handed people in England was 3 percent in 1900; it is 11 percent now (McManus & Hartigan, 2007).

A disproportionate number of famous artists, musicians, political leaders, and athletes were/are left-handed, including Pele, Babe Ruth, Monica Seles, Bill Gates, Oprah Winfrey, Jimi Hendrix, Lady Gaga, Tina Fey, Jennifer Lawrence, and Justin Bieber. Six of the past 10 U.S. presidents were/are lefties: Harry Truman, Gerald Ford, Ronald Reagan, George H.W. Bush, Bill Clinton, and Barack Obama. Did their ability to combine logic and creativity help them?

My two left-handed children are lawyers, as was my husband; I and my other two children are neither lefties nor lawyers. Coincidence?

---

that they become circus stars. Most of us would fall off a rope but can still balance the left and right sides well enough to stand steady on two feet.

Practice matters in coordinating the left and right hemispheres, because all important brain functions, from those that support the infant's first attempts to crawl to those that allow the president to negotiate an international agreement, require both sides of the brain. As one leader in split-brain research explains, humans have "multiple minds" in one skull. The left and right hemispheres are confederates, not competitors (Gazzaniga, 2015).

Thanks to the corpus callosum, if one brain region cannot handle a task, other regions assist. That may explain why left-handed people often have more axons in their corpus callosum than right-handed people: The culture requires more coordination of both sides of their bodies. (See A Case to Study, above.)

The need for using the entire brain may also explain a curious finding: The elderly use more parts of their brains, typically on both sides, to perform tasks that are localized among younger adults (Hatta et al., 2015). If age reduces efficiency in one brain area, other parts may help.

Of course, understanding the parts of the brain is only the beginning of neuroscience. The crucial activity is in the cells, which send and receive messages. That activity can be measured in many ways (see Inside the Brain).

WHAT HAVE YOU LEARNED?

1. How does the prenatal human brain compare to the brains of other animals?
2. What are three ways to describe the parts of the brain?
3. Why does the human brain appear lumpy on the surface?
4. Where is each of the four lobes of the brain?
5. What does the left side of the brain control?
6. Why do people need a corpus callosum?

INSIDE THE BRAIN

Measuring Mental Activity

A hundred years ago, people thought that emotions came from the heart. That's why we send hearts on Valentine's Day, why we speak of broken hearts, of a soft spot in the heart, or of a hardened heart. But now we know that everything begins in the brain. Never say, dismissively, "It's all in your head." Of course it is in your head; everything is.

Until quite recently, the only way scientists could estimate brain activity was to measure skulls. That led to some false ideas, now discredited. In the nineteenth and early twentieth centuries, some said that women could never be professors because their brains were too small (Swaab & Hofman, 1984). Many people believed in *phrenology*, that bumps on the head reflected intelligence and character. Psychiatrists would run their hands over a person's skull to measure 27 traits, including spirituality, loyalty, and aggression.

Within the past half-century, neuroscientists learned to use electrodes, magnets, light, and computers to measure brain activity (see **Table 5.1**). Bumps on the head and head size (within limits) were proven irrelevant. Instead, small changes in light absorption, or magnetism, or oxygenated blood flow are analyzed to indicate brain function.

These new techniques have led to many significant discoveries. People with schizophrenia, depression, and other disorders often have neurological patterns that reflect their condition, and that reveal when particular treatments are effective. In another example, fMRI on adolescents has found that a full-size brain is not necessarily a fully functioning brain: The prefrontal cortex is not completely connected to the rest of the brain until adulthood.

At every age, notable individual differences over the life span are apparent. For instance, the brains of some adolescents are more mature than others (Foulkes & Blakemore, 2018), the brains of some new mothers change with birth and newborn care (P. Kim et al., 2016), and the brains of some older adults are much more active than others.

All the tools indicate brain plasticity and variations not imagined in earlier decades. However, although technology reveals activity in parts of the brain, technology cannot yet measure the depth and wisdom of that activity (Horien et al., 2019). Required is "thoughtful selection of fMRI measures . . . to come ever closer to understanding how our brains make us who we are" (Horien et al., 2019).

This confirms the need for theory: Without an idea of what to look for or what results might mean, the millions of data points from all brain images can lead to the same trap as earlier measurements of the skull—human bias.

TABLE 5.1

Some Techniques Used by Neuroscientists to Understand Brain Function

EEG (electroencephalogram)	ERP (event-related potential)
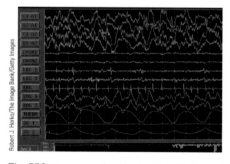	
The EEG measures electrical activity in the cortex. This can differentiate active brains (beta brain waves—very rapid, 12 to 30 per second) from sleeping brains (delta waves—1 to 3 per second) and brain states that are half-awake, or dreaming. Complete lack of brain waves, called flat-line, indicates brain death.	The amplitude and frequency of brain electrical activity changes when a particular stimulus (called an event) occurs. First, the ERP establishes the usual patterns, and then researchers present a stimulus (such as a sound, an image, a word) that causes a blip in electrical activity. ERP indicates how quickly and extensively people react—although this method requires many repetitions to distinguish the response from the usual brain activity.
MRI (magnetic resonance imaging)	**fMRI (functional magnetic resonance imaging)**
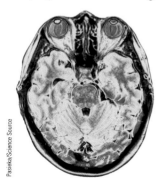 The water molecules in various parts of the brain each have a magnetic current, and measuring that current allows measurement of myelin, neurons, and fluid in the brain.	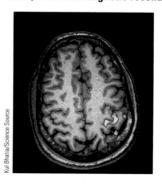 In advanced MRI, function is measured as more oxygen is added to the blood flow when specific neurons are activated. The presumption is that increased blood flow means that the person is using that part of the brain. fMRI has revealed that several parts of the brain are active at once—seeing something activates parts of the visual cortex, but it also may activate other parts of the brain far from the visual areas.

Robert J. Herko/The Image Bank/Getty Images

William Taufic/Getty Images

Pasieka/Science Source

Kul Bhatia/Science Source

TABLE 5.1

Some Techniques Used by Neuroscientists to Understand Brain Function (*continued*)

PET (positron emission tomography)

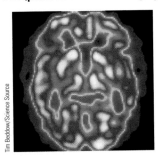

When a specific part of the brain is active, the blood flows more rapidly in that part. If radioactive dye is injected into the bloodstream and a person lies very still within a scanner while seeing pictures or other stimuli, changes in blood flow indicate thought. PET can reveal the volume of neurotransmitters; the rise or fall of brain oxygen, glucose, amino acids; and more. PET is almost impossible to use with children (who cannot stay still) and is very expensive with adults.

fNIRS (functional near infrared spectroscopy)

This method also measures changes in blood flow. But, it depends on light rather than magnetic charge and can be done with children, who merely wear a special cap connected to electrodes and do not need to lie still in a noisy machine (as they do for PET or fMRI). By measuring how each area of the brain absorbs light, neuroscientists infer activity of the brain (Ferrari & Quaresima, 2012).

DTI (diffusion tensor imaging)

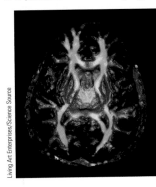

DTI is another technique that builds on the MRI. It measures the flow (diffusion) of water molecules within the brain, which shows connections between one area and another. This is particularly interesting to developmentalists because life experiences affect which brain areas connect with which other ones. Thus, DTI is increasingly being used by clinicians who want to individualize treatment and monitor progress (Van Hecke et al., 2016).

For both practical and ethical reasons, it is difficult to use these techniques on large, representative samples. One of the challenges of neuroscience is to develop methods that are harmless, quick, acceptable to parents and babies, and comprehensive. A more immediate challenge is to depict the data in ways that are easy to interpret and understand.

Communication in the Brain

Now that the overall configuration of the brain (the cerebral cortex, the lobes, the sides) has been described, we need to explain how the 86 billion brain cells become active, communicating with one another, allowing thought and action.

Brain Cells

A **neuron** is a specialized cell that transmits messages, activating movement, senses, memories, and more. Neurons are found in the peripheral as well as the central nervous system, but they are particularly numerous and significant in the brain.

Axons and Dendrites

Neurons transmit messages via fibers that reach toward other neurons. Those fibers are either **dendrites** (which bring messages to the cell body) or **axons** (which extend outward but do not quite touch the dendrites of other cells). Most neurons have one axon and several dendrites. The tiny gap between an axon and dendrite is called a **synapse**.

neuron One of billions of nerve cells in the central nervous system, especially in the brain.

dendrite A fiber that extends from a neuron and receives electrochemical impulses transmitted from other neurons via their axons.

axon A fiber that extends from a neuron and transmits electrochemical impulses from that neuron to the dendrites of other neurons.

synapse The intersection between the axon of one neuron and the dendrites of other neurons.

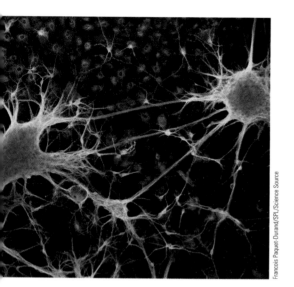

Connecting The color staining on this photo makes it obvious that the two cell bodies of neurons (stained chartreuse) grow axons and dendrites to each other's neurons. This tangle is repeated thousands of times in every human brain. Throughout life, those fragile dendrites will grow or disappear as the person continues thinking.

automatization A process in which repetition of a sequence of thoughts and actions makes the sequence routine so that it no longer requires conscious thought.

Axons can be short or long, reaching distant regions of the brain or body. An axon from a neuron in the spine extends to the big toe! Touch my toe, and I might not notice—the message from my toe to my spine to my brain may be so faint that I do not detect it. But if my toe breaks when I stub it, the pain message activates many neurons and will get through.

On/Off Messaging

There is one situation when the pain of a broken toe is not felt. Suppose someone deliberately hurts a person, breaking their arm as well as their toe. Then that arm pain message, or the victim's fear or fury, might blot out the toe pain. (The brain does not receive messages about multiple stimuli simultaneously.)

That is useful knowledge. If a person has an unbearable itch, the itch neurons might switch off if the person scratches so hard that a pain neuron takes over (some people prefer pain to itch). Another way to halt an itch is to put a frozen apple on it (the cold sensation overtakes the itch).

Because neurons are either on or off, activated or inhibited, effective psychotherapy may be cognitive, teaching people to replace negative thoughts with positive ones, or behavioral, getting people to do one thing that prevents them from doing another. Ideally, both involve changes in the brain, blocking some neurons by activating others.

Similarly, if a young child's temper tantrum perseverates, the best strategy may not be to explain why crying should stop (logic won't stop intense emotion) but to find a distraction that captures the child's attention, thus short-circuiting the prior neuronal activation.

Automatization

If a particular message has been transmitted many times, travel across the synapse seems instantaneous, giving rise to the phrase "Neurons that fire together wire together." This underlies another characteristic of the brain over the years: **automatization**. A sequence of thoughts and actions that is oft repeated becomes habitual, automatic, as the firing of one neuron sets off a chain reaction, with impulses crossing hundreds of synaptic gaps in an instance.

To be specific, when the cell body of a particular neuron is sufficiently activated to reach a threshold, it passes that excitement on down the line via its lone axon, which reaches synapses of the dendrites of other neurons. As you might imagine, some messages are so strong that they are like a tidal wave, impossible to ignore, involving many synapses, dendrites, and neurons; others are faint, disappearing instead of being sent. Often the message activates other neurons, but sometimes the message is to inhibit action: It signals "stop," "wait," "don't act."

Automatic responses can involve many neurons, all combining their messages and thus leading to an overpowering impulse. Or the messages can all be inhibitory, so the thought of a certain action produces intense fear and repulsion. A problem occurs when both action and inhibition occur, so the person is stuck between approach and avoidance, unable to act but also unable to ignore the act. That conflict leads to anxiety and depression (Struijs et al., 2018).

Examples of Automatization

Usually automatic processes make the tasks and routines of daily life easier. Brushing your teeth, putting on your socks, and turning the steering wheel of the car are all tasks that take much thought from children, becoming automatic by adulthood.

Reading becomes automatic as well. As you remember, reading requires coordination of many parts of the brain, more than a thousand neurons. For children, reading is painstakingly slow, as sight, sound, and thought must all connect, but adults see a billboard and automatically read it — even when they do not want to.

Children gradually become fluent readers, as extensive practice allows neurons from all four lobes to fire together automatically when a word is seen. This also explains misreading: If a glance omits a letter, the word flashed to the mind is not the one on the page. People then stop, think "that can't be right," and reread.

Likewise, learning to speak a second language, to recite the multiplication tables, and to write some words, gradually becomes automatic. When you sign your name, you do not need to think about how to spell it. Bilingual adults do not translate: They automatically think and respond in one language or another, depending on which language is activated.

Automatization Over the Life Span

Over the years of adulthood, vocabulary is the intellectual ability most likely to be maintained or increased. The reason is thought to be that, since talking and listening occur often every day, language becomes automatic. Some of the oldest-old still speak and understand well, even if they have forgotten most of the math, or history, or other knowledge they once knew.

Early learning is particularly likely to became automatic. If a bilingual elder loses some linguistic ability, it usually is in their second language, even if their first language was rarely spoken for decades.

This works for bad habits as well as good ones: Children who were often hit may later decide, based on thoughtful reflection and new information, that physical force should not be used on children. However, that person may "lose it" under emotional stress and hit a child. Similarly, adults feel anger at hearing certain words, or shame at making certain mistakes, or joy at tasting certain foods, because of long-buried automatic responses.

Following Instructions In middle childhood, children become quite capable of following adults' instructions, as these children in Tallinn, Estonia, are. Their teacher told them to put out their right hand, so that Pope Francis could greet each child quickly. The teacher must not have given the most important instruction about greeting a pope: Keep your eyes open.

Neurotransmitters

At synapses, axons release **neurotransmitters**, which are tiny bits of chemicals that transmit impulses from one neuron to be picked up by the dendrites of receiving neurons. The first neurotransmitter was discovered less than a century ago; now we know there are hundreds of them. Common neurotransmitters are *dopamine*, *serotonin*, *acetylcholine*, *glutamate*, *GABA*, *norepinephrine*, and *endorphins*.

Neurotransmitters are the brain's communicators, and without them we could not think. Many aspects of diet, genes, and experience affect them. For instance, caffeine reduces the neurotransmission of adenosine making sleep difficult; glucose feeds several neurotransmitters and thus sugar activates the brain.

Abnormalities in neurotransmitters (both too much and too little) impair brains, affecting movement and thought. Among the specifics: Parkinson's disease is characterized by insufficient dopamine, schizophrenia by too much dopamine, depression by insufficient serotonin, Alzheimer's by inadequate acetylcholine.

Every psychoactive drug and every emotional experience affect neurotransmitters, either increasing or inhibiting them (Contreras et al., 2018). Often various drugs work in concert, aiding or inhibiting neurotransmitters and affecting dendrite growth (Hamdy et al., 2018; Gray et al., 2013). Much remains to be discovered.

Some professionals specialize in psychopharmacology: They continually discover variable and unexpected impacts of each drug and neurotransmitter. Many neurocognitive disorders respond to judicious use of neurotransmitters.

neurotransmitter A brain chemical that carries information from the axon of a sending neuron to the dendrites of a receiving neuron.

Generally *morphine* relieves pain by increasing endorphins; *fluoxetine* (brand name: Prozac) is a *selective serotonin reuptake inhibitor (SSRI)*, reducing depression by keeping serotonin in the synapse longer; *alprazolam* (brand name: Xanax) increases GABA, thereby reducing anxiety; and so on.

Yet the connections just mentioned are disputed by some experts, and the impact of any drug depends on an individual's genes, experiences, circumstances, and age (Pritchard et al., 2020). New research will add, subtract, or modify what is known.

Overall, brains and behaviors adapt to whatever neurotransmitters are available. This is a warning for psychoactive drug users, whether the drug is a common one such as caffeine, or a less common one such as heroin. For instance, if a drug increases dopamine, the brain reduces natural dopamine neurotransmitters. Consequently, people who originally felt pleasure with a drug might soon feel depressed without it, because no natural dopamine eases withdrawal.

Since brains adjust to experience, more of any addictive drug is needed for the same result. If a person daily drinks one cup of coffee to stay awake, soon two cups are needed. If a person takes cocaine for the high, soon no high is felt, but the pain of the low intensifies.

This brain adjustment is particularly ominous with opioids, whether legal (morphine), illegal (heroin), prescription (oxycodone), or synthetic (fentanyl). Gradually more of the drug is needed to reduce pain signals. If the amount reaches the point of halting all signals, breathing stops. In the United States, every day from 2016 to 2019, about a hundred people died from opioid overdose: They hoped the dose was enough to stop pain, not realizing all sensation would stop.

Myelination

Sending messages from one neuron to another depends not only on synapses, dendrites, axons, and neurotransmitters but also on **myelin**, a fatty coating on the axons that speeds signals from the cell body (see **Figure 5.3**). Myelination allows faster **reaction time**—that is, the time it takes to respond to a stimulus. Increasing myelination over childhood allows better and faster cognition; myelin breakdown in late adulthood slows down thinking (Lu et al., 2013; Scantlebury et al., 2014).

At first, myelination occurs mostly in the motor and sensory cortexes: Babies react more quickly to sights and sounds with every passing month. Over the years of childhood, increasing myelination allows older children to be better game players: Batters swing, soccer players kick, video players score by clicking and toggling, all more rapidly with age.

Reaction time is pivotal, not only for physical actions but also for social and academic skills. For instance, deciding when to talk and when to stay quiet is something few young children do. Instead, they talk when told to be quiet, perhaps blurting out embarrassing questions, because it takes too long for them to process a thought. But by age 12, some children can, within a split-second, hear a remark and

1. realize that a comment could be made;
2. decide what clever words might be said;
3. imagine the response; and
4. speak or stay quiet.

We all sometimes regret what we said or did not say. Fortunately, people learn many automatic responses: please, thank you, sorry, excuse me, good morning. Adults prepare their response even while the other person is still talking. Children are much slower (Lindsay et al., 2019). Myelination helps with that.

The elderly walk more slowly, talk more slowly, and think more slowly. Less myelin is part of the reason. This affects thinking because speed is crucial for

myelin The coating on axons that speeds transmission of signals from one neuron to another.

reaction time The time it takes to respond to a stimulus, either physically (with a reflexive movement such as an eyeblink) or cognitively (with a thought).

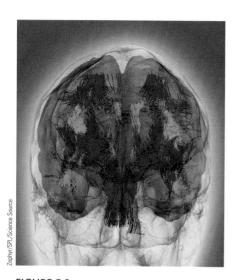

FIGURE 5.3

Mental Coordination? This brain scan of a 38-year-old depicts areas of myelination (the various colors) within the brain. As you see, the two hemispheres are quite similar, but not identical. For most important skills and concepts, both halves of the brain are activated.

many aspects of cognition. In fact, some experts believe that reaction time is pivotal for intelligence (Schubert et al., 2017). Slow walking predicts cognitive impairment and brain disease (Montero-Odasso et al., 2017).

The Limbic System

A crucial aspect of development is emotional regulation, the ability to regulate emotions so that anger does not automatically lead to hitting, that fear does not always result in flight, that disappointment does not evoke unbidden tears. Adults regulate their rage, fear, and sorrow, an ability that starts with a region deep within the forebrain called the **limbic system**.

The term *limbic system* was first used about 75 years ago to refer to several crucial parts of the brain that specialize in emotions. Now that neuroimaging has revealed more about brain circuitry, it no longer seems accurate to locate emotions exclusively in one region of the brain. Instead, more than a dozen brain regions are involved with emotions, and those brain areas that once were thought to be solely emotional are now known to have many other functions.

Nonetheless, certain parts of the so-called limbic system are crucial for emotions. Adolescent depression, for instance, can be traced to deficiencies in the limbic system (Redlich et al., 2018). We now describe several parts of the brain that are central for emotions.

> **limbic system** The parts of the brain that interact to produce emotions, including the amygdala, the hypothalamus, and the hippocampus. Many other parts of the brain also are involved with emotions.

The Amygdala

The **amygdala** is a tiny structure, about the same shape and size as an almond. It registers strong emotions, both positive and negative, especially fear. Increased amygdala activity causes some people to have terrifying nightmares or sudden terrors, and an overactive amygdala may explain why some adults seem consumed by rage or paralyzed by fear. Murderous outbursts and panic attacks can be traced to the amygdala.

The amygdala is present in infancy and grows as the child grows. Almost every toddler sometimes hits and cries (displaying the infamous toddler temper), and almost every young child has moments of irrational fear originating in the amygdala. My youngest daughter, at age 4, clung to me at bedtime; she was terrified that a tidal wave would drown her as she slept. I did not explain why that was ridiculous (her bedroom was on the third floor). Her amygdala needed comforting touch, not logic.

Specific evidence of that the amygdala can overwhelm logic came from the first (1966) of the infamous school shooters. Charles Whitman murdered his mother and then wrote, "let there be no doubt that I loved this woman with all my heart." Whitman then climbed a tower at the University of Texas in Austin to gun down and kill 14 strangers. He was shot and killed; an autopsy revealed a brain tumor pressing against his amygdala.

> **amygdala** A tiny brain structure that registers emotions, particularly fear and anxiety.

The Hippocampus

Another structure in the traditional limbic system is the **hippocampus**, located next to the amygdala. A central processor of memory, especially memory for locations, the hippocampus connects places with emotions. For example, if a person was once mugged on a particular street corner, later that person might be frightened when walking past that corner.

For all of us, some places feel comforting (perhaps a childhood home) and others evoke fear (perhaps a hospital), even when the experiences that originated those emotions are long gone. Phobias—of a doctor in a white coat, of a rat, of an airplane—arise when the hippocampus signals the amygdala.

We now know that the hippocampus remembers much more than emotions: It is thought to be the prime repository of memories of all kinds. Nonetheless,

> **hippocampus** A brain structure that is a central processor of memory, especially memory for locations.

emotional memories, especially terrors as with *posttraumatic stress disorder (PTSD)* or sudden panic attacks, involve buried memories in the hippocampus.

The Hypothalamus

The **hypothalamus** is another part of the brain that was traditionally considered part of the limbic system. The hypothalamus responds to signals from the amygdala and to memories from the hippocampus by sending messages to a crucial gland, the **pituitary**, adjacent to the hypothalamus. Together they manufacture over 50 distinct **hormones**, which are chemicals that are distributed throughout the body via the bloodstream.

Hormones

Hormones affect every emotion, as well as appetite, stress, sleep, and lust. Here we highlight several hormones that directly affect emotions. Often people think that emotions spring from something outside us, typically someone who makes us feel love, anxiety, rage, and so on. However, emotions may begin with internal hormones.

Oxytocin

You love your partner, your children, and your parents because of their wonderful qualities and your many experiences with them, right? No! Or, at least, only somewhat. The reason might be **oxytocin**, nicknamed "the love hormone" because it increases love for other people. That also is an oversimplification (Aguilar-Raab et al., 2019). Neither experience nor oxytocin always produce love.

Research on the psychological effects of oxytocin began with voles (a mouse-like creature that scampers in the wild). Montane voles, with very little natural oxytocin, are selfish, promiscuous. They are not dedicated caregivers (no love?) of their own children, who sometimes starve for lack of nurturance. Prairie voles (another species) have abundant oxytocin. They are devoted mates and parents. They stick with one partner lifelong, and fathers and mothers tend their offspring with admirable, cooperative solicitude (much love?).

Scientists blocked oxytocin in some Prairie voles (Keebaugh et al., 2015). Bonding and caregiving disappeared. The opposite worked, too: Adding oxytocin to Montane voles increased caregiving. For people, oxytocin in a person's bloodstream usually increases trust and solicitude.

Deep within every human brain are genes and receptors that produce and distribute oxytocin, signaling the hypothalamus to produce the hormone and then the pituitary to spread it throughout the body and brain, especially the amygdala and prefrontal cortex (Jurek & Neumann, 2018). Some people have more receptors than others.

Experiences increase or decrease oxytocin (Gangestad & Grebe, 2017). Touch helps: Having sex, holding babies, experiencing massage, hugging strangers, and even petting dogs increase oxytocin, unless those events provoke stress (such as a growling dog might). Past experiences matter, too: Adults who had loving mothers have more oxytocin (Perkeybile et al., 2019).

Oxytocin is not always benign: It can increase fear of strangers and even hostility. This is thought to be an outgrowth of love for one's own kin, tribe, and nation (Sapolsky, 2019).

Cortisol

The second hormone with profound emotional effects is **cortisol** (the main *glucocorticoid*), which increases with stress and reduces immunity. Cortisol levels vary daily, higher in the morning and lower at night.

hypothalamus A brain area that responds to the amygdala and the hippocampus and directs the pituitary to produce hormones that activate other parts of the brain and body.

pituitary A gland in the brain that responds to a signal from the hypothalamus by producing many hormones, including those that regulate growth and sexual maturation.

hormones Chemicals in the bloodstream that originate in the brain and affect many aspects of life, including sleep, hunger, lust, rage, and love.

oxytocin The primary bonding hormone, evident lifelong but particularly high at birth and in lactation.

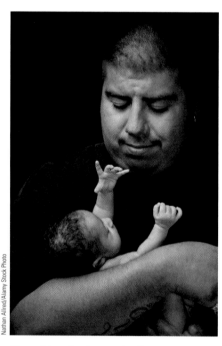

Mutual Joy For thousands of years, hormones and instincts have propelled fathers and babies to reach out to each other, developing lifelong connections.

cortisol The primary stress hormone; fluctuations in the body's cortisol level affect human emotions.

Cortisol affects the brain, in paradoxical ways. To think clearly, humans need some cortisol but not too much. If an infant is chronically stressed (parents yelling, hitting), high cortisol overloads normal functioning, harming the hypothalamus. Later, in adolescence, both too much and too little cortisol correlate with severe depression (Ford et al., 2019). In adulthood, someone overstressed in childhood might be hyperalert, overwhelmed by fear, stress, and anxiety, or the opposite, steely cold when most people would be emotional.

Sex Hormones

Why do some teenagers take dangerous risks, feel suicidal, believe they are geniuses, lust after the wrong person, and so on? Overall, adolescents are beset by strong emotions. As one team of experts writes:

> Adolescence is often considered a period of emotional turmoil. Although this label appears to overstate the difficulties of most adolescents, adolescence is nonetheless a critical period for emotional development, with emotional reactivity becoming more frequent and more intense.
>
> *[Coe-Odess et al., 2019, p. 595]*

Overstating, yes (Conklin, 2018; Pechmann et al., 2020). But the core idea that "raging hormones" affect adolescent moods is at least partly true. The physical changes of adolescence begin with a surge of sex hormones (*androgens* and *estrogens*) sent from the hypothalamus to the pituitary to the adrenal glands (see **Figure 5.4**). All children increase in estradiol and testosterone at puberty, with boys increasing dramatically in testosterone (45 times higher than before puberty) and girls increasing in estradiol (8 times higher) (Herting & Sowell, 2017).

Pubertal hormones not only stimulate the gonads but also target the amygdala directly (Romeo, 2013), while development of the prefrontal cortex is more a result of time than of hormones. Since hormones cause the instinctual, sexual, and emotional areas of the brain to develop years ahead of the reflective, analytical areas, emotional rushes (the limbic system) are unchecked by caution, reflection, and planning (the prefrontal cortex).

This was recently recognized in a U.S. Supreme Court ruling that held that adolescents should not be held to the same standards as adult criminals because their brains were not as mature as those of adults, as summarized in an article titled "Kids Are Different" (Levick, 2019). This is also apparent to parents, teachers, and playwrights. Remember Romeo and 13-year-old Juliet: Their passionate love and deep despair led to their tragic death.

The timing gap between the hormonal activation of the amygdala and the maturation of the prefrontal cortex explains why, despite quicker reflexes, better vision, and stronger bodies than adults, teenage drivers have more deadly motor-vehicle accidents. Blame the slow prefrontal cortex, while other parts of the brain are fully myelinated and automatic (Luna et al., 2013).

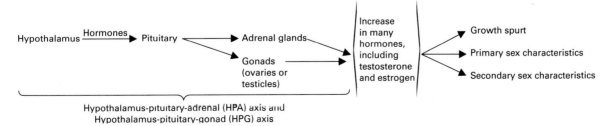

FIGURE 5.4

Biological Sequence of Puberty Puberty begins with a hormonal signal from the hypothalamus to the pituitary gland, both deep within the brain. The pituitary, in turn, sends a hormonal message through the bloodstream to the adrenal glands and the gonads to produce more hormones.

Plasticity

Now that we have described the parts of the brain and how brain cells communicate, we can focus on the most remarkable characteristic of the human brain: *plasticity*, a concept so central to human development that it was explained in Chapter 1.

Plasticity is apparent in the brain. Lobes, regions, and hemispheres connect; the corpus callosum thickens; the prefrontal cortex interprets; neurons that fire together, wire together; dendrites and axons become myelinated, parts of the limbic system grow, emotions become regulated—all because of experiences. We now explore four examples of plasticity: early in life (pruning), in adolescence (onset of puberty), in adulthood (expertise), and in late adulthood (neurogenesis).

The Early Months: Pruning

Fetal brains grow rapidly, as already explained, but another rapid prenatal process involves dying, not growing. Many healthy, newly formed neurons present in the 6-month-old fetus are gone before birth. This programmed cell death is called *apoptosis* (Underwood, 2013).

Perhaps the final three months require cell death to create space in the brain for the remaining neurons, which will coordinate thinking, remembering, and responding.

In other words, some brain space is saved for new neurons and dendrites, because humans must survive within a vast diversity of living conditions, each of which requires specific brain connections. Ours is the only species that thrives in every part of the earth, with diverse climates, cultures, and family types (from single parents with one child to extended families with 20 children). The plasticity of our brains makes adaptation possible.

Thus, early cell death—not too much, not too little—is protective. As one team writes:

> Plasticity is particularly important during embryonic development, enabling an organism to adapt to the demands of the environment in which it develops and will eventually inhabit.
>
> [Hsiao & Patterson, 2012, p. 1317]

At birth, even after apoptosis, the brain still contains more neurons than needed, but far fewer dendrites and synapses than a person will eventually possess. An estimated fivefold increase in dendrites in the cortex occurs in the next 24 months, with about 100 trillion synapses present by age 2. Meanwhile, apoptosis (or *pruning*) continues. All told, according to one expert, about half of all neurons self-destruct in the months immediately before or after birth (Cavallaro, 2015).

This is by design: For humans, lack of pruning causes neurological obstacles. Just as a gardener might prune a rose bush by cutting away some growth to enable more, or more beautiful, roses to bloom, unused brain connections atrophy and disappear to enable more efficient brain function.

As another expert explains it, in the first years of life, all children undergo an "exuberant overproduction of cells and connections followed by a several-year sculpting of pathways by massive elimination of much of the neural architecture" (Insel, 2014, p. 1727). If pruning does not occur, that might be an underlying cause of *autism spectrum disorder (ASD)* (Dong et al., 2018).

To understand the balance between growth and death, developmentalists categorize some infant experiences as essential and some not (Greenough et al., 1987).

- **Experience-expectant.** Certain experiences are needed for the brain to develop, just as a tree requires water. Those experiences are part of almost every infant's life, allowing human brains to grow as genes direct.
- **Experience-dependent.** Some experiences are not essential: They happen to infants in some families and cultures but not in others, and brains are molded accordingly.

Experience-expectant brain development means that certain experiences *must* happen for normal brain maturation to occur. In all cultures and places, in deserts and in the Arctic, on isolated farms and in crowded cities, babies are given things to see, objects to manipulate, and people to love. Caregivers provide whatever the baby's brain needs at the time. For example, parents provide more stimulation (toys, outdoor sights, social play) for 10-month-olds than 2-month-olds because that is what their brains need (Bornstein et al., 2015).

Babies respond. They listen and look around, they grab for faces and objects, they babble at people and toys. As a result, the plasticity of their brains allows their neurons to sprout dendrites. Without such expected experiences, brains wither.

In contrast, certain facets of brain development are experience-dependent. These experiences differ for each infant. Because of plasticity, infant brains adjust to their specific context. What language is heard, whose faces are seen, or how emotions are expressed—from slight pursing of the lips to throwing oneself on the ground—vary from one home to another. *Depending* on such variations, infants' neurons connect in particular ways; some dendrites grow while others disappear (Stiles & Jernigan, 2010).

Thus, experience-expectant events make all people similar, and experience-dependent events make each person unique. To give a specific example, all babies develop language: Social communication is characteristic of *Homo sapiens*, so it is experience-expectant.

However, the specific language could be spoken or signed and could be Tajik, Tamil, Thai, or Twi—that is experience-dependent. If a baby's brain never heard the sounds of English, for instance, but heard only a quite different cadence, tone, and sound, the neurons that allow hearing and producing English would die to make room for learning the mother tongue.

Thus, plasticity allows learning a specific language. If the brain had to maintain the young infant's ability to learn all 6,000 of the world's languages, 2-year-olds would not be able to master the complex intonation and pronunciation of their first language. Some children successfully learn two or three languages, but no adult can master several unrelated languages: Brain plasticity does not allow openness to linguistic sounds never heard in childhood.

experience-expectant Brain functions that require certain basic common experiences (which an infant can be expected to have) in order to develop normally.

experience-dependent Brain functions that depend on particular, variable experiences and therefore may or may not develop in a particular infant.

Face Lit Up, Brain Too Thanks to scientists at the University of Washington, this young boy enjoys the EEG of his brain activity. Such research has found that babies respond to language long before they speak. Experiences of all sorts connect neurons and grow dendrites.

Aaron McCoy/Photolibrary/Getty Images

That explains why, if you have friends who can discuss complex ideas in English but who never heard English until they were teenagers, their accent reveals that English was not their first language. The requisite experience-dependent brain development did not occur, so apoptosis pruned the neurons that enable flawless English pronunciation. The same is true, of course, for people whose first language was English but who study a "foreign" language in adulthood. Even with great effort, they have lost the neurons that allow native pronunciation.

Variable Age of Puberty

The second example of plasticity comes from something often thought to be entirely under genetic control—puberty. As you read, puberty is triggered via hormones produced by the hypothalamus and pituitary. However, the onset of puberty is determined, not solely by genes and hormones but also by experience, which includes diet (heavier girls reach menarche earlier than those with less body fat) and external hormones, either in food (given to farm animals to increase meat or milk) or medically prescribed (if a child is unusually short or late).

Scientists have discovered the power of another experience, specifically stress, which increases cortisol. Cortisol may shrink the hippocampus (Teicher et al., 2018), which affects the hypothalamus and the pituitary, thus affecting the onset of puberty.

ESPECIALLY FOR Parents Worried About Early Puberty Suppose your cousin's 9-year-old daughter has just had her first period, and your cousin blames hormones in the food supply for this "precocious" puberty. Should you change your young daughter's diet? (see response, page 147)

A VIEW FROM SCIENCE

Stress and Puberty

Emotional stress, particularly when it has a sexual component, often precipitates puberty. The underlying mechanism is thought to be hormonal. As already explained, hormones vary by age, genes, and gender. That may explain why the link between stress and puberty is more apparent in some children than others, in girls more often than boys (Ellis & Del Giudice, 2019).

For example, a large longitudinal study in England compared girls whose biological fathers lived at home with girls whose fathers were absent. Typically, in that community, when the father was not present, the mother was stressed and was dating other men. The daughters had higher rates of depression and earlier menarche than other girls (Culpin et al., 2015).

The connection between sexual stress and early puberty is found in developing nations as well as developed ones. A study of girls in Peru reported that girls who were physically and sexually abused were more likely (odds ratio 1.56) than other Peruvian girls to reach menarche before age 11 (Barrios et al., 2015).

That research was cross-sectional, but similar findings come from longitudinal studies. For example, one longitudinal study found that a decade after parents demanded respect, often spanked, and rarely hugged their young children, their daughters reached puberty earlier than other girls in the same study (Belsky et al., 2007). A follow-up of the same girls at age 15, controlling for genetic differences, found that the strict treatment in childhood increased their rate of sexual problems (more sex partners, pregnancies, sexually transmitted infections) but *not* other problems (drugs, crime) (Belsky et al., 2010). This suggests that stress triggers earlier increases of sex hormones, but not generalized rebellion. That is evidence of brain plasticity.

Why would higher cortisol accelerate puberty? The opposite effect—delayed puberty—makes more sense. It would be beneficial if stressed teens were late to reach puberty. At age 14, they might still look and act childlike, which might evoke adult protection rather than lust or anger. Protection is especially needed in conflict-ridden or single-parent homes, yet such homes produce earlier puberty and less parental nurturance. Is this a biological mistake? Not according to evolutionary theory:

> Maturing quickly and breeding promiscuously would enhance reproductive fitness more than would delaying development, mating cautiously, and investing heavily in parenting. The latter strategy, in contrast, would make biological sense, for virtually the same reproductive-fitness-enhancing reasons, under conditions of contextual support and nurturance.
>
> *[Belsky et al., 2010, p. 121]*

In other words, thousands of years ago, when harsh conditions threatened survival of the species, adolescents needed to reproduce early and often, lest the entire community become extinct. By contrast, in past peaceful times, puberty could occur later, allowing children to postpone maturity and instead enjoy extra years of nurturance from their biological parents and grandparents. Genes evolved to allow the plasticity required for differential responses to war and peace.

Of course, this evolutionary benefit no longer applies. Today, early sexual activity and reproduction are more destructive than protective of communities. However, since the brain has been shaped over millennia, plasticity allows the same variations in age of puberty today as occurred thousands of years ago. The mismatch is in the century, not in the plasticity of the brain.

One study of sexually abused girls found that they began puberty as much as a year earlier than they otherwise would have (Noll et al., 2017). Particularly for girls who are genetically sensitive, puberty comes early if their family interaction is stressful but late if their family is supportive. The brain, specifically the hypothalamus and the pituitary, responds to how a child is raised. That is plasticity.

Plasticity in Adulthood: Expertise

As you have read, human brains are far more specialized than the brains of any other animal. That is why they are large: There is so much to learn. Plasticity allows adults to mold their brains to suit their particular interests.

Adults shape their brains by choosing activities. They become experts, evident in anything from playing chess to performing surgery (Tracey et al., 2014). Their brains reflect their choice, with particular connections (automaticity), lobes, and hemispheres growing or shrinking.

A detailed neurological example comes from taxi drivers. They must find the best routes (factoring in traffic, construction, time of day, and many other details), know where new fares might be, respond to passengers who are talkative, who are silent, or whose remarks seem ignorant and biased. Expert drivers are faster, busier, and earn bigger tips than novices; they have learned from experience. That is evident in their brains.

Research in England—where taxi drivers "have to learn the layout of 25,000 streets in London and the locations of thousands of places of interest, and pass stringent examinations" (Woollett et al., 2009, p. 1407)—found not only that the drivers became more expert with experience but also that their brains adjusted. Those brain areas that are dedicated to spatial representation were far more developed than in the brains of the ordinary Brit. On IQ tests, the taxi drivers' scores were average, but in navigating London, expertise was apparent.

Other research finds that expanded brain areas and new neurons are particularly likely to emerge in the olfactory cortex, which is "highly plastic" (Huart et al., 2019, p. 77). Usually the sense of smell is reduced with age, because that sense is rarely used.

Professional perfumers, however, must detect differences in odors, long past the age when most adults can no longer do so (Delon-Martin et al., 2013). Smell is also crucial for firefighters who must sense a whiff of smoke and discern what is smoldering, or chefs who must sense when something is cooking properly. Those experts maintain smell sensitivity in their brains that most other people do not. Plasticity allows that.

Slowness in Late Adulthood

Our final example begins with a question: Might plasticity allow adult brains to overcome the decrements of age? There is much to overcome. Researchers report that, with age, myelination, neurotransmitters, neural fluid, and blood circulation are all reduced.

Even brain size decreases, by a fraction of a percent through most years of adulthood, then faster after age 65 or so. By age 80, a typical brain is 20-percent smaller than at age 30 (Hedman et al., 2012).

Consequently, elders are slower in everything. However, plasticity means that practice affects brain functioning. Education and intellectual activity are protective, especially if older adults challenge their brains by socializing with other people. New dendrites and neurons develop, particularly in the hippocampus, the brain structure most prominent in memory (Bergmann et al., 2015).

Expertise Illustrated Vivian Howard is chef and creator of Chef and the Farmer, a North Carolina restaurant that gained rave reviews and national attention.

Observation Quiz What do you see that signifies an expert chef? (see answer, page 147) ↑

Travis Dove/The New York Times/Redux

Atrophy Ranking

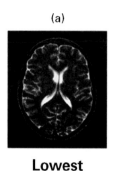
(a)
Lowest

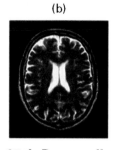
(b)
25th Percentile

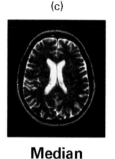
(c)
Median

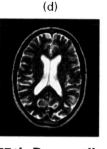
(d)
75th Percentile

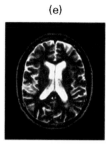
(e)
Highest

Republish with permission from Springer Science anc Bus Media B V. from Farrell C, et al. Development and initial testing of normal reference MR images for the brain at ages 65-70 and 75-80 years. European Radiology 2009;19: 177-183; permission conveyed through Copyright Clearance Center, Inc.

Not All Average A team of neuroscientists in Scotland (Farrell et al., 2009) published these images of the brains of healthy 65- to 70-year-olds. The images show normal brain loss (the white areas) from the lowest (5th percentile) to the highest (95th percentile). Some atrophy is inevitable (even younger brains atrophy), but few elders are merely average.

Is brain plasticity sufficient to compensate for neuronal loss? Some scientists say no. One team of 19 scientists reported that few neurons develop after age 13 (Sorrells et al., 2018). Other scientists say yes, that neurogenesis "appears to contribute significantly to hippocampal plasticity across the life span" (Kempermann et al., 2015). A third team of 12 scientists reported that new neurons form even after age 70 (Boldrini et al., 2018).

As you see, how much plasticity is apparent during late adulthood is debatable. Many older people experience **mild cognitive impairment (MCI)**, characterized by occasional forgetfulness or confusion. With MCI, people need to write down appointments, set alarms, wait for names to come to mind, and so on. Stress and worry make it worse. However, new habits can remedy much of the problem.

Some experts say that all brains become impaired if a person lives long enough. But everyone agrees that the brain is sufficiently plastic to benefit from what people do: Exercise, avoiding drugs, reducing hypertension, and engaging in social activities that challenge one's ideas and habits are as important at age 80 as at age 18. That means playing bridge, not solitaire; joining a book club, not doing crossword puzzles; discussing politics, not answering yes/no internet surveys; planning finances with the family, not doing Sudoku puzzles alone.

This leads to the final, and most feared topic in life-span neuroscience: diseases and conditions that destroy the brain.

mild cognitive impairment (MCI)
When a person is somewhat more confused and forgetful than they were, but still able to function well.

WHAT HAVE YOU LEARNED?

1. How does plasticity make it possible for humans to live in a variety of places?
2. When does death and birth of neurons occur, and how might this affect a person's development?
3. What factors in a child's environment cause puberty to occur?
4. What have taxi drivers contributed to our understanding of plasticity?
5. What agreement and disagreement are there regarding brain development in late adulthood?

Attacks on the Brain

Thus far, we have discussed the healthy brain, which is typical for most people, most of the time, even at age 100. But brains do not always function well. Injury, drugs, and disease can harm them, as we now describe.

Traumatic Brain Injury

One common brain disorder is likely to occur before age 30, although the outcome is most apparent much later (Silver et al., 2019). **Traumatic brain injury (TBI)** is the umbrella term for brain damage caused by a blow, by an extremely loud noise, or by rapid acceleration or deceleration of the head. A *concussion* is a sign of a TBI, but the effects (slurred speech, pounding headaches, slower thinking) may not be readily apparent and may be ignored or denied by the person who experiences the TBI.

The most common causes are whiplash in a car accident, a hit on the head in a game, or a loud explosion in a war. Soon the victim seems okay. However, TBI is called the "silent epidemic," because every year an estimated 69 million people worldwide sustain one (Dewan et al., 2019). Plasticity allows most to recover with rest and time.

However, one TBI makes the brain more vulnerable later on. TBIs may become **chronic traumatic encephalopathy (CTE)**. CTE it is difficult to diagnosis, because:

> The first clinical manifestations are insidious, but typically marked by deterioration in attention, concentration and memory that are often accompanied by disorientation, dizziness, headaches, and mood disorders. As the disease progresses, more prominent symptoms begin to manifest including impulsivity, mood lability, impaired judgment, and overt dementia. In later phases of CTE, these symptoms continue to worsen and are accompanied by impaired motor control.
>
> *[Sundman et al., 2015]*

CTE is especially common in athletes who experienced multiple blows. Although the headlines focus on professional football and hockey players, researchers scanned the brains of nonprofessional college football and track stars. The frontal cortexes of the former were thinner than the latter (Adler et al., 2018).

Most people who might develop CTE do not realize they are at risk. Everyone needs to avoid loud explosions and blows to the head, especially if they had a concussion in the past. That seems obvious, but when contact sports were first popular, even football players and boxers wore no helmets. Not until 1969 in the United States were new cars required to have headrests, which make whiplash injuries less likely to cause CTE. Older cars do not have head rests. Many school buses still do not.

Posttraumatic Stress Disorder

Since about 1990, more and more people have been diagnosed with **posttraumatic stress disorder (PTSD)**, which begins with a life-threatening or profoundly frightening event, such as rape, severe beating, active combat, or major earthquake. A victim may not function normally for months or years after the event. Many adults experience some trauma; afterward (post-) about 10 percent develop PTSD.

People with PTSD have trouble sleeping, are quick to anger, relate poorly to family and friends, have disabling flashbacks. Their brains reveal the problem (Hughes & Shin, 2011). Two structures have become smaller and less active, the hippocampus, which controls the amygdala, and the *anterior cingulate cortex*, the part of the prefrontal cortex that specializes in empathy. Thus, memories are not processed well (hippocampus), and compassion declines (anterior cingulate cortex).

By contrast, the insula and the amygdala are hyperactive, allowing raw fear and extreme disgust to overwhelm the prefrontal cortex.

Although some brains are genetically vulnerable to PTSD, a monozygotic twin study confirms that PTSD is acquired, not innate, because the twin who experienced trauma was much more likely to suffer years later (Dahlgren et al., 2018). A direct personal threat, not merely witnessing a threat, precipitates PTSD. Combat soldiers, not medics, torture victims, not perpetrators, develop PTSD (Weisleder & Rublee, 2018).

Modern medicine saves many soldiers who would have died in earlier wars. Yet TBI, CTE, PTSD, and chronic pain all correlate. That may be why the greatest death risk for those in the armed forces is now suicide, not combat (Blakey et al., 2018; Nock et al., 2013).

traumatic brain injury (TBI) An injury to the brain caused by a sudden blow, explosion, or a rapid jerk of the head. This trauma may cause a concussion, with momentary dizziness or unconsciousness. Recovery is likely with rest and quiet, although repeated TBIs can cause chronic traumatic encephalopathy (CTE).

chronic traumatic encephalopathy (CTE) An ongoing disease (chronic) that destroys the brain, caused by repeated concussions or sudden blows to the head (TBIs).

Team Victory and Players' Defeat Both these professional football players from the Chicago Bears (shown here in 1935) experienced multiple TBIs, which increased their risk of memory loss and mood disturbances later on.

Observation Quiz Football players in former times had special articles of clothing to wear. What were they? (see answer, page 147) ↑

posttraumatic stress disorder (PTSD) An anxiety disorder that develops as a delayed reaction to exposure to actual or threatened death, serious injury, or sexual violence. Its symptoms may include flashbacks to the event, hyperactivity and hypervigilance, displaced anger, sleeplessness, nightmares, sudden terror or anxiety, and confusion between fantasy and reality.

FIGURE 5.5
Substance Use and the Brain Every psychoactive substance affects the brain, but some substances and some brain functions are affected more than others. In one study, people seeking treatment for substance abuse were tested on the Montreal Cognitive Assessment, which was designed to measure neurocognitive disorders in late adulthood. Participants were asked to draw a clock at 2:30 and received full, half, or no credit *(a)*. The average was 25.5, which is low normal. (The score of the general population is 27.5; the highest possible is 30.) Thirty-one percent of the individuals were so low as to be rated cognitively impaired. Memory and visuospatial ability were especially poor, with some variation depending on which substance they abused *(b)*.

Clock Drawing as a Measure of
Cognitive Decline

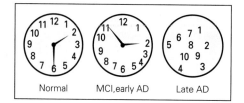

Normal   MCI,early AD   Late AD

(a)
Data from Bruijnen et al., 2019.

Visuospatial Ability on a Scale of 0 to 4

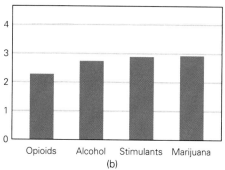

(b)

Drug Abuse

Every drug that affects the brain has the potential to be abused, destroying neurons and shrinking various regions. The best evidence comes from the two legal drugs most commonly used by adults, cigarettes and alcohol.

Cigarettes

Chronic cigarette smokers are at risk for every brain disease. The main reason is that smoking cuts down on oxygen reaching the lungs, and that slows down the circulation of blood everywhere in the body, including the brain.

The effects begin long before late adulthood, as evident in hundreds of 50-year-olds who had been followed for 25 years (the CARDIA study). The researchers reported that "smokers had significantly smaller GM [gray matter] volume in the temporal, occipital, and frontal lobes, and in the amygdala" but not in other regions, notably the hippocampus (Elbejjani et al., 2019). In other words, their brains were less able to process emotions, sounds, and motor skills, but they could still remember—unlike those with other types of brain damage.

Alcohol

Alcohol abuse harms the brain directly by destroying neurons, and indirectly by impairing judgment, causing suicide, homicide, HIV infection, and accidents, which are the four leading causes of death before age 50. Further, chronic alcohol abuse results in a deficiency of vitamin B1 (thiamine), which causes *Wernicke-Korsakoff syndrome*, a disease that destroys the brain.

Other Drugs

Research on marijuana and illegal drugs also finds brain destruction from chronic use. Specifics, such as which brain areas are harmed by which drugs, at what dose or frequency, are not known, because solid research, with longitudinal studies of matched control and experimental groups, is impossible with illegal drugs.

Fortunately, most addicts quit by age 30. If not, many die before they reach the age when the combination of age and chronic drug abuse might reveal neuronal loss. As best we know, every psychoactive drug, legally prescribed or not, may harm the brain (Birkenhäger-Gillesse et al., 2018; Brick & Erickson, 2013), although much more science is needed.

Brain Diseases

neurocognitive disorder (NCD) Any of a number of brain diseases that affect a person's ability to remember, analyze, plan, or interact with other people.

A **neurocognitive disorder (NCD)** (the term, used by DSM-5, for what was formerly called dementia) can occur at any age. The causes may be a virus, such as those that cause syphilis, AIDS, or *bovine spongiform encephalopathy* (BSE or *mad cow disease*).

Income, Gender, and NCD

The main risk factor for a neurocognitive disorder is age. About 3 percent of 65- to 75-year-olds and 25 percent of those over age 85 have an NCD (Koller & Bynum, 2014). That translates, worldwide, to an estimated 50 million with an

NCD, which directly affects at least another 150 million family members (World Health Organization, September, 2015).

In the United States, rates rise as income falls, because malnutrition, stress, TBIs, pollution, and inadequate medical care are all more common among the poor. The opposite is true in other nations, because most poor people die before age 70. Thus, wealth correlates with longevity, and longevity correlates with neurocognitive disorders.

In China, for example, twice as many people had an NCD in 2010 compared to two decades earlier (Chan et al., 2013). Because longevity is now common throughout China, aged people living in rural areas who experienced deprivation when they were younger now have higher rates of NCDs (Ji et al., 2015; Jia et al., 2014). Women are more likely to develop an NCD than men, attributed to two facts: Women live longer and have less education.

There is good news here, as better health and more education in children and young adults result in better brain health in late adulthood. In every developed nation, the rate (not the number) of NCDs is lower than it was. Careful nationwide data from England and Wales found that, in 1991, 8.3 percent of the people over age 65 had an NCD. Two decades later, only 6.5 percent did (Matthews et al., 2013). The U.S. rate has also declined in the twenty-first century (Sullivan et al., 2019).

Alzheimer's Disease

In the past century, millions of people in every large nation have been diagnosed with **Alzheimer's disease (AD)** (now formally referred to as *major NCD due to Alzheimer's disease*). Severe and worsening memory loss is the main symptom, but diagnosis was not definitive until an autopsy found extensive plaques and tangles in the cerebral cortex (see **Table 5.2**).

Plaques are clumps of a protein called *beta-amyloid* in tissues surrounding the neurons; **tangles** are twisted masses of threads made of a protein called *tau* within the neurons. A normal brain contains some beta-amyloid and tau, but these proliferate in brains with AD, especially in the hippocampus. Forgetfulness is the dominant symptom, from momentary lapses to—after years of progressive disease—forgetting the names and faces of one's own children.

Alzheimer's disease is partly genetic. If it develops in middle age, the affected person either has trisomy-21 (Down syndrome) or has inherited one of three

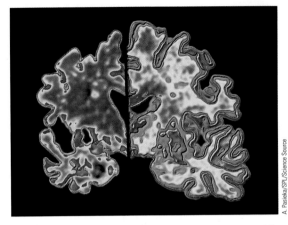

The Alzheimer's Brain This computer graphic shows a vertical slice through a brain ravaged by Alzheimer's disease *(left)* compared with a similar slice of a normal brain *(right)*. The diseased brain is shrunken because neurons have degenerated. The red indicates plaques and tangles.

A. Pasieka/SPL/Science Source

Alzheimer's disease (AD) The most common cause of major NCD, characterized by gradual deterioration of memory and personality and marked by the formation of plaques of beta-amyloid protein and tangles of tau in the brain.

plaques Clumps of a protein called beta-amyloid, found in brain tissue surrounding the neurons.

tangles Twisted masses of threads made of a protein called tau within the neurons of the brain.

TABLE 5.2

Stages of Alzheimer's Disease

Stage 1. People in the first stage forget recent events or new information, particularly names and places. For example, they might forget the name of a famous film star or how to get home from a familiar place. This first stage is similar to mild cognitive impairment—even experts cannot always tell the difference. In retrospect, it seems clear that President Ronald Reagan had early AD while in office, but no doctor diagnosed it.

Stage 2. Generalized confusion develops, with deficits in concentration and short-term memory. Speech becomes aimless and repetitious, vocabulary is limited, words get mixed up. Personality traits are not curbed by rational thought. For example, suspicious people may decide that others have stolen the things that they themselves have mislaid.

Stage 3. Memory loss becomes dangerous. Although people at stage 3 can care for themselves, they might leave a lit stove or hot iron on or might forget whether they took essential medicine and thus take it twice—or not at all.

Stage 4. At this stage, full-time care is needed. People cannot communicate well. They might not recognize their closest loved ones.

Stage 5. Finally, people with AD become unresponsive. Identity and personality have disappeared. When former president Ronald Reagan was at this stage, a longtime friend who visited him was asked, "Did he recognize you?" The friend answered, "Worse than that—I didn't recognize him." Death comes 10 to 15 years after the first signs appear.

dominant genes: amyloid precursor protein (APP), presenilin 1, or presenilin 2. When a dominant gene is the cause, AD progresses quickly, destroying the brain and causing death within three to five years.

Most cases begin much later, at age 75 or so. Many genes have some impact, including SORL1 and APOE4 (allele 4 of the APOE gene), but none is determinative. People who inherit one copy of APOE4 (as about one-fifth of all U.S. residents do) have about a 50/50 chance of developing AD, with women more at risk than men (Altmann et al., 2014). Those who inherit two copies almost always develop the disorder if they live long enough.

Vascular Disease

The second most common cause of neurocognitive disorder is a stroke (a temporary obstruction of a blood vessel in the brain) or a series of strokes, called *transient ischemic attacks (TIAs, or ministrokes)*. The interrupted blood flow reduces oxygen, destroying part of the brain. Symptoms (blurred vision, weak limbs, slurred speech, and confusion) suddenly appear.

vascular disease Formerly called vascular or multi-infarct dementia, vascular disease is characterized by sporadic, and progressive, loss of intellectual functioning caused by repeated infarcts, or temporary obstructions of blood vessels, which prevent sufficient blood from reaching the brain.

In a TIA, symptoms may vanish quickly, unnoticed. However, another TIA is likely, eventually causing **vascular disease**, also called *vascular* or *multi-infarct dementia* (Kalaria, 2018). Poor decisions and uncontrolled impulses are as prevalent as memory loss.

Vascular disease correlates with the APOE4 allele, as well as other genetic precursors (Vittner et al., 2018). For some elderly people, vascular disease is caused by surgery that requires general anesthesia. They suffer a ministroke, which damages their brains, especially when their cognitive reserve is depleted.

Frontotemporal Disorders

Several types of neurocognitive disorders affect the frontal and temporal lobes and thus are called **frontotemporal NCDs**, or *frontotemporal lobar degeneration*. (Pick disease is the most common form.) These disorders cause perhaps 15 percent of all cases of NCDs.

frontotemporal NCDs Deterioration of the amygdala and frontal lobes that may be the cause of 15 percent of all major neurocognitive disorders. (Also called *frontotemporal lobar degeneration*.)

In frontotemporal NCDs, parts of the brain that regulate emotions and social behavior (especially the amygdala and prefrontal cortex) deteriorate. Emotional and personality changes are the main symptoms. A loving mother with a frontotemporal NCD might reject her children, or a formerly astute businessman might invest in a hare-brained scheme. As you can imagine, caregivers of people with this disorder are more stressed, and less supported, than caregivers of people with Alzheimer's (Nowaskie et al., 2019).

Frontotemporal NCDs tend to occur before age 70. Diagnosis is difficult for two reasons. First, symptoms appear at younger ages (the 60s more than the 80s), so doctors are less likely to notice and expect them. Second, memory loss is not the primary symptom, so family members also are slower to recognize the problem.

One wife was furious because her husband

> threw away tax documents, got a ticket for trying to pass an ambulance and bought stock in companies that were obviously in trouble. Once a good cook, he burned every pot in the house. He became withdrawn and silent, and no longer spoke to his wife over dinner. That same failure to communicate got him fired from his job.
>
> [D. Grady, 2012, p. A1]

Finally, he was diagnosed with a frontotemporal NCD. His wife asked him to forgive her fury. He understood neither her anger nor her apology.

There are many forms and causes of frontotemporal NCDs—including a dozen or so alleles. All usually progress rapidly, leading to death in about five years.

DATA CONNECTIONS: Prevalence of Major NCD Among Older Adults explores the rates at which older people are diagnosed with major neurocognitive disorder. **LaunchPad**

VISUALIZING DEVELOPMENT   Major NCD

The map below shows the number of people ages 60 and over in each world region, and the percentage of those people who have a major neurocognitive disorder. Population data come from the United Nations, where skilled statisticians compile data on all 193 member nations. Therefore, the numbers are quite accurate. Prevalence data (shown in orange) come from *The Lancet*, a highly respected British medical journal, and are as accurate as possible. However, those numbers are affected by cultural variations, not only in definition and diagnosis but also in survival rates. Thus, a low percentage of people living with major NCD is not necessarily a sign of regional health. Comparisons between regions may be unfair, but one conclusion is clear: Nowhere in the world are more than 8 percent of the elderly suffering from severe brain disease.

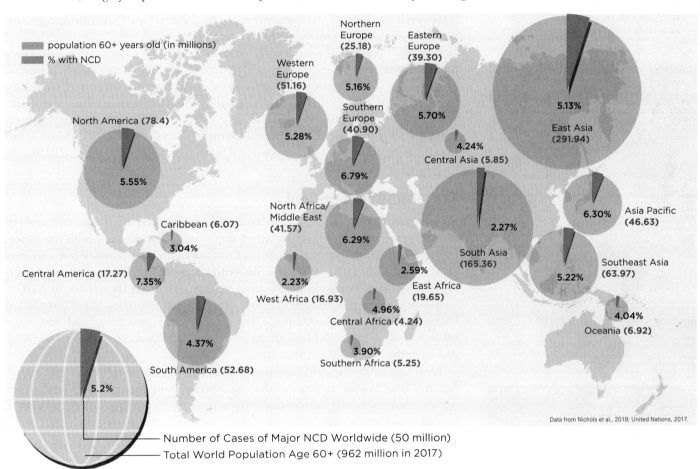

population 60+ years old (in millions)
% with NCD

Northern Europe (25.18)   5.16%
Western Europe (51.16)   5.28%
Eastern Europe (39.30)   5.70%
Southern Europe (40.90)   6.79%
East Asia (291.94)   5.13%
Central Asia (5.85)   4.24%
North America (78.4)   5.55%
Caribbean (6.07)   3.04%
Central America (17.27)   7.35%
North Africa/Middle East (41.57)   6.29%
West Africa (16.93)   2.23%
Central Africa (4.24)   4.96%
East Africa (19.65)   2.59%
South Asia (165.36)   2.27%
Asia Pacific (46.63)   6.30%
Southeast Asia (63.97)   5.22%
Oceania (6.92)   4.04%
Southern Africa (5.25)   3.90%
South America (52.68)   4.37%
5.2%

Number of Cases of Major NCD Worldwide (50 million)
Total World Population Age 60+ (962 million in 2017)

Data from Nichols et al., 2019; United Nations, 2017.

HEALTH CARE COSTS ASSOCIATED WITH MAJOR NCD

Alzheimer's disease and other major neurocognitive disorders are among the costliest chronic diseases to society: Individuals with a major NCD have more hospital and skilled nursing facility stays and home health care visits than other older people. However, the human cost may be greater than these estimates: Many family members spend substantial time caring for people with a major NCD, but often that time is not calculated until the disorder is severe.

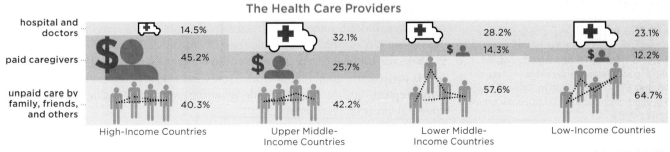

The Health Care Providers

	High-Income Countries	Upper Middle-Income Countries	Lower Middle-Income Countries	Low-Income Countries
hospital and doctors	14.5%	32.1%	28.2%	23.1%
paid caregivers	45.2%	25.7%	14.3%	12.2%
unpaid care by family, friends, and others	40.3%	42.2%	57.6%	64.7%

Data from World Health Organization, 2012; United Nations, 2015.

Parkinson's disease A chronic, progressive disease that is characterized by muscle tremor and rigidity and sometimes major neurocognitive disorder; caused by reduced dopamine production in the brain.

Lewy body disease A form of major neurocognitive disorder characterized by an increase in Lewy body cells in the brain. Symptoms include visual hallucinations, momentary loss of attention, falling, and fainting.

Exercise for Elders In every nation, those who exercise have healthier hearts, lungs, brains, and lives than those who do not. Two contrasting examples are the exercise class in a Michigan Senior Center led by Diane Evans (foreground) and the stepper machine on a beach in Greece.

● **Observation Quiz** Both are beneficial, but neither is ideal. Why not? (see answer, page 147) ↑

Other Disorders

Many other brain diseases begin with impaired motor control (shaking when picking up a cup of coffee, falling when trying to walk), not with impaired thinking. The most common of these is **Parkinson's disease**, the cause of about 3 percent of all cases of NCDs.

Parkinson's disease starts with rigidity or tremor of the muscles as dopamine-producing neurons degenerate, affecting movement long before cognition (Jankovic, 2018). Middle-aged adults with Parkinson's disease usually have sufficient cognitive reserve to avoid major intellectual loss, although about one-third have mild cognitive decline, sometimes in advance of more obvious symptoms (Darweesh et al., 2017). If someone over age 65 develops Parkinson's, cognitive problems are likely to emerge within a few years.

Another 3 percent of people with NCD in the United States suffer from **Lewy body disease**: excessive deposits of a particular kind of protein in their brains. Lewy bodies are also present in Parkinson's disease, but in Lewy body disease they are more numerous and dispersed throughout the brain, interfering with communication between neurons. The main symptom is loss of inhibition: A person might gamble or become hypersexual. Symptoms are similar to Parkinson's, but brain damage is more comprehensive and begins sooner (Walker et al., 2019).

Preventing Impairment

Severe brain damage cannot be reversed, although the rate of decline and some of the symptoms can be treated. However, diet, exercise, and good health (no hypertension, diabetes, smoking, or obesity) not only ameliorate losses but also may prevent them (Amin et al., 2019). Recently, fewer adults have untreated hypertension, diabetes, or cigarette addiction, which may explain the decline in NCDs.

Because brain plasticity is lifelong, exercise that improves blood circulation builds capacity and repairs damage, but also prevents, postpones, and slows cognitive loss of all kinds. A Mediterranean diet, restorative sleep, halting infections, and an active social life are protective.

Most current research focuses on those already experiencing brain impairment. Yet, it is much easier to prevent than to reverse brain destruction. The case for earlier research is clear. As one team stressed:

> Diversifying and exploring new treatment ideas is essential, as these diseases are inherently complex and not terribly well understood. . . . interventions can be started prior to neuronal loss, which likely would result in the highest chance for success.
>
> [Baker & Petersen, 2018, p. 1214]

Depression

Not every cognitive problem in late adulthood indicates brain damage or disease. The most common reversible condition that is mistaken for major NCD is depression. Typically, older people tend to be quite happy; frequent sadness or anxiety is not normal. Indeed, some research suggests that life satisfaction increases with age. This is contrary to what most people think about late adulthood (Lacey et al., 2012).

However, untreated depression at any age increases the risk of major NCD, and this is particularly notable if doctors, family members, and the elderly themselves think depression is normal. The elderly tend to resist medication and psychotherapy for depression (Nair et al., 2020).

Ironically, people with untreated anxiety or depression may exaggerate minor memory losses or refuse to talk. Quite the opposite reaction occurs with early Alzheimer's disease, when victims are often surprised that they cannot answer questions, or with Lewy body disease or frontotemporal NCDs, when people talk too much without thinking. Talking, or lack of it, provides an important clue.

Specifics provide other clues. People with neurocognitive loss might forget what they just said, heard, or did because current brain activity is impaired, but they might repeatedly describe details of something that happened long ago. The opposite may be true for emotional disorders.

Polypharmacy

At home as well as in the hospital, most elderly people take numerous drugs—not only prescribed medications but also over-the-counter preparations and herbal remedies—a situation known as **polypharmacy**. The rate of polypharmacy is increasing in the United States. For instance, the rate of people over age 65 who took five drugs or more was 13 percent in 1988. By 2015, that rate had tripled to 39 percent (National Center for Health Statistics, 2018).

Unfortunately, recommended drug doses are determined primarily by clinical trials with younger adults, for whom homeostasis usually eliminates excess medication. When homeostasis slows down, excess lingers. In addition, most trials to test new drugs exclude people who have more than one disease. As a result, drugs are not tested on people who will use them most.

Drug interactions can cause confusion and memory loss. Almost any drug affects the brain, with neurological effects obvious with drugs intended to reduce anxiety and depression. The simple solution seems to be to discontinue drugs, but that may not only increase disease but also harm the brain. For instance, untreated diabetes and hypertension cause cognitive decline. Lack of drug treatment for those conditions may be one reason why low-income elders experience more illness, more cognitive impairment, and earlier death than do high-income elders.

As this chapter has made abundantly clear, brains are precious, but understanding and protecting them is complicated. Good nutrition; constructive coping with stress; seat belts and helmets; stopping child abuse and domestic violence—all these measures are recommended. Although brain shrinkage occurs over time, individual variations in when and how much are vast.

One team explains, "the human brain is arguably the most complex entity in the known universe, and this complexity is best reflected by the fact that the brain strives to understand itself" (Huang & Luo, 2015, p. 42). "Striving to understand" is a challenge for all of us. We need to follow the advice of that prenatal instructor: "Use your BRAIN."

polypharmacy A situation in which elderly people are prescribed several medications. The various side effects and interactions of those medications can result in dementia symptoms.

CHAPTER APP 5

 Medisafe

iOS: https://tinyurl.com/y3x7fk75
ANDROID: https://tinyurl.com/96fvedt
RELEVANT TOPIC: Polypharmacy

This app reminds users when it's time to take medication and when prescriptions are running low. (A "Medifriend" can be designated by the user to receive these reminders as well.) A drug interaction checker notifies users if they have been prescribed medications that aren't supposed to be taken together.

WHAT HAVE YOU LEARNED?

1. What are common causes of traumatic brain injury and chronic traumatic encephalopathy?
2. How does chronic drug use affect the brain?
3. Which neurocognitive disorders are characterized by memory loss and which are not?
4. What factors increase or decrease the incidence of brain diseases?
5. How is depression unlike a neurocognitive disorder?

SUMMARY

Naming the Parts of the Brain

1. The brain develops from the brainstem to the prefrontal cortex, becoming much larger in humans than in other animals.

2. In most living creatures, the cerebellum (for basic body functions) and the midbrain (for emotions and communication among brain parts) are the largest parts of the brain. For humans, the forebrain (called the cerebrum) is the largest part.

3. The cerebral cortex has six layers and many specialized parts, each with particular functions. Most of our conscious thought arises from the cortex.

4. The brain is organized into four lobes, the occipital, temporal, parietal, and frontal. Each specializes in particular functions.

5. The bodies and brains of every living creature have a left and right side. Each brain hemisphere controls the opposite side of the body. Many cognitive functions are on one hemisphere or the other, but no one is exclusively left- or right-brained.

6. Most important skills use both sides of the brain. The corpus callosum transmits messages from one hemisphere to the other.

Communication in the Brain

7. Neurons send messages to other neurons via dendrites, neurotransmitters, and axons. This process is affected by past experience and drugs, medically prescribed or not.

8. The limbic system includes regions of the brain that are crucial for human emotions, the amygdala, the hippocampus, and the hypothalamus. Hormones that originate in the brain, particularly oxytocin and cortisol, are crucial for love, fear, rage, anxiety, and so on.

9. The maturation of the brain is uneven, dependent on age and experience. Adolescent brains develop more slowly than adolescent bodies.

Plasticity

10. The human brain is not only larger, proportionally, than the brains of other animals, it is also more adaptable to whatever the environment demands of a person. This involves cell death and cell growth. In a word, brains are *plastic*.

11. Examples of plasticity include, infants learning language, adolescent girls reaching puberty, adults becoming experts at their chosen job or hobby, and older adults developing new neurons.

Attacks on the Brain

12. Some brain damage is more likely in adolescence or early adulthood than later on. Traumatic brain injury can lead to severe problems in middle age or later. Drug abuse is more likely among younger adults and also harms the brain.

13. Earlier brain loss from CTE may not be noticed until combined with the typical brain changes in later adulthood. Then symptoms are manifest. In general, age is the most common risk factor for a neurocognitive disorder.

14. The two most common causes of late adulthood brain disease are Alzheimer's disease and multiple strokes. Memory loss is evident, as is mental confusion.

15. Less common is frontotemporal disorder (as in Pick's disease), and many conditions that begin with impaired movement (as in Parkinson's disease). These also cause massive cognitive loss over time, but memory loss is not the dominant sign.

16. Brain disease can be forestalled or prevented if depression is treated, and if diet, sleep, social activities, and exercise are optimal. Brain health is important lifelong, although severe harm may not be evident until late in life.

KEY TERMS

central nervous system (p. 119)
hindbrain (p. 119)
midbrain (p. 119)
forebrain (p. 119)
brainstem (p. 119)
cerebellum (p. 120)
cerebrum (p. 120)
cerebral cortex (p. 120)
prefrontal cortex (p. 122)
impulse control (p. 123)
perseverate (p. 123)
left hemisphere (p. 124)
right hemisphere (p. 124)

corpus callosum (p. 124)
neuron (p. 127)
dendrite (p. 127)
axon (p. 127)
synapse (p. 127)
automatization (p. 128)
neurotransmitters (p. 129)
myelin (p. 130)
reaction time (p. 130)
limbic system (p. 131)
amygdala (p. 131)
hippocampus (p. 131)
hypothalamus (p. 132)

pituitary (p. 132)
hormones (p. 132)
oxytocin (p. 132)
cortisol (p. 132)
experience-expectant (p. 135)
experience-dependent (p. 135)
mild cognitive impairment (MCI) (p. 138)
traumatic brain injury (TBI) (p. 139)
chronic traumatic encephalopathy (CTE) (p. 139)

posttraumatic stress disorder (PTSD) (p. 139)
neurocognitive disorder (NCD) (p. 140)
Alzheimer's disease (p. 141)
plaques (p. 141)
tangles (p. 141)
vascular disease (p. 142)
frontotemporal NCDs (p. 142)
Parkinson's disease (p. 144)
Lewy body disease (p. 144)
polypharmacy (p. 145)

APPLICATIONS

1. Many factors affect intellectual sharpness. Think of an occasion when you felt inept and an occasion when you felt smart. How did the contexts of the two experiences differ? How might those differences affect the performance of elderly and young adults who go to a university laboratory for testing?

2. Some people mistakenly assume that almost any high school graduate can become a teacher, since most adults know the basic reading and math skills that elementary children need to learn.

Describe aspects of expertise that experienced teachers need to master, with examples from your own experience.

3. Test your own brain by comparing how your mind works in two contrasting conditions. For example, you could spend two hours reading this text and taking notes, each hour in a different condition, such as before and after dinner, or exercise, or a cup of coffee. Compare the two conditions, such as pages read, ideas remembered, connections made to things you know from other parts of your life.

ESPECIALLY FOR ANSWERS

Response for Early-Childhood Teachers (from p. 122) One solution is to remind yourself that the children's brains are not yet myelinated enough to enable them to quickly walk, talk, or even button their jackets. Maturation has a major effect, as you will observe if you can schedule excursions in September and again in November. Progress, while still slow, will be a few seconds faster.

Response for Parents Worried About Early Puberty (from p. 136) Probably not. If she is overweight, her diet should change, but the hormone hypothesis is speculative. Genes are the main factor; she shares only one-eighth of her genes with her cousin.

OBSERVATION QUIZ ANSWERS

Answer to Observation Quiz (from p. 137) At least nine things! Full apron, hair in bun (not in eyes), gas flame, tilt of pan, moving pan partly off to adjust heat, long handle on pan, the pan itself (durable, heat-conducting, expensive), constant stirring, and most important of all—intense concentration on the task.

Answer to Observation Quiz (from p. 139) Shoes with cleats. Not helmets, shoulder pads, or knee braces.

Answer to Observation Quiz (from p. 144) Neither photo depicts exercise that is likely to become an enjoyable routine. The teacher is not facing the class, so she may not know when someone cannot follow her pose, and the beach exerciser is unlikely to return every day, because exercise machines are often symbols of good intentions that do not last longer than a few days.

CHAPTER 6

Sensation, Perception, and Movement

148

I was walking along a busy avenue, midday, as were hundreds of strangers. Parents were smiling at babies or admonishing children; friends were laughing or pointing at clothes on store manikins; vehicles of all sizes were honking, or accelerating, or braking.

I glanced at a sidewalk fruit stand (three large navel oranges for $2 — better than in my neighborhood). I noticed a man carrying a bouquet of roses. I wondered: wife? sweetheart? mother? I then noticed my sexism; the flowers could be for himself or some other man.

I spotted someone 50 feet ahead. "Peter," I yelled. He turned, I waved, he waved back and waited. We walked together for a block, chatting about nothing special.

"Nothing special," because Peter is my colleague at work, not my friend; we exchange greetings, not much more.

But there *was* something special. I recognized his back among all the strangers, he heard his name amid all the noises, and we walked together because we connected on a busy sidewalk. An everyday miracle.

This chapter is about the development of that miracle. Unless something is wrong, every adult can do what Peter and I did. We used our eyes and ears; we walked, waved, and talked, just as 6 billion older children and adults on Earth already do, and as the other 2 billion or so babies and younger children are learning to do. In this chapter we describe the development of the senses and motor skills, from birth to old age.

Every sense connects people with each other, as well as allowing experience to lead to thought. That is how people grow, families develop, and our humanity survives: stimulus → sensation → perception → cognition.

What Will You Know?

1. Would your sensory skills at birth be better if you were a kitten?
2. What is the connection between touch, smell, and sex?
3. Why do people avoid getting hearing aids?
4. When should you stop rough-and-tumble play?

The First Two Years

It was once thought that infants were bombarded with "blooming, buzzing confusion" of all the senses (James, 1890), but we now know that is not true. To understand this, we must explain the sequence just mentioned, stimulus → sensation → perception → cognition.

A *stimulus* is something that *could* be sensed. The **sensation** occurs when a sensory system detects a stimulus, as when the hairs of the inner ear vibrate with sound or the eye's pupil intercepts waves of light. Thus, sensations traditionally begin when some stimulus affects a sense organ—the ear, eye, tongue, nose, or skin.

Perception occurs when the brain—the auditory cortex, the visual cortex, the somatosensory cortex, and so on—becomes aware of the sensation. Neurons need to reach a threshold that makes perception possible. Then *cognition* occurs if that awareness becomes conscious, processed by the neurons to become a thought.

Those links are not automatic, and they change over the life span. Most stimuli never reach the sense organs; most sensations never become perceptions; many of our perceptions never lead to cognitions. The entire process begins in infancy, when the senses are amazingly sharp, as we now explain.

Precocial or Altricial?

Biologists categorize species as either **precocial**, when newborns have relatively mature sensory and motor skills, or **altricial**, when newborns need maturation to manifest those skills. The precocial colt stands on its spindly legs almost before amniotic fluid dries on its already hairy coat; some fish are so precocial that they need no maternal care at all. Birds vary: Ducks can swim almost immediately (precocial), but some songbirds stay in the nest for weeks before they can fly or feed themselves (altricial).

Primates are altricial in motor skills, with humans the most altricial of all. Because of that, caregivers must carry children from place to place. Adults spoon-feed infants, cut up food for preschoolers, and button, zip, snap, or tie for young children.

By contrast, human senses are precocial; they all function at birth, unlike many other mammals who are born with eyes sealed shut. This combination of active senses and immature motor abilities requires newborns to connect with families and communities, making humans social creatures from the very start (Konner, 2010).

That social dependence is why newborns have open eyes, sensitive ears, and responsive noses, tongues, and skin. Minutes-old infants stare, bewildered and fascinated, seeming to search for their parents. In the first days of life, the senses are hypersensitive to caregivers, probably more than they will be in a week or two (Zeifman, 2013). The specifics differ for each of the senses, as we now detail.

Hearing

Many adults, upon first seeing a baby, notice the ears, shaped to reflect a unique combination of genes. But they could be equally impressed with the universals: Every ear, no matter what the particulars, is shaped with round edges and

sensation The response of a sensory organ (eyes, ears, skin, tongue, nose) when it detects a stimulus.

perception When the brain is conscious of a sensation or idea. Perception sometimes combines several senses and ideas: You might suddenly perceive that your mother is angry because of her face and voice and your past experience of her anger.

precocial When the senses and motor skills are developed before (pre-) birth. A precocial newborn creature can immediately see, hear, smell, and move as an older infant could.

altricial When the senses and motor skills do not develop until days or months after birth. An altricial newborn creature is virtually blind, deaf, and immobile.

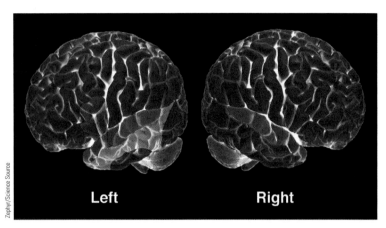

Left Right

From Sound to Language Hearing occurs in the temporal lobe, in both hemispheres, the green and some of the orange parts of these brain images. Language comprehension, however, is mostly in the left hemisphere (the region shaded yellow) and in Broca's area (shaded orange), which produces speech. A person could hear but not understand (as is true in infancy) or understand but not speak (as is true if Broca's area is damaged).

ESPECIALLY FOR Nurses and Pediatricians The parents of a 6-month-old have just been told that their child is deaf. They don't believe it because, as they tell you, the baby babbles as much as their other children did. What do you tell them? (see response, page 180)

indentations to cup vibrations (sound waves) and direct them to the ear canal. Then those sound waves vibrate the *tympanic membrane* (the eardrum), which makes three *ossicles* (the tiniest bones of the body) move, and they conduct sound to the *cochlea*, itself formed of many parts, including about 15,000 hair cells, within the skull.

The tympanic membrane, ossicles, cochlea, and hair cells begin to transmit sound before birth, as the fetus listens to the mother's speech, startles at loud sounds, quiets with rhythmic music. Babies a few hours old listen more carefully to their mother's voice than to the voice of a stranger, preferring to hear the language they heard before birth.

Early Language Learning

Infants respond to pitch, including crying at shouts and listening attentively to whispers. They like rhythms, not only the familiar heartbeat but also the steady rhythm of a lullaby, or of soothing music. They particularly prefer speech sounds, especially when directed to them (Ramírez-Esparza, 2017). By 6 months, they begin to understand what a caregiver says, especially if the words are simple, animated, and inviting.

Many studies find that infants are primed to learn language, beginning at birth when they begin to distinguish when one word begins and another ends (Fló et al., 2019). Certainly by 8 months their hearing is particularly attuned to one of the approximately 6,000 human languages (Fecher & Johnson, 2018), and then they zoom in to the language they hear. By 18 months they are less able to distinguish sounds that are not part of their mother tongue.

Infants quickly grasp the rhythm, tone, and frequency of particular sounds (e.g., some languages use *th*, some do not). One-year-olds imitate the actions of strangers who speak their native language, with words not yet understood, more than the actions of someone speaking another language (Buttelmann et al., 2013).

Infants perceive not only nuances of pronunciation, such as the way the *r* or *ch* is pronounced, but also patterns and rhythms, such as rising and falling tones (Hay et al., 2019). Changes in pitch are crucial in some languages, not for English. Infant perception reflects that.

Cochlear Implants

Because auditory perceptions are crucial for early learning, newborn hearing is tested in every U.S. hospital. Deaf babies may get hearing aids, and parents are taught sign language. By age 1, delicate brain surgery provides cochlear implants, bypassing the deaf ear, and providing sound waves directly to the auditory cortex (Kral et al., 2019).

A cochlear implant involves surgery on the brain, connecting a tiny microphone on the surface of the head to a receptor implanted inside the skull that transmits sound directly to the auditory cortex, avoiding the ossicles and the cochlea. That seems radical, but infants with implants quickly utter sounds similar to the early vocalizations of hearing infants (Välimaa et al., 2019).

Cochlear implants and infant hearing aids are not chosen by every parent of a deaf infant, particularly if the parents are deaf themselves, in part because the implication is that technology can "cure" hearing loss. That idea ignores the thriving deaf culture, which prioritizes visual and motor skills over auditory ones. Ideally, even with implants, a deaf child becomes bilingual, proficient in signed and spoken language.

Measuring the Senses

How do we know what a preverbal baby can hear, or, for that matter, see, feel, smell, or taste? One way is to watch closely. Close observation should be part of every adult interaction with an infant.

Newborns visibly relax when held snugly with their ear pressed to someone's chest, listening to the heartbeat. Within the first weeks, babies turn their heads toward sounds they like, people they know, smells they prefer. On the other hand, they spit out unpleasant tastes, cry at distressing touches, turn away from what they do not want.

The sense of hearing is particularly acute: Infants look at people who speak their language, who sing their favorite songs, who say their name. The sense of vision catches up: By 3 months, babies smile more broadly at people they love, follow moving objects with their eyes, focus on preferred objects.

All that can be observed by an attentive caregiver. How can scientists improve on that? To demonstrate infant senses scientifically, beyond observation, researchers have devised several methods, first for hearing and then for the other senses (de Groot & Hagoort, 2018). One method is to connect a rubber nipple to a tape recorder in such a way that the strength of sucking plays a recording or connects to a screen image that comes into focus as babies suck more vigorously. This method not only detects preferences, but also determines if a baby can hear the difference between similar sensations.

Often research takes advantage of *habituation*, which is the process of becoming less interested in repeated exposure to the same old sound, sight, taste, and so on. (Think of listening to your teacher's voice after several hours of a lecture, or of school lunches that serve macaroni and cheese day after day.) Once habituation has occurred, people pay less attention; interest perks up when something new occurs.

Babies habituate to sounds: They are less attentive to the tenth or twentieth time a particular sound is heard. If they perceive a new sound, they react via brain waves, or sucking strength, or eye-gaze. That reveals that they can hear a difference between two similar sounds.

Habituation was crucial for a classic study that showed that, even by 1 month, babies can distinguish "pah" from "bah" (Eimas et al., 1971). Thousands of studies over the past decades use habituation to learn what preverbal infants can sense. It is evident that all the senses are present at birth, becoming more acute and perceptive over the early months and years.

Vision

People notice the color of the newborn *iris*, but whether a baby has blue or brown eyes matters little for vision. Two other visible parts of the eye, specifically the *pupil* (the dark circle in the middle of the iris) and the *sclera* (the white area around the iris) are important. The crucial factor is not whether or not they are present (virtually every human has them) but what they indicate to the astute observer.

The pupil adjusts to light and emotion by changing size, becoming smaller with light and arousal, such as anger. The white sclera indicates where someone is looking. People notice if their conversation partner is emotionally relaxed (larger pupil) and attentive (the sclera indicates that) (Palmer & Clifford, 2018).

Do newborns notice the pupils and sclera in people who look at them? Probably not: Vision is the least mature sense at birth. Indeed, one scientist writes that newborns seem "apparently blind" (Brodsky, 2016).

Experience and Perception

The reason for newborn's poor visual perception is lack of prenatal experience. Unlike for sounds, which are heard by the fetus, there is nothing much for the fetus to see. Thus, sensation is present, but perception is not. Initially, infants focus only on things close to their eyes, such as the face of their breast-feeding mother, and even that is blurry.

Almost immediately, however, experience combines with maturation of the visual cortex to improve vision. By 2 months, infants see colors, shapes, contrasts. They focus on faces and smile at them. (Smiling can occur earlier, but not because of vision.)

As experience builds, dendrites grow and scanning improves. Thus, 1-month-olds might stare at the hairline, but 3-month-olds look closely at the eyes and

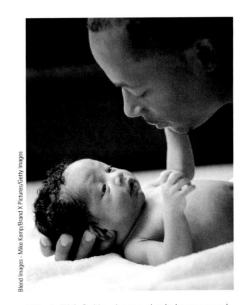

Blend Images - Mike Kemp/Brand X Pictures/Getty Images

Who's This? Newborns don't know much, but they look intensely at faces. Repeated sensations become perceptions, so in about six weeks this baby will smile at Dad, Mom, a stranger, the dog, and every other face. If this father in Utah responds like typical fathers everywhere, cognition will be apparent by 6 months: The baby will chortle with joy at seeing him but become wary of unfamiliar faces.

mouth, smiling more at happy faces than at angry or expressionless ones. They pay attention to patterns, colors, and motion—the mobile above the crib, for instance. They smile more broadly at people they know. Each month they are better able to *track* (follow with their eyes) a moving object, allowing researchers to know what interests them (Stone & Bosworth, 2019).

Because of this rapid development, babies enjoy new sights. A crying baby might be distracted by being taken outside to watch passing cars. If feasible, *cataracts* (present in about 1 newborn in 2,000) are surgically removed in the early months so the cornea is clear and sights can reach the brain, allowing activation (Medsinge & Nischal, 2015). Without that, pruning might erase some neurons in the visual cortex that are primed (expectant) for sight.

Using Two Eyes

Binocular vision (coordinating both eyes to see one image) cannot develop in the womb (nothing is far enough away). Consequently, many newborns use their two eyes independently, momentarily appearing wall-eyed or cross-eyed. Usually, experience allows both eyes to focus on one thing between 2 and 4 months (Seemiller et al., 2018).

For eye muscles to develop, distant sights need to be seen. Caregivers should not keep infants in a white crib in a pale room or put a blanket over the carriage when taking them out. Of course, a sleeping infant outside on a cold day may need such a blanket, but focusing and binocular vision are sensory skills, and they need practice to develop.

We know this because of research on newborn kittens whose eyes were sutured shut. Later, with eyes open, they could not see as well as other cats. Depth perception (required for leaping up or down from a table, as cats often do) was particularly impaired if one eye had not been used (Hubel & Wiesel, 2004). Cats scrambled, tumbled, fell.

Human babies show evidence of depth perception (which requires binocular vision) by 3 months, but they do not understand the hazards of falling over a "visual cliff" until they practice creeping, crawling, and walking. Nor do they yet know if a surface is best traversed upright, sitting, or on their stomachs (Kretch & Adolph, 2013). Precocial and altricial, again: It takes time for senses to inform perception and cognition.

Touch

Touch, in its literal, traditional meaning, is the ability of the skin to detect indentations and pressure, such as a poke, a caress, or a rough surface. The *epidermis* (the outer layer of the skin) and the *dermis* (several layers beneath the epidermis) are sensitive to touch because those layers are connected to dendrites and axons below the surface—more on some areas, such as the fingertips, less in others.

Touch is present in very young infants. This is most evident in newborn reflexes. These are described later, but one (rooting) merits mention now. If a cheek is brushed, infants turn their head toward that cheek, a reflex that helps the baby finding a nipple. Overall, infants are soothed by wrapping, rubbing, massaging, cuddling, and cradling. Gentle and rhythmic stroking on their arms relaxes them (Fairhurst et al., 2014).

Some touch is experience-expectant, essential for normal growth. Beyond that, touch is experience-dependent, varying by culture. In some places, daily massage begins soon after birth (Trivedi, 2015). For example, in rural India, mothers immediately bathe and massage their newborns.

binocular vision The ability to focus the two eyes in a coordinated manner in order to see one image.

THINK CRITICALLY: Which is most important in the first year of life, accurate hearing or seeing?

This cultural tradition harms fragile infants; public health workers teach mothers to wipe their newborns gently with a dry cloth and breast-feed immediately—preserving body heat and reducing death (Acharya et al., 2015).

Body heat is vital for newborns, who must quickly adjust to many new sensory experiences. They are less able to warm up or cool down themselves, an ability called *thermoregulation*, which explains why they are vulnerable to death when they are too cold or too hot (Schinasi et al., 2020). Holding a baby, skin-to-skin, lets the baby attain the temperature of a healthy adult.

By contrast, some mothers in Western nations need encouragement to touch their babies. Touch communicates, facilitating bonding between caregiver and baby. Many infants want the feel of a favorite blanket, or stuffed toy, to help them sleep. One of my daughters was comforted when her tiny hands held onto my hair; she connected that sensation with maternal nurturance.

Taste and Smell

The senses of taste and smell are present at birth but are shaped by experience. Infants may tolerate, or even enjoy, many tastes or smells that an older child might dislike or that might make an adult gag.

Taste arises from thousands of taste buds, most of which are on the *papillae* (bumps) on the tongue (you can see them). Each taste bud has hundreds of cells that can detect various tastes—definitely the five basic ones (sweet, sour, bitter, salty, and umami or savory) and perhaps several more, including astringent and fat. Those cells are present (although there are fewer of them) at birth, and become increasingly sensitive and selective in the early months (Mennella & Castor, 2012).

Smell may be our oldest sense, arising from deep within the brain. Smell results from molecules wafting through the air from a smelly source to the odor receptacles in the nose. In the very back of the nasal cavity, behind the eyes, the molecules of smell reach neurons.

Unlike vision, which travels at the speed of light, smell molecules take time to reach the brain. Since the infant brain has yet to be well-myelinated and connected, smell is particularly dependent on the reactions of other people, and on experiences that make a particular smell pleasant or not.

Newborns can smell (they turn away from a whiff of ammonia, for instance), and taste hundreds of substances, from disgusting to delicious, but even the

Learning About a Lime As with every other normal infant, Jacqueline's curiosity leads to taste and then to a slow reaction, from puzzlement to tongue-out disgust. Jacqueline's responses demonstrate that the sense of taste is acute in infancy and that quick brain perceptions are still to come.

newborn prefers the mothers' diet, spices and all, which they swallowed as amniotic fluid (part of preparing the lungs to function).

The very young infant learns to like breast milk with the flavors of the mother's diet. Some research suggests that breast-fed babies are more likely to tolerate a variety of tastes later on because their mother ate a variety of foods, unlike formula-fed babies who have only one early taste (Mennella & Castor, 2012).

Preferences for mother's diet may aid survival, as each culture prioritizes foods that were consumed by past generations who lived in that place. For example, bitter foods provide some defense against malaria, hot spices help preserve food, some spices slow cancer, high-fat foods reduce starvation, and so on (Aggarwal & Yost, 2011; Kuete, 2017; Prasad et al., 2012). Thus, for infants, developing a preference for certain tastes may facilitate more than affinity to their family and culture; it may save their lives.

All children tend to like sweets more than adults do, but the strength of that preference depends partly on whether or not their mother added sugar to their food (Mennella & Bobowski, 2015). Early taste preferences endure when a person migrates to another culture. Immigrants from Africa or Asia to North America or Europe purchase costly, imported delicacies if those foods were plentiful when they were infants.

Adaptation also occurs for the sense of smell. Adults traveling to their homeland, having left decades earlier, often express joy at the smell of the place. Because babies recognize each person's scent, they prefer to sleep next to their favorite caregivers and nuzzle into their caregivers' cheeks and chests—especially when the adults are shirtless. Often the smells of infancy (cut grass, baking bread, flowers, an open market) become indelible, evoking memories decades later.

In infancy, as well as later, smell, color, and texture make foods tasty or not (as in Dr. Seuss's *Green Eggs and Ham*). Part of the brain—the *gustatory cortex*—receives taste messages, combines them with smell, texture (slimy, crunchy, silky, creamy), and temperature (hot soup, ice water), and then renders a judgment, affected by the opinions of others.

Parents say "yum, yum" when they spoon mush into their infants' mouths, toddlers look at what others eat and want some. Taste and smell, just like vision and audition, are not solely biological; they are social as well.

Combining Senses

Not every sense requires an organ dedicated to it; what is required is that the brain, consciously or not, reacts to a particular kind of sensation. Scientists agree that humans have more than the traditional five senses, just described, although they disagree as to how many other senses there are and how acute they are in infancy. We will discuss the senses of temperature, body position (proprioception), pain, and motion soon. But now we emphasize that, particularly in infancy, the senses all work together.

Sensory connections allow **cross-modal sensations**, when a sensation from one mode (such as hearing) is also experienced in another mode (such as vision). Many of our spoken words (e.g., slimy, poop, zigzag) convey appearance, and thus are cross-modal. This is innate: When 4-month-old infants hear "kiki," they are more likely to look at an angular shape than a round one (Ozturk et al., 2013).

Cross-modal perception is evident from what we now know about the brain: The prefrontal cortex receives messages from every sensory region. Each sense can connect to others. When an infant is blind or deaf, the corresponding visual

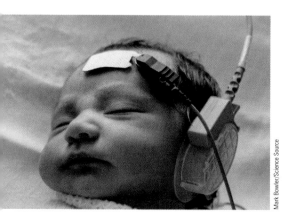

Mark Bowler/Science Source

Click, Click Laws require the hearing of every newborn to be tested, because brain response to the clicks and beeps of the audiometer indicate that a baby will learn spoken language within a year. If the baby is deaf (as is about one in a thousand), then sign language, hearing aids, or surgery will be recommended.

cross-modal sensations When a sense from one mode (e.g., hearing or touch) evokes a sense in another mode. If a person hears a voice and envisions what the person looks like, that is cross-modal.

or auditory cortex takes on some of the abilities of the intact sense, making infants who are blind, for instance, extraordinarily alert to sounds.

That may help explain why Helen Keller, blind and deaf, became one of the noted intellectuals of her era. For the first 19 months of her life, she used all her senses—she was seeing, hearing, and talking. Then her illness made her blind and deaf. That early experience may have allowed the sense of touch to connect to the other parts of her brain.

For every infant, all the senses work together. Sometimes this is literally true, neurologically and anatomically. For instance, smell and taste both feed into the upper throat: Food becomes delicious when both senses combine to send a joint message to the brain.

Synesthesia

Closely related to cross-modal perception is **synesthesia**, when one sense triggers another in the brain—a number or letter may evoke a color, a sound, a texture. This is not simply that two distinct sensory modes are used on one object, but that two modes are fused as one.

According to a dominant hypothesis, synesthesia is common in infants because the boundaries between the sensory parts of the cortex are still forming. Pruning (explained soon) has not yet eliminated unnecessary connections (Maurer et al., 2013).

For many babies, textures are associated with vision, sounds with smells, and the infant's own body merges with those of their caregiver. One psychoanalyst contends that every infant needs to "hatch": Not until at about 4 months do they begin to experience themselves as distinct sensory beings, separate from their mothers (Mahler et al., 2000).

synesthesia When one sense triggers another. For example, a number written in black print might be seen as a color. Synesthesia can occur with every sense, not just vision.

An Example: Kangaroo Care

Now we consider an example that highlights the combinations of all the infant senses and the reciprocal sensations of the adult. That is *kangaroo care*, with a baby resting on the mother's naked chest (see photo). The experience is cross-modal: The infant hears the mother's heartbeat, touches her skin, sees her face, smells her scent, and tastes her milk.

The history of kangaroo care illustrates why the difference-equals-deficit idea is an error. Before modern medical care that included incubators and bright lights, newborns were routinely placed on their mothers' chest to keep warm. By the middle of the twentieth century, babies were born in hospitals. They were routinely separated from their mothers at birth and placed in the nursery, where doctors and nurses could care for them day and night.

Those hospital babies were more likely to survive than the babies born at home. People concluded that letting mothers hold their newborns immediately was a primitive custom that might increase mortality. But remember that correlation is not causation. The fact that hospital care decreased newborn deaths did not mean that every aspect of home birth was harmful.

In about 1960, research began to accumulate that suggested that, in hospital births, bonding between mother and baby was more likely if the mothers held their babies against their skin soon after birth (Klaus & Kennell, 1976). Some hospitals began to let some mothers (especially

Better Care Kangaroo care benefits mothers, babies, and hospitals, saving space and medical costs in this ward in Manila. Kangaroo care is one reason Filipino infant mortality in 2010 was only one-fifth of what it was in 1950.

single parents) hold their babies. That skin-to-skin care seemed to improve bonding and infant health.

Mothers who were not particularly needy, with infants who were not particularly fragile, began to want to hold their newborns, too. Some hospitals allowed this, a practice now labeled kangaroo care, because mother kangaroos keep their newborns in their pouch for weeks after birth. Now this practice, once forbidden, is common in many hospitals.

A summary of 124 studies found that kangaroo care reduces newborn stress: Compared to other newborns, kangaroo-care babies gain more weight, come home from the hospital sooner, and benefit in every other measured way (Boundy et al., 2016). This is not because of a single sense; the combination is needed. When newborns and new mothers see and hear each other, they bond more quickly; when newborns are warmed by a mother's body, they shiver less.

Fathers and other partners can also provide kangaroo care, again with good results (Kostandy & Ludington-Hoe, 2019). Worldwide, about 3 million newborns die each year: Public health experts believe that early parent–infant contact, including kangaroo care, could save hundreds of thousands of them (Smith et al., 2017).

Cross-modal perception is evident for parents as well as for infants. Imagine a newborn nestled on your chest — your mind and your senses would be activated. Parents who use every sense to care for their newborns (talking to them, inhaling the baby smell, caressing them, watching them closely) tend to be happier and more responsive caregivers. Kangaroo care is dramatic evidence for the interaction of the senses, as the combination reduces stress for everyone — mother, father, and baby.

Indeed, because of mutually reinforcing senses, mothers whose babies are in the newborn intensive-care unit (NICU) and who experience kangaroo care are much less likely (9 to 34 percent) to fear that they will be unable to care for their fragile babies at home (Sweeney et al., 2017). It may be that separating mothers and newborns in the intensive-care nurseries is one reason for the high rate of neurocognitive disorders in those NICU survivors, because the brain needs loving sensory care (Császár-Nagy & Bókkon, 2018).

All babies sometimes cry, and all caregivers want to comfort them. Since all the senses function, and since the brain fires only one thought at a time, every sense could provide a distraction from crying. That is illustrated in **Table 6.1**.

WHAT HAVE YOU LEARNED?

1. What does *altricial* mean? (Give an example.)

2. What does *precocial* mean? (Give an example.)

3. What aspects of the human visual system are apparent at birth, and what aspects take time to appear?

4. What aspects of the human auditory system are apparent at birth?

5. How does early hearing relate to language acquisition?

6. What evidence shows that the human infant can taste and smell?

7. What is the difference between synesthesia and cross-modal perception?

8. What is a sensory explanation for the benefits of kangaroo care?

TABLE 6.1

Practical Implications of Infant Sensation

Audition

- *Sh, sh, sh* is heard prenatally (from the mother's gastrointestinal or cardiovascular systems). Therefore, whispering "hush" is comforting.

- The heartbeat is a familiar rhythm before birth. Newborns may be soothed if held with an ear over the left side of the caregiver's chest.

- Infants are attuned to the human voice; quiet talk helps.

- The varied tones and rhythms of music are distracting. Babies are not critics: Off-key lullabies are appreciated more than speech (Tsang et al., 2017).

- Background "white noise"—an air conditioner, a vacuum cleaner, a fan, an audio recording of waves slowly lapping the shore—is soothing.

Vision

- Faces and motion are particularly interesting, such as a caregiver making faces that include head shaking, wide open and blinking eyes, mouths open and shut.

- Moving (not too fast) a toy animal with big eyes may distract a fussy baby.

- Taking the baby to the window, or outside to watch people and cars, may stop the crying.

Touch

- Being securely wrapped (swaddled) is reminiscent of the womb. Experienced caregivers fold young babies snuggly inside blankets, creating a "baby burrito," as my son-in-law expressed it.

- Gentle rubbing of the arms, legs, and so on (massage) is relaxing.

- Pressure on the stomach may also help. My husband sometimes held my infant daughters in the air, his big hand on their tiny bellies, small legs dangling as they looked around. I said, "don't drop them." He never did; they stopped crying.

Taste and Smell

- A drop of water with sugar, ginger, or other ingredients ("gripe water") is not recommended for frequent use, but worth an occasional try.

- Breast milk contains some substances that reduce pain. Even when a baby is not hungry, nursing can be soothing.

From Age 2 to 25

All the senses are at their most acute during childhood and early adulthood, and all are extraordinarily plastic, affected by experiences, as we soon describe. But before those specifics, notice the ages above (2 to 25), a marked departure from the standard chronological demarcations of the life span (early childhood, middle childhood, adolescence, emerging adulthood, middle adulthood, late adulthood).

However, when describing the senses, three age-based stages seem best. The links of stimulus → sensation → perception → cognition continue to develop every year from age 2 to 25.

Hearing

The ability to hear probably peaks in mid adolescence, when a teenager might be able to hear tones that are imperceptible to older people, or to understand a whispered conversation in the next room that the adults assumed would not be heard.

It Was a Blast Blinding light, deafening noise, crushing crowds, lost identity, "out-of-body" — all words of praise for this 2018 concert in Dallas, Texas. With such immediate ecstasy, why think about the long-term damage?

In developed nations, this also is the time when serious damage is likely, as many teenagers and young adults listen to loud music on their headphones, socialize where people shout to be heard, and attend deafening concerts. That has led to a new worry (Gopal et al., 2019; Hussain et al., 2018). Younger adults ignore symptoms of hearing loss (ringing, muffled sounds, temporary deafness), in part because their overall hearing is so good that they do not imagine that losses are occurring.

Many younger adults dismiss warnings about auditory damage. As one said, "There are more important things to worry about" (Hunter, 2018). Of course, global problems may be more critical, but the best way to avoid worrying about one's senses is to automatically protect them.

There is some careful research on portable listening devices that reports that most adolescent users do NOT damage their hearing by occasional headphone listening. Damage appears when the devices are loud and the listening frequent, such as more than two hours a day for five years or more (Portnuff, 2016). Overall, hearing is designed to sometimes be subject to loud noises, but not to endure too much.

Unfortunately, some adolescents are particularly vulnerable to hearing loss for three reasons (Portnuff, 2016).

1. The sense of invincibility. Many are unaware that temporary signs, such as *tinnitus* (ringing in the ears), suggest notable loss later on.
2. The power of social norms. If teenagers think everyone listens to loud music, or if high-decibel music at a concert makes them feel connected to hundreds of others, they ignore warning signs of hearing damage.
3. The need for emotional respite. Music affects moods and relieves stress. Some young adults are addicted to that relief, many hours a day.

Sometimes studies of hearing measure only pure tone hearing, such as how loud a sound must be before it is heard. But the crucial factor from age 2 to 25 is perception, not sensation, specifically how adept a person is at hearing a conversation. This ability improves with experience. When speech is "degraded," that is, rapid, muffled, with background noise, or so on, despite their better sensory ability, adolescents (ages 12–16) are not as adept as young adults (e.g., Hillock-Dunn & Wallace, 2012; Tangkhpanya et al., 2019). Ideally, by age 20, people can perceive as well as hear so they can appreciate music, respond to conversation, and even listen to the birds sing.

Vision

Checking vision needs to be part of routine health care for every child, because young children do not know if they cannot see as well as everyone else. A study of Irish schoolchildren found that in first grade, about 1 in 9 children had vision problems (O'Donoghue et al., 2012).

You just read that hearing becomes its most acute in adolescence, and, unless noise damage occurs, stays strong until at least age 25. That is not true for vision. Children see better every year, and then, at puberty, the shape of the eyeball changes, becoming rounder. Near objects are easy to see (*nearsightedness*) but distance vision (*farsightedness*) is a little less acute.

Usually this is no problem: There is no need to read street signs a few blocks away, or to see the faintest stars in the sky. For most people age 2 to 25, eyes adjust to variations in distance. But for some adolescents, changes in the eyeball impair vision, such as reading the PowerPoint presentation from the back of the classroom, or knowing where a fly baseball is likely to land.

That same study in Ireland found that the rate of vision problems in adolescence was twice as high as for younger children, entirely because the rate of nearsightedness increased. Only about 1 in 400 6-year-olds was nearsighted; but about 45 in 400 12-year-olds were (O'Donoghue et al., 2012).

Many young adults rely on their visual sense, not only in obvious ways (reading a book) but in other ways, such as looking at a friend's face to detect their mood. The sense of vision may dominate all the other senses. In one study, emerging adults who focused on a difficult visual task were oblivious to a strong smell that was noticed by another group of emerging adults who had a much easier task (Forster & Spence, 2018).

Smart Glasses An estimated one million U.S. children learn less because their vision is impaired. Fifteen thousand of them were public school students in Baltimore, Maryland, but Rashad Solomon, age 9, is no longer among them. Every Baltimore child is screened, and then a nonprofit (Vision for Baltimore, funded in part by Johns Hopkins University), provides free exams and glasses.

People believe their eyes more than their ears. Probably everyone who says "fine" when asked "How are you?" has been told "You don't look fine; what is wrong?" Young adults may be especially perceptive in social interpretation, which is one reason many prefer face-to-face communication—attending a party; talking privately, in person, with a close friend; listening in class to an effective teacher—instead of phone, text, or e-mail. The latter are useful to confirm, plan, and schedule face-to-face encounters, but they do not replace what a person can see by looking at the face and body position of a friend.

Touch

The sense of touch remains acute throughout childhood and early adulthood, but interpretation is powerfully influenced by experience. The easiest example regards efforts to prevent sexual abuse, in which children are taught the difference between good touch and bad touch (Manheim et al., 2019).

For preschoolers, this means that no one should touch parts of the body that a bathing suit covers; for adolescence, this means teaching boys and girls the importance of asking a partner if a certain sexual touch is okay. Some parents are very concerned about sexual abuse and communicate that fear to the children. Some children are abused sexually, and others experience affectionate care, with reassuring and welcome touch.

Because of their past experience and their parents teaching, some young adults are hypersensitive to any touch. Others welcome hugs from anyone. Learning boundaries for touch is a crucial aspect of cultural education. Ideally, by adulthood, people have learned to appreciate touch that expresses comfort, concern, and respect and to stop unwelcome touch immediately.

A discussion of the role of touch in social work explains:

> Positive touch [is] . . . highly significant for effective communication, secure attachments/relationships and optimum physical and mental health throughout the life course. Much research revealed negative or absent touch can have a cumulative adverse effect on people's lives, and others around them, if they deploy or accept destructive touch interactions or withdraw emotionally.
>
> [Green, 2017, p. 785]

Ideally, children are touched often, lovingly, with care. Communication via touch may be natural to humans, a hypothesis that arises from watching children

THINK CRITICALLY: In some cultures, men and women never touch each other unless they are husband and wife; in other cultures, adults routinely greet each other by hugging, bumping shoulders, slapping hands. Are your culture's touch customs what you want them to be?

with each other: They often hug, tap, bump, grab, and otherwise touch each other, spontaneously and with mutual joy. Similarly, adolescent romance also includes much touching—teenagers thrill at holding hands, sitting close, caressing a cheek, a first kiss. Is it strange that "playing footsie" is romantic?

Emerging adults are more reticent and selective than children. In the United States, a sports victory is sometimes celebrated by athletes' back-slapping each other; work stress sometimes leads employees to pay for deep massage; sexual touching before or without intercourse is sometimes part of the sexual script for adolescents and adults. Interestingly, for many teenagers, holding hands and a first kiss are as sexually exciting as coitus.

Consider the variations in handshakes and hugs: Some adults welcome, and some reject, anything more than slight, glancing touch. A cross-cultural study of romantic kissing (lip-to-lip touch, either superficially or deeply) found that kissing is part of romance in only about half of all cultures (Jankowiak et al., 2015).

All of these examples show not only that adults are selective regarding touch but also that cultural norms regarding touch are taught to children and then become part of adult expectations and perceptions.

Taste and Smell

Remember that taste and smell are profoundly affected by experience, with smell the slowest sense to react. That allows substantial social influence on these senses.

Picky eating is a trait of many children, partly because their taste buds are more sensitive to bitter and more receptive to sweet than is true for adults (Mennella & Bobowski, 2015). A change may occur at puberty: Many adolescents begin to like coffee (bitter) and reject bubble gum (sweet), in part because of changes in the taste buds, but also because of changes in cognition.

Researchers do not agree on the definition, measurement, and consequences of being a picky eater, but it seems that age 3 may be the peak of being "very choosy." Parent example is influential (Taylor et al., 2015). If picky eating continues into adolescence and early adulthood, it may interfere with nutrition and be a sign of an eating disorder, but this is less true in early childhood.

Smell is also a sense that shows great variety, affected by social context. For example, the smell of urine and bowel movements does not seem to bother many children, but becomes offensive to many adults. A smoldering fire, a gas leak, or even burnt toast is not detected easily by some children or adults, but others (firefighters, gas company employees, chefs) become very sensitive to such smells by early adulthood.

Habituation is evident. That's why people douse themselves with perfume, thinking they use enough to be attractive, unaware that too much makes them repulsive.

Remember that infants experience cross-modal perception. This continues after age 2: The smell or sight of some foods stimulates taste buds; voices evoke images. Beyond that, about 3 percent of adults experience synesthesia: Their brains still combine sensory stimuli, hearing sounds as colors, tasting letters, or feeling numbers (Cytowic, 2018).

Sexual smells are particularly evocative. Consider a series of studies involving heterosexual young men who sniffed T-shirts worn by young women who were either ovulating or at the end of their cycle (Miller & Maner, 2011; Tan & Goldman, 2015). The T-shirts were placed in plastic bags, sealed, and inhaled by the men, who were told they were evaluating the smell of a detergent.

Nonetheless, after they rendered their judgment and were asked to sit and wait in a room with several empty chairs, the men who had a whiff of fertility were more likely to sit near a woman! Most research on smell and sex has been done with men, but as scientists have become aware of women's sexual urges, they are

Dave Carpenter/Cartoonstock

" IT SAYS RIGHT HERE IN THE INGREDIENTS, THIS PRODUCT CONTAINS NO YUCKY STUFF!"

Who Is Fooling Whom? He doesn't believe her, but maybe she shouldn't believe what the label says, either. For example, "low fat" might also mean high sugar.

discovering that women respond to male smells. Both sexes drink more alcohol when they smell fertility, even when no actual men or women are nearby (Tan & Goldman, 2015, 2017).

Some scientists question those studies, as that research does not always replicate and because people do not want to be guided by smell (Mostafa et al., 2012; Wyatt, 2015). No one doubts, however, that most other mammals are powerfully influenced by sexual smells (Liberles, 2014).

Other Senses

In the discussion of infancy, you read that experts describe several senses beyond the traditional five. Now we describe three of them: Each is apparent in childhood and beyond.

Pain

Pain is the most obvious other sense. Whether or not infants feel pain, with similar intensity as older children and young adults, is a matter of intense study and dispute, not only among scientists but also among politicians. However, it is clear that, by age 2 and beyond, people feel pain.

Two kinds of fibers in the body communicate pain. *A-delta fibers* register quick, sudden pain; *C fibers* are slower. Pain can be sharp (A-delta) or throbbing (C). Curiously, some parts of the body have more pain receptors than others. A toothache can be excruciating; a cut on the leg might be hardly felt; brain surgery is painless (although cutting the surface of the skull is painful).

Generally, pain begins when some body part experiences damage. A pain sensation is carried by axons to the spine and then the brain. Many parts of the brain, not only the location of that particular body part but also the *insula* and the *anterior cingulate*, assess the pain message. Then the prefrontal cortex decides on action.

Sometimes no analysis is needed. A hand is quickly moved from a hot stove. But more often, the prefrontal cortex (which reaches full functioning at about age 25) must counteract the message: When a nurse draws blood for analysis, the patient must not move when the needle punctures the skin.

Pain processing in the brain is strongly affected by interpretation and learning: A slap may be felt as a welcome caress or as an insult that leads to murderous rage. When a child falls, observers must wait before comforting: Many falls are not painful. Many adolescents and young adults seem to welcome pain (as in tattoos, sports, exercise).

The link between cognition and sensation is apparent with bleeding. Soldiers may not know they are shot until they see their blood. Athletes might not realize they are injured until a post-game shower reveals a scrape. Many people, athletes or not, see a bruise on their body and wonder how they got it. Children connect visible blood with injury. They feel better as soon as a Band-Aid covers a cut.

Distraction and sympathy help. Young children want a parent to kiss a bump; hospitalized children want to hold a parent's hand and hear a song; young adults want a doctor to name an illness. The benefits of diagnosis and sympathy explain what had been a puzzle, the *placebo effect*. People who are given an inert pill (such as a sugar pill with no medicine in it) often feel better! (Colagiuri et al., 2015).

Because interpretation is crucial, no one knows how much pain another person experiences. Doctors and nurses ask patients to rate their pain, from zero (none at all) to 10 (so intense they might pass out). But sensations do not lead directly to cognitions: interpretation varies. Some people moan and cry; others hide their pain; others say, "I didn't feel anything."

All senses benefit people in some way, which makes it not surprising that pain is protective. A few rare people lack the genes for the sense of pain. But instead of having happy, pain-free lives, they may become severely injured and die young. For

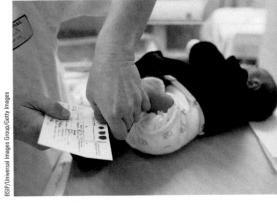

The First Blood Test This baby will cry, but most experts believe the heel prick shown here is well worth it. The drops of blood will reveal the presence of any of several genetic diseases, including sickle-cell disease, cystic fibrosis, and phenylketonuria. Early diagnosis allows early treatment, and the cries subside quickly with a drop of sugar water or a suck of breast milk.

THINK CRITICALLY: What political controversy makes objective research on newborn pain difficult?

instance, they move their hands off a fire only when they see their red, blistering skin; they might not seek treatment when cancer destroys their organs.

Hot and Cold

Temperature is also considered a sense. We perceive hot or cold, not only on our skin (a burn, or ice) but also in the air we breathe and in our bodies at rest, as we feel flushed, sweaty, chilled. Experienced caregivers can feel a child's forehead and realize, not only a fever, but also temperature. The difference between 103 and 101 can be felt!

Some other creatures have an extraordinary sense of temperature. Some reptile embryos become male or female depending on the temperature of incubation (Refsnider et al., 2014). Some snakes have, quite literally, an organ that detects heat waves (Goris, 2011). Boa constrictors use their sense of warmth to detect prey.

There is good reason why the sense of temperature is a topic for ages 2 to 25. Children and young adults probably feel temperature more acutely than infants and the aged. Again, it is hard to assess, objectively, how hot or cold someone else feels, but we do know that bodies of people at both ends of the life span do not *thermoregulate* (react to temperature by warming up or cooling down) very well. One consequence is that the death rate of the very old and very young rises during a heat spell (Gronlund et al., 2014; Schinasi et al., 2020).

Proprioception

proprioception The sense of where the parts of the body are, both when they are in one spot and when they are moving.

Not every scientist agrees that temperature merits recognition as a distinct sense (it may be part of touch) but all acknowledge another sense called **proprioception**, the sense of body position. People know, for instance, if their feet are on the ground or dangling in the air. That is proprioception.

Unlike the other senses, no specific organ is dedicated to proprioception, but this sense reaches the brain, affecting perception, cognition, and action as other senses do. This is particularly apparent when damage to proprioception occurs. When that sense is lost, a person cannot grab something without looking at their hands, cannot walk (much less dance) without falling, cannot even get out of bed and stand up in the dark. The sense of balance is often considered part of proprioception.

Proprioception develops with maturation. Crawling and toddling children may topple over; children improve on their ability to balance. That may explain why children like to walk on a ledge, pump on a swing, climb on a rocky hill or playground gym. Mastery of proprioception is usually reached by adolescence, and then declines over the decades of adulthood (Henry & Baudry, 2019).

For many young athletes, however, continued improvement in proprioception is possible as well as instrumental in, for instance, aiming a soccer ball, blocking the basket-shooting of the opposing team, avoiding a football tackle. Have you noticed that, in concerts attended by emerging adults, hundreds stand and sway with the music, while concerts for older adults include comfortable seats? Credit proprioception.

Advancing and Advanced At 8 months, she is already an adept crawler, alternating hands and knees, intent on progress. She will probably be walking before a year.

onebluelight/E+/Getty Images

WHAT HAVE YOU LEARNED?

1. Exactly how is later deafness affected by hearing in early adulthood?
2. How are the senses of audition and vision similar and different?
3. Why do more adolescents than children need glasses?
4. How does touch vary by culture?
5. What is the connection between smell and sexual attractiveness?
6. How is pain connected to cognition?
7. What happens when proprioception is damaged?

Age 25 and Up

Over adulthood every sense becomes less acute, beginning as early as age 25. The rate of decline is barely perceptible at first and accelerates in late adulthood. The age when any specific loss noticeably affects functioning depends on genes and past health.

Remember the sequence: stimulus → sensation → perception → cognition? Stimuli do not change, and sensation becomes strong in infancy, with perception powerful in childhood and early adulthood. Children, adolescents, and young adults develop preferences, antipathies, and interpretations of their sensations.

In adulthood, cognition comes to the fore, as adults evaluate, compensate, and interpret their perceptions. Reduced sensory acuteness in the second half of life may not be devastating.

Regarding age-related sensory loss, two facts need to be kept in mind:

1. Plasticity. As one team wrote, "mental imagery can lead to cross-modal cortical plasticity" (Berger & Ehrsson, 2018, p. 927). Practice helps, losses may be mitigated by other senses, and clarity of interpretation can compensate for clarity of sensation.
2. Aids to the senses. A crucial factor in all the sensations is the use of appropriate technology, and other innovations.

Of course, losses do not disappear, but most older adults can see, hear, and so on much better than was the case a few decades ago. Cheap reading glasses are available in drug stores, the volume on every electronic device is adjustable, smoke alarms are in every home. Literally hundreds of other compensatory aids are readily available.

A problem is that many people with sensory losses do not use every useful device, but that is not primarily due to the equipment but to the people. Instead, problems arise from reluctant individuals and unhelpful societies (e.g., public and private insurance may not pay for technology, nor for the professionals who can adapt them to each person). Consequently, we now explain the losses and their effects.

Hearing

Remember that hearing begins prenatally? That may be why hearing is the first sense to fade: "signs of [age-related hearing impairment] in males may already be evident at an age of 30–39" (Yang et al., 2015, p. 2). **Presbycusis** (literally, "aging hearing") is rarely diagnosed until about age 60, but whispers become inaudible years earlier. (See **Figure 6.1**.)

One reason people do not realize that their hearing is less acute is that no one knows what is not heard until the loss becomes extreme. People simply turn up the volume on the TV and ask, "What did you say?"—blaming someone's soft voice or odd accent rather than their own hearing.

This is harmful in many ways. Some younger people assume that people with hearing losses are incompetent. They yell, simplify, and infantilize, using *elderspeak*, a form of speech, similar to babytalk, that reduces complexity ("The doctor will see you now, dear"). One result is that people with poor hearing risk low self-esteem, social isolation, and cognitive loss—including, by late adulthood, major neurocognitive impairment (often called *dementia*) (Loughrey et al., 2018).

The most common reason for hearing loss is destruction of the tiny hairs in the cochlea that reverberate with sound and send messages to the brain. The first cochlea hairs that are damaged are those that respond to high frequencies, which may explain why rock concerts have pounding drums (consider the implications of "heavy metal").

presbycusis Hearing loss that is related to aging. At earlier ages, a few people lose hearing because of disease or injury, but everyone experiences presbycusis in late adulthood.

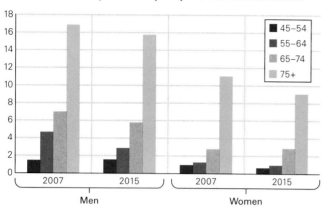

Percent of People Who Say They Are Deaf or Almost Deaf

FIGURE 6.1

Cohort and Gender Why the improvement, especially for men aged 55–64? Laws mandating protective earphones began in about 1990, which means that the 2007 cohort of construction workers usually did not have protective headgear, but the 2015 cohort did.

presbyopia Visual loss that is related to aging. Usually this is the result of one or more of three conditions that become more common with age: cataracts, glaucoma, and macular degeneration.

Everyone loses some hearing with age, with men more vulnerable than women. For both genders, health, nutrition, and protection against loud noise (jackhammers, explosions, ear-splitting music) slow down loss. Protective headphones are now legally required for soldiers, construction workers, and many other occupations, which is a major reason that workers who entered the labor force after 1990 hear better than those before the law went into effect.

This may be one reason rates of major neurocognitive disorders are lower today than earlier, since hearing loss reduces cognition (Sarant et al., 2019). Because people are now living longer, millions in the United States (and millions more elsewhere) have notable hearing loss.

Tiny, effective hearing aids, unlike the crude and bulky ones of a few generations ago, are available. Those with severe losses benefit from cochlear implants, which not only allow better hearing but aid executive function (the master cognitive ability, further explained in Chapter 7) (Sarant et al., 2019).

Aids and implants do not solve all age-related deafness, in part because few insurance policies pay for these expensive remedies. Added to that, adults connect hearing aids with aging. In an ageist culture, no one wants to appear "old." The sad consequence: Many older adults become isolated and less aware because of hearing losses.

Vision

Vision also changes over adulthood, with **presbyopia** (age-related visual loss) part of the aging process. There are many physiological causes. One is that the shape of the eyeball changes, from convex in adolescence to concave in middle age. Many adults become farsighted, holding their newspapers farther away than 20-year-olds do. The eye muscles no longer change the shape of the lens to allow near focus (Aldwin & Gilmer, 2013).

Unlike hearing losses, many visual losses are disease-related, and can be prevented or treated if they are recognized early. The three most common are cataracts, glaucoma, and macular degeneration (see **Table 6.2**).

TABLE 6.2

Common Vision Impairments Among the Elderly

- *Cataracts.* As early as age 50, about 10 percent of adults have cataracts, a thickening of the lens, causing vision to become cloudy, opaque, and distorted. By age 70, 30 percent have cataracts, which can be removed in outpatient surgery and replaced with an artificial lens.

- *Glaucoma.* About 1 percent of those in their 70s and 10 percent of those in their 90s have glaucoma, a buildup of fluid within the eye that damages the optic nerve. Early stages have no symptoms. Without treatment, glaucoma causes blindness, but the damage can be prevented. Testing is crucial, particularly for African Americans and people with diabetes, since the first signs of glaucoma may occur for them as early as age 40.

- *Macular degeneration.* About 4 percent of those in their 60s and about 12 percent of those over age 80 have a deterioration of the retina, called macular degeneration. An early warning occurs when vision is spotty (e.g., some letters missing when reading). Again, early treatment—in this case, medication—can restore some vision, but without treatment, blindness occurs about five years after macular degeneration starts.

Cataracts are almost inevitable with age. Other factors (cigarette smoking, ultraviolet light) accelerate the age-related decline. Cataracts are a haze on the surface of the lens, which decreases the light reaching the retina and increases glare. In developed nations, surgery to replace cataracts with clear lenses is routine. Sadly, cataracts are the leading cause of blindness in poor nations, where such surgery is a luxury (Y.-C. Liu et al., 2017).

Glaucoma is less common but more serious. It is caused by increasing fluid in the eye, which damages the retina and the optic nerve. Glaucoma is the leading cause of blindness in the United States—particularly tragic since early detection and then eye drops can relieve the pressure on the retina before irreversible damage occurs.

Macular degeneration is the third visual disease, a common cause of blindness in late adulthood. At present, there is no cure, but drugs, diets, brain stimulation, and surgery are all under study.

As with all the senses, genes are influential, but many factors slow down vision loss. Stopping smoking, exercising to maintain blood circulation, and maintaining a healthy diet are among them (McGuinness et al., 2017). Since early signs are not noticed by the person, everyone needs to have their eyes checked long before losses occur.

In addition to acuity, every other aspect of vision also changes. Flexibility slows and adjustment to bright or dark takes longer. Adults are blinded when leaving a dark theater and going outside, or when driving at night with oncoming headlights. Motion perception (How fast is that car approaching?) and contrast sensitivity (Is that a bear, a tree, or a person?) slow down. Color vision fades (Is that sock black or navy blue?).

Family history and ethnic background provide a warning. For instance, African Americans are less likely to develop macular degeneration but more likely to develop glaucoma (D. Fisher et al., 2016; Ladapo et al., 2012). But with every sense, family history is a better guide to inheritance than any ethnic category, and lifestyle can outweigh many familial vulnerabilities.

cataracts A surface covering on the eye's lens that clouds vision by decreasing the light that reaches the retina. Makes sight dimmer and increases glare.

glaucoma An increase in fluid in the eye, which damages the retina and the optic nerve. Can be mitigated with eye drops but, left untreated, can cause blindness.

macular degeneration The loss of functioning in the macula of the eye, which results in blind spots.

(a)

(b)

(c)

(d)

Through Different Eyes These photographs depict the same scene as it would be perceived by a person with (a) normal vision, (b) cataracts, (c) glaucoma, and (d) macular degeneration. Think about how difficult it would be to find your own car if you had one of these disorders. That may help you to remember to have your vision checked regularly.

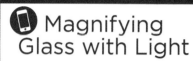

There are many ways that people can compensate for vision loss. Among them:

- large-print books and newspapers;
- large and bold fonts on electronic devices;
- special lights, filters, telescopes, and magnifiers;
- sounds, such as a stick that beeps when a cup is full; and
- touch, Braille, and raised stars on elevator buttons.

Touch

Touch is a powerful lifelong sense. A hug, a pat on the hand, a kiss on the cheek from a longtime partner may express affection more than words. When people are dying and no longer can see, hear, or talk, a touch may still express care.

Although most of the research on how touch affects people has involved infants, touch may be even more important in late adulthood. Touch carries meaning that can reduce the sense of isolation, mitigate pain, and confirm affection—all particularly important for older adults (Field, 2019).

Medical professionals currently understand the value of *therapeutic touch*, which is stroking or massaging someone to improve health, reduce pain, relieve anxiety. Many scientists are skeptical of claims for therapeutic touch, but generally, patients who are touched as well as medicated improve (e.g., Mueller et al., 2019).

What about people who are not particularly stressed, isolated, or in pain? It seems that the sense of touch communicates social support that is beneficial at every age. One line of research finds that many forms of touch (hugging, petting a dog, having sex) increase oxytocin, a hormone nicknamed "the love hormone" because it fosters social connections.

Researchers asked married couples to play a board game or join an art class. They each were assessed on the frequency of touching each other, and on the level of oxytocin in their system. Oxytocin levels rose as touching increased (Melton et al., 2019).

Research on touch is nowhere near as extensive as research on hearing and seeing. However, there seems to be no doubt that the sense of touch communicates throughout life, and that we all should "reach out and touch someone."

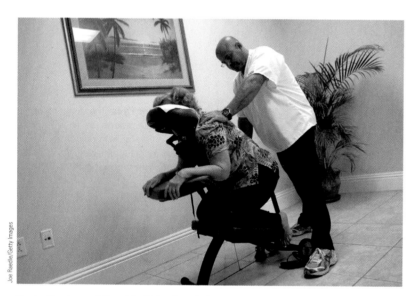

Body Knots and Psychic Pain Revolution, immigration, communism, capitalism—all these stresses and forces are felt in the body as well as the brain. Here at the Clinica Asociacion Cubana in Miami, Florida, Gustavo Bella releases tension in Odilia Poruen, an example of the close connection between touch and health. At this center for Cuban émigrés, music, games, and food connect Cuban childhood to U.S. adulthood.

Smell and Taste

The senses of smell and taste remain important throughout adulthood, even as they become less strong. Unfortunately, most of what is known about these senses comes from research on what happens when they are impaired. Diminished acuteness of taste and smell not only decreases enjoyment, but it also can seriously harm health.

Indeed, one of the hallmarks of frailty in old age is that the appetite is reduced. Weight loss is a symptom, and may be a cause, of many health problems in late adulthood. Further, if adults become accustomed to sweet or salty foods (easy to do, given advertisements and cultural values), when taste fades, that person might add more sugar to their tea or salt to their vegetables. By age 65, those habits increase many ailments. Among adults over 65 in the United States, 26 percent have diabetes, and 67 percent have hypertension (Centers for

Disease Control and Prevention, 2017), with too much sugar and salt among the reasons.

Smell, as already explained, is physiologically connected to taste. Moreover, smell is designed to prevent toxins — rotten food, smoldering wood, leaking gas from the stove, a dead mouse under the radiator, dinner burning in the oven. The fact of declines with age alerts younger adults to use their superior sense of smell to protect their older relatives.

Pain

Remember that pain is subjective: It is hard to know what amount of pain someone else feels. Pain, especially lower back pain, becomes more common with age, but attitudes about pain become increasingly important.

At every age, pain interacts with thought: Humans invent "compensations, corrections, or radically effective solutions" to pain (Damasio, 2018, p. 11). Some sources suggest that pain decreases with age. It is hard to know if this is true, but it seems that, although minor aches and pains increase with age, people become better able to tolerate them (Lautenbacher et al., 2017).

Pain correlates with depression; treatment for depression may relieve pain (Zis et al., 2017). However, the elderly may resist pain medication because they do not want anything to interfere with their thinking. Some are so accustomed to chronic pain that they seek medication only when pain is intense.

My father in his 90s walked haltingly because each step hurt; it pained me to watch.

"Get a knee replacement," I said.

"My doctor said I could wait until the pain is unbearable. I can bear it," he said.

He died at age 93, with the knees he was born with.

WHAT HAVE YOU LEARNED?

1. How do the senses interact with cognition in adulthood?

2. How does hearing change with age?

3. What are the benefits and problems with hearing aids and cochlear implants?

4. What are the effects of age on eyeball shape?

5. What are the differences among the three age-related diseases in vision?

6. Why is touch especially important in later years?

7. How can changes in taste and smell affect life and health?

8. Does the sense of pain become more or less significant in later life? Why?

Motor Skills: Birth to Old Age

At every age, the ability to move the body (called *motor skills*) is closely related to every other aspect of development. Motor and sensory skills are reciprocal, each affecting the other.

Infants crawl because they want to touch something; ailing elders walk because someone calls them, and everyone between those ages moves because they sense, or perceive, or think something that compels them to use their motor abilities. Then, movement expands their sensory awareness and cognitive ability. Motor development is "embodied, embedded, enculturated, and enabling" (Adolph & Hoch, 2019, p. 143).

Moving the Body Before Age 2

As already mentioned, motor skills are altricial: Of all mammals, humans are slowest to be able to walk. This aids bonding: The helpless infant elicits care. Nonetheless, infants move their bodies as much as they can. Babies only a few days old turn their heads toward the source of a sound; the eyes of very young babies move to follow slowly moving objects, a tracking ability that advances month by month.

Progress is evident month by month, from the 2-month-old who inches to a corner of the crib to the 12-month-old who takes a step, falls, and gets up to step again, to the 2-year-old who runs in the park, with the caregiver trying to keep up.

Reflexes

Motor skills begin with reflexes, which seem instinctual and automatic. Newborns have dozens of them, 20 of which are listed here in italics.

- *Reflexes that maintain oxygen supply.*
  The *breathing reflex* begins even before the umbilical cord, with its supply of oxygen, is cut. Additional reflexes that maintain oxygen are reflexive *hiccups* and *sneezes*, as well as *thrashing* (moving the arms and legs about) to escape something that covers the face. *Coughing* and *sneezing* are reflexes to clear the throat.

- *Reflexes that maintain constant body temperature.*
  When infants are cold, they *cry*, *shiver*, and *tuck their legs* close to their bodies. When they are hot, they try to *push away* blankets and then stay still.

- *Reflexes that manage feeding.*
  The *sucking reflex* causes newborns to suck anything that touches their lips—fingers, toes, blankets, and rattles, as well as natural and artificial nipples of various textures and shapes. In the *rooting reflex*, babies turn their mouths toward anything that brushes against their cheeks—a reflexive search for a nipple—and start to suck. *Swallowing* also aids feeding, as does *crying* when the stomach is empty and *spitting up* when too much is swallowed quickly.

- *Reflexes that signify brain functions.*
  Babinski reflex. When a newborn's feet are stroked, the toes fan upward.
  Stepping reflex. When newborns are held upright, feet touching a flat surface, they move their legs as if to walk.
  Swimming reflex. When held horizontally on their stomachs, newborns stretch out their arms and legs.
  Palmar grasping reflex. When something touches the palms, newborns grip it tightly.
  Moro reflex. When someone bangs on the table they are lying on, newborns fling their arms out and then bring them together on their chests, crying with wide-open eyes.

The strength and duration of reflexes vary from one baby to another. Many reflexes disappear by 3 months, but some morph into motor skills if the social context encourages them.

VIDEO: Newborn Reflexes shows several infants displaying the reflexes discussed in this section.

The stepping reflex reveals the power of context. Some cultures discourage walking; others encourage it. Babies respond, some walking at 10 months, others at 15 months.

Much depends on what caregivers do. Indeed, 1-year-olds can swim! Usually the swimming reflex disappears by 6 months, but if an infant is held, stomach down and head up, in warm water and a caregiver encourages spontaneous paddling, infants move their arms in a swimming motion. (Of course, the young child's prefrontal cortex is not ready for safe water movement: Toddler swimmers need a life jacket and an adult very close by.)

Gross Motor Skills

Deliberate actions that use many parts of the body, producing large movements, are called **gross motor skills**. They emerge from reflexes and proceed in a *cephalocaudal* (head-down) and *proximodistal* (center-out) direction. (See **At About This Time**.)

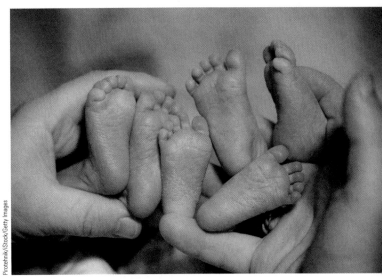

Pirotehnik/iStock/Getty Images

Miracles, Old and New For millennia, every newborn has been considered a miracle, evident in the old proverb "Every new baby is evidence that God has not yet given up on the world." This twenty-first-century mother holds the feet of her triplets, born in Ukraine, a center for unrestricted fertility miracles.

gross motor skills Physical abilities involving large body movements, such as walking and jumping. (The word *gross* here means "big.")

AT ABOUT THIS TIME

Age Norms (in Months) for Gross Motor Skills

	When 50% of All Babies Master the Skill	When 90% of All Babies Master the Skill
Sits unsupported	6	7.5
Stands holding on	7.4	9.4
Crawls (creeps)	8	10
Stands not holding	10.8	13.4
Walks well	12.0	14.4
Walks backward	15	17
Runs	18	20
Jumps up	26	29

Note: As the text explains, age norms are affected by culture and cohort. The first five norms are based on babies from countries on five continents [Brazil, Ghana, Norway, United States, Oman, and India] (World Health Organization, 2006). The next three are from a U.S.-only source [Coovadia & Wittenberg, 2004; based on Denver II (Frankenburg et al., 1992)]. Mastering skills a few weeks earlier or later does not indicate health or intelligence. Being very late, however, is a cause for concern.

Observation Quiz Which of these skills has the greatest variation in age of acquisition? Why? (see answer, page 180) ←

Thus, infants first control their heads, lifting them up to look around. Control moves downward—upper bodies, arms, and finally legs and feet. Rolling over is the first gross motor skill to develop; babies lying prone push themselves onto their backs. (Back-to-front rollovers take another month or two.)

The role of practice in evident in new norms for rolling over. Most babies used to roll from back to front by 3 months. Since about 1990, conscientious caregivers have put infants to sleep on their backs to prevent *sudden infant death syndrome (SIDS)*, a situation where a seemingly healthy infant dies in their sleep because they stop breathing. One factor that markedly reduces the risk of SIDS is sleeping on one's back.

A side effect of this safer sleep position is that babies roll over later than they once did. Caregivers now provide *tummy time*, placing a wide-awake infant on the floor, belly-down, to practice moving in that position. Some babies fuss at the

No Stopping Him Something compels infants to roll over, sit, stand, and walk as soon as their bodies allow it. This boy will fall often, despite his balancing arms, but he will get up and try again. Soon he will run and climb. What will his cautious mother (behind him) do then?

fine motor skills Physical abilities involving small body movements, especially of the hands and fingers, such as drawing and picking up a coin. (The word *fine* here means "small.")

unfamiliar position, and some caregivers do not insist, so currently rolling over is later than it was.

Similarly, sitting depends on both maturation and experience. By 3 months, most babies can sit propped up in a lap. By 6 months, they can usually sit unsupported. Infants who are never propped up (as in some institutions for abandoned babies) sit much later.

Most 8- to 10-month-olds can lift their midsections and crawl (or creep, as the British call it) on "all fours," coordinating the movements of their hands and knees. Crawling also depends on experience. Some babies never do it, especially if the floor is cold, hot, or rough, or if they have always lain on their backs. It is not true that babies must crawl to develop normally.

As soon as they are able, babies take independent steps, falling frequently at first, about 32 times per hour. They persevere because walking is quicker than crawling, and it benefits all the senses, providing better sight lines and free hands to touch, grab, and taste (Adolph & Tamis-LeMonda, 2014).

Once toddlers take those first unsteady steps, they practice obsessively, barefoot or not, at home or in stores, on sidewalks or streets, on lawns or in mud. They "immediately go more, see more, play more, and interact more" (Adolph & Tamis-LeMonda, 2014, p. 191). Experienced parents are glad babies are altricial, staying in one place as newborns and moving slowly until age 1. It is exhausting to follow a walking infant who is driven to explore.

Fine Motor Skills

Fine motor skills (small movements, like finger control) develop after gross motor skills. Newborns have a strong reflexive grasp and 2-month-olds wave their arms at objects dangling within reach. By 3 months, they can usually touch such objects, but their limited eye–hand coordination prevents grabbing. In other words, motor ability (arm and hand control, altricial) has not yet coordinated with the senses (precocial).

By 4 months, infants sometimes grab, but their timing is off: Many close their hands too early or too late. Finally, by 6 months, with a concentrated, deliberate stare, most babies can reach, grab, and grasp almost any object that is of the right size. Some can even transfer an object from one hand to the other, an advanced motor skill. Almost all can hold a bottle, shake a rattle, and yank a sister's braids. (See **At About This Time.**)

Toward the end of the first year, finger skills improve as babies master the pincer movement (using thumb and forefinger to pick up tiny objects) and self-feeding (first with hands, then fingers, then, at age 2 or so, with utensils).

As with gross motor skills, fine motor skills are shaped by culture and opportunity. This was already explained with the sense of vision.

Age 2 to 25

Motor skills develop from age 2 to 25, depending on both maturation and practice. Young children can run but not hop, use a wide marker but not a regular pencil, spot tiny marks on paper (and sometimes name the letters) but cannot move their eyes in an organized and consistent direction across a page in order to read. They can hear speech sounds, but even at

AT ABOUT THIS TIME

Age Norms (in Months) for Fine Motor Skills

	When 50% of All Babies Master the Skill	When 90% of All Babies Master the Skill
Grasps rattle when placed in hand	3	4
Reaches to hold an object	4.5	6
Graps with thumb and finger	8	10
Stacks two blocks	15	21
Imitates vertical line (drawing)	30	39

Data from World Health Organization, 2006.

A CASE TO STUDY

My Late Walkers

I know firsthand the relationship between reflexes, culture, and practice. I once thought that genes caused variations in the age at which children acquire motor skills, a comforting thought because my first three children did not walk until 14 months.

Our oldest child, Bethany, was born when I was in graduate school. At 14 months, she was talking, and at the 80th percentile in height and weight. But she had not yet taken her first step. I told my husband that genes are more influential than anything we did. I had read that babies in Paris are late walkers; my grandmother was French.

To my relief, Bethany soon began walking, and she became the fastest runner in her kindergarten class. My genetic explanation was bolstered when our next two children, Rachel and Elissa, were also slow to walk. My students with Guatemalan and Ghanaian ancestors bragged about their infants who walked before a year; those from China and France had later walkers. Genetic, I thought.

Fourteen years after Bethany, Sarah was born. I could finally afford a full-time caregiver, Mrs. Todd, from Jamaica. She thought Sarah was the most advanced baby she had ever known, except for her own daughter, Gillian.

"She'll be walking by a year," Mrs. Todd told me. "Gillian walked at 10 months."

"We'll see," I graciously replied.

I underestimated culture, Sarah, and Mrs. Todd. She bounced my delighted baby on her lap, day after day, and spent hours giving her "walking practice." Sarah took her first step at 12 months—late for a Todd, early for a Berger, and a humbling lesson for me.

As a scientist, I know that a single case proves nothing. My genetic explanation might be valid, especially since Sarah shares only half her genes with Bethany and since my daughters are only one-eighth French, a fraction I conveniently ignored when I needed reassurance about my late-walking firstborn.

Nonetheless, I now know that practice influences every aspect of sensory and motor growth. Genes provide the scaffold, and brain maturation is crucial, but specifics of nurture affect nature at every stage.

age 6 many children cannot yet control the movement of their lips and tongue (a fine motor skill) to pronounce every word correctly. The ability to blow bubbles, to make clicking sounds (essential in some languages), and to whistle takes even longer.

Sheer physical growth of body and brain and changed proportions are prerequisites for motor skills, but opportunity, practice, and motivation are crucial. Swimming, playing the violin, and cliff climbing are all possible by age 6, but most children cannot do them.

Over time, the center of gravity moves downward, enabling many new gross motor skills, and proximodistal control improves eye–hand coordination, advancing fine motor skills. Athletic skills develop: With opportunity, peers, and encouragement children learn to aim a soccer ball, throw a basketball, swing a bat—if that is what they or their culture expects.

Practice continues to refine skills. Camps allow adolescents to refine their skills; Spring Training is scheduled for every professional baseball team. Motivation and practice are evident with a crucial fine motor skill—penmanship. Many children write sloppily until they decide they want a distinctive and artistic signature. Many teenagers refine their writing and then "tag" public spaces. That requires advanced motor skills.

Active Play

Throughout childhood, play with peers is the foundation for development of the senses and motor skills. Children want and need to log in hours of practice, and that means that adults with young children need to be patient, because even on a routine walk to the store children run, jump, smell a flower, balance on a ledge, and kick leaves or a bit of garbage.

VIDEO: Fine Motor Skills in Infancy and Toddlerhood shows the sequence in which babies and toddlers acquire fine motor skills.

VISUALIZING DEVELOPMENT Developing Motor Skills

Every child can do more with each passing year. These examples detail what one child might be expected to accomplish from ages 2 to 6. But each child is unique, and much depends on culture, practice, and maturity.

Skills

Average height in inches
Boys 45.5   Girls 45.0

Boys 43.0   Girls 42.5

Boys 40.5   Girls 40.0

Boys 37.5   Girls 37.0

Boys 34.1   Girls 33.5

Draw and paint recognizable images
Write simple words
Read a page of print
Tie shoes
Catch a small ball

6 years

Skip and gallop in rhythm
Clap, bang, sing in rhythm
Copy difficult shapes and letters
Climb trees, jump over things
Use a knife to cut
Wash face, comb hair

5 years

Catch a beach ball
Use scissors
Hop on either foot
Feed self with fork
Dress self
Copy most letters
Pour juice without spilling
Brush teeth

4 years

Kick and throw a ball
Jump with both feet
Pedal a tricycle
Copy simple shapes
Walk down stairs
Climb ladders

3 years

Run without falling
Climb out of crib
Walk up stairs
Feed self with spoon
Draw spirals

2 years

Sources & credits listed on p. SC-1

Same Situation, Far Apart Given the contrast between the Russian children in front of their rural school *(left)* and the Japanese girls beside their urban school *(right)*, you might see the differences here. But child psychologists notice that children everywhere chase and catch, kick and throw, and as in these photos, jump rope while chanting rhymes.

The adult's job is to ensure safety while allowing exploration. Thus, children must learn to stop at the curb, and to hold an adult's hand when crossing the street — a child's impulse is to keep running. But it is a mistake to insist that the child always walk beside the adult. Children need to move to develop their bodies. This is particularly evident when they are with other children, who also love to run, climb, and so on.

Play takes different forms as people mature. Many 2-year-olds fall down and bump clumsily into each other, but that does not stop them. By age 5, some children are quite adept, and by age 10, children can master virtually every skill that adults can do. They enjoy throwing balls, or pumping legs on swings, or climbing ladders with other children.

Size and judgment limits children, not their bodies. Some children are able to shoot a basketball, walk a tightrope, dive a jackknife, catch a softball, ski a mountain, cook a meal, knit a scarf. Since practice and motivation matter, no child can do all these behaviors. But all children need hours of activity every day.

The best teachers, and the prime motivators, are other children. Peers provide an audience, role models, and challenge. For instance, running skills develop best when children chase or race each other; almost no child goes out for a run alone. As an added bonus, active social play — not solitary play — correlates with peer acceptance, a healthy self-concept, and emotional regulation (Becker et al., 2014; Sutton-Smith, 2011).

Think of team sports in adolescence. Many young people practice daily, sometimes enduring pain and discomfort, in order to play with other adolescents. Ideally, schools have many teams, for all genders, abilities, and interests, so that every child develops their senses and motor skills.

Practicing and developing motor skills does not stop in adulthood. Many adults not only exercise, they work to improve their running speed, or tennis game, or batting accuracy, often with other people to motivate them. Teams of adults form and compete with one another; runners enter races; couples make tennis dates with other couples; and so on.

All that is fun, but it may also be crucial for healthy development. Among nonhuman primates, deprivation of social play warps development in later life, rendering some monkeys unable to mate, to make friends, or even to survive alongside

Henrik Weis/Corbis

Idyllic Two 8-year-olds, each with a 6-year-old sister, all four daydreaming or exploring in a very old tree beside a lake in Denmark—what could be better? Ideally, all of the world's children would be so fortunate, but most are not.

Observation Quiz Which of the senses is most evident here? (see answer, page 180) ↑

other monkeys (Gray, 2018). The same may be true for human primates, but, of course, controlled experiments are ethically impossible.

Play in the Neighborhood

Think now about neighborhood play. Ideally, everyone has a safe, nearby space to play, with ample time, appropriate equipment, and people to play with. This was the case a century ago, when children with varied skills played together in empty lots or fields without adult supervision. Adults gathered in pickup games or sports contests at church socials, at the local YMCA, at neighborhood community centers. Members of U.S. Congress have sports teams, which temporarily blur the partisan divides.

These arenas for the mastery of motor skills are flexible. Rules and boundaries are adapted to the context (out of bounds was "past the tree" or "behind the truck"). For children, stickball, touch football, tag, hide-and-seek, and dozens of other running and catching games can last forever—or at least until dark. Ideally, play is active, interactive, and everyone does it.

Traditionally, outdoor play was not solely physical; it involved all the senses: Children listened for cars, checked the clouds, squeezed dirt, tasted berries, poked ant holes. Now, more than half the world's children live in cities, often with crowded streets and no nearby green space. Gone are the days when parents said, "Go out and play," expecting their children back when hunger, rain, or nightfall brought them home.

Currently, not only have vacant lots and empty fields disappeared, but parents fear *stranger danger*—thinking that a stranger will hurt their child (which is exceedingly rare), ignoring the benefits of outdoor play. As one advocate of unsupervised, creative play sadly noted:

> Actions that would have been considered paranoid in the '70s—walking third-graders to school, forbidding your kid to play ball in the street, going down the slide with your child in your lap—are now routine.
>
> *[Rosin, 2014]*

Some communities have organized sports that vary by culture—tennis, karate, cricket, yoga, rugby, baseball, soccer, or others. However, few children from poor families or with disabilities are in private sports leagues, which require advance planning, adult transportation, and payment.

Activities that depend on adult volunteers, such as Little League baseball, are less common in low-income neighborhoods. Children avoid sports if they judge themselves as clumsy, and many schools prioritize one varsity team per season, with good grades a prerequisite for participation. As a result, the children most likely to benefit are least likely to engage, even when enrollment is free. The reasons are many, the consequences sad, for developmental scholars as well as children (Dearing et al., 2009).

The same factors are relevant for adult play. George Bernard Shaw said, "We don't stop playing because we grow old; we grow old because we stop playing." That is relevant to our understanding of motor skills in adulthood. They continue to develop, or atrophy, based on how much we use them. Some communities have many opportunities for adults to play. Adults engage in yoga, dancing, and hundreds of possible sports—and then the requisite motor skills continue to improve.

Rough-and-Tumble Play

One form of play highlights how play advances sensory and motor skills. That is **rough-and-tumble play**, which looks rough, with children seeming to tumble over one another. Shortsighted adults might intervene ("Stop it, someone's going to get hurt!").

The term "rough-and-tumble" was coined by British scientists who studied animals in East Africa (Blurton-Jones, 1976). They noticed that young monkeys often chased, attacked, rolled over in the dirt, and wrestled each other, but never hurt each other. If a monkey wanted to play, he would catch the eye of a peer and then run a few feet away. This invitation to rough-and-tumble play was almost always accepted with a *play face* (smiling, not angry). Puppies, kittens, and young baboons behave similarly.

When these scientists returned home, they were surprised to notice what they had seen many times but now perceived. Their own children, like baby monkeys, engaged in rough-and-tumble play. Once they alerted other scientists, it became apparent that children chase, wrestle, and grab each other, developing games like tag and cops-and-robbers, with various conventions, expressions, and gestures that children use to signify "just pretend."

Rough-and-tumble play has occurred worldwide for centuries (Fry, 2014). It is more common among boys than girls and flourishes in ample space with minimal supervision (Pellegrini, 2013). It helps the prefrontal cortex develop, as children learn to regulate emotions, coordinate sensations, practice social skills, and strengthen their bodies (Pellis et al., 2018).

Note that all the senses can be involved and carefully calibrated: Words, facial expressions, and touches are all regulated by the children, so no one is hurt. This is particularly evident when one child is notably older: Typically, they are careful not to hurt the younger one.

The lessons learned in rough-and-tumble play extend lifelong. For example, as you just read, the sense of touch in adulthood is an outgrowth of the experiences of childhood.

rough-and-tumble play Play that seems to be rough, as in play wrestling or chasing, but in which there is no intent to harm.

Fine Motor Skills

Children take years to control their fine motor skills. They might know how to spell their name at age 4, but writing it neatly often does not occur until age 9 or so—with much variation. Likewise, sewing, knitting, and drawing all take time to master. Throughout childhood, a source of variation is one's sex: Girls master fine motor skills about six months ahead of boys.

The fine motor skills most valued are often finger movements, enabling humans to write, draw, type, tie, and so on. Movements of the tongue, jaw, lips, and toes are fine movements, too. Actually, cephalocaudal development means that mouth skills precede hand skills by many months.

Since every culture encourages finger dexterity, children practice finger movements, and adults teach how to use spoons, or chopsticks, or pencils. By contrast, mouth skills such as spitting or biting are not praised. (Only other children admire skill with bubble gum.)

Currently, some children practice writing skills for years, proceeding from scribbles with a large marker, to writing their names in block letters, to artistic penmanship by age 10—if that is what their culture encourages. Adults need to make sure children use writing to facilitate reading: Without that awareness, children may develop writing that is artistic but illegible.

Unfortunately, penmanship is allotted much less time during the school day in the twenty-first century than in earlier times—evident in the neat cursive writing

Same Situation, Far Apart: Finger Skills Children learn whatever motor skills their culture teaches. Some master chopsticks, with fingers to spare; others cut sausage with a knife and fork. Unlike children in Japan *(left)* and Germany *(right)*, some never master either, because about one-third of adults worldwide eat directly with their hands.

of many older adults, unlike what most teenagers now produce. Some scholars worry that without penmanship practice, hand skills will not advance (Zubrzycki, 2012).

Today, finger skills are practiced as children manipulate keyboards, but typing is not an adequate replacement for handwriting. Seeing the hand move on the paper activates parts of the brain that are dormant with keyboarding. Every person of every age remembers better what they write by hand (Velay & Longcamp, 2012).

Other fine motor skills that also engage the senses, such as pounding a nail, sewing a seam, and playing an instrument, were once part of the school curriculum but have been eliminated. Those skills can be useful for adults, too: Many adult classes center around learning a fine motor skill.

Adulthood: Age 25 Onward

Remember that in adulthood, the senses gradually become less acute every decade. The same is true for motor skills. Most adults gradually lose their ability to move quickly and with precision. The range of motion decreases, so elders are less able to turn the neck to the side, twist the torso, or swing the legs above the waist.

Nonetheless, every motor skill responds to use. For instance, range of motion depends more on practice than on age. Some people still can touch their toes and strike yoga positions in later adulthood. Swimming, tai chi, and simply walking daily with a longer step, all make a difference—but a sudden twist is a mistake. Slow movements, repeated often, are needed.

Balance depends partly on exercise that keeps leg muscles strong, maintaining proprioception. Neurons and axons from the extremities to the brain, as well as with vision, mean slower reactions, so age slows down a person's ability to catch themselves when momentary imbalance occurs.

Over the decades, even before a person officially reaches late adulthood, muscles shrink; joints lose flexibility; stiffness is more evident; bending is harder. As a result, every motor skill is reduced. Rising from sitting on the floor, twisting in a dance, or even walking "with a spring in your step" is more difficult.

A strained back, neck, or other muscle occurs for almost every adult long before old age. People who exercise regularly, including weight bearing, muscle strengthening, and overall stretching, are less likely to strain a muscle. However, lower back pain is second only to the common cold for reasons employees miss work (Goode et al., 2013).

After age 40 adults are shorter than they were, because back muscles, connective tissue, and bones lose density, making less space between the vertebrae in the spine. On average, people lose about an inch (2 to 3 centimeters) before age 65 and continue to shrink after that. The loss is in the trunk, not the leg bones, because cushioning between spinal disks is reduced. Among the consequences are wider waists and changes in balance, both strongly influenced by physical activity, as is shrinkage overall.

Muscles depend on use—a few weeks of bedrest results in notable weakness. The fibers for Type II muscles (the fast ones needed for forceful actions) are reduced much faster than Type I muscle fibers (for slower, more routine movement) (Nilwik et al., 2013).

Thus, adults may be less likely to win a 100-meter dash than a marathon, or they may be unable to lift heavy rocks for a few minutes but can pick vegetables for hours. The inner organs also depend on muscles: The heart is a muscle that benefits from regular exercise but is strained by sudden, extreme exertion. These abilities decline so slightly over most adult decades that few people notice their loss.

World's Record for Centenarians Can you sprint 100 meters in less than 30 seconds? Almost until his death in 2019, this man, Hidekichi Miyazaki, could. Maybe you need more practice. Hidekichi had been running for 105 years!

The one domain in which early losses of motor abilities is noticeable is sports. Some professional athletes are "old" at age 30. The aging of the body is most evident in skills that require strength, agility, and speed: Gymnasts, boxers, and basketball players are among the athletes who benefit from youth but who experience slowdowns by age 25. Fine motor skills endure longer, as evident with golfers, billiard players, and archers. The intellectual and emotional gains of adulthood may compensate; some older adults are more valuable teammates than athletes a decade younger.

For gross motor skills particularly, muscle strength is crucial. Muscles all weaken with age, a condition called *sarcopenia* first mentioned in Chapter 4. Each muscle develops as it is used—some people have strong hands but weak legs, or vice versa. Since internal muscles keep a person alive, they function well in old age unless pollution, inactivity, or drug abuse has weakened them. Many older adults who never leave their beds still have strong hearts, even though their legs may become too weak to support them.

In considering motor skills, we focus most on skeletal muscles, connected to the bones and activated by motor neurons. They signal that the muscle should move, in a rhythmic gait when walking, in a directed reach when picking something up, and so on.

If the muscles and neurotransmitters can no longer do a basic task, as when hands picking up a cup shake, or when feet shuffle instead of walk, that is a sign that something is seriously wrong—Parkinson's disease perhaps, or a brain tumor. Muscles, like the rest of the body, slow down with age, but people of every age need to keep moving and continue to do so even at age 100. (See Career Alert.)

Putting It All Together

Increasingly with age, all of a person's senses and motor abilities combine to improve perception and cognition. Many scientists go beyond cross-modal perception and motor skill ability. They find evidence for **embodied cognition**, that body sensations and movements affect thoughts and behavior even when people are unaware of it (Foglia & Wilson, 2013).

embodied cognition An idea or concept that is expressed in the body as well as with words. This connection between mind and body is expressed in many phrases, postures, and actions.

CAREER ALERT | The Physical Therapist

Almost every adult will, at some point, need physical therapy. Bodies age, and with aging comes reduced physical ability. Moreover, dozens of diseases, including diabetes, arthritis, osteoporosis, and heart disease, affect strength, agility, and the senses. People are living longer, but get less exercise in their daily work. Cars, riding lawnmowers, and vacuum cleaners have replaced walking, pushing a mower, sweeping the floor; much employment involves sitting and operating a machine.

Thus, for many reasons, physical therapy is among the fastest growing occupations in the United States today. The U.S. Bureau of Labor Statistics projects a 25-percent increase over the next 10 years in the number of *physical therapists* (PTs). That does not include the closely related, and also expanding, profession of *occupational therapy* (OT).

Salaries are high — in 2019 the median annual salary was $89,440. Education requirements are also high. A physical therapist needs to know how to advise people with every kind of disability.

I admire those in PT, in part because of my personal experience. I had very minor surgery (one toe kept sticking up, making it hard to wear dress shoes, so the bone needed to be realigned). The surgeon warned me that it would be painful, advising me not to walk much for weeks. I was defiant, discarding most of my pain medication and walking two days after the surgery.

I reluctantly followed the surgeon's advice to see a physical therapist. I was ready for the PT to laugh and tell me that physical therapy was for legs, arms, and backs, not for toes. But instead she used special lotion and massage on my toes and taught me six exercises to do every day. When I told her that I was amazed that she knew exercises for a toe, she explained that she was taught what to do for every part of the body, and added, "Your toe is connected to the rest of you."

I realized that she knew about my whole body, and that every part might affect the rest of it. I needed her to help me make sure the total body would continue to do what I wanted it to do. A much-needed profession, indeed.

Neuroscientists suggest that sensations in the hindbrain that never reach the prefrontal cortex nonetheless affect emotions and judgments (Damasio, 2005). Much of this is captured in our speech.

Consider these metaphors.

- Hearing: An idea makes *alarms* ring, or *sounds* great.
- Vision: We see the *light*, something is *rosy* or *dark*, someone is *dazzled*, or *blinded*.
- Touch: We have *rough* day; someone is a *smooth* operator. Reach out to *touch* someone; we need a *pat* on the back or a *shoulder* to cry on.
- Smell: The *sweet* smell of success, an idea *stinks*, something smells *fishy*.
- Taste: The past made us *bitter*; we have *soured* on a dream.
- Proprioception: A *balanced* approach; *stand* your ground; something is *shaky*.
- Motor actions: A *heavy* heart, don't take this *lightly*, *grasp* a new idea, *kick* someone who is down, *walk* in my shoes.

Embodied cognition goes beyond recognition that our speech is peppered with metaphors from the senses and motor skills. The idea is that bodies and brains are intertwined, that our senses communicate ideas, that "sensorimotor factors serve as the groundwork for cognition" (Costello & Bloesch, 2017).

As evident throughout this chapter, senses and motor skills are intimately related to the thoughts and social connections of the rest of development. As you remember from Chapter 2, Piaget called the first stage of cognition "sensorimotor." A strong foundation of senses and motor skills endures and protects body and mind lifelong.

Every disability risks isolation and illness. Individuals and communities need to protect abilities and compensate — with technology as well as the other senses — for losses. Exercise of the body and of the senses protects the mind and the spirit.

Thus, the everyday miracle of senses and motor skills is not only worth celebrating, it is worth protecting. Remember the opening anecdote: I hope Peter and I continue to hear our names, see each other, and walk down the street — and if those abilities fade, we need hearing aids, glasses, exercise. If we chance to meet at age 100, we might again chat about nothing special.

WHAT HAVE YOU LEARNED?

1. How do the immature motor skills of the infant aid in bonding to caregivers?

2. What reflexes protect infant survival?

3. When does an infant develop gross motor skills?

4. What fine motor skills appear before age 2?

5. What are the benefits of interactive play?

6. Why does handwriting take years to develop?

7. What athletic skills peak in early adulthood, and what ones later? Why?

8. How does aging affect the development of muscles, and of fine motor skills?

9. What is the connection between mind and body evident in embodied cognition?

SUMMARY

The First Two Years

1. Newborn humans are altricial in motor skills but precocial in senses. All the senses function at birth, attuned especially to the social world.

2. The ears are shaped and connected to the cochlea in the brain, transmitting sound waves even before birth. An infant's hearing is sensitive to the sound of voices, especially to their own mother's voice speaking the native language.

3. Infants look avidly at everything they see, first at lights but soon at faces about a foot away. Movement captures attention.

4. Touch, taste, and smell all function in early infancy. Experiences quickly build into expectations, which makes the first two years crucial for lifelong preferences.

5. Cross-modal perception, when several senses each inform the other to recognize objects, is evident in infancy. This may be the reason kangaroo care protects the health of fragile newborns.

From Age 2 to 25

6. Hearing may be at its most acute during mid-adolescence. However, many older adolescents and emerging adults listen to music so loud that it is deafening, with the consequences of hearing loss experienced decades later.

7. Vision changes at puberty, as many children become nearsighted teenagers. Humans rely on vision more than on the other senses; from age 2 on people read others' emotions by looking at facial expressions, especially eyes.

8. Touch is comforting, exciting, or aversive depending on experiences and lessons learned in childhood. Cultures and individuals vary in what is perceived as appropriate touch, especially sexual touch.

9. Smell and taste are profoundly affected by experience. For some adults, smell is a sexual turn-on or turn-off.

10. Interpretation and habituation are crucial for the senses of pain and temperature. Proprioception is another sense that may be vital. It develops in childhood, allowing adults to keep their balance and to keep from bumping into each other.

Age 25 and Beyond

11. All the senses fade with age, but plasticity, cognition, and technology can compensate. This is apparent with hearing, which decreases notably, particularly in men, but can be remedied with hearing aids.

12. Visual losses begin with the eyeball changing shape so that reading glasses are often needed. Many adults develop cataracts, which can be corrected by routine surgery, and some experience glaucoma, pressure that is relieved with eye drops.

13. Touch, taste, and smell also fade with age. Each of these may need awareness and compensation. It is difficult to know how age affects pain: It seems that more aches appear but that the sense of pain is reduced.

Motor Skills: Birth to Old Age

14. At birth, human motor skills are altricial, with many survival and instinctual reflexes but little deliberate control. Gross and fine motor skills advance as soon as maturation allows.

15. Infants move and control their bodies as best they can, sitting up and grasping objects at 6 months, walking and using finger movements by a year.

16. In play with peers, not only motor skills but also social skills develop. This is evident in rough-and-tumble play.

17. By age 10, the major limitations are body size and practice. Adolescents develop many skills, including athletic abilities, penmanship, and dance moves.

18. Generally people are at their strongest in early adulthood and become progressively weaker by late adulthood, as muscles shrink. However, practice is more influential than maturation alone.

19. Many words and phrases suggest that movement, the senses, and emotions are closely connected, as the term embodied cognition attests.

KEY TERMS

sensation (p. 149)
perception (p. 149)
precocial (p. 149)
altricial (p. 149)
binocular vision (p. 152)

cross-modal sensations (p. 154)
synesthesia (p. 155)
proprioception (p. 162)
presbycusis (p. 163)
presbyopia (p. 164)

cataracts (p. 165)
glaucoma (p. 165)
macular degeneration (p. 165)
gross motor skills (p. 169)
fine motor skills (p. 170)

rough-and-tumble play (p. 175)
embodied cognition (p. 177)

APPLICATIONS

1. Observe three infants (whom you do not know) in public places such as a store, playground, or bus. Look closely at body size and motor skills, especially how much control each baby has over their legs and hands. From that, estimate the baby's age in months, and then ask the caregiver how old the infant is.

2. Go to a playground or another place where young children play. Note the motor skills that the children demonstrate, including abilities and inabilities, and keep track of age and sex. What differences do you see among the children?

3. Compare play spaces and school design for children in different neighborhoods—ideally, urban, suburban, and rural areas. Note size, safety, and use. How might this affect children's health and learning?

4. Compensating for sensory losses is difficult because it involves learning new habits. To better understand the experience, reduce your hearing or vision for a day by wearing earplugs or dark glasses that let in only bright lights. (Use caution and common sense: Don't drive a car while wearing earplugs or cross streets while wearing dark glasses.) Report on your emotions, the responses of others, and your conclusions.

ESPECIALLY FOR ANSWER

Response for Nurses and Pediatricians (from p. 150) Urge the parents to begin learning sign language and investigating the possibility of cochlear implants. Babbling has a biological basis and begins at a specified time in deaf as well as hearing babies. If their infant can hear, sign language does no harm. If the child is deaf, however, lack of communication may be destructive.

OBSERVATION QUIZ ANSWERS

Answer to Observation Quiz (from p. 169) Jumping up, with a 3-month age-range for acquisition. The reason is that the older an infant is, the more impact both nature and nurture have.

Answer to Observation Quiz (from p. 174) Proprioception. All four seem to take balance for granted, including the girl at the right whose feet dangle but seems in no risk of falling.

CHAPTER 7

Memory and Information Processing

The dentist said that Bethany (our daughter, then age 10) needed braces. I was surprised: I thought she was well-formed in every way, including her teeth. But many of our friends were parents of children with braces, so we followed their example and the advice of our dentist.

In retrospect, we should have waited a few years. She remembers throwing her retainer in the trash when she emptied her lunch tray at school; I remember not being diligent at reminding her to brush her teeth and wear that retainer. Instead, my attention was focused on a discussion my husband and I were having about whether to have a fourth child. I thought yes, fondly remembering my joy with my babies; he was more hesitant, remembering his youth in a family where dentistry was a major expense. He asked me whether we could afford a fourth round of orthodontia.

Fast forward, we had a fourth child, and she turned out not to need braces. Our oldest daughter and I have opposite memories of her braces: I remember my negligence, and she remembers hers. (I still think her teeth are fine; she decided recently to try again, paying for adult orthodontia herself.) It is not unusual for people to have different memories of the past. I also remember how our second child felt at our first child's braces: She was jealous, eager to get braces, too. She remembers nothing of her jealousy.

However, my mother's reaction at the time is the one I remember best.

"Bethany needs braces? No one in my family ever needed braces," Mom told me.

That triggered a memory of mine, when I was 5. I replied, "Glen [my brother, six years older] had braces."

"No," Mom said. "He never did."

I asked Glen.

"Yes, I had braces for two years," he remembered.

This chapter explores many aspects of memory, including my retrospective fondness for infants, my husband's prospective worries about the cost of another child, my mother's selective memory of her son's braces. As you will read, everyone has personal memories and reactions, even about the same thing.

What Will You Know?

1. Do children with ADHD have problems in how they read faces?
2. Can people remember anything they experienced before age 2?
3. Is it true that the more you know, the more you learn?
4. Should witnesses to a crime be believed?

Studying Memory

Hundreds of thousands of studies have led to two new conclusions about memory:

1. Memory is not one ability but many: explicit and implicit, semantic and episodic, flashbulb and face, procedural and prospective, sensory and source, and more.
2. Memory abilities vary lifelong. They are not fixed at birth nor the same for everyone; personal experiences, genetic strengths, private motives, and, of course, age, matter for every kind of memory.

Most of this chapter illustrates these two facts by describing the development of memory at various ages. At each age, some types and variations of memory are explained, but the basics are true lifelong—many kinds, much diversity, changing from one year to the next, always crucial, because "just about everything we do or say depends on the smooth and efficient operation of our memory systems" (Schacter, 1996, p. 2).

information processing A perspective that compares human thinking processes, by analogy, to computer analysis of data, including sensory input, connections, stored memories, and output.

Information Processing

Before diving deep into the memory ocean, we need to understand how memory became a pivotal topic in human development. It began with the approach to cognitive science called **information processing**.

Like a Computer

The term *information processing* came from what computers do, processing vast quantities of data, with input, then analysis, and finally output. The human mind also processes information. Brain activity varies depending on strength and location of activated neurons, influenced by age, genes, and history.

Technological advances, including digital cameras with millisecond measurements, computer programs that crunch a million numbers instantly, detailed molecular analysis, and stunning neurological imagery, have revealed brain activity never before known. That allows scientists inspired by the cognitive revolution to go beyond Piaget's stages or Vygotsky's generalizations (Dobson et al., 2018; Liben & Muller, 2015; Núñez et al., 2019).

Steps in Processing

Like computers, people can (1) perceive large amounts of information (as described in Chapter 6). They then (2) select relevant units of information (as a search engine does); (3) analyze (as software programs do); and (4) express conclusions so that another person can understand them (as a computer printout might). By tracing the paths and links between these four steps (attention,

Fly Me to the Moon Before computer programs, all information-processing was done by gifted mathematicians. Here is Katherine Johnson at her desk in 1962, one of the African American "Hidden Figures" whose calculations were essential for early space flight. Six years later, John Glenn insisted that she personally confirm the computer output before he agreed to the first moon landing in 1969.

input, program, and output), scientists can better understand cognition. Computers can encode, store, and retrieve more material with greater speed than any person, but they cannot match the depth and creativity of human memory.

Strategies

Processing information depends on memory. All four steps are needed: Humans need to (1) perceive information, (2) encode it, (3) store it, and (4) retrieve it. Because we all have "islands of memory in a sea of forgetfulness" (Baddeley, 2020), strategies for memory are more crucial than knowing facts (Lemaire, 2017). In computers, those strategies are programs that operate automatically and invariably. For humans, however, strategies do not appear suddenly nor affect all data at once. Their use, and efficiency, may be the crucial developmental difference between infants, children, adults, and older adults.

Siegler and Math

Although complex, innovative, state-of-the-art technology is used by information-processing scientists, this research is often quite practical. Robert Siegler provided a useful understanding of day-by-day strategies used by children as they learn math (Siegler & Chen, 2008; Siegler et al., 2011).

Understanding numbers, for instance, develops slowly. Young children can count: Many 3-year-olds have memorized the numbers from 1 to 10. But understanding that each number represents an object takes longer: Asked to count five cookies, a young child might be mystified or may simply repeat the memorized list. They do not grasp one-to-one correspondence, so they might say there are nine cookies because they pointed at the cookies while they recited numbers, and they were saying "nine" when they finished pointing.

Later, they may know that each cookie gets one number, but adding two more cookies to a group of three cookies requires counting them all: The idea of 2 + 3 equals 5, or even starting at 3 and saying 4 and then 5, is beyond them. They need 1-2-3-4-5, usually with a finger pointing to each one. It is easier if the cookies are arranged in a straight line; if they are in a circle, the child might not know where to begin and end.

Ebb and Flow

We know this from Siegler's research: Children do not suddenly grasp the logic of the number system. Instead, their understanding accrues gradually, with new and better strategies for calculation tried, ignored, half-used, abandoned, and finally adopted. Siegler compared the acquisition of knowledge to waves on a beach when the tide is rising. There is substantial ebb and flow; eventually a new level is reached.

Another math example is estimating where a number might fall on the number line, such as where the number 53 would be placed on a line from zero to 100. Proficiency gradually builds, predicting math skills years later (Schneider et al., 2018). Many information-processing experts advocate giving 5-year-olds practice with simple number lines so that, by age 10, they can do multiplication and division.

Similarly, understanding fractions (e.g., that 3/16 is smaller than 1/4) is connected to a previous grasp of the relationship between one number and another. A kindergartner who understands where to put a number on the number line is likely, five years later, to be a fifth-grader who has a good grasp of how one fraction compares to another.

Note how this relates to memory. It is not that suddenly a new idea is presented and then remembered. If that were true, teachers would simply explain a new bit

VIDEO: Arithmetic Strategies: The Research of Robert Siegler demonstrates how children acquire math understanding.

A Boy in Memphis Moziah Bridges (known as Mo Morris) created colorful bowties, which he first traded for rocks in elementary school. He then created his own company (Mo's Bows) at age 9, selling $300,000 worth of ties to major retailers by age 14. He is shown here with his mother, who encouraged his math ability and entrepreneurship.

ABC/Photofest

ESPECIALLY FOR Teachers of 3-Year-Olds What should you do if a child counts 5-6-9-8? (see answer, page 211)

Learn more about how children are affected by dyslexia in **VIDEO: Dyslexia: Expert and Children.**

of information and then students would understand it. But that does not happen, as every parent knows when a child answers "I forgot" in response to the parent's "I told you to … bring your lunch box home . . . say thank you to Grandpa . . . not go out of this yard."

Instead of occurring instantly, experiences gradually form new habits and insights. One experience, a taste of a new food, for instance, does not change a person's memory of that food. Just as waves gradually reach high tide, repeated tastings accumulate: Adults prefer tastes and smells that they frequently experienced in childhood, even if they no longer remember any childhood meal. That is information processing.

Children with Learning Differences

Another major set of practical contributions from information processing occurs regarding learning difficulties. For instance, *dyslexia* (unusual difficulty in reading) was assumed to be primarily a visual problem, a logical assumption since looking at letters is visual. But information-processing research discovered that dyslexia begins with hearing. Children are slow to read if they do not hear spoken differences (Steinbrink et al., 2014).

Knowing this, speech therapists focus on articulation during early childhood, years before children develop dyslexia. Repeated practice hearing and talking, emphasizing final consonants, distinctions between words that sound similar, and subtle spoken differences (such as between an *s* and a *z*) all foster later reading.

Note the importance of repeated practice. That is how memory builds, in this case the child's hearing, watching the therapists' lips, and then saying the sounds. This is sensory memory, a crucial foundation for reading. You probably have noticed that many children at first say the words, in a whisper, to themselves: That helps them read.

In another example, it has long been recognized that children with *attention-deficit/hyperactivity disorder (ADHD)* have difficulty in social contexts: They find it hard to learn in class with other students, to obey their parents, to make friends.

Information-processing research has led to the discovery that certain brain circuits (called *fronto-striatal systems*) do not function normally in children with ADHD. Consequently, some children are impaired when reading facial expressions and interpreting voice tones in order to understand others' emotions (Uekermann et al., 2010).

For this reason, a child with ADHD may not know whether their father's "Come here" is an angry command or a loving suggestion. No wonder adults consider those children disobedient. A child with ADHD may miss the clues that tell if a classmate is hostile or friendly, or when it is time to listen quietly and when it is time to talk. Information processing suggests remediation: If the specific brain function can be activated, or if children can find other ways to understand emotions, they learn more, obey more, and gain friends.

The effort to help children learn strategies to process information is ongoing—no obvious treatment is effective for every child—but intervention for children with many disorders benefits from information-processing research (Sonuga-Barke & Cortese, 2018; Rapport et al., 2013).

Educators and therapists find that teaching specific skills, connected to particular neurological areas, overcomes disorders. And memory is often crucial. As information processing has discovered, each type of memory at each age, repeated until it becomes established, provides a foundation for later learning.

Happy Reading Those large prism glasses keep the letters from jumping around on the page, a boon for this 8-year-old French boy. Unfortunately, each child with dyslexia needs individualized treatment: These glasses help some, but not most, children who find reading difficult.

BSIP/UIG/Getty Images

1. What are the two facts about memory that everyone agrees on?

2. How is information processing in people like information processing in a computer?

3. What do computers do better than the human mind?

4. What does the human mind do better than computers?

5. How does Siegler's metaphor of waves on a beach describe knowledge of math?

6. How has information processing helped children with dyslexia?

7. What information might be misunderstood by children with ADHD?

Memory in Infancy

Memory in the first two years was once assumed to be completely absent. Then an explosion of research asserted the opposite. As you will see, both those contrasting conclusions are true, depending on which memory (implicit or explicit) is measured.

Developmentalists now see extensive evidence of early memories. Chapter 8 will present details of language development before age 1. For now, all you need to know is that the first spoken word is the culmination of a year of memories. Hearing speech, or seeing gestures, in the early months leads to the language their family speaks, as well as to lifelong unconscious memories.

Infant Amnesia?

Freud and Piaget thought that people remember nothing from the early years of their lives. This was called *infant amnesia*, an idea that is not totally wrong.

Two memory researchers explained:

> We are the proud parents of a little girl who just turned 2. . . . we threw a party with all the trimmings (Elmo birthday cards, presents, sparkly birthday hats, and a chocolate cake topped with two pink candles). When we dimmed the lights and lit the candles, the birthday girl burst into tears. . . . she will not explicitly remember the "birthday candle incident" when she is an adult. This phenomenon, in which adults are unable to remember specific events from our first few years of life, was named infantile amnesia by Sigmund Freud.
>
> [Josselyn & Frankland, 2012, p. 423]

Selective Amnesia As we grow older, we forget about spitting up, nursing, crying, and almost everything else from our early years. However, strong emotions (love, fear, mistrust) leave lifelong traces.

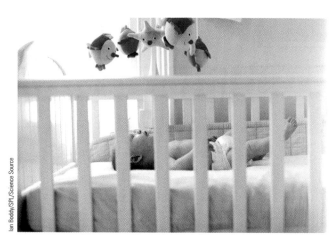

Ian Boddy/SPL/Science Source

He Remembers! Infants are fascinated by moving objects within a few feet of their eyes—that's why parents buy mobiles for cribs and why Rovee-Collier tied a string to a mobile and a baby's leg to test memory. Babies not in her experiment, like this one, sometimes flail their limbs to make their cribs shake and thus make their mobiles move. Piaget's stage of "making interesting sights last" is evident to every careful observer.

⬤ **Observation Quiz** Do you see anything here that is less than ideal? (see answer, page 211) ↑

reminder session An experience (sight, word, smell, and so forth) that evokes a memory, which was not available before the reminder.

macmillan learning

VIDEO: Contingency Learning in Young Infants shows Carolyn Rovee-Collier's procedure for studying instrumental learning during infancy.

This is quite different from adult memory. Those proud parents wrote, "This event seems permanently etched in our memories, and we can vividly recall many details of the not-so-happy birthday" (Josselyn & Frankland, 2012, p. 423). That divergence between adult and infant memory is the reason the term "infant amnesia" was used.

Research confirms that young children recall very few facts or details of early events, especially when asked to put memories into words. A 6-month-old who had major surgery, for instance, cannot recount anything about that event when asked at age 2, or at any later time. By contrast, if major surgery occurs in adulthood, it is remembered for months, years, decades. My tonsils were removed when I was 20; I still remember some aspects of that event.

Unfortunately, the term "infant amnesia" implies that infants remember nothing. We now know that infants can remember a great deal.

Remember to Kick

Evidence comes from a scientist who studied babies too young to grab, sit, or crawl, much less talk about their memories (Rovee-Collier, 1987, 1990; Rovee-Collier et al., 2013).

Infants aged 2 months to 6 months lay on their backs in a crib. One end of a ribbon was tied to a mobile above them and the other end to their foot. Virtually every baby made random kicks and realized that kicking made the mobile move. That led to vigorous, frequent kicking, and laughter. So far, no memory was needed: Self-activated movement is immediately reinforcing.

Could such young infants remember that kicking made the mobile move? Yes! A day later when their foot was tied again to the mobile, some 2-month-olds quickly kicked. So did 6-month-olds two weeks after the kick/mobile experience.

Particularly interesting were the results for the 3-month-olds. If the mobile-and-ribbon apparatus was reinstalled and tied to their foot one week later, most started to kick immediately. But when other 3-month-old infants were retested after a two-week interlude, they began with only random kicks. Apparently they had forgotten. Amnesia? Not quite.

The lead researcher in the mobile experiments thought of a way to awaken memory. She gave 3-month-olds a reminder session before being retested (Rovee-Collier & Hayne, 1987). A **reminder session** is any experience that helps recollection.

In this particular reminder session, at the age when infants had forgotten how to make the mobile move (for 3-month-olds, two weeks after their first experience), babies watched the mobile move but were *not* tied to it and could *not* kick. The next day, when they were again connected to the identical mobile, some kicked vigorously.

Apparently, watching the mobile on the previous day had revived memory. The information was stored in their brains, but they needed processing time to retrieve it. Later research revealed that memory is strengthened by repeated reminders and experiences. Factors that seem irrelevant (such as the pattern on crib sheets, the exact appearance of the mobile) matter (Rovee-Collier & Cuevas, 2009).

The overall conclusion is that, in the first years of life, babies remember. They learn from their own movements, from watching other people, even from picture books and videos (Hayne & Simcock, 2009). The dendrites and neurons of several areas of the brain change. Early memory comes from old parts of the brain—including the cerebellum and the amygdala (Vöhringer et al., 2018). Those brain parts develop in the first months of life.

That is one explanation for the phenomenon called *déjà vu*, when people suddenly feel, upon entering a new place, that they have been there before. Memory, reminders, and unconscious brain traces begin early in life.

Explicit and Implicit Memory

To understand why some people thought infants had no memory and others disagreed, it is useful to recognize the distinction between implicit and explicit memory. **Explicit memory** refers to memories that are verbal, easily recalled, and conscious. **Implicit memory** is not accessible to words and conscious thought. Explicit memory is fragile or absent during infancy; implicit memory is strong even in the first weeks of life.

Research on adults regarding this implicit/explicit distinction often begins with *priming*, which is putting an idea or word in someone's mind, distracting them, and later asking them a seemingly unrelated request, such as to write or do something that might reflect that implicit memory.

For example, suppose you must fill in the blanks on some words, including KI__ __, an explicit task. One study of the *weapons effect* (when seeing a gun primes aggression) found that adults who were primed by viewing photos of gun-toting criminals, soldiers, or police were more likely to write KILL than KISS (Benjamin & Bushman, 2016).

Implicit memory is typically rooted in a different part of the brain from explicit memory (Norman & Schacter, 2014). Implicit memory is strong lifelong; explicit memory improves markedly every year of childhood beginning at about age 2 and decreases very gradually over the years of adulthood.

Procedural Memory

One kind of implicit memory is *procedural memory*, also called *motor memory* because it is memory for movement. Many motor skills, such as riding a bike, hammering a nail, and knitting a stitch, are implicit—if they have become habitual.

For example, do you remember how to tie your shoes? Of course you do, implicitly. You can do it in the dark, and you usually tie without thinking, a useful skill if you are talking to someone or planning your route as you don your running shoes.

However, can you describe the process explicitly, for someone who has never tied shoes? Probably not. To explain it, you need to tie your shoes, watching and narrating what you do. You might miss some crucial detail. Words fail; implicit memory does not.

Habits Endure

People of all ages develop habits that are implicit and therefore hard to break. This is true even in infancy.

For example, the fastest, most efficient way for an infant to crawl is on "all fours" with hands and knees. But many babies start out some other way, "bear-walking" (hands and feet), scooting (on their bottoms and hands), lopsided (one side moving, the other side dragging along). Some never crawl but "cruise," holding on to tables and chairs while walking. All of these alternates originate when 6- to 10-month-olds first try to move. Some babies quickly figure out that conventional crawling is more efficient, but some continue crawling oddly, because their early motor memory has become habitual.

For children and adults, implicit motor memory is evident in the swing of a bat or racket, in the finger action of a musician, or the feet of an experienced driver (who might slam the floor while sitting in the passenger seat if they see a sudden need to brake). Some athletes have learned one way to kick, catch, throw, or swing, and later realize that another way is better. At that point it is hard to learn the new move: Implicit memory interferes.

explicit memory Memory that can be recalled in the conscious mind, usually factual memories that are expressed with words.

implicit memory Memory that is not verbal, often unconscious. Many motor and emotional memories are implicit.

ESPECIALLY FOR Students If you want to remember something that you learn in class for the rest of your life, what should you do? (see answer, page 211)

Dance the Damage Away Memory for movement, music, and touch endures when semantic memory does not, as these elderly couples illustrate. The pair in downtown Hanoi *(right)* have much to forget about their childhood during the war in Vietnam, and the couple in Florida *(left)* (he is 86, she 75) are learning dance in a class for elders with memory loss.

A final example arises when you watch your elders dance. New dance moves emerge with each generation. Teenagers practice various regional and historical dances, salsa and the jitterbug, the twist and tango, jerking and krumping, typically at home with a mirror, talking to themselves to harness explicit memory. Then implicit memory takes over; no need for conscious thought about whether to move the hips sideways, or back to front, or in circles. Decades later, middle-aged parents dance with dated moves, as their laughing teenagers tell them.

Emotional Memory

Another type of implicit memory is *emotional memory*, which starts in infancy and endures lifelong. An adult might be drawn to one stranger or feel a chill at first sight of another one. In both cases, implicit memories rise up, for reasons hidden from the conscious mind. Likewise, people prefer certain colors, shapes, tastes, sounds, and smells without knowing why. Many people find it hard to sleep in a dark room without a light on, or in a secure house without checking the locks, because of emotional memory.

Some of my students told me that their mothers made them wear pajamas at night because they might need to leave the house quickly in a fire, and put on clean underwear every morning in case they were in a car crash and taken to the hospital! As adults, they realize how illogical that is, but the fear (an emotional memory) endures and they cannot sleep naked, even in a hot room.

Think again about the example of early surgery, which 2-year-olds seem to have forgotten completely. If infants are frequently subjected to painful medical procedures, they may, years later, be phobic of hospitals, doctors, and injections, without knowing why (Noel et al., 2015). Similarly, infants who are often frightened by yelling or abuse may, decades later, find it hard to love and trust anyone.

Positive early memories also persist. Sounds, sights, and smells are remembered implicitly. Memories of people endure. Newborns quickly recognize their caregivers by face, voice, and smell (Sullivan et al., 2011). If the same loving person provided care and comfort every day in infancy, and then left for a year, their return would cause less fear than would the sudden appearance of a stranger.

Infant memory for caregivers continues to solidify month by month (Mullally & Maguire, 2014). Babies smile broader, laugh louder, and are comforted more quickly by their favorite persons compared to strangers who are equally solicitous. Indeed, by about 9 months, a friendly stranger might provoke tears, not laughter.

I can confirm this. I once went jogging, leaving my youngest daughter, Sarah, then 5 months old, with my oldest daughter, Bethany, and her best friend, Julie, both adolescents. Sarah was asleep when I left, but she awoke, crying. Bethany and Julie tried to comfort her, but I heard wailing as I approached the house, sweating profusely. Sweat did not bother Sarah; she quieted as soon as she was in my arms.

Bethany asked Julie, "How did Mom do that?," and Julie shook her head. They were bewildered, since Bethany had done exactly what I did. Apparently, deep in her being, Sarah remembered me. She still does. We hug each other in greeting, a comforting touch that evokes implicit memory. Do you hug anyone? Does someone try to hug you, but you resist? If you do not know why, consider childhood.

WHAT HAVE YOU LEARNED?

1. What do people usually forget from infancy?

2. What do people usually remember from infancy?

3. What is a reminder session?

4. How did Rovee-Collier prove that early memories exist?

5. What does déjà vu suggest about memory?

6. How does hugging in adulthood reflect early memories?

Memory in Childhood

Some memories from infancy, particularly implicit memories, endure lifelong. But other aspects of memory seem to begin at about age 2 and then continue to develop. The youngest children need to be reminded to put on socks before shoes, to brush teeth before bed, to use the bathroom before their bladder suddenly releases. Older children remember to do so.

Each type of memory follows a particular pattern. Young children learn some things quickly and well (vocabulary, for instance) but have a harder time with other things. For example, children do best with visible, present memories, not disembodied ones. A 3-year-old might name the colors of a dozen crayons in front of them but cannot name even six colors when none are visible.

Young brains can connect one current event with another but have trouble distinguishing reality from imagination. Children might believe that a dream is real, for instance, becoming terrified by nightmares because the memory of the dream invades the memory in real life.

Working Memory

The advances of memory from age 2 to 20 are most evident in **working memory**, which is memory that is active at any given moment. Working memory is a temporary and conscious manipulation of various bits of information.

working memory Memory that is active at any given moment.

Short- and Long-Term Memory

At first the term "working memory" was thought to be the same as *short-term memory*, which is memory for whatever was just heard or seen (Atkinson & Shiffrin, 1968). Short-term memory is measured by presenting a number of items (words, numbers, letters) and asking the person to repeat them back. If the list is too long, some elements fade from the mind before the person has a chance to repeat them.

For example, many intelligence tests ask a child to repeat numbers in sequence, first two numbers, then three, then four, and so on. As they mature, children improve in how much they recall. This example of short-term memory is often used in IQ tests, because it correlates with advancing cognition.

A problem appeared when researchers tried to determine the boundary between short- and long-term memory. How short is short? A few seconds? A minute? And how long is long? If a memory lasted two minutes and then decayed, that was called long-term memory, which seemed odd. Some memories decay instantly (very short), some memories endure for 100 years (very long term), and most are between the two. Instead of those terms, working memory (which may include aspects of both short- and long-term memory) currently is considered the most important measure.

Measuring Memory

Working memory requires more than repeating what was just heard; it requires that items can be connected to each other and analyzed (Krasny-Pacini et al., 2018, p. 76). One oft-used measure is called the *n-back*, when a person must remember a previous item on a list. For example, if the person hears 4-8-7-3-9, and is asked for the number that was two (the *n*) before the 9, they would say 7.

Many researchers now believe that working memory might include information that was learned months ago, recalled from storage (Barrouillet & Camos, 2012; Miyake & Shah, 1999; Schweppe & Rummer, 2014). If a person remembers many bits (some embedded from long-term, some recent from short-term), that signifies a large working memory.

A child's working memory is quite small. Typical 5-year-olds can remember three digits in sequence (e.g., 4-8-2) and might have trouble with a working memory challenge, such as saying those three in reverse order. Because young children have limited working memory, they say "I never said that" or "I always knew that," even when neither is true.

Adolescent short-term memory is longer. It might be seven digits (e.g., 7-3-5-2-9-1-6), with tests of working memory such as asking repetition of only odd numbers (7-3-5-9-1) or rearranging them all by size (1-2-3-5-6-7-9). These examples are only possibilities: Tests and memories vary a great deal. However, progress is universal: From age 2 to 20, those at both the bottom and the top of the memory ladder improve every year in short-term, long-term, and working memory.

The Brain in Childhood

As you read in Chapter 5, with maturation, brain size increases, especially before age 6. By middle childhood, most brain growth, and most memory capacity, has already occurred. From then on, new dendrites, synapses, and stronger connections, between one part of the brain and another, allow memory advances. New memories become possible, older memories become more durable, and working memory improves every year.

Myelination also increases in childhood, allowing faster encoding and less decay. As always, the brain responds to experience: New projections appear in the hippocampus, with better connections to the cortex (Ghetti & Bunge, 2012; Riggins et al., 2018).

Instead of one memory site in the brain, there are dozens. Some areas are for one sense, such as for touch and for smell, but some memories are located in a particular neuron. For instance, the region for touch has specific neurons dedicated to each body part; the area for names has one spot for the names of fruits, another for the names of tools, and another for names of close family members (which explains why mothers sometimes call their son by their daughter's name but never call him a banana.) One book describes 14 distinct types of memory, each with subcategories (Slotnick, 2017).

The content, structure, and connection of each region of the brain depend, in part, on experience. For example, children who learn to play the violin have

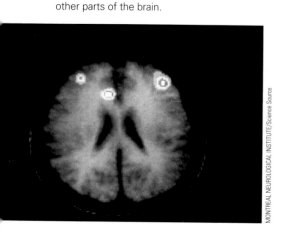

Many Memories The lit areas are regions of the brain that are activated when a person is asked to remember. Note that all of the activated areas are in the prefrontal cortex (top of picture), not in areas for sensory input at the bottom (vision, occipital lobe), sides (audition, temporal lobes), or middle (touch, parietal lobe). Thinking begins with sensations, but input is forgotten unless it is transferred to other parts of the brain.

MONTREAL NEUROLOGICAL INSTITUTE/Science Source

more connections in the brain region for fingers. Indeed, the structure of the brain is affected by musical training, as shown by a study that began with 5-year-olds who all had similar brains. Then some learned to play an instrument for two years, and at that point, their brains differed from their peers (Habibi et al., 2018).

After age 6, three of the four lobes of the brain have reached almost full size, but one lobe still shows marked growth. That is the frontal cortex, especially the most forward part, the prefrontal cortex. Consequently, adults are better than children at planning ahead (remembering what groceries to buy for a future dinner) and coordinating distinct thoughts (remembering past learning, future goals, present needs).

Semantic Versus Episodic Memory

One way to understand the components of memory begins by noticing that some children are adept at academic learning, scoring high on achievement tests, and others are not. These abilities are distinct: High scorers are not necessarily best at recalling details of their personal experiences. When asked, "What did you do this summer?" some children might be able to provide only a few facts, such as "I went to Texas"; others might talk for hours.

This is an example of the difference between **semantic memory** and **episodic memory**. The word *semantic* comes from *sema*, the Greek word for sign or symbol. Piaget wrote that the onset of symbolic thought is what separates the thinking of infants (sensorimotor) and young children.

Memory researchers find the same thing: As children become more verbal, their semantic memory improves. Further, once children's brains allow them to be more deliberate and less impulsive (see Chapter 5), they are more selective, better able to remember the facts and definition adults teach them.

The word *episodic* comes from the word *episode*, originally an interlude or transition in Greek drama or music. For the Greeks, episodes could be understood by themselves, although they were connected to what came before and after. A scholar named Tulving (Tulving, 1983; Tulving et al., 1972) was first to use semantic and episodic to contrast memories that were primarily verbal and factual, which he called "semantic," from memories that were sensorial (often visual), emotional, and personal, which he called "episodic."

For example, semantic memory includes:

- Rain is wet.
- 2 plus 2 equals 4.
- This book was written by Kathleen Berger.

Episodic memory includes:

- how drenched you got in a recent sudden downpour;
- your anxiety at a math exam; and
- the time you wanted to study this chapter but forgot where you put the book!

Tulving's terms are now standard in memory research.

Background Knowledge
Crucial for semantic memory is the **knowledge base**, which is basic knowledge. The knowledge base varies from subject to subject: Someone well versed in basketball, for instance, may not have much knowledge in astronomy. Essentially, the more a person knows, the better able they are to remember new semantic information, because they can link it to what they know.

semantic memory Memory that depends on words and numbers, and that presents facts that are agreed on by many people. Contrasts with episodic memory.

episodic memory Memory for a particular episode, or experience, usually remembered with the senses and emotions, not with words and facts. Each person's episodic memory is theirs alone, even when two people share the same experience.

knowledge base A body of knowledge in a particular area that makes it easier to master new information in that area.

Carol Yepes/Getty Images

What Does She See? It depends on her knowledge base and personal experiences. Perhaps this trip to an aquarium in Spain is no more than a break from the school routine, with the teachers merely shepherding the children to keep them safe. Or, perhaps she has learned about sharks and dorsal fins, about scales and gills, about warm-blooded mammals and cold-blooded fish, so she is fascinated by the swimming creatures she watches. Or, if her personal emotions shape her perceptions, perhaps she feels sad about the fish in their watery cage or finds joy in their serenity and beauty.

metamemory Knowledge about how to remember, such as how to create mnemonics.

For example, if you know other people named Kathleen, or Berger, you will remember my name more easily. This fact is especially apparent if you have a textbook written by someone from another culture and language, whose name is unlike any you know. It may be hard to remember who wrote that book.

Much of the education of children, both in school and out of it, builds the knowledge base. One reason children can learn in fifth grade, for instance, is that they remember what they learned in fourth grade. Conversations at home and at school, books and newspapers read, television and videos viewed, and classroom learning, all contribute to the knowledge base. Thus, school curriculum, religious teachings, museum visits, internet games, interactions with friends, exploration of nature . . . all of these affect what new information a child can remember.

Attention and motivation are crucial for building the knowledge base. A child might memorize words and rhythms of hit songs, know "recipes" in *Animal Crossings* and *Minecraft*, recite names and histories of star athletes, and yet not know whether World War I was in the nineteenth or twentieth century, or whether Pakistan is in Asia or Africa.

Some semantic memory facts (rain is wet) are widely known by almost everyone by age 2. Other facts take years and education to learn (2 + 2), and some are known only by a few people (Berger wrote this book). But all are semantic memory because they are based on facts and can be expressed in words. Expanding a student's semantic memory is a goal of many schools and colleges, and the results are measured on tests with right and wrong answers.

Episodic memory is personal. Even when two people experience the same episode, one may forget it and another remembers it. Think of what your mother said to you as a child: You might remember her words, but she might not. Such episodic memory is affected not only by the individual but also by other people: If you told a friend what your mother said, and the friend reacted and repeated what you said, that memory is likely to endure.

Other people cannot mark your memory right or wrong, although they can deny it happened and you yourself can revise it. But episodic memory belongs to the person who experienced it, not to the culture.

Every episodic memory depends partly on a person's emotions and partly on other people: A shared memory, told and retold, is likely to stick. Listener responses solidify and distort memories.

Teaching to Remember

Metamemory is knowledge about how to remember. Children's first attempt at metamemory is usually to repeat whatever is to be remembered over and over and over, an ineffective strategy because it relies on short-term memory, not working memory. A distraction can interfere with the memory, erasing it.

Adults can use metamemory to teach children what to remember. For example, after a trip to the zoo, an adult might say to a 4-year-old, "Remember when we saw the tiger, and you held on to the fence, counted the stripes, and heard the tiger roar? Why is your cat called a "tiger kitty?" Even better would be to take a picture of the child near the tiger and paste it in a scrapbook with a cutout tiger, and with the child's words describing the event. Then the zoo trip may be remembered years later.

Memory is consolidated best using several modalities (in this example, sight, touch, hearing), with new experiences connected with familiar ones (the cat at home). Metamemory methods include reminder sessions: Repetition works best, not as rote, but as when a memory is connected to other experiences or used in new ways. Learning the alphabet, for instance, benefits from other images (A is for apple, or alligators all around), or using a dictionary, or alphabetizing a list.

TABLE 7.1

Advances in Memory from Infancy to Age 11

Child's Age	Memory Capabilities
Under 2 years	Infants remember actions and routines that involve them. Memory is implicit, triggered by sights and sounds (an interactive toy, a caregiver's voice).
2–5 years	Young children use words to encode and retrieve memories. Explicit memory begins, although children do not yet use memory strategies. Children remember things by rote (their phone number, nursery rhymes).
5–7 years	Children realize that they need to remember some things, and they try to do so, usually via rehearsal (repeating an item again and again). This is not the most efficient strategy, but repetition can lead to automatization.
7–9 years	Children can be taught new strategies, including visual clues (remembering how a particular spelling word looks) and auditory hints (rhymes, letters). Children benefit from organizing things to be remembered.
9–11 years	Memory becomes adaptive and strategic as children continue to learn various memory techniques from teachers and other children. They can organize material themselves, developing their own memory aids.

Singing, rhyming, and movement also helps, as every teacher knows. Preschoolers touch and move their bodies as they sing "head, shoulders, knees, and toes / head, shoulders, knees, and toes / And eyes and ears and mouth and nose." That helps with vocabulary.

Rhymes help older children learn spelling rules ("*i* before *e* except after *c*") and ways to screw in a lightbulb ("lefty, loosey, righty, tighty"). Sentences are used to remember musical notes, planets, and so on. Children gradually learn such rules, and eventually create their own (see **Table 7.1**).

Memory techniques, developed spontaneously by children or taught to them by adults, aid cognition of all kinds. Students who achieve the highest grades are not necessarily those with high IQ scores, or those who study longest, but those who are best at metamemory.

Culture matters, as do the demands of specific teachers. For example, many Muslim children are taught strategies to remember long passages because they memorize all 80,000 words of the Quran. Some U.S. teachers require memorization of poems, or national texts (such as the Gettysburg Address or the Declaration of Independence), or math facts. Some professions, such as stage acting, require memory of many lines of dialogue. Each adult profession requires detailed procedural and semantic memory, which leads to the next phase of development.

WHAT HAVE YOU LEARNED?

1. Why are some people better at semantic than episodic memory, and others the opposite?
2. Why does semantic memory improve when vocabulary advances?
3. How does what a child already knows make it easier to learn more?
4. How can adults improve a child's metamemory?
5. How is memory affected by culture?

Memory in Adulthood

Memory is essential in adulthood, no less so than food, water, and air. Adults need to remember how to do their work, to care for their bodies, to relate to others, to navigate neighborhoods. Children need adults to accomplish these things; they would die without adult memory.

The Reminiscence Bump

The first years of adulthood may be prime time for memory. When adults of any age recall the past, they are most likely to remember events that occurred when they were emerging adults, ages 18–25 (Munawar et al., 2018). This is called the *reminiscence bump*, which is found for autobiographical memories (perhaps because people establish their own identity, via leaving home, choosing a life partner, starting a new job).

The reminiscence bump is also evident for generational memories: People tend to think that events that occurred when they were young adults were world-changing (Corning & Schuman, 2015). A U.S. veteran who fought during World War II is likely to think the United States must intervene in international conflicts; someone who was 20 during the Vietnam or Iraq wars is much more hesitant. How a person thinks about racism, or sexism, or health care, or immigration, depends not only on direct experience but also how old the person was when newspapers, television, and politicians focused on those issues.

People establish their political and social values in early adulthood, and the memory of them endures throughout life. It is not surprising that adults viewed LGBTQ individuals more favorably after the U.S. Supreme Court decided that same-sex marriage was permissible, nor that each younger generation was more positive.

What *is* surprising is that in the two years after the decision, positive attitudes continued to increase among young adults, but adults born before 1981 demonstrated a slight decrease in their support (Pew Research Center, May 14, 2019) (see **Figure 7.1**). The explanation: the reminiscence bump, which pushed older adults back to their opinions when they were 20.

Implicit Memory in Adulthood

In the discussion of infant memory, you learned that everyone remembers implicitly without knowing it. People might honestly say, "I don't remember," meaning "I cannot recall it." However, people may unwittingly lie if they experienced something and then say, "I have no memory of that."

FIGURE 7.1

Echoes of 1996 The U.S. Congress passed the Defense of Marriage Act (DOMA) in 1996, when attitudes about same-sex couples were fervent. Which generation's reminiscence bump occurred during those years? This chart suggests it: Gen Xers were aged 16–30.

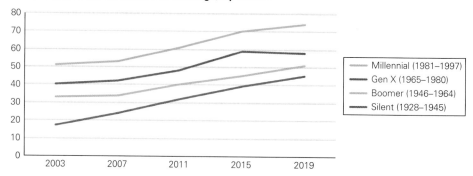

Percent Who Support Same-Sex Marriage, by Cohort

Millennial (1981–1997)
Gen X (1965–1980)
Boomer (1946–1964)
Silent (1928–1945)

Data from Pew Research Center, May 14, 2019.

Learning in College

The distinction between implicit and explicit memory is useful if you are puzzled as to why some students find certain classes difficult that other students find easy. Much depends on implicit memory. You may think you have forgotten everything you learned in the fourth grade, or whatever your parents discussed at dinner when you were a child. But it still may be in your brain.

For example, perhaps last semester you took introductory Spanish, a class exclusively for beginners who must assert that they do not know any Spanish. One student might have been cared for by a Spanish-speaking grandmother who died before she was 2. From then on, she never heard Spanish: She does not understand it, which is why she enrolled in the class. But she effortlessly earns an A. Do not credit genes or heritage; do not suspect lying or teacher favoritism. Instead, credit (or blame) implicit memory.

More generally, if you find some college classes particularly easy or hard, it could be that your implicit memory and knowledge base are the reasons. That does not mean, of course, that you should avoid hard classes; you might learn more from them. But don't expect yourself to understand every new idea easily.

Adults with Amnesia

The clearest evidence that explicit and implicit memory arise from different brain regions comes from adults with amnesia. Some have explicit memory loss yet intact implicit memory. Indeed, some have no conscious memory at all, but nonetheless exhibit extensive past learning (MacPherson & Sala, 2019).

In extreme cases, all explicit memory is destroyed, but implicit memory remains. One famous example is Clive Wearing, a gifted musicologist, perhaps the world expert on seventeenth-, eighteenth-, and nineteenth-century British music. He is able to play music so well that it makes the heart leap; the sounds plumb the depths of the listener's soul.

In 1985, Clive was director of a famous choir and a respected employee of the BBC, when he contracted viral encephalitis that destroyed part of his brain. From then on, his explicit memory decays almost immediately. He forgets what happened half a minute ago, as well as everything else in explicit memory that occurred before his illness.

Clive had remarried a year before his illness. When he became conscious, he greeted his new wife with delight, telling her he had just awakened from a coma. But when she returned after leaving for a minute, he greeted her again with surprise and joy, saying that he is now awake and that she is beautiful. He repeats that every few moments, day after day, year after year.

How would you feel if your love repeatedly said they were thrilled to see you? Would you tire of that? Probably: A shared past is part of close relationships. Clive's wife reflected on this in *Forever Today*, a book about his memory and her emotions (Wearing, 2005).

Clive no longer remembers the names of his children or of any composers. But, when seated at the piano, viewing a complex musical score, he plays flawlessly, bringing joy and heartbreak to his wife. He can direct the singing of his choir, but he does not know who they are.

Distortions of Memory

Not only implicit memory but also explicit semantic and episodic memory can be biased. For instance, probably every reader knows one fact about September 11, 2001, specifically that a plane hit the World Trade Center, causing collapse and death. That is in semantic memory. Particularly people who were young adults at the time (the reminiscence bump) are likely to have other semantic memories of 9/11, that two planes hit the twin towers, and that two other planes were part of

A Happy Couple? Clive and Deborah Wearing share fleeting moments of joy, but he forgets everything that happened a few seconds ago, and she remembers his profound memory loss that makes him greet her with surprise every time he sees her. If you had to choose, would you rather be him or her?

IAT Revelations or Speculations?

Researchers have developed the *Implicit Association Test (IAT)* to measure implicit memory. Thousands of studies and an estimated 20 million people worldwide have taken some version of the IAT (Yen et al., 2018).

The IAT measures how long it takes for someone to push a button when they see a category (such as old or young adults, immigrants or native-born people, African Americans or European Americans, alcohol or fish, and so on) on the left side of a computer screen and a particular adjective on the right. The person is not supposed to push the button for some categories, but sometimes should push when a designated category is paired with positive words (for people, "beautiful," "good," "trustworthy") or later, negative ("ugly," "evil," "dishonest") ones. The time between the screen display and the push is recorded.

If the time is the same for positive and negative adjectives, there is no implicit prejudice for or against that category. Typically, however, the time differs by a millisecond or more.

For example, if a person is told to press whenever a positive adjective appears, yet "trustworthy" is pushed a millisecond quicker when Sweden is on the other side of the screen than when Nigeria is, then the person has some implicit prejudice. (This particular example is for illustration; the actual tests have dozens of versions, all based on the idea that implicit memory slows down certain associations.)

This basic way to measure implicit memory has many uses. Some form of the IAT has been used to detect implicit reactions to hundreds of objects, people, and behaviors, indicating how likely a person is to commit suicide, take drugs, or forgive someone (Chan et al., 2018, Goldring & Strelan, 2017).

The most controversial application is when the IAT is used to measure implicit prejudice about people of a particular race, age, gender, sexual orientation, or disability. Essentially, people must indicate when one category — say older woman, Black student, overweight man, disabled child — is paired with a positive, and, later, negative, word.

For example, when seeing "overweight man" on the left side of the screen, people are told to push the button whenever a positive adjective appears on the right. Then instructions switch, telling people to push whenever "overweight man" is presented with a negative adjective. If a person who sees "overweight man" takes a millisecond longer to push "handsome" than "ugly," that delay may indicate implicit bias.

Thousands of IAT experiments have taken place. One meta-analysis finds that this method of assessing implicit prejudice is accurate (Greenwald et al., 2009) and another not (Oswald et al., 2013). Public opinions are divided: Some complain that the IAT is "tiny bits of data" that distract from fighting prejudice, and others praise it for revealing "racism bubbling just below the surface of our national psyche" (Yen et al., 2018, p. 515).

The underlying question is whether implicit biases affect behavior. If so, can we counteract that? People disagree: Hence, opposing perspectives.

---

the attack. Some remember how many deaths occurred, and that President Bush was reading to second-grade children in Florida at the time.

However, how many of those facts are in your semantic memory? In 2002, a year after the attack, I asked a group of about 300 students how many people died. (I intended to illustrate that semantic memory is affected by one's worldview; many people "remember" far too many or too few deaths.) The first student to answer was a young man who said "343 firefighters." "But how many overall?" I asked. He said he did not know or care. Like him, our semantic memory is selective. (The actual number was 2,977.)

Episodic memory is even more selective. Almost every adult remembers where they were and how they learned of the collapse of the twin towers. Many of them, now middle-aged, are quite confident that their memories are accurate. Yet researchers interviewed people immediately after the event and then years later, discovering many inaccuracies, such as how the person learned of the attack.

Some people are quite confident of a distorted memory. Inaccuracies are durable, and, according to one view, inaccurate episodic memories may help people define themselves! (Sullivan-Bissett, 2018; Puddifoot & Bortolotti, 2019)

This is particularly apparent when someone with a neurocognitive disorder or mental illness remembers past successes that did not actually occur, but everyone is vulnerable to *hindsight bias*, when a person thinks they predicted something that later happened. People think they were wiser than they really were. Hindsight bias is especially likely in older compared to younger adults (Groß & Pachur, 2019). That encourages self-respect—is that harmful?

Semantic memories also vary: People are selective in remembered facts. When teachers tell their students about 9/11 (as required in some school districts) (Duckworth, 2018), some stress the need for intercultural understanding, others for increased security. Some highlight the willingness of strangers to help each other, others the evil that others do. That incident was used to support the U.S. war on Iraq, a nation that was not connected to the attack. The student who knew how many firefighters died in 9/11 was planning a career as a firefighter; did his selective memory help him?

Witnessing a Crime

A team of scholars introduced their discussion of false memory by stating:

> The human cognitive system is capable of impressive feats. Synthesizing information over time, drawing inferences, detecting patterns, speculating, abstracting implications, and creating new ideas—going beyond the perceived world and imagining what could be—these are the very cognitive capabilities that underlie some of humanity's most important intellectual achievements and scientific advances.
>
> *[Zaragoza et al., 2019, p. 182]*

In order to do all that, working memory must combine bits of semantic and episodic memory to produce new ideas for all humanity, as well as for personal plans, fantasies, and joys.

But after praising the "human cognitive system," these scholars wrote:

> Somewhat paradoxically, the very skills and predilections that contribute to human intelligence can sometimes undermine people's ability to serve as accurate eyewitnesses.
>
> *[Zaragoza et al., 2019, p. 182]*

No one of any age is always an accurate witness, nor necessarily a false one (see A View from Science). Repeated events are remembered better than one-time events, so asking the particular date of a memory is not a fair indication of veracity. The interviewer must listen respectfully and attentively, not encouraging or suggesting. Otherwise people might want to please the interviewer or might want to get away from an unpleasant situation by agreeing to everything—both problems particularly likely in children. For everyone, memories of events long past are neither always accurate nor always distorted.

This became a national issue when members of the U.S. Senate Judiciary Committee interviewed Brett Kavanaugh to decide if he should be confirmed as a Supreme Court justice. Christine Blasey Ford was "a hundred percent certain" that he sexually assaulted her decades ago, and he denied that it could have happened. The entire nation was caught up in whether he could have forgotten (yes, he could) or she could have misremembered details (yes, she could). Thus, both might have told their truth. Although both accounts cannot be true, both may have believed that the other lied.

The Sequence of Memory

To better understand how old memories return and new memories appear, it helps to know the various steps in the memory process. Although there are many descriptions, a classic one that still is relevant follows the process from first awareness to permanent memory (Atkinson & Shiffrin, 1968; Plancher & Barrouillet, 2019).

A VIEW FROM SCIENCE

False Witnesses

Thanks to extensive work by Elizabeth Loftus (2005), it is now apparent that people may be certain that something happened, which, in fact, never did. In hundreds of studies, replicated with adults of many ages and backgrounds, an interviewer first talks with the parents of an adult. Then the researcher recounts to the unsuspecting adult several experiences that actually happened in childhood and adds one that never occurred.

Later, some people are quite sure that the fictional event occurred. Indeed, some recount details and emotions that were not suggested by the interviewer.

Among the remembered childhood events that never happened:

- Being lost in a mall
- Spilling punch on the parents of the bride at a wedding reception
- Being hospitalized
- Surviving a car accident
- Riding in a hot air balloon
- Pulling a specific prank on a teacher
- Being attacked by an animal
- Being frightened by a clown

This research has helped many judges, juries, and therapists listen to memories of sexual abuse, both abuse that actually occurred and abuse that did not. Actual events are rarely completely forgotten, although they often are kept secret, because shame and confusion surround sexual abuse. At the same time, adults can misremember, especially if someone else encourages them to "recover" a memory because a therapist thinks that is the reason a person has problems with depression, or intimacy, or anger. Innocent parents have been falsely accused of "satanic ritual abuse, babies being sacrificed, group sex, and horrible torture" (Schacter, 1996).

The current consensus of those who study memory is that it is quite possible to implant inaccurate memories. This became tragic in the 1980s, when judges, juries, and journalists wanted to prove that day care was harmful. In one case, preschoolers were led to say that adults in their nursery school performed bizarre sexual acts, such as licking peanut butter from the child's genitals. In this case, day-care workers were convicted and imprisoned. Years later, they were found to be innocent (Ceci & Bruck, 1995).

If a crime occurs and a child may be a witness, current best practices are that children are interviewed immediately after the crime was committed by a friendly adult who does not ask leading questions (Lyon et al., 2019). The interview is videotaped to ensure fair questioning. No cross examination is allowed, because children might be pressured to agree to whatever an adult says.

This research has not only helped lawyers in court cases but also has advised those who interview unaccompanied minors who fled Latin American nations, hoping to enter the United States. Unless interviewers understand the research, "immigrant children are at high risk for reluctance, incomplete reporting, and errors" (Quas & Lyon, 2019). This is one of many examples when understanding the science of human development can benefit children as well as adults.

From Sensation to Perception

Sensory acuity builds over childhood. The *sensory register* is the name for all the stimuli that reach the brain and are then heard, seen, and so forth.

Most sensations are registered for a moment but never become perceptions. They are not remembered unless motivation and repeated experiences make them memorable. Some adults spot a small coin on a trash-filled sidewalk or hear their baby's cry among many other noises, senses that most people do not perceive.

One leading expert described two basic components of memory: the **visuospatial sketchpad** and the **phonological loop** (Baddeley, 2003; Baddeley & Hitch, 1994). The sketchpad records visual images; the phonological loop echoes sounds.

Encoding

The expert who described the visual sketchpad and the auditory loop added a third component, *the central executive*, to coordinate those seen and heard impressions into a coherent whole, forgetting some and saving others.

Thus, after the sensory register notices a sensation (usually visual or auditory), the central executive may consolidate those sensations into a memory. That process is called **encoding**. Encoding occurs, primarily, as the various sensory inputs reach the hippocampus, a crucial part of the brain for initial memory.

visuospatial sketchpad The metaphorical area of the brain where memories of sights and places are briefly stored. Most items disappear unless they are put into more enduring storage.

phonological loop The mind's echoing of what was just heard. That echo can then be put in storage, or it can be forgotten.

encoding To put into memory something that was thought or experienced. Encoding requires perception and interpretation, and thus is not completely accurate.

Encoding takes time and repetition: One hypothesis is that, to avoid decay, a memory needs to be held in mind at least seven seconds. Visual memories come first through the occipital lobe (the visuospatial sketchpad), and auditory memories via the phonological loop. If a particular item comes to the hippocampus both ways (you see a person and hear their name), it is more likely to be remembered.

The seven-second rule has led to suggestions to increase the time the brain focuses on each item to be remembered. A person might meet someone, look directly at them, and say and write their name several times — Mike, Mike, Mike — either in reality or in imagination, such as writing MIKE on his forehead or on your forearm with your finger.

Encoding techniques can be taught. Indeed, here is one tip: Don't use the camera on your cell phone! Many students take a picture of the notes on the board or skip class but get the PowerPoint slides from the lecture. That is far less effective for encoding than physically writing notes describing whatever seems significant in what the professor said. Physical note taking requires time and movement, using both sight and sound, and thus, is more likely to be encoded than the click of a smartphone.

Storage

Storage is the next step in the memory process: Encoded material is stored in the brain. It is not known how much one adult mind can hold, nor exactly how storage is affected by aging (Jaroslawska & Rhodes, 2019). People cannot store too many things at once: Distractions, powerful emotions, and competing cognitive tasks all reduce storage.

Nonetheless, storage capacity is vast; people over 100 years old can add new memories while retaining old ones. Some people speak several languages and remember so many facts and experiences that it seems possible that brains have unlimited capacity. Storage is not like a suitcase that cannot be stuffed with one more item; it is more like the sky, so vast that the limits are beyond our experience.

It is also apparent that, although memory consolidation seems to first occur in the hippocampus, the most durable memories are lodged elsewhere in the brain, a process that is enhanced with a good night's sleep. If the hippocampus is damaged (as happens with some brain injuries and with Alzheimer's disease), people may no longer encode new memories, but may have preserved old ones.

Specifics of storage matter. The amount of material in storage increases when memories are linked together. To remember a specific fact, it helps to know where you first read that fact (what book, where on the page), or who told you. That allows *deep processing*, which increases storage (sometimes said to be in long-term memory).

Discrete items are remembered better if they are learned in chunks, with repetitions, rhymes, tunes, links, and connections. That is why phone numbers, Social Security numbers, birth dates, and so on are separated by hyphens. (The phone number of the Association for Psychological Science is (202) 293-9300. Obviously, the psychologists who chose these numbers understood storage.)

Retrieval

Retrieval is the final step in the memory process, when people recollect what they remember. How material is stored, such as whether it was linked to other stored material when it was encoded, affects how effectively it can be retrieved.

Recall doesn't always occur on command. One example is called the *tip of the-tongue phenomenon*, when someone thinks they know a word or a name but cannot say it, as if it were stuck on the tongue (Brown, 2012). Another example is freezing when taking a test: Students may know more than they can recall during a test, perhaps remembering it minutes after they hand in their exam.

storage All memories that are somewhere in the brain are said to be in storage. Most of this material is buried, not easy to retrieve.

retrieval Bringing something in memory back to the conscious mind. Humans store much more than they can retrieve.

Push the Face Faces are remembered better than names, so even when someone cannot tell the phone to call their son, they can push a button to call him. However, technology is not always designed for reality. If memory is severely impaired, someone might forget that they just spoke to their son ten minutes before.

For everyone, the distant past is harder to remember than the immediate past. If you forgot your first-grade teacher's name, for example, that does not mean that you had a poor memory when you were 6. Recall might be better: If you were presented with three names, one of them your first-grade teacher, you could identify it.

In another example, you can recognize someone in a crowd, because matching a face in front of you with stored visual memory is far easier than linking that face with stored auditory memory. That is why almost everyone says they have a better memory for faces than names. Retrieval depends on the earlier steps of the process: If a memory is not encoded or stored, it cannot be retrieved.

One clue for retrieval is that a memory is like a carrot, growing underground, with a few visible green leaves to pull to unearth the entire carrot. Remembering one aspect of something to be remembered, such as the first letter of a name, or the place when that memory was first implanted, or a smell, a photo, a sensation of any kind, can retrieve the memory.

In Marcel Proust's famous tome *Remembrance of Times Past (La recherché du temps perdus)*, a bite of a pastry (a madeleine) dipped in tea triggered a feeling of intense joy, because it evoked the memory of a long dead, much beloved aunt. She gave him madeleines dipped in that same kind of tea.

Repetition aids memory. Daily memory exercises, such as doing crossword puzzles or remembering a series of numbers interleaved with math tasks, lead to faster and more accurate memory, for crosswords or math.

This is useful in analyzing games and video programs that claim to improve memory. If there is a pretest and posttest, you will do much better on the posttest. However, that improvement is only for that specific task (Redick, 2019).

Thus, a person who is gradually able to complete a crossword puzzle in half an hour might not be any faster than before in doing math, or in reading comprehension, or remembering the name of someone just met. To improve at a particular memory task, practice that task, but don't expect overall benefits.

Expert Memory

Many developmentalists agree that abstract working memory may not be the best way to measure memory in adulthood, because every year the knowledge base continues to build and that benefits memory for specific tasks and topics, not abstract memory.

In many professions, from violin players to jet pilots, adults do not become experts until they have extensive practice. Working memory, using material stored over the years, is crucial (Ericsson, 2014). The relationship between age (which slows down abstract memory) and experience (which builds practical memory) is complex: Many factors influence memory over the decades (Krampe & Charness, 2018).

Remembered and reassessed experience is particularly important in professions that combine explicit and implicit memory. Presidents, premiers, and popes are usually quite old, in part because accumulated memories are required for extraordinary judgment.

In adulthood, the many variations between one person and another are less affected by age than by other factors (motivation, experience, culture, genes) that impact memory. Consider another example, driving a car. Teenagers have acute senses and quick reactions, and they are adept at explicit memory. They can, and do, memorize rules of the road in order to get their driver's license, knowing how many feet away from a fire hydrant to park legally, how to adjust their mirror before driving, the amount of the fine for not wearing a seatbelt.

VISUALIZING DEVELOPMENT Many Kinds of Memory

Memory is not one thing but many, as diagrammed below. Yet all memories combine to make us who we are, who we were, and who we will be. If you were offered a day with anyone, anywhere, any experience of your choice, but you were told that day would be completely erased from memory, would you take it?

EXTERNAL INPUTS

ENCODING
Information is placed in memory.

STORAGE
Information is retained in memory.

RETRIEVAL
Information stored in memory is found as needed.

SENSORY REGISTER
Temporary storage of sensory information.

SHORT-TERM MEMORY
Memory for whatever was just heard or seen.

LONG-TERM MEMORY
Memory responsible for the storage of information for an extended period of time.

CENTRAL EXECUTIVE
A component of working memory that manages the activities of the phonological loop and visuospatial sketchpad. The central executive directs attention and prioritizes particular activities rather than acts as a memory store.

Working Memory

Phonological Loop
The mind's echoing of what was just heard or read, which can then be stored or forgotten.

Visuospatial Sketchpad
The metaphorical area of the brain that briefly stores information about the appearance and location of objects.

IMPLICIT MEMORY
Memory that is not verbal, often unconscious.

Procedural Memory
A type of implicit memory—Memory for movement (also called *motor memory*).

EXPLICIT MEMORY
Memory that can be recalled in the conscious mind.

Semantic Memory
Memory that depends on words and numbers, and presents facts that are agreed on by many people. Contrasts with episodic memory.

Episodic Memory
Memory for a particular episode, or experience, usually recalled with senses and emotions, not words and facts.

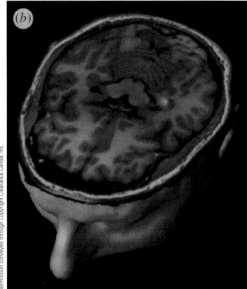

Never Lost The red in this image shows the activated brain areas of London taxi drivers as they navigated the busy London streets. Those areas were more developed, even when the drivers were not working, than in the typical brain. Brains respond to practice: The longer a cabby had been driving, the more brain growth was evident in regions dedicated to spatial representation. As explained in the text, we all become experts, with particular brain connections at whatever we do again and again.

Yet teenagers and young adults have the highest rate per mile driven of motor vehicle crashes. Why? One reason is experience aids memory. A study of drivers' eye movements found that teenage drivers look straight ahead as they grip the wheel, but older, experienced drivers also scan the sides of the road (Robbins & Chapman, 2019). Closely related are benefits of implicit motor memory. Practiced movements become locked in automatic memory: The mind does not need to think about how to turn the steering wheel or apply the brake, and can instead attend to a car unexpectedly speeding through a red light.

Face Memory

The role of experience, and the need for compensation for whatever memory problems an adult might have, is evident with memory for faces. Two tiny brain areas (one in each hemisphere) called the *fusiform face area*, enables face recognition. This is a remarkable ability: Stop to think how miraculous it is that you can recognize someone you knew well five years ago if you chance to see them where you never expected they would be, perhaps in the audience of a concert, or among thousands at a political rally, or in Tokyo.

Unless you have *prosopagnosia* (face blindness), the fusiform face area of the brain remembers tiny differences between one face and another that allows this miracle. Newborns are quicker to recognize a face that they have seen just once than are older children and adults (Zeifman, 2013).

For newborns, every face is fascinating: Babies stare at pictures of monkey faces and photos of human ones, at drawings and toys with faces, as well as at live faces. At 6 weeks, they smile at any face about 2 feet away. Memory soon is evident: Babies smile more readily at familiar people, differentiate men from women, and distinguish among faces from their own ethnic group (called the *own-race effect*).

The own-race effect raises a worrisome question: Are people naturally racist? No: Experience, not inherent racism, is the reason, because most babies see only people who are the same ethnic background as they are. Consequently, they notice small differences in appearance among people from their own ethnic background but are less adept at noticing such nuances in others.

When babies have more experience with people of many hues, the own-race effect is not evident. Babies in Malaysia (a multiracial nation) are able to recognize people of many races, but they have another facial bias: They distinguish women much more easily than men. In that nation, men are rarely active caregivers of babies (Tham et al., 2019).

Children of one ethnicity who are adopted and raised exclusively among people of another ethnicity may recognize differences among people of their adopted group more readily than differences among people of their biological group (McKone et al., 2019).

The importance of experience is confirmed by two studies. In the first study, parents repeatedly "read" a book to their 6-month-old infants (Scott & Monesson, 2010). The book depicted six monkey faces. One-third of the infants' parents read the name of each monkey while showing the pictures; another one-third said only "monkey" as they turned each page; the final one-third simply turned the pages with no verbal labeling.

At 9 months, infants in all three groups viewed pictures of six *unfamiliar* monkeys. The infants who had heard names of monkeys were better at distinguishing one new monkey from another than were the infants who saw the same picture book but did not hear each monkey's name (Scott & Monesson, 2010).

Evidently, hearing names taught babies that each monkey is unique. This applies to humans' understanding of racial and national groups as well. Interacting with several named people of any group helps people avoid stereotypes (Thorup et al., 2018).

Prosopagnosia

I know a man who has severe prosopagnosia. He recognizes his wife and his children because he has an emotional and auditory memory of them: He is a responsive husband and father, a much-loved member of the family.

However, he was once in an electronics store in midtown Manhattan, and another customer smiled broadly at him. He was suspicious; strangers do not usually interact so quickly in New York, especially not smiling as this stranger did. He looked wary until the man said, "Dad. I am your son." The problem, of course, is that he knew his son very well at home, but not by sight in a strange place.

I have another friend with a milder version of prosopagnosia. She deliberately encodes features—hairstyles, facial features, voices (which are as distinct as faces, but few of us need to know that). This woman has a romantic partner of another race who is blind. Interracial couples are no longer rare, but most people still fall in love with people similar to them. Does my friend have a particular affinity for people who are visually impaired?

Finally, I remember another incident, this time of an adult with typical face recognition. She had grown up exclusively with people of her own ethnicity and was a teacher in her local, segregated school. Suddenly she was transferred to another school, where most students were of another ethnicity. She told me that her transfer was unfair, because she could not individualize instruction, since "All _____'s look alike."

I was stunned by her prejudice, but I remembered memory research. We each can improve our memory ability if we are motivated to do so, compensating for any deficits related to age or experience. The teacher needed to stop complaining and focus on the facial individuality of her students.

The general lesson of these three cases is that we all have memory weaknesses and strengths, part of the variability mentioned in the start of this chapter. The answer to "What is memory for?" depends on what each of us wants our memory to be for, and then we need to use our strengths and shore up our weaknesses. Our memory can be trained to remember what is important to us.

What Harms Memory

As you see, memory improves with deep processing and practice. However, unlike childhood, memory improvement over the years of adulthood is not inevitable. Several specific factors impair memory.

Sleep

For decades, people have wondered why living things sleep. Historically, some adults believed the unconscious mind, or spirits, or ancestors communicate to sleeping adults. Dreams have been interpreted as warnings, or unconscious urges, or repressed wishes.

Many adults consider sleep to be wasted time. People sometimes brag about not needing much sleep, as did President Reagan and Prime Minister Thatcher before they developed Alzheimer's (Walker, 2017). Presidents Obama and Trump also averaged less than six hours of sleep each night, both believing they accomplished more that way.

Recently, however, the relation of sleep to mental processes has been studied in detail, and sleep is now recognized as a memory aid (Klinzing & Diekelmann, 2019; Xie et al., 2019). When people sleep, their brain reviews the day, discarding most memories and consolidating others (Peter-Derex, 2019).

An early sign of sleep deprivation is impaired memory. That means that adults who want to boost their achievement should not sleep less, but more—at least seven hours or so, with enough deep sleep (called *alpha sleep*). Many researchers and therapists seek to understand, and implement, good *sleep hygiene*, habits that improve sleep quality and reduce insomnia (Trauer et al., 2015).

Stress

The relationship between stress and memory is complicated, because some stress actually aids memory (Lotan et al., 2018). Stress awakens emotions (joy, anger, fear) that put the person on high alert. Thus, emotional experiences make sights and sounds enter the sensory register, allowing the brain to encode and store the memory.

But too much stress, for too long, is destructive of memory neurons. If daily life is filled with stress—financial, academic, social—then an excess of *glucocorticoids* (several hormones, including cortisol) destroys the neurons of the hippocampus, the brain area that is crucial for memory consolidation. The damage is most evident in childhood: Abused girls and neglected boys have smaller hippocampi, reducing adult memory capacity they otherwise would have (Teicher et al., 2018).

People who are terrified in adulthood may remember too well! *Posttraumatic stress disorder (PTSD)* results from flashbacks to a frightening experience (as already explained in Chapter 5). Many victims of PTSD were in combat. For veterans, gunfire and explosions are remembered vividly, disturbing sleep, ruining relationships, and intruding on normal life long after the return to civilian life. Other traumas (rape, torture, climate disasters) also cause PTSD.

It seems that memory needs some stress but not too much for too long. How can that be achieved, given that every adult has reasons to be worried and anxious at times? Current answers include prayer, exercise, nature (viewing trees, active gardening), and meditation, all of which aid executive function, particularly memory (Diamond, 2013).

Meditation

Recent research on meditation (as practiced by Buddhists, Christian monks, and dedicated but nonreligious adults) is intriguing. Memory and mood benefits have been established in many studies comparing experienced meditators with people who do not meditate (Tang & Posner, 2015). Somewhat paradoxically, a focus on the present moment (called *mindfulness*) helps people remember the past without anxiety (Creswell, 2017).

The research on meditation and mindfulness is not accepted by every scientist, partly because of problems with replication, procedures, and participants (Davidson & Kaszniak, 2015). For example, people who meditate regularly are a select group, perhaps more religious or more intelligent than average.

To overcome those background factors, one study began with people, aged 18–45, who were not meditators. The volunteers were divided randomly into three groups: One group had no special treatment, one listened to 13-minute podcasts every day for eight weeks, and a third listened to a 13-minute guided meditation. After eight weeks, not only did the mood of the meditators improve but also scores on some (not all) measures of recall and working memory rose (Basso et al., 2019) (see **Figure 7.2**). One experiment is not enough to convince everyone, but all three factors (sleep, stress, and meditation) point in the same direction, that memory is not fixed but plastic.

Drugs and Health

The major discussion of diseases that destroy memory neurons is in Chapter 5. Here we briefly mention drugs and health conditions that seem to target memory.

The most common memory-destroying drug is alcohol. Many a person who has drunk too much experiences a *blackout*, later wondering, with dread, what they did the night before. Lesser amounts can cause a *brownout*, when memories are fuzzy and imprecise. The same effect can occur for many other drugs, because "the addicted brain co-opts the neural mechanisms of learning and memory" (Cushman & Byrne, 2018).

Medical conditions that slow down blood circulation also slow down memory; hypertension, obesity, and heart

Observation Quiz Did the students become twice or three times as good on the n-back after eight weeks of meditation? (see answer, page 211) ⬇

FIGURE 7.2
Mood and Memory Other data show that college students who meditate every night for eight weeks become less depressed and less anxious. But this figure shows memory improvement. Students listened to a series of numbers and then were asked what number was one, two, or three back from the last number spoken. The control group was quite good at this, but they did not improve much. The meditators, however, became significantly better.

Percent of Correct Trials (All Conditions)

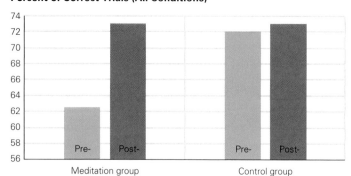

Data from Basso et al., 2019.

disease are particularly harmful. On the plus side, factors that protect the heart, such as regular exercise and a healthy diet, benefit memory.

Memory in Late Adulthood

Memory decline is gradual, almost imperceptible, but by late adulthood notable memory loss is evident. Nonetheless, the two general principles from the beginning of this chapter bear repeating. First, memory is not one thing but many: Some aspects of memory fade with age, but not all of them. Second, variation is evident; some older people remember very well.

Of course, severe memory loss is a symptom of major neurocognitive disorder (dementia). The rate of Alzheimer's and other neurocognitive disorders increases with age, described in Chapter 5. In this chapter, we focus on typical, not disease-related, changes in memory with age.

Types of Memory That Decline

Some memes about memory reflect ageism, not reality. The word "senile" for instance, means old, but it has come to mean mental confusion and memory loss. When adults mislay their keys, or forget where their car is parked, they usually attribute that to a distraction, unless they are old. Then they might call it a "senior moment."

Ageism is not the sole explanation: It is undeniable that some memory loss, especially working memory, occurs with age. Explicit memory fades faster than implicit memory; semantic memory fades faster than episodic memory (Fraundorf et al., 2019; Ward et al., 2013). Thus, for elders it is harder to remember names than actions. Old-old people may still swim, bike, and drive, and can tell exactly what their childhood bedroom looked like, even if they cannot name both U.S. senators from their state.

In a recent measure called *alpha memory*, a person hears several words and is told to repeat them in alphabetical order. That requires encoding (the phonological loop), storage (the alphabet), and then retrieval. A study of people aged 17–87 found that success (words correctly remembered and alphabetized) peaked in the 20s and then gradually declined (Zaragoza et al., 2019).

And I Always Respected My Elders The good old days? Long-term memory forgets some details.

Planning Ahead People of every age put their pills beside their toothbrush, coffee pot, or bed to remind them when to take their medicine. To keep from forgetting or doubling up, they use pill cases labeled with days of the week and times of day. Because many older people use such methods, the prospective memory paradox is that memory in daily life is much better than in laboratory experiments.

Source Amnesia

One memory deficit is *source amnesia*—forgetting the origin of a fact, idea, or snippet of conversation. Source amnesia is particularly problematic currently, with social media, many channels of television, and many printed sources bombarding the mind.

In practical terms, source amnesia means that a person might believe "fake news," a rumor, or a political advertisement because they forgot that the information came from a biased source. Deficits in source amnesia are particularly apparent in those over age 70. Compensation requires attending to the reason behind a message before accepting a con artist's promises or the polarizing politics of a TV ad. Analyzing, or even noticing, who said what and why is less likely be done by an older person, who might repeat what their political hero, or next-door neighbor, or Facebook feed, said (Devitt & Schacter, 2016).

Prospective Memory

Another crucial type of memory is called *prospective memory*—remembering to do something in the future (to take a pill, to meet someone for lunch, to buy milk). Prospective memory also fades notably with age. This may become dangerous if, for instance, a person cooking dinner forgets to turn off the stove, or if a driver is in the far lane of the highway when the exit appears.

The crucial aspect of prospective memory seems to be the ability to shift the mind quickly from one task to another: Older adults get immersed in one thought and have trouble changing gears (Schnitzspahn et al., 2013). For that reason, many elders have learned to follow routines (brush teeth, take medicine, get the paper) and to set an alarm to remind them to leave for a doctor's appointment.

One aspect of prospective memory is called *proactive cognitive control*, which requires sustained attention to possibilities that have not yet occurred. That is increasingly difficult with age (Lamichhane et al., 2018). Planning how to make a move to a new home, or what to do if the COVID-19 virus requires quarantine is difficult, making it more likely to cause denial or panic in someone 80 than in someone 18.

Declining Senses

Every sense is less sharp with age, as noted in Chapter 6. Some sensations never reach perception. Small sensory losses—not noticed by the person or family—affect memory. Added to normal aging, some experiences that impair memory are more common among the old, including death of a spouse, moving to a new residence, or surgery. Hospitalization reduces memory, temporarily, in everyone (Loughrey et al., 2018).

The brain automatically fills in missed sights and sounds, but not always accurately. For example, elders may guess at what was said. With age, adults become less accurate at knowing where someone is looking or whether they appear sad, happy, or angry (Grainger et al., 2017; Hughes & Devine, 2015).

Small hearing losses make a difference. The cognition and the hearing of almost 2,000 adults (average age 77) were repeatedly tested (Lin et al., 2013). Eleven years later, retesting found that the cognitive scores of the adults with hearing loss (often unaware of it) were down 7 percent; those with no hearing impairment were down 5 percent.

That 2-percent difference is small, but statistically it was highly significant (.004). That means that losing hearing, only a little, matters. In that study, those whose hearing loss was more notable also declined more in cognition (Lin et al., 2013).

One study of visual information processing began with point-light walkers (people who walk in the dark with lights on their hands, feet, elbows, knees, and so on). Only the lights, not the person, are visible. Older adults were less accurate at judging the emotions of those point-light walkers, particularly when the walkers expressed anger (stamping feet and so on) or sadness (slower movement) (Spencer et al., 2016).

Multiple Sensations

There is an important qualifier here. Although every study of each sense in isolation finds significant input loss with age, one recent study found no loss in perception of emotion when the emotion was genuine (not produced by an actor, as in the point-light tests) and when participants could use three input sources (seeing facial expressions, hearing words, listening to tones) (Wieck & Kunzmann, 2017).

In other words, input from each sense is reduced with age, but using all of the senses together may allow adequate information processing and memory. No wonder that elders prefer to talk face-to-face instead of via e-mail, or, when a close friend dies, that comforting touch, talk, and gestures are better than a mailed sympathy card.

Memory Improvement with Age

Thus far, we have focused on what elders do not remember. But some things are remembered well. Vocabulary is one example: Cross-sectional, longitudinal, and cross-sequential studies all show that vocabulary increases over most of adulthood. Even at age 90 vocabulary is larger, on average, than from ages 20 to 40 (Salthouse, 2019). Older people remember words and languages that they learned decades ago, and they continually learn new words and phrases.

For instance, the words *internet*, *smartphone*, *e-mail*, and *fax* appeared long after today's elders were young. Most very old people understand and use these words. Tests show that older adults may know what a word means, but have difficulty recalling a word on command, a task that requires explicit memory.

Control strategies are particularly useful in that case: allowing time ("it will come to me"), reducing stress (deep and slow breathing), and using clues (remembering the first letter, remembering when that word was used) to compensate for momentary loss. Many studies find that memory strategies are particularly crucial in late adulthood. Wise elders link one memory with another to aid retrieval (Mitchell et al., 2018).

Past experiences may also contribute to memory improvement. Thus, the current cohort of the elderly is more proficient in vocabulary than earlier generations of older adults were, probably because words—in the media and in social interaction—are increasingly important in daily life (Hartshorne & Germine, 2015).

If people suffer a stroke, or a neurocognitive disorder, they may lose recent explicit and semantic memory but not older, implicit and episodic ones. I know an aged Holocaust survivor who suffered a stroke. At first, he spoke only his childhood language (Polish), was terrified of nurses because they might be Nazis, and did not recognize his own adult children. With time, his more recent types of memory returned: He spoke English, thanked his caregivers, and was happy to see his daughter.

Emotional Memories

As already noted, the sensory inputs that begin the memory process are less acute with age, and that affects the ability of older adults to read emotions by looking at someone's face or listening to someone's voice. However, it is also true that a lifetime of experience may allow older adults to compensate for these sensory losses. A team decided to measure empathy when visual contact was impossible (Rauers et al., 2013).

They studied a hundred couples who had been together for years. All participants were repeatedly asked to indicate their own emotions (how happy, enthusiastic, balanced, content, angry, downcast, disappointed, nervous they were) and to

Measuring Partner Empathy

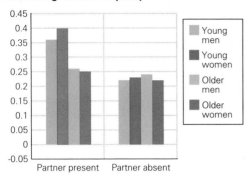

Data from Rauers et al., 2013.

FIGURE 7.3

Do You Know How Angry I Am? Partners are quite good at knowing how their mate is feeling, especially if they can see their partner and they are in their 20s, not their 70s. Separation makes this task more difficult for the young ones, but not the old ones, whose guesses about their distant partner's mood are just as accurate as the guesses of those fifty years younger.

guess the emotions of their partner at that moment. Technology helped: The participants were beeped at various times and indicated their answers on a smartphone that they kept with them. Sometimes they happened to be with their partner, sometimes not.

When the partner was present, accuracy was higher for the younger couples: because they could see and hear their mate. But when the partner was absent, the older participants were as good as the younger ones (see **Figure 7.3**). The researchers wrote,

> [Could you] predict a social partner's feelings when that person is absent? Your judgment would probably be better than chance, and although many abilities deteriorate with aging, this particular ability may remain reliable throughout your life.
>
> *[Rauers et al., 2013, p. 2215]*

As information processing has discovered, the brain is an active organ, changing every day. The particulars of early experiences and memory are critically important for later cognition. At every age, "people perceive more of a visual scene than was presented to them," developing expectations for what they observe, filling in the unseen parts (Mullally & Maguire, 2014). For some of the elderly, that "filling in" process is on target, because of a lifetime of remembered experiences.

Brain Growth in Later Adulthood

Parts of the brain grow and gain neurons during adulthood. Not only do dendrites form and pathways strengthen, but new neurons are born. One area that gains brain cells is the hippocampus, the brain structure that is most prominent in memory (Bergmann et al., 2015).

Those new cells appear to "contribute significantly to hippocampal plasticity across the life span" (Kempermann et al., 2015). As you remember, stress affects the hippocampus even more than other areas of the brain, making the cortisol produced by *stereotype threat* (see Chapter 9) a crucial problem in late adulthood.

A classic example of stereotype threat occurs when elders are told they are taking a memory test: Their anxiety makes them perform less well than their peers who took the same test but were not told it was a memory test (Hughes et al., 2013). These results depend partly on a self-fulfilling prophecy: Because elders fear that their memory declines with age, they experience anxiety, which makes it so.

By contrast, instead of becoming anxious in response to stereotype threat, some elders are motivated to prove the predictions wrong and excel (Hess et al., 2019). (Remember that some stress enhances memory, too much reduces it.)

Memory Requirements Across the Life Span

Now for the concluding part of this section, as well as the chapter overall. We have seen that memory abilities change as people grow older. Now we must note that memory in old age may work well enough, because each stage calls forth whatever kind of memory is needed at that age.

Newborns need to respond to every face, to develop attachment to their primary caregiver. Therefore, they need memory of the sight, sound, smell, and feel of whomever their caregiver might be—woman or man, biological relative or not.

Infants also need to remember the sounds of their native language so they can talk by age 1; preschoolers need to remember emotions so they can regulate them; schoolchildren need to specialize in semantic and explicit memory so they can learn in school; adolescents need to remember personal experiences so they can establish their identity; the reminiscence bump helps young adults connect with their own nation and culture.

ESPECIALLY FOR People Who Are Proud of Their Intellect What can you do to keep your mind sharp all your life? (see answer, page 211)

Ecological Validity

At every age, memory needs to be understood in context, and thus we need to consider what memory abilities need to function well at what age. Measurement of memory needs to reflect developmental stage.

Traditionally, memory was measured in isolation from practical uses. Researchers studied memory for nonsense words, or a string of numbers repeated forward and backward, or drawing an unusual shape, viewed for a minute. All that measures "pure" memory, unrelated to the knowledge base, and all that led to the conclusion that memory abilities increased over childhood and gradually faded in adulthood.

The life-span perspective caused researchers to rethink memory assessment. When multicultural, multicontextual, and plastic perspectives are understood, that makes abstraction and speed (e.g., how many words beginning with a certain letter can be written in a minute) less significant. Many researchers now seek **ecological validity**, determining the function of memory in daily life. Do people remember what they need to remember in order to function well?

This might change research details. For example, because of changes in their circadian rhythm, older adults are at their best in the early morning, when adolescents are half asleep. If a study were to compare the memories of 85-year-olds and 15-year-olds, both tested at 7 A.M., the teenagers would be at a disadvantage. The opposite would occur if the test were at 7 P.M.

Similarly, memory is often assessed via a timed test. For example, in the study already mentioned of older adults and hospitalization, the participants were asked to write down all the animal names they could think of in a minute. In such conditions, faster thinkers (usually young) would score higher than slower thinkers (usually old), although the slower ones might be accurate if they had a few more seconds to think.

Indeed, age differences in prospective memory are readily apparent in laboratory tests but disappear in some naturalistic settings, a phenomenon called the *prospective memory paradox* (Schnitzspahn et al., 2011). Motivation is crucial; elders are less likely to forget whatever they believe is important—phoning a child to say "happy birthday," for instance.

Awareness of the need for ecological validity has led to restructuring some memory tests. The results are that older people lose less memory ability than once was thought. Of course, any test may overestimate or underestimate ability. For instance, how can the accuracy of episodic memory be measured? Many older people recount in vivid detail some events that occurred decades ago. That is impressive . . . if the memories are accurate. As noted, eyewitnesses of any age sometimes misremember.

Many people think that some memories are so-called **flashbulb memories**, as if the mind were a camera that recorded a photo of exactly what happened. It turns out, however, that "people tend to be overconfident in the accuracy of their flashbulb memories" (Kensinger & Kark, 2018).

Unfortunately, "there is no objective way to evaluate the degree of ecological validity . . . because ecological validity is a subjective concept" (Salthouse, 2010, p. 77). It is impossible to be totally objective in assessing memory; memory and tests of memory always have a subjective component.

That raises the question "What is memory for?" Older adults usually think they remember well enough. Fear of memory loss is more typical at age 60 than at age 80, even though actual memory loss increases with age. Crucial for everyone is how to remember what is important to remember.

Active in the Community One of the best ways for the elderly to stay mentally active is to be active in their neighborhoods. Registering new voters, as this man is doing, benefits the community while also helping seniors to maintain their control processes.

ecological validity The idea that cognition should be measured in settings that are as realistic as possible and that the abilities measured should be those needed in real life.

flashbulb memories Named after a camera's flash that reveals every detail in a photo. The hypothesis is that the surprise and intense emotion of some experiences cause every detail to be seared into the mind.

executive function A combination of memory, inhibition, and cognitive flexibility that allows better thinking, so people can anticipate, strategize, and plan behavior.

VIDEO: Old Age: Thinking and Moving at the Same Time features a research study demonstrating how older brains are quite adaptable.

Executive Function

Developmentalists believe that the most important cognitive ability is not abstract intelligence but **executive function**, the ability to use the mind to plan, remember, inhibit some impulses, and execute others. This is an ability that develops throughout life.

Executive function is comprised of (1) memory, (2) inhibition, and (3) flexibility. This combination makes people happier, healthier, and more successful at every age. Executive function advances learning in childhood (Diamond, 2016), protects adolescents from destructive emotional outbursts (Poon, 2018), promotes coping skills in adulthood (Nieto et al., 2019), and forestalls death in old age (Reimann et al., 2018).

Memory is essential for executive function, not only as one of the three components but also interwoven with the other two. An active and extensive working memory is needed for inhibition, because the person "must be able to resist focusing exclusively on just one thing." Similarly, flexible thought requires a supple memory "to recombine ideas and facts in new, creative ways" (Krasny-Pacini et al., 2018, p. 76).

Thus, we have something to add to the two generalities that opened this chapter. Memory is not only (1) several distinct things and (2) variable, it is also (3) foundational at every life stage. It enables people to think, act, and be uniquely themselves. That is no less true at the end of life than at the beginning.

WHAT HAVE YOU LEARNED?

1. What is lost in encoding in later adulthood?
2. How does stress affect older adults differently from younger adults?
3. What is the danger in failing source memory?
4. What is the danger in failing prospective memory?
5. What evidence suggests memory improvement in later adulthood?
6. What conclusions about memory are valid lifelong?

SUMMARY

Studying Memory

1. There are many kinds of memory, all changing with experience, genes, motivation, and age. Memory is plastic, not fixed.

2. One approach to studying cognition is information processing, using advanced technology. This approach reveals how human memory works, both similar to and different from computer processing.

3. Experience builds memory, not suddenly but with an ebb and flow, as evident from Siegler's research on math. Understanding this process is particularly beneficial for children with special learning needs.

Memory in Infancy

4. Infant amnesia is selective, evident for explicit memory but not for implicit memory, which explains why early habits are surprisingly durable.

5. Repetition and reminders aid memory, even in the first months of life. Infants remember motor sequences, such as when to kick, sensations such as taste, and emotions, such as attachment to caregivers.

Memory in Childhood

6. Children gradually develop explicit memories, including short-term, long-term, and working memory. Motivation is crucial for building the knowledge base.

7. Metamemory techniques can be used to help children remember. These methods can be taught to children, so they advance from simple repetition to remembering rules, experiences, strategies, and facts.

Memory in Adulthood

8. Early adulthood may be a particularly fertile time for autobiographical memories, according to the reminiscence bump. This also is the time when political values are set, bolstered by memories of particular experiences.

9. At every age, memories of past experiences can be distorted, either shaded in favor of a person or completely false.

10. Memories follow a sequence from encoding, to storage, to retrieval. Problems can occur at each step, including the frustrating tip-of-the-tongue experience.

11. Adults become experts, remembering particular skills, strategies, or information unusually well because of motivation and practice. Face recognition can be seen as an example of expertise, evident in people of all ages.

12. Sleep loss, too much stress, poor diet, alcohol, and slow blood circulation can all impair memory.

Memory in Late Adulthood

13. In late adulthood, many types of memory are less acute than in younger adults. This includes working memory, source amnesia, prospective memory, and sensory perception.

14. In some ways, however, older adults remember very well. That is evident in vocabulary, implicit memory, and emotional sensitivity.

15. What people need to remember varies depending on their age and social context. Ecological validity is crucial for measuring memory over the life span.

KEY TERMS

information processing (p. 182)	semantic memory (p. 191)	visuospatial sketchpad (p. 198)	retrieval (p. 199)
reminder session (p. 186)	episodic memory (p. 191)	phonological loop (p. 198)	ecological validity (p. 209)
explicit memory (p. 187)	knowledge base (p. 191)	encoding (p. 198)	flashbulb memories (p. 209)
implicit memory (p. 187)	metamemory (p. 192)	storage (p. 199)	executive function (p. 210)
working memory (p. 189)			

APPLICATIONS

1. At all ages, memory is selective. People forget much more than they remember. Choose someone—a sibling, a former classmate, or a current friend—who went through some public event that you did, too. Sit down together, write separate lists of all details that each of you remembers about the event, and then compare your accounts. What insight does this exercise give you into the kinds of things adults remember and forget?

2. Memories are powerfully affected by the age of the person who remembers them. Write down everything you remember about an incident from your childhood—including details of the place, time, people present. Then ask your parent or sibling to write down what they remember about it. Analyze similarities and differences.

3. Everyone is forgetful sometimes. Describe something you forgot and why. If you forgot the same thing at age 80, would you still make the same attribution?

ESPECIALLY FOR ANSWERS

Response for Teachers of 3-Year-Olds (from p. 184) Don't say "wrong." You might just nod, or say "Yes, 5-6-7-8-9." But accept that that learning is a process, with ebb and flow.

Response for Students (from p. 187) Review it several times over the next days and weeks, and you will probably remember it in 50 years, with a little review.

Response for People Who Are Proud of Their Intellect (from p. 208) If you answered "Use it or lose it" or "Do crossword puzzles," you need to read more carefully. No specific brain activity has proved to prevent brain slowdown. Overall health is good for the brain as well as for the body, so exercise, a balanced diet, and well-controlled blood pressure are some smart answers.

OBSERVATION QUIZ ANSWERS

Answer to Observation Quiz (from p. 186) The mobile is a good addition—colorful and too high for the baby to reach. (Let's hope it is securely fastened and those strings are strong and tight!) But two things are not what a cognitive developmentalist would recommend: (1) The crib and the wall are both plain white, limiting what the baby can focus on, and (2) the crib bumper is a SIDS risk.

Answer to Observation Quiz (from p. 204) Did you see that the x-axis is from 56 to 74 percent? The meditators improved about 15 percent, 62.4 to 73.4, a significant result but not double or triple.

Language: Communication from Birth to Death

"Mama, mama," my 16-month-old grandson said. I was caring for him while his parents worked. He looked directly at me; his tone was commanding, not complaining.

At that age he spoke very few words. But I thought I knew what he meant. Since babies comprehend much more than they express, I nodded, smiled, looked at him, and replied, "Mommy will come soon."

"Mama, mama," he insisted, looking at me. He could see that I wanted to help, but apparently my response was not helpful.

He does not understand Japanese, but some sounds are universal. "Mama" is milk in Japanese baby talk (*miruku* is Japanese for milk), so I offered milk in his sippy cup.

"No, no, no," he shook his head.

I was bewildered. Fortunately, his father came soon. The boy grinned broadly, repeating "mama, mama." His father scooped him up, and he cuddled happily in his arms.

I asked what "mama" means.

"Pick me up."

This was communication—successful, failed, and then successful. My grandson said what he wanted, I replied with attention and encouragement. But then communication failed because of a word that I did not understand.

Much of language is like that: We humans communicate often, with words, facial expressions, and body movements. Our efforts are not always successful, but ideally we persist. The process is mutual: the boy and father communicate well, with shared understanding. Since my grandson and I were both trying our best to communicate, I think I would, eventually, have picked him up. He probably would have lifted his arms to show me what he wanted.

This chapter is about that process. It describes communication, from first cries to final words, and theories regarding language development in every culture.

Sometimes the word "language" is used narrowly, as a specific set of spoken words and grammar that is used in one part of the world. By that definition, the people of the world speak more than 6,000 languages, with the English language only one of many.

In this chapter, language is defined more broadly, as any form of communication between one creature and another. This includes spoken language and much more—hand gestures, facial expressions, sign language, body language, and so on. The function of language is to communicate, and the development of communication is the topic of this chapter.

- **Theories of Communication and Language**
  Theory One: People Need to Be Taught
  Theory Two: Social Impulses Foster Communication
  Theory Three: People Teach Themselves
  Theory Four: Neuroscience

What Will You Know?

1. How do people communicate without talking?
2. Is speaking two languages better than speaking only one?
3. When are words insulting and when are they comforting?
4. Do people need to be taught to talk?

The First Two Years

Exactly how language develops, propelled by both the brain and the environment, is a topic of great interest to many theorists and researchers, as described at the end of this chapter. But first, we need to detail specifics, beginning the first two years, "from burping to grammar" as one scholar described it (Saxton, 2010, p. 2). (See At About This Time.)

Touching and Looking

The first communication is via touch and facial expression. Parents feel compelled to hold their babies, who relax when held securely. Communication by sight is also instantaneous: Newborns stare and parents stare back.

A few decades ago, babies born in hospitals were *not* handed to their parents at birth, but were cleaned, weighed, wrapped, and medicated with eye drops to prevent infection. Then they were taken to be put behind glass in the nursery, where parents could gaze at them.

Two psychologists began a revolution (Klaus & Kennel, 1976). They learned from shepherds that newborn lambs needed to be licked and nuzzled by their mothers in the first moments after birth. If a naive farmer removed a newborn lamb to be vaccinated, tested, or cleaned before returning it to the mother, she might reject it, refusing to let it feed despite pitiful bleating.

Based on studies of domestic animals, those psychologists insisted that mother–child bonding required newborns to be held by their mothers immediately. Mothers who held their newborns, skin to skin, were more responsive to their infants later on.

Subsequent research found that early contact is not essential for bonding, but fortunately those psychologists changed human birth practices before the more nuanced research with human babies was published. Now babies are put on the breast immediately so

AT ABOUT THIS TIME

The Development of Spoken Language in the First Two Years

Age*	Means of Communication
Newborn	Reflexive communication—cries, movements, facial expressions.
2 months	A range of meaningful noises—cooing, fussing, crying, laughing.
3–6 months	New sounds, including squeals, growls, croons, trills, vowel sounds.
6–10 months	Babbling, including both consonant and vowel sounds repeated in syllables.
10–12 months	Comprehension of simple words; speechlike intonations; specific vocalizations that have meaning to those who know the infant well. Deaf babies express their first signs; hearing babies also use specific gestures (e.g., pointing) to communicate.
12 months	First spoken words that are recognizably part of the native language.
13–18 months	Slow growth of vocabulary, up to about 50 words.
18 months	Naming explosion—three or more words learned per day. Much variation: Some toddlers do not yet speak.
21 months	First two-word sentence.
24 months	Multiword sentences. Half of the toddler's utterances are two or more words long.

*The ages in this table reflect norms. Many healthy, intelligent children attain each linguistic accomplishment earlier or later than indicated here.

mothers can hold them, communicating before drops impede vision. Those early communications matter for later language: babies with skin-to-skin contact with their mothers become babies who vocalize more at 3 months (Bigelow & Power, 2012).

Skin-to-skin connection immediately is now recommended, even when birth was by c-section or in hospitals in poor nations (Widström et al., 2019). Fathers, married or not, are encouraged to massage the birthing mother and then hold their newborns. Ideally, all three (mother, baby, father) communicate immediately with sight, sound, touch, and smell. That is the beginning of language!

Crying and Talking

New infants make noises, mostly crying, which activates neurons in their parents' brains (Swain et al., 2011). In the past few decades, many experts have analyzed early cries (Manfredi et al., 2018). Babies have multiple cries, not just one, and the cries vary in loudness and tone. All babies communicate as best as they can. Adults listen to pitch, rhythm, and intensity, and interpret those cries—a cry of hunger, loneliness, tiredness, or pain. Medical professionals listen for odd cries, which alert them when something is seriously wrong. One condition is called "crie de chat" (French for "cat's cry"), because the first symptom is a cat-like cry.

Caregivers respond with touch, of course, but also verbally. New parents talk to their babies, even in that first hour of skin-to-skin contact. Their talk is designed for infant appeal: Caregivers use higher, softer, and more varied pitch, simpler words, repetition, varied speeds, and exaggerated emotional tones. This special language mode is sometimes called *motherese*, but non-mothers do it as well, so scientists prefer a more formal term: *child-directed speech*.

Infants respond. They prefer child-directed speech, in their home language, as well as the particular touch and face that they experience. Some adults are much more animated than others; babies come to expect whatever communication mode their parents provide. However, if a mother is distant and unexpressive, as might happen if she is sick, depressed, exhausted, or overwhelmed, the baby becomes less responsive as well.

This process means that babies are "acquiring much of their native language before they utter their first word" (Aslin, 2012, p. 191). Infants learn more than spoken language; they learn all forms of communication.

Maternal Depression and Language Development

Sadly, this mutual responsiveness (called *synchrony*, discussed in Chapter 13), is lacking when caregivers are depressed. They convey, via gaze, tone, expression, and gesture, that life contains little joy, and that their infant's attempts to communicate are unwelcome (Shapiro et al., 2018). As a result, infants become depressed; adult responses become "pathways for the cross-generational transfer of emotional maladjustment from depressed mothers to their infants" (Granat et al., 2017, p. 11).

Imagine two dyads: In one pair, a mother dances with her delighted 3-month-old infant, swinging, dipping, swaying, and singing, while both people laugh and bob their heads. In another, the mother, stone-faced, changes a diaper with neither caress nor sound, ignoring a baby's smile or cry, or worse, with an expression of disgust and a rough wipe. Communication begins early; not all early messages are good ones.

Depressed mothers talk less, sigh more, smile rarely—and their babies imitate them. This may continue: Children of depressed mothers are less verbal, with reduced communication skills (De Luca et al., 2018; Goodman et al., 2011).

THINK CRITICALLY: What will happen if no one plays with an infant?

Consequently, caregiver depression impairs language learning. Details reveal exactly how this occurs. For example, one study analyzed a particular feature of child-directed speech, the range of pitch (e.g., from high to low) when 281 mothers showed their 3- to 14-month-olds a plush gorilla and said "Pet the gorilla" (Porritt et al., 2014).

These mothers were volunteers from the community, none diagnosed with major depression. However, a screening questionnaire (the Beck Depression Inventory) found that some had symptoms of depression. When those mothers said, "Pet the gorilla," their speech was flatter, with less varied pitch. Their infants had more limited vocabularies.

Many studies link maternal depression and child depression. Five possible causes have been suggested for this correlation: (1) genes, (2) maternal hormones during prenatal development, (3) postpartum depression in mothers, (4) postpartum depression in fathers, and (5) depression of either or both parents during childhood.

Thousands of studies have explored these questions, and the answer is that all five have an impact. Depression in children is certainly not all genetic. This is apparent because although both parents contribute equally to a child's genes, depression correlates more strongly with the mother's depression than the father's.

One massive study (8,937 children, from birth to emerging adulthood) found that the depression of 18-year-olds was much more influenced by the mothers than the fathers, with maternal prenatal and postnatal depression influential. Postpartum depression was especially influential if parents were low in education (Pearson et al., 2013).

Why would education make a difference? The authors suggest that educated parents are more able to hire another caregiver to provide the stimulation the infant needs (Pearson et al., 2013). There may be a more direct reason: Parents with more education, even if they are depressed, talk to their babies.

Babbling and Signing

As you read, babies and caregivers communicate from the very beginning. Then, at about 6 months, infants **babble**, as repetition of speech-like sounds is called. That "ma-ma-ma," "da-da-da," "ba-ba-ba," is experience-expectant; all babies babble, including deaf babies.

Babies expect a response. If they hear one, they babble again, pause to listen, and repeat the babble. That is the beginning of conversation! The sounds they make echo whatever they hear. By 10 months, their babble is called *expressive jargon*, and astute listeners can detect what language the baby has been hearing, since the infant echoes the tones, cadence, and phonemes of that language.

In childhood, vocabulary correlates with maternal education, probably because educated mothers often talk to their infants. However, no matter what the mother's SES, the best predictor of later language is how much the baby babbles at 6 months (McGillion et al., 2017), which reflects how much others talk to the baby. Those early noises are communicative: ideally, other people communicate back, which increases babbling.

babbling An infant's repetition of certain syllables, such as *ba-ba-ba*, that begins when babies are between 6 and 9 months old.

Who Is Babbling? Probably both the 6-month-old and the 27-year-old. During every day of infancy, mothers and babies communicate with noises, movements, and expressions.

Show Me Where Pointing is one of the earliest forms of communication, emerging at about 10 months. As you see here, pointing is useful lifelong for humans.

holophrase A single word that is used to express a complete, meaningful thought.

naming explosion A sudden increase in an infant's vocabulary, especially in the number of nouns, that begins at about 18 months of age.

Some caregivers teach *baby signs* to their 6- to 12-month-olds, who use hand signs before they can control their tongues, lips, and jaws to say words. There is no evidence that baby signing accelerates talking (as had been claimed), but it increases early communication, itself an advantage (Kirk et al., 2013). For deaf babies, early signing is crucial, predicting later cognition and sign language (M. Hall et al., 2017).

Indeed, gestures are a powerful means of communication lifelong (Goldin-Meadow, 2015). Preverbal infants lift their arms to be picked up, shake their head to indicate no, point to objects, and even look where someone else is pointing. Pointing requires something remarkable — understanding another person's point of view. Most animals cannot do that: Most 10-month-old humans can, especially if the pointer uses words and tone ("look at that!") (Daum et al., 2013).

First Spoken Words

Finally, at about a year, the average infant utters a few words. Strangers might not understand: Good caregivers are master interpreters. For example, at 13 months, a child named Kyle knew standard words such as *mama*, but he also knew *da*, *ba*, *tam*, *opma*, and *daes*, which his parents knew to be, respectively, "downstairs," "bottle," "tummy," "oatmeal," and "starfish." He also had a special sound that he used to call squirrels (Lewis et al., 1999).

Soon after the first birthday, spoken vocabulary increases gradually (perhaps one new word a week). Initially, words are merely labels for familiar things (*mama* and *dada* are common), but then each word becomes a **holophrase**, a single word to convey emotions, expectations, hopes. A holophrase (*holo-* comes from "whole") is accompanied by gestures, facial expressions, and nuances of tone, loudness, and cadence. Imagine three distinct messages in "Dada," "Dada?" or "Dada!"

At every age, people understand much more than they can say. The toddler who speaks only five holophrases can respond to multiword sentences, such as "Where is the ball?" or "Give it to Daddy." All the senses are used to communicate: People understand best if they can see the facial expression and body position of the speaker. Voice itself uses tone and speed to communicate. Think of your mother saying your name. Can you imagine it said with joy, with sorrow, and with anger? Likewise, the toddler's tone is expressive, even when the child speaks very few words.

The Naming Explosion

Spoken vocabulary builds rapidly once the first 50 words are mastered, with 21-month-olds typically saying twice as many words as 18-month-olds. This language spurt is called the **naming explosion**; many children ask, "What's that?" and want to know the name of everything they see. Of course, if they live in a large family with many pets, they will tend to learn many names, but another child's explosion might be with names of objects, actions, and events (Rudman & Titjen, 2018).

Even before the explosion, nouns are already favored. Infants name each significant caregiver (often *dada*, *mama*, *nana*, *papa*, *baba*, *tata*), each sibling, and sometimes each pet. Other words refer to the child's favorite foods (*nana* can mean banana, *baba* can mean bottle) and to elimination (*pee-pee*, *wee-wee*, *poo-poo*, *ka-ka*, *doo-doo*).

Notice that these words have two identical syllables, a consonant followed by a vowel. Many words follow that pattern — not just *baba* but also *bobo*, *bebe*, *bubu*, *bibi*. Other early words are only slightly more complicated — *ma-me*, *ama*, and so on.

The meaning varies by language, but every baby says such words, and every culture assigns meanings to the sounds babies can easily say. That's why rabbits are bunnies and stomachs are tummies.

An interesting question is whether the naming explosion should be called, instead, a vocabulary explosion. Do children learning every language learn more nouns than non-nouns, or is this true only for children learning English? What evidence we have shows more similarities than differences in the early language learning process: It seems that 2-year-olds everywhere realize that objects have names, and that names are easier to learn than actions. Milk, juice, and water are usually learned before drink, swallow, and suck.

Early Grammar

Word order, prefixes, suffixes, intonation, verb forms, pronouns and negations, prepositions and articles—all of these are aspects of **grammar**, which includes all of the methods that languages use to communicate meaning. Grammar is dramatically evident at 18 months, when two words are combined.

For example, "Baby cry" and "More juice" follow grammatical word order. At the one-word stage, a child might say "juice" and then sign or say "more," but once two-word sentences begin at about 18–21 months, children do not typically say "Juice more."

Likewise, even toddlers know that "cry baby" is not the same as "baby cry." By age 2, children use grammar when they combine three words, using subject–verb–object word order if they are speaking English. Two-year-olds say "Mommy read book" rather than any of the five other possible sequences of those words. Other languages use different grammatical order, and their toddlers follow suit.

Proficiency with grammar correlates with sentence length, which is why **mean length of utterance (MLU)** is used to measure a child's language progress (e.g., Miyata et al., 2013). "Baby is crying" is more advanced than "Baby crying" or simply "Baby!"

Social References

The fact that communication is not necessarily verbal is especially apparent in **social referencing**: Toddlers often consult other people, much as a student might consult a dictionary or other reference work. A reassuring glance, a deliberate movement, or a facial expression of alarm, pleasure, or dismay—those are used as references.

Social references tell toddlers if something is interesting or important, fun or forbidden. Even at 8 months, infants notice where other people are looking and use that information to look in the same direction themselves (Tummeltshammer et al., 2014).

Social referencing has many practical applications. Consider mealtime. Caregivers the world over pretend to taste and say "yum-yum," encouraging toddlers to eat beets, liver, or spinach. Toddlers read expressions, insisting on the foods that the adults *really* like. Some tastes (spicy, bitter, sour) are rejected by very young infants, but children might develop a taste for raw fish or curried goat or smelly cheese—foods that children in other cultures refuse. If they see their caregivers eat it with evident delight, they learn to like it (Forestell & Mennella, 2017).

Once they can walk and explore, the need to consult others becomes urgent, and infants check back to other people often. One-year-olds seek clues in gazes, faces, and body position, paying close attention to emotions and intentions. Indeed, long before they understand what someone means when they tell them to look at something, they notice where someone is looking and look at the same object—including when the looker did not want them to see (Gredebäck et al., 2018).

grammar All of the methods—word order, verb forms, and so on—that languages use to communicate meaning, apart from the words themselves.

mean length of utterance (MLU) The average number of words in a typical sentence (called utterance because children may not talk in complete sentences). MLU is often used to measure language development.

social referencing Seeking information about how to react to an unfamiliar or ambiguous object or event by observing someone else's expressions and reactions. That other person becomes a social reference.

Rotini Pasta? Look again. Every family teaches their children to relish delicacies that other people avoid. Examples are bacon (not in Arab nations), hamburgers (not in India), and, as shown here, a witchetty grub. This Australian aboriginal boy is about to swallow an insect larva.

VISUALIZING DEVELOPMENT Early Communication and Language

Communication Milestones: The First Two Years

These are norms. Many intelligent and healthy babies vary in the age at which they reach these milestones.

Months	Communication Milestone
0	Reflexive communication—cries, movements, facial expressions
1	Recognizes some sounds Makes several different cries and sounds Turns toward familiar sounds
3	A range of meaningful noises—cooing, fussing, crying, laughing Social smile well established Laughter begins Imitates movements Enjoys interaction with others
6	New sounds, including squeals, growls, croons, trills, vowel sounds Meaningful gestures, including showing excitement (waving arms and legs) Expresses negative feelings (with face and arms) Capable of distinguishing emotion by tone of voice Responds to noises by making sounds Uses noise to express joy and unhappiness Babbles, including both consonant and vowel sounds repeated in syllables
10	Makes simple gestures, like raising arms for "pick me up" Recognizes pointing Makes a sound (not in recognizable language) to indicate a particular thing Responds to simple requests Deaf babies express their first signs
12	More gestures, such as shaking head for "no" Babbles with inflection, intonation Names familiar people (like "mama," "dada," "nana") Uses exclamations, such as "uh-oh!" Tries to imitate words Points and responds to pointing First spoken words
18	Combines two words (like "Daddy bye-bye") Slow growth of vocabulary, up to about 50 words Language use focuses on 10–30 holophrases Uses nouns and verbs Uses movement, including running and throwing, to indicate emotion Naming explosion may begin, three or more words learned per day Much variation: Some toddlers do not yet speak
24	Combines three or four words together; half the toddler's utterances are two or more words long Uses adjectives and adverbs ("blue," "big," "gentle") Sings simple songs

Information from American Academy of Pediatrics

Universal First Words

Across cultures, babies' first words are remarkably similar. The words for mother and father are recognizable in almost any language. Most children will learn to name their immediate family and caregivers between the ages of 12 and 18 months.

Language	Mother	Father
English	mama, mommy	dada, daddy
Spanish	mama	papa
French	maman, mama	papa
Italian	mamma	bebbo, papa
Latvian	mama	te-te
Syrian Arabic	mama	babe
Bantu	be-mama	taata
Swahili	mama	baba
Sanskrit	nana	tata
Hebrew	ema	abba
Korean	oma	apa

ampyang/iStock/Getty Images

Mastering Language

Children's use of language becomes more complex as they acquire more words and begin to master grammar and usage. A child's spoken words or sounds (utterances) are broken down into the smallest units of language to determine their length and complexity:

MEAN LENGTH OF UTTERANCE (MLU), ILLUSTRATED

"Baby!" = 1

"Baby + Sleep" = 2

"Baby + Sleep + ing" = 3

"Shh! + Baby + Sleep + ing" = 4

"Shh! + Baby + is + Sleep + ing" = 5

"Shh! + The + Baby + is + Sleep + ing" = 6

A toddler's favorite references are their parents, but they also use relatives, other children, and even strangers. They are remarkably selective, noticing who is a reliable reference and who is not (Fusaro & Harris, 2013). For example, by 18 months, children check expressions and body positions when a dog approaches. They learn joy or fear, depending on what others convey. Adults communicate which objects are not be touched, who is to be welcomed with a hug and who is to be avoided, what emotions can be expressed and what not.

Of course, communication may be misunderstood at any age. One child, who spoke only a few words, said a loud "No" and then deliberately pushed a plate from their highchair onto the floor (Rudman & Titjen, 2018). The mother's response: "No." What did the baby think "No" meant? Notice that communication of emotions is central to early speech.

WHAT HAVE YOU LEARNED?

1. Before they understand words, how do babies communicate?
2. What are the tools of communication for caregivers and infants?
3. What is the relationship between babbling and the first spoken words?
4. How does caregiver depression affect infant language?
5. What is the typical pattern of language development from 12 months to 24 months?

Language from Age 2 to 20

Communication improves every year (see At About This Time). Most children learn not only their family language but also the more formal language used in school. (Most of the world's home languages are not school languages.) Even when the home and school languages are ostensibly the same, communication is distinct at home, at school, and with friends. Children master all three.

Thousands of scientists have studied communication skills; hundreds of thousands of educators worldwide teach language; at this very moment more than 2 billion 2- to 19-year-olds (the United Nations' estimate of total child population in 2020) are learning new words, mastering complicated grammar, and communicating ideas, emotions, and memories.

Scientists are awed, teachers are impressed, and most of the 2 billion take communication for granted. This book is about the science, so we describe the awesome.

The Drive to Communicate

Human children have a powerful need to communicate. The youngest children talk to themselves, to their toys, and especially to people, even when the people are not listening. They make eye contact and smile at other children whom they do not know but who happen to be on the same bus, same grocery store, same sidewalk. If a young child at the playground does not know the language of the other children, that child nonetheless

AT ABOUT THIS TIME

Language in Early Childhood

Approximate Age	Characteristic or Achievement in First Language
2 years	*Vocabulary:* 100–2,000 words
	Average sentence length: 2–6 words
	Grammar: Plurals; pronouns; many nouns, verbs, adjectives
	Questions: Many "What's that?" questions
3 years	*Vocabulary:* 1,000–5,000 words
	Average sentence length: 3–8 words
	Grammar: Conjunctions, adverbs, articles
	Questions: Many "Why?" questions
4 years	*Vocabulary:* 3,000–10,000 words
	Average sentence length: 5–20 words
	Grammar: Dependent clauses, tags at sentence end ("…didn't I?" "…won't you?")
	Questions: Peak of "Why?" questions; many "How?" and "When?" questions
6 years and up	*Vocabulary:* 5,000–30,000 words
	Average sentence length: Some seem unending ("…and…who…and…that…and…")
	Grammar: Complex, depending on what the child has heard, with some children correctly using the passive voice ("Man bitten by dog") and subjunctive ("If I were…")
	Questions: Some about social differences (male–female, old–young, rich–poor) and many other issues

communicates, listens, and soon speaks the basics of whatever language their playmates understand.

Young children are not perturbed by mispronunciation, in part because no young child says the sounds of their native language the way adults do. Eventually they speak with the same accent as their language community, but mispronunciation before age 6 does not necessarily mean hearing problems.

Older children and adolescents hesitate to talk to strangers but continue to communicate with their friends, sometimes on the phone for hours, sometimes texting hundreds of times a day with a close friend they saw just a few hours before. Especially with friends before age 20, language is more expressive than referential: It communicates emotions more than facts.

Building Vocabulary

The crucial measure of early language is not pronunciation but vocabulary, a mainstay of every test of intelligence, and a predictor of both a kindergartener's later success and an older child's IQ. Remember that the first word appears at about 12 months. Then, by about 18 months, the rate accelerates. From that point on, vocabulary builds, from about 500 words at age 2 to more than 10,000 at age 6, and 20,000 at age 10.

These are averages. Estimates of vocabulary size at age 6 range from 5,000 to 30,000. The process continues: By age 20, the *average* person knows 42,000 basic words, with some knowing twice that and some only half.

Variations by Socioeconomic Status and Gender

A much-cited study found that vocabulary was directly related to how much language a child heard, and found that, before age 3, children in families low in SES heard 30,000 fewer words than higher-SES children (Hart & Risley, 1995). That study led to a nationwide campaign to encourage low-income parents to talk more to their children.

Many later studies also found that low-SES parents talk less to their young children, and that meant the children entered kindergarten already behind other children in their ability to learn in school. That language deficit is thought to be the crucial reason some children score lower on achievement tests, and why they are much more likely to drop out of high school and find only low-income employment lifelong.

Some research disputes those findings, suggesting that young children from low-SES families overhear much more language than other children. As a result, there is much more variation within each strata of socioeconomic status, with some low-SES children hearing more words than some high-SES children (Sperry et al., 2019). Their eventual achievement gaps should not be blamed on their parents, but should instead be blamed on the quality of their preschools and primary schools.

Some of the leading scholars in child development argue against that interpretation, contending that overheard speech is not nearly as useful to children as child-directed speech (Golinkoff et al., 2019). They argue that adults need to spend hours every day listening and talking directly to young children. This can occur no matter what the parents SES. Then the children will develop language, and do well in school.

Another controversy involves gender differences in children's verbal proficiency. Generally, girls are ahead of boys in every aspect of language, with some studies finding this less apparent once children begin first grade (B. Lange et al., 2016). Boys, however, show more variation, with some quite high in language skills and others quite low. This may be a direct influence of female hormones, or may be the result of parents and schools, a topic explored in Chapter 12.

ESPECIALLY FOR Parents You've had an exhausting day but are setting out to buy groceries. Your 7-year-old wants to go with you. Should you explain that you are so tired that you want to make the trip to the supermarket solo this time? (see response, page 238)

How to Count Words

How large is vocabulary by age 20? About half a million words are in a full-size English dictionary, but that includes names, technical terms, and words that are really several forms or spellings of a basic word. A better estimate comes from a team of vocabulary experts, who listed 61,800 distinct words that might reasonably be known to non-specialists (Brysbaert et al., 2016). No one knows them all.

The basic *spoken* vocabulary is typically about 20,000 words, most learned before age 20. By late adolescence, people understand about three times as many words as they speak, although estimates vary. There is marked variation in how vocabulary is measured (Hoffman et al., 2014).

The quickest tests of vocabulary simply ask people to check words that they know from a list. (The lists include some nonwords; when people check those, their total of correct words is reduced.) This method assumes reading ability.

Other tests require the tester to say a word, and the testee to define it. This is complicated in two ways. First, only particular definitions are accepted. For example, the word "orange" is on a standard IQ test. Orange is correctly defined as a citrus fruit, or a color between red and yellow, but not as "like an apple," "related to a grapefruit," or "the sun at sunset." The examiner is allowed to say "tell me more," but unless the person then provides one of the listed meanings, the answer is wrong. Another complication is pronunciation. Is orange one syllable or two? If the examiner pronounces a word in an unfamiliar way, is that a valid measure?

Consider what children actually know. In one study, children listened to a story about a raccoon that saw its reflection in the water, and were asked what "reflection" means. Here are five answers:

1. "It means that your reflection is yourself. It means that there is another person that looks just like you."
2. "Means if you see yourself in stuff and you see your reflection."
3. "Is like when you look in something, like water, you can see yourself."
4. "It mean your face go in the water."
5. "That means if you the same skin as him, you blend in."

[Hoffman et al., 2014, pp. 471–472]

Which child was right? Technically, none of them! In the same study, another story included "a chill ran down his spine," and children were asked what chill meant. One answered, "When you want to lay down and watch TV—and eat nachos" (Hoffman et al., 2014, p. 473). Again wrong.

This illustrates another problem with measuring vocabulary. Meanings change, and new words and phrases appear. Many additions originate among adolescents, who often repurpose words (e.g., bad, cool, woke), creating meanings and phrases that are not on the list of accepted definitions.

Given that new words appear every year, perhaps there is no limit to how many words a person can know. For many reasons, it may be unfair to expect people to know a certain number by a certain age. No matter how vocabulary is measured, however, it is apparent that children add new words every day.

What Is It? These two children at the Mississippi River Museum in Iowa might call this a crocodile, but really it is an alligator. Fast-mapping allows that mistake, and egocentrism might make them angry if someone tells them they chose the wrong name.

Fast-Mapping

How are all those words learned? Sometimes slowly, sometimes quickly.

After painstakingly learning one word at a time in toddlerhood, children develop interconnected categories for words, a kind of mental map to aid learning

fast-mapping The speedy and sometimes imprecise way in which children learn new words by tentatively placing them in mental categories according to their perceived meaning.

new words. A child can then learn a word after one exposure via **fast-mapping** (Woodward & Markman, 1998), because, rather than waiting for several exposures and contexts, children hear a word once and immediately stick it into their mental language grid.

Language mapping is not precise. For example, children rapidly connect new animal names to known animal names. Thus, *tiger* is easy to map if you know *lion*, but a leopard might be called a tiger unless someone has already introduced the word *leopard*. A trip to the zoo facilitates fast-mapping, because zoos place similar animals near each other.

Books offer many opportunities to advance vocabulary, which is one reason developmentalists urge parents to read to their children, and later with their children, every day. A mentor reading a picture book might point out the stripes on tigers and spots on leopards, or an older child might read about felines (the cat family), learning about dozens of species with details such as that calico cats are almost always female.

Motivation and opportunity are crucial here: Some adolescents read books that are beyond their teachers' knowledge or forbidden by their parents. By the end of adolescence, those teenagers who are avid readers know about 52,000 basic words, double that of the nonreaders (Brysbaert et al., 2016).

Over- and Underextension

The problem with fast-mapping is that new words may be misinterpreted and new ideas misunderstood (Coutanche & Thompson-Schill, 2015). One problem is **overextension**, using a word to mean more than it actually means. For example, many young children use "mommy" to mean any caregiver or any woman. Red could be used for purple; all cats might be called kitties.

overextension Using a word to mean more than most people think it means.

The opposite problem is **underextension**, excluding some meanings that belong with that word. I once heard two 3-year-olds argue over whether they wore coats or jackets; neither agreed with me that it was both. Many children insist that each object has one name, and one name only.

underextension Limiting the meaning of a word, and failing to recognize that some words can be correctly used with many referents.

To accurately delineate a word requires time and many examples, a process called *slow-mapping* (K. Wagner et al., 2013). That is not what children do. Even in adolescence, people expand their vocabulary without understanding the limits of the word. Many misuse polysyllabic words, in an attempt to sound intelligent.

Using words precisely requires ongoing learning, since meanings change, undertones emerge, and new words appear. Ideally, the school curriculum teaches the specific meanings of words that belong to each academic discipline. In psychology, for instance, *nature*, *punishment*, *integrity*, and much more have specific meanings unlike those in fast-mapping.

Home communication may be crucial. In one longitudinal study of adolescent language ability, the researchers had, decades earlier, assessed their parents' and grandparents' communication patterns (Sohr-Preston et al., 2013). Not surprisingly, parents who were college graduates had teenagers with bigger vocabularies. But education was only an indirect influence; the parents' past communication with their children was the direct correlate.

In this study, parents and children were videoed discussing a family problem. Researchers years later viewed the tapes and rated the family interaction for clarifications, explanations, responsiveness, and respect. Nonverbal communication, such as slouching or leaning forward, smiling or shaking one's head, looking at the person talking or at the floor, was evident. When parents were good communicators, their children's communication, including spoken words, was advanced. In other words, mutual communication—both listening and talking—is crucial for children and adolescents to become language proficient.

Impaired Language Learning

Some children of every linguistic community have language difficulties. Instead of blaming their homes or culture, the problem originates in their brains (Brookshire & McNeil, 2015). They need speech therapy to overcome the problems, ideally before kindergarten.

Specific language impairment (SLI) is a common disability for about 7 percent of all 5-year-olds. The details of their difficulties are affected by the challenges of their particular language (some languages are more regular or easier to pronounce than others), but the problem appears in every community (Leonard, 2014).

Although it might seem logical to blame language impairment on the added difficulty of learning two languages, the opposite may be more accurate. Indeed, learning two languages sometimes makes it easier to help children with SLI (Grasso et al., 2018). The teacher needs to know both languages, and know exactly how to help.

There are dozens of causes of SLI (Brookshire & McNeil, 2015). Trouble with hearing is often the origin of the problem, but some children hear well and nonetheless have speech problems. Language impairments typically begin with speech, but later involve *dyslexia* (trouble reading) (Hayiou-Thomas et al., 2017).

Similarly, it is a mistake to blame the child's home environment, or gender, for language difficulties. Any child might need targeted, sequential help to overcome a language disability. Ideally, dyslexia is diagnosed and remedied before the child is actually expected to read.

Grammar

Grammar helps people express ideas that otherwise would be impossible to communicate. During childhood, children learn prefixes, suffixes, modifiers, and compound words. For instance, 2-year-olds know *jump*, but teenagers also know *jumped*, *jumping*, *jump start*, *jumpsuit*, *ski jump*, *high jump*, and both meanings of *jumper*.

Language Variations

With grammar, as with vocabulary, comprehension is ahead of production. People can understand what someone else is saying, even when they cannot use the same grammatical forms themselves. This is obvious if a person understands a "foreign" language but cannot speak it, but it also appears in less apparent ways.

CAREER ALERT   The Speech Therapist

Language disorders are evident during infancy, and speech therapy can be life changing for young children who have trouble making themselves understood, but they are not usually diagnosed until the child enters school. Consequently, speech therapists can help people of every age, but they are most in demand for school-age children.

A major problem is that parents and teachers may not recognize the problem until it has become a major impediment. Compared to children with normal speech, those who stutter report poorer relationships with their parents, sometimes with mothers too accepting and fathers too angry (Lau et al., 2012). Speech therapists are needed to help families, not just preschoolers with speech problems.

In the United States, there are about 130,000 speech pathologists. Most of them are certified by the American Speech, Language, and Hearing Association; half of them work in schools, but relatively few of them are fluent in the home languages of bilingual children. Thus, if you are bilingual and trained as a speech therapist,

you would be very much in demand. Current annual salary is about $70,000, with marked variation from one state to another. The demand for speech therapists is growing faster than for almost any other profession.

In the United States and many other nations, public funds pay for the diagnosis and treatment of speech disorders. However, most people with such problems never receive help—in part because parents and teachers may not recognize the problem, nor realize how effective a good therapist can be. Many children with speech problems can overcome them completely; adults with SLI can almost always be helped, although after years of problematic speech, usually some problems remain.

When people use language more effectively, self-esteem, academic competence, and social relationships improve. As a result, speech therapists sometimes gain much more than money: They have the joy of knowing they have brightened an entire life.

Camels Protected, People Confused Why the contrasting signs? Does everyone read English at the international airport in Chicago (O'Hare) but not on the main road in Tunisia?

For example, every language has *function words*, which are words that have no meaning in isolation but that function to make sentences meaningful. In English, *the, a,* and *an* are function words, understood by everyone who speaks English, long before they use them (Shi, 2014). People who learn a language as adults have great difficulty with function words, sometimes omitting them completely, because they do not translate.

Another problem is that every language has words and phrases that are puzzling (Leonard, 2014). English-learning children often have trouble with knowing when to use *who/whom, have been/had been, here/there, yesterday/tomorrow*. Many children tell what they did tomorrow, or will do yesterday. Sometimes these words are difficult in comprehension as well as production. A child told to "stay there" or "come here" may be confused, and not follow instructions. Better to say, "Stay there on that bench," or "Come here to hold my hand."

A third problem is that some grammar requires careful learning. For example, English has easy markers to denote past and future (*-ed, had, did, will*), but children learning Chinese have more difficulty with tense; Hungarian children may need to focus more on verbs, because they change depending on the object of the sentence; English-speaking children need to learn to add the *s* to a verb for third person *singular* but not the third person plural (he comes, they come), which contradicts what they have already learned about added *s*.

All young children make grammar and pronunciation mistakes. Many repeat themselves, or repeat syllables or sounds, in stuttering. Developmentalists need to know when those errors are an early sign of a specific language impairment, so targeting remediation can occur.

Grammar Mistakes in Every Language

No matter what the native language, a common problem with grammar is called **overregularization**, making the language more "regular" than it really is. Once children learn that, in English, adding *-ed* makes a verb past tense, they say they "comed" and "goed" instead of came and went. This error is a sign of advanced learning: The child knows and applies the rules of grammar. The problem, of course, is that English has many exceptions, so that this advance is heard as ungrammatical.

Grammar continues to develop every year. By the end of adolescence, people say and understand sentences of 20 words or more, with subordinate clauses, conditionals, past perfect tenses, subjunctive propositions, odd rules, and even odder exceptions—if they have been exposed to such constructions.

overregularization The application of rules of grammar even when exceptions occur, making the language seem more "regular" than it actually is.

Pragmatics

Probably the most difficult aspect of language is **pragmatics**, which is knowing which words, tones, and grammatical forms to use when, and with whom (Siegal & Surian, 2012). Young children often blurt out words that embarrass their parents ("Why is that lady so fat?" or "I won't kiss grandpa because his breath smells.") The pragmatics of polite speech require nuanced social understanding, beyond that of most young children.

In some languages, pragmatics includes using proper words to address someone who is older, or who is not a close friend or family member. Many languages designate objects as male or female, and a few distinguish paternal from maternal grandparents, or signify birth order. Children master such distinctions, which are quite difficult if an adult is learning them as a new language.

Pragmatics are particularly difficult for people on the autism spectrum. Often such people are quite verbal, with extensive vocabularies, but they are bewildered when language reflects social relationships (Klinger et al., 2014). Sadly, children may bully, mock, or shun peers who fail at the social nuances of communication. That worsens the social difficulties of people on the spectrum (Maïano et al., 2016).

Humor

One specific aspect of pragmatics occurs with linguistic jokes. Younger children may not understand standard jokes and teenagers find them lame and stale, but 6- to 11-year-olds delight in puns and unexpected answers to normal questions.

Some traditional jokes ("What is black and white and red (read) all over?"; "Why did the chicken cross the road?") bring laughter only for a year or two. Then, jokes that build on those standard jokes become funny—temporarily. Someone asked my grandson, "Why did the chicken cross the playground?" He laughed at the answer: "To get to the other slide."

In adolescence, metaphors, irony, aphorisms, and sarcasm become better understood. When 7-year-olds are asked the meaning of "Birds of a feather flock together," for instance, most say that birds like to be with other birds of the same kind. Only after puberty can most children apply such aphorisms to people.

Similarly, a sardonic "I see that you decided to grace us with your presence" might be taken literally by a younger child. Understanding irony, figures of speech, and so on is difficult for all young children, especially for those who are deaf or on the autism spectrum (O'Reilly et al., 2014). Communication is much more than vocabulary.

Many attempts at humor are appreciated by one group and offensive to another. This is particularly obvious in the joy that children have in telling "poop jokes," or slightly older children in humor that refers to sexual body parts. Adults often forbid such humor. Of course, adults themselves must know who will be offended by a joke that someone else will enjoy. That is pragmatics.

Code Switching

Mastery of pragmatics allows people to change styles of speech, or *linguistic codes*, depending on their audience. Each code includes many aspects of verbal and nonverbal communication—tone, pronunciation, sentence length, idioms, vocabulary, grammar, gestures, body position. Code switching is part of the social awareness that humans need to function well. Someone who uses academic speech on the street is out of touch.

Sometimes the switch is between *formal code* (used in academic contexts) and *informal code* (used with friends); sometimes it is between standard (or proper) speech and dialect or slang (used on

pragmatics The practical use of language that includes the ability to adjust language communication according to audience and context.

Go With the Flow This boat classroom in Bangladesh picks up students on shore and then uses solar energy to power computers linked to the internet as part of instruction. The educational context will teach skills and metaphors that peers of these students will not understand.

the street). Code in texting—numbers (411), abbreviations (LOL), emoticons (:-D), and spelling (r u ok?)—demonstrate pragmatics if the user knows when such uses are appropriate and when not.

Some children are unaware that slang, curses, and even contractions are not used in formal language. Ideally, schools provide language instruction in the formal code as well as grammar (*who* or *whom?*), pronunciation, and spelling. Peers provide the informal code; local communities transmit dialect, metaphors, and pronunciation.

Many U.S. children speak one of the 20 or so regional or ethnic English dialects, each with particular word use, pronunciation, and grammar. Code switching correlates with school achievement, and pride in origins correlates with motivation, so teachers need to respect the child while teaching the formal code (Terry et al., 2016). As you will now see, the same approach is crucial when a child's home language is not the school language.

Bilingual Communication

Ideally, everyone would speak, understand, read, and write at least two languages. This would bridge linguistic barriers, boost self-confidence, and, since language and culture are intertwined, facilitate multicultural understanding. Childhood is the best time to accomplish this.

Fortunately, young children are quite capable of learning two languages if they hear both often and are encouraged to speak. Before age 2, some bilingual children confuse their two languages, but after age 2 they add thousands of vocabulary words, master grammar, and speak in multiword sentences in two languages as easily as in one.

Bilingual Brains

Bilingual children switch languages easily, speaking the appropriate language to someone who is monolingual. If a child knows that an adult understands both, sometimes when they are questioned in one language they reply in the other—with no mixing of languages (Ribot et al., 2018). The young child's innate drive to communicate, and the brain regions that are primed for language, allow fluency (Höhle et al., 2020).

Brain imagery reveals that when two languages are learned early in life, both are located in the same brain areas. As a result, early bilingualism allows adults speak fluently, with native accents (Berken et al., 2017). As one team contends, the infant brain has "only one linguistic system," quite capable of holding several languages in that one system. Then "dynamic bilingualism" advances cognition (Garcia & Wei, 2014).

That does not mean that language is solely in one part of the brain. Many brain areas are involved in language, and they all are activated in bilingual children. What happens is the language areas are expanded, not that new ones are created (DeLuca et al., 2019).

Why might knowing two languages aid cognition? Perhaps speakers learn to inhibit unwanted impulses (in order not to blurt out the wrong word to a monolingual person), or to attend to details (to use the grammar peculiar to each language), or to advance memory (to learn twice as many words) (Bialystok, 2015, 2018; Morales et al., 2013). All this is part of what is called *executive function* (a collection of abilities that aid learning, as explained in the previous chapter).

Not everyone agrees that bilingualism advances overall cognition, in part because some comparison studies do not find those advances (Spätgens & Schoonen, 2018; Nichols et al., 2020). Scholars on both sides of this disagreement criticize the research of the others. The underlying problem for scientists is

THINK CRITICALLY: Do children from some backgrounds need to become especially adept at code switching? Does this challenge advance cognitive development?

Bilingual Learners These are Chinese children learning a second language. Could this be in the United States? No, this is a class in the first Chinese-Hungarian school in Budapest. There are three clues: the spacious classroom, the letters on the book, and the trees outside.

ATTILA KISBENEDEK/AFP/Getty Images

that political policies make it impossible to find two groups of children, identical in every way except in how many languages they speak. Thus, finding valid experimental and control groups is virtually impossible.

Nonetheless, no study finds that fluency in two languages impairs learning. It was prejudice, not evidence, that led a prominent psychologist a century ago to write that children hearing two languages would suffer "mental confusion" (Saer, 1923, p. 1).

In the United States, most children are raised in homes and communities where one language is all they hear (see **Figure 8.1**). Since the first years of life are the best for learning language, many children enter kindergarten with only a rudimentary understanding of the school language if it is not their home language, and those who already speak the school language might not befriend those who do not.

It may be unfair to blame the parents for not introducing young children to two languages. Before research showed advantages of bilingualism, some parents were told to talk to their children only in the dominant language. If they did not know the dominant language, and if their children were not in preschool, the result was a child who was neither bilingual nor monolingual. That child did not speak any language well. Such children were behind their peers in kindergarten, and, unless they had teachers who recognized the problem and helped them, stayed behind during their academic career.

If parents live in a community where everyone speaks the same language, the children have another problem: They may struggle with the language requirement in high school and college, and they may be handicapped in our increasingly multicultural world.

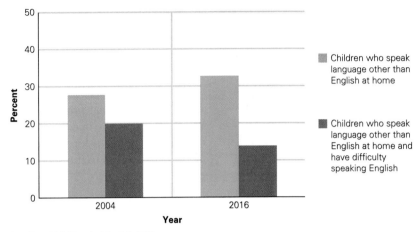

Bilingual 5- to 17-Year-Olds in the United States

Data from Child Trends, March 7, 2019.

Legend: Children who speak language other than English at home; Children who speak language other than English at home and have difficulty speaking English

FIGURE 8.1

Home and Country Do you see good news, or do you see trouble? A dramatic increase in the number of bilingual children is a benefit for the nation, but the hundreds of thousands of children who still have trouble with English suggests that more education is needed.

Teaching a Second Language

Since most children of the world speak a language at home that differs from the official language, a critical question is how best to teach a second language. Various nations have quite different approaches.

In the United States

In the United States, children below average in English proficiency are called **English language learners (ELLs)**. Family background, especially SES, is one reason a child is ELL, but even high-SES children who struggled to learn English become less proficient readers (Howard et al., 2014). This is not inevitable: Many educators seek the best way to teach children a second language while still protecting the first.

Methods for teaching children a new language range from **immersion**, in which instruction occurs entirely in a language they do not know, to the opposite, in which children are instructed in their first language until the second language is taught as a "foreign" tongue. Between these extremes lies **bilingual education**, with instruction in two languages.

When children come from many nations, each with a separate language, bilingual education is impossible. In the United States, another method is used, called **English as a second language (ESL)**, with all non-English speakers taught in one multilingual group. ESL teachers use gestures, pictures, and pantomime to communicate—and then help children learn the English words that express those ideas.

English language learners (ELLs) Children in the United States whose proficiency in English is low—usually below a cutoff score on an oral or written test. Many children who speak a non-English language at home are also capable in English; they are not ELLs.

immersion A strategy in which instruction in all school subjects occurs in the second (usually the majority) language that a child is learning.

bilingual education A strategy in which school subjects are taught in both the learner's original language and the second (majority) language.

English as a second language (ESL) A U.S. approach to teaching English that gathers all of the non-English speakers together and provides intense instruction in English. Students' first languages are never used; the goal is to prepare students for regular classes in English.

Prove That You Speak English At Eagleton Middle School in Maryville, Tennessee, 140 students learn English as a second language. Graduation requires proven fluency, such as writing and reading a speech in English. That is what Jessica Hunt and Omar Andrade are about to do.

Each of these methods has advocates, and each sometimes succeeds. The key variable may be emotional, not pedagogical. Teachers need to understand that the child's home language should be seen not as a deficit but instead as a tool to help the child learn (MacSwan et al., 2017). The research finds that children need active social interaction and encouragement, talking (not just listening) to foster communication.

If parents speak only one language with their young children, ideally they find a preschool that provides a second language. This applies to children whose first language is the majority language. It is contrary to what we know about children's brains to begin foreign language instruction in high school, when the brain no longer adjusts to the sound and structure of a new language.

In Canada

Canada has had two official languages (English and French) for decades. Adults who work for the government are expected to be bilingual, but many find it hard to become fluent in the language they did not learn as children. Outside Quebec, only 10 percent of Canadian adults are fluent in both languages.

However, an estimated 300,000 Canadian children whose home language is English are now in French immersion schools, and many French-speaking children are in English schools. They eventually score well on tests of French, English, math, science, and so on (Hayday, 2015; Sénéchal & LeFevre, 2014).

A Canadian official, noting the linguistic successes of bilingual Canadian young adults, contends "It is easier to learn a third language than it is to learn a second language; learning French is not a barrier but a bridge to the rest of the world" (Fraser, 2015, p. xiii). He may be right: In a *foreign language effect*, bilingual adults are more rational, less self-centered, and more open to reason when thinking and speaking about something in their second language (Costa et al., 2017).

The Language Shift

One problem has been identified with early second-language learning, especially if education is only in the majority language. Some children lose the ability to speak their home language when they learn the school language, a phenomenon called the *language shift*. This shift is common in South America among those who speak an indigenous language (they switch to Spanish), or among Spanish-speaking immigrants in the United States (they switch to English); or, in Canada, among the indigenous people whose home language is neither English nor French.

A language shift is particularly likely if children conclude that their original language is inferior to the dominant language. That undercuts parental communication and authority, adding to the cultural tragedy if children are unaware of the past glories of their heritage. A language shift is less common among families who are successful economically and educationally: Children are less ashamed of their background. This may explain why, in the United States, some children of Asian heritage switch, but most do not (Cho, 2015).

WHAT HAVE YOU LEARNED?

1. Why is it hard to know the vocabulary size of a child or adolescent?
2. What indicates that children are learning grammar?
3. When do people learn what language is appropriate for specific people, such as peers, teachers, people who understand one language or another?
4. What do linguists mean when they talk about language codes?
5. What is the best time and method to teach a child a second language?

Communication in Adulthood

Most of the research on adult communication in adulthood is quite positive. Adults become better communicators every year. But first we must consider one problem that many adults have—pronunciation!

Replacing the Accent

The infant brain is exquisitely attuned to speech, hearing exactly how words are pronounced. Even before the first word is spoken, an astute listener can detect that babies are babbling the sounds and cadences of the language they hear. Then, over the first years of childhood, pronunciation improves, dendrites and synapses form, unused neurons are pruned away.

That is beneficial, in that adults can hear in others' voices whether they are angry, tired, or happy. But that exquisite sensitivity comes at a price. In psychological terms, we gain perceptual depth at the price of perceptual narrowing. We can no longer produce nuances of pronunciation in languages never heard during our early years.

The easiest example is with the 30 or so languages that use a click sound as part of speech. Children in those communities become adept at clicking, but if someone never clicked in their early years, they cannot do so later on. Similarly, the rolled *r*, the enunciated *l* or *th*, the difference between *b* and *v*, are mastered by children learning some languages but not others, and very difficult for adults who never learned them.

Most languages use tone (high, low, or varied) to mark meaning. For example, in Mandarin Chinese, */ma/* means "mother" or "horse," depending on how it is said. People who grew up speaking non-tonal languages, such as English, have difficulty reproducing tonal distinctions (Hay et al., 2015).

Of course, adults can hear accents. Probably every reader of this book can distinguish whether an English-speaking adult grew up in Alabama, Jamaica, Scotland, or India. Further nuances are possible: Those from India can distinguish Delhi from Dhanbad, those from New England can distinguish Boston from Brooklyn, and those who grew up in Brooklyn can distinguish Canarsie from Carroll Gardens (neighborhoods a few miles apart in Brooklyn). Actors taking on the persona of someone from a particular region practice extensively before they pass muster—except to people actually from that place.

Differences are evident not only in accent but also in word choice and phrases. Did you understand the phrase "pass muster"? It means adequate to a particular standard. The phrase originally came from a military officer who reviewed the troops, who had to stand at attention, which was called muster.

If a recruit's dress, posture, and expression were acceptable, they would pass muster. The phrase came to my mind to express what I wanted to convey, but I suspect I got it from my father, who was a captain in the Navy. People sometimes misstate it and say "pass mustard"—a mistake I would not make because of my dad.

Thousands of phrases arise from a particular place and time. Then people from that place might pass it on to others, who may reproduce it accurately or not.

This influences communication in ways that adults may not realize. If an adult wants to erase traces of their childhood and speak a new language like a native, they probably cannot. Adults immersed in one language may be unaware of the many metaphors that are localized. In the United States, baseball metaphors abound: Teachers who tell their students to keep their eye on the ball might wonder why their students look everywhere but on the paper in front of them.

Observation Quiz Pinker's tie and white shirt are traditional; they would be understood by an academic audience a century ago. But three visible aspects would not be understood. What are they? (see answer, page 238) ↓

English as a Second Language Can people comprehend complex ideas in their second language? Steven Pinker, a linguist from Harvard University in Massachusetts, lectured in English at the Jaipur Literature Festival in India, where Hindi and 121 other languages are first languages. Almost no infant learns English first, but about 150 million Indians learn English as a second language. Despite his accent, Pinker's audience understood him well.

Language Advances

Although pronunciation learned in adulthood falls short of what children learn in the early years, every other aspect of language development continues to improve past levels attained by age 20.

Vocabulary

A detailed longitudinal study found that, for people of every social class, vocabulary increases from adolescence through midlife, even if the person did not attend college and does very little reading (Sullivan & Brown, 2015). Advances were more dramatic for those who frequently read a variety of books and newspapers: Their vocabulary at age 42 was a third higher than that of the average 16-year-old.

In that study, researchers found that reading added to vocabulary, but content mattered. Those whose newspapers were mostly tabloids did not advance as much as those who read more detailed, comprehensive newspapers.

Improvement continues into old age. When language skills are measured in standard intelligence tests, vocabulary increases every decade, for almost everyone until about age 65 or 70, and then variation is notable. Vocabulary declines every year of late adulthood in some people but not in everyone: Some people continue to add new words at age 80 and 90 (Salthouse, 2015).

The data on overall numbers include only basic words that any adult might understand. Specialists in every profession and hobby add hundreds of other words that refer to their particular interests.

- Is international politics or global trade your specialty? If so, you can probably name far more of the world's 195 nations than most people.
- Are you someone who builds or designs cars? Then you probably know far more of the 400 automobile parts listed on Wikipedia than I do.

Many words and phrases now understood did not exist when today's adults were children, including one in the previous bullet (itself a new meaning for an old word), or the hundreds added to the Oxford Dictionary in 2017, including *precariat*, *sharrow*, *spoiler alert*, *binge-watch*, and *microaggression*. We all add new words as current events require it: I did not know *coronavirus*, *pandemic*, or the phrases "flatten the curve" and "social distancing" a few months ago.

Among scientists who study human development, the fact that adults continue to gain vocabulary lifelong is good news. The assumption is that more extensive and elaborate language use indicates intelligence. However, that assumption may not be universally accepted: Sometimes knowing when to keep quiet is valued. Culture may differ in this regard, as A View from Science explains.

Nonverbal Communication

A crucial part of communication is not with words; it is with gestures, facial expressions, and body positions. Adults learn that nonverbal communication is potent: Most adults become better at communicating with movements every year. Culture matters.

For example, a study of gestures discovered over 100 meaningful hand gestures. A few had the same meaning across cultures, but many had distinct local meanings, recognized by people within one group but unknown to others—including to the scientists who did the research (Matsumoto & Hwang, 2013).

Consider the meaning of two raised and separated fingers (the index finger and the middle finger). It can mean peace, victory, an insult, or merely number two. In a now classic example, in 1992 then President Bush visited Australia, and was photographed raising those two fingers to indicate his approval of a group of protesters as his motorcade passed. To Australians, that gesture meant "up yours."

Observation Quiz Beyond the open hands, what else shows that this is a close moment between teammates? (see answer, page 238) ↓

What Did You Say? Nothing. No words needed as Ichiro Suzuki and Martin Prado are about to shake hands before the Miami Marlins beat the Washington Nationals.

G Flume/Getty Images

The Good Blabbermouth

Traditionally, especially in small, poor, communities, a good child was a quiet child, and adults were admired for being "strong and silent." If adults talked too much, they were shunned as blabbermouths, gossip was called sinful, good workers did not waste time in "idle talk." Note the implications of each of those phrases.

This may add insight to conflicts in close romantic relationships. Remember that, generally, females develop language skills in advance of males. It is also true that women are more likely to seek to "talk it out" when conflicts arise. If a man does not want to talk about a conflict, that does not necessarily mean that he does not care about the relationship. This may be a particular problem in older couples, who grew up when men were not supposed to talk about feelings (Nice et al., 2020).

This was recognized by one older man, who thought that he did not know how to communicate with his wife. He wished he had learned it as a boy, explaining:

> I think we can all learn as teenage boys to communicate more with either the girl we're dating or the girl we're marrying or the grandma you're living with about what's going on. Maybe that will need to be taught in school somewhere, 'cause I didn't have it when I was growing up.
>
> [Quoted in Nice et al., 2020, p. 203]

The variability in communication may be partly cultural. In some cultures, too much talk was a problem, not a benefit. Families had secrets, emotions were unexpressed, it was thought that some things were better unsaid. In one cartoon, a wife tells her husband, "We should stop talking about this, so we don't say something to each other that we mean."

In some rural areas of the world, the antitalk meme continues. In Senegal, for instance, it was feared that talking to babies or even making eye contact might encourage evil spirits to take over the child (Zeitlin, 2011).

However, in the twenty-first-century global economy, all forms of communication are crucial. People talk, read, and write—in person or via the internet—and those who are better communicators earn more money, have happier relationships, and experience high self-esteem. Most developmentalists now believe that, to succeed in adulthood, infants need to be encouraged to talk.

In one study in rural Senegal, professionals from the region (fluent in Wolof, the language spoken by the people) taught mothers in some villages about infant care, including responsive communication via gestures, facial expressions, and words.

A crucial aspect of the curriculum was that infants learn language even before they begin speaking, and that verbal ability predicts later intelligence and adult success. Other similar villages were a control group: No classes for new mothers were offered.

Those who designed this study did not challenge traditional notions directly; instead, they explained exactly how early responses led to smarter babies. The mothers drew their own conclusions.

The results were clear. Those mothers talked more to their babies, who, after a year, uttered nine more words in five minutes of mother–infant play than did babies in the control group (Weber et al., 2017). A success in applied science!

Pragmatics

Counting vocabulary words is an easy way to notice that adult communication continues to grow, but a better measure of communication skills is increasing awareness of the sensitivities of other people. Of course, everyone is sometimes oblivious to how their verbal and nonverbal communications are understood by people of another sexual orientation, or religion, or ethnicity, or background (Brown, 2015; Gasman et al., 2015). In fact, all of us have said something insensitive; we may still be unaware of such mistakes. Pragmatics is a lifelong challenge.

As you already read, children may not know when a particular comment is rude, or humorous, or spot on (a phrase from England that means exactly right). Most people from cultures with a heavy dose of British English understand "spot on," but those who learned English as adults might not.

Are Languages Sexist?

In general, adults have difficulty with conventions and idioms of a language that were not learned from daily interactions in childhood. One intriguing aspect is whether the language assigns gender to inanimate objects, as about half of the world languages do. For instance, in French and Spanish, inanimate objects are masculine or feminine; in German, they are masculine, feminine, or neuter; in English they have no gender. Does that indicate something about the culture, as some suggest? (Chiu & Hong, 2013).

When U.S. hurricanes were first named, the names were always female. Then women objected, and since 1979, female and male names alternate. One study suggested that hurricanes with female names are deadlier, because people do not take them as seriously as ones with male names, a gender bias (Jung et al., 2014).

Other scientists strongly disagreed, not only with those conclusions but also with the statistical analysis. The original authors defended their research. This dispute highlights that the conventions of science do not obliterate the human factors in communication. Remember, disagreement, replication, and re-analysis are part of the scientific method. But all agree: Language reflects gender.

Cultural Differences

That dispute about hurricane names is a small example of the larger issue of communication. Miscommunication abounds, contributing to divorce, lawsuits, elections, airplane crashes, homicides, medical errors . . . in fact, almost everything that can go wrong in human life can be attributed to communication mistakes. Pragmatics is especially difficult when communicating with someone of another gender, age, or culture, because there are forms, implications, and connotations in words and phrases that have meaning to one group but not to others.

For example, a White woman told a Black woman that some White people were intimidated by the dreadlocks of another Black woman. The speaker intended her comment to show that she was not as racist as some of her peers, but her listener was offended. The listener, however, did not immediately communicate her emotional reaction. When a third party later told the White woman, she realized why her comment was disrespectful, and she apologized (DiAngelo, 2018).

As I write this, I imagine some readers consider me insensitive to put this in print, and other readers wonder why the woman apologized. But that is the point: The same comment can be considered benign or hostile, and adults continually learn from other people's reactions to communication.

Communication is particularly challenging when people raised in different cultures work together. There are specific ways for "requesting, refusing, apologizing, complimenting, and complaining in various languages" (Ishihara & Cohen, 2014, p. ix). Even people who speak the same language may nonetheless offend each other with phases or expressions. One of the advantages of living in a multiethnic nation is that adults become aware of such microaggressions, but pragmatic sensitivity is a lifelong goal.

Recently many men are stunned to hear that what they thought was a compliment was understood as an insult and a power play by some women. I experienced this first-hand. I walk my dog each morning, usually saying "Good morning" to an older neighbor who often stands outside his home to smoke an early-morning cigarette. Recently he began to reply, "Good morning, darling." After several days, I gathered my courage and told him, "I am not your darling, I am your friend." He said "I am sorry. I hope I have not offended you." This was culture clash: My interpretation was a surprise to him.

Adults become more sensitive and precise in their use of words every year. We all tend to underextend and overextend because we are unaware of the implications of the words we use. Are some immigrants "undocumented," or are they "illegal aliens"? Are criminals people who have committed serious crimes, or people who have been arrested and convicted, or anyone who has violated any law? If someone is a criminal by any of those measures, are they always a criminal, or can they become a noncriminal?

Over my adult life, as a student of human development, I have noticed many changes in terminology. For example, the disability community insists that we should use "people-first" language. No one *is* a schizophrenic, but some people have been diagnosed with schizophrenia; no child *is* autistic, but some children are on the autism spectrum. Maybe no one is a criminal, although some people have broken the law.

As every textbook author knows, accepted uses and boundaries of words change over the decades. I now cringe when someone refers to women as girls, I avoid using *America* as a synonym for the United States, I think it insulting to call someone "retarded." Yet I am sure that some of my words are misleading or offensive to some people. (That is inadvertent. If you are one of those people, I apologize. Please tell me.)

For the Very Old

As you have just seen, communication continues to develop throughout life. Language is usually the last ability to fade with age. Vocabulary continues to hold steady long after reaction time, or short-term memory, or spatial estimate, declines.

At every age, people understand more than they express. Many older people have trouble recalling names. However, recognition memory for words is markedly better in later life than recall. For instance, an older person might not immediately call a particular utensil a spatula, but they may be well aware that a spatula is not a whisk. They also may reach for it in a drawer jumbled with utensils and use it appropriately.

Even when recall fades, pragmatics may continue to improve. Wisdom is often defined as the ability to respond appropriately to many people, circumstances, and situations—a definition that evokes pragmatics. A survey of people from 26 nations in every corner of the world found that people consider wisdom more common in the old than the young (Löckenhoff et al., 2009).

Most esteemed religious leaders, whose words are considered insightful by millions of younger people, are quite old. (Pope Francis was born in 1936; the Dalai Lama in 1935; they are both in their mid-80s). All these are masters of communication.

If brain diseases erase memories and distort emotions, many elders retain their ability to communicate. People with neurocognitive disorders sometimes can still play word games (Scrabble is one example), and people who no longer talk can nonetheless sing. They may even know all the words to familiar songs, with each song evoking a memory and a mood. I have a friend who was a death doula for an aged, religious person. She found that singing hymns was comforting to the person in ways that words were not.

When people are dying, communication is crucial. Many dying people want to hear familiar prayers and poems, or to be read to—from a current newspaper, a well-loved novel, a sacred book. Hospice workers say that the brain responds to words even when a person is unable to respond. Much attention is paid to a dying person's last words, words that often take great effort to articulate. And many mourners regret that they did not say "I love you" to a dying relative, even though they may have said those words many times before.

Long Past Warring Many of the oldest men in Mali, like this imam, are revered. Unfortunately, Mali has experienced violent civil wars and two national coups in recent years, perhaps because 75 percent of the male population are under age 30 and less than 2 percent are over age 70. In 2019, the British newspaper *The Guardian* described Mali as the most dangerous nation in the world. Too few of the young can hear the words of the old.

WHAT HAVE YOU LEARNED?

1. What differences in pronunciation are easy to hear but difficult to produce?
2. How does verbal ability change with age?
3. What is conveyed in nonverbal communication?
4. What evidence suggests that there are gender and ethnic differences in adult communication?
5. What is "people first" language, and why do some people insist on it?
6. What communication abilities decrease and what ones are maintained in later adulthood.
7. How is communication relevant when people are dying?

Theories of Communication and Language

As you have read, in every part of the world, people communicate their hopes, fears, and memories—sometimes in more than one language—and their fellow humans understand them. By adolescence, people communicate with nuanced words and gestures, some writing poems and lyrics that move thousands of their co-linguists. Adults continue to advance in vocabulary and social communication. Even people who are dying communicate, sometimes only with a movement of the eyes or a squeeze of the hand.

FIGURE 8.2

Maternal Responsiveness and Infants' Language Acquisition Learning the first 50 words is a milestone in early language acquisition, as it predicts the arrival of the naming explosion and the multiword sentence a few weeks later. Researchers found that half of the infants of highly responsive mothers (top 10 percent) reached this milestone at 15 months. The infants of less responsive mothers (bottom 10 percent) lagged significantly behind, with half of them at the 50-word level at 21 months.

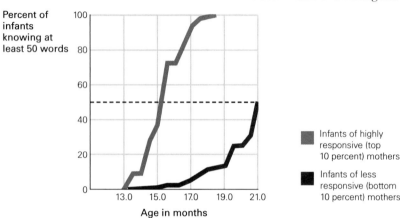

Data from Tamis-LeMonda et al., 2001, p. 761.

How and why do people learn language so easily and continue to communicate lifelong? Answers begin again with infants, since communication seems to arise from the first months of life. Four divergent theories have attempted to answer this question.

Theory One: People Need to Be Taught

One idea arises from behaviorism. The essential idea is that learning to communicate is acquired, step by step, through association and reinforcement.

B. F. Skinner (1957) noticed that spontaneous babbling is usually reinforced. Typically, when a baby says "ma-ma-ma-ma," a grinning mother appears, repeating the sound and showering the baby with attention, praise, and perhaps food. Repetition strengthens associations, so infants learn language faster if parents speak to them often (see **Figure 8.2**). Few parents know this theory, but many use behaviorist techniques by praising and responding to the toddler's simple, mispronounced speech, thus teaching language.

Behaviorists note that some 3-year-olds converse in elaborate sentences; others just barely put one simple word with another. Such variations correlate with the amount of language each child has heard. That continues throughout life. As you read, vocabulary is directly related to reading, as reading to young children helps with fast mapping, and reading in adulthood increases vocabulary.

As you also learned, some cultures discourage talking. People in those places may try not to communicate. They avoid being "blabbermouths" or "gossips" (words that convey cultural values), and do not express emotions. Some cultures teach people to cover their mouths when they laugh, and never to lose their temper or even talk too loudly. Behaviorists describe direct results in language proficiency, arising from practices that reinforce, or punish, language.

According to this theory, people learn language because others teach it to them via repetition, encouragement, or not. There is some empirical support for this theory, in that infants can be seen as "statistical learners" of language, deciding the meanings and boundaries of words based on how often those sounds are heard (Saffran & Kirkham, 2018).

Parents of the most verbal children teach language from infancy onward—singing, explaining, listening, responding, and reading to their babies every day, giving their children a rich trove of verbal data, allowing older children to interrupt adults because they have something to say, giving students in school credit for "participation," encouraging adults to express their opinions through "freedom of expression." Thus, this theory seems supported in the culture, but, as you soon will see, not everyone agrees.

Theory Two: Social Impulses Foster Communication

The second theory arises directly from the sociocultural reason for language: communication. According to this perspective, humans are, above all, social beings, dependent on one another for survival and joy. Thus, for all people of every age, the drive to be part of the community leads to a powerful need to communicate and to understand the communications of others.

That explains why all human infants (and no chimpanzees) seek to master words and grammar in order to join the social world (Tomasello & Herrmann, 2010). According to this perspective, it is the social function of speech, not the words, that undergirds early language. This theory notes that all the other forms of communication, with body position, gestures, and the like, are also part of the social impulse. We strive to connect with others, and language is one manifestation of that.

This theory challenges child-directed videos, CDs, and downloads named to appeal to parents (*Baby Einstein, Brainy Baby,* and *Mozart for Mommies and Daddies—Jumpstart your Newborn's I.Q.*). Since all babies naturally strive to communicate, and since early language development is impressive, even explosive (as in the naming explosion), such videos are unnecessary and may even be an impediment. If parents allow infants to watch such programs, they might mistakenly believe that language learning is aided by video.

However, developmental research finds that screen time may be harmful, because it avoids the social interaction that is essential for learning to communicate. One study found that toddlers could learn a word from either a book or a video but that only book-learning, not video-learning, enabled children to use the new word in another context (Strouse & Ganea, 2017).

Another study focused particularly on teaching 18 baby signs that refer to particular objects (Dayanim & Namy, 2015). The babies in this study were 15 months old, an age at which all babies use gestures and are poised to learn object names. The 18 signs referred to common early words, such as *baby, ball, banana, bird, cat,* and *dog.*

In this study, the toddlers were divided into four groups: video only, video with parent watching and reinforcing, book instruction with parent reading and reinforcing, and no instruction. Not surprisingly, the no-instruction group learned words (as every normal toddler does) but not signs, and the other three groups learned some signs. The two groups with parent instruction learned most, with the book-reading group remembering signs better than either video group. Why?

The crucial factor seemed to be parent communication. When parents watch a video with their infants, they tend to sit passively, talking less than when they read a book or play with toys (Anderson & Hanson, 2016). Since adult input is essential for language learning, cognitive development is reduced by video time. Infants are most likely to understand and apply what they have learned when they learn directly from another person (Barr, 2013). Screen time cannot "substitute for *responsive,* loving face-to-face relationships" (Lemish & Kolucki, 2013, p. 335).

The same principals apply to communication in the workplace, in family life, and in old age. People need direct social communication in order to flourish, because humans are, at the core, social beings. Language is an outgrowth of that.

"Keep in mind, this all counts as screen time."

Caught in the Middle Parents try to limit screen time, but children are beguiled and bombarded from many sides.

ESPECIALLY FOR Nurses and Pediatricians Eric and Jennifer have been reading about language development in children. They are convinced that because language develops naturally, they need not talk to their 6-month-old son. How do you respond? (see response, page 238)

Theory Three: People Teach Themselves

A third theory holds that language learning is genetically programmed. Adults need not teach it (theory one), nor is it a by-product of social interaction (theory two). Instead, it arises from a particular gene (FOXP2), brain maturation, and the overall human impulse to imitate.

You already learned about function words, such as the English articles (*the, an, a*). They are not taught to children, they are learned as children strive to understand language. Such words signal that the next word will be the name of an object, and since babies have "an innate base" that primes them to learn, articles facilitate learning nouns (Shi, 2014, p. 9). It is difficult to teach the proper use of such words, even to highly intelligent and motivated adults learning a new language, because their language-learning genes are past the sensitive learning time. "The," "an," and "a" help young children but are confusing to English-learning adults.

Our ancestors were genetically programmed to imitate for survival, but until a few millennia ago, no one needed to learn languages other than their own.

⬤ **Observation Quiz** If this is a typical scene, what family values are evident? (see answer, page 238) ↓

Family Values Every family encourages the values and abilities that their children need to be successful adults. For this family in Ecuador, that means strong legs and lungs to climb the Andes, respecting their parents, and keeping quiet unless spoken to. A "man of few words" is admired. By contrast, many North American parents babble in response to infant babble, celebrate the first spoken word, and stop their conversation to listen to an interrupting child. If a student never talks in class, or another student blurts out irrelevant questions, perhaps the professor should consider cultural influences.

Steven J. Kazlowski/Alamy

language acquisition device (LAD)
Chomsky's term for a hypothesized mental structure that enables humans to learn language, including the basic aspects of grammar, vocabulary, and intonation.

Thus, human genes allow experience-dependent language learning, pruning the connections that our particular language does not need. If they are needed by another language that we want to learn in adulthood, our brains cannot resurrect them, because of our genes, according to this theory.

The prime spokesman for this perspective was Noam Chomsky (1968, 1980). Although behaviorists focus on variations among children in vocabulary size, Chomsky focused on similarities in language acquisition—the evolutionary universals, not the differences.

Noting that all children master basic grammar according to a schedule, and that at puberty learning a new language is increasingly difficult, Chomsky hypothesized that people have an innate **language acquisition device (LAD)** in the brain. The LAD allows humans to derive the rules of grammar quickly and effectively from the speech they hear every day.

For example, everywhere, a raised tone indicates a question, and infants prefer questions to declarative statements (Soderstrom et al., 2011). This suggests that infants are wired to talk, and caregivers universally ask them questions long before they can answer back.

According to theory three, language is experience-expectant, as the developing brain quickly and efficiently connects neurons to support whichever language the infant hears. Because of this experience-expectancy, the various languages of the world are all logical, coherent, and systematic. Then some experience-dependent learning occurs as each brain adjusts to a particular language, and schools teach the finer points, such as the subjunctive and the proper use of pronouns.

The surface structures of language need to be learned by each person, and these change as the chronosystem differs for each cohort of adults. For example, in many languages, pronouns indicated gender and number, with the male pronouns used when gender was unknown. Now writers no longer use "he" and "him" as a generic pronoun, instead using "he or she" and "hers or his," or "they" and "theirs." Likewise, "Latino," which once meant people of Latin heritage of both genders or exclusively male, has become "Latinx."

Such changes are explained by this third theory because the surface structures of languages respond to culture, unlike the deep structures that all languages follow. The central idea is that all humans are innately driven to communicate—and they do so with noises, gestures, body positions—whatever they can. Cultures then teach which of the more than 6,000 world languages, and which of the many body and facial variations, are to be mastered.

Theory Four: Neuroscience

Neuroscience is the most recent method to investigate the development of language. It was once thought that language was located in two specific regions of the brain (Wernicke's area and Broca's area). Both those areas are usually in the left hemisphere, which led to the notion that language and communication were functions of the left brain.

But now neuroscientists are convinced that language arises from both sides and many brain regions. The entire brain is involved in communication, with body movements (parietal cortex), social understanding (prefrontal cortex), physiological signs (smaller pupils and faster breathing that might mean anger). Some genes and regions are crucial for language, but hundreds of genes and many brain regions contribute to communication (Hahn et al., 2019).

Neuroscientists write about "connections," "networks," "circuits," and "hubs" to capture the idea that communication, including language, is interrelated and complex (Dehaene-Lambertz, 2017; Pulvermüller, 2018). Even when the focus is simply on talking, one neuroscientist notes that "speech is encoded at multiple levels in different parallel pathways" (Dehaene-Lambertz, 2017, p. 52).

That neuroscientist began a detailed description of the infant brain and language with the same amazement that traditional linguists have expressed for decades:

> For thousands of years and across numerous cultures, human infants are able to perfectly master oral or signed language in only a few years. No other machine, be it silicon or carbon based, is able to reach the same level of expertise.
>
> [Dehaene-Lambertz, 2017, p. 48]

A worldwide bestseller, first published in Israel and then translated and published in English, is *Sapiens: A Brief History of Humankind*. Harari (2015) contends that the reason our particular human species (*homo sapiens*) survived amidst other species of humans and many bigger, fiercer, mammals is that our ancestors learned to communicate and cooperate. That occurred because of a "cognitive revolution," something in our brains that chanced to occur and then allowed language, not only via speech and gestures, but with written ledgers, laws, proclamations, and, recently, books.

The current understanding from neuroscience is that the entire developmental process, as just reviewed, for language is directed, both enhanced and constrained, by brain maturation (D'Souza & D'Souza, 2019).

Perhaps. In any case, as this chapter makes clear, communication and language are crucial human abilities lifelong. Scientists are awed by this human ability, crediting it for our special status among all the creatures of the world. This chapter has tried to explain the what, how, and why of language and communication lifelong, but many questions remain. What does seem evident, however, is that we are fortunate that we can communicate with our fellow humans.

Evidently, humans are born to communicate and do so lifelong. Specific aspects of language are diverse and varied; each of us tries to discern what someone of another age or culture is communicating. I think I would have, eventually, understood what Isaac meant by "mama," even if his father had not arrived to tell me.

WHAT HAVE YOU LEARNED?

1. According to behaviorism, how do adults teach infants to talk?

2. According to sociocultural theory, why do infants try to communicate?

3. Do people really have a language acquisition device?

4. How does the neuroscience explanation of language learning differ from the other three theories?

SUMMARY

The First Two Years

1. Communication is the essence of language. Thus language begins at birth, expressed in touch, facial expressions, and tone. Babies communicate at first with cries, and adults with child-directed speech.

2. In the first year of life, infants attend to sounds that caregivers make, and proceed from cries, to babbling, to gestures, to expressive sounds, to a first word or two.

3. In the second year of life, toddlers communicate with holophrases, and gradually add words until a language spurt at about 18 months, putting two or more words together before age 2. Babies understand much more than they can say.

Language from Age 2 to 20

4. Vocabulary builds rapidly in childhood, as children learn several new words a day, via fast-mapping new words. Variation is evident: Some children and adolescents know twice as much as others.

5. Grammar allows much more extensive communication. Children tend to overextend the rules of grammar, and to believe that each word has one and only one exclusive meaning.

6. The practical (pragmatic) function of language is difficult to learn. Schools teach formal language; peers teach informal codes.

7. Learning two languages is easier in childhood than later on. Bilingualism may foster cognition, but the danger is a language shift if the new language is thought to be better than the original one.

Communication in Adulthood

8. Language abilities continue to advance in adulthood, but it is difficult for adults to produce the exact pronunciation and the idioms of an unfamiliar language.

9. Communication occurs in many ways. Nonverbal communication, via gestures, body position, and tone, is especially important in conveying emotions.

10. The most difficult aspect of language is sensitivity to the nuances of words and phrases that may be offensive to some people in ways that the speaker does not realize.

Theories of Communication and Language

11. Theories differ in explaining how infants learn language — whether infants must be taught or that social impulses foster language learning or that brains are genetically attuned to language as soon as the requisite maturation occurs.

12. Neuroscience finds that language abilities arise from many parts of the brain. The former notion that language was solely a left-brain function is no longer believed.

13. Each theory of language learning is confirmed by research. Developmental scientists find that many parts of the brain, and many strategies for learning, result in early language accomplishments. Current research, with the benefit of advances in neuroscience, reaches the same conclusion.

KEY TERMS

babbling (p. 215)
holophrase (p. 216)
naming explosion (p. 216)
grammar (p. 217)
mean length of utterance
  (MLU) (p. 217)

social referencing (p. 217)
fast-mapping (p. 222)
overextension (p. 222)
underextension (p. 222)
overregularization
  (p. 224)

pragmatics (p. 225)
English language learners
  (ELLs) (p. 227)
immersion (p. 227)
bilingual education
  (p. 227)

ESL (English as a second
  language) (p. 227)
language acquisition device
  (LAD) (p. 236)

APPLICATIONS

1. Elicit vocalizations from an infant—babbling if the baby is under age 1, using words if the baby is older. Write down all of the baby's communication for 10 minutes. Then ask the primary caregiver to elicit vocalizations for 10 minutes, and write these down. What differences are apparent between the baby's two attempts at communication? Compare your findings with the norms described in the chapter.

2. Many educators recommend that parents read to babies every day, even before 1 year of age. What theory of language development does this reflect and why? Ask several parents whether they did so, and why or why not.

3. To demonstrate how rapidly language is learned, show a preschool child several objects and label one with a nonsense word that the child has never heard. (*Toma* is often used; so is *wug*.) Or choose a word that the child does not know, such as *wrench*, *spatula*, or the name of a coin from another nation. Test the child's fast-mapping.

ESPECIALLY FOR ANSWERS

Response for Parents (from p. 220) Your son would understand your explanation, but you should take him along if you can do so without losing patience. You wouldn't ignore his need for food or medicine, so don't ignore his need for learning. While shopping, you can teach vocabulary (does he know pimientos, pepperoni, polenta?), categories (root vegetables, freshwater fish), and math (which size box of cereal is cheaper?). Explain in advance that you need him to help you find items and carry them and that he can choose only one item that you wouldn't normally buy. Seven-year-olds can understand rules, and they enjoy being helpful.

Response for Nurses and Pediatricians (from p. 235) Although humans may be naturally inclined to communicate with words, exposure to language is necessary. You may not convince Eric and Jennifer about this, but at least convince them that their baby will be happier if they talk to him.

OBSERVATION QUIZ ANSWERS

Answer to Observation Quiz (from p. 229) Pinker is reading from a small laptop, using a device to change slides of a PowerPoint presentation, and has hair that would not have been acceptable for scholars a few decades ago.

Answer to Observation Quiz (from p. 230) Their mouths are open and their bodies are tilted toward each other.

Answer to Observation Quiz (from p. 236) There is no social interaction, no talking. All family members quietly stare at sky and terrain; awe of nature may be a family value. Hierarchy and gender seem significant: The father looks distant and above all the other family members, the mother is busy, and the children are below the parents. Do only males wear hats?

Copyright Crezalyn Nerona Uratsuji/Getty Images

CHAPTER 9

Intelligence and Cognition

*C*ogito ergo sum ("I think therefore I am") was on the sweatshirt I wore my sophomore year. I was not alone. Hundreds of my dormmates proudly wore the same shirt. Our elder dormmates (about age 21) chose Descartes' famous dictum to broadcast that women (dorms were single-sex back then) had minds.

As I reflect on it now, our slogan (in Latin!) was arrogant, snobbish, and defensive. But Descartes was right. As explained in Chapter 2, a cognitive revolution occurred in about 1980; most developmentalists now agree that how people think influences how they are. Beliefs affect behavior.

This chapter describes insights that led to that revolution, first by discussing intelligence, and then explaining Piaget, Vygotsky, and information processing. Is it true that *cogito ergo sum*, or instead, is cognition peripheral to who we are?

What Will You Know?

1. What does an IQ test really measure?
2. When does a child stop being egocentric?
3. How can teachers insure that students are neither bored nor lost?
4. Do adults think better, or worse, than smart adolescents'?

Intelligence

What is intelligence? Is there such a thing, and do some people have more of it than others? The answer, historically and in modern day, seems to be yes.

A Historical View

In *Theaetetucs*, Plato writes about a student who compares intelligence to a lump of wax. In that ancient text, the lump may be bigger or smaller, harder or softer, pure or less pure, and thus people vary in their intelligence. In the nineteenth century, many British psychologists thought that intelligence, just like height and appearance, was a trait that children inherited from their parents (Galton, 1869).

Current Perspectives

One leader in psychological research on intelligence over the past four decades is Robert Sternberg, who recently reiterated his summary of the study of intelligence by writing:

> Some people are better at some things than others, some of those people who are better are better not only at some things, but at lots of things. The study of intelligence evolved, in part, to explain these individual differences.
>
> [Sternberg, 2020, p. xxi]

Another current explanation notes that:

> Intuitively we all know what it is to be intelligent, although definitions of intelligence can be very diverse. It is something that helps us plan, reason, solve problems, quickly learn, think on our feet, make decisions and, ultimately, survive in the fast, modern world.
>
> [Goriounova & Mansvelder, 2019]

Thus, people have always noted that some people are more intelligent than others. Many have wondered how intelligence can be measured, and what the implications are if someone is highly intelligent or the opposite.

Cognitive Artifacts

In the first half of the twentieth century it was thought that too much intelligence might be harmful ("too smart for his own good"). Galton himself wrote, "Men who leave their mark on the world are very often those who, being gifted and full of nervous power, are at the same time haunted and driven by a dominant idea, and are therefore within a measurable distance of insanity."

But research begun in 1921 on genius children (IQ above 130) found that they learned more in school and college, and they were more likely to have happy and successful adult lives (Terman & Oden, 1959). Not always, of course. Longitudinal studies of those children found that intelligence does not guarantee happiness, but it helps (Shurkin, 1992).

In the twenty-first century, many people not only believe that there is such a thing as intelligence, but they also find that intelligence helps people adapt to whatever environment they find themselves. Over the millennia, when nations encourage intellectual growth, everyone benefits.

For example, written language, the number system, universities, and the scientific method are **cognitive artifacts**—that is, ways to amplify and extend general cognitive ability. A psychologist who studies intelligence believes that the nations with the most advanced economies and greatest national wealth are those that make best use of cognitive artifacts (Hunt, 2012).

The germ theory of disease, for instance, was developed because doctors were able to research, write, publish, and then learn from each other (Hunt, 2011a). Those people who understood and benefited from that theory had longer and healthier lives, and that advanced entire nations. In more recent times, preventive health care, clean water, electricity, global travel, and the internet have resulted in advanced societies.

According to this idea, smart people are better able to use the cognitive artifacts of their society to advance their own intelligence. People who are high in intelligence benefit from education, and then teach others. That makes education a cognitive

cognitive artifacts An idea or mental creation that becomes a powerful social construction, influencing the thinking of everyone. The number system, the germ theory of disease, and the idea of the nation-state are all cognitive artifacts.

artifact, producing the Age of Enlightenment in the seventeenth century, which has meant less suffering, less violence, and longer lives for everyone (Pinker, 2018).

What IQ Is

The basic premise of intelligence testing is that some people are quicker to learn than others, and that measuring those differences will guide educators and everyone else. Over the past 150 years, tests of intelligence were developed, exalted, criticized, and scorned. As you will see, they remain controversial.

Originally an IQ (intelligence quotient) score was literally a quotient (the answer to a division problem). A person taking an IQ test was asked many questions, and their score was used to figure out their *mental age*, which was the age at which the average person attained that score. For test-takers under age 18, their mental age was divided by their *chronological age* (the actual age) and multiplied by 100, and that number was the IQ.

General Intelligence

Those who developed IQ tests assumed that scores on many kinds of questions could be combined to indicate **general intelligence (*g*)**. *g* cannot be measured directly, but *g* could be calculated indirectly by measuring language, memory, reasoning, and so on.

Of course, young children do not know as much as older children—that is why mental age was divided by chronological age. But children who were above average in intelligence would learn faster than other children, and hence their mental age would be ahead of their chronological age and their IQ would be above average.

Psychologists thought that, by age 18, intelligence was as high as it ever would be. Adults of any age who scored as well as an average 18-year-old would score 100; those who were more or less ahead of 18-year-olds would be above or below 100.

The underlying idea of *g* was explained by an American, Spearman (1923), who wrote a 358-page book titled *The Nature of "Intelligence" and the Principles of Cognition*. Many educators still believe Spearman's basic idea.

A child who scores 100 is exactly average, a child who scores below 70 (about 2 percent of all children) is thought to need special education for slow learners, and a child who scores above 130 (another 2 percent) is a genius and may need gifted education. To further understand IQ scores, consider the examples in **Table 9.1**.

From Rescue to Discrimination

Originally, IQ tests were used to prevent cruel punishment of low-IQ children who could not learn as fast as other children. If a schoolchild did not know the times

> **general intelligence (*g*)** The idea that intelligence is one basic trait, underlying all cognitive abilities. According to *g*, people have varying levels of this general ability.

TABLE 9.1

Calculating IQ Scores

If 9-year-olds, on average, answer exactly 60 questions correctly, then everyone who answers 60 questions correctly—no matter what their chronological age—has a mental age of 9.

1. The IQ of children whose mental age was the same as their chronological age would be 100. Thus, a 9-year-old who got 60 questions right would have an IQ of **9 ÷ 9 = 1 × 100 = 100**, exactly average.

2. If a child answered far more questions correctly than most children their age, their IQ would be over 100. For example, if a 6-year-old answered 60 questions correctly, the IQ would be **133 (9 ÷ 6 × 100)**.

3. If a child answered far fewer questions correctly than most children their age, then their IQ would be less than 100. For example, if a 12-year-old answered only 60 questions correctly, the IQ would be **75 (9 ÷ 12 × 100)**.

The current method of calculating IQ is more complex, but the basic idea is the same: IQ is calculated based on the average mental age of people of a particular chronological age. (See **Figure 9.1**.)

FIGURE 9.1

In Theory, Most People Are Average Almost 70 percent of IQ scores fall within the "average" range. Note, however, that this is a norm-referenced test. In fact, actual IQ scores have risen in many nations; 100 is no longer exactly the midpoint. Furthermore, in practice, scores below 50 are slightly more frequent than indicated by the normal curve (shown here) because severe disability is the result not of normal distribution but of genetic and prenatal factors.

⬤ **Observation Quiz** If a person's IQ is 110, in what category are they? (see answer, page 270) ➔

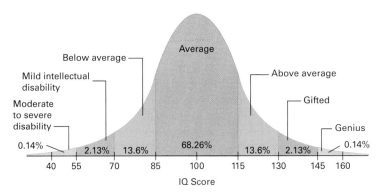

Theoretical Distribution of IQ Scores

tables, or spell words correctly, that child had to kneel for hours on rice, stand in the corner wearing a dunce cap, or suffer blows (with a ruler, a paddle, or a hand).

That is no longer true (19 U.S. states allow corporal punishment in schools, but the reason is misbehavior, not low achievement). Credit goes to Albert Binet, who developed the first IQ test in France in 1905, to spare children from unfair punishment.

Binet's test was adapted in United States, becoming the *Stanford-Binet*, joined by another set of IQ tests developed by David Wechsler, the *WISC (Wechsler Intelligence Scale for Children)*, and later the *WAIS (Wechsler Adult Intelligence Scale)* and the *WPPSI (Wechsler Preschool and Primary Scale of Intelligence)*.

All these IQ tests have been updated many times. Current versions of the Stanford-Binet and the WISC are still in use, not only saving children from impossible demands but also saving lives of criminals whose IQs are so low that they are spared execution because they are deemed unable to understand their crimes.

Early testers assumed that intelligence was a fixed characteristic, present at birth. Those researchers were not surprised that women often scored lower than men, and that African Americans scored lower than European Americans, because they thought that White European men, on average, were a little smarter than others. It did not occur to them that the environment, as well as the nature of the tests, caused those differences.

Low scores have relegated some children to classes where no one learns to read, kept some immigrants out of the United States, and justified racial, sexual, and ethnic discrimination. Terman himself thought that genes justified his prejudices against women, African Americans, and poor Whites (Shurkin, 1992).

The Flynn Effect

It is true that IQ scores usually remain relatively stable over the life span (Sauce & Matzel, 2018). Stability occurs partly because genes endure lifelong, but also because most people remain in their social milieu lifelong. Each person is raised by responsive or neglectful parents, taught in excellent or substandard schools, experiences good health and stimulating work or poor health and mind-numbing jobs.

The advantages a child has early on are likely to continue, so stability of IQ is a consequence of nurture, not just nature. Some individuals experience dramatically higher or lower scores from one decade to the next, and average IQ can rise for an entire group, as it did for women toward the end of the twentieth century, when millions of women were hired for paid jobs (Schaie, 1996).

The fact that experience can change IQ was doubted until evidence showed increases in IQ over the decades of the twentieth century in nation after nation. In 2000, an *average* 18-year-old from the Netherlands, for instance, scored at the same level that a high-IQ Dutch 18-year-old did in 1950. That is the **Flynn effect**,

Flynn effect The rise in average IQ scores that has occurred over the decades in many nations.

named after the researcher who described it (Flynn, 1999, 2012). The Flynn effect is apparent in every nation with longitudinal data. It is more apparent for women than for men and in southern Europe more than northern Europe, probably because educational opportunities for women and southern Europeans improved markedly in the twentieth century (D. Weber et al., 2017).

Most psychologists now agree that the brain is like a muscle, affected by mental exercise—which often is encouraged or discouraged by the social context. The preceding two chapters explain how that occurs for memory (Chapter 7) and language (Chapter 8). As you just read, it probably occurs for every aspect of intellectual development.

Many Intelligences

Scores change over time, depending on which intellectual muscles a particular culture emphasizes. Consequently, IQ tests are considered much less definitive than they were once thought to be. Another late-twentieth-century criticism goes farther: Perhaps no single test can measure the complexities of human intellectual development. According to some experts, children inherit and develop **multiple intelligences**, some high and some low, and those abilities cannot be combined into one score.

Gardner's Nine

One leading developmentalist, Howard Gardner, originally described seven intelligences: *linguistic, logical-mathematical, musical, spatial, bodily-kinesthetic* (movement), *interpersonal* (social understanding), and *intrapersonal* (self-understanding), each associated with a particular brain region (Gardner, 1983). He subsequently added an eighth, *naturalistic* (understanding nature, as in biology, zoology, or farming), and a ninth, *spiritual* (thinking about life and death) (Gardner, 1999, 2006; Gardner & Moran, 2006).

Although everyone has some of all nine intelligences, Gardner believes that each individual excels in particular ones. There is no overarching *g*; instead everyone has some strengths and weaknesses, and cultures encourage some of those abilities.

For example, someone might be gifted spatially but not linguistically (a visual artist who cannot describe her work) or might have interpersonal but not naturalistic intelligence (an astute clinical psychologist whose houseplants die). Gardner's concepts influence teachers in many primary schools, where children might demonstrate their understanding of a historical event via a poster with drawings instead of writing a paper with a bibliography.

Schools, cultures, and families dampen or expand particular intelligences. If two children are born with musical aptitude, the child whose parents are musicians is more likely to develop musical intelligence than the child whose parents are tone deaf. But if a child happens to be very low in musical aptitude but born in a musicians' family, that child can learn to play an instrument (as can almost any child) but will never reach concert quality.

Gardner believes that schools and IQ tests may be too narrow, teaching only some aspects of intelligence and thus stunting children's learning. The standard IQ test relies heavily on verbal and mathematical intelligence, thus shortchanging many children. Other IQ tests have been published, each useful in some situations. However, every test is the product of a particular culture, and thus reflects only some of the gifts a person might have.

Currently in the United States, of Gardner's nine intelligences, linguistic and mathematical intelligence are the core of most tests of aptitude and achievement. But in some other cultures, the ability to dance (kinesthetic intelligence), or to

multiple intelligences The idea that human intelligence is composed of a varied set of abilities rather than a single, all-encompassing one.

A Gifted Child Gardner believes every person is naturally better at some of his nine intelligences, and then the social context may or may not appreciate the talent. In the twenty-first century, verbal and mathematical intelligence is usually prized far more than artistic intelligence, but Georgie Pocheptsov was drawing before he learned to speak. The reason is tragic: His father suffered and died of brain cancer when Georgie was a toddler, and his mother bought paints and canvases to help her son cope with his loss. By middle childhood (shown here), Pocheptsov was already a world-famous artist. Now as an adult, his works sell for hundreds of thousands of dollars—often donated to brain tumor research.

Brownie Harris/Corbis/Gett• Images

analytic intelligence A form of intelligence that involves such mental processes as abstract planning, strategy selection, focused attention, and information processing, as well as verbal and logical skills.

creative intelligence A form of intelligence that involves the capacity to be intellectually flexible and innovative.

practical intelligence The intellectual skills used in everyday problem solving. (Sometimes called *tacit intelligence*.)

grow herbs (naturalistic intelligence), or to pray (spiritual intelligence) might be a more crucial indicator of intelligence in that community.

Sternberg's Three

Robert Sternberg agrees that a single intelligence score is misleading. Instead of nine intelligences, Sternberg (1988) proposed three fundamental forms: analytic, creative, and practical. (See **Table 9.2**.)

Analytic intelligence includes all of the mental processes that foster academic proficiency by making efficient learning, remembering, and thinking possible. Thus, it draws on abstract planning, strategy selection, focused attention, and information processing, as well as on verbal and logical skills.

Strengths in those areas are valuable in emerging adulthood, particularly in college and in graduate school. Multiple-choice tests and brief essays that call forth remembered information, with only one right answer, indicate analytic intelligence.

Creative intelligence involves the capacity to be intellectually flexible and innovative. Creative thinking is divergent rather than convergent, valuing the unexpected, imaginative, and unusual rather than standard and conventional answers.

Sternberg developed tests of creative intelligence that include writing a short story titled "The Octopus's Sneakers" or planning an advertising campaign for a new doorknob. Those with many novel ideas earn high scores. Some famous innovators in the technological revolution (Steve Jobs, Mark Zuckerberg) never graduated from college, because they had creative ideas that did not fit with the standard college curriculum.

Practical intelligence involves the capacity to adapt one's behavior to the demands of a given situation. This capacity includes an accurate grasp of the expectations and needs of the people involved and an awareness of the particular skills that are called for, along with the ability to use these insights effectively.

Practical intelligence is sometimes called *tacit intelligence* because it is not obvious on tests. Instead, it comes from "the school of hard knocks" and is

TABLE 9.2

Sternberg's Three Forms of Intelligence

	Analytic Intelligence	**Creative Intelligence**	**Practical Intelligence**
Mental processes	• Abstract planning • Strategizing • Focused attention • Verbal skills • Logic	• Imagination • Appreciation of the unexpected or unusual • Originality • Vision	• Adaptive actions • Understanding and assessing daily problems • Applied skills and knowledge
Valued for	• Analyzing • Learning and understanding • Remembering • Thinking	• Intellectual flexibility • Originality • Future hopes	• Adaptability • Concrete knowledge • Real-world experience
Indicated by	• Multiple-choice tests • Brief essays • Recall of information	• Inventiveness • Innovation • Resourcefulness • Ingenuity	• Performance in real situations • "Street smarts"

Information from Sternberg, 1988, 2003, 2011, 2015.

sometimes called "street smarts," not "book smarts." The stereotype of the absent-minded professor arises from the fact that not everyone who is high in analytic intelligence is high in practical intelligence.

Think about what cognitive abilities are needed in adulthood. Analytic intelligence is useful in higher education, but practical intelligence aids daily life.

After college, few adults need to define obscure words or deduce the next element in a number sequence (analytic intelligence), and few need to compose new music, restructure local government, or invent a new gadget (creative intelligence). Ideally, those few find people with practical intelligence to implement their analytic or creative ideas.

Practical intelligence helps adults maintain a home, advance a career, manage money, distinguish real news from false news, respond to the emotional needs of lovers, relatives, neighbors, and coworkers. A longitudinal study of adults, aged 22 to 101, found that scores on tests of practical intelligence were steadier than scores on other kinds of tests over the years of adulthood, with no notable decrement until very old age, in part because these skills are needed throughout life (Schaie, 2005/2013).

How might those three forms of intelligence work for a president or prime minister faced with a national or international crisis? Ideally the leader listens to scientists who have analytic intelligence, not dismissing them because they are impractical. And the leader encourages creative individuals, who suggest some impossible actions but others that illuminate a new perspective. Then, the leader has the practical intelligence to combine those two streams to convince an entire nation.

In Adulthood

In the 1960s, a leading researcher, Raymond Cattell, teamed up with a promising graduate student, John Horn, to study intelligence tests. They concluded that adult intelligence is best understood by grouping various measures into two categories, which they called *fluid* and *crystallized*.

Fluid Intelligence

As its name implies, **fluid intelligence** is like water, flowing to its own level no matter where it happens to be. Fluid intelligence is quick and flexible, enabling people to learn anything, even things that are unfamiliar and unconnected to what they already know. Curiosity, learning for the joy of it, solving abstract puzzles, and the thrill at discovery are marks of fluid intelligence.

People who are high in fluid abilities are quick and flexible, drawing inferences and grasping relationships between concepts, with large working memories. Questions that test fluid intelligence among Western adults might be:

What comes next in each of these two series?*

4 9 1 6 2 5 3

V X Z B D

Puzzles are often used to measure fluid intelligence, with bonus points for speedy solutions (as on many IQ tests). Immediate recall—of nonsense words, of numbers, of a sentence just read—is one indicator because working memory is crucial for fluid intelligence, especially in timed tests (Singh et al., 2018). However, whether working memory is the underlying cause for high fluid intelligence, or merely a correlate, is still questioned (Burgoyne et al., 2019).

---

*The correct answers are 6 and F. The clue is to think of multiplication (squares) and the alphabet: Some series are much more difficult to complete.

fluid intelligence Those types of basic intelligence that make learning of all sorts quick and thorough. Abilities such as short-term memory, abstract thought, and speed of thinking are all usually considered part of fluid intelligence.

Intelligence in Action Lin-Manuel Miranda created and starred in *Hamilton: An American Musical*, which has been one of the hottest tickets on Broadway for six years. His creative intelligence is obvious, but his analytic and practical intelligence are also part of his success.

crystallized intelligence Those types of intellectual ability that reflect accumulated learning. Vocabulary and general information are examples. Some developmental psychologists think crystallized intelligence increases with age, while fluid intelligence declines.

Crystallized Intelligence

The accumulation of facts, information, and knowledge as a result of education and experience is called **crystallized intelligence**. The size of a person's vocabulary, the knowledge of chemical formulas, and long-term memory for dates in history all indicate crystallized intelligence. Tests designed to measure this intelligence might include questions like these:

> What is the meaning of the word *eleemosynary*?
>
> Who was Descartes?
>
> Explain the difference between a tangent and a triangle.
>
> Why does the city of Peking no longer exist?

Although such questions seem to measure achievement more than aptitude, these two are connected, especially in adulthood. Intelligent adults read widely, think deeply, and remember what they learn—so their achievement reflects their aptitude. Crystallized intelligence is an outgrowth of fluid intelligence.

Thus, someone who is high in fluid intelligence is likely to become high in crystallized intelligence. Neurological research finds that network connections in the brain underlie both kinds of intelligence (Barbey, 2018).

Both Together Now

To reflect the total picture of a person's intellectual aptitude, both fluid and crystallized intelligence must be measured. Scores on items measuring fluid intelligence decrease with age, whereas scores on items measuring crystallized intelligence increase.

This distinction is useful, not only for typically developing individuals but also for those with intellectual disability (I. Chen et al., 2017). They also show similar patterns of fluid and crystallized intelligence over time.

For everyone, combining these two types of intelligence makes total IQ scores fairly steady from age 30 to age 70. Although brain slowdown begins at age 20 or so, it is rarely apparent until massive declines in fluid intelligence affect crystallized intelligence. Only then do overall IQ scores fall.

This brings us to highlight a final point in our understanding of intelligence. It is not an abstract lump of wax, as Plato surmised, but a cluster of abilities that develop within a particular person, affected by experience, culture, and age. Intelligence is dynamic, not static, and thus tests reflect the values of parents, schools, and cultures. Any test is limited, a snapshot, not a permanent record. We must consider the process of cognition, not merely the product. It is time for Piaget!

WHAT HAVE YOU LEARNED?

1. What was the original reason for the development of IQ tests?
2. What is the difference between mental age and chronological age?
3. Why do scientists seek to find *g*?
4. What cultural ideas are evident in traditional IQ tests?
5. Why does Gardner differ from the idea that there is a general intelligence?
6. When is it beneficial to be high in analytic intelligence?
7. When is it beneficial to be high in creative intelligence?
8. When is it beneficial to be high in practical intelligence?

Piaget's Stages of Intelligence

Jean Piaget (1896–1980) was, perhaps, "the greatest developmental psychologist of all time" (Haidt, 2013, p. 6). He revolutionized our understanding of cognition, recognizing that not only ideas but also ways of thinking change as people grow older, and that those thoughts shape, frame, and direct human emotions and actions.

Piaget became interested in human thought when his first professional job was to standardize an early version of the Stanford-Binet IQ test. He asked children standard questions, such as "How many fingers are on a hand?" (a question on a current test) and tally how old the children were who answered correctly. Either of two answers was acceptable: "five" or "four and a thumb." Six-year-olds usually know; 3-year-olds usually do not. The data on the age of the children who answered correctly were used to establish norms for the intelligence test.

But Piaget was a scientist by training (remember, his Ph.D. was in the study of shellfish); he observed closely and listened carefully. Consequently, he became intrigued by the wrong answers. For instance, some children looked at their own hands, counted, but came up with the wrong number.

He asked other questions, and again was struck by the answers. Some boys said that they had a brother, and that their brother had no brother. Some children thought the clouds were alive, some thought daisies were not flowers, some thought ice was not water.

How and *why* children think as they do reveals much more, Piaget concluded, than *what* they know. In Piagetian terms, people *construct* new ideas. Each person builds their understanding, not always accurately. He called a person's understanding of a particular concept a **scheme**. (In French, the word "scheme" is more comprehensive than the usual English meaning.)

As they mature, people adapt their thoughts to their experiences, rebuilding their schemes. As you remember from Chapter 2, at every age humans seek **cognitive equilibrium**—a state of mental balance. People construct that equilibrium either by **assimilation**, when new experiences are reinterpreted to fit into old ideas, or by **accommodation**, when old ideas are restructured because of new experiences.

Also explained in Chapter 2 is that Piaget believed that cognition could be characterized in four major stages. Now we describe those stages in detail (see **Table 9.3**).

scheme According to Piaget, a scheme is a cognitive framework for understanding an idea.

cognitive equilibrium In cognitive theory, a state of mental balance in which a person is able to reconcile new experiences with existing understanding.

assimilation The reinterpretation of new experiences to fit into old ideas.

accommodation The restructuring of old ideas to include new experiences.

VIDEO ACTIVITY: Sensorimotor Intelligence in Infancy and Toddlerhood shows how senses and motor skills fuel infant cognition.

TABLE 9.3

Piaget's Periods of Cognitive Development

	Name of Period	Characteristics of the Period	Major Gains During the Period
Birth to 2 years	Sensorimotor	Infants use senses and motor abilities to understand the world. Learning is active, without reflection.	Infants learn that objects still exist when out of sight (*object permanence*) and begin to think through mental actions. (The sensorimotor period is discussed in Chapter 6.)
2–6 years	Preoperational	Children think symbolically, with language, yet children are *egocentric*, perceiving from their own perspective.	The imagination flourishes, and language becomes a significant means of self-expression and social influence. (The preoperational period is discussed in Chapter 9.)
6–11 years	Concrete operational	Children understand and apply logic. Thinking is limited by direct experience.	By applying logic, children grasp concepts of conservation, number, classification, and many other scientific ideas. (The concrete-operational period is discussed in Chapter 12.)
12 years through adulthood	Formal operational	Adolescents and adults use abstract and hypothetical concepts. They can use analysis, not only emotion.	Ethics, politics, and social and moral issues become fascinating as adolescents and adults use abstract, theoretical reasoning. (The formal-operational period is discussed in Chapter 15.)

Stage One: Sensorimotor

Piaget called cognition in the first two years **sensorimotor intelligence**, because an infant's only way to understand early experiences is via senses and motor skills. He described the interplay of sensation, perception, action, and cognition as *circular reactions*, emphasizing that, as in a circle, there is no beginning and no end. Each experience leads to the next, which loops back (see **Figure 9.2**).

Adapting Reflexes: Substages One and Two

In **primary circular reactions**, the circle is within the infant's body. Substage one, called *reflexes*, lasts only a month. It includes senses as well as motor reflexes, the foundations of sensorimotor thought. As you remember from Chapter 4, babies are born with dozens of reflexes. They use them to understand their world.

Substage two, *first acquired adaptations* (also called *stage of first habits*), occurs because reflexes adjust to whatever responses occur. Sensation leads to perception, perception to cognition, and then cognition leads back to sensation. Infants adapt their reflexes as their movements teach them what their body can do and how each action feels.

The interplay of sensation, perception, and cognition causes *circular reactions*. As in a circle, there is no beginning and no end of cognition. Each experience leads to the next thought, which loops back. Circular reactions occur at every stage of cognitive development, according to Piaget, but they are especially evident in sensorimotor thought.

Here is one example. In a powerful reflex, full-term newborns suck anything that touches their lips. A newborn's first challenge is to suck, swallow, and suck again without spitting up—a major intellectual and motor task that takes practice. Soon the sucking reflex adapts to bottles or breasts, pacifiers or fingers, each

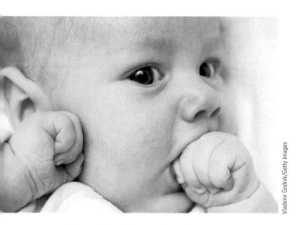

Vladimir Godnik/Getty Images

Time for Adaptation Sucking is a reflex at first, but adaptation begins as soon as an infant differentiates a pacifier from her mother's breast or realizes that her hand has grown too big to fit into her mouth. This infant's expression of concentration suggests that she is about to make that adaptation and suck just her thumb from now on.

sensorimotor intelligence Piaget's term for the way infants think—by using their senses and motor skills—during the first period of cognitive development.

primary circular reactions The first of three types of feedback loops in sensorimotor intelligence, this one involving the infant's own body. The infant senses motion, sucking, noise, and other stimuli and tries to understand them.

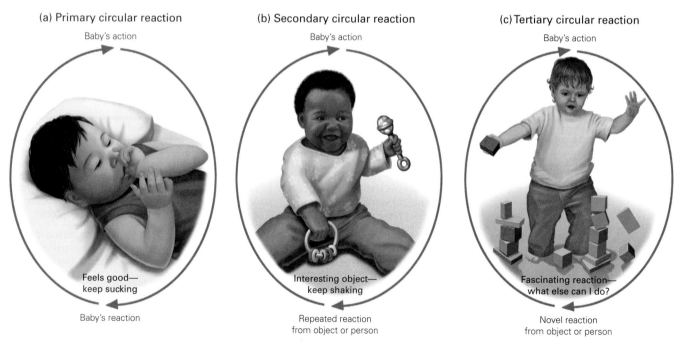

(a) Primary circular reaction

Baby's action

Feels good— keep sucking

Baby's reaction

(b) Secondary circular reaction

Baby's action

Interesting object— keep shaking

Repeated reaction from object or person

(c) Tertiary circular reaction

Baby's action

Fascinating reaction— what else can I do?

Novel reaction from object or person

FIGURE 9.2

Never Ending Circular reactions keep going because each action produces pleasure that encourages more action.

requiring specific types of tongue-pushing. This early adaptation (substage two) signifies that infants have begun to interpret sensations; as they accommodate, they are "thinking."

Exciting Experiences: Substages Three and Four

In stages three and four, development advances from primary to **secondary circular reactions**. These reactions extend beyond the infant's body; this circular reaction is between the baby and something else.

During substage three (4 to 8 months), infants try to continue exciting experiences, *making interesting sights last*. Realizing that rattles make noise, for example, they wave their arms and laugh whenever someone puts one in their hand.

Then, at substage four (8 months to 1 year), *new adaptation and anticipation* occur. Babies ask for help (fussing, pointing, gesturing) to accomplish what they want, reaching out for the rattle, for instance. Adaptation becomes more complex. Substage three babies know how to continue an experience; substage four babies initiate and anticipate.

For example, before age 1, babies anticipate being fed. At first, they open their mouths happily (an interesting experience, substage three), but a few months later they adapt—keeping their mouths firmly shut if the food on the spoon is something they do not like. If caregivers teach signs, by 10 months babies sign "eat" and "more."

Piaget thought that, at about 8 months, babies first understand **object permanence**—the concept that objects or people continue to exist when they are no longer in sight (see **Table 9.4**). Not until then do infants search for toys that have fallen from the crib, rolled under a couch, or disappeared under a blanket. Blind babies also demonstrate object permanence before they are 1 year old, reaching for something that they hear nearby (Fazzi et al., 2011).

As one developmentalist noted:

> Many parents in our typical American middle-class households have tried out Piaget's experiment in situ: Take an adorable, drooling 7-month-old baby, show her a toy she loves to play with, then cover it with a piece of cloth right in front of her eyes. What do you observe next? The baby does not know what to do to get the toy! She looks around, oblivious to the object's continuing existence under the cloth cover, and turns her attention to something else interesting in her environment. A few months later, the same baby will readily reach out and yank away the cloth cover to retrieve the highly desirable toy. This experiment has been done thousands of times and the phenomenon remains one of the most compelling in all of developmental psychology.
>
> *[Xu, 2013, p. 167]*

secondary circular reactions The second of three types of feedback loops in sensorimotor intelligence, involving the infant and an object or another person, as with shaking a rattle or playing peek-a-boo.

ESPECIALLY FOR Parents When should parents decide whether to feed their baby only by breast, only by bottle, or using some combination of the two? When should they decide whether or not to let their baby use a pacifier? (see response, page 269)

object permanence The realization that objects (including people) still exist when they can no longer be seen, touched, or heard.

TABLE 9.4

The Timing of Object Permanence

In tracing the development of object permanence, Piaget found:

- Infants younger than 8 months do not search for an object that disappeared.
- At 8 months, infants search immediately, but not if they must wait.
- At 18 months, they search after a wait, but not if they have seen the object put first in one place and then moved to another. Instead, they search in the first place, not the second, a mistake called the A-not-B error.
- By 2 years, children understand object permanence, including A-not-B. They progress over the next years through several stages of ever-advanced cognition.

This research provides practical suggestions. If infants under 8 months reach for something they cannot have (keys, candy), caregivers can put the coveted object out of sight. Fussing stops, because object permanence is not yet understood. For older infants, hiding is not enough. It must be locked up or discarded, lest the child who grasps object permanence later retrieves it, climbing onto a table or under a chair to do so.

Experimenting: Substages Five and Six

tertiary circular reaction Piaget's description of the cognitive processes of the 1-year-old, who gathers information from experiences with the wider world and then acts on it. The response to those actions leads to further understanding, which makes this circular.

After their first birthday, infants start experimenting, a cognitive advance. **Tertiary circular reactions** begin when 1-year-olds take independent actions to discover the properties of other people, animals, and things. Infants no longer respond only to their own bodies (primary reactions) or to other people or objects (secondary reactions). Their cognition is more like a spiral than a closed circle, increasingly creative with each discovery.

In Piaget's substage five (ages 12 to 18 months), *new means through active experimentation*, goal-directed and purposeful activities become more elaborate and self-motivated.

Toddlers are delighted to squeeze all the toothpaste out of the tube, or draw on the wall, or uncover an anthill—activities they have never seen adults do. Piaget referred to toddlers as "**little scientists**" who "experiment in order to see." Such curiosity advances cognition. This devotion to discovery is familiar to every scientist—and to every parent.

little scientist Piaget's term for toddlers' insatiable curiosity and active experimentation as they engage in various actions to understand their world.

ESPECIALLY FOR Parents One parent wants to put all breakable or dangerous objects away because the toddler is able to move around independently. The other parent says that the baby should learn not to touch certain things. Who is right? (see response, page 269)

Finally, in the sixth substage (ages 18 to 24 months), toddlers use *mental combinations*, intellectual experimentation via imagination. Thinking can supersede the active experimentation of a few months earlier.

Because they combine ideas, substage-six toddlers think about the consequences of their experimental drive, hesitating before yanking the cat's tail or dropping a raw egg on the floor. Of course, the urge to explore may overtake caution: Things that are truly dangerous (cleaning fluids, swimming pools, open windows) need to be securely locked, at least until age 6, when logic begins at Piaget's third stage, concrete operational thought.

The ability to combine ideas allows toddlers to pretend. They know that a doll is not a real baby, but they can belt it into a stroller and take it for a walk.

Piaget describes another substage-six intellectual accomplishment involving both thinking and memory, **deferred imitation**, which occurs when infants copy behavior they noticed hours or even days earlier (Piaget, 1962/2013c). Piaget described his daughter, Jacqueline, who observed another child

> who got into a terrible temper. He screamed as he tried to get out of a playpen and pushed it backward, stamping his feet. J. stood watching him in amazement, never having witnessed such a scene before. The next day, she herself screamed in her playpen and tried to move it, stamping her foot lightly several times in succession.
>
> *[Piaget, 1962/2013c, p. 63]*

deferred imitation A sequence in which an infant first perceives something that someone else does and then performs the same action a few hours or even days later.

As you will soon read, recent research recognizes the six substages of sensorimotor development at younger ages than Piaget described. Piaget may have underestimated how rapidly infant learning occurs. But he was right to describe babies as avid and active learners who "learn so fast and so well" (Xu & Kushnir, 2013, p. 28).

preoperational intelligence Piaget's term for cognitive development between the ages of about 2 and 6; it includes language and imagination (which involve symbolic thought), but logical, operational thinking is not yet possible at this stage.

Stage Two: Words But Not Logic

symbolic thought A major accomplishment of preoperational intelligence that allows a child to think symbolically, including understanding that words can refer to things not seen and that an item, such as a flag, can symbolize something else (in this case, a country).

Ages 2–6 are the years of **preoperational intelligence**, Piaget's second period of cognitive development. Preoperational children use **symbolic thought**, when an object or word stands for something else, including something out of sight or imagined.

During the sensorimotor stage, the word *dog*, for instance, is only the furry, friendly, family dog, licking and sniffing at the infant, not yet a symbol (Callaghan, 2013). By age 2, the word becomes a symbol: It can refer to a remembered dog, or a plastic dog, or an imagined dog.

Language is a prime example of symbolic thought; words make it easier to think and remember. That's why young children explode into language: Once they grasp symbolic thought, that propels them to learn thousands of words. However, although vocabulary and imagination soar during preoperational intelligence, logical connections between ideas are not yet active. That's why Piaget called this stage *pre*operational.

Obstacles to Logic

Piaget noted four limitations that make logic difficult until middle childhood:

1. centration;
2. focus on appearance;
3. static reasoning; and
4. irreversibility.

Centration is the tendency to focus on one aspect of a situation to the exclusion of all others. Young children may, for example, insist that Daddy is a father, not a brother, because they center on his role in their lives. They seem unaware that they themselves are a brother or sister to their sibling.

Those examples illustrate a particular type of centration that Piaget called **egocentrism**—literally, "self-centeredness." Egocentric children contemplate the world exclusively from their personal perspective. Preoperational children ask adults to play with them, expecting that adults will enjoy moving trucks or dressing dolls as much as they do. Egocentric, but not selfish.

A second characteristic of illogical preoperational thought is a **focus on appearance**. For instance, a girl given a short haircut might worry that she has turned into a boy. In preoperational thought, a thing is whatever it appears to be—evident in the joy young children have in wearing the hats or shoes of a grown-up, clomping noisily and unsteadily around the living room.

Third, preoperational children use **static reasoning**. They believe that the world is stable, unchanging, always in the state in which they currently encounter it. They do not understand that their own parents were once children, or that their parents' relationship with their own parents has changed.

One told his grandmother to tell his mother not to spank him, because "she has to do what her mother says." If a preschooler wants a bottle because a baby brother or sister has one, that child is not swayed by an adult who says "You had a bottle when you were little, now you are a big kid."

The fourth characteristic of preoperational thought is **irreversibility**. Preoperational thinkers fail to recognize that reversing a process sometimes restores whatever existed before. A child who is upset because there is lettuce on her sandwich might still reject the food when the lettuce is removed, believing that what is done cannot be undone.

Conservation Not Yet

Piaget investigated several ways in which preoperational intelligence disregards logic. A famous set of experiments involved **conservation**, the notion that the amount of something remains the same (is *conserved*) despite changes in its appearance.

centration A characteristic of preoperational thought in which a young child focuses (centers) on one idea, excluding all others.

egocentrism Piaget's term for children's tendency to think about the world entirely from their own personal perspective.

focus on appearance A characteristic of preoperational thought in which a young child ignores all attributes that are not apparent.

static reasoning A characteristic of preoperational thought in which a young child thinks that nothing changes. Whatever is now has always been and always will be.

irreversibility A characteristic of preoperational thought in which a young child thinks that nothing can be undone. A thing cannot be restored to the way it was before a change occurred.

conservation The principle that the amount of a substance remains the same (i.e., is conserved) even when its appearance changes.

VIDEO ACTIVITY: Achieving Conservation focuses on the cognitive changes that enable older children to pass Piaget's conservation-of-liquid task.

Tests of Various Types of Conservation

Type of Conservation	Initial Presentation	Transformation	Question	Preoperational Child's Answer
Volume	Two equal glasses of pink lemonade.	Pour one into a taller, narrower glass.	Which glass contains more?	The taller one.
Number	Two equal lines of candy.	Increase spacing of candy in one line.	Which line has more candy?	The longer one.
Matter	Two equal balls of cookie dough.	Squeeze one ball into a long, thin shape.	Which piece has more dough?	The long one.
Length	Two pencils of equal length.	Move one pencil.	Which pencil is longer?	The one that is farther to the right.

FIGURE 9.3

Conservation, Please According to Piaget, until children grasp the concept of conservation at (he believed) about age 6 or 7, they cannot understand that the transformations shown here do not change the total amount of liquid, candies, cookie dough, and pencils.

Suppose two identical glasses contain the same amount of milk, and the milk from one glass is poured into a taller, narrower glass. If young children are then asked whether one glass contains more, or both glasses contain the same amount, they insist that the narrower glass (with the higher level) has more. (See **Figure 9.3** for other examples.)

All four characteristics of preoperational thought are evident in this mistake. Young children fail to understand conservation because they focus (*center*) on what they see (*appearance*), noticing only the immediate (*static*) condition. It does not occur to them that they could pour the milk back into the empty glass and recreate the level of a moment earlier (*irreversibility*).

Piaget's original tests of conservation required children to respond verbally to questions. Later research has found that when the tests of logic are simplified or made playful, young children may succeed. Some indicate via eye movements (recorded by high-resolution cameras and computer analysis) that they know something before they say it in words (Goldin-Meadow & Alibali, 2013). This is another example of Piaget underestimating what children can understand.

Stage Three: Logic About Experiences

concrete operational thought Piaget's term for the ability to reason logically about direct experiences and perceptions.

Piaget called the next stage **concrete operational thought**. Children are no longer limited by egocentrism; they can think using logic. (An *operation* is arranging ideas to reach conclusions.) Children have new reasoning skills; they apply logic to *concrete* situations, which are situations grounded in experience.

How to Think About Flowers A person's stage of cognitive growth influences how he or she thinks about everything, including flowers. (a) To an infant in Piaget's sensorimotor stage, flowers are "known" through pulling, smelling, and even biting. (b) At the concrete operational stage, children become more logical. This boy can understand that flowers need sunlight, water, and time to grow. (c) At the adult's formal operational stage, flowers can be part of a larger, logical scheme—for instance, to earn money while cultivating beauty. As illustrated by all three photos, thinking is an active process from the beginning of life until the end.

Concrete thinking arises from what is visible, tangible, and real, not abstract and theoretical (as at the next stage, *formal operational thought*). Children shift from preoperational to concrete operational thinking between ages 5 and 7, becoming more systematic, objective, and scientific, no longer caught up in egocentric, magical thinking.

You just read about one logical operation that becomes possible during middle childhood: *conservation*. By age 7, most children know that the quantity of water does not change when it is in another container.

Another logical concept is **classification**, the schemes that objects can be organized into subgroups (or *categories* or *classes*) according to some characteristic that they share. For example, *family* includes parents, siblings, and cousins. Other common classes are animals, toys, and food. Each class includes some elements and excludes others; each is part of a hierarchy, a logical understanding that is beyond most younger children.

Food, for instance, is an overarching category, with the next-lower level of the hierarchy being meat, grains, fruits, and so on. Most subclasses can be further divided: Meat includes poultry, beef, and pork, each of which can be divided again. Adults (but not young children) realize that items at the bottom of a classification hierarchy belong to every higher level, yet also know the boundaries of the various levels: Bacon is always pork, meat, and food, but most food, meat, and pork are not bacon.

The mental operation of moving up and down the hierarchy becomes possible in middle childhood, although with help it can occur earlier. Some young children can classify if they are told the categories (e.g., which of these are transportation?). Older children (about age 9) sometimes spontaneously sort things into categories (Guimarães & Oliveira, 2018).

Piaget devised many classification experiments. For example, a child is shown a bouquet of nine flowers—seven yellow daisies and two white roses. Then the child is asked, "Are there more daisies or more flowers?"

Until about age 7, most children answer, "More daisies." The youngest children offer no justification, but some 6-year-olds explain that "there are more yellow ones than white ones" or "because daisies are daisies, they aren't flowers" (Piaget et al., 2015). By age 8, most children can classify: "More flowers than daisies," they confidently reply.

classification The logical principle that things can be organized into groups (or categories or classes) according to some characteristic that they have in common.

Stage Four: Logic About Things Unseen

In his fourth stage, Piaget described a shift to **formal operational intelligence** as adolescents move past concrete operational thinking and consider

formal operational intelligence In Piaget's theory, the fourth and final stage of cognitive development, characterized by more systematic logical thinking and by the ability to understand and systematically manipulate abstract concepts.

abstractions, including "assumptions that have no necessary relation to reality" (Piaget, 1950/2001, p. 163). Utopias and dystopia, zombies and space aliens, are in books, TV shows, movies — all riveting to some formal operational thinkers.

Measuring Logic

Piaget and his colleagues devised a number of tasks to assess formal operational thought (Inhelder & Piaget, 1958/2013b). This is most apparent in appreciation of logic, of advanced math, or the scientific method:

> in contrast to concrete operational children, formal operational adolescents imagine all possible determinants . . . [and] systematically vary the factors one by one, observe the results correctly, keep track of the results, and draw the appropriate conclusions.
>
> *[Miller, 2016]*

One of Piaget's experiments (diagrammed in **Figure 9.4**) required balancing a scale by hooking weights onto the scale's arms. To master this task, a person must consider the reciprocal interaction between distance from the center and heaviness of the weight. Therefore, a heavy weight close to the center can be counterbalanced with a light weight far from the center on the other side.

Piaget reported that balancing was not understood by the 3- to 5-year-olds. Then, by age 7, children balanced the scale by putting the same amount of weight on each arm, but they didn't realize that the distance from the center mattered. By age 10, children experimented with the weights, using trial and error.

Thus, before puberty, children are concrete thinkers, needing to tinker with the scale to find the balance. Finally, by about age 13 or 14, some children hypothesized about reciprocity, developing the correct formula which they then used to balance the scale (Piaget & Inhelder, 1972).

VIDEO ACTIVITY: The Balance Scale Task shows children of various ages completing the task and gives students a chance to try it as well.

(a)

(b)

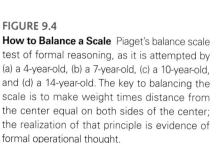

(c)

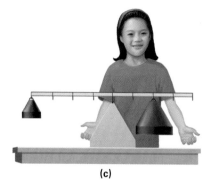

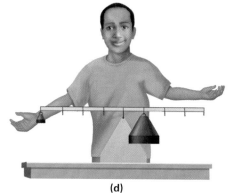

(d)

FIGURE 9.4

How to Balance a Scale Piaget's balance scale test of formal reasoning, as it is attempted by (a) a 4-year-old, (b) a 7-year-old, (c) a 10-year-old, and (d) a 14-year-old. The key to balancing the scale is to make weight times distance from the center equal on both sides of the center; the realization of that principle is evidence of formal operational thought.

What If?

One hallmark of formal operational thought is the capacity to think of possibility, not just reality. "Here and now" is only one of many possibilities, including "there and then," "long, long ago," "not yet," and "never." As Piaget said:

> The adolescent . . . thinks beyond the present and forms theories about everything, delighting especially in considerations of that which is not.
> [Piaget, 1950/2001, p. 163]

Adolescents are therefore primed to engage in **hypothetical thought**, reasoning about *if–then* propositions that do not reflect reality. For example, consider this question:

> If all mammals can walk,
> And whales are mammals,
> Can whales walk?

Children answer "No!" They know that whales swim, not walk; the logic escapes them. Some adolescents answer "Yes." They understand the conditional *if*, and therefore the counterfactual phrase "if all mammals":

> *Possibility* no longer appears merely as an extension of an empirical situation or of action actually performed. Instead, it is *reality* that is now secondary to *possibility*.
> [Inhelder & Piaget, 1958/2013b, p. 251; emphasis in original]

In other words, adolescents can think about thinking, an epistemological approach to reality that allows almost any possibility to be conceptualized—even ones that older generations never dreamed of (Moshman, 2018). Hypothetical thought transforms perceptions, not necessarily for the better.

Adolescents might criticize everything from their mother's spaghetti (it's not *al dente*) to the Gregorian calendar (it's not the Chinese or Jewish one). They criticize what *is* because of their hypothetical thinking about what might be, and because of their growing awareness of other families and cultures. That complicates decision making when it comes to immediate, practical questions, although it enables counterarguments to many statements their parents or teachers might make.

In developing the capacity to think hypothetically, by age 14 or so adolescents become more capable of **deductive reasoning**, or *top-down reasoning*, which begins with an abstract idea or premise and then uses logic to draw specific conclusions. In the example above, "if all mammals can walk" is a premise.

By contrast, **inductive reasoning**, or *bottom-up reasoning*, predominates during the school years. Children accumulate facts and experiences (the *knowledge base*) to aid thinking. Since they know whales cannot walk; knowledge trumps the logic.

Thinking About Poverty and Racism

Social scientists make a distinction between two ways to interpret social problems, either as caused by individuals or as caused by social structures. Younger children focus on individuals; adolescents begin to see structures.

An example of the progress toward deductive reasoning comes from developmental changes in understanding racism. Preoperational children attending preschools with children of many backgrounds may be oblivious to ethnic differences. Their friends are usually of the same sex (they notice gender differences by age 2) but of many ethnicities (they do not categorize people by race) (Weisman et al., 2015).

By middle childhood, they become aware of race—and they have been taught that it is bad to be racist. Overt prejudice declines with concrete operational thought,

hypothetical thought Reasoning that includes propositions and possibilities that may not reflect reality.

deductive reasoning Reasoning from a general statement, premise, or principle, through logical steps, to figure out (deduce) specifics. (Also called *top-down reasoning*.)

inductive reasoning Reasoning from one or more specific experiences or facts to reach (induce) a general conclusion. (Also called *bottom-up reasoning*.)

Fire Your Trebuchet! Denis Mujanovic, Anna Dim, Ahmed Kamaludeen, and Ghaden Asad are all high school students participating in the Western Kentucky Physics Olympics. Here they compete with their carefully designed trebuchets, a kind of catapult related to the slingshot.

especially among elementary schoolchildren who have contact with children of other races (Raabe & Beelmann, 2011). Adolescents become increasingly aware of racism, especially if they personally have experienced it (Seider et al., 2019).

However, concrete operational children tend to think the core problem is that some people are prejudiced. That leads them to a conclusion: People need to be enlightened, and parents might be blamed if they did not teach their children tolerance. By contrast, some older adolescents think, deductively, that racism requires policy solutions.

This is one conclusion from a study of adolescent opinions regarding policies to remedy racial discrimination (Hughes & Bigler, 2011). Not surprisingly, most students of all ages in an ethnically diverse U.S. high school recognized disparities between African and European Americans and believed that racism was a major cause.

However, age made a difference. Among those who recognized marked inequalities, older adolescents (ages 16 to 17) more often supported systemic solutions (e.g., affirmative action and desegregation) than did younger students.

The researchers wrote: "[D]uring adolescence, cognitive development facilitates the understanding that discrimination exists at the social-systemic level . . . [and] racial awareness begins to inform views of race-conscious policies during middle adolescence" (Hughes & Bigler, 2011, p. 489). Studies of how children allocate resources to those of another ethnic group find that adolescents are more likely to consider past inequities and current needs, again a broader and less self-centered perspective (Hitti et al., 2017).

That study was primarily of White youth. Similar findings come from a longitudinal study that analyzed how African American and Latinx high school students understand poverty and racism. Younger children blame individuals, either the poor person (lazy or unskilled), the greedy landlord, the inept social worker, the wealthy president. Formal operational thinkers recognize structural problems (poor schools, reduced job opportunities, and so on) (Flanagan et al., 2013; Seider et al., 2019).

This shift is apparent in many studies, although the change is not as dramatic as a strict switch from concrete to formal thinking might imply: Older adolescents are marginally more aware of social structures. That awareness does not always inspire individual accomplishment; adolescents do not always believe that they can change those structures (Godfrey et al., 2019).

Update on Piaget

Piaget was a brilliant, creative scientist. His research on cognition began an innovative view of children's thinking. Thousands of researchers have followed his lead, many confirming and elaborating his discoveries. Many still do. The Jean Piaget Society, a thriving group of researchers, had their 49th annual conference in Oregon in 2019. (Their 50th was planned for May 2020, but was postponed due to COVID-19.)

However, in the past several decades, many scientists have documented limitations and problems with Piaget's view. We soon discuss a possible fifth stage, called *postformal*, not recognized by Piaget but described by many scholars of adult cognition.

Alternate perspectives on cognitive development, specifically Vygotsky's ideas, and the information-processing perspective, are also considered. But first we need to highlight two problems with Piaget's theory of child development: He described stages instead of continuity, and he relied on motor skills, not brain waves.

Continuity, Not Stages

Many researchers now find more continuity than discontinuity in cognitive development. A strict stage theory, as Piaget seemed to provide, is not accurate. For example, object permanence, conservation, and many other ideas are understood bit by bit, at younger ages than Piaget found. Indeed, with active, guided experience, glimmers of conservation are apparent at age 4 (Sophian, 2013).

There is no sudden cognitive shift between one stage and the next, as Piaget seemed to imply. People of all ages sometimes think like young children, magically and egocentrically. As you have doubtless noticed when you discuss racism or any other hot-button issue, adults sometimes use preoperational or concrete operational reasoning. An age-based view of cognition is mistaken.

Early Object Permanence

Object permanence is one of Piaget's most often cited discoveries. His research that discovered that infants younger than 8 months do not search for missing toys—even if covered momentarily by an easily removable cloth—astonished and then convinced thousands of developmentalists. They agreed with Piaget that infant cognition gradually increases with maturation.

However, Piaget's discovery of object permanence rests on the second problem with Piaget: He relied on actions, not on physiological measures such as brain activity, gaze duration, or heartbeat. Two widely respected researchers, Renee Baillargeon and Elizabeth Spelke, challenged Piaget, suggesting that infants begin to understand object permanence as early as 4 months (Baillargeon, 1987; Spelke et al., 1983; Baillargeon & DeVos, 1991).

Family Fun Peek-a-boo makes all three happy, each for cognitive reasons. The 9-month-old is discovering object permanence, his sister (at the concrete operational stage) enjoys making her brother laugh, and their mother understands more abstract ideas—such as family bonding.

In dozens of experiments over the past two decades, young infants view objects on a screen, or on a puppet stage, and then something temporarily covers the object. When the cover is removed and the object is still there, the babies show no indication of surprise. But if the object is gone, or if another one is in its place, when the cover is removed, young infants are surprised.

Infant surprise is measured by advanced technology, calibrating gaze (looking time, pupil dilation), heartbeat (changed rhythm), or brain waves. Baillargeon, Spelke, and many others consider those physiological reactions as evidence that infants understand object permanence long before they can act on it.

Thus, Piaget may have relied too much on an infant's ability to pull a cover off an object, something very young infants cannot do because they cannot yet control their hands. Piaget may have been testing a motor skill, not a cognitive one.

Later, with older children, he listened to what they said, again not measuring their physiological reactions. This was not his fault: He did his research before advanced computer analysis of gaze, heartbeat, and brain scans was available. Nonetheless, he was led astray by depending on motor skills and language proficiency.

Remember that the scientific method encourages researchers to reexamine the data and conclusions of other scientists, so questioning Piaget is now common. So is questioning those who question! Some defenders of Piaget argue that the wide-eyed looking Baillargeon found in those 4- to 6-month-olds was not evidence of object permanence, but merely evidence that novelty was noticed (Bremner et al., 2015). Perhaps Piaget was more right than wrong.

WHAT HAVE YOU LEARNED?

1. What did scientists think about infant cognition before Piaget?

2. Why is Piaget's first stage called sensorimotor?

3. What evidence did Piaget find of cognition in infants younger than 4 months?

4. Why are 1-year-olds called little scientists?

5. What cognitive ability makes 2- to 6-year-olds more advanced than infants?

6. What do 7- to 11-year-olds understand that younger children do not?

7. What is different between the thinking of an adolescent and of a younger child?

8. What are two common criticisms of Piaget's theory?

Hero Images/Getty Images

Learning to Button Most shirts for 4-year-olds are wide-necked without buttons, so preschoolers can put them on themselves. But the skill of buttoning is best learned from a mentor, who knows how to increase motivation.

apprentice in thinking Vygotsky's term for the young child whose intellectual growth is stimulated and directed by older and more skilled members of society.

Vygotsky: Cognition as a Social Experience

Piaget's legacy continues. Current researchers in cognitive development refer to his stages, either to nestle within them or to bounce off in another direction. In 2019, published articles referring to him numbered 27,100. But Piaget's vision was not the only one in the twentieth century. Another prominent theorist, with 22,600 referrals in 2019, wrote in Russia.

Lev Vygotsky (1896–1934) had much in common with Piaget. Both grew up in Europe in the first half of the twentieth century, and both advanced our understanding of education and cognition. They observed children's thinking and concluded that a child's mind was far more active than most of their contemporaries imagined.

But there is one major difference. Vygotsky emphasized the sociocultural aspects of cognition, whereas Piaget stressed individual exploration and discovery. Why did they not describe cognition in the same way? The reason is that they both lived and studied in very different circumstances.

The Social Context

Vygotsky lived in the multiethnic, politically turbulent nation of Russia, which became the Soviet Union after the 1917 revolution. His research included how farmers think about tools, how illiterate people contemplate abstract ideas, how deaf children learn in school.

His personal experience and his scientific research made Vygotsky conclude, unlike Piaget, that there are no universal ages and stages. Instead, he thought the social and cultural context was pivotal in guiding cognition. Because of international politics—the Soviet Union was first embraced, then opposed, by the political leaders of Western Europe and the United States—Vygotsky's views did not reach mainstream developmental psychology until decades after his death.

Currently, however, Vygotsky's insistence that social forces are as powerful as private ones in affecting cognitive processes—is increasingly supported by recent research in many nations (Miller & Aloise-Young, 2018).

Mentors

Vygotsky thought that each person, schooled or not, learns from mentors in the community (Vygotsky, 2012). Just as, in earlier centuries, a young person wanting to repair shoes might become an apprentice to an experienced cobbler, thereby learning to fix shoes while observing and assisting an expert, children become an **apprentice in thinking**. They watch and work with the adults of their community, who ask questions, explain ideas, and demonstrate beliefs.

The customs and artifacts of the society are also part of the curriculum for the apprentice. For example, what, where, and how people eat teaches children not only about nutrition and manners, but also about human relationships (sharing, status, respect, and so on) (Poulain, 2017).

This process continues in adulthood. Marriages, workplaces, churches, temples, stores, political gatherings, neighborhood parties, community centers, and so on are all learning environments.

As you read in Chapter 2, Vygotsky highlighted *guided participation*, the method used by parents, teachers, and entire societies to teach the skills and habits expected within their culture. Mentors offer not only instruction but also "mutual involvement in several widespread cultural practices with great importance for learning: narratives, routines, and play" (Rogoff, 2003, p. 285). Active apprenticeship and sensitive guidance are central for Vygotsky because people depend on others to teach them. Learning is informal, pervasive, and social.

The Zone of Proximal Development

As part of the apprenticeship of thinking, a mentor (parent, peer, or professional) finds the **zone of proximal development**, an imaginary area (zone) surrounding the learner, which contains the skills, knowledge, and concepts that the learner is close to (proximal) acquiring but cannot yet master independently.

Learning occurs when mentors and mentees interact in that zone in a "process of joint construction" (Valsiner, 2006). They develop knowledge together, which means that the mentor must not be too simplistic nor too confusing—the zone is between what is already known and what is beyond comprehension.

For example, when adults read a book to a child, they might point to a picture and help the child name something in it, or repeat a phrase and ask the child what it means. Children's responses indicate whether the mentor has found the zone.

College professors do the same thing. They look at student's faces to see if their words are understood or if they are too far from the zone (students look blank, or fall asleep) or if the words are so well understood that the students are bored (perhaps doodling, perhaps checking their phones). Before the COVID-19 pandemic, it was not hard to see if a joke fell flat or struck home, an indication of whether the zone was correctly assessed.

Vygotsky's insights are useful to every educator. An example is coaches of sports teams. As one explained, "I need to get into the brain, I need to get into the mind, I need to understand mentally, physically, emotionally, spiritually, where my players are" (Mary, quoted in Vinson & Parker, 2019, p. 98). The team she coached reached international success.

How and when people enter their learning zone depends, in part, on the wisdom and willingness of mentors to provide **scaffolding**, or temporary sensitive support. The original meaning of the word "scaffold" relates to construction, a set of beams outside a structure that enables workers to climb up to the next level to build the next level. (See photo.) In the same way, mentors create a scaffold to allow learners to master a new concept.

This is obvious when a parent teaches a child to cross the street. Good mentors stop at the curb, hold the child's hand with a firm grasp, point out the stoplights and speeding cars, and explain every step of the way. After months or years, a hand on the shoulder is enough. Then a mere warning—"look both ways"; "wait for the light"—suffices. Finally, grown children cross a street, and, eventually, a busy highway, themselves.

The idea of scaffolding was never explicitly explained by Vygotsky. However, many Western theorists consider "scaffold" an apt metaphor for how a mentor helps a learner in the zone of proximal develop (Shvarts & Bakker, 2019).

For example, Jerome Bruner wrote:

> How can the competent adult "lend" consciousness to a child who does not "have" it on his own? What is it that makes possible this implanting of vicarious consciousness in the child by his adult tutor? It is as if there were a kind of scaffolding erected for the learner by the tutor. But how? Nowhere in Vygotsky's writings is there any concrete spelling out of what he means by such scaffolding. But I think I can reconstruct his intentions.
>
> *[Bruner, 1986, p. 74]*

Even in adulthood, mentoring and context continue to teach. To stick with the street-crossing example, anyone who has traveled to a distant city has noticed that people differ in when and how they cross the street. Waiting for a green light is the rule in some cities, not in others. Indeed, some places have lights that display how many seconds before turning to red; other busy intersections in other cities have no lights at all. A wise tourist crosses with a local mentor, perhaps a friend who takes them by the arm, or, if not, a stranger who becomes an unwitting guide.

zone of proximal development (ZPD) Vygotsky's term for the skills—cognitive as well as physical—that a person can exercise only with assistance, not yet independently.

scaffolding Temporary support that is tailored to a learner's needs and abilities and aimed at helping the learner master the next task in a given learning process.

⬤ **Observation Quiz** Is the girl below right-handed or left-handed? (see answer, page 270) ↓

Tim Hall/The Image Bank/Getty Images

Count by Tens A large, attractive abacus could be a scaffold. However, in this toy store the position of the balls suggests that no mentor is nearby. Children are unlikely to grasp the number system without a motivating guide.

I became aware of this when I was walking with a new colleague in the Bronx. The light was red on a busy street we had to cross, but there were no cars coming. I stepped off the curb, and noticed than she was not beside me. I took her arm, felt her hesitate, saw her troubled expression. I said, "You are not from New York, are you?"

In this example, I can imagine some readers thinking I was foolish, and others agreeing with my "big city" mentality, which chooses speed over caution. But the point is not who was right; the point is that each of us has been influenced by our context.

Everyday Scaffolding

Hundreds of applications of Vygotsky's ideas are evident. Human cognition is shaped by other people, both those in the immediate surroundings and those who mentored each person as a child. This is reciprocal. Humans adjust to others, parents are shaped by their children, education is interactive. That process advances cognition, according to Vygotsky.

This occurs in adulthood as well as childhood. Every work environment is a sociocultural influence on the thoughts and actions of people who work there. For example, physical therapists have been taught specific exercises, but they tailor those exercises to the personality of the particular patient and to the social context. When they treat severely ill patients in hospitals, therapists find the zone of proximal development for the patient's illness and personality, while reflecting the culture of the specific intensive care unit (ICU) (Pawlik & Kress, 2013).

Past experiences with guided participation affect current thinking. For example, when we were children, if our pediatricians were respectful and friendly, and our caregivers guided our responses and asked pointed questions that were answered respectfully, then as adults we will quickly seek medical diagnosis and question our doctors. Other adults avoid doctors and refuse medication because of childhood mentoring.

Extensive research on teaching language follows Vygotsky's principles. Consider what might happen when an adult enrolls in a class that encourages learning Spanish. The teacher might begin class with "Como estas?," teaching students to answer "muy bien." Scaffolding to the next step within the zone occurs when that teacher elicits students to ask "Como estas?" Once that is understood, the teacher might reply to the students' "Como estas?" with "Enfermo," coughing. That cough would scaffold "sick."

By contrast, if a learner's attempt to speak Spanish is met with laughter, then no scaffolding, no apprenticing, and—no learning. According to Vygotsky, education is a social event that occurs within the learning zone (Adamson et al., 2014). We all teach each other; we all learn from what we see others do.

What Mentors Do

In general, mentors are attuned to ever-shifting abilities and motivation, recognizing past accomplishments and urging progress to the next level, not to the moon. Learners ask questions, show interest, and demonstrate progress, which guides and inspires the mentors. When education goes well, both are fully engaged and productive within the zone of proximal development. Particular skills and goals vary enormously, but the overall interaction is the same.

In every culture, mentors:

- Present challenges, knowing each step of cognitive development, tailoring instruction to what the learner already knows, and finding the zone.
- Offer assistance but do not take over, thus guiding participation.

Observation Quiz What can you see that indicates that this man is an excellent mentor? (see answer, page 270) ↓

Building a Mind These middle school students in Richmond, Virginia, think they are building a robot, and that is what their hands are doing. But their teacher is using words to help them understand how their creation works.

Ariel Skelley/DigitalVision/Getty Images

- Add crucial information, scaffolding that will allow understanding.
- Encourage motivation.

Overall, a person's ability to learn from mentors indicates intelligence. According to Vygotsky, "What children can do with the assistance of others might be . . . even more indicative of their mental development than what they can do alone" (Vygotsky, 1980, p. 85).

Vygotsky recognized that good mentors are sometimes slightly older peers, rather than established authorities. This was recognized by one acclaimed coach, Peter, who spoke about the 16-year-old he hired as assistant coach.

> I would say Ali is a better coach than me; not because he has any qualifications but because the children connect with him much more. So what I have kind of said to him is that the children are watching you for clues: a) of how to behave and also b) your passion for football. And he's very, very good because he is a child himself; he may be a few years older but he is basically a child himself and so they look up to him and, without knowing it, he is coaching them. It's not a specific thing but they are always kind of watching what he does and the way he does a specific turn or whatever but also they get a lot of feedback from him in terms of encouragement and I think those coaches, the young coaches, are really, really important.
>
> *[Vinson & Parker, 2019, p. 103]*

Ali, not surprisingly, considered Peter an outstanding coach, praising his ability to notice small details as he intently watched his players, intervening only occasionally.

Boundary Spanners

As you have seen, Vygotsky's ideas are applied in many situations. One group that illustrates the reach of Vygotsky's approach are bankers in South Korea.

A group of researchers studied *boundary spanners* in large Korean financial firms (Roberts & Beamish, 2017). In this study, a boundary spanner was a Korean person who had worked in North America and returned to mentor their colleagues. These researchers referred to scaffolding to explain how the returnees help their companies cross the boundary between Korean tradition and North American practice.

One boundary spanner reported, "When I approach my colleagues with a fresh idea, they often buy it the first time. 'WOW! That's a great idea.' But when it comes time for implementation, they tend to still believe in what they know." The idea was beyond their zone.

These researchers reported that successful boundary spanners used scaffolding to get the Korean employees to understand, adapt, and adopt new methods. For example, one had seminars every morning at 8 A.M. at which he explained the financial news reported in that day's *Wall Street Journal*. That newspaper was the scaffold—a useful tool that he used as a ladder to allow climbing to new understanding (Roberts & Beamish, 2017).

Language as a Cognitive Tool

All objects of a culture guide education. However, Vygotsky believed that language is especially pivotal, advancing thinking in two ways.

The first is with internal dialogue, or **private speech**, in which people talk without expecting anyone to listen (Vygotsky, 2012). Young children often talk out loud to review, decide, and explain events to themselves (Al-Namlah et al., 2012).

Observation Quiz Where is this? (see answer, page 270) ↓

Teaching Health Daniel Garcia is a health professional, providing medical information at this Buddhist temple. His challenge is to find the zone. He seems to be off to a good start: His smile, clipboard, and shirt are all tools that help him teach.

Marcus Yam/Los Angeles Times/Getty Images

private speech The internal dialogue that occurs when people talk to themselves (either silently or out loud).

social mediation Human interaction that expands and advances understanding, often through words that one person uses to explain something to another.

THINK CRITICALLY: Are you aware of any misconceptions you learned in childhood that still linger in your adult thinking?

Older children are more circumspect, sometimes whispering to themselves, sometimes thinking quietly. Audible or not, private speech aids cognition and self-reflection (de Guerrero, 2018). Many adults talk aloud when alone or write down ideas to help them think. That is exactly what Vygotsky would expect.

The second way in which language advances thinking, according to Vygotsky, is by facilitating social interaction (Vygotsky, 2012). This **social mediation** function of speech occurs during both formal instruction (when teachers explain things) and casual conversation. Words entice people into the zone of proximal development. The employees in that Korean firm discussed those *Wall Street Journal* articles, and their talking and listening advanced their thinking.

Both private speech and social mediation, as Vygotsky described them, build with age. Each aspect of language facilitates the other. For example, a study of children aged 4–8 found that as their private speech increased, so did sensitivity to each other's thinking, making conversation more informative (San Martin et al., 2014).

One arena of human development in which private speech (sometimes called *self-talk*) has proven particularly useful is in sports. Young children just play, hoping to win. Adults do more than that. Especially in stressful, competitive play, professional athletes talk to themselves in order to perform at their best (Van Raalte et al., 2017). Social mediation is also evident: Team members shout at each other, with both compliments and commands.

Both Vygotsky and Piaget emphasized the process of cognition. Sometimes Piaget's approach is called inside-out, in that the maturation of the child allows new thinking about all the external experiences of life, while Vygotsky's approach is called outside-in, in that the social world is incorporated into the child's mind.

But both were less interested in measuring the results (as in intelligence tests) and more interested in *how* children learn. Neither was explicit about learning in adulthood, but as you read the next section, you will again see an emphasis on how adults learn, not on what they know.

WHAT HAVE YOU LEARNED?

1. What do Piaget and Vygotsky have in common?
2. How do Piaget and Vygotsky differ?
3. Explain an example that illustrate the zone of proximal development.
4. How is the scaffolding metaphor relevant for learning?
5. What did Vygotsky consider the two functions of language?
6. What are the characteristics of a good mentor?

Adult Thinking

Most developmentalists in the first half of the twentieth century, like Piaget, thought that when the body was fully grown, the mind would be fully grown as well. However, as you read in Chapter 1, current research finds that development continues lifelong.

As one researcher wrote:

> since about 1980, a number of researchers offered critiques of the implication that cognitive growth abated in adolescence. Instead, a number of proposals appeared that, though independent, converged on an extension of Piaget's theory. These extensions proposed that thinking needs to be integrated with emotional and pragmatic aspects, rather than only dealing with the purely abstract.
>
> *[Labouvie-Vief, 2015, p. 89]*

Postformal Thought

Although *formal operational* thought was the final stage of Piaget's theory, many cognitive psychologists find that postadolescent thinking is a cut above that. Adults are more practical and flexible, combining intuition and analysis.

Some developmentalists propose a fifth stage, called **postformal thought**, a "type of logical, adaptive problem-solving that is a step more complex than scientific formal-level Piagetian tasks" (Sinnott, 2014, p. 3). In postformal cognition, "thinking needs to be integrated with emotional and pragmatic aspects, rather than only dealing with the purely abstract" (Labouvie-Vief, 2015, p. 89).

As they integrate emotion and pragmatics, postformal thinkers are flexible, with a "more complex, nuanced, and paradoxical" mode of thinking (Gidley, 2016). They consider all aspects of a situation, anticipating problems and dealing with them rather than denying, avoiding, or procrastinating.

Postformal thinking is especially useful in the dilemmas of daily life. For example, one advocate of postformal thought asked herself:

> how can I create and hold a unified concept of my self and my identity at the same time I hold a concept of my self and my identity as growing, evolving, and changing?

[Sinnott, 2017, p. 19]

Her answer was postformal thought.

postformal thought A proposed adult stage of cognitive development, following Piaget's four stages, that goes beyond adolescent thinking by being more practical, more flexible, and more dialectical (i.e., more capable of combining contradictory elements into a comprehensive whole).

Stereotype Threat

Unfortunately, many people do not recognize their own stereotypes. One of the most pernicious is **stereotype threat**, arising in people who worry that other people might judge them as stupid, inept, lazy, oversexed, or worse because of their

stereotype threat The thought in a person's mind that one's appearance or behavior will be misread to confirm another person's oversimplified, prejudiced attitudes.

A VIEW FROM SCIENCE

Rejecting Stereotypes

Stereotypes are common in concrete operational thought. Children seek simple, factual answers to complex, philosophical questions. Concrete thinking does not end in childhood. Every adult (including me and you) holds beliefs that others consider stereotypical.

Ideally, postformal thinking allows adults to move past simplistic ideas (Chang & Chiou, 2014). The goal is to combine personal experience and logic, which, as just explained, is characteristic of postformal thinking at its best.

Is this possible? That question was explored in an experiment that involved voters in South Florida (Broockman & Kalla, 2016). Canvassers sought to reduce transphobia (fear regarding transgender people), a common prejudice that follows naturally from the concrete operational thought that male and female are opposites (discussed in Chapter 11). This research was a field study, based on what had been learned in laboratory studies (Flores et al., 2018).

The study began with a list of registered voters in South Florida. Half the names and addresses were allocated to the experimental group; half to the control group. Canvassers rang the doorbells of the voters. The experimental half were asked to talk about a time when they had been marginalized because of

some characteristic (ethnicity, age, religion and so on) they were thought to have.

The voters were then asked how their experiences and emotions might apply to transgender people. Canvassers were encouraged to listen respectfully and to facilitate "deep processing" of the information. This meant the voters were encouraged to reflect, and were not told counterarguments.

For the other half of the voters, in the control group, the canvassers focused on climate change and recycling. Three days, three weeks, and three months later, both groups answered a questionnaire that they did not know was related to the canvassing encounter. The questionnaire asked for opinions on many issues, including recycling and transgender individuals.

Those who had a brief conversation about transgender concerns became somewhat more positive toward trans people, especially if the canvassers had identified themselves as transgender. The control group did not change their opinion on that topic.

The scientists believe that the crucial difference was cognitive: An encounter that made them connect their own experience to an issue that was new to them allowed postformal thinking and reduced the stereotype.

THINK CRITICALLY: What imagined criticisms impair your own achievement, and how can you overcome them?

dialectical thought The most advanced cognitive process, characterized by the ability to consider a thesis and its antithesis simultaneously and thus to arrive at a synthesis. Dialectical thought makes possible an ongoing awareness of pros and cons, advantages and disadvantages, possibilities and limitations.

thesis A proposition or statement of belief; the first stage of the process of dialectical thinking.

antithesis A proposition or statement of belief that opposes the thesis; the second stage of the process of dialectical thinking.

synthesis A new idea that integrates the thesis and its antithesis, thus representing a new and more comprehensive level of truth; the third stage of the process of dialectical thinking.

THINK CRITICALLY Can you see dialectical thinking when you remember what you believed as a child?

ethnicity, gender, age, or appearance. Stereotype threat is increasingly apparent as children grow into adults, because people become more aware of what other people might think. It is an imagined but nonetheless powerful threat, and envisioned idea, a "threat in the air" (Steele, 1997).

Thus, some people have a stereotype that other people have a stereotype about them. Then the *possibility* of being stereotyped arouses emotions and hijacks memory, disrupting cognition. Most of the research on stereotype threat has been on college students, who do not perform as well when they are thinking about other people's opinions about them.

Over the years of adulthood, people may confront their internalized self-doubts. Success in college or on the job, or years of affirmation from a partner, or coping with a health or family crisis, may undercut stereotype threat. Postformal thinking allows a combination of emotions and logic, enabling some people to replace debilitating anxiety with cognitive focus (Popham & Hess, 2015). That is a postformal achievement.

Dialectical Thought

Cross-cultural research suggests that formal operational adult thought, at its best, becomes **dialectical thought**, which may be the most advanced cognitive process (Basseches, 1984, 1989; Grossmann, 2018; Riegel, 1975). The word *dialectic* refers to the philosophical concept, developed by Hegel two centuries ago, that every idea or truth bears within itself the opposite idea or truth.

To use the words of philosophers, each idea, or **thesis**, implies an opposing idea, or **antithesis**. Dialectical thought involves considering both these poles simultaneously and then forging them into a **synthesis**—that is, a new idea that integrates the original and its opposite. Note that the synthesis is not a compromise; it is a new concept that incorporates both original ones in some transformative way (Lemieux, 2012).

For example, many young children idolize their parents (thesis), many adolescents are highly critical of their parents (antithesis). Ideally adults appreciate their parents and forgive their shortcomings, which they attribute to their parents' background, historical conditions, and age. Thus, with postformal thinking, adults gain a more nuanced respect for their parents (synthesis).

A "Broken" Marriage

Now consider an example of dialectical thought familiar to many: the end of a love affair. A nondialectical thinker might believe that each person has stable, enduring, independent traits. Faced with a troubled romance, then, a nondialectical thinker concludes that one partner (or the other) is at fault, or perhaps the relationship was a mistake from the beginning because the two were a bad match.

By contrast, dialectical thinkers see people and relationships as constantly evolving; time as well as social interaction changes both partners. Therefore, a romance becomes troubled not because the partners are fundamentally incompatible, or because one or the other is fatally flawed, but because they have not adapted to the changes in the other.

As dialectical thinking assesses it, marriages do not "break"; relationships do not "fail." Instead, relationships either grow as circumstances change or they stagnate as the two people move apart. Partners who think dialectically can move from the initial thesis ("I love you because you are perfect") to the antithesis ("I hate you—you are selfish") to a new synthesis ("Neither of us is perfect, but together we can grow").

A dialectic perspective not only encourages adults to work together on their relationships but also helps them cope if they break up. Many adults feel guilty after divorce, switching from blaming their partner to blaming themselves (Kiiski et al., 2013; Leonoff, 2015). Children are caught in the middle (van der Wal et al., 2019).

Ideally, adults achieve a dialectical understanding, seeing divorce as an opportunity to look at themselves more closely and make necessary changes. They move from the thesis ("My partner was bad") and antithesis ("I was bad") to synthesis ("I have learned from this"). This is the goal of two modern practices, the no-fault divorce, when the former spouses do not need to blame each other, and the joint custody arrangement, when the parents need to cooperate to raise the children.

Without such postformal thinking, problems arise in emerging adults whose parents divorced. They tend to blame one parent and idealize the other, which impairs their ability to develop partnerships of their own. Worse is blaming themselves, as children sometimes do. Hopefully adult thinking helps the children understand more clearly what happened to their parents' marriage (Shanholtz et al., 2019).

If people do not reach a synthesis of intellect and emotion, behavioral extremes (such as those that lead to binge eating, anorexia, obesity, addiction, and violence) and cognitive extremes (such as believing that one is the best or the worst person on earth) are common. Those are typical of the egocentrism of adolescence—and of some adults. By contrast, dialectical thinkers balance personal experience with knowledge.

As an example of such balance, an adult student of mine wrote:

> Unfortunately, alcoholism runs in my family. . . . I have seen it tear apart not only my uncle but my family also. . . . I have gotten sick from drinking, and it was the most horrifying night of my life. I know that I didn't have alcohol poisoning or anything, but I drank too quickly and was getting sick. All of these images flooded my head about how I didn't want to ever end up the way my uncle was. From that point on, whenever I have touched alcohol, it has been with extreme caution. . . . When I am old and gray, the last thing I want to be thinking about is where my next beer will come from or how I'll need a liver transplant.
>
> *[Laura, personal communication]*

Laura's thinking about alcohol is postformal in that it combines knowledge (e.g., of alcohol poisoning) with emotions (images flooding her head). Note that she is cautious, not abstinent; she has both objective awareness of her genetic potential and subjective experience of wanting to be part of the crowd.

She combines both modes of thought to reach a conclusion that works for her. She does not need searing personal experiences (becoming an uncontrollable drinker and reaching despair). If she did, she would need to go to the other extreme (avoiding even one sip).

Like Laura, most adults think about their own drug and alcohol use, combine experience, emotions, and knowledge, and no longer abuse drugs. The data shows a marked drop off in the frequency of binging by about age 25 or 30 (Philbin & Mauro, 2019).

Some, for both genetic and social reasons, have become addicts and must stop completely, but most adults can drink a glass or two on occasion because they have moved past the extremes of binging and abstinence of their younger selves. They have achieved a new synthesis.

The exception here is opioid addiction, which peaks after age 25. One possible explanation is that use often begins with a medical prescription to reduce pain. For that reason, addiction precedes thought. Postformal thinking has not yet focused on this form of drug abuse.

Dual Processing

Much of our understanding of advanced adult thought focuses on the integration of two distinct processes in the brain, the analysis of the prefrontal cortex and the emotions of the limbic system. Thus, thinking occurs in two ways, called **dual processing** (Evans & Stanovich, 2013). (See **Figure 9.5**.)

ESPECIALLY FOR Someone Who Has to Make an Important Decision Which is better, to go with your gut feelings or to consider pros and cons as objectively as you can? (see response, page 270)

dual processing The notion that two networks exist within the human brain, one for emotional processing of stimuli and one for analytical reasoning.

Dual Processing

System 1	System 2
Intuitive	Analytic
Hot	Cold
Implicit	Explicit
Creative	Factual
Gist	Specific
Experiential	Rational
Qualitative	Quantitative
Contextualized	Decontextualized

FIGURE 9.5
Two Modes Each pair describes two modes of thought. Although researchers who use each pair differ in what they emphasize, all see two contrasting ways to think.

A College Professor

Remember that postformal thinking and dialectical reasoning apply to adults of every age, not simply because of maturation but because of experience. In every profession, experience sometimes allows better understanding than knowledge alone.

One of the leading thinkers in adult cognition is Jan Sinnott, a professor and past editor of the *Journal of Adult Development*. She describes the first course she taught:

> I did not think in a postformal way. . . . Teaching was good for passing information from the informed to the uninformed. . . . I decided to create a course in the psychology of aging . . . with a fellow graduate student. Being compulsive graduate students had paid off in our careers so far, so my colleague and I continued on that path. Articles and books and photocopies began to take over my house. And having found all this information, we seem to have unconsciously sworn to use all of it. . . .
>
> Each class day, my colleague and I would arrive with reams of notes and articles and lecture, lecture, lecture. Rapidly! . . .
>
> The discussion of death and dying came close to the end of the term (naturally). As I gave my usual jam-packed lecture, the sound of note taking was intense. But toward the end of the

class . . . an extremely capable student burst into tears and said she had to drop the class. . . . Unknown to me, she had been the caretaker of an older relative who had just died in the past few days. She had not said anything about this significant experience when we lectured on caretaking. . . . How could she? . . . We never stopped talking. "I wish I could tell people what it's really like," she said.

> [*Sinnott, 2008, pp. 54–55*]

Sinnott changed her lesson plan. In the next class, she asked that student to share her experiences.

> In the end, the students agreed that this was a class when they . . . synthesized material and analyzed research and theory critically.
>
> [*Sinnott, 2008, p. 56*]

Sinnott wrote that she still lectures and gives multiple-choice exams, but she also realizes the impact of the personal story. She combines analysis and emotion; she includes the personal experiences of the students. Her teaching became postformal, dialectical, and responsive.

The terms and descriptions that scientists use to describe these two processes vary, including *intuitive/analytic*, *implicit/explicit*, *contextualized/decontextualized*, *creative/factual*, *unconscious/conscious*, *gist/quantitative*, *emotional/intellectual*, *experiential/rational*, *hot/cold*, and *systems 1 and 2*. Although they interact and can overlap, each mode is often considered independent (Kuhn, 2013).

The thinking described by the first half of each pair is easier and quicker, which makes it preferred in daily life. Sometimes, however, circumstances necessitate the second mode, because deeper thought is needed. The teenage lag between the maturation of the limbic system and of the prefrontal cortex reflects this duality.

In this chapter, when describing these two processes, we use the terms *intuitive* and *analytic*, defined as follows:

intuitive thought Thought that arises from an emotion or a hunch, beyond rational explanation, and is influenced by past experiences and cultural assumptions.

analytic thought Thought that results from analysis, such as a systematic ranking of pros and cons, risks and consequences, possibilities and facts. Analytic thought depends on logic and rationality.

- **Intuitive thought** begins with a belief, assumption, or general rule (called a *heuristic*) rather than logic. Intuition is quick and powerful; it feels "right."
- **Analytic thought** is the abstract, logical, hypothetical-deductive thinking described by Piaget in formal operational thought. It involves rational and systematic analysis of many interacting factors, as in the scale-balancing problem.

Intuitive and Analytic Processing

The challenge for adults is to combine the two forms of thought. That is another way to describe postformal thought.

To test yourself on intuitive and analytic thinking, answer the following:

1. A bat and a ball cost $1.10 in total. The bat costs $1 more than the ball. How much does the ball cost?
2. If it takes 5 minutes for 5 machines to make 5 widgets, how long would it take 100 machines to make 100 widgets?
3. In a lake, there is a patch of lily pads. Every day the patch doubles in size. If it takes 48 days for the patch to cover the entire lake, how long would it take for the patch to cover half the lake?

> [*from Gervais & Norenzayan, 2012, p. 494*]

VISUALIZING DEVELOPMENT Thinking in Adulthood

In adulthood, we are able to think both intuitively and analytically, but adolescents tend to rely more on intuitive thinking.

INDUCTIVE vs. DEDUCTIVE REASONING

INDUCTIVE: Conclusion reached after many of the following. Note that the problem is that the adolescent's nimble mind can rationalize many specifics. Only when the evidence is overwhelming is the conclusion reached.

DEDUCTIVE: The principle is the starting point, not the end point.

Drug addiction is destructive.

GENERAL CONCLUSION

GENERAL PRINCIPLE

APPLICATION
Say no to every drug.

EXAMPLE
Stay away from drug users; they are losers.

HYPOTHETICAL CASE
If I use drugs, I won't get into the college I want.

IDEAS FROM AUTHORITY
Mom says drugs are bad (but Mom may not know).

My religion says drugs are sinful (but religion may not be right).

OBSERVATION
A relative smoked cigarettes and died of lung cancer (but he was old).

A friend crashed a car when drunk (but he was speeding).

A fellow student was arrested for having cocaine (he shouldn't have carried it).

PAST EXPERIENCES
Personally smoked a few cigarettes; now want more (maybe try other drugs).

Got drunk, threw up, blacked out (maybe stick to beer).

EXTENSION
Reliance on substances of any kind is suspect; avoid energy drinks, e-cigs, etc.

TEST CASE
Sports hero used steroids; was stripped of his Olympic medals.

CHANGES IN AGE

theshots.co/Shutterstock

INTUITIVE THINKING

age

YOUNGER

This singer is cute and fun ≡ **I'll listen to her**

ANALYTICAL THINKING

OLDER

This singer is very popular
+ She sometimes writes her own songs
+ She makes creative videos
+ I agree with her morals ≡ **I'll listen to her music**

As people age, their thinking tends to move from intuitive processing to more analytic processing. Virtually all cognitive psychologists note these two alternative processes and describe a developmental progression toward more dispassionate logic with maturity. However, the terms used and the boundaries between the two vary. They are roughly analogous to the traditional distinction between inductive and deductive reasoning, and to Piaget's concrete operational versus formal operational thought. Although experts vary in their descriptions, and individuals vary in when and how they use these two processes, adolescents tend to favor intuitive rather than analytic thinking. Postformal thinkers can combine them, becoming more flexible as well as more practical.

Answers are on page 270. As you see, the quick, intuitive responses may be wrong. That is understood by postformal thinkers.

When the two modes of thinking conflict, people of all ages sometimes use one and sometimes the other: We are all "predictably irrational" at times (Ariely, 2010). Fortunately, by about age 25, the brain is better balanced, and the rapid connections within the limbic system are joined by rapid processing elsewhere in the brain.

A postformal approach to the topic of cognition recognizes that there are many aspects and alternative approaches to the study of cognition. Many other chapters of this book explore some aspect of thinking.

Indeed, this entire book is about cognition, in that one goal is to further every reader's intellectual growth. Recall the basic insight of the cognitive revolution: The way people think affects everything they say, do, and feel. With that we end this chapter, recognizing that cognitive development never ends.

WHAT HAVE YOU LEARNED?

1. Why do scholars of adult development think Piaget should have a fifth stage?

2. What are the three characteristics of postformal thought?

3. How can a good marriage be considered a synthesis?

4. How does postformal thinking make it more difficult to hold a stereotype?

5. What is the difference between *stereotype* and *stereotype threat*?

6. Is dialectical thinking the same as duel-process thinking?

7. When is analytic thought best and when is intuitive thought best?

SUMMARY

Intelligence

1. People have wondered about intelligence for centuries, as some people are much quicker learners and seem smarter than others. Intelligent innovations (cognitive artifacts) have advanced cognition among entire populations.

2. In the past century, many psychologists have sought to measure intelligence, via the IQ test. IQ is an abbreviation of intelligence quotient, the result of dividing a child's mental age by their chronological age.

3. Contrary to earlier assumption that g (general intelligence) was the result of genes, and thus did not change over the life span, we now see intelligence as more plastic in individuals as they mature. In the Flynn effect, average intelligence has increased in entire nations over the past decades.

4. Critics of IQ testing contend that intelligence is manifested in multiple ways, which makes g too narrow and limited. Gardner describes nine distinct intelligences, and noted that North American culture is heavily focused on only two, linguistic and mathematical.

5. Sternberg proposed three fundamental forms of intelligence: analytic, creative, and practical. Most research finds that although analytic and creative abilities decline with age, practical intelligence may improve. In daily life, practical intelligence may be most important.

Piaget's Stages of Intelligence

6. Piaget revolutionized our understanding of cognition, first by detailed study of his own three infants and then by listening to older children in order to understand their thinking processes. He discovered that how people think affects what they do, and that children do not think as adults do.

7. The first stage of cognitive development, according to Piaget, is sensorimotor intelligence. Infant cognition advances through six substages, from reflexes to mental combinations.

8. From ages 2–6, symbolic thought characterizes cognition, according to Piaget. Imagination and language flourish at this stage. Children's cognition is limited because, at this stage, children are egocentric and focused on appearance. Thinking is static, which makes reversibility not understood.

9. Concrete operational thinking (ages 7–11) is logical about real experiences. Children are eager to understand facts and can grasps concepts including conservation and classification.

10. Piaget believed that formal operational thought begins at adolescence and continues in adulthood. People in this stage can understand abstractions and possibilities, inductive as well as deductive reasoning.

11. Piaget was limited by the experimental methods of his day, which led him to underestimate the age of object permanence

and many other ideas. The limitations of his stage theory are now recognized, but developmentalists praise his insights about the development of active cognition.

Vygotsky: Cognition as a Social Experience

12. Vygotsky emphasized that learning is a social experience, embedded in culture. That contrasts with Piaget's stress on individual discovery made possible by maturation.

13. The mentor's challenge is to find the zone of proximal development for each learner, and then to scaffold learning opportunities so that the apprentice learner can enter that zone.

14. Language is an essential tool for cognition, according to Vygotsky. This occurs in two ways: private speech as a person teaches themselves, and social mediation as mentor and mentee use language to tell each other the next steps in education.

Adult Thinking

15. Many developmentalists suggest that there is a fifth stage of cognitive development, sometimes called postformal thought. It combines emotions and practical thinking, in a flexible way, to deal with the problems of life.

16. One benefit of postformal thinking is that adults can move past the stereotypes of their youth. Combining emotions and facts leads to keeping only those ideas from childhood that still make sense in adulthood.

17. Dialectical thought allows people to see beyond thesis and antithesis to reach a synthesis. This helps with marriages, divorces, and all relationships.

18. People have two modes of thinking: intuitive and analytic, or system 1 and system 2. In adulthood, dual processing allows more advanced, dialectical thought. The two processes can combine, creating a more reflective, practical thinker.

KEY TERMS

cognitive artifacts (p. 240)
general intelligence (*g*) (p. 241)
Flynn effect (p. 242)
multiple intelligences (p. 243)
analytic intelligence (p. 244)
creative intelligence (p. 244)
practical intelligence (p. 244)
fluid intelligence (p. 245)
crystallized intelligence (p. 246)
scheme (p. 247)
cognitive equilibrium (p. 247)
assimilation (p. 247)
accommodation (p. 247)
sensorimotor intelligence (p. 248)

primary circular reactions (p. 248)
secondary circular reactions (p. 249)
object permanence (p. 249)
tertiary circular reactions (p. 250)
little scientists (p. 250)
deferred imitation (p. 250)
preoperational intelligence (p. 250)
symbolic thought (p. 250)
centration (p. 251)
egocentrism (p. 251)

focus on appearance (p. 251)
static reasoning (p. 251)
irreversibility (p. 251)
conservation (p. 251)
concrete operational thought (p. 252)
classification (p. 253)
formal operational intelligence (p. 253)
hypothetical thought (p. 255)
deductive reasoning (p. 255)
inductive reasoning (p. 255)
apprentice in thinking (p. 258)

zone of proximal development (p. 259)
scaffolding (p. 259)
private speech (p. 261)
social mediation (p. 262)
postformal thought (p. 263)
stereotype threat (p. 263)
dialectical thought (p. 264)
thesis (p. 264)
antithesis (p. 264)
synthesis (p. 264)
dual processing (p. 265)
intuitive thought (p. 266)
analytic thought (p. 266)

APPLICATIONS

1. Test a toddler's ability to pretend and to imitate, as Piaget would expect. Use a doll or a toy car and pretend with it, such as feeding the doll or making the car travel. Then see whether the child will do it. This experiment can be more elaborate if the child succeeds.

2. Replicate one of Piaget's conservation experiments. The easiest one is conservation of liquids (see Figure 9.3). Work with a child under age 5 who tells you that two identically shaped glasses contain

the same amount of liquid. Then carefully pour one glass of liquid into a narrower, taller glass. Ask the child whether one glass now contains more, or the glasses contain the same amount.

3. Read a biography or an autobiography that includes information about the person's thinking from age 18 to age 60, paying particular attention to practical, flexible, or dialectical thought. How did personal experiences, education, and ideas affect the person's thinking?

ESPECIALLY FOR ANSWERS

Response for Parents (from p. 249) Both decisions should be made within the first month, during the stage of reflexes. If parents wait until the infant is 4 months or older, they may discover that they are too late. It is difficult to introduce a bottle to a 4-month-old who has never sucked on an artificial nipple or a pacifier to a baby who has already adapted the sucking reflex to a thumb.

Response for Parents (from p. 250) It is easier and safer to baby-proof the house because toddlers, being "little scientists," want to explore. However, it is important for both parents to encourage and guide the baby. If having untouchable items prevents a major conflict between the adults, that might be the best choice.

Response for Someone Who Has to Make an Important Decision (from p. 265) Both are necessary. Mature thinking requires a combination of emotions and logic. To make sure you use both, take your time (don't act on your first impulse) and talk with people you trust. Ultimately, you will have to live with your decision, so do not ignore either intuitive or logical thought.

OBSERVATION QUIZ ANSWERS

Answer to Observation Quiz (from p. 242) The person is average. Anyone with a score between 85 and 115 has an average IQ.

Answer to Observation Quiz (from p. 259) Right-handed. Her dominant hand is engaged in something more comforting than exploring the abacus.

Answer to Observation Quiz (from p. 260) Body position (leaning over) and facial expression (intense interest) suggest that he is actively engaged in mentoring. And notice—no hands on the robot. He is guiding, but not taking over.

Answer to Observation Quiz (from p. 261) Los Angeles, California. Garcia is an undergraduate at the University of California at Los Angeles. Clues—ethnic diversity and the temple's architecture.

Answers to questions on p. 266

	Intuitive	Analytic
1.	10 cents	5 cents
2.	100 minutes	5 minutes
3.	24 days	47 days

The correct answer is the analytic one, but few adolescents take the time to figure it out.

CHAPTER 10

Personality, Identity, and Self

"**Y**our backpack is open."
        I hear that several times a day from strangers on sidewalks, at street corners, in stores. "Thank you. I know," I usually reply. Sometimes I smile, make eye contact, and add "it gives me a chance to say thank you to strangers." Then the stranger is surprised, and usually smiles. But I never react as expected, taking my backpack off and zipping it shut.

The backpack is large, with three deep pockets. I zip it only halfway, leaving the top open so that I can see each section. That saves time when I must find something. Nothing visible is valuable; nothing ever falls out, which I explain to strangers if they tell me I might lose something.

Once, as I was waiting for the subway, next to me sat a boy. His father sat on his other side. The man said, "Your backpack is open."

"Thank you. I know."

"Do you want me to zip it for you?"

I smiled and shook my head.

"You must be tired and busy," he said. "My son could zip it for you."

He seemed upset, and the boy was looking at me, ready to zip. I did not want to be rude.

"OK."

The son zipped; the father was happy. I thanked them both, as if I were grateful.

The merits of open backpacks can be argued either way, but this chapter begins with my backpack because it reveals three characteristics of personality. First, each person has a distinct identity, which reflects the way that particular person thinks and acts. That man and I have quite different attitudes about things being closed. (I keep kitchen cabinets, closet doors, and jackets open, too.)

Second, unless people recognize personality differences, they misinterpret what other people do. That father assumed that my backpack was open because I was tired, not because I prefer it open. That could have led to a disagreement, but fortunately most humans are polite to other people, certainly to family members and often, as in this case, to strangers. That is the third trait: We all have an identity based on what we do and who we think we are; we each have a self-concept, and we try to be who we hope to be.

My identity as a professor of psychology leads me to appreciate "all kinds of people" (see Chapter 1), and my self-concept makes me inclined to be helpful. I did not want my backpack zipped, but I recognized the father's wish to help me, and the boy's wish to please his father. I decided to help them by letting them help me.

Personality, *identity*, and *self* are three constructs that all refer to a basic truth: All people are uniquely themselves, developing as life goes on. This chapter explains that.

What Will You Know?

1. What causes personality—genes, childhood, or life experiences?
2. If children are abused, will that damage them lifelong?
3. Do adults have the same personality at age 60 as at age 30?
4. Do older adults see the world in an overly positive light?

Theories of Personality

personality An individual's characteristic way of thinking, feeling, and acting.

We all are ourselves, with distinct personalities. **Personality** is each person's characteristic way of thinking, feeling, and acting. Our thoughts, emotions, and behaviors are part of our cherished individuality, our unique self.

At the same time, we also are all human, with a shared identity as people. To understand both aspects, the unique and the universal, we begin with theories to frame what we see.

Three major frameworks are apparent. Does our unique self arise from (1) genes, (2) early childhood, or (3) circumstances that change over the life span? Each of these three possibilities has advocates. We need to emphasize that no one believes that personality comes exclusively from only one of these and not at all from the other two, but we deepen and expand our understanding to consider all three.

THINK CRITICALLY: Would your personality fit better in another culture?

Genes

Personality may arise from genes, which direct the formation of neurons, dendrites, neurotransmitters, and hormones. This theory notes that every trait arises from distinctive brain patterns and then leads to behavior. Extensive research confirms that innate, biological factors make one person fearful and another foolhardy, one outgoing and another shy, one angry and another sanguine.

A precursor to the genetic theory of personality was called the *trait theory*, developed by Allport (1961) who wrote about dispositions, and Cattell and Child (1975) who wrote about endowment. Trait theorists contended that traits were enduring: A person who was shy, or honest, or aggressive would be so lifelong. Originally that theory did not specify where those traits came from, but now there is extensive evidence that many traits originate from genes.

Specific Codes

Of course, you remember that each gene is a bundle of connections, and that, although almost all codes are the same for every human, some tiny polymorphic variations make each of us unique. Some of those specific alleles that characterize emotions are apparent in the first weeks of life.

For example, infants with a particular version of the MAOA gene are quick to anger (Sung et al., 2015). The 7-repeat allele of the DRD4 VNTR gene, when combined with the 5-HTTLPR genotype, results in 6-month-olds who are difficult—often crying, hard to distract, slow to laugh (Holmboe et al., 2011; Windhorst et al., 2015).

Another gene, AVPR1A, correlates with singing in a choir (Morley et al., 2012) and having a satisfying sex life (Acevedo et al., 2019). The particulars of these effects are not "robust," which means they are not yet confirmed. Much more research is needed.

You need not remember the letters of these alleles, but such data have convinced almost everyone that personality traits begin with genetic variations.

Research on genetic variations that affect personality is complex, because alleles on some genes code for certain thoughts and emotions, and then those particular alleles depend on other codes in other genes to transcribe and receive them. The mitochondria, inherited directly from the mother, affect this, as do thousands of other genetic factors that are passed down from either parent to each zygote (Meijer et al., 2019).

The biological explanation of the self leads to treatment for psychopathology. Suppose a person is weirdly delusional, or irrationally aggressive, or deeply sad. These are symptoms of schizophrenia, oppositional defiance disorder, and depression, all of which are serious psychological disorders. If the cause is in the chemicals produced by the genetic structure of the brain, treatment might be a drug to alter that biochemistry.

Some people with symptoms of psychopathology refuse to take their medication, because they don't feel like themselves! That suggests that each of us may have come to accept aspects of our identity that others might find troubling.

The research on the precise path and influence of genes on the self is an exciting area of neuroscience, but much remains unknown. Most current research is on nonhuman animals, because ethical concerns limit invasive techniques, and practical concerns make it hard to gather longitudinal data on human moods and brains. Consequently, details of the genetic impact on human personality are not yet clear. However, one general finding is confirmed many times over: Hormones affect human personality, and these result, at least in part, from the genes.

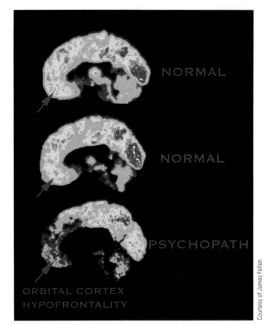

Ax Murderer? That blue area on the left is ominous. When a missing orbital cortex is accompanied by the MAOA gene, a person may become a homicidal maniac, as was true for seven ancestors of Jim Fallon, a neuroscientist. One was the infamous Lizzie Borden, who murdered her father and step-mother. Jim was shocked to discover that he himself inherited both those biological traits. However, Diane, his wife and the mother of his three children, has known him for 30 years and said, "Fortunately, he wasn't abused as a young person, so I've lived to be a ripe old age so far." Brains and genes do not act in isolation: Childhood matters.

Hormones

To probe the link between genes and personality, consider that genes increase neurotransmitters and hormones, which are chemicals in the cerebral fluid and the blood that affect thinking, emotions, and behavior (the three components of personality). They push everyone toward anxiety, lust, sleep, hunger, fear, depression, and happiness, and predispose some people to homicide, suicide, anorexia, or schizophrenia.

As already explained in Chapter 5, one hormone, *oxytocin*, affects many aspects of personality, decreasing anxiety and increasing trust, making people more loving, loyal, and generous. Sometimes oxytocin increases aggression, especially to defend one's family and friends.

The personality effects of oxytocin, and indeed of all the hormones, are pervasive and complex. One detailed review (103 pages) concludes that there is "a high level of uncertainty" regarding the connections between oxytocin and "various behavioral traits . . . including . . . loneliness . . . emotional withdrawal . . . empathy . . . maternal sensitivity . . . aggression and antisocial behavior" (Jurek & Neumann, 2018, p. 1877).

Another crucial hormone that may affect personality is *cortisol*, known as the stress hormone. In infancy and throughout life, people high in cortisol are quickly worried when something seems amiss; those with lower cortisol are calm when unexpected threats appear. Newborns vary substantially in how much cortisol is in their saliva, which suggests that cortisol levels are partly inherited (Ivars et al., 2015).

Similarly, the sex hormones (estrogens, androgens, testosterone, and more) affect reactions, sometimes in paradoxical ways (Arnold, 2020). The hormones in women's bodies fluctuate over the menstrual cycle, a reaction partly governed by genetic factors. Many women notice that their moods fluctuate as well—further evidence that hormones affect personality.

Of course, people can, and often do, behave in ways contrary to the emotions arising from their hormones. But this first theory holds that genetic variations affect our personality traits lifelong.

Early Childhood and Personality

Now we consider the second cluster of theories about personality. Some believe that personality is formed in the first five years of life. This cluster arose from psychoanalytic theory, which was once a prominent personality theory in the United States (Engler, 2006).

That is no longer true in this country, but many scholars in Europe and the Middle East still emphasize personality formation in the first years of life. According to one European reviewer, "the psychoanalytic view of personality remains the most comprehensive and influential personality theory of all time" (Susanu, 2020, p. 341).

Freud and Personality

The patriarch of the idea that early-childhood experiences determine traits was Sigmund Freud. You already read in Chapter 2 about Freud's developmental stages, which set the stage for personality. Now we explain another of Freud's core ideas, his view of the self. He thought that each individual has three parts: *ego*, *id*, and *superego*, all shaped by early caregiving.

ego The conscious self. *Ego* is the Latin word for "I."

The word **ego** (Latin for *I*) means "self." Merriam-Webster defines ego as "the self especially as contrasted with another self," and the Oxford dictionary defines it as "a person's sense of self-esteem or self-importance." The psychoanalytic ideal is a person with a strong ego, who is confident and comfortable with themselves, and therefore has no need to demean other people nor a tendency to twist reality in self-defense.

id The primitive, animal-like drives and emotions that humans have. Much of the id concerns sex and aggression.

The ego controls the **id**, which is what Freud called those instincts that humans share with all other animals, especially the drive for sex and the fear of death. The id is most evident in infants, who demand food immediately, who move when and where they wish, who grab and hit to get what they want. As the ego develops during the first years of life, young children learn to wait for dinner, to avoid hitting Mother, and so on. Parents are instrumental in this process; they guide children to develop their ego and control their id.

superego A strict sense of right and wrong, imposed and nurtured in the young child by parents and culture.

The **superego** is the third part of the self. It imposes a very strict morality, a sense of right and wrong. It develops primarily in the phallic stage, at age 5 or so. The superego internalizes the moral teachings of parents, pastors, and everyone else, believing in serious punishment (castration in life, hell after death) for immorality.

In Freud's theory, the ego employs *defense mechanisms*, such as forgetting traumatic experiences (repression) or blaming someone else for one's own emotions (displacement), to defend against attacks from the id and the superego.

The interaction among these three forces — an ongoing war between good and evil — makes the personality (Freud, 1927/1990).

Ideally, during the first five years of life, parents help their offspring control instincts and follow moral norms without being overwhelmed by either selfish impulses or fear of sin. Thus, a strong ego allows a happy and productive life, with neither the id nor the superego in control.

Psychodynamic Theory Since Freud

Few contemporary developmentalists endorse Freud's specific concept of ego/id/superego, but many believe that the experiences of early childhood have a powerful influence on adult personality. The term **psychodynamic** reflects the view, that the forces of the psyche are dynamic, actively repressing, tempering, and expressing lessons learned long ago in childhood. This view is evident in a recent study of kindergarten children in Jordan. The teams of researchers believe that "if childhood years were appropriately constructed, the individual will be more mature and productive during adolescence and adulthood stages, vice versa is also true" (Al-Darabah et al., 2019, p. 70).

Freud's theories were revised and extended by many neo-Freudians (Jung, Adler, Horney and others), and criticized by many others, who thought he overstressed early life, sex, and the unconscious, and did not understand women (Burston, 2020; Whitebook, 2017; Roudinesco, 2017; Mills, 2004).

psychodynamic A view of adult emotional difficulties that stresses the interaction of early experiences and current life.

Erikson and the Self

For developmental psychologists, the most famous neo-Freudian was Erik Erikson, who worked for six years with Freud's daughter Anna and other disciples of Freud, until Hitler's rise forced them all to leave Austria. Freud went to England; Erikson went to the United States, where he extended Freudian insights, developing his own eight-stage theory of human development.

Erikson agreed with Freud that adults carry the legacy of childhood experiences (the first four of Erikson's stages) into adulthood, and hence we describe the specifics of those childhood stages now. Erikson also extended Freud's theory, with four more stages in adulthood (see **Table 10.1**). Those four are described later in this chapter.

TABLE 10.1

Erikson's Eight Stages of Development

Stage	Virtue/Pathology	Possible If Not Successfully Resolved
Trust vs. mistrust	Hope/withdrawal	Suspicious of others, making close relationships difficult
Autonomy vs. shame and doubt	Will/compulsion	Obsessively driven, single-minded, not socially responsive
Initiative vs. guilt	Purpose/inhibition	Fearful, regretful (e.g., very homesick in college)
Industry vs. inferiority	Competence/inertia	Self-critical of any endeavor, procrastinating, perfectionistic
Identity vs. role diffusion	Fidelity/repudiation	Uncertain and negative about values, lifestyle, friendships
Intimacy vs. isolation	Love/exclusivity	Anxious about close relationships, jealous, lonely
Generativity vs. stagnation	Care/rejection	[In the future] Fear of failure
Integrity vs. despair	Wisdom/disdain	[In the future] No "mindfulness," no life plan

Information from Erikson, 1982/1998.

Same Situation, Far Apart: Helping at Home Sichuan, in China *(right)*, and Virginia, in the United States *(left)*, provide vastly different contexts for child development. Children everywhere help their families with household chores, as these two do, but gender expectations vary a great deal.

⬤ **Observation Quiz** What do you see that suggests vast socioeconomic differences in the homes of these two children? (see answer, page 299) ↑

The first of Erikson's stages is *trust versus mistrust*. In this stage, attentive caregiving is crucial, because "the child's first geography and the basic maps acquired in such interplay with the mother no doubt remain guides for the ego's first orientation in the world" (Erikson, 1993a, p. 220). In other words, a child who develops trust will become an adult characterized by hope for the future.

The next of Erikson's stages is *autonomy versus shame and doubt*. The toddler's natural bent is to be self-willed (the "terrible twos," or the "no" stage). If the child is never allowed to do what they want (for instance, punished for crying, for running, for exploring) then the personality trait of self-doubt will dominate adulthood.

Then comes *initiative versus guilt*. Ideally, the child experiences the joy of play because "play allows the child to feel that he is master of his life" (Erikson, 1993a, p. 40). On the other hand, guilt is internalized if, for instance, children build a tower but someone knocks it down, draw a picture but someone discards it, try to dress themselves but someone takes over, saying they are doing it all wrong. That someone could be a parent, a teacher, or another child. The point is that children want to do things, and they should be proud of what they have done.

Erikson's final childhood stage is *industry versus inferiority*, when schoolchildren learn whether their efforts will allow them to master reading, math, sports, or whatever. Because of these early experiences, some adults believe in themselves, overcoming whatever problems they experience (sometimes called *self-efficacy*). They need and want to stay busy, active, industrious. Other adults are passive, never feeling worthy of any praise or achievement. For them, the sense of inferiority echoes lifelong.

Overall, the perspective that early-childhood experiences are crucial is a popular one for many people who are not familiar with current perspectives in psychology (Susanu, 2020). However, Freud relied heavily on what he gleaned from his patients, and he and other neo-Freudians seemed to appreciate history and mythology more than the rigors of scientific experiments. Accordingly, another perspective that arose from thousands of experiments has come to the fore.

Ongoing Learning

Now the third perspective. In opposition to the psychodynamic theories, behaviorism dominated psychology in the latter half of the twentieth century. As explained in Chapter 2, the basic idea was that people are reinforced or punished by their experiences. This begins in childhood but continues lifelong, which means that if the environmental circumstances change, personality will change (Skinner, 1974).

Adulthood, according to behaviorists, can be as influential as childhood in shaping the self. Accordingly, personality traits, such as being outgoing or shy, and punctual or tardy, do not arise from genes (theory one) or childhood experiences (theory two), but from repeated reinforcement or punishment.

In 1945, it was recognized that the Great Depression, the Holocaust, and World War II profoundly shaped the personality of adults who experienced them. Psychologists thought of "personality and individuality as something passive that can be broken by these raging forces that intrude from the outside world" (Mroczek, 2020, p. 472).

Over the past 75 years, behaviorists developed a "radically different conception of personality" from the one they had originally (Mroczek, 2020, p. 471). It is now thought that adults choose the social environments of their lives, selecting their vocation, their spouse, their neighborhood, and so on. Their personalities influence those choices, which then determine what reinforcements and punishments they are likely to encounter.

Behaviorists also extended their understanding, as evident in *social learning theory* (Bandura, 1986) (see Chapter 2). Personality, and all other behaviors and emotions, are not only the product of direct reinforcement but also the result of the social context, including what people learn from observing other people.

Most adults arrange their lives to reinforce the personality patterns already set early on. This makes it seem as if the psychodynamic theory is correct, that childhood factors are crucial. However, that is not necessarily true. Instead, adult self-concept, self-esteem, and personality are affected by the social context.

This behaviorist perspective is easier to understand when adult life is unlike childhood. Consider attitudes about money. Some adults are called spendthrifts because they spend money as soon as they get it; others are criticized as misers because they spend too little. These are personality characteristics that begin in childhood but are affected by adult experiences.

For example, a person who grew up in poverty but then becomes wealthy might become quite generous if new beliefs and circumstances push them to be so. Thus, attitudes about poverty and wealth are the result of influences lifelong, because of the "social inequalities that contribute heavily to differences in self-processes" (Spencer et al., 2015, p. 750). If inequalities change, personalities change.

Similarly, someone with a substance use disorder who becomes clean, a nonreligious person who becomes a believer, an immigrant who arrives in a new nation, a juvenile delinquent who joins the U.S. Marines—all of these people may develop a new sense of self, with habits, emotions, and beliefs they did not have before. One of their new friends might describe their personality with words unlike those of someone who knew them earlier and then lost touch. Both would be accurate; this theory holds that adults can change.

New traits do not develop easily or quickly, but psychologists have documented many examples of personality change in adulthood (Specht et al., 2014; Schwaba & Bleidorn, 2018). In each case above, new personality patterns emerge over the years because the person entered a community (recovery group, church, nation, military) with other people who exemplify and reinforce new behavior. But childhood personality traits are not chiseled in stone.

macmillan learning

VIDEO ACTIVITY: Modeling: Learning by Observation features the original footage of Albert Bandura's famous experiment.

Footage by Dr. Albert Bandura

THINK CRITICALLY: Is your attitude about money more affected by your childhood experiences or by your current financial situation?

WHAT HAVE YOU LEARNED?

1. What is the connection between genes and traits?

2. Is oxytocin a "love hormone"?

3. Does the ego always control the id and superego?

4. How was Erikson connected to Freud?

5. How have the behaviorist concepts of personality changed since 1945?

6. What would be an example of someone whose personality changed in adulthood?

The Self in Childhood

As you see, each of these perspectives on personality is plausible, yet developmentalists tend to emphasize one or the other. Now we go beyond theory to consider what is known about selfhood and personality over infancy and childhood.

Infancy

Some babies are harder to care for than others because of their personality as well as their physical needs. That was not obvious to scientists until the publication of a book titled *Your Child Is a Person*, which detailed the results of the *New York Longitudinal Study* (NYLS) (Chess et al., 1965). Nine characteristics were assessed longitudinally from the first weeks of life: Babies were Easy (40 percent), Difficult (10 percent), Slow-to-warm-up (15 percent), or Hard-to-classify (35 percent).

The NYLS was the first large study to recognize that each newborn has distinct inborn personality traits (Thomas & Chess, 1977). The difficult ones were irregular, fearful, and cried a lot; the easy ones were the opposite. It was unfair, according to these researchers, to blame parents for the traits of their babies.

Later research recognized that infants affect their parents as much as vice versa (Lengua et al., 2019). If a mother had a hard pregnancy and was naturally depressed or anxious, and then her baby was difficult, that infant often became a child with emotional problems. The reason was the personality of both the mother and the infant (Garthus-Niegel et al., 2017).

But difficult babies do not always become anxious or aggressive children. If a difficult infant happens to have an insecure parent, the baby may be blamed for crying, and then that infant becomes an antisocial child. However, if the parents are loving and patient, despite the infant's temperament, that child is less likely to develop hostile traits later on (Pickles et al., 2013).

temperament Inborn differences between one person and another in emotions, activity, and self-regulation. It is measured by the person's typical responses to the environment.

Many recent studies have confirmed that personality begins with inborn **temperament**, defined as the "biologically based core of individual differences in style of approach and response to the environment that is stable across time and situations" (van den Akker et al., 2010, p. 485). Then, in differential susceptibility, parenting matters.

Studies of on temperament generally finds three clusters of personal traits:

- Negative mood (fearful, angry, unhappy);
- Exuberance (active, social, not shy); and
- Effortful control (regulating attention and emotion, self-soothing).

[Lengua et al., 2019]

Temperament over the Years

The best evidence for the relationship between infant temperament and later life comes from another longitudinal study. Scientists analyzed temperament eight times, at 4, 9, 14, 24, and 48 months and again in middle childhood, adolescence, and adulthood (Fox et al., 2001, 2005, 2013; Jarcho et al., 2013; Tang et al., 2020).

This study not only followed the same infants for decades, it was also multi-method. Scientists designed experiments to evoke emotions appropriate for the age of the participants, collected detailed narratives and questionnaires from mothers and, later, directly from participants, gathered observational data, and added physiological measures, including brain scans.

In early childhood, change was most likely for the inhibited, fearful infants and least likely for the exuberant ones (see **Figure 10.1**). Why would that be? Perhaps when parents realize that their infant is often frightened, they encourage bravery, thus modifying the innate emotion. On the other hand, if parents see that their baby is exuberant, they allow that characteristic to continue.

Or it may be the brain structures of some infants protect them from continuing to be fearful. Other research finds that children with a relatively large limbic system (specifically the *insula*) and a relatively small *ventrolateral prefrontal cortex* are more likely to develop severe social anxiety later on (Auday & Pérez-Edgar, 2019).

Children from the original longitudinal study varied in how much they were affected by peers. Those who were inhibited as infants were particularly likely to take risks if their peers encouraged them (Nozadi et al., 2020).

Unexpected gender differences emerged. As teenagers, boys who were inhibited infants had relatively high rates of drug abuse, but that was not as apparent for the girls (Williams et al., 2010). This could be directly biological, related to increased testosterone in pubescent boys. Or it could be cultural: Shy boys may drink and smoke to mask their social anxiety, but socially anxious girls may be accepted as they are.

When the fearful children from this study grew up, those who were inhibited in childhood still showed, in brain scans, evidence of their infant temperament. They also were more likely to be seriously depressed or anxious (Tang et al., 2020). That confirms that biology affected their traits.

In behavior, however, only about half were still fearful, but the other half acted like those without temperamental inhibition. They still had brain patterns that signaled anxiety, but another part of their brains (the *anterior cingulate cortex*, which signals safety) was also active (Shechner et al., 2018).

Perhaps some fearful children are quickly comforted and reassured by their caregivers, which establishes a neurological link between fear and comfort. As a result, if their temperamental anxiety rises in adulthood, their brains counteract it. They are not stopped by fear. Core personality endures, but other factors affect expression (which is evidence for all three theories of personality development).

Affordances

To further understand this, it is useful to understand that the environment (people, places, and objects) *affords*, or offers, opportunities for self-expression. Each is called an **affordance** (Gibson, 1997). Which particular affordance

ESPECIALLY FOR Nurses Parents come to you with their fussy 3-month-old. They have read that temperament is "fixed" before birth, and they are worried that their child will always be difficult. What do you tell them? (see response, page 299)

affordance Something offered (afforded) by the environment. People do not necessary follow up on affordances, but they could. For example, someone might be offered a glass of water but say, "No, thank you."

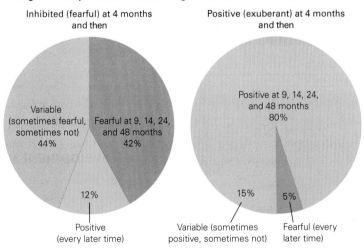

Changes in Temperament Between Ages 4 Months and 4 Years

Inhibited (fearful) at 4 months and then

Variable (sometimes fearful, sometimes not) 44%

Fearful at 9, 14, 24, and 48 months 42%

12%

Positive (every later time)

Positive (exuberant) at 4 months and then

Positive at 9, 14, 24, and 48 months 80%

15%

Variable (sometimes positive, sometimes not)

5%

Fearful (every later time)

Data from Fox et al., 2001.

FIGURE 10.1

Do Babies' Temperaments Change? Sometimes it is possible—especially if they were fearful babies. Adults who are reassuring help children overcome fearfulness. If fearful children do not change, it is not known whether that's because their parents are not sufficiently reassuring (nurture) or because the babies themselves are temperamentally more fearful (nature).

is perceived and acted on depends on four factors: awareness, motivation, maturation, and experience.

It begins with perception: People view their environment differently depending on their personality. "Perceiving is active, a process of obtaining information about the world . . . We don't simply see, we look" (Gibson, 1988, p. 5).

Humans always seek to be themselves. This is obvious in 2-year-olds, for whom every open space affords running: a meadow, a building's long hall, a highway. To adults, affordance of running is limited: They notice a bull grazing in the meadow, neighbors behind the hallway doors, traffic on the road.

Similarly, if adults want to sit, they seek affordances. That may be an empty chair, but if no chair is available, people seek something that affords sitting—perhaps a low table, perhaps a carpeted floor, perhaps a tree stump. Affordances are affected by culture as well as by personality traits. An adult with a reticent personality at a formal gathering might want to sit, but they do not sink to the floor.

I once sat on the floor at a busy airport (there were no seats in the waiting area) while waiting to welcome my deplaning daughter. A guard told me, "You cannot sit there." I asked, "Why?"

We both repeated ourselves several times, and then he said in exasperation, "I told you not to sit, and you just keep asking why." Obviously, his affordances differed with mine for reasons of personality, circumstances, and vocation (scientists ask why, security officers want people to do as they are told).

In the same way, everyone has particular personality traits that they want to express, or hope to change, and then our parents, our culture, or our circumstances afford some expressions and not others. We all need to recognize that in each other, as well as in our children. If a child seems too shy, or too aggressive, or too emotional, adults may curb or redirect those characteristics, but they need first to recognize and appreciate them.

This is much easier for some parents than others, in part because of the parents' personality and culture. Ideally, the child's personality fits in the social context, which developmentalists call **goodness of fit**.

For example, if a child is shy, and the parent is also shy, a good fit may occur because the parent understands that emotion, not blaming the child for it but teaching the child how to cope with it. That was the theme of a best-selling book, *Quiet*, written by an introvert to explain the value of introversion, and to tell other introverts how to avoid problems with their temperament (Cain, 2012).

As you see, goodness of fit occurs with shared personality traits, but it also varies by culture and by circumstances. That affects the parent's patience and responsiveness, which affects the child's personality. Sometimes a parent identifies or rejects a child, and the mismatched child reciprocates (see A Case to Study).

Development of the Self-Concept

As children mature, they develop their **self-concept**, which is a person's idea about themselves, including their intelligence, personality, abilities, gender, and ethnic background. Self-concept continues to form lifelong, becoming more complex and logical as cognitive development and social awareness increase.

Social Comparison

Contrary to what many young children believe, older children realize they are *not* the fastest, smartest, prettiest, best. At some point between ages 6 and 11, when they win a race with their mother, it dawns on them that she could have run faster if she had tried! They also notice that some other children are unlike themselves, perhaps chosen more quickly on the team for kickball, or more likely to know the answer in class, or bigger, stronger, or whatever.

Feliz Navidad Not only is every language and culture distinct, but each individual also has their own temperament. Here children watch the Cortylandia Christmas show in Madrid, Spain, where the Christmas holiday begins on December 24 and lasts through January 6, which is Three Kings Day. As you see from the fathers and children, each person has their own reaction to the same event.

Observation Quiz What indicates that each father has his own child on his shoulders? (see answer, page 299) ↑

goodness of fit When the personality and impulses of the parents mesh with those of the children, such as an outgoing parent having outgoing children.

self-concept A person's understanding of who they are, in relation to self-esteem, appearance, personality, and various traits.

Goodness of Fit

The mother of twin boys, Mike and Jeff, felt that she was not recognized for herself. Mike came home from the hospital soon after birth, but Jeff was small and fragile, and

> He was in the hospital and everyone was all "poor Jeff, poor Jeff" and I started thinking, "Well, what about me? I'm the one's just had twins. I'm the one's going through this, he's a seven-week-old baby and doesn't know a thing about it" . . . I sort of detached and plowed my emotions into Mike.

This continued as the twins grew, with this woman's husband favoring Jeff while the mother continued favoring Mike. That became a problem, not only for the twins but for the marriage, which became "acrimonious." When the boys were five, the mother said

> Jeff and his dad really relate to each other. We all knew Don [her husband] had a connection with Jeff and I had a connection with

Mike . . . Jeff would do everything for Don but he wouldn't for me, and no matter what I did for either of them it wouldn't be right.

The mother recognized herself in Mike.

> I think he's always been like me, more sort of abrupt [laughs], I'll sort of say what I think and then think about the consequences after . . . he's got to that stage where he just doesn't really care who he sort of hurts and he doesn't think about the consequences after, that's it.
>
> [quoted in Caspi et al., 2004, p. 156, 157]

Each boy modeled his behavior after one of the parents, whose arguments about them escalated. The boys also developed distinct personalities, evident to their kindergarten teachers. Jeff was more of a misfit than Mike. How did that happen? It was not genetic: They were monozygotic twins.

Hopefully, they also recognize some of their own positive traits. Crucial to this awareness is **social comparison**—comparing one's self to others (Suls et al., 2020).

Ideally, social comparison helps children value themselves and abandon the imaginary, rosy self-evaluation of preschoolers. Until about age 7, children confuse their actual self and their ideal self and cannot reliably "compare their competencies with those of others as a basis for self-conception" (Thomaes et al., 2017, p. 1874). But at school age, the self-concept becomes more realistic, incorporating comparison to peers and judgments from the overall society.

Some children—especially those from minority ethnic or religious groups—become newly aware of social prejudices that they need to overcome. Children also become aware of gender discrimination, with girls complaining that they are not allowed to play tougher sports and boys complaining that teachers favor the girls (C. Brown et al., 2011).

Self-Esteem

A person's view of themselves, whether they accept and like who they are, is called **self-esteem**. It requires some awareness of oneself and of other people.

Thus, social comparison is part of the process. Encouragement from parents, affection from friends, and school success all bolster self-esteem. These protect and produce self-confidence, which results in more effort, which leads to more self-esteem.

Generally, family trouble such as divorce reduces self-esteem, but when divorce leads to joint physical custody (the child alternates living with each parent), self-esteem is as high as when both parents live together (Turunen et al., 2017). The reason may be that parents who know a child well are more realistic about the child. It is known that "overly positive, inflated praise" reduces self-esteem (Brummelman et al., 2017, p. 1799).

Over the years of middle childhood, children who affirm pride in their gender and ethnicity are likely to develop healthy self-esteem (Corenblum, 2014). Transgender children particularly experience discrimination. For them, parental support is crucial, but parents themselves experience stress (Hidalgo & Chen, 2019). Overall, parents who feel supported by their community are better able to affirm their own children.

social comparison The tendency to assess one's abilities, achievements, social status, and other attributes by measuring them against those of other people, especially one's peers.

self-esteem How a person values themselves. It could be high ("I am the smartest") or low ("I am the dumbest"), but it is best to be realistic and on the high side.

Pictorial Press Ltd/Alamy

Black Panther Mythical superheroes, and the perpetual battle between good and evil, are especially attractive to boys in middle childhood but resonate with people of all ages, genders, and ethnic groups. *Black Panther* was first a comic-book hero in 1966 and then became a 2018 movie that broke records for attendance and impact. It features not only African American heroes but also an army of strong women — busting stereotypes and generating self-esteem for many children.

Especially when the outside world seems hostile, parents and schools, ideally, provide *racial socialization*, teaching their African American, Latinx, or American Indian children about leaders of their group, as well as providing instruction as to how to overcome prejudice (M.-T. Wang et al., 2020). Similarly, girls, or low-SES children, or children of same-sex marriages, or children with various differences and disorders, need to understand their strengths, lest social comparison makes them devalue who they are.

High self-esteem is distinguished from *narcissism*, the belief that one is the best, the greatest, the most wonderful person, and that everyone else is less than that. Narcissism can be association with high or low self-esteem, and in both cases is destructive of mental health (X. Xu et al., 2020). Narcissism is a personality disorder in adulthood.

Every child needs to be proud of their personal accomplishments — a spelling worksheet with a gold star, getting up and dressed on time, saving their allowance, hitting a softball, or protecting a younger sibling. Such pride develops in part because of family support (Orth, 2018) and in part because of friends. Interestingly, not only do children with supportive social relationships have higher self-esteem, but also the link is reciprocal: Higher self-esteem leads to better social relationships (Harris & Orth, 2019).

Bullies and Friendship

An example of the impact of social relationships on selfhood and personality is illustrated by school bullies. Everyone involved — bullies, victims, and bystanders — is at risk for a distorted self-concept, impaired social understanding, and lower school achievement. Decades later, victims have higher rates of mental illness, and bullies have higher rates of imprisonment and death. Thus, the damage to the self-concept can be long-lasting (deLara, 2016).

However, longitudinal data show that not every victim is permanently harmed; not every bully is stuck in a dangerous trajectory; not every bystander remains indifferent. Some people learn from their childhood trauma, becoming empathic, self-confident adults.

What seems crucial is friendship. For victims, that could mean having a friend who is also a victim. Such friends cannot physically protect another victim, but they provide psychological defense — reassuring victims that their condition is not their fault and that the bully is mean, stupid, racist, or whatever (Schacter & Juvonen, 2018). That reduces the worst harm: loss of self-respect.

Self-respect can be nurtured by family members. However, if children are bullied by peers in school *and* siblings at home, they are four times more likely to develop serious psychological disorders by age 18 (Dantchev et al., 2018).

Adverse Childhood Experiences

adverse childhood experiences (ACEs) A range of potentially traumatic childhood stresses, including abuse, neglect, family disruption and dysfunction, and parental incarceration, that can have lasting, negative effects on health and well-being.

Thousands of researchers have now demonstrated that an accumulation of harmful events in childhood is devastating in adulthood. Nine possible **adverse childhood experiences (ACEs)** are almost always included in this research:

- Abuse of the child (physical, sexual, verbal);
- Problems of someone else in the household (mental illness, addiction, prison); and
- Parental conflict (separation, divorce, domestic violence).

Other ACEs that are often included are poverty, frequent change of residence, and neighborhood conditions (Hughes et al., 2017).

Adverse experiences in childhood affect people decades later, even if the person has left them behind. ACEs are common (60 percent of U.S. adults have experienced at least one), but the lifelong damage is most evident when a child experiences four or more. That is the case for about 15 percent of adults (Merrick et al., 2019). Four ACEs double the rate of deadly adult diseases (cancer, heart disease, and so on) and increase sixfold the rate of adult sexual abuse, mental illness, substance abuse, and self-inflicted harm (Hughes et al., 2017).

We have known for decades that childhood abuse may have long-term effects, but the research on ACEs has added three new discoveries:

- A multiplier effect: Accumulated ACEs magnify the impact more than simply adding them together.
- Psychosocial impact exceeds biological impact. The increased risk of suicide, for instance, is greater than the increased risk of cancer. Devastation to self-esteem is profound, reducing later education, employment, and relationships.
- Problems should not be blamed on ethnic, immigrant, or racial status. Although prejudice and poverty increase the incidence of ACEs, background factors are not the cause. Instead, actual childhood experiences are. Thus, many children from low-SES, immigrant, or non-White families escape ACEs, and some middle-class, native-born, White children experience four or more.

resilience The capacity to adapt well to significant adversity and to overcome serious stress.

The research on ACEs comprises a mandate for pediatricians, parents, and political leaders: Avoid stereotypes and protect every child from the direct conditions that increase harm (Jones et al., 2020; McEwen & Gregerson, 2019; Rasmussen et al., 2020).

Resilience

The devastation of adverse childhood experiences may seem, at first, contrary to research on resilience, which finds some children unscathed by early experiences. They have been called "resilient" or even "invincible."

However, current thinking about resilience (see **Table 10.2**), finds that no one is truly untouched by past history or current context: Some weather early storms, and a few not only survive but become stronger because of them (Luthar, 2015; Masten, 2014; Rutter, 2012).

Defining Resilience

Resilience has been defined as "a dynamic process encompassing positive adaptation within the context of significant adversity" (Luthar et al., 2000, p. 543) and "the capacity of a dynamic system to adapt successfully to disturbances that threaten system function, viability, or development" (Masten, 2014, p. 30). Note that resilience is recognized in the context of *significant* adversity, a *threat* to development. Researchers emphasize two aspects of resilience:

- Resilience is *dynamic*, not a stable trait. That means that someone may be resilient at some periods but not others, and the effects from one period reverberate as time goes on.

TABLE 10.2

Dominant Ideas About Resilience, 1965 to Present

1965	All children have the same needs for healthy development.
1970	Some conditions or circumstances — such as "absent father," "teenage mother," "working mom," and "day care" — are harmful for every child.
1975	All children are *not* the same. Some children are resilient, coping easily with stressors that cause harm in other children.
1980	Nothing inevitably causes harm. Both maternal employment and preschool education, once thought to be risks, are often helpful.
1985	Factors beyond the family, both in the child (low birthweight, prenatal alcohol exposure, aggressive temperament) and in the community (poverty, violence), can be very risky for children.
1990	Risk–benefit analysis finds that some children are "invulnerable" to, or even benefit from, circumstances that destroy others.
1995	No child is invincible. Risks are always harmful — if not in education, then in emotions; if not immediately, then long term.
2000	Risk–benefit analysis involves the interplay among many biological, cognitive, and social factors.
2008	Focus on strengths, not risks. Assets in child (intelligence, personality), family (secure attachment, warmth), community (schools, after-school programs), and nation (income support, health care) must be nurtured.
2010	Strengths vary by culture and national values. Both universal ideals and local variations must be recognized and respected.
2015	Genes as well as cultural practices can be either strengths or weaknesses. Differential susceptibility: Identical stressors can benefit one child and harm another.
2020	Resilience is seen more broadly as a characteristic of mothers and communities.

Same Situation, Far Apart: Praying Hands
Differences are obvious between the northern Indian girls entering their Hindu school *(left)* and the West African boy in a Christian church *(right)*, even in their clothes and hand positions. But underlying similarities are more important. In every culture, many 8-year-olds are more devout than their elders. That is especially true if their community is under stress. Faith aids resilience.

- Resilience is a *positive adaptation* to stress. For example, if parental rejection leads a child to a closer relationship with another adult, that is positive resilience, not passive endurance.

The social context, especially supportive adults who do not blame the child, allow positive adaptation to occur. A chilling example comes from the "child soldiers" in the 1991–2002 civil war in Sierra Leone (Betancourt et al., 2013). Children witnessed, and often participated in, murder, rape, and other traumas. When the war was over, 529 war-affected youth, then aged 10 to 17, were interviewed. Many were severely depressed, with crippling anxiety.

These war-damaged children were interviewed again two and six years later. Surprisingly, many were functioning well. Resilience was more likely if:

- The war occurred when they were in middle childhood, not adolescence;
- At least one caregiver survived and was reunited with the child;
- Their communities did not reject them, no matter which side of the civil war they had joined; and
- Daily routines (school, family responsibilities) were restored.

Cognitive Coping

Disasters take a toll, but resilience is possible. Factors in the child (especially problem-solving ability), in the family (consistency and care), and in the community (good schools and welcoming religious institutions) all foster resilience (Masten, 2014).

The child's developing self-concept may be crucial, because self-concept affects how the child interprets whatever occurs (Lagattuta, 2014). Some low-SES children do not feel personally to blame, and their family has predictable routines: Then they may be resilient. However, cortisol increases *if* they interpret events connected to their family's poverty as a personal threat and *if* the family circumstances are chaotic (Coe et al., 2018).

In general, how children think of family situations (poverty, divorce, and so on) affects how they see themselves. Do you know adults from low-SES families who seem quite capable and confident? Chances are they did not feel deprived. Only later did they realize that sleeping in the same bed with siblings, eating macaroni night after night, wearing worn hand-me-downs, signified poverty. Therefore, their low-income childhood did not cast a shadow over adulthood.

Some children consider the family they were born into a temporary hardship; they look forward to the day when they can leave childhood behind. A future orientation protects self-esteem (Cui et al., 2020). If a child also has personal strengths, they may shine in adulthood—evident in the United States in thousands of success stories, from Abraham Lincoln to Oprah Winfrey.

Another example occurs when children serve as *language brokers*, when they must interpret for their immigrant parents who do not understand the language or the culture. Children become depressed if they feel burdened by their role, or they become proud of themselves if they feel they are vital for their family's well-being (Weisskirch, 2017b).

Resilience research can be reconciled with the research just mentioned on ACEs, on social comparison, and on self-esteem. Overall, the child's temperament and self-concept, the parent's ability to protect the child from psychic harm, and the community's support via friends, neighbors, schools, and other institutions, allow children in difficult circumstances to survive and even thrive (Masten, 2014). But lifelong damage may occur if too few protections, and too many adverse experiences, occur.

The crucial role of family is illustrated by the basketball star LeBron James. He never met his father and moved 12 times between the ages of 5 and 8 (Luthar et al., 2015, p. 275). James said:

> Whatever my mom could do or could not do, I also knew that nobody was more important in her life than I was. You have no idea how much that means when you grow up without so many of the basic things you should have. You have no idea of the security it gives you, how it makes you think "Man, I can get through this, I can survive."
>
> *[Manfred, 2013]*

All this raises the question: What will the final outcome be for the millions of children who missed regular school in 2020 because of COVID-19? Predictions are for a "social crisis" (Van Lancker & Parolin, 2020). Maybe not. Perhaps this will strengthen their family relationships, and thus eventually lead to resilience? Or will this be a final blow to self-esteem, crushing some children? We will not know until careful, longitudinal studies are done.

VIDEO ACTIVITY: Child Soldiers and Child Peacemakers examines the state of child soldiers in the world and then explores how adolescent cognition impacts the decisions of five teenage peace activists.

WHAT HAVE YOU LEARNED?

1. What temperamental characteristics of infants seem to continue in childhood and adulthood?

2. What evidence is for and against the idea that fearfulness in childhood continues in adulthood?

3. How do affordances of the environment, and goodness of fit within a family, affect how children develop?

4. How does the self-concept develop?

5. What is the difference between self-esteem and narcissism?

6. What new ideas come from research on adverse childhood experiences?

7. When are children resilient to childhood conditions?

8. How does the research on bullies apply to our understanding of self-esteem, of family, and of friendship?

Adolescence and Adulthood

In many chapters of this book, adolescence is presented as a discrete stage of life, when children's bodies become adult bodies, when young minds question adult traditions, when teenage emotions skitter from euphoria to despair and back.

Regarding personality, however, adolescence is best seen not as a separate garden path, but as the first stretch of a long road. Accordingly, here we discuss adolescence and adulthood together.

Achieving Identity

In discussing adolescence and adulthood, we use Erik Erikson's psychosocial descriptions. As you will see, his framework for adult development remains useful. Although originally Erikson pegged adolescence as the time for the identity crisis, he later explained that the search for identity continued to echo lifelong (Erikson, 1968/1994).

identity versus role confusion Erikson's term for the fifth stage of development, in which the person tries to figure out "Who am I?" but is confused as to which of many possible roles to adopt.

identity achievement Erikson's term for the attainment of identity, or the point at which a person understands who he or she is as a unique individual, in accord with past experiences and future plans.

role confusion A situation in which an adolescent does not seem to know or care what their identity is. (Sometimes called *identity diffusion* or *role diffusion*.)

foreclosure Erikson's term for premature identity formation, which occurs when an adolescent adopts his or her parents' or society's roles and values wholesale, without questioning or analysis.

moratorium An adolescent's choice of a socially acceptable way to postpone making identity-achievement decisions. Going to college is a common example.

Identity versus role confusion is Erikson's most famous stage. This crisis is resolved with **identity achievement**, when a person has reconsidered the goals and values of their childhood, accepting some and discarding others, while forging their own identity, a difficult psychosocial task (Sugimura et al., 2018).

One developmental scholar outlined four steps of the search for identity: (1) role confusion, (2) foreclosure, and (3) moratorium. Ideally, people then reach (4) achievement, the final stage (Kroger & Marcia, 2011; Marcia, 1966).

Role confusion is the opposite of achievement. It is characterized by lack of commitment to any goals or values. It arises early in adolescence, when the hormones of puberty awaken sexual impulses and the cognitive advances of hypothetical thought trigger reexamination of values that were once accepted. Children who thought the other gender was stupid, or who learned that sexual impulses were "dirty" or "nasty" might question themselves.

Identity **foreclosure** occurs when, in order to avoid the confusion of sorting through all the nuances of who they are and what they believe, people lump traditional roles and values together, to be swallowed whole or rejected totally. They might follow every custom from their parents or culture, not exploring alternatives. Or they might foreclose on an oppositional, *negative identity*—rejecting all their elders' values and routines, again without thoughtful questioning.

Foreclosure is comfortable but limiting, a temporary shelter. A more mature shelter is **moratorium**, a time-out that includes exploration, either in breadth (trying many things) or in depth (following one path but with only tentative commitment). Finally, adults reach *identity achievement*: They know who they are, their true self.

The early 20s are "the period of life that offers the most opportunities for identity exploration" (Luyckx et al., 2013, p. 703). Many people continue their search for identity in adulthood.

No Role Confusion These are high school students in Junior ROTC training camp. For many youths who cannot afford college, the military offers a temporary identity—complete with haircut, uniform, and comrades.

Sara Caldwell/Staff/The Augusta Chronicle/ZUMAPRESS.com/Alamy

Arenas of Identity Formation

Erikson (1968/1994) highlighted four aspects of identity: religious, political, vocational, and sexual, and later added a fifth identity (ethnic). Over the past decades, gender identity has become particularly crucial and complex. Consequently, it is a major topic in Chapter 11 (Sex and Gender). We now consider the other four.

Religious Identity

Most adolescents question some aspects of their faith, but their *religious identity* is similar to that of their parents. Few reject their religion totally if they have been raised in it, especially if they have a good relationship with their parents (Kim-Spoon et al., 2012).

The search for religious identity may be universal, as a study of youth in eight nations suggests (Benson et al., 2012). Most of the research has been on Christian youth in Western nations. However, a recent study in Japan reported that Buddhist adolescents also seek to establish their own religious beliefs and practices (Sugimura et al., 2019).

Adults seeking a religious identity may adopt a completely different faith, but usually they continue within their broad religious heritage, perhaps identifying with another branch but nonetheless remaining Christian, Jewish, Muslim, and so on. Attendance at churches, synagogues, temples, and mosques decreases from adolescence on but increases with parenthood.

Sometimes religious identity is thought to conflict with college education, but the data say otherwise. Among U.S. residents who identify as Christian, college graduates are more likely to attend church services once a week (52 percent) than nongraduates (45 percent). They are less certain of their faith, however (Pew Research Center, April 26, 2017).

Some aspects of religious identity change with age, according to a multigenerational, longitudinal U.S. study. Younger adults are more likely to say that they are "spiritual," older adults to identify as "religious." Younger adults are more likely to feel personally connected with God, whereas older adults see God as more transcendent—as "out there" (Bengtson et al., 2015).

An increasing number of adults, especially younger adults, identify with no religion. Nonetheless, if they were raised with a strong religious background, they behave and believe in ways more similar to religious people than to those raised without religion (Van Tongeren et al., 2020). Thus, if religious identity is taken to include moral values, then adults still seek a religious identity, and childhood influences that.

 DATA CONNECTIONS: Religious Identity: Young Adults Versus Older Cohorts explores the religious affiliations, practices, and beliefs of U.S. adults, focusing on cohort-specific data.

Political Identity

In the twenty-first century, more U.S. adults identify as independent (38 percent) than Republican (26 percent), or Democrat (26 percent), or any other party (5 percent) (Pew Research Center, March 14, 2019). However, most vote as their family does. Some boast that they vote for the person, not the party, or that they do not care about politics, but those opinions usually echo their parents.

Nonetheless, political involvement of all kinds is influenced by maturation, events, and parents. This was obvious in the protests after the 2020 deaths of George Floyd and Breonna Taylor at the hands of police officers: The protesters were all ages, but more were under 30 than over 60. On the other hand, in every presidential election in the twenty-first century, about 70 percent of those over age 60 voted, but only about 50 percent of citizens under age 30 did. Do those facts suggest that political identity is more, or less, important with age?

Ethnic Identity

Related to religious and political identity is *ethnic identity*, which is how a person connects with their heritage. As you remember from Chapter 1, ethnicity is not the same as race. Ethnic identity is "not a matter of one's idiosyncratic self-perception but, rather, [is] profoundly shaped by one's social context, including one's social role and place in society" (Seaton et al., 2017, p. 683). Ethnic pride is a buffer against depression and low achievement (Huguley et al., 2019; Umaña-Taylor & Hill, 2020), although the relationship in adulthood between pride and ethnicity is "complex and nuanced" (Miller-Cotto & Byrnes, 2016).

Currently, almost every young adult wonders about their ancestral roots. Those who have indigenous ancestors (about 1 percent of the population) may refer to a particular group (Diné, Dakota, Lakota); those with ancestors who fought in the American Revolution or Civil War, or who were enslaved and brought from

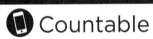

CHAPTER APP 10

Countable

IOS:
https://tinyurl.com/jeh8m6y

ANDROID:
https://tinyurl.com/y8rb3q5b

RELEVANT TOPIC:
Political choices in emerging adulthood

This app informs users of pending U.S. federal legislation (and soon, state and local legislation) with succinct, nonpartisan, sourced writeups that include pro and con arguments. Countable also enables users to give instant feedback on pending bills and see how their representatives voted.

Happy and Proud Before the colonists came, at least 600 distinct indigenous nations thrived in North America. Then their land was taken, livelihood destroyed, and culture denigrated. Death from wars, starvation, and disease resulted in fewer than 1 percent of the current population of the United States claiming tribal membership. One reason for hope: Now members of those 600 nations often identify with each other. Evidence is Jessa Rae Growing Thunder, 2012–2013 Miss Indian World, shown here making her entrance at the 30th Annual Gathering of Nations in Albuquerque, New Mexico.

Africa, or were part of the great immigration wave a century ago, want to trace their lineage. Such efforts may lead to DNA testing, which is becoming popular as well as fraught with uncertainty (Bettinger, 2019; Bull, 2019).

Apparently, ethnic identity is not a private, personal choice but a community one. Adults with more education are likely to seek specifics, such as a particular indigenous group instead of just Mexican or American Indian. National politics also has an impact, so many adults who considered themselves White now want to know more about their background and family history. Ethnic identity is complicated, varied, and crucial (Feliciano & Rumbaut, 2018).

Vocational Identity

As just explained, many kinds of identity require the young person to reconcile family influences and personality with cultural mandates. Adults reject, foreclose, and reconsider whatever parents have taught about religious, political, and ethnic identity, finally achieving their own combination of past and present.

However, that process is not possible for vocational identity, because the entire job market has transformed over the past century. Once, many boys expected to work in the same vocation as their fathers did, with family farms, family businesses, family professions. Girls planned to be housewives and mothers as their female ancestors did.

Now, less than 1 percent of families live and work on farms, only 10 percent work in manufacturing, and the rate of female employment is close to the male rate. Work itself has changed in many ways, with education increasingly important in hiring and raises (Ackerman & Kanfer, 2020).

Adults do not have one vocational identity, but many. Longitudinal data on a large sample of adults born in about 1970 found that the average man or woman held 12 jobs by age 50 (U.S. Bureau of Labor Statistics, January 18, 2019). The youth changed jobs more often than the middle aged, but even those over age 35 changed jobs, on average, about once every 5 years. (Those numbers predate the massive job losses in 2020.)

A realistic answer to "What do you want to be?" is difficult at every age. A meta-analysis found that many people are hampered in decisions about careers because of a lack of knowledge of themselves, especially what they can do (Urbanaviciute et al., 2020). And adults of every age underestimate themselves and misunderstand what various jobs entail, especially if their knowledge comes from television portrayals.

Part of the problem is that vocation is connected to self-concept, which means that people want to figure out what they value before they choose a vocation. As one developmentalist explains:

> Career choices faced by individuals inevitably raise the question of the meaning that they intend to give their lives. To choose their work or sector in which they want to evolve is also to consider the purpose of their existence, the priorities (physical, spiritual, social, aesthetic, etc.) that they want to give, the choices that they wish to operate, the overall style of life that they wish to give themselves.
>
> [Bernaud, 2014, p. 36]

No wonder vocational identity is difficult to achieve!

Erikson's Adult Stages

As we have just seen, Erikson's fifth stage, identity versus role confusion, can extend into adulthood. Beyond that are two more adult stages—*intimacy versus isolation*, and *generativity versus stagnation*, with many social and cultural factors influencing them (see **Table 10.3**).

TABLE 10.3

Erikson's Stages of Adulthood

Unlike Freud or other early theorists who thought adults simply worked through the legacy of their childhood, four of Erikson's eight psychosocial stages occur after puberty. His most famous book, *Childhood and Society* (1993a), devoted only two pages to each adult stage, but elaborations in later works have led to a much richer depiction (Hoare, 2002).

Identity Versus Role Confusion

Although Erikson originally situated the identity crisis during adolescence, he realized that identity concerns could be lifelong. Identity combines values and traditions from childhood with the current social context. Since contexts keep evolving, many adults reassess all four types of identity (sexual/gender, vocational/work, religious/spiritual, and political/ethnic).

Intimacy Versus Isolation

Adults seek intimacy—a close, reciprocal connection with another human being. Intimacy is mutual, not self-absorbed, which means that adults need to devote time and energy to one another. This process begins in emerging adulthood and continues lifelong. Isolation is especially likely when divorce or death disrupts established intimate relationships.

Generativity Versus Stagnation

Adults need to care for the next generation, either by raising their own children or by mentoring, teaching, and helping others. Erikson's first description of this stage focused on parenthood, but later he included other ways to achieve generativity. Adults extend the legacy of their culture and their generation with ongoing care, creativity, and sacrifice.

Integrity Versus Despair

When Erikson himself reached his 70s, he decided that integrity, with the goal of combating prejudice and helping all humanity, was too important to be left to the elderly. He also thought that each person's entire life could be directed toward connecting a personal journey with the historical and cultural purpose of human society, the ultimate achievement of integrity.

Intimacy

Intimacy refers to the adult need to find a person or persons to share their life with. There is no doubt that social affiliation is a basic human need, recognized by everyone who has studied adult development (Baumeister & Leary, 1995).

Much of the discussion of intimacy is in Chapter 12, which covers attachment and social relationships, and in Chapter 13, which covers family. Here, however, we need to highlight that people choose their friends and mates in part as reflections of themselves. This is most obvious in the relationship between selection and facilitation.

Selection is crucial at several pivotal times—adolescence, emerging adulthood, and mate selection. Friends and romantic partners are selected for their similar values and interests. Then, a person's social context facilitates destructive or constructive behaviors.

This is readily apparent in adolescence. Happy, energetic, and successful teens choose friends who themselves are high achievers, with no major emotional problems. A student's grade-point average and IQ increase if their friends are highly intelligent (Meldrum et al., 2019). This works the other way as well. Those who are drug users, sexually active, and alienated from school choose compatible friends. In general, peers provide opportunity, companionship, and encouragement for what young adolescents already might do.

Selection and facilitation are evident lifelong, but the balance between the two shifts. Early adolescence is a time of selection; facilitation is more evident in later adolescence. After age 18 or so, selection becomes important again, as young adults abandon some high-school friends and establish new ones (Samek et al., 2016).

In adulthood, selection is crucial for friends as well as romantic partners, and then chosen intimates facilitate development of some aspects of one's self.

Being Intimate The word "intimacy" was traditionally a euphemism for sexual intercourse, but to developmentalists it is much more than that. Look closely at these two couples, one in Spain *(left)* and one in Malaysia *(right)*. Whether or not they are having sex does not matter: They are intimate in their touching, emotions, and even clothing.

People are attracted to people who are similar to themselves, not too much better and not too much worse on various measures, with values and background with which they identify (Cemalcilar et al., 2018; Laakasuo et al., 2017).

Dozens of factors have an influence: People tend to choose others of similar education, ethnicity, personality, drug use, eating, religious values, politics. And then the chosen person reinforces whatever characteristics a person has. For example, if an adult becomes friends with a person who is an extrovert, that adult is likely to become more outgoing (van Zalk et al., 2020).

The fact that people tend to choose mates similar to themselves is call *homogamy*, which once referred solely to ethnic, educational, and economic factors. Now similarities in personality and shared values matter (Brandén & Bernhardt, 2020).

Outsiders may not see this at first: I know many long-married couples who seem unlike each other. For instance, one pair almost always support opposite political candidates. That puzzled me. Then the wife said, "We sit on the fence, debating both sides before we vote." I knew who would fall on which side of the fence, but I realized that their shared joy of debate was part of their marital glue: Their final choice mattered less.

Generativity

Generativity is often expressed by caring for the younger generation, but it can be expressed in other ways. This is particularly crucial today, since many adults do not have children.

Meaningful employment, important creative production, and caregiving of other adults also are generative ways to avoid stagnation. This is the theme of a new concept, *reproductive identity*, which captures the idea that, while generatively continues to be a basic need for adults, the expression of it has changed (Athan, 2020).

Often, employment becomes a source of generativity. Salary and benefits are only one part of the rewards of employment. Also crucial are:

- Developing and using personal skills, becoming experts;
- Aiding and advising coworkers, as mentors or friends;
- Enhancing education and health; and
- Contributing to the community by providing goods or services.

extrinsic rewards of work The tangible benefits, usually in salary, insurance, pension, and status, that come with employment.

intrinsic rewards of work The personal gratifications, such as pleasure in a job well done or friendships with coworkers, that accompany employment.

These facts highlight the distinction between the **extrinsic rewards of work** (the tangible benefits such as salary, health insurance, and pension) and the **intrinsic rewards of work** (the intangible gratifications of actually doing the job). These two types of rewards may be negatively correlated, if employers increase pay *instead* of creating working conditions that improve intrinsic rewards. That is a mistake, as intrinsic rewards correlate with worker satisfaction, worker effort, less burnout, and fewer workers who quit to find another job (Kuvaas et al., 2017).

We need to recognize that some people work primarily because their salary and benefits allow their family to thrive, but for others, "the intrinsic rewards associated with the work experience are often more salient than the paycheck" (Ackerman & Kanfer, 2020, p. 494).

Especially early in adulthood, some people work in the *gig economy*, which includes all of the temporary, episodic, or independent jobs that are not part of a regular contract with benefits. They drive cars for hire, tutor children, sell items online, care for the elderly, clean houses, work as actors or musicians, act as social media "influencers," and much more.

Temporary and independent workers are preferred by employers, who do not need to provide job security or health care, and by governments, since unemployment insurance does not include independent workers. They may be exploited, especially in nations of Asia and Africa where laws do not protect labor (Hua & Ray, 2018). Thus, young adult workers suffered disproportionally during the COVID-19 pandemic.

Indeed, the gig economy is the subject of much analysis (Wood et al., 2019; Gleim et al., 2019; Vallas & Schor, 2020). Is it a boon to workers, who can function as independent entrepreneurs, working as much or as little as they want on their own schedule? Or is it less like "an assemblage of freely acting entrepreneurs but rather a herd that, like livestock, can be milked or sheared to extract revenue" (Vallas & Schor, 2020)?

From a personality perspective, gig work may encourage some traits (ambitious, independent) and discourage others (cooperative, docile). This depends on how they find work. In some aspects of the gig economy (car-for-hire, odd jobs, personal care) companies (e.g., Uber, TaskRabbit, SeniorCare) reward those who are friendly and reliable, so those traits are nurtured.

Older adults have other problems if they lose their jobs:

1. Seniority brings higher salaries, more respect, and greater expertise; that makes losing a job more painful.
2. Available work requires skills that they never learned.
3. Age discrimination and stereotype threat undercut hiring.
4. If relocation is needed, intimacy may suffer.

Unemployment

Remember that, universally, adults seek to use whatever skills and abilities they have. That helps explain why unemployment is destructive of mental and physical health, increasing the rates of domestic abuse, substance use disorder, depression, and many other social and mental health problems (Sumner & Gallagher, 2017; Wanberg, 2012). In addition to loss of income, uncertainty about future work adds significantly to family stress (Schneider et al., 2017).

A meta-analysis of research on eight stressful events found that losing a job was even worse for mental health than the death of a parent. The stress of unemployment lingered after finding a job (Luhmann et al., 2012).

Worst may be job loss when adults have a partner and children. That causes a "cascade" of family stresses, harming every family member, with trouble reverberating within the family and adding new stresses and increasing problems for everyone (McKee-Ryan & Maitoza, 2018). Adults of all ages find a purpose in life in their family, and work can facilitate or impede that.

A major concern for all working adults is conflict between the demands of employment and family life, called *work–life balance*. Couples have various ways to achieve this, with personality, gender, and culture affecting each partner. Ideally, the family finds an equilibrium that works for them, but then job loss can lead to imbalance, resentment, and abuse.

THINK CRITICALLY: Should adults "work to live" or "live to work"? Is income and status more important than time with family and close relationships? Should fathers and mothers both scale back on employment to meet the needs of children or to have time for each other?

It is also possible that workers' dependence on income is itself a problem. Some of that is justified: Poverty reduces happiness and increases stress for everyone. If job loss means insufficient income for food and shelter, that affects the whole family.

However, at a certain level of wealth, happiness does not increase (D'Ambrosio et al., 2020; Ward & King, 2016). One study found that people are increasingly happy as they get richer until they reach $100,000, then more money doesn't necessarily mean more happiness, and above $250,000 happiness might actually decrease with income (Jebb et al., 2018).

This is based on average life satisfaction based on thousands of people at each income level. When these data are analyzed in terms of self-concept and personality, individual differences appear. Are some people temperamentally inclined to equate their pride with their income and others not?

How valuable wealth is to people varies not only by culture and personality but also by relative deprivation: If people compare themselves with other people who are similar to them but notably richer, income matters.

Retirement

The relationship between work, income, and identity may be highlighted in retirement. Many nations mandate a particular age for retirement; the United States does not, except in some occupations, such as firefighters and airplane pilots. Many older adults continue working until they believe that their retirement income is adequate, or until health concerns prompt them to quit.

However, given that senior employees often earn more pay and benefits, many employers want their oldest employees to retire. Retirees who felt they chose to leave are likely to enjoy having time for family and hobbies; those who felt forced often experience identity problems similar to those of the unemployed (Ryan et al., 2017).

Some retirees work part time or become self-employed, with small businesses or consulting work. Some employers provide bridge jobs, enabling older workers to transition from full employment. Crafting an employment bridge, or doing consulting work, is an option that is more available to highly educated, long-term employees; thus, SES continues to impact older people (Calvo et al., 2018).

When employers do not provide bridge jobs, many older workers join the gig economy, taking on part-time work as handymen, car drivers, craft workers, and so on. Overall, less than half of all workers in the United States stop working completely after quitting full-time jobs (Hudomiet et al., 2018).

A longitudinal study of older adults in the Netherlands before and after retirement found that self-esteem decreased in the five years before retirement (Bleidorn & Schwaba, 2018). Then, for many, self-esteem rose after retirement because they no longer experienced work–family conflicts: Apparently many older workers found it hard to be a good worker, spouse, and grandparent simultaneously, and they were happy to stop working.

Note that in the Netherlands, where this study took place, public support for retirees is extensive. The social context (particularly culture, pensions, and health care) makes a difference everywhere in how older adults feel about retirement. For those reasons, retirement often increases self-esteem in many nations of Europe and North America but decreases it in many Asian nations (Mukku et al., 2018). But again, personality and work–life balance make a difference.

The Big Five

Big Five The five basic clusters of personality traits that remain quite stable throughout adulthood: openness, conscientiousness, extroversion, agreeableness, and neuroticism.

A major description of personality begins with analysis of data, organized by advanced statistical programs to discover that human personality traits can be grouped into five clusters called the **Big Five**:

- *Openness*: imaginative, curious, artistic, creative, open to new experiences
- *Conscientiousness*: organized, deliberate, conforming, self-disciplined
- *Extroversion*: outgoing, assertive, active
- *Agreeableness*: kind, helpful, easygoing, generous
- *Neuroticism*: anxious, moody, self-punishing, critical

(To remember the Big Five, the acronym OCEAN is useful.)

Each person is somewhere on a continuum on each of these five. The low end might be described, in the same order as above, with these five adjectives: *closed, careless, introverted, hard to please,* and *placid.*

Adults choose vocations, hobbies, health habits, mates, and neighborhoods to reflect their personality. Those high in extroversion might work in sales, those high in openness might be artists, and so on.

Sometimes major events in adulthood, either expected events (marriage, birth, new job) or unexpected ones (divorce, disease, sudden wealth) affect the Big Five, and sometimes events that are expected but do not occur (e.g., infertility when a child was planned) affect personality traits. However, usually those effects are relatively minor: The Big Five endure (Denissen et al., 2019; Luhmann et al., 2020).

Age Changes

When adults are followed longitudinally, stability of the Big Five is evident. Change is more likely in emerging adulthood or late adulthood than for 25- to 64-year-olds (Wagner et al., 2019).

The general age trend seems to be positive, as people align with the norms of their community. People under the age of 30 "actively try to change their environment," moving away from home and finding new friends, changing their nurture. Later in life, context shapes traits; once adults have chosen their vocation, family, and neighborhoods, they "change the self to fit the environment" (Kandler, 2012, p. 294).

Several longitudinal studies published in the twentieth century found not only considerable stability in personality, but also that traits tended to improve as adults became more mature (e.g., Vaillant, 1977). Divorce and job loss reduced self-esteem, but middle-aged adults were less depressed, anxious, and more nurturant and conscientious than younger adults. However, that no longer seems true: Anxiety and depression have increased among adults in recent years, especially among those aged 45–64 (Almeida et al., 2020).

Cultural Influences

As in these examples, culture shapes personality. As one team phrased it, "personality may acculturate" (Güngör et al., 2013, p. 713). A study of well-being and self-esteem in 28 nations found that people are happiest if their personality traits match their social context. This has implications for immigrants, who might feel (and be) less appreciated when the personality values of their home culture clash with their new community.

For example, extroversion is valued in Canada and less so in Japan; consequently, Canadians and Japanese have a stronger sense of well-being if their personal ratings on extroversion (high or low) are consistent with their culture (Fulmer et al., 2010). Many people criticize immigrants for the very traits that are valued in their home cultures.

Within the United States, people move to, or away from, cities or rural areas or suburbs, partly to be with other people with similar personality variables.

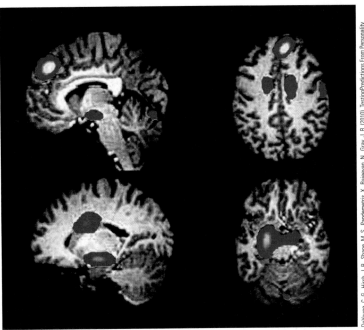

DeYoung, C. G., Hirsh, J. B., Shane, M. S., Papdemetris, X., Rajeevan, N., Gray, J. R. (2010). Testing Predictions From Personality Neuroscience: Brain Structure and the Big Five. Psychological Science Vol. 21(6) pp. 820-828. Copyright © 2010 by Association for Psychological Science. Reprinted by permission of SAGE Publications, Inc.

Active Brains, Active Personality The hypothesis that individual personality traits originate in the brain was tested by scientists who sought to find correlations between brain activity (shown in red) and personality traits. People who rated themselves high in four of the Big Five (conscientiousness, extroversion, agreeableness, neuroticism—but not openness) also had more activity in brain regions that are known to relate to those traits. Here are two side views *(left)* and a top and bottom view *(right)* of the brains of people high in neuroticism. Their brain regions known to be especially sensitive to stress, depression, threat, and punishment (yellow bullseyes) were more active than the same brain regions in people low in neuroticism (DeYoung et al., 2010).

ESPECIALLY FOR Immigrants and Children of Immigrants Poverty and persecution are the main reasons why some people leave their home for another country, but personality is also influential. Which of the Big Five personality traits do you think is most characteristic of immigrants? (see response, page 299)

Even within cities in the United States, self-esteem is enhanced if others in that city are similar in openness, agreeableness, and conscientiousness (Bleidorn et al., 2016).

Common Themes

Universal trends are more significant than cultural differences. Regarding the Big Five, adults who are low in neuroticism and high in agreeableness tend to be happier than the opposite. Personal experiences matter, affecting individuals everywhere more than nations anywhere. For example, people who personally experience a happy marriage become less neurotic over time; people in unhappy marriages become more neurotic (O'Meara & South, 2019).

Many researchers find that personality shifts slightly with age, but the rank order of various traits of the Big Five stays the same. Thus, 20-year-old extroverts are still extroverts at age 50 and 80, more outgoing than most people their age, although not necessarily than most 20-year-olds.

WHAT HAVE YOU LEARNED?

1. Is it better to have a confused or a foreclosed identity?
2. What usually happens with religious identity during adulthood?
3. Is political identity stronger early or late in adulthood?
4. How does ethnic identity affect a person's success in life?
5. Why is vocational identity particularly difficult in today's economy?
6. How do selection and facilitation characterize adult relationships?
7. What are the intrinsic rewards of work?
8. Why is unemployment hard on self-esteem?
9. What are the Big Five personality traits?
10. How does age and culture affect the Big Five?

Personality, Identity, and Older Adults

What happens to the self when people grow old? As you just read, personality tends to stay the same, although marked contextual changes, such as retirement or death of a spouse, have some effect. However, current scholarship suggests that for some people, late adulthood is a time of personality change.

Stereotypes

At every age, social discrimination and stereotypes reduce self-esteem, limit effort, and increase depression. The worst aspect may be that stereotypes can be internalized, either believing them about oneself or believing that other people hold stereotypes that they do not hold (stereotype threat is explained in Chapter 9).

This is true for racism, sexism, classism, ableism, and all the other *-isms*. For example, many sources have noted that the increased rate of hypertension among African Americans is directly tied to their experiences of discrimination (Barajas et al., 2019; Dolezsar et al., 2014). Current research explores whether this is as true for other groups, and whether specific groups within the Black community are more often harmed. It seems that low-SES, older men might be especially vulnerable.

Ageism

Ageism "shares parallels with other prejudices, such as racism and sexism. Like any form of bias, ageism effectively reduces individuals to broad, stereotypical categories" (North, 2015). Because it is part of the culture, it is particularly hard to combat, as found in a program that attempted to dislodge ageism from the implicit thoughts of children (Babcock et al., 2018).

Ironically, both perpetrators and victims of ageism may think it is benevolent (Kagan, 2018). For example, describing someone as a "sweet old lady" who "still has all her marbles" is ageist. People of all ages tend to shape their personality to fit the social context, as you have seen. Thus, an older adult might identify as confused or forgetful ("a senior moment"), and that itself might undercut independence. If older people themselves are ageist, they may avoid the company of other older people, thus removing the social experiences that could benefit them all.

Ageism has, at least, been named and recognized when it applies to older adults. However, some sources suggest that ageism may be even worse in regard to younger adults, who are sometimes thought to be irresponsible (Bratt et al., 2020; Chasteen et al., 2020). This is a caution for everyone seeking to understand people from a developmental perspective.

It is evident, of course, that people of every age differ in their personality, self-concept, and identity in part because of their age. On the other hand, we need to keep in mind that each person is unique, and that stereotypes of any kind may obscure that reality. For example, of the Big Five, on average conscientiousness and extroversion decline and neuroticism builds. But personal and national differences matter as much (or more) than age (Graham et al., 2020).

Self-Concept

Self-awareness begins, as you remember, before age 2, and it builds throughout childhood and adolescence. In the early decades, self-image is greatly affected by physical appearance and by other people's perceptions (Harter, 2012). In late adulthood, this creates a problem: Not only does appearance fade, but prejudice about the old increases.

One task of older adults is to maintain their self-concept despite senescence, which alters appearance and social status in ways that might undercut self-esteem. In late adulthood, the "creation and maintenance of identity is a key aspect of healthy living" (Resnick et al., 2011, p. 10). One factor is whether the demands of work and family are reduced in late adulthood, encouraging personality traits such as happiness and personal choice, dubbed the *la dolce vita effect*. On the other hand, poverty and health problems may change a person's self-concept and self-esteem (Schwaba & Bleidorn, 2018).

Integrity

We return again to Erikson for an explanation of the self-concept of older adults. His eighth and final stage of development is **integrity versus despair** (Erikson et al., 1986/1994). The word *integrity* is often used to mean honesty, but here it means a feeling of being whole, not scattered, comfortable with oneself. The virtue of old age, according to Erikson, is wisdom, which implies a broad perspective.

As an example of integrity, many older people are proud of their personal history. They glorify their past. This is true for national past, such as considering the generation who fought

ageism A prejudice whereby people are categorized and judged solely on the basis of their chronological age.

integrity versus despair The final stage of Erik Erikson's developmental sequence, in which older adults seek to integrate their unique experiences with their vision of community.

Twice Fortunate Ageism takes many forms. Some cultures are youth-oriented and devalue the old, while others are the opposite. These twin sisters were lucky to be alive when this photo was taken: They were born in rural China in 1905, a period when most female twins died. When this photo was taken, they were age 103, and fortunate again, venerated because they have lived so long.

in World War II the "greatest generation," ignoring the racism and sexism that were evident at the time.

On a personal level, many boast about bad experiences such as skipping school, taking drugs, escaping arrest, or being physically beaten. As Erikson explained it, such acceptance of the past is far better than despair, because "time is now short, too short for the attempt to start another life" (Erikson, 1993a, p. 269). For every stage, the tension between the two opposing aspects (here integrity versus despair) propels growth. In this final stage,

> life brings many, quite realistic reasons for experiencing despair: aspects of a past we fervently wish had been different; aspects of a future that are uncertain and frightening. And, of course, there remains inescapable death, that one aspect of the future which is both wholly certain and wholly unknowable. Thus, some despair must be acknowledged and integrated as a component of old age.
>
> *[Erikson et al., 1994, p. 72]*

Holding On to the Self

Most older people consider their personalities and attitudes quite stable over their life span, even as they acknowledge physical changes of their bodies and gaps in their memory (Klein, 2012). One 103-year-old woman, wrinkled, shrunken, and severely crippled by arthritis, displayed a photo of herself as a beautiful young woman. She said, "My core has stayed the same. Everything else has changed" (quoted in Troll & Skaff, 1997, p. 166).

Her statement echoes what people of all ages and cultures believe. As one review wrote:

> The baby and the senior citizen have none of the same memories, preferences, or knowledge, they look entirely different from one another, and they are not even made up of the same physical stuff, since most of the baby's cells have died and been replace by new cells.
>
> *[Starmans, 2017, p. 1777]*

Yet this scientist, and scientists everywhere, agree that there is a self and that it continues lifelong. People of all ages typically seek to become better, to become closer to their ideal self, and with age, people are more likely to think they have done so.

For example, many older people refuse to move from drafty, dangerous dwellings into smaller, safer apartments, because leaving familiar places means abandoning personal history. That is explained by the need to be oneself, which is affirmed by all the personal memories of life. Likewise, an older person may avoid surgery or refuse medicine because they fear anything that might distort their thinking or emotions: Their priority is self-protection, even if it shortens life (Miller, 2011–2012).

compulsive hoarding The urge to accumulate and hold on to familiar objects and possessions, sometimes to the point of their becoming health and/or safety hazards. This impulse tends to increase with age.

The insistence on protecting the self may explain **compulsive hoarding**, saving old papers, books, mementos . . . even junk. The rationale is that someone, someday, might find the stuff useful. Many elderly hoarders were children in the Great Depression and World War II, when saving scraps and reusing products meant survival and patriotism.

Thinking Positive

Socioemotional selectivity theory, first explained in Chapter 2, further explains that older people select social contexts that reinforce their generativity, pride, and joy. As socioemotional theory predicts, when people believe that their future time is limited, they think about the meaning of their life and then decide that they should cherish family and friends, thus furthering their happiness.

positivity effect The tendency for elderly people to perceive, prefer, and remember positive images and experiences more than negative ones.

For that reason, the personality of older adults tilts toward optimism, as they see the bright side of things. This is known as the **positivity effect**. A meta-analysis

A VIEW FROM SCIENCE

Attitudes About Others

A pair of researchers wondered if the positivity effect occurred because older adults simply avoided unpleasant people (Luong & Charles, 2014). Accordingly, they assigned younger and older adults to work on a task with a disagreeable partner.

In fact, that partner was an actor, trained to be equally nasty with everyone. For example, the actor never smiled and would say, "I really don't see where you're coming from." True to expectations, compared to the younger participants, the older adults more often reported that they liked the partner and enjoyed the task. They did not try to change their partner or feel resentful, as many of the younger adults did.

Moreover, with the disagreeable partner, compared to the younger adults, the elders' blood pressure rose less and came down more quickly. The pulse of the older participants hardly

changed at all (Luong & Charles, 2014). The conclusion: Having a positive outlook not only makes a person happier, it also makes them healthier.

I like that conclusion, but that itself raises my concern. I think about my daughter, my mother, and me. When I was young, I liked movies that were gritty, dramatic, violent. My mother questioned my choices; I told her I hated sugarcoated fluff.

Now my youngest daughter wants me to read dystopian novels and watch disturbing movies. I tell her the world has enough poverty and conflict; I don't need to read about imaginary killing. Is this the positivity effect? Am I too optimistic about climate change, about war, about the devastation of the global COVID-19 lockdown, the resulting economic depression? Have I become my mother?

---

of more than 115 comparisons between younger and older adults found that the elderly perceive, prefer, and remember positive images and experiences more than negative ones (Reed et al., 2014).

Because of the positivity effect, unpleasant experiences are ignored, forgotten, or reinterpreted. Stressful events (economic loss, serious illness, death of friends or relatives) become less central to identity with age. Self-efficacy (the idea that a person has the power to control and change a situation) correlates with a happier and longer life (Gerstorf et al., 2014).

The positivity effect may explain why, in every nation and religion, older people tend to describe themselves as patriotic and devout. They see their national history and religious beliefs in positive terms, and they are proud to be themselves — Canadian, Czech, Chinese, or whatever. Of course, this same trait can keep them mired in their earlier prejudices — racism, or sexism, or homophobia, for instance.

The positivity effect correlates with believing that life is meaningful. Elders who are happy, not frustrated or depressed, agree strongly that their life has a purpose (e.g., "I have a system of values that guides my daily activities" and "I am at peace with my past") (Hicks et al., 2012).

Sometimes this positivity effect feeds into the ageist thought that older people are unable to see problems that might occur. A study refuted that idea: Older adults are quite able to evaluate risks of various activities. They prefer to look at the bright side, but they are not oblivious to problems (Rolison, 2019).

Conclusion

Where does the discussion of personality, identity, and the self lead? Let us return to the beginning. It is apparent that each of us has a unique self, enclosed within our body, reflecting our genes, our brain activity, our experiences — perhaps especially those from early childhood, perhaps not. Ancient sages recognized the self and the soul; current researchers also acknowledge that people have selves that develop throughout life; even children believe each of them has a self (they put it near the eyes) (Starmans, 2017).

Theories suggest that we become ourselves because of genes, childhood experiences, or adult social contexts. All seem partly true.

As people age, many specifics change, but people are still themselves. Adults accept who they are—a radical acceptance that is hard-won, after the struggle to form an identity and the need to harmonize that personal self with all the other selves. The study of development, and the research reported in this chapter, suggests not only that we are who we are, but also that we are still becoming who we will be.

WHAT HAVE YOU LEARNED?

1. How is ageism similar to racism and sexism?

2. How does the self-concept change with age?

3. What is needed for an older person to experience integrity rather than despair?

4. Why is hoarding more common among the old than the young?

5. What is the positivity effect?

SUMMARY

Theories of Personality

1. A major personality theory traces differences in traits to differences in genetic codes. Genes produce hormones, including oxytocin, cortisol, and the sex hormones, all of which affect human emotions and behavior lifelong.

2. Freud believed that personality occurred because of ongoing conflict between the ego, id, and superego. Early-childhood experiences set the stage for this conflict, affecting personality lifelong.

3. Erikson agreed with Freud that family influences in childhood profoundly affect adult personality. What happens at the stages of trust, autonomy, initiative, and industry affects how suspicious, brave, creative, and self-confident a person will be.

4. Behaviorists emphasize the importance of ongoing reinforcement and punishment in determining personality.

5. Often adult personality reflects childhood personality because adults choose their adult social context; however, sometimes historical events intervene, changing adult reinforcement and thus personality.

The Self in Childhood

6. Children differ in temperament, being easy or difficult depending on how fearful, outgoing, and emotionally controlled they are. Some environments afford certain emotions and actions more than others. Ideally, goodness of fit means that parents afford self-expression to their children.

7. The self-concept develops as children compare themselves to others. Self-esteem and social relationships each affect the other.

8. Four or more adverse childhood experiences (abuse, family trouble) have a lifelong impact. The specific circumstances of a child's life, not their general ethnic or economic background, are crucial.

9. Some children seem resilient to harm from significant problems of their lives. The wider community (schools, neighborhood) and the child's interpretation of the situation are crucial. Having a steady and supportive caregiver is also crucial for resilience.

Adolescence and Adulthood

10. The search for identity begins in adolescence and continues into adulthood. Many people experience confusion, foreclosure, and moratorium before achievement.

11. Religious identity continues to follow in the direction set in childhood, with younger adults attending services less often and considering themselves personally spiritual and less part of an organized religion than older adults.

12. Political concerns, such as racial justice, climate change, and LGBTQ rights, are motivating to younger adults, but voting increases with maturation. Ethnic identity is increasingly important for all adults. It correlates with adult achievement.

13. Vocational identity is difficult, as most young adults change jobs several times, yet consider employment a way to express their personal values.

14. Intimacy is important for adults at every age. Adults choose friends who facilitate the activities and values they hold.

15. Generativity includes finding work that has intrinsic as well as extrinsic rewards. The social aspects of employment may be crucial, which is one reason unemployment is particularly difficult.

16. Personality traits have been clustered into five clusters: openness, conscientiousness, extraversion, agreeableness, and neuroticism. These Big Five are fairly stable throughout adulthood, although dramatic experiences can affect them.

Personality, Identity, and Older Adults

17. Ageism can reduce self-esteem and limit personality expression in late adulthood. In the stage of integrity and despair, older adults seek to maintain their identity despite changes in health and circumstances.

18. Older adults tend to cherish friends and memories. The positivity effect helps them focus on experiences that make them happy.

KEY TERMS

personality (p. 272)	goodness of fit (p. 280)	identity versus role confusion (p. 286)	intrinsic rewards of work (p. 290)
ego (p. 274)	self-concept (p. 280)	identity achievement (p. 286)	Big Five (p. 292)
id (p. 274)	social comparison (p. 281)	role confusion (p. 286)	ageism (p. 295)
superego (p. 274)	self-esteem (p. 281)	foreclosure (p. 286)	integrity versus despair (p. 295)
psychodynamic (p. 275)	adverse childhood experiences	moratorium (p. 286)	compulsive hoarding (p. 296)
temperament (p. 278)	(ACEs) (p. 282)	extrinsic rewards of work (p. 290)	positivity effect (p. 296)
affordance (p. 279)	resilience (p. 283)		

APPLICATIONS

1. Ask several people how their personalities have changed in the past decade. The research suggests that changes are usually minor. Is that what you found?

2. Ask three people who are not from your ethnic group about their ethnic identity. Discuss when and how they became aware of their ethnicity and if their ethnicity is connected to their religion, their habits, their values. Ask how their thoughts about ethnicity are similar to, and different from, their parents, as well as what they know about their grandparents, and other ancestors. Write about these individuals and your own ethnicity, addressing similarities and differences.

3. Vocational identity is fluid in early adulthood. Talk with several people over age 30 about their work history. Are they doing what they expected they would be doing when they were younger? Are they settled in their vocation and job? Pay attention to their age when they decided on their jobs. Was age 25 a turning point?

ESPECIALLY FOR ANSWERS

Response for Nurses (from p. 279) It's too soon to tell. Temperament is not truly "fixed" but variable, especially in the first few months. Many "difficult" infants become happy, successful adolescents and adults, if their parents are responsive.

Response for Immigrants and Children of Immigrants (from p. 293) Extroversion and neuroticism, according to one study (Silventoinen et al., 2008). Because these traits decrease over adulthood, fewer older adults migrate.

OBSERVATION QUIZ ANSWERS

Answer to Observation Quiz (from p. 276) The Virginia home has a large double sink, glass doors to the outside, and smooth white walls. The Chinese home has no dryer, no clothesline, no grassy yard. (Some U.S. communities forbid hanging clothes outside to dry, and some require a lawn, not just dirt.) The Chinese home also has an uneven natural roof.

Answer to Observation Quiz (from p. 280) Look at the facial expressions.

Peathegee Inc/Blend Images/Getty Images

CHAPTER 11

Sex and Gender

"This one is a boy," proclaimed a smiling, self-assured older woman, pointing to my very pregnant body, as I walked on a public sidewalk with my young daughters.

Strangers rarely talk to strangers on the street, but privacy norms do not apply during pregnancy. People I had never met asked me when I was due, and patted my belly, even though they would never touch the body of any nonpregnant woman.

Acquaintances were worse. Some assumed that my husband and I conceived our second, third, and fourth child because we were "trying for a boy." Many proclaimed that a "balanced" family is best, ignoring the statistic that only half of all two-child families are one boy and one girl. My own mother told me she had a perfect family, first a son and then a daughter. When her son had three boys and no girls, and I had four daughters and no sons, she no longer bragged about her perfect family.

She did, however, tell me of a newspaper ad asking prospective parents to send a few dollars to obtain a sure-fire diet that would produce a boy or a girl, "money back if not satisfied." That was a great scam, not only because the babies born to half of those who followed the diet were the desired sex, but also because the others might be ashamed to demand a refund, because that would signal disappointment with their own child.

Fortunately, prenatal diagnosis had told me that this fetus had the usual number of chromosomes (46) and no Y, so I knew I was carrying a girl. I defended my unborn daughter from that stranger's sexism with a loud and angry "No! A girl, and I am glad." I was pleased to see her startled expression.

She was indeed misguided and sexist. But I fear that my angry response was sexist as well. As this chapter explains, sex and gender are far more complicated than the emotional responses of that woman, or my mother, or me. Only one of 46 chromosomes made my brother male and me female. But gender is more significant than one chromosome.

What Will You Know?

1. Are male and female polar opposites, like on and off, or more varied, like hot and cold?

2. Do boys and girls have different play preferences?

3. Why would anyone worry that young adults are having less sex than people their age a decade ago?

4. Why do women live five years longer than men?

5. Are men more aggressive than women?

Using Words

The first words new parents once heard were "It's a boy!" or "It's a girl!" Now many parents hear those words months before birth, perhaps throwing a "gender reveal" party to announce to all. Why are those words more eagerly sought than critical information such as pulse, oxygen, and weight?

Words frame how people understand reality. We have already seen this with difference/deficit, race/ethnicity, implicit/explicit, sensation/perception. This chapter begins with definitions referring to sex and gender, because to understand the shifting concepts of this topic, we need to understand the language.

Nature and Nurture

As noted in Chapter 1, some developmental characteristics arise from biology and some from culture. Since about 1960, social scientists have used the word **sex** to refer to physiological differences that begin with the XX or XY chromosomes and the word **gender** to refer to characteristics that result from culture.

That was a useful distinction, because some sex differences are better understood as gender differences. Indeed, some scientists thought that all male/female differences were the result of early childhood socialization, an idea that led to tragedy.

sex In the social sciences, the term used to designate male or female characteristics that are present at birth, not cultural.

gender In the social sciences, the term that refers to the social and cultural construct of being male or female, some variation of the two, or neither.

An Example

In 1965, identical twin boys were born to the Reimer family in Canada. Their parents named them Bruce and Brian, following the then-common idea that twins should have similar names. At 6 months, the boys seemed to have a problem with urination, and surgery was scheduled. Bruce's surgery went terribly wrong, destroying his penis. Brian's surgery was canceled (Colapinto, 2006).

How should parents raise a boy who had no penis? At that time, some people thought that children became whatever gender their parents and society set out for them in infancy. Girls learned to be girls, and boys learned to be boys.

The parents consulted a world-renowned doctor, John Money. He advised further surgery to construct female genitals for Bruce, and to raise him as a girl. They did so, changing the baby named Bruce to Brenda. The famous doctor studied the twins throughout childhood, citing them as proof that male/female differences are cultural, not biological (Money & Ehrhardt, 1972).

As the twins navigated childhood, an opposing perspective gradually took hold among scholars. Social scientists began to believe that a person's gender is in their brain, regardless of the sex they were assigned at birth, and that having a body that doesn't match their self-perception leads to distress.

Indeed, the twin who had been raised as a girl felt odd during childhood and was puzzled as an adolescent that the physical changes girls typically experience did not occur. The child who had been raised as Brenda was told the truth and soon assumed a male identity and name, David (Diamond & Sigmundson, 1997).

Current Perspectives

Opinions have changed. Today, if the penis of an XY infant were destroyed, he would be raised as a boy. Most social scientists now believe that some male and female differences are inborn, not a matter of upbringing, although disagreement remains regarding exactly which differences are innate and which are not.

Scientists no longer think that gender makes sex irrelevant. They also realize that defining sex and gender has become far more complex than scientists once thought. Nature is affected by nurture and vice versa; sexual characteristics are shaped by culture, and then gender affects sex. To grasp a bit of this complexity, consider what one of the leaders of the field wrote two decades ago:

> Developmental scientists view outcomes, such as gender-related behavior, as the product of a developmental system that involves numerous factors interacting over time to produce stability or change. In the case of gender, the influences of interest include sex chromosome genes, early testosterone exposure, socialization by external forces (such as parents and broader society), and self-socialization.
>
> *[Hines, 2020, p. 39]*

As you see, two of the factors that Hines mentions (chromosomes and testosterone) are from nature, two (parents and society) are nurture, and the fifth (self-socialization) is from the person themselves. Given the interaction of five powerful influences, no wonder experts continue to debate the relative impact of each.

Moreover, neither sex nor gender are what they were when humans first evolved: Both change not only over the centuries but also over each person's life. Yet neither is easy to change. For example, some sociocultural forces are deeply embedded in social customs and remain strong even when tradition is outdated and harmful (such as female circumcision, common in 30 nations).

Recent research suggests a *gender similarities hypothesis*, that the emphasis on differences ignores the reality that the two sexes have far more in common than traditional theories recognize (Hyde, 2016). Similarities outweigh differences in the brain, body, and behavior (Hyde et al., 2019; Roseberry & Roos, 2016; Xiong et al., 2018).

Given such complications, some scholars prefer to stress the interaction between sex and gender rather than trying to separate them. Indeed, the distinction that was useful a few decades ago has become so complex that some scholars combine them into one term, *sex/gender* (Hyde et al., 2019).

The current consensus is that scientists need to "treat culture and biology not as separate influences but as interacting components of nature and nurture" (Eagly & Wood, 2013, p. 349). Nonetheless, some traits evident at certain stages of life seem more affected by biology and others by culture, so in this chapter *sex* refers to physiological influences and *gender* to social ones.

The Opposite Sex?

An added complication in terminology is that male and female used to be considered opposites, like on/off, in/out. Now it is recognized that **gender identity** is more of a *continuum*. Just like temperature is a matter of degree, not hot/cold, most traits within most people are not at the extremes, but somewhere between.

But that may be inaccurate because the word *between* implies "two," a concept called **gender binary**. (The prefix *bi-* means "two," as in *bicycle, bifurcate, bisexual*.) The gender binary assumes sexual *dimorphism*, a term that literally means "divided (*di-*) into distinct forms (*morphs*)."

Gender is now considered more fluid than binary. That is certainly indicated by the growing awareness of **nonbinary** people, who sometimes refer to themselves as *gender queer*. But it also true for everyone else, of whatever gender. Every aspect of brains, behavior, and bodies zigzags along that continuum, changing not only from one person to another but also within the same person over time.

Another false binary regards the direction of one's sexuality, once thought to be either/or. In the middle of the twentieth century, Kinsey shocked people by proposing that humans can be mostly, or only sometimes, straight or gay, rather than exclusively one or the other (Kinsey, 1948, 1953). Kinsey found that same-sex experiences were common among adolescents, who usually settled into heterosexuality by adulthood.

Kinsey did not simply ask people about their sexuality. He measured genital arousal, which sometimes revealed more than what people said. Recently other measures, such as heart rate, pupil dilation, or blood pressure when a person sees photographs, confirm that sexual arousal varies in strength as well as in direction. (Sarlo & Buodo, 2017).

Sexual Orientation

The direction of one's sexual attraction, or **sexual orientation**, is not either/or, same-gender, or another gender. Orientation means "turned toward," and when it refers to sexuality it refers to who is attracted to whom. People could be strongly or weakly turned on by some people and not by others.

Traditionally, sexual orientation was thought to be simple: A person could be attracted to people of their own sex, another sex, or both male and female sexes. But that can be too narrow; it assumes the gender binary. Sexual orientation and gender identity may be more fluid, sometimes changing as life changes.

On the other hand, this definition can be too wide. For example, I am attracted, sexually, to very few people, not to all men, or all women, or all people.

Likewise, some people are strongly oriented, and some are weakly attracted, to one sex and/or gender. Further, some are attracted to multiple sexes or genders, some seem attracted to no one, and some were oriented in one direction and then shifted.

Given the diversity of gender identities and sexual orientations, scientists question surveys such as the U.S. Census that assume the binary, asking if a person is male or female (Westbrook & Saperstein, 2015).

A step toward a broader understanding is found in some medical surveys that include "other" as an option. Some demographers wonder if people might be offended if a nonbinary choice is offered, or other participants might be troubled if only two choices are allowed.

Remember that step 3 of the scientific method requires collecting data before drawing conclusions. Accordingly, some scientists gave a survey to 1,000 individuals in each of three nations (Sweden, Canada, United States). Half the surveys offered

The Opposite Sex? Every cohort of adolescents rebels against the conventions of the older generations. Earlier generations of boys grew their hair long. A decade later, some girls shaved their heads. Now many teenagers do not see male and female as opposites, choosing instead a nonbinary approach to gender expression.

gender identity A person's emotional and psychological sense of being a man, a woman, both, or neither. Gender identity may or may not align with an individual's sex at birth.

gender binary The idea that gender comes in two—and only two—forms, male and female.

nonbinary The rejection of the binary. When applied to gender, this means that sexual characteristics, identity, roles, and orientation are all fluid, not male/female.

sexual orientation A term that describes an individual's sense of enduring romantic, emotional, and/or sexual attraction to other people.

the binary choice (male or female) and half the nonbinary choice (male, female, or other). When offered three choices, almost everyone chose male or female, but no one objected to the "other" option (Medeiros et al., 2020). Next time you answer a questionnaire, notice if whoever wrote the questions is aware of the nonbinary.

Identity, Role, and Behavior

An added complication with definitions is that gender identities, public roles, and private behavior may differ. How people define themselves, how they behave publicly, and what they do privately, are three separate expressions of gender.

In 1982, two books were published—*Real Women Don't Pump Gas* and *Real Men Don't Eat Quiche*—to make fun of the common tendency to confuse identity with behavior. Nonetheless, those identities sometimes surprise people.

A person can identify as male or female but work at a job that is more common for another gender. Imagine a woman who identifies as female but who is the boss of a construction crew. She wears stained overalls, work boots, and a helmet covering her tied-back hair. She shouts orders using words that are not ladylike, and her male crew responds with deference or resentment, as they would with a male boss.

Then she goes home to her husband and children, takes her hair down, showers, applies fragrant lotion, and acts as mothers and wives traditionally do. Her identity, public role, and private actions are what she, her crew, and her family expect.

This example is not unusual. Considerable research finds that many adults take on public roles that once were exclusive to another gender, but "ample evidence shows greater support for gender equality in the public sphere of employment than in the private sphere of the family" (Dernberger & Pepin, 2020, pp. 36–37).

The fact that identity, roles, and activity are distinct was one reason the U.S. military, from 1994 to 2011, had a policy of "Don't ask, don't tell," which enabled gay and lesbian soldiers to serve in the army as long as their sexual orientation was secret. That particular schism between private and public identity is no longer military policy, but many people still separate identity, role, and action. The specifics of each of these three vary over the life span, as well as among males and females, as we now describe.

THINK CRITICALLY: Since identity is formed lifelong, is your current identity different from what it was five years ago?

WHAT HAVE YOU LEARNED?

1. What is the difference between sex and gender?
2. What is learned from the example of David Reimer?
3. Why is the idea of the gender binary inaccurate?
4. What are the varieties of sexual orientation?
5. What is the difference between gender identity, public gender role, and private gender action?

Before Puberty

Sex and gender matter to people lifelong, but the manifestations differ before and after puberty. First we consider boys and girls before the rush of hormones that make them men and women.

Prenatal: Conception to Birth

Biology is most powerful before a developing person is born. At conception, the 23rd pair of chromosomes is either XX or XY, or, rarely, XYY, XXY, a lone X, or even XXX. An embryo cannot grow without at least one X.

Since every ovum carries an X, the crucial factor in sex determination is whether the sperm carries a Y or an X. The Y is the only chromosome that contains the SRY gene, which produces massive amounts of testosterone, especially in the third and fourth prenatal month and again at puberty.

Organs in the Embryo

Every embryo develops a bladder, intestines, a urethra, and an anus to rid the body of waste products, and two gonads that produce gametes to eventually create a new human. Those essential organs begin to form during the embryonic period, as do the facial features, brain, heart, lungs, and bones.

Genital organs (the penis, the vagina, etc.) do not form during those first eight weeks. Instead the embryo has an *indifferent gonad*, a sex organ than will morph early in the fetal period. Embryos are unisex.

Thus, every embryo has both male and female potential, via the *Wolffian ducts* (male) and *Müllerian ducts* (female). At about 8 weeks after conception, one or the other of the two ducts shrinks (Zhao et al., 2017). Then the SRY gene instructs the indifferent gonad to place sex organs outside the body, and a flood of hormones are produced, affecting fetal bodies and brains.

All this illustrates a general fact: Males and females are alike in most ways. However, one trait of our human brains is to notice differences more than similarities (a tendency the gender similarities hypothesis tries to combat). This is evident when we think of the human body. We ignore similarities and, instead, seem obsessed with how urine is expelled and if gamete-producing organs are inside (ovaries) or outside (testicles) the body.

These differences can be viewed in sonograms in mid-pregnancy. An obstetrician said she asks future parents if they want to know sex: Most say yes, because that makes choosing a name easier. However, if a pregnant women does not seem to protect the health of the fetus, the doctor tells sex, describes activity, and does whatever else she can to help the future mother realize that the future baby is not an "it" but a person.

Hormones and the Fetal Brain

In fetal development, one hormone, *testosterone*, may be particularly significant. As one expert states, "To describe the organizational effects of testosterone as profound is to rather understate the case" (Hardy, 2019, p. 108). Because of that Y chromosome, testosterone is much more prevalent in the male than the female fetus, affecting brain and skeleton.

Recently some researchers have focused on the 2D:4D ratio, comparing the length of the second and fourth digits. According to some, testosterone early in prenatal development makes longer ring fingers (4D) in males and longer index fingers (2D) in females. This difference in length is miniscule; many men and women have a contrary digit ratio. Partly for that reason, many scientists dispute digit ratio to indicate the presence of early hormones (Leslie, 2019).

Nonetheless, decades of research have confirmed sex differences in the fetal body and brain (Wheelock et al., 2019; McCarthy et al., 2017). Among the prenatal, hormonal effects are that parts of the hippocampus are larger in females; parts of the amygdala are larger in males.

The significance of prenatal sex differences is controversial. According to one scholar, neuroscientists are susceptible to *neurosexism*, attributing gender differences to brain differences "in the absence of data" (Fine, 2014, p. 915). People disagree about the impact of the relatively minor dimorphism in male and female bodies and brains.

To make it more complicated, although sex differences appear when the *average* male is compared to the *average* female, overlap is common. Some males have

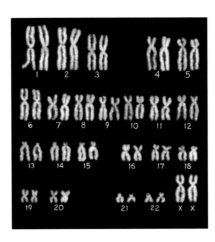

Biophoto Associates/Science Source

Intersex Every now and then, a baby is born with "ambiguous genitals," meaning that the child's sex is not abundantly clear. When this happens, analysis of the chromosomes may reveal that the zygote was XX or XY. The karyotypes shown here indicate a typical baby boy *(left)* and girl *(right)*.

intersex A broad term describing people born with reproductive or sexual anatomy and/or a chromosome pattern that isn't typically male or female.

neurological characteristics typical for females, and vice versa. Very few adults (less than 10 percent) are typical for their sex in every one of a dozen traits that distinguish male and female brains (Joel et al., 2015). Most brains are a male/female mosaic.

The Intersex Fetus

The most dramatic evidence for the male/female mosaic are people who are **intersex**. They are born with genitalia that are ambiguous, or with genitalia that appear male or female, unlike their chromosomes, or with a chromosome pattern that is not typically male or female. Incidence of intersex conditions is unknown: Estimates vary from 1 in 50 to 1 in 2,000.

Intersex conditions occur for many reasons. The most common one is an allele that impedes prenatal hormones, leading to *congenital adrenal hyperplasia (CAH)*, which affects the brain and the body (Herting et al., 2020).

If an intersex condition is apparent at birth, many parents choose surgery to make the genitals conform to one sex. Following the gender binary, such children are usually raised as either a boy or a girl. But some intersex adults feel that such surgery violated their human rights, because when parents choose surgery for intersex infants, that denies part of who they are (Bauer et al., 2019; Davis, 2015).

The Vulnerable Male

Hormones influence other aspects of prenatal development. For example, XY newborns are heavier and longer than XX newborns, an average difference of 4 ounces and a half inch. However, XYs are at higher risk of spontaneous abortion (miscarriage), of still or preterm birth, and of developmental anomalies, such as those that cause autism and learning disorders (Alur, 2019).

Among newborns, sex differences are apparent only when thousands of babies are compared. For instance, a study of 30 million births, worldwide, reported a stillborn rate of 1 in 200, about 35 million per year. Of those 35 million, the male/female ratio is about 55:45 (Mondal et al., 2014).

The fact that males are slightly more often born dead or preterm seems insignificant when compared to other differences in prenatal development. For example, in nations where many women are malnourished, the 2009 stillborn rate was a tragic 1 in 28, compared to 1 in 500 in nations when nutrition and medical care are optimal (Cousens et al., 2011). But remember, humans focus on sex differences more than on commonalities.

Birth to 2 Years

Gender differences begin at birth, when nurses put a blue or pink cap on the newborn's head. Parents describe the newborn girl as "sweet"; the newborn boy as "strong."

Early Maturation

Girls mature slightly faster than boys do, and they do not cry as much, on average. They are quicker to sleep through the night. Of course, all babies cry and spit up, but immature digestion makes boys cry more and gain weight more slowly. By 6 months girls have caught up to boys in weight (Fields et al., 2009). Girls also talk sooner, on average, a verbal advantage that continues throughout life.

Any male/female differences evident in the early months must be nature, not nurture, right? Not necessarily. Almost every development is affected by external influences, from the moment of birth.

For instance, immature digestion requires more frequent feeding, which may be one reason that infant boys are slower to "sleep through the night" (Kaley et al., 2012; Lundqvist et al., 2000). But is that entirely physiology?

Could baby boys who initially cry because of stomach pain, quickly learn that crying at 2 A.M. results in being picked up and fed? If so, when he is half-awake in the early hours, he might remember that he will be cuddled if he cries, so he cries.

A half-awake infant girl might go back to sleep. Her parents may notice that their daughter sleeps through the night earlier than their son did, but they are unlikely to realize that their responses in the first weeks of life is the reason.

On the female verbal advantage: Mothers talk more to their daughters than to their sons (K. Johnson et al., 2014). Why? Is that because infant girls babble more, or vice versa? That girls are more advanced in language development is not disputed, but the reason is.

People and Objects

All babies are social from the first hours of life, yet close examination of averages finds some sex differences. Infant girls tend to look longer at people; boys are more interested in mechanical things (Connellan et al., 2000). Throughout infancy, girls stare at faces longer, smile more, and prefer to play with dolls more than trucks (Lauer et al., 2015).

Girls also play with smaller objects, perhaps because finger control is faster in girls, who attain the *pincer grasp* (using the thumb and forefinger to pick up an object), on average, at 10 months; boys at 11 months.

In one study, 1-year-olds could play however they wanted with an array of toys (Alexander & Saenz, 2012). Some toys were traditionally for boys (blocks, vehicles, tools), some for girls (doll, cosmetics, tea sets), and some neutral (books, puzzles). The boys showed a slight preference for the "boy" toys, and the girls had a decided preference for the "girl" toys.

Do these preferences arise from innate forces or from early learning? The researchers measured finger length (Alexander & Saenz, 2012). Those children (girls as well as boys) with a more masculine 2D:4D ratio were less likely to choose "girl" toys. The researchers suspect that play preferences reflect early hormones in the brain.

Another study that suggests that sex differences are innate involved point-light walkers, who are people in the dark, wearing lights on hands, feet, elbows, and knees. Only the lights can be seen, not the people. When 4- to 18-month-old infants watched a point-light walker, they noticed gender differences. Boys, particularly, preferred to look at point-light men (Tsang et al., 2018). Perhaps they recognized a gender similarity, maybe something in their brains was attracted to the movement of the men.

By age 2, most infants use gender labels (*Mrs., Mr., lady, man*). They might call any woman *mama* and any man *dada*, but they know that *mama* is female. That difference could be nature—perhaps humans are primed to perceive sex differences.

A Contrary Perspective

However, not everyone is convinced. The social context differs for infant boys and girls, even when the adults try to react the same to every infant. Fathers sing and talk more to their daughters but describe shapes and motion more with their sons, as well as use more words of achievement, such as *proud* and *win* (Mascaro et al., 2017).

Caregivers are much more often female (mothers, grandmothers, babysitters), and infants notice that. That could explain why those boys looked more intently at

Gender-Nonconforming The dad, not the daughter. Like many 6-year-olds, she loves wearing her frilly dress, and like many fathers he allows her to follow traditional roles, here by letting her put a tiara on his head.

the male point-light walkers: It was a novelty. That also could explain early learning of gender labels: If steady caregivers are all female, and men are more likely to interact by playing for a few minutes and then the women do the feeding, diapering and so on, then infants may notice that gender matters and therefore learn gender words.

Childhood: Age 2–10

Both sex and gender continue to make a difference as children grow older. Boys and girls become increasingly divergent, in clothes, playmates, and aspirations.

Many 2-year-olds have a favorite playmate of another sex; by age 6, that is unusual. Six-year-old girls, whose mothers wear jeans and no make-up, may insist on wearing pink and purple, skirts and lipstick, called the "frilly pink dress" effect (Halim et al., 2014). Boys typically play with other boys if given a choice, wearing boots, stripes, and military camouflage.

As you see, each year makes a difference. By age 3, children know whether they are boys or girls; by age 4, they insist that certain toys (such as dolls or trucks), activities (dress-up for girls and balls for boys), and roles (Daddy, Mommy, nurse, teacher, police officer, soldier) are for one gender or the other. As one expert states:

> . . . four year olds say that girls will always be girls and will never become boys. . . . They are often more absolute about gender than adults are. They'll tell their very own pantssuited doctor mother that girls wear dresses and women are nurses.
>
> *[Gopnik, 2016, p. 140]*

In one preschool, the young children themselves decided that one wash-up basin was for boys and the other for girls. That fits the early cognitive binary that everything can be divided into male and female.

But another cognitive mandate for 3-year-olds is to do whatever it takes to get what you want. A young girl started to use the boys' basin.

> **Boy:** This is for the boys.
> **Girl:** Stop it. I'm not a girl and a boy, so I'm here.
> **Boy:** What?
> **Girl:** I'm a boy and also a girl.
> **Boy:** You, now, are you today a boy?
> **Girl:** Yes.
> **Boy:** And tomorrow what will you be?
> **Girl:** A girl. Tomorrow I'll be a girl. Today I'll be a boy.
> **Boy:** And after tomorrow?
> **Girl:** I'll be a girl.
>
> *[Ehrlich & Blum-Kulka, 2014, p. 31]*

This incident occurred in Israel, where women are drafted into the army and have served as national leaders for decades. Probably this girl had been told that some gender restrictions are unfair to females, and she appropriated that message when she wanted to wash up. Neither she nor the boy questioned the overall binary, however. Ages 5 and 6 is the period of peak rigidity about male and female: Children assert that boys and girls are opposites (Halim, 2016). Every major theory of human development has sought to explain this early awareness of gender.

By age 6, children are astute "gender detectives," seeking out ways that males and females differ in their society. They try to conform to their culture, as do all humans of every age. Mia is one example:

> On her first day of school, Mia sits at the lunch table eating a peanut butter and jelly sandwich. She notices that a few boys are eating peanut butter and jelly, but not one girl is. When her father picks her up from school, Mia runs up to him and exclaims, "Peanut butter and jelly is for boys! I want a turkey sandwich tomorrow."
>
> *[Quoted in C. Miller et al., 2013, p. 307]*

Children Encouraged to Play with Toys and Engage in Activities Associated with Another Sex

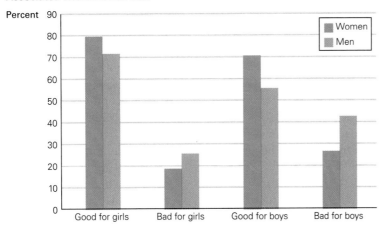

Data from Parker et al., 2017.

FIGURE 11.1
Similarities? What is more remarkable — that most people think girls should be encouraged to play with trucks and boys encouraged to play with dolls, or that some people do not? Your answer probably depends on whether you thought gender equality was achieved or is still far away.

By age 7, both boys and girls may be intolerant of each other, saying "girls [or boys] are stupid" or "boys [or girls] stink."

Fathers and Mothers

Most parents believe they treat their sons and daughters the same, but in practice many follow long-standing, unconscious gender norms. A 2017 survey found that most adults thought parents should encourage their children to play with toys associated with another sex, but a sizable minority disagreed (Parker et al., 2017).

The strongest disagreement was expressed by men regarding boys: 43 percent of the men thought boys should *not* be encouraged to do things usually stereotyped for girls, such as care for dolls, jump rope, or wear bracelets (see **Figure 11.1**).

Fathers, more than mothers, behave differently with the boys. For instance, a massive study of 41 low- and middle-income nations found that fathers took their young boys outside more often than their girls. They also were more likely to read to, tell stories to, and count with their sons (Bornstein & Putnick, 2016).

However, fathers may have good reasons for what they do. They may be more aware of subtle gender restrictions than mothers are, because cultural norms give them more power but less leeway. At least in Western democracies, women can wear pants *or* skirts, apply eyeshadow *and/or* lipstick *or* no makeup, crop their hair *or* grow it shoulder length. Men have fewer choices. Fathers may feel their boys need to be guided to fill the male role: Mothers may be less aware of the need to do so.

Transgender Children

Both parents may be challenged when their child is **transgender**, expressing a consistent, insistent, and persistent awareness that their gender identity is not the same as the one assigned at birth. Such children are contrasted with children who are *cisgender*, when their gender identity is the one on their birth certificate.

One mother, who chose not to use the pronoun that reflected her child's gender identity, said:

> Since he was two, all he can say is that he wants to be a girl, or that he is a girl. He knows that he is not, but there is no way to change his mind. He is 6 now, and he still asks me everyday "Mom, can I be a girl when I grow up?"
> [*quoted in Malpas, 2011, p. 453*]

A study of 36 transgender children, whose parents accepted their transition to their gender identity before age 6, compared them with their cisgender siblings

THINK CRITICALLY: Why do more people encourage girls to do "boy things" than boys to do "girl things"?

transgender A broad term for people whose gender identity and/or gender expression differs from what is typically expected of the sex they were assigned at birth. Some (but not all) transgender people take hormones or undergo surgery to make their bodies align with their gender identity.

Not Emma In a North Carolina kindergarten, each child had an "All About Me" day, in which the teacher would draw a picture of the child for all of the other children to copy. Emma's birth certificate assigned her as male, but she identifies as a girl. On her day, she proudly wore a light-pink shirt with a heart, pink glittery shoes, and long hair—and she came home bawling because the teacher drew this picture with her "boy name" (barely visible here). Her parents consoled her, had her edit her name and draw longer hair, with some other additions.

and with gender-conforming peers from other families. All the children had definite preferences for clothes, toys, and activities. The transgender children selected whatever conformed to their chosen gender, just as the cisgender children did to the gender they always had (Fast & Olson, 2018).

Parental and social acceptance is far from guaranteed. One study of 129 transgender adolescents found that only a third of the mothers and a fourth of the fathers responded positively when their children first expressed their gender identity. As time went on, some parents became more accepting, but even when the children were age 15 to 21, most (64 percent) fathers did not accept their transgender children (Grossman et al., 2019).

Here definitions again become useful. A transgender girl is someone who was thought to be a boy at birth, but who identifies as a girl and follows female norms. In adulthood, this includes aspects of female identity that are neither necessary nor easy, such as wearing high heels and pantyhose. Like a cisgender woman, she may identify as a straight woman, or a lesbian, or as bisexual.

The same is true for a transgender man: He may identify as a straight man, a gay man, or a bisexual man. The crucial fact that makes someone transgender, either M→F or F→M, is that they *transi*tioned from the identity assigned at birth to who they now are.

Spontaneous Play

Children in all cultures and centuries like to play, developing their own games. Especially after age 6, play patterns reflect gender roles. A meta-analysis of 75 studies found that girls had strong preferences for "girl" toys, especially dolls, and boys for "boy" toys, especially trucks (Davis & Hines, 2020).

Activities also diverge. Boys tend to do more rough-and-tumble play, chasing and wrestling, running all around the playground during recess, developing their gross motor skills in group games with several players on each side. Girls are more likely to stay in one area, talking with a friend, playing jacks or foursquare, taking turns at hopscotch or jump rope. They develop balance and fine motor skills.

A detailed study of age and motor skills confirmed these gender differences but also found that the exact skill and age of the child mattered (Kokštejn et al., 2017). That suggests, of course, that adults influence what skills children master at which age, and that they need to consider each child as an individual.

Children of both sexes "self-socialize"; they seek to fit it with their friends, so from age 4 to 14 girls get more girlish and boys more boyish. This process is particularly evident in boys, who hate to be called "sissies." (Girls are more tolerant of being called "tomboys.")

By age 9, children not only practice gender segregation, they are comfortable with it. If a child is excluded because of ethnicity or race, schoolchildren call that unfair, but if a group of boys or girls excludes a child because of gender, most children consider that acceptable (Møller & Tenenbaum, 2011). Schools are sometimes segregated by sex, a practice controversial among adults but not usually among children.

Children voluntarily segregate by sex even when the activity is gender neutral (books, clay, computers) (Martin et al., 2013). For example, if a girl is at the computer, another girl is likely to join; if a boy is creating with clay, another boy might do likewise. Indeed, throughout childhood, gender distinctions are so powerful that every theory tries to explain why that is (see **Table 11.1**).

For their part, parents may be astonished at the power of gender preferences in young children. I know that I was (see A Case to Study).

TABLE 11.1

Theory	Essential Idea
Psychoanalytic theory	During the *phallic stage* (age 3–5), children notice whether or not they have a penis (*phallus* is the Greek word for penis). Boys experience *castration anxiety* and girls, *penis envy*. Both sexes masturbate and adore the parent of the other sex, named the *Oedipus* or *Electra complex*, both after the characters in ancient Greek dramas. Adoration of the other-sex parent leads to wanting to replace the same-sex parent. That desire is so frightening that it ushers in *latency* (age 6–10), a stage characterized by repression of sexual feelings.
Behaviorism	Children are conditioned to follow gender roles because they are reinforced or punished. For example, boys are called "handsome," girls called "pretty," and they are told "Boys don't cry" or "Girls don't fight." Peers reinforce gender-typical behavior: If a boy brings his doll to school, his classmates will punish him, not physically, but with words and laughter. He quickly learns.
Social learning theory	Children model themselves after their parents and their older siblings. Generally, mothers become more domestic when they have young children, and fathers tend to work longer hours. Children follow the examples they see, unaware that their very existence caused gender divergence.
Cognitive theory	Young children's immature cognition leads them to think in simple, egocentric categories, when appearance trumps logic. This is apparent in all children, including those who are transgender: Children want their hair and clothes to register their gender.
Sociocultural theory	Every culture distinguishes male and female, and children aspire to join adult society. Cultures vary by era and region, but children do not know that. In contemporary North America, girls want to be teachers and nurses; boys to be firefighters and police officers, because that is what they see.
Evolutionary theory	Evolutionary theory holds that sexual passion is a basic human drive, because all creatures must reproduce. Males and females follow that evolutionary mandate by seeking to attract the other sex—walking, talking, and laughing in traditional feminine or masculine ways. This evolutionary drive is born into our species, with genes, chromosomes, and hormones dictating that young boys gravitate toward rough-and-tumble play while girls care for their dolls.
Selectivity theories	As explained in Chapter 2, the newest set of theories emphasizes selection. Adults make choices, and distinguishing people by sex and gender is a choice that can change. For instance, consider politics. Female suffrage was a choice, made first in New Zealand in 1893, in the United States in 1920, and in Saudi Arabia in 2015. Recognition of same-sex marriage was a recent choice, not yet selected in about 50 nations. Unlike the other theories, selectivity theory suggests that most of our sex and gender distinctions could easily change.

WHAT HAVE YOU LEARNED?

1. When does a fetus become male or female?

2. What suggests that males are more vulnerable than females?

3. What suggests that females mature more quickly than males?

4. What is the difference between having an intersex condition and being transgender?

5. How and why do infants respond differently to men and women?

6. What gender differences are found in children's play?

7. How would boys and girls respond to gender segregation?

A CASE TO STUDY

The Berger Daughters

I dressed my baby girls in blue, trying to create a unisex world for them. I wanted to free them from gender stereotypes. I failed.

My eldest, Bethany, at about 4 years old told me:

Bethany: When I grow up, I'm going to marry Daddy.
    Me: But Daddy's married to me.
Bethany: That's all right. When I grow up, you'll probably be dead.
    Me: *[Determined to stick up for myself]* Daddy's older than me, so when I'm dead, he'll probably be dead, too.
Bethany: That's OK. I'll marry him when he gets born again.

I was dumbfounded, stunned by how Freudian this sounded. Bethany saw my face fall, and pitied me:

Bethany: Don't worry, Mommy. After you get born again, you can be our baby.

A few years later, my second-born daughter Rachel told me:

Rachel: When I get married, I'm going to marry Daddy.
    Me: Daddy's already married to me.
Rachel: *[With joy at her wonderful solution]* Then we can have a double wedding!

My third daughter, Elissa, left a valentine on my husband's pillow on February 14th (see **Figure 11.2**).

Finally, when Sarah turned 5, she also said she would marry her father. I told her she couldn't, because he was married to me. Her response revealed one more hazard of screen time: "Oh, yes, a man can have two wives. I saw it on television."

FIGURE 11.2
Pillow Talk Elissa placed this artwork on my husband's pillow. My pillow, beside it, had a less colorful, less elaborate note—an afterthought. It read, "Dear Mom, I love you too."

As you remember from Chapter 1, a single example (one family with four daughters) does not prove that Freud was correct. I still think Freud was wrong on many counts, and I am proud that all four girls became college-educated, professionally employed women. But in many ways, they are following gender-specific paths. Freud's description of the phallic stage seems less bizarre than I once thought.

Adolescence and Early Adulthood

As you just read, the bodies of boys and girls are quite similar during childhood. Although gender differences are apparent, physiological ones are less so. Then puberty!

It begins with hormones. Although the adrenal glands produce estrogens and androgens in everyone, *estrogens* (from the ovaries) are far greater in females while *androgens* (from the testes) are far greater in males. Those hormones affect the entire body, from hairline to foot width, in sex-specific ways.

The most obvious changes are in body shape and sex organs, which increase in size many times over. Those hormones also affect the psyche, causing thoughts and urges, fantasies and actions. Children become adults, first in identity, and then, in early adulthood, in roles and activities.

Gender and Sexuality

Remember from Chapter 10 that Erikson termed the fourth type of identity *sexual identity*, now called gender identity. As with the other aspects of identity, adolescents figure out who they are, so they can move forward in their lives.

The hormones of puberty awaken teens to sexual interest and arousal. Many middle schoolers imagine sexual encounters, first at a distance, perhaps staring at a magazine, a screen, a celebrity on a distant stage. Soon, closer people become the object of sexual interest, and exchanging glances, text messages, and short conversations may begin a romance. By ninth grade, about half of adolescents have begun dating (Kreager et al., 2016b).

Then, "progression of sexual events among adolescents follows a fairly consistent sequence: kissing and holding hands, breast and chest fondling, manual genital contact, touching under or without clothes, touching genitals directly, oral sex, and penile–vaginal intercourse, followed by less common variations, such as anal sex" (Efrati & Gola, 2019, pp. 420–421). That progression typically takes years, often extending past high school.

Every two years, the Youth Risk Behavior Survey (YRBS) asks dozens of questions of students throughout the United States. About one-fifth of ninth-graders and almost three-fifths of all high school seniors have had sexual intercourse (MMWR, June 15, 2018). Among seniors, boys and girls have similar rates (59 and 56 percent)

Every year from 2005 to 2019, the number of adolescents who chose a sexual orientation other than heterosexual increased, to over 15 percent. Gay or lesbian orientation was relatively uncommon (2.5 percent), with 8.7 percent choosing bisexual, and 4.5 percent "not sure" (see **Figure 11.3**).

The data suggest what the researchers called *dissonance*: Many heterosexual adolescents had sexual contact with people of the same gender, and many lesbian or gay adolescents had sexual contact with people of another gender. Adolescents do not equate sexual activity and sexual orientation.

Other surveys also find that gender diversity is increasing. This is most evident with transgender identity. In 2016, researchers estimated that 1.4 million people in the United States identified as transgender. That is about 0.6 percent, twice the rate a decade earlier (Flores et al., 2016).

The reason for the increase is not without controversy. Between 2014 and 2016, three times as many U.S. adolescents who had been designated female at birth identified as male (Littman, 2018; Marchiano, 2017). Some blamed that increase on an encouraging, but mistaken, peer culture. Transgender advocates object to that interpretation, claiming that celebration (not blame) is in order, because more young people can express their identity (Short, 2019; Wadman, 2018).

Identity and Health

The experiences and complexities of gender identity and sexual orientation precipitate emotions. The rates of substance abuse, anxiety, and depression rise for everyone in adolescence, male and female, but gender disparities are apparent. Depression and eating disorders increase dramatically among females, while delinquency and abuse of illegal drugs is higher for males (Miech et al., 2020).

Youth who are lesbian, gay, bisexual, transgender, or queer/questioning (LGBTQ) have higher rates of depression, anxiety, and substance abuse than other people their age. They are more likely to be suicidal and victims of bullying (Hatchel et al., 2019; Jun et al., 2019; O'Brien et al., 2019; Strutz et al., 2015).

Most medical and psychological professionals recognize that being LGBTQ is a risk factor for mental and physical health problems. That is why doctors are advised to ask patients about sexual orientation and gender identity to guide them in providing treatment. However, many are reluctant to do so, which may

Everywhere Glancing, staring, and—when emotions are overwhelming—averting one's eyes are part of the universal language of love. Although the rate of intercourse among teenagers is lower than it was, passion is expressed in simple words, touches, and, as shown here, the eyes on a cold day.

THINK CRITICALLY: Why are girls four times as likely to say they are bisexual than boys are?

FIGURE 11.3
These data come from the answers of high school students throughout the United States, to questions on the Youth Risk Behavior Survey (YRBS). Many had had no sexual experiences, and many had sexual experiences that differed from the orientation they chose for themselves.

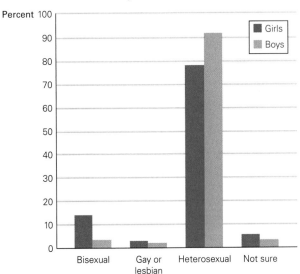

Data from Johns et al., 2020.

indicate more about attitudes among the older generations than the younger ones (Grasso et al., 2019).

Professional views are shifting. Evidence comes from the *Diagnostic and Statistical Manual of Mental Disorders (DSM)*. The fourth edition of that manual diagnosed *gender identity disorder* in people with "a strong and persistent cross-gender identification" (American Psychiatric Association, 2004). The fifth edition instead described *gender dysphoria*, which is a conflict between a person's assigned gender and the gender with which they identify. (American Psychiatric Association, 2013).

This is not simply a vocabulary change. A *disorder* means that something is seriously wrong, no matter how a person feels about it, whereas *dysphoria* may be caused by society, family, peers, or the individual. Dysphoria can occur in anyone of any gender.

VIDEO: Romantic Relationships in Adolescence explores teens' attitudes and assumptions about romance and sexuality.

Changing Times

Cohort differences are evident. Being a young adult now is quite different in terms of ideas about sex than was true a generation ago. Same-sex experiences, and openness about female sexuality, are much more common in 2020 than a few decades ago.

There is widespread recognition of *sexism*, as prejudice against people because of their sex is called. The term was first used in the 1960s, when women realized that stereotypes about women were keeping women down, similar to the racism that led to discrimination against African Americans. Soon it became apparent that sexism stereotyped men as well, and that some attitudes that seem benevolent were, in fact, sexist (Hopkins-Doyle et al., 2019).

This has changed behavior of young adults, as reflected in data on college attendance. In 1950, 24 percent of the college students were female (they were "co-eds," a term that implied "add-ons"). In 2020, 56 percent were female. Put another way, in 1950, there was one co-ed for every three college men; now there are four women for every three men.

Another cohort change is more cohabitation with less pressure to marry. In former years, the goal for many young adults was to marry by age 21 or so. No longer. For many emerging adults, the ideal is *serial monogamy*, which means a series of several relationships, each exclusive for months or years (Olmstead, 2020).

Consequently, cohabitation has become is a common experience, beginning at about the same age as marriage once did. Most (an estimated range of 60–90 percent) young adults live with a sexual partner at some point (Sassler & Lichter, 2020).

Another example of cohort changes is decline in the once common *double standard*, with one set of rules for sexual activity for girls and another for boys. To be specific, boys were supposed to "make the first move" and to "score," which meant to have sex. Girls did not want "a reputation," which meant that they did not want boys talking about scoring with them. Parents enforced the double standard, with stricter curfews, supervision, and expectations for their daughters than for their sons.

The double standard is much reduced. Both genders are expected to be sexual, at about the same rate. The Me Too movement has exposed the double standard of earlier years, although neither sexism nor the double standard have totally disappeared.

Benefits and Costs

None of the three cohort changes—reductions in sexism, in pressure to marry, and in the double standard—are totally successful. Although there are many college students who are female, sexism is thought to be one reason that far fewer women enter STEM curricula. Cohabiting couples seem more likely to divorce

(Rosenfeld & Roesler, 2019); the double standard is still apparent in some ways (Guo, 2019), and sexual harassment still occurs.

Many researchers describe sexism in health care (Homan, 2019). Men do not go to doctors as often for preventive care, which increases their rate of prostate cancer and heart disease; health problems specific to women (e.g., contraception, prenatal care) are sometimes not covered by insurance. Sexism is also evident in salaries, promotions, and specialties of doctors and nurses.

Positive Change

That said, we should acknowledge the benefits that results from a greater acceptance of sexuality among young people, with more experiencing the joy of sex and with fewer ashamed or secretive. As sexual activity has become a shared experience, some of the problems of adolescent sex are less common. To be specific:

- *Teen births have decreased.* In the United States, the 2018 rate of births to teenage mothers (aged 15 to 19)was less than one-fourth the rate when sexism was first named, with the biggest drop among Hispanic teens (J. Martin et al., November 27, 2019). Similar declines are evident in other nations. The most dramatic results are from China, where the 2015 teen pregnancy rate was one-tenth of the rate 50 years ago (reducing the projection of the world's population by about 1 billion).

- *The use of "protection" has risen.* Contraception, particularly condom use among adolescent boys, has increased markedly in most nations since 1990. The U.S. YRBS found that 60 percent of sexually active high school boys used a condom during their most recent intercourse (Johns et al., 2020) (see **Table 11.2**). When girls are treated as partners, not conquests, contraception becomes more prevalent.

- *The teen abortion rate is down.* In the United States, the teen abortion rate has declined every year since abortion became legal. The rate today is about half that of 20 years earlier. Likewise, teen abortion rates are decreasing in every nation with reliable data, whether or not that nation has liberal or restrictive abortion laws (Sedgh et al., 2015).

Sexually Transmitted Diseases

However, increasing sexual freedom has another problem, increasing rates of **sexually transmitted infection (STI)**, which is any infection transmitted through sexual contact. In the United States, half of all new STIs occur in people

sexually transmitted infection (STI)
A disease spread by sexual contact, including syphilis, gonorrhea, genital herpes, chlamydia, and HIV.

TABLE 11.2

Condom Use Among High School Students

Country	Sexually Active (% of Total)	Used Condom at Last Intercourse (% of Those Sexually Active)
France	20	84
England	29	83
Canada	23	78
Russia	33	75
Israel	14	72
United States	29	54

Data from Currie et al., 2009; Centers for Disease Control and Prevention, October 9, 2018.

ESPECIALLY FOR Health Practitioners
How might you encourage adolescents to seek treatment for STIs? (see response, page 331)

ages 15 to 25, even though this age group has less than one-fourth of the sexually active people (Centers for Disease Control and Prevention, 2018).

A survey of adolescents in a U.S. pediatric emergency department found that half of the teenagers (average age 15) were sexually active and 20 percent of those had an STI—although that was not why they came for medical help (Miller et al., 2015).

There are hundreds of STIs. *Chlamydia* is the most frequently reported one; it often begins without symptoms, yet it can cause permanent infertility.

Another common one is *human papillomavirus (HPV)*, which has no immediate consequences but increases the risk of cancer. Fortunately, in about 1990, an effective vaccine was developed that should be given before sexual activity.

However, less than half of all U.S. adolescents are fully immunized (Hirth, 2019). Among the reasons: Some state health departments do not promote it, the vaccine was originally recommended only for girls (sexism again?), and full immunization requires three doses, so a person needs regular medical care, which is particularly scarce among those aged 15–25.

Syphilis may be the worst STI of all, because mothers transmit the virus to their newborns, who develop lifelong disabilities (and sometimes early death). The U.S. rate of *congenital syphilis* has been increasing since 2009, with the 2017 rate twice as high as the 2014 rate (Umapathi et al., 2019). Fortunately, this STI is still rare, but good (and early) prenatal care can prevent it. Thus, the increase indicates that health care does not reach the most vulnerable pregnant women.

Not rare is *HIV/AIDS*, the cause of death for an estimated 35 million people worldwide. Untreated, AIDS victims die a painful death, with multiple organ failure. HIV can now can be controlled with medication and good medical care that halts transmission of the virus, allowing women with HIV to give birth to healthy babies, and men and women who are HIV-positive to live a long life. However, many people with HIV do not know they are infected, and 16,000 of them died in the United States in 2018. Both sexism and homophobia are among the reasons HIV continues to be transmitted.

 DATA CONNECTIONS: Major Sexually Transmitted Infections: Some Basics offers more information about the causes, symptoms, and rates of various STIs.

Casual Sex

Another reason STIs are increasing is that, especially in adolescence and early adulthood, sex may occur with no other connection between the people (Olmstead, 2020). This is called, in an apt term used by college students, a **hookup**: a sexual interaction between partners who know and care little about each other, perhaps having met at a party just a few hours before. Hookups are more common among first-year college students than among those about to graduate, perhaps because older students are more likely to seek a steady partner (James-Kangal et al., 2018).

The desire for physical sex without emotional commitment is stronger in young men than in young women, either for hormonal (testosterone) or cultural (women want committed fathers if children are born) reasons. In a U.S. survey of 18- to 24-year-olds who had completed at least one year of college, 56 percent of the men but only 31 percent of the women said they had had a hookup (Monto & Carey, 2014).

That men and women have different expectations regarding a relationship may be reflected in what makes them jealous. Women are more likely to be upset if

hookup A sexual encounter between two people who are not in a romantic relationship. Neither intimacy nor commitment is expected.

their mate has a close, emotional connection with another woman; men are more upset if their partner has sex with someone else (Buss & Schmitt, 2019).

DATA CONNECTIONS: Sexual Behaviors of U.S. High School Students examines how sexually active teens really are.

Physical Contact

Thus far we have focused on words and attitudes more than on physical, sexual, interaction. That focus is important, of course. Deemphasizing categories such as straight and gay, male and female, are needed to help us notice the similarities in all people as well as the individuality of each one. But we should not ignore male/female differences in sexual activity, a particularly important topic during this age period, when people discover their own sexuality and that of their partners.

At puberty and then increasing during adolescence, sexual impulses trigger physiological arousal, evident in the genitals, the heart rate, and many other body reactions. That is universal, but there are also significant differences between males and females that need to be recognized as people seek a mutually satisfying interaction.

In adolescence and young adulthood, arousal is quicker and more evident in males than females. The expression varies by culture: Caressing, oral sex, nipple stimulation, and kissing are all taboo in some cultures, expected in others.

The classic manual on sex (Comfort, 2013) notes many male/female differences. Males seem more compelled toward intercourse and oral sex; women may want more caressing and kissing. Men experience a refractory period after orgasm when orgasm is not possible; women desire more foreplay and afterplay.

The urge to masturbate is stronger in males than females (Driemeyer et al., 2016), with culture being influential: Some religions consider masturbation a shameful sin, others a God-given pleasure; some cultures expect mutual masturbation, others do not.

Men are more likely to feel addicted to pornography and distressed by sexual fantasies, compulsions, and actions (Dickenson et al., 2018; Rowland et al., 2020). Such distress is more likely under age 25, especially if the young man is no longer closely connected to his parents (Astle et al., 2019; Efrati & Gola, 2019).

In every culture with good data, males have more sexual partners than females do. That begins in high school, when the 2017 YRBS study found that students who had had four or more partners were more often male than female (12 and 8 percent) (MMWR, June 15, 2018). That pattern, with more young men than young women but relatively few overall having multiple partners, is also the case in early adulthood, with men more likely to seek casual sex than women.

It is useful for everyone to recognize these male/female differences, not only for a happy relationship but also to avoid date rape and sexual assault. That aggression may begin with both sexes seeking mutual pleasure, but women wanting to avoid casual sex, and men assuming that women share their sexual desires.

This topic is complicated by many old myths: about men (they can't control themselves), about women (they want sex but don't admit it), and about rape itself (an attack by a stranger, or involving a woman who is drugged). All three of these are false, but historically men did not recognize that sex without consent is an aggressive act.

To probe the differences in perception, one team wrote a sequence, beginning when a man and woman met in a bar and ending with her reporting rape. In the United States and the Philippines, 407 college women were asked when they would have stopped the interaction (Tuliao et al., 2017). Cultural trends as well as many individual differences were found. You can imagine some people saying that the woman should not have invited the man to her apartment, and others saying she should not have accused him of rape.

Overall, young men may be distressed if they do not have a sexual partner. Young women may have the opposite problem. They may be distressed if they do have a partner! That is one possible conclusion of the next study.

A study of 3,923 adult women in the United States found that those who *voluntarily* had sex before age 16 were more likely to divorce later on, whether or not they became pregnant or later married their first sexual partner. The same study found that adolescent girls whose first sexual experience was unwanted (either "really didn't want [it]" or "had mixed feelings") were also likely to divorce (Paik, 2011, p. 477).

To summarize, both sexes can be aroused, both can respond to touch, words, and sights, both can experience the intense pleasure of orgasm. Yet mutual understanding and communication is needed for both to be happy.

Everyone needs to realize that men and women might differ but also that each individual has a particular body and mind. As one wag said, "the most important sexual organ for both men and women is not between their legs but between their ears."

Less Sexual Activity

The final topic regarding problems among adolescents and young adults may be surprising: too little sexual activity. Over the past decades in the United States, every gender, ethnic, and age group is *less* sexually active than the previous cohort. Between 1993 and 2017, intercourse experience among African American high school students decreased 42 percent (to 46 percent) among European Americans, down 18 percent (to 39 percent); and among Latinos, down 27 percent (to 41 percent) (MMWR, June 15, 2018) (see **Figure 11.4**).

That is usually seen positively, as fewer babies are born to teenage mothers. The overall birth rate is down among people under age 30. That reduces overpopulation, energy consumption, and unwanted children.

But there is a downside as well. As already mentioned, the intimacy of sex connects one human with another. If young adults have fewer sexual experiences, that may mean they also have fewer social connections and more loneliness. Between 2000 and 2018, the percentage of men who had no sexual activity in the past year increased from 20 percent to 31 percent, and women from 15 percent to 19 percent (Ueda et al., 2020).

FIGURE 11.4

Boys and Girls Together Boys tend to be somewhat more sexually experienced than girls during the high school years, but since the YRBS began in 1991, the overall U.S. trend has been toward equality in rates of sexual activity.

Percent of U.S. Ninth- to Twelfth-Graders Who Say They Have Had Sexual Intercourse

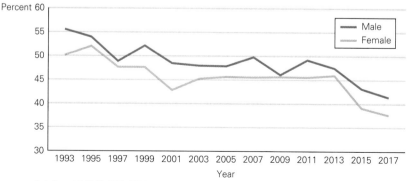

Data from MMWR, 1992–2018.

Since sex fosters the social bonding that humans need, promoting health and happiness lifelong, lack of sexual interaction may mean lack of social relationships. Among young adults, rates are particularly low among female college students and among unemployed men (Ueda et al., 2020).

To address this problem, we need to know why it occurs. Many reasons have been suggested: fear of disease, fear of pregnancy, more female assertion, more male unemployment, more male imprisonment for nonviolent crimes. One commentator blames technology:

> Between the 24-hour availability of entertainment and the temptation to use smartphones and social media, sexual activity may not be as attractive as it once was. Put simply, there are now many more choices of things to do in the late evening than there once were and fewer opportunities to initiate sexual activity if both partners are engrossed in social media, electronic gaming, or binge watching.
>
> [Twenge, 2020, p. e203889]

Ironically, many young adults seek partners via online dating sites that match preferences (some have dozens of questions, asking about everything from pets to kissing) and suggest who would like whom. Those sites include photographs, religious beliefs, ethnicity, and much more—which some argue are the surface aspects of a relationship. That may lead to a "rejection mind-set," a focus on superficial aspects of a person and not the deeper bonding needed for commitment (Pronk & Denissen, 2020).

Many readers of this text are young adults. Do you agree that the lack of sex among your generation signifies a problem?

WHAT HAVE YOU LEARNED?

1. What changes in gender identity have occurred in recent years?
2. What sex differences are apparent in depression and delinquency?
3. What is the double standard and how has it changed over time?
4. What has gotten better in the sexual activities of adolescents in the past decades?
5. Why are sexuality transmitted diseases increasing?
6. What male/female differences are there in sexual drives and actions?
7. Why might less sexual activity be a problem?

Adulthood

In adulthood, men and woman follow many paths, described in other chapters. Here we consider only two aspects of adulthood that are specifically and profoundly influenced by gender: employment and child care. Then we look at late adulthood, a time of life when gender matters a great deal.

Employment

Once men hoped to find a wife who would take care of him and his children, and women hoped to become a wife and mother. Adult women were not expected to be employed: If a married woman worked, that meant that her husband was not "a good provider." In the 1930s, when many men could not find work, laws were passed to make it illegal to hire a married woman.

In 1950, only 28 percent of women aged 45–54 (past the age when many mothers thought they should be home with their young children) were employed.

Maskot/Getty Images

Family Balance Work–life balance is much easier if governments and families adjust to the demands of work and parenthood. This family is in Sweden, where fathers are granted paternity leave, and thus are more comfortable taking care of young infants.

⬤ **Observation Quiz:** What can you see in the photo that suggests that this family is committed to raising a family together? (see answer, page 331) ⬆

Unmarried women sometimes worked, but their jobs were in vocations that were thought to be suited for women: Nurses and secretaries were almost always women. Only men could be police*men*, fire*men*, or post*men*.

By 2018, that flipped. Only 26 percent of the women aged 45–54 were *not* in the labor market. The employed 74 percent were usually married. As part of the feminist revolution, some adults filled jobs that once were exclusively for another sex.

As current college students are well aware, gender equity is not yet attained, but progress is apparent. Overall, women earned, on average, a third less than men in 1980; they earned a seventh less in 2018 (Kochhar, 2020). No job is exclusive to one gender: 9 percent of the nurses are men and 13 percent of police officers are women.

A new problem has appeared, called *work–life balance*, which is how to combine employment and personal life in such a way as to enhance, rather than diminish, human development. No matter the work entails, those who achieve balance are happier and healthier (Brauner et al., 2019).

This dilemma first arose with mothers who had to balance work and caring for children: Employers instituted on-site day care, or flexible schedules for mothers. It soon became obvious, as found in a survey of 33 nations, that work–life balance could be a problem for men as for women (Noda, 2020). Soon, adults without children realized that their work sometimes interfered with the rest of their life, such as their leisure, community involvement, and social interactions.

Thus, work–life balance is now recognized as a problem for everyone, with or without children, employees or employers (Kelliher et al., 2019). Currently, work–life imbalance requires many solutions, including flexible scheduling, remote work, paternal as well as maternal leave, paid leave to care for a needy family member, part-time work, self-employment, and so on.

Family Life

Many researchers describe the women's liberation movement as a "stalled revolution," with progress evident in the public sphere (employment, education, politics) but not in the domestic one (Scarborough et al., 2019). Women still do much more home care—cleaning, cooking, washing—than men do.

Caregiving

The male–female differences in domestic work are most evident in caregiving. Mothers do most of the child care, and when young children are grown, women still are more often caregivers for their adult children who are ill or disabled and for older adults, especially their aged parents or parents-in-law. They care for grandchildren and for unrelated children.

When older partners need care, "it's the wife who has to look after the man" (Williams et al., 2017). When a wife needs care, husbands find other caregivers (a daughter, a paid helper). Indeed, a detailed study of caregiving found not only that women are more often caregivers of husbands than vice versa (in part because brides are younger than grooms) but also that their husbands, on average, need more intense care, in part because they are less likely to enter nursing homes (Swinkels et al., 2019).

This caregiving disparity was evident in a large U.S. study (the Health and Retirement Study) that queried grandparents and found that of those who were not married (because of divorce or death), 52 percent of the women and 20 percent of the men provided some grandchild care (Ho, 2015). For older married couples, the grandfathers said they provided as much care as the grandmothers, but usually they were with their wife when they were providing care, and she did most of the work.

Many studies also consider financial support for family members. Here men may provide more help, in part because of cultural norms and in part because of income. Wives may quit work when babies are born; husbands may take on overtime.

Currently, both grandparents are usually employed (the first grandchild arrives at about age 50) when grandchildren are born. Grandmothers often reduce employment to care for grandchildren; grandfathers may postpone retirement if their descendants need financial support.

Of course, this gender difference does not always hold true. Fathers may provide significant guidance as well as caregiving, and many grandfathers are instrumental in the lives of their grandchildren (Coall et al., 2016). Individual differences in caregiving sometimes override the gender norms.

Custody After Divorce

Traditionally, women avoided divorce unless they were desperate, because they needed a man's income to support the family. Then, in the 70s, divorces became more common, in part because women found jobs. Currently, women are more likely to want a divorce than men are.

Until recently, custody decisions assumed that children in their "tender years" needed mothers' care and fathers' income. Women were considered to be naturally, genetically, and hormonally more nurturing, and fathers were required to pay child support. Fathers were awarded custody only when a man could prove that the mother was unfit (because of drug addiction, child abuse, or some other behavior thought to be inappropriate for a mother).

Fortunately, that has changed, certainly in the research on child development and hopefully in the courts. Children benefit from both parents, who both can provide nurturance and financial support. That has led to a movement toward joint physical (not just legal) custody, when children spend at least a fourth of the time living with their fathers and the rest with their mothers.

That seems to benefit children, because each parent contributes to child welfare (Nielsen, 2018). Many studies find that joint custody is better for the parents as well (Sodermans et al., 2015). However, one study questions this conclusion.

Sweden was one of the first nations to mandate joint custody after divorce, unless there was a compelling reason not to do so. A major study asked 4,000 Swedish parents how worried and anxious they were (Fritzell et al., 2020). It was not surprising that fathers and mothers who were living together and raising their own children were lowest in worry and anxiety. What was surprising is that single parents with joint custody were more troubled than single parents who were solo.

The authors suggest that some fathers in joint custody do not know how to care for their children alone, day after day, and that, when the children are with the fathers, some mothers suffer from "loneliness, longing, and of not always knowing how the child fares . . . [because of] the internalized ideal of mothers and fathers" (Fritzell et al., 2020, p. 8).

One scholar suggests that the effects of joint custody depends on the education and income of the spouses (Steinbach, 2019). When researchers study highly educated adults, joint custody seems best, because fathers know how to relate to their children and mothers welcome some time for their own pursuits. The Swedish study found that low-SES immigrant mothers were most anxious in joint custody.

This is an example of a need for an intersectional perspective, as described in Chapter 1. The impact of various norms and policies (not just on custody but on every aspect of sex and gender) may depend on income, ethnicity, and

VISUALIZING DEVELOPMENT Marital Status in the United States

Adults seek committed partners but do not always find them—age, cohort, and culture are always influential. Some choose to avoid marriage, more commonly in northern Europe and less commonly in North Africa than in the United States. As you see, in 2018, U.S. emerging adults were unlikely to marry, middle-aged adults had the highest rates of separation or divorce, and widows often chose to stay alone while widowers often remarried.

MARITAL STATUS IN THE UNITED STATES

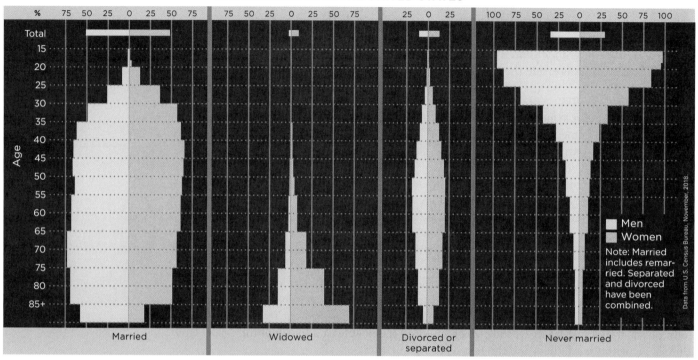

TOP REASONS FOR GETTING MARRIED, ACCORDING TO U.S. ADULTS

NEARLY HALF OF NEW MARRIAGES INVOLVE REMARRIAGES

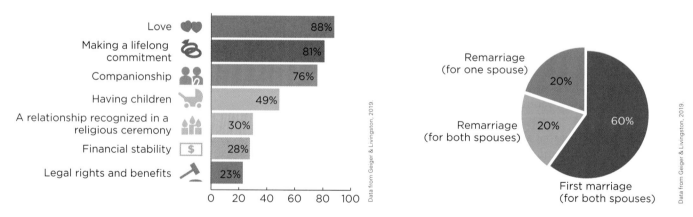

LIVING ARRANGEMENTS OF 25 TO 34 YEAR OLDS

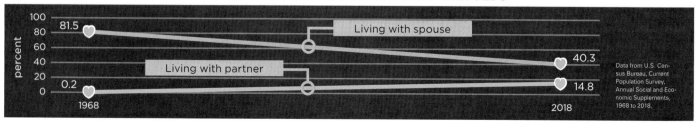

sexual orientation. The next generation of studies will, hopefully, take that into account.

Later Adulthood

Gender matters in late adulthood, sometimes in surprising ways. Sex is one example.

Hormones and Sexual Activity

With age, the level of sex hormones circulating in the adult bloodstream declines—suddenly in women, gradually in men. As a result, sexual desire, arousal and frequency of intercourse decrease. Reproduction becomes impossible for women, less likely in men, as described in Chapter 4.

However, adult sexual bonding and satisfaction does not correlate with hormones or intercourse. Instead, a study of older adults in Britain found that being in reasonably good health, having a partner, and experiencing a range of affectionate activities—kissing, cuddling, handholding—correlates with sexual satisfaction much less than age or frequency of intercourse does (Erens et al., 2019). Similarly, a study in five other nations (Brazil, Germany, Japan, Spain, United States) found that although sexual activity decreased during each decade of adulthood, most couples had a "high level of physical affection and relationship happiness" (Rosen et al., 2016, p. 159).

The data suggest that even though frequency of intercourse declines with age, sexual satisfaction often increases *after* middle age. How can that be? Consider the view from science.

Physical Touch Older couples, including this one in New York City, develop many ways to express love, beyond the sexual intercourse that may be the focus for younger couples.

Observation Quiz: What three signs of synchrony are visible here? (see answer, page 331) ↑

A VIEW FROM SCIENCE

Sex After Age 70

Sexual needs and interactions vary extremely from one person, one cohort, and one context to another. Further, questionnaires and physiological measures designed for young bodies may be inappropriate for the aged (Erens et al., 2019). Accordingly, two researchers studied elderly sex using a method called *grounded theory*.

They found 34 people (17 couples, aged 50 to 86, married an average of 34 years), interviewing each privately and extensively. They read and reread all the transcripts, tallying responses and topics by age and gender (that was the grounded part). Then they analyzed common topics, interpreting trends (that was theory).

They concluded that sexual activity is more a social construction than a biological event (Lodge & Umberson, 2012). All their informants said that intercourse was less frequent with age, including four couples for whom intercourse stopped completely because of the husband's health. Nonetheless, more respondents said that their sex life had improved than said it deteriorated (44 percent compared to 30 percent). Those 44 percent who reported improvement were more likely to be older (age 65–86) than middle-aged (50–65). How could that be?

The authors write that the reason might be that "images of masculine sexuality are premised on high, almost uncontrollable levels of penis-driven sexual desire" (Lodge & Umberson, 2012, p. 430). Meanwhile, the culture "implore[s] women to be both desirable and receptive to men's sexual desires and impulses," deeming "older women and their bodies unattractive" (Lodge & Umberson, 2012, p. 430).

According to that interpretation, middle-aged adults are distressed when they first realize that aging has changed their sexual interactions. Both genders feel inadequate. But after another decade or so, they then conclude that the young idea of good sex (frequent intercourse) is too limited. Instead they enjoy other aspects of their sex lives, and that advances their love for each other. As one man over age 70 said:

> I think the intimacy is a lot stronger . . . more often now we do things like holding hands and wanting to be close to each other or touch each other.
>
> *[Jim, quoted in Lodge & Umberson, 2012, p. 438]*

An older woman said her marriage improved because

> We have more opportunities and more motivation. Sex was wonderful. It got thwarted, with . . . the medication he is on. And he hasn't been functional since. The doctors just said that it is going to be this way, so we have learned to accept that. But we have also learned long before that there are more ways than one to share your love.
>
> *[Helen, quoted in Lodge & Umberson, 2012, p. 437]*

Gender and Personality

Some observers suggest that each gender takes on traits that earlier were exclusive to another gender. Indeed, one observer describes a *gender crossover* (Guttman, 1987), suggesting that roles switch, with older women becoming assertive and older men become nurturant, each gender "reclaiming" the positive characteristics that had been reserved for another gender.

That idea does not seem supported by research. For the most part, longitudinal research finds that people keep the personality traits they had earlier, with older people slightly less open to new experiences, slightly less outgoing, slightly more agreeable (Specht, 2017). If an older woman seems more assertive, or an older man seems more nurturant, instead of a crossover, perhaps they had those traits all along but could not express them because of restrictive gender norms.

There is, however, one difference that varies with gender: feelings of isolation and despair. As you remember, depression is more common among adolescent girls than boys. Then, average self-esteem rises in all genders, including those who are LGBTQ, with men averaging higher levels than women. Self-esteem reaches a peak at about age 60, and then decreases a little, more in men than women. Extroversion and openness also decline, and neuroticism increases. Optimism increases, particularly in women.

During most of adulthood, U.S. males are about three times as likely to die by suicide (see **Figure 11.5**). That finding is explained either by available means (specifically that males have more access to guns, which are the primary suicide weapon in the United States) or by hormones (testosterone again, that increases sudden, destructive rage). But it could be a lifetime of gender conformity, making men less able to deal with their emotions by talking with someone else.

Age has a marked impact, for both men and women, in opposite ways. With each decade after age 50, women are less likely to die by suicide than younger women, but over the same decades, men are more likely to kill themselves than younger men. These two trends result in an astonishing sex difference: Among the oldest people, the male suicide rate is 10 times the female rate (National Institute of Mental Health, September, 2020).

Understanding the reason may help in reducing male suicides. The fact that women are caregivers may be significant, in that caregiving requires some social interaction and provides a reason for living. Without that, an older person is at risk. This suggestion arises from data showing that the older men who are most likely to kill themselves are the ones who are alone, either widowed or never married.

Health

Every disease is more common in one sex or another, with men more likely to have lethal diseases and women more likely to have chronic ones. A few diseases are

FIGURE 11.5

Despairing Men, Hopeful Women? The gender differences in suicide are puzzling at every age, but the rates going in opposite directions in late adulthood are particularly astonishing. It is hard to think of a biological explanation, but many sociological hypotheses need exploration.

Suicide Rate by Age Group—United States

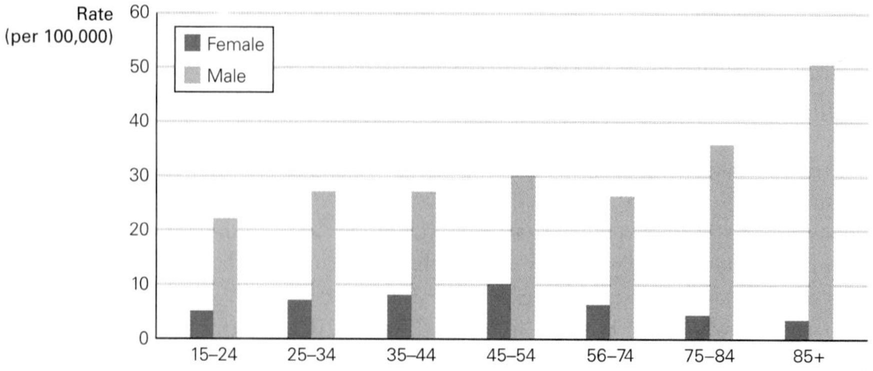

Data from National Institute of Mental Health, September, 2020.

sex-specific, including two of the most common cancers, breast and prostate. Both occur to about one in seven adults, and both were once always fatal but now at least three of every four adults diagnosed with these cancers survives, sometimes to live decades longer.

Most other diseases occur in people of any gender, but differ in rate and treatment. For example, heart attacks were once far more common in middle-aged men than women, but reduction of those rates has meant that cardiovascular deaths now tend to occur at age 70 or later, and are the leading cause of death for both men and women. There is one significant gender difference, however: Men's cardiovascular deaths tend to be sudden, while women's are chronic; they live with failing cardiovascular systems for years.

Sex differences are apparent for other diseases as well. Women have higher rates of autoimmune (e.g., lupus) and chronic (e.g., arthritis and Alzheimer's) diseases than men, but men are more likely to die of COVID-19.

When nations are compared, sex differences vary in ways that are not understood. For example, diabetes is known to be a risk factor for death in late adulthood, and incidence, diagnosis, and treatment are affected by gender, genes, and weight. In the United States, rates are far higher among African Americans than European Americans, with gender differences as well: Rates are higher in African American women than African American men.

However, diabetes rates are increasing in Africa in ways that raise questions about sex differences. Women have higher rates of diabetes in Cameroon, South Africa, and Uganda, but men have higher rates in Ghana, Nigeria, and Sierra Leone (Hilawe et al., 2013).

Longevity

Finally, longevity clearly favors women (see **Figure 11.6**). In 1900 this was not necessarily the case, because the death rate of childbearing woman was high, before safe abortions, before sterilization prevented childbirth fever, before cesareans with anesthesia and infection control allowed safe nonvaginal birth if the fetal head was too large.

None of those problems need occur today, although they still do in nations with few doctors, and inadequate public health. In advanced nations less than 1 birth in 10,000 results in maternal death. (The United States is the highest among developed nations, at about 2 deaths per 10,000). Now that maternal mortality is rare, women live an average five years longer than men.

These discrepancies seem to originate from chromosomes, not culture. But given what we have learned in the past 50 years, as reviewed in this chapter, we cannot be so sure.

Men, for instance, do not go to the doctor as often as women do—is that a sex or gender difference, and would men live longer if they had more medical help?

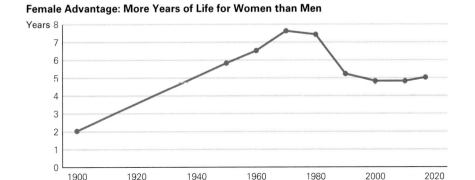

Female Advantage: More Years of Life for Women than Men

FIGURE 11.6

New Challenges in Every Generation Two cohort changes explain these fluctuations: first, safer childbirth, then reduced heart attack deaths. In future years, the female advantage will increase again, because of opioid deaths, suicide, and COVID, all of which are more frequent in men than women.

They do not eat as healthy a diet, they do not have as many social connections, they smoke and drink more and hike less.

Those five years that men lose by being male seem substantial, until we look at other factors that influence life expectancy. National wealth seems the most glaring: The average life span in the wealthiest nations is 21 years longer than the average in the poorest nations (85 compared to 54). This again suggests a problem noted in the beginning of this chapter: We humans may focus more on sex and gender differences than on other, more critical, differences among humans.

WHAT HAVE YOU LEARNED?

1. For whom is work–life balance a problem and why?
2. What are the typical caregiving differences between men and women?
3. Why is joint custody after divorce more common now than it was?
4. How and why does sexual activity change in late adulthood?
5. What happens to personality traits as people grow older?
6. How and why do suicide rates differ for men and women in late adulthood?
7. What suggests that male/female differences in health and longevity are the result of nature?
8. What suggests that male/female differences in health and longevity are the result of nurture?

Aggression

To wrap up this chapter, we now focus on aggression, a topic that provides a window on sex and gender at every stage of life. Aggression could be discussed in many chapters, but it is here because some people assume that males are the aggressors and females are the victims.

What Is Aggression?

Aggression is actively and needlessly harming someone else. It is beyond self-assertion, beyond self-defense, beyond saving someone from worse harm. Some aggressive acts seem small, called *microaggressions*, and some are huge, like dropping a bomb on a city.

People justify aggression, which raises more issues and long-term effects. But that is not our focus here. Instead, we ask a smaller question: Is one gender more aggressive than another? To answer that question, we need to recognize that aggression varies by motives and methods.

Motives for Aggression

instrumental aggression Hurtful behavior that is intended to get something that another person has.

reactive aggression An impulsive retaliation for another person's intentional or accidental hurtful action.

relational aggression Nonphysical acts, such as insults or social rejection, aimed at harming the social connection between the victim and other people.

bullying aggression Unprovoked, repeated physical or verbal attack, especially on victims who are unlikely to defend themselves.

- **Instrumental aggression** When someone wants something and uses aggression to get it. For example, a toddler grabs a toy from another child, a child pushes to be first in line, or an adult raises the price of a lifesaving drug to become richer.
- **Reactive aggression** When people react to a hurt, such as an insult or a physical attack, by insulting, hitting, or in some other aggressive way.
- **Relational aggression** When people try to improve their own social standing by demeaning or rejecting others. A child might say, "You can't be my friend," or someone of any age might spread rumors or gossip to damage someone's reputation.
- **Bullying aggression** When people harm someone else for their own pleasure.

Methods of Aggression

- **Physical aggression** With physical force—hitting, kicking, biting, shooting.
- **Verbal aggression** With words, either directly or indirectly.
- **Material aggression** With objects, such as defacing another's books or papers, or stealing, destroying, or hiding something.
- **Cyber Aggression** With technology, such as sending embarrassing smartphone photographs to many people, or posting slurs and attacks on social media.

Aggressive Children

All babies use instrumental and reactive aggression. Boy and girl infants are equally likely to grab toys, push people, and throw objects (Hay, 2017). Temperament is more influential on infant aggression than XX or XY chromosomes. Some babies seem quick to anger, and then they act on it (Hay et al., 2011).

Over the years of childhood, the brain matures and empathy increases. Gender differences in aggression begin to appear, as children learn what is expected and effective for their gender. By age 6 if not earlier, boys are more likely to use physical aggression, whereas girls use verbal aggression. Both can be bullies, usually bullying others of the same gender.

Indirect aggression, including cyberattacks or destroying possessions, becomes more common as children approach adolescence, in part because access to technology and appreciation of objects increases. Puberty also leads to more relational aggression, because social status among peers is crucial, and popularity entails targeted aggression (Cillessen & Mayeux, 2004). This varies by classroom norms or community standards, but less by gender, as both boys and girls use indirect aggression to increase popularity.

Teachers accept relational aggression much more readily than physical aggression (Swit, 2019). The saying "Sticks and stones will hurt my bones, but words will never hurt me" is false, but many adults believe it. Consequently, school bullies are less likely to pummel someone and more likely to destroy their self-esteem.

Female researchers in the United States noticed that much aggression is relational, not physical (Coyne & Ostrov, 2018). Especially in early adolescence, girls increase in relational and cyber aggression: Their overall rates of aggression are close to the boys' rates, or maybe higher (P. Smith et al., 2019; Zimmer-Gembeck et al., 2013). No researcher now thinks that aggression is a "uniquely masculine trait" (Been et al., 2019).

Aggressive Adults

Although most adults, most of the time, help rather than harm each other, and although girls can be as aggressive as boys when all forms of aggression are considered, we also must note that men are expected to be more aggressive than women, and they are so. If one man confronts another on the street or in the boardroom, the man often counterattacks. If a woman is confronted, aggression is less likely. She may deflect, defer, joke, or apologize.

The gender divide in aggression among adults is starkly evident in physical aggression. Worldwide, 96 percent of murderers are men (UNODC, 2013), who usually kill other men. Further, in every nation men are much more likely to rape and attack, either in international wars or in local communities (Evans et al., 2019; Hudson & Hodgson, 2020).

Domestic Aggression

In the privacy of the home, as well, women are far more likely to be physically harmed by their sexual partner than vice versa. Rates are declining, but twice as

Would You Stop It? Children teach each other when physical play becomes aggression. A clue for adults: Look at facial expressions. These boys may be playing.

physical aggression Using physical force to harm someone.

verbal aggression Using words to harm someone.

material aggression Harming someone by defacing or destroying something that belongs to them.

cyber aggression Harming someone by using technology, such as social media.

ESPECIALLY FOR Teachers How can a teacher reduce aggression among students? (see answer, page 331)

situational couple violence Fighting between romantic partners that is brought on more by the situation than by the deep personality problems of the individuals. Both partners are typically victims and abusers.

intimate terrorism A violent and demeaning form of abuse in a romantic relationship, in which the victim (usually female) is frightened to fight back, seek help, or withdraw. In this case, the victim is in danger of physical as well as psychological harm.

many wives as husbands are killed by their spouse (Fridel & Fox, 2019). Thankfully, such partner murders are rare.

When all forms of aggression are considered, fewer gender differences appear. Although men are more publicly aggressive, women may be more likely to be aggressive within their homes, hurling insults, shunning intimacy, destroying possessions (Archer, 2004). Among teenagers, daughters seem as likely to yell at their parents as sons.

Given that, it becomes obvious that gendered assumptions of aggression miss the mark. This is evident in the social response to spousal abuse. There are hundreds of shelters for women who are victims of violent husbands. That is a good thing: Women sometimes need a safe place. But it is a mistake to assume that men are more aggressive than women because of their genes and hormones (Furtuna, 2014, 2016). Some men need a safe place!

Remember that adults of every age and gender are not usually aggressive. One reason for the survival of our species is that humans tend to forgive their friends, befriend strangers, and tolerate enemies (Bregman, 2020). Only a minority are markedly aggressive, and that minority includes males and females. How many people are aggressive, and how often they are, depends not only on nature but also nurture—frustration, stress, pain, and so on.

Common Couple Aggression

To protect both men and women, we need to recognize two forms of couple aggression, each with distinct causes, patterns, and means of prevention.

Situational couple violence occurs when both partners fight—with words, slaps, and exclusion (leaving home, refusing sex, and so on). The *situation* causes stress, and then the partners attack each other. When coping methods are destructive (such as substance abuse) and external stress is high, such as for many low-income, non-White, or same-sex couples, adults may turn on those closest to them.

Regarding intimate partner violence, rates between adults who are same-sex partners are equal or higher than among mixed-sex couples. Lesbian couples may be more likely to abuse each other than gay couples (Longobardi & Badenes-Ribera, 2017; Rollè et al., 2018). This is another bit of evidence that women can be as aggressive as men, when all forms of aggression are considered and when the location is home.

In situational violence, aggression is mutual. One partner utters an aggressive comment and the other slaps them, for instance. Often the roots are in the culture, in financial stress, and in childhood patterns, not primarily in the adults. That is a hopeful finding: Adults who care for each other but are caught in reciprocal domestic abuse can learn to overcome the culture of violence.

This explains something that surprised some social workers: Many abused partners say they love each other and want to stay together. They seek counseling to help their relationship, rather than to end it (Visser et al., 2020).

Effective treatment may be particularly important if children are involved, because children are harmed if they witness their parents fight. Furthermore, couple violence may spill over to child maltreatment. This may explain another surprise: Children are more often abused by mothers than by fathers (U.S. Department of Health and Human Services, 2020). Here again, most parents love their children and want to learn how to guide them without harming them.

Intimate Terrorism

The other type of couple abuse is **intimate terrorism**. It is less common but more violent; instead of mutual aggression there is a power imbalance. Usually intimate terrorism involves a male abuser and female victim, although the sex roles can be reversed (Dutton, 2012). (See **Figure 11.7**.) It is dangerous to the victim and to anyone who intervenes.

Age at First Experience of Sexual Violence, Physical Violence, or Stalking

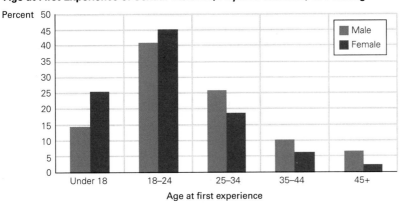

Data from Smith et al., 2018.

FIGURE 11.7

When Did It Begin? These data are from the U.S. Centers for Disease Control and Prevention, a reputable source. As you see, when victims are asked when the first incident of sexual violence, physical violence, or stalking occurred, emerging adulthood is the most likely time. For a sizable minority, the first incidence occurred before age 18 (especially for females) or after age 25 (especially for men). Almost never does intimate partner violence begin after age 45 (although victimization, once started, often continues). Not shown here are other data from this report, which shows that, over their lifetime, about a third of all adults have been victimized in some way (raped, physically abused, threatened, stalked). Rates are similar for both women (36 percent) and men (34 percent), although more women sought medical, legal, or psychological help in recovery than men did (25 percent of all women versus 11 percent of all men).

With intimate terrorism, the victim needs to be immediately separated from the abuser, relocated to a safe place, and given social support that restores independence. Both partners may resist that, because the terrorist gets some satisfaction from abuse, and the victim often submits and apologizes.

One strategy used by intimate terrorists is to isolate the victim from family and friends. That helps explain domestic violence among Latinx couples. Especially if they live far from other Latinx couples, women are more often perpetrators of spouse abuse than men are, in part because boys are taught "never hit a girl."

If a Latinx couple live in a neighborhood with many other Latinx people, another cultural value, *familism*, reduces domestic violence toward children and toward mates, in both partners (Soller & Kuhlemeier, 2019).

Revenge Porn

The crucial role of the social context is also evident in what is sometimes called revenge porn, which is posting in social media naked photos or videos of one's partner, to shame them in front of strangers (Eaton et al., 2020). Revenge porn tilts the aggressive balance, because women are much more vulnerable than men. Note, however, the problem would not occur without gendered emotions regarding sex.

What can be concluded from the research on gender and aggression? All children and adults can harm other people, and some of them do. How they do it, after age 2, is affected by their age, gender, and what they have been taught. We should not blame one sex: Everyone needs to learn, ideally in childhood but certainly by adulthood, how to express frustration, disagreement, and conflict.

That can be extended to this entire chapter. Although it may sound simplistic, especially given the complicated interpretations and variations of human sex and gender, we all need to learn how to respect and love each other.

WHAT HAVE YOU LEARNED?

1. What are four motives for aggression?

2. What are four varieties of aggression?

3. What are the sex/gender differences in aggression in infancy?

4. What are the sex/gender differences in aggression in childhood?

5. What are the sex/gender differences in aggression in adulthood?

6. What is the best outcome for situational couple violence?

7. What is the best outcome for intimate terrorism?

SUMMARY

Using Words

1. Sex refers to biological differences and gender to sociocultural differences between males and females. Sex and gender are interactive and intertwined, making a clear distinction between the two impossible.

2. The gender similarities hypothesis is that males and females are alike in most ways. Masculinity and femininity can be seen as extremes on a continuum, with most people, and most traits within any individual, somewhere on that line.

3. Sexual orientation refers to sexual attraction. People can be attracted to people of any sex or gender.

4. A nonbinary perspective means that gender identity is fluid and multifaceted, not either/or categories implied by the gender binary.

Before Puberty

5. Usually, the 23rd pair of chromosomes is XX (female) or XY (male) at conception, and then hormones at the beginning of the fetal stage shape the body and brain to be a boy or girl.

6. As fetuses and infants, males are more vulnerable, slower to mature, with language development faster in females. These effects are evident throughout childhood and are affected by parental nurture as well as nature.

7. By age 5, gender differences are strong, with children having definite ideas of activities, aspirations, and toys that are appropriate for girls or boys. Gender segregation continues throughout childhood.

Adolescence and Early Adulthood

8. Gender identity becomes a complex issue in adolescence, with about 15 percent of high school students not identifying as heterosexual.

9. Sexism and the double standard are increasingly recognized as problematic, although gender discrimination, both personal and institutional, has not disappeared.

10. Many problems that once were common in adolescence are less common today, include teen pregnancy and avoidance of condoms.

11. However, STIs and casual sex are increasingly common, and committed sexual partnerships are decreasing.

Adulthood

12. Employment of adult women has flipped, from one-fourth employed to one-fourth not employed. This has highlighted problems in work–life balance, which now is understood as a problem for fathers, for adults without children, and for employers, as well as for mothers.

13. Women are the prime caregivers, in childhood as well as later on. Fathers are increasingly recognized as important for children. This is leading to an increase in joint custody after divorce.

14. Older adults can continue their sexual interactions, although intercourse becomes less frequent. Personality patterns also continue. However, older women tend to be less despondent, while older men tend to be more so, as evident in suicide data.

15. Disease and death patterns differ for older men and women, with the latter living five years longer, on average. Both nature and nurture may be the reason.

Aggression

16. Aggression is harming someone else needlessly. There are many motives and types of aggression.

17. Infant boys and girls tend to be equally aggressive. In childhood, however, boys engage in more physical aggression and property destruction, while girls engage in verbal and relational aggression.

18. Most adults are kind to each other, not aggressive. However, when violent aggression occurs, men are more often the perpetrators.

19. In situational couple violence, both partners are aggressive, with women using words more than physical force. Couples want to learn how to relate to each other with less mutual attacking.

20. In intimate terrorism, the victim needs to be protected, and reconciliation is less likely. The social context is crucial, not only to protect the victim but also to avoid the social norms that allow this pattern to occur.

KEY TERMS

sex (p. 301)
gender (p. 301)
gender identity
  (p. 303)
gender binary
  (p. 303)
nonbinary (p. 303)

sexual orientation
  (p. 303)
intersex (p. 306)
transgender (p. 309)
sexually transmitted infection
  (STI) (p. 315)
hookup (p. 316)

instrumental aggression
  (p. 326)
reactive aggression (p. 326)
relational aggression
  (p. 326)
bullying aggression (p. 326)
physical aggression (p. 327)

verbal aggression (p. 327)
material aggression
  (p. 327)
cyber aggression (p. 327)
situational couple violence
  (p. 328)
intimate terrorism (p. 328)

APPLICATIONS

1. Gender indicators often go unnoticed. Go to a public place (park, restaurant, busy street) and spend at least 10 minutes recording examples of gender differentiation, such as articles of clothing, mannerisms, interaction patterns, and activities. Quantify what you see, such as baseball hats on eight males and two females. Or (better, but more difficult) describe four male–female conversations, indicating gender differences in length and frequency of talking, interruptions, vocabulary, and so on.

2. Talk with someone who became a teenage parent. Were there any problems with the pregnancy, the birth, or the first years of parenthood? Would the person recommend teen parenthood? What would have been different had the baby been born three years earlier or three years later? Were there differences in the reactions and behavior of the mother and father?

3. Talk to three people you would expect to have contrasting views on love and marriage (differences in age, gender, upbringing, experience, and religion affect attitudes). Ask each the same questions, and then compare their answers, paying particular attention to male/female differences.

ESPECIALLY FOR ANSWERS

Response for Health Practitioners (from p. 316) Many adolescents are intensely concerned about privacy and fearful of adult interference. This means that your first task is to convince the teenagers that you are nonjudgmental and that everything is confidential.

Response for Teachers (from p. 327) Teachers need to recognize verbal and relational aggression. In addition, the social context is crucial, so the class needs to be structured to be helpful and cooperative with each other.

OBSERVATION QUIZ ANSWERS

Answer to Observation Quiz (from p. 320) Part of it is in the facial expressions. This goodbye looks like a normal routine that all three are comfortable with.

Answer to Observation Quiz (from p. 323) Three signs: facial expressions, holding their drinks, and bending their bodies so their heads touch.

Emotional and Moral Development

B one-tired after a day of teaching, I was grateful to find a seat on the crowded downtown subway. At the next stop, more people boarded, including a tense mother who stood near me. She held a baby, about 18 months old, in one arm; her other arm was wrapped around a pole as she balanced several heavy bags. I thought of offering my seat. Too tired. But I could, at least, hold her bags on my lap.

"Can I help you?" I asked, offering a hand. Wordlessly she handed me . . . the baby! The little girl sat quiet and listened as I talked about her socks, pointing to the red and blue stripes. I sang a soft lullaby. Her body relaxed, her emotions shifting from fear to contentment. Her eyes stayed on her mother.

I felt surprise and joy, that the mother trusted me and that I once again had a small human on my lap. The mother's expression changed from stress to relief.

Should I have been surprised? Mothers everywhere need help with infant care, and strangers everywhere are *allomothers*. We bring gifts to newborns, attend to infant cries, and become caregivers, teachers, helpers. That is part of the moral mandate that binds humanity together. Other passengers were watching me, perhaps making sure that I was not harming the child, perhaps wishing they had been chosen.

This chapter is about the development of human emotions and morals. The emotions of everyone on that train were influenced by our personal needs: my tiredness, the mother's stress, the baby's wariness. And like every moment of our lives, moral choices were made. I could have offered my seat; the mother could have given me a package; other passengers could have acted or protested. Emotions and morals are expressed lifelong, as you will now read. Understanding them is the goal of this chapter.

What Will You Know?

1. Do children learn to express or hide their emotions?
2. Can adults tell what someone is feeling just by seeing or hearing them?
3. Why is telling a good lie considered a cognitive advance?

Emotions from Birth to Age 10

The emotional life of children is rich and varied. Each stage of development is characterized by emotional depth and discovery.

Primary Emotions

Emotions are often categorized as *primary* or *secondary*. **Primary emotions** are called "natural kinds," which means they are innate and universal. Four emotions are primary: happiness, sadness, fear, and anger. Some scholars include two more: surprise and disgust.

The facial expressions that people use to express primary emotions are recognized universally, even by people who have no contact with Western culture (Izard, 1977). Indeed, blind babies have similar (not identical) facial expressions as seeing infants when something makes them happy, sad, angry, or afraid (Valente et al., 2018).

Many scholars deem that as evidence that primary emotions arise from the brain, not from what they learn from other people (TenHouten, 2018), although later in childhood and adulthood, everyone in every culture, blind or not, learns how and when to express those emotions (Barrett et al., 2019).

Secondary emotions are more clearly the result of learning and experience, both in how they are expressed and in what triggers them. Shame, guilt, and confusion are secondary emotions. The distinction between primary and secondary emotions was first explained decades ago (Plutchik, 1958, 1991) and continues to be useful (Montag & Panksepp, 2017; Wang et al., 2020).

primary emotions Basic emotions that originate from innate, neurological impulses. Such emotions are experienced universally, lifelong, including in early infancy. These include happiness, sadness, and fear.

secondary emotions Emotions that build on primary emotions, but also include experience, learning, and culture. These include pride and shame.

social smile A smile evoked by a human face, normally first evident in infants about 6 weeks after birth.

Emotions in Infancy

In the first days after birth, emotions are almost entirely internal, with the two basic primary emotions, pleasure and pain. Newborns are content when fed and drifting off to sleep. Discomfort is also evident: Newborns cry when hurt or hungry, tired or frightened (as by a loud noise or a sudden loss of support), or if something external evokes internal pain (such as a heel stick, circumcision).

Crying and Smiling

By the second week and increasing to 6 weeks, about one infant in five has bouts of uncontrollable crying, called *colic*. Colic may be the result of immature digestion, or reflux, or the infant version of a migraine headache (Gelfand, 2018).

Soon, additional emotions become recognizable. Happiness is expressed by a fleeting **social smile**, evoked by any face at about 6 weeks (Wörmann et al., 2012). (See At About This Time.) Preterm babies smile later, because the social smile requires neurological maturation, about 42 to 44 weeks after conception (White-Traut et al., 2018). All infants smile at any face at first, evidence of the human social impulse. Everyone smiles back.

By about 3 months, uncontrollable crying decreases and joy builds, often in tandem with curiosity: A typical 3- to 9-month-old chortles upon discovering

AT ABOUT THIS TIME

Developing Emotions

Birth	Distress; contentment
6 weeks	Social smile
3 months	Laughter; curiosity
4 months	Full, responsive smiles
4–8 months	Anger
9–14 months	Fear of social events (strangers, separation from caregiver)
12 months	Fear of unexpected sights and sounds
18 months	Self-awareness; pride; shame; embarrassment

As always, culture and experience influence the norms of development. This is especially true for emotional development after the first 8 months.

new things, particularly experiences that balance familiarity and surprise, such as Daddy making a funny face, or a colorful, musical mobile.

A study of infant laughter found that not only Daddy, but also every adult can encourage emotional expressions. One example occurred with a 10-month-old:

> The first time she laughed hysterically was when a friend pretended she had smelly feet. My little girl kept putting her feet to everyone's noses, laughing so much, this went on for about 20 mins.
>
> *[quoted in Addyman & Addyman, 2013, p. 150]*

When adults mirror infant emotions, reacting to them (as did these parents by laughing with their daughter), babies learn what is funny, frightening, sad, and so on. That recognition helps them understand the connection between experiences and feelings.

Happiness becomes more discriminating over the first year. Babies smile more quickly and broadly at familiar caregivers. They still smile at strangers, but not as readily.

In one study, infants first enjoyed a video of people dancing to music as it normally occurs, on the beat. Then they watched a video in which the soundtrack was mismatched with dancing. Eight- to 12-month-old babies, compared to younger ones, were quite curious—but less delighted—about offbeat dancing. The researchers concluded "babies know bad dancing when they see it" (Hannon et al., 2017).

Anger and Sadness

In the early months, anger, sadness, frustration, and surprise are added to pleasure and pain, and emotions become responsive to external experiences. Excitement is evident when joy is anticipated. Many babies kick their legs when a smiling mother approaches, taking off her bra to reveal a full breast.

Anger is also elicited, deliberately or not. For example, to study infant emotions, researchers "crouched behind the child and gently restrained his or her arms for 2 min[utes] or until 20 s[econds] of hard crying ensued" (Mills-Koonce et al., 2011, p. 390). "Hard crying" was common: Infants hate to be strapped in, caged in, closed in, or just held in place when they want to explore. Curiosity is strong, and impeding that arouses anger.

Developmentally Correct Both Santa's smile and Olivia's grimace are appropriate reactions for people of their age. Adults playing Santa must smile no matter what, and if Olivia smiled, that would be troubling to anyone who knows about 7-month-olds. Yet every Christmas, thousands of parents wait in line to put their infants on the laps of oddly dressed, bearded strangers.

In infancy, anger is a healthy response, unlike sadness, which also may appear in the first months (Thiam et al., 2017). The crucial question is "How do caregivers respond to anger or sadness?" Ideally, they recognize the emotion and then try to mitigate it: Then anger does not beget more anger, sadness more sadness.

For example, one study began with mothers of 4-month-olds reacting to crying. Some mothers responded by acknowledging and sympathizing with the emotion, and then with comforting words and soothing touch. When mothers did that, at 12 months their babies were less often sad or angry (McKay et al., 2019),

Fear

Fear as a primary emotion begins with unexpected physical sensations, such as a sudden chill, or loss of support, or a loud noise. By a year, fear is also secondary: Babies can be afraid of a thing, from snakes to strangers, not just of a sensation. Fear among 1-year-olds depends on three factors: discrepancy, temperament, and social context.

Two kinds of social fear are typical, increasing from the middle of the first year:

- **Separation anxiety**—clinging and crying when a familiar caregiver is about to leave. Separation anxiety is expected at age 1, intensifies by age 2, and then usually subsides.
- **Stranger wariness**—fear of unfamiliar people, expressed in various ways, from a nervous smile to a loud cry

These two expressions of social fear (anxiety and wariness) are evident in babies worldwide, reflecting the evolutionary need for babies to stay with familiar caregivers. Which particular strangers provoke anxiety varies depending on how much the culture expects mothers to be exclusive caregivers (Morelli et al., 2017).

In some cultures, every adult in the community comforts a distressed infant. Then unfamiliar people evoke much less fear. This is an example of cultural variations in infant attachment, a topic explored in Chapter 13.

Curiosity also builds over the first year. Many 1-year-olds are curious but wary of anything unexpected, from the flush of the toilet to the pop of a jack-in-the-box, from the closing of an elevator door to the tail-wagging approach of a dog. With repeated experience and reassurance, toddlers might enjoy flushing the toilet (again and again) or calling the dog (crying if the dog does *not* come). A stroller ride in a busy store becomes fascinating, not frightening.

Note the transition from instinct to learning to thought, from the amygdala to the cortex. Emotions travel in the body, gaining or losing power as they do so.

Some manifestations of emotion are expected at age 1 but are possible problems later. If separation anxiety and stranger fear remain intense after age 3, impairing a child's ability to leave home, to go to school, or to play with other children, that is an emotional disorder, according to the *DSM-5* (American Psychiatric Association, 2013). Likewise, stranger wariness may become a social phobia or general anxiety if it continues intensely (Rudaz et al., 2017).

As you remember from Chapter 10, some variation in social fear is caused by inborn temperament, influenced by early-childhood experiences. But beyond that, all babies are somewhat wary, somewhat fearful, and, with encouragement and maturation, they overcome those emotions and make friends. Eventually, unless something is seriously amiss, everyone leaves home alone for school, work, and social gatherings.

Early-Childhood Emotions

Emotions take on new strength from ages 1 to 6, as both memory and mobility advance. Context is crucial, with noteworthy interaction between primary fears and secondary learning. As one team expressed it, "Fear can be an adaptive emotional response if it leads to behaviors that promote safety—avoiding traversal over the edge of a cliff or recoiling from a poisonous snake or spider" (LoBue & Adolph, 2019).

But that team also stressed that two other infant emotions, curiosity and interest, can be more compelling than fear. At age 1 babies are as likely to grab for a snake as they are to recoil. Adults teach them to be afraid!

Throughout the second year and beyond, primary emotions become more focused, targeted toward experiences that are infuriating, terrifying, or exhilarating. Laughing and crying are louder and more discriminating.

Temper Tantrums

The new strength of emotions is apparent in temper tantrums. Toddlers and "terrible twos" are famous for fury. When something angers them, they might yell, scream, cry, hit, and throw themselves on the floor. Logic is beyond them: If adults

separation anxiety An infant's distress when a familiar caregiver leaves; most obvious between 9 and 14 months.

stranger wariness An infant's expression of concern—a quiet stare while clinging to a familiar person, or a look of fear—when a stranger appears.

ESPECIALLY FOR Nurses and Pediatricians Parents come to you concerned that their 1-year-old hides her face and holds onto them tightly whenever a stranger appears. What do you tell them? (see response, page 361)

Learning Emotion Regulation Like this girl in Hong Kong, all 2-year-olds burst into tears when something upsets them—a toy breaks, a pet refuses to play, or it's time to go home. Mothers who comfort young children and help them calm down are teaching them to regulate their emotions.

tease or get angry, if parents insist on obedience or command the child to stop crying, that makes it worse (Cierpka & Cierpka, 2016).

One child said, "I don't want my feet. Take my feet off. I don't want my feet." Her mother tried logic, to no avail, and then offered to get scissors and cut off the offending feet. A new wail erupted, with a loud shriek "Nooooo!" (Katrina, quoted in Vedantam, 2011).

With tantrums, soon sadness comes to the fore. Then comfort — not punishment — is helpful. Angry outbursts are typical in early childhood, but if they persist and become destructive, that signifies trouble, in parent or child (Cierpka & Cierpka, 2016).

Secondary Emotions

As with these examples, innate reactions may evolve into moral values and psychic responses, with specifics depending on parents and experiences. For example, many children take off their clothes in public, unaware that nakedness is taboo. Children are curious and uninhibited: Shame and self-consciousness are secondary emotions.

As children become more aware of other people, other secondary emotions appear, including shame, pride, jealousy, embarrassment, and guilt. All those emotions require social awareness. Such awareness typically emerges from family interaction, especially the relationship between caregiver and baby.

Positive emotions also show social awareness and learning. Many toddlers try to help a stranger who has dropped something or who is searching for a hidden object, and some express sympathy for someone who hurt themselves (Aitken et al., 2019).

Over time, children learn when and whom to help by watching adults. Some adults donate to panhandlers, others look away, and still others complain to the police. Attitudes about ethnicity, or immigration, or clothing, begin with the infant's innate preference for the familiar balanced by interest in novelty. Then caregivers shape attitudes (see A View from Science).

Theory of Mind

Egocentrism (described in Chapter 9) leads young children to think that the thoughts and emotions or other people are just like their own. At some point, however, children grasp a new idea, that other people have their own ideas and feelings. That is **theory of mind**.

Many young children say "I love you" when a caregiver says that to them, or they express sympathy for someone who is hurt (Aitken et al., 2019). But early in life, such commendable emotions occur because the young child knows how that feels. They can be *sympathetic*, which means to share emotions, but not *empathetic*, which is to understand someone's emotions that are not like one's own.

Empathy requires theory of mind, an emergent ability, slow to develop but evident in most children by age 4 (S. Carlson et al., 2013). Although the terms are not yet crisply defined, "the ability to switch from ego-centered perspective" is basic for empathy (Quesque & Rossetti, 2020).

Theory of mind and empathy continue to develop lifelong. Adults wonder why people fall in love with the particular persons they do, why they vote for the political leaders they choose, or why they make foolish decisions, from signing for a huge mortgage to buying an overripe cucumber. Children are likewise puzzled about a playmate's anger, a sibling's generosity, or an aunt's too-wet kiss.

theory of mind A person's theory of what other people might be thinking. In order to have a theory of mind, children must realize that other people are not necessarily thinking the same thoughts that they themselves are. That realization seldom occurs before age 4.

Candies in the Crayon Box Anyone would expect crayons in a crayon box, but once a child sees that candy is inside, he expects that everyone else will also know that candies are inside!

Macmillan Publishers

A VIEW FROM SCIENCE

The Origins of Jealousy

With all emotions, scientists wonder how and why they develop over time. To illustrate the science behind this quest, consider jealousy, a secondary emotion. Jealousy arises when people feel they have a special bond with someone that might be broken by a third person.

Newborns do not know enough to be jealous, but infants do (Hart, 2015). In a series of studies, when mothers ignored their 9-month-olds and showered attention on another baby, the infants looked more at their mothers, touching them and moving closer. An electroencephalogram (EEG) showed activity in the same part of the infant brain that already was associated with jealousy in adults (Mize et al., 2014; Mize & Jones, 2012).

By 2010, many studies had confirmed that infants can be jealous. Then scientists wondered about individual differences. Is jealousy related to maternal responsiveness, to infant temperament, or to having a sibling who is a rival for parental love?

The research is less definitive on these questions, but it seems that having a sibling, or being temperamentally negative, is less influential on jealousy than the relationship with the caregiver (Hart, 2015). Crucial, however, is feeling secure in one's bond: Secure children become less jealous when their mother attends to another person (Murphy et al., 2020).

Remember that new questions arise from every scientific finding. Why does jealousy exist in children or adults? It can be argued that jealousy is adaptive, that it protects human relationships (Yong & Li, 2018). But sometimes jealousy is pathological, called the "green-eyed monster" because it fuels domestic abuse: One lover might destroy another, or kill a rival in homicidal rage.

Overall, many emotions exist for good reasons, yet they can be destructive. Consider the primary emotions: Happiness makes life satisfying but can lead to drug addiction; sadness prompts us to repair problems but can become depression; fear keeps us safe but can become a phobia; anger leads to reform but can also lead to violence. What about jealousy?

An interesting speculation has emerged: Strong jealousy appears at about age 1 because at that age our fertile foremothers sometimes had a new baby. In ancient times, toddlers with younger siblings needed to assert their need for attention and breast milk or risk death (Hart, 2018). Within a few years, jealousy could subside because children were secure in maternal love. Then siblings could be buddies, not rivals. Thus, if adults are irrationally jealous, perhaps they had insecure and hostile family relationships.

Remember the scientific method. Interesting hypotheses need to be tested, not simply accepted. Nonetheless, insight into infant emotions might help us understand the implicit emotions of older children, adolescents, and adults.

Of course, infant survival no longer requires jealousy. However, as is evident in love, lust, hate, disgust, and many other feelings, human emotions are not rational responses to current reality, but reflect inborn needs, fears, and attachments. As with much of the research on emotional development, these studies raise questions that are relevant to adults. Are you jealous of anyone? Does that emotion serve you well?

Where Is the Chocolate?

The classic experiments that indicate theory of mind measure the child's realization that someone else might believe something the child knows is not true. Hundreds of studies begin with a puppet show in which someone does not see that something is moved from one location to another. The child is asked where that someone will look for the object.

If children have a firm theory of mind, they will realize that the other person does not know the new location, and thus that the person will look where he thought it was, not where it really is.

One of the first experiments (Wimmer & Perner, 1983) regarding theory of mind is reported below. The set for this experiment included a blue box, a green box, a piece of chocolate, and two puppets, a mother and her son, Maxi.

Mother returns from her shopping trip. She bought chocolate for a cake. Maxi may help her put away the things. He asks her: "Where should I put the chocolate?" "In the blue cupboard," says the mother.

Maxi puts the chocolate into the blue cupboard. [A toy chocolate is put into the blue box.] Maxi remembers exactly where he put the chocolate so that he can come back and get some later. He loves chocolate. Then he leaves for the playground. [The boy doll is removed.]

Mother starts to prepare the cake and takes the chocolate out of the blue cupboard. She grates a bit into the dough and then she does <u>not</u> put it back into the blue *but puts it into the green cupboard. [Toy chocolate is thereby transferred from the blue to the green box.]*

Now she realizes that she forgot to buy eggs. So she goes to her neighbor for some eggs. [Mother puppet leaves.]

Then Maxi comes back from the playground, hungry, and he wants to get some chocolate. [Boy doll reappears.] He still remembers where he had put the chocolate. Where will Maxi look for the chocolate?

ESPECIALLY FOR Social Scientists Can you think of any connection between Piaget's theory of preoperational thought and 3-year-olds' errors in this theory-of-mind task? (see response, page 361)

The actual experiment included other characters (grandfather, older sibling) and other scenarios, but the results of all the questions was the same. Only half of the 4- to 5-year-olds correctly answered that Maxi will look for the chocolate where he thought it was rather than where it really was, but all of the children age 6 and older got it right (Wimmer & Perner, 1983).

Age Variations in Theory of Mind

The classic studies of theory of mind, like the one above, find that at about age 3 or 4 children begin to understand that someone else might not know what they themselves know. By age 5, most children have a firm theory of mind, at least as it was measured in the early studies. Some newer research with other measures finds theory of mind earlier or later. Part of the reason for conflicting results is in the definitions of theory of mind as well as the details of the experiments (Quesque & Rossetti, 2020).

The studies that find theory of mind before age 3 do not require children to respond verbally to a detailed puppet show. Instead, children's gaze is tracked as they look at where an object is actually hidden, and where someone might think it is hidden. Studies that find theory of mind before age 3 are hard to replicate (Powell et al., 2018).

As more and more studies of theory of mind occur, it is apparent that culture, age, and experience all matter. Theory of mind is enhanced if caregivers respond to the child's emotions and share some emotions of their own. Children who have siblings develop theory of mind more quickly. Children who are neurologically impaired, and thus slower to understand the social world (perhaps with autism, or deafness), are also slower to develop theory of mind.

This emotion has become the topic of many studies of older children, adolescents, adults, and older adults (Henry et al., 2013). Apparently, theory of mind begins by age 4, but empathy builds lifelong, enhanced by discussion of emotions, role-playing and drama, and reading literary fiction (Goldstein & Winner, 2012; Kidd & Castano, 2013).

VIDEO: Theory of Mind: False-Belief Tasks demonstrates how children's theory of mind develops with age.

Emotion Regulation

emotion regulation The ability to control when and how emotions are expressed.

Controlling the expression of feelings, called **emotion regulation**, is a lifelong endeavor, with rapid development during early childhood (Hu et al., 2017).

Babies learn to "self-soothe" via thumb sucking, blanket holding, or rocking, for instance, and then children gradually develop more mature ways to control the primary emotions of fear, anger, and sadness, and the secondary emotions such as guilt and envy. At every stage, parents help children learn emotion regulation (Morawska et al., 2019).

Children learn when and how to express their emotions. Thus, emotion regulation actually has two steps, first regulating the emotion (anger at someone might be turned to empathy) and then regulating what to do with the emotion (hitting someone might be turned to a scowl).

Think of what happens when someone gets a gift. If the receiver is a young child, everyone can probably tell whether the child liked the present, because emotions are visible (Galak et al., 2016). If the receiver is an adult, others may not know, because adults may tell themselves that "it's the thought that counts" and have learned to disguise their reactions. This is an example of emotion regulation: Adults hide disappointment, cry only in private, stifle laughter in church.

Already by age 6, most children can feel angry, frightened, sad, anxious, or proud without the explosive outbursts of temper, or terror, or tears of 2-year-olds. Depending on a child's training and temperament, some emotions are easier to control than others, but even temperamentally angry or fearful children learn to regulate their emotions (Moran et al., 2013; Suurland et al., 2016; Tan et al., 2013). Self-regulation of emotions continues throughout childhood, aiding friendships and academics (McKown et al., 2016).

Notice the role of maturation. The primary emotions, such as sadness and joy, develop in infancy. However, brain maturation and social awareness are needed for secondary emotions, such as pride, envy, and guilt (Frydenberg, 2017). Normally, both primary and secondary emotions become more evident by age 4 or 5. Then emotion regulation begins in earnest.

Among adults in the United States, postponement of emotional pleasure is a sign of maturity: Dieters resist cake today so they will be thinner next summer; students study in advance for exams next week; adults save for retirement. Children who regulate their emotions, including postponing gratification, become successful adults, who continue to invest in the future, in work as well as in family life (see A View from Science).

VIDEO ACTIVITY: Can Young Children Delay Gratification? illustrates how most young children are unable to overcome temptation even when promised a reward.

Feeling Guilty

Postponing pleasure is one example of ongoing emotion regulation. Regulating guilt is another emotion that requires internalizing social standards.

Erikson's third developmental stage (about age 3 to 6) is **initiative versus guilt**. *Initiative* includes saying something new, beginning a project, expressing an emotion. Depending on how others react, children feel proud or guilty. Ideally, they learn to rein in boundless pride and avoid crushing guilt.

initiative versus guilt Erikson's third psychosocial crisis, in which young children undertake new skills and activities and feel guilty when they do not succeed at them.

A VIEW FROM SCIENCE

Waiting for the Marshmallow

You probably have heard of the famous marshmallow test (Mischel et al., 1972; Mischel, 2014). Young children were seated in front of a marshmallow and told they could eat it immediately or wait—sometimes as long as 15 minutes—while the researcher left the room. They were promised another marshmallow if they didn't eat the first one before the adult returned.

Those who waited used various tactics—they looked away, closed their eyes, or sang to themselves. Decades later, the researchers contacted the children to see how their lives turned out. Those who delayed gobbling up one marshmallow in order to get two became more accomplished as teenagers, young adults, and even middle-aged adults—doing well in college, for instance, and having happy marriages.

This experiment has been replicated many times. The average child waits about six minutes. Few 4-year-olds can sit for long in front of a marshmallow without eating it, but those who wait are likely to be more successful years later (Shoda et al., 1990).

Some cultures encourage instant gratification; others teach patience. In a replication of the marshmallow test, children of the Nso people in Cameroon waited longer than the California children in Mischel's original experiment (Lamm et al., 2018). Well-traveled adults notice that waiting in long lines is more expected in some cultures than in others.

In another replication of the marshmallow test, this one in the United States, children experienced a reliable or unreliable examiner. Specifically, children were told they should wait for better crayons, and better stickers, but after two minutes, the examiner returned to tell half of them that no better crayons or stickers was available. The other half got wonderful crayons or stickers.

Then all the children were given the marshmallow test. Those with the reliable examiner waited, on average, 12 minutes, with 64 percent waiting the full 15 minutes. Those with the unreliable experimenter, waited an average of only three minutes, with only 7 percent waiting 15 minutes (Kidd et al., 2013). Emotions—disappointment or trust—matter.

Both Accomplished Note the joy and pride in this father and daughter in West New York, New Jersey. Who has achieved more?

THINK CRITICALLY: At what age, if ever, do people understand when pride becomes prejudice?

Pride is common in early childhood. As one team expressed it:

> Compared to older children and adults, young children are the optimists of the world, believing they have greater physical abilities, better memories, are more skilled at imitating models, are smarter, know more about how things work, and rate themselves as stronger, tougher, and of higher social standing than is actually the case.

[Bjorklund & Ellis, 2014, p. 244]

Protective optimism helps young children try new things, and thus, initiative advances learning. As Erikson predicted, that emotion protects young children from the guilt and shame and encourages them to learn. This does not mean that children should never feel shame or guilt. Guilt can be crushing, a reason for depression (Donohue et al., 2020), but it can motivate children and adults to reduce the guilt by caring for other people (Donohue & Tully, 2019).

Adults learn to take responsibility for their mistakes, and then fix them. That reduces guilt. Shame is harder to reduce, for it is a feeling of social disapproval for something done that cannot be undone.

The connection between pride and guilt develops over childhood. Young children often brag about what they have accomplished. As long as the boast is not a lie, other young children like them for it. At about age 7, a developmental shift occurs, and children as well as adults appreciate modesty more than boasting (Lockhart et al., 2018). By then, children have usually learned some emotion regulation.

The Reciprocity of Emotions

Children strengthen and develop their neuronal connections in response to the emotions of other people. The process is reciprocal and dynamic: Anger begets anger, which leads to more anger; joy begets joy, and so on.

This reciprocity is not just a matter of words and facial expression, it also directly involves the brain. For instance, researchers scanned the brains of mothers and children as they did a difficult puzzle together. When the mothers became frustrated, the children did, too—and vice versa. As the scientists explain, "mothers and children regulate or deregulate each other" (Atzaba-Poria et al., 2017, p. 551).

The practical application of shared emotionality benefits adults as well as children. If a happy young boy runs to you, you might laugh, pick him up, and swing him around; if a grinning young girl drums on the table, you might catch the rhythm and pound in return, smiling broadly. In both adults and children, laughter and happiness increase endorphins and lower cortisol. Emotions are infectious: Catch the good ones, and drop the bad ones.

As Children Grow Older

Throughout the centuries and in every culture, school-age children have been industrious. New sources of emotions arise. Older children savor the pleasure of mastering whatever skills their culture values; they feel competent (see At About This Time).

Erikson noted that the 6-to 10-year-old "must forget past hopes and wishes, while his exuberant imagination is tamed and harnessed to the laws of impersonal things," becoming "ready to apply himself to given skills and tasks" (Erikson, 1993a, pp. 258, 259). Simply trying new things (initiative) is no longer sufficient. Sustained activity that leads to pride is the goal.

AT ABOUT THIS TIME

Signs of Psychosocial Maturation During Middle Childhood*

Children responsibly perform specific chores.

Children make decisions about a weekly allowance.

Children can tell time and have set times for various activities.

Children have homework, including some assignments over several days.

Children are punished less often than when they were younger.

Children try to conform to peers in clothes, language, and so on.

Children voice preferences about their after-school care, lessons, and activities.

Children are responsible for younger children, pets, and, in some places, work.

Children strive for independence from parents.

*Of course, culture is crucial. For example, giving a child an allowance is typical for middle-class children in developed nations since about 1960. It was rare, or completely absent, in earlier times and other places.

Think of learning to read and to add, both of which are painstaking and tedious. For instance, slowly sounding out "Jane has a dog" or writing "3 + 4 = 7" for the hundredth time is not exciting. Yet school-age children busily practice reading and math: They are intrinsically motivated to read a page, finish a worksheet, memorize a spelling word, color a map. They also can be furious at themselves if they make a mistake.

According to Erikson, children judge themselves as either *industrious* or *inferior*—deciding whether they are competent or incompetent, productive or useless, winners or losers. Self-pride depends not necessarily on actual accomplishments but on how others, especially peers, view one's accomplishments. Social rejection is both a cause and a consequence of feeling inferior (Rubin et al., 2013).

As you see, emotions may arise within someone, but they are guided by the social context. Many scientists agree that executive control processes (with many names: *grit, emotion regulation, conscientiousness, resilience, executive function, effortful control*) develop over the years of middle childhood. Those emotions may be crucial for achievement, although developmentalists do not all agree as to how this occurs (Duckworth, 2016; Lam & Zhou, 2019). (See A Case to Study.)

A CASE TO STUDY

Pride in Schoolwork

Consider children in two cultures, 12,000 miles apart: New England in the United States and Taiwan, just east of China. More than 200 mothers were asked to discuss with their child two learning-related incidents that they knew their child had experienced. One incident was when the child had a "good attitude or behavior in learning"; and the other was when the child was "not perfect" (J. Li et al., 2014).

All of the mothers were married and middle-class, and all believed in the value of education and wanted their child to do well in school. However, a cultural difference was evident in the emotions they wanted their children to feel. The Taiwanese mothers were far more likely to mention what the researchers called "learning virtues," such as practice, persistence, and concentration. The American mothers were more likely to mention "positive affect," such as happiness and pride.

This distinction is evident in the following two excepts:

First, Tim and his American mother discussed a "not perfect" incident.

Mother: I wanted to talk to you about . . . that time when you had that one math paper that . . . mostly everything was wrong and you never bring home papers like that. . . .

Tim: I just had a clumsy day.

Mother: You had a clumsy day. You sure did, but there was, when we finally figured out what it was that you were doing wrong, you were pretty happy about it . . . and then you were happy to practice it, right? . . . Why do you think that was?

Tim: I don't know, because I was frustrated, and then you sat down and went over it with me, and I figured it out right with no distraction and then I got it right.

Mother: So it made you feel good to do well?

Tim: Uh-huh.

Mother: And it's okay to get some wrong sometimes.

Tim: And I, I never got that again, didn't I?

The next excerpt occurred when Ren and his Taiwanese mother discuss a "good attitude or behavior."

Mother: Oh, why does your teacher think that you behave well?

Ren: It's that I concentrate well in class.

Mother: Is your good concentration the concentration to talk to your peer at the next desk?

Ren: I listen to teachers.

Mother: Oh, is it so only for Mr. Chang's class or is it for all classes?

Ren: Almost all classes like that. . . .

Mother: So you want to behave well because you want to get an . . . honor award. Is that so?

Ren: Yes.

Mother: Or is it also that you yourself want to behave better?

Ren: Yes. I also want to behave better myself.

[J. Li et al., 2014, p. 1218]

Other studies also find that parents in Asia emphasize hard work, and their children feel upset with themselves if they do not meet a standard, while parents in North America stress the joy of learning. One group of researchers contends that these emotions make U.S. children happier but less accomplished than Asian ones (F. Ng et al., 2014). True?

Emotions from Age 11 to 25

Adolescents and emerging adults are famous (infamous) for emotional outbursts, for good reason. Their emotions are "more frequent, intense, and volatile. . . . more euphoric and more depressed" compared to either adults or children (Guyer et al., 2016, pp. 75–76).

Emotional Control

We wrote about gradually developing emotion regulation in childhood. That may loosen in adolescence, because hormones, brain growth, and social circumstances are all disruptive. As summarized by one team, "in emotional contexts, adolescents' impulse-control ability is severely taxed relative to that of children and adults" (Casey & Caudle, 2013, p. 86).

Instead of controlling their emotions, some adolescents use drugs, exercise, diet, and sleep deprivation to increase them. They listen to music that is loud and angry, or sad and in a minor key. Some brag about being high, or smashed, or floating, all feelings that most adults avoid if possible, or are ashamed to admit.

This gradually gets better in the 20s: "A peak of emotionality in early adolescence is followed by a slowly emerging ability to exert greater self-directed control over behaviors and emotions" (Guyer et al., 2016, p. 77).

Many researchers have focused on adolescent risk-taking, in part because risks cause more deaths from ages 11–25 than all the diseases combined. Both positive and negative risks are common in adolescence (Duell & Steinberg, 2019). Emotions—excitement, joy, courage—precede, accompany, and follow risks.

These emotions are adaptive, helping adolescents enter the adult world of work, higher education, and romance. There is "a functional role for adolescent hyper-emotionality. Risk-taking may serve to integrate individuals within new social networks in adolescence" (Guyer et al., 2016, p. 80). However too much risk-taking is destructive.

Part of the reason emotions change during adolescence is increasing desire for attention from peers. One way to get that attention is to take risks, which may explain the results of one study that found that risk-taking escalates with troubled peer relationships (Telzer et al., 2015). That study measured activity in various parts of the brain, and found many links between adolescent emotions, peer influence, and adolescent behavior.

You might wonder how researchers measure risk-taking. Of course, they ask about behavior (did you ever steal, shoplift, break a parental rule, drive too fast, etc.), but how do we know that the adolescents are telling the truth? If they lied, then the correlations between high risk and peer conflicts is invalid.

Accordingly, many scientists have developed ways to measure risk in a laboratory environment. For example, in the study cited above, adolescents pumped air

In Every Nation Everywhere, older adolescents are most likely to protest against government authority. Here, younger adolescents in Alabama celebrate the 50-year anniversary of the historic Selma-to-Montgomery march across the Pettus Bridge. In that historic movement, most of those beaten and killed were under age 25.

Justin Sullivan/Getty Images News/Getty Images

into balloons until they "cashed-out" by stopping and earning 25 cents per pump, or until the balloon burst, when they earned nothing. They had 36 balloon trials, preprogramed to pop after 1 to 12 pumps. Some adolescents were very cautious, cashing out at fewer than 6 pumps, and some usually kept pumping much longer (and thus had more pops). Total earnings ranged from $8.25 to $26.75.

The participants who had more popped balloons, and earned less money, were also the ones who said they took more risks (Telzer et al., 2015). That suggests that the participants were truthful, and the correlation between risk, conflict, and low social support is valid.

Gradually, the thrill of risk-taking is reduced and the emotions of reflection, caution, and fear increase. This was evident in another study, in which 10- to 30-year-olds judged "how good or bad an idea is it to . . ." do various risky things (such as riding a bicycle down the stairs or taking pills at a party) (Shulman & Cauffman, 2014, p. 170). The participants had to make quick judgments on a sliding scale from 0 to 100.

For instance, the bicycle-riding could be rated at 70 (a rather bad idea) and the pills at 95 (a very bad idea). There also were eight items that were not risky at all, such as eating a sandwich. Intriguing age differences were found. As children aged from 10 to 20, items were rated less risky (closer to a good idea). Then, at age 20, the trend went in the other direction: Every year from 20 to 30, items were considered closer to 100.

 DATA CONNECTIONS: Risk-Taking Behaviors Among Adolescents in the United States explores the risky behaviors U.S. teens are most likely to undertake, according to data compiled by the Youth Risk Behavior Surveillance (YRBS) questionnaire.

Major Emotional Harm

The brain and hormonal development of adolescence (described in Chapters 4 and 5) increase emotionality. As just explained, this fuels emotions. It also explains why adolescence is the time when many serious emotional disorders appear. Early adolescence is particularly hazardous for depression and anxiety (Hamlat et al., 2019), later adolescence and early adulthood for substance abuse and schizophrenia. As always with emotions, some regulation is needed.

> Emotional reactions can become maladaptive when the type, strength, or coordination across neurophysiological systems is not optimal for a particular context. Indeed, the onset of psychiatric disorders during the adolescent years is high, particularly for mood, anxiety, and substance use disorders.
>
> *[Guyer et al., 2016, p. 76]*

Thus, puberty puts some vulnerable children over an emotional cliff. Of course, family stress, school pressure, and genes also matter. Brain activity and hormones are never the sole cause (Roberts & Lopez-Duran, 2019). [Major depression, substance use disorder, and schizophrenia are described in Chapter 15.]

Love

Many of the emotions of adolescence and emerging adulthood are connected to romance. Sexual partnerships are the cause of much joy and excitement, or sadness and despair.

"Falling in love" is a common experience for older adolescents. But exactly what that means is affected by many particulars—personality, age, cohort, and gender among them. The classic love story, Romeo and Juliet, echoes through the ages because it illustrates many themes that are recognizable today. Juliet was 13 years old; Romeo was probably a few years older. Their love killed them both.

The emotions of love are wonderful: joy, excitement, and happiness among them. But there may also be strong negative emotions: despair, jealousy, and revenge. For those under age 25, many emotions regarding romance, for good or ill, are evident (Gómez-López et al., 2019).

Sadly, youth correlates with couple abuse: Young lovers are more likely to hurt each other, during the relationship or after it is over, than older couples. If a young person has several romantic relationships early in adolescence, they are likely to have emotionally fraught romantic relationships later on (Loeb et al., 2020).

Another correlate of partner violence in emerging adulthood is substance abuse (Low et al., 2017). All substances affect emotions, and this is another reason that the emotions of anger, jealousy, and hostility are particularly common among young couples.

That explains why, currently, since marriage does not occur until about age 30, partner abuse is more common among dating and cohabiting couples than among married ones. The statistics and reports focus on physical abuse, but close relationships are also the prime source of hurt feelings, anger, and sadness.

broaden-and-build model The idea that positive emotions, such as joy, hope, happiness, and gratitude, each increase each other and build a foundation for other positive perspectives and experiences.

◉ Observation Quiz It looks as if men's well-being more than doubled between age 18 and the early 20s. Is that right? (see answer, page 361) ↓

FIGURE 12.1
Worthy People This graph shows a steady, although small, rise in young adults' sense of well-being from age 18 to age 24, as measured by respondents' ratings of statements such as "I feel I am a person of worth." The ratings ranged from 1 (complete disagreement) to 5 (complete agreement). The average rating was actually quite high at age 18, and it increased steadily over the years of emerging adulthood.

Emerging Adults' Sense of Well-Being

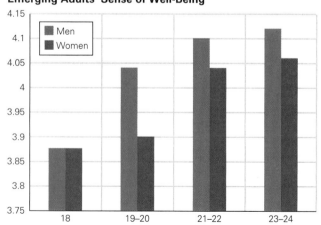

Data from Schulenberg et al., 2005.

WHAT HAVE YOU LEARNED?

1. What happens with emotional control in adolescence?
2. Why are adolescents more emotional than children?
3. What factors increase risk-taking?
4. How is risk-taking measured?
5. Why do many serious mental disorders begin with adolescent emotions?
6. What is the relationship between adolescent emotions and romance?
7. Why is partner abuse more likely in younger adults than older ones?

Emotions After Age 25

In some ways, emotional development quiets in adulthood. Adults do not develop new emotions, and the emotions they have are less volatile (see **Figure 12.1**).

Many emotional extremes of adolescence are modified. Depression becomes less frequent; homicide rates (both as victims and killers) are down; risk-taking decreases as caution rises. As you remember from Chapter 9, in postformal thought the dual processes of emotion and logic come together more often, modifying impulsive, destructive reactions.

Clusters of Emotions

One advance that might happen in adulthood is that emotions cluster together, with each component advancing the other, instead of popping up, singly and suddenly, like popcorn. Social scientists have described two such clusters, one positive and one negative.

The positive cluster has been identified by Barbara Fredrickson, who advocates a **broaden-and-build model**. The idea is that repeated experiences of positive emotions broaden out to cause other positive responses, and then build toward future well-being.

Fredrickson (2013) names 10 positive emotions: joy, gratitude, serenity, interest, hope, pride, amusement, inspiration, awe, and love. Her research has convinced her that these emotions tend to work together, with each increasing the others, and then the combination forming a foundation for future positivity, with resilience to stress, undoing the harm of fear, sadness, and anger.

This theory suggests that adults can work to increase their positive emotions, which will make them more alert to the good things in life (Thompson et al., 2020). How might they do that? By beginning meditation or mindfulness, or appreciating nature. Laughter and loving are healing. The goal of broaden and build is to increase our compassion for ourselves and others (Fredrickson & Siegel, 2017).

Although this theory is not without critics, many psychologists, personnel directors, and social workers apply it. For example, when college students are contemplating suicide, successful intervention inspired by the broaden-and-build model encourages them to think of the positive aspects of their life (Kaniuka et al., 2020).

The negative cluster has been investigated by several others, as they explore what is called the **dark triad**: *psychopathy*, *narcissism*, and *Machiavellianism*. Each overlaps with the other two. Consequently, some adults are far more destructive than if they were characterized by only one of this triad (Paulhus & Williams, 2002).

Similar to the broaden-and-build 10, there are 10 distinct emotions that characterize the dark triad: selfish, impulsive, manipulative, pessimistic, untrustworthy, egotistic, dishonest, grandiose, superficial, and shameless. Again, each of these emotions makes the others stronger, so having one trait of the triad makes the others more likely (Vize et al., 2018).

Both clusters capture the attention of many researchers, who find that, especially in adulthood, some traits tend to spill over to other similar traits, affecting behavior. For example, a study of 755 people in Poland during the COVID-19 pandemic found that those with the dark triad were less likely to prevent the spread of the virus, and more likely to hoard food, protective equipment, and so on (Nowak et al., 2020).

Emotional Intelligence

Another development of emotions during adulthood is **emotional intelligence**, which includes not only awareness of one's own and other's emotions, but also an understanding of how to regulate them. The concept of emotional intelligence was first described decades ago (Goleman, 2005) and has since been applied in many fields, from clergy who want to inspire their congregations, to sales managers who seek to instruct their teams (Stanley, 2020; West et al., 2018).

For example, emotional intelligence guides an adult who is feeling down to take a walk, call a friend, write in a journal—whatever they have learned that helps them. Adults also learn how to assess the moods of other people: If someone is getting angry, a person with emotional intelligence avoids adding fuel to the fire. Overall, it seems that emotional intelligence helps adults have a more social and satisfying life (Petrides et al., 2016).

The research on emotional intelligence highlights the difference between personality (Chapter 10), cognition (Chapter 9), and emotions (this chapter). Of course, there is much overlap, but generally emotions are more transitory, affected by fluctuating hormones, diet, stress, and exercise, whereas personality traits are more durable. Both are influenced by cognition, specifically understanding oneself and others.

Thus, emotions are volatile; they change from day to day or even minute to minute. For instance, happiness is strongly affected by whether or not a person

Maybe Next Year Self-acceptance is a gradual process over the years of adulthood, aided by the appreciation of friends and family. At some point in adulthood, people shift from striving to fulfill their potential to accepting their limitations.

dark triad Three personality traits—psychopathology, narcissism, and Machiavellianism—that, when combined, make a person selfish and destructive.

emotional intelligence The ability to recognize, understand, and regulate emotions. This includes both awareness of the emotions of others and awareness of one's own emotions. Ideally, those high in emotional intelligence have both.

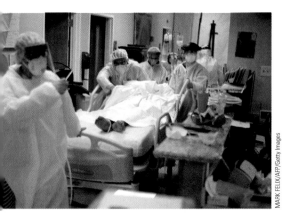

Emotional Intelligence at Work This COVID-19 patient is fortunate to be in Houston, Texas, a world-renowned hub with many research hospitals and medical professionals. Timing is also fortunate: This photo was taken in July 2020, after doctors had learned from the pandemic in China (in January) and New York (in April). However, those two circumstances did not save every-one: 16,000 Texans had died from the virus by October 2020, more in July than in any other month to date.

is well fed and rested, and that may change by the hour. As people move through adulthood, emotional intelligence increasingly allows them to recognize their own and other people's emotions, and then to regulate them.

Emotional Intelligence Throughout Adulthood

Maturation correlates with improved emotional intelligence, as people become experienced with family life and job requirements. Emotional intelligence correlates not only with age, but also with less self-destructive behavior (Saraiva et al., 2018). One large study found that emotional intelligence improved from early adulthood through middle age (Cabello et al., 2016).

Many corporations, schools, and industries have tried to improve the emotional intelligence of their employees. The data suggest success: Adults can, indeed, become more astute regarding emotions (Kotsou et al., 2019). That is especially likely if the training program is personally engaging, with discussion among the trainees (Mattingly & Kraiger, 2019).

Emotional Understanding

Although adults are better at detecting emotions than children, everyone misses some emotional signs. It is remarkable how many cues there are. In one study, people looked at hundreds of full-body photographs, and could distinguish, better than chance, which of 28 emotions was depicted (Cowen & Keltner, 2020).

Auditory clues are understood as well. Those adept at emotional recognition can detect 24 emotions in the sounds (not words) that people utter (Cowen et al., 2019). Some of that may be innate, but much of it is learned via careful listening in adulthood. Consider how parents can understand a baby's cry, or how partners who know each other well can detect emotions that strangers do not notice.

Late Adulthood

Earlier chapters explained many of the forces that affect the emotions of the older adult. Three possible reasons for a decline in emotional awareness are obvious: Neurocognitive losses (Chapter 5) make some older people confused or depressed; ageism (Chapter 10) reduces their confidence; hormones (Chapter 11) affect the emotions at every age; and many hormones are reduced with age.

However, there are two factors that suggest that decline is not the best way to describe emotional development in late adulthood: ecological validity and the positivity effect.

Ecological Validity

Many studies find that adults over age 65 miss some emotional clues that younger adults notice, especially clues regarding negative emotions (Guarnera et al., 2017, 2018). Seeing and hearing are less acute with age. That diminished sensory acuteness renders older adults less accurate than younger adults when tested on the ability to read emotions by looking at someone's face or listening to someone's voice.

This has been confirmed by dozens of tests of emotional recognition, when older and younger adults look at photos of faces, or watch videos, or hear audiotapes. Scientists in laboratories are careful to standardize the measurement of emotions: People of different ages see exactly the same photos, and the lighting, air temperature, and ambient noise are the same for everyone.

Care is taken to make sure that the participants have no sensory impairments or cognitive difficulties that might affect the results. The conclusions are always the same: Older adults are less accurate at emotional detection than younger adults.

However, such careful research may not be the best way to measure emotions in older adults. As you already read in the memory chapter, some people suggest that the abilities of elders should be measured with awareness of how they are needed in daily life. Might emotions in daily life be unlike those found in carefully calibrated experiments?

That question led a team to measure empathy between partners in a hundred couples who had been together for years (Rauers et al., 2013). The participants were repeatedly asked how they felt (how happy, enthusiastic, balanced, content, angry, downcast, disappointed, nervous they were) and to guess the emotions of their partner at that very moment. Technology helped: The participants were beeped at various times on a pager, and they indicated their answers on a smartphone. Sometimes they happened to be with their partner, sometimes not.

When the partner was present, accuracy was higher for the younger couples, presumably because they could see and hear their mate. But when the partner was absent, the older participants were as good as the younger ones (see **Figure 12.2**). The researchers asked a question of those who read this study.

> [Could you] predict a social partner's feelings when that person is absent? Your judgment would probably be better than chance, and although many abilities deteriorate with aging, this particular ability may remain reliable throughout your life.
>
> [*Rauers et al., 2013, p. 2215*]

The Positivity Effect

You remember from Chapter 2 that the *positivity effect* is part of socioemotional selectivity, that older people perceive, prefer, and remember positive images, memories and experiences more than negative ones (Reed et al., 2014). Unpleasant experiences are ignored, forgotten, or reinterpreted.

Now we explore that in more detail, because elders prefer happy emotions. Doesn't everyone? No! Younger adults have what is called a *negativity bias*. They notice and remember negative photos, experiences, and emotions more readily than positive ones. That flips in late adulthood (Carstensen & DeLiema, 2018).

For example, if younger and older adults are asked to look at a series of pictures, some positive (a smiling baby), some negative (a hospital surgery), and some neutral (an ordinary chair), and later are asked which pictures they remembered, the older adults remember more of the positive ones, and the younger adults more of the negative ones.

Older people are not unable to remember negatives; they just are not as motivated to think about them. We know this because many studies find that when the positivity effect is not helpful, it is not present.

For example, one study asked older and younger adults to list the possible advantages and disadvantages of various behaviors, and then to indicate how likely they would be to do them. One behavior was visiting another country. Participants listed many benefits (e.g., learning about another culture) and risks (e.g., a suitcase might be lost).

In that study, older adults were slightly more likely to notice risks—the positivity effect did not blind them to that (Rolison, 2019). Why? Probably because the study found that they were less likely to do those behaviors, so they were quite able to list what the negative possibilities were.

Measuring Partner Empathy

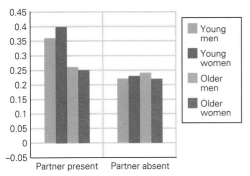

Data from Rauers et al., 2013.

FIGURE 12.2

Always on My Mind When they were together, younger partners were more accurate than older ones at knowing their partner's emotions, but older partners were as good as younger ones when they were apart. This study used "smartphone experience sampling," buzzing both partners simultaneously to ask how they and their partner felt. Interestingly, differences were found with age but not length of relationship—5, 10, 20, or 30 years of togetherness did not necessarily increase empathy when apart, but men who were in their 70s were better at absent mood assessment than men in their 20s.

THINK CRITICALLY: Does the positivity effect avoid reality?

Moral Development

Understanding moral development is important for everyone who wants to understand how maturation affects humans. As one leader said, "Of all the topics debated in courtrooms, dining rooms, boardrooms, and bedrooms, few issues affect people more profoundly than questions of morality" (Schein, 2020, p. 213).

How do people learn **morality**? Or perhaps people do not *learn* morals; perhaps they simply discover them as they become aware of mores (the origin of the word *moral*), which are the social norms and habits of their particular place and time. Added to that complexity is how religion connects with morality.

morality The ability to distinguish between right and wrong.

Religion and Morality

Many people—theologians, believers, and atheists among them—have wondered how religion and morality are connected. As one source explains "the notion that religion is a precondition for morality is widespread and deeply ingrained" (McKay & Whitehouse, 2015, p. 447). A contrary view is that religion is a source of immorality, in that religious wars have harmed many people, and in that believers still hurt those who do not believe as they do. Younger adults are more likely to be critical of religion (see **Figure 12.3**).

Universally, however, religious principles and moral prescriptions often motivate individuals to care for each other. Although it is not hard to notice when religions and morals are destructive, it also is apparent that the need for morality is universal, and religion undergirds morality in many cultures.

Parents recognize this. They often teach both moral and religious values, and children are more likely to be prosocial and to avoid delinquency and self-harm if they have a religious/moral upbringing (Hardy et al., 2019).

FIGURE 12.3

No Religion, No Morals? Not so! Forty percent of Milennials (born between 1981 and 1996) say "no religious affiliation" when asked. However, many consider themselves more moral than than their elders. Some consider themselves spiritual, not religious; they believe in God and pray, but never attend their local church, mosque, or synagogue. The problem, of course, is that people of different cohorts disagree about what is immoral, especially regarding race, the environment, and sexuality.

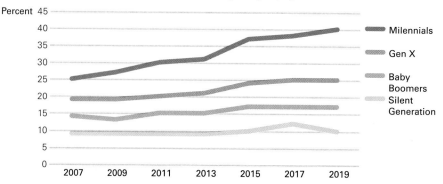

U.S. Adults Who Say They Are Not Affliated with Any Religion, by Cohort

Data from Pew Research Center, October 17, 2019.

With maturation, religious beliefs may move from a narrow, self-centered view of religion and morality toward a broader, universal one. This was described by James Fowler (1981, 1986) in a now-classic sequence of six stages of faith.

Before any thought occurs, according to Fowler, a person is at "zero," when religion simply reflects children's relationship with their parents. Then thought begins.

- *Stage one: Intuitive-projective faith*. Faith is magical, illogical, imaginative, and filled with fantasy, especially about the power of God and the mysteries of birth and death. It is typical of children ages 3 to 7.
- *Stage two: Mythic-literal faith*. Individuals take the myths and stories of religion literally, believing simplistically in the power of symbols. God is seen as rewarding those who follow divine laws and punishing others. Stage two is typical from ages 7 to 11, but it also characterizes some adults. Fowler cites a woman who says extra prayers at every opportunity, to put them "in the bank."
- *Stage three: Synthetic-conventional faith*. This is a conformist stage. Faith is conventional, reflecting concern about other people and favoring "what feels right" over what makes intellectual sense. Fowler quotes a man whose personal rules include "being truthful with my family. Not trying to cheat them out of anything. . . . I'm not saying that God or anybody else set my rules. I really don't know. It's what I feel is right."
- *Stage four: Individual-reflective faith*. Faith is characterized by intellectual detachment from the values of the culture and from the approval of other people. College may be a springboard to stage four, as young people learn to question the authority of parents, professors, and others and to rely instead on their own understanding of the world. Faith becomes an active commitment.
- *Stage five: Conjunctive faith*. Faith incorporates both powerful emotional ideas (such as the power of prayer and the love of God) and rational conscious values (such as the worth of life compared with that of property). People are willing to accept contradictions, obviously a postformal manner of thinking. Fowler says that this perspective is seldom achieved before middle age.
- *Stage six: Universalizing faith*. People at this stage have a powerful vision of universal compassion, justice, and love that compels them to live their lives in a way that others may think is either saintly or foolish. A transforming experience is often the gateway to stage six, as happened to Moses, Muhammad, the Buddha, and Saul/Paul of Tarsus, as well as more recently to Mohandas Gandhi, Martin Luther King, Jr., and Mother Teresa.

  As you know, these seven named people were compelled by their religious faith to act not only according to the highest principals of their religion but also according to the highest principles of morality.

These stages of faith are not accepted by every scholar of religion and morality, in part because "The relationship between religion and morality is a deep and emotive topic . . . [with] bewildering theoretical and methodological complexity." It is apparent that religion and morality are interwoven, and that one group's terrorist is another group's freedom fighter; the religion and morality of one person may clash with that of another. We cannot untangle this issue here, nor decide which religious values and moral principles are the right ones.

What we can do is consider what scholars have learned about moral development over the life span, beginning with babies. This chapter concludes by raising the question again: what is right and wrong?

Moral Infants

A dozen 6-month-old infants astonished thousands of social scientists and philosophers more than a decade ago (Hamlin et al., 2007). They did it by reaching for a blue square or a yellow triangle.

The specifics were as follows: Infants watched a puppet show. They saw a red circle try to climb a green mountain. The circle began at the bottom, got halfway up to a resting place, and then tried, but failed, to reach the top.

At that point a helper or hinderer appeared, either a blue square or a yellow triangle. The helper gave two upward shoves that pushed the red circle to the top. The hinderer gave two downward shoves that pushed the circle back. After watching both episodes, the infants were offered a choice of puppets (helper or hinderer) to play with.

To make sure the choice wasn't influenced by color, shape, or sequence, half of the infants saw the blue square as the helper and half saw it as hinderer; half saw the upward push first, half the downward. All 12 infants chose the helper!

That experiment has been replicated over a hundred times, sometimes with slightly older infants, sometimes with a video instead of puppets. The results have never been as absolute as that first report; some infants choose the hinderer. However, overall, more infants choose the helper (Margoni & Surian, 2018).

The original scientist concluded that infants have "an innate moral core" (Hamlin, 2013). He believes that humans are born with a sense of fairness, of justice, of helping. That conclusion is supported by other research. By measuring how long they look at contrasting scenes, preverbal infants seem to expect:

- a fair distribution of cookies between two dolls;
- an owl puppet to help another owl puppet
- one puppet not to hit another.

The evidence is mixed regarding how universal and strong that early moral core might be, but apparently some infants, some of the time, recognize what is fair and unfair (Ting et al., 2020). This extends to behavior. Even before they can talk, infants might share a favorite toy, comfort a crying child, give a blanket to a shivering adult (Hammond & Drummond, 2019).

Moral Young Children

By early childhood, children have an understanding of moral behavior, and adults try to shape that behavior. As you will see, children's perceptions are not necessarily astute, and adults, attempts to teach are not always successful.

Empathy and Antipathy

Moral behavior at every age begins with awareness of the needs and emotions of others. Some children develop **empathy**, an understanding of other people's feelings and concerns. Empathy leads to compassion and **prosocial behavior** — helpfulness and kindness without any obvious personal benefit. Prosocial actions and preferences increase from ages 1 to 6. Empathetic preschoolers become first-graders who are likely to share, help, and play with other children (Z. Taylor et al., 2013).

This process continues as children mature: Empathy, prosocial behavior, and moral reasoning often arise together, each increasing the other two (Mestre et al., 2019). In older children, those who are high in empathy are also most likely to care for people from other groups (Taylor et al., 2020).

The opposite can also happen. Some children dislike other children, especially those who are mean, or who insist on their own way in sociodramatic play. Antipathy may lead to **antisocial behavior**, which includes verbal insults, social exclusion, and physical assault. Such behavior begins in childhood, but continues in adulthood. A longitudinal study of abused and neglected children found that, throughout adulthood, they were likely to be antisocial (Esposti et al., 2020).

empathy Feeling the same emotions as someone else. Empathy is not the same as *sympathy*, a less personal feeling, such feeling sorry for someone (pity).

prosocial behavior Literally, "for other people" — doing something for others without expecting any reward. In early childhood, prosocial behavior is sharing something or caring for someone who needs help.

antisocial behavior Literally, "against other people" — doing something that needlessly hurts others. In childhood, this may be physical (hitting, kicking), or verbal (with insults or rejection). Antisocial is not *asocial*, which is being less involved with other people.

Both prosocial and antisocial behavior are innate, but then are affected by what parents and other children do (Spinrad & Gal, 2018). The fact that such behaviors are in every child, and probably every adult, means that circumstances and morality are relevant lifelong.

Generally, antisocial behavior diminishes over the preschool years, especially as social understanding increases. Religious development can parallel this development. Indeed, many scholars believe that faith also grows in stages, from the young child's belief that God punishes and blesses them for what they do, to stages of adult religious development. Religion can encourage prosocial actions, with mature adults believing in universal principles, such as respect for all people, helping the poor, protecting life (Day, 2017). Of course, this is far from inevitable.

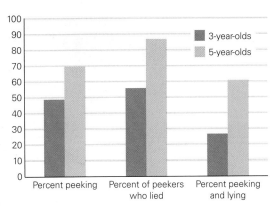

Data from Evans et al., 2011.

Telling Lies

Evidence of increasing sense of morality is increasing willingness to tell a lie. Children not only know when they have done something wrong, they try to lie about it. One team contends that, by age 4, most (80 percent) children have lied to avoid admitting a transgression (O'Connor et al., 2020). Lying requires some theory of mind, because children need to understand that someone else might not know what they know. With cognitive advancement, older children are better liars (Alloway et al., 2015).

The details of one of the many experiments in lying illustrate the point. Children (aged 3 to 5) were seated in front of an upside-down cup covering dozens of candies (Evans et al., 2011). They were told *not* to peek; the experimenter then left them alone.

For 142 children (57 percent), curiosity overcame obedience (see **Figure 12.4**). They peeked, spilling so many candies onto the table that they could not put them back under the cup. The examiner returned, asking how the candies got on the table. Only one-fourth of the participants (more often the younger ones) told the truth.

The rest lied, and their skill increased with age.

- The 3-year-olds typically told hopeless lies (e.g., "The candies came out by themselves").
- The 4-year-olds told unlikely lies (e.g., "Other children came in and knocked over the cup").
- Some 5-year-olds, however, told plausible lies (e.g., "My elbow knocked over the cup accidentally").

In this study, skill at lying not only improved with age, it also improved with cognition: Those who were more advanced in theory of mind told better lies.

Surprisingly, parents are not accurate at knowing whether a child is telling the truth or not (Evans et al., 2011, p. 42). Parents are more likely to think a child is telling the truth when that is not the case, than the opposite. That is probably a good strategy, since accusing a truth-teller of lying is likely to damage the parent–child trust.

Better lying may signal advanced morality as well as advanced cognition. A study of 6- to 12-year-olds telling prosocial lies (such as saying that a disappointing gift was appreciated) found that the better liars were advanced in theory of mind and in executive control (Williams et al., 2016).

Learning from Punishment

Parents often hope to teach their children morals. Children are most likely to be punished during early childhood, because that is when they do many things that parents find wrong, and that is also when parents have most power. However, like the research on lying, the research on punishment may be surprising.

FIGURE 12.4
Better with Age? Could an obedient and honest 3-year-old become a disobedient and lying 5-year-old? Apparently yes, as the proportion of peekers and liars in this study more than doubled over those two years. Does maturation make children more able to think for themselves or less trustworthy?

Smack Will the doll learn never to disobey her mother again?

ESPECIALLY FOR Parents Suppose you agree that spanking is destructive, but you sometimes get so angry at your child's behavior that you hit him or her. Is your reaction appropriate? (see response, page 361)

psychological control A disciplinary technique that involves threatening to withdraw love and support, using a child's feelings of guilt and gratitude to the parents.

time-out A disciplinary technique in which a person is separated from other people and activities for a specified time.

induction A disciplinary technique in which the parent tries to get the child to understand why a certain behavior was wrong. Listening, not lecturing, is crucial.

In the United States, young children are slapped, spanked, or beaten more often than are infants or older children, and more often than children in Canada or western Europe. Does that teach them morality?

Not according to most Europeans. In many nations of Europe, physical punishment is illegal. However, people in other many other nations disagree. A massive international study in low- and moderate-income nations found that 63 percent of 2- to 5-year-olds had been corporally punished (slapped, spanked, hit with an object) in the past month (Deater-Deckard & Lansford, 2016). Older children are less often physically punished, perhaps because they are better at hiding their transgressions.

Given a multicultural, multicontextual perspective, it is not surprising that many of those spanked children become fine adults, who believe they were not harmed by spanking. Nonetheless, a correlation between spanking and aggression is found everywhere (Lansford et al., 2014; Wang & Liu, 2018). Children who are *not* spanked are *more* likely to develop emotion regulation.

Although some adults believe that physical punishment will "teach a lesson," others contend that the lesson learned is an immoral one, that "might makes right." Children who were physically disciplined more often use corporal punishment on others—first on their classmates, and later on their lovers, then on their children (Thompson et al., 2017).

If spanking is harmful but morals need to be taught, what is a parent to do? Some employ **psychological control**, using shame, guilt, and gratitude to teach moral behavior (Barber, 2002). Adults might ask "How could you do that after all I have done for you?" But psychological control has its own problems, including making the child feel less competent, less loved, and less independent (Scharf & Goldner, 2018).

Consider a study in Finland, where corporal punishment is forbidden, but psychological control is not. The more parents used psychological control, the lower the children's math scores, a correlation that increased over time. Further, the children tended to have negative emotions (depression, anger, shame) (Aunola et al., 2013). Other research finds that, years later, shame, more than guilt, increases feelings of low self-esteem, and the wish to hurt oneself (Sheehy et al., 2019).

Another disciplinary technique is the **time-out**, in which a misbehaving child is required to sit quietly, without toys or playmates. The morality of time-out depends on specifics. Time-out is not to be done in anger, or for too long; it is recommended that parents use a calm voice and limit time-out to less than five minutes.

Many experts favor time-out, especially when it is part of a close parent–child relationship and is used to punish a behavior that the child knows is wrong (Dadds & Tully, 2019). Thus, time-out is not a teaching tool; it is a reinforcing tool.

Often combined with the time-out, either preceding or following it, is another alternative to physical punishment and psychological control—**induction**. In this method, parents discuss the infraction with their child. Ideally, a strong and affectionate parent–child relationship allows the child to express emotions, the parent to listen, and then the child to understand the moral lapse.

Induction takes time and patience, and, like other discipline measures, it does not always succeed. One problem is that young children confuse causes with consequences; they tend to think they behaved properly, given the situation. Simple induction ("Why did he cry?") may be effective in that it encourages empathy, but as already explained, empathy requires some theory of mind. Nonetheless, children whose parents used induction when they were 3-year-olds became less likely to disobey teachers or to bully other children in elementary school (Choe et al., 2013b).

As long as punishment is not abusive, the particular method chosen seems less crucial than the authority's morality. This is a lesson for outsiders: If a particular parent seems too strict, or too lenient, that may not matter if the children consider the discipline morally just and fair and know that "Love your children" is a prime moral rule (Grusec et al., 2017). If so, they are likely to develop well, morally and intellectually (Pinquart & Kauser, 2018). With older children, as you will now see, induction may be crucial.

Moral Older Children

A developmental view of morality finds that children, on their own, develop moral standards, disapproving of cheating in a game, or of a bully harming other children, or of a teacher favoring one child over another. As Piaget noted a century ago, children play games together, with rules of conduct that they develop and enforce. Children also consider loyalty to peers a crucial moral value (don't "snitch" or "rat").

Good Intentions

On example of the development of morality among children is the understanding of intentions. A lie is much worse than the same statement that is unknowingly false (Rizzo et al., 2019).

In one study, 5- to 11-year-olds heard about one child pushing another. Sometimes the push was selfish (because the child wanted to use the swing), sometimes not (to keep the other child from harm). Younger children judged based on results (the pushed child might be injured), but the older children considered intention. They accepted justifiable harm but thought unjustifiable harm was far worse (Jambon & Smetana, 2014).

I saw this in my grandson, at age 8. A stopped subway made me late to pick him up from school one day. It was not much problem; he was safe, and I was not very late. I told him the reason and said, "I'm sorry."

"I forgive you," he replied, to my surprise.

I had done nothing that merited forgiveness, but he knew that not every child understood intentions. He wanted me to know that he did, and that he did not blame me.

Maturation Matters

One indicator of advances in moral judgment during childhood may be how willing a child is to consider the needs of other children. This increases with age.

For example, one study measured generosity in 5- to 12-year-olds from five nations (United States, Canada, China, Turkey, and South Africa). They had chosen 10 stickers for themselves, and then were told of an unknown child who had no stickers. Would they give some to that child? Generosity increased with age: On average, 5-year-olds gave away two and kept eight, while 12-year-olds gave away five and kept five (Cowell et al., 2017).

Culture had an impact. Children from Toronto were most generous, and children from Cape Town, least, a difference thought to reflect national wealth (Cowell et al., 2017). An interesting detail is that those cultural differences were not evident in every child: Some children from each of the five nations kept all or almost all stickers to themselves, and some from each nation gave more than half away.

The fact that children who came from wealthier nations were more likely to donate is an example of a lifelong principle called "feel good, be good." When

Universal Morality Remarkable? Not really. By the end of middle childhood, many children are eager to express their moral convictions, especially with a friend. Chaim Ifrah and Shai Reef believe that welcoming refugees is part of being a patriotic Canadian and a devout person of Jewish faith, so they brought a welcoming sign to the Toronto airport where Syrian refugees (mostly Muslim) were about to deplane.

THINK CRITICALLY: If one of your moral values differs from that of your spouse, your parents, or your community, should you still try to teach it to your children? Why or why not?

people of any age feel happy and secure, they are more generous to others (Kushlev et al., 2020).

Considering Goals

How do children develop morality? Piaget studied punishment. The goal could be *retribution* (hurting the transgressor) or *restitution* (restoring what was lost). He found that children advance from retribution to restitution between ages 8 and 10 (Piaget, 1932/2013b). Ethicists consider that a moral advance (Claessen, 2017).

To learn how this occurs, researchers asked 133 children, all around age 9:

> Late one afternoon there was a boy who was playing with a ball on his own in the garden. His dad saw him playing with it and asked him not to play with it so near the house because it might break a window. The boy didn't really listen to his dad, and carried on playing near the house. Then suddenly, the ball bounced up high and broke the window in the boy's room. His dad heard the noise and came to see what had happened. The father wonders what would be the fairest way to punish the boy. He thinks of two punishments. The first is to say: "Now, you didn't do as I asked. You will have to pay for the window to be mended, and I am going to take the money from your pocket money." [Restitution]. The second is to say: "Now, you didn't do as I asked. As a punishment you have to go to your room and stay there for the rest of the evening." [Retribution]. Which of these punishments do you think is the fairest?
>
> *[Leman & Björnberg, 2010, p. 962]*

The children were split almost equally in their answers. Then, 24 pairs of children who had opposite views were formed. Each pair was asked to discuss the issue, trying to reach agreement. (The other 85 children did not discuss it.) Six pairs were boy–boy, six were boy–girl with the boy favoring restitution, six were boy–girl with the girl favoring restitution, and six were girl–girl.

The conversations typically took only five minutes, and the retribution side was more often chosen. Piaget would consider that a moral back-slide, since more advocates of restitution than retribution switched. Gender was not a factor: About as many girls as boys chose the less mature answer.

Two weeks and eight weeks later, the children were queried again. Many had switched, toward restitution, and many of those who initially favored retribution also switched (see **Figure 12.5**). This advance occurred even among the children who merely thought about the dilemma again, but children who had discussed it with another child were particularly likely to decide that restitution was better.

FIGURE 12.5

Benefits of Time and Talking The graph on the left shows that most children, immediately after their initial punitive response, became even more likely to seek punishment rather than to repair damage. However, after some time and reflection, they affirmed the response that Piaget would consider more mature. The graph on the right indicates that children who had talked about the broken window example moved toward restorative justice even in examples that they had not heard before, which was not true for those who had not talked about the first story.

Repair Harm or Hurt the Transgressor? Nine-Year-Olds' Responses

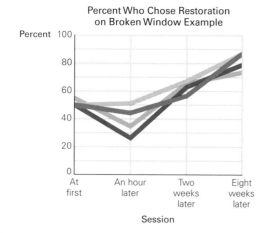

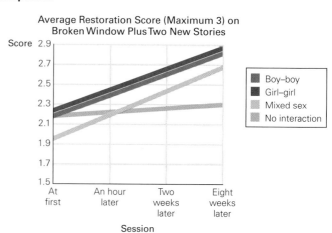

Data from Leman & Björnberg, 2010.

The main conclusion from this study was that "conversation on a topic may stimulate a process of individual reflection that triggers developmental advances" (Leman & Björnberg, 2010, p. 969). Parents and teachers take note: Raising moral issues and letting children talk about them may advance morality—not immediately, but soon.

Considering Reasons

The most famous studies of the relationship between thinking and morality were undertaken by Lawrence Kohlberg. He described three levels of moral reasoning, with two stages at each level (see **Table 12.1**). For Kohlberg, the crucial issue is *why* a person reaches the moral conclusion that they do. His three levels are:

- **Preconventional moral reasoning**. This is similar to preoperational thought in that it is egocentric. Preconventional thinkers are most interested in their personal pleasure or avoiding punishment.
- **Conventional moral reasoning** parallels concrete operational thought in that it relates to current, observable practices: Children watch what their parents, teachers, and friends do and try to follow suit.
- **Postconventional moral reasoning** is similar to formal operational thought because it uses abstractions, going beyond what is concretely observed, willing to question "what is" in order to decide "what should be."

According to Kohlberg, the cognitive advances that occur with maturation also advance moral thinking. During middle childhood, children's answers shift from being primarily preconventional to being more conventional: Concrete thought and peer experiences help children move past the first two stages (level I) to the

preconventional moral reasoning
Kohlberg's first level of moral reasoning, emphasizing rewards and punishments.

conventional moral reasoning
Kohlberg's second level of moral reasoning, emphasizing social rules.

postconventional moral reasoning
Kohlberg's third level of moral reasoning, emphasizing moral principles.

TABLE 12.1

Kohlberg's Three Levels and Six Stages of Moral Reasoning

Level I: Preconventional Moral Reasoning
The goal is to get rewards and avoid punishments; this is a self-centered level.

- *Stage one: Might makes right* (a punishment-and-obedience orientation). The most important value is to maintain the appearance of obedience to authority, avoiding punishment while still advancing self-interest. Don't get caught!
- *Stage two: Look out for number one* (an instrumental and relativist orientation). Everyone prioritizes their own needs. The reason to be nice to other people is so that they will be nice to you.

Level II: Conventional Moral Reasoning
Emphasis is placed on social rules; this is a parent- and community-centered level.

- *Stage three: Good girl and nice boy.* The goal is to please other people. Social approval is more important than any specific reward.
- *Stage four: Law and order.* Everyone must be a dutiful and law-abiding citizen, even when no police are nearby.

Level III: Postconventional Moral Reasoning
Emphasis is placed on moral principles; this level is centered on ideals.

- *Stage five: Social contract.* Obey social rules because they benefit everyone and are established by mutual agreement. If the rules become destructive or if one party doesn't live up to the agreement, the contract is no longer binding. Under some circumstances, disobeying the law is moral.
- *Stage six: Universal ethical principles.* Universal principles, not individual situations (level I) or community practices (level II), determine right and wrong. Ethical values (such as "life is sacred") are established by individual reflection and religious ideas, which may contradict egocentric (level I) or social and community (level II) values.

next two (level II). Postconventional reasoning is not usually present until adolescence or adulthood, if then.

Kohlberg posed moral dilemmas to boys in the United States beginning at age 10. Eventually he also interviewed girls, teenagers, and adults from other U.S. places and other nations. The most famous example of these dilemmas involves a poor man named Heinz, whose wife was dying. Heinz could not pay for the only drug that could cure his wife, a drug that a local druggist sold for 10 times what it cost to make.

> Heinz went to everyone he knew to borrow the money, but he could only get together about half of what it cost. He told the druggist that his wife was dying and asked him to sell it cheaper or let him pay later. But the druggist said "no." The husband got desperate and broke into the man's store to steal the drug for his wife. Should the husband have done that? Why?
>
> [Kohlberg, 1963, p. 19]

Kohlberg's assessment of morality depends not on what a person answers but why an answer is chosen. For instance, suppose a child says that Heinz should steal the drug. That itself does not indicate a moral stage. The reason could be that Heinz needs his wife to care for him (preconventional), or that people will blame him if he lets his wife die (conventional), or that a human life is more valuable than the law (postconventional).

Or suppose another child says Heinz should not steal. Again, the reason is crucial. If the reason not to steal is to avoid jail, that is preconventional; if it is that the community will label him a criminal, that is conventional; if it is that business owners should be able to set their own prices, that is postconventional.

Kohlberg was acclaimed for suggesting that a school's curriculum should include discussions of moral issues, but he also was criticized for not appreciating cultural or gender differences. For example, loyalty to family overrides other values in some cultures, so some people might avoid postconventional actions that hurt their family. Also, Kohlberg's original participants were all boys, which may have led him to discount female values of nurturance and relationships (Gilligan, 1982).

Moral Adolescents and Young Adults

Although Kohlberg's original research participants were middle school students, he and many others believe that high school and college students should be encouraged to reflect on their moral values. This can be done via formal classes or can simply be understood as an examination of issues and priorities.

Defining Issues

One scholar who studies moral development wrote:

> Dramatic and extensive changes occur in young adulthood (the 20s and 30s) in the basic problem-solving strategies used to deal with ethical issues. . . . These changes are linked to fundamental reconceptualizations in how the person understands society and his or her stake in it.
>
> [Rest, 1993, p. 201]

Defining Issues Test (DIT) A series of questions developed by James Rest and designed to assess respondents' level of moral development by having them rank possible solutions to moral dilemmas.

Rest developed a multi-choice measure of moral reasoning called the **Defining Issues Test (DIT)**. The person reads situations and then must choose priorities. For example, in one DIT dilemma, a news reporter must decide whether to publish some old personal information that will damage a political candidate. Respondents rank their priorities from personal benefits ("credit for investigative reporting") to higher goals ("serving society").

The DIT continues to be used in thousands of studies, in almost every nation, and is a valid measure of Kohlberg's stages (van den Enden et al., 2019). It seems that the DIT correlates with how a person functions in their profession, whether they engage in political action, and how they live (Han et al., 2019; Moreira et al., 2018).

Rest wrote that college education may propel a shift in moral reasoning. This is especially likely if coursework includes extensive discussion of ethics or if the student's future profession (such as law, business, or medicine) requires ethical decisions. Students in those curricula are often taught ethical guidelines (Carrese et al., 2015; Kalshoven & Taylor, 2018; Shapiro & Stefkovich, 2016). For example, psychotherapists lose their license if they have sex with a client.

Age and Priorities

Another way to think about the morals of people as they age from adolescence to adulthood is to think first about their values. Rank the following 10 according to what you think important at age 20, and then at age 80.

1. *Self-direction:* wanting autonomy, ignoring others' opinions
2. *Stimulation:* seeking excitement, novelty, adventure
3. *Hedonism:* keeping comfort, enjoying sensory pleasure
4. *Power:* seeking status, prestige, and dominance
5. *Achievement:* feeling competent, successful
6. *Security:* keeping yourself, your family, and your society safe
7. *Conformity:* respecting social norms, curbing odd impulses
8. *Tradition:* valuing culture and religious beliefs, rituals
9. *Benevolence:* sacrifice for people in your immediate circle
10. *Universalism:* care and protect everyone, all nations

[list adapted from Schwartz et al., 2012; Schwartz, 2015, 2017]

People from 29 countries and of all ages have ranked these 10. In every nation, older adults value security, conformity, and tradition more than stimulation and hedonism, which are valued by younger adults. (Did you guess that?) Local economy and culture affect the other five, although generally, universalism and benevolence become more important than self-direction and power as people mature.

This list is included here because, contrary to Kohlberg, many scholars think moral judgments are not cognitive abstractions but rather are part of a personal value system that responds to biological factors, such as hunger, tiredness, hormones [Have you ever done something you later thought was immoral because you were exhausted and stressed?] or in the brain (see Inside the Brain).

The list of values provides insight for many moral differences between generations. Is it immoral for a young person to have sex with someone they would never marry, to skip school to go to the beach, to drink alcohol to get drunk?

Each of those behaviors may reflect a value system that prioritizes stimulation over security, autonomy over tradition. Older, or more devout, people may consider those actions immoral, but younger people may defend them on moral grounds. Think of the moral mandates of "Freedom from tyranny" or "Don't be swayed by public opinion," and you will understand.

Moral Adults

As with emotions, new morals do not appear after age 25. Long-standing values continue to be held strongly. Adults justify what they do, even though the situation may, in fact, override the principle.

Context

A classic moral dilemma is called "the trolley." The original situation is that a runaway trolley is racing toward four people who will be killed (Foot, 1978). You can pull a switch

ESPECIALLY FOR Someone Who Has to Make an Important Decision Which is better, to go with your gut feelings or to consider pros and cons as objectively as you can? (see response, page 361)

INSIDE THE BRAIN

Morally Disgusting?

Moral principles may arise from deep within the human brain, which is why people may defend their morals so passionately when logic and facts do not support them. Particular attention has focused on the regions primed for disgust (Haidt et al., 1997; Kavaliers et al., 2019; Moll et al., 2005). These include the *anterior insula*, *basal ganglia*, *superior temporal gyrus*, and *anterior cingulate cortex*—all names of specific parts of the brain.

You do not need to know exactly where those parts are, but you do need to know that neuroscience finds activation of those parts when a person smells or sees something disgusting, whether that something is a physical thing or a moral behavior (Chapman & Anderson, 2013).

To understand how strong the visceral reaction to immorality can be, we need to begin by understanding the reason for the ancient aversion to toxins. Millennia ago, highly sensitized and coordinated neurological disgust was essential for human survival. That kept our ancestors from ingesting poison, as with dead bodies, or rotten food, or polluted water. Each of those substances creates a smell and visceral reaction such as nausea, diarrhea, loss of appetite.

But the center for substance disgust has been repurposed for moral disgust. Notice that some of the worst human prejudices involve a visceral reaction against people of another ethnicity, or sexuality, or physical condition, which we justify by calling them "dirty," or "unclean." This immoral disgust arises when leaders use dehumanizing terms, such as comparing a group to animals or insects.

A particularly striking example occurred at a political rally in Rwanda in 1992, when a Hutu legislator named Léon Mugesera called the Tutsi people "cockroaches." That dehumanization led to genocide in 1994, when the Hutu slaughtered as many as a million Tutsi. After a lengthy legal battle, Mugesera was convicted and jailed for life in 2016.

Moral psychologists are on high alert when any group is accused of bringing diseases to a nation, or when any group is referred to as animals, insects, or words of disgust. We now know that emotions can be triggered by such words, and that actions that seem unthinkable somehow become moral (Strohminger & Kumar, 2018).

Observation Quiz What do you see that is positive, and what is problematic? (see answer, page 361) ⬇

Who Is My Neighbor? Hunger is a worldwide problem, but people are more likely to care for people in their community than elsewhere. During the COVID-19 pandemic, farmers in upstate New York sent food to downstate New York. This photo is from Brooklyn, where one volunteer is delivering food to another, part of a church that feeds people who live nearby.

AP Photo/Frank Franklin II

that will divert the trolley to another track, but that track has one person who would be killed. Would you push the switch? Most people say yes. They reason that saving four people is better than killing one, and that they have a moral obligation to act.

This question is followed by another: same trolley, same four versus one, but no switch. Instead, you are standing on a footbridge next to an overweight man whom you could shove down to the track. His body would stop the trolley, saving four by killing him. Would you push? Most people say no, following another moral principle deep within the psyche: Do not, directly, kill another human being.

This dilemma has become a classic example of the idea that a person's willingness to take a moral action depends, in part, on what the person must do. Humans are much more willing to drop a bomb from a plane than to directly kill people in an enemy city, or to murder someone with a rifle—especially from a distance—than with a knife.

The continued popularity of this dilemma, despite the antiquated words (trolley, footbridge), occurs because dozens of variations have revealed that moral decisions vary, not by principle, but by context. What if the four people are convicted murderers, or the overweight man is a child pornographer, or if some of the people are your neighbors, or strangers from another nation, or of another race, or very old? What if that one person is your child or your mother?

Indeed, some people would hesitate if the one creature was not a person but their very own dog (Sapolsky, 2018)! Many scholars now conclude that Kohlberg missed the point of moral actions, that the choices we make in daily life are heavily influenced by context, not principles or logic (Schein, 2020). In the COVID-19 pandemic, hospitals were compelled to postpone some surgeries that would have occurred in normal times, making choices that echoed the trolley dilemma (Al-Balas et al., 2020).

Moral Foundations

A clash between morality and cognition is highlighted in the work of Jonathan Haidt, who has studied morals in many religions, cultures, and nations. He believes that both training and context are crucial, and, like many others, he thinks that religions have been developed to reinforce morality.

To be more specific, many scholars have found that, if morality includes caring for strangers, religions do not necessarily make a person more or less moral. However, scholars also agree that religions can instill morality (Bloom, 2012; Shariff, 2015).

Haidt wrote many imaginary situations to highlight the clash between morals and logic:

- A family dog dies, and the family cooks the meat and eats it for dinner.
- A brother and sister alone in a distant land decide to have sex.
- Someone drinks water from a glass that had a dead, sterilized cockroach in it.

Each of these was explained to a participant in detail, and it was made clear that no one would be harmed. For example, the brother/sister sex story included the information that both used very effective contraception, both agreed they would tell no one, both knew this sex would happen only once, both were sure that no one in that land knew them.

Nonetheless, each of these three imagined situations was highly offensive to most adults. They disapproved on moral grounds, often referring to religious principles to back up their feelings. When they tried to explain logical reasons, they failed. However, they still insisted that these were immoral.

Haidt contends that people have five deep moral values, which are learned within each culture in childhood and which guide adults. The five moral foundations are:

1. Care for others; harm no one.
2. Promote freedom; avoid oppression.
3. Be fair; do not cheat.
4. Seek purity; avoid contamination.
5. Respect authority; do not break laws.

The importance of these five varies by nation and religion. Purity, for instance, is more crucial in India, and freedom is more crucial in the United States. The current political polarization in the United States may be essentially a clash of moral priorities, with each political party ranking these five differently (Clifford, 2019; Tappin & McKay, 2019).

If one group prioritizes the first two and another group the last two, then each group will interpret the middle one, fairness, differently. This may explain why people of different religious, political, or cultural backgrounds consider each other not merely mistaken, but also immoral (Haidt, 2013).

For instance, in 2011 a law was passed in France forbidding covering one's face in public. The reason was said to be protection (avoiding harm #1) from masked bandits, but the regulation made no exception for devout Muslim women (some of whom wear burkas in order to avoid contamination and obey religious authority [#4 and #5]) or skiers who want to cover their face in subzero temperatures (personal freedom #2). No wonder the law was considered immoral by some but fair (#3) by others.

Similarly, think about public health measures in 2020 to contain COVID-19. Some contend that compulsory mask-wearing is needed to protect community health (#1) while others see it as a restriction of freedom (#2).

Difficult Choices

Although empathy is needed lifelong, adults need to temper it by a more comprehensive moral understanding (Bloom, 2017). Adults in the helping professions are

burnout The state of exhaustion and depression that may overcome professional helpers, when they lose their empathy for people who are suffering.

vulnerable to **burnout**, a term that originally referred to fighting fire with another fire. Now emotional burnout renders adults exhausted and depressed. This reduces effective care for anyone, including themselves (Shanafelt et al., 2020; Koutsimani et al., 2019; Willard-Grace et al., 2019). As you see, moral development in adulthood requires a combination of cognition and emotion. Moral issues are profound, influencing us every day. To repeat the quote that began this discussion, "Of all the topics debated in courtrooms, dining rooms, boardrooms, and bedrooms, few issues affect people more profoundly than questions of morality" (Schein, 2020, p. 213).

At first people might think that their own morals are clear and correct, but a deeper consideration reveals complexity in even the simplest issues. That is evident in the opening anecdote of this chapter, in the trolley/footbridge dilemma, in the Kohlberg and Haidt questions, and in the actions of other nations.

It is easy to see that, in Rwanda, the Hutu who murdered their Tutsi neighbors thought they were moral warriors but in fact were committing crimes against humanity. Moral ideas are weaponized to allow immoral acts.

It is not hard to see other examples in earlier eras and other nations, from the Roman gladiators and lions who killed early Christians, to the Germans who killed 6 million Jewish, socialist, and LGBTQ individuals, to Pol Pot and the Khmer Rouge in Cambodia to the treatment of the Uighur people in China. Indeed, probably someone in your class can cite another, more recent, example. But it is not easy to see how that might be occurring now, here, in us.

Would the moral thing for me, on that subway ride described in the chapter opener, to have been to give up my seat for that stressed mother, so she and her daughter could both sit happily together? That might have made both of them have a happier time together that evening, and might have inspired other passengers to consider what they could do for their fellow riders. In retrospect, that is what I should have done.

WHAT HAVE YOU LEARNED?

1. How does telling a lie indicate intellectual growth?
2. How does parental punishment advance moral development?
3. How effective is psychological control?
4. What factors are needed to make time-out effective?
5. How does punishment vary internationally?
6. What are the characteristics of Kohlberg's preconventional, conventional, and postconventional moral stages?
7. How does the trolley dilemma reveal the limits of logic?
8. What are the five moral principles that Haidt recognizes?
9. What do Haidt's stories highlight regarding moral values?

SUMMARY

Emotions from Birth to Age 10

1. Some primary emotions—happiness, sadness, and fear—are present at birth. Smiling, laughing, and preference for a familiar caregiver become evident in the early months.

2. A baby's eagerness to explore is accompanied by fear and frustration. These emotions build during early childhood, as children learn what is joyful to them, and what makes them angry.

3. Theory of mind, which traditionally is said to begin at about age 4, allows children to experience empathy. This emotion continues lifelong. All the secondary emotions—shame, guilt, and pride among them—are affected by the child's experiences.

4. Emotion regulation is the ability to control, and then express, and not express, emotions. Pride, shame, and guilt develop with maturation, as evident in Erikson's third and fourth stages.

Emotions from Age 11 to 25

5. Adolescents and emerging adults tend to have volatile and frequent emotions. These emotions accompany risk-taking, for good or ill.

6. Relationships with peers, and romantic partnerships, are the source of many adolescent emotions. Joy and excitement, as well as sadness and despair, are often part of these relationships.

Emotions After Age 25

7. Emotions may cluster together in adulthood, as suggested by the broaden-and-build model or the dark triad.

8. Emotional intelligence increases in adulthood, as people are better able to understand their own emotions and those of others.

9. Understanding and interpreting emotional clues are abilities that adults gain from experience, and also abilities that can be taught. These abilities may diminish in late adulthood, but sensitivity to the emotions of one's partner may be maintained.

10. The positivity effect suggests that older adults are more attuned to some emotions, such as happiness and love, than to others, such as anger and fear.

Moral Development

11. Infants may have an innate "moral core" that guides them to care for others. Then, during childhood, children learn to lie, or stay mum, in order to avoid punishment.

12. Spanked children tend to become more aggressive, which suggests that corporal punishment may teach the wrong lesson. Listening and talking with children seems to be more effective.

13. Discussing moral issues, either with parents and peers, advances children's moral thinking. Kohlberg's three levels and six stages of moral thinking tied morality to Piaget's stages.

14. The hierarchy of moral values suggests that, over the years of adulthood, people become more concerned with tradition and less concerned with excitement.

15. The trolley dilemma, and Haidt's moral questions, suggest that context and gut feelings can override cognitive analysis of moral issues.

KEY TERMS

primary emotions (p. 333)
secondary emotions (p. 333)
social smile (p. 333)
separation anxiety (p. 335)
stranger wariness (p. 335)
theory of mind (p. 336)
emotion regulation (p. 338)

initiative versus guilt (p. 339)
broaden-and-build model (p. 344)
dark triad (p. 345)
emotional intelligence (p. 345)
morality (p. 348)
empathy (p. 350)

prosocial behavior (p. 350)
antisocial behavior (p. 350)
psychological control (p. 352)
time-out (p. 352)
induction (p. 352)
preconventional moral reasoning (p. 355)

conventional moral reasoning (p. 355)
postconventional moral reasoning (p. 355)
Defining Issues Test (DIT) (p. 356)
burnout (p. 360)

APPLICATIONS

1. Theory of mind emerges at about age 4, but many adults still have trouble understanding other people's thoughts and motives. Ask several people why someone in the news did whatever they did (e.g., a scandal, a crime, a heroic act). Then ask your informants how sure they are of their explanation. Compare and analyze the reasons as well as the degrees of certainty. (One person may be sure of an explanation that someone else thinks is impossible.)

2. Think of a life-changing decision you have made. How did logic and emotion interact? What would have changed if you had given the matter more thought—or less?

3. Ask three parents about punishment, including their preferred type, at what age, for what misdeeds, and by whom. Ask your three informants how they were punished as children and how that affected them. If your sources all agree, find a parent (or a classmate) who has a different view.

ESPECIALLY FOR ANSWERS

Response for Nurses and Pediatricians (from p. 335) Stranger wariness is normal up to about 14 months. This baby's behavior actually might indicate secure attachment.

Response for Social Scientists (from p. 338) According to Piaget, preschool children focus on appearance and on static conditions (so they cannot mentally reverse a process). Furthermore, they are egocentric, believing that everyone shares their point of view. No wonder they believe that they had always known the puppy was in the blue box and that Maxi would know that, too.

Response for Parents (from p. 352) No. The worst time to spank a child is when you are angry. You might seriously hurt the child, and the child will associate anger with violence. You would do better to learn to control your anger and develop other strategies for discipline and for prevention of misbehavior.

Response for Someone Who Has to Make an Important Decision (from p. 357) Both are necessary. Mature thinking requires a combination of emotions and logic. To make sure you use both, take your time (don't act on your first impulse) and talk with people you trust. Ultimately, you will have to live with your decision, so do not ignore either intuitive or logical thought.

OBSERVATION QUIZ ANSWERS

Answer to Observation Quiz (from p. 344) No. Read the caption and the scale on the *y* axis. Well-being rose, on average, about 4 percent—a significant rise, but not a dramatic one.

Answer to Observation Quiz (from p. 358) Comforting is that five professionals are present, and concerning is the lack of face shields and supplemental oxygen. At this point in Texas, no medical center had all the personal protective equipment that they needed.

CHAPTER 13

Leren Lu/DigitalVision/Getty Images

Attachment: Family and Friends

M y daughter, Bethany, came to visit her nephew, Isaac, then 7 months old. She had often come before, and Isaac had always smiled broadly, waving his arms when he saw her animated voice, face, and body. But this time he looked away, nuzzling his mother.

Later, Bethany tried again, and Isaac looked and laughed.

"You like me now," she said.

"He always liked you, he was just tired," said Elissa, his mother.

"I know," Bethany told her. "I didn't take it personally."

I appreciated both daughters. Elissa sought to reassure Bethany, and Bethany understood Isaac's reaction. But the person I appreciated most was Isaac, with evident attachment to his mother, yet open to other relationships as securely attached babies are.

I also appreciate Oscar, Asa, Rachel, Sarah, and me (father, brother, aunts, and grandmother). We all tried to capture Isaac's attention: we sang, we jumped, we shook our heads, we made odd noises, we pretended to fall down. Isaac rewarded us with heart-warming, love-sustaining, laughter. Family attachments were evident.

One time, after I babysat for several hours, I told Oscar, "It is hard work. I admire that you and Elissa do it 24/7."

"Yes," he said. "When we find his parents, they will be grateful to us."

I laughed, realizing again that human bonds are the foundation of our lives.

This chapter is about attachments. As you will see, the term as it used in psychology originated half a century ago with John Bowlby, a British psychologist. He inspired an American, Mary Ainsworth, and many others, to explore early relationships between caregivers and infants. That led to thousands of extensions, refinements, and replications, eventually studying all the human relationships that characterize the life span, from cradle to grave.

Accordingly, with this chapter we begin with the traditional theory of attachment, and grow from there to all the family and friendship relationships of the developing person. You will read about how humans satisfy their universal need to connect with each other, via myriad family structures and age-related actions, from the crawling infant, to the caregiving octogenarian.

The theme of this chapter is what Isaac, with his very real family and his hypothetical parents, illustrated: Humans are social creatures.

- **Other Social Connections**
  People Without Families
  Late Adulthood

What Will You Know?

1. Do mothers and infants naturally develop strong attachments to each other?
2. Is one style of parenting better than the others?
3. Is the "standard North American family" the ideal family structure?
4. In adulthood, can close friends replace family connections?

Attachment

Attachment—the social bonds that glue one person to another—is a lifelong process, evident among humans and other mammals of every age for 200,000 years. However, the scientific study of attachment is relatively new, flourishing in the past half century.

attachment According to Ainsworth, "an affectional tie" that an infant forms with a caregiver—a tie that binds them together in space and endures over time.

Origins of the Theory

Attachment theory and research is the "joint work" of an unlikely pair, John Bowlby and Mary Ainsworth (Bretherton, 1992).

In 1950, Mary Ainsworth went to London because her new husband, Leonard Ainsworth, needed to finish his Ph.D. studies. Bowlby was already a leading psychiatrist, deputy director of the prestigious Tavistock Institute.

Ainsworth decided to learn more about the research British psychologists were conducting. She met Bowlby, who became her teacher, her mentor, and finally her collaborator. He encouraged her to do field research on mother–infant relationships in six villages in Uganda, which led to a detailed book (Ainsworth, 1967).

Attachment Theory

John Bowlby had worked with children who were separated from their mothers during World War II. As he tried to help them, he realized that their emotional deprivation went far deeper than the physical trauma they experienced (Bowlby, 1951). Some of them withdrew from human relationships, becoming emotionally stunted. That observation led to a seminal paper on the mother–child relationship (Bowlby, 1958).

As a psychoanalyst himself, Bowlby agreed with Freud's emphasis on the early mother–child relationship. But he found Freud's understanding of development to be "unsatisfactory," in part because it was not based on careful observation of infants and their mothers.

Bowlby wrote that his "point of view" was opposite to Freud's (Bowlby, 1969, p. 3), because he began by observing very young children instead of extrapolating from adults who, Freud theorized, were damaged by their mothers. Maternal absence, Bowlby discovered, was worse than maternal action.

Bowlby respected Freud, but he also was impressed with the work of Harry Harlow, a scientist from the United States. Harlow was not a behaviorist, but he was strongly influenced by the behaviorist emphasis on experimental evidence

Connecting to Mary Ainsworth Notice the infant's facial expression and body position. Secure infants, when their mothers are present, are primed to learn from other people. This photo was taken in 1973, a year when Ainsworth published a dozen articles on early attachments.

from nonhuman animals. He conducted thousands of experiments with baby monkeys, eventually demonstrating that caregiver love during infancy was essential for healthy development.

Harlow's findings echoed what Bowlby was thinking about human children. When monkeys were reared in isolation they became psychologically damaged for life, unable to establish relationships. In adulthood they could not mate; their social ineptness made them vulnerable to vicious attacks from other monkeys (Harlow, 1986).

The third scholarly influence on Bowlby was from *ethology*, the discipline that studies the behavior of nonhuman species. The ethological research that most captured Bowlby's attention was that of Konrad Lorenz (1979), who found that goslings instinctively follow the movements of the first living creature they see.

That instinct meant that they usually bonded with their mother goose, but Lorenz famously became "mother" to a gaggle of geese, who followed him wherever he went. From that, Bowlby concluded that human animals might also be born with an instinct to seek connections with a caregiver.

Many other academic psychologists in London in the 1960s were familiar with the work of Freud, Harlow, and Lorenz, but Bowlby's genius was to go beyond that. He combined the theories of those three with observations: His own experiences with children sent away from their mothers in the war, his collaborators' reports on other children in Europe, and Mary Ainsworth's detailed notes from Uganda.

That mix of theory and observation led to Bowlby's master work, the three-volume *Attachment and Loss*. The initial volume (more than 400 pages), was on attachment.

Mary Ainsworth "read [the] first draft of this book and suggested many improvements" (Bowlby, 1969, p. xxxiii). By that time, she had become a professor at Johns Hopkins, in Maryland, and was "most generous" in sharing her research results, not only from Uganda but also from mothers and infants in Baltimore.

Signs of Attachment

Ainsworth categorized varieties of attachment (Ainsworth et al., 1978). She wrote that two clusters of behaviors, *proximity-seeking* (wanting to be close to someone) and *contact-maintaining* (wanting to see, hear, and touch someone) signify attachment.

Psychologists and others quickly realized the validity of Ainsworth's clusters. Anyone who watches babies closely now recognizes attachment: Infants might cry if their mother closes the door when going to the bathroom, or if she leaves home without them. Infants protest if they are awake when their mother puts them in their crib to sleep; toddlers fuss if a back-facing car seat prevents them from seeing the driver.

Young children are upset when proximity or contact is lost; they seek to restore it. In the first weeks of life, babies snuggles into the body of someone holding them; 3-month-olds follow their mother with their eyes; 10-month-olds crawl to another room to be with their caregiver; 2-year-olds run down the sidewalk to greet a parent.

When they are tired, young children lean on legs, grab hands, and climb up on laps. The early research was on mothers, as in these examples, but later research found the same thing with fathers and other attachment figures.

Attachment is mutual. Parents engage in proximity-seeking and contact-maintaining when they tiptoe to the crib to gaze at their sleeping infant, or absent-mindedly smooth a child's hair. When their children are a little older, they attend school concerts, plays, and sports events with their eyes and camera focused on their own children.

Details depend on culture. For instance, Ainsworth reported that Ugandan mothers never kissed their infants but often massaged them. In some cultures, infants are not hugged in greeting but instead a hand is taken to shake (Mesman et al., 2016).

Cultural adaptions are evident in the United States as well. Many caregivers take the baby into the bathroom (one mother said she hadn't been alone in the bathroom for two years [Senior, 2014]), or rig a mirror in the car so the back-facing baby sees the driver.

Four Types of Attachment

Attachment is classified into four types: A, B, C, and D (see Visualizing Development, page 366). **Secure attachment (type B)** is evident when an infant is comfortable in the presence of a caregiver. Confidence that they are loved allows them to explore when the caregiver is in sight. Type B is in the middle of two extremes, A and C, both insecure.

Some insecure infants play independently without maintaining contact; they do not look at their caregiver or crawl to them when upset. This is **insecure-avoidant attachment (type A)**.

Other children have the opposite reaction: their attachment is **insecure-resistant/ ambivalent attachment (type C)**. Children with type C cling to the caregiver, fear separation, and are angry at being left.

Ainsworth considered A, B, and C as three strategies that infants develop to deal with their experiences. Likely Bowlby, she thought the infant's need to attach was instinctual, and that infants then develop whatever strategy (A, B, or C) works for them.

Ideally, they are secure (type B), but insecure attachment (A or C) is also strategic. Type A infants have learned that their mother is unavailable, so they ignore her until or unless she instigates contact. Type C infants have learned that, if they cling tightly and cry loud enough, their mothers might attend to them.

One of Ainsworth's students, Mary Main, realized that some infants have no strategy at all, because their mothers are unpredictable and erratic, affectionate one moment and punitive the next. Main described a fourth category, **disorganized attachment (type D)**. Type D infants may shift suddenly from hitting to kissing, from staring blankly to crying hysterically, from pinching themselves to freezing in place.

Many studies report that almost two-thirds of 1-year-olds are secure (type B) (Cassidy & Shaver, 2016). When their caregiver is present, they happily play; when the caregiver leaves, they are distressed. They welcome the caregiver's return, reestablishing contact. Then they explore again. The caregiver is a *base for exploration*, providing assurance and enabling discovery. This balanced reaction—concerned but not overwhelmed by comings and goings—indicates security.

About one-third of infants are insecure, either indifferent (type A) or unduly anxious (type C), and about 5 to 10 percent are disorganized (type D). Type D is especially worrisome, because those infants have no consistent strategy for social interaction, even avoidance or resistance. (See **Table 13.1**.)

Type D toddlers are at risk for later psychopathology, including severe aggression and major depression (Cicchetti, 2016; Gazzillo et al., 2020). Indeed, the connection between type D, inadequate care, and later problems sometimes leads to removal of infants from their parents—a practice that is problematic (White et al., 2019).

No single assessment of attachment type is definitive: Secure infants sometimes behave in insecure ways. It is the *pattern* of interaction, not one moment,

secure attachment (type B) A relationship in which an infant obtains both comfort and confidence from the presence of the caregiver.

insecure-avoidant attachment (type A) A pattern of attachment in which an infant avoids connection with the caregiver, as when the infant seems not to care about the caregiver's presence, departure, or return.

insecure-resistant/ambivalent attachment (type C) A pattern of attachment in which an infant's anxiety and uncertainty are evident, as when the infant becomes very upset at separation from the caregiver and both resists and seeks contact on reunion.

disorganized attachment (type D) A type of attachment that is marked by an infant's inconsistent reactions to the caregiver's departure and return.

VISUALIZING DEVELOPMENT Developing Attachment

Attachment begins at birth and continues lifelong. Much depends not only on the ways in which parents and babies bond, but also on the quality and consistency of caregiving, the safety and security of the home environment, and individual and family experience. While the patterns set in infancy may echo in later life, they are not determinative.

How Many Children are Securely Attached?

The specific percentages of children who are secure and insecure vary by culture, parent responsiveness, context, and specific temperament and needs of both the child and the caregiver. Generally, about a third of all 1-year-olds seem insecure.

50–70%	10–20%	10–20%	5–10%
Secure Attachment (Type B)	Avoidant Attachment (Type A)	Ambivalent Attachment (Type C)	Disorganized Attachment (Type D)

Attachment in the Strange Situation May Influence Relationships Through the Life Span

Attachment patterns formed in infancy affect adults lifelong, but later experiences of love and rejection may change early patterns. Researchers measure attachment by examining children's behaviors in the Strange Situation where they are separated from their parent and play in a room with an unfamiliar caregiver. These early patterns can influence later adult relationships. As life goes on, people become more or less secure, avoidant, or disorganized.

Securely Attached [Type B]
In the Strange Situation, children are able to separate from caregiver but prefer caregiver to strangers.

> Later in life, they tend to have supportive relationships and positive self-concept.

Insecure-Avoidant [Type A]
In the Strange Situation, children avoid caregiver.

> Later in life, they tend to be aloof in personal relationships, loners who are lonely.

Insecure-Resistant/Ambivalent [Type C]
In the Strange Situation, children appear upset and worried when separated from caregiver; they may hit or cling.

> Later in life, their relationships may be angry, stormy, unpredictable. They have few long-term friendships.

Disorganized [Type D]
In the Strange Situation, children appear angry, confused, erratic, or fearful.

> Later in life, they can demonstrate odd behavior—including sudden emotions. They are at risk for serious psychological disorders.

The Continuum of Attachment

Avoidance and anxiety occur along a continuum. Neither genes nor cultural variations were understood when the Strange Situation was first developed (in 1965). Some contemporary researchers believe the link between childhood attachment and adult personality is less straightforward than this table suggests.

Low Avoidance

Secure   Resistant

Low Anxiety   High Anxiety

Avoidant   Disorganized

High Avoidance

Darq/Shutterstock

TABLE 13.1

Predictors of Attachment Type

Secure attachment (type B) is more likely if:

- The parent is usually sensitive and responsive to the infant's needs.
- The infant–parent relationship is high in synchrony.
- The infant's temperament is "easy."
- The parent is not stressed about income, other children, or their marriage.
- The parent has a working model of secure attachment to their own parents.

Insecure attachment is more likely if:

- The parent mistreats the child. (Neglect increases type A; abuse increases types C and D.)
- The mother is mentally ill. (Paranoia increases type D; depression increases type C.)
- The parent is highly stressed about income, other children, or their marriage. (Parental stress increases types A and D.)
- The parent is intrusive and controlling. (Parental domination increases type A.)
- The parent has alcohol use disorder. (Father with alcoholism increases type A; mother with alcoholism increases type D.)
- The child's temperament is "difficult." (Difficult children tend to be type C.)
- The child's temperament is "slow-to-warm-up." (This correlates with type A.)

that is crucial (Mikulincer & Shaver, 2019). It makes sense to assess and foster secure attachment between infants and caregivers, but relationships between children and their parents sometimes change over time (Fearon & Roisman, 2017).

Attachment Parenting

Recently some people have begun advocating *attachment parenting*, which prioritizes the mother–infant relationship during the first three years of life far more than Ainsworth or Bowlby did (Komisar, 2017; Sears & Sears, 2001). Attachment parenting mandates that mothers should always be near their infants (co-sleeping, "wearing" the baby in a wrap or sling, breast-feeding on demand for months or years).

Some experts suggest that attachment parenting is distant from the theory and research (Ennis, 2015). It also requires intensive mother devotion to the infant, which may clash with the mother's wish to share caregiving responsibilities with their partner and others (Sánchez-Mira & Saura, 2020), as well as the partner's wish to be intimately connected to the mother and baby (Faircloth, 2020).

Measuring Attachment

Measuring the security of the mother–infant relationship once seemed impossible, because babies cannot talk, and caregivers might not tell how they feel. Fortunately, Mary Ainsworth developed a laboratory procedure called the **Strange Situation**, which measures 1-year-olds' reactions to stress, with and without the caregiver.

The specifics of the Strange Situation, as designed by Ainsworth, are as follows: In a well-equipped playroom, an infant is observed for eight episodes, each lasting no more than three minutes. First, the child and mother are together. Next, according to a set sequence, a stranger and the mother come and go. The infants' responses indicate which type of attachment (A, B, C, or D) they have formed.

Researchers focus on the following:

> *Exploration of the toys.* A secure infant plays happily.
> *Reaction to the caregiver's departure.* A secure infant is somewhat distressed when the caregiver leaves (a pause in playing, a plaintive sound, a worried expression).

Strange Situation The eight-episode measurement of attachment designed by Mary Ainsworth. In a mildly stressful ("strange") playroom, the infant reacts as the mother and a stranger enter and leave.

Same or Different? A theme of this chapter is that babies and mothers are the same worldwide, yet dramatically different in each culture. Do you see similarities between the Huastec mother in Mexico and mothers in the United States?

Reaction to the caregiver's return. A secure infant welcomes the caregiver's return, seeking contact, and then plays again. Typically a secure infant gets a comforting hug, and resumes playing.

THINK CRITICALLY: Is the Strange Situation a valid way to measure attachment in every culture, or is it biased toward the Western idea of the ideal mother–child relationship?

Scientists are carefully trained: watching videos, calibrating ratings, and studying manuals. They are certified to measure attachment only when they have reached a high level of accuracy. It is especially crucial to recognize common behaviors that signify insecurity, because many are contrary to what untrained observers might think. For instance, clinging to caregivers may be type C; too friendly to strangers, type A.

Other scientists have developed measures to signify secure or insecure attachment in older children and adults. For example, the Adult Attachment Interview (AAI) asks adults to talk about their childhood. They can be type B (balanced memories), type A ("I never want to see her again"), or type C ("she was a saint"). It is especially troubling if they are type D, confused and incoherent, remembering few details.

However, measures of attachment after infancy may not be reliably connected to early attachment, in part because attachment itself is more fluid than it was originally thought to be, and in part because each assessment indicates only some aspects of the parent–child relationship (Jewell et al., 2019). An entire issue of a psychology journal explores the complexities of measuring attachment in adulthood (Simpson & Karantzas, 2019).

Nonetheless, assessing infant attachment via the Strange Situation has made longitudinal studies possible. It is evident that early attachment affects the brain and the immune system lifelong (Bernard et al., 2019). New circumstances, such as domestic violence, affect the link between childhood attachment and adult behavior, but early attachment forms connections that do not disappear, although they may be later broken or strengthened (Fearon & Roisman, 2017).

Attachment continues to be studied by thousands of scientists, in many nations, ages, and cultures. Caregivers who are not parents, as well as children who are not typical, nonetheless demonstrate attachment.

At first, attachment was thought to be exclusive to infants, but now attachment in older children and in adults is extensively explored (e.g., Pinto & Figueiredo, 2019; Voges et al., 2019; Cassidy & Shaver, 2016). Attachment between people and pets, or between adults and God, has also been studied (Leman et al., 2018; Meehan et al., 2017).

International Research

Culture and cohort matter. Research at the end of the twentieth century found that insecure German infants were more often avoidant (type A) and insecure Japanese children were more often resistant (type C) (Rothbaum et al., 2000; Sagi et al., 1991). Everywhere, however, secure attachment is the usual pattern.

Many families in developing nations are severely stressed. Family income may be low, homes crowded, and several children may be born a year or two apart, all of which decrease the likelihood of secure attachment. Type D attachment seems more common in Africa than elsewhere. Even so, secure attachment is the norm (Voges et al., 2019).

Details of one specific study in Kenya of Gusii infants, aged 8–27 months, confirm this (Kermoian & Leiderman, 1986). In that culture, *exclusive* maternal care is rare. Instead, although the mothers breast-feed their babies, other people do most of the infant care. Usually a child under age 10 is tasked to be the infant caregiver.

This study used a modified Strange Situation: 61 percent of the Gusii infants were securely attached to their mothers, and 54 percent were securely attached to their child caregivers. Only 23 percent were insecurely attached to both, a rate somewhat lower than the rate of insecure attachment in the United States. Some of those 23 percent had good reason to be anxious: They had been recently weaned, and a new baby was at their mother's breast.

International research confirms that each child needs at least one dedicated caregiver, and that disrupting that relationship causes lifelong harm. That is why developmentalists of every political stripe are horrified that thousands of children of immigrants are separated from their parents at the border between Mexico and the United States (Roth et al., 2020; Upchurch et al., 2020).

Assumptions of the Theory

Four major questions (originally listed by Van IJzendoorn, 1990), are (1) whether attachment is basic to humans (in much the same way language is), (2) whether secure attachment is typical, (3) whether healthy attachment is the result of good caregiving, and (4) whether there are consequences of early attachments. Many developmentalist now believe that the answer to these four is yes. It seems that there is:

1. Universality. The infant's urge to attach is instinctual, part of human nature.
2. Normality. Secure attachments are typical for most infants.
3. Sensitivity. Secure attachment is produced by sensitive and responsive caregiving.
4. Later development. Infant attachments affect later health, cognition, and emotions.

A valid question regarding all of social science research is whether some behaviors assumed to be universal are, in fact, only true for *WEIRD* nations, which are Western, Educated, Industrialized, Rich Democracies. One correction to attachment theory from cross-cultural research is that Bowlby's WEIRD assumption that mothers were the exclusive caregiver was too restrictive: Many infants of the world develop secure attachments to nonmothers.

Beyond that, however, these four basic tenants of attachment theory have proven valid with many populations in many nations (Mesman et al., 2016). All humans seek social connection (item 1); secure attachments are likely in poor nations as well as rich ones (item 2), and attachment depends more on social interaction than on the specifics of birth or temperament (item 3).

The old idea of maternal instinct has been replaced by a newer idea that giving birth is only one of several factors that bond mother to child. Indeed, a study of children born via a surrogate (a woman who gestates a fetus for someone else) and then given to the parents found that attachment was similar to children raised by both biological parents (Carone et al., 2017).

Infants can be attached to both parents, or to a sibling, another relative, or a nonrelated caregiver (see A Case to Study). Exclusive attachment to the biological mother, and intensive attachment parenting, is *not* found in most families in most cultures.

Finally, early attachment relationships do seem to affect later friendships, romances, and parenting (item 4) (Feeney & Fitzgerald, 2019) You will read many examples later in this chapter, when we explain the family structures humans have created. First, we note how the attachment impulse is manifest as people develop.

A CASE TO STUDY

Can We Bear This Commitment?

I notice signs of secure or insecure attachment within families, even in families I see at the park, on the street, in the grocery store. I particularly observe families I know. I see parent–child attachment at least as strong in adoptive families as in genetic ones.

One adoptive couple is Macky and Nick, who adopted their daughters at birth. They echo my responses to my biological children. Two examples:

- When Alice was a few days old, I overheard Nick phone another parent, asking which detergent is best for washing baby clothes. That reminded me that I also switched detergents for my newborn.
- Years later, when Macky was engrossed in conversation, Nick interrupted to say they needed to stop talking because the girls needed to get home for their naps. I remembered times when I said exactly that to my loquacious husband.

My appreciation of their attachment was cemented by a third incident. In Macky's words:

I'll never forget the Fourth of July at the spacious home of my mother-in-law's best friend. It was a perfect celebration on a perfect day. Kids frolicked in the pool. Parents socialized nearby, on the sun-drenched lawn or inside the cool house. Many guests had published books on parenting; we imagined they admired our happy, thriving family.

My husband and I have two daughters, Alice who was then 7 and Penelope who was 4. They learned to swim early and are always the first to jump in the pool and the last to leave. Great children, and doesn't that mean great parents?

After hours of swimming, the four of us scrambled up to dry land. I went inside to the library to talk with my father, while most people enjoyed hot dogs, relish, mustard, and juicy watermelon.

Suddenly we heard a heart-chilling wail. Panicked, I raced to the pool's edge to see the motionless body of a small child who had gone unnoticed underwater for too long. His blue-face was still. Someone was giving CPR. His mother kept wailing, panicked, pleading, destroyed. I had a shameful thought—thank God that is not my child.

He lived. He regained his breath and was whisked away by ambulance. The party came to a quick close. We four, skin tingling from the summer sun, hearts beating from the near-death of a child who was my kids' playmate an hour before, drove away.

Turning to Nick, I asked, "Can we bear this commitment we have made? Can we raise our children in the face of all hazards—some we try to prevent, others beyond our control?"

That was five years ago. Our children are flourishing. Our confidence is strong and so are our emotions. But it takes only a moment to recognize just how entwined our well-being is with our children and how fragile life is. We are deeply grateful.

A Grateful Family This family photo shows *(from left to right)* Nick, Penelope, Macky, and Alice with their dog Cooper. When they adopted Alice as a newborn, the parents said, "This is a miracle we feared would never happen."

WHAT HAVE YOU LEARNED?

1. Why are John Bowlby and Mary Ainsworth called "an unlikely pair?"
2. What did Bowlby learn from Freud, Harlow, and Lorenz?
3. Why did Bowlby disagree with Freud's "point of view"?
4. What are the two sets of behaviors that indicate attachment?
5. Why are both secure and insecure attachments called strategies?
6. What is the difference between types of insecure attachment?
7. How is attachment measured in infancy?
8. What is universal, and what is cultural, in attachment?

Social Connections over the Life Span

Scientists have much to learn about human development. The pace of brain, body, and language development in infancy inspires awe, but many details and variations in infancy and beyond are unexplored. However, the main theme of this chapter is well established: Humans are social creatures. Babies develop attachments to survive, and then everyone needs to attach lifelong. This is apparent at every stage.

Infancy

Attachment, as Bowlby and Ainsworth described it, is evident at about age 1. But as you will now see, parent–child bonding begins before that, is evident in the first months of life, and extends beyond the standard Strange Situation measures of attachment.

Prenatal Attachment

Many pregnant women are thrilled to feel the first movement in the womb (called *quickening*, at about four months past conception). When kicks become more palpable and visible, fathers may put a hand on the spot, celebrating the new human.

Prenatal care typically includes a sonogram, printed out as a blurry photo that the pregnant couple cherish. Many prospective parents are eager to know the gender, size, and activity of their fetus. They often name, and bond with, the baby. If the fetus dies before birth, or if a newborn does not survive, the parents mourn a person, not merely a failed pregnancy.

This is important for outsiders to understand, as one account notes that friends sometimes say, "don't feel sad, you are young and can have another baby" (Malacrida, 2017, p. 27). The reality is that the mourning is for a particular baby, not a generic fetus; attachment is not a generality, it is a connection between two persons and it can begin as soon as the new creature makes its presence known.

The Newborn

Babies begin their part of the attachment effort as soon as they are born. It takes months, even years, for motor skills to develop, but newborns are ready to attach, their version of the imprinting Lorenz found in his goslings. Human babies prefer seeing, hearing, smelling, and touching people more than anything else.

The early appearance and actions of the baby are also a powerful trigger for adult attachment. This was expressed by one scientist:

> When a neonate turns to focus gaze on you, it can be an irresistible invitation to engage, to respond, to explore. Other people's responses to the flattery of these invitations can be the start of a developmental path of mutuality and connection. Prosocial feelings are a two-way business: infant interest cannot go anywhere on its own.
> *[Reddy, 2019, p. 2021]*

It was also expressed by a great aunt, who had already raised two grandnieces.

> I'm gonna take care of no more babies. . . . I'm too old. . . . But I was there when she was born. See, this is the thing that really hooked me. I was there when she took her first breaths. . . . she opened her eyes, looked at me, and started hollerin'. I was hooked like a fish. That was it.
> *[quoted in Stahl, 2016, p. 102]*

A few days later, she took that baby home, and mothered her for years. More generally, an infant's stare, or cry, or smile activates a caregiver, not always right after birth but usually in the days and weeks after that. This is evident neurologically: Adult brain waves coordinate with infant brains (Piazza et al., 2020; Wass et al., 2018).

Synchrony

Ideally, early caregiver–child relationships are characterized by **synchrony**, a mutual exchange that requires split-second timing. Metaphors for synchrony are

synchrony A coordinated, rapid, and smooth exchange of responses between a caregiver and an infant.

Open Wide Synchrony is evident worldwide. Everywhere, babies watch their parents carefully, hoping for exactly what these three parents—each from quite different cultures—express, and responding with such delight that adults relish these moments.

Observation Quiz The universality of synchrony is evident here, not only in the babies but also in the parents, each of whom began at birth with a quite different relationship to the baby. Can you guess what those differences are? (see answer, page 397) ↑

THINK CRITICALLY: What will happen if no one plays with an infant?

often musical—a waltz, a jazz duet—to emphasize that each partner is attuned to the other, with moment-by-moment responses. Synchrony is evident in the first three months: The first smiles at about 2 months have "enormous" power (Reddy, 2019), typically triggering strong reactions in every onlooker. Synchrony becomes more frequent and elaborate as the infant matures.

Long before they can reach out and grab, infants respond excitedly to caregiver attention by waving their arms. They are delighted if someone moves closer so that a small arm touches the face or, even better, a small hand can grab hair. In response, caregivers open their eyes wide, raise their eyebrows, smack their lips, and emit nonsense sounds. Hair grabbing might make adults bob their heads back and forth, in a playful attempt to shake off the grab, to the infants' delight.

Synchrony is a sign of attachment between partners of every age. It is evident in older children and adults, facilitating social interactions lifelong (Cirelli, 2018; Reddy, 2019). Do you know a couple who have a long and happy relationship? Watch for synchrony. They might mirror each other in facial expressions, body positions, tone of voice, even completing the sentences of the other.

Or imagine a staid patriarch with an infant grandchild: He might make noises, smile, shake his head. The stone-faced grandpa is transformed, and the baby responds. Synchrony again.

Childhood and Adolescence

Parents, grandparents, and other relatives continue to be attachment partners long past infancy. From age 2 to 20, however, social connections expand; peers and nonparent adults can have major impact, for good or ill.

Who Plays with You?

The influence of nonfamily members is evident in the two most important activities of children: play and education. Remember rough-and-tumble and sociodramatic play, both teaching children about their own selves and about the larger world? Both require playmates.

This was recognized almost a century ago, when Mildred Parten (1932) explained the development of social play during early childhood.

1. *Solitary play*: A child plays alone, unaware of any other children playing nearby.
2. *Onlooker play*: A child watches other children play.
3. *Parallel play*: Children play with similar objects in similar ways but not together.
4. *Associative play*: Children interact, sharing material, but their play is not reciprocal.
5. *Cooperative play*: Children play together, creating dramas or taking turns.

This last step, cooperative play, advances as children grow older, with team sports, dramatic performances, marching bands, and so on. Group activities teach cooperation, self-control, and emotional regulation—all essential lessons. A review confirmed that social play, but not one-person play, benefited learning (Lillard et al., 2013).

The need for peers became particularly evident when schools closed because of COVID-19. Although concerns about remote learning, food programs, and so on were noted immediately (e.g., Masonbrink & Hurley, 2020), psychologists worry about long-term impairment from absent social networks (Xin et al., 2020).

Learning Together

Social interactions lead to academic achievements, as recognized by both Vygotsky and Piaget, who said that "play is the work of childhood." Both theorists were well aware of the connection between play, learning, and the social influence of other students on each child, as they explained decades ago (Nicolopoulou, 1993). Having a good relationship with a teacher is the most powerful motivation for learning.

Friends are important for nonacademic learning, too. One example is that friends are the best defense against school bullies, not because they can stop the hurtful act (often they cannot) but because they drain the pain.

The fact that schooling is social is evident in bullies themselves. They need other children, not only as victims, but as admirers. School bullies almost never act alone: An audience is sought, because, especially by age 10 or so, bullies gain fear and respect from bystanders (Guy et al., 2019).

Bullies learn to be better bullies because of social learning: By age 10 they rarely do physical bullying (they might get hurt in a fight) and have learned to do verbal and relational harm, which is much more hurtful, again because the victims have become more attuned to social relationships as well.

Peers and Parents

Sometimes it is thought that, in the second decade of life, children switch from depending on parents to depending on friends. But that is not true: Peers do not supplant parents, they supplement them. Parents need to understand the influence of peers, while still maintaining supportive relationships with their children.

A longitudinal study of all U.S. middle school students (almost 800 of them) in one community found that three-fourths had healthy relationships with their parents *and* their peers. The two were correlated: A positive relationship with both groups provided some protection from serious problems during adolescence and early adulthood (Dishion et al., 2019).

Another study of 13-year-olds focused particularly on coping with stress, such as moving from one school to another, or problems in the family. Those best able to cope were those with supportive parents and friends (McMahon et al., 2020).

One stress for adolescents is talking with potential romantic partners. For this direct peer support is vital: Friends help friends to cope with ups and downs, encouraging them to talk to a special someone, or reassuring them if that someone rejects them.

Peer culture makes physical touch more, or less, likely. There is substantial variability in whether and when a teenager is dating, and what the dating relationship entails (Kindelberger et al., 2020) Their friends' actual experience is less influential than their perception of their friends' activity.

This is evident in sexting (sending sexual photos of oneself to a romantic partner). A study of older high school students (average age, 17) found that they misperceived how often their popular classmates sent sexts (Maheux et al., 2020).

Good over Evil or Evil over Good? Boys everywhere enjoy "strong man" fantasy play, as the continued popularity of Spider-Man and Superman attests. These boys follow that script. Both are Afghan refugees living in Pakistan.

ESPECIALLY FOR Parents of a Teenager Your 13-year-old comes home after a sleepover at a friend's house with a new, weird hairstyle—perhaps cut or colored in a bizarre manner. What do you say and do? (see response, page 397)

They thought that almost all (87 percent) of their popular peers were sexting, although a confidential survey found no significant differences in sexting among the popular compared to the less popular students (overall rate was 55 percent). The students who were more likely to send sexts were also those who imagined that popular students did more sexting than was actually the case (Maheux et al., 2020).

Siblings

The peers who are most immediate, of course, are brothers and sisters. Siblings influence each other to be more empathic or deviant (Daniel et al., 2018; Jambon et al., 2019). That influence is reciprocal. Parents sometimes favor the oldest or youngest, the boys or the girls. That complicates the interactions: Better is for the parents to try to structure fair and equitable interaction and let the siblings develop their own bonds (Pike & Oliver, 2017).

In childhood, some sibling rivalry seems inevitable, teaching negotiating skills. In adolescence, if the environment and genes push a teen toward negative behavior, a successful and admired older sibling can be crucial, advising the younger one to stay in school, avoid drugs, and so on (Aizpitarte et al., 2019; Gallagher et al., 2018). On the other hand, one sibling can lead another into trouble.

A few decades ago, children without siblings were thought to be selfish and lonely. But a study of 20,000 adults concluded "beliefs about only children appear to contradict actual group differences" (Stronge et al., 2019), and another study found no evidence that single-born children are unusually selfish or asocial (Foster et al., 2020).

Changing social contexts might be the reason. Perhaps in the nineteenth century, when 90 percent of the economy was devoted to agriculture and many families lived on isolated farms, a child without brothers or sisters might not learn how to interact with other children. Currently, however, parents of a single child find playmates, day-care centers, and early education: Their children are not loners.

The importance of sibling influence is apparent in a study of twins. A study of drug use and delinquency found that—even controlling for genes and environment—when one twin broke the law, the other was likely to break the *same* law (Laursen et al., 2017).

Peer Influence

Throughout childhood, children compare themselves to each other, in the social comparison described in Chapter 10. What they wear, what slang they used, what skills they learn, depend on what they see and hear from other children.

The role of social attachments is useful in understanding teenagers who break the law (see Inside the Brain). Many researchers distinguish between two kinds of young lawbreakers (Levey et al., 2019; Monahan et al., 2013), as first proposed by Terri Moffitt (2001, 2003). Both types are arrested for the first time in adolescence for similar crimes, but their futures diverge.

Those who break the law with friends are usually **adolescence-limited offenders**, whose criminal activity stops by age 21. If they also have healthy relationships with their parents, they are unlikely to use drugs or to commit crimes later on (Dishion et al., 2019).

Those who break the law alone may be **life-course-persistent offenders**. They are not attached to peers or adults, which bodes

adolescence-limited offenders A person whose criminal activity stops by age 21.

life-course-persistent offenders A person whose criminal activity typically begins in early adolescence and continues throughout life; a career criminal.

● **Observation Quiz** What evidence do you see that traditional norms remain in this culture? (see answer, page 397) ↓

More Familiar Than Foreign? Even in cultures with strong and traditional family influence, teenagers choose to be with peers whenever they can. These boys play at Cherai Beach in India.

EyesWideOpen/Getty Images News/Getty Images

INSIDE THE BRAIN

Lopsided Growth

Laurence Steinberg is a noted expert on adolescence (e.g., Steinberg, 2014, 2015). He is also a father.

When my son, Benjamin, was 14, he and three of his friends decided to sneak out of the house where they were spending the night and visit one of their girlfriends at around two in the morning. When they arrived at the girl's house, they positioned themselves under her bedroom window, threw pebbles against her windowpanes, and tried to scale the side of the house. Modern technology, unfortunately, has made it harder to play Romeo these days. The boys set off the house's burglar alarm, which activated a siren and simultaneously sent a direct notification to the local police station, which dispatched a patrol car. When the siren went off, the boys ran down the street and right smack into the police car, which was heading to the girl's home. Instead of stopping and explaining their activity, Ben and his friends scattered and ran off in different directions through the neighborhood. One of the boys was caught by the police and taken back to his home, where his parents were awakened and the boy questioned.

I found out about this affair the following morning, when the girl's mother called our home to tell us what Ben had done. . . . After his near brush with the local police, Ben had returned to the house out of which he had snuck, where he slept soundly until I awakened him with an angry telephone call, telling him to gather his clothes and wait for me in front of his friend's house. On our drive home, after delivering a long lecture about what he had done and about the dangers of running from armed police in the dark when they believe they may have interrupted a burglary, I paused.

"What were you thinking?" I asked.

"That's the problem, Dad," Ben replied, "I wasn't."

[Steinberg, 2004, pp. 51, 52]

Steinberg's son was right: When emotions are intense, especially when friends are nearby, cortisol floods the brain, causing the prefrontal cortex to shut down. This shutdown is not reflected in questionnaires that require teenagers to respond to paper-and-pencil questions regarding hypothetical dilemmas. On those tests, most teenagers think carefully and answer correctly. In fact, when strong emotions are not activated, teenagers may be more logical than adults (Casey & Caudle, 2013). They remember facts that they have learned in biology or health class about sex and drugs. They know exactly how HIV is transmitted, how pregnancy occurs, and how alcohol affects the brain. However,

the prospect of visiting a hypothetical girl from class cannot possibly carry the excitement about the possibility of surprising someone you have a crush on with a visit in the middle of the night. It is easier to put on a hypothetical condom during an act of hypothetical sex than it is to put on a real one when one is in the throes of passion. It is easier to just say no to a hypothetical beer than it is to a cold frosty one on a summer night.

[Steinberg, 2004, p. 53]

Ben reached adulthood safely. Other teenagers, with less cautious police or less diligent parents, do not. Brain immaturity makes teenagers vulnerable to social pressures and stresses, which typically bombard young people today. Emotional control, revealed by fMRI studies, is not fully developed until adulthood, because the prefrontal cortex is less connected to the limbic system (Hartley & Somerville, 2015). Thoughtful reappraisal of emotional impulses is slower in adolescence than later on (Schweizer et al., 2020; Silvers et al., 2015).

Longitudinal research finds that heightened arousal occurs in the brain's reward centers — specifically the *nucleus accumbens*, a region of the ventral striatum that is connected to the limbic system — when adolescent brains are compared to their own brains earlier or later in development (Braams et al., 2015). Further, when other teens are watching, adolescents are thrilled to take dramatic risks that produce social acclaim, risks they would not dare take alone. Interestingly, the reward regions that are highly activated when peers are watching decrease in activation when the adolescent's mother is nearby (Telzer et al., 2015).

The research on adolescent brain development confirms two insights regarding adolescent growth in general. First, physiological changes triggered by puberty are dramatic, unlike those of either childhood or adulthood. Second, the social context matters — the body and brain of humans respond not only to hormones and physical maturation but also to friends and family.

Most states in the United States now restrict drivers under age 18, such as mandating no passengers under age 20, or only family members as passengers. That saves lives, because teenagers are less likely to race a train, pass a truck, or zoom around a blind curve when alone.

---

ill for their future. The hope for them is that they will develop attachments in adulthood: marriage and parenthood reduce criminality, particularly in men (Zoutewelle-Terovan et al., 2014).

Peer pressure occurs when someone is pushed by friends to do something that they would not do alone. Peer pressure is especially strong in early adolescence, when adults seem clueless about biological and social stresses, but peers empathize.

peer pressure Encouragement to conform to one's friends or contemporaries in behavior, dress, and attitude; usually considered a negative force, as when adolescent peers encourage one another to defy adult authority.

A VIEW FROM SCIENCE

Your Classmates

An intriguing study began with all eleventh-graders in several public schools in Los Angeles, that had some honors and some nonhonors classes. Researchers visited every class to offer a free course, worth $200, to prepare for the Scholastic Aptitude Test (SAT) (often a factor in college admission). Students were not allowed to discuss the offer: They had to decide on the spot whether to accept the free course, signing a paper to indicate yes or no (Bursztyn & Jensen, 2015).

It is important to understand that individual students were not honors or nonhonors (as happens in some schools that have two tracks); the classes in each subject were tracked but many students chose some honors and some nonhonors classes.

Although all of the papers had identical, detailed descriptions of the SAT program, one word differed regarding who would learn of their decision—either no other students or only the students in that particular class.

The two versions were:

Your decision to sign up for the course will be kept completely private from everyone, <u>except</u> the other students in the room.

Your decision to sign up for the course will be kept completely private from everyone, <u>including</u> the other students in the room.

That word mattered. When they thought their classmates would know what they did, being in an honors class made a student more likely to sign up, and being in nonhonors class, less likely.

To make sure this was a peer effect, not just divergent motivation between honors and nonhonors students, the researchers compared students who took two, and only two honors classes. There were 107 such students. Some of them happened to be in their honors class when they decided whether or not to sign up for SAT prep and some happened to be in their nonhonors class.

When the decisions of those 107 were kept totally private, acceptance rates were similar (72 and 79 percent) no matter which class students were in at the moment. But, if students thought their classmates might know their decision, *imagined* peer pressure affected them. When in an honors class, 97 percent signed up for the SAT program; when in a nonhonors class, only 54 percent signed up (Bursztyn & Jensen, 2015).

Having friends is beneficial: Peers pressure each other to study and to plan for their future. The peers with the strongest influence are those in the immediate social circle. Two forces guide peer relationships: *selection* and *facilitation*. Children select friends with similar values and interests. Then, imagined or actual peer pressure facilitates destructive or constructive behaviors (see A View from Science).

It is easier to do wrong ("Let's all skip school on Friday") or right ("Let's study together for the chem exam") with friends. Happy, energetic, and successful children have high-achieving friends, and vice versa. Parents should not blame "a wrong crowd" for their child's behavior, because those friends were chosen and then facilitated.

Attachments in Adulthood

Adults have many attachments, not originally proposed by Bowlby and Ainsworth, but studied by many researchers. Friends, lovers, and strangers influence everyone.

Love and Romance

Most adults seek romantic partners. Variations in family constellations are discussed later in this chapter, but a general trend is that adult partnerships are influenced by attachments formed in infancy (Hazan & Shaver, 1987; Levy et al., 2015).

For example, those who were securely attached (type B) are more likely to have supportive partnerships; those who were avoidant (type A) are likely to fear

VIDEO ACTIVITY: Marriage in Adulthood features researcher Ronald Sabatelli and interviews of people discussing the joys and challenges of marriage.

commitment; and those who were anxious (type C) are likely to be overly dependent. Worst of all, again, may be those who experienced disorganized attachment (type D): They may switch from adoration to loathing and back again, making it almost impossible for their partner to continue the relationship (Beeney et al., 2017).

The partner has a role in this. For example, if a partner expresses gratitude, an adult is likely to feel less anxious about the relationship (Park et al., 2019).

Robert Sternberg (1988) described three distinct aspects of love, which is the glue that attaches one partner to another (see **Table 13.2**). The first, passion, is evident early in a relationship, with intense physical, cognitive, and emotional arousal characterized by excitement, ecstasy, and euphoria. The entire body and mind, hormones and neurons, are activated; the person is obsessed (Sanz Cruces et al., 2015).

Passionate love is difficult to measure. In fact, 33 scales attempt to measure it; each of these is distinct, although overlap is also common (Hatfield et al., 2012). For current young adults, passion does not usually lead to marriage.

Intimacy is knowing someone well. This aspect of love is reciprocal, with each partner gradually revealing more as well as accepting more of the other's revelations. The moonstruck joy of passionate love can become bittersweet as intimacy increases. As one observer explains, "Falling in love is absolutely no way of getting to know someone" (Sullivan, 1999, p. 225).

The research is not clear about the best schedule for passion and intimacy, whether they should progress slowly or quickly, for instance. According to some research, they may be disconnected, as lust arises from a different part of the brain than affection (Fisher, 2016a; Langeslag et al., 2013).

The third aspect, commitment, is enshrined in marriage and childbearing. Social forces, especially families, strengthen or undermine commitment.

TABLE 13.2

Sternberg's Seven Forms of Love

Present in the Relationship?

Form of Love	Passion	Intimacy	Commitment
Liking	No	Yes	No
Infatuation	Yes	No	No
Empty love	No	No	Yes
Romantic love	Yes	Yes	No
Fatuous love	Yes	No	Yes
Companionate love	No	Yes	Yes
Consummate love	Yes	Yes	Yes

Information from Sternberg, 1988.

A Lover's Kiss Ralph Young awakens Ruth *(left)* with a kiss each day, as he has for most of the 78 years of their marriage. Here they are both 99, sharing a room in their Indiana residence, "more in love than ever." Half a world away, in Ukraine *(right)*, more kisses occur, with 70 newly married couples and one couple celebrating their golden anniversary. Developmental data suggest that now, several years after these photos, the two old couples (if both partners are still alive) are more likely to be happily married than the 70 young ones.

Apparently, once adults make a commitment, they expect to be devoted to that person's well-being for years, which explains why contemporary young adults take almost a decade longer to marry and have children than was the case historically.

When passion, intimacy, and commitment are all present, Sternberg called that *consummate love*. The ideal that can be reached in any partnership but is more likely to occur in long-term relationships.

Conflict

Serious conflict among partners and family members is less evident in cultures that stress **familism**, the belief that family members should sacrifice individualism to care for one another. Specifics of who should sacrifice what for whom varies by culture.

familism The belief that family members should support one another, sacrificing individual freedom and success, if necessary, in order to preserve family unity and protect the family from outside forces.

For example, most refugee youth (Palestinian, Syrian, Iraqi) in Jordan agree that parents have the right to decide their children's hairstyles, clothes, and music—contrary to what most U.S. teenagers believe (Smetana et al., 2016).

Among U.S. Latinx families, familism means that parents should ask what their children do and with whom, and that children should reply honestly with respect. That is called a "high-monitoring" family, with everyone expecting shared information. However, many Latinx parents avoid conflict by not criticizing their children, especially regarding hair or clothes. Then, high-monitoring, low-conflict families have happy, helpful, high-performing adolescents. The opposite is true for high-monitoring, high-conflict families (Roche et al., 2019).

Pivotal is how conflict is handled. For example, one study began by asking 101 couples to discuss a conflict in their marriage (Low et al., 2019). Then they were videoed helping their 5-year-olds build a tower. The discussion and the helping were analyzed by independent judges.

Three strategies to deal with conflict were observed: *disengagement* (avoiding discussion of the conflict, a type A strategy), *aversive cognitive perseveration* (escalating, taking opposite sides, with great intensity, a type C strategy), and *adaptive engagement* (seeking to understand the other, finding a compromise, a type B strategy). Only the third strategy reduced the conflict.

Conflict affected their later interaction with the child. Some parents expressed anger (those who were disengaged or aversive), and some expressed delight (more often those with adaptive engagement) at their child's immature skill at tower-building. This is an example of a general finding: Parents' attachment style with their partner is likely to reflect their attachment style with their children.

Not My Fault Humans always seem to find it easier to blame someone else, but this is particularly true when teenage girls talk to their mothers.

Resolving Conflicts

If conflict is rife and ongoing, that destroys not only the marriage but also the children's well-being. Unresolved, open conflict harms all family relationships, yet "conflict is natural and inevitable, and it has functional, positive aspects" (Gottman & Gottman, 2017, p. 17). People disagree, but that need not break social bonds.

How should conflict be resolved? Some guidelines that apply to all conflicts, at every age, are:

- Use humor;
- Stick to the issue at hand (don't bring up past problems);
- Express respect;

"So I blame you for everything—whose fault is that?"

B. Smaller

- Seek understanding; and
- Remember that the relationship is more important than winning an argument.

One particularly devastating pattern in adult relationships is **demand/withdraw**, when one partner insists on explanations while the other retreats. "We need to talk about this" is met with "No—not now" or simply *stonewalling*, a complete lack of response. This begins a downward spiral: Demanding becomes yelling, and stone-walling leads to slammed doors and angry exits (Merrill & Afifi, 2012).

Think of this in attachment terms. The demanding partner is using a type C strategy, and the withdrawing partner is using type A. No wonder such couples are likely to separate if they cannot reach a type B middle.

demand/withdraw A pattern of social interaction in which one partner increasingly demands response, and the other increasingly withdraws from the relationship.

How to Relate to Children

One of the most common conflicts between parents is how to raise the children.

Fifty years ago Diana Baumrind studied 100 preschool children (Baumrind, 1967, 1971). She found that parents differed on four dimensions:

1. *Expressions of warmth.* Some were warm and affectionate; others, cold and critical.
2. *Strategies for social interaction.* Parents varied in responding, attending, punishing.
3. *Communication.* Some listened patiently; others demanded silence.
4. *Expectations.* Some expected maturity and self-control; others did not.

On the basis of these dimensions, Baumrind identified three parenting styles (summarized in **Table 13.3**).

- **Authoritarian parenting.** The authoritarian parent's word is law, not to be questioned, a style called *power-assertive*. Misconduct brings strict punishment, usually physical. Authoritarian parents set rules and hold high standards. Children are expected to obey, not disagree.
- **Permissive parenting.** Permissive parents (also called *indulgent*) make few demands, accepting immaturity. Discipline is rare. Permissive parents listen to their offspring, even if they curse the parent (never allowed in an authoritarian family).
- **Authoritative parenting.** Authoritative parents set limits, and encourage maturity, but they usually listen and forgive (not punish) if the child falls

authoritarian parenting An approach to child rearing that is characterized by high behavioral standards, strict punishment of misconduct, and little communication from child to parent.

permissive parenting An approach to child rearing that is characterized by high nurturance and communication but little discipline, guidance, or control.

authoritative parenting An approach to child rearing in which the parents set limits and enforce rules but are flexible and listen to their children.

TABLE 13.3

Characteristics of Parenting Styles Identified by Baumrind

Parenting Style	Warmth	Discipline	Expectations of Maturity	Communication Style	
				Parent to Child	Child to Parent
Authoritarian	Low	Strict, often physical	High	High	Low
Permissive	High	Rare	Low	Low	High
Authoritative	High	Moderate, with much discussion	Moderate	High	High

neglectful/uninvolved parenting An approach to child rearing in which the parents seem indifferent toward their children, not knowing or caring about their children's lives.

short. They consider themselves guides, not authorities (unlike authoritarian parents) and not friends (unlike permissive parents).

- **Neglectful/uninvolved parenting** is a fourth style, described by other researchers. Neglectful parents ignore their children's behavior; their children do whatever they want. But notice a crucial contrast between uninvolved parents and permissive parents. The former seems not to care; the latter cares very much.

Long-term consequences of these parenting styles have been reported in many nations (Baumrind, 2013; Deater-Deckard, 2013; Gülseven et al., 2018; Lawrence et al., 2019; Nelson et al., 2019; Xu et al., 2019). Cultural variations are evident, but trends are:

- *Authoritarian* parents raise children who become conscientious, obedient, and quiet but not especially happy. Such children tend to feel guilty or depressed, internalizing their frustrations and blaming themselves when things don't go well. As adolescents, they sometimes rebel, leaving home before age 20.
- *Permissive* parents raise children who lack self-control, especially in the give-and-take of peer relationships. Inadequate emotional regulation makes them immature and impedes friendships; they are unhappy. They tend to continue to live at home, still dependent on their parents in adulthood.
- *Authoritative* parents raise children who are successful, articulate, happy with themselves, and generous with others. These children are usually liked by teachers and peers, especially in cultures that value individual initiative (e.g., the United States).
- *Neglectful/uninvolved* parents raise children who are immature, sad, lonely, and at risk of injury and abuse, not only in early childhood but also lifelong.

Notice that each of these parenting styles influences how children interact with other people. Humans learn social skills and values from their early experiences. Each can be seen as an outgrowth of a particular attachment style, with the authoritative style encouraging the mutual interaction characterized by secure attachment (Ebrahimi et al., 2017; Ming & Baharudin, 2017).

So far, the research on the connection between parenting style and attachment type is more prevalent in the Middle East than in the Americas, again raising the question of how universal attachment and parenting styles are. More research is needed!

Disagreement between parents about how to raise the children arises partly because every adult is influenced by how they themselves were raised. Since cultural differences are evident, and since ethnic, religious, regional, and economic diversity in the United States make "every marriage . . . a cross-cultural experience" (Gottman & Gottman, 2017, p. 19), it is not surprising that parents disagree.

Ideally, the parents discuss their disagreements and present a united front. But this does not always happen. One of my students wrote:

> My mother externalized her feelings with outbursts of rage, lashing out and breaking things, while my father internalized his feelings by withdrawing, being silent and looking the other way. One could say I was being raised by bipolar parents. Growing up, I would describe my mom as the Tasmanian devil and my

Protect Me from the Water Buffalo These two are at the Carabao Kneeling Festival. In rural Philippines, hundreds of these large but docile animals kneel on the steps of the church, part of a day of gratitude for the harvest.

REUTERS/Erik de Castro

father as the ostrich, with his head in the sand. . . . My mother disciplined with corporal punishment as well as with psychological control, while my father was permissive. What a pair.

[C., 2013]

This student is now a single parent, having twice married, given birth, and divorced. She is one example of a general finding: The effects of childhood linger.

The right balance between demand and affection depends on the child and the culture. As evident many times in this chapter, human attachment involves two people, each connected to the other. Parents and children develop their relationship together. Although good parenting takes many forms, which means that outsiders should not be too quick to judge other families, it is also evident that hostile, punitive parenting has never helped children, and every child needs protection and guidance. This leads to a sad topic.

Child Maltreatment

The most glaring example of failed attachment occurs with **child abuse**, deliberate action that harms physical, emotional, or sexual well-being, and **child neglect**, failure to meet essential needs, such as for food, medical care, or learning. These are extremes of authoritarian or neglectful parenting. Both forms of maltreatment are social experiences: Someone else does, or does not, do something.

In 2018, 677,529 children in the United States were reported, investigated, and verified as maltreated. Of those, 61 percent were neglected, 11 percent physically abused, 2 percent psychologically abused, 7 percent sexually abused (see **Figure 13.1**). Worst of all, 15 percent experienced multiple abuses (Department of Health and Human Services, January 15, 2020). (The remaining 4 percent were medical, educational, or unclassified.)

The problem is complex, with many overlapping causes, but lack of attachment is often at the core. A meta-analysis of 16 studies found that parents with insecure attachments—to their mothers, to their romantic partners, to their children—were about three times more likely to mistreat their children than adults who had experienced secure attachment. The most chilling statistic: Parents who were insecurely attached were five times more likely to kill their children (Lo et al., 2019).

child abuse Deliberate action that is harmful to a child's physical, emotional, or sexual well-being.

child neglect Failure to meet a child's basic physical, educational, or emotional needs.

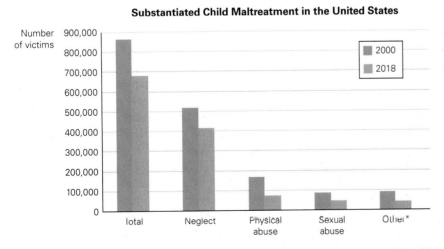

Substantiated Child Maltreatment in the United States

Data from U.S. Department of Health and Human Services, December 31, 2000, p. 24, January 15, 2020, p. 38.
*Includes emotional and medical abuse, educational neglect, and maltreatment not specified by the state records.

FIGURE 13.1

Not Good News It might seem to be good news that physical and sexual abuse are increasingly unusual. But the continued high rate of neglect is ominous. Adults can overcome memories of abuse, but neglect is likely to leave enduring traces on the brain.

Fortunately, most adults with past insecure attachment or even past maltreatment do _not_ abuse their children (Widom et al., 2015a). As you read, infants are primed to evoke care: Some adults who seem detached from other adults may become strongly attached to their children. Psychologists recognize the "central role of attachment" and work to strengthen early parent–child attachment (Toth & Manly, 2019).

One insight from attachment theory is that the early months and years are crucial. Even if maltreatment stops at age 5, emotional problems (externalizing for the boys and internalizing for the girls) linger (Godinet et al., 2014). As stressed in Chapter 10, drug abuse, social isolation, and poor health can be traced to _adverse childhood experiences_, including maltreatment, family chaos, and father absence.

All is not lost, however. Hate is corrosive; love is healing. A warm and enduring adult relationship can repair some childhood damage. A secure attachment to a loving romantic partner may allow secure attachment with one's child (Dion et al., 2019).

Parenting over the Life Span

Maltreatment occurs far too often, but much more often, parents are dedicated to their children lifelong. This is dramatically evident when an adult has a serious disability that makes independence impossible (Solomon, 2012). Many parents continue to care for their disabled adult children, asserting that this caregiving is a positive aspect of their life (Howson & McKay, 2020).

Such parents are the most striking example of the attachment many parents feel to their grown children. Moreover, past attachments affect adults when neither generation is particularly needy. One 80-year-old "watches her middle-aged children for signs of improvement," because a mother "never outgrows the burden of love" (Scott-Maxwell, 1968, p. 16).

The commitment of parents to their children is also evident in how many adult children are independent from their parents. About two-thirds (64 percent) of all Americans believe that by age 22, young adults should be financially independent, but less than one-fourth (24 percent) of 22-year-olds actually are (Barroso et al., 2019).

U.S. statistics show more multigenerational families, which some people mistakenly assume that means that more grandparents live with their grandchildren. But that is not true: The two adult generations who are increasingly likely to live together are young adults and their middle-aged parents. In July 2020, 52 percent of all 18- to 29-year-olds lived with one or both of their parents, a rate that was already high but that increased with the COVID-19 pandemic (Fry et al., 2020).

This raises the topic of _helicopter parenting_, when parents hover over a grown child, ready to swoop in when needed, or worse, _snowplow parenting_, removing obstacles in their children's path. It is not easy to determine when family support is restrictive and when it is liberating (Wolbert et al., 2018). Families and cultures vary, often for good reasons (Son & Padilla-Walker, 2019). But it is easy to recognize that many parents are attached to their children, lifelong.

Not only are parents attached to their children, but also adult children are attached to their parents, trying to convince them to change their diet, to go to the doctor, to move to a safer home. Family caregivers shoulder most of the burden of care for aged parents who suffer from severe physical or cognitive losses. Why? The impulse goes beyond social norms or past history. Instead, there may be "a longstanding loving relationship that has value in itself; a value so deep that it cannot be effaced even by horrific disease" (Lang & Fowers, 2019, p. 204).

Family Systems

Every family member is connected to every other, a phenomenon called **linked lives** (e.g., Wickrama et al., 2013a; Settersten, 2015). Proponents of this idea explain:

> Because of the linked, or interdependent, lives of individuals within a family system, the events, trajectories, or transitions occurring within one family member's life may have reverberating effects on the lives of the other members. . . . Children's, parents', and grandparents' lives are intricately and dependently intertwined across each generation's life course.
>
> *[Gilligan et al., 2018, pp. 115–116]*

Thus, if one family member graduates from college, or is hospitalized, or gains or loses a job, everyone else is affected. Imagine three sisters walking along, arm-in-arm, and the middle one stumbles. The sisters on either side hold her up until she regains her balance. Linked arms is a metaphor for linked lives.

This concept underlies **family systems theory**. A family is a system, like systems in the body (the reproductive system, for instance) or in public life (the transportation system). The idea is that several parts work together to allow smooth functioning. Thus, relationships between any subsystem of a family touches everyone else: A child is affected by the parents' relationship, or by how the older siblings cooperate, even if the child is unaware of those interactions. The grandparents, who may live elsewhere, are part of the family system as well.

linked lives Lives in which the success, health, and well-being of each family member are connected to those of other members, including those of another generation, as in the relationship between parents and children.

family systems theory The idea that a family is a dynamic, interactive system, with each part affecting the other parts, and the entire interaction making the whole greater than the parts.

Fortunate Boys This single father *(left)* in Pennsylvania takes his three sons to the playground almost every day, and this family *(right)* in Mali invests time and money in their only child's education. All four boys have loving fathers. Does family function make family structure irrelevant?

Rules, Routines, and Rituals

Each family develops a culture that sustains them (Fiese et al., 2019). Rules and routines keep chaos and confusion away: Everyone knows that they must remove their shoes at the door (or not), or come to dinner at 6 (or 7), or brush their teeth in the morning and at night (or after every meal).

Rules and routines vary from one family to another and are designed to make life easier for everyone. They are practical; they change if circumstances change. In some families, one parent sets them (a patriarch or matriarch); in some families they are set by a family meeting. But families need rules and rituals to keep the family system working. If they become outdated as outside forces change what is needed, a new routine can be established.

For instance, suppose an adolescent joins the soccer team, requiring afterschool practice that has them arriving home, dirty and sweaty, minutes before 6. The dinner rule changes: The new routine might be "shower after outdoor play; dinner at 6:30." No chaos. The particulars matter less than having regular rules and routines that everyone knows.

Researchers have focused on low-income families, because they are buffeted with stresses that might impede good functioning. However, if a financially stressed family has well-established routines for eating, sleeping, and so on, dysfunction is less likely (Fiese et al, 2016; Philbrook et al., 2020). Lights out for everyone at the same time, after snacks, or books, or prayers, or whatever, makes bedtime arguments disappear.

Unlike rules and routines, which adjust with circumstances, rituals are embedded deeply within the family. They do not readily change, because they give the family identity and coherence. Birthdays often become rituals. Some cultures have a major celebration at age 1 (e.g., mundan in South Asia, when the hair is shaved); others when a child reaches age 13 (e.g., the bat or bar mitzvah for a Jewish child); others when a girl turns 15 (e.g., la quinceañera in Latin American nations and cultures). Those events are maintained, even when the family is far from their native land where the celebration originated.

As with these examples, many rituals arise from religions. Other signify roots: Immigrant families often have a song, or phrase, from the "old country"; Asian American families may have a corner of the house with photos of ancestors, or organize their home according to feng shui, even if they deny being religious at all (Jeung et al., 2019).

Socioeconomic Status

You just read that much of the research on the harmful effects of family chaos has focused on low-income families. We need to delve deeper into the impact of SES on family systems.

Marriage rates fall with economic recession, while rates of divorce and domestic violence rise, especially if someone loses a job. Low SES correlates with other problems, so "risk factors pile up in the lives of some children, particularly among the most disadvantaged" (Masten, 2014, p. 95).

Several scholars have developed the *family stress model*, which holds that any risk, such as poverty, divorce, or unemployment, damages a family if, and only if, it increases stress on the parents, making them less patient and responsive (Masarik & Conger, 2017).

If parents fear that they cannot provide food and shelter for the children, then worry may render them tense and hostile. The parents' *reaction* to low income may exacerbate or minimize the actual deprivation. Some events that are usually stressful can be benign if the parents are not troubled. For instance, reframing a job loss as an opportunity for something better protects the children.

Family rules and rituals may help family pride and cohesion, and that may be protective.

An unexpected correlation is evident: Adolescents in high-income families are more likely to develop problems related to suicide, drug addiction, or eating disorders than those in middle-SES families (Luthar et al., 2018). Family stress and lax routines may be the explanation: Wealthy parents who worry about their own status may pressure their children to excel, and may be so engrossed in their own struggles that they do not provide the ongoing support that the children need. That may lead the children to crushing fear of failure, causing loneliness, depression, and drug use.

Two-Parent Families

There are dozens of family systems, each with strengths and weaknesses. Often family structures are organized simply by whether they are headed by two parents or one. This does not take into account all the practical variations, as we soon explain. Nonetheless, we begin with the binary, two parents or one.

The "Standard North American Family"

A **nuclear family** has two parents, at least one child, and no other relatives. Traditionally the children are biological progeny, from the father's sperm and the mother's ova. That family type was formerly called the *Standard North American Family (SNAF)* (Smith, 1993), because it once was the U.S. norm, more common than any other family type.

Perhaps because it is often considered "standard," children in those families, on average, achieve most educationally, from preschool through college, and they are less likely to be depressed, aggressive, or have other psychological problems. The parents also benefit: In middle age and beyond, long-married men and women tend to be happier and healthier than their divorced contemporaries (Mikucka, 2016).

However, there are good reasons to examine that correlation. The data confirm the advantages of the nuclear family, but there are two questions. First, do children fare best in such families because societies are structured to support those families more than other families? Second, are nuclear families *always* best for children?

The answer to the first question is maybe, and to the second question, no. Some benefits of standard nuclear families are correlates, not causes.

Every comparison of high- and low-SES adults suggests "close to two different subsystems" of family organization in the United States today (Cherlin, 2020, p. 69). Married parents raising their own children also tend to be wealthier and better educated before they married, and then tax codes, health care, housing, and so on favors them. Thus, children in nuclear families tend to fare well, but interpreting that correlation is complex.

Adoptive Families

Children who are raised by two adoptive parents have a major advantage: Adopted children are much wanted, whereas many (estimates range from 30 to 50 percent) of the children born in biological families are mistimed or unwanted (Guzzo & Hayford, 2020). Adoptive parents not only choose to have their children, but they also average fewer divorces and more education.

Domestic adoptions are usually *open*, which means that the birth mother decided that someone else would be a better parent, but she still wanted to know that her child was growing and learning. Most adopted children develop as well or better than other children their age, especially when they are under age 12. During adolescence, concerns about identity (Chapter 10) may add stress to the family (Farr & Grotevant, 2019).

Shared Environment? All three children live in the same home in Brooklyn, New York, with loving, middle-class parents. But, it is not hard to imagine that family life is quite different for the 9-year-old girl than for her sister, born a year later, or their little brother, age 3.

Observation Quiz Are significant gender differences evident here? (see answer, page 397) ↑

nuclear family A family that consists of a father, a mother, and their biological children under age 18.

Structure or Function? This mother and her child could be half of a nuclear family, or a single mother with one adoptive child, or part of four other family structures. That does not matter as much as family function: If this scene is typical, with both enjoying physical closeness in the great outdoors, this family functions well.

Living Arrangements of U.S. Adults—Age 18 and Older

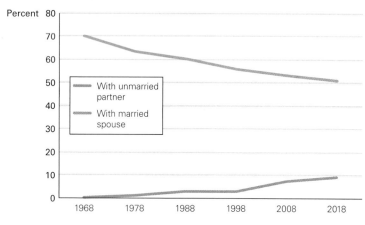

Data from Current Population Survey, Annual Social and Economic Supplement, 1967–2019.

FIGURE 13.2

Rise and Fall Note that this chart shows all adults, of every age. That makes the 20-percent reduction in married couples, and the 10 percent increase in cohabiting couples, a significant change in the entire culture, not just a change for those in their 20's—who are more often living together than married.

cohabitation When a couple live together in a committed romantic relationship but are not formally married.

Middle American Family This photo shows a typical breakfast in Brunswick, Ohio—Cheerios for 1-year-old Carson, pancakes that 7-year-old Carter does not finish eating, and happy family photos crowded on the far table.

DAVID MAXWELL/The New York Times/Redux

Parents Who Do Not Marry

Cohabitation (when unmarried couples live together) has become the norm in the United States among young adults, as well as common among older adults who have new partners after divorce (Sassler & Lichter, 2020). Most (59 percent) of all U.S. adults under age 45 have cohabited (Graf, 2019) (see **Figure 13.2**). Some cohabiting couples eventually marry, but many do not. If they stay together for years, they function like a married couple, and they may bear and raise children.

This family structure has many advantages for the adults. It provides some independence, makes sexual and emotional interaction easier, and saves housing costs. In some European nations, children of cohabiting parents fare as well as those of married parents (Rijken & Liefbroer, 2016).

Surprisingly, in many African and Latin American nations, children of cohabiting parents are healthier and better educated than other children. The reason is that cohabiting mothers tend to be of higher SES than married mothers, and they pass these advantages on to their children (Pierce & Heaton, 2019).

However, in the United States, children whose parents cohabit rather than marry fare less well than children in married nuclear families. The reason may be that, in the United States, cohabiting couple tend to be lower SES and less committed to each other. They are more likely to separate, even if they have children together.

Same-Sex Parents

In 29 nations, a married couple family can be headed by two men or two women. In the United States, about half a million same-sex couples have married. Before legalization of that family structure, opponents said that their children would have troubled childhoods. Those fears were unfounded.

For example, a large study in Europe comparing children in male–female, female–female, and male–male couples found, unexpectedly, that the major predictor of a child's well-being was not the parents' sexual orientation but their income and marital status (Cenegy et al., 2018). Married parents had more successful children than unmarried parents.

Another study twice (in 2008 and 2015) compared how children of same-sex couples in the United States fared compared to other-sex couples. In 2008, neighborhoods mattered. If the community was hostile to same-sex couples, the children averaged lower grades in school. By 2015, in every neighborhood, children did equally well no matter what their parents' sexual orientation (Boertien & Bernardi, 2019). Obviously, national culture had changed, which meant that the local community mattered less.

Stepfamilies

Another type of two parent family is also vulnerable to the specifics of culture and income. That is the stepfamily. Remarried adults benefit from having a mate who loves them, but stepchildren have higher rates of illness, injury, or, in adolescence, pregnancy, drug addiction, and arrest, than other children their age.

The problem is that every new living arrangement is disruptive, especially if it involves new schools, friends, siblings, and parents. Further, the rules, routines, and rituals change: New dining and sleeping arrangements can be disconcerting.

Children need clear routines, yet parents often disagree. Ideally, in all two-parent families, parents discuss discipline, develop compromises, and present a solid front early on—not easy, but worth the effort to have stable family rules.

But consensus is difficult when three adults—two of whom had such marital difficulty that they divorced, and a third who does not know the history of the child—must agree. Remember that strategies to resolve conflicts are crucial for every family: This is particularly hard for stepparents. Disengagement is easier; not better.

One study using family systems theory focused on children born to parents who had remarried after one or both had had children from another relationship. Those new, shared children were the biological offspring of both married parents, but they "scored lower than other groups of siblings on several outcomes, such as educational attainment, antisocial behavior, and depressive symptoms (Sanner et al., 2020, p. 608).

As family systems theory would predict, they were powerfully influenced by their parents' relationships with their older half-siblings, even when they did not realize the genetic and nongenetic links.

For example, Sam, a shared child living with both his parents, explained:

> my dad has a temper, and my brother has a temper, so they would get into huge arguments. Rob was always the scapegoat for my dad's anger. . . . I think the fact that he wasn't his biological child put strain on their relationship, which spilled over into other relationships. . . . [While] my mom . . . was in the "white picket fences, perfect home, nothing's wrong with us" kind of mind-set.
>
> *[Sanner et al., 2020, pp. 613–614]*

Single-Parent Families

Compared to two-parent households, single parents have three potential problems: less income, less stability, and too much to do. Nonetheless, some parents find that living with a partner is more difficult than living without one. One result: The number of single parents is increasing worldwide.

In 2019, about 40 percent of U.S. births were to unmarried mothers, and almost half of all marriages ended in divorce. The combination of marriage avoidance, divorce, unstable cohabitation, and, less often, parental death or imprisonment, means that, unlike 50 years ago when any family except the standard one was unusual, now most U.S. children live, at least for a year or two, with only one parent (see **Figure 13.3**).

Some single parents overcome the three problems just mentioned. When there is too much to do, single parents may prioritize spending time with their children. They might spend less time with friends and never stay late at work. They may also find helpers: a grandparent, an adult sibling, or the other parent frequently helps with child care and material support.

Regarding instability, children are stressed whenever their schools, neighborhoods, and primary caregivers change. If their single parent lives with a new partner, then leaves that partner, and then cohabits with another partner, those repeated adjustments make daily life harder for the children, because rules, routines, and rituals change.

Any change is disruptive, no matter what the family structure. When schools, bedrooms, teachers, friends, mealtimes, discipline, and so on keep changing, children suffer.

FIGURE 13.3

At Any Given Moment This chart shows that, at any given moment, most children live with two parents, who could be biological, adoptive, or step-. However, many have spent or will spend time with a single parent. These data do not record who else is in the household. For instance, almost half of the infants who live with a single parent also live with a grandmother.

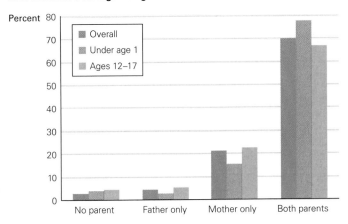

U.S. Children's Living Arrangements—2019

Data from U.S. Bureau of the Census, Current Population Survey, 2019 Annual Social and Economic Supplement.

THINK CRITICALLY: Can you describe a situation in which having a single parent would be better than having two parents?

As you remember, some stress is inevitable and even beneficial, but too much impedes development. Some single parents manage to provide stability; that benefits the children.

The most difficult problem for many single parents may be poverty, since family income is reduced when one only adult in the household is working. However, in some communities, relatives, neighbors, community organizations, and public programs provide nutritious food, health care, recreation, and so on. Overall, single parents have many obstacles to overcome, and they need help from other people, but some children in such families thrive.

Looking closely at the data, interesting ethnic differences are found. Children in African American and Latinx single-parent families are less likely to be impaired by their family structure than European or Asian American families. The suggested reason is that neighbors and relatives are more likely to help (Cross, 2020).

Courts are increasingly likely to mandate joint physical custody of children after a divorce. This makes neither parent exactly a single parent, since the other parent is also an active partner. In general, when both parents are directly involved in caregiving, children are healthier, physically and emotionally (Baude et al., 2016; Braver & Votruba, 2018).

The same result is sometimes achieved when single parenthood is not the result of divorce but rather of a union that never involved marriage. Parents who do not live with their children can be a major source of child care as well as financial support. This requires something hard for both parents: recognition that children benefit when both parents love them, putting aside their emotions about each other.

Some adults become a *single parent by choice* (Carone, 2017; Van Gasse & Mortelmans, 2020). Less than 1 percent of all men or women deliberately decide to become a single parent, but the fact that thousands have done so reminds us that the impulse to care for children characterizes our species. Just as infants seek attachments, many adults do as well.

The Extended Family

extended family A family of relatives in addition to the nuclear family, usually three or more generations living in one household.

An **extended family** includes relatives in addition to parents and children. Usually the additional persons are grandparents, sometimes with uncles, aunts, and cousins. In times of crises such as deep poverty, a troubled divorce, or a teenage birth, a three-generation home may seem best.

Of course, "relationships between grandparents and grandchildren can offer tremendous benefits to family members of each generation" (Margolis & Arpino, 2018, p. 23). But that does not require living together: Sharing a home with grandparents does not usually work out well (Berger, 2019).

We need to dispel three myths:

Myth 1. Extended families are formed to help feeble, lonely grandparents. NOT usually. More often, unlike 50 years ago, the middle generation is the needy one. Usually, grandparents are employed and pay housing expenses. Younger generations move in.

Myth 2. Extended families foster family harmony. NOT usually. Often, shared kitchens and child rearing lead to disputes.

Myth 3. Grandmothers are primary caregivers in extended families. NOT usually. Typically, the primary caregiver is the grandchild's mother.

Most extended families are a temporary solution to a serious problem. Although many grandchildren live with grandparents for vacations, it is unusual for an extended family household to last five years or more.

Twenty years ago, a detailed study exploded the myth that extended families are ideal (Black et al., 2002). This research began with 194 young African American mothers of preschoolers. Prior research had repeatedly reported poor grandmother health in three-generation households: These researchers were not surprised to confirm that. However, given "the enthusiasm of policy-makers for three generation households," they expected benefits for the younger generations. Not so.

Compared to the mothers who lived apart from their mothers, the young women in extended families were more depressed, and their children were more disobedient or withdrawn, as well as less advanced in language. Even worse, rates of mistreatment were higher. One suggested reason: Grandmother criticism accompanied grandmother care. That increased conflict and reduced attachment.

Other studies also suggest that extended families are not ideal. For example, every pediatrician now agrees that the ideal nutrition for infants is breast milk. However, if young mothers are living with their own mothers, they are *less* likely to breast-feed their babies (Pilkauskas, 2014).

Households in China and the United States

Sometimes Westerners idealize Asian culture, praising China for respect for the aged and prevalence of extended families. But that was true decades ago, not today. Asia has experienced a "rapid decline of intergenerational coresidence." In China, adults with higher education and more income are particularly unlikely to live with their aged parents (Gruijters & Ermisch, 2019).

This is not a reason to be critical of China. Filial devotion is still evident. Families in Asia, like those in the rest of the world, remain interconnected: The rapid decline in co-residence correlates with a dramatic increase in living nearby.

This is relevant for other nations as well. We need to clarify the distinction between households and families. The U.S. Census counts households, specifically who lives together under one roof (see **Figure 13.4** for recent household tallies).

U.S. Households with Children Under Age 18—2019

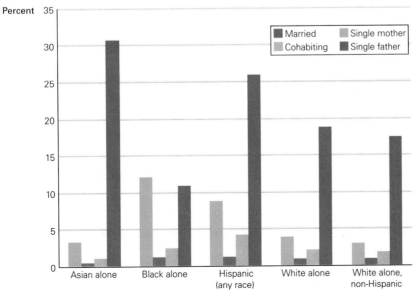

Data from U.S. Census Bureau, 2016a, 2016b.

FIGURE 13.4

Possible Problems As the text makes clear, structure does not determine function, but raising children is more difficult as a single parent, in part because income is lower. African American families have at least one asset, however. They are more likely to have grandparents who are actively helping with child care.

But household structures do not reflect family functions. Many adults live near, but not with, their parents, and many single parents live near, but not with, the other parent. Those nearby relatives often provide caregiving, emotional support, and material help. Thus, single parents are less often alone, and extended families are more common than household data suggests.

Census categories are particularly misleading with single-occupant households. Between 2010 and 2020, more than one-fourth of U.S. households were comprised of one person, triple the rate 50 years ago. Most (61 percent) of those adults who live alone are age 55 or older (U.S. Census Bureau, November, 2019). Many are widows who are integral to well-functioning families: They are active caregivers.

Does the rise in single adult households signify family breakdown, or increased loneliness? Not at all! The factor that correlates most with single-person households is not loneliness but income: People who can afford it prefer their own homes. Many people who live alone are strongly attached to family and friends. That makes them no less, and perhaps more, happy than other people.

The Skipped-Generation Household

A particular version of grandparent household is called *skipped generation*, because one or both grandparents (half the time it is the grandmother alone) care for grandchildren when the middle generation is usually absent. About 2 percent of all U.S. households are skipped generation. That is a solution of last resort, when the middle generation is in prison, dead, abusive, or severely neglectful. It is better than foster care with a stranger, but neither grandparents nor grandchildren do as well as in other family structures (Berger, 2019; Pilkauskas & Dunifon, 2016).

Because of shrinking rural wealth and a restricted school policy in cities, an estimated 22 percent of Chinese children (61 million children) are *left behind*, the term used for children left with rural grandparents when parents work in cities (Zhao et al., 2017). Those children do poorly, in education and emotions, especially if both parents have left (Hu et al., 2020; Lan et al., 2019). However, the grandparents tend to be healthier, emotionally and physically, than other grandparents (Xu, 2019). The reasons include that the middle generation provides income and emotional support, unlike the usual case in skipped-generation families in North America.

 DATA CONNECTIONS: Family Structure in the United States and Around the World examines how rates of different types of families vary nationally and internationally.

WHAT HAVE YOU LEARNED?

1. How is a family system similar to a body system (such as the cardiovascular system)?
2. What are the differences between family rules, routines, and rituals?
3. What is the "Standard North American Family"?
4. Why do children in two-parent families fare well, on average?
5. What are the advantages and disadvantages of adoptive families?
6. What makes children of same-sex couples similar to, and different from, children of other-sex couples?
7. What are the advantages and problems of stepfamilies?
8. What are the advantages and disadvantages of single-parent families?
9. Who benefits, and who is harmed, by extended families?
10. Why is household structure a misleading way to measure family function?

Other Social Connections

Social connections are pivotal lifelong (Padilla-Walker et al., 2017), as evident in the many names for it. Maslow called it *love and belonging*, Erikson's stage six refers to *intimacy*; other social scientists write about *affiliation, interdependence, communion,* or *attachment*.

People Without Families

We have focused thus far on families, because humans organize themselves into families. Attempts to raise children without parents, even when the children are well cared for, have not been successful.

We know how important families are not only because abandoned children suffer in many ways, but also because well-loved children suffer if they are not in families. One example of this occurred in the 1950s on the Israeli kibbutzim (cooperative communities, typically comprised of more than 100 adults who shared values and work, usually in agriculture), which provided excellent care for the children in the "children's house," one of the best buildings on the kibbutz.

Since both parents needed to work, and since the Holocaust meant that many adults had no experience in functioning families when they were young, the pioneers decided that it would be better for children to live together, day and night, with each other and with a loving and well-trained caregiver.

That made ideological and practical sense. However, the practice was abandoned because it became apparent that both generations, children and parents, suffered emotionally (Aviezer et al., 2002). Similar (but less well-studied) results are found everywhere when children are raised without parents.

However, while almost every child has a family, and while most adults are attached, for better or for worse, to the parents who raised them, it is also true that attachment to friends can supplement, and sometimes substitute for, family attachment.

Adults always combine new and old social connections, finding the best balance between family and friends (Jorgensen & Nelson, 2018). Each person is part of a **social convoy**. The word *convoy* originally referred to a group of travelers in hostile territory, such as the pioneers in ox-drawn wagons headed for California or soldiers marching across unfamiliar terrain. Individuals were strengthened by their convoy, sharing difficult conditions and defending one another.

Friends are a crucial part of the social convoy; they are chosen for the traits that make them reliable fellow travelers. Mutual loyalty and aid characterize friendship (Rawlins, 2016). An unbalanced friendship (one giving and the other taking) often ends because *both* parties are uncomfortable.

Early Adulthood

Early adulthood is the time of life when people have the most friends and acquaintances, a conclusion drawn from a study of 29 nations (Wrzus et al., 2013). Some high-school friends are lost and others kept, as dependence on parents is reduced.

In addition, young adults add many new acquaintances, from college, from work, or from the neighborhood. They share apartments, go to parties where they meet new people, eat lunch or go for a drink with work colleagues, or arrange study dates at college. The size of their networks is usually in the hundreds, sometimes the thousands.

Most friendships throughout adulthood are asexual. Young men and women typically have some platonic friends of the same sex, as well as some of the other sex.

social convoy Collectively, the family members, friends, acquaintances, and even strangers who move through the years of life with a person.

Fellow Travelers Here that phrase is not a metaphor for life's journey but a literal description of a good friend, Tom, carrying 30-year-old Kevan Chandler, from Fort Wayne, Indiana, as they view the Paris Opera House. Kevan was born with spinal muscular atrophy because both his parents are carriers of the recessive gene. He cannot walk, but three of his friends agreed to take him on a three-week backpacking adventure through Europe. The trip was funded by hundreds of people who read about Kevan's plans online.

Luke Thompson

FIGURE 13.5

Same, Yet Different The authors of this study were struck by how similar the friendship patterns of sexual minority and majority people were. As you see, the one noticeable trend is age, not sexuality. People over 30 reported fewer friends overall, and fewer other-sex friends in particular, from an average of 2.6 to an average of 2.1.

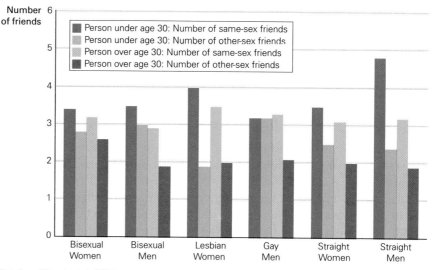

Friends You Could Call If In Trouble Late at Night

Number of friends

- Person under age 30: Number of same-sex friends
- Person under age 30: Number of other-sex friends
- Person over age 30: Number of same-sex friends
- Person over age 30: Number of other-sex friends

Bisexual Women | Bisexual Men | Lesbian Women | Gay Men | Straight Women | Straight Men

Data from Gillespie et al., 2015.

ESPECIALLY FOR Young Men Why would you want at least one close friend who is a woman? (see response, page 397)

In fact, in the United States the number of friends is affected more by the person's age than by their sexuality.

This was confirmed in a detailed study of friendship that included 25,185 adults, 1,361 of whom were sexual minorities (Gillespie et al., 2015). The number of friends was quite similar among people of every sexual orientation and gender identity.

Most people had at least three same-sex friendships and at least two of the other sex. Gay men under age 30 tended to have the highest number of cross-sex friends, perhaps because their cross-sex friendships avoided sexual tension that heterosexual cross-sex friendships might entail.

In this study, participants were asked how many friends they could discuss sex with, celebrate their birthdays with, or call if in trouble late at night. Not surprisingly, all groups thought of more people for celebrating birthdays than talking sex. Generally, the number of friends to call in late-night emergencies was between the other two (see **Figure 13.5**). Almost everyone had a least one friend in every category.

Reciprocity

The number of friends does not correlate with life satisfaction, but the quality of friendship does (Gillespie et al., 2015). As found in every study, all adults benefit from good friends, in part because friendships are reciprocal, between people who are similar in background, values, and personalities. Extraverts are particularly likely to have many friends, and their friends tend to already be quite extraverted but become more extraverted because of the friendship (van Zalk et al., 2020).

Other studies also show that friends tend to become more similar to each other, not only in personality but also in religion, politics, and behavior. Thus, people choose friends largely because of what they have in common, but they differ in some ways, too. Friends often admire some aspect of another person, and instigate friendship to develop that desired trait (anything from book-reading to hiking) in themselves.

This illustrates one of the benefits of close relationships. Friendships increase each person's understanding of their world via *self-expansion* (Aron et al., 2013), which means that other people's experiences and ideas expand each person's understanding.

When a friend is unlike oneself (perhaps from another ethnic group yet sharing the same politics, religion, and personality), then friendship adds insight beyond that from family relationships. Indeed, even having close friends who themselves had close friends from another group decreases prejudice (Zhou et al., 2019).

Fictive Kin

A crucial role for friends occurs when adults find their interactions with their childhood family to be toxic. They may become **fictive kin** in another family, considered "like a sister," "my brother," or "my second mother." They are not technically related (hence *fictive*), but they are treated like a family member (hence *kin*).

Fictive kin can be a lifeline for adults who are rejected by their original family (perhaps because of sexual orientation or gender identity), or are unable to visit family (perhaps because of prohibitive immigration policies), or resist family practices (perhaps by stopping addiction, or by joining a religious group).

Fictive kin can provide personal support. For example, when hostility and prejudice segregated and marginalized them, many African American neighbors became fictive kin to each other. Many adults within that community guided and helped the younger generation, allowing survival and success and also giving the adults pride and social connections (Glover et al., 2018).

It is obvious that the younger generation benefits from being included in a loving family other than the one they were born into; it may not be as obvious that the patriarch or matriarch who adds unrelated children to their social network also benefits. Yet a detailed study of the Filipino community in Canada found the fictive kin relationships were reciprocal, benefiting all the generations (Ferrer et al., 2017). That illustrates a general theme: Adults of all ages need social connections, with family, friends, and/or fictive kin.

Strangers or Twins? Both. Aysha Lord *(left)* is a "genetic twin" to Peter Milburn *(right)*, a father of four who had a fatal blood cancer. He was saved by stem cells donated by a stranger—Aysha—whose cells were a perfect match.

fictive kin People who become accepted as part of a family in which they are not genetically or legally members.

Late Adulthood

The need for attachment is evident lifelong. Intimacy and generativity continue. Beyond this continuity, a new question arises regarding friends and family in late adulthood. Is this period a time for gradual withdrawal from the social word, or for more intense involvement with it?

Activity Versus Disengagement

That question is at the core of a virulent debate that began about 50 years ago. According to **disengagement theory**, aging leads elders to gradually disconnect from social interaction (Cumming & Henry, 1961). The process was thought to be a mutual interaction between the old and young. Evidence for disengagement was:

disengagement theory The view that aging makes a person's social sphere increasingly narrow, resulting in role relinquishment, withdrawal, and passivity.

- The social circle shrinks, as older adults are less likely to leave home to attend parties, to join marches, to go to cultural events.
- Coworkers withdraw, because of retirement and because elders are less current about technology, modes of production, changing world markets.
- Adult children marry and become parents, so child-rearing becomes more pressing than relationships with their aging parents.
- Physical disabilities make socialization harder: Older adults do not hear, see, or move as well as they did.

As a result, disengagement from social interaction occurs as children move away, retirement begins, and involvement in politics, or religious institutions, or community centers becomes difficult. Added to that, spouses and siblings die, leaving the surviving elder with fewer social connections.

Disengagement theory provoked a storm of protest. Many gerontologists insisted that older people need and want new involvements. They proposed **activity theory**, that elders seek to remain socially involved. If they disengage, they do so unwillingly and suffer because of it (Kelly, 1993; Rosow, 1985).

activity theory The view that older people want and need to remain active in a variety of social spheres—with relatives, friends, and community groups—and become withdrawn only unwillingly, as a result of ageism.

Activity theory highlighted that older adults replaced disengagement from some spheres with increased engagement in others. Five examples are:

- Family involvement increases. Married couples increase their interaction, elders engage with family members via meals together, phone calls, social media, connecting with siblings, children, and grandchildren more than ever.
- Older people are *more*, not less, politically and socially engaged than younger generations (Ang, 2019). They attend fewer mass marches, but they vote more often, write letters to public officials, keep up with the news.
- Many remain productive, sometimes with part-time work, or bridge jobs, or self-employment, but the notion that most retire is inaccurate.
- Many become pillars of churches, community groups, neighborhood networks.

All these activities benefit physical and mental health (Kahana et al., 2013; Russell et al., 2019; Tabassum et al., 2016), with active elders living longer.

Ongoing discussion of disengagement and activity now emphasizes that older adults need

> a social environment that is rich in opportunities for maintaining engagement and avoiding unnecessary dependence on others. . . . Active ageing strategies should encompass and interact with many different specific policy areas: fostering employment, promoting engagement, reducing poverty, improving health and well-being, lifelong learning, and much more.
>
> *[Zaidi & Howse, 2017]*

Further study of disengagement and activity suggest that much depends on the social context of a particular person's life, as well as on the national culture. For instance, a study found that the social circle shrinks with age in the United States but not in Mexico or Japan, and actually increases in Lebanon (Ajrouch et al., 2018).

When older adults are asked to define successful aging, neither disengagement nor activity theory seems accurate. Instead, older adults may disengage from some social situations and become active in others (Teater & Chonody, 2019). Efforts to keep elders active, as might be found in some senior centers or other programs designed by younger adults for older ones, fall short of the needs of older people.

Single Older Adults

Decades together usually means a happy old age, but not always.

For many reasons, as longevity increases, so does the number of older adults who are single (Reher & Requena, 2018). Some have been unmarried for years; they have usually established friendship networks that meet their social needs. In addition, every developed nation is experiencing a rise of the "gray divorce," as divorces after decades of marriage are called (Brown & Lin, 2012; Tang et al., 2020).

If they are unmarried because of death of a spouse, as half of all older married people will be eventually, that may be worst of all. The best data on this, controlling not only for age but also for emotions and preexisting conditions, come from Scandinavia (Brenn & Ytterstad, 2016; Möller et al., 2011). After the death of a spouse, odds of death increase by about 50 percent, especially in three situations:

- the survivor is the husband, not the wife;
- the bereaved spouse is relatively young (age 60 or so); and
- the death is recent (with highest risk in the first week after the death).

Friends of the Earth Protection of the land and connection to the younger generations are values for many of the oldest generation. But, as shown here, people of all ages express their political passions best when they are among like-minded, same-cohort activists. Otherwise they might disengage.

To understand this, consider the perspective of three people (quoted in Koren, 2016).

First, a man who became a widower at age 64:

> my life changed drastically [with my wife's death] from being full to being empty. Empty, empty, I functioned like a machine.

Then, his 41-year-old son:

> I didn't want to lose him too, he simply withered away, and the worst was when he sent us pictures of a dead rose; a rose that withered along with him.

Fortunately, this man met a woman who filled the void left by his wife's death. Like many widows, she was not expecting to find a new partner, and her life was not empty.

> I didn't expect to find someone, I wasn't looking at all. When my husband died, . . . there are things I like to do. I do this kind of art work, for example, it gives me a lot of satisfaction, and I like to work in the garden, and I love my children and grandchildren. I thought I'd continue like this. And then I met him, only a year after my husband died [. . .] and then our relationship began.

This repartnering was good for everyone, particularly the widower. He says:

> now that she [my partner] is here, my heart is somewhat full. I feel like a person, before I felt I was in transition waiting to leave [the world]. That's it; now I feel like a whole person.

As with this widower, one solution for the divorced or widowed older adult is to find a new partner. That is easier for the men, in part because after age 75, there are about twice as many single older women than men. Women satisfy their need for social connection in other ways, with more involvement with their relatives (especially younger ones), with their social community, and with friendship.

Friendship in Late Adulthood

As one team of scientists stresses, "friend relationships are as important as family ties in predicting psychological well-being in adulthood and old age" (Blieszner et al., 2019).

The friendship circle shrinks every decade of adult life, but quality, not quantity, characterizes friendships in late adulthood (Wrzus et al., 2013). Many adults nurture close ties with their best friends (English & Carstensen, 2014). This is more true now than it was in former years: Because more women have had significant jobs, and have been leaders in their churches, their political groups, and their communities, they have more social connections with people who are not relatives (Fiori et al., 2020).

That bodes well, because "Late-life adults report liking and caring about their friends, laughing together and having fun, feeling satisfied with their relationships, being able to confide in each other, and reminding each other to stay healthy" (Blieszner et al., 2019). Friendship brings many benefits: Not only are older adults with several close friends happier than others, they also tend to be cognitively and physically healthier.

As you see, the social needs of humans at every stage of life, from the newest baby to the oldest adult, are powerful. Satisfying the need for attachment varies with age, family structures, and culture. However, to understand the development of any one person, it is necessary to understand and appreciate the social interactions that person might have. For me, writing this book is one way I connect to other people. I hope reading this chapter, and maybe participating in a class that studies human development over the life span, does that for you!

WHAT HAVE YOU LEARNED?

1. What was learned about children from the kibbutzim in Israel?

2. Why do people have more friends in early adulthood than later?

3. Why would someone become fictive kin?

4. What is the basic idea of disengagement theory?

5. Why did developmentalists object to disengagement theory?

6. Are friends more, or less, needed in late adulthood?

SUMMARY

Attachment

1. Bowlby and Ainsworth developed attachment theory, which holds that infants need to connect with a caregiver and vice versa.

2. Of the four types of attachment, one (type B) is secure, in which the infant explores happily as long as the mother is nearby. Three (A,C,D) are insecure, each reflecting the infant's response if a caregiver is not reliably responsive.

3. Attachment in infancy is measured by the Strange Situation, in which the caregiver and a stranger come and go while the infant remains in a playroom.

4. Manifestations of attachment vary by culture, with other caregivers—such as fathers, grandmothers, non-relatives—sometimes providing secure attachment.

Social Connections over the Life Span

5. Attachment is evident in every stage of life. Parents often bond with their child before birth.

6. Infants are primed to use all their senses and motor skills to develop synchrony and to connect with their caregivers.

7. Children's play, education, and social relationships (including bullying) are influenced by attachment. Adolescents select their peers, who influence them for good or ill, sometimes becoming delinquents.

8. Adults as parents can be authoritarian, authoritative, permissive, or neglectful. Each expresses an attachment style.

9. Caregiving between parents and their adult children continue lifelong. Indeed, family connections that begin when children are small are strong in old age.

Family Systems

10. Family systems theory considers how families function as a unit. That is affected by linked lives, whether or not family members live together.

11. Children in every two-parent structure ("standard," cohabiting, same sex, step-, adoptive) experience benefits and problems. School achievement and emotional health benefit from parental education, income, and stability.

12. Single parents tend to have lower income and higher stress than other adults. However, some single-parent households function well, especially when the other parent (or the grandparents) and the overall community are supportive.

13. Extended families—when adults of several generations live together—signify family stress or poverty rather than family harmony. Skipped-generation families are unusual, but they may be needed when something is seriously problematic in the middle generation.

Other Social Connections

14. Everyone needs social connections in order to live a happy and healthy life. Whenever people have tried to raise children without families, or whenever adults have tried to live in social isolation, problems emerge.

15. Friends are also important lifelong. Young adults typically have more friends than later on. Over the years of adulthood, quality, not quantity, of friendships seem crucial.

16. When family members do not, or cannot, provide needed social support, adults may become fictive kin, becoming "like family" with other people.

17. In late adulthood, friends may become crucial for physical and mental health than ever. The theory that adults voluntarily and naturally disengage from social connections in later life seems untrue.

KEY TERMS

attachment (p. 363)
secure attachment (type B) (p. 365)
insecure-avoidant attachment (type A) (p. 365)
insecure-resistant/ambivalent attachment (type C) (p. 365)
disorganized attachment (type D) (p. 365)

Strange Situation (p. 367)
synchrony (p. 371)
adolescence-limited offenders (p. 374)
life-course-persistent offenders (p. 374)
peer pressure (p. 375)
familism (p. 378)
demand/withdraw (p. 379)

authoritarian parenting (p. 379)
permissive parenting (p. 379)
authoritative parenting (p. 379)
neglectful/uninvolved parenting (p. 380)
child abuse (p. 381)
child neglect (p. 381)
linked lives (p. 383)

family systems theory (p. 383)
nuclear family (p. 385)
cohabitation (p. 386)
extended family (p. 388)
social convoy (p. 391)
fictive kin (p. 393)
disengagement theory (p. 393)
activity theory (p. 393)

APPLICATIONS

1. How would your childhood have been different if your family structure had been different, such as if you had (or had not) lived with your grandparents, if your parents had (or had not) gotten divorced, if you had (or had not) been adopted, if you had lived with one parent (or two), if your parents were both the same sex (or not)? Avoid blanket statements: Appreciate that every structure has advantages and disadvantages.

2. One cultural factor that influences infant development is how infants are carried from place to place. Ask four mothers whose infants were born in each of the past four decades how they transported them—front or back carriers, facing out or in, strollers or carriages, in car seats or on mother's laps, and so on. Why did

they choose the mode(s) they chose? What are their opinions and yours on how such cultural practices might affect infants' development?

3. Record video of synchrony for three minutes. Ideally, ask the parent of an infant under 8 months of age to play with the infant. If no infant is available, observe a pair of lovers as they converse. Note the sequence and timing of every facial expression, sound, and gesture of both partners.

4. Did your parents' marital and employment status affect you? How would you have fared if they had chosen other marriage or work patterns?

ESPECIALLY FOR ANSWERS

Response for Parents of a Teenager (from p. 373) Remember: Communicate, do not control. Let your child talk about the meaning of the hairstyle. Remind yourself that a hairstyle in itself is harmless. Don't say, "What will people think?" or "Are you on drugs?" or anything that might give your child reason to stop communicating.

Response for Young Men (from p. 392) Not for sex! Women friends are particularly responsive to deep conversations about family relationships, personal weaknesses, and emotional confusion. But women friends might be offended by sexual advances, bragging, or advice giving. Save these for a future romance.

OBSERVATION QUIZ ANSWERS

Answer to Observation Quiz (from p. 372) The first baby is adopted, the second was born at home, and the third is with the father, not the mother. Synchrony is universal! Although not evident here, it is also true that each is in a different nation: United States, Ethiopia, and England.

Answer to Observation Quiz (from p. 374) The girls are only observers, keeping a respectful distance.

Answer to Observation Quiz (from p. 385) Did you notice that the two males are first, and that the father carries the boy? Everyone should notice gender, ethnic, and age differences, but interpretation of such differences is not straightforward. This scene may or may not reflect male–female roles.

Lifelong Learning

On a long-ago summer day at Grandma and Grandpa's house, my 2-year-old daughter wanted to go outside. My mother had taken her out earlier, to the garden. Grandma reported, "Bethany pulled up some carrots. She was amazed that carrots were buried in the ground."

But when I opened the door, Bethany was not interested in carrots. She spied another child about her size on a distant yard and ran to her. I followed, carrying my 10-month-old. The mother of that neighbor child was also watching an older girl, Johanna, age, 4. As our children played, we mothers exchanged pleasantries, about weather, naps, learning to share. She admired my children; I admired hers.

Then I asked, "Where is Johanna going to school?"

"Oh, I'm not sending her to school yet. It's easier to keep her home, I need to be here anyway with her little sister."

I kept my thoughts and opinions to myself.

That conversation stays with me because it reveals widely diverse assumptions and circumstances. In the decades since, as I learn about schools worldwide, I am often struck by assumptions about education. Should school begin at age 2 or 6? What is best: public or private, single-sex or coed, strict or permissive, religious or secular? Should everyone go to college or only a few? Can people still learn in old age? This chapter discusses the research for all those possibilities.

What Will You Know?

1. What should children learn before kindergarten?
2. Why are curriculum issues particularly controversial in the United States?
3. Is college education still a good investment?

Learning Before First Grade

The word *education* comes from the Latin word *educare*, which means to draw out, or to lead forth, as one might lead a donkey that wants to stay put, or, better yet, as one might pull a carrot from the ground as Bethany did. Education elicits, activates, and guides what is already there.

That explains why learning is lifelong; why everyone, at every age, can be educated. You have read about plasticity of the brain (Chapter 5), language learning before the first words (Chapter 8), object understanding in infancy (Chapter 9). We still use terms — first grade, preschool — that originated in earlier centuries. But we now know that education begins at birth.

Birth to Age 3

A cliché is that "mothers are the first teachers." Early mothering teaches infants about emotions, actions, people, and things. Mothers are the first, but not necessarily the best, teachers. When mothers (or anyone else) abuse or neglect a baby, cognition is impaired lifelong (King et al., 2019).

Home-Visiting Programs

One solution to early neglect is called **home visiting**, when professionals visit new mothers. Originally, the emphasis was on physical health and preventing abuse, but more recently, early learning is stressed. In hundreds of home-visiting programs, professionals bring toys and books, teaching mothers how to respond to infant noises, gestures, and emotions (Berlin et al., 2018).

Programs in the United States target young or low-SES mothers who sometimes resist outside advice. That undercuts the program and explains why some home-visiting programs are not effective. The most successful programs begin before birth, train the visitors well, and emphasize cultural sensitivity (Baudry et al., 2017).

Crucial is that the mothers are seen as individuals, with varying needs and values. Visiting nurses in New Zealand (where every mother is visited, thus reducing some suspicion) are taught to individualize their work, sometimes focusing on medical needs, sometimes on education, sometimes on emotions (de Haan & Connolly, 2019).

In the United States, more than a hundred versions of home visiting have been implemented, some successful and some not. Too often, one community service agency administers a program that they think will help, for 100 or so babies, with no longitudinal data. (About 4 million babies are born in the United States each year.)

A promising effort used a proven curriculum (called Welcome Baby) and attempted to coordinate all the service providers in Los Angeles, public and private. Every mother who gave birth in any of 14 hospitals that served many low-income families was offered the program, and about a third (13,000 per year) agreed (Altmayer & DuBransky, 2019). Because the program was voluntary, culturally responsive, and inclusive, the stigma and resistance that undercut mandated programs was reduced.

The Los Angeles effort was stellar in many other ways. The program targeted both health and education, linking families to other services. Repeated evaluation, including experimental and control groups as well as focus groups and official statistics, were used to improve training and coordination among dozens of agencies.

Among the lessons learned: Health professionals are crucial; the most successful visitors are nurses from the community who are trained to do this work. Programs are most effective if they begin before birth (although participants could sign up within one month after birth if they choose).

home visiting Hundreds of programs in the United States involving nurses and other trained adults visiting new mothers in their homes, with the overall goal of improving the mother's interaction with her baby. Specifics vary: The goal is sometimes health, sometimes education, and sometimes attachment.

Total Weeks of Paid Leave Available to Mothers and Fathers—Selected Nations

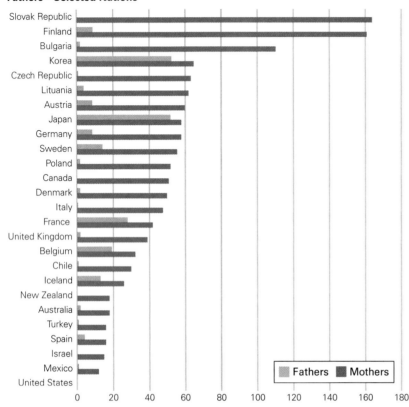

Data from OECD Family Database, August, 2019.

FIGURE 14.1

Out of Date? Laws requiring paid maternity leave are changing every year. For some of these nations, these numbers will soon need updating. Change may occur in the United States, because more women are in the 117th Congress. Current U.S. laws are more reflective of the 1950s, when most new mothers were married and expected to quit employment when their babies were born.

Data were collected on the achievements of the infants. They learned to communicate and to solve problems better than similar children who did not enroll. Although this home-visiting program continued only until the babies were 9 months old, cognitive benefits were still evident years later. This is found in other programs as well (Baudry et al., 2017; Kitzman et al., 2019).

Group Care for Infants

For cultural, ideological, and economic reasons, nations have markedly different policies regarding publicly funded group care for infants. Such care is rare in most nations of South Asia, sub-Saharan Africa, and South America, where many adults believe it is harmful. Some of those nations mandate, instead, that every employer pay for maternal leave when a baby is born (see **Figure 14.1**). The United States has no mandated paid leave, nor readily available group care.

By contrast, people in other nations believe that infant care is a public right, like police and fire protection. Government subsidies and regulations for infant care were instituted at least 20 years ago in France, Israel, China, Chile, Norway, Sweden, Denmark, Finland, Iceland, and the Netherlands. Australia and Germany have recently started such programs.

International Variations

Quality of care varies. In the Scandinavian nations, teachers are required to earn advanced degrees and have internship experience before they teach infants (King et al., 2019). That is less true in Germany and Australia, because those nations instituted low-cost day care primarily to increase the birth rate (Harrison et al., 2014).

In France, publicly subsidized care begins at 12 weeks, but only about 10 percent of all infants receive it. The waiting list is long, and the adult–infant ratio is 1:5 under age 1 and 1:8 from age 1 until 3. According to one critic, "ensuring high-quality provision seems at odds with affordability and availability of places for under threes" (Fagnani, 2013, p. 92).

Norway takes an opposite course. Norwegians believe that mothers are the best teachers of young infants, so employed women receive full salary to stay home with their babies for 47 weeks after birth (see **Figure 14.2**). Fathers are granted some paid leave as well. Beginning at age 1, high-quality, center day care is available for everyone, even in the sparsely populated rural counties where only two or three 1-year-olds live. In 2016, most Norwegian 1-year-olds (72 percent) were in center care, as were almost all 2- and 3-year-olds (92 and 96 percent) (Statistics Norway, 2018).

Possible Harm

Many educators worry that early group care might undercut attachment and emotional regulation. The first worry is unfounded. The research finds that secure mother–infant attachment (as measured by the *Strange Situation*, discussed in Chapter 13) is as common for infants in high-quality day care as with exclusive maternal care. In retrospect, this makes sense. Even if infants are in day care 40 hours a week, mothers can still spend more hours (128, including every night

Variations in Types of Child Care, by Nation and Age

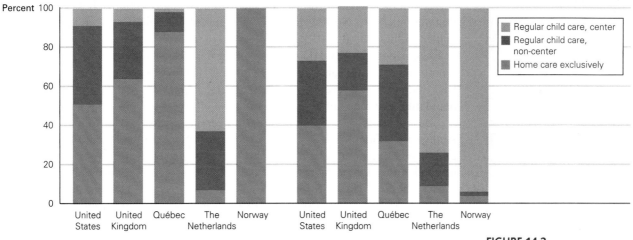

6 months   **36 months**

FIGURE 14.2

Who Cares for the Baby? Infants are the same everywhere, but cultures and governments differ dramatically. Does a 6-month-old need their mother more than a 3-year-old? Norway and Québec say yes; the United States, United Kingdom, and the Netherlands say no.

Observation Quiz Which nation has the most extreme shift at age 1? (see answer, page 436) ↑

and weekend) with their babies. As you read in Chapter 13, some mother–infant dyads are not securely attached, but group care is not the reason.

Regarding emotional regulation, the evidence is not as clear. A meta-analysis of research on infant caregiving (Dearing & Zachrisson, 2017) reported that half of the studies of group infant care found higher rates of aggression among those children (sometimes only for the boys), later on. All of those studies were in North America.

The other half of the studies (some North American and some not) found no effects. Indeed, some studies reported better social skills and emotional regulation in early-day-care children (Broekhuizen et al., 2018; Crosby et al., 2010).

A longitudinal study in Canada found that early enrollment (before age 2) in an educational day care was especially beneficial for boys. Thirty years later, they were more likely to be high school graduates earning a good salary than were boys who had not attended day care. Organized child care before kindergarten did not seem to affect the girls, either for good or for ill (Domond et al., 2020).

Quality Care

Low-quality day care usually means too few teachers, who spend most of their time controlling behavior (the opposite of education), rather than encouraging talk, creativity, and curiosity. Those children are less likely to learn how to interact with others. The opposite is true for high-quality care.

The most often-cited longitudinal research comes from the Early Child Care Research Network of the National Institute of Child Health and Human Development (NICHD), which followed over 1,300 children born in 1991 from birth through adolescence. Early day care correlated with many cognitive advances, especially in language. Children who were enrolled in high-quality day care had higher achievement in primary school and high school.

A summary of that research found:

> higher quality of child care was linked to higher academic-cognitive skills in primary school and again at age 15. [But] higher hours of child care were associated with teacher reports of behavior problems in early primary school and youth reports of greater impulsivity and risk taking at age 15.
>
> *[Burchinal et al., 2014, p. 542]*

Why do studies reach opposite conclusions about behavior problems? Perhaps the adults, not the children, are the deciding factor. Most studies measure

Double Winner These parents brought their babies to the San Francisco legislature to advocate for paid parental leave. They won! The San Francisco Board of Supervisors voted yes, making this the first jurisdiction in the United States to mandate fully paid leave. The law went into effect in 2017—too late for both the mother and father shown here. Perhaps their next babies?

behavior problems by asking teachers. If kindergarten teachers want quiet students, and children who had early group care are more talkative, the teacher may consider that a problem. In Norway, infant care is praised for helping shy children become bolder (Solheim et al., 2013).

Reconsider the NICHD comment that early day care correlated with "youth reports of greater impulsivity and risk taking." That worries adults, not adolescents. Risk-taking is admired by some teenagers; if past day care increases current popularity, that may not be a problem.

Another issue is when and where the research was done. Many longitudinal studies, including NICHD, began 40 years ago. Since much has changed in early-childhood education as well as in the society, with some improvements from the research and some problems from new public pressures, the results may differ for today's children (Haslip & Gullo, 2018).

The National Association for the Education of Young Children (NAEYC, the leading professional organization) updated their standards for infant care (birth to 15 months) (NAEYC, 2014). Those new guidelines include: no more than four babies per adult, no more than eight in a group, strict hygiene practices, an individualized curriculum that emphasizes emotional and intellectual growth, and teachers who "engage infants in frequent face-to-face social interactions"—including talking, singing, smiling, and touching (NAEYC, 2014, p. 4) (see **Table 14.1**).

Early-Childhood Schooling

As you just read, not everyone advocates infant group care. However, virtually every expert agrees that 3- to 6-year-olds benefit from high-quality group education (McCoy et al., 2017; Reynolds & Temple, 2019).

Longitudinal Studies

In 1965 many educators and political leaders (including the U.S. president) thought that early education was a potent weapon in the "war on poverty." A huge nationwide program, called *Head Start*, was created to advance education before first grade. At first Head Start was an eight-week summer program with half a million children and stellar results, including dramatic increases in IQ scores. But the

---

TABLE 14.1

High-Quality Day Care

High-quality day care during infancy has five essential characteristics:

1. *Adequate attention to each infant*

   A small group of infants (no more than five) needs two reliable, familiar, loving caregivers. Continuity of care is crucial.

2. *Encouragement of language and sensorimotor development*

   Infants need language—songs, conversations, and positive talk—and easily manipulated toys.

3. *Attention to health and safety*

   Cleanliness routines (e.g., handwashing), accident prevention (e.g., no small objects), and safe areas to explore are essential.

4. *Professional caregivers*

   Caregivers should have experience and degrees/certificates in early-childhood education. Turnover should be low, morale high, and enthusiasm evident.

5. *Warm and responsive caregivers*

   Providers should engage the children in active play and guide them in problem solving. Quiet, obedient children may indicate unresponsive care.

IQ benefits seemed to fade by third grade (Westinghouse Learning Corporation, 1969).

Fortunately, three small programs began during the same era. Unlike Head Start, they were all-day programs that educated young children for years. Instead of enrolling 4-year-olds, they began earlier (sometimes in infancy), employed well-trained teachers, and stressed play and language, individualized teaching, and actively involved parents. Those three were *Perry* (or *High/Scope*), in Wisconsin; *Abecedarian*, in North Carolina; and *Child–Parent Centers*, in Chicago. The first two had matched control groups, the third compared children of the same demographic. All three had long-term follow up.

Those three boosted learning throughout childhood and adulthood. Graduates were less likely to repeat grades or be designated as slow learners. In adolescence, they were more likely to attend high school and college; in adulthood more of them had good jobs and fewer of them were arrested; and in middle age, they were healthier—as measured by blood work, hypertension, and disease diagnosis (Campbell et al., 2014; Reynolds & Ou, 2011; Reynolds & Temple, 2019; Schweinhart et al., 2005).

The quality of early schooling made a difference, as did the quality of the next school the children attended. That conclusion has been corroborated with more recent research, not only among low-income children (as in the three studies above) but also for more fortunate children. For instance, one study followed 1,307 children, mostly middle class, from 10 cities. The researchers concluded that attending a high-quality preschool, and then a good primary school, led to higher scores on achievement tests compared to other children from the same neighborhoods and backgrounds (Ansari & Pianta, 2018).

Head Start continues to be funded, educating about a million children per year. The first children were 4-year-olds, enrolled in half-day or summer programs. But by 2017, almost all were full-day programs and about a fourth of the students were age 3 or younger. Outcomes vary. Children who are homeless, or have a disability, or are learning English are particularly likely to benefit (U.S. Department of Health and Human Services, 2010). The reason is thought to be that Head Start is their only preschool option. For more privileged children, Head Start seems to be no better, and sometimes worse, than other programs of early education (Crosnoe et al., 2016; Garcia, 2018).

Currently in the United States, 54 percent of 3- to 4-year-olds are in some early-education program—about half of them in private programs, half in public ones (National Center for Education Statistics, 2018). That is the lowest rate among developed nations, but it is five times higher than in 1965 (see **Figure 14.3**).

FIGURE 14.3

Who Misses Out? The children least likely to be in educational programs are from families who speak Spanish, or whose income is slightly above poverty level, or whose mothers are unemployed. In all three situations, high-quality early education would be especially helpful.

Lifetime Achievement The baby in the framed photograph escaped the grip of poverty. The woman holding the photograph proved that early education can transform children. She is Frances Campbell, who spearheaded the Abecedarian Project. The baby's accomplishments may be the more impressive of the two.

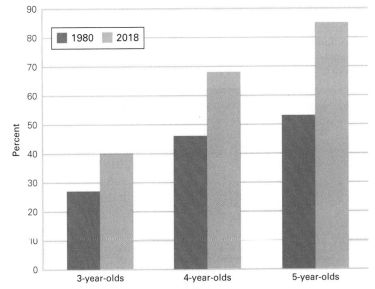

U.S. Preschool Enrollment by Age

Data from Digest of Education Statistics, 2019.

Quality matters and is not indicated by cost or sponsorship—such as public or private, state or federal, corporate or religious. The crucial factor is teacher training and behavior. Teachers who talk, listen, laugh, guide, and play with the children provide quality education; teachers who sit, watch, and command ("Stop hitting"; "Stay in line") do not. Remember that to educate means to pull forth what is already in the person: Too many commands do the opposite.

It seems beneficial if the program has a defined curriculum that everyone understands and teaches. The goal could be to encourage individuality (*child-centered*) or to prepare children for formal education (*teacher-directed*). Both are now explained. Either way, adults need to structure learning as part of a team: They are educators, not babysitters.

Child-Centered Programs

Schools that are child-centered, or *developmental*, stress each child's personal growth. Teachers in such programs believe children need to follow their own interests. For example, they agree that "children should be allowed to select many of their own activities from a variety of learning areas that the teacher has prepared" (Lara-Cinisomo et al., 2011, p. 101). The physical space and the materials (dress-up clothes, art supplies, puzzles, blocks) are arranged to allow exploration.

Most child-centered programs encourage artistic expression (Bassok et al., 2016). According to advocates of child-centered programs, children need to tell stories, draw pictures, dance, and make music for both joy and learning. Child-centered programs are influenced by Piaget, who thought that children will discover new ideas if given a chance, and by Vygotsky, who thought that children learn from playing, especially with other children.

Long before Piaget and Vygotsky, one type of child-centered school began in the slums of Rome in 1907, when Maria Montessori opened a nursery school (Standing, 1998). She believed that children needed structured, individualized projects. Her students completed puzzles, cleaned tables with sponges and water, traced shapes, and so on.

Contemporary **Montessori schools** still emphasize individual pride and achievement, presenting many literacy-related tasks (e.g., outlining letters and looking at books). Specific materials differ from those that Montessori designed, but the underlying philosophy is the same. Children seek out learning tasks; they do not sit quietly listening to a teacher. That makes Montessori programs child-centered (Lillard, 2013).

Another form of early-childhood education is **Reggio Emilia**, named after the town in Italy where it began. In Reggio Emilia, 3- to 5-year-olds master skills that are not usually taught in North American schools until age 7 or so, such as writing and using tools. Reggio schools do not provide large-group instruction, with lessons in, say, forming letters or cutting paper. Instead, hands-on activities are chosen by each child, perhaps drawing, cooking, building, or gardening.

Measurement of achievement, such as tests of letters and numbers, is antithetical to the Reggio conviction that children learn at their own pace and direction (Harris, 2019). Learning is documented for each child via scrapbooks, photos, and daily notes.

A third type of child-centered school is **Waldorf**, first developed by Rudolf Steiner in Austria in 1919. The emphasis again is on creativity and individuality—with no homework, no tests, and no worksheets. As much as possible, children play outdoors—appreciation of nature is part of Waldorf. Children of several ages learn together, because older children serve as mentors for younger ones, and the curriculum follows the children's interests, not their age.

Most Waldorf schools have a set schedule—usually circle time in the beginning and particular activities on certain days (always baking on Tuesdays,

Montessori schools Schools that offer early-childhood education based on the philosophy of Maria Montessori, which emphasizes careful work and tasks that each young child can do.

Reggio Emilia A program of early-childhood education that originated in the town of Reggio Emilia, Italy, and that encourages each child's creativity in a carefully designed setting.

Waldorf schools An early-childhood education program that emphasizes creativity, social understanding, and emotional growth. It originated in Germany with Rudolf Steiner and now is used in thousands of schools throughout the world.

Child-Centered Pride Why does Rachel Koepke, a 3-year-old from a Wisconsin town called Pleasant Prairie, seem so pleased that her hands (and cuffs) are blue? The answer arises from northern Italy—Rachel attended a Reggio Emilia preschool that encourages creative expression.

ELIZABETH FLORES/Tribune News Service/PLEASANT PRAIRIE/WI/USA/Newscom

for instance)—but children are not expected to master specific skills at certain ages. Imagination is prized (Kirkham & Kidd, 2017).

Teacher-Directed Programs

The goal of teacher-directed programs is to make all children "ready to learn" when they enter primary school. For that reason, basic skills are stressed, including precursors to reading, writing, and arithmetic. Behavior is also taught, as children learn to respect adults, to follow schedules, to hold hands when they go on outings, and so on.

The curriculum includes learning the names of letters, numbers, shapes, and colors, with age-related expectations. Orderly, scheduled activities teach routines: Children nap, eat, and go to the bathroom at certain times. Children learn to sit quietly and listen. Good behavior is reinforced with praise and other rewards; misbehavior is punished with time-outs (brief separation from activities).

Children practice forming letters, sounding out words, counting objects, and writing their names. If a 4-year-old learns to read, that is success. (In a child-centered program, that might arouse suspicion that play or socialization was neglected.) Many teacher-directed programs were inspired by behaviorism, which emphasizes step-by-step learning, with reinforcement (praise, gold stars, prizes) for accomplishment.

Another inspiration for teacher-directed programs comes from information-processing research that finds that children who enter kindergarten without knowing names and sounds of letters are likely to become first-graders who cannot read (Ozernov-Palchik et al., 2017). Literacy depends on connecting symbols and sounds, a connection unlikely to result from creative play (Gellert & Elbro, 2017).

That is one reason many state legislatures mandate that the goal of education before age 6 is mastery of specifics, such as the sound and shape of letters. This outcome is best achieved by teacher-directed learning. Because teachers are sensitive to student needs and policy directives, Head Start programs have become more teacher-directed over the past three decades, to the distress of many developmentalists (Walter & Lippard, 2017).

If You're Happy and You Know It Gabby Osborne (pink shirt) has her own way of showing happiness, not the hand-clapping that Lizalia Garcia tries to teach. The curriculum of this Head Start class in Florida includes learning about emotions, contrary to the wishes of some legislators, who want proof of academics.

ESPECIALLY FOR Teachers In trying to find a preschool program, what should parents look for? (see response, page 436)

 DATA CONNECTIONS: A Look at Early Child Care in the United States explores how various maternal demographics affect child-care arrangements and describes some of the standards of the National Association for the Education of Young Children (NAEYC).

Education and Money

This discussion of philosophies, practices, and programs may give the impression that the research on early-childhood cognition is contradictory. That is not true. Specifics are debated, but empirical evidence and longitudinal evaluation find that preschool education advances learning. Ideally, each program has a curriculum that guides practice, all the adults collaborate, and experienced teachers respond to each child.

Sometimes the debate about early education seems to be more about money than about learning. Those three small programs that had a lifelong effect were expensive, ranging from $7,000 to $20,000 per year per child [in 2020 dollars]. From a life-span perspective, later savings in less special education, prison, and health care, and more tax revenue (because of more employment) make early education a wise investment. However, legislators are elected based on immediate costs, not long-term results, so long-term investment may be ignored.

The other evidence that suggests that early education is worth the cost comes from families with high income and education. Private preschools may be very expensive—as much as $40,000 a year. Yet, although they could afford home care, wealthy families are more likely to enroll their 3- and 4-year-olds in an educational program than are low-income families, even when the latter are offered subsidized programs. Apparently, those who can afford it decide that preschool is money well spent.

In the past decade, some states (e.g., Oklahoma, Georgia, Florida, New Jersey, and Illinois) and some cities (e.g., New York, Boston, Cleveland, San Antonio, and Los Angeles) have offered preschool to every 4-year-old (although restrictions may apply). Although this investment results in fewer children needing special education later on, some aspects of implementation are controversial—a topic for further longitudinal research (McCoy et al., 2017).

WHAT HAVE YOU LEARNED?

1. What makes a home-visiting program successful or not?
2. What is distinctive about infant education in Scandinavia?
3. What is the evidence for possible harm from group infant care?
4. What are the long-term effects of early-childhood education?
5. How has Head Start changed since it began?
6. What is an example of how child-centered programs achieve their goal?
7. What is an example of how teacher-directed programs achieve their goal?
8. Why isn't preschool funded by governments, like school for older children is?

From First Grade Through High School

As you just read, education before age 6 may or may not be in an organized program, paid by the government. By contrast, *primary* (ages 6–11) education is not only subsidized by every nation, it is required almost everywhere. Often, *secondary* (ages 12–18) education is provided as well, although not necessarily required.

This was not true two decades ago, but now every national leader understands that educated citizens are a national strength (Patrinos & Psacharopoulos, 2020). Traditionally, boys were more often educated than girls, but that was before the data showed that educated women, even more than men, improve the long-term health and wealth of a nation.

In the twenty-first century in many developing nations, the number of students in primary school exceeds the number of children ages 6–11. The reason is that many people older than 11 seek basic education that was not available when they were young. Ghana, El Salvador, and China are among the nations with more students in primary school than the population of school-age children (UNESCO, 2014).

School Organization

Before describing specifics of curriculum, we need to note the relationship between national, state, and local authority over schools. As you just read, most nations set curriculum and school funding by a national department of education, and usually schools are funded primarily by the national government. That is not true in the United States.

Although the U.S. federal government has some influence, most of the control of education rests with local school boards, one for each district (the United States has 14,000 school districts). School districts must conform to standards set by the states, but many rely on funds from local property taxes. As a result, some school districts in wealthy neighborhoods have much more income than in poor neighborhoods, which affects teacher salaries, adult–child ratio, buildings, after-school programs, and much more.

Where Do U.S. Children Go to School?

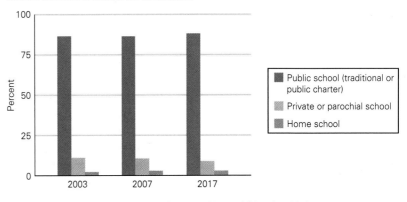

Data from National Center for Education Statistics, Digest of Education, 2019.

FIGURE 14.4
Where'd You Go to School? Note that although home schooling is still the least-chosen option, the number of home-schooled children may be increasing. Not shown is the percentage of children attending the nearest public school, which is decreasing slightly because of charter schools and magnet schools. More detailed data indicate that the child most likely to be home-schooled is a 7-year-old European American girl living in a rural area of the South with an employed father and a stay-at-home mother.

This varies by state. For example, two states next to each other in the middle of the United States, Kansas and Nebraska, have quite different funding sources for public education. In Kansas, 17 percent is property taxes and 63 percent is state funding, whereas in Nebraska, 52 percent is property taxes and 33 percent is state funding (McFarland et al., 2018). When each local community pays a substantial amount of their property taxes to their local public schools, as in Nebraska, the funding of the local schools varies substantially by neighborhood.

Community members may suddenly balk at taxes, or may insist that a certain book be removed from the library, or that curriculum reflect an ideology. The third U.S. funding source is the federal government, which typically targets certain school programs more than others, and thus federal money does not flow equally to all schools.

As a result of this mix, issues regarding education are part of local, state, and national politics, unlike in most other nations. From a developmental perspective, that has advantages and disadvantages: The benefit is that the general public considers their local schools to be part of the macrosystem that supports everyone, and the problem is that the public are less likely to care about the education of children in other communities. Primary and secondary education are more a political issue than a developmental issue.

Most (about 80 percent) of U.S. parents choose to send their children to their local public school (see **Figure 14.4**). They think that their school is educating their children well, although many are critical of public schools in general.

One public option chosen by about 8 percent of parents in the United States is a *charter school*, funded and licensed by the state but exempt from some regulations, such as hours, class size, admissions, and expulsions. Parents tend to be more satisfied and to volunteer more in charter schools, perhaps because they have chosen that school or because many such schools require parental volunteering (Oberfield, 2020).

Every state provides funds and regulations for charter schools, with the specifics controversial. Charter schools are more often in cities than in rural areas. Unlike traditional public schools, they can reject students, so they have fewer children with disabilities or non-English-speaking backgrounds than the nearest noncharter public school. On the other hand, since many are in cities, they have a higher percent of students of color than the nation as a whole.

Another alternative is a *private school*, attended by about 10 percent of students in the United States. Three-fourths of private schools are church-sponsored, funded by tuition and religious institutions. Half of those religious private schools are sponsored by the Catholic church and half by other religious groups. Those schools tend to be smaller than the public schools; many are struggling financially.

The other one-fourth of private schools are not religious but rely on endowments and tuition, sometimes more than $50,000 per child per year. In those schools, class size is smaller, curriculum is more specialized (e.g., Chinese or French offered in the early grades), and facilities are more elaborate (e.g., a well-equipped science lab, a stage, a pool, a garden).

Many parents who send their children to private schools want their taxes to pay for them. In about a third of all U.S. states, legislatures have approved *vouchers*, a certain amount of money granted to each child for education. Parents can assign that money to any private school.

Some parents decide to avoid all schools, and instead to teach their children at home, because the parents are dissatisfied with the religious, moral, or social environment of their local school. For home schooling to succeed, the family needs an adult to provide intensive, daily instruction.

About 3 percent of all children in the United States were home-schooled in 2015. As you might imagine, the quality of their education varies: Some home-schooled children score high academically, although they miss the social aspects of school. States vary in what they require from home schooling, but all mandate that children be educated: It is maltreatment not to do so.

This variation in schools for children helps to explain the vast differences in formal and informal curriculum that we now explore.

The Formal Curriculum

What should children learn? Every nation teaches reading, writing, and arithmetic—the classic "three R's" (See the **At About This Time** tables for some of the

---

AT ABOUT THIS TIME

Math

Age	Norms and Expectations
6 years	• Count to 100. • Understand *bigger* and *smaller*. • Add and subtract one-digit numbers.
8 years	• Add and subtract two-digit numbers. • Understand simple multiplication and division. • Understand word problems with two variables.
10 years	• Add, subtract, multiply, and divide multidigit numbers. • Understand simple fractions, percentages, area, and perimeter of shapes. • Understand word problems with three variables.
12 years	• Begin to use abstract concepts, such as formulas and algebra.

Math learning depends heavily on direct instruction and repeated practice, which means that some children advance more quickly than others. This list is only a rough guide meant to illustrate the importance of sequence.

AT ABOUT THIS TIME

Reading

Age	Norms and Expectations
6–7 years	• Know the sounds of the consonants and vowels, including those that have two sounds (e.g., *c, g, o*). • Use sounds to figure out words. • Read simple words, such as *cat, sit, ball, jump*.
8 years	• Read simple sentences out loud, 50 words per minute, including words of two syllables. • Understand basic punctuation, consonant–vowel blends. • Comprehend what is read.
9–10 years	• Read and understand paragraphs and chapters, including advanced punctuation (e.g., the colon). • Answer comprehension questions about concepts as well as facts. • Read polysyllabic words (e.g., *vegetarian, population, multiplication*).
11–12 years	• Demonstrate rapid and fluent oral reading (more than 100 words per minute). • Vocabulary includes words that have specialized meaning in various fields. For example, in civics, *liberties, federal, parliament*, and *environment* all have special meanings. • Comprehend paragraphs about unfamiliar topics. • Sound out new words, figuring out meaning using cognates and context. • Read for pleasure.
13+ years	• Continue to build vocabulary, with greater emphasis on comprehension than on speech. Understand textbooks.

Reading is a complex mix of skills, dependent on brain maturation, education, and culture. The sequence given here is approximate; it should not be taken as a standard to measure any particular child.

universally recognized sequences of learning to read and do arithmetic.) Increasingly in the past decade, children in the United States are also taught to work well with other people, a prosocial goal that also advances academic learning (Wiedermann et al., 2020).

One-question is the sequence of learning. Some researchers suggests that learning math skills advances learning in the other disciplines, and thus math should be emphasized in the early grades. Others say that the first three years should focus on learning to read, and that then children can read to learn. Still others argue that latent learning (memory skills, emotional regulation, curiosity) is more important and will help with every skill (Bailey et al., 2020).

Specifics of curriculum — exactly what skills should be taught in each grade and how — are intensely studied among educators, and thus are not our purview here. Sequence is crucial: Education needs to be aligned with the sequence of cognition, language, and memory (see Chapters 7, 8, and 9).

Beyond that, a general finding from research on family development is key: Schools and classrooms benefit from rules, routines, and rituals that every student and teacher understands. Underlying achievement in every subject may be language, memory, emotional regulation, intellectual curiosity, and so on, and schools that emphasize these skills, and teachers that impart them consistently and systematically, have students who learn more (Valiente et al., 2020; Wiedermann et. al., 2020).

As already explained, parents, politicians, and the public often disagree about curriculum. Here we raise five controversial topics — religion, the arts, physical education, science, and international perspective — each emphasized in some schools, not in others.

Teaching Religion

Should schools teach religion? In many nations of the Middle East, learning the Koran is part of children's education. In many Northern European nations, schools are sponsored either by Lutheran or Roman Catholic churches, and clergy of those faiths teach religion in public school. That historical practice creates a "mismatch" between traditional school curricula and contemporary Europeans, who are of many faiths or no faith (Smyth et al., 2013).

Many colonists came to America to escape religious persecution, so separation of church and state is enshrined in the U.S. Constitution. Of course, children can and do pray, express beliefs, and wear religious symbols. But no single religion is taught in public schools.

In the early twentieth century, anti-Catholic rhetoric in schools and national politics (Gordon, 2017) led most parishes to open parochial schools (*parochial* comes from "parish"), where children learned from nuns. For similar reasons, some Jewish schools were founded.

In the past 20 years, many Catholic schools have closed, but new religious schools have opened, sometimes because the local public school seemed to undercut their faith (see **Figure 14.5**). Of course, parents choose such schools for other reasons as well, both academic and social. Traditionally, students in religious schools outperformed children in public schools, including charter schools (Jeynes, 2012). Is that because such schools tend to have clear-cut rules, routines, and rituals, which might differ from other schools?

Arts Education

Music, drama, dance, and the visual arts are central in some nations, not in others. Schools in Finland consider arts education essential, with a positive impact on learning (Nevanen et al., 2014). By contrast, in the United States, half of all 18- to

FIGURE 14.5
Diversity of Religion Unlike a century ago, most contemporary religious schools in the United States are quite small, with fewer than 150 students in the entire school, from first to twelfth grade. Most (90 percent) children receive religious education after school, on weekends, or not at all.

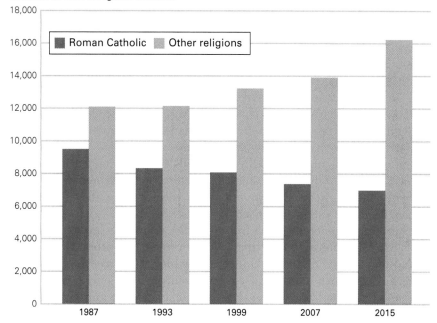

Number of U.S. Religious Schools

Data from Education Statistics, 2019.

24-year-olds said that they had no arts education in childhood, either in school or anywhere else (Rabkin & Hedberg, 2011). That may have changed: More than half of all schools report that they offer music and art education at least three times every week (64 percent for music, 55 percent for art) (National Center for Education Statistics, 2018).

Currently, music education is of particular interest, because of a now-discredited report that listening to Mozart improved cognition (Rauscher et al., 1993). Later research found that listening to music does not affect brain connections, but that learning to play an instrument might advance intelligence and learning overall (Herholz & Zatorre, 2012; Rose et al., 2019).

The evidence is mixed. One study compared 202 kindergartners, half with less than an hour per week of music, and half with 4 hours per week. At the end of the year, no significant differences in intellectual skills were found (Hogan et al., 2018).

Another study found contrary results. This began with 6-year-olds, divided into three groups, each assigned a distinct after-school activity.

- 6–7 hours learning to play an instrument (usually the violin);
- 3–4 hours in a special sports program (soccer or swimming); or
- no special after school programing.

To make the groups as equal as possible, many in the third group had applied for the music training but randomly had not been selected. The family income of all three groups was low, averaging between $10,000 and $20,000, and IQ was about average and equal in all groups.

Many in the music group not only were given individual lessons, but also learned to play in an ensemble with other children. After two years, the researchers found that children in the music group improved on several measure of brain development and cognition, including the connections between the two hemispheres via the corpus collosum (Habibi et al., 2018). The sports group also benefited more than the control group. The researchers suggest that

THINK CRITICALLY: Can you think of three possible explanations for the discrepancy between school report and student reports in the frequency of arts education?

participation in activities other than music may in fact be associated with . . . [cognitive skills] . . . provided that the activities are socially interactive and comparably motivating and engaging.

[Habibi et al., 2018, p. 79]

This study suggests what other studies have also found, that individual training matters, but that learning with peers may matter more. One overall conclusion was that learning to play an instrument, and connecting that skill with other people, benefited overall education.

Physical Education

That experiment in music raises the third issue, physical education. In the past two decades, many U.S. schools reduced time for sports, recess, and gym to devote more time for reading and math. The assumption was that more time on reading was needed for better scores (Van Dyke et al., 2018).

These data test of your understanding of correlation (from Chapter 1). Remember that correlation is not causation. Instead of more physical education leading to less reading, might reduced reading be caused by *less* physical education? (Kern et al., 2018)? Or might a third variable cause both?

In Japan, children score well on international tests of math, science, and literature. School children have several recess breaks totaling more than an hour each day, in addition to gym classes. Japanese public schools often have well-equipped outdoor yards, indoor gyms, and swimming pools. The Japanese believe physical activity promotes learning and character development (Webster & Suzuki, 2014). Are they right? Or is there a third variable?

Science Learning

A major concern in many nations is how to develop more experts in STEM (science, technology, engineering, and math). More science instruction, early on, is one strategy.

Educational systems vary in how much time they spend on STEM-related activities. For example, in the fourth grade, U.S. children spent about 100 hours learning science, more than South Korea (76 hours) but less than Spain (124 hours). But scores on international tests of science knowledge (TIMSS) are the opposite of that (the scores are South Korea, 589; United States, 546; and Spain, 518).

Why doesn't time spent correlate with science scores? Do official estimates reflect actual instruction? Or is student engagement disconnected for the curriculum (Kim et al., 2018)?

To improve engagement, some advocate connecting classrooms to the internet and providing laptops to each child. Many schools have done that. However, outcome data are inconclusive. The most hopeful experiment came from Australia, where specially trained teachers, well-designed software, and advanced computers taught integral calculus to sixth-graders in 19 schools. When the special curriculum ended, many 11- to 13-year-olds could solve problems usually given to university students (Fluck et al., 2020).

In general, some lessons awaken student engagement in STEM; others do not. One summary of the literature reported that students are distracted between 10 percent and 50 percent of the time when they are supposed to be learning (Godwin et al., 2016).

Those researchers studied exactly when students were distracted. They found that interest was higher in group work than in whole-class instruction (Godwin et al., 2016). Thus, having the students work with each other on a math problem, or personally conduct an experiment, or fix a technical problem, may be better than watching the teacher show or tell something to the entire class.

ESPECIALLY FOR Future School Administrators Imagine that you are a school principal, and you see that reading scores are low and physical education is scarce. What third variable might be relevant? (see answer, page 436)

THINK CRITICALLY: What third variable might explain the correlation of academics and physical activity in Japan?

Future Engineers After-school clubs now encourage boys to learn cooking and girls to play chess, and both sexes are active in every sport. The most recent push is for STEM (science, technology, engineering, and math) education—as in this after-school robotics club.

International Perspective

The final curriculum issue is whether schools should foster a local, national, or international perspective. An example of the difference-equals-deficit error explained in Chapter 1 is that people tend to think that their region is superior to other regions, and that their language and culture are best.

This is evident in how the United States presents international comparisons. The annual federal report on the condition of education says that the United States is in the top 15 nations in various assessments, without noting that it is sometimes fifteenth, and never in the first five.

In many U.S. states, the history of that particular state is part of the required curriculum. In every nation, national history is taught, often quite narrowly. This was made clear to me when my 22-year-old friend spoke of her college year abroad in Italy. Her Italian classmates asked what her parents did. She told them they were professors who taught U.S. history. Some Italians laughed and said, "That is an easy job. There is not much history in such a new nation."

The same narrow perspective is evident in the course called "world history." When I took that course in high school, it began with ancient Greece. Why not ancient Egypt, China, India, or Central America? Why was I required to memorize the succession of kings in England? School can help students understand other perspectives; many schools do not.

International perspective, or lack of it, is evident in learning a language. We know that language mastery is easiest before puberty, and that international understanding advances with linguistic knowledge. We also know that learning a second language advances overall learning in many ways (Bialystock, 2018). Yet few English-speaking students in the United States study another language until high school.

In high school, when another language is finally required, most often it is Spanish (69 percent), sometimes French or Italian (15 percent), rarely Latin (4 percent), almost never languages chosen to advance a global perspective, such as Japanese, Chinese, Arabic, Swahili, or any other language (each less than 1 percent) (Snyder et al., 2019).

Regarding national narrowness in history and language, every nation has their own version. For example, Colombia has about a dozen heritage languages, as well as several dialects of Spanish. Colombian teachers of Spanish as a second language say that "Spanish gives us an opportunity to communicate with each other," and that people "had to learn Spanish to demand their rights, so they were not robbed anymore" (quoted in Benavides-Jimenez & Mora-Acosta, 2019).

These two statements could be said by people in any nation who speak a language that is not the majority one (see **Figure 14.6**). Such people live in every nation of the world. Both statements are valid goals, but the broader goal of international understanding is not evident.

In the United States, the first language for about 7 percent of the children is Spanish, with a significant minority speaking Arabic, Chinese, or one of a dozen other languages at home. The main educational push is to advance knowledge of English, which is almost always the language of instruction.

The United States is not the only nation that teaches children to fit in with the dominant group. Schools in

VIDEO ACTIVITY: Educating the Girls of the World examines the situation of girls' education around the world while stressing the importance of education for all children.

FIGURE 14.6

A Learning Opportunity This increasing diversity suggests that U.S. children can learn from children of many backgrounds, especially since each of these categories is diverse in itself. However, most schools are quite segregated, which is a lost opportunity.

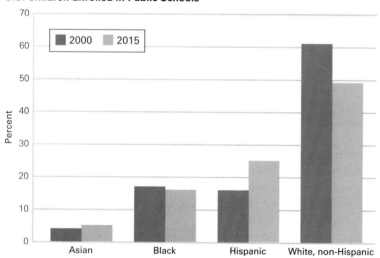

U.S. Children Enrolled in Public Schools

Data from Digest of Education Statistics, 2019.

China also stress standard Chinese, despite a large minority whose heritage language is not the standard Chinese (Gao & Ren, 2019).

To truly foster a wider perspective, young children might all be taught another language. Canada has done this with some success. Seventeen percent of Canadians in 2011 said they can carry on a conversation in both English and French, an improvement over the rate in 1961 (12 percent) (Lepage & Corbeil, 2013).

Hundreds of studies in dozens of nations have compared children who are taught in two languages versus children who are taught only in one. For some of them, the second language is the majority language within their community; for others it is a minority language that their parents hope they will learn. In general, children taught bilingually master two languages as well as children taught exclusively in one language master that one language (Bialystok, 2018).

Young children in bilingual programs are better at social skills, presumably because they need to be attentive to background differences in classmates (Chamorro & Janke, 2020). By puberty, they have an another advantage: They are ahead of their peers in math and other subjects because of better executive function. As you remember from Chapter 7, executive function includes the ability to switch from one task to another—which is exactly what the brains of bilingual children must do (Barac et al., 2014).

The Hidden Curriculum

The five controversies of the overt curriculum just mentioned sometimes pale compared to controversies about the **hidden curriculum**, the implicit values and assumptions of a school. Schedules, class composition, teacher characteristics, discipline, methods, sports, student government, building design, school climate, and extracurricular activities all may teach more lessons than the formal, published curriculum.

Tracking

Schools differ markedly in how children are grouped. Most schools separate children by age, so that 9-year-olds, for instance, are in the fourth grade unless they have been "held back." Beyond that, within each grade, some schools are tightly "tracked," with students assigned to classes based on reading scores.

This was the case in the first school where I taught, a large, all-boys public school. My homeroom was 7-14, which meant that the students were in the next-to-lowest track of 15 sections of seventh grade. I did not know the implications of tracking; my students did. One of them told me angrily, "I don't belong here." He then grabbed a newspaper and read it flawlessly. Another student could not read at all.

As in this case, some schools track students within the school. More crucial may be tracking between one school and another, which is the result of the local school district funding. Since local property taxes are the primary support in many U.S. school districts, schools in some districts are far better funded than those in other districts. Internationally as well, some nations invest heavily in public education, others do not. Children who move from one nation to another are often far ahead or far behind their new classmates.

Some schools have spacious classrooms, wide hallways, and large, grassy playgrounds; others have cramped, poorly equipped classrooms and barren, cramped play yards. Some schools have guidance counselors, sports teams, and a wealth of after-school activities; some have none. Those aspects of the hidden curriculum teach students about how much they, and their education, are valued by their community.

hidden curriculum The unofficial, unstated, or implicit patterns within a school that influence what children learn. For instance, teacher background, organization of the play space, and tracking are all part of the hidden curriculum—not formally prescribed, but instructive to the children.

Room to Learn? In the elementary school classroom in Florida *(left)*, the teacher is guiding two students who are working to discover concepts in physics—a stark contrast to the Filipino classroom *(right)* in a former storeroom. Sometimes the hidden curriculum determines the overt curriculum, as shown here.

Observation Quiz How many children are in the classroom in the Philippines? (see answer, page 436) ↑

Teacher Characteristics

A crucial demonstration of the hidden curriculum is the background and training of the teachers. If their gender, ethnicity, or economic background is unlike their students, children may believe that education is irrelevant for them. Likewise, the teachers may not understand the culture of their students. A study of student achievement in all the schools of Florida found that students learned more when the teacher was the same ethnicity as they were (Egalite et al., 2015).

Currently in the United States, about half of all public-school students are male (52 percent), and half are Latinx, Asian, Native American, or Black (51 percent). However, most experienced teachers are older European American women. Few children ever have a young, male teacher who is not European American.

Of course, many of those older women are excellent educators, but schools also need excellent men of color to be educators—for all students, regardless of their ethnicity. Every student needs to learn that caring teachers of many backgrounds work together to foster learning. Does the hidden curriculum teach that?

Teacher Expectations

Less visible but more influential are attitudes. If a teacher expects a child to be disruptive, or unable to learn, that child may confirm those expectations. The reason is that teacher behavior—quick criticism, rare praise, inadequate help—becomes a self-fulfilling prophecy.

This was first shown in a classic study (Rosenthal & Jacobson, 1968). Teachers were told that results of an IQ test suggested that certain students would to do particularly well that year. In fact, the test did not exist, and those students were randomly chosen. Nonetheless, the first- and second-graders who were predicted to bloom did so. Their average achievement was higher than the average for their classmates. This was not true for the older children: Apparently expectations had already solidified for them.

That study has been replicated thousands of times, not always with the same results. However, the general conclusion is confirmed. Expectations matter, leading teachers to smile, listen, and respond more to some students. Students reciprocate.

For example, one recent study assessed math achievement five times between kindergarten and eighth grade (Jamil et al., 2018). Teacher expectations were influential for the girls and the students of color, but not for the White boys. For them, teacher expectations mattered less, perhaps because their parents and culture already expected them to do well in math.

Fortunately, teachers can be taught to raise their expectations. Then they encourage every child (Sparks, 2016). Parental expectations matter also. The most dramatic evidence comes from parents who are immigrants to the United States: They typically expect schools to teach and children to learn. That may explain why immigrant children average higher grades and more achievement than their classmates (De Feyter et al., 2020).

Cultures also have expectations. In the United States, people are expected to express their opinions, even when they are contrary to fact. Consequently, teachers often welcome student questions, call on quiet children, assign children to work in pairs, and reward those who talk. By contrast, in some cultures, children are expected to be quiet, and teachers punish outspoken pupils. One mother, new to the United States, was told in her parent–teacher conference that her son was adjusting well, as evidenced by his talking more in class. The mother apologized!

Children absorb the lessons of their culture. In one study, middle-class children asked questions and requested help from their teachers more often than low-SES students did (Calarco, 2014). The researchers suggested that low-SES students had learned at home to be quiet, and that they were afraid that asking for help would earn unwanted attention and criticism. The sad consequence of this culture clash is that teachers might conclude that quiet students don't care.

Adults teach students not only to express opinions but how to neutralize those in power. In the protests after George Floyd's death in May of 2020, I learned that many African American parents taught their children to keep their hands visible and say "yes, sir" if stopped by a police officer. As explained in Chapter 10, many parents of minority groups provide racial socialization, especially if the school does not do it.

In a telling example of learned expectations, Aarti Shahani describes her interview to become a citizen of the United States. She had spent all her life in New York City, but her passport still said she was from India.

> My language makes me American. I don't mean English. I mean the certainty with which I say things I do not know, the inclination to lead in groups, the visceral joy in crass humor.
>
> Also my bright-eyed assumption that the world is supposed to be fair.

Children in U.S. schools not only learn to talk, they learn how to complain ("that's not fair"), when to keep quiet, and how relate to authorities. Aarti had learned all these lessons well, and she used her facial expressions, eye contact, and tone to get the interviewer on her side. After answering easy questions about American history and geography, Aarti and her examiner smiled at each other, and the interviewer checked that she answered the questions correctly and looked over her application. Arti described what the interviewer said next.

> "OK, so like, um, I don't wanna, um, tell you what to do. But, um, like, if you're gonna say you won't bear arms, [question 48 on the form] I mean—I get it! But, like, you should just change your answer." . . .
>
> I had checked the box for no—though I really meant maybe. . . . Because maybe wasn't an option, I erred on the side of caution.
>
> "Listen. You're not, like, the first one to check no. I've, like, seen other people do it. But, um, like, it's just gonna slow everything down. So, like, if ya want my advice, let's just change that answer. . . . [The examiner erased No and checked Yes.] OK. That OK with you?!"
>
> I shrugged.
>
> "Good." "Congratulations! You're, like, an American."

> *[Shahani, 2019]*

School Climate

In some schools, children help each other, laugh together, and cooperate with their teachers. In other schools, children compete for grades and teacher attention. Those variations are called *school climate*. That aspect of the hidden curriculum reflects an attitude toward learning, either a growth mindset or fixed mindset (also called *incremental* or *entity*) (Dweck, 2016).

- The **growth mindset** is that learning develops with effort, with one person's growth likely to advance another's. Mistakes are "learning opportunities"; sharing ideas and strategies does not diminish one's own education—quite the opposite.

- The **fixed mindset** is the belief that ability is determined early on, perhaps at conception, so failure is evidence of inborn inadequacy. People compete to prove they are smarter than the others on a hierarchy.

With a fixed mindset, children who realize that they are not good at math, for instance, or that writing is hard, stop trying, because they believe they will never be good at math, writing, or whatever. They deflect attention from their failure ("school sucks"; "the teacher is unfair").

Teachers reciprocate with a fixed mindset of their own. They attribute poor student performance to low intelligence, or to innate temperament, or to a particular neighborhood or family. That gets them off the hook: No one could expect them to change the student's nature.

On the other hand, children with a growth mindset seek challenges. They work hard at learning, enjoy discussions with their classmates, change their opinions, and choose difficult courses. Teachers with growth mindset believe that every child can succeed; they encourage effort, curiously, collaboration. A resistant student is a challenge (see A Case to Study).

The growth and fixed mindset may be relevant in deciding if schools should be segregated by gender. A fixed mindset suggests that biology affects learning style, so boys and girls need instruction tailored to them. A growth mindset suggests that everyone can learn in various ways if they try and that people of all ages and genders benefit from those who think and learn differently. Learning with others helps people understand themselves, and opens them to learning in modes that are new for them (Stephens et al., 2019).

growth mindset An approach to understanding intelligence that holds that intelligence grows incrementally, and thus can be increased by effort. Those who subscribe to this view believe they can master whatever they seek to learn if they pay attention, participate in class, study, complete their homework, and so on.

fixed mindset An approach to understanding intelligence that sees ability as an innate entity, a fixed quantity present at birth. Those who hold this view do not believe that effort enhances achievement.

Now Learn This Educators and parents disagree among themselves about how and what middle school children need to learn. Accordingly, some parents send their children to a school where biology is taught via dissecting a squid *(left)*, others where obedience is taught via white shirts and lining up *(right)*.

One Teacher in Finland

How do the growth and fixed mindset work in the classroom? A researcher was tasked to answer that question by observing Anne, an experienced teacher in Finland (Rissanen et al., 2019). Anne's class had 21 first-grade students, including three who spoke another language.

Growth mindset was apparent when Anne divided the children into groups. She did not put the most able in one group and the least able in another; she instead mixed them so that they could work together. She and her aide (the student/teacher ratio in Finland is about 10:1) worked closely with each group, challenging them to learn from each other.

The goals for the class also indicated a growth mindset: Anne sought to teach process, not facts. She said:

> I try to communicate that mistakes are ok and it's not very serious if you make them and somehow through that encourage them, like, let's just do this again and let's give it another try.

Anne herself sometimes deliberately made mistakes, so she could demonstrate that mistakes are an opportunity to learn. She encouraged students to try what was hard for them, after first appreciating what they had done so far. For example, she said to one child:

> Let's look back a bit, because you were absent when we worked with these . . . well, you can start. You already draw such beautiful numbers so there's no point in practicing them now, but you can start from here. Tell me, how many balloons are here?

If she had told that child he was a good artist, she would be praising him for a fixed quality. Instead, she praised him for practicing at drawing "such beautiful numbers." She then presented the new challenge in a way that allowed the child to blame his failure on an external reason ("You were absent") and pushed him to stop doing what was easy and to "start from here" to master the new task. She scaffolded education by beginning with counting balloons.

However, the observer described times when Anne might have challenged a child's fixed mindset. One boy was lying on his desk, and Anne asked him to sit up. He sat up but soon lay down again. Anne said:

> He is the kind of student who is not very open to receiving any kind of support or help, and he has a strong conviction that he is very able and knows everything and, in reality, quite often he does not. So I have to be very sensitive with him, and, like now, this posture of his is one indication that he is not very willing to work.

Rather than being "very sensitive," should Anne have challenged him? The observer noted other times when Anne too readily blamed lack of effort on innate personality. She said of a shy student, "I usually don't ask her anything unless I really see she is willing to answer," and she left another anxious student alone, deciding that she should be sensitive to his anxiety.

With every teacher/student interaction, many responses and interpretations are possible. This observer thought that teachers should push every student. Anne disagreed.

A meta-analysis found some academic advantage to single-sex education at puberty but none in high school (Pahlke et al., 2014). The temporary advantage may occur because children are distracted by the other sex when they first experience hormonal fluctuations. With maturation, boys and girls can learn together. That may be why almost all colleges that once were all male or all female are now open to both.

Beliefs about growth or fixed potential matter at every age, but early adolescence, when children decide whether to study hard or to quit trying, is particularly pivotal. In the first year of middle school, students with a fixed mindset do not achieve much, whereas those with mastery motivation improve academically. Growth beliefs lead to better coping—solving problems rather than self-blame (Monti et al., 2017).

Other research finds that, especially in adolescence, the relationship between goals and achievement is reciprocal, with each affecting the other. Schools that are well structured recognize this reciprocity, so adolescents "will develop their full potential" (Scherrer et al., 2020). Aspiration is met with an opportunity to do the work, and to be successful at it.

Trends in Math and Science Study (TIMSS) An international assessment of the math and science skills of fourth-graders and eighth-graders. Although the TIMSS is very useful, different countries' scores are not always comparable because sample selection, test administration, and content validity are hard to keep uniform.

Progress in International Reading Literacy Study (PIRLS) Inaugurated in 2001, a planned five-year cycle of international trend studies in the reading ability of fourth-graders.

Program for International Student Assessment (PISA) An international test taken by 15-year-olds in 50 nations that is designed to measure problem solving and cognition in daily life.

TABLE 14.2

PIRLS Distribution of Reading Achievement for Fourth-Graders

	2011	2016
Hong Kong	571	569
Russian Federation	568	581
Finland	568	566
Singapore	567	576
N. Ireland	558	565
United States	556	549
Denmark	554	547
Chinese Taipei	553	559
Ireland	552	567
England	552	559
Canada	548	543
Italy	541	548
Germany	541	537
Israel	541	530
New Zealand	531	523
Australia	527	544
Poland	526	565
France	520	511
Spain	513	528
Iran	457	428

Data from Mullis et al., 2012b, 2017b.

TABLE 14.3

2018 PISA Scores for 15-Year-Olds

Singapore	556
Hong Kong	530
Japan	520
Finland	516
Canada	516
United Kingdom	504
Netherlands	502
Germany	500
United States	495
France	493
Australia	491
Russia	487
Italy	477
Israel	465
Chile	438
Mexico	416
Jordan	416
Colombia	405
Brazil	400
Philippines	350

Data from OECD, 2019.

For instance, if a teenager hopes to become a scientist, that goal will motivate them to take a challenging science class. Then the teacher and school must make sure that the class encourages inquiry, insight, and experimentation, leading to success in that science class. Then, achievement leads back to the goal.

International Testing

Every nation seeks to improve education, because longitudinal data find that when achievement rises, the national economy advances (Hanushek & Woessmann, 2015). Educated children become productive and healthier adults. As nations wonder how well their education system functions, many (about 100 nations) have turned to international tests. The most common tests are:

- **Trends in Math and Science Study (TIMSS)**;
- **Progress in International Reading Literacy Study (PIRLS)**; and
- **Program for International Student Assessment (PISA)**.

The first two are, obviously, for math, science, reading, and thinking, and are given in fourth, eighth, and twelfth grade. They measure the kinds of knowledge that are usually taught in schools (see **Table 14.2**). The third test, the PISA, is given to 15-year-olds and measures the application of learning to everyday issues (see **Table 14.3**). Financial literacy, digital understanding, and analytic reasoning are part of the PISA.

In these tests, East Asian nations rank high, and scores of about a dozen nations (some in Europe, most in Asia) surpass the United States, which generally is in about the middle of the developed nations. Poor nations are much lower, because universal education of children is relatively new. One surprise is Finland, which generally is in the top 10, bested only by East Asian nations (Singapore is often at the top).

Scores in Finland increased dramatically after reform of its public education system to encourage collaboration and active learning. Finland avoids tracking: Teachers learn to challenge the high achievers and to help those who struggle. Teachers are granted more autonomy than most other nations allow. They must, however, collaborate with colleagues; they are assigned time and space to do so (Sahlberg, 2011, 2015).

Finland has strict requirements for teacher certification, including five years at university, learning educational theory as well as practice. Tuition is free for future teachers, but only the top 3 percent of high school graduates are admitted to teacher's colleges.

Educators praise the Finnish school system, although some suggest that reform is easier in small nations. (Finland has 5.6 million residents, the United States, 330 million). Others say that success occurs because Finland allows teachers to think about teaching, and then to do what they already know is best (Andere, 2020).

Problems with International Comparisons

Those who create, implement, and score the PIRLS, TIMSS, and PISA use extensive measures to make the tests fair and culture-free. One requirement is that participating children represent the diversity (economic, ethnic, etc.) of each nation's population. Thousands work to ensure validity and reliability. Consequently, most social scientists respect the results of these tests.

The tests are far from perfect, however. Creating questions that are valid for everyone is impossible. For example, in math, should fourth-graders be expected to understand fractions, graphs, decimals, and simple geometry? Nations introduce these concepts at different ages.

Further, every question reflects culture, despite the testers attempt to make them universal. Consider this item:

> Three thousand tickets for a basketball game are numbered 1 to 3,000. People with ticket numbers ending with 112 receive a prize. Write down all the prize-winning numbers.

Only 26 percent of fourth-graders worldwide got this one right (112; 1,112; 2,112—with no additional numbers). About half of the children in East Asian nations and 36 percent of the U.S. children were correct. Those national scores are not surprising; children in Singapore, Japan, and China have been close to the top on every international test for 20 years, and the United States has been above average but not by much.

However, children from North Africa did especially poorly; only 2 percent of Moroccan fourth-graders were correct. Is basketball, or 3,000 tickets for one game, or random prizes as common in North Africa as in North America?

Here is another math item. A recipe—4 eggs, 8 cups of flour, ½ cup of milk—is given, and then the children are asked:

> The above ingredients are used to make a recipe for 6 people. Sam wants to make this recipe for only 3 people. Complete the table below to show what Sam needs to make the recipe for 3 people. The number of eggs he needs is shown.

Eggs	2
Flour	? ___
Milk	? ___

The table lists 2 eggs, and the child needs to fill in amounts of flour and milk. Fourth-grade children in Ireland and England scored highest on this item (about half got it right), while those in Korea, China, and Japan scored lower (about 33 percent). The United States scored higher than East Asian nations but lower than England.

This is puzzling. Why aren't East Asians ahead? Are English and Irish children experienced with recipes that include eggs, flour, and milk, unlike Japanese children? Or are Asian children distracted by reading about a boy cooking?

DATA CONNECTIONS: Motivation or Achievement?: A Look at Various Nations' PISA Scores demonstrates with an interactive map how U.S. students' PISA scores compare to those of other nations.

Gender Differences

In addition to marked national, ethnic, and economic differences, gender differences in achievement scores are reported. In reading, girls are ahead of boys in every nation, at every age. The largest gender gap is in Saudi Arabia, where girls score about 15 percent higher. In the United States, France, Spain, and Hong Kong the gap is quite small, less than 2 percent.

THINK CRITICALLY: Finland's success has been attributed to many factors, some mentioned here and some regarding the geography and population of the nation. What do you think is the most influential reason?

By contrast, boys have often been ahead of girls in math and science. In the past decades of the TIMSS, these gender differences have narrowed, disappeared, or reversed. For example, in TIMSS math, fourth-grade U.S. boys are only slightly ahead of girls (less than 2 percent). In some nations, girls are higher than boys, such as 10 percent in Indonesia and 20 percent in Jordan. Why?

Some scientists thought that girls and boys would be closer in scores in nations with greater gender equality, as indicated by laws against discrimination and by proportions of female doctors, lawyers, and political leaders. But the data do not always support that explanation (Reilly et al., 2019; Stoet & Geary, 2013).

A new explanation has emerged (Eriksson et al., 2020). This begins by noting that laws and employment reflect norms a few decades ago, but that children respond to the current values of their parents, teachers, and peers. Accordingly, researchers compared values in many nations with the male/female gap in scores on international tests. Adults were asked if they agreed with three statements:

- Jobs: When jobs are scarce, men should have more right to a job than women.
- Politics: On the whole, men make better political leaders than women do.
- Education: Education is more important for a boy than a girl.

[Adapted from Welzel, 2013, p. 67]

When people strongly disagreed, that indicated gender equality. Those nations with a higher endorsement of gender equality were nations with smaller gender gaps in reading, math, and science. Thus, nationally, legal equality mattered less than the attitudes of the parents and teachers. The equality in reading surprised many social scientists. Why could this be?

Many hypotheses are suggested; boys may no longer curb language skills in order to be more manly, girls may no longer reject STEM careers, girls may spend less time and boys more time studying when sports include them equally, parents may encourage sons to read and daughters to study math when they believe that college and employment should be gender fair. Even in early childhood, adults now encourage girls to think of STEM careers (Sullivan, 2019).

Economic Equity

The question of gender equity in education raises another issue, ethnic and economic equity. International tests show that achievement falls as family and school income falls. This is true even in nations with guaranteed health care, housing, and food for everyone, but it is especially apparent in the United States, where low-income families struggle to obtain medical care, shelter, and nutrition.

In the United States, achievement scores of Latinx and African American children are significantly lower than those of European and Asian American children. This troubles everyone who cares about children's education, but the explanations vary, from culture to discrimination, from economics to systemic racism.

The data suggest that the causes interact. Ethnicity plus income plus family practices plus school policies plus community culture all interact to result in some children learning more than others (Morrissey et al., 2014; Paschall et al., 2018; Reardon et al., 2019). When income is taken into account, ethnic disparities are much reduced, but they do not disappear.

This explanation is buttressed by another test, the **National Assessment of Educational Progress (NAEP)**, a group of tests designed to measure achievement in the United States. Nationwide, the NAEP finds that Latinx and African American fourth-graders are about 12 percent lower than their European American peers in reading and 9 percent lower in math (National Center for Education Statistics, 2018).

National Assessment of Educational Progress (NAEP) An ongoing and nationally representative measure of U.S. children's achievement in reading, mathematics, and other subjects over time; nicknamed "the Nation's Report Card."

On many NAEP measures, Asian American children score higher than European Americans. Among Asians, children with East Asian (Japan, Korea, China) heritage score higher than those from South Asia (Bangladesh, India, Cambodia) (Cherng & Liu, 2017). Similar disparities are found between children who are from wealthy or poor White or Black families.

The economic explanation is further bolstered by comparing states within the United States. Some states spend more than twice as much money to educate a child as other states do. The highest is Massachusetts ($17,000). NAEP scores of students of color in Massachusetts are comparable to scores for White students in some other states.

No one thinks that money alone is the reason some schools provide better education than others. For example, schools in Utah spend relatively little per student, but the children do quite well on achievement tests. Every educator knows that much needs to be done before education in one location is as good as in another, and equity begins with income but does not stop there.

Special Education

In the United States, about one child in eight is designated as having learning, language, or emotional disabilities that affect their education. Equity issues may be particularly salient for those children. Not all such children need targeted educational intervention (many types of psychopathology are further discussed in Chapter 15), but here we focus on their schooling.

In the middle of the twentieth century, most such children were educated in a separate class, or were not in school. However, many of these children never learned basic academic or social skills. Nor did other children learn how to appreciate them as individuals.

Parent advocacy led to a series of federal laws, mandating that every child be educated in the **least restrictive environment**. That means that all children with learning disabilities are educated within regular classes unless a restrictive learning situation (such as a separate class) is essential.

For that reason, most children with disabilities in the U.S. are included in the general classroom, with "appropriate aids and services." This is a shift: In 1990–1991, only a third of children with disabilities spent most of the day in a regular classroom; in 2017 that percentage had doubled. This is especially true for children with learning or language disabilities, which are the most common disabilities among children.

A recent educational strategy is called **response to intervention** (Al Otaiba et al., 2019; Miciak et al., 2019). All children are taught specific skills, such as learning the sounds that various letters make. If some children do not master sounds and letters, *intervention* occurs within the regular class. The child's *response* is usually to learn whatever the curriculum mandates, because in-class, one-on-one tutoring works.

Only if repeated intervention fails is a child formally tested, diagnosed, and given an **individual education plan (IEP)**, which specifies particular special services either within the classroom or outside it. For instance, children with a language disability might work with a trained speech therapist several times a week.

Early Intervention

Sometimes the current approach is called "wait to fail," because learning problems may not be noticed or diagnosed until a child has been struggling for years. As one expert says, "We need early identification, and. . . . early intervention. If you wait until third grade, kids give up" (Shaywitz, quoted in Stern, 2015, p. 1466).

least restrictive environment A legal requirement that children with disabilities be assigned to the most general educational context in which they can be expected to learn.

response to intervention An educational strategy intended to help children who demonstrate below-average achievement in early grades, using special intervention.

individual education plan (IEP) A document that specifies educational goals and plans for a child with a disability.

How It Should Be but Rarely Is In this well-equipped classroom in Centennial, Colorado, two teachers are attentively working with three young children, indicating that each child regularly receives individualized instruction. At this school, students with developmental disabilities learn alongside typical kids, so the earlier a child's education begins the better. Sadly, few nations have classrooms like this, and in the United States, few parents can find or afford special help for their children. Indeed, most children with disabilities are not diagnosed until middle childhood.

Kathryn Scott/The Denver Post/Getty Images

This is dramatically apparent with *autism spectrum disorder*, when children have impaired social skills, often evident in early language development and play patterns. Some signs are apparent in infancy (see Chapter 15), but children are not usually diagnosed until age 4, on average (MMWR, March 28, 2014). A sizable group are not diagnosed until age 7 or so, when problems with social interaction has led to victimization and emotional outbursts. This is years after effective intervention could begin.

In fact, some children diagnosed with autism spectrum disorder before age 4 no longer have it later on—an outcome that seems to be related to targeted education in the early years (Kroncke et al., 2016). Even with early intervention, most children with autism have some deficits in adulthood, but the fact that some children overcome social and cognitive symptoms is another argument for early intervention. Plasticity of the brain and behavior is especially evident.

Early diagnosis is also needed for all learning disabilities. For example, *dyslexia* (problems with reading) is apparent in early childhood, before children are expected to read. As explained to pediatricians, dyslexia

> is commonly undiagnosed until a child has repeatedly failed to learn to read in elementary school; this late diagnosis not only places the child at an academic disadvantage but also can be a precursor to psychiatric comorbidities such as anxiety and depression.
>
> [*Sanfilippo et al., 2020*]

Screening before first grade makes sense, but few school systems do it.

Culture and Cohort

Culture and cohort affect not only when but also which disabilities are recognized, what they are called, and how schools intervene. As **Figure 14.7** shows, the proportion of children designated as having a disability rose in the United States from 10 percent in 1980 to 14 percent in 2018, not because

FIGURE 14.7

Changing Labels Note that while fewer children have intellectual disability, more have autism. Many experts think that is a change in name, not substance.

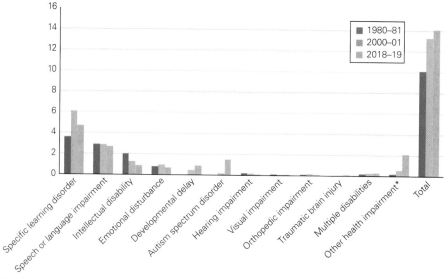

Percent of 3- to 21-Year-Olds with Disabilities (Compared to Total Public School Enrollment)

Data from National Center for Education Statistics, May, 2019.
*Other health impairments include having limited strength, vitality, or alertness due to chronic or acute health problems such as a heart condition, tuberculosis, rheumatic fever, nephritis, asthma, sickle cell anemia, hemophilia, epilepsy, lead poisoning, leukemia, or diabetes.

more children have disabilities, but because more disabilities are recognized. In 2015, 60 percent of children who had an IEP were considered learning disabled, speech impaired, or on the autism spectrum. None of these categories was recognized by schools 50 years ago (National Center for Education Statistics, May, 2020).

To further understand this, consider autism spectrum disorder again. Not until 2000 were children with autism recognized as needing special education. In that year, 93,000 children with autism were designated as needing special education; in 2017, 710,000 were, an eightfold increase.

Overall, the U.S. school system designates more children as having disabilities than any other nation: Whether or not this is a reason for national pride depends on whether one considers special education a benefit to children, to parents, or to teachers.

OPPOSING PERSPECTIVES

Education of the Gifted and Talented

Questions abound regarding special education for children who are considered gifted and talented. How should they be designated, and how should they be taught?

Some argue that because brains develop during childhood, children who have special intellectual or artistic talents should be encouraged to develop those gifts instead of having to spend boring hours with children who are not gifted. Others argue that every child should be challenged and taught, which entails special education for everyone while all are learning to respect the abilities of everyone else. Part of the question is "Who is really gifted?"

A hundred years ago, the definition of gifted was simple: high IQ. A famous longitudinal study followed 1,000 "genius" children, who scored above 140 on the Stanford-Binet IQ test (Terman, 1925). Although many criticize IQ tests (see Chapter 9) for favoring some abilities more than others, some school systems still define gifted as an IQ of 130 or above.

School placement of gifted children once seemed simple, too. Children were grouped by mental age, defined as scoring on an IQ test in the way most children of a particular age might score. Because of their mental age, some children skipped grades, and others were held back.

This was easy in a one-room schoolhouse, when all the children were educated together. My brilliant father completed the first- to eighth-grade curriculum in 4 years in his rural one-room school, because the teacher gave him work that the older children had.

But problems appeared in larger schools, because a bright younger child in a class of many older children was often shunned or bullied. Today children rarely skip grades, because mental age does not indicate social maturity. My father almost failed his freshman year of college: He was prepared intellectually but not emotionally.

One woman who skipped grades remembers:

> Nine-year-old little girls are so cruel to younger girls. I was much smaller than them, of course, and would have done anything to have a friend. Although I could cope with the academic work very easily,

emotionally I wasn't up to it. Maybe it was my fault and I was asking to be picked on. I was a weed at the edge of the playground.
>
> [Rachel, quoted in Freeman, 2010, p. 27]

Note that even in adulthood she calls herself a weed. Her self-concept was damaged lifelong.

Mental Age: 18. Chronological Age: 10. Gregory Smith was a student at Randolph-Macon College in Virginia, shown here in 1999 attending physics class. At age 10, he was quite capable of understanding force and mass, and was one of the best at performing the complicated calculations required in college science. Was he ready to learn all the other things that college teaches?

An alternative in many school districts is educating gifted children of the same age together, in their own separate class. Ideally, they avoid the social problems of skipping grades: They are not lonely because they are appreciated by classmates and teachers.

Their brain structures are not slowed down but develop to support their talents, which is the rationale for special education (Moreno et al., 2015). Since plasticity means that children learn whatever their context teaches, perhaps some children need gifted-and-talented classes.

The problem is that each such child is gifted in a particular way, in music, or math, or sports, for instance. Consequently, such classes require unusual teachers, themselves bright and creative, not troubled by children who have extraordinary talents, or who know more than they do. Teachers need to be flexible, self-assured, and able to individualize the curriculum.

For example, a 7-year-old artist may need freedom, guidance, and inspiration for magnificent art but also need patient, step-by-step instruction in sounding out simple words. Similarly, a 7-year-old classmate who already reads at the twelfth-grade level might have immature social skills, so the teacher must find another child to befriend them and then must teach both to share, compromise, and take turns.

A teacher of gifted children must be ready to discuss books that most children cannot read until college, must offer advanced math puzzles to other children, must guide science inquiry far beyond the usual interests of young children, and must encourage whatever a particular child might want to learn, while making sure all children master basic academic and social skills.

This raises many political and moral questions. Some school districts refuse to have gifted classes because they consider that unfair to the other children, perhaps even racist, sexist, or elitist. They argue that every child needs great teachers, no matter what the child's abilities or disabilities.

If each school district (and sometimes each school principal) hires and assigns teachers, as occurs in the United States, then the best teachers may have the most able students, and the school districts with the most money (the most expensive homes) have the highest-paid teachers. Should it be the opposite?

Charter schools may exclude children with disabilities and may select only high achievers. Private schools may do the same. Often in large cities, one school building contains two schools, a regular one and a charter. Then all of the students suffer: Some feel inferior and others superior—with neither group motivated to try new challenges and no one learning how to work together (Herrmann et al., 2016; Van Houtte, 2016).

Some nations (China, Finland, Scotland, and many others) educate all children together, assuming that all children could become high achievers if they put in the effort and are guided by effective teachers. That is a growth mindset. Since every child is special, should every child have special education?

CAREER ALERT The Teacher

Many people who study human development hope to become teachers, for good reason. Teachers can make a huge impact on a child's life. Probably every adult remembers a teacher or two whose interest and insight still affects them.

The need is great, and the demand huge. In the United States in 2018 there were 3,170,000 public school and 488,000 private school teachers—and that does not include preschool teachers, college professors, school administrators, after-school teachers, or paraprofessionals. Every year more than 100,000 teachers need to be replaced because they leave the profession—some retire, some quit, some die. Further, many specialties within the teaching profession are chronically understaffed: Anyone who is trained as a teacher in math, science, bilingual education, or special education will find work—if they are willing to relocate or commute to the districts that need them.

Those interested in teaching probably already know that the salary is not that great, but the benefits are adequate, and the job includes more vacation days than most professions. However, outsiders may not realize that good teachers spend as much time preparing and planning as they do in direct teaching. Further, some students are responsive, but others are unaffected or hostile. Some students have problems the teacher cannot solve: abusive or neglectful parents, learning disabilities, severe poverty, chronic depression. That makes the work emotionally draining.

The openings in the profession are in areas that require special training. Novices may hope to teach high school English or the early grades, in affluent suburbs, but such jobs are coveted by experienced teachers and are rarely filled by new recruits. Instead, prepare for the areas of high need: math teachers in cities, teachers for children with disabilities, bilingual teachers who are fluent in at least two languages, speech teachers who can relate well to children and parents of many backgrounds.

I know all this myself. When I was a girl, my uncle told me I was smart and therefore could become a teacher. I bristled, thinking he was pigeon-holing me. But my first graduate degree was a Master of Arts in teaching (MAT), and I have now taught at every level, from preschool through graduate school. I am thrilled when I see students learn new skills, ideas, or perceptions. I still learn and make mistakes, and every day I try to figure out how best to convey what I know.

I encourage readers of this book to consider teaching as a career. However, be forewarned: This profession is more challenging than it may seem. As one leading educator wrote, "Teaching is not rocket science—it is much harder than that" (Sahlberg, 2015, p. 133).

WHAT HAVE YOU LEARNED?

1. How are schools funded in the United States?

2. Who decides what is taught, or not taught, in primary school?

3. What alternatives to public education are available in the United States, and how are they funded?

4. What international differences are found in teaching religion, art, music, physical education, and science?

5. Which aspects of the hidden curriculum are taken for granted in the United States?

6. Why would anyone object to tracking children by age and ability?

7. How do expectations affect learning?

8. Why is a growth mindset considered better than a fixed mindset?

9. How valid or invalid are international tests?

10. What disabilities are most common among children who have an IEP?

Education in Adulthood

Some education programs are designed to help adults master what children learn in primary or secondary schools. As you already read, in several nations the number of students in primary school exceeds the number of children in that age group, because adults want to learn what they never did decades ago. For the most part, classes are separate from children's classes, because pedagogy for adults requires more explicit, logical, and targeted education.

Still Learning, Not in College

In the United States, many young adults learn various vocational skills, often earning a certificate that will qualify them for a job as a plumber, bartender, home health worker, or one of hundreds of other specific jobs. Quality of such programs varies, since there is no national policy regarding certification.

Some unions, companies, cities, and states have apprenticeship programs, again varying in equity and usefulness. Crucial seems to be integrated training, so that the skills learned are the ones that employers need (Bragg et al., 2019).

Some nations have national programs of certification via apprenticing or on-the-job training. Norway is one such nation, where earning a certificate correlates with increased income and responsibility (Bratsberg et al., 2020).

The GED

The U.S. government has published detailed curriculum goals for adult education (Pimentel, 2013) and offers an exam, the *GED* (*General Education Diploma* or *General Equivalency Development*), for those who want to master what high school students learn. More than half a million adults in the United States earn a GED each year, which is about two-thirds of those who take the test. With a GED, adults can enroll in most colleges or find work that requires a high school diploma.

About two-thirds of those who take the tests pass it. Some of the others try again, and pass on the second try. However, some critics contend that the GED is the "easy way out" for students who do not want the discipline of high school classes, and others say that the GED is not as valid as a high school diploma (Heckman et al., 2012). Others say that the test is more difficult than what high school requires.

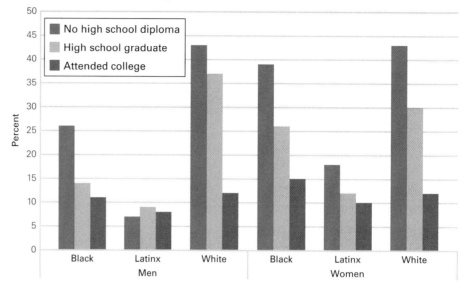

Current Smokers—United States

Data from National Center for Health Statistics, 2019.

FIGURE 14.8

College and Health These are rates for adults over age 25. Rates for current college students are far less dramatic. Apparently, the benefits of higher education accumulate over the decades, including knowing how to understand the science, as well as personal knowledge of how to change oneself.

● **Observation Quiz** Which education and ethnic group has the most and least effects of college on smoking rates? (see page 436) ↑

Learning in College

College education improves both wealth and health. Few explicit job skills or health practices are taught, but the general benefits are apparent when adults who are the same age, from the same communities, are compared. For example, cigarette smoking is less than half as high among people who have been to college, presumably because college teaches people to consider evidence, to plan for the long term, and to control their own behavior (see **Figure 14.8**).

On almost every measure of adult development, college graduates are ahead of those who merely graduated from high school. This is dramatically evident in employment. Compared to someone who stopped after high school, a Bachelor's degree results in earning an additional $23,972 per year. Unemployment is almost twice as high for high school graduates as for college graduates (Torpey, 2018) (see **Table 14.4**).

TABLE 14.4

Median Weekly Earnings (in Dollars) and Unemployment Rate (in Percent) by Educational Attainment, 2017

Educational Attainment	Median Usual Weekly Earnings	Unemployment Rate
Doctoral degree	$1,743	1.5%
Professional degree	1,836	1.5
Master's degree	1,401	2.2
Bachelor's degree	1,173	2.5
Associate's degree	836	3.4
Some college, no degree	774	4.0
High school diploma, no college	712	4.6
Less than a high school diploma	520	6.5

College advances not only health and wealth, but also many cognitive abilities. According to one comprehensive review:

> Compared to freshmen, seniors have better oral and written communication skills, are better abstract reasoners or critical thinkers, are more skilled at using reason and evidence to address ill-structured problems for which there are no verifiably correct answers, have greater intellectual flexibility in that they are better able to understand more than one side of a complex issue, and can develop more sophisticated abstract frameworks to deal with complexity.
>
> *[Pascarella & Terenzini, 1991, p. 155]*

Sometimes people scoff at the benefits of college. Remember to apply the scientific method, seeking evidence, not sheer opinion. Three aspects seem crucial.

1. A single case proves nothing. Instead of focusing on someone you know who did not find work after college, consider the data for a large, representative sample.
2. Consider the effects of context and culture. The financial benefits of a college degree are greatest for those from ethnic minorities or low-income families. Ironically, they are least likely to enter or graduate from college (Kena et al., 2015).
3. Remember a life-span perspective. Many of the benefits of college are not obvious until a decade or more after graduation, when college graduates are healthier and have more income, happier marriages, and better jobs than their peers.

There is an important caveat here. Many of the income benefits of college degree come years after graduation, but the effort and expenses begin at enrollment. A pay jump occurs after earning a degree, yet student loans need to be repaid with or without a degree. Keep that in mind when choosing a college: Private, for-profit institutions are popular; they encourage students to take student loans because that is their main income. However, only a third of their students graduate. Graduation rates are highest at the most expensive colleges, which also have the most scholarships, so students and their parents need to explore and plan the budget before enrolling.

College for the Masses

Every nation has increased the number of students enrolled in college. A policy of **massification**, that college could benefit everyone (the masses), was first enacted in the United States. Every state opened a state university in the nineteenth century, and many more public colleges (about half of them, community colleges) opened since then.

In 2019, a total of 1,636 public colleges were subsidized by state and local governments. About three-fourths of all college students attend a public institution. The 2,406 private colleges are smaller than the public colleges: Only one-fourth of all U.S. college students attend them.

The United States no longer leads in massification. One indicator is how many 25- to 34-year-olds have earned a post-high school degree (see **Figure 14.9**)

massification The idea that establishing institutions of higher learning and encouraging college enrollment can benefit everyone (the masses).

FIGURE 14.9
Too Many or Not Enough? Adults in every nation debate whether almost everyone needs to graduate from college. Does your opinion depend on your national origin?

Percent of 25-to 34-Year-Olds with College Degrees—Selected Nations

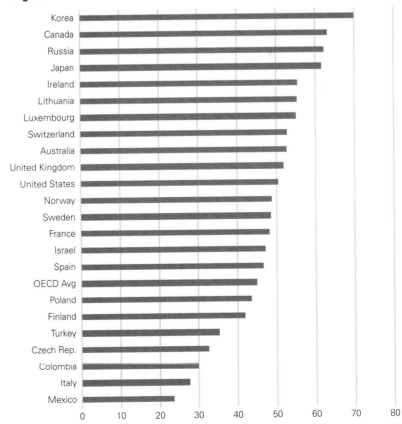

Data from OECD, 2020.

50 percent in the United States, 63 percent in Canada, 62 percent in Japan (OECD, 2020). Rates are lower in China, but since 2010, China has had more college graduates than the United States.

Some nations are moving beyond massification toward universal participation, with college available for everyone, in the same way earlier education is open to anyone. Two questions arise. Will there be enough college-level jobs for all the graduates? Does increasing enrollment reduce the quality of education? These questions have been raised in many nations (e.g., Marginson, 2016; Wu & Hawkins, 2018).

Perhaps college no longer provides the education and employment benefits it once did. Or perhaps the benefits come from a selection advantage, that the more motivated and able students are more likely to enroll in challenging colleges, while most students do not gain from college education. If that is so, then massification is not the solution. Instead, to improve college education, nations need to provide better preschool education, increase college rigor, and support low-income students so that they can devote more time to study (Zhou, 2019).

A disturbing study compared current U.S. college students and those 30 years ago. The data suggest that four years of college now imparts only half as much critical thinking, analysis, and communication skills as it once did. Indeed, in the first two years of college, 45 percent of the students did not advance in those metrics at all (Arum & Roksa, 2011).

The reasons cited were many. Compared to decades ago, the research found that students study less, professors expect less, and classes that require reading at least 40 pages a week, or writing 20 pages a semester, are often optional or canceled. Small seminar classes have been replaced by large lecture classes; students avoid the classes that require intellectual effort, evident in that far fewer major in English or history than was the case decades ago. Business is now the most popular major.

The authors of that study followed the students after graduation. Those who did more socializing than studying, choosing easy courses rather than ones requiring extensive reading and writing, were more likely to be unemployed or have low-income jobs. College taught them to expect fulfilling lives but did not give them the critical-thinking skills or the self-discipline that employers sought (Arum & Roksa, 2014).

From a developmental perspective, every advance in education is the product of two forces: the individual and the social context. Thus, blaming college students for their lack of discipline is only half right. The macrosystem and exosystem are also at fault. The outcome of this combination varies for each student, as most readers of this book know personally.

Although most students enroll in college because they want good jobs, few college classes impart job-related skills. Instead, longitudinal research suggests that college teaches life skills. A well-educated person is not necessarily a wealthy person.

A study of academic rigor (teachers ask challenging questions in class and require difficult assignments) suggests that rigor increases motivation to learn more and to think critically (Culver et al., 2019). That study did not find dramatic effects, but at least there was a nudge in the right direction. Apparently, college is not the glorious educational experience that some hope, but it is another step toward lifelong learning.

Professional Education

Many dedicated professional schools—for nurses, teachers, police officers, lawyers, doctors, and others—provide education after the basics of college. Often, not only advanced education but also on-the-job experience, professional

VISUALIZING DEVELOPMENT   Why Study?

From a life-span perspective, college graduation is a good investment, for individuals (they become healthier and wealthier) and for nations (national income rises). However, when the effort and cost of higher education depend on immediate choices made by students and families, as in the United States, many decide it is not worth it, as illustrated by the number of people who earn Bachelor's degrees.

CURRENT COLLEGE ENROLLMENT AMONG U.S. 18- TO 24-YEAR-OLDS

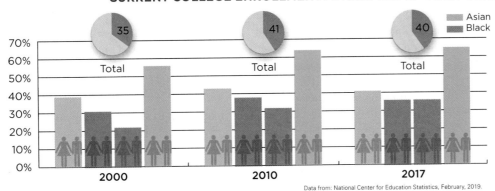

If this graph showed how many in each group *ever* attended college, the numbers for Black and Hispanic people would be closer to the numbers for Asian people, many of whom earn both Bachelor's and advanced degrees during this six-year period.

Data from: National Center for Education Statistics, February, 2019.

HIGHEST LEVEL OF EDUCATION ATTAINED BY U.S. ADULTS

The percentage of U.S. residents with high school and college diplomas is increasing as more of the oldest cohort (often without degrees) dies and the youngest cohorts aim for college. The data below are for people ages 25 and older. In 1968, half of them reached high school age when education past eighth grade was a luxury, expected for those who were rich, native-born, and white, not for the general population.

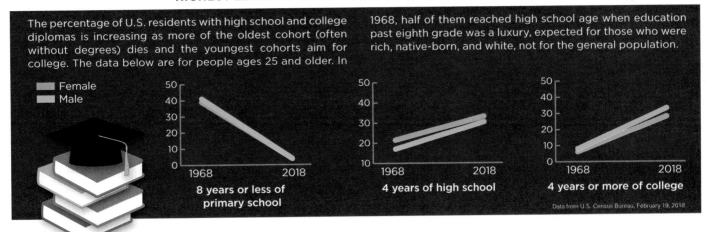

Data from U.S. Census Bureau, February 19, 2018.

INCOME IMPACT

Over an average of 40 years of employment, someone who completes at least a Master's degree earns 1.5 million dollars more than someone who leaves school in eleventh grade. That translates into more than $200,000 for each year of education from twelfth grade to a Master's. The earnings gap is even wider than those numbers indicate because this chart includes only adults who have jobs, yet finding work is more difficult for those with less education.

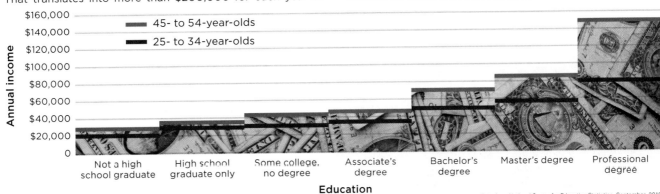

Data from National Center for Education Statistics, September, 2018.
Photo: Jupiterimages/Thinkstock/Photos.com/Getty Images Plus.

exams, and licenses are prerequisites for employment. An overall problem is the gap between theory and practice, between classroom education and demands of the work, between traditional education and needs of future workers.

This is not the place to detail all the problems in bridging theory and practice. Instead, we cite one profession, nursing. In 2009, the Carnegie Foundation for the Advancement of Teaching published *Educating Nurses: A Call for Radical Transformation*.

The need for transformation is apparent, as nurses have increasing responsibilities in today's medical professions. They are counselors for the deepest human emotions, advocates for people at their most vulnerable, as well as professionals who do many jobs that were once exclusive to physicians. Thus, nurses need clinical insight and medical knowledge, as well as technical skill in using many devices and medicines, all the time working closely with other medical professions with varied training and personality.

That requires human relations skills in addition to advanced education. According to the Carnegie publication, every college course for nurses needs to focus on how academic knowledge impacts human health. For instance:

> The Chemistry course introduces students to relevant unfolding case studies enabling them to use newly gained knowledge on diffusion of gasses in a case of Decompression Sickness (DCS, or Bends) experienced in deep sea diving, as well as fluid shifts between intracellular and extracellular spaces, acid-base balance, and other conditions.
>
> *[Benner, 2012, p. 183]*

In other words, formal education and practical application are intimately connected. Then, once on the job, nurses need to learn from doctors, other nurses, and patients in continuous improvement — a characteristic of many professions. Similarly, ongoing education in nursing as well as in many other professions is "evidence-based," requiring the same critical thinking described in Chapter 1 (Mackey & Bassendowski, 2017).

Overall, human relationships and technical knowledge are crucial for every job: That is why many primary, secondary, and tertiary schools included cooperation and intercultural understanding as one of their learning goals. The increasing diversity of colleges, corporations, and communities makes this possible and important, as now discussed.

Diversity

One challenge for all adults is how to thrive in an increasingly diverse world. Immigration, travel, technology, and better laws have all given adults more interaction with people of other backgrounds. Learning how to respect everyone, to understand and appreciate many cultures, is a major challenge.

This learning begins in college. In the United States, when undergraduate and graduate students are tallied by ethnicity, almost half (48 percent) are "minorities" of some kind (Black, Hispanic, Asian, American Indian, Pacific Islander, two or more races) (see **Figure 14.10**). Faculty are also more diverse; 24 percent are people of color (Snyder et al., 2019).

Consequently, for the first time, many students meet atheists, Muslims, immigrants, or people whose ancestors came from Africa, or Asia, or South America. Almost no college has students only of one ethnic or cultural

And Millions More When few U.S. colleges enrolled African Americans, many historically Black colleges and universities (HBCUs) educated millions of young adults, benefiting the entire society. This is graduation day at Howard University, chartered by U.S. Congress in 1867.

Cheriss May/NurPhoto via Getty Images

background. Colleges that, historically, were exclusively Black or Catholic, for instance, now have students who are White, Protestant, or of other ethnic and religious backgrounds. Diversity does not stop there: Within every ethnic or religious group, students in college and in the workplace realize the limitations of their particular upbringing.

Colleges that make use of their diversity—via curricula, assignments, discussions, cooperative education, learning communities, and so on—stretch student understanding and advance moral thinking (E. T. Parker et al., 2016; Pascarella et al., 2014). Some colleges require every student to take a course that promotes understanding of people from other backgrounds. The impact of such courses is positive, but not large. Much depends on the students' willingness to engage and the professors' ability to listen (Denson et al., 2020).

College diversity begins a learning process that continues on the job. Of course, simply working with someone of another background does not result in deeper thought. Instead, a broader understanding of people unlike oneself comes from honest conversations, shared projects, teamwork when the diverse strengths of each member are recognized. Professors, bosses, administrators, and the students and workers themselves all can facilitate intercultural understanding.

This can occur at work, although less research is available. Employers who create teams of diverse workers can reap the benefits of different perspectives. This is particularly true if the task is not routine but requires innovation. Then "diversity can be beneficial to idea generation and implementation" (Thayer et al., 2018, p. 368).

Lest this sound too sanguine, we should also note that everyone learns and works better when they feel appreciated and understood by the other people with them. In two arenas, diverse team members can work well: in the military, where each soldier's life depends on the team, and in hospital emergency rooms, where a patient's survival depends on cooperation among all professionals (Ervin et al., 2018; Goodwin et al., 2018). In those work situations, diversity can advance effectiveness, but it can also reduce it.

Team leaders can be crucial in making sure each team member feels able to contribute. For example, the head of the U.S. National Science Foundation, which is the main source of public funds for research and training in science and engineering, noticed that more female scientists than male scientists left their profession. He decided that one reason was unrecognized sexual harassment and developed a policy that he hoped would not only reduce overt harassment but also send a message to all scientists (Córdova, 2020).

Some research finds that cities thrive, economically, when many specialized workers are interdependent (Bettencourt et al., 2014). But there is no guarantee: Ethnic rivalry and even riots erupt in cities more often than in small, less diverse, towns. Political leaders and heads of companies can be polarizing or unifying; diversity is problematic or beneficial. The crucial factor, of course, is learning how to work with people of various backgrounds, a learning task that might come with experience.

Learning on the Job

Beyond general human relations skills, every job requires certain skills and knowledge that are peculiar to that job. Education that is broad enough to focus on process and communication helps when specific knowledge needs to be mastered.

Percent of U.S. College Students of Non-European Ancestry

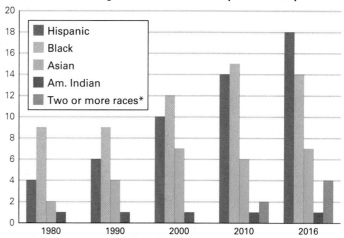

*Before the twenty-first century, the U.S. government did not allow people to identify with more than one race.

Data from U.S. Department of Education, National Center for Education Statistics, 2019.

FIGURE 14.10

Increasing Diversity Note that the total proportion of "minority" students has increased from 16 percent to 44 percent. This makes it likely that all emerging adults will have personal experience with peers of other backgrounds, which may help them throughout their future lives. Most college students in the United States, now and in prior years, are European American.

expert Someone with specialized skills and knowledge developed around a particular activity or area.

In **VIDEO: Expertise in Adulthood: An Expert Discusses His Work**, Kenneth Davis explains his research on how the neurotransmitter acetylcholine affects memory.

Beyond that, seeking a specific vocational identity, as described in Chapter 10, is a step toward wanting to learn whatever is needed to do the job well.

This is particularly evident as people become *experts* in a particular skill, career, or avocation. An **expert**, as defined by cognitive scientists, is not necessarily someone with rare and outstanding knowledge. Developmentalists consider experts to be more—and less—than that. Expertise is learned, the product of years of education (usually self-taught), and experience (usually at work) in adulthood.

After time and effort, some people have accumulated knowledge, practice, and experience that transform them—they enter a higher league than most people. That is expertise. Because they have mastered knowledge of generalities and many exceptions, experts are more flexible than the novice.

The role of experience, education, and intuition is evident, for example, in surgery (Norman et al., 2018). Data on physicians indicate that the single most important question to ask a surgeon is "How often have you performed this operation?" The novice, even with the best, most recent training, is less skilled than the expert.

Expertise is also evident in cooking. One study asked expert chefs to describe how they conceived their extraordinarily sumptuous dishes. They spoke of sudden insight, not step-by-step analysis (Stierand & Dörfler, 2016). Consider how a chef adjusts ingredients, temperature, technique, and timing as a dish develops, tasting to decide whether a little more spice is needed, seldom following a recipe exactly. Standards are high: Expert chefs throw food away, even when many less-expert people would happily eat it.

In psychotherapy as well, experience matters as much or more than formal education. One study asked therapists to talk aloud as they analyzed a hypothetical client. Novices and experts all had the requisite academic knowledge. The experts did more *forward thinking*, using inferences and developing a possible treatment plan. The novices were less likely to think about the person's social relationships, focusing more on the individual and a description of what is—rather than imagine what might be (Eells et al., 2011).

Overall, experts process incoming information quickly, analyze it efficiently, and then act in well-rehearsed ways that make their efforts appear unconscious. In fact, some automatic actions are no longer accessible to the conscious mind. The brains of expert musicians, for instance, have developed in such a way that they are better at hearing sounds (with "perfect pitch") and moving their hands with speed and sensitivity (Altenmuller & Furuya, 2018).

Motivation is crucial. A study of adults seeking to become professional pianists found that the difference between those who would be experts was not in the hours of practice or the physiology of the hands but in the dedication to understanding exactly what practice was needed (McPherson et al., 2019).

Expertise among chess players has been studied intensely, in part because international rankings define levels of expertise. The general finding is that, although chess-playing adults show age-related decrements and slowdowns on general tests of cognition, age seems to have no effect on chess ability. This is particularly apparent for speedy recognition that the king has been threatened: Older experts do that almost as quickly as younger adults (in a fraction of a second), despite steep, age-related declines on standard tests (Gobet & Charness, 2018).

The expert artist, musician, or scientist is creative and curious, deliberately experimenting and enjoying the challenge when unexpected things occur (Csikszentmihalyi, 2013). Remember Pavlov (Chapter 2). He already had won the Nobel Prize when he noticed his dogs' unexpected reaction to being fed. His expertise made him notice, then investigate, and eventually develop insights that opened a new perspective in psychology.

In order to be a flexible expert, many options need to be understood. It is estimated that expert chess players have memorized 100,000 possible opening sequences (Chassy & Gobet, 2011). Major airlines usually require pilots to have thousands of hours of flight experience before they can become a captain (Durso et al., 2018).

Education, Age, and Experience

To understand learning over the life span, we need to focus more deeply on the relationship between expertise and age. This is not straightforward, but one requirement for expertise is time. People who become experts need months—or even years—of learning to develop that expertise.

In some arenas, a decade of deliberate practice is needed. Circumstances, training, genes, ability, and age all affect matter. As expertise builds, brains change. This occurs not only for motor skills—playing the violin, dancing, driving—but also for reasoning and judgment (Zatorre et al., 2012).

One oft-cited example of the relationship between age, education, and expertise comes from taxi drivers. They must find the best route (factoring in traffic, construction, time of day, and many other details), must know where new passengers are likely to be, and must understand how to relate to customers, some of whom might want to talk, others not.

Research in England—where taxi drivers "have to learn the layout of 25,000 streets in London and the locations of thousands of places of interest, and pass stringent examinations" (Woollett et al., 2009, p. 1407)—found not only that the drivers became more expert with time but also that their brains adjusted to the need for particular knowledge. Some regions of their brains (areas dedicated to spatial representation) were more extensive and active than those of an average person. On ordinary IQ tests, the taxi drivers' scores were average, but in navigating London, their expertise was apparent.

Learning in Daily Life

Adults often spend many hours learning what they want to know. One example is learning how to fix things, such as what to do when the toilet doesn't flush, or the lights flicker, or the car doesn't start. Another example is the domestic arts that once were considered "women's work"—knitting, sewing, baking—all now learned by people of every age, gender, and background. It is now typical for adults with an unexpected pain, or odd body malfunction, to first turn to the internet and to friends to learn about the problem before consulting a specialist.

A major domain of learning is political. Many adults read and analyze the words of people running for political office, from the president down to the county clerk. They discuss this with each other, ideally seeking out those who might disagree in order to learn more. Details of pipelines, or water pollution, or police action are studied by many adults, who not only learn about them but then try to persuade others. Voting increases with every age group, a measure of adult education! (See **Figure 14.11**.)

Learning in Late Adulthood

Is it possible to educate older adults? The traditional answer was no, as in the oft repeated (and demeaning) saying, "You can't teach an old

FIGURE 14.11
Education Lifelong One measure of adult education is whether a person is aware of matters beyond their own life. You can see that both life experience and past schooling make a person more likely to understand enough about their local congressperson to vote for or against them. Young adults who left high school are most likely to say "they are all the same," a sentiment often expressed by older adults who graduated college 50 years ago.

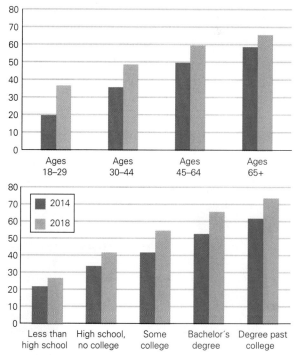

Percent of U.S. Citizens Voting in Midterm Elections

Data from U.S. Census Bureau, 2020.

dog new tricks." In the first half of the twentieth century, everyone assumed that people gradually lost intellectual ability starting at about age 20, so that by age 70 or so people were in their "second childhood," closed to new learning. But now it is apparent that although education may take more time and practice in late adulthood, learning continues. (See Chapter 5 about brain changes in later life.)

DATA CONNECTIONS: The Link Between Education and Longevity shows how, for men and women alike and for people of all ethnic groups, more education often means a longer, healthier life.

Exercise and the Mind Creative activity may improve the intellect, especially when it involves social activity. Both the woman in a French ceramics class *(top)*, subsidized by the government for residents of Grenoble over age 60, and the men in the Fourth of July Parade in Amherst, New Hampshire *(bottom)*, are doing what every senior should do—engaging in creative work with other people. Finger dexterity and lung capacity are, in general, impaired with age, but that does not stop these two, nor should it. Everyone has abilities that remain strong in late adulthood, despite the ageism of stereotypes.

Cumulative Advantage

Life-span psychologists are struck by a fact already cited in Chapter 5, that the rate of *major neurocognitive disorders* (Alzheimer's and the like) is declining. Why?

Dozens of factors have been hypothesized, including diet and exercise. Now we highlight another factor that seems to be influential: education.

Having graduated from college, even if it was 60 years ago, correlates with lower rates of major neurocognitive disorders. A college degree seems more protective than several health factors (Finkel & Bravell, 2018).

This is the result not merely of a diploma 60 years earlier, but of a *cumulative advantage* from college education (Blossfeld et al., 2019). When curiosity and critical thinking are encouraged in emerging adulthood, those traits lead to cognitively stimulating jobs, marriages, and community involvement. Every year those advantages from past education build.

Consequently, much of the current intellectual potential of elders is a result of ongoing education over the many decades, such as reading books and newspapers, attending concerts and lectures, learning languages, and seeking challenges (Schwaba et al., 2018; Wettstein et al., 2017). Indeed, age itself is less predictive of death than a decline in openness to new learning (Sharp et al., 2019).

Universities of the Third Age

Should there be schools and classes that are targeted for older adults? Some people answer yes. A movement called *University of the Third Age* (U3A) has taken root in dozens of nations (Formosa, 2019).

Specifics vary. In France and many nations of eastern Europe, a university provides a professor and curriculum. In the United Kingdom and Australia, elders themselves organize the topics, teaching, and learning. In some nations (China), the government encourages U3A groups; in other nations (e.g., the United States), private organizations are the sponsors.

The phrase "third age" comes from the idea that there is an age between retirement and very old age when education is not only possible, it is fulfilling. One easy example is learning computer and internet skills, something no older person was taught in school. Many elders want to master the computer, and classes in computer skills for older people often have waiting lists. The results of that education are evident: Those who are able to navigate the internet become healthier and more alert (Kamin & Lang, 2020). This is especially evident with the COVID-19 pandemic.

Rapid growth is evident in U3A groups. China is said to have 66,867 groups with almost 8 million members, the United Kingdom has over 1,000 with 400,000 members (Formosa, 2019). This expansion is evidence that elders want to learn, and they are willing to go the places where they will do so.

The travel and tourism industries recognize this and have developed many trips targeted to elders eager to experience new sights and understand different societies. It is not unusual for those who are about to travel to study a new language, read a new history book, and ask many questions.

Older tourists have particular preferences and interests that reflect their needs and desires at this point in the life span, but many want to keep learning as they age and welcome the fact that they now have time and money to do so (Huber, 2019). This is counter to the stereotypes of elders. In fact, to the surprise of many, there is a rise of interest in "adventure tourism" among older adults, who want to do more than passively observe new places (Gross & Sand, 2019).

That raises the question of the purpose of education. In schools and colleges, much of the learning is geared toward skills that people will need later on, either basic skills such as the three R's, or job-related skills such as learning to be a nurse, an accountant, a teacher, and so on. In late adulthood, education occurs primarily for the love of learning, with the ancillary benefits of happiness, community connection, and intellectual challenge.

Think back to the beginning of this chapter, as infants begin to learn about the world. The same eagerness to learn is evident lifelong.

WHAT HAVE YOU LEARNED?

1. What are the possibilities and problems with noncollege education for young adults?

2. What does a college degree provide for adults?

3. How has college education changed in the past decades?

4. How does diversity in a college student body affect education?

5. What qualifies someone as an expert?

6. How does college education affect health and cognition in late adulthood?

7. What characteristics of older adults are revealed by University of the Third Age?

SUMMARY

Before First Grade

1. Nations differ in what they think is the best way to educate infants. Some have extensive, publicly supported group education, and some believe mothers should stay home with their children.

2. In the United States, an extensive program of home visits is designed to help low-SES mothers teach their babies. Some have long-term success; some have no impact.

3. Whereas infant day care is controversial, longitudinal evidence shows that good preschool programs have a lasting impact on cognition and self-esteem. Funding is uncertain, since the benefits are long term but the cost is immediate.

4. Child-centered programs, such as Montessori, Reggio Emilia, and Waldorf, stress the growth of each individual child. They are in accord with theories of Piaget and Vygotsky.

5. Teacher-directed programs emphasize skills that children will need in kindergarten. They are in accord with theories of behaviorism and information processing.

From First Grade Through High School

6. In most nations, school policies and funding are set by the federal government. In the United States, these are determined primarily by states and local school districts, 14,000 of them.

7. Most parents send their children to the local public school, but the United States offers many alternatives—charter schools, private religious schools, private nonreligious schools, and home schooling, each with advantages and disadvantages.

8. The overt curriculum always includes reading, writing, and math, as well as some behavioral goals, but many other aspects of primary education are controversial.

9. U.S. schools do not teach any particular religion, but some adults create private schools that teach religion. Often they have strict rules regarding behavior as well.

10. Controversies are evident in the best way to teach the arts, physical education, science, and a second language.

11. About one child in eight is designated as needing special education, codified in an independent educational plan (IEP).

Most of these children are now educated with the regular students, but have special help.

Education in Adulthood

12. Adults who do not go to college often earn certificates in various occupations, or undergo on-the-job training. When such educational programs are aligned with the market, income and expertise increases.

13. College degrees correlate with greater income over a lifetime. This is less because of specific skills learned than of advanced thinking and communicating skills.

14. Current college education is less rigorous than in the past, and may therefore be less transformative over adulthood. However, increased diversity may expand social and intellectual skills.

15. Expertise develops over the years of adulthood, as people become experts in whatever they are motivated to learn and practice.

16. Older adults continue learning. Some nations have extensive learning opportunities designed for elders, such as in University of the Third Age.

KEY TERMS

home visiting (p. 399)
Montessori (p. 404)
Reggio Emilia (p. 404)
Waldorf (p. 404)
hidden curriculum (p. 413)
growth mindset (p. 416)
fixed mindset (p. 416)

Trends in Math and Science Study (TIMSS) (p. 418)
Progress in International Reading Literacy Study (PIRLS) (p. 418)
Program for International Student Assessment (PISA) (p. 418)

National Assessment of Educational Progress (NAEP) (p. 420)
least restrictive environment (p. 421)
response to intervention (p. 421)

individual education plan (IEP) (p. 421)
massification (p. 427)
expert (p. 432)

APPLICATIONS

1. Contact several day-care centers to try to assess the quality of care they provide. Ask about factors such as adult/child ratio, group size, and training for caregivers of children of various ages. Is there a minimum age? Why or why not? Analyze the answers, using Table 14.1 as a guide.

2. Talk to two parents of primary school children. What do they think are the best and worst parts of their children's education? Ask specific questions and analyze the results.

3. Describe what happened and what you thought in the first year you attended a middle school or a high school. What made it better or worse than later years in that school?

4. Some people mistakenly assume that almost any high school graduate can become a teacher, since most adults know the basic reading and math skills that elementary children need to learn. Describe aspects of expertise that experienced teachers need to master, with examples from your own experience.

ESPECIALLY FOR ANSWERS

Response for Teachers (from p. 405) Tell parents to look at the people more than the program. Parents should see the children in action and note whether the teachers show warmth and respect for each child.

Response for Future School Administrators (from p. 411) Less funding for coaches, a school with no grassy fields, no library in the school or nearby.

OBSERVATION QUIZ ANSWERS

Answer to Observation Quiz (from p. 401) Norway. Almost every mother stays home with her infant for the first year (she is paid her salary to do so), and almost every mother enrolls her 1-year-old in public day care.

Answer to Observation Quiz (from p. 414) About 60 (6 rows, 10 in a row). Did trying to count make you realize that the children

at the back cannot see or hear the teacher very well? None of them have glasses, so some of them cannot read the board.

Answer to Observation Quiz (from p. 426) Most: White men. Least: Latinx women.

CHAPTER 15

Health, Wellness, and Developmental Psychopathology

"I explained to your friend that the technician might want to see the prior mammogram, which might help in case there is an anomaly."

"Might want?" "Might help in case?" "Anomaly?"

I hadn't asked any questions before the aide told me what she had already told my "friend" who was standing beside us, still clad in her pink patient gown. I was surprised that the aide decided to address me, but since she did, I tried to understand what she said. I asked questions. Her answers only added to my confusion.

Perhaps she was confused, too; perhaps she was required to utter those words for liability reasons. But the more I thought about it, the phrase "explained to your friend" seemed to insult Diana, as if she could not understand what had been told to her.

In fact, Diana is one of the most cogent, insightful people I know. For 20 years we have talked deeply about politics, education, our children, our emotions. Over the past decade, her sight has deteriorated; now she is blind. She compensates, walking with her white-tipped cane, organizing her refrigerator so she can find, by touch, the food she wants; talking to her phone; listening to the radio and to audiobooks to stay informed and thoughtful.

Four of her five basic senses are sharp. She detects nuances in words and tones (she is a psychotherapist); she appreciates smell, taste, and touch.

Diana refuses pity, saying, "Blindness is not life-threatening." She tap-taps with her stick when she walks alone in her neighborhood; strangers help her cross the streets.

She asked me to take her to a routine mammogram, in a huge building ten blocks away, because she needed help finding the building, the elevator, the floor, and the room, and then filling out the electronic forms.

After I did all that, the aide ushered her into the changing room, saying "clean gowns are up there," pointing to a shelf that Diana could not see. I was a few feet away, so I retrieved a pink gown and handed it to her, telling the aide, "She is very capable, but she is blind." Then Diana closed the door, changed, had the mammogram, and was ushered back into the waiting room. That is when the aide told me everything she had already "told my friend," with Diana silent beside us.

I thought about the prejudices and assumptions, not only about people who cannot see, but about people of another race, culture, nation, gender, sexual orientation, mobility, age, ability. Those prejudices make people sick.

This chapter describes health, including what it is, how to protect it, and how to reduce or avoid problems that occur. The goal is for everyone to be strong and capable, as Diana is.

No one should expect others to do what they cannot (find the pink gown) but, more importantly, no one should assume that people with disabilities are impaired overall. Instead, as stressed at the end of this chapter, neurodiversity and plasticity make us all disabled and able, sick and well, impaired and vital.

What Will You Know?

1. Is saving a life more important than reducing a disability?
2. What disorders are less common as people grow older?
3. What is the most important thing a person can do to protect their health?

Measuring Health

Every stage of life has gains and losses, and every person has weaknesses and strengths. Unfortunately, people tend to notice what is wrong instead of what is right, the sprained toe or the toothache instead of the steadily beating heart or pain-free hands. Some say that people wear tight shoes in order to feel relief when they take them off.

There are sound evolutionary reasons for that tendency. Survival over the millennia depended on avoiding snakes in the grass more than on seeing birds in the tree. But it may be destructive to ignore gains when we focus on losses. If investors are too "risk-averse," they lose income. If couples divorce because of habits that annoy each other, they might later remember the good qualities that led to marriage. After death, mourners say, "I wish I told him how much I loved him."

In order to evaluate health and illness, we need a clear and accurate measurement of the good and the bad. There are four metrics: *mortality*, *morbidity*, *disability*, and *well-being*: We need to attend to them all, the losses (mortality) and the gains (wellness).

Mortality

Death, or **mortality**, is probably the most straightforward way to measure health. Death within a population can be indicated by either life expectancy or death rate.

Life Expectancy

Average life expectancy indicates how long a baby born in a particular place and time is expected to live. In 1950, the average, worldwide, was 47; in 2020, 72. That means babies born today are expected to live 25 more years than their great-grandparents. Nations vary, from 54 in Nigeria, to 85 in Japan. (The 2020 life expectancy in the United States is 79.) Everywhere life is much longer than it was even a few decades ago (see **Figure 15.1**). (Some of the reasons for national differences are explained at the end of this chapter.)

mortality Another word for a person's susceptibility to death.

average life expectancy The number of years the average newborn in a particular population group is likely to live.

◑ Observation Quiz Can you see four ways that Diana achieves selective optimization with compensation? (see answer, page 471) ↓

Walking Alone Diana walks alone, day and night, on her block in Manhattan, protected by strangers and her own determination.

Daniel Arnold

Average Life Expectancy—Selected Nations

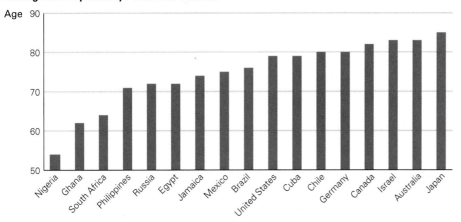

Data from United Nations, Department of Economic and Social Affairs, Population Division, 2019.

FIGURE 15.1
Individuals May Vary Everywhere, some newborns die, and some people live past 100, but the nations with lower average life expectancy have fewer centenarians and more early deaths. This chart shows average life span in only 18 of the 202 nations reported by the World Health Organization; most other nations in the same region have similar death rates. Nigeria, at 54, is among the lowest, and Japan, at 85, is the highest.

In most nations, life expectancy increased by a month or so each year of the twenty-first century, but that is not true in the United States, where it has not changed much over the past 15 years. The main reason: Although mortality from cancer and heart disease continues to decrease, deaths from suicide and opioid addiction in middle age have risen. Those "deaths of despair" keep the U.S. mortality rate steady (Knapp et al., 2019).

Maximum life expectancy is how long a creature of a particular species might live under ideal conditions (Wolf, 2010). For rats that is 4 years; rabbits, 13; tigers, 26; house cats, 30; brown bats, 34; brown bears, 37; chimpanzees, 55; Indian elephants, 70; finback whales, 80; lake sturgeon, 150; giant tortoises, 180.

The oldest well-documented human life ended at age 122, when Jeanne Calment died in southern France in 1997. That is several years longer than the previous record or the age that other very old people have attained. Some researchers consider it implausible and suggest that Calment actually died in her 70s, and her identity was taken by her daughter, Yvonne, in order to escape serious debt (Zak, 2019).

Be that as it may, it is certain that no one has yet been proven to have outlived her, despite documented birth dates for over a billion people who have died since then. This suggests that the maximum is not more than 122 (Medford & Vaupel, 2019).

maximum life expectancy The oldest possible age to which members of a species can live under ideal circumstances. For humans, that age is approximately 120 years.

Death Rate

The other way to measure mortality is to consider the annual number of deaths per thousand people in a particular population, which can be categorized by age, gender, ethnicity, or cause. Death rates provide clues about increasing wellness.

For example, in the United States death rates range from about 0.08 (Asian American girls aged 5 to 9) to 155 (White men over age 85) (Kochanek et al., 2019). Some disparities in death rate are caused by age and genes, but some pinpoint ways to reduce mortality. For example, looking closely at the death rate in old men reveals inadequate self-care and increased isolation: Better social outreach is needed.

COVID-Related Deaths

These data precede COVID-19, which will reduce life expectancy as well as increase the death rate. The accurate 2020 rate will not be known until 2022, because epidemiologists need to gather and verify the data, and some states and nations report only definite, not probable, COVID-related deaths.

Already, however, COVID-19 death rates provide useful information. For example, the data reveal that ventilators should be used only for patients with extreme breathing difficulties, that high fever is not inevitable in people with the virus, that loss of taste and smell and white toes are symptoms, and that hydroxy-chloroquine does not reduce deaths (Cavalcanti et al., 2020).

None of that could be recognized by considering only individual cases. By analyzing death rates per thousand, urgent care improved. People who contracted the virus in August of 2020 were much more likely to survive than those who contracted it in April 2020 because mortality data led to better treatment.

Another set of insights comes from ethnic differences in COVID-19 death rates. Compared to White Americans, Black and Latinx Americans were much more likely to die. That alerted everyone to disparities in housing, employment, and health care, as well as to differences in preexisting conditions.

Mortality statistics also revealed "excess deaths," which are non-COVID deaths that would not have occurred pre-pandemic. In March and April of 2020, in New York City, non-COVID deaths were 22 percent higher than a year earlier (MMWR, May 15, 2020). Excess deaths were even higher in Madrid, Spain (26 percent), much lower in Paris, France (7 percent), and down by 4 percent in Copenhagen, Denmark (Griffith, 2020; Vandoros, 2020).

The rise in excess deaths is not surprising. People with life-threatening illnesses might not get medical help, or hospitals might be overwhelmed with COVID cases, or increased depression might lead to more suicides and homicides.

But what happened in Denmark? Fewer motor vehicle crashes? Less pollution because of fewer cars, trucks, or planes? Better control of the pandemic so, unlike Madrid or New York, hospitals saved more non-COVID patients? Better universal health care? Answers can prevent excess deaths in the future.

Morbidity

morbidity Illness or disease, which can be acute (such as a sudden pain that indicates a heart attack) or chronic (such as decades of shortness of breath caused by lung disease).

The second major way to measure health is **morbidity**, which refers to illnesses and impairments of all kinds—acute and chronic, physical and psychological. Morbidity does not necessarily correlate with mortality.

This lack of correlation is evident in the *gender paradox* (Di Lego et al., 2020). Compared to men, women have lower rates of mortality but higher rates of morbidity. Even in nations with excellent medical care, women live longer but sicker lives than men do (Freedman et al., 2016; Hoogendijk et al., 2019).

An easy example is arthritis, which is not fatal: Arthritis is morbidity, not mortality (Barbour et al., 2017). More than half of all older women have it, but less than half of older men do (56 percent compared to 44 percent).

Ironically, reduced mortality has increased morbidity. For example, heart disease is still the leading cause of death, but by postponing cardiovascular death via drugs and surgery, more people live for years with pacemakers and medication.

Obesity

Adults in the United States gain an average of 1 to 2 pounds each year, much more than prior generations did. Over the 40 years of adulthood, that adds 40 to 80 pounds. Thus, two-thirds of U.S. adults are overweight, defined as a body mass index (BMI) of 25 or more.

A meta-analysis found that mortality rates by age for adults who were overweight but not obese were *lower* than for those of average weight (Flegal et al., 2013). An explanation is that some people have a high BMI because they are actually very fit: Muscle weighs more than fat, so their BMI is high while the fat content of their body is not.

Obesity increases mortality, morbidity, and disability, and reduces well-being, correlating with many specific kinds of psychopathology. For example, obesity increases pain from back and joint problems, and that is one reason that opioids are more often prescribed for those who are obese than for other adults (Stokes et al., 2020).

Adults who are obese are targets of scorn and prejudice. They are less likely to be chosen as marriage partners, as employees, and even as friends. The stigma leads them to avoid medical checkups, to eat more, and to exercise less—impairing their health far more than their weight alone (Puhl et al., 2020).

For the morbidly obese, who are 100 pounds or more over their ideal body weight or have a BMI of 40 or more, surgery may be the best option. Each year, about 200,000 U.S. residents undergo bariatric surgery to restrict weight gain. The rate of complications is high: About 2 percent die during or soon after the operation, and about 10 percent need additional surgery.

However, morbidity is markedly reduced. Ten years after the surgery, the rate of obesity-related diseases, including diabetes, is much lower, and weight loss of 50 pounds or more is usually maintained (O'Brien et al., 2019).

AP Images/Adrian Kraus

Explaining Her Cancer Dr. Magnuson is a specialist in geriatric oncology, so she knows how to explain treatment options to Nancy Simpson. Older adults are quite capable of making informed decisions, as long as their doctors do not oversimplify or use elderspeak.

DATA CONNECTIONS: Body Mass Index (BMI) demonstrates how body mass index is determined and gives students an opportunity to measure theirs.

Breast and Prostate Cancer

A detailed example of the importance of recognizing morbidity as well as mortality comes from breast and prostate cancer, each affecting about one in seven women or men. At one time, virtually everyone with either of these cancers died of it, but currently, with advanced medical care, at least 80 percent survive.

Screening and treatment reduce mortality but increase morbidity. Indeed, some women who carry genes that put them at risk decided to surgically remove healthy breasts to avoid the chance of cancer. Might screening and treatment do more harm than good?

This question is especially pertinent for prostate cancer, because screening is often misleading. A blood test provides a PSA number: Below 4 is usually cancer free, from 4–10 suggests cancer. However, screening increases morbidity and adds only a day to two to the average man's life (Ilic, 2018). Why?

Anxiety, false positives, and overdiagnosis may lead to needless surgery or radiation. If the biopsy was accurate, and treatment meant a cure, that still might not reduce mortality because prostate cancer usually grows slowly: Most men with a positive diagnosis die of some other cause before prostate cancer becomes lethal.

Screening increases treatment, which increases morbidity (in the short term because of recovery from surgery, plus long-term incontinence and impotence) but does not reduce mortality. The American Council of Physicians warns of "limited potential benefits and substantial harms of screening for prostate cancer" (Qaseem et al., 2013, p. 761), and the U.S. Preventive Services Taskforce recommended against routine screening for prostate cancer.

This is not to say that screening is *always* harmful. Some forms of prostate cancer grow quickly, and rising PSA levels can indicate treatment that averts serious harm. Some men, because of genes and family history, are at high risk for prostate cancer, and screening can prevent death. But for the general population, screening may cause more harm than good (Callender et al., 2019).

A similar problem is evident with mammograms: Many scientists try to reduce the morbidity caused by false positives from mammograms while acknowledging that accurate diagnosis may be lifesaving (Mayo et al., 2019). Always, both morbidity and mortality need to be considered.

Comorbidity

comorbid Refers to the presence of two or more unrelated disease conditions at the same time in the same person.

Many diseases and disorders are **comorbid**. The prefix *co-* means "together," so a comorbid condition means that two or more morbidities occur together.

For instance, diabetes increases the risk of heart disease and dementia; autism increases major depression; a child with one learning disability is likely to have another; hearing impairment correlates with attention-deficit/hyperactivity disorder; poor heart health risks late-onset depression (Antoine et al., 2017; Armstrong et al., 2017; Farrell et al., 2020; Read et al., 2020; Srikanth et al., 2020).

In fact, comorbidity is more often the rule than the exception, either because of a common prenatal cause or because of early childhood abuse or neglect. The biological aspects of brain development affect learning, which influences the emotions, and the physical strains on one body system affect the other systems lifelong.

Disability

disability A physical, mental, or emotional impairment that makes one or more major life activity difficult or impossible.

The third way to measure health is **disability**, which refers to difficulty or inability to do something because of a "physical, mental, or emotional condition." Limitation in function (not severity of disease) is the hallmark of disability.

Physical disabilities are often measured by inability to perform the *activities of daily life (ADLs)*; cognitive disabilities occur when people cannot perform the *instrumental activities of daily life (IADLs)*. For example, people who cannot feed themselves have an ADL, people who cannot plan and prepare dinner have an IADL (see **Table 15.1**).

In general, physical disabilities (such as with the senses and mobility) are rated more disabling by people who do *not* have disabilities than by those with them.

TABLE 15.1

Instrumental Activities of Daily Life

Domain	Exemplar Task
Managing medical care	Keeping current on checkups, including teeth, ears, and eyes Assessing supplements as good, worthless, or harmful
Food preparation	Evaluating nutritional information on food labels Preparing and storing food to prevent spoilage
Transportation	Comparing costs of car, taxi, bus, and train Determining quick and safe walking routes
Communication	Knowing when, whether, and how to use landline, cell, texting, mail, and e-mail Programming speed dial for friends and emergencies
Maintaining household	Following instructions for operating an appliance Keeping safety devices (fire extinguishers, CO_2 alarms) active
Managing one's finances	Budgeting future expenses (housing, utilities, etc.) Completing timely income tax returns Avoiding costly scams, unread magazines

By contrast, psychological illnesses (such as depression) are considered less disabling by outsiders than by the people who experience them (Vigo et al., 2016).

The severity of a disability depends on both the individual and the society. Consider again prostate cancer surgery. Is impotency a disability? "Yes" for some young men, but "no" for some older men who stopped having intercourse years earlier, and who hope never to have sex again.

Societies reduce disabilities via **universal design**, when objects and environments are designed to be accessible to everyone, with or without a handicap. For example, universal design results in entrance ramps; in large, legible signs; and in microphones that accurately convey speech that is clearly spoken (Williamson, 2019).

universal design The creation of settings and equipment that can be used by everyone, whether or not they are able-bodied and sensory-acute.

Well-Being

The fourth measure of health, **well-being**, is probably the most important, and yet is most difficult to measure. Well-being indicates how vital and energetic — physically, intellectually, and socially — an individual feels. Well-being is *joie de vivre*, the zest for living, the love of life. A person can be vital despite disease or disability.

well-being The feeling of happiness and health that makes life satisfying.

THINK CRITICALLY: How do you compare with other people your age?

Many psychologists agree that well-being is the goal. They call it *happiness*, or *satisfaction*, or *flow*, or *flourishing*, terms that refer to slightly different aspects of well-being. All agree, however, that something beyond mortality, morbidity, and disability is needed for a good life (Csikszentmihalyi, 1990; Diener, 2009; Seligman, 2011).

Consider how this applies to treatment for cancer. An oncologist might assess only whether a particular treatment shrinks a tumor or adds a year to life. Instead, attention to well-being means telling patients the personal costs, such as tiredness, or pain, or depression, of every intervention. Doctors can increase well-being by explaining how other patients have coped with that cancer.

The need for well-being is evident for every disease and disability. For example, many college students sometimes drink too much alcohol, and they experience a "hangover" the next day, a disabling condition usually with headache and stomachache. By contrast, every college student has had moments of joy and high alert, perhaps when their thoughts suddenly came together with clarity and insight. In both cases, students learn how to avoid loss, or gain, of well-being.

Cost-Benefit Analysis

If none of these four measures (mortality, morbidity, disability, well-being) is known, individuals pay for what they hope is the best care for themselves, and donate to charities that have provided a "warm glow" in the past (O'Brien & Kassirer, 2019). That is not always the wisest choice (Fiennes, 2017).

One "oft-used example. . . . Trachoma surgeries to prevent blindness have been estimated to cost less than $50, whereas training a guide dog to help a person who is already blind has been estimated to cost $50,000" (Caviola, 2020, p. 509).

Without a cost-benefit analysis, people donate to provide for one dog, and not to prevent blindness in 100. To make wise choices, especially regarding public health, we need an objective method to weigh costs and benefits. Two common ways to do that are *DALYs* and *QALYs*.

Reach Wide for Wellness One of the impediments to life and health is the notion that people who exercise must look young and attractive. This man is wise and brave, as well as admirably balanced.

Melanie Stetson Freeman/The Christian Science Monitor/Getty Images

Years Lost and Gained As a young man, John Lewis was beaten many times over five years, including suffering a broken skull when he tried to walk across an Alabama bridge on Bloody Sunday, 1965. Did his lost DALYs lead to gains in QALYs? When he died at age 80, he was a national hero.

disability-adjusted life years (DALYs)
A number that indicates how many years of total well-being are lost because of a disability. The idea is that each year of a disabled person's life is a fraction of what it could have been.

quality-adjusted life years (QALYs)
A number that indicates quality years added because of a full life.

Years of Disability

Disability-adjusted life years, or **DALYs**, indicate how much and how long a disability impairs people. The assumption is that a disabled person has somewhat less than a full life; thus, a person born in Chile who dies at age 80 (the average life expectancy there), with a lifelong disability that reduces functioning by about 30 percent, would lose 24 DALYs ($.3 \times 80$). If that same person died at age 50 because of the disability, that would be a loss of 45 DALYs. ($80 - 50 = 30 + .3 \times 50$).

DALYs have been used by the World Health Organization to assess the Global Burden of Disease, which helps nations decide how to spend public health money. It is used particularly in low-income nations to assess basic health measures.

One benefit of DALYs is that various strategies can be compared. For instance, is it more effective to provide drugs to treat malaria or to give everyone mosquito nets for their beds? DALYs consider local mortality and disability rates: Ethiopia needs bed nets as well as drugs, but Canada needs only malaria drugs.

DALYs consider all the costs of any treatment and any condition. For example, kidney disease is a significant, but rarely direct, cause of mortality and morbidity. Calculating DALYs make the case that treating kidney disease saves health costs (Cockwell & Fisher, 2020).

DALYs also consider conditions that affect the mind. Depression is "a major human blight." It is not the leading cause of mortality or morbidity (heart disease is), but it is the leading cause of DALYs because people who are depressed usually have that disorder for decades, thus accumulating a lifetime of lost functioning (K. Smith, 2014).

Quality of Life

Another cost-benefit measure is more often used in developed nations: **QALYs (quality-adjusted life years)**. If well-being is as high as possible, quality of life is 100 percent, which means that each year equals one QALY. Someone who lives 80 healthy, happy, energetic years has 80 QALYs. If one of those years includes surgery and painful recovery, reducing well-being by half, then that person's QALY would be 79½.

DALYs and QALYs Together

When global health is considered, both DALYs and QALYs are useful (Feng et al., 2020). The following are among the findings now widely accepted based on such measures:

- Community health improvements, such as clean water and widespread immunization, are cost effective, because they benefit millions, each by a small amount.
- Noncommunicable diseases (cancer, heart disease, schizophrenia) are now the most common causes of morbidity, even in poor nations.
- Nutritional deficiencies, especially of iron, iodine, and vitamin A, are not listed on death certificates but cause chronic disabilities, especially for the fetus and infant.
- Psychopathologies, such as depression and autism, rarely affect mortality directly, but they often increase DALYs and decrease QALYs.
  [Hassen et al., 2020; Juma et al., 2019; Ogbo et al., 2018; Vigo et al., 2016]

Thus, all four ways to measure health, using DALYs, QALYs, and other indicators, move us closer to the goal first mentioned on the last page of Chapter 1, "to help everyone reach their potential."

INSIDE THE BRAIN

Body Disease Versus Brain Disease

It makes sense to assess the costs and benefits of various interventions that are designed to improve health, but exactly how that should be done is controversial. QALYs were explicitly forbidden from consideration by the U.S. Congress in national health care (Neumann & Cohen, 2018).

QALYs make decisions about national health care easier, which is why they are extensively used in England, but they are not individualized, which is why they are less used in the United States. Neither nation, however, considers the effect of brain disorders on life years.

Yet, as you just read, diseases of the brain, such as depression and schizophrenia, are the cause of more lost QALYs than any disease of the rest of the body. Thousands of scientists seek to improve the function of the brain.

Some of the research is promising. Drugs have many proven impacts on the brain. One specific example is that antidepressants relieve depression by their effect on new neurons formed in the hippocampus (Planchez et al., 2020).

In addition, many psychotherapists seek to help people think about, and then act on, their daily lives, increasing QALY's and reducing DALYs. Many other possibilities, not well-researched but requiring investigation, are that various foods, pollutants, aerobic exercise, and gut microbes affect mental health (Martirosyan, 2019; Zu et al., 2020; Maurus et al., 2019).

It is apparent that the focus on mortality rather than morbidity, on direct and immediate causes of harm rather than the ongoing impairment of a malfunctioning brain, results in less joy and energy over the years of life.

Worldwide, most research in this area is sponsored by the drug industry. Their goal is to find drugs that will profit the particular company. That is not bad, but that does not improve QALYs for the general population.

This is apparent in the public health funds for research on Alzheimer's disease. As you remember, most people never experience that disease, but those who do often live a decade or more with severe reduction in quality of life. Moreover, their caregivers often experience depression and disability, again with increased DALYs. Attention to quality of life, for those with the disease and for their caregivers, is much needed (Lin et al., 2019).

However, although drugs and therapies to improve QALY's and reduce DALY's are proven to help people with neurocognitive disorders, it is also apparent that public health funding is much more likely to be devoted to physical ills—cardiovascular diseases, cancers, and so on—than to brain disorders (Lund, 2020). More attention to DALYs or QALYs might remedy that.

WHAT HAVE YOU LEARNED?

1. Why are people more likely to avoid risks than to seek benefits?

2. How long is an average newborn expected to live?

3. What is an "excess" death?

4. Why might morbidity increase when mortality falls?

5. What are gender differences in morbidity and mortality?

6. How do physical disabilities compare to psychological disabilities?

7. How could a severely disabled person be high in well-being?

8. When are DALYs and QALYs useful?

Developmental Psychopathology

The word "pathology" refers to sickness, and thus pathologies are the diseases and conditions that increase mortality, morbidity, and disability. Many affect the body more than the mind; pathologists look for signs of sickness in the tissues, bones, and organs of the body more than in behavior.

Instead, here we consider **psychopathology**, the illnesses (*-pathology*) that impair behavior (*psycho-*). They are the subject of a massive tome from the American Psychiatric Association, now in its fifth edition, the ***Diagnostic and Statistical Manual of Mental Disorders (DSM-5)***, with about 20 major categories and hundreds of subcategories.

psychopathology Illnesses that primarily affect the mind and behavior, not the physical body. Schizophrenia is an example.

Diagnostic and Statistical Manual of Mental Disorders (DSM-5) Revised about every 12 years by hundreds of U.S. psychiatrists to name and diagnose psychological disorders, this 991-page book is in its fifth edition.

Another major classification list is used internationally: the World Health Organization's *International Statistical Classification of Diseases and Related Health Problems (ICD-10)*. The *DSM-5* and the *ICD-10* are largely in agreement, with some variation in certain diagnoses.

developmental psychopathology A perspective on psychological disorders that reflects changes as people grow older. For example, many childhood experiences can cause or mitigate mental disorders.

Developmental psychopathology links typical with atypical development. This topic is relevant lifelong, because "[e]ach period of life, from the prenatal period through senescence, ushers in new biological and psychological challenges, strengths, and vulnerabilities" (Cicchetti, 2013b, p. 458). Turning points, opportunities, and past influences are always apparent.

At the outset, four general principles should be emphasized.

1. *Abnormality is normal*, meaning that everyone has some aspects of behavior that are quite atypical. Thus, most people sometimes act oddly. The opposite is also true: Everyone with a diagnosed disorder is, in many respects, like everyone else.
2. *Disorders change year by year.* Most disorders are comorbid, with more than one problem in the same person. The disorder that seems most severe in one year may become much milder, but another problem may appear.
3. *Life may get better or worse.* Prognosis is uncertain. Many children with severe disabilities (e.g., blindness, dyslexia) become productive adults. Conversely, some conditions (e.g., conduct disorder) become more disabling.
4. *Diagnosis and treatment reflect the social context.* Each individual interacts with the surrounding setting—including family, school, community, and culture—to modify, worsen, or even create psychopathology.

We focus on only a few of the many psychological disorders, organized here by the age at which they commonly arise. That is one logical way to categorize them, but do not be misled: Every condition is influenced by genes, so they could be said to originate at conception, and every condition affects people at many ages. Indeed, a prominent theory of psychopathology is that an underlying vulnerability is at the root of many manifestations of pathology, and then specifics of culture and experience shape that foundation into particular problems (Smith et al., 2020).

Disorders Arising in Childhood

Three major disorders—autism, attention-deficit/hyperactivity disorder (ADHD), and learning disorders—typically are apparent before adolescence. A fourth, anxiety, increasingly affects children. Although their symptoms and expressions change with age, they usually affect adults as well.

Autism Spectrum Disorder

Autism was once thought to affect fewer than 1 in 1,000 children, who exhibited "an extreme aloneness that, whenever possible, disregards, ignores, shuts out anything . . . from the outside" (Kanner, 1943). Children with autism were usually nonverbal and severely impaired: They died young.

VIDEO: Current Research into Autism Spectrum Disorder explores why the causes of ASD are still mostly unknown.

autism spectrum disorder (ASD) A developmental disorder marked by difficulty with social communication and interaction—including difficulty seeing things from another person's point of view—and restricted, repetitive patterns of behavior, interests, or activities.

That is no longer true. In the United States, among all 3- to 17-year-olds, 1 child in every 36 has been diagnosed as having ASD (G. Xu et al., 2019). The defining symptom is still impaired social interaction, making children with autism less adept at conversation, at social play, and at understanding emotions. Other common symptoms include slow language development, repetitive play, and sensitivity to smells and sounds.

DSM-5 changed the terminology from *autism* in *DSM-IV* to **autism spectrum disorder (ASD)**. People "on the spectrum" may have a severe, moderate, or mild form, with the mild version formerly called *Asperger's syndrome*. Some very successful people probably have or had ASD, from the eighteenth-century philosopher who founded utilitarianism (Jeremy Bentham) to a 2020 hero of climate change (Greta Thunberg, who proclaims her autism as well as her trenchant criticism of world leaders).

Many scientists are searching for biological ways to detect autism with blood tests or brain scans before age 1. Other scientists seek behavioral signs in the early months, such as the absence of the social smile, or reduced gazing at faces and eyes (Macari et al., 2020).

Definitive diagnosis of ASD in infancy is not yet available, but it is known that younger siblings of children with autism have about a 20 percent chance of later being diagnosed on the spectrum. For that reason, many researchers study infants who are high risk (with a sibling) or low risk (with no relatives on the spectrum).

Will parents be troubled if they learn that their baby might be on the spectrum? To answer that, one study included 88 infants, half high risk and half not. All were given many neurological and behavioral tests at 5, 10, 14, 18, 24, and 36 months. Almost all the parents were grateful for the study. They appreciated learning about their infant's development, even when the child was atypical (Achermann et al., 2020).

This confirms what we know about psychopathology: People want to know what problems they or their loved ones have. They prefer accurate knowledge to uncertainty; recognizing symptoms makes it easier to treat.

Why is ASD so much more common that it once was? Two former hypotheses are now proven false. One was that unaffectionate mothers (the so-called refrigerator mother) caused children to withdraw from social interaction (Bettelheim, 1975). Before that idea was proven wrong, caregivers were blamed.

The second disproven hypothesis was that infant vaccinations cause autism. Thousands of studies in many nations refute this idea (only one discredited, fraudulent study backed it). Some of the best data come from Denmark, where detailed medical records for every resident have been analyzed. Between 1999 and 2010, Danish births totaled 657,461. Those infants who were fully vaccinated were slightly *less* likely to be among the 6,517 who were diagnosed with autism before age 10 (Hviid et al., 2019).

Four new hypotheses have arisen:

1. Something that occurs prenatally, such as exposure to drugs, viruses, or pesticides, may harm the fetus.
2. Something in the environment, such as new chemicals in food, air, or water, may affect the developing brain.
3. More children are now diagnosed, because their parents seek special education, which was not publicly funded for children with autism until 2000.
4. More children are diagnosed, because *DSM*-5 expanded the definition to include many more children.

Many experts seek to understand why the prevalence of ASD seems to be increasing. They have discovered that ASD is not one disorder but a cluster of similar disorders, which means that one gene or toxin that increases the incidence of one type of autism may not be relevant for another.

Attention Deficit/Hyperactivity Disorder (ADHD)

A child with **attention-deficit/hyperactivity disorder (ADHD)** is inattentive, overactive, and/or impulsive. That describes almost every 2-year-old, but even at age 5 those with ADHD "are so active and impulsive that they cannot sit still, are constantly fidgeting, talk when they should be listening, interrupt people all the time,

THINK CRITICALLY: Many adults are socially awkward, insensitive to other people's emotions, and poor at communication—might they have been diagnosed as on the spectrum if they had been born more recently?

attention-deficit/hyperactivity disorder (ADHD) A condition characterized by a persistent pattern of inattention and/or by hyperactive or impulsive behaviors; ADHD interferes with a person's functioning or development.

Not a Cartoon At age 3, Owen Suskind was diagnosed with autism. He stopped talking and spent hour after hour watching Disney movies. His father said his little boy "vanished," as chronicled in the Oscar-nominated documentary *Life Animated*. Now, at age 23 (shown here), Owen still loves cartoons, and he still has many symptoms of autism spectrum disorder. However, he also has learned to speak and has written a movie that reveals his understanding of himself, *The Land of the Lost Sidekicks*.

can't stay on task, . . . accidentally injure themselves." They are "difficult to parent or teach" (Nigg & Barkley, 2014, p. 75). It is also possible to have an attention deficit but no hyperactivity, as with a child who is easily distracted and seems to daydream often.

In 1980, about 5 percent of U.S. 4- to 17-year-olds were diagnosed with ADHD. More recently, the rate was 11 percent (Xu et al., 2018). The rate has also increased in other nations, especially wealthy ones, but not as much (Fayyad et al., 2017; Polanczyk et al., 2014).

As with ASD, some people attribute the increase in ADHD to greater awareness and expanded definitions, not to children themselves. In *DSM-IV*, the criteria for diagnosis mandated that symptoms must *impair* daily life and start before age 7; *DSM-5* allows onset up to age 12, with symptoms that *impact* life.

The growth in ADHD diagnosis concerns experts who see three problems:

- *Misdiagnosis.* If ADHD is diagnosed when another disorder is the problem, treatment might make the problem worse. A child with *disruptive mood dysregulation disorder* (once commonly misdiagnosed as childhood bipolar disorder), an *anxiety disorder,* or Tourette's syndrome, might be negatively affected by ADHD medication (Strawn et al., 2017). Indeed, the entire issue of which medication is appropriate for which child is a complicated one, especially since many disorders are comorbid and since symptoms change with age. Always, accurate diagnosis and careful, individualized treatment are important.

- *Drug abuse.* Some adolescents seek a diagnosis of ADHD, because that will give them special accommodations and drugs that are thought to enhance concentration. The U.S. rates rise at adolescence, with 14 percent of 12- to 17-year-olds diagnosed with the disorder (Xu et al., 2018). College students who have earlier been diagnosed with ADHD have higher rates of substance abuse, especially marijuana and alcohol, but this seems more likely a consequence of the disease than a consequence of misdiagnosis (Mochrie et al., 2020).

- *Typical behavior considered pathological.* If activity, impulsiveness, and curiosity are diagnosed as ADHD, and treatment reduces that, the result may be less exuberant children. (On the other hand, if children who are unfairly bullied and blamed for behavior that would respond to appropriate treatment, then children suffer because the adults hesitate. Many children *do* have the disorder, and treatment can be transformative.)

"Typical considered pathological" is one interpretation of data on 378,000 children in Taiwan, a Chinese nation whose rates of ADHD are increasing (M.-H. Chen et al., 2016). Boys born in August, and who therefore entered kindergarten when they had just turned 5, were diagnosed with ADHD at the rate of 4.5 percent, whereas boys born in September, starting kindergarten when they were almost 6, were diagnosed at the rate of 2.8 percent.

Diagnosis for these Chinese boys typically occurred years after kindergarten, but August birthday boys were at risk throughout their school years (see **Figure 15.2**). The data suggest that a year of maturation would have reduced the rate of ADHD by over a third. Note, however, that two-thirds of the more mature children nonetheless were diagnosed with ADHD.

◀)) Observation Quiz This chart also shows medication rate. Are those August birthdays more likely to be medicated than the September birthdays? (see answer, page 471) ↓

FIGURE 15.2

One Month Is One Year In the Taiwanese school system, the cutoff for kindergarten is September 1, so some boys enter school a year later because they were born a few days later than others. Those who are relatively young among their classmates are less able to sit still and listen. They are almost twice as likely to be given drugs to quiet them down.

Diagnosed with Attention-Deficit/Hyperactivity Disorder (ADHD)

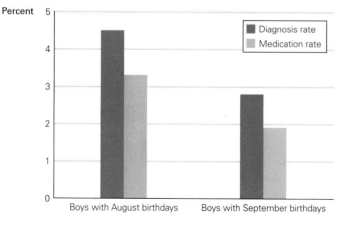

Data from M.-H. Chen et al., 2016.

This example highlights a related concern. Traditionally, in ADHD "boys outnumber girls 3-to-1 in community samples and 9-to-1 in clinical samples" (Hasson & Fine, 2012, p. 190). (Clinical samples are those children whose ADHD receives ongoing professional care.) Could typical "boy activity" be troubling to mothers and female teachers? Could that be the reason for this male/female ratio? Are girls underdiagnosed?

Many experts have become more aware of girls with ADHD, including the inattentive type (not hyperactive). A recent U.S. report finds the male/female ratio close to 2:1, not 3:1. In a national survey, parents report that 14 percent of all 4- to 17-year-old boys and 6 percent of all 4-to 17-year-old girls have been diagnosed with ADHD (Xu et al., 2018). Often a girl's main symptom is inattentiveness, not hyperactivity. When should a daydreaming, distracted child be diagnosed with ADHD?

The question of proper diagnosis and treatment is controversial (Gordon-Hollingsworth et al., 2015; Storebø & Gluud, 2020). A leading book argues that drug companies and doctors are far too quick to push pills, making ADHD "by far the most misdiagnosed condition in American medicine" (Schwarz, 2016, p. 2). A critical review of that book notes that millions of people "have experienced life-changing, positive results" from treatment — including medication (Zametkin & Solanto, 2017, p. 9).

Many children in the United States who are diagnosed with ADHD are medicated; in England and Europe, less than half are (Polanczyk et al., 2014); in mainland China almost none are because Chinese children who do not pay attention are thought to need correction, not medication (Yang et al., 2013). In certain African nations, an inattentive, overactive child is more likely to be punished than sent to a psychiatrist.

Medication and Treatment

How best to treat disorders in children and adults is a fascinating and often frustrating issue. Both overdiagnosis and underdiagnosis occur, and certainly some children and adults find that their lives are much improved by accurate diagnosis and effective treatment, while others seem not to benefit.

The drug most commonly prescribed for children with ADHD is *Ritalin (methylphenidate)*, but at least 20 other psychoactive drugs are prescribed for children to treat depression, anxiety, intellectual disability, autism spectrum disorder, disruptive mood dysregulation disorder, childhood bipolar disorder, tics, and other conditions (Strawn et al., 2017).

Many studies have found mixed results from the various drugs for children and adolescents, so prescribers must proceed with trial and error, in not only whether and what to prescribe but also how much. One review notes "numerous divergent pathways between medication/medication dose and clinical response and side effects" (Wehry et al., 2018, p. 40) and another that "individual patients appear to have a unique dose response curve" (Strawn et al., 2017).

A meta-analysis finds that medication is likely to help when it is combined with cognitive-behavioral therapy, but also that the specifics of various disorders vary from one child, one context, and one nation to another. Thus, no particular drug, and no particular therapy, works for every child (López-Pinar et al., 2018).

Most professionals believe that contextual interventions (instructing caregivers and schools on child management, changing the diet, increasing outdoor play, eliminating screens) should be tried before drugs. Good advice, but not easy to take if a parent or teacher is trying to manage an overactive, disruptive child every day.

Specific Learning Disorders

From ages 6 to 11, children are expected to master all the basic school skills that are needed in adulthood. Chapter 14 advocated universal early screening to assess

specific learning disorder A marked deficit in a particular area of learning that is not caused by an apparent physical disability, by an intellectual disability, or by an unusually stressful home environment.

dyslexia Unusual difficulty with reading; thought to be the result of some neurological underdevelopment.

dyscalculia Unusual difficulty with math, probably originating from a distinct part of the brain.

learning problems and to individualize education. What might those learning problems be?

The *DSM-5* diagnosis of **specific learning disorders** includes problems in perception or information-processing that cause low achievement in reading, math, or writing (including spelling), as well as in other skills (Grigorenko et al., 2020). Deficiencies undercut academic achievement, destroy self-esteem, and qualify a child for special education (according to U.S. law) or formal diagnosis (according to *DSM*-5).

The learning disorder that is most often diagnosed is **dyslexia**—unusual difficulty with reading. Historically, some children with dyslexia figured out themselves how to cope—as did Hans Christian Andersen and Winston Churchill.

Early theories of dyslexia hypothesized visual difficulties—for example, reversals of letters (reading *god* instead of *dog*) and mirror writing (*b* instead of *d*). That hypothesis was tested and disproven. Instead, dyslexia more often manifests as speech and hearing difficulties (Hulme & Snowling, 2016). Language development in the early years correlates with reading development later on.

Another common learning disorder is **dyscalculia**, unusual difficulty with math. For example, when asked to estimate the height of a normal room, second-graders with dyscalculia might answer "200 feet," or, when shown both the 5 and 8 of hearts from a deck of playing cards and asked which is higher, schoolchildren might use their fingers to count the hearts on each card (Butterworth et al., 2011).

DSM-5 recognizes a third learning disability, *dysgraphia*, difficulty in writing. Few children write neatly at age 5, but practice allows most children to write easily and legibly by age 10. Some cultures and schools stress penmanship; others do not. For example, a team in Saudi Arabia considered it "foundational expertise" (Rao et al., 2017).

For all learning disorders, family history is a factor, because genes affect many aspects of learning. And for all of them, early, targeted attention, without blame, allows most children to master basic skills by age 8 (Grigorenko et al., 2020). Without that, learning disorders underlie other problems, as now explained.

Childhood Anxiety

Some children have emotional reactions that seem extreme to adults, and some of those are diagnosed with anxiety disorders if the ability to go to school, make friends, or sleep is hindered. One study found that the parents of about 4 percent of all 6- to 11-year-olds had been told by a doctor that their child had an anxiety disorder (Bitsko et al., 2018). One type of anxiety disorder that children experience is a *phobia*, an irrational fear of an object or experience that makes them especially anxious.

Social scientists and educators are concerned about the impact on some children of practices such as "active shooter drills," in which children are taught to go to the floor, or into the closet, to escape gunfire. A national study of high school students found that almost two-thirds of all children say that such drills make them feel "scared and hopeless" (Moore-Petinak et al., 2020). How to prevent gun violence while preventing anxiety is crucial for educators and parents, lest schools "make a bad situation worse" (Limber & Kowalski, 2020).

Another contextual influence on anxiety among children occurred with COVID-19. A large-scale study in China found that about one in every four children experienced severe anxiety, including being frightened of leaving home, of other people, and of getting sick themselves (Duan et al., 2020).

Remember the fourth principle of the generalities about psychopathology: The social context is always crucial. Instead of focusing only on the anxious, or overactive, or asocial child, the community may need to reconsider some norms and policies.

Disorders Arising in Adolescence

Before discussing specific disorders that arise in adolescence, we need to reiterate that age is only one of many variables that affect the risk of psychopathology. As emphasized in the second and third general principles on page 444, disorders may change in severity and expression, but they rarely stop or start at a particular age.

Certainly, the disorders of childhood just mentioned continue into adolescence and adulthood, and depression, conduct disorder, and oppositional defiant disorder, soon described, are evident before and after adolescence. Placement here is not meant to imply that they are exclusive to adolescence.

Furthermore, the manifestations of psychopathology can be expressed either in outward behavior (*externalizing*) or private distress (*internalizing*). This distinction is useful but also sometimes misleading, especially in children. Sometimes external activity is a sign of internal distress, and sometimes it is a cause of internal distress, with demographic and cultural factors influencing the symptoms.

One study of the co-occurrence of externalizing and internalizing disorders explains the complications thus:

> the patterns of associations between externalizing and internalizing problems may differ across population subgroups defined by, for example, gender, race/ethnicity, socioeconomic status, clinical status, birth conditions. The patterns of associations may also change as children age and transition into adolescence.
>
> *[Oh et al., 2020, p. 478]*

Externalizing Disorders

Externalizing actions are obvious when teenagers slam doors, curse parents, and tell friends exactly how badly others have behaved. Some "act out" by breaking laws. They steal, damage property, or injure others, often in rage (Ghosh et al., 2017). Crime rates escalate and then peak in late adolescence, a phenomenon evident in every nation, with boys much more likely to be arrested than girls (Liu & Miller, 2020).

A frequently diagnosed externalizing disorder is **conduct disorder**, when a person (typically an adolescent) seems to defy any authority or age-appropriate social norm, and to seek revenge for any provocation. People with this condition may even seem callous and unemotional, lacking empathy. In adulthood, conduct disorder may lead to criminal behavior and a diagnosis of *antisocial personality disorder*.

Considered a developmental precursor to conduct disorder, **oppositional defiant disorder (ODD)** is typically diagnosed during childhood. It is characterized by frequent and persistent irritability and anger, with outbursts of temper that are reactive, not rational. Children with ODD often argue with adults or refuse to comply with their rules and requests, and their social functioning is significantly impaired.

As early as age 3, oppositional defiant disorder is often comorbid with ADHD (Harvey et al., 2016). A longitudinal study of 662 children with ODD found that, by age 29, they were less successful in employment and higher education. The authors suggest that counselors could have helped them develop

> strategies for coping with irritability (i.e., obtaining adequate sleep, stress reduction, avoiding caffeine, emotion regulation, and anger management) and managing workplace conflict without resorting to anger and defiance.
>
> *[Leadbeater & Ames, 2017, p. 762]*

A developmental perspective is crucial for parents and other authority figures when they confront a defiant teenager. As you read in Chapter 13, here are two kinds of young lawbreakers, *adolescence-limited offenders,* and *life-course-persistent offenders* (Levey, 2019; Monahan et al., 2013), as first proposed by

conduct disorder When a person has great difficulty following social norms and rules and also is destructive, deliberately aggressive, calculating, and/or cruel.

oppositional defiant disorder (ODD) When a child refuses to comply with rules and instead is quick to get angry at every request.

Terri Moffitt (2001, 2003). Both types could be diagnosed as conduct disorder or oppositional defiance disorder, and are often arrested in adolescence for destroying property, disregarding laws, or fighting someone who they think is disrespectful.

If adolescence-limited offenders can be protected from various snares (quitting school, entering prison, drug addiction) that stop supportive friendships, and if parents and other authorities teach self-control, neither dismissing the crime nor overreacting, delinquents may outgrow their defiance or learn to channel it. In adulthood they might oppose systemic injustice rather than challenge every authority.

A recent longitudinal study finds some validity in separating delinquents into limited and persistent categories, but also finds many more paths than these two. This and many other studies conclude that the social context is crucial, with neighborhood, families, and particularly friends very influential (Ahonen et al., 2020).

Depression

The social context is also crucial for depression. Depression is marked by significant sadness, lack of energy, and sometimes low self-worth or related symptoms. This disorder increased worldwide by around 30 percent from 1970 to 2017, from 162 million to 241 million people (Q. Liu et al., 2020). Everywhere, age and gender matter: Rates "skyrocket in adolescence" (Hankin, 2020), and females are about twice as often depressed as males.

Depression is sometimes called "the common cold of mood disorders," since almost everyone experiences depression sometimes. But when sadness and hopelessness disrupt all normal, regular activities for two weeks or more, that is **major depressive disorder (MDD)** (Lorenzo-Luaces, 2015). MDD is a severe, disabling pattern of depression that causes significant impairment in daily life and may be experienced by one-fifth of all 17-year-olds (Hankin, 2020).

major depressive disorder Deep and long-lasting (two weeks or more) depression, with problems with mood, sleep, appetite, and so on.

Among adolescent girls, depression is comorbid with serious self-harm, such as cutting (Plener et al., 2015) and eating disorders, including anorexia and bulimia (noted in Chapter 4). Sexual abuse contributes to depression, again higher in girls (see Chapter 11).

Treatment for teenage depression may need to be targeted to the particular underlying psychological problem, either distorted thinking ("It's all my fault and things will never get better") or impaired social connections (rejection from family, no close friends) (Hankin, 2020). In general, many factors are associated with adolescent depression, with gender, age, and severity all significant influences on what treatment (antidepressants, cognitive-behavioral therapy, psychodynamic therapy) works best for which adolescents (Scott et al., 2019).

suicidal ideation Thinking about suicide, usually with some serious emotional and intellectual or cognitive overtones.

Serious, distressing thoughts about killing oneself (called **suicidal ideation**) are one sign of depression and are most common at about age 15. Among U.S. high school students, nearly one-fourth (24 percent) of the girls and one-eighth (13 percent) of the boys thought seriously about suicide within the past year (Johns et al., 2020). (See **Figure 15.3**.)

Also prevalent is deliberate self-harm, such as cutting oneself, exercising in pain, or starving oneself. Each of these behaviors is distinct, but various forms of self-injury correlate with suicidal thought (Klonsky et al., 2013).

parasuicide Any potentially lethal action against the self that does not result in death. (Also called attempted suicide or failed suicide.)

Suicidal ideation can lead to **parasuicide**, any deliberate self-harm that could have been lethal, also called *attempted suicide* or *failed suicide*. Parasuicide is the preferred term, because "failed" suicide implies that to die is to succeed (!), and the difference between attempt and completion may be luck, immaturity, and

Suicidal Ideation and Parasuicide Among U.S. High School Students

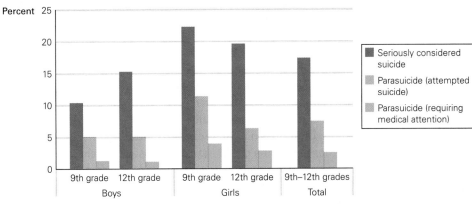

Data from MMWR, June 15, 2018.

FIGURE 15.3

Sad Thoughts Completed suicide is rare in adolescence, but serious thoughts about killing oneself are frequent. More girls than boys say they have thought about, or attempted, suicide. The rate for boys may be underestimated for three reasons: (1) boys are less forthcoming about their emotions; (2) boys consider it unmanly to try suicide and fail; and (3) more males than females die by suicide. Other sources show even higher rates of parasuicide.

Observation Quiz Does thinking seriously about suicide increase or decrease during high school? (see answer, page 471) ↑

treatment, not intent. In 2019, among U.S. high school students, 11 percent of the girls and 7 percent of the boys *tried* to kill themselves (Johns et al., 2020).

Although suicidal ideation and parasuicide are common during adolescence, completed suicides are not. In the United States in 2018, the rate of completed suicide for teenagers, aged 10 to 19 (in school or not), was about 7 per 100,000, or 0.007 percent. (Rates rise notably for the next age group, ages 20–24.)

There are two disparate indications that, for adolescents, sexuality is connected to depression and suicide. One sign is that couple suicides, when both lovers kill themselves, are most common during adolescence. The second indicator is that the rate of parasuicide is four times higher among LGBTQ youth, especially if they experienced "conversion therapy" (illegal in many but not all states), in an attempt to make them heterosexual (Green et al., 2020).

Depression is discussed here, because the harm is great, especially if the teenager misses school or develops other self-destructive behaviors. But it could easily have been discussed later. Major depression can be a serious mental illness lifelong, and severe depression in adolescence increases the risk of an episode of major depression later in life (Johnson et al., 2018). This is one reason many psychologists fear the lifelong consequences of the COVID-related increase in teen depression (Racine et al., 2020).

Disorders Arising in Adulthood

Here we discuss suicide, anxiety disorders, schizophrenia, and drug abuse. These all are apparent before adulthood, but they are discussed in this section because they are most severe in adulthood. According to the *DSM-5*, personality disorders cannot be diagnosed in children or adolescents, in part because of the outmoded view that personality is solidified in adulthood.

Suicide

You just read about the distinction between suicidal ideation, parasuicide, and completed suicide. Remember that depression increases much more in girls than in boys. That gender disparity continues for women and men. As you remember from Chapter 11, completed suicide is much more common in males.

Many people wonder why men are more often suicidal but less likely than women to be depressed. Among the reasons suggested are access to guns, the effects of hormones, and the harm of the strong, silent, image of masculinity. Regarding this macho mandate, it is possible that men are as often depressed as women, but are less likely to seek help for it (Oliffe et al., 2019; Kuehner, 2017).

CHAPTER APP 15

My3-Support Network

iOS:
https://tinyurl.com/yyzlpmqo

ANDROID:
https://tinyurl.com/qgsd6qb

RELEVANT TOPIC:
Suicidal ideation among adolescents

My3-Support Network is a crisis-support app for people who experience suicidal thoughts. Users choose three trusted people from their contacts list to place on the app (911 and the National Suicide Hotline are automatically listed). Users create their own safety plan, listing warning signs, coping strategies, distractions, and their "reasons to live." The app also links users to organizations that address the needs of specific groups, such as suicide attempt survivors, LGBTQ youth, and more.

If you or someone you know needs help, call the National Suicide Prevention Lifeline at **1-800-273-8255**. You can also text HOME to **741-741** for free, 24-hour support from the Crisis Text Line.

Recovering A young Japanese man sits alone in his room, which until recently was his self-imposed prison. He is one of thousands of Japanese young people (80 percent of whom are male) who have the anxiety disorder known as hikikomori.

social anxiety disorder Fear of social situations, especially when other people might judge one negatively, as with public speaking.

hikikomori An anxiety disorder first evident among emerging adults in Japan, when a person refuses to leave their room.

ESPECIALLY FOR Immigrants What can you do in your adopted country to avoid or relieve the psychological stresses of immigration? (see response, page 471)

Anxiety Disorders

A major set of disorders, evident in about one-fifth of all U.S. adults, is anxiety disorders (U.S. Department of Health and Human Services, National Institute of Mental Health, 2017). These include *panic disorder, social anxiety disorder, separation anxiety disorder, generalized anxiety disorder,* and *specific phobia.*

As you remember, a sizable number of children experience anxiety disorders, but epidemiologists find them even more prevalent than depression among adults. Incidence statistics vary from study to study, as well as nation to nation depending partly on definition and cutoff score. Generally, anxiety disorders begin in childhood, and become more disabling in adolescence and adulthood. They are often comorbid with depression, and thus could have been discussed among the disorders that arise in adolescence (Ohayon & Schatzberg, 2010; Wersebe et al., 2018).

However, although anxiety disorders appear before adulthood, they are more likely to be debilitating in adulthood, especially obvious when young adults are expected to become independent of their parents and establish their own families, jobs, and homes. Those who suffer from anxiety disorders often have great difficulty with these adult roles. For example, one of the most common anxiety disorders is **social anxiety disorder** (sometimes called *social phobia*), the fear of being judged or rejected by others, which makes everyday human interactions distressing.

Many young adults with this anxiety disorder cannot take the first step in finding a marriage partner or securing a job. A 10-year longitudinal study found that emerging adults with social anxiety disorder became 30-year-olds with less income and less success than other adults (Mojtabai et al., 2015).

In Japan, a severe social anxiety disorder, affecting an estimated 100,000 young adults, is **hikikomori**, which means "pull away" (Kato et al., 2019). The person with hikikomori stays in his (or, less often, her) room almost all the time for six months or more, a reaction to extreme anxiety. Usually the person is a young man, fearful of the social and academic pressures of high school and college, but women and those past college age also can experience hikikomori.

The close connection between Japanese mothers and children, and the fact that most families have only one or two children, makes this particular disorder more common in Japan than elsewhere. Hikikomori also occurs in other nations (Frankova, 2019).

Once classified as an anxiety disorder but now called a "trauma- and stressor-related disorder," *posttraumatic stress disorder (PTSD)* begins when a person has had a terrifying experience—such as a near-death encounter in battle or a rape.

Terrifying experiences, usually in the form of abuse, occur in childhood, although they may not fully develop into PTSD (Margolin & Vickerman, 2007). But trauma also occurs in adulthood. Young adults, especially if they have no support from close friends or relatives, as might occur if they are soldiers in a foreign land, are especially vulnerable to this disorder (Grant & Potenza, 2010).

Sometimes witnessing such an experience, and identifying with the victim, can be the start of PTSD. Most people with such experiences gradually recover, but some people have flashbacks, vivid nightmares, or sudden panics. That seems to be the case for some health care workers who worked in hospitals treating COVID-19 patients. Those who did not become sick themselves nonetheless had higher rates of PTSD, especially if they felt untrained, unsupported, and at risk themselves (Carmassi et al., 2020).

Schizophrenia

About 1 percent of all adults experience schizophrenia, becoming overwhelmed by disorganized and bizarre thoughts, delusions, hallucinations, and emotions (American Psychiatric Association, 2013). The psychotic episodes that characterize schizophrenia occur at every age and in every nation, but, again, some cultures, ages, and contexts have much higher rates than others. Half of all sufferers had their first serious episode at the start of adulthood (McGrath et al., 2016).

No doubt schizophrenia is partly genetic. A study of 31,000 twin pairs born in Denmark found that if one monozygotic twin develops schizophrenia, the other twin, with the same genes, has a 33 percent chance of developing schizophrenia also. For dizygotic twins (half the same genes), the rate is 7 percent (Hilker et al., 2018).

Nonetheless, most people with this disorder have no immediate family members diagnosed with it (McCutcheon et al., 2020). Among the many non-genetic factors that tip vulnerable people over the edge are: "pregnancy and birth complications, childhood trauma, migration, social isolation, urbanicity, and substance abuse, alone and in combination, acting at a number of levels over time" (Stilo & Murray, 2019).

Diagnosis is most common between ages 18 to 24, with men particularly vulnerable. After a first hospitalization, another is likely. If a person develops schizophrenia after age 40, they are less likely to have a strong genetic risk and more likely to have experienced stressful environmental influences (L. Chen et al., 2018).

Substance Use Disorder

You might be surprised to see this topic in adulthood rather than adolescence, because you know that many teenagers *try* psychoactive drugs. Rates are down in recent years: 2019 data show alcohol at 59 percent, vaping at 47 percent, and marijuana at 44 percent. For the most part, that is experimentation, not addiction (Miech et al., 2020). (See **Figure 15.4**.)

However, this topic appears in adulthood, not adolescence, because that is the most common period when experimental use becomes abuse, defined as harmful to body and mind. Adults, more than adolescents, are likely to suffer from **substance use disorder (SUD)**, recognized by *DSM-5* and by every global indicator of mental health. SUD is a common cause of mortality, morbidity, and disability, with the individual unwilling or unable to stop using a drug even when it damages their health. At that point it is pathological, a disorder.

From the perspective of psychopathology, legality is not the question. Indeed, most adults take drugs that affect their mood. Almost 90 percent drink caffeinated soda, tea, or coffee; 58 percent of North Americans drink alcohol; about 14 percent use marijuana; and about 3 percent take other mood-altering drugs. For SUD, the questions are whether, which, and when drug use is destructive.

Nations, religions, and individuals provide different answers. In many Muslim nations, alcohol is forbidden. In France, more people smoke cigarettes, unlike in the United States, where cigarettes are banned from airplanes, bars, and many other places. (A joke in Europe is that if a person wants to quit smoking, they should visit the United States.)

Generally, in North America, adults with more education are less likely to abuse drugs, but that is not true for current college students. For example, the rate of marijuana vaping among U.S. college students in 2018 was 12 percent, compared to 8 percent for their age-mates not in college (Schulenberg et al., 2020).

When is psychoactive drug use merely preference, not disorder? The facts vary by substance.

Tobacco is always destructive. It is a leading risk factor for many diseases. The World Health Organization calls tobacco

substance use disorder (SUD) A pattern of maladaptive behavior resulting from the repeated use of a substance, often to the point of tolerance to the substance and withdrawal reactions.

THINK CRITICALLY: How would you apportion blame for drug addiction?

FIGURE 15.4
Too Old for That As you can see, emerging adults are the biggest substance abusers, but illegal drug use drops much faster than does cigarette use or binge drinking.

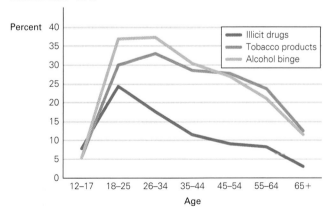

Data from SAMHSA, 2018.

Cigarette Smokers Among U.S. Adults Over Age 18

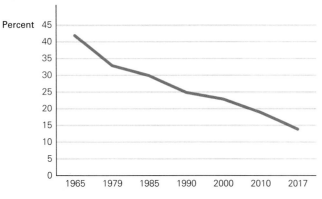

FIGURE 15.5

And Rates Continue to Fall in 2020 Cynics say that people never change, or that corporate profits rule human behavior, but the data on cigarette smoking prove otherwise. Both population and personal reduction in cigarette smoking occurred, despite massive advertising and corporate efforts to hide the data, as it became evident that smoking is substance abuse.

VIDEO: College Binge Drinking shows college students engaging in (and rationalizing) this risky behavior.

FIGURE 15.6

Why? This chart puzzles public health workers, because opioid deaths rose during the years when smoking deaths fell. Further, more deaths were adults in midlife, rather than older or younger people. What are the possible reasons: drug companies, unemployment, lack of effective drug treatment?

Drug Overdose Deaths Involving Synthetic Opioids — United States

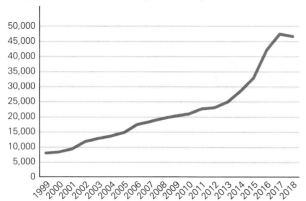

Data from Hedegaard et al., 2020.

"the single largest preventable cause of death and chronic disease," yet smoking is increasing in low-income nations where rates of abject poverty are declining (Yang & Dong, 2019).

By contrast, in the United States, in the first half of the twentieth century, smoking rose with SES, such as that by 1960, most adults smoked. Then it fell (see **Figure 15.5**), most precipitously in those with more education. That is a victory for public health, especially evident among the young. Only 10 percent of those 18–24 are current smokers, as are 17 percent of those aged 55–64. Of the oldest adults, more are former smokers than current smokers (National Center for Health Statistics, 2019).

The harm from cigarettes is dose-related: Each puff, each day, each breath of secondhand smoke makes cancer, heart disease, strokes, and emphysema more likely. No such linear harm results from drinking *alcohol*. In fact, adults who drink wine, beer, or spirits *in moderation*—never more than two drinks a day—live longer than abstainers (Goel et al., 2018).

This may be a misleading correlation because some of those abstainers were formerly heavy drinkers, so their death rate reflects earlier damage done by alcohol (Chikritzhs et al., 2015; Knott et al., 2015). The truth of that is debatable, but no one disputes the harm from excessive drinking. Certainly, abstainers should not start (Goel et al., 2018).

Alcohol use disorder, which entails both alcohol abuse and alcohol dependence, destroys brain cells, is a major cause of liver damage and several cancers, contributes to osteoporosis, decreases fertility, and accompanies many suicides, homicides, and accidents—all while wreaking havoc in families. Even moderate consumption is unhealthy if it leads to smoking, overeating, casual sex, or other destructive habits.

Alcohol abuse also shows age, gender, cohort, and cultural differences. For example, the risk of accidental death while drunk is most common among young men: Law enforcement in the United States has cut their drunk driving in half. However, middle-aged parents who abuse alcohol are more harmful to other people, because of their neglect and irrational rage (Blas & Kurup, 2010).

Many scientists, public health doctors, and political leaders are concerned about the epidemic of deaths from *opioid* abuse in the United States. Rates have risen dramatically in the past decade (see **Figure 15.6**), resulting in lower life expectancy in 2018 than in 2010.

Here mortality data, and cost-benefit analysis, are needed. Most states in the United States passed laws that would reduce how often doctors prescribe opioids. What is the effect? Do decreases in mortality outweigh the increases in morbidity and disability (such as pain in those with cancer).

Those laws successfully reduced legal opioid prescriptions, but increased pain and abuse of heroin and fentanyl. Of ten studies on the effect of the restrictive laws, six reported no effect, three found reduced deaths, and one found increased deaths (Fink et al., 2018).

Are there better ways to reduce addiction? Needle exchange and treatment programs are expensive, so definitive cost-benefit analysis is needed. One study found that needle exchange programs reduce mortality from HIV/AIDS and hepatitis A and C but may not reduce addiction (Motie et al., 2020). One study, of course, is *not* definitive.

Can we prevent drug abuse before it begins? Suggestions include changes in arrest and conviction practices, improvements in public schools, increased employment opportunities and wages, and much more. An objective analysis of cost and benefits might help!

Clues come from the geographic distribution of opioid addictions. Some states (New Hampshire, Ohio, West Virginia, Massachusetts) have death rates four times higher than in others (Iowa, Oregon, Texas, Hawaii). Local policies and norms matter; again more research, including cost-benefit analysis, is needed.

We have already mentioned the problem of older adults and polypharmacy (Chapter 4), and that drugs can increase neurocognitive disorders in adults. But we also need to note the effects on the brains of younger adults.

Every psychoactive drug excites the limbic system and interferes with the prefrontal cortex. Because of these neurological reactions, drug users are less rational and more emotional (varying from euphoria to terror, from paranoia to rage) than they would otherwise be. Remember that brain development lags behind outward maturation. If brain development in stalled in adolescence and early adulthood, every hazard—including car crashes, unsafe sex, and suicide—increases in adulthood when compared to those who are drug-free.

Further, at every age, drug overuse temporarily shuts down the prefrontal cortex. Did you notice that the suicide rate is higher in middle adulthood than earlier? One suggested reason is that drug addiction that continues into middle age leads to "deaths of despair" (Shanahan et al., 2019).

Neurocognitive Disorders

Many of the psychopathologies just reviewed, including substance abuse, become less common in late adulthood. However, elders are vulnerable to a variety of brain diseases, including Parkinson's, Alzheimer's, vascular disease, and Lewy body disease. These diseases impair much more than memory; they affect emotions and impulses. Many adults who seemed to have their behavior and emotions under control experience depression, anxiety, and antisocial behavior.

DSM-5 includes many psychopathologies that are more common in late adulthood. Since Chapter 5 discussed brain diseases, we will not review the details here. However, we close this section of this chapter by noting that, with every manifestation of psychopathology, recognizing the signs, symptoms, and causes is the first step toward effective treatment. Even better, once people know how to nurture the strengths of the human body, mind, and spirit, many problems can be prevented before they start.

Remember, the goal is health. We need to move past mortality, morbidity, and disability and seek well-being. How to do that is the focus of the rest of this chapter.

Pain Killer "Never meant to cause you any pain," sang Prince in his classic song, "Purple Rain." But his own pain led to an opioid addiction and then to an accidental overdose of fentanyl, a synthetic opioid that is 50 times more powerful than heroin. His death at age 57 hurt us all.

ESPECIALLY FOR Doctors and Nurses If you had to choose between recommending various screening tests and recommending lifestyle changes to a 35-year-old, which would you do? (see answer, page 471)

WHAT HAVE YOU LEARNED?

1. What is *DSM-5*?
2. How has the diagnosis of autism changed?
3. What are the four possible hypotheses for the increase in autism?
4. Why are developmentalists particularly worried about the increases in ADHD among adolescents?
5. What is suggested by the study of ADHD in Taiwan?
6. What three specific learning disabilities are recognized by *DSM-5*?
7. What is the difference between parasuicide and attempted suicide?
8. When does opposition defiance become a disorder?
9. Why is depression discussed in adolescence, but anxiety discussed in adulthood?
10. Which substance is most commonly abused in adulthood?
11. What disorders become more common as adults grow older?

FRANCK FIFE/AFP/Getty Images

What a Body Can Do Here at age 27, Tobin Heath leaps to celebrate her goal at the soccer World Cup Final in Vancouver, her most recent of seven years of star performances. All young adults can have moments when their bodies and minds crescendo to new heights.

medical model Considering mental illness to be similar to physical illness, with definite signs, diagnoses, and cures. Many psychologists disagree with that model of psychopathology.

neurodiversity The idea that each person has neurological strengths and weaknesses that should be appreciated, in much the same way diverse cultures and ethnicities are welcomed. Neurodiversity seems particularly relevant for children with disorders on the autism spectrum.

Protecting Health

As emphasized in the first part of this chapter, mortality and morbidity data need to consider rates per thousand, not merely whether one individual is sick or well. Accordingly, after we describe choices that individuals can make to protect their own health, we consider changes that can affect the entire community.

Attitudes and Health

Adding life to years may begin with attitudes more than with genes. Individuals differ regarding what they think makes them happy, but everyone seeks their own well-being, each in their own way. Thus, we begin to explain what protects health by exploring variations in attitudes.

Some prioritize comfort and immediate pleasure; others want more money and more friends; some care about how they look and endure pain for appearance; some believe strongly in religious mandates and are glad to avoid sin—which may be not what someone else considers sin.

The Medical Model

One of the differences in people is how much they agree with what is called the **medical model** of mental illness. Essentially, the medical model tends to conceptualize psychological differences as problems to be cured. Psychologists question this model, in that the term mental *illness* implies that people with psychological abnormalities are sick. Instead, "heterogeneity, comorbidity, fuzzy boundaries between normal and pathological" make psychological disorders distinct from physical ones (Nesse & Stein, 2012).

The problem is particularly evident with mood and anxiety disorders, the most commonly diagnosed psychopathologies. Anxiety might be adaptive, if it helps someone find a better job or leave a dangerous situation. Depression is normal when a loved one dies, not something to be cured with a pill or a stiff drink. Some great artists (e.g., van Gogh) had schizophrenia. If he could have been cured of his condition, would the world have suffered?

This problem with the medical model becomes apparent when a person resists treatment. At what point is "involuntary confinement" necessary? If a person is ill, they may need to be hospitalized, medicated, and restrained, but who decides that—when and how?

Many people with disabilities resist the idea that they have a problem that needs to be cured (Hogan, 2019). Instead, they suggest that society needs to design the environment to accommodate the differently abled.

Neurodiversity

One general lesson regarding attitude arises from studies of autism. **Neurodiversity** means that each person's brain functions differently (Kapp et al., 2020; Silberman, 2015). As explained, people with autism are slow to develop theory of mind: They are not as adept at understanding the emotions of other people. However, the brains of some children with autism function extraordinarily well in math, music, or art, even though social perceptions are difficult.

Thus, people on the spectrum have a mixture of perceptions, abilities, and deficiencies that are unlike most neurotypical people. That means that, because of their diverse abilities, adults should neither be dazzled by the talents nor despondent by the deficits of those on the autism spectrum. The medical model makes people try to "cure" people with autism instead of appreciating them for the distinct people they are.

The idea of neurodiversity is insightful for every disorder. A person who is overly anxious encourages everyone to escape a hurricane at first warning, where someone else might stay and drown. A person who enjoys writing down what they are doing every minute can be diagnosed as obsessive, or they can be lauded as a lawyer who is accurate in billing. As shown in the movie *A Beautiful Mind*, John Nash was both hospitalized with schizophrenia and awarded the Nobel prize in math.

Ageism and Attitude

One example of the importance of attitude is found in the research on aging. If an older person thinks that age means lost mental and physical ability, they will not get hearing aids, or glasses, or even consult a doctor if they are in pain.

Ageism is particularly likely to become a *self-fulfilling prophecy,* a prediction that comes true because people believe it. There are three harmful consequences:

- If older people are treated as frail and confused, they become less independent.
- If the norms for younger adults are taken as universal, people try to make older adults fit them.
- If older people themselves think that their age makes them feeble, they may stop self-care, avoid social interaction, or not consult a doctor.

Of course, every *-ism* is destructive, but ageism is distinctly harmful. One reason is that its victims are unprepared for it, without decades of recognizing and counteracting it. Another reason is that both perpetrators and victims of ageism may think it is benevolent (Kagan, 2018).

For example, describing someone as a "sweet old lady" who "still has all her marbles" is ageist; so is describing a man who is interested in sex a "dirty old man." If elders themselves avoid other older people, they remove the social experiences that could benefit them all. My mother did that, as described in A Case to Study.

In an ageist culture, "feeling youthful is more strongly predictive of health than any other factors including commonly noted ones like chronological age, gender,

Shame on You Greta Thunberg spoke these words to world leaders in her 2019 speech on climate change at the United Nations General Assembly. Does her autism and neurodiversity enable her to say what many people think but are afraid to say?

A CASE TO STUDY

I'm Not Like Those Other Old People

My mother, in her 80s, was reluctant to enter an assisted-living apartment. She told me that she did not want to live there because too many of the people were old. Her attitude was not unusual: Many older people believe that "they" are old, but "I" am younger (Weiss & Lang, 2012).

Asked how old they feel, most 80-year-olds lop a decade or more off their age (Pew Research Center, June 29, 2009). Think of the logical lapse here. If *most* 80-year-olds feel how they imagine the average 70-year-old feels, then that feeling is, in fact, typical of 80-year-olds. Thus, 80-year-olds have a stereotype of 80-year-olds, and they believe it does not apply to them.

This same phenomenon is apparent for every aspect of functioning in late adulthood. One study asked people to estimate trajectories over the life span of six cognitive functions and four social ones (Riediger et al., 2014). People of all age groups estimated that most people would decline, usually by age 60 and clearly by age 80. That is accurate: Many declines occur.

However, that study found that, on every measure, older people were most likely to estimate that their own functioning was better than that of the average older person (see **Table 15.2**). This was particularly true for memory, speed, and making new friends—the three abilities most often stereotyped as dropping markedly with age.

They endorsed a cultural stereotype and then rejected it when it applied to them. So did my mother.

TABLE 15.2

How Do You Compare to Other People Your Age?

	9-Year-Olds	13- to 15-Year-Olds	21- to 26-Year-Olds	70- to 76-Year-Olds
Memory	Better	Same	Worse	Better
Cognitive speed	Same	Worse	Worse	Better
Mental math	Better	Same	Worse	Better
Concentration	Same	Same	Worse	Better
New friends	Same	Worse	Worse	Better
Self-assertion	Better	Same	Same	Better

marital status and socioeconomic status" (Barrett, 2012, p. 3). Thus, attitudes are crucial. Another study found that:

> Perceptions are a strong predictor of psychological wellbeing in later life . . . [and] older adults with negative self-perceptions of aging also have greater levels of disability, ill health, worse physical function and a higher risk of mortality over time.
>
> *[Robertson et al., 2016, p. 71]*

Ideally, older people would not be ageist, but if they are, it is better for them to believe that the stereotypes of elders do not apply to them. Self-perceived age correlates with health and happiness (Kotter-Grühn et al., 2016). This is true lifelong, although it takes different forms. Emerging adults are more likely to say they feel older than they actually are, and for them that indicates maturity. Ageism regarding other old people is harmful, but worse may be ageism about oneself.

Selective Optimization with Compensation

selective optimization with compensation The theory, developed by Paul and Margaret Baltes, that people try to maintain a balance in their lives by looking for the best way to compensate for physical and cognitive losses and to become more proficient in activities they can already do well.

Paul and Margret Baltes (1990) developed a theory called **selective optimization with compensation** to describe the "general process of systematic functioning" (Baltes, 2003, p. 25), by which people maintain a balance in their lives as they grow older. They believe that people seek to *optimize* their development, *selecting* the best way to *compensate* for physical and cognitive losses, becoming more proficient at activities they want to perform well.

Selective optimization with compensation applies to every aspect of life, ranging from choosing friends to playing baseball. Each adult seeks to maximize gains and minimize losses, practicing some abilities and ignoring others. Choices are critical, because any ability can be enhanced or diminished, depending on how, when, and why a person uses it. It is possible to "teach an old dog new tricks," but learning requires that adults *want* to learn those new tricks.

This is a step beyond denying that ageist stereotypes apply to oneself. It requires choosing (selection) which abilities to protect (optimization) and then adjusting (compensating) other aspects of life to allow those chosen abilities to stay strong.

One example is with technology. Older adults who use cell phones, the internet, personal computers, and so on are, on average, much more outgoing, healthy, and satisfied with their lives than elders who do not. Yet many older people are quickly frustrated with technology, refusing to learn how to use computers (Nimrod, 2019).

On technology, it is evident that older adults themselves have stereotypes about those who do not use it. As one 76-year-old said:

> I search everything by myself and find everything I need. One must be in the loop. Technology is rapidly developing, and you must develop yourself accordingly. If you fail to do so, you go downhill. If I see a woman my age who has no idea about technology, I will think that she is a little dumb, even if it's not true.
>
> *[quoted in Nimrod, 2019]*

Adults of many ages would be much happier if they selected what they wanted to do, compensating (larger print, voice activated phones, redesigned keyboards) as need be. Many younger people learn to block certain people, access new social media sites, evaluate websites. Older people also need to be selective. As one said;

> I learned how to use the things that interest me, such as WhatsApp and Facebook. I know that there are lots of other applications, but I'm not interested. I'm not going to complicate my life by putting more things in my head that I don't need, I've learned what I needed to learn.
>
> *[quoted in Nimrod, 2019]*

Health Habits

Every day, each person eats, sleeps, moves, and socializes. The specifics of those four affect every aspect of mortality, morbidity, disability, and well-being.

Eating Well

Maintaining a healthy weight is crucial for every aspect of health. As you know, eating disorders (anorexia, bulimia, and binge-eating disorder) are psychopathological, reducing life and well-being. But diet involves much more than quantity; the specific elements matter, too.

One easy example is the interaction of drug abuse and diet. Specifics vary by drug. The so-called wet brain is not directly caused by chronic alcohol abuse, but instead by deficiencies in thiamine, which often result from heavy drinking over the years. That causes *Korsakoff's syndrome*, with memory loss and confusion (Arts et al., 2017). The compulsion to eat food that is high in fat and sugar is evident in the "munchies" of marijuana use (Baggio & Chong, 2020), which crowds out healthy foods. By contrast, loss of appetite is common with many drugs, especially cigarettes (Bloom et al., 2019), and that also makes a healthy diet less likely.

Specifics vary by person. For example, coffee is usually, but not always, beneficial, depending on genes, sleep patterns, and expectations (Del Coso et al., 2020; Gökcen & Şanlier, 2019). Similarly, diet profoundly affects the microbiome, which influences mood, cognition, and appetite, but again details vary from one person to another (Zmora et al., 2019).

There is controversy about particulars. Some advocate specific foods, such as blueberries, red wine, garlic, ample water, and avocados, that might make dementia less likely. Some believe psychopathology would be less common if people ate diets free of gluten (wheat), or without salt or sugar, or no animal products, or no food additives.

The counterargument is that a varied diet is what people need. When scientists compare popular diets, the evidence favors the so-called *Mediterranean diet*, with many and varied vegetables, whole grains, fish, nuts, and olive oil (D'Alessandro & De Pergola, 2018; Dinu et al., 2018; Galbete et al., 2018; Schwingshackl et al., 2020)

The evidence also confirms that too much animal fat, from red meat, full-fat cheese, saturated fat, and cream is harmful. For instance, in premenopausal women, a high-fat diet increases breast cancer (Farvid et al., 2014), although no fat may also be harmful.

Compensation All of the senses decline with age. Some people accept these losses as inevitable, becoming socially isolated and depressed. Instead, compensation is possible in two ways. One is to increase use of the other senses and abilities. Stevie Wonder illustrates this well—he relies on hearing and touch, which have enabled him to sell over 100 million records and win 25 Grammys. The other way is more direct: Many technological and medical interventions are available for every sensory loss.

Just Keep Rowing Along After four years in Iraq and two in Afghanistan, Jared McCallum sought new challenges. He hiked the Appalachian Trail (2,180 miles) and, on September 1, 2014, began rowing the Mississippi River. Here, on October 1, 2014, he is at Rock Island, Iowa.

One particular condition, called *frailty*, is an underlying cause of many of the disabilities of late adulthood. Frailty is diagnosed by symptoms, such as lack of energy and loss of weight. As you already read, obesity interferes with a healthy body and mind, but so does being too thin (below 20 BMI), a key symptom of frailty, systemic cancer, and many illnesses. Good eating habits prevent both overweight and underweight.

Exercise

Many people have sought the secret sauce, the fountain of youth, the magic bullet that will slow, or stop, or even reverse morbidity and disability, while increasing well-being. Few realize that it has already been found. Thousands of scientists, studying every disease of aging, have found something that helps every condition — exercise.

Exercise reduces blood pressure, strengthens the heart and lungs, promotes digestion, and makes depression, diabetes, osteoporosis, strokes, arthritis, and several cancers less likely. It also strengthens the immune system (Davison et al., 2014), and protects against cognitive decline (Rashid et al., 2020).

Health benefits from exercise are substantial for men and women, old and young, former sports stars and those who never joined a team. Protection against depression is particularly evident among older adults, who, sadly, are the age group least likely to exercise much (Pauly et al., 2019).

Moving the body protects both mental health and physical health. Surroundings are key. Neighborhoods high in walkability (paths, sidewalks, etc.) reduce time driving and watching television (Kozo et al., 2012). This relationship between the surroundings, movement, and health is causal, not merely correlational. Moreover, active people feel energetic, which increases other good habits. Exercise in midlife reduces depression later in life (Willis et al., 2018).

Even a little movement — gardening, light housework, walking up the stairs or to the bus — helps. Intensity is unnecessary: Regular exercise is. For example, a 10-year study of 4,840 older adults measured how many steps they took each day and how quickly they walked. Speed did not matter much but distance did: Those who took less than 4,000 steps per day died at 3 times the rate of those who averaged 12,000 steps (Saint-Maurice et al., 2020).

Ideally, exercise is varied — working on overall fitness and specific muscle groups — and is part of daily life, not something that occurs on vacation or in a particular season of the year. Unused muscles atrophy quickly — even a few weeks of bedrest weakens the legs.

Adults today do not move their legs, arms, or even hands as much in daily life as adults did a century ago, thanks to many modern devices, from the automobile to the TV remote. A counterdevelopment in advanced nations is the proliferation of gyms and personal trainers (Brighton et al., 2020).

Overall, more than half (57 percent) of all adults, age 18 and older meet *either* of the two U.S. weekly goals of 150 minutes of aerobic exercise *or* muscle-strengthening exercise at least two days a week. That is much better than 20 years ago, when only 41 percent met either benchmark (National Center for Health Statistics, 2019). Rates improved in every age, ethnic, and gender group.

Of course, it is better to meet both goals, and only 25 percent did so — with lower rates with age. That 25 percent is nonetheless almost twice what it was: In 1998, only 14 percent of adults met both goals (National Center for Health Statistics, 2019).

The cohort evidence is encouraging, but the age evidence is not. People exercise less as they grow older. Most young adults are quite active, getting aerobic exercise by climbing stairs, jogging to the store, joining intramural college and company athletic teams, playing at local parks, biking, hiking, swimming, and so on. In the United States, emerging adults walk more and drive less than older adults.

In 2017, of the youngest adults, 34 percent meet both the aerobic and muscle strengthening standards, compared to only 21 percent of middle-aged adults and 13 percent of the oldest adults (U.S. Department of Health and Human Services, 2018) (see **Figure 15.7**).

For everyone, movement should be part of daily life, walking or biking (not driving), climbing stairs (not taking elevators), stretching while making the bed, squatting and standing while gardening, and the like. Labor-saving devices may also be disability-promoting devices!

Heavy people who exercise regularly reduce their risk for the diseases of aging, unlike those who are thinner but do not move much. A meta-analysis showed that physical activity reduced the risk of breast cancer, no matter how heavy the woman was (Pizot et al., 2016).

Sleep

Vitality and immunity increase with adequate sleep. One night's poor sleep makes a person tired and irritable the next day—that is homeostasis, the body's way to maintain equilibrium. But if poor sleep quality is typical every day in youth, then appetite, mood, and activity adjust (more, down, less) to achieve homeostasis, while allostatic load rises and organ reserve declines.

The exact amount and schedule of sleep varies by individuals as well as by age. For example, the "heterogeneity among naps, nappers, and napping" means that health and cognition sometimes benefit from naps and sometimes suffer (Spira, 2018). This is true culturally as well. A midday nap (a *siesta*) remained part of daily life for people in Southern Europe and South America when it was no longer possible in the industrialized North, because factories in the North, and therefore jobs, were located far from bedrooms.

Some variability is part of human diversity. People vary in how much sleep they need (D. Patel et al., 2018). But too much or too little sleep cause (not just correlate with) anxiety, depression, and many other problems.

Sleep (and everything else) changes with age. Only babies should "sleep like a baby." The circadian rhythm that shifts at adolescence shifts again, in the other direction, in late adulthood. Elders are often sleepy in the early evening and up before dawn. Many wake often during the night and nap every day (Gulia & Kumar, 2018).

Sleep problems worsen with age, because many elders have restless legs, muscle pain, breathing difficulties, and snoring. Then disturbed and inadequate sleep makes every other problem worse, causing anxiety and depression (D. Patel et al., 2018).

The key at every age is to find a routine that works well, allowing a person to wake without an alarm and to stay alert without caffeine. Stress about sleep is itself a problem: the *DSM-5* defines *insomnia* as being distressed with sleep patterns. Some people "self-medicate" by drinking alcohol at bedtime, which increases night-time falls, disturbing dreams, and early waking. Note that self-medication may makes the insomnia worse.

Doctors may make the same mistake. If a patient complains about sleep, they might prescribe

> drugs that are commonly used to manage insomnia, such as benzodiazepines and non-benzodiazepines, [which] can lead to several residual side-effects like drug dependence, tolerance, rebound insomnia, muscle relaxation, hallucinations, depression, and amnesia.
>
> *[Gulia & Kumar, 2018, p. 161]*

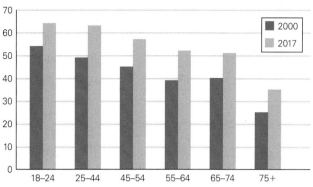

Percent of U.S. Adults Meeting Either the Aerobic or Strengthening Exercise Goals

FIGURE 15.7

Getting Better Every Decade? This figure shows that American adults are becoming more active, not only compared to adults their age 17 years ago, but also compared to their own activity when they were younger. Thus, those who were aged 18–24 in 2000 became more active than they were (from 54 to 63 percent). However, look closely: Many of the oldest people became less active than they themselves were a decade earlier.

Instead, to protect both physical and mental well-being, at every age, people need good *sleep hygiene*. That includes, several hours before bedtime, (1) turning off television and other screens, (2) exercising, and (3) no more substances (alcohol, caffeine, nicotine, hard-to-digest foods) that might interfere with sleep. Bodies adjust to patterns, so regular exercise, set bedtimes, routine meditation and relaxation practices, and maybe a midday nap might all increase health.

Social Relationships

Thousands of studies have confirmed that social relationships are closely connected to every measure of health: People who are in touch with friends, family members, neighbors, and community groups live longer, feel better, and have fewer disabilities lifelong. One summary states it well:

> Social isolation and loneliness among young (18–40 years), middle-aged (41–64), and older adults (65 years and older) is thus a serious public health concern of our time because of its strong connection with cardiovascular, autoimmune, neurocognitive, and mental health problems.
>
> *[Newman & Zainal, 2020, p. e12]*

Scientists not only have many ways to measure health (as described in the beginning of this chapter); they also have many ways to measure social connections. Some focus on loneliness, some on social outreach; some on social cohesion; some on involvement with churches, block associations, political groups; and so on. Separately and together, those foster health for children, adolescents, and adults, as found in thousands of studies and summarized in several meta-analyses (Cramm et al., 2013; Haslam et al., 2021; Holt-Lunstad, 2017; Martino et al., 2017; O'Connor et al., 2021).

One finding is that each type of social connection improves the others. For example, people who feel less lonely are also, in the next 10 years, more involved in activities that require social engagement; people who are socially engaged, are, in the next 10 years, less likely to be lonely. The converse is also true: A downward spiral occurs (McHugh Power et al., 2019).

Why is this a health *habit*, not simply a fact of life? Because people become more active socially by choice, just as they can choose to develop better eating, sleeping, and exercise habits. Further, people can help others become more social. This begins with children who do better, physically, emotionally, and cognitively, if they have at least one teacher with whom they connect. Schools can foster this in how they are organized (Allen et al., 2018). At the other end of the life span, older adults can phone friends, join groups, share food, help neighbors.

We need not describe this vast body of research now. Instead, to illustrate, we describe one study, a meta-analysis of deaths by heart attack and stroke, so that you can see the precision and detail of this body of research. A team began by searching 16 electronic databases, checking reference lists to find unpublished articles, and asking experts if they knew of any studies that had not been published.

They found 35,925 articles that might be relevant. This is the first step in meta-analysis: Find every relevant study, even those in obscure journals or that are never published. Two researchers examined all those, looking for those that reported correlations between social isolation or loneliness, heart disease or strokes, longitudinal data, comparison groups, and solid empirical results.

They found 23 that met all the criteria. Then they calibrated the results of these 23, taking into account how many participants were in each. The final result, after careful calculations, was that lack of social connections increase heart disease by 29 percent and stroke by 31 percent (Valtorta et al., 2016).

Note that health habits decrease risk of poor health but do not eliminate it. There are no guarantees, but a combination of all the attitudes and health habits listed here markedly increase the likelihood of a long and happy life.

---

macmillan learning

Many of the older adults in **VIDEO: Active and Healthy Aging: The Importance of Community** frequent senior centers for daily social contact, and some benefit from volunteering.

Policy and Health

Many aspects of public health begin with improving the living conditions for everyone. Climate contributes to health, in floods, hot temperatures, hurricanes, wildfires, and more, and no one person can change that.

Health Habits Depend on Other People

For all the measures above that are personal actions that people can take to improve their health, there is a public, social component. People eat better if they eat with someone who also is trying to increase vegetables and reduce fat, people exercise more if they meet a friend for walking or join a gym or a team; people sleep better if they have a partner who is quietly sleeping as well. Screens and social media keep people awake: Ideally, they are off, and in another room, at night.

Neighborhoods matter, too. Some have walking and biking paths, safe fields and parks, and subsidized pools and gyms. Some have farmers' markets, with fresh local produce; others are *food deserts*, with no healthy food nearby. Some are quiet; others are noisy all night.

Health experts cite extensive research showing that community design, safety, and neighbor friendliness promotes walking and biking, reducing obesity, hypertension, and depression (Nehme et al., 2016; Yu & Lippert, 2016).

Childhood poverty, abuse, and hunger affect all functions of the body and brain, impairing health in middle age even if the childhood problems stopped decades ago (Duncan & Kawachi, 2018; Widom et al., 2015b). Some of this is directly biological, but much is psychological. Sleep, for instance, is influenced by anxiety and depression as much as specifics of light and sound.

The stunning mortality statistics in the beginning of this chapter make it obvious that the worldwide average of 25 additional years for everyone was the result of public health measures, not of individuals who decided to eat better, exercise more, and so on. To better understand the connection between public health and private morbidity, we look at two examples: immunization and lead.

Immunization

Humans have an immune system that fights off every disease with three levels of protection: the outer defenses such as the skin, the general immune system that attacks every pathogen (something harmful, like a virus or bacteria), and the adaptive immune system that develops antibodies to any specific disease that the other two levels did not destroy.

That third level takes time to identify a new pathogen and develop targeted antibodies. For many deadly diseases, such as smallpox, chicken pox, and measles, if a person has survived the disease, the immune system "remembers" and has latent antibodies from years ago that are ready to resist that same disease.

Immunization can now occur with vaccination, which usually involves giving the person a small dose of the live virus, or a small dose of the deactivated virus, which triggers the body's natural immune system. For COVID-19, another way to create a vaccine is to deactivate the molecular elements that allow the virus to spread. Ideally, vaccination provides total protection without any side effects.

Immunization protects those who cannot be safely vaccinated, such as infants under 3 months and people with impaired immune systems (HIV-positive, aged, or undergoing chemotherapy). **Herd immunity** is protective of these individuals: Usually, if almost all the people in a community (a herd) are immunized, no one dies of that disease.

The specific percentage that needs to be immunized varies by disease. Measles, for instance, is highly contagious, so public health experts believe herd immunity requires successful vaccination of about 95 percent of the population. The lack of herd immunity is the reason COVID-19 is so dangerous: No one is already immune.

immunization A process that stimulates the body's immune system by causing production of antibodies to defend against attack by a particular contagious disease. Creation of antibodies may be accomplished either naturally (by having the disease), by injection, by drops that are swallowed, or by a nasal spray.

herd immunity When a sufficient proportion of a population is immune to an infectious disease (through vaccination and/or prior illness) to make its spread from person to person unlikely.

True Dedication This young Buddhist monk lives in a remote region of Nepal, where until recently measles was a common, fatal disease. Fortunately, a UNICEF porter carried the vaccine over mountain trails for two days so that this boy—and his whole community—could be immunized.

Scott Eells/Redux

Personal Choice and Public Harm

None of the U.S. states require vaccination for people who have medical reasons to avoid vaccines. Fortunately, their numbers are few, less than 3 percent, so herd immunity of the other 97 percent protects them. In the past 50 years, scientists have developed many safe vaccines that have saved millions of lives, especially of young children and older adults. Usually it takes at least two years of development and testing to find a safe and effective vaccine.

Stunning successes in my lifetime include the following:

- Smallpox, the most lethal disease for children in the past, was eradicated worldwide as of 1980. Vaccination against smallpox is no longer needed.
- Polio, a crippling and sometimes fatal disease, has been virtually eliminated in the Americas.
- Varicella (chicken pox) killed 100–150 people (mostly under age 5) in the United States each year, and 4 million were itchy and feverish for a week. Then, in 1995, a vaccine was developed. Currently, the U.S. death rate from chicken pox is under 10 a year, usually of those not fully vaccinated (two doses, age 1 and age 5).
- Measles (rubeola, not rubella) is disappearing, thanks to a vaccine developed in 1963. Prior to that time, 3–4 million cases occurred each year in the United States alone (Centers for Disease Control and Prevention, May 15, 2015). In 2012

in the United States, only 55 people had measles, although globally about 20 million measles cases occurred that year.

Given those successes, it seems logical that no one would suffer or die of those diseases again. But some children are not vaccinated. Without herd immunity, the disease could infect everyone who cannot be immunized, such as infants in the first week of life, or anyone without a natural immune system.

Then, if a tourist from a nation without widespread immunity brings measles, for instance, back to the United States, and if too many parents do not immunize their children, outbreaks occur. That happened in 2019, where at least 1,249 people in the United States had measles (including a newborn who caught it from the mother)—the highest rate since 1994 (Patel et al., 2019). (See Visualizing Development.)

This is a classic case where individual choices harm the community. Fifteen U.S. states allow parents to refuse vaccination because of "personal belief," and 45 states allow religious exemptions. Together, that reduces herd immunity. After a measles outbreak in 2015 at Disneyland, California no longer allows "philosophical" refusal of immunization. However, religious exemptions are still permitted, and many Californians found clergy who were willing to accept them as new members of the religion, confirming religious objections.

Immunization is particularly important for young children who have baby brothers or sisters, because babies are too young to be fully protected. Other unvaccinated people who benefit from herd immunity are those with unusual medical conditions that might cause an overreaction to vaccination, or people whose treatment for cancer or an organ transplant has temporarily disabled their immune systems.

Lead in the Brain

Lead was recognized as a poison a century ago (Hamilton, 1914). The symptoms of *plumbism*, as lead poisoning is called, were obvious—intellectual disability, hyperactivity, and even death if the level reached 70 micrograms per deciliter of blood.

The lead industry defended the heavy metal. Manufacturers argued that low levels were harmless, and they blamed parents for letting their children eat flaking chips of lead paint (which tastes sweet).

Lead remained a major ingredient in paint (it speeds drying) and in gasoline (it raises octane) for most of the twentieth century. Finally, chemical analyses of blood and teeth, with careful longitudinal and replicated research, proved that lead indeed poisoned the brain (Needleman et al., 1990; Needleman & Gatsonis, 1990).

The United States banned lead in paint (in 1978) and automobile fuel (in 1996). The blood level that caused plumbism was set at 40 micrograms per deciliter, then 20, and then 10. Danger is now thought to begin at 5 micrograms, but no level has been proven to be risk-free (MMWR, April 5, 2013). Part of the

VISUALIZING DEVELOPMENT   Immunization

Before the measles vaccine was introduced in 1963, 30 million people globally contracted measles each year. About 2 million of them died, usually because they were both malnourished and sick. (World Health Organization, April 28, 2017). Thankfully, worldwide vaccination efforts now mean that no child need die of measles.

Measles is highly infectious, so 95 percent of the population must be immunized in order for herd immunity to protect the entire community. The United States achieved that: A decade ago, measles incidence was close to zero. Experts thought it would soon be eliminated in all developed countries, so public health workers focused on the very poorest nations.

ESTIMATED MEASLES VACCINE COVERAGE — SELECTED NATIONS

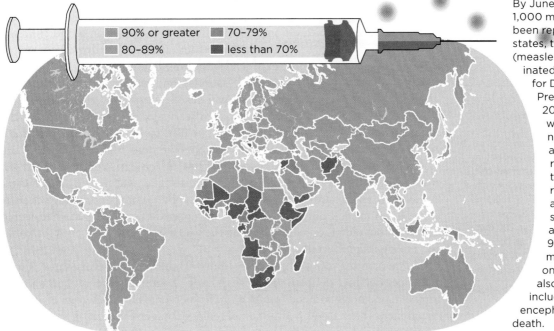

90% or greater
80-89%
70-79%
less than 70%

By June 2019, more than 1,000 measles cases had been reported in 28 U.S. states, the most since 1992 (measles was declared eliminated in 2000) (Centers for Disease Control and Prevention, June 17, 2019). To understand what went wrong, note that many states allow personal or religious exemptions to immunization requirements. Thus, as the U.S. map below shows, several states are not at that safe 95 percent — leaving many vulnerable, not only to discomfort but also to complications, including pneumonia, encephalitis, and even death.

Data from World Health Organization, May 29, 2019.

VACCINE EXEMPTION AND HERD IMMUNITY — UNITED STATES

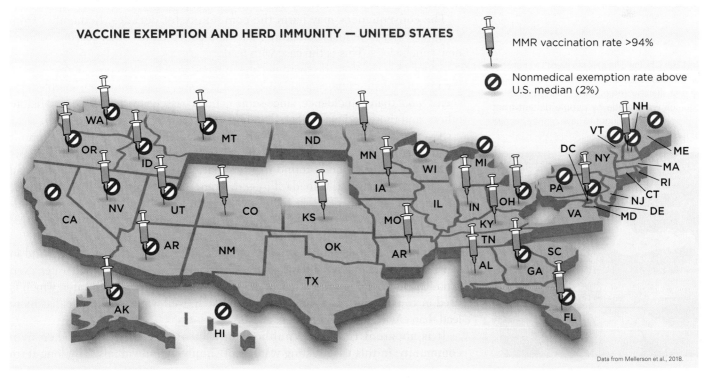

MMR vaccination rate >94%

Nonmedical exemption rate above U.S. median (2%)

Data from Mellerson et al., 2018.

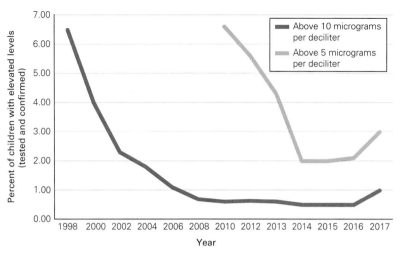

Data from Child Trends Data Bank, 2015; Centers for Disease Control and Prevention, 2018.

FIGURE 15.8

Dramatic Improvement in a Decade When legislators finally accepted the research establishing the damage from lead in paint, gasoline, and water, they passed laws that helped to make it exceedingly rare for any child to die or suffer intellectual disability because of plumbism. A decade ago, 10 micrograms per deciliter of blood was thought to be completely safe; now less than 1 child in 200 tests at that level, and even 5 micrograms per deciliter alerts pediatricians and parents to find the source. These national data make the tragedy in Flint, Michigan, especially shocking.

Not His Choice His parents want to know his blood lead level, and this nurse volunteered to test the children of Flint, Michigan. Earlier choices were made by people distant from this scene, who sought to save money instead of health.

problem is that the fetus and infant absorb lead at a much higher rate than adults do, so lead's neurotoxicity is especially destructive of developing brains (Hanna-Attisha et al., 2016).

Regulation has made a difference: The percentage of U.S. 1- to 5-year-olds with more than 5 micrograms of lead per deciliter of blood was 8.6 percent in 1999–2001, 4.1 percent in 2003–2006, and 2.6 percent in 2007–2010 (see **Figure 15.8**). Children who are young, low-SES, and/or living in old housing tend to have higher levels (MMWR, April 5, 2013).

Many parents increase their children's calcium intake, wipe window ledges clean, avoid child exposure to construction dust, test drinking water, discard lead-based medicines and crockery (available in some nations), and make sure children never eat chips of lead-based paint.

However, this topic is in the public health section of this chapter because private actions alone are not sufficient to protect health. Parents are blamed for obesity, injury, abuse, and neglect, but often the larger community is also to blame.

A stark recent example occurred in Flint, Michigan, where in April 2014 cost-saving officials (appointed by the state to take over the city when the tax base shrunk as the auto industry left) changed the municipal drinking water from Lake Huron to the Flint River. That river contained chemicals that increased lead leaching from old pipes, contaminating the water supply—often used for drinking and mixing infant formula.

The percent of young children in Flint with blood lead levels above 5 micrograms per deciliter doubled in two years, from 2.4 to 4.9 percent, and more than tripled in one neighborhood from 4.6 to 15.7 percent (Hanna-Attisha et al., 2016). Apparently, the state-appointed emergency manager focused on saving money, ignoring possible brain damage to children, an oversight representing an "abject failure to protect public health" (Bellinger, 2016, p. 1101).

The consequences may harm the community for decades. Remember from Chapter 1 that scientists sometimes use data collected for other reasons to draw new conclusions. This is the case with lead.

About 15 years after the sharp decline in blood lead levels in preschool children, the rate of violent crime committed by teenagers and young adults fell sharply. This seems more than coincidence, since some nations passed laws to reduce lead before others, and those nations saw a reduction in teenage crime earlier than others.

A scientist comparing these trends concluded that some teenagers commit impulsive, violent crimes because their brains were poisoned by lead years earlier. The correlation is found in every nation that has reliable data on lead and crime—Australia, Canada, Finland, France, Germany, Italy, New Zealand, and the United States (Nevin, 2007). Moreover, blood lead levels in early childhood predict later attention deficits and school suspensions (Amato et al., 2013; Goodlad et al., 2013).

The Flint example horrified many parents and educators. Lead was found in some schools, and many cautious parents give their children only bottled water, even if no lead has been found in their water sources. Some prefer well water, which is used in 13 percent of U.S. homes. Unfortunately, well water, on average, has more lead than city water (Gibson et al., 2020).

It is apparent that some public health measures need to be taken by a community, in this case testing water, not simply by individuals. The long-term results of lead in children's brains raises questions about the effects of hundreds, perhaps thousands, of chemicals in the air, water, or soil. Population data on mortality, morbidity, and disability make it apparent that protecting well-being is not entirely a matter of each person for themselves, but of people helping each other protect everyone.

Conclusion

We have described how health is measured, many forms of psychopathology, and several ways that individuals and communities can increase health for everyone. But moving from words to understanding and then to action are not simple steps. Personally, I do not do all the health steps that I described.

Back to the opening of this chapter: I said that Diana was very competent, but the aide did not understand my words. That is why she spoke to me as if Diana could not comprehend her words about anomalies.

I did not correct her; I replied. Only later did I realize what had happened. When I mentioned it to Diana, she said she was not upset with the aide or me because she has become accustomed to people who think her loss of sight means a loss of mind. I hope that this chapter has made us better informed, and then will motivate us to protect our own well-being and that of everyone else.

WHAT HAVE YOU LEARNED?

1. What attitudes result from the medical model of mental illness?
2. What are the implications of neurodiversity for autism spectrum disorder?
3. How is agism a self-fulfilling prophecy?
4. What specifics are recommended for a healthy diet?
5. What are the symptoms of frailty in old age?
6. How do exercise habits change with age?
7. What diseases and disorders does exercise prevent?
8. How does culture affect sleep and insomnia?
9. How is social activity both a cause and a consequence of depression?
10. Who is protected by herd immunity?
11. How does lead get into old buildings, into the water supply, into the air?
12. Why did it take a century for plumbism to be recognized?

SUMMARY

Measuring Health

1. Mortality is measured either with life expectancy (averaging about 80 in the United States, about 72 worldwide) or by death rate per thousand in particular group. Maximum life expectancy for the human species is about 120; average life expectancy per group provides insight into how to increase longevity.

2. Mortality data, comparing nations and treatments, has helped doctors prevent some COVID-19 deaths. Excess deaths are higher than the usual average for a group. Many non-COVID-19 excess deaths occurred during the pandemic.

3. Morbidity is disease. A gender paradox is that women have higher rates of morbidity but lower rates of mortality than men do. Many illnesses and conditions are comorbid; obesity is an important example.

4. Disability is inability to perform basic tasks, either the physical activities of daily life (ADLs) or the cognitive activities of daily life (IADLs). Disability over a lifetime can be measured with disability adjusted life years (DALYs).

5. Well-being is the feeling of energy, joy, and vitality that makes life worth living. It is measured with quality adjusted life years

(QALYs). Cost-benefit analysis is useful for public health but may not reflect individual values.

Developmental Psychopathology

6. Some serious psychological disorders arise in childhood. Many of these seem to be increasing. One example is autism spectrum disorder.

7. Other disorders of childhood include attention deficit/hyperactivity disorder (ADHD) and learning disorders, such as in reading (dyslexia), in math (dyscalculia), and in writing (dysgraphia).

8. In adolescence, rates of depression escalate, especially in girls, and oppositional defiant disorder increases, especially in boys. Parasuicide is common, but suicide is not.

9. In adulthood, rates of suicide increase. Posttraumatic stress disorder is most common in early adulthood. Anxiety disorders are also common.

10. Substance use often begins in adolescence, but addiction is more common in adulthood. Alcohol and cigarettes are the drugs most often abused, both contributing to almost every disease. Opioid addiction is increasing, causing many deaths.

11. While many disorders become less common in old age, some increase, particularly neurocognitive disorders. With all disorders, knowing the causes and consequences helps with prevention and treatment.

Protecting Health

12. The medical model conceptualizes disorders as problems to be cured. This concept is resisted by many psychologists, who seek to modify the excesses of various disorders but who also appreciate diversity in emotions, values, and behavior.

13. Neurodiversity means that some people may have unusual attitudes, brain functions, and beliefs that nonetheless benefit society. Stereotypes about age and pathology can be destructive of health.

14. Individual selection of what talents and interests one wants to pursue, as one compensates for whatever weaknesses one has, leads to greater health and well-being.

15. What a person eats influences their physical and psychological health. Every drug affects nutrition as well as the mind. In general, variety of diet seems best, avoiding most drugs and fat.

16. Exercise is pivotal in protecting health at every age. Improvements are evident with increased exercise over the past decades. However, older adults exercise less than younger adults, even though they benefit more.

17. Sleep is essential for physical and psychological health. Patterns change with age, but the immune system and the brain require adequate sleep.

18. The immune system fights off disease, either naturally or because of immunization, which has added decades of life to people worldwide. Herd immunity protects the most vulnerable—the very young, the very old, and the very sick.

19. Especially early in life, lead impairs the brain, making people more impulsive and less thoughtful than they would otherwise be. Over the past century, public health measures have gradually reduced lead in paint, pollution, and the soil.

KEY TERMS

mortality (p. 438)
average life expectancy (p. 438)
maximum life expectancy (p. 439)
morbidity (p. 440)
comorbid (p. 442)
disability (p. 442)
universal design (p. 443)
well-being (p. 443)
disability-adjusted life years (DALYs) (p. 444)

quality-adjusted life years (QALYs) (p. 444)
psychopathology (p. 445)
Diagnostic and Statistical Manual of Mental Disorders (DSM-5) (p. 445)
developmental psychopathology (p. 446)
autism spectrum disorder (ASD) (p. 446)
attention-deficit/hyperactivity disorder (ADHD) (p. 447)

specific learning disorders (p. 450)
dyslexia (p. 450)
dyscalculia (p. 450)
conduct disorder (p. 451)
oppositional defiant disorder (ODD) (p. 451)
major depressive disorder (MDD) (p. 452)
suicidal ideation (p. 452)
parasuicide (p. 452)

social anxiety disorder (p. 454)
hikikomori (p. 454)
substance use disorder (SUD) (p. 455)
medical model (p. 458)
neurodiversity (p. 458)
selective optimization with compensation (p. 460)
immunization (p. 465)
herd immunity (p. 465)

APPLICATIONS

1. A major expense for many older people is health care, both routine and catastrophic. Government payment for health care expenses (hospitals, drugs, and preventive care) varies widely from nation to nation. Compare two nations, your own and one other, on specifics of coverage and on data that indicate the health of older people (rates of longevity, diseases, etc.).

2. Ask five people of various ages whether they want to live to age 100, and record their responses. Would they be willing to eat half as much, exercise much more, experience weekly dialysis, or undergo other procedures in order to extend life? Analyze the responses.

ESPECIALLY FOR ANSWERS

Response for Immigrants (from p. 454): Maintain your social supports. Ideally, emigrate with members of your close family, and join a religious or cultural community where you will find emotional understanding.

Response for Doctors and Nurses (from p. 457): Obviously, much depends on the specific patient. Overall, however, far more people develop a disease or die because of years of poor health habits than because of various illnesses not spotted early. With some exceptions, age 35 is too early to detect incipient cancers or circulatory problems, but it's prime time for stopping cigarette smoking, curbing alcohol abuse, and improving exercise and diet.

OBSERVATION QUIZ ANSWERS

Answer to Observation Quiz (from p. 438): To enable walking, Diana has flat, rubber-soled shoes and taps with her cane, and to prevent COVID-19 she wears gloves and a mask. There is a fifth sign here of her optimization. Since she cannot attend mass demonstrations, her mask says "VOTE."

Answer to Observation Quiz (from p. 448): Yes, not only overall but also in response to the diagnosis. When a September birthday boy is diagnosed with ADHD, he is less likely to be medicated than an August birthday boy—the opposite of what would be expected if only boys with real problems were diagnosed.

Answer to Observation Quiz (from p. 453): Both. It increases for boys but decreases for girls.

CHAPTER 16

Death and Dying

Pascal Deloche/Godong/Getty Images

"When is Pappy going to die?" asked a 4-year-old when he was in the car with Pappy (his grandfather), his grandmother, and his parents. The grandmother and parents hesitated and then answered, "A lot of years"; "Not for a long, long time"; "We hope he never does." Pappy was silent.

That quieted the boy for a while. He had his birthday a week before and was acutely aware of time passing. He was no longer 3; he now had a new number, 4. That evening he asked his parents, "What is Pappy's last number?" And then, "What is my last number?"

The answer came after a pause. "We don't know" (Sekeres, 2013).

This chapter explores what we know and do not know about death. Everyone will have a "last number" and Pappy's number is likely to come sooner than the boy's, but we do not know the duration of anyone's life span. Humans, everywhere and for hundreds of thousands of years, have thought about death, buried their dead, and hoped for longer and better lives, but we do not know whether new customs will replace the old ones.

Here we describe ancient practices and new dilemmas, among them defining when death occurs and what makes a good death. You will read how people "work through the contradictions of a loss, and go on to experience significant growth following a traumatic event" (Tedeschi et al., 2017). There is *hope* in death, *choice* in dying, and *affirmation* in mourning, each described in a major section of this final chapter, and each with new understanding of this enduring topic.

What Will You Know?

1. Why is death a topic of hope, not despair?
2. What is the difference between a good death and a bad one?
3. How does mourning help with grief?

Death and Hope

A multicultural life-span perspective reveals that reactions to death are filtered through many cultural prisms, affected by historical changes and regional variations as well as by the age of both the dying and the bereaved.

One emotion is constant, however: hope. It appears in many ways: hope for life after death, hope that the world is better because someone lived, hope that death occurred for a reason, hope that survivors rededicate themselves to whatever they deem meaningful in life. Immortality of some kind seems evident as people think about death (Robben, 2018).

Cultures, Epochs, and Death

Many people in developed nations have never witnessed someone die. This was not always the case (see **Table 16.1**).

If someone reached age 50 in 1900 in the United States and had had 20 high school classmates, at least six of those fellow students would have already died. The survivors would visit and reassure their dying friends at home, promising to see them in heaven.

People today are less sure about an afterlife but still have hope. Before noting how this can be, we describe traditional responses when familiarity with death was common.

Ancient Times

Paleontologists have evidence from 120,000 years ago that the Neanderthals buried their dead with tools, bowls, or jewelry, signifying belief in an afterlife (Stiner, 2017). The date is controversial: Burial with objects could have begun earlier, but it is certain that death long ago was an occasion for hope, mourning, and remembrance.

Two Western civilizations with written records — Egypt and Greece — had elaborate death rituals millennia ago. The ancient Egyptians built magnificent pyramids, refined mummification, and scripted instructions (called the *Book of the Dead*) to help the soul (*ka*), personality (*ba*), and shadow (*akh*) reunite after death so that the dead could protect the living (Taylor, 2010).

Another set of beliefs came from the ancient Greeks. Again, continuity between life and death was evident, with hope for this world and the next. The fate of a dead person depended on their life. A few would have a blissful afterlife, a few were condemned to torture in Hades, and most would enter a shadow world until they were reincarnated.

Ancient Chinese, Mayan, Indian, and African cultures also had rituals about death, and they venerated ancestors, who they believed were still connected to the living in some way (Hill & Hageman, 2016). That gave survivors hope for themselves.

Everywhere:

- Actions during life were thought to affect destiny after death.
- An afterlife was assumed.
- Mourners said prayers and made offerings to prevent the spirit of the dead from haunting and hurting them, and to gain blessing and strength from the ancestors.

TABLE 16.1

How Death Has Changed in the Past 100 Years

Death occurs later. A century ago, the average life span worldwide was less than 40 years (47 in the rapidly industrializing United States). Half of the world's babies died before age 5. Now newborns are expected to live to age 72 (79 in the United States); in many nations, centenarians are the fastest-growing age group.

Dying takes longer. In the early 1900s, death was usually fast and unstoppable; once the brain, the heart, or any other vital organ failed, the rest of the body quickly followed. Now death can often be postponed through medical technology: Hearts can beat for years after the brain stops functioning, respirators can replace lungs, and dialysis does the work of failing kidneys.

Death often occurs in hospitals. For most of our ancestors, death occurred at home, with family nearby. Now most deaths occur in hospitals or other institutions, with the dying surrounded by medical personnel and machines.

The causes of death have changed. People of all ages once usually died of infectious diseases (tuberculosis, typhoid, smallpox), or, for many women and most infants, in childbirth. Now disease deaths before age 50 are rare, and in developed nations most newborns (99 percent) and their mothers (99.99 percent) live.

And after death . . . People once knew about life after death. Some believed in heaven and hell; others, in reincarnation; others, in the spirit world. Prayers were repeated — some on behalf of the souls of the deceased, some for remembrance, some to the dead asking for protection. Believers were certain that their prayers were heard. People now are aware of cultural and religious diversity; many raise doubts that never occurred to their ancestors.

Conversation Who is talking here? Unless you are an Egyptologist, you would not guess that this depicts a dead man conversing with the gods of the Underworld. Note that the deceased is relatively young and does not seem afraid — both typical for people in ancient Egypt.

HIP/Art Resource, NY

Contemporary Beliefs

Now consider contemporary beliefs. Diversity of customs and beliefs is apparent, yet common themes are also evident. It is now recognized that connections between the living and the dead continue, so each person and each community memorializes the dead in a way to help the survivors live on (Klass & Steffen, 2017).

This is evident in beliefs in life after death. Heaven? Purgatory? Hell? Rebirth and reincarnation? Continued presence on Earth as a spirit? Despite such differences, it also is true that in all cultures and religions, death brings communities together, affirming sacrifice, continuity, and compassion. An international study of 890 people from four Asian cultures and 695 from North America found that most (including the 295 who said they were not religious) believed in life after death (Nichols et al., 2018).

Understanding Death Throughout the Life Span

Thoughts about death—as about everything else—are influenced by each person's age, cognitive maturation, and past experiences. Here are some of the specifics.

Death in Childhood

Some adults think children are oblivious to death; others believe children should participate in funerals and other rituals, just as adults do. You know from your study of childhood cognition that neither view is completely correct.

Children are affected by the attitudes of others. They may be upset if they see grown-ups cry or if grown-ups keep them away from death rituals for someone they loved. Thus, adults should neither ignore the child's emotions nor expect mature reactions. Because the limbic system matures more rapidly than the prefrontal cortex, children may seem happy one day and depressed the next.

Young children who themselves are fatally ill typically fear that death means being abandoned (Wolchik et al., 2008). Consequently, parents should stay with a dying child—holding, reading, singing, and sleeping. A frequent and caring presence is more important than logic. Children are much better at dealing with facts than fears, so they continue to rely on adults to care for them (Stein et al., 2019).

By school age, many children seek independence. Parents and professionals can be too solicitous; older children do not want to be babied if they are dying or if someone else is dying. They want facts and a role in "management of illness and treatment decisions" (Varga & Paletti, 2013, p. 27). Doctors, nurses, and parents now are advised to listen to sick children, allow them to ask questions, and answer in words they understand—not in medical terminology that puts a barrier between the child and the facts (Stein et al., 2019).

That is true when the children themselves are seriously ill, and also when someone the child knows has died. Lies and platitudes are the opposite of what the child needs (Stevenson, 2017). Children who lose a friend, a relative, or a pet might, or might not, seem sad, lonely, or angry.

If a child is told that Grandma is sleeping, that God wanted a sibling in heaven, or that Grandpa went on a trip, there are two possibilities, neither of them good. The first possibility is that the child believes the explanation and insists on waking up Grandma, complaining to God, or phoning Grandpa to say, "Come home." The second is worse. If adults lie, the child may conclude that death is so terrifying to adults that they cannot be trusted to talk about it.

As children become concrete operational thinkers, they seek facts, such as exactly how a person died and where that person is now. They want something to do: bring flowers, repeat a prayer, write a letter. Interestingly, older children are better able to understand that death is a biological event and that the dead cannot come back to life.

Observation Quiz Beyond the coffin, do you see any other signs of ritual? (see answer, page 494) ↓

Sorrow All Around When a 5-day-old baby died in Santa Rosa, Guatemala, the entire neighborhood mourned. Symbols and a procession help with grief: The coffin is white to indicate that the infant was without sin and will therefore be in heaven.

JOHAN ORDONEZ/AFP/Getty Images

But simultaneously they also are more likely to accept a religious/spiritual understanding. They see no contradiction in that (Harris, 2018).

Death in Adolescence and Emerging Adulthood

Remember that adolescent emotions are powerful and erratic, changing quickly. Adolescents may be self-absorbed, philosophical, analytic, or distraught—or all four at different moments. Self-expression is part of the search for identity; death of a loved one does not put an end to that search. Some adolescents use social media to write to the dead person or to vent their grief—an effective way to express their personal identity concerns (Balk & Varga, 2017).

"Live fast, die young, and leave a good-looking corpse" is advice often attributed to actor James Dean, who died in a car crash at age 24. At what stage would a person be most likely to agree? Emerging adulthood, of course (see **Figure 16.1**).

Terror management theory explains some illogical responses to death. The idea is that people who fear death become more defensive of their own culture, more ageist, and more likely to take risks (Burke et al., 2010). They manage their terror by defying death. Terror management is particularly evident among college students and seems to disappear when people are middle-aged or older (Maxfield et al., 2007).

Terror management may explain an illogical action by some adolescents in Florida who suffer from asthma. Compared to high school students without asthma, they are *more* likely to use tobacco products (28 percent versus 24 percent). That includes higher rates of smoking cigarettes and cigars, which they know are harmful for their lungs (Reid et al., 2018).

Death in Adulthood

When adults become responsible for work and family, attitudes shift. Death is not romanticized. Many adults quit addictive drugs, start wearing seat belts, and adopt other death-avoiding behaviors when they reach age 30 or so. Unfortunately, this is not always true, Some adults, especially men in their 30s, continue to take risks and die from it—at twice the rate of women.

Adults who are dying may be less concerned about themselves than about the other people they will leave, especially children. It helps if they write a letter to the child to be opened at some age—such as 18—so they know that their love and care will continue after they die.

Many adults seek comfort in religious values. That helps many but not everyone. Research finds that religious beliefs sometimes increase death anxiety, although they usually decrease it (Jong et al., 2018). Variation occurs partly because religions differ in attitudes about death.

To defend against their own fears, adults do not accept the death of others. When Dylan Thomas was about age 30, he wrote to his dying father: "Do not go gentle into that good night/Rage, rage against the dying of the light" (Thomas, 2003, p. 239). Adults also do not accept their own death. A woman diagnosed at age 42 with a rare and almost always fatal cancer (a sarcoma) wrote:

> I hate stories about people dying of cancer, no matter how graceful, noble, or beautiful. . . . I refuse to accept I am dying; I prefer denial, anger, even desperation.
>
> *[Robson, 2010, pp. 19, 27]*

Adult reactions to the death of someone else depend partly on the age of the deceased. Millions of people mourned James Dean, Prince, and Whitney Houston

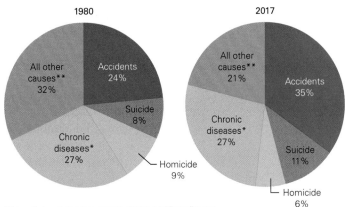

Causes of Death for 15- to 24-Year-Olds—United States

1980

All other causes** 32%
Accidents 24%
Suicide 8%
Chronic diseases* 27%
Homicide 9%

2017

All other causes** 21%
Accidents 35%
Chronic diseases* 27%
Suicide 11%
Homicide 6%

*Primarily heart disease, cancer, stroke, and liver disease.
**Includes most infectious diseases, such as HIV/AIDS, pneumonia, flu. These data predate COVID-19, but even so, accidents kill more adults than all infectious diseases.
Data from National Center for Health Statistics, 2019.

FIGURE 16.1

Tuberculosis Versus Driving into a Tree Medical science has become better at curing cancer, preventing heart disease, controlling HIV, and treating gunshot wounds. But more adults drive dangerously or despair of living. Better psychological science needed!

terror management theory The idea that people adopt cultural values and moral principles in order to cope with their fear of death. This system of beliefs protects individuals from anxiety about their mortality and bolsters their self-esteem.

(ages 24, 57, and 48, respectively). Equally talented entertainers who die at age 80 or 90 are less mourned. In terms of the COVID-19 pandemic, the fact that older adults were most likely to die is thought to be one reason that younger adults were less concerned about mask-wearing, social distancing, and inside dining at restaurants.

Logically, adults should work to change social factors that increase the risk of mortality—such as air pollution, junk food, and unsafe cars. Instead, many react more strongly to rare causes of death, such as anthrax and avalanches. They particularly fear deaths beyond their control.

For example, people fear travel by plane more than by car. In fact, flying is safer: In 2019 in the entire world, only 287 people were killed in air traffic accidents; but in the United States alone, 40,100 were killed by motor vehicles, according to the National Safety Council.

Ironically, when four airplanes were hijacked by terrorists on September 11, 2001, many North Americans drove long distances because they were afraid to fly. In the next few months, 2,300 more U.S. residents died in car crashes than usual (Blalock et al., 2009). Not logical, but certainly very human.

Death in Late Adulthood

In late adulthood, attitudes shift again. Anxiety decreases; hope rises (De Raedt et al., 2013).

Some older people remain happy when they are fatally ill. Many developmentalists believe that one sign of mental health among older adults is acceptance of mortality, which increases concern for others. Some elders engage in *legacy work*, trying to leave something meaningful for later generations (Lattanzi-Licht, 2013).

As evidence of this attitude change, older people seek to reconcile with estranged family members and tie up loose ends. Do not be troubled if grandparents allocate heirlooms, discuss end-of-life wishes, or buy a burial plot: All of those actions are developmentally appropriate.

Acceptance of death does not mean that elders give up on living; rather, their priorities shift. In an intriguing series of studies (Carstensen, 2011), people were presented with the following scenario:

> Imagine that in carrying out the activities of everyday life, you find that you have half an hour of free time, with no pressing commitments. You have decided that you'd like to spend this time with another person. Assuming that the following three persons are available to you, whom would you want to spend that time with?
> • A member of your immediate family
> • The author of a book you have just read
> • An acquaintance with whom you seem to have much in common

Older adults, more than younger ones, choose the family member (see **Figure 16.2**). The researchers explain that family becomes more important when death seems near.

Near-Death Experiences

At every age, coming close to death may be an occasion for hope. This is most obvious in what is called a *near-death experience*, in which a person almost dies. Survivors sometimes report having left the body and moved toward a bright light while feeling peace and joy. The following classic report is typical:

> I was in a coma for approximately a week. . . . I felt as though I were lifted right up, just as though I didn't have a physical body at all. A brilliant white light appeared. . . . The most wonderful feelings came over me—feelings of peace, tranquility, a vanishing of all worries.
>
> *[quoted in Moody, 1975, p. 56]*

FIGURE 16.2

Turning to Family as Death Approaches Both young and old people diagnosed with cancer (one-fourth of whom died within five years) more often preferred to spend a free half-hour with a family member rather than with an interesting person whom they did not know well.

Would you spend a free half-hour with a family member, a book author, or an acquaintance?

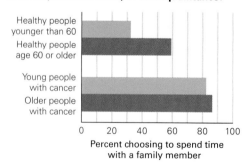

Data from Pinquart & Silbereisen, 2006.

Near-death experiences often include religious elements (angels seen, celestial music heard). Survivors often become more spiritual, less materialistic.

A reviewer of near-death experiences is struck by their endorsement of religious beliefs. In every culture, "all varieties of the dying experience" move people toward the same realizations: (1) the limitations of social status, (2) the insignificance of material possessions, and (3) the narrowness of self-centeredness (Greyson, 2009).

In fact, people who have merely heard about near-death experiences from other people tend to have some of the same emotions, feeling more spiritual and less materialistic (Tassell-Matamua et al., 2017). That brings us back to a general theme. Thinking about death can make people more hopeful about the future—their own and that of others.

THINK CRITICALLY: When a person is almost dead, might thoughts occur that are not limited by the neuronal connections in the brain?

WHAT HAVE YOU LEARNED?

1. In ancient cultures, how did people deal with death?

2. What are the common themes in religious understanding about death?

3. How do children respond to death?

4. Why might fear of death lead to more risk taking?

5. How does being closer to one's own death affect a person's attitudes?

6. In what ways do people change after a near-death experience?

Choices in Dying

Do you recoil at the heading "Choices in Dying"? If so, you may be living in the wrong century. Every twenty-first-century death involves choices, beginning with risks taken or avoided, habits sustained, and specific measures to postpone or hasten death.

A Good Death

People everywhere hope for a good death, one that is:

- At the end of a long life
- Peaceful
- Quick
- In familiar surroundings
- With family and friends present
- Without pain, confusion, or discomfort

Many would add that *control over circumstances* and *acceptance of the outcome* are also characteristic of a good death, but cultures and individuals differ. Some dying individuals willingly cede control to doctors or caregivers, and others fight every sign that death is near.

A review finds that family, medical personnel, and the dying person emphasize different aspects of "a good death" (Meier et al., 2016). One issue is psychological and spiritual well-being, which is important for many patients but less so for physicians.

Another issue is predictions about the timing of death and the benefits of treatment. Even when patients are severely ill, doctors currently are reluctant to make predictions and promises, because it is well known that they are sometimes

Where Death Occured in the United States, 2018

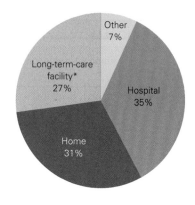

Data from MMWR, May 15, 2020.
*Includes hospice, nursing homes, and similar long-term-care facilities.

FIGURE 16.3

Not with Family Almost everyone prefers to die at home, yet most people die in an institution, surrounded by medical personnel and high-tech equipment, not by the soft voices and gentle touch of loved ones. The "other" category is even worse, as it includes most lethal accidents or homicides. But don't be too saddened by this chart—improvement is possible. Twenty years ago, the proportion of home deaths was notably lower.

VIDEO: End of Life: Interview with Laura Rothenberg features a young woman with a terminal illness discussing her feelings about death.

ESPECIALLY FOR Relatives of a Person Who Is Dying Why would a healthy person want the attention of hospice caregivers? (see response, page 494)

wrong. That makes them hesitate to discuss such issues, but patients and family members are eager for such information, imperfect as it is (Thomas et al., 2019; White et al., 2016).

Medical Care

In some ways, modern medicine makes a good death more likely. The first item on the list has become the norm: Death usually occurs at the end of a long life. Younger people still get sick, but surgery, drugs, radiation, and rehabilitation typically mean that the ill enter a hospital and then return home. If young people die, their death is typically quick (a fatal accident or suicide) and without pain, although painful for their loved ones.

In other ways, however, medical advances make a bad death more likely. When a cure is impossible, physical and emotional comfort deteriorate. Nurses and doctors are slower to respond to a bell, explain less when they come, and use medical measures that increase pain. Hospitals may exclude visitors when a person is about to die; patients may become delirious or unconscious.

Although people want to die at home, only about a third of all deaths in developed nations occur at home (see **Figure 16.3**). In England, where one published goal of public medicine is a good death, half of the deaths occur in hospitals, one-fourth in *care homes* (called *nursing homes* in the United States), and only one-fourth at home (Bone et al., 2018).

The underlying problem may be medical care itself, which is so focused on lifesaving that dying is resisted (Lee, 2019). Medical staff members are taught about drugs, surgeries, and other actions that treat the body; they may ignore the emotions. As one pastor said, "Cancer is a family disease; dying is not a solo experience."

During the COVID-19 pandemic, most hospitals and nursing homes did not allow family members to be with sick or dying people, because visitors might spread the virus. However, that concern for physical health came at the expense of psychological health: Those who died did not have a good death.

Stages of Dying

Emotions were the focus of Elisabeth Kübler-Ross (1975, 1997). In about 1960, she asked the administrator of a large hospital for permission to speak with dying patients. He told her that no one was dying! Eventually, she found a few terminally ill patients who wanted very much to talk.

From ongoing interviews, Kübler-Ross identified reactions of dying people. She divided their emotions into five sequential stages.

1. Denial ("I am not really dying.")
2. Anger ("I blame my doctors, or my family, or my God.")
3. Bargaining ("I will be good from now on if I can live.")
4. Depression ("I don't care; nothing matters anymore.")
5. Acceptance ("I accept my death as part of life.")

Another set of stages of dying is based on Maslow's hierarchy (Zalenski & Raspa, 2006):

1. Physiological needs (freedom from pain)
2. Safety (no abandonment)
3. Love and acceptance (from close family and friends)
4. Respect (from caregivers)
5. Self-actualization (appreciating one's unique past and present)

Maslow later suggested a possible sixth stage, *self-transcendence* (Koltko-Rivera, 2006), which emphasizes the acceptance of death.

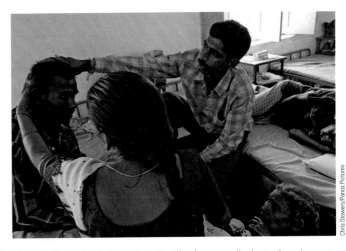

Same Situation, Far Apart: As It Should Be Dying individuals and their families benefit from physical touch and suffer from medical practices (gowns, tubes, isolation) that restrict movement and prevent contact. A good death is likely for these two patients—a husband with his wife in their renovated hotel/hospital room in North Carolina *(left),* and a man with his family in a Catholic hospice in Andhra Pradesh, India *(right).*

Other researchers have *not* found stages of dying. Remember the woman dying of a sarcoma, cited earlier? She said that she would never *accept* death and that Kübler-Ross should have included desperation as a stage. Kübler-Ross said that her stages have been misunderstood, as "our grief is as individual as our lives. . . . Not everyone goes through all of them or goes in a prescribed order" (Kübler-Ross & Kessler, 2005, p. 7).

Nevertheless, both lists remind caregivers that each dying person has strong emotions and needs that may be unlike that same person's emotions and needs a few days or weeks earlier. These emotions differ from those of the person's doctors and loved ones, who themselves have varied emotions. A good death recognizes dynamic changes in everyone's thoughts.

Telling the Truth

Many wise contemporary physicians stress honest conversations regarding medical care (Gawande, 2014; Kalanithi, 2016). Knowing the truth allows the dying to choose appropriate care (including addictive painkillers, music or prayers that are personal to the individual, favorite foods, visits from distant relatives, and so on (Lundquist et al., 2011).

The ideal caregiving is difficult, because patients misunderstand, symptoms change, priorities shift. Some dying people do *not* want visitors, music, medical intervention, or the truth about their condition. And then they may change their mind. Ideally, conversation among all concerned is ongoing, occurring over weeks and months (Cripe & Frankel, 2017).

Better Ways to Die

Several practices have become more prevalent since the contrast between a good death and the usual hospital death has become clear. Hospice and palliative care are examples.

Hospice

In London in the 1950s, Cecily Saunders opened the first modern **hospice**, where terminally ill people could spend their last days in comfort. Since then, thousands of hospices have opened in many nations, and hundreds of thousands of caregivers bring hospice care to dying people in hospitals and in homes. Most hospice deaths occur at home.

Observation Quiz One of the five senses is particularly important for the dying, even when sight and hearing are fading. What is it? (see answer, page 494) ↑

hospice An institution or program in which terminally ill patients receive palliative care to reduce suffering; family and friends of the dying are helped as well.

TABLE 16.2

Barriers to Entering Hospice Care

- Hospice patients must be terminally ill, with death anticipated within six months, but predictions are difficult, even for physicians. Research confirms that "death is highly unpredictable" (Einav et al., 2018, p. 1462).

- Patients and caregivers must accept death. Traditionally, entering a hospice meant the end of curative treatment (chemotherapy, dialysis, and so on). This is no longer true. Now treatment can continue. Many hospice patients survive for months, and some are discharged because they have recovered (Salpeter et al., 2012).

- Hospice care is costly. Skilled workers—doctors, nurses, psychologists, social workers, clergy, music therapists, and so on—provide individualized care day and night.

- Availability varies. Hospice care is more common in England than in mainland Europe and is a luxury in poor nations. In the United States, western states have more hospices than midwestern states do. Even in one region (northern California) and among clients of one insurance company (Kaiser), the likelihood that people with terminal cancer will enter hospice depends on exactly where they live (Keating et al., 2006).

THINK CRITICALLY: What are the possible reasons that fewer people in hospice are from non-European backgrounds?

Two principles characterize hospice care:

- Each patient's autonomy is respected. For example, pain medication is readily available, not on a schedule or set dosage.

- Family members and friends are counseled before the death, taught to provide care, and guided in mourning afterward. Death is thought to happen to a family, not just to an individual.

Hospice allows measures that hospitals may forbid: acupuncture, special foods, flexible schedules, visitors at midnight, excursions outside, massage, aromatic oils, religious rituals, and so on (Doka, 2013). Comfort takes precedence over cure, but that reduces stress and may extend life. Curative treatments are also allowed, although paying for them is complex.

About 20 percent of U.S. hospice patients are discharged alive, usually because they want more intensive care (many were admitted to a hospital), but one in every seven was discharged because their condition improved, and they were no longer likely to die soon (Russell et al., 2017).

Unfortunately, hospice does not reach everyone (see **Table 16.2**). It is more common in England than in mainland Europe, more common in the western part of the United States than the Southeast, and rare in poor nations.

Everywhere, hospice care correlates with higher income. Only recently have Medicare and Medicaid covered some hospice care, but if a person chooses hospice, payment for curative care may stop, and room and board expenses are not covered. Thus, in many regions, a poor person seeking hospice care must live at home and must agree that a cure is no longer possible.

Ethnic differences are apparent. For example, African Americans choose hospice about half as often as European Americans do. They are more likely to seek aggressive hospital care—which, ironically, means more pain and distress. One team suggests that African American churches should explain the spiritual benefits of hospice (Townsend et al., 2017).

Some private insurance policies pay for hospice *only* if a doctor certifies that the patient has less than six months to live, a judgment doctors are reluctant to render. One sad consequence: Hospice care usually begins within two weeks of death—too late for ideal personalized care.

 DATA CONNECTIONS: How Death Has Changed in the Last 100 Years presents several graphs that show increases in life expectancy over the past century while also addressing the importance of a "good death."

palliative care Medical treatment designed primarily to provide physical and emotional comfort to the dying patient and guidance to his or her loved ones.

Palliative Care

In 2006 the American Medical Association approved a new specialty, **palliative care**, which focuses on relieving pain and suffering. Palliative measures are not only for the dying; everyone may benefit. Palliative-care doctors prescribe powerful drugs and procedures that make patients comfortable, and they can treat nonlethal symptoms, such as rashes, muscle soreness, and nausea, with salves, foods, exercise, and meditation.

The benefits of palliative care are particularly clear for patients who are seriously ill. In one study, such patients were asked, "Which would you prefer?":

- Five more years of life, with three hospitalizations in the last two months and death in intensive care, with moderate pain and discomfort; OR
- Four more years of life, with one hospitalization in the last two months, to be discharged to die at home with mild pain and discomfort.

Almost all (86 percent) chose death at home (Rubin et al., 2020).

The need for skilled palliative care is obvious when one considers pain relief. Doctors hesitate to prescribe addictive opioids, yet high doses are the best way to mitigate severe pain from cancer, surgery, and other conditions. Morphine and other opiates have a **double effect**: They relieve pain (a positive effect), but slow down respiration (a negative effect). Laws and ethics require weighing pain reduction versus the hastening of death (Woods & Graven, 2020).

Indeed, almost any medical measure has several effects. Surgery itself removes or repairs something harmful, but causes pain, infection, and sometimes death. On the other hand, heavy sedation may delay death more than extend life, since an unconscious patient cannot think or feel. Is being unconscious, with no chance of recovery, worse than death itself?

double effect When an action (such as administering opiates) has both a positive effect (relieving a terminally ill person's pain) and a negative effect (hastening death by suppressing respiration).

Ethical Issues

As you see, medical successes create new dilemmas. Death is no longer the natural outcome of age and disease; when and how death occurs involves human choices. (See A Case to Study.)

Deciding When Death Occurs

One difficult ethical decision is deciding when a person is dead. This used to be simple: A person was dead when the heart stopped beating and the lungs no longer took in air. Now stopped hearts are restarted, breathing continues with respirators, feeding tubes provide calories, drugs fight pneumonia. At what point, if ever, should those interventions stop?

A CASE TO STUDY

What Is Your Intention?

The law focuses on intent: If a drug or surgery is intended to relieve suffering, then it is morally and legally justifiable if death occurs. Otherwise, it is not (Sulmasy, 2018).

However, people disagree as to whether a drug, or surgery, or any other medical measure is, on balance, more positive than negative. About half of all palliative care physicians have been accused of killing a patient. The accusation usually comes from a grief-stricken loved one, and then medical facts exonerate the doctors. Sometimes the accusation comes from another medical person, and judgment become more complicated.

Consider a court case. A man with terminal cancer was terrified of future pain and loss of control, so his doctor privately gave him a drug to take if he reached the point where he could not bear living. That man told another doctor, who accused the first doctor of

breaking the law as well as defying medical ethics. The first doctor argued that this was double effect: He was relieving the "existential suffering" of the patient (a positive effect), knowing that death might be the result (the negative effect). The first court found him guilty, but he appealed and was exonerated, because his intent was to stop the terror, not stop the life.

This troubled many others. One wrote:

> The offer to provide the drug was described as a palliative treatment in that it gave reassurance and comfort to the patient. Double effect reasoning was extended in this instance to encompass potentially facilitating a patient's death. This extension further muddies the murky double effect reasoning waters.
>
> *[Duckett, 2018, p. 33]*

Almost every life-threatening condition results in treatments started, stopped, or avoided, with death postponed, prevented, or welcomed. This has fostered impassioned moral arguments, between nations (evidenced by radically different laws) and within them.

Religious advisers, doctors, and lawyers disagree with colleagues within their respective professions; family members have opposite opinions; and people within each group diverge. For example, outsiders might imagine that all Roman Catholic leaders share the same views, but that is far from the truth (Bedford et al., 2017).

Evidence of Death

Historically, death was determined by listening to a person's chest: No heartbeat meant death. To make sure, a feather was put to the person's nose to indicate respiration—a person who had no heartbeat and did not exhale was pronounced dead. Very rarely, but widely publicized when it happened, death was declared when the person was still alive.

Modern medicine has changed that: Hearts and lungs need not function on their own. Many life-support measures and medical interventions circumvent the organ failures that once caused death. Checking breathing with feathers is a curiosity that, thankfully, is never used today.

But how do we know that a person is dead? The lungs and heart can be compelled to continue functioning with machines, even when the brain has ceased to function. It is possible for a person to appear dead but actually be *locked in*, that is, unable to communicate (see **Table 16.3**). Doctors are horrified about the possibility of taking someone off life support who might recover, but they are also troubled at keeping a heart beating artificially when the person is dead.

Accordingly, most nations of the world have standards that determine brain death. When details are compared, almost never is one national standard exactly like another: 78 different sets of standards and tests are used (Lewis et al., 2020).

Fortunately, recent international discussion has led to a broad consensus. A group of 45 experts from many nations defined death as "a complete and permanent loss of brain function as defined by an unresponsive coma with loss of capacity for consciousness, brainstem reflexes, and the ability to breathe independently." Nations differ in which, and how many, tests are used to determine brain death, including not only neurological evidence but also attempts to trigger a gag reflex, and to evoke some reaction of the eyes when touched (Greer et al., 2020).

Family members may cling to hope long after medical experts are convinced that recovery is impossible. Beyond the cost and psychic distress of this divide, people who want to donate their organs after death cannot do so if too much time elapses between brain death and procurement of the organs. Thus, standards need to be clearly defined, agreed on by medical and theological experts, and then communicated to the general public.

Euthanasia

Ethical dilemmas are particularly apparent with *euthanasia* (sometimes called *mercy-killing*). There are two kinds of euthanasia.

In **passive euthanasia**, a person near death is allowed to die. The person's medical chart may include a **DNR (do not resuscitate) order**, instructing medical staff not to restore breathing or restart the heart if breathing or pulsating stops.

THINK CRITICALLY: At what point, if ever, should intervention stop to allow death?

---

passive euthanasia When a seriously ill person is allowed to die naturally, without active attempts to prolong life.

DNR (do not resuscitate) order A written order from a physician (sometimes initiated by a patient's advance directive or by a health care proxy's request) that no attempt should be made to revive a patient if he or she suffers cardiac or respiratory arrest.

TABLE 16.3

Dead or Not? Yes, No, and Maybe

Brain death: Prolonged cessation of all brain activity with complete absence of voluntary movements; no spontaneous breathing; no response to pain, noise, and other stimuli. Brain waves have ceased; the electroencephalogram is flat; *the person is dead.*

Locked-in syndrome: The person cannot move, except for the eyes, but normal brain waves are still apparent; *the person is not dead.*

Coma: A state of deep unconsciousness from which the person cannot be aroused. Some people awaken spontaneously from a coma; others enter a vegetative state; *the person is not yet dead.*

Vegetative state: A state of deep unconsciousness in which all cognitive functions are absent, although eyes may open, sounds may be emitted, and breathing may continue; *the person is not yet dead.* The vegetative state can be *transient, persistent,* or *permanent.* No one has ever recovered after two years; most who recover (about 15 percent) improve within three weeks. After sufficient time has elapsed, the person may, effectively, be dead, although nations vary in how much time must elapse between lack of response and declaration of death (Lewis et al., 2020).

A more detailed version is the **POLST (physician-ordered life-sustaining treatment)**, which describes when antibiotics, feeding tubes, and so on should be used.

Passive euthanasia is legal everywhere, but many emergency personnel automatically start artificial respiration and stimulate hearts. POLSTs are not always followed as the doctor intended. About a third of the time, when a doctor has prescribed only comfort care, the hospital personnel nevertheless institute intensive, life-prolonging measures (Lee et al., 2020). Similarly, some patients and family members do not want passive euthanasia, but more often the opposite occurs: People want a peaceful death, but medical measures prolong life and pain.

Active euthanasia is deliberate action to cause death, such as turning off a respirator or giving a lethal drug. Some physicians accept active euthanasia when three conditions occur: (1) Suffering cannot be relieved, (2) the illness is incurable, and (3) the patient wants to die. Active euthanasia is legal in the Netherlands, Belgium, Luxembourg, Switzerland, Colombia, and Canada (each nation has different requirements) and illegal (but rarely prosecuted) elsewhere.

In every nation, some physicians would never perform active euthanasia (even in nations in which it is legal); but others have done so (even in nations where it is illegal). Acceptance of active euthanasia seems to be increasing among physicians. For example, in 1999 and again in 2015, hundreds of doctors in Finland were given the following situation:

> A 60-year-old male patient is suffering from prostatic cancer with metastases. Metastases in the thoracic spine led to total paraparesis [paralysis of the legs] 1 month earlier. There is no hope for a cure. The patient is well aware of the situation. He has totally lost his will to live. When you are together with him alone, he asks for a sufficient dose of morphine to "get away." You have denied the overdose, explaining that it is against your ethical principles. During the following days, you notice that the patient asks you to double his morphine dose because of unbearable pain. You suppose that increasing the dose in such a way would lead to the patient's death.

The doctors were asked, anonymously, what they would do. Most declined to give the deadly dose, but the percentage of those who would double the morphine increased over the 16 years, from 25 percent to 34 percent. Interestingly, rates were higher among older men than younger women (Piili et al., 2018). The thought is that if a doctor could identify with the man, they were more likely to do what he wanted.

Physician Help with Death

Between passive and active euthanasia is another option: A doctor may provide the means for patients to end their own lives in **physician-assisted suicide**, typically by prescribing lethal medication that a patient can choose to take when they are ready to die. Oregon was the first U.S. state to legalize this practice, asserting that such deaths are "death with dignity," not suicide. This practice is now legal in, Montana, Vermont, Colorado, Hawaii, Maine, New Jersey, California, and both the state and the city of Washington.

The Oregon law requires the following:

- The dying person must be an Oregon resident, over age 17.
- The dying person must request the lethal drugs three times, twice spoken and once in writing,
- Fifteen days must elapse between the first request and the prescription.
- Two physicians must confirm that the person is terminally ill, has less than six months to live, and is competent (i.e., not mentally impaired or depressed).

POLST (physician-ordered life-sustaining treatment) This is an order from a doctor regarding end of life care. It advises nurses and other medical staff which treatments (e.g., feeding, antibiotics, respirators) should be used and which not. It is similar to a living will, but it is written for medical professionals and thus is more specific.

active euthanasia When someone does something that hastens another person's death, with the intention of ending that person's suffering.

physician-assisted suicide A form of active euthanasia in which a doctor provides the means for someone to end his or her own life, usually by prescribing lethal drugs.

Too Late for Her When Brittany Maynard was diagnosed with progressive brain cancer that would render her unable to function before killing her, she moved from her native California to establish residence in Oregon so that she could die with dignity. A year later, the California Senate Health Committee debated a similar law, with Brittany's photo on a desk. They approved the law, 5–2.

TABLE 16.4

Oregon Residents' Reasons for Requesting Physician Assistance in Dying, 2018

Percent of Patients Giving Reason (most had several reasons)	
Less able to enjoy life	90
Loss of autonomy	87
Loss of dignity	72
Burden on others	59
Loss of control over body	39
Pain	33
Financial implications of treatment	7

Data from Oregon Public Health Division, 2020.

THINK CRITICALLY: Why would someone take all of the steps to obtain a lethal prescription and then not use it?

Even if all of this occurs, approval is not automatic. Only about one-third of the initial requests are granted.

Opposite opinions are deeply held. Some people believe that suicide can be noble. Buddhist monks publicly burned themselves to death to advocate Tibetan independence from China; one individual's suicide set off the Arab Spring; one terminally ill woman (Brittany Maynard) pleading to die changed the laws of California. (She moved to Oregon to die before the law changed.) Everywhere, some people die for the honor of their nation, their family, or themselves.

However, some religions oppose the practice. Physician-assisted suicide is anathema in Islamic nations; in North America, many people who consider themselves devout Christians are strongly opposed (Bulmer et al., 2017). In many U.S. states, dying with dignity laws have been proposed and defeated.

Pain: Physical and Psychological

The Netherlands has permitted active euthanasia since 1980. The patient must be clear and aware in making the request, and the goal is to halt "unbearable suffering" (Buiting et al., 2009). Dutch physicians first try to make the suffering bearable via medication.

The Netherlands' law was revised in 2002 to allow euthanasia not only when a person is terminally ill but also when a person is chronically ill and in pain. A qualitative analysis found that Dutch physicians considered "unbearable suffering" to include "fatigue, pain, decline, negative feelings, loss of self, fear of future suffering, dependency, loss of autonomy, being worn out, being a burden, loneliness, loss of all that makes life worth living, hopelessness, pointlessness and being tired of living" (Dees et al., 2011, p. 727).

Oregon residents also request lethal drugs primarily for psychological, not physiological, pain (see **Table 16.4**). That raises additional ethical questions, as Opposing Perspectives explains. Many people make a distinction between physical and psychological pain.

OPPOSING PERSPECTIVES

The "Right to Die"?

Some legal scholars believe that people have a right to choose their death, but others believe that the right to life forbids the right to die (Wicks, 2012). Indeed, some people fear that legalizing euthanasia or physician-assisted suicide creates a *slippery slope*, leading toward ending life for people who are disabled, poor, or non-White.

The data refute that concern. In Oregon and elsewhere, the oldest-old, the poor, and those of non-European heritage are *less* likely to use fatal prescriptions. In Oregon, almost everyone who chooses "death with dignity" is European American (97 percent), has health insurance, is educated (74 percent had some college), and has lived a long life (see **Figure 16.4**). Most died at home, with friends or family.

The number of Dutch people (again tilted toward those with higher SES) choosing euthanasia is increasing. Is this a slippery slope? Some people think so; others think it shows that people welcome a choice about dying.

Addressing the slippery-slope argument, a cancer specialist writes:

> To be forced to continue living a life that one deems intolerable when there are doctors who are willing either to end one's life or to assist one in ending one's own life, is an unspeakable violation of an individual's freedom to live — and to die — as he or she sees fit. Those who would deny patients a legal right to euthanasia or assisted suicide typically appeal to two arguments: a "slippery slope" argument, and an argument about the dangers of abuse. Both are scare tactics, the rhetorical force of which exceeds their logical strength.
>
> *[Benatar, 2011, p. 206]*

Not everyone agrees with that doctor. Might deciding to die be a sign of depression? Should physicians consult with a psychiatrist rather than prescribe lethal drugs (Finlay & George, 2011)? Declining ability to enjoy life was cited by 90 percent of Oregonians who requested physician-assisted suicide in 2019 (see Table 16.4). Is that sanity or depression?

Characteristics of Oregon Patients Who Chose to Die with Death With Dignity Act (DWDA) Medications—1998–2019*

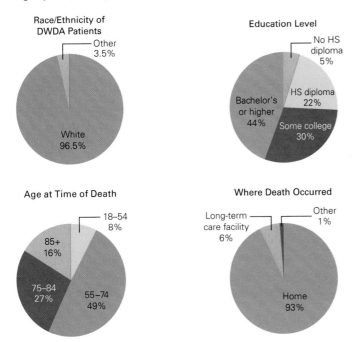

Data from Oregon Public Health Division, 2020.
*Percentages may not add up to 100% due to a small number of cases marked "unknown" in cited study.

FIGURE 16.4

Death with Dignity? The data do not suggest that people of low SES are unfairly pushed to die. Quite the opposite—people who choose physician-assisted suicide tend to be among the better-educated, more affluent citizens.

Might acceptance of death be mentally healthy in the old but not in the young? If only those over age 54 were allowed the right to die, that would exclude 8 percent of Oregonians who opted to die with dignity. Might age-based restrictions an example of reverse ageism, in that an age cutoff assumes that the young are not capable of choice, but that life matters less for the old?

In 2019, 290 Oregonians obtained lethal prescriptions, and 188 legally used drugs to die. Most of the others died naturally, but some were alive in January 2020, keeping the drugs for possible future use (in the past, about 10 percent used their prescriptions the year after obtaining them). These numbers have increased every year: Only 16 died with physician assistance in 1998.

An increase is also evident in the Netherlands, where some form of euthanasia accounted for about 1 in 50 deaths when the law was first in place but 1 in 25 deaths in 2019. Some might interpret these data as evidence of a slippery slope; others see it as proof that the law is useful, allowing both the 4 percent and the 96 percent to die as they wish.

There is another argument against physician-assisted suicide: It distracts from care for the dying. In the words of one doctor:

> We still need to deal with the problem that confronts most dying patients: how to get optimal symptom relief, and how to avoid the hospital and stay at home in the final weeks. Legalizing euthanasia and PAS is really a sideshow in end-of-life care—championed by the few for the few, extensively covered by the media, but not targeted to improve the care for most dying patients who still suffer.
> [Emanuel, 2017]

Could a law designed to allow death with dignity actually undercut death with dignity? A position statement from the International Association of Hospice and Palliative Care says:

> [N]o country or state should consider the legalization of euthanasia or PAS until it ensures universal access to palliative care services and to appropriate medications, including opioids for pain and dyspnea.
> [De Lima et al., 2017, p. 8]

Since no state or nation has "universal access to palliative care," by that standard, no nation is ready to offer physician-assisted suicide. A contrary opinion is evident in Canada, where its Supreme Court unanimously approved physician-assisted suicide after the Canadian Medical Association withdrew their objection to it (Attaran, 2015).

Since then, the Canadian experience has been similar to Oregon: Canadians who obtained physician-assisted suicide tended to be more educated and wealthier than other dying Canadians (Downar et al., 2020). That leads to a new question: Is physician-assisted suicide less available to those of low SES?

Advance Directives

Recognizing that people differ, many professionals hope everyone has **advance directives**. A person can specify desired medical treatment, where and how death occurs, what should happen to the body (cremation or burial, traditional or "green"), and details of the funeral or memorial.

The legality of such directives varies by jurisdiction: Sometimes a lawyer must ensure that documents are legal; sometimes a written request, signed and witnessed, is adequate. (A website, PREPAREforyourcare.org, is keyed to each state.)

Many people approve of personal choice and advance directives in theory, but they are uncertain about specifics, which vary because of other circumstances. For example, restarting the heart may extend life for decades in a young, healthy adult but may cause a major neurocognitive disorder in an older person. Is it fair to continue life while damaging the mind?

advance directives Any description of what a person wants to happen as they die and after death. This can include medical measures, visitors, funeral arrangements, cremation, and so on.

Adding to the dilemma is that predictions are not definitive. It is hard to know in advance when artificial feeding, breathing, or heart stimulation results in only a temporary respite, or when antibiotics or pain medication causes irreversible coma, terrifying hallucinations, or permanent damage. Even if this is known, people make opposite choices.

Wills and Proxies

Advance directives often include a living will and/or a health care proxy. A **living will** indicates what medical intervention is desired if a person is unable to express preferences. (If the person is conscious, hospital personnel ask about each specific procedure, often requiring written consent. Patients who are lucid can override any instructions of their living will.)

Why would anyone override their own earlier wishes? Because living wills include phrases such as "incurable," "reasonable chance of recovery," and "extraordinary measures," and it is difficult to know what those phrases mean until a specific issue arises. Even then, doctors and family members disagree about what is "extraordinary" or "reasonable."

A **health care proxy** is another person delegated to make medical decisions if someone becomes unable to do so. That seems logical, but unfortunately neither a living will nor a health care proxy guarantees that medical care will be exactly what a person would choose.

For one thing, proxies often find it difficult to allow a loved one to die, unless the living will demands it. A larger problem is that few people — experts included — understand the risks, benefits, and alternatives to every medical procedure. That makes it difficult to decide when the risks outweigh the benefits.

Medical professionals know that advance directives are not simple. As one couple wrote:

> Working within the reality of mortality, coming to death is then an inevitable part of life, an event to be lived rather than a problem to be solved. Ideally, we would live the end of our life from the same values that have given meaning to the story of our life up to that time. But in a medical crisis, there is little time, language, or ritual to guide patients and families in conceptualizing or expressing their values and goals.
>
> [Farber & Farber, 2014, p. 109]

living will A document that indicates what medical intervention an individual prefers if he or she is not conscious when a decision is to be expressed. For example, some do not want mechanical breathing.

health care proxy A person chosen to make medical decisions if a patient is unable to do so, as when in a coma.

ESPECIALLY FOR People Without Advance Directives Why do very few young adults have advance directives? (see response, page 494)

WHAT HAVE YOU LEARNED?

1. What is a good death?
2. What are Kübler-Ross's five stages of dying, and why doesn't everyone agree with them?
3. What determines whether or not a person will receive hospice care?
4. Why is the double effect legal, even though it speeds death?
5. How is it determined that death has occurred?
6. What is the difference between passive and active euthanasia?
7. What are the four prerequisites of "death with dignity" in Oregon?
8. Why would a person who has a living will also need a health care proxy?

Affirmation of Life

Human relationships are life sustaining, but all adults lose someone they love. Grief and mourning are part of living.

Grief

Grief is the powerful sorrow felt after a profound loss, especially when a loved one dies. Grief is deep and personal, an anguish that can overtake daily life.

Normal Grief

Grief is normal, even when it includes odd actions and thoughts. The specifics vary from person to person, but uncontrollable sobbing, sleeplessness, and irrational and delusional thoughts are common (Doka, 2016).

Sheryl Sandberg described her grief a year after her husband died:

> I was swallowed up in the deep fog of grief—what I think of as the void. An emptiness that fills your heart and your lungs, constricts your ability to think, or even to breathe.
>
> [Sandberg & UC Berkeley, 2016, 05:07–05:19]

Joan Didion remembers her reaction after her husband's sudden death. She refused the offers of her friends to come stay with her:

> Grief has no distance. Grief comes in waves, paroxysms, sudden apprehensions that weaken the knees and blind the eyes and obliterate the dailiness of life. . . . I see now that my insistence on spending that first night alone was more complicated than it seemed, a primitive instinct. . . . There was a level on which I believed that what had happened remained reversible. . . . I needed to be alone so that he could come back.
>
> [Didion, 2005, pp. 27, 32, 33]

When a loved one dies, loneliness, denial, anger, and sorrow come in sudden torrents. Many people want some time alone, yet everyone also needs to be with other people, because other people are a reminder that life continues. Grief typically hits hardest in the first week, but unexpected rushes can occur months or years later.

VIDEO: Bereavement: Grief in Early and Late Adulthood presents the views of a young-adult daughter and middle-aged mother on the death of the mother's brother, to whom they were both close.

Complicated Grief

Sometimes grief festers, becoming what is called **complicated grief**, impeding life over a long period. The DSM-IV had a "bereavement exclusion," stating that major depression could not be diagnosed within two months of a death, but DSM-5 changed that. Major depression can begin soon after someone dies (LeBlanc et al., 2019).

Depression may begin with **absent grief**, when a bereaved person does not seem to grieve. This is a common first reaction, but ongoing unexpressed grief can trigger physical or psychological symptoms, such as trouble breathing, panic attacks, or crippling sorrow.

Another kind of complicated grief is **disenfranchised grief**, "not merely unnoticed, forgotten, or hidden; it is socially disallowed and unsupported" (Corr & Corr, 2013b, p. 135). Some people experience deep grief but are forbidden by social norms to express it.

For instance, often only a current spouse or close blood relative is legally allowed to decide on funeral arrangements, disposal of the body, and other matters. This made sense when all family members were close, but it may now result in "gagged grief and beleaguered bereavement" (Green & Grant, 2008, p. 275).

Sometimes a longtime but unmarried partner is excluded, especially when the partner is of the same sex (Curtin & Garrison, 2018). Relatives, especially those who live far away, may not know who are the deceased person's friends. Thus, some mourners are disenfranchised—not informed about the funeral, unable to grieve with fellow mourners.

incomplete grief When circumstances, such as a police investigation or an autopsy, interfere with the process of grieving.

Incomplete Grief

Grief is a process, usually intense at first, diminishing over time, and eventually reaching closure. Customs such as viewing the dead, or throwing dirt on the grave, or scattering ashes, all allow expression and then closure. However, many circumstances can interfere, creating **incomplete grief**.

Traumatic death is always unexpected, and then denial, anger, and depression undercut the emotions of grief (Kauffman, 2013). Murders and suicides often trigger police, judges, and the press, so mourners who need time to grieve instead must answer questions. An autopsy may prevent grief if someone believes that the body will rise or that the soul remains in the body.

Inability to recover a body, as with soldiers who are missing in action or with victims of a major flood or fire, may prevent grief from being expressed and thereby hinder completion. That explains why, after destruction of the World Trade Center on 9/11, when DNA identified a fragment of bone, families often had a funeral and burial to allow grieving.

In natural or human-caused disasters such as hurricanes and wars, incomplete grief is common, because survival — food, shelter, medical care — takes precedence. In the days and weeks after disasters, the death rate of causes not directly attributable to the trauma increases, as people suffer from the indifference of others and of their own diminished self-care.

Those hundreds of thousands of Americans who lost a loved one to COVID-19 often speak of the circumstances of the death, specifically their inability to visit their family member, and of the tragedy of the person dying alone. The mourners may have been more troubled by the circumstances than by the death itself: In any case, the unmet psychological needs of everyone are part of the long legacy of the virus.

A team of four physicians describes a woman who tried desperately to see her dying husband. In the hours before his death, she went through all five of Kübler-Ross's stages, including anger (threatening a lawsuit), then bargaining, pleading "for just five minutes." She was rejected at every turn. Her wail when he died alone led the doctors to call for some compassionate solution, perhaps via telemedicine, that recognizes the needs of both patient and mourners (Wakam et al., 2020).

The reality that grief is a process suggests that other people should not try to cut it short or prescribe its course. No one should tell parents who lost a baby that "You never knew that baby; you can have another," or pet owners that "It was only a cat," or those with aged relatives that "It was time for them to die." All that may ring true for outsiders, but loss rings louder than logic. Each grief has its own expressions; others should not decide what is appropriate (Doka, 2016).

People who live and work where no one knows their personal lives may lack customs to help them grieve. The laws of some nations — China, Chile, and Spain, for example — mandate paid bereavement leave, but this is not true in the United States (Meagher, 2013).

Indeed, for workers at large corporations or students in universities, grief may become "an unwelcome intrusion (or violent intercession) into the normal efficient running of everyday life" (M. Anderson, 2001, p. 141). Many college professors (me included) wish students would not miss classes or delay assignments because of a death. I may be wrong. My rationale is that people should not be stopped by death, and that activity aids recovery. But I know that incomplete grief impedes recovery, and that my path is mine, not everyone else's.

Rest in Peace? COVID-19 not only disrupted life for everyone, it also disrupted death. Here, Brazilians are about to be buried in a mass grave after dying alone. Many of the living are as troubled by their exclusion from the bedside and the grave as they are by the loss of a loved one.

MICHAEL DANTAS/AFP via Getty Images

Mourning

Grief splinters people into jumbled pieces, making them vulnerable. Mourning reassembles them, making them whole again and able to rejoin the larger community. To be more specific, **mourning** is the public and ritualistic expression of bereavement, the ceremonies and behaviors that a religion or culture prescribes to honor the dead and allow recovery in the living.

How Mourning Helps

Mourning customs are a buffer between normal and complicated grief. That is needed because the grief-stricken are vulnerable to irrational thoughts and self-destructive acts. Some eat too little or drink too much; some forget caution as they drive or even as they walk across the street. Physical and mental health dips in the recently bereaved; the rate of suicide increases.

Sometimes death continues to impact life years later. The death of a child is particularly hard on the parents, who need each other but, in the irrationality of grief, may blame each other. Years after the loss of a child, illness and death rates of parents rise (Brooten et al., 2018).

A large study in Sweden found that adults whose brother or sister died long ago were more likely to die than other Swedes their age. This was true no matter how the sibling died, but if suicide was the cause, adult survivors were three times more likely to die by suicide than were other Swedes of the same age and background (Rostila et al., 2013).

Similarly, after the suicide of a celebrity, rates rise for ordinary people. This alerts us that shared mourning is especially important when suicide occurs. Survivors tend to blame themselves, feel angry at the deceased, or consider following the example. Outsiders may stay away because they do not know what to say. All of this adds difficulty to expressions of grief and rituals of mourning, yet both are especially crucial.

Many customs are designed to help people move from grief toward reaffirmation. For example, eulogies emphasize the dead person's good qualities; people who did not personally know the deceased attend wakes, funerals, or memorial services to comfort the survivors.

Public expression of grief channels and contains private grief. Examples include the Jewish custom of sitting shiva at home for a week and then walking around the block to signify a return to life, or the three days of active sorrow among some Muslim groups, or the 10 days of ceremonies beginning at the next full moon following a Hindu death. In many cultures, the continuity of life is symbolized by flowers, or ashes, or long-lasting candle flames, or a baby named after a dead person. Many cultures set a day aside each year to honor the dead.

One example of cultural differences compares individualistic cultures (e.g., the United States and Western Europe) and community cultures (e.g., most Asian and African cultures). In an individualistic culture, the person is memorialized, and mourners take action—with gravestones, black armbands, and so on to remember that particular person. A photo is framed and placed where everyone can see it.

By contrast, Asians see people as interdependent. Therefore, mourning is a family and group event, when a dead person joins the ancestors, reflecting continuity over the generations (Valentine, 2017). A family area is designated for all the ancestors.

The Western practice of building a memorial, dedicating a plaque, or naming a location for a dead person is antithetical to some Eastern cultures. Indeed, some Asian cultures believe that the spirit should be allowed to rest in peace, and thus all possessions, signs, and other evidence of a particular dead person are removed after proper prayers.

mourning The ceremonies and behaviors that a religion or culture prescribes for people to express their grief after a death.

Honor Your Father Worldwide, children mourn their deceased parents by performing rituals developed by their community, as these four young men do while they spread ashes in the sea. Some secular adults, born and raised in Western Europe or North America, fly thousands of miles back to India with their Hindu fathers' ashes, comforted by thus respecting their heritage.

dbimages/Alamy Stock Photo

John Moore/Getty Images

The Human Touch Benetha Coleman fights Ebola in this treatment center by taking temperatures, washing bodies, and drawing blood, but she also comforts those with symptoms. Why would anyone risk working here? Benetha has recovered from Ebola, and, like many survivors of a disaster, she wants to help others who suffer.

THINK CRITICALLY: Do you think current wars are fueled by a misguided impulse to assign blame?

This created a cultural clash when terrorist bombs in Bali killed 38 Indonesians and 164 foreigners (mostly Australian and British). The Indonesians prayed intensely and then destroyed all reminders; the Australians raised money to build a memorial (de Jonge, 2011). Indonesian officials posed many obstacles to prevent construction; the Australians were frustrated; the memorial was never built. Neither group understood the deep emotions of the other.

Growth After Death

In recent decades, many people everywhere have become less religiously devout, and mourning practices are now less ritualized. Has death become a source of despair, not hope? Maybe not. People worldwide become more spiritual when confronted with death (Lattanzi-Licht, 2013).

If the dead person was a public figure, mourners may include thousands, even millions. They express their sorrow to one another, stare at photos, and listen to music that reminds them of the dead person, weeping as they watch funerals on television. Mourners often pledge to affirm the best of the deceased, forgetting any criticisms that they might have had in the past.

Some observers suggest that mourning can lead people to *posttraumatic growth* (the opposite of posttraumatic stress disorder, or PTSD) (Tedeschi et al., 2017). As you remember, Kübler-Ross found that reactions to death eventually lead to acceptance. Finding meaning may be crucial to the reaffirmation that follows grief. In some cases, this search starts with preserving memories: Displaying photographs and personal effects and telling anecdotes about the deceased person are central to many memorial services in the United States.

Organizations that are devoted to combating a particular problem (such as breast cancer or AIDS) find their most dedicated donors, demonstrators, and advocates among people who have lost a loved one to that specific danger. That also explains why, when someone dies, survivors often designate a charity that is connected to the deceased. Then mourners contribute, hoping the death has led to good.

Placing Blame and Seeking Meaning

A common impulse after death is for the survivors to assess blame—for medical measures not taken, for laws not enforced, for unhealthy habits not changed. The bereaved sometimes blame the dead person, sometimes themselves, and sometimes others. Blame is especially common when death is unexpected: It is a human reaction to the question "why?"

The medical establishment is often blamed. In November 2011, Michael Jackson's personal doctor, Conrad Murray, was found guilty and jailed for prescribing the drugs that led to the singer's death. Many fans and family members cheered at the verdict; Murray was one of the few who blamed Jackson, not himself.

In 2018, the doctor who prescribed painkillers to Prince was fined $30,000, but he was not prosecuted because he was not the source of the illegal drugs that killed Prince. Many of Prince's friends knew about his addiction: They blamed themselves and each other.

In 2020, over a million people worldwide died of COVID-19. Who to blame? Every nation blamed outsiders. U.S. President Trump blamed the Chinese, not his own policies. A woman whose father died said "his only preexisting condition was trusting Trump." The fact that African Americans died at twice the rate of others is blamed by some on systemic racism and the ideology of caste (Wilkerson, 2020). Others blamed health habits that increased rates of conditions known to worsen the effects of COVID-19.

For public tragedies, nations accuse one another. Blame is not rational or proportional to guilt. For instance, outrage at the assassination of Archduke

Francis Ferdinand of Austria by a lone Serbian terrorist in 1914 provoked a conflict between Austria and Serbia—soon joined by a dozen other nations—that led to the four years and 16 million deaths of World War I.

When death occurs from a major disaster, survivors often seek to honor the memory of the dead. Many people believe that Israel would not have been created without the Holocaust, or that same-sex marriage would not have been be legalized if the AIDS epidemic had not occurred.

Mourners often resolve to bring those responsible to justice. Blame can land on many people. After 17 people died in a gun massacre at a high school in Parkland, Florida, surviving students accused adults of not curbing the National Rifle Association (NRA), and they successfully persuaded major companies to discontinue discounts for NRA members. Florida enacted a law to raise the age for gun purchase to 21 and to require a wait period before a person can buy a gun. The NRA opposed that law, and the students thought it did not go far enough.

The search for blame in Parkland included:

- the school resource officer who stayed outside during the shooting,
- the mental health workers who did not hospitalize the gunman,
- the design of the school classrooms that made killing easier,
- the specifics of gun manufacture (e.g., assault weapons, bump stocks),
- the sheriff,
- the FBI,
- the school superintendent (who almost was fired),
- the Republican president (Trump),
- the former Democratic president (Obama).

Childish Response? The survivors of the high school shooting in Parkland, Florida, sparked a nationwide protest against the National Rifle Association and the lawmakers and corporations who support it. Are these protestors in Washington, D.C., naive?

Humans seek to blame someone—and the response may not be logical. The students who became spokespeople for gun laws were both lauded and derided.

Ideally, counselors, politicians, and clergy can steer grief-stricken survivors toward beneficial ends. That may have happened in 2015, when a gunman killed nine people in a prayer group at Emanuel African Methodist Episcopal Church in Charleston, South Carolina. Some people noted that the killer identified with the Confederate soldiers who fought in the Civil War.

Within a month, the state Senate voted to remove the Confederate flag from the center of Charleston, and major retailers stopped selling that flag. The church members chose forgiveness.

Those church members may have had the right idea. When homicides occur, some family members want revenge, and others forgive. More generally, some people forgive the dead for past misdeeds rather than blaming them, a practice more likely to lead to psychological well-being (Gassin et al., 2017). Ideally, irrational blame subsides, and mourners reach a deep awareness of the root cause of a death, resolving to prevent it in the future.

Diversity of Reactions

As you see, the specifics of bereavement and blame vary. Social scientists hesitate to claim that one particular reaction is best. Culture matters. Should mourners keep the dead person's possessions, talk to the deceased, and frequently review memories? Maybe, or maybe not. Those practices correlate with worse adjustment in the United States but better adjustment in China (Lalande & Bonanno, 2006).

Past experiences affect bereavement. Children who lost their parents might be more distraught decades later when someone else dies. Past attachment also

In **VIDEO: Bereavement and Grief: Late Adulthood**, people discuss their experiences with the loss of beloved family members and friends—and all agree that these losses have been very difficult experiences.

AP Photo/The Daily News. Todd Maisel, Pool

She Didn't Forget Eleven years after planes crashed into the World Trade Center, the field in Pennsylvania, and the Pentagon, killing 2,977 innocent people, several memorial ceremonies were held. Alice Watkins attended one of them to remember a friend who died. Are continuing bonds an expression of our connection to heritage and history, or a sign that some people are stuck in the past?

continuing bonds The ongoing attachment and connection that the living have with the dead. Currently, continuing bonds are considered common and often beneficial.

matters (Kosminsky, 2017). Older adults who were securely attached as children are likely to experience normal grief; those whose attachment was insecure-avoidant are likely to have absent grief; and those who were insecure-resistant may become stuck, focusing on blame, unable to reaffirm their own lives.

Continuing Bonds

Reaffirmation does not mean forgetting; **continuing bonds** are evident years after death (Klass & Steffen, 2017; Stroebe et al., 2012). Such bonds are memories and connections that link the living and the dead. They may help or hinder ongoing life, depending on past relationship to the dead person and on the circumstances of death. Often survivors write letters or talk to the deceased person, or consider events — a sunrise, a butterfly, a rainstorm — as messages of comfort.

Bereavement theory once held an "unquestioned assumption" that mourners should grieve and then move on, accepting that the dead person is gone forever (Neimeyer, 2017). It was thought that if this progression did not take place, pathological grief could result, with the person either not grieving enough (absent grief) or grieving too long (incomplete grief).

But now a much wider variety of reactions are recognized. Continuing bonds are not only normal but, as one researcher notes, the "centrality of relations between the living and the dead" is helpful to the mourner and to everyone else (Neimeyer, 2017).

A bereaved person *might or might not* want to visit the grave, light a candle, cherish a memento, pray, or sob. Mourners may want time alone or may want company. Those who have been taught to bear grief stoically may be distressed if a friend advises them to cry but they cannot. Conversely, those whose cultures expect loud wailing may resent being told to hush.

Don't Assume

Assumptions arising from one culture or religion might be inaccurate; people's reactions about death and hope vary for many reasons. One example came from a 13-year-old girl who refused to leave home after her 17-year-old brother was shot dead on his way to school. The therapist was supposed to get her to go to school again.

> It would have been easy to assume that she was afraid of dying on the street, and to arrange for a friend to accompany her on her way to school. But careful listening revealed the real reason she stayed home: She worried that her depressed mother might kill herself if she were left alone.
>
> [Crenshaw, 2013]

To help the daughter, the mother had to be helped.

No matter what fears arise, what rituals are followed, or what grief entails, mourning gives the living a deeper appreciation of themselves and others. In fact, a theme frequently sounded by those who work with the dying and the bereaved is that death leads to a greater appreciation of life, especially of the value of intimate, caring relationships.

It is fitting to end this book with a reminder of the creative work of living. As first described in **Chapter 1**, the study of human development is a science, with topics to be researched, understood, and explained.

But the process of living is an art as well as a science, with strands of love and sorrow woven into each person's unique tapestry. Death, when it leads to hope; dying, when it is accepted; blame, when it leads to prevention; and grief, when it fosters affirmation — all add meaning to birth, growth, development, and love.

SUMMARY

Death and Hope

1. In ancient times, death connected the living, the dead, and the spirit world. People respected the dead and tried to live their lives so that their own death and afterlife would be good.

2. Every modern religion includes rituals and beliefs about death. These vary a great deal, but all bring hope to the living and strengthen the community.

3. Death has various meanings, depending partly on the age of the person involved. For example, young children want companionship; older children want to know specifics of death.

4. Terror management theory finds that many adults cope with death anxiety by defiantly doing whatever is risky. In adulthood, people tend to worry about leaving something undone or abandoning family members; older adults are more accepting of death.

Choices in Dying

5. A death that is painless and that comes at the end of a long life may be more possible currently than a century ago. However, other aspects of a good death—quick, at home, surrounded by loved ones—are less likely than in earlier times.

6. The emotions of people who are dying change over time. Some may move from denial to acceptance, although stages of dying are much more variable than originally proposed. Honest conversation helps many, but not all, dying persons.

7. Hospice caregivers meet the biological and psychological needs of terminally ill people and their families. Comfort is prioritized over cure, especially when attempts to cure prolong suffering and keep families away.

8. Palliative care relieves pain and suffering. This is now an important part of care in most hospitals and every hospice.

9. Drugs that reduce pain may decrease breathing, producing a double effect. That is legal everywhere. However, euthanasia and physician-assisted suicide are controversial. Several nations and U.S. states allow some forms of these; most do not.

10. Since 1980, death has been defined as occurring when brain waves stop; however, many measures now prolong life when no conscious thinking occurs.

11. Advance directives, such as a living will and a health care proxy, are recommended for everyone. However, no one can anticipate the specifics of possible interventions. Family members as well as professionals and nations often disagree.

Affirmation of Life

12. Grief is overwhelming sorrow. It may be irrational and complicated, absent, disenfranchised, or incomplete.

13. Mourning rituals channel human grief, helping people move to affirm life. Specifics vary by culture and cohort. Everywhere, bereavement is a community experience, not borne by the individual alone. COVID-19 makes this more difficult, as people die alone and family members are kept away.

14. The impulse to blame someone for an unexpected death is a common human reaction. Ideally that leads to a better understand of causes and prevention of future harm. Posttraumatic growth is possible.

15. Continuing bonds with the deceased are no longer thought to be pathological. Past attachment history affects how a person responds to death.

KEY TERMS

terror management theory (p. 475)
hospice (p. 479)
palliative care (p. 480)
double effect (p. 481)
passive euthanasia (p. 482)

DNR (do not resuscitate) order (p. 482)
POLST (physician-ordered life-sustaining treatment) (p. 483)
active euthanasia (p. 483)

physician-assisted suicide (p. 483)
advance directives (p. 485)
living will (p. 486)
health care proxy (p. 486)
grief (p. 487)

complicated grief (p. 487)
absent grief (p. 487)
disenfranchised grief (p. 487)
incomplete grief (p. 488)
mourning (p. 489)
continuing bonds (p. 492)

APPLICATIONS

1. The text recommends that everyone should have a health care proxy and a living will. Ask 10 people if they have these, and why or why not. Analyze the reasons—including your own.

2. Find quotes about death in *Bartlett's Familiar Quotations* or a similar collection that includes many centuries and cultures. Do you see any historical or cultural patterns of acceptance, denial, or fear?

3. People of varying ages have different attitudes toward death. Ask someone younger than 20, someone between 20 and 60, and someone over 60 what thoughts they have about their own death. What differences do you find?

ESPECIALLY FOR ANSWERS

Response for Relatives of a Person Who Is Dying (from p. 478): Death affects the entire family, including children and grandchildren. I learned this myself when my mother was dying. A hospice nurse not only administered my mother's pain medication (which made it easier for me to be with her) but also counseled me. At the nurse's suggestion, I asked for forgiveness. My mother indicated that there was nothing to forgive. We both felt a peace that would have eluded us without hospice care.

Response for People Without Advance Directives (from p. 486): Young adults tend to avoid thinking realistically about their own deaths. This attitude is emotional, not rational. The actual task of preparing the documents may be easy (the forms can be downloaded; no lawyer is needed). Young adults have no trouble doing other future-oriented things, such as getting a tetanus shot or enrolling in a pension plan.

OBSERVATION QUIZ ANSWERS

Answer to Observation Quiz (from p. 474): The chief mourners are wearing white (unlike the others) and the grandmother has red roses—a luxury often reserved for weddings and funerals.

Answer to Observation Quiz (from p. 479): Touch. That is why the exclusion of family when a patient has COVID-19 is so devastating for the dying and the family.

More About Research Methods

This appendix explains how to learn about any topic. One of the most important lessons from the recent COVID-19 pandemic is that we need accurate information, reported honestly and analyzed carefully, to protect our mental and physical health. Science is essential to keep speculation and wishful thinking from destroying us.

Remember that almost no conclusion is entirely certain, now and forever. That is why the scientific method requires testing every hypothesis, basing conclusions on evidence, and reporting methods and statistics so that others can confirm, dispute, and replicate.

One of the most important aspects is in the selection of the participants in a study. Ideally, they are diverse in gender, ethnicity, race, and economic background, but if not, the biases and limitations of a restricted sample must be acknowledged.

Beyond that, when doing research connected with your own study in learning about human development, here are several suggestions.

Make It Personal

Think about your life, observe your behavior, and watch the people around you. Pay careful attention to details of expression, emotion, and behavior. The more you see, the more fascinated, curious, and reflective you will become. Ask questions and listen carefully and respectfully to what other people say regarding development.

Whenever you ask specific questions as part of an assignment, remember that observing ethical standards (see Chapter 1) comes first. *Before* you interview anyone, inform the person of your purpose and assure them of confidentiality. Promise not to identify the person in your report (use a pseudonym), and do not repeat any personal details that emerge in the interview to anyone (friends or strangers). Your instructor will provide further ethical guidance. If you might publish what you've learned, get in touch with your college's Institutional Review Board (IRB).

Read the Research

No matter how deeply you think about your own experiences, and no matter how intently you listen to others whose background is unlike yours, you also need to read scholarly published work in order to fully understand any topic that interests you. Be skeptical about magazine or newspaper reports; some are bound to be simplified, exaggerated, or biased.

Professional Journals and Books

Part of the process of science is that conclusions are not considered solid until they are corroborated in many studies, which means that you should consult several sources on any topic. Five journals in human development are:

- *Developmental Psychology* (published by the American Psychological Association)
- *Child Development* (Society for Research in Child Development)
- *Developmental Review* (Elsevier)
- *Human Development* (Karger)
- *Developmental Science* (Wiley)

These journals differ in the types of articles and studies they publish, but all are well respected and peer-reviewed, which means that other scholars review each article submitted and recommend that it be accepted, rejected, or revised. Every article includes references to other recent work.

Also look at journals that specialize in longer reviews from the perspective of a researcher.

- *Child Development Perspectives* (from Society for Research in Child Development)
- *Perspectives on Psychological Science* (This is published by the Association for Psychological Science. APS publishes several excellent journals, none specifically on development but every issue has at least one article that is directly relevant.)

Beyond these seven are literally thousands of other professional journals, each with a particular perspective or topic, including many in sociology, family studies, economics, medicine, demography, education, and more. To judge them, look for journals that are peer-reviewed. Also consider the following details: the background of the author (research funded by corporations tends to favor their products); the nature of the publisher (professional organizations, as in the first two journals above, protect their reputations); and how long the journal has been published (the volume number tells you that). Some interesting work does not meet these criteria, so be careful before believing what you read.

Many *books* cover some aspect of development. Single-author books are likely to present only one viewpoint. That view may be insightful, but it is limited. You might consult a *handbook*, which is a book that includes many authors and many topics. One good handbook in development, now in its seventh edition (a sign that past scholars have found it useful) is:

- *Handbook of Child Psychology and Developmental Science* (7th ed.), edited by Richard M. Lerner, 2015, Hoboken, NJ: Wiley.
- Another set of handbooks—*Handbook of the Biology of Aging, Handbook of the Psychology of Aging,* and *Handbook of Aging and the Social Sciences*—is now in its eighth edition, published by the Academic Press in 2016.

Both of these handbooks are updated about every five years, so a new edition might be out soon. Check on it, and use the newest one. Dozens of other good handbooks are available, many of which focus on a particular age, perspective, or topic.

The Internet

The *internet* is a mixed blessing, useful to every novice and experienced researcher but dangerous as well. Every library worldwide and most homes in North America, Western Europe, and East Asia have computers that provide access to journals and other information. If you're doing research in a library, ask for help from the librarians; many of them can guide you in the most effective ways to conduct online searches. In addition, other students, friends, and even strangers can be helpful.

Virtually everything is on the internet, not only massive national and international statistics but also accounts of very personal experiences. Photos, charts, quizzes, ongoing experiments, newspapers from around the world, videos, and much more are available at a click. Every journal has a website, with tables of contents, abstracts, and sometimes full texts. (An abstract gives the key findings; for the full text, most colleges and universities have access. Again, ask librarians for help.)

Unfortunately, you can spend many frustrating hours sifting through information that is useless, tangential, or trash. *Directories* (which list general topics or areas and then move you step by step in the direction you choose) and *search engines* (which give you all the sites that use a particular word or words) can help you select appropriate information. Each directory or search engine provides somewhat different lists; none provides only the most comprehensive and accurate sites. Sometimes organizations pay, or find other ways, to make their links appear first, even though they are biased. With experience and help, you will find quality on the internet, but you will also encounter some junk no matter how experienced you are.

Anybody can put anything online, regardless of its truth or fairness, so you need a very critical eye. Make sure you have several divergent sources for every "fact" you find; consider who provided the information and why. Every controversial issue has sites that forcefully advocate opposite viewpoints, sometimes with biased statistics and narrow perspectives.

Here are four internet sites that are quite reliable:

- *childtrends.org* A leading U.S. research organization focusing on improving children's lives. Their site contains a wealth of data and evidence-based research.
- *childdevelopmentinfo.com* Child Development Institute. A useful site, with links and articles on child development and information on common childhood psychological disorders.
- *eric.ed.gov* Education Resources Information Center (ERIC). Provides links to many education-related sites and includes brief descriptions of each.
- *www.cdc.gov/nchs/hus.htm* The National Center for Health Statistics issues an annual report on health trends, called *Health, United States.*

Every source—you, your interviewees, journals, books, and the internet—is helpful. Do not depend on any particular one. Avoid plagiarism and prejudice by citing every source and noting objectivity, validity, and credibility. Your own analysis, opinions, words, and conclusions are crucial, backed up by science.

Additional Terms and Concepts

As emphasized throughout the text, the study of development is a science. Social scientists spend years in graduate school, studying methods and statistics. Chapter 1 touches on some of these matters (observation and experiments, correlation and causation, independent and dependent variables; experimental and control groups; cross-sectional, longitudinal, and cross-sequential research), but there is much more. A few additional aspects of research are presented here to help you evaluate research wherever you find it.

Who Participates?

The entire group of people about whom a scientist wants to learn is called a **population**. Generally, a research population is quite large—not usually the world's entire population of more than 7 billion, but for statistics on birthweight or unwed mothers of all of the 3,788,235 babies born in the United States in 2019.

The particular individuals who are studied in a specific research project are called the **participants**. They are usually a **sample** of the population. Ideally, the participants are a **representative sample**, that is, a sample that reflects the population. Every peer-reviewed, published study reports details on the sample.

Selection of the sample is crucial. People who volunteer, or people who have telephones, or people who have some particular condition are not a *random sample*; in a random sample, everyone in a particular population is equally likely to be selected. To avoid *selection bias*, some studies are *prospective*, beginning with an entire cluster of people (for instance, every baby born on a particular day) and then tracing the development of some particular characteristic. Ideally, the sample is diverse in gender, ethnicity, and other ways: If it is not, the bias must be explained.

For example, prospective studies find the antecedents of heart disease, or child abuse, or high school dropout rates—all of which are much harder to find if the study is *retrospective*, beginning with those who had heart attacks, experienced abuse, or left school. Thus, although retrospective research finds that most high school dropouts say they disliked school, prospective research finds that some who like school still decide to drop out and then later say they hated school, while others dislike school but stay to graduate. Prospective research discovers how many students are in these last two categories; retrospective research on people who have already dropped out does not.

Research Design

Every researcher begins not only by formulating a hypothesis but also by learning what other scientists have discovered about the topic in question and what methods might be useful and ethical in designing research. Often they include measures to prevent inadvertently finding only the results they expect. For example, the people who actually gather the data may not know the purpose of the research. Scientists say that these data gatherers are **blind** to the hypothesized outcome. Participants are sometimes "blind" as well, because otherwise they might, for instance, respond the way they think they should.

Another crucial aspect of research design is to define exactly what is to be studied. Researchers establish an **operational definition** of whatever phenomenon they will be examining, defining each variable by describing specific, observable behavior. This is essential in quantitative research, but it is also useful in qualitative research.

For example, if a researcher wants to know when babies begin to walk, does walking include steps taken while holding on? Is one unsteady step enough? Some parents say yes, but the usual operational definition of *walking* is "takes at least three steps without holding on." This operational definition allows comparisons worldwide, making it possible to discover, for example, that well-fed African babies tend to walk earlier than well-fed European babies.

When emotions or personality traits are studied, operational definitions are difficult to formulate but crucial for interpretation of results. How should *aggression* or *sharing* or *shyness* be defined? Lack of an operational definition leads to contradictory results. For instance, critics report that infant day care makes children more aggressive, but advocates report that it makes them more assertive and outgoing. In this case, both may be seeing the same behavior but defining it differently.

For any scientist, operational definitions are crucial, and studies usually include descriptions of how they measured attitudes or behavior.

Reporting Results

You already know that results should be reported in sufficient detail so that another scientist can analyze the conclusions and replicate the research. Various methods, populations, and research designs may produce divergent conclusions. For that reason, handbooks, some journals, and some articles are called *reviews*: They summarize past research. Often, when studies are similar in operational definitions and methods, the review is a **meta-analysis**, which combines the findings of many studies to present an overall conclusion.

Table App.1 describes some other statistical measures. One of them is *statistical significance*, which indicates whether or not a particular result could have occurred by chance.

A crucial statistic is **effect size**, a way of measuring how much impact one variable has on another. Effect size ranges from 0 (no effect) to 1 (total transformation, never found in actual studies). Effect size may be particularly important when the sample size is large, because a large sample often leads to highly "significant" results (results that are unlikely to have occurred by chance) that have only a tiny effect on the variable of interest.

Hundreds of statistical measures are used by developmentalists. Often the same data can be presented in many ways: Some scientists examine statistical analysis intently before they accept conclusions as valid. A specific example

meta-analysis A technique of combining results of many studies to come to an overall conclusion. Meta-analysis is powerful, in that small samples can be added together to lead to significant conclusions, although variations from study to study sometimes make combining them impossible.

effect size A way of indicating statistically how much of an impact the independent variable in an experiment had on the dependent variable.

TABLE App.1

Statistical Measures Often Used to Analyze Search Results

Measure	Use
Effect size	There are many kinds, but the most useful in reporting studies of development is called *Cohen's d*, which can indicate the power of an intervention. An effect size of 0.2 is called small, 0.5 moderate, and 0.8 large.
Significance	Indicates whether the results might have occurred by chance. If chance would produce the results only 5 times in 100, that is significant at the 0.05 level; once in 100 times is 0.01; once in 1,000 is 0.001.
Cost-benefit analysis	Calculates how much a particular independent variable costs versus how much it saves. This is useful for analyzing public spending, such as finding that preschool education programs or preventative health measures save money.
Odds ratio	Indicates how a particular variable compares to a standard, set at 1. For example, one study found that although less than 1 percent of all child homicides occurred at school, the odds were similar for public and private schools. The odds of it in high schools, however, were 18.47 times that of elementary or middle schools (set at 1.0) (MMWR, January 18, 2008).
Factor analysis	Hundreds of variables could affect any given behavior. In addition, many variables (such as family income and parental education) overlap. To take this into account, analysis reveals variables that can be clustered together to form a factor, which is a composite of many variables. For example, SES might become one factor, child personality another.
Meta-analysis	A "study of studies." Researchers use statistical tools to synthesize the results of previous, separate studies. Then they analyze the accumulated results, using criteria that weigh each study fairly. This approach improves data analysis by combining studies that were too small, or too narrow, to lead to solid conclusions.

involved methods to improve students' writing ability between grades 4 and 12. A meta-analysis found that many methods of writing instruction have a significant impact, but effect size is much larger for some methods (teaching strategies and summarizing) than for others (prewriting exercises and studying models). For teachers, this statistic is crucial, for they want to know what has a big effect, not merely what is better than chance (significant).

Numerous articles published in the past decade are meta-analyses that combine similar studies to search for general trends. Often effect sizes are also reported, which is especially helpful for meta-analyses since standard calculations almost always find some significance if the number of participants is in the thousands.

An added problem is the *file drawer problem*—that studies without significant results tend to be filed away rather than published. Thus, an accurate effect size may be much smaller than the published meta-analysis finds, or may be nonexistent. For this reason, replication is an important step.

Overall, then, designing and conducting valid research is complex yet crucial. Remember that with your own opinions: As this appendix advises, it is good to "make it personal," but do not stop there.

GLOSSARY

A

absent grief When mourners do not grieve, either because other people do not allow expressions of grief or because the mourners do not allow themselves to feel sadness. 487

accommodation The restructuring of old ideas to include new experiences. 247

active euthanasia When someone does something that hastens another person's death, with the intention of ending that person's suffering. 483

activity theory The view that elderly people want and need to remain active in a variety of social spheres—with relatives, friends, and community groups—and become withdrawn only unwillingly, as a result of ageism. 393

adolescence-limited offenders A person whose criminal activity stops by age 21. 374, 451

advance directives Any description of what a person wants to happen as they die and after death. This can include medical measures, visitors, funeral arrangements, cremation, and so on. 485

adverse childhood experiences (ACEs) A range of potentially traumatic childhood stresses, including abuse, neglect, family disruption and dysfunction, and parental incarceration, that can have lasting, negative effects on health and well-being. 282

affordance Something offered (afforded) by the environment. People do not necessary follow up on affordances, but they could. For example, someone might be offered a glass of water but say, "No, thank you." 279

ageism A prejudice whereby people are categorized and judged solely on the basis of their chronological age. 295

allele A variation that makes a gene different in some way from other genes for the same characteristics. Many genes never vary; others have several possible alleles. 59

allostasis A dynamic body adjustment, related to homeostasis, that affects overall physiology over time. The main difference is that homeostasis requires an immediate response, whereas allostasis requires longer-term adjustment. 105

altricial When the senses and motor skills do not develop until days or months after birth. An altricial newborn creature is virtually blind, deaf, and immobile. 149

Alzheimer's disease (AD) The most common cause of major NCD, characterized by gradual deterioration of memory and personality and marked by the formation of plaques of beta-amyloid protein and tangles of tau in the brain. 141

amygdala A tiny brain structure that registers emotions, particularly fear and anxiety. 131

analytic intelligence A form of intelligence that involves such mental processes as abstract planning, strategy selection, focused attention, and information processing, as well as verbal and logical skills. 244

analytic thought Thought that results from analysis, such as a systematic ranking of pros and cons, risks and consequences, possibilities and facts. Analytic thought depends on logic and rationality. 266

andropause A term coined to signify a drop in testosterone levels in older men, which typically results in reduced sexual desire, erections, and muscle mass. (Also called *male menopause*.) 112

anorexia nervosa An eating disorder characterized by distorted body image, severe calorie restriction, and intense fear of weight gain. Affected individuals voluntarily undereat or binge and purge, depriving their vital organs of nutrition. Anorexia can be fatal. 103

antisocial behavior Literally, "against other people"—doing something that needlessly hurts others. In childhood, this may be physical (hitting, kicking), or verbal (with insults or rejection). Antisocial is not *asocial*, which is being less involved with other people. 350

antithesis A proposition or statement of belief that opposes the thesis; the second stage of the process of dialectical thinking. 264

apprenticeship in thinking Vygotsky's term for how cognition is stimulated and developed in people by more skilled members of society. 42

apprentice in thinking Vygotsky's term for the young child whose intellectual growth is stimulated and directed by older and more skilled members of society. 258

assimilation The reinterpretation of new experiences to fit into old ideas. 247

asthma A chronic disease of the respiratory system in which inflammation narrows the airways from the nose and mouth to the lungs, causing difficulty in breathing. Signs and symptoms include wheezing, shortness of breath, chest tightness, and coughing. 75

attachment According to Ainsworth, "an affectional tie" that an infant forms with a caregiver—a tie that binds them together in space and endures over time. 363

attention-deficit/hyperactivity disorder (ADHD) A condition characterized by a persistent pattern of inattention and/or by hyperactive or impulsive behaviors; ADHD interferes with a person's functioning or development. 447

authoritarian parenting An approach to child rearing that is characterized by high behavioral standards, strict punishment of misconduct, and little communication from child to parent. 379

authoritative parenting An approach to child rearing in which the parents set limits and enforce rules but are flexible and listen to their children. 379

autism spectrum disorder (ASD) A developmental disorder marked by difficulty with social communication and interaction—including difficulty seeing things from another person's point of view—and restricted, repetitive patterns of behavior, interests, or activities. 446

automatization A process in which repetition of a sequence of thoughts and actions makes the sequence routine so that it no longer requires conscious thought. 128

average life expectancy The number of years the average newborn in a particular population group is likely to live. 438

axon A fiber that extends from a neuron and transmits electrochemical impulses from that neuron to the dendrites of other neurons. 127

B

babbling An infant's repetition of certain syllables, such as *ba-ba-ba*, that begins when babies are between 6 and 9 months old. 215

behaviorism A grand theory of human development that studies observable behavior. Behaviorism is also called *learning theory* because it describes the laws and processes by which behavior is learned. 36

Big Five The five basic clusters of personality traits that remain quite stable throughout adulthood: openness, conscientiousness, extroversion, agreeableness, and neuroticism. 292

bilingual education A strategy in which school subjects are taught in both the learner's original language and the second (majority) language. 227

binge eating disorder An eating disorder common in adolescence, which involves compulsive overeating. 103

binocular vision The ability to focus the two eyes in a coordinated manner in order to see one image. 152

body image A person's idea of how their body looks. 102

body mass index (BMI) The ratio of a person's weight in kilograms divided by height in meters squared. 92

brainstem The part of the brain in the very back of the head, which connects to the spinal cord (the backbone). The hindbrain and the midbrain are considered part of the brainstem. 119

broaden-and-build model The idea that positive emotions, such as joy, hope, happiness, and gratitude, each increase each other and build a foundation for other positive perspectives and experiences. 344

bulimia nervosa An eating disorder characterized by binge eating and subsequent purging, usually by induced vomiting and/or use of laxatives. 103

bullying aggression Unprovoked, repeated physical or verbal attack, especially on victims who are unlikely to defend themselves. 326

burnout The state of exhaustion and depression that may overcome professional helpers, when they lose their empathy for people who are suffering. 360

C

calorie restriction The practice of limiting dietary energy intake (while consuming sufficient quantities of vitamins, minerals, and other important nutrients) for the purpose of improving health and slowing down the aging process. 115

carrier A person whose genotype includes a gene that is not expressed in the phenotype. The carried gene occurs in half of the carrier's gametes and thus is passed on to half of the carrier's children. If such a gene is inherited from both parents, the characteristic appears in the phenotype. 65

cataracts A surface covering on the eye's lens that clouds vision by decreasing the light that reaches the retina. Makes sight dimmer and increases glare. 165

central nervous system The brain and the spinal cord, crucial for our senses, thoughts, and emotions. The central nervous system is often distinguished from the peripheral nervous system, the noncentral parts such as the arms and legs. 119

centration A characteristic of preoperational thought in which a young child focuses (centers) on one idea, excluding all others. 251

cerebellum A structure of the hindbrain that is particularly crucial for movement. 120

cerebral cortex The outer layers of the brain, which are the location of most human sensations and thoughts. 120

cerebrum The forebrain, small in some animals but huge in humans. The cerebrum is the location of emotions as well as sensations. It grows rapidly in prenatal life, infancy, and childhood, and is not fully grown and connected until early adulthood. 120

child abuse Deliberate action that is harmful to a child's physical, emotional, or sexual well-being. 381

child neglect Failure to meet a child's basic physical, educational, or emotional needs. 381

chromosome One of the 46 molecules of DNA (in 23 pairs) that virtually every cell of the human body contains and that, together, contain all the genes. Other species have more or fewer chromosomes. 58

chronic traumatic encephalopathy (CTE) An ongoing disease (chronic) that destroys the brain, caused by repeated concussions or sudden blows to the head (TBIs). 139

classical conditioning The learning process in which a meaningful stimulus (such as the smell of food to a hungry animal) is connected with a neutral stimulus (such as the sound of a tone) that had no special meaning before conditioning. (Also called *respondent conditioning*.) 37

classification The logical principle that things can be organized into groups (or categories or classes) according to some characteristic that they have in common. 253

cognitive artifacts An idea or mental creation that becomes a powerful social construction, influencing the thinking of everyone. The number system, the germ theory of disease, and the idea of the nation-state are all cognitive artifacts. 240

cognitive equilibrium In cognitive theory, a state of mental balance in which a person is able to reconcile new experiences with existing understanding. 247

cognitive theory A grand theory of human development that focuses on changes in how people think over time. According to this theory, our thoughts shape our attitudes, beliefs, and behaviors. 39

cohabitation When a couple live together in a committed romantic relationship but are not formally married. 386

cohort People born within the same historical period who therefore move through life together, experiencing events, technologies, and cultural shifts at the same ages. For example, the effect of the internet varies depending on what cohort a person belongs to. 5

comorbid Refers to the presence of two or more unrelated disease conditions at the same time in the same person. 442

complicated grief A type of grief that impedes a person's future life, usually because the person clings to sorrow or is buffeted by contradictory emotions. 487

compression of morbidity A shortening of the time a person spends ill or infirm, accomplished by postponing illness. 114

compulsive hoarding The urge to accumulate and hold on to familiar objects and possessions, sometimes to the point of their becoming health and/or safety hazards. This impulse tends to increase with age. 296

concrete operational thought Piaget's term for the ability to reason logically about direct experiences and perceptions. 252

conduct disorder When a person has great difficulty following social norms and rules and also is destructive, deliberately aggressive, calculating, and/or cruel. 451

conservation The principle that the amount of a substance remains the same (i.e., is conserved) even when its appearance changes. 251

continuing bonds The ongoing attachment and connection that the living have with the dead. Currently, continuing bonds are considered common and often beneficial. 490

conventional moral reasoning Kohlberg's second level of moral reasoning, emphasizing social rules. 355

copy number variations Genes with various repeats or deletions of base pairs. 60

corpus callosum A long, thick band of nerve fibers that connects the left and right hemispheres of the brain and allows communication between them. 124

correlation A number between +1.0 and −1.0 that indicates the degree of relationship between two variables, expressed in terms of the likelihood that one variable will (or will not) occur when the other variable does (or does not). A correlation indicates only that two variables are somehow related, not that one variable causes the other to occur. 26

cortisol The primary stress hormone; fluctuations in the body's cortisol level affect human emotions. 132

creative intelligence A form of intelligence that involves the capacity to be intellectually flexible and innovative. 244

critical period A crucial time when a particular type of developmental growth (in body or behavior) *must* happen for normal development to occur, or when harm (such as from a toxic substance or destructive event) can occur. 3

cross-modal sensations When a sense from one mode (e.g., hearing or touch) evokes a sense in another mode. If a person hears a voice and envisions what the person looks like, that is cross-modal. 154

cross-sectional research A research design that compares groups of people who differ in age but are similar in other important characteristics. 23

cross-sequential research A hybrid research design in which researchers first study several groups of people of different ages (a cross-sectional approach) and then follow those groups over the years (a longitudinal approach). (Also called *cohort-sequential research* or *time-sequential research*.) 24

crystallized intelligence Those types of intellectual ability that reflect accumulated learning. Vocabulary and general information are examples. Some developmental psychologists think crystallized intelligence increases with age, while fluid intelligence declines. 246

culture A system of shared beliefs, norms, behaviors, and expectations that persist over time and prescribe social behavior and assumptions. 7

cyber aggression Harming someone by using technology, such as social media. 327

D

dark triad Three personality traits—psychopathology, narcissism, and Machiavellianism—that, when combined, make a person selfish and destructive. 345

deductive reasoning Reasoning from a general statement, premise, or principle, through logical steps, to figure out (deduce) specifics. (Also called *top-down reasoning*.) 255

deferred imitation A sequence in which an infant first perceives something that someone else does and then performs the same action a few hours or even days later. 250

Defining Issues Test (DIT) A series of questions developed by James Rest and designed to assess respondents' level of moral development by having them rank possible solutions to moral dilemmas. 356

demand/withdraw A pattern of social interaction in which one partner increasingly demands response, and the other increasingly withdraws from the relationship. 379

dendrite A fiber that extends from a neuron and receives electrochemical impulses transmitted from other neurons via their axons. 127

deoxyribonucleic acid (DNA) The chemical composition of the molecules that contain the genes, which are the chemical instructions for cells to manufacture various proteins. 58

dependent variable In an experiment, the variable that may change as a result of whatever new condition or situation the experimenter adds. In other words, the dependent variable *depends* on the independent variable. 21

developmental psychopathology A perspective on psychological disorders that reflects changes as people grow older. For example, many childhood experiences can cause or mitigate mental disorders. 446

developmental theory A group of ideas, assumptions, and generalizations that interpret and illuminate the thousands of observations that have been made about human growth. A developmental theory provides a framework for explaining the patterns and problems of development. 33

Diagnostic and Statistical Manual of Mental Disorders (DSM-5) Revised about every 12 years by hundreds of U.S. psychiatrists to name and diagnose psychological disorders, this 991-page book is in its fifth edition. 445

dialectical thought The most advanced cognitive process, characterized by the ability to consider a thesis and its antithesis simultaneously and thus to arrive at a synthesis. Dialectical thought makes possible an ongoing awareness of pros and cons, advantages and disadvantages, possibilities and limitations. 264

difference-equals-deficit error The mistaken belief that a deviation from some norm is necessarily inferior to behavior or characteristics that meet the standard. 8

differential susceptibility The idea that people vary in how sensitive they are to particular experiences. Often such differences are genetic, which makes some people affected "for better or for worse" by life events. (Also called *differential sensitivity*.) 15

disability A physical, mental, or emotional impairment that makes one or more major life activity difficult or impossible. 442

disability-adjusted life years (DALYs) A number that indicates how many years of total well-being are lost because of a disability. The idea is that each year of a disabled person's life is a fraction of what it could have been. 444

disenfranchised grief A situation in which certain people, although they are bereaved, are prevented from mourning publicly by cultural customs or social restrictions. 487

disengagement theory The view that aging makes a person's social sphere increasingly narrow, resulting in role relinquishment, withdrawal, and passivity. 393

disorganized attachment (type D) A type of attachment that is marked by an infant's inconsistent reactions to the caregiver's departure and return. 365

dizygotic (DZ) twins Twins who are formed when two separate ova are fertilized by two separate sperm at roughly the same time. (Also called *fraternal* twins.) 69

DNR (do not resuscitate) order A written order from a physician (sometimes initiated by a patient's advance directive or by a health care proxy's request) that no attempt should be made to revive a patient if he or she suffers cardiac or respiratory arrest. 482

dominant–recessive pattern The interaction of a heterozygous pair of alleles in such a way that the phenotype reflects one allele (the dominant gene) more than the other (the recessive gene). 65

double effect When an action (such as administering opiates) has both a positive effect (relieving a terminally ill person's pain) and a negative effect (hastening death by suppressing respiration). 481

Down syndrome A condition in which a person has 47 chromosomes instead of the usual 46, with 3 rather than 2 chromosomes at the 21st site. People with Down syndrome typically have distinctive characteristics, including unusual facial features, heart abnormalities, and language difficulties. (Also called *trisomy-21*.) 79

dual processing The notion that two networks exist within the human brain, one for emotional processing of stimuli and one for analytical reasoning. 265

dynamic-systems approach A view of human development as an ongoing, ever-changing interaction between the physical, cognitive, and psychosocial influences. The crucial understanding is that development is never static but is always affected by, and affects, many systems of development. 5

dyscalculia Unusual difficulty with math, probably originating from a distinct part of the brain. 450

dyslexia Unusual difficulty with reading; thought to be the result of some neurological underdevelopment. 450

E

eclectic perspective The approach taken by most developmentalists, in which they apply aspects of each of the various theories of development rather than adhering exclusively to one theory. 54

ecological-systems approach A perspective on human development that considers all of the influences from the various contexts of development. (Later renamed *bioecological theory*.) 4

ecological validity The idea that cognition should be measured in settings that are as realistic as possible and that the abilities measured should be those needed in real life. 209

ego The conscious self. *Ego* is the Latin word for "I." 274

egocentrism Piaget's term for children's tendency to think about the world entirely from their own personal perspective. 251

embodied cognition An idea or concept that is expressed in the body as well as with words. This connection between mind and body is expressed in many phrases, postures, and actions. 177

embryo The name for a developing human organism from about the third week through the eighth week after conception. 89

embryonic period The stage of prenatal development from approximately the third week through the eighth week after conception, during which the basic forms of all body structures, including internal organs, develop. 87

emotion regulation The ability to control when and how emotions are expressed. 338

emotional intelligence The ability to recognize, understand, and regulate emotions.

This includes both awareness of the emotions of others and awareness of one's own emotions. Ideally, those high in emotional intelligence have both. 345

empathy Feeling the same emotions as someone else. Empathy is not the same as *sympathy*, a less personal feeling, such feeling sorry for someone (pity). 350

empirical evidence Evidence that is based on observation, experience, or experiment; not theoretical. 18

encoding To put into memory something that was thought or experienced. Encoding requires perception and interpretation, and thus is not completely accurate. 198

English as a second language (ESL) A U.S. approach to teaching English that gathers all of the non-English speakers together and provides intense instruction in English. Students' first languages are never used; the goal is to prepare students for regular classes in English. 227

English language learners (ELLs) Children in the United States whose proficiency in English is low—usually below a cutoff score on an oral or written test. Many children who speak a non-English language at home are also capable in English; they are not ELLs. 227

episodic memory Memory for a particular episode, or experience, usually remembered with the senses and emotions, not with words and facts. Each person's episodic memory is theirs alone, even when two people share the same experience. 191

ethnic group People whose ancestors were born in the same region and who often share a language, culture, and religion. 10

evolutionary theory When used in human development, the idea that many current human emotions and impulses are a legacy from thousands of years ago. 44

executive function A combination of memory, inhibition, and cognitive flexibility that allows better thinking, so people can anticipate, strategize, and plan behavior. 210

experience-dependent Brain functions that depend on particular, variable experiences and therefore may or may not develop in a particular infant. 135

experience-expectant Brain functions that require certain basic common experiences (which an infant can be expected to have) in order to develop normally. 135

experiment A research method in which the researcher tries to determine the cause-and-effect relationship between two variables by manipulating one (called the

independent variable) and then observing and recording the ensuing changes in the other (called the *dependent variable*). 21

expert Someone with specialized skills and knowledge developed around a particular activity or area. 432

explicit memory Memory that can be recalled in the conscious mind, usually factual memories that are expressed with words. 187

extended family A family of relatives in addition to the nuclear family, usually three or more generations living in one household. 388

extremely low birthweight (ELBW) A body weight at birth of less than 1,000 grams (2 pounds, 3 ounces). 92

extrinsic rewards of work The tangible benefits, usually in salary, insurance, pension, and status, that come with employment. 290

F

familism The belief that family members should support one another, sacrificing individual freedom and success, if necessary, in order to preserve family unity and protect the family from outside forces. 378

family systems theory The idea that a family is a dynamic, interactive system, with each part affecting the other parts, and the entire interaction making the whole greater than the parts. 383

fast-mapping The speedy and sometimes imprecise way in which children learn new words by tentatively placing them in mental categories according to their perceived meaning. 222

fetal alcohol syndrome (FAS) A cluster of birth defects, including abnormal facial characteristics, slow physical growth, and reduced intellectual ability, that may occur in the fetus of a woman who drinks alcohol while pregnant. 89

fetal period The stage of prenatal development from the ninth week after conception until birth, during which the fetus gains about 7 pounds (more than 3,000 grams) and organs become more mature, gradually able to function on their own. 87

fetus The name for a developing human organism from the start of the ninth week after conception until birth. 91

fictive kin People who become accepted as part of a family in which they are not genetically or legally members. 393

fine motor skills Physical abilities involving small body movements, especially of the hands and fingers, such as drawing and picking up a coin. (The word *fine* here means "small.") 170

fixed mindset An approach to understanding intelligence that sees ability as an innate entity, a fixed quantity present at birth. Those who hold this view do not believe that effort enhances achievement. 416

flashbulb memories Named after a camera's flash that reveals every detail in a photo. The hypothesis is that the surprise and intense emotion of some experiences cause every detail to be seared into the mind. 209

fluid intelligence Those types of basic intelligence that make learning of all sorts quick and thorough. Abilities such as short-term memory, abstract thought, and speed of thinking are all usually considered part of fluid intelligence. 245

Flynn effect The rise in average IQ scores that has occurred over the decades in many nations. 242

focus on appearance A characteristic of preoperational thought in which a young child ignores all attributes that are not apparent. 251

forebrain Another name for the cerebrum. 119

foreclosure Erikson's term for premature identity formation, which occurs when an adolescent adopts his or her parents' or society's roles and values wholesale, without questioning or analysis. 286

formal operational intelligence In Piaget's theory, the fourth and final stage of cognitive development, characterized by more systematic logical thinking and by the ability to understand and systematically manipulate abstract concepts. 253

fragile X syndrome A genetic disorder in which part of the X chromosome seems to be attached to the rest of it by a very thin string of molecules. The cause is a single gene that has more than 200 repetitions of one triplet. 81

frontotemporal NCDs Deterioration of the amygdala and frontal lobes that may be the cause of 15 percent of all major neurocognitive disorders. (Also called *frontotemporal lobar degeneration*.) 142

G

gamete A reproductive cell. These sperm (for males) and ova (for females) each contain 23 chromosomes, so the zygote will contain 46 chromosomes, in 23 pairs. 61

gender In the social sciences, the term that refers to the social and cultural construct of being male or female, some variation of the two, or neither. 301

gender binary The idea that gender comes in two—and only two—forms, male and female. 303

gender identity A person's emotional and psychological sense of being a man, a woman, both, or neither. Gender identity may or may not align with an individual's sex at birth. 303

gene A small section of a chromosome; the basic unit for the transmission of heredity. A gene consists of a string of chemicals that provide instructions for the cell to manufacture certain proteins. 58

general intelligence (g) The idea that intelligence is one basic trait, underlying all cognitive abilities. According to g, people have varying levels of this general ability. 241

genotype An organism's entire genetic inheritance, or genetic potential. 63

germinal period The first two weeks of prenatal development after conception, characterized by rapid cell division and the beginning of cell differentiation. 87

glaucoma An increase in fluid in the eye, which damages the retina and the optic nerve. Can be mitigated with eye drops but, left untreated, can cause blindness. 165

goodness of fit When the personality and impulses of the parents mesh with those of the children, such as an outgoing parent having outgoing children. 280

grammar All of the methods—word order, verb forms, and so on—that languages use to communicate meaning, apart from the words themselves. 217

grief The deep sorrow that people feel at the death of another. Grief is personal and unpredictable. 487

gross motor skills Physical abilities involving large body movements, such as walking and jumping. (The word *gross* here means "big.") 169

growth mindset An approach to understanding intelligence that holds that intelligence grows incrementally, and thus can be increased by effort. Those who subscribe to this view believe they can master whatever they seek to learn if they pay attention, participate in class, study, complete their homework, and so on. 416

guided participation The process by which people learn from others who guide their experiences and explorations. 42

H

health care proxy A person chosen to make medical decisions if a patient is unable to do so, as when in a coma. 486

herd immunity When a sufficient proportion of a population is immune to an infectious disease (through vaccination and/or prior illness) to make its spread from person to person unlikely. 465

heritability A statistic that indicates what percentage of the variation in a particular trait within a particular population, in a particular context and era, can be traced to genes. 72

hidden curriculum The unofficial, unstated, or implicit patterns within a school that influence what children learn. For instance, teacher background, organization of the play space, and tracking are all part of the hidden curriculum—not formally prescribed, but instructive to the children. 413

hikikomori An anxiety disorder first evident among emerging adults in Japan, when a person refuses to leave their room. 454

hindbrain The very back of the brain, part of the brainstem. 119

hippocampus A brain structure that is a central processor of memory, especially memory for locations. 131

holophrase A single word that is used to express a complete, meaningful thought. 216

home visiting Hundreds of programs in the United States involving nurses and other trained adults visiting new mothers in their homes, with the overall goal of improving the mother's interaction with her baby. Specifics vary: The goal is sometimes health, sometimes education, and sometimes attachment. 399

homeostasis The adjustment of all of the body's systems to keep physiological functions in a state of equilibrium. As the body ages, it takes longer for these homeostatic adjustments to occur, so it becomes harder for older bodies to adapt to stress. 105

hookup A sexual encounter between two people who are not in a romantic relationship. Neither intimacy nor commitment is expected. 316

hormone replacement therapy (HRT) Taking hormones (in pills, patches, or injections) to compensate for hormone reduction. HRT is most common in women at menopause or after removal of the ovaries, but it is also used by men as their testosterone decreases. HRT has some medical uses but also carries health risks. 111

hormones Chemicals in the bloodstream that originate in the brain and affect many aspects of life, including sleep, hunger, lust, rage, and love. 132

hospice An institution or program in which terminally ill patients receive palliative care to reduce suffering; family and friends of the dying are helped as well. 479

humanism A theory that stresses the potential of all humans, who have the same basic needs regardless of culture, gender, or basic background. 48

hypothalamus A brain area that responds to the amygdala and the hippocampus and directs the pituitary to produce hormones that activate other parts of the brain and body. 132

hypothesis A specific prediction that can be tested. 18

hypothetical thought Reasoning that includes propositions and possibilities that may not reflect reality. 255

I

id The primitive, animal-like drives and emotions that humans have. Much of the id concerns sex and aggression. 274

identity achievement Erikson's term for the attainment of identity, or the point at which a person understands who he or she is as a unique individual, in accord with past experiences and future plans. 286

identity versus role confusion Erikson's term for the fifth stage of development, in which the person tries to figure out "Who am I?" but is confused as to which of many possible roles to adopt. 286

immersion A strategy in which instruction in all school subjects occurs in the second (usually the majority) language that a child is learning. 227

immunization A process that stimulates the body's immune system by causing production of antibodies to defend against attack by a particular contagious disease. Creation of antibodies may be accomplished either naturally (by having the disease), by injection, by drops that are swallowed, or by a nasal spray. 465

implicit memory Memory that is not verbal, often unconscious. Many motor and emotional memories are implicit. 187

impulse control The ability to postpone or deny the immediate response to an idea or behavior. 123

incomplete grief When circumstances, such as a police investigation or an autopsy, interfere with the process of grieving. 488

independent variable In an experiment, the variable that is introduced to see what effect it has on the dependent variable. (Also called *experimental variable*.) 21

individual education plan (IEP) A document that specifies educational goals and plans for a child with special needs. 421

induction A disciplinary technique in which the parent tries to get the child to understand why a certain behavior was wrong. Listening, not lecturing, is crucial. 352

inductive reasoning Reasoning from one or more specific experiences or facts to reach (induce) a general conclusion. (Also called *bottom-up reasoning*.) 255

infertility The inability to conceive a child after trying for at least a year. 109

information processing A perspective that compares human thinking processes, by analogy, to computer analysis of data, including sensory input, connections, stored memories, and output. 182

information-processing theory A perspective that compares human thinking processes, by analogy, to computer analysis of data, including sensory input, connections, stored memories, and output. 41

initiative versus guilt Erikson's third psychosocial crisis, in which young children undertake new skills and activities and feel guilty when they do not succeed at them. 339

insecure-avoidant attachment (type A) A pattern of attachment in which an infant avoids connection with the caregiver, as when the infant seems not to care about the caregiver's presence, departure, or return. 365

insecure-resistant/ambivalent attachment (type C) A pattern of attachment in which an infant's anxiety and uncertainty are evident, as when the infant becomes very upset at separation from the caregiver and both resists and seeks contact on reunion. 365

instrumental aggression Hurtful behavior that is intended to get something that another person has. 326

integrity versus despair The final stage of Erik Erikson's developmental sequence, in which older adults seek to integrate their unique experiences with their vision of community. 295

intermittent fasting A pattern of eating that includes periods of restricted eating interspersed with usual consumption. The most popular pattern is two days per week eating less than 750 calories and five days of normal eating, all while drinking plenty of water. 115

intersectionality The idea that the various identities need to be combined. This is especially important in determining if discrimination occurs. 11

intersex A broad term describing people born with reproductive or sexual anatomy and/or a chromosome pattern that isn't typically male or female. 306

intimate terrorism A violent and demeaning form of abuse in a romantic relationship, in which the victim (usually female) is frightened to fight back, seek help, or withdraw. In this case, the victim is in danger of physical as well as psychological harm. 328

intrinsic rewards of work The personal gratifications, such as pleasure in a job well done or friendships with coworkers, that accompany employment. 290

intuitive thought Thought that arises from an emotion or a hunch, beyond rational explanation, and is influenced by past experiences and cultural assumptions. 266

irreversibility A characteristic of preoperational thought in which a young child thinks that nothing can be undone. A thing cannot be restored to the way it was before a change occurred. 251

K

knowledge base A body of knowledge in a particular area that makes it easier to master new information in that area. 191

L

language acquisition device (LAD) Chomsky's term for a hypothesized mental structure that enables humans to learn language, including the basic aspects of grammar, vocabulary, and intonation. 236

least restrictive environment A legal requirement that children with special needs be assigned to the most general educational context in which they can be expected to learn. 421

left hemisphere The left half of the brain. This half controls the right side of the body. 124

Lewy body disease A form of major neurocognitive disorder characterized by an increase in Lewy body cells in the brain. Symptoms include visual hallucinations, momentary loss of attention, falling, and fainting. 144

life-course-persistent offenders A person whose criminal activity typically begins in early adolescence and continues throughout life; a career criminal. 374, 451

life-span perspective An approach to the study of human development that takes into account all phases of life, not just childhood or adulthood. 2

limbic system The parts of the brain that interact to produce emotions, including the amygdala, the hypothalamus, and the hippocampus. Many other parts of the brain also are involved with emotions. 131

linked lives Lives in which the success, health, and well-being of each family member are connected to those of other members, including those of another generation, as in the relationship between parents and children. 383

little scientist Piaget's term for toddlers' insatiable curiosity and active experimentation as they engage in various actions to understand their world. 250

living will A document that indicates what medical intervention an individual prefers if he or she is not conscious when a decision is to be expressed. For example, some do not want mechanical breathing. 486

longitudinal research A research design in which the same individuals are followed over time, as their development is repeatedly assessed. 24

low birthweight (LBW) A body weight at birth of less than 2,500 grams (5½ pounds). 92

M

macular degeneration The loss of functioning in the macula of the eye, which results in blind spots. 165

major depressive disorder Deep and long-lasting (two weeks of more) depression, with problems with mood, sleep, appetite, and so on. 452

massification The idea that establishing institutions of higher learning and encouraging college enrollment can benefit everyone (the masses). 427

material aggression Harming someone by defacing or destroying something that belongs to them. 327

maximum life span The oldest possible age to which members of a species can live under ideal circumstances. For humans, that age is approximately 122 years. 76, 439

mean length of utterance (MLU) The average number of words in a typical sentence (called utterance because children may not talk in complete sentences). MLU

is often used to measure language development. 217

medical model Considering mental illness to be similar to physical illness, with definite signs, diagnoses, and cures. Many psychologists disagree with that model of psychopathology. 458

menarche A girl's first menstrual period, signaling that she has begun ovulation. Pregnancy is biologically possible, but ovulation and menstruation are often irregular for years after menarche. 100

menopause The time in middle age, usually around age 50, when a woman's menstrual periods cease and the production of estrogen, progesterone, and testosterone drops. Strictly speaking, menopause is dated one year after a woman's last menstrual period, although many months before and after that date are menopausal. 110

metamemory Knowledge about how to remember, such as how to create mnemonics. 192

microbiome All the microbes (bacteria, viruses, and so on) with all their genes in a community; here, the millions of microbes of the human body. 60

midbrain In humans, a relatively small cluster of brain regions that aid in movement and the senses, although the primary site for these functions is in the cerebral cortex. 119

mild cognitive impairment (MCI) When a person is somewhat more confused and forgetful than they were, but still able to function well. 138

modeling The central process of social learning, by which a person observes the actions of others and then copies them. 39

monozygotic (MZ) twins Twins who originate from one zygote that splits apart very early in development. (Also called *identical twins*.) Other monozygotic multiple births (such as triplets and quadruplets) can occur as well. 69

Montessori schools Schools that offer early-childhood education based on the philosophy of Maria Montessori, which emphasizes careful work and tasks that each young child can do. 404

morality The ability to distinguish between right and wrong. 348

moratorium An adolescent's choice of a socially acceptable way to postpone making identity-achievement decisions. Going to college is a common example. 286

morbidity Illness or disease, which can be acute (such as a sudden pain that indicates a

heart attack) or chronic (such as decades of shortness of breath caused by lung disease). 440

mortality Another word for a person's susceptibility to death. 438

mourning The ceremonies and behaviors that a religion or culture prescribes for people to express their grief after a death. 489

multifactorial Referring to a trait that is affected by many factors, both genetic and environmental, that enhance, halt, shape, or alter the expression of genes, resulting in a phenotype that may differ markedly from the genotype. 69

multiple intelligences The idea that human intelligence is composed of a varied set of abilities rather than a single, all-encompassing one. 243

myelin The coating on axons that speeds transmission of signals from one neuron to another. 130

N

naming explosion A sudden increase in an infant's vocabulary, especially in the number of nouns, that begins at about 18 months of age. 216

National Assessment of Educational Progress (NAEP) An ongoing and nationally representative measure of U.S. children's achievement in reading, mathematics, and other subjects over time; nicknamed "the Nation's Report Card." 420

nature In development, nature refers to the traits, capacities, and limitations that each individual inherits genetically from his or her parents at the moment of conception. 14

neglectful/uninvolved parenting An approach to child rearing in which the parents seem indifferent toward their children, not knowing or caring about their children's lives. 380

neurocognitive disorder (NCD) Any of a number of brain diseases that affect a person's ability to remember, analyze, plan, or interact with other people. 140

neurodiversity The idea that each person has neurological strengths and weaknesses that should be appreciated, in much the same way diverse cultures and ethnicities are welcomed. Neurodiversity seems particularly relevant for children with disorders on the autism spectrum. 458

neuron One of billions of nerve cells in the central nervous system, especially in the brain. 127

neurotransmitter A brain chemical that carries information from the axon of a sending neuron to the dendrites of a receiving neuron. 129

nonbinary The rejection of the binary. When applied to gender, this means that sexual characteristics, identity, roles, and orientation are all fluid, not male/female. 303

nuclear family A family that consists of a father, a mother, and their biological children under age 18. 385

nurture In development, nurture includes all of the environmental influences that affect the individual after conception. This includes everything from the mother's nutrition while pregnant to the cultural influences in the nation. 14

O

obesity Weighing as much or more than U.S. children of the same age in about 1990 who were in the top 5 percent as indicated by the 2000 CDC growth charts. Far more than 5 percent of U.S. children are now obese. 97

object permanence The realization that objects (including people) still exist when they can no longer be seen, touched, or heard. 249

operant conditioning The learning process by which a particular action is followed by something desired (which makes the person or animal more likely to repeat the action) or by something unwanted (which makes the action less likely to be repeated). (Also called *instrumental conditioning*.) 38

oppositional defiant disorder (ODD) When a child refuses to comply with rules and instead is quick to get angry at every request. 451

organ reserve The capacity of organs to allow the body to cope with stress, via extra, unused functioning ability. 105

overextension Using a word to mean more than most people think it means. 222

overregularization The application of rules of grammar even when exceptions occur, making the language seem more "regular" than it actually is. 224

overweight Weighing as much or more than the top 15 percent of U.S. children of the same age in about 1990 as indicated by the 2000 CDC growth charts. Far more than 15 percent of U.S. children now exceed the earlier norms. 97

oxytocin The primary bonding hormone, evident lifelong but particularly high at birth and in lactation. 132

P

palliative care Medical treatment designed primarily to provide physical and emotional comfort to the dying patient and guidance to his or her loved ones. 480

parasuicide Any potentially lethal action against the self that does not result in death. (Also called attempted suicide or failed suicide.) 452

parental imprinting Some genes, or absence of needed genes, reflect whether that genetic condition came from the father or the mother. The concept is that the influence of the XX or XY chromosomes extends past the 23rd pair, as if the parent tattoos (imprints) a particular signature on them. 67

Parkinson's disease A chronic, progressive disease that is characterized by muscle tremor and rigidity and sometimes major neurocognitive disorder; caused by reduced dopamine production in the brain. 144

passive euthanasia When a seriously ill person is allowed to die naturally, without active attempts to prolong life. 482

peer pressure Encouragement to conform to one's friends or contemporaries in behavior, dress, and attitude; usually considered a negative force, as when adolescent peers encourage one another to defy adult authority. 375

percentile A point on a ranking scale of 0 to 100. The 50th percentile is the midpoint; half of the people in the population being studied rank higher and half rank lower. 93

perception When the brain is conscious of a sensation or idea. Perception sometimes combines several senses and ideas: You might suddenly perceive that your mother is angry because of her face and voice and your past experience of her anger. 149

permissive parenting An approach to child rearing that is characterized by high nurturance and communication but little discipline, guidance, or control. 379

personality An individual's characteristic way of thinking, feeling, and acting. 272

perseverate To stay stuck, or persevere, in one thought or action for a long time. The ability to be flexible, switching from one task to another, is beyond most young children. 123

phenotype The observable characteristics of a person, including appearance, personality, intelligence, and all other traits. 63

phonological loop The mind's echoing of what was just heard. That echo can then be put in storage, or it can be forgotten. 198

physical aggression Using physical force to harm someone. 327

physician-assisted suicide A form of active euthanasia in which a doctor provides the means for someone to end his or her own life, usually by prescribing lethal drugs. 483

pituitary A gland in the brain that responds to a signal from the hypothalamus by producing many hormones, including those that regulate growth and sexual maturation. 132

plaques Clumps of a protein called beta-amyloid, found in brain tissue surrounding the neurons. 141

plasticity The idea that abilities, personality, and other human characteristics can change over time. Plasticity is particularly evident during childhood, but even older adults are not always "set in their ways." 14

POLST (physician-ordered life-sustaining treatment) This is an order from a doctor regarding end of life care. It advises nurses and other medical staff which treatments (e.g., feeding, antibiotics, respirators) should be used and which not. It is similar to a living will, but it is written for medical professionals and thus is more specific. 483

polygenic Referring to a trait that is influenced by many genes. 69

polypharmacy A situation in which elderly people are prescribed several medications. The various side effects and interactions of those medications can result in dementia symptoms. 145

positivity effect The tendency for elderly people to perceive, prefer, and remember positive images and experiences more than negative ones. 296

postconventional moral reasoning Kohlberg's third level of moral reasoning, emphasizing moral principles. 355

postformal thought A proposed adult stage of cognitive development, following Piaget's four stages, that goes beyond adolescent thinking by being more practical, more flexible, and more dialectical (i.e., more capable of combining contradictory elements into a comprehensive whole). 263

posttraumatic stress disorder (PTSD) An anxiety disorder that develops as a delayed reaction to exposure to actual or threatened death, serious injury, or sexual violence. Its symptoms may include flashbacks to the event, hyperactivity and hypervigilance, displaced anger, sleeplessness, nightmares, sudden terror or anxiety, and confusion between fantasy and reality. 139

practical intelligence The intellectual skills used in everyday problem solving. (Sometimes called *tacit intelligence*.) 244

pragmatics The practical use of language that includes the ability to adjust language communication according to audience and context. 225

precocial When the senses and motor skills are developed before (pre-) birth. A precocial newborn creature can immediately see, hear, smell, and move as an older infant could. 149

preconventional moral reasoning Kohlberg's first level of moral reasoning, emphasizing rewards and punishments. 355

prefrontal cortex The area of the cortex at the very front of the brain that specializes in anticipation, planning, and impulse control. 122

preoperational intelligence Piaget's term for cognitive development between the ages of about 2 and 6; it includes language and imagination (which involve symbolic thought), but logical, operational thinking is not yet possible at this stage. 250

presbycusis Hearing loss that is related to aging. At earlier ages, a few people lose hearing because of disease or injury, but everyone experiences presbycusis in late adulthood. 163

presbyopia Visual loss that is related to aging. Usually this is the result of one or more of three conditions that become more common with age: cataracts, glaucoma, and macular degeneration. 164

preterm A birth that occurs two or more weeks before the full 38 weeks of the typical pregnancy—that is, at 36 or fewer weeks after conception. 92

primary circular reactions The first of three types of feedback loops in sensorimotor intelligence, this one involving the infant's own body. The infant senses motion, sucking, noise, and other stimuli and tries to understand them. 248

primary emotions Basic emotions that originate from innate, neurological impulses. Such emotions are experienced universally, lifelong, including in early infancy. These include happiness, sadness, and fear. 333

primary sex characteristics The parts of the body that are directly involved in reproduction, including the vagina, uterus, ovaries, testicles, and penis. 102

private speech The internal dialogue that occurs when people talk to themselves (either silently or out loud). 261

Program for International Student Assessment (PISA) An international test taken by 15-year-olds in 50 nations that is designed to measure problem solving and cognition in daily life. 418

Progress in International Reading Literacy Study (PIRLS) Inaugurated in 2001, a planned five-year cycle of international trend studies in the reading ability of fourth-graders. 418

proprioception The sense of where the parts of the body are, both when they are in one spot and when they are moving. 162

prosocial behavior Literally, "for other people"—doing something for others without expecting any reward. In early childhood, prosocial behavior is sharing something or caring for someone who needs help. 350

psychoanalytic theory A theory of human development that contends that irrational, unconscious drives and motives underlie human behavior. 34

psychodynamic A view of adult emotional difficulties that stresses the interaction of early experiences and current life. 275

psychological control A disciplinary technique that involves threatening to withdraw love and support, using a child's feelings of guilt and gratitude to the parents. 352

psychopathology Illnesses that primarily affect the mind and behavior, not the physical body. Schizophrenia is an example. 445

Q

qualitative research Research that considers qualities instead of quantities. Descriptions of particular conditions and participants' expressed ideas are often part of qualitative studies. 27

quality-adjusted life years (QALYs) A number that indicates quality years added because of a full life. 442

quantitative research Research that provides data that can be expressed with numbers, such as ranks or scales. 27

R

race A group of people who are regarded by themselves, or by others, as distinct from other groups on the basis of physical appearance, typically skin color. Social scientists think race is a misleading concept, as biological differences are not signified by outward appearance. 10

reaction time The time it takes to respond to a stimulus, either physically (with a reflexive movement such as an eyeblink) or cognitively (with a thought). 130

reactive aggression An impulsive retaliation for another person's intentional or accidental hurtful action. 326

Reggio Emilia A program of early-childhood education that originated in the town of Reggio Emilia, Italy, and that encourages each child's creativity in a carefully designed setting. 404

relational aggression Nonphysical acts, such as insults or social rejection, aimed at harming the social connection between the victim and other people. 326

reminder session An experience (sight, word, smell, and so forth) that evokes a memory, which was not available before the reminder. 186

replication Repeating a study, usually using different participants, perhaps of another age, SES, or culture. 18

resilience The capacity to adapt well to significant adversity and to overcome serious stress. 283

response to intervention An educational strategy intended to help children who demonstrate below-average achievement in early grades, using special intervention. 421

retrieval Bringing something in memory back to the conscious mind. Humans store much more than they can retrieve. 199

right hemisphere The right half of the brain, which controls the left side of the body. 124

role confusion A situation in which an adolescent does not seem to know or care what their identity is. (Sometimes called *identity diffusion* or *role diffusion*.) 286

rough-and-tumble play Play that seems to be rough, as in play wrestling or chasing, but in which there is no intent to harm. 175

S

scaffolding Temporary support that is tailored to a learner's needs and abilities and aimed at helping the learner master the next task in a given learning process. 259

scheme According to Piaget, a scheme is a cognitive framework for understanding an idea. 247

science of human development The science that seeks to understand how and why people of all ages and circumstances change or remain the same over time. 16

scientific method A way to answer questions using empirical research and data-based conclusions. 18

scientific observation A method of testing a hypothesis by unobtrusively watching and recording participants' behavior in a systematic and objective manner—in a natural setting, in a laboratory, or in searches of archival data. 20

secondary circular reactions The second of three types of feedback loops in sensorimotor intelligence, involving the infant and an object or another person, as with shaking a rattle or playing peek-a-boo. 249

secondary emotions Emotions that build on primary emotions, but also include experience, learning, and culture. These include pride and shame. 333

secondary sex characteristics Physical traits that are not directly involved in reproduction but that indicate sexual maturity, such as a man's beard and a woman's breasts. 102

secure attachment (type B) A relationship in which an infant obtains both comfort and confidence from the presence of the caregiver. 365

selective optimization with compensation The theory, developed by Paul and Margaret Baltes, that people try to maintain a balance in their lives by looking for the best way to compensate for physical and cognitive losses and to become more proficient in activities they can already do well. 48, 460

self-concept A person's understanding of who they are, in relation to self-esteem, appearance, personality, and various traits. 280

self-esteem How a person values themselves. It could be high ("I am the smartest") or low ("I am the dumbest"), but it is best to be realistic and on the high side. 281

semantic memory Memory that depends on words and numbers, and that presents facts that are agreed on by many people. Contrasts with episodic memory. 191

sensation The response of a sensory organ (eyes, ears, skin, tongue, nose) when it detects a stimulus. 149

senescence The process of aging, whereby the body becomes less strong and efficient. 104

sensitive period A time when a certain type of development is most likely, although it may still happen later with more difficulty. For example, early childhood is considered a sensitive period for language learning. 3

sensorimotor intelligence Piaget's term for the way infants think—by using their senses and motor skills—during the first period of cognitive development. 248

separation anxiety An infant's distress when a familiar caregiver leaves; most obvious between 9 and 14 months. 335

sex In the social sciences, the term used to designate male or female characteristics that are present at birth, not cultural. 301

sexual orientation A term that describes an individual's sense of enduring romantic, emotional, and/or sexual attraction to other people. 303

sexually transmitted infection (STI) A disease spread by sexual contact, including syphilis, gonorrhea, genital herpes, chlamydia, and HIV. 315

situational couple violence Fighting between romantic partners that is brought on more by the situation than by the deep personality problems of the individuals. Both partners are typically victims and abusers. 328

small-for-gestational age (SGA) A term for a baby whose birthweight is significantly lower than expected, given the time since conception. For example, a 5-pound (2,265-gram) newborn is considered SGA if born on time but not SGA if born two months early. (Also called *small-for-dates.*) 92

social anxiety disorder Fear of social situations, especially when other people might judge one negatively, as with public speaking. (Also called *social anxiety disorder.*) 454

social comparison The tendency to assess one's abilities, achievements, social status, and other attributes by measuring them against those of other people, especially one's peers. 281

social construction An idea that is built on shared perceptions, not on objective reality. Many age-related terms (such as *childhood, adolescence, yuppie,* and *senior citizen*) are social constructions, connected to biological traits but strongly influenced by social assumptions. 7

social convoy Collectively, the family members, friends, acquaintances, and even strangers who move through the years of life with a person. 391

social learning theory An extension of behaviorism that emphasizes the influence that other people have over a person's behavior. Even without specific reinforcement, every individual learns many things through observation and imitation of other people. (Also called *observational learning.*) 39

social mediation Human interaction that expands and advances understanding, often through words that one person uses to explain something to another. 262

social referencing Seeking information about how to react to an unfamiliar or ambiguous object or event by observing someone else's expressions and reactions. That other person becomes a social reference. 217

social smile A smile evoked by a human face, normally first evident in infants about 6 weeks after birth. 333

sociocultural theory A newer theory that holds that development results from the dynamic interaction of each person with the surrounding social and cultural forces. 42

socioeconomic status (SES) A person's position in society as determined by income, occupation, education, and place of residence. (Sometimes called *social class.*) 6

socioemotional selectivity theory The theory that older people prioritize regulation of their own emotions and seek familiar social contacts who reinforce generativity, pride, and joy. 49

specific learning disorder A marked deficit in a particular area of learning that is not caused by an apparent physical disability, by an intellectual disability, or by an unusually stressful home environment. 450

spermarche A boy's first ejaculation of sperm. Erections can occur as early as infancy, but ejaculation signals sperm production. Spermarche may occur during sleep (in a "wet dream") or via direct stimulation. 100

static reasoning A characteristic of preoperational thought in which a young child thinks that nothing changes. Whatever is now has always been and always will be. 251

stem cells Cells from which any other specialized type of cell can form. 87

stereotype threat The thought in a person's mind that one's appearance or behavior will be misread to confirm another person's oversimplified, prejudiced attitudes. 263

storage All memories that are somewhere in the brain are said to be in storage. Most of this material is buried, not easy to retrieve. 199

Strange Situation The eight-episode measurement of attachment designed by Mary Ainsworth. In a mildly stressful ("strange") playroom, the infant reacts as the mother and a stranger enter and leave. 367

stranger wariness An infant's expression of concern—a quiet stare while clinging to a familiar person, or a look of fear—when a stranger appears. 335

stunting The failure of children to grow to a normal height for their age due to severe and chronic malnutrition. 96

substance use disorder (SUD) A pattern of maladaptive behavior resulting from the repeated use of a substance, often to the point of tolerance to the substance and withdrawal reactions. 455

suicidal ideation Thinking about suicide, usually with some serious emotional and intellectual or cognitive overtones. 452

superego A strict sense of right and wrong, imposed and nurtured in the young child by parents and culture. 274

survey A research method in which information is collected from a large number of people by interviews, written questionnaires, or some other means. 22

symbolic thought A major accomplishment of preoperational intelligence that allows a child to think symbolically, including understanding that words can refer to things not seen and that an item, such as a flag, can symbolize something else (in this case, a country). 250

synapse The intersection between the axon of one neuron and the dendrites of other neurons. 127

synchrony A coordinated, rapid, and smooth exchange of responses between a caregiver and an infant. 371

synesthesia When one sense triggers another. For example, a number written in black print might be seen as a color. Synesthesia can occur with every sense, not just vision. 155

synthesis A new idea that integrates the thesis and its antithesis, thus representing a new and more comprehensive level of truth; the third stage of the process of dialectical thinking. 264

T

tangles Twisted masses of threads made of a protein called tau within the neurons of the brain. 141

temperament Inborn differences between one person and another in emotions, activity, and self-regulation. It is measured by the person's typical responses to the environment. 278

teratogen An agent or condition, including viruses, drugs, and chemicals, that can impair prenatal development and result in birth defects or even death. 89

terror management theory The idea that people adopt cultural values and moral principles in order to cope with their fear of

death. This system of beliefs protects individuals from anxiety about their mortality and bolsters their self-esteem. 475

tertiary circular reaction Piaget's description of the cognitive processes of the 1-year-old, who gathers information from experiences with the wider world and then acts on it. The response to those actions leads to further understanding, which makes this circular. 250

theory of mind A person's theory of what other people might be thinking. In order to have a theory of mind, children must realize that other people are not necessarily thinking the same thoughts that they themselves are. That realization seldom occurs before age 4. 336

thesis A proposition or statement of belief; the first stage of the process of dialectical thinking. 264

time-out A disciplinary technique in which a person is separated from other people and activities for a specified time. 352

transgender A broad term for people whose gender identity and/or gender expression differs from what is typically expected of the sex they were assigned at birth. Some (but not all) transgender people take hormones or undergo surgery to make their bodies align with their gender identity. 309

traumatic brain injury (TBI) An injury to the brain caused by a sudden blow, explosion, or a rapid jerk of the head. This trauma may cause a concussion, with momentary dizziness or unconsciousness. Recovery is likely with rest and quiet, although repeated TBIs can cause chronic traumatic encephalopathy (CTE). 139

Trends in Math and Science Study (TIMSS) An international assessment of the math and science skills of fourth-graders and eighth-graders. Although the TIMSS is very useful, different countries' scores are not always comparable because sample selection, test administration, and content validity are hard to keep uniform. 418

U

underextension Limiting the meaning of a word, and failing to recognize that some words can be correctly used with many referents. 222

universal design The creation of settings and equipment that can be used by everyone, whether or not they are able bodied and sensory-acute. 443

V

vascular disease Formerly called vascular or multi-infarct dementia, vascular disease

is characterized by sporadic, and progressive, loss of intellectual functioning caused by repeated infarcts, or temporary obstructions of blood vessels, which prevent sufficient blood from reaching the brain. 142

verbal aggression Using words to harm someone. 327

very low birthweight (VLBW) A body weight at birth of less than 1,500 grams (3 pounds, 5 ounces). 92

visuospatial sketchpad The metaphorical area of the brain where memories of sights and places are briefly stored. Most items disappear unless they are put into more enduring storage. 198

W

Waldorf schools An early-childhood education program that emphasizes creativity, social understanding, and emotional growth. It originated in Germany with Rudolf Steiner and now is used in thousands of schools throughout the world. 404

wasting The tendency for children to be severely underweight for their age as a result of malnutrition. 96

well-being The feeling of happiness and health that makes life satisfying. 443

working memory Memory that is active at any given moment. 189

X

X-linked A gene carried on the X chromosome. If a male inherits an X-linked recessive trait from his mother, he expresses that trait because the Y from his father has no counteracting gene. Females are more likely to be carriers of X-linked traits but are less likely to express them. 66

XX A 23rd chromosome pair that consists of two X-shaped chromosomes, one each from the mother and the father. XX zygotes become females. 63

XY A 23rd chromosome pair that consists of an X-shaped chromosome from the mother and a Y-shaped chromosome from the father. XY zygotes become males. 63

Z

zone of proximal development (ZPD) Vygotsky's term for the skills—cognitive as well as physical—that a person can exercise only with assistance, not yet independently. 259

zygote The single cell formed from the union of two gametes, a sperm and an ovum. 58

REFERENCES

Accardo, Pasquale. (2006). Who's training whom? *The Journal of Pediatrics, 149*(2), 151–152.

Acevedo, Bianca P.; Poulin, Michael J.; Geher, Glenn; Grafton, Scott & Brown, Lucy L. (2019). The neural and genetic correlates of satisfying sexual activity in heterosexual pair-bonds. *Brain and Behavior, 9*(6), e01289.

Acharya, Arnab; Lalwani, Tanya; Dutta, Rahul; Knoll Rajaratnam, Julie; Ruducha, Jenny; Varkey, Leila Caleb; . . . Bernson, Jeff. (2015). Evaluating a large-scale community-based intervention to improve pregnancy and newborn health among the rural poor in India. *American Journal of Public Health, 105*(1), 144–152.

Achermann, Sheila; Bölte, Sven & Falck-Ytter, Terje. (2020). Parents' experiences from participating in an infant sibling study of autism spectrum disorder. *Research in Autism Spectrum Disorders, 69*(101454).

Ackerman, Phillip L. & Kanfer, Ruth. (2020). Work in the 21st century: New directions for aging and adult development. *American Psychologist, 75*(4), 486–498.

Adamson, Lauren B.; Bakeman, Roger; Deckner, Deborah F. & Nelson, P. Brooke. (2014). From interactions to conversations: The development of joint engagement during early childhood. *Child Development, 85*(3), 941–955.

Addyman, Caspar & Addyman, Ishbel. (2013). The science of baby laughter. *Comedy Studies, 4*(2), 143–153.

Adler, Caleb; DelBello, Melissa, P; Weber, Wade; Williams, Miranda; Duran, Luis Rodrigo Patino; Fleck, David; . . . Divine, Jon. (2018). MRI evidence of neuropathic changes in former college football players. *Clinical Journal of Sport Medicine, 28*(2), 100–105.

Adolph, Karen E. & Hoch, Justine E. (2019). Motor development: Embodied, embedded, enculturated, and enabling. *Annual Review of Psychology, 70*, 141–164.

Adolph, Karen E. & Tamis-LeMonda, Catherine S. (2014). The costs and benefits of development: The transition from crawling to walking. *Child Development Perspectives, 8*(4), 187–192.

Aggarwal, Bharat B. & Yost, Debora. (2011). *Healing spices: How to use 50 everyday and exotic spices to boost health and beat disease.* Sterling.

Aguilar-Raab, Corina; Eckstein, Monika; Geracitano, Susanne; Prevost, Marie; Gold, Ian; Heinrichs, Markus & Bilderbeck, Amy. (2019). Oxytocin modulates the cognitive appraisal of the own and others close intimate relationships. *Frontiers in Neuroscience, 13*(714).

Ahonen, Lia; FitzGerald, Douglas; Klingensmith, Kaylee & Farrington, David P. (2020). Criminal career duration: Predictability from self-reports and official records. *Criminal Behaviour and Mental Health, 30*(4), 172–182.

Ainsworth, Mary D. Salter. (1967). *Infancy in Uganda: Infant care and the growth of love.* Johns Hopkins Press.

Ainsworth, Mary D. Salter; Blehar, Mary C.; Waters, Everett & Wall, Sally N. (1978). *Patterns of attachment: A psychological study of the strange situation.* Lawrence Erlbaum.

Aitken, Jess; Ruffman, Ted & Taumoepeau, Mele. (2019). Toddlers' self-recognition and progression from goal- to emotion-based helping: A longitudinal study. *Child Development*, (In Press).

Aizpitarte, Alazne; Atherton, Olivia E.; Zheng, Lucy R.; Alonso-Arbiol, Itziar & Robins, Richard W. (2019). Developmental precursors of relational aggression from late childhood through adolescence. *Child Development, 90*(1), 117–126.

Ajrouch, Kristine J.; Fuller, Heather R.; Akiyama, Hiroko & Antonucci, Toni C. (2018). Convoys of social relations in cross-national context. *The Gerontologist, 58*(3), 488–499.

Akhtar, Nameera & Jaswal, Vikram K. (2013). Deficit or difference? Interpreting diverse developmental paths: An introduction to the special section. *Developmental Psychology, 49*(1), 1–3.

Akombi, Blessing J.; Agho, Kingsley E.; Hall, John J.; Wali, Nidhi; Renzaho, Andre M. N. & Merom, Dafna. (2017). Stunting, wasting and underweight in sub-Saharan Africa: A systematic review. *International Journal of Environmental Research and Public Health, 14*(8).

Aksglaede, Lise; Link, Katarina; Giwercman, Aleksander; Jørgensen, Niels; Skakkebæk, Niels E. & Juul, Anders. (2013). 47, XXY Klinefelter syndrome: Clinical characteristics and age-specific recommendations for medical management. *American Journal of Medical Genetics Part C: Seminars in Medical Genetics, 163*(1), 55–63.

Al Otaiba, Stephanie; Baker, Kristi; Lan, Patrick; Allor, Jill; Rivas, Brenna; Yovanoff, Paul & Kamata, Akihito. (2019). Elementary teacher's knowledge of response to intervention implementation: A preliminary factor analysis. *Annals of Dyslexia, 69*(1), 34–53.

Al-Balas, Mahmoud; Al-Balas, Hasan Ibrahim & Al-Balas, Hamzeh. (2020). Surgery during the COVID-19 pandemic: A comprehensive overview and perioperative care. *American Journal of Surgery, 219*(6), 903–906.

Al-Darabah, Intisar Turki; Almohtadi, Reham; Jwaifell, Mustafa & Dib, Fahima. (2019). Parental upbringing styles and their relationship with social withdrawal among a sample of kindergarten children: The forgotten victim. *Journal of Education and Practice, 10*(18).

Al-Namlah, Abdulrahman S.; Meins, Elizabeth & Fernyhough, Charles. (2012). Self-regulatory private speech relates to children's recall and organization of autobiographical memories. *Early Childhood Research Quarterly, 27*(3), 441–446.

Aldwin, Carolyn M. & Gilmer, Diane Fox. (2013). *Health, illness, and optimal aging: Biological and psychosocial perspectives* (2nd ed.). Springer.

Alexander, Gerianne M. & Saenz, Janet. (2012). Early androgens, activity levels and toy choices of children in the second year of life. *Hormones and Behavior, 62*(4), 500–504.

Ali, Marwan & Parekh, Neel. (2020). Male age and andropause: Contemporary clinical approaches, andrology, ART and antioxidants. In Parekattil, Sijo J.; Esteves, Sandro C. & Agarwal, Ashok (Eds.), *Male infertility* (pp. 469–477). Springer.

Allen, Kelly; Kern, Margaret L.; Vella-Brodrick, Dianne; Hattie, John & Waters, Lea. (2018). What schools need to know about fostering school belonging: A meta-analysis. *Educational Psychology Review, 30*, 1–34.

Allendorf, Keera & Pandian, Roshan K. (2016). The decline of arranged marriage? Marital change and continuity in India. *Population and Development Review, 42*(3), 435–464.

Alloway, Tracy Packiam; McCallum, Fiona; Alloway, Ross G. & Hoicka, Elena. (2015). Liar, liar, working memory on fire: Investigating the role of working memory in childhood verbal deception. *Journal of Experimental Child Psychology, 137*, 30–38.

Allport, Gordon W. (1961). *Pattern and growth in personality.* Holt, Rinehart and Winston.

Almeida, David M.; Charles, Susan T.; Mogle, Jacqueline; Drewelies, Johanna; Aldwin, Carolyn M.; Spiro, Avron & Gerstorf, Denis. (2020). Charting adult development through (historically changing) daily stress processes. *American Psychologist, 75*(4), 511–524.

Altenhoevel, A.; Norman, K.; Smoliner, C. & Peroz, I. (2012). The impact of self-perceived masticatory function on nutrition and gastrointestinal complaints in the elderly. *JNHA: Geriatric Science, 16*(2), 175–178.

Altenmüller, Eckart & Furuya, Shinichi. (2018). Brain changes associated with acquisition of musical expertise. In Ericsson, K. Anders; Hoffman, Robert R.; Kozbelt, Aaron & Williams, A. Mark (Eds.), *The Cambridge handbook of expertise and expert performance* (2nd ed., pp. 550–575). Cambridge University Press.

Altmann, Andre; Tian, Lu; Henderson, Victor W. & Greicius, Michael D. (2014). Sex modifies the *APOE*-related risk of developing Alzheimer disease. *Annals of Neurology, 75*(4), 563–573.

Altmayer, Christina & DuBransky, Barbara Andrade. (2019). Strengthening home visiting: Partnership and innovation in Los Angeles County. *The Future of Children, 29*(1), 61–79.

Alur, Pradeep. (2019). Sex differences in nutrition, growth, and metabolism in preterm infants. *Frontiers in Pediatrics, 7*(22).

Amato, Michael S.; Magzamen, Sheryl; Imm, Pamela; Havlena, Jeffrey A.; Anderson, Henry A.; Kanarek, Marty S. & Moore, Colleen F. (2013). Early lead exposure (<3 years old) prospectively predicts fourth grade school suspension in Milwaukee, Wisconsin (USA). *Environmental Research, 126,* 60–65.

American College of Obstetricians and Gynecologists Committee on Obstetric Practice. (2011). Committee opinion no. 476: Planned home birth. *Obstetrics & Gynecology, 117*(2), 425–428.

American Psychiatric Association. (2004). *Diagnostic and statistical manual of mental disorders: DSM-IV* (4th ed.). American Psychiatric Association.

American Psychiatric Association. (2013). *Diagnostic and statistical manual of mental disorders: DSM-5* (5th ed.). American Psychiatric Association.

Amin, Fakhra; Amin, Anas; Asghar, Muhammad Nadeem; Khaki, Peerzada Shariq Shaheen; Khan, Mohd Shahnawaz; Tabrez, Shams; . . . Bano, Bilqees. (2019). Alzheimer's: A progressive brain disease: Causes, symptoms, and prevention. In Ashraf, Ghulam Md & Alexiou, Athanasios (Eds.), *Biological, diagnostic and therapeutic advances in Alzheimer's disease: Non-pharmacological therapies for Alzheimer's disease* (pp. 31–51). Springer.

Andere, Eduardo. (2020). *The future of schools and teacher education: How far ahead is Finland?* Oxford University Press.

Anderson, Daniel R. & Hanson, Katherine G. (2016). Screen media and parent–child interactions. In Barr, Rachel & Linebarger, Deborah Nichols (Eds.), *Media exposure during infancy and early childhood: The effects of content and context on learning and development* (pp. 173–194). Springer.

Anderson, Michael. (2001). 'You have to get inside the person' or making grief private: Image and metaphor in the therapeutic reconstruction of bereavement. In Hockey, Jenny; Katz, Jeanne & Small, Neil (Eds.), *Grief, mourning, and death ritual* (pp. 135–143). Open University Press.

Andreas, Nicholas J.; Kampmann, Beate & Le-Doare, Kirsty Mehring. (2015). Human breast milk: A review on its composition and bioactivity. *Early Human Development, 91*(11), 629–635.

Ang, Shannon. (2019). Life course social connectedness: Age-cohort trends in social participation. *Advances in Life Course Research, 39,* 13–22.

Ansari, Arya & Pianta, Robert C. (2018). Variation in the long-term benefits of child care: The role of classroom quality in elementary school. *Developmental Psychology, 54*(10), 1854–1867.

Antenucci, Antonio. (2013, November 26). Cop who bought homeless man boots promoted. *New York Post.*

Antoine, Michelle W.; Vijayakumar, Sarath; McKeehan, Nicholas; Jones, Sherri M. & Hébert, Jean M. (2017). The severity of vestibular dysfunction in deafness as a determinant of comorbid hyperactivity or anxiety. *Journal of Neuroscience, 37*(20), 5144–5154.

Archer, John. (2004). Sex differences in aggression in real-world settings: A meta-analytic review. *Review of General Psychology, 8*(4), 291–322.

Ariely, Dan. (2010). *Predictably irrational: The hidden forces that shape our decisions* (Revised and Expanded ed.). Harper Perennial.

Ariès, Philippe. (1965). *Centuries of childhood: A social history of family life.* Vintage.

Armstrong, Nicole M.; Meoni, Lucy A.; Carlson, Michelle C.; Xue, Qian-Li; Bandeen-Roche, Karen; Gallo, Joseph J. & Gross, Alden L. (2017). Cardiovascular risk factors and risk of incident depression throughout adulthood among men: The Johns Hopkins Precursors study. *Journal of Affective Disorders, 214,* 60–66.

Arnold, Arthur P. (2020). Sexual differentiation of brain and other tissues: Five questions for the next 50 years. *Hormones and Behavior, 120,* 104691.

Aron, Arthur; Lewandowski, Gary W.; Mashek, Debra & Aron, Elaine N. (2013). The self-expansion model of motivation and cognition in close relationships. In Simpson, Jeffry A. & Campbell, Lorne (Eds.), *The Oxford handbook of close relationships* (pp. 90–115). Oxford University Press.

Arts, Nicolaas; Walvoort, Serge & Kessels, Roy. (2017). Korsakoff's syndrome: A critical review. *Neuropsychiatric Disease and Treatment, 13,* 2875–2890.

Arum, Richard & Roksa, Josipa. (2011). *Academically adrift: Limited learning on college campuses.* University of Chicago Press.

Arum, Richard & Roksa, Josipa. (2014). *Aspiring adults adrift: Tentative transitions of college graduates.* University of Chicago Press.

Ash, Caroline & Mueller, Kristen. (2016). Manipulating the microbiota. *Science, 352*(6285), 530–531.

Ashraf, Quamrul & Galor, Oded. (2013). The 'Out of Africa' hypothesis, human genetic diversity, and comparative economic development. *American Economic Review, 103*(1), 1–46.

Aslin, Richard N. (2012). Language development: Revisiting Eimas et al.'s /ba/ and /pa/ study. In Slater, Alan M. & Quinn, Paul C. (Eds.), *Developmental psychology: Revisiting the classic studies* (pp. 191–203). Sage.

Astle, Shelby; Leonhardt, Nathan & Willoughby, Brian. (2019). Home base: Family of origin factors and the debut of vaginal sex, anal sex, oral sex, masturbation, and pornography use in a national sample of adolescents. *The Journal of Sex Research,* (In Press).

Atamna, Hani; Tenore, Alfred; Lui, Forshing & Dhabi, Joseph M. (2018). Organ reserve, excess metabolic capacity, and aging. *Biogerontology, 19*(2), 171–184.

Athan, Aurélie M. (2020). Reproductive identity: An emerging concept. *American Psychologist, 75*(4), 445–456.

Atkinson, Richard C. & Shiffrin, Richard M. (1968). *Human memory: A proposed system and its control processes.* Academic Press.

Attaran, Amir. (2015). Unanimity on death with dignity—Legalizing physician-assisted dying in Canada. *New England Journal of Medicine, 372,* 2080–2082.

Atzaba-Poria, Naama; Deater-Deckard, Kirby & Bell, Martha Ann. (2017). Mother-child interaction: Links between mother and child frontal electroencephalograph asymmetry and negative behavior. *Child Development, 88*(2), 544–554.

Auday, Eran S. & Pérez-Edgar, Koraly E. (2019). Limbic and prefrontal neural volume modulate social anxiety in children at temperamental risk. *Depression and Anxiety, 36*(8), 690–700.

Augustine, Vineet; Gokce, Sertan Kutal & Oka, Yuki. (2018). Peripheral and central nutrient sensing underlying appetite regulation. *Trends in Neurosciences, 41*(8), 526–539.

Aunola, Kaisa; Tolvanen, Asko; Viljaranta, Jaana & Nurmi, Jari-Erik. (2013). Psychological control in daily parent–child interactions increases children's negative emotions. *Journal of Family Psychology, 27*(3), 453–462.

Austad, Steven N. (2010). Methusaleh's zoo: How nature provides us with clues for extending human health span. *Journal of Comparative Pathology, 142*(Suppl. 1), S10–S21.

Aviezer, Ora; Sagi, Abraham & Van Ijzendoorn, Marinus. (2002). Balancing the family and the collective in raising children: Why communal sleeping in kibbutzim was predestined to end. *Family Process, 41*(3), 435–454.

Azrin, Nathan H. & Foxx, Richard M. (1974). *Toilet training in less than a day.* Simon & Schuster.

Babcock, Renée L.; Malonebeach, Eileen E. & Salomon, Hannah M. (2018). A quantitative and qualitative evaluation of the impact of an intergenerational program on children's biases toward older adults. *Journal of Intergenerational Relationships, 16*(1/2), 123–138.

Babineau, Vanessa; Green, Cathryn Gordon; Jolicoeur-Martineau, Alexis; Minde, Klaus; Sassi, Roberto; St-André, Martin; . . . Wazana, Ashley. (2015). Prenatal depression and 5-HTTLPR interact to predict dysregulation from 3 to 36 months—A differential susceptibility model. *Journal of Child Psychology and Psychiatry, 56*(1), 21–29.

Baddeley, Alan. (2003). Working memory and language: An overview. *Journal of Communication Disorders, 36*(3), 189–208.

Baddeley, Alan; Eysenck, Michael W. & Anderson, Michael C. (Eds.). (2020). *Memory* (3rd ed.). Routledge.

Baddeley, Alan D. & Hitch, Graham J. (1994). Developments in the concept of working memory. *Neuropsychology, 8*(4), 485–493.

Baggio, Michele & Chong, Alberto. (2020). Recreational marijuana laws and junk food consumption. *Economics & Human Biology, 39*(100922).

Bailey, Drew H.; Oh, Yoonkyung; Farkas, George; Morgan, Paul & Hillemeier, Marianne M. (2020). Reciprocal effects of reading and mathematics? Beyond the cross-lagged panel model. *Developmental Psychology, 56*(5), 912–921.

Baillargeon, Jacques; Urban, Randall James; Zhang, Wei; Zaiden, Mohammed Fathi; Javed, Zulqarnain; Sheffield-Moore, Melinda; . . . Sharma, Gulshan. (2019). Testosterone replacement therapy and hospitalization rates in men with COPD. *Chronic Respiratory Disease, 16.*

Baillargeon, Renée. (1987). Object permanence in 3½- and 4½-month-old infants. *Developmental Psychology, 23*(5), 655–664.

Baillargeon, Renée & DeVos, Julie. (1991). Object permanence in young infants: Further evidence. *Child Development, 62*(6), 1227–1246.

Baker, Darren J. & Petersen, Ronald C. (2018). Cellular senescence in brain aging and neurodegenerative diseases: Evidence and perspectives. *The Journal of Clinical Investigation, 128*(4), 1208–1216.

Balk, David & Varga, Mary Alice. (2017). Continuing bonds and social media in the lives of bereaved college students. In Klass, Dennis & Steffen, Edith Maria (Eds.), *Continuing bonds in bereavement: New directions for research and practice.* Routledge.

Baltes, Boris; Zhdanova, Ludmila & Clark, Malissa. (2011). Examining the relationships between personality, coping strategies, and work–family conflict. *Journal of Business and Psychology, 26*(4), 517–530.

Baltes, Paul B. (1987). Theoretical propositions of life-span developmental psychology: On the dynamics between growth and decline. *Developmental Psychology, 23*(5), 611–626.

Baltes, Paul B. (2003). On the incomplete architecture of human ontogeny: Selection, optimization and compensation as foundation of developmental theory. In Staudinger, Ursula M. & Lindenberger, Ulman (Eds.), *Understanding human development: Dialogues with lifespan psychology* (pp. 17–43). Kluwer Academic Publishers.

Baltes, Paul B. & Baltes, Margret M. (1990). Psychological perspectives on successful aging: The model of selective optimization with compensation. In Baltes, Paul B. & Baltes, Margret M. (Eds.), *Successful aging: Perspectives from the behavioral sciences* (pp. 1–34). Cambridge University Press.

Bandura, Albert. (1986). *Social foundations of thought and action: A social cognitive theory.* Prentice-Hall.

Bandura, Albert. (1997). The anatomy of stages of change. *American Journal of Health Promotion, 12*(1), 8–10.

Bandura, Albert. (2006). Toward a psychology of human agency. *Perspectives on Psychological Science, 1*(2), 164–180.

Bandura, Albert. (2016). *Moral disengagement: How people do harm and live with themselves.* Worth.

Barac, Raluca; Bialystok, Ellen; Castro, Dina C. & Sanchez, Marta. (2014). The cognitive development of young dual language learners: A critical review. *Early Childhood Research Quarterly, 29*(4), 699–714.

Barajas, Clara B.; Jones, Shawn C. T.; Milam, Adam J.; Thorpe Jr, Roland J.; Gaskin, Darrell J.; LaVeist, Thomas A. & Furr-Holden, C. Debra M. (2019). Coping, discrimination, and physical health conditions among predominantly poor, urban African Americans: Implications for community-level health services. *Journal of Community Health, 44*(5), 954–962.

Barber, Brian K. (Ed.) (2002). *Intrusive parenting: How psychological control affects children and adolescents.* American Psychological Association.

Barbey, Aron K. (2018). Network neuroscience theory of human intelligence. *Trends in Cognitive Sciences, 22*(1), 8–20.

Barbour, Kamil E.; Helmick, Charles G.; Boring, Michael & Brady, Teresa J. (2017, March 10). *Vital signs: Prevalence of doctor-diagnosed arthritis and arthritis-attributable activity limitation—United States, 2013–2015. Morbidity and Mortality Weekly Report, 66*(9), 246–253. Atlanta, GA: Centers for Disease Control and Prevention.

Barone, Joseph. (2015). *It's not your fault!: Strategies for solving toilet training and bedwetting problems.* Rutgers University Press.

Barr, Rachel. (2013). Memory constraints on infant learning from picture books, television, and touchscreens. *Child Development Perspectives, 7*(4), 205–210.

Barrett, Anne E. (2012). Feeling young—A prescription for growing older? *Aging Today, 33,* 3–4.

Barrett, Lisa Feldman; Adolphs, Ralph; Marsella, Stacy; Martinez, Aleix M. & Pollak, Seth D. (2019). Emotional expressions reconsidered: Challenges to inferring emotion from human facial movements. *Psychological Science in the Public Interest, 20*(1), 1–68.

Barrios, Yasmin V.; Sanchez, Sixto E.; Nicolaidis, Christina; Garcia, Pedro J.; Gelaye, Bizu; Zhong, Qiuyue & Williams, Michelle A. (2015). Childhood abuse and early menarche among Peruvian women. *Journal of Adolescent Health, 56*(2), 197–202.

Barroso, Amanda; Parker, Kim & Fry, Richard. (2019, October 23). *Majority of Americans say parents are doing too much for their young adult children: Young men are taking longer to reach financial independence, as young women have gained ground. Social & Demographic Trends.* Washington, DC: Pew Research Center.

Barrouillet, Pierre & Camos, Valérie. (2012). As time goes by: Temporal constraints in working memory. *Current Directions in Psychological Science, 21*(6), 413–419.

Barthel, Michael & Stocking, Galen. (2020, April 6). *Older people account for large shares of poll workers and voters in U.S. general elections. Fact Tank.* Washington, DC: Pew Research Center.

Basseches, Michael. (1984). *Dialectical thinking and adult development.* Ablex.

Basseches, Michael. (1989). Dialectical thinking as an organized whole: Comments on Irwin and Kramer. In Commons, Michael L.; Sinnott, Jan D.; Richards, Francis A. & Armon, Cheryl (Eds.), *Adult development* (Vol. 1, pp. 161–178). Praeger.

Basso, Julia C.; McHale, Alexandra; Ende, Victoria; Oberlin, Douglas J. & Suzuki, Wendy A. (2019). Brief, daily meditation enhances attention, memory, mood, and emotional regulation in non-experienced meditators. *Behavioural Brain Research, 356,* 208–220.

Bassok, Daphna; Latham, Scott & Rorem, Anna. (2016). Is kindergarten the new first grade? *AERA Open, 2*(1).

Baude, Amandine; Pearson, Jessica & Drapeau, Sylvie. (2016). Child adjustment in joint physical custody versus sole custody: A meta-analytic review. *Journal of Divorce & Remarriage, 57*(5), 338–360.

Baudry, Claire; Tarabulsy, George M.; Atkinson, Leslie; Pearson, Jessica & St-Pierre, Audrey. (2017). Intervention with adolescent mother–child dyads and cognitive development in early childhood: A meta-analysis. *Prevention Science, 18*(1), 116–130.

Bauer, Markus; Truffer, Daniela & Crocetti, Daniela. (2019). Intersex human rights. *International Journal of Human Rights, 24*(6), 1–26.

Baumeister, Roy F. & Leary, Mark R. (1995). The need to belong: Desire for interpersonal attachments as a fundamental human motivation. *Psychological Bulletin, 117*(3), 497–529.

Baumrind, Diana. (1967). Child care practices anteceding three patterns of preschool behavior. *Genetic Psychology Monographs, 75*(1), 43–88.

Baumrind, Diana. (1971). Current patterns of parental authority. *Developmental Psychology, 4*(1, Pt. 2), 1–103.

Baumrind, Diana. (2013). Authoritative parenting revisited: History and current status. In Larzelere, Robert E.; Morris, Amanda Sheffield & Harrist, Amanda W. (Eds.), *Authoritative parenting: Synthesizing nurturance and discipline for optimal child development* (pp. 11–34). American Psychological Association.

Bavineni, Mahesh; Wassenaar, Trudy M.; Agnihotri, Kanishk; Ussery, David W.; Lüscher, Thomas F. & Mehta, Jawahar L. (2019). Mechanisms linking preterm birth to onset of cardiovascular disease later in adulthood. *European Heart Journal, 40*(14), 1107–1112.

Beck, Andrew F.; Bradley, Courtney L.; Huang, Bin; Simmons, Jeffrey M.; Heaton, Pamela C. & Kahn, Robert S. (2015). The pharmacy-level asthma medication ratio and population health. *Pediatrics, 135*(6), 1009–1017.

Becker, Derek R.; McClelland, Megan M.; Loprinzi, Paul & Trost, Stewart G. (2014). Physical activity, self-regulation, and early academic achievement in preschool children. *Early Education and Development, 25*(1), 56–70.

Beckwith, Jon & Pierce, Robin. (2018). Genes and human behavior: Ethical implications. In Gerlai, Robert T. (Ed.), *Molecular-genetic and statistical techniques for behavioral and neural research* (pp. 599–622). Elsevier.

Bedford, Elliott Louis; Blaire, Stephen; Carney, John G.; Hamel, Ron; Mindling, J. Daniel & Sullivan, M. C. (2017). Advance care planning, palliative care, and end-of-life care. *The National Catholic Bioethics Quarterly, 17*(3), 489–501.

Been, Laura E.; Gibbons, Alison B. & Meisel, Robert L. (2019). Towards a neurobiology of female aggression. *Neuropharmacology, 156*(107451).

Beeney, Joseph E.; Wright, Aidan G. C.; Stepp, Stephanie D.; Hallquist, Michael N.; Lazarus, Sophie A.; Beeney, Julie R. S., . . . A., Pilkonis Paul. (2017). Disorganized attachment and personality functioning in adults: A latent class analysis. *Personality Disorders: Theory, Research, and Treatment, 8*(3), 206–216.

Bellinger, David C. (2016). Lead contamination in Flint—An abject failure to protect public health. *New England Journal of Medicine, 374*(12), 1101–1103.

Belsky, Daniel W.; Caspi, Avshalom; Houts, Renate; Cohen, Harvey J.; Corcoran, David L.; Danese, Andrea; . . . Moffitt, Terrie E. (2015). Quantification of biological aging in young adults. *Proceedings of the National Academy of Sciences of the United States of America, 112*(30), e4104–e4110.

Belsky, Jay; Bakermans-Kranenburg, Marian J. & van IJzendoorn, Marinus H. (2007). For better and for worse: Differential susceptibility to environmental influences. *Current Directions in Psychological Science, 16*(6), 300–304.

Belsky, Jay; Steinberg, Laurence; Houts, Renate M. & Halpern-Felsher, Bonnie L. (2010). The development of reproductive strategy in females: Early maternal harshness → earlier menarche → increased sexual risk taking. *Developmental Psychology, 46*(1), 120–128.

Benatar, David. (2011). A legal right to die: Responding to slippery slope and abuse arguments. *Current Oncology, 18*(5), 206–207.

Benavides-Jimenez, Fabián & Lisbeth Mora-Acosta, Yenny. (2019). Beliefs of two culturally diverse groups of teachers about intercultural bilingual education. *Profile: Issues in Teachers' Professional Development, 21*(2), 63–77.

Bengtson, Vern L.; Silverstein, Merril; Putney, Norella M. & Harris, Susan C. (2015). Does religiousness increase with age? Age changes and generational differences over 35 years. *Journal for the Scientific Study of Religion, 54*(2), 363–379.

Benjamin, Arlin James & Bushman, Brad J. (2016). The weapons priming effect. *Current Opinion in Psychology, 12*, 45–48.

Benjamin, Christopher F. A.; Li, Alexa X.; Blumenfeld, Hal; Constable, R. Todd; Alkawadri, Rafeed; Bickel, Stephan; . . . Hirsch, Lawrence J. (2018). Presurgical language fMRI: Clinical practices and patient outcomes in epilepsy surgical planning. *Human Brain Mapping, 39*(7), 2777–2785.

Benn, Peter. (2016). Prenatal diagnosis of chromosomal abnormalities through chorionic villus sampling and amniocentesis. In Milunsky, Aubrey & Milunsky, Jeff M. (Eds.), *Genetic disorders and the fetus: Diagnosis, prevention, and treatment* (7th ed., pp. 178–266). Wiley-Blackwell.

Benner, Patricia. (2012). Educating nurses: A call for radical transformation—how far have we come? *Journal of Nursing Education, 51*(4), 183–184.

Benson, Peter L.; Scales, Peter C.; Syvertsen, Amy K. & Roehlkepartain, Eugene C. (2012). Is youth spiritual development a universal developmental process? An international exploration. *The Journal of Positive Psychology, 7*(6), 453–470.

Berg, Jeremy. (2018). Imagine a world without facts. *Science, 362*(6413), 379.

Berger, Christopher C. & Ehrsson, H. Henrik. (2018). Mental imagery induces cross-modal sensory plasticity and changes future auditory perception. *Psychological Science, 29*(6).

Berger, Kathleen S. (2019). *Grandmothering: Building strong ties with every generation.* Rowman & Littlefield.

Bergmann, Olaf; Spalding, Kirsty L. & Frisén, Jonas. (2015). Adult neurogenesis in humans. *Cold Spring Harbor Perspectives in Biology, 7*, a018994.

Berken, Jonathan A.; Gracco, Vincent L. & Klein, Denise. (2017). Early bilingualism, language attainment, and brain development. *Neuropsychologia, 98*, 220–227.

Berlin, Lisa J.; Martoccio, Tiffany L. & Jones Harden, Brenda. (2018). Improving early Head Start's impacts on parenting through attachment-based intervention: A randomized controlled trial. *Developmental Psychology, 54*(12), 2316–2327.

Bernard, Kristin; Hostinar, Camelia E. & Dozier, Mary. (2019). Longitudinal associations between attachment quality in infancy, C-reactive protein in early childhood, and BMI in middle childhood: Preliminary evidence from a CPS-referred sample. *Attachment & Human Development, 21*(1), 5–22.

Bernaud, Jean-Luc. (2014). Career counseling and life meaning: A new perspective of life designing for research and applications. In Di, Fabio A. & Bernaud, J- L. (Eds.), *The construction of the identity in 21st century: A Festschrift for Jean Guichard* (pp. 29–40). Nova Science.

Betancourt, Theresa S.; McBain, Ryan; Newnham, Elizabeth A. & Brennan, Robert T. (2013). Trajectories of internalizing problems in war-affected Sierra Leonean youth: Examining conflict and postconflict factors. *Child Development, 84*(2), 455–470.

Bettelheim, Bruno. (1975). *The empty fortress: Infantile autism and the birth of the self.* Free Press.

Bettencourt, Luís M. A.; Samaniego, Horacio & Youn, Hyejin. (2014). Professional diversity and the productivity of cities. *Scientific Reports, 4*(5393).

Bettinger, Blaine T. (2019). *The family tree guide to DNA testing and genetic genealogy* (2nd ed.). Penguin.

Bialik, Kristen. (2017, June 12). *Key facts about race and marriage, 50 years after Loving v. Virginia. Fact Tank.* Washington, DC: Pew Research Center.

Bialystok, Ellen. (2015). Bilingualism and the development of executive function: The role of attention. *Child Development Perspectives, 9*(2), 117–121.

Bialystok, Ellen. (2018). Bilingualism and executive function: What's the connection? In Miller, David; Bayram, Fatih; Rothman, Jason & Serratrice, Ludovica (Eds.), *Bilingual cognition and language: The state of the science across its subfields* (pp. 283–306). John Benjamins.

Bigelow, Ann E. & Power, Michelle. (2012). The effect of mother–infant skin-to-skin contact on infants' response to the Still Face Task from newborn to three months of age. *Infant Behavior and Development, 35*(2), 240–251.

Birdsong, David. (2018). Plasticity, variability and age in second language acquisition and bilingualism. *Frontiers in Psychology, 9*(81).

Birkenhäger-Gillesse, Elizabeth G.; Kollen, Boudewijn J.; Achterberg, Wilco P.; Boersma, Froukje; Jongman, Lydia & Zuidema, Sytse U. (2018). Effects of psychosocial interventions for behavioral and psychological symptoms in dementia on the prescription of psychotropic drugs: A systematic review and meta-analyses. *Journal of the American Medical Directors, 19*(3), 276.e1–276.e9.

Birkett, D. Peter. (2008). *The psychiatry of stroke* (2nd ed.). Haworth Press.

Biro, Frank M.; Greenspan, Louise C.; Galvez, Maida P.; Pinney, Susan M.; Teitelbaum, Susan; Windham, Gayle C.; . . . Wolff, Mary S. (2013). Onset of breast development in a longitudinal cohort. *Pediatrics, 132*(6), 1019–1027.

Bitsko, Rebecca H.; Holbrook, Joseph R.; Ghandour, Reem M.; Blumberg, Stephen J.; Visser, Susanna N.; Perou, Ruth & Walkup, John T. (2018). Epidemiology and impact of health care provider–diagnosed anxiety and depression among US children. *Journal of Developmental & Behavioral Pediatrics, 39*(5), 395–403.

Bjorklund, David F. & Ellis, Bruce J. (2014). Children, childhood, and development in evolutionary perspective. *Developmental Review, 34*(3), 225–264.

Black, Maureen M.; Papas, Mia A.; Hussey, Jon M.; Hunter, Wanda; Dubowitz, Howard; Kotch, Jonathan B.; . . . Schneider, Mary. (2002). Behavior and development of preschool children born to adolescent mothers: Risk and 3-generation households. *Pediatrics, 109*(4), 573–580.

Blakey, Shannon M.; Wagner, H. Ryan; Naylor, Jennifer; Brancu, Mira; Lane, Ilana; Sallee, Meghann; . . . Elbogen, Eric B. (2018). Chronic pain, TBI, and PTSD in military veterans: A link to suicidal ideation and violent impulses? *Journal of Pain, 19*(7), 797–806.

Blalock, Garrick; Kadiyali, Vrinda & Simon, Daniel H. (2009). Driving fatalities after 9/11: A hidden cost of terrorism. *Applied Economics, 41*(14), 1717–1729.

Blas, Erik & Kurup, Anand Sivasankara (Eds.). (2010). *Equity, social determinants, and public health programmes.* World Health Organization.

Bleidorn, Wiebke; Schönbrodt, Felix; Gebauer, Jochen E.; Rentfrow, Peter J.; Potter, Jeff & Gosling, Samuel D. (2016). To live among like-minded others: Exploring the links between person-city personality fit and self-esteem. *Psychological Science, 27*(3), 419–427.

Bleidorn, Wiebke & Schwaba, Ted. (2018). Retirement is associated with change in self-esteem. *Psychology and Aging, 33*(4), 586–594.

Blieszner, Rosemary; Ogletree, Aaron M. & Adams, Rebecca G. (2019). Friendship in later life: A research agenda. *Innovation in Aging, 3*(1), igz005.

Bloom, Erika Litvin; Farris, Samantha G.; DiBello, Angelo M. & Abrantes, Ana M. (2019). Smoking-related weight and appetite concerns and use of electronic cigarettes among daily cigarette smokers. *Psychology, Health & Medicine*, 24(2), 221–228.

Bloom, Paul. (2012). Religion, morality, evolution. *Annual Review of Psychology*, 63, 179–199.

Bloom, Paul. (2017). *Against empathy: The case for rational compassion.* Random House.

Blossfeld, Gwendolin Josephine; Blossfeld, Pia Nicoletta & Blossfeld, Hans-Peter. (2019). A sociological perspective on education as a lifelong process. In Becker, Rolf (Ed.), *Research handbook on the sociology of education.* Edward Elgar.

Blurton-Jones, Nicholas G. (1976). Rough-and-tumble play among nursery school children. In Bruner, Jerome S.; Jolly, Alison & Sylva, Kathy (Eds.), *Play: Its role in development and evolution* (pp. 352–363). Basic Books.

Boertien, Diederik & Bernardi, Fabrizio. (2019). Same-sex parents and children's school progress: An association that disappeared over time. *Demography*, 56, 477–501.

Boldrini, Maura; Fulmore, Camille A.; Tartt, Alexandria N.; Simeon, Laika R.; Pavlova, Ina; Poposka, Verica; . . . Mann, John. (2018). Human hippocampal neurogenesis persists throughout aging. *Cell Stem Cell*, 22(4), 589–599.e5.

Bone, Anna E.; Gomes, Barbara; Etkind, Simon N.; Verne, Julia; Murtagh, Fliss Em; Evans, Catherine J. & Higginson, Irene J. (2018). What is the impact of population ageing on the future provision of end-of-life care? Population-based projections of place of death. *Palliative Medicine*, 32(2), 329–336.

Bonilla-Silva, Eduardo. (2018). *Racism without racists: Color-blind racism and the persistence of racial inequality in America* (5th ed.). Rowman & Littlefield.

Borja, Sharon; Nurius, Paula S.; Song, Chiho & Lengua, Liliana J. (2019). Adverse childhood experiences to adult adversity trends among parents: Socioeconomic, health, and developmental implications. *Children and Youth Services Review*, 100, 258–266.

Bornstein, Marc H. (2015). Children's parents. In Lerner, Richard M. (Ed.), *Handbook of child psychology and developmental science* (7th ed., Vol. 4, pp. 55–132). Wiley.

Bornstein, Marc H.; Mortimer, Jeylan T.; Lutfey, Karen & Bradley, Robert. (2011). Theories and processes in life-span socialization. In Fingerman, Karen L.; Berg, Cynthia; Smith, Jacqui & Antonucci, Toni (Eds.), *Handbook of life-span development* (pp. 27–56). Springer.

Bornstein, Marc H. & Putnick, Diane L. (2016). Mothers' and fathers' parenting practices with their daughters and sons in low- and middle-income countries. *Monographs of the Society for Research in Child Development*, 81(1), 60–77.

Bouchard, Thomas J.; Lykken, David T.; McGue, Matthew; Segal, Nancy L. & Tellegen, Auke. (1990). Sources of human psychological differences: The Minnesota Study of Twins Reared Apart. *Science*, 250(4978), 223–228.

Boundy, Ellen O.; Dastjerdi, Roya; Spiegelman, Donna; Fawzi, Wafaie W.; Missmer, Stacey A.; Lieberman, Ellice; . . . Chan, Grace J. (2016). Kangaroo mother care and neonatal outcomes: A meta-analysis. *Pediatrics*, 137(1), e20152238.

Bowlby, John. (1951). Maternal care and mental health. *Bulletin of the World Health Organization*, 3(3), 355–533.

Bowlby, John. (1958). Separation of mother and child. *The Lancet*, 271(7018), 480.

Bowlby, John. (1969). *Attachment and loss* (Vol. 1). Basic Books.

Bowlby, John. (1983). *Attachment* (2nd ed.). Basic Books.

Braams, Barbara R.; van Duijvenvoorde, Anna C. K.; Peper, Jiska S. & Crone, Eveline A. (2015). Longitudinal changes in adolescent risk-taking: A comprehensive study of neural responses to rewards, pubertal development, and risk-taking behavior. *The Journal of Neuroscience*, 35(18), 7226–7238.

Bragg, Debra D.; Endel, Barbara; Anderson, Nate; Soricone, Lisa & Acevedo, Erica. (2019, July 10). *What works for adult learners: Lessons from career pathway evaluations.* JJF.

Brainard, Jeffrey. (2018). Rethinking retractions. *Science*, 362(6413), 390–393.

Braithwaite, Dawn O.; Marsh, Jaclyn S.; Tschampl-Diesing, Carol L. & Leach, Margaret S. (2017). "Love needs to be exchanged": A diary study of interaction and enactment of the family kinkeeper role. *Western Journal of Communication*, 81(5), 601–618.

Brame, Robert; Bushway, Shawn D.; Paternoster, Ray & Turner, Michael G. (2014). Demographic patterns of cumulative arrest prevalence by ages 18 and 23. *Crime & Delinquency*, 60(3), 471–486.

Brandén, Maria & Bernhardt, Eva. (2020). Does similarity in work-family related attitudes improve relationship quality? Evidence from Sweden. *Journal of Family Studies*, (In Press).

Brandt, Hella E.; Ooms, Marcel E.; Ribbe, Miel W.; van der Wal, Gerrit & Deliens, Luc. (2006). Predicted survival vs. actual survival in terminally ill noncancer patients in Dutch nursing homes. *Journal of Pain and Symptom Management*, 32(6), 560–566.

Bratsberg, Bernt; Nyen, Torgeir & Raaum, Oddbjørn. (2020). Economic returns to adult vocational qualifications. *Journal of Education and Work*, 33(2), 99–114.

Bratt, Christopher; Abrams, Dominic & Swift, Hannah J. (2020). Supporting the old but neglecting the young? The two faces of ageism. *Developmental Psychology*, 56(5), 1029–1039.

Brauner, Corinna; Wöhrmann, Anne M.; Frank, Kilian & Michel, Alexandra. (2019). Health and work-life balance across types of work schedules: A latent class analysis. *Applied Ergonomics*, 81(102906).

Braver, Sanford L. & Votruba, Ashley M. (2018). Does joint physical custody "cause" children's better outcomes? *Journal of Divorce & Remarriage*, 59(5), 452–468.

Brazelton, T. Berry & Sparrow, Joshua D. (2006). *Touchpoints, birth to 3: Your child's emotional and behavioral development* (2nd ed.). Da Capo Press.

Bregman, Rutger. (2020). *Humankind: A hopeful history.* Little, Brown.

Bremner, J. Gavin; Slater, Alan M. & Johnson, Scott P. (2015). Perception of object persistence: The origins of object permanence in infancy. *Child Development Perspectives*, 9(1), 7–13.

Brenn, Tormod & Ytterstad, Elinor. (2016). Increased risk of death immediately after losing a spouse: Cause-specific mortality following widowhood in Norway. *Preventive Medicine*, 89, 251–256.

Bretherton, Inge. (1992). The origins of attachment theory: John Bowlby and Mary Ainsworth. *Developmental Psychology*, 28(5), 759–775.

Brick, John & Erickson, Carlton K. (2013). *Drugs, the brain, and behavior: The pharmacology of drug use disorders.* Routledge.

Brighton, James; Wellard, Ian & Clark, Amy. (2020). *Gym bodies: Exploring fitness cultures.* Routledge.

Brodsky, Michael C. (2016). *Pediatric neuro-ophthalmology* (3rd ed.). Springer.

Broekhuizen, Martine L.; Aken, Marcel A. G.; Dubas, Judith S. & Leseman, Paul P. M. (2018). Child care quality and Dutch 2- and 3-year-olds' socio-emotional outcomes: Does the amount of care matter? *Infant and Child Development*, 27(1), e2043.

Bronfenbrenner, Urie & Morris, Pamela A. (2006). The bioecological model of human development. In Damon, William & Lerner, Richard M. (Eds.), *Handbook of child psychology* (6th ed., Vol. 1, pp. 793–828). Wiley.

Broockman, David & Kalla, Joshua. (2016). Durably reducing transphobia: A field experiment on door-to-door canvassing. *Science*, 352(6282), 220–204.

Brookshire, Robert H. & McNeil, Malcolm R. (2015). *Introduction to neurogenic communication disorders* (8th ed.). Mosby.

Brooten, Dorothy; Youngblut, Joanne M.; Caicedo, Carmen; Del Moral, Teresa; Cantwell, G. Patricia & Totapally, Balagangadhar. (2018). Parents' acute illnesses, hospitalizations, and medication changes during the difficult first year after infant or child NICU/PICU death. *American Journal of Hospice and Palliative Medicine*, 35(1), 75–82.

Brown, Alan S. (2012). *The tip of the tongue state.* Psychology Press.

Brown, Christia Spears; Alabi, Basirat O.; Huynh, Virginia W. & Masten, Carrie L. (2011). Ethnicity and gender in late childhood and early adolescence: Group identity and awareness of bias. *Developmental Psychology*, 47(2), 463–471.

Brown, Sarah. (2015). At Kansas, student leaders take the blame for racial-climate concerns. *Chronicle of Higher Education*, 62(13).

Brown, Susan L. & Lin, I-Fen. (2012). The gray divorce revolution: Rising divorce among middle-aged and older adults, 1990–2010. *The Journals of Gerontology: Series B*, 67(6), 731–741.

Brown, Susan L. & Lin, I-Fen. (2013). The gray divorce revolution. *Family Focus, National Council on Family Relations*, (FF57), F4–F5.

Bruijnen, Carolien J. W. H.; Dijkstra, Boukje A. G.; Walvoort, Serge J. W.; Markus, Wiebren; VanDerNagel, Joanne E. L.; Kessels, Roy P. C. & DE Jong, Cornelis A. J. (2019). Prevalence of cognitive impairment in patients with substance use disorder. *Drug and Alcohol Review, 38*(4), 435–442.

Brummelman, Eddie; Nelemans, Stefanie A.; Thomaes, Sander & Orobio De Castro, Bram. (2017). When parents' praise inflates, children's self-esteem deflates. *Child Development, 88*(6), 1799–1809.

Bruner, Jerome S. (1986). *Actual minds, possible worlds.* Harvard University Press.

Brunham, Robert C.; Gottlieb, Sami L. & Paavonen, Jorma. (2015). Pelvic inflammatory disease. *New England Journal of Medicine, 372,* 2039–2048.

Brysbaert, Marc; Stevens, Michaël; Mandera, Paweł & Keuleers, Emmanuel. (2016). How many words do we know? Practical estimates of vocabulary size dependent on word definition, the degree of language input and the participant's age. *Frontiers in Psychology, 7*(1116).

Buehler, Cheryl. (2020). Family processes and children's and adolescents' well-being. *Journal of Marriage and Family, 82*(1), 145–174.

Buiting, Hilde; van Delden, Johannes; Onwuteaka-Philpsen, Bregje; Rietjens, Judith; Rurup, Mette; van Tol, Donald; . . . van der Heide, Agnes. (2009). Reporting of euthanasia and physician-assisted suicide in the Netherlands: Descriptive study. *BMC Medical Ethics, 10*(18).

Bull, Sofia. (2019). *Television and the genetic imaginary.* Palgrave Macmillan.

Bulmer, Maria; Böhnke, Jan R. & Lewis, Gary J. (2017). Predicting moral sentiment towards physician-assisted suicide: The role of religion, conservatism, authoritarianism, and Big Five personality. *Personality and Individual Differences, 105,* 244–251.

Burchinal, Margaret R.; Lowe Vandell, Deborah & Belsky, Jay. (2014). Is the prediction of adolescent outcomes from early child care moderated by later maternal sensitivity? Results from the NICHD study of early child care and youth development. *Developmental Psychology, 50*(2), 542–553.

Burgoyne, Alexander P.; Hambrick, David Z. & Altmann, Erik M. (2019). Is working memory capacity a causal factor in fluid intelligence? *Psychonomic Bulletin & Review, 26,* 1333–1339.

Burke, Brian L.; Martens, Andy & Faucher, Erik H. (2010). Two decades of terror management theory: A meta-analysis of mortality salience research. *Personality and Social Psychology Review, 14*(2), 155–195.

Burston, Daniel. (2020). Freud in America: The golden age, the Freud wars, and beyond. In *Psychoanalysis, politics and the postmodern university* (pp. 19–44). Palgrave Macmillan.

Bursztyn, Leonardo & Jensezn, Robert. (2015). How does peer pressure affect educational investments? *Quarterly Journal of Economics, 130*(3), 1329–1367.

Buss, David M. (2015). *Evolutionary psychology: The new science of the mind* (5th ed.). Routledge.

Buss, David M. & Schmitt, David P. (2019). Mate preferences and their behavioral manifestations. *Annual Review of Psychology, 70*(1), 77–110.

Buss, Kristin A.; Jaffee, Sara; Wadsworth, Martha E. & Kliewer, Wendy. (2018). Impact of psychophysiological stress-response systems on psychological development: Moving beyond the single biomarker approach. *Developmental Psychology, 54*(9), 1601–1605.

Buttelmann, David; Zmyj, Norbert; Daum, Moritz & Carpenter, Malinda. (2013). Selective imitation of in-group over out-group members in 14-month-old infants. *Child Development, 84*(2), 422–428.

Butterworth, Brian; Varma, Sashank & Laurillard, Diana. (2011). Dyscalculia: From brain to education. *Science, 332*(6033), 1049–1053.

Byers-Heinlein, Krista; Burns, Tracey C. & Werker, Janet F. (2010). The roots of bilingualism in newborns. *Psychological Science, 21*(3), 343–348.

Cabello, Rosario; Sorrel, Miguel A.; Fernández-Pinto, Irene; Extremera, Natalio & Fernández-Berrocal, Pablo. (2016). Age and gender differences in ability emotional intelligence in adults: A cross-sectional study. *Developmental Psychology, 52*(9), 1486–1492.

Cain, Susan. (2012). *Quiet: The power of introverts in a world that can't stop talking.* Crown Publishers.

Calarco, Jessica McCrory. (2014). The inconsistent curriculum: Cultural tool kits and student interpretations of ambiguous expectations. *Social Psychology Quarterly, 77*(2), 185–209.

Callaghan, Tara. (2013). Symbols and symbolic thought. In Zelazo, Philip D. (Ed.), *The Oxford handbook of developmental psychology* (Vol. 1). Oxford University Press.

Callender, Tom; Emberton, Mark; Morris, Steve; Eeles, Ros; Kote-Jarai, Zsofia; Pharoah, Paul D. P. & Pashayan, Nora. (2019). Polygenic risk-tailored screening for prostate cancer: A benefit–harm and cost-effectiveness modelling study. *PloS Medicine, 16*(12), e1002998.

Calvo, Esteban; Madero-Cabib, Ignacio & Staudinger, Ursula M. (2018). Retirement sequences of older Americans: Moderately destandardized and highly stratified across gender, class, and race. *The Gerontologist, 58*(6), 1166–1176.

Camhi, Sarah M.; Katzmarzyk, Peter T.; Broyles, Stephanie; Church, Timothy S.; Hankinson, Arlene L.; Carnethon, Mercedes R.; . . . Lewis, Cora E. (2013). Association of metabolic risk with longitudinal physical activity and fitness: Coronary artery risk development in young adults (CARDIA). *Metabolic Syndrome and Related Disorders, 11*(3), 195–204.

Campbell, Frances; Conti, Gabriella; Heckman, James J.; Moon, Seong H.; Pinto, Rodrigo; Pungello, Elizabeth & Pan, Yi. (2014). Early childhood investments substantially boost adult health. *Science, 343*(6178), 1478–1485.

Campo, Juan Eduardo. (2015). Muslim ways of death: Between the prescribed and the performed. In Garces-Foley, Kathleen (Ed.), *Death and religion in a changing world.* Routledge.

Cardozo, Eden R.; Thomson, Alexcis P.; Karmon, Anatte E.; Dickinson, Kristy A.; Wright, Diane L. & Sabatini, Mary E. (2015). Ovarian stimulation and in-vitro fertilization outcomes of cancer patients undergoing fertility preservation compared to age matched controls: A 17-year experience. *Journal of Assisted Reproduction and Genetics, 32*(4), 587–596.

Carlson, Robert G.; Nahhas, Ramzi W.; Martins, Silvia S. & Daniulaityte, Raminta. (2016). Predictors of transition to heroin use among initially non-opioid dependent illicit pharmaceutical opioid users: A natural history study. *Drug & Alcohol Dependence, 160,* 127–134.

Carlson, Stephanie M.; Koenig, Melissa A. & Harms, Madeline B. (2013). Theory of mind. *Wiley Interdisciplinary Reviews: Cognitive Science, 4*(4), 391–402.

Carmassi, Claudia; Foghi, Claudia; Dell'Oste, Valerio; Cordone, Annalisa; Bertelloni, Carlo Antonio; Bui, Eric & Dell'Osso, Liliana. (2020). PTSD symptoms in healthcare workers facing the three coronavirus outbreaks: What can we expect after the COVID-19 pandemic. *Psychiatry Research, 292*(113312).

Carone, Nicola; Baiocco, Roberto & Lingiardi, Vittorio. (2017). Single fathers by choice using surrogacy: Why men decide to have a child as a single parent. *Human Reproduction, 32*(9), 1871–1879.

Carr, Deborah; Freedman, Vicki A.; Cornman, Jennifer C. & Schwarz, Norbert. (2014). Happy marriage, happy life? Marital quality and subjective well-being in later life. *Journal of Marriage and Family, 76*(5), 930–948.

Carrese, A., Joseph; Malek, Soleymani, Janet; Watson, J., Katie; Lehmann, B., Lisa; Green, H., Michael; Mccullough, J., Laurence; . . . Doukas, J., David. (2015). The essential role of medical ethics education in achieving professionalism: The Romanell report. *Academic Medicine, 90*(6), 744–752.

Carstensen, Laura L. (2011). *A long bright future: Happiness, health, and financial security in an age of increased longevity.* PublicAffairs.

Carstensen, Laura L. & DeLiema, Marguerite. (2018). The positivity effect: A negativity bias in youth fades with age. *Current Opinion in Behavioral Sciences, 19,* 7–12.

Carvalho, Maria Eduarda S.; Justo, João M. R. M; Gratier, Maya; Tomé, Teresa; Pereira, Esmeralda & Rodrigues, Helena. (2019). Vocal responsiveness of preterm infants to maternal infant-directed speaking and singing during skin-to-skin contact (Kangaroo Care) in the NICU. *Infant Behavior and Development, 57*(101332).

Casey, B. J. & Caudle, Kristina. (2013). The teenage brain: Self control. *Current Directions in Psychological Science, 22*(2), 82–87.

Caspi, Avshalom; Moffitt, Terrie E.; Morgan, Julia; Rutter, Michael; Taylor, Alan; Arseneault, Louise; . . . Polo-Tomas,

Monica. (2004). Maternal expressed emotion predicts children's antisocial behavior problems: Using monozygotic-twin differences to identify environmental effects on behavioral development. *Developmental Psychology*, 40(2), 149–161.

Cassidy, Féaron C. & Charalambous, Marika. (2018). Genomic imprinting, growth and maternal–fetal interactions. *Journal of Experimental Biology*, 221(Suppl. 1).

Cassidy, Jude & Shaver, Phillip R. (Eds.). (2016). *Handbook of attachment: Theory, research, and clinical applications*. Guilford Press.

Cattell, Raymond B. & Child, Dennis. (1975). *Motivation and dynamic structure*. Wiley.

Cavalcanti, Alexandre B.; Zampieri, Fernando G.; Rosa, Regis G.; Azevedo, Luciano C. P.; Veiga, Viviane C.; Avezum, Alvaro; . . . Berwanger, Otavio. (2020). Hydroxychloroquine with or without azithromycin in mild-to-moderate COVID-19. *New England Journal of Medicine*, 383, 2041–2052.

Cavallaro, Sebastiano. (2015). Cracking the code of neuronal apoptosis and survival. *Cell Death & Disease*, 6(e1963).

Cavanagh, Shannon E. & Fomby, Paula. (2019). Family instability in the lives of American children. *Annual Review of Sociology*, 45, 493–513.

Caviola, Lucius; Schubert, Stefan; Teperman, Elliot; Moss, David; Greenberg, Spencer & Faber, Nadira S. (2020). Donors vastly underestimate differences in charities' effectiveness. *Judgment and Decision Making*, 15(4), 509–516.

Ceci, Stephen J. & Bruck, Maggie. (1995). *Jeopardy in the courtroom: A scientific analysis of children's testimony*. American Psychological Association.

Cemalcilar, Zeynep; Baruh, Lemi; Kezer, Murat; Kamiloglu, Roza Gizem & Nigdeli, Bihter. (2018). Role of personality traits in first impressions: An investigation of actual and perceived personality similarity effects on interpersonal attraction across communication modalities. *Journal of Research in Personality*, 76, 139–149.

Cenegy, Laura Freeman; Denney, Justin T. & Kimbro, Rachel Tolbert. (2018). Family diversity and child health: Where do same-sex couple families fit. *Journal of Marriage and Family*, 80(1), 198–218.

Centers for Disease Control and Prevention. (2015, May 15). *Epidemiology and prevention of vaccine-preventable diseases* (Hamborsky, Jennifer; Kroger, Andrew & Wolfe, Charles Eds. 13th ed.). Public Health Foundation.

Centers for Disease Control and Prevention. (2018, June 29). *Blood lead levels (μg/dl) among U.S. children < 72 months of age, by state, year, and blood lead level (bll) group. CDC's National Surveillance Data (2012–2016)*. Atlanta, GA: U.S. Department of Health and Human Services.

Centers for Disease Control and Prevention. (2018, October 9). *Youth risk behavior survey: Data summary & trends report 2007–2017*. Atlanta, GA: National Center for HIV/AIDS, Viral Hepatitis, STD, and TB Prevention, Division of Adolescent and School Health. 328447.

Centers for Disease Control and Prevention. (2019, June 17). Measles cases and outbreaks. Centers for Disease Control and Prevention.

Centers for Disease Control and Prevention. (2019, May 30). Diabetes: Type 2 diabetes. Centers for Disease Control and Prevention.

Centers for Disease Control and Prevention, National Center for Health Statistics. (2017). *Underlying cause of death 1999–2016 on CDC WONDER Online Database, released December, 2017. Data are from the Multiple Cause of Death Files, 1999–2016, as compiled from data provided by the 57 vital statistics jurisdictions through the Vital Statistics Cooperative Program* [Data set]. CDC WONDER.

Centers for Disease Control and Prevention, National Center for Health Statistics. (2018, July 3). *Underlying cause of death, 1999–2017 on CDC WONDER Online Database* [Data set]. CDC WONDER.

Chamorro, Gloria & Janke, Vikki. (2020). Investigating the bilingual advantage: The impact of L2 exposure on the social and cognitive skills of monolingually-raised children in bilingual education. *International Journal of Bilingual Education and Bilingualism*, (In Press).

Chan, Derwin King Chung; Keatley, David A.; Tang, Tracy C. W.; Dimmock, James A. & Hagger, Martin S. (2018). Implicit versus explicit attitude to doping: Which better predicts athletes' vigilance towards unintentional doping?, 21(3), 238–244.

Chan, Kit Yee; Wang, Wei; Wu, Jing Jing; Liu, Li; Theodoratou, Evropi; Car, Josip; . . . Rudan, Igor. (2013). Epidemiology of Alzheimer's disease and other forms of dementia in China, 1990–2010: A systematic review and analysis. *The Lancet*, 381(9882), 2016–2023.

Chang, Yevvon Yi-Chi & Chiou, Wen-Bin. (2014). Diversity beliefs and postformal thinking in late adolescence: A cognitive basis of multicultural literacy. *Asia Pacific Education Review*, 15(4), 585–592.

Chapman, Hanah A. & Anderson, Adam K. (2013). Things rank and gross in nature: A review and synthesis of moral disgust. *Psychological Bulletin*, 139(2), 300–327.

Chartier, Karen G.; Scott, Denise M.; Wall, Tamara L.; Covault, Jonathan; Karriker-Jaffe, Katherine J.; Mills, Britain A.; . . . Arroyo, Judith A. (2014). Framing ethnic variations in alcohol outcomes from biological pathways to neighborhood context. *Alcoholism: Clinical and Experimental Research*, 38(3), 611–618.

Chassy, Philippe & Gobet, Fernand. (2011). Measuring chess experts' single-use sequence knowledge: An archival study of departure from 'theoretical' openings. *PLoS ONE*, 6(11), e26692.

Chasteen, Alison L.; Horhota, Michelle & Crumley-Branyon, Jessica J. (2020). Overlooked and underestimated: Experiences of ageism in young, middle-aged, and older adults. *The Journals of Gerontology: Series B*, (In Press), gbaa043.

Chen, Frances R.; Fung, Annis Lai Chu & Raine, Adrian. (2019). The cognitive, affective, and somatic empathy scales (CASES). Cross-cultural replication and specificity to different forms of aggression and victimization. *Journal of Personality Assessment*, (In Press).

Chen, Irit; Lifshitz, Hefziba & Vakil, Eli. (2017). Crystallized and fluid intelligence of adolescents and adults with intellectual disability and with typical development: Impaired, stable or compensatory trajectories? *Grant Medical Journals*, 2(5), 104–115.

Chen, Laura; Selvendra, Ajit; Stewart, Anne & Castle, David J. (2018). Risk factors in early and late onset schizophrenia. *Comprehensive Psychiatry*, 80, 155–162.

Chen, Mu-Hong; Lan, Wen-Hsuan; Bai, Ya-Mei; Huang, Kai-Lin; Su, Tung-Ping; Tsai, Shih-Jen; . . . Hsu, Ju-Wei. (2016). Influence of relative age on diagnosis and treatment of Attention-deficit hyperactivity disorder in Taiwanese children. *The Journal of Pediatrics*, 172, 162–167.e1.

Cherlin, Andrew J. (2020). Degrees of change: An assessment of the deinstitutionalization of marriage thesis. *Journal of Marriage and Family*, 82(1), 62–80.

Cherng, Hua-Yu Sebastian & Liu, Jia-Lin. (2017). Academic social support and student expectations: The case of second-generation Asian Americans. *Asian American Journal of Psychology*, 8(1), 16–30.

Chess, Stella; Thomas, Alexander & Birch, Herbert G. (1965). *Your child is a person: A psychological approach to parenthood without guilt*. Viking.

Chikritzhs, Tanya; Stockwell, Tim; Naimi, Timothy; Andreasson, Sven; Dangardt, Frida & Liang, Wenbin. (2015). Has the leaning tower of presumed health benefits from 'moderate' alcohol use finally collapsed? *Addiction*, 110(5), 726–727.

Child Trends. (2019, March 7). Dual language learners. Child Trends.

Child Trends Databank. (2015, March). *Lead poisoning: Indicators on children and youth*. Bethesda, MD: Child Trends.

Chiu, Chi-Yue & Hong, Ying-Yi. (2013). *Social psychology of culture*. Routledge.

Chiu, Maria; Rahman, Farah; Vigod, Simone; Lau, Cindy; Cairney, John & Kurdyak, Paul. (2018). Mortality in single fathers compared with single mothers and partnered parents: A population-based cohort study. *The Lancet Public Health*, 3(3), e115–e123.

Chlebowski, Rowan T.; Manson, JoAnn E.; Anderson, Garnet L.; Cauley, Jane A.; Aragaki, Aaron K.; Stefanick, Marcia L.; . . . Prentice, Ross L. (2013). Estrogen plus progestin and breast cancer incidence and mortality in the Women's Health Initiative observational study. *Journal of the National Cancer Institute*, 105(8), 526–535.

Cho, Grace. (2015). Perspectives vs. reality of heritage language development. *Multicultural Education*, 22(2), 30–38.

Choe, Daniel E.; Lane, Jonathan D.; Grabell, Adam S. & Olson, Sheryl L. (2013a). Developmental precursors of young school-age children's hostile attribution bias. *Developmental Psychology*, 49(12), 2245–2256.

Choe, Daniel E.; Olson, Sheryl L. & Sameroff, Arnold J. (2013b). The interplay of externalizing problems and physical and inductive discipline during childhood. *Developmental Psychology*, 49(11), 2029–2039.

Choi, Hyunkyung; Van Riper, Marcia & Thoyre, Suzanne. (2012). Decision making following a prenatal diagnosis of Down syndrome: An integrative review. *Journal of Midwifery & Women's Health, 57*(2), 156–164.

Chomsky, Noam. (1968). *Language and mind.* Harcourt Brace & World.

Chomsky, Noam. (1980). *Rules and representations.* Columbia University Press.

Christ, Anette & Latz, Eicke. (2019). The Western lifestyle has lasting effects on meta-flammation. *Nature Reviews Immunology, 19*(5), 267–269.

Christian, Hayley; Knuiman, Matthew; Divitini, Mark; Foster, Sarah; Hooper, Paula; Boruff, Bryan; . . . Giles-Corti, Billie. (2017). A longitudinal analysis of the influence of the neighborhood environment on recreational walking within the neighborhood: Results from RESIDE. *Environmental Health Perspectives, 125*(7).

Cicchetti, Dante. (2013a). Annual research review: Resilient functioning in maltreated children—past, present, and future perspectives. *Journal of Child Psychology and Psychiatry, 54*(4), 402–422.

Cicchetti, Dante. (2013b). An overview of developmental psychopathology. In Zelazo, Philip D. (Ed.), *The Oxford handbook of developmental psychology* (Vol. 2, pp. 455–480). Oxford University Press.

Cicchetti, Dante. (2016). Socioemotional, personality, and biological development: Illustrations from a multilevel developmental psychopathology perspective on child maltreatment. *Annual Review of Psychology, 67*, 187–211.

Cierpka, Manfred & Cierpka, Astrid. (2016). Developmentally appropriate vs. persistent defiant and aggressive behavior. In Cierpka, Manfred (Ed.), *Regulatory disorders in infants.* Springer.

Cillessen, Antonius H. N. & Mayeux, Lara. (2004). From censure to reinforcement: Developmental changes in the association between aggression and social status. *Child Development, 75*(1), 147–163.

Cirelli, Laura K. (2018). How interpersonal synchrony facilitates early prosocial behavior. *Current Opinion in Psychology, 20*, 35–39.

Cirelli, Laura K.; Jurewicz, Zuzanna B. & Trehub, Sandra E. (2020). Effects of maternal singing style on mother–infant arousal and behavior. *Journal of Cognitive Neuroscience, 32*(7), 1213–1220.

Claessen, Jacques. (2017). *Forgiveness in criminal law through incorporating restorative mediation.* Wolf Legal Publishers.

Clark, D. Angus; Durbin, C. Emily; Heitzeg, Mary M.; Iacono, William G.; McGue, Matt & Hicks, Brian M. (2020). Sexual development in adolescence: An examination of genetic and environmental influences. *Journal of Research on Adolescence, 30*(2), 502–520.

Clifford, Scott. (2019). How emotional frames moralize and polarize political attitudes. *Political Psychology, 40*(1), 75–91.

Coall, David A.; Hilbrand, Sonja; Sear, Rebecca & Hertwig, Raplh. (2016). A new

niche? The theory of grandfather involvement. In Buchanan, Ann & Rotkirch, Anna (Eds.), *Grandfathers: Global perspectives* (pp. 21–44). Palgrave.

Cockwell, Paul & Fisher, Lori-Ann. (2020). The global burden of chronic kidney disease. *The Lancet, 395*(10225), 662–664.

Coe, Jesse L.; Davies, Patrick T. & Sturge-Apple, Melissa L. (2018). Family instability and young children's school adjustment: Callousness and negative internal representations as mediators. *Child Development, 89*(4), 1193–1208.

Coe-Odess, Sarah J.; Narr, Rachel K. & Allen, Joseph P. (2019). Emergent emotions in adolescence. In LoBue, Vanessa; Pérez-Edgar, Koraly & Buss, Kristin A. (Eds.), *Handbook of emotional development* (pp. 595–625). Springer.

Cohen, Jon. (2014). Saving lives without new drugs. *Science, 346*(6212), 911.

Colaco, Marc; Johnson, Kelly; Schneider, Dona & Barone, Joseph. (2013). Toilet training method is not related to dysfunctional voiding. *Clinical Pediatrics, 52*(1), 49–53.

Colagiuri, B.; Schenk, L. A.; Kessler, M. D.; Dorsey, S. G. & Colloca, L. (2015). The placebo effect: From concepts to genes. *Neuroscience, 307*, 171–190.

Colapinto, John. (2006). *As nature made him: The boy who was raised as a girl.* Harper Perennial.

Collin-Vézina, Delphine; De La Sablonnière-Griffin, Mireille; Palmer, Andrea M. & Milne, Lise. (2015). A preliminary mapping of individual, relational, and social factors that impede disclosure of childhood sexual abuse. *Child Abuse & Neglect, 43*, 123–134.

Comfort, Alex. (2013). *The joy of sex* (The ultimate revised ed.). Crown.

Condon, John; Corkindale, Carolyn; Luszcz, Mary & Gamble, Elizabeth. (2013). The Australian first-time grandparents study: Time spent with the grandchild and its predictors. *Australasian Journal on Ageing, 32*(1), 21–27.

Confer, Jaime C.; Easton, Judith A.; Fleischman, Diana S.; Goetz, Cari D.; Lewis, David M. G.; Perilloux, Carin & Buss, David M. (2010). Evolutionary psychology: Controversies, questions, prospects, and limitations. *American Psychologist, 65*(2), 110–126.

Conklin, Hilary G. (2018). Caring and critical thinking in the teaching of young adolescents. *Theory Into Practice, 57*(4), 289–297.

Connellan, Jennifer; Baron-Cohen, Simon; Wheelwright, Sally; Batki, Anna & Ahluwalia, Jag. (2000). Sex differences in human neonatal social perception. *Infant Behavior and Development, 23*(1), 113–118.

Contreras, Carlos M.; Gutiérrez-García, Ana G. & Sánchez-Salcedo, José A. (2018). Fluoxetine and stress inversely modify lateral septal nucleus-mpfc neuronal responsivity. *Behavioural Brain Research, 351*, 114–120.

Coon, Carleton S. (1962). *The origin of races.* Knopf.

Coovadia, Hoosen M. & Wittenberg, Dankwart F. (Eds.). (2004). *Paediatrics and child health: A manual for health professionals in developing countries* (5th ed.). Oxford University Press.

Córdova, France. (2020). Leadership to change a culture of sexual harassment. *Science, 367*(6485), 1430–1431.

Corenblum, Barry. (2014). Relationships between racial–ethnic identity, self-esteem and in-group attitudes among First Nation children. *Journal of Youth and Adolescence, 43*(3), 387–404.

Corning, Amy & Schuman, Howard. (2015). *Generations and collective memory.* University of Chicago Press.

Corr, Charles A. & Corr, Donna M. (2013a). Culture, socialization, and dying. In Meagher, David K. & Balk, David E. (Eds.), *Handbook of thanatology: The essential body of knowledge for the study of death, dying, and bereavement* (2nd ed., pp. 3–8). Routledge.

Corr, Charles A. & Corr, Donna M. (2013b). Historical and contemporary perspectives on loss, grief, and mourning. In Meagher, David & Balk, David E. (Eds.), *Handbook of thanatology: The essential body of knowledge for the study of death, dying, and bereavement* (2nd ed., pp. 135–148). Routledge.

Costa, Albert; Vives, Marc–Lluís & Corey, Joanna D. (2017). On language processing shaping decision making. *Current Directions in Psychological Science, 26*(2), 146–151.

Costello, Matthew C. & Bloesch, Emily K. (2017). Are older adults less embodied? A review of age effects through the lens of embodied cognition. *Frontiers in Psychology, 8*(267).

Council on Communications and Media. (2011). Policy statement—Children, adolescents, obesity, and the media. *Pediatrics, 128*(1), 201–208.

Council on Community Pediatrics. (2015). Promoting food security for all children: Policy statement. *Pediatrics, 136*(5), e1431–e1438.

Cousens, Simon; Blencowe, Hannah; Stanton, Cynthia; Chou, Doris; Ahmed, Saifuddin; Steinhardt, Laura; . . . Lawn, Joy E. (2011). National, regional, and worldwide estimates of stillbirth rates in 2009 with trends since 1995: A systematic analysis. *The Lancet, 377*(9774), 1319–1330.

Coutanche, Marc N. & Thompson-Schill, Sharon L. (2015). Rapid consolidation of new knowledge in adulthood via fast mapping. *Trends in Cognitive Sciences, 19*(9), 486–488.

Couzin-Frankel, Jennifer. (2019). Experimental drug holds off type 1 diabetes. *Science, 364*(6445), 1021.

Coviltir, Valeria; Burcel, Miruna; Cherecheanu, Alina Popa; Ionescu, Catalina; Dascalescu, Dana; Potop, Vasile & Burcea, Marian. (2019). Update on myopia risk factors and microenvironmental changes. *Journal of Ophthalmology, 2019*(4960852).

Cowell, Jason M.; Lee, Kang; Malcolm-Smith, Susan; Selcuk, Bilge; Zhou, Xinyue & Decety, Jean. (2017). The development of generosity and moral cognition across five cultures. *Developmental Science, 20*(4), e12403.

Cowen, Alan S.; Elfenbein, Hillary Anger; Laukka, Petri & Keltner, Dacher. (2019). Mapping 24 emotions conveyed by brief human vocalization. *American Psychologist*, 74(6), 698–712.

Cowen, Alan S. & Keltner, Dacher. (2020). What the face displays: Mapping 28 emotions conveyed by naturalistic expression. *American Psychologist*, 75(3), 349–364.

Coyne, Sarah M. & Ostrov, Jamie M. (2018). *The development of relational aggression*. Oxford University Press.

Cramm, Jane M.; van Dijk, Hanna M. & Nieboer, Aanna P. (2013). The importance of neighborhood social cohesion and social capital for the well being of older adults in the community. *The Gerontologist*, 53(1), 142–152.

Crenshaw, David A. (2013). The family, larger systems, and traumatic death. In Meagher, David K. & Balk, David E. (Eds.), *Handbook of thanatology: The essential body of knowledge for the study of death, dying, and bereavement* (2nd ed., pp. 305–309). Routledge.

Crenshaw, Kimberle. (1989). Demarginalizing the intersection of race and sex: A Black feminist critique of antidiscrimination doctrine, feminist theory and antiracist politics. *University of Chicago Legal Forum*, 139–167.

Creswell, J. David. (2017). Mindfulness interventions. *Annual Review of Psychology*, 68, 491–516.

Cripe, Larry D. & Frankel, Richard M. (2017). Dying from cancer: Communication, empathy, and the clinical imagination. *Journal of Patient Experience*, 4(2), 69–73.

Crosby, Danielle A.; Dowsett, Chantelle J.; Gennetian, Lisa A. & Huston, Aletha C. (2010). A tale of two methods: Comparing regression and instrumental variables estimates of the effects of preschool child care type on the subsequent externalizing behavior of children in low-income families. *Developmental Psychology*, 46(5), 1030–1048.

Crosnoe, Robert & Johnson, Monica Kirkpatrick. (2011). Research on adolescence in the twenty-first century. *Annual Review of Sociology*, 37(1), 439–460.

Crosnoe, Robert; Purtell, Kelly M.; Davis-Kean, Pamela; Ansari, Arya & Benner, Aprile D. (2016). The selection of children from low-income families into preschool. *Developmental Psychology*, 52(4), 599–612.

Cross, Christina J. (2020). Racial/ethnic differences in the association between family structure and children's education. *Journal of Marriage and Family*, 82(2), 691–712.

Császár-Nagy, Noémi & Bókkon, István. (2018). Mother-newborn separation at birth in hospitals: A possible risk for neurodevelopmental disorders? *Neuroscience and Biobehavioral Reviews*, 84, 337–351.

Csikszentmihalyi, Mihaly. (1990). *Flow: The psychology of optimal experience*. Harper Perennial.

Csikszentmihalyi, Mihaly. (2013). *Creativity: Flow and the psychology of discovery and invention*. Harper Perennial.

Cui, Zehua; Oshri, Assaf; Liu, Sihong; Smith, Emilie P. & Kogan, Steven M. (2020). Child maltreatment and resilience: The promotive and protective role of future orientation. *Journal of Youth and Adolescence*, 49, 2075–2089.

Culpin, Iryna; Heron, Jon; Araya, Ricardo & Joinson, Carol. (2015). Early childhood father absence and depressive symptoms in adolescent girls from a UK cohort: The mediating role of early menarche. *Journal of Abnormal Child Psychology*, 43(5), 921–931.

Culver, K. C.; Braxton, John & Pascarella, Ernie. (2019). Does teaching rigorously really enhance undergraduates' intellectual development? The relationship of academic rigor with critical thinking skills and lifelong learning motivations. *Higher Education*, 78, 611–627.

Cumming, Elaine & Henry, William Earl. (1961). *Growing old: The process of disengagement*. Basic Books.

Currie, Candace; Nic Gabhainn, Saoirse; Godeau, Emmanuelle & International HBSC Network Coordinating Committee. (2009). The health behaviour in school-aged children: WHO Collaborative Cross-National (HBSC) study: Origins, concept, history and development 1982–2008. *International Journal of Public Health*, 54, 131–139.

Curtin, Nancy & Garrison, Mary. (2018). "She was more than a friend": Clinical intervention strategies for effectively addressing disenfranchised grief issues for same-sex couples. *Journal of Gay & Lesbian Social Services*, 30(3), 261–281.

Curtindale, Lori M.; Bahrick, Lorraine E.; Lickliter, Robert & Colombo, John. (2019). Effects of multimodal synchrony on infant attention and heart rate during events with social and nonsocial stimuli. *Journal of Experimental Child Psychology*, 178, 283–294.

Cushman, Susan & Byrne, John H. (2018). Special issue covering the relationship between mechanisms of addiction and learning. *Learning and Memory*, 25.

Cutts, Diana & Cook, John. (2017). Screening for food insecurity: Short-term alleviation and long-term prevention. *American Journal of Public Health*, 107(11), 1699–1700.

Cuzzolaro, Massimo & Fassino, Secondo (Eds.). (2018). *Body image, eating, and weight: A guide to assessment, treatment, and prevention*. Springer.

Cytowic, Richard E. (2018). *Synesthesia*. MIT Press.

D'Alessandro, Annunziata & De Pergola, Giovanni. (2018). The Mediterranean diet: Its definition and evaluation of a priori dietary indexes in primary cardiovascular prevention. *International Journal of Food Sciences and Nutrition*, 69(6), 647–659.

D'Ambrosio, Conchita; Jäntti, Markus & Lepinteur, Anthony. (2020). Money and happiness: Income, wealth and subjective well-being. *Social Indicators Research*, 148(1), 47–66.

D'Souza, Dean & D'Souza, Hana. (2019) Emergent and constrained: Understanding brain and cognitive development. *Journal of Neurolinguistics*, 49, 228–231.

Dadds, Mark R. & Tully, Lucy A. (2019). What is it to discipline a child: What should it be? A reanalysis of time-out from the perspective of child mental health, attachment, and trauma. *American Psychologist*, 74(7), 794–808.

Dahlgren, M. Kathryn; Laifer, Lauren M.; Van Elzakker, Michael B.; Offringa, Reid; Hughes, Katherine C.; Chan, T. H.; . . . Shin, Lisa M. (2018). Diminished medial prefrontal cortex activation during the recollection of stressful events is an acquired characteristic of PTSD. *Psychological Medicine*, 48(7), 1128–1138.

Damasio, Antonio. (2005). *Descartes' error: Emotion, reason, and the human brain*. Penguin.

Damasio, Antonio R. (2018). *The strange order of things: Life, feeling, and the making of cultures*. Pantheon.

Daniel, Ella; Plamondon, André & Jenkins, Jennifer M. (2018). An examination of the sibling training hypothesis for disruptive behavior in early childhood. *Child Development*, 89(1), 235–247.

Danks, Kelly A.; Pohlig, Ryan & Reisman, Darcy S. (2016). Combining fast-walking training and a step activity monitoring program to improve daily walking activity after stroke: A preliminary study. *Archives of Physical Medicine and Rehabilitation*, 97(9, Suppl.), S185–S193.

Dantchev, Slava; Zammit, Stanley & Wolke, Dieter. (2018). Sibling bullying in middle childhood and psychotic disorder at 18 years: A prospective cohort study. *Psychological Medicine*, 48(14), 2321–2328.

Darweesh, Sirwan K. L.; Wolters, Frank J.; Postuma, Ronald B.; Stricker, Bruno H.; Hofman, Albert; Koudstaal, Peter J.; . . . Ikram, M. Arfan. (2017). Association between poor cognitive functioning and risk of incident Parkinsonism: The Rotterdam study. *JAMA Neurology*, 74(12), 1431–1438.

Darwin, Charles. (1859). *On the origin of species by means of natural selection*. J. Murray.

Dasgupta, Rajib; Sinha, Dipa & Yumnam, Veda. (2016). Rapid survey of wasting and stunting in children: What's new, what's old and what's the buzz? *Indian Pediatrics*, 53(1), 47–49.

Daum, Moritz M.; Ulber, Julia & Gredebäck, Gustaf. (2013). The development of pointing perception in infancy: Effects of communicative signals on covert shifts of attention. *Developmental Psychology*, 49(10), 1898–1908.

Davidson, Richard J. & Kaszniak, Alfred W. (2015). Conceptual and methodological issues in research on mindfulness and meditation. *American Psychologist*, 70(7), 581–592.

Davis, Georgiann. (2015). *Contesting intersex: The dubious diagnosis*. New York University Press.

Davis, Jac T. M. & Hines, Melissa. (2020). How large are gender differences in toy preferences? A systematic review and meta-analysis of toy preference research. *Archives of Sexual Behavior*, 49, 373–394.

Davison, Glen; Kehaya, Corinna & Jones, Arwel Wyn. (2014). Nutritional and physical activity interventions to improve immunity. *American Journal of Lifestyle Medicine*.

Daw, Jonathan; Guo, Guang & Harris, Kathie Mullan. (2015). Nurture net of nature:

Re-evaluating the role of shared environments in academic achievement and verbal intelligence. *Social Science Research*, 52, 422–439.

Day, James Meredith. (2017). Religion and human development in adulthood: Well-being, prosocial behavior, and religious and spiritual development. *Behavioral Development Bulletin*, 22(2), 298–313.

Dayanim, Shoshana & Namy, Laura L. (2015). Infants learn baby signs from video. *Child Development*, 86(3), 800–811.

De Boeck, Paul & Jeon, Minjeong. (2018). Perceived crisis and reforms: Issues, explanations, and remedies. *Psychological Bulletin*, 144(7), 757–777.

de Bruin, Joyce J. & Schaefer, Rebecca S. (2017). Musical activities and cognitive enhancement in dementia. In Colzato, Lorenza S. (Ed.), *Theory-driven approaches to cognitive enhancement* (pp. 273–280). Springer.

De Feyter, Jessica J.; Parada, Mayra D.; Hartman, Suzanne C.; Curby, Timothy W. & Winsler, Adam. (2020). The early academic resilience of children from low-income, immigrant families. *Early Childhood Research Quarterly*, 51, 446–461.

de Groot, Annette M. B. & Hagoort, Peter (Eds.). (2018). *Research methods in psycholinguistics and the neurobiology of language: A practical guide*. Wiley Blackwell.

de Guerrero, María C. M. (2018). Going covert: Inner and private speech in language learning. *Language Teaching*, 51(1), 1–35.

de Haan, Irene & Connolly, Marie. (2019). More nuanced universal services for new parents: Avoiding assumptions of homogeneity. *Journal of Social Service Research*, 45(5), 727–738.

de Jonge, Huub. (2011). Purification and remembrance: Eastern and Western ways to deal with the Bali bombing. In Margry, Peter Jan & Sánchez-Carretero, Cristina (Eds.), *Grassroots memorials: The politics of memorializing traumatic death* (pp. 262–284). Berghahn Books.

De Lima, Liliana; Woodruff, Roger; Pettus, Katherine; Downing, Julia; Buitrago, Rosa; Munyoro, Esther; . . . Radbruch, Lukas. (2017). International Association for Hospice and Palliative Care position statement: Euthanasia and physician-assisted suicide. *Journal of Palliative Medicine*, 20(1), 8–14.

De Luca, Susan M.; Yueqi, Yan; Dicorcia, Daley & Padilla, Yolanda. (2018). A longitudinal study of Latino and non-Hispanic mothers' and fathers' depressive symptoms and its association with parent-child communication. *Journal of Affective Disorders*, 227, 580–587.

De Raedt, Rudi; Koster, Ernst H. W. & Ryckewaert, Ruben. (2013). Aging and attentional bias for death related and general threat-related information: Less avoidance in older as compared with middle-aged adults. *The Journals of Gerontology Series B: Psychological Sciences and Social Sciences*, 68(1), 41–48.

Dearing, Eric; Wimer, Christopher; Simpkins, Sandra D.; Lund, Terese; Bouffard, Suzanne M.; Caronongan, Pia; . . . Weiss, Heather. (2009). Do neighborhood and home contexts help explain why low-income children miss opportunities to participate in activities outside of school? *Developmental Psychology*, 45(6), 1545–1562.

Dearing, Eric & Zachrisson, Henrik D. (2017). Concern over internal, external, and incidence validity in studies of child-care quantity and externalizing behavior problems. *Child Development Perspectives*, 11(2), 133–138.

Deater-Deckard, Kirby. (2013). The social environment and the development of psychopathology. In Zelazo, Philip D. (Ed.), *The Oxford handbook of developmental psychology* (Vol. 2, pp. 527–548). Oxford University Press.

Deater-Deckard, Kirby & Lansford, Jennifer E. (2016). Daughters' and sons' exposure to childrearing discipline and violence in low- and middle-income countries. *Monographs of the Society for Research in Child Development*, 81(1), 78–103.

Dees, Marianne K.; Vernooij-Dassen, Myrra J.; Dekkers, Wim J.; Vissers, Kris C. & van Weel, Chris. (2011). 'Unbearable suffering': A qualitative study on the perspectives of patients who request assistance in dying. *Journal of Medical Ethics*, 37(12), 727–734.

Dehaene-Lambertz, Ghislaine. (2017). The human infant brain: A neural architecture able to learn language. *Psychonomic Bulletin & Review*, 24(1), 48–55.

Del Coso, Juan; Salinero, Juan José & Lara, Beatriz. (2020). Effects of caffeine and coffee on human functioning. *Nutrients*, 12(1), 125.

deLara, Ellen Walser. (2016). *Bullying scars: The impact on adult life and relationships*. Oxford University Press.

Delon-Martin, Chantal; Plailly, Jane; Fonlupt, Pierre; Veyrac, Alexandra & Roye, Jean-Pierre. (2013). Perfumers' expertise induces structural reorganization in olfactory brain regions. *NeuroImage*, 68, 55–62.

DeLuca, Vincent; Rothman, Jason & Pliatsikas, Christos. (2019). Linguistic immersion and structural effects on the bilingual brain: A longitudinal study. *Bilingualism: Language and Cognition*, 22(5), 1160–1175.

Demartini, Julie K.; Casa, Douglas; Stearns, Rebecca; Belval, Luke; Crago, Arthur; Davis, Rob & Jardine, John. (2015). Effectiveness of cold water immersion in the treatment of exertional heat stroke at the Falmouth Road Race. *Medicine & Science in Sports & Exercise*, 47(2), 240–245.

Deming, Michelle E.; Covan, Eleanor Krassen; Swan, Suzanne C. & Billings, Deborah L. (2013). Exploring rape myths, gendered norms, group processing, and the social context of rape among college women a qualitative analysis. *Violence Against Women*, 19(4), 465–485.

Demir, Melikşah; Haynes, Andrew & Potts, Shannon K. (2017). My friends are my estate: Friendship experiences mediate the relationship between perceived responses to capitalization attempts and happiness. *Journal of Happiness Studies*, 18(4), 1161–1190.

Denhardt, David T. (2018). Effect of stress on human biology: Epigenetics, adaptation, inheritance, and social significance. *Journal of Cellular Physiology*, 233(3), 1975–1984.

Denissen, Jaap J. A.; Luhmann, Maike; Chung, Joanne M. & Bleidorn, Wiebke. (2019). Transactions between life events and personality traits across the adult lifespan. *Journal of Personality and Social Psychology*, 116(4), 612–633.

Denson, Nida; Bowman, Nicholas A.; Ovenden, Georgia; Culver, K. C. & Holmes, Joshua M. (2020). Do diversity courses improve college student outcomes? A meta-analysis. *Journal of Diversity in Higher Education*, (In Press).

Dernberger, Brittany N. & Pepin, Joanna R. (2020). Gender flexibility, but not equality: Young adults' division of labor preferences. *Sociological Science*, 7(2), 36–56.

Devitt, Aleea L. & Schacter, Daniel L. (2016). False memories with age: Neural and cognitive underpinnings. *Neuropsychologia*, 91, 346–359.

Dewan, Michael C.; Rattani, Abbas; Gupta, Saksham; Baticulon, Ronnie E.; Hung, Ya-Ching; Punchak, Maria; . . . Park, Kee B. (2019). Estimating the global incidence of traumatic brain injury. *Journal of Neurosurgery*, 130(4), 1039–1408.

DeYoung, Colin G.; Hirsh, Jacob B.; Shane, Matthew S.; Papademetris, Xenophon; Rajeevan, Nallakkandi & Gray, Jeremy R. (2010). Testing predictions from personality neuroscience. *Psychological Science*, 21(6), 820–828.

Di Lego, Vanessa; Di Giulio, Paola & Luy, Marc. (2020). Gender differences in healthy and unhealthy life expectancy. In Jagger, Carol; Crimmins, Eileen M.; Saito, Yasuhiko; De Carvalho Yokota, Renata Tiene; Van Oyen, Herman & Robine, Jean-Marie (Eds.), *International handbook of health expectancies* (pp. 151–172). Springer.

Diamond, Adele. (2013). Executive functions. *Annual Review of Psychology*, 64, 135–168.

Diamond, Adele. (2016). Why improving and assessing executive functions early in life is critical. In Griffin, James Alan; McCardle, Peggy D. & Freund, Lisa (Eds.), *Executive function in preschool-age children: Integrating measurement, neurodevelopment, and translational research* (pp. 11–43). American Psychological Association.

Diamond, Milton & Sigmundson, H. Keith. (1997). Sex reassignment at birth: Long-term review and clinical implications. *Archives of Pediatric Adolescent Medicine*, 151(3), 298–304.

DiAngelo, Robin. (2018). *White fragility: Why it's so hard for white people to talk about racism*. Beacon.

Dickenson, Janna A.; Gleason, Neil; Coleman, Eli & Miner, Michael H. (2018). Prevalence of distress associated with difficulty controlling sexual urges, feelings, and behaviors in the United States. *JAMA Network Open*, 1(7), e184468.

Didion, Joan. (2005). *The year of magical thinking*. Knopf.

Diener, Ed (Ed.) (2009). *The science of well-being: The collected works of Ed Diener*. Springer.

Dinu, M.; Pagliai, G.; Casini, A. & F., Sofi. (2018). Mediterranean diet and multiple health outcomes: An umbrella review of meta-analyses of observational studies and randomised trials. *European Journal of Clinical Nutrition, 72*, 30–43.

Dion, Jacinthe; Gervais, Jennifer; Bigras, Noémie; Blackburn, Marie-Eve & Godbout, Natacha. (2019). A longitudinal study of the mediating role of romantic attachment in the relation between child maltreatment and psychological adaptation in emerging adults. *Journal of Youth and Adolescence, 48*, 2391–2402.

DiPietro, Janet A.; Costigan, Kathleen A. & Voegtline, Kristin M. (2015a). Fetal motor activity. *Monographs of the Society for Research in Child Development, 80*(3), 33–42.

DiPietro, Janet A.; Costigan, Kathleen A. & Voegtline, Kristin M. (2015b). Sex differences in fetal development. *Monographs of the Society for Research in Child Development, 80*(3), 59–65.

Dishion, Thomas J.; Mun, Chung; Ha, Thao & Tein, Jenn-Yun. (2019). Observed family and friendship dynamics in adolescence: A latent profile approach to identifying "mesosystem" adaptation for intervention tailoring. *Prevention Science, 20*(1), 41–55.

Dobson, Keith S.; Poole, Julia C. & Beck, Judith S. (2018). The fundamental cognitive model. In Leahy, Robert L. (Ed.), *Science and practice in cognitive therapy: Foundations, mechanisms, and applications.* Guilford.

Doka, Kenneth J. (2013). Historical and contemporary perspectives on dying. In Meagher, David K. & Balk, David E. (Eds.), *Handbook of thanatology: The essential body of knowledge for the study of death, dying, and bereavement* (2nd ed., pp. 17–23). Routledge.

Doka, Kenneth J. (2016). *Grief is a journey: Finding your path through loss.* Atria.

Dolezsar, Cynthia M.; McGrath, Jennifer J.; Herzig, Alyssa J. M. & Miller, Sydney B. (2014). Perceived racial discrimination and hypertension: A comprehensive systematic review. *Health Psychology, 33*(1), 20–34.

Dolgin, Elie. (2015). The myopia boom. *Nature, 519*(7543), 276–278.

Domond, Pascale; Orri, Massimiliano; Algan, Yann; Findlay, Leanne; Kohen, Dafna; Vitaro, Frank; . . . Côté, Sylvana M. (2020). Child care attendance and educational and economic outcomes in adulthood. *Pediatrics, 146*(1), e20193880.

Dong, Daoyin; Zielke, Horst Ronald; Yeh, David & Yang, Peixin. (2018). Cellular stress and apoptosis contribute to the pathogenesis of autism spectrum disorder. *Autism Research, 11*(7), 1076–1090.

Donohue, Meghan Rose; Tillman, Rebecca; Perino, Michael T.; Whalen, Diana J.; Luby, Joan & Barch, Deanna M. (2020). Prevalence and correlates of maladaptive guilt in middle childhood. *Journal of Affective Disorders, 263*, 64–71.

Donohue, Meghan Rose & Tully, Erin C. (2019). Reparative prosocial behaviors alleviate children's guilt. *Developmental Psychology, 55*(10), 2102–2113.

Dougherty, Ilona & Clarke, Amelia. (2018). Wired for innovation: Valuing the unique innovation abilities of emerging adults. *Emerging Adulthood, 6*(5), 358–365.

Douglas, Angela E. (2018). *Fundamentals of microbiome science: How microbes shape animal biology.* Princeton University Press.

Downar, James; Fowler, Robert A.; Halko, Roxanne; Huyer, Larkin Davenport; Hill, Andrea D. & Gibson, Jennifer L. (2020). Early experience with medical assistance in dying in Ontario, Canada: A cohort study. *CMAJ, 192*(8), E173–E181.

Downar, James; Goldman, Russell; Pinto, Ruxandra; Englesakis, Marina & Adhikari, Neill K. J. (2017). The "surprise question" for predicting death in seriously ill patients: A systematic review and meta-analysis. *CMAJ, 189*(13), E484–E493.

Driemeyer, Wiebke; Janssen, Erick; Wiltfang, Jens & Elmerstig, Eva. (2016). Masturbation experiences of Swedish senior high school students: Gender differences and similarities. *The Journal of Sex Research.*

Duan, Li; Shao, Xiaojun; Wang, Yuan; Huang, Yinglin; Miao, Junxiao; Yang, Xueping & Zhu, Gang. (2020). An investigation of mental health status of children and adolescents in China during the outbreak of COVID-19. *Journal of Affective Disorders, 275*, 112–118.

Duckett, Stephen. (2018). Knowing, anticipating, even facilitating but still not intending: Another challenge to double effect reasoning. *Journal of Bioethical Inquiry, 15*(1), 33–37.

Duckworth, Angela L. (2016). *Grit: The power of passion and perseverance.* Scribner.

Duckworth, Cheryl Lynn. (2018). *9/11 and collective memory in US classrooms: Teaching about terror.* Routledge.

Duell, Natasha & Steinberg, Laurence. (2019). Positive risk taking in adolescence. *Child Development Perspectives, 13*(1), 48–52.

Duffey, Kiyah J.; Steffen, Lyn M.; Van Horn, Linda; Jacobs, David R. & Popkin, Barry M. (2012). Dietary patterns matter: Diet beverages and cardiometabolic risks in the longitudinal Coronary Artery Risk Development in Young Adults (CARDIA) Study. *American Journal of Clinical Nutrition, 95*(4), 909–915.

Dugas, Lara R.; Fuller, Miles; Gilbert, Jack & Layden, Brian T. (2016). The obese gut microbiome across the epidemiologic transition. *Emerging Themes in Epidemiology, 13*(1).

Duncan, Dustin T. & Kawachi, Ichiro (Eds.). (2018). *Neighborhoods and health* (2nd ed.). Oxford University Press.

Durso, Francis T.; Dattel, Andrew R. & Pop, Vlad L. (2018). Expertise and transportation. In Ericsson, K. Anders; Hoffman, Robert R.; Kozbelt, Aaron & Williams, A. Mark (Eds.), *The Cambridge handbook of expertise and expert performance* (2nd ed., pp. 356–371). Cambridge University Press.

Dutton, Donald G. (2012). The case against the role of gender in intimate partner violence. *Aggression and Violent Behavior, 17*(1), 99–104.

Dvornyk, Volodymyr & Waqar-ul-Haq. (2012). Genetics of age at menarche: A systematic review. *Human Reproduction Update, 18*(2), 198–210.

Dweck, Carol S. (2016). *Mindset: The new psychology of success.* Random House.

Eagly, Alice H. & Wood, Wendy. (2013). The nature–nurture debates: 25 years of challenges in understanding the psychology of gender. *Perspectives on Psychological Science, 8*(3), 340–357.

Eaton, Asia A.; Noori, Sofia; Bonomi, Amy; Stephens, Dionne P. & Gillum, Tameka L. (2020). Nonconsensual porn as a form of intimate partner violence: Using the power and control wheel to understand nonconsensual porn perpetration in intimate relationships. *Trauma, Violence, & Abuse,* (In Press).

Ebrahimi, Loghman; Amiri, Mohsen; Mohamadlou, Maryam & Rezapur, Roya. (2017). Attachment styles, parenting styles, and depression. *International Journal of Mental Health and Addiction, 15*, 1064–1068.

Ecker, Simone & Beck, Stephan. (2019). The epigenetic clock: A molecular crystal ball for human aging. *Aging, 11*(2), 833–835.

Eells, Tracy D.; Lombart, Kenneth G.; Salsman, Nicholas; Kendjelic, Edward M.; Schneiderman, Carolyn T. & Lucas, Cynthia P. (2011). Expert reasoning in psychotherapy case formulation. *Psychotherapy Research, 21*(4), 385–399.

Efrati, Yaniv & Gola, Mateusz. (2019). Adolescents' compulsive sexual behavior: The role of parental competence, parents' psychopathology, and quality of parent–child communication about sex. *Journal of Behavioral Addictions, 8*(3), 420–431.

Egalite, Anna J.; Kisida, Brian & Winters, Marcus A. (2015). Representation in the classroom: The effect of own-race teachers on student achievement. *Economics of Education Review, 45*, 44–52.

Ehrlich, Sara Z. & Blum-Kulka, Shoshana. (2014). 'Now I said that Danny becomes Danny again': A multifaceted view of kindergarten children's peer argumentative discourse. In Cekaite, Asta; Blum-Kulka, Shoshana; Grøver, Vibeke & Teubal, Eva (Eds.), *Children's peer talk: Learning from each other* (pp. 23–41). Cambridge University Press.

Eimas, Peter D.; Siqueland, Einar R.; Jusczyk, Peter & Vigorito, James. (1971). Speech perception in infants. *Science, 171*(3968), 303–306.

Einav, Liran; Finkelstein, Amy; Mullainathan, Sendhil & Obermeyer, Ziad. (2018). Predictive modeling of U.S. health care spending in late life. *Science, 360*(6396), 1462–1465.

Elbejjani, Martine; Auer, Reto; Jacobs, David R.; Haight, Thaddeus; Davatzikos, Christos; Goff, David C.; . . . Launer, Lenore J. (2019). Cigarette smoking and gray matter brain volumes in middle age adults: The CARDIA Brain MRI sub-study. *Translational Psychiatry, 9*(1), 78.

Ellis, Bruce J. & Boyce, W. Thomas. (2008). Biological sensitivity to context. *Current Directions in Psychological Science, 17*(3), 183–187.

Ellis, Bruce J. & Del Giudice, Marco. (2019). Developmental adaptation to stress: An evolutionary perspective. *Annual Review of Psychology, 70*(1), 111–139.

Emanuel, Ezekiel J. (2017). Euthanasia and physician-assisted suicide: Focus on the data. *Medical Journal of Australia, 206*(8), 1–2e1.

Engler, Barbara. (2006). *Personality theories: An introduction* (7th ed.). Houghton Mifflin.

English, Tammy & Carstensen, Laura L. (2014). Selective narrowing of social networks across adulthood is associated with improved emotional experience in daily life. *International Journal of Behavioral Development, 38*(2), 195–202.

Ennis, Linda Rose. (2015). *Intensive mothering: The cultural contradictions of modern motherhood.* Demeter Press.

Epstein, Robert; Pandit, Mayuri & Thakar, Mansi. (2013). How love emerges in arranged marriages: Two cross-cultural studies. *Journal of Comparative Family Studies, 44*(3), 341–360.

Erens, Bob; Mitchell, Kirstin R.; Gibson, Lorna; Datta, Jessica; Lewis, Ruth; Field, Nigel & Wellings, Kaye. (2019). Health status, sexual activity and satisfaction among older people in Britain: A mixed methods study. *PLoS ONE, 14*(3), e0213835.

Erickson, Anders C.; Ostry, Aleck; Chan, Hing Man & Arbour, Laura. (2016). Air pollution, neighbourhood and maternal-level factors modify the effect of smoking on birth weight: A multilevel analysis in British Columbia, Canada. *BMC Public Health, 16*(1).

Ericsson, K. Anders (Ed.) (2014). *The road to excellence: The acquisition of expert performance in the arts and sciences, sports, and games.* Psychology Press.

Erikson, Erik H. (1968). *Identity: Youth and crisis.* Norton.

Erikson, Erik H. (1982). *The life cycle completed: A review.* Norton.

Erikson, Erik H. (1993a). *Childhood and society* (2nd ed.). Norton.

Erikson, Erik H. (1993b). *Gandhi's truth: On the origins of militant nonviolence.* Norton.

Erikson, Erik H. (1994). *Identity: Youth and crisis.* Norton.

Erikson, Erik H. (1994). *Identity and the life cycle.* Norton.

Erikson, Erik H. (1998). *The life cycle completed.* Norton.

Erikson, Erik H.; Erikson, Joan M. & Kivnick, Helen Q. (1986). *Vital involvement in old age.* Norton.

Erikson, Erik H.; Erikson, Joan M. & Kivnick, Helen Q. (1994). *Vital involvement in old age.* Norton.

Eriksson, Kimmo; Björnstjerna, Marie & Vartanova, Irina. (2020). The relation between gender egalitarian values and gender differences in academic achievement. *Frontiers in Psychology, 11*(236).

Ervin, Jennifer N.; Kahn, Jeremy M.; Cohen, Taya R. & Weingart, Laurie R. (2018). Teamwork in the intensive care unit. *American Psychologist, 73*(4), 468–477.

Esposti, Michelle Degli; Pereira, Snehal M. Pinto; Humphreys, David K.; Sale, Richard D. & Bowes, Lucy. (2020). Child maltreatment and the risk of antisocial behaviour: A population-based cohort study spanning 50 years. *Child Abuse & Neglect, 99*(104281).

Evans, Angela D.; Xu, Fen & Lee, Kang. (2011). When all signs point to you: Lies told in the face of evidence. *Developmental Psychology, 47*(1), 39–49.

Evans, Jonathan St. B. T. & Stanovich, Keith E. (2013). Dual-process theories of higher cognition: Advancing the debate. *Perspectives on Psychological Science, 8*(3), 223–241.

Evans, Spencer C.; Frazer, Andrew L.; Blossom, Jennifer B. & Fite, Paula J. (2019). Forms and functions of aggression in early childhood. *Journal of Clinical Child & Adolescent Psychology, 48*(5), 790–798.

Fagnani, Jeanne. (2013). Equal access to quality care: Lessons from France on providing high quality and affordable early childhood education and care. In *Equal access to childcare: Providing quality early childhood education and care to disadvantaged families* (pp. 77–99). Policy Press.

Faircloth, Charlotte. (2020). Parenting and social solidarity in cross-cultural perspective. *Families, Relationships and Societies, 9*(1), 143–159.

Fairhurst, Merle T.; Löken, Line & Grossmann, Tobias. (2014). Physiological and behavioral responses reveal 9-month-old infants' sensitivity to pleasant touch. *Psychological Science, 25*(5), 1124–1131.

Farber, Stu & Farber, Annalu. (2014). It ain't easy: Making life and death decisions before the crisis. In Rogne, Leah & McCune, Susana Lauraine (Eds.), *Advance care planning: Communicating about matters of life and death* (pp. 109–122). Springer.

Fareed, Mohd; Anwar, Malik Azeem & Afzal, Mohammad. (2015). Prevalence and gene frequency of color vision impairments among children of six populations from North Indian region. *Genes & Diseases, 2*(2), 211–218.

Farr, Rachel H. & Grotevant, Harold D. (2019). Adoption. In Fiese, Barbara H.; Celano, Marianne; Deater-Deckard, Kirby; Jouriles, Ernest N. & Whisman, Mark A. (Eds.), *APA handbook of contemporary family psychology: Foundations, methods, and contemporary issues across the lifespan* (pp. 725–741). American Psychological Association.

Farrell, C.; Chappell, F.; Armitage, P. A.; Keston, P.; MacLullich, A.; Shenkin, S. & Wardlaw, J. M. (2009). Development and initial testing of normal reference MR images for the brain at ages 65–70 and 75–80 years. *European Radiology, 19*(1), 177–183.

Farrell, Lara J.; Lavell, Cassie; Baras, Eden; Zimmer-Gembeck, Melanie J. & Waters, Allison M. (2020). Clinical expression and treatment response among children with comorbid obsessive compulsive disorder and attention-deficit/hyperactivity disorder. *Journal of Affective Disorders, 266*, 585–594.

Farvid, Maryam S.; Cho, Eunyoung; Chen, Wendy Y.; Eliassen, A Heather & Willett, Walter C. (2014). Premenopausal dietary fat in relation to pre- and post-menopausal breast cancer. *Breast Cancer Research and Treatment, 145*, 255–265.

Fast, Anne A. & Olson, Kristina R. (2018). Gender development in transgender preschool children. *Child Development, 89*(2), 620–637.

Fayyad, John; Sampson, Nancy A.; Hwang, Irving; Adamowski, Tomasz; Aguilar-Gaxiola, Sergio; Al-Hamzawi, Ali; . . . Kessler, Ronald C. (2017). The descriptive epidemiology of DSM-IV Adult ADHD in the World Health Organization World Mental Health Surveys. *ADHD Attention Deficit and Hyperactivity Disorders, 9*, 47–65.

Fazzi, Elisa; Signorini, Sabrina G.; Bomba, Monica; Luparia, Antonella; Lanners, Josée & Balottin, Umberto. (2011). Reach on sound: A key to object permanence in visually impaired children. *Early Human Development, 87*(4), 289–296.

Fearon, R. M. Pasco & Roisman, Glenn I. (2017). Attachment theory: Progress and future directions. *Current Opinion in Psychology, 15*, 131–136.

Fecher, Natalie & Johnson, Elizabeth K. (2018). The native-language benefit for talker identification is robust in 7.5-month-old infants. *Journal of Experimental Psychology: Learning, Memory, and Cognition, 44*(12), 1911–1920.

Feeney, Judith & Fitzgerald, Jennifer. (2019). Attachment, conflict and relationship quality: Laboratory-based and clinical insights. *Current Opinion in Psychology, 25*, 127–131.

Feld, Barry C. (2013). *Kids, cops, and confessions: Inside the interrogation room.* New York University Press.

Feldman, Ruth. (2012a). Oxytocin and social affiliation in humans. *Hormones and Behavior, 61*(3), 380–391.

Feldman, Ruth. (2012b). Parent-infant synchrony: A biobehavioral model of mutual influences in the formation of affiliative bonds. *Monographs of the Society for Research in Child Development, 77*(2), 42–51.

Feliciano, Cynthia & Rumbaut, Rubén G. (2018). Varieties of ethnic self-identities: Children of immigrants in middle adulthood. *RSF: The Russell Sage Foundation Journal of the Social Sciences, 4*(5), 26–46.

Feng, Xue; Kim, David D.; Cohen, Joshua T.; Neumann, Peter J. & Ollendorf, Daniel A. (2020). Using QALYs versus DALYs to measure cost-effectiveness: How much does it matter? *International Journal of Technology Assessment in Health Care, 36*(2), 96–103.

Ferrari, Marco & Quaresima, Valentina. (2012). A brief review on the history of human functional near-infrared spectroscopy (fNIRS) development and fields of application. *NeuroImage, 63*(2), 921–935.

Ferraris, Pauline; Yssel, Hans & Missé, Dorothée. (2019). Zika virus infection: An update. *Microbes and Infection, 21*(8/9), 353–360.

Ferraro, Kenneth F. & Schafer, Markus H. (2017). Visions of the life course: Risks, resources, and vulnerability. *Research in Human Development, 14*(1), 88–93.

Ferreira, Manuel A. R.; Jansen, Rick; Willemsen, Gonneke; Penninx, Brenda; Bain, Lisa M.; Vicente, Cristina T.; . . . Phipps, Simon. (2017). Gene-based analysis of regulatory variants identifies 4 putative novel asthma risk genes related to nucleotide synthesis and signaling. *Journal of Allergy and Clinical Immunology, 139*(4), 1148–1157.

Ferrer, Ilyan; Brotman, Shari & Grenier, Amanda. (2017). The experiences of reciprocity among Filipino older adults in Canada: Intergenerational, transnational, and community consideration. *Journal of Gerontological Social Work, 60*(4), 313–327.

Fiedler, John L.; Afidra, Ronald; Mugambi, Gladys; Tehinse, John; Kabaghe, Gladys; Zulu, Rodah; . . . Bermudez, Odilia. (2014). Maize flour fortification in Africa: Markets, feasibility, coverage, and costs. *Annals of the New York Academy of Sciences, 1312*, 26–39.

Field, Tiffany. (2019). Social touch, CT touch and massage therapy: A narrative review. *Developmental Review, 51*, 123–145.

Fields, David A.; Krishnan, Sowmya & Wisniewski, Amy B. (2009). Sex differences in body composition early in life. *Gender Medicine, 6*(2), 369–375.

Fiennes, Caroline. (2017). We need a science of philanthropy. *Nature, 546*(7657), 187.

Fiese, Barbara H.; Gundersen, Craig; Koester, Brenda & Jones, Blake L. (2016). Family chaos and lack of mealtime planning is associated with food insecurity in low income households. *Economics & Human Biology, 21*, 147–155.

Fiese, Barbara H.; Jones, Blake L. & Saltzman, Jaclyn A. (2019). Systems unify family psychology. In Fiese, Barbara H.; Celano, Marianne; Deater-Deckard, Kirby; Jouriles, Ernest N. & Whisman, Mark A. (Eds.), *APA handbook of contemporary family psychology: Foundations, methods, and contemporary issues across the lifespan*. American Psychological Association.

Finch, Caleb E. (2010). Evolution of the human lifespan and diseases of aging: Roles of infection, inflammation, and nutrition. *Proceedings of the National Academy of Sciences, 107*(Suppl. 1), 1718–1724.

Fine, Cordelia. (2014). His brain, her brain? *Science, 346*(6212), 915–916.

Fink, David S.; Schleimer, Julia P.; Sarvet, Aaron; Grover, Kiran K.; Delcher, Chris; Castillo-Carniglia, Alvaro; . . . Cerdá, Magdalena. (2018). Association between prescription drug monitoring programs and nonfatal and fatal drug overdoses: A systematic review. *Annals of Internal Medicine, 168*(11), 783–790.

Finkel, Deborah & Bravell, Marie Ernsth. (2018). Cohort by education interactions in longitudinal changes in functional abilities. *Journal of Aging and Health, 32*(3/4), 208–215.

Finlay, Ilora G. & George, R. (2011). Legal physician-assisted suicide in Oregon and the Netherlands: Evidence concerning the impact on patients in vulnerable groups—Another perspective on Oregon's data. *Journal of Medical Ethics, 37*(3), 171–174.

Fins, Joseph J. & Bernat, James L. (2018). Ethical, palliative, and policy considerations in disorders of consciousness. *Archives of Physical Medicine and Rehabilitation, 99*(9), 1927–1931.

Fiori, Katherine L.; Windsor, Tim D. & Huxhold, Oliver. (2020). The increasing importance of friendship in late life: Understanding the role of sociohistorical context in social development. *Gerontology, 66*, 286–294.

Fisher, Diana E.; Klein, Barbara E. K.; Wong, Tien Y.; Rotter, Jerome I.; Li, Xiaohui; Shrager, Sandi; . . . Cotch, Mary Frances. (2016). Incidence of age-related macular degeneration in a multi-ethnic United States population. *Ophthalmology, 123*(6), 1297–1308.

Fisher, Helen E. (2016a). *Anatomy of love: A natural history of mating, marriage, and why we stray*. Norton.

Fisher, Helen E. (2016b). Broken hearts: The nature and risks of romantic rejection. In Booth, Alan; Crouter, Ann C. & Snyder, Anastasia (Eds.), *Romance and sex in adolescence and emerging adulthood* (pp. 3–28). Routledge.

Flanagan, Constance A. (2013). *Teenage citizens: The political theories of the young*. Harvard University Press.

Flegal, Katherine M.; Kit, Brian K.; Orpana, Heather & Graubard, Barry I. (2013). Association of all-cause mortality with overweight and obesity using standard body mass index categories: A systematic review and meta-analysis. *JAMA, 309*(1), 71–82.

Fló, Ana; Brusini, Perrine; Macagno, Francesco; Nespor, Marina; Mehler, Jacques & Ferry, Alissa L. (2019). Newborns are sensitive to multiple cues for word segmentation in continuous speech. *Developmental Science, 22*(4), e12802.

Flores, Andrew R.; Haider-Markel, Donald P.; Lewis, Daniel C.; Miller, Patrick R.; Tadlock, Barry L. & Taylor, Jami K. (2018). Transgender prejudice reduction and opinions on transgender rights: Results from a mediation analysis on experimental data. *Research & Politics, 5*(1).

Flores, Andrew R.; Herman, Jody L.; Gates, Gary J. & Brown, Taylor N. T. (2016, June). *How many adults identify as transgender in the United States?* Los Angeles, CA: Williams Institute.

Fluck, Andrew E.; Ranmuthugala, Dev; Chin, C. K. H.; Penesis, Irene; Chong, Jacky; Yang, Yang & Ghous, Asim. (2020). Transforming learning with computers: Calculus for kids. *Education and Information Technologies, 25*, 3779–3796.

Flynn, James R. (1999). Searching for justice: The discovery of IQ gains over time. *American Psychologist, 54*(1), 5–20.

Flynn, James R. (2012). *Are we getting smarter?: Rising IQ in the twenty-first century*. Cambridge University Press.

Foglia, Lucia & Wilson, Robert A. (2013). Embodied cognition. *Wiley Interdisciplinary Reviews: Cognitive Science, 4*(**3**), 319–325.

Fontana, Luigi; Colman, Ricki J.; Holloszy, John O. & Weindruch, Richard. (2011). Calorie restriction in nonhuman and human primates. In Edward, J. Masoro & Steven, N. Austad (Eds.), *Handbook of the biology of aging* (7th ed., pp. 447–461). Academic Press.

Foot, Philippa. (1978). *Virtues and vices and other essays in moral philosophy*. University of California Press.

Ford, Jodi L.; Boch, Samantha J. & Browning, Christopher R. (2019). Hair cortisol and depressive symptoms in youth: An investigation of curvilinear relationships. *Psychoneuroendocrinology, 109*(104376).

Forestell, Catherine A. & Mennella, Julie A. (2017). The relationship between infant facial expressions and food acceptance. *Current Nutrition Reports, 6*(2), 141–147.

Formosa, Marvin (Ed.) (2019). *The University of the Third Age and active ageing: European and Asian-Pacific perspectives*. Springer.

Forster, Sophie & Spence, Charles. (2018). "What smell?" Temporarily loading visual attention induces a prolonged loss of olfactory awareness. *Psychological Science, 29*(10), 1642–1652.

Foster, Joshua D.; Raley, Jennifer R. & Isen, Joshua D. (2020). Further evidence that only children are not more narcissistic than individuals with siblings. *Personality and Individual Differences, 161*(109977).

Foulkes, Lucy & Blakemore, Sarah-Jayne. (2018). Studying individual differences in human adolescent brain development. *Nature Neuroscience, 21*, 315–323.

Fowler, James W. (1981). *Stages of faith: The psychology of human development and the quest for meaning*. Harper & Row.

Fowler, James W. (1986). Faith and the structuring of meaning. In Dykstra, Craig & Parks, Sharon (Eds.), *Faith development and Fowler* (pp. 15–42). Religious Education Press.

Fox, Nathan A.; Henderson, Heather A.; Marshall, Peter J.; Nichols, Kate E. & Ghera, Melissa M. (2005). Behavioral inhibition: Linking biology and behavior within a developmental framework. *Annual Review of Psychology, 56*, 235–262.

Fox, Nathan A.; Henderson, Heather A.; Rubin, Kenneth H.; Calkins, Susan D. & Schmidt, Louis A. (2001). Continuity and discontinuity of behavioral inhibition and exuberance: Psychophysiological and behavioral influences across the first four years of life. *Child Development, 72*(1), 1–21.

Fox, Nathan A.; Reeb-Sutherland, Bethany C. & Degnan, Kathryn A. (2013). Personality and emotional development. In Zelazo, Philip D. (Ed.), *The Oxford handbook of developmental psychology* (Vol. 2, pp. 15–44). Oxford University Press.

Fradkin, Chris; Wallander, Jan L.; Elliott, Marc N.; Tortolero, Susan; Cuccaro, Paula & Schuster, Mark A. (2015). Associations between socioeconomic status and obesity in diverse, young adolescents: Variation across race/ethnicity and gender. *Health Psychology, 34*(1), 1–9.

Franco, Manuel; Bilal, Usama; Orduñez, Pedro; Benet, Mikhail; Alain, Morejón; Benjamín, Caballero; . . . Cooper, Richard S. (2013). Population-wide weight loss and regain in relation to diabetes burden and cardiovascular mortality in Cuba 1980–2010: Repeated cross sectional surveys and ecological comparison of secular trends. *BMJ, 346*(7903), f1515.

Frankenburg, William K.; Dodds, Josiah; Archer, Philip; Shapiro, Howard & Bresnick,

Beverly. (1992). The Denver II: A major revision and restandardization of the Denver Developmental Screening Test. *Pediatrics*, 89(1), 91–97.

Frankova, Iryna. (2019). Similar but different: Psychological and psychopathological features of primary and secondary hikikomori. *Frontiers in Psychiatry*, 10(558).

Fraser, Graham. (2015). Preface. In Hayday, Matthew, *So they want us to learn French: Promoting and opposing bilingualism in English-speaking Canada*. University of British Columbia Press.

Fraundorf, Scott H.; Hourihan, Kathleen L.; Peters, Rachel A. & Benjamin, Aaron S. (2019). Aging and recognition memory: A meta-analysis. *Psychological Bulletin*, 145(4), 339–371.

Frederick, David A.; Lever, Janet; Gillespie, Brian Joseph & Garcia, Justin R. (2017). What keeps passion alive? Sexual satisfaction is associated with sexual communication, mood setting, sexual variety, oral sex, orgasm, and sex frequency in a national U.S. study. *The Journal of Sex Research*, 54(2), 186–201.

Fredrickson, Barbara L. (2013). Positive emotions broaden and build. In Devine, Patricia & Plant, Ashby (Eds.), *Advances in experimental social psychology* (Vol. 47, pp. 1–53). Academic Press.

Fredrickson, Barbara L. & Siegel, Daniel J. (2017). Broaden-and-build theory meets interpersonal neurobiology as a lens on compassion and positivity resonance. In Gilbert, Paul (Ed.), *Compassion: Concepts, research and applications*. Routledge.

Freedman, Vicki A.; Wolf, Douglas A. & Spillman, Brenda C. (2016). Disability-free life expectancy over 30 years: A growing female disadvantage in the US population. *American Journal of Public Health*, 106(6), 1079–1085.

Freeman, Joan. (2010). *Gifted lives: What happens when gifted children grow up?* Routledge.

Freerks, Lisa; Papadatou Soulou, Eleni; Batchelor, Hannah & Klein, Sandra. (2019). A review of GI conditions critical to oral drug absorption in malnourished children. *European Journal of Pharmaceutics and Biopharmaceutics*, 137, 9–22.

Freud, Sigmund. (1927). *The ego and the id.* Hogarth Press.

Freud, Sigmund. (1990). *The ego and the id.* W. W. Norton & Co.

Fridel, Emma E. & Fox, James Alan. (2019). Gender differences in patterns and trends in U.S. homicide, 1976–2017. *Violence and Gender*, 6(1).

Fritzell, Sara; Gähler, Michael & Fransson, Emma. (2020). Child living arrangements following separation and mental health of parents in Sweden. *SSM—Population Health*, 10(100511).

Fry, Douglas P. (2014). Environment of evolutionary adaptedness, rough-and-tumble play, and the selection of restraint in human aggression. In Narvaez, Darcia; Valentino, Kristin; Fuentes, Agustin; McKenna, James J. & Gray, Peter (Eds.), *Ancestral landscapes in human evolution: Culture, childrearing and social wellbeing* (pp. 169–188). Oxford University Press.

Fry, Richard; Passel, Jeffrey S. & Cohn, D'Vera. (2020, September 4). *A majority of young adults in the U.S. live with their parents for the first time since the Great Depression. Fact Tank.* Washington, DC: Pew Research Center.

Frydenberg, Erica. (2017). *Coping and the challenge of resilience.* Palgrave.

Fulmer, C. Ashley; Gelfand, Micheke J.; Kruglanski, Arie W.; Kim-Prieto, Chu; Diener, Ed; Pierro, Antonio & Higgins, E. Tory. (2010). On "feeling right" in cultural contexts: How person-culture match affects self-esteem and subjective well-being. *Psychological Science*, 21(11), 1563–1569.

Furtuna, Dorian. (2014, September 22). Male aggression: Why are men more violent? *Psychology Today.*

Furtuna, Dorian. (2016, January 18). Why young men join ISIS? The psychology of terrorists. *Social Ethology: Human Instincts in Modern Society.*

Fury, Gail; Carlson, Elizabeth A. & Sroufe, Alan. (1997). Children's representations of attachment relationships in family drawings. *Child Development*, 68(6), 1154–1164.

Fusaro, Maria & Harris, Paul L. (2013). Dax gets the nod: Toddlers detect and use social cues to evaluate testimony. *Developmental Psychology*, 49(3), 514–522.

Fuster, Joaquin. (2015). *The prefrontal cortex* (5th ed.). Academic Press.

Galak, Jeff; Givi, Julian & Williams, Elanor F. (2016). Why certain gifts are great to give but not to get: A framework for understanding errors in gift giving. *Current Directions in Psychological Science*, 25(6), 380–385.

Galbete, Cecilia; Schwingshackl, Lukas; Schwedhelm, Carolina; Boeing, Heiner & Schulze, Matthias B. (2018). Evaluating Mediterranean diet and risk of chronic disease in cohort studies: An umbrella review of meta-analyses. *European Journal of Epidemiology*, 33, 909–931.

Gallagher, Annabella; Updegraff, Kimberly; Padilla, Jenny & McHale, Susan M. (2018). Longitudinal associations between sibling relational aggression and adolescent adjustment. *Journal of Youth and Adolescence*, 47(10), 2100–2113.

Galton, Francis. (1896). *Hereditary genius: An inquiry into its laws and consequences.* London, UK: Macmillan.

Gangestad, Steven W. & Grebe, Nicholas M. (2017). Hormonal systems, human social bonding, and affiliation. *Hormones and Behavior*, 91, 122–135.

Gao, Xuesong & Ren, Wei. (2019). Controversies of bilingual education in China. *International Journal of Bilingual Education and Bilingualism*, 22(3), 267–273.

Gao, Yuan; Huang, Changquan; Zhao, Kexiang; Ma, Louyan; Qiu, Xuan; Zhang, Lei; . . . Xiao, Qian. (2013). Depression as a risk factor for dementia and mild cognitive impairment: A meta-analysis of longitudinal studies. *International Journal of Geriatric Psychiatry*, 28(5), 441–449.

Garcia, Elisa B. (2018). The classroom language context and English and Spanish vocabulary development among dual language learners attending Head Start. *Early Childhood Research Quarterly*, 42, 148–157.

García, Ofelia & Wei, Li. (2014). *Translanguaging: Language, bilingualism and education.* Palgrave MacMillan.

Gardner, Howard. (1983). *Frames of mind: The theory of multiple intelligences.* Basic Books.

Gardner, Howard. (1999). Are there additional intelligences? The case for naturalist, spiritual, and existential intelligences. In Kane, Jeffrey (Ed.), *Education, information, and transformation: Essays on learning and thinking* (pp. 111–131). Merrill.

Gardner, Howard. (2006). *Multiple intelligences: New horizons in theory and practice.* Basic Books.

Gardner, Howard & Moran, Seana. (2006). The science of multiple intelligences theory: A response to Lynn Waterhouse. *Educational Psychologist*, 41(4), 227–232.

Garthus-Niegel, Susan; Ayers, Susan; Martini, Julia; von Soest, Tilmann & Eberhard-Gran, Malin. (2017). The impact of postpartum posttraumatic stress disorder symptoms on child development: A population-based, 2-year follow-up study. *Psychological Medicine*, 47(1), 161–170.

Gaskins, Audrey Jane; Mendiola, Jaime; Afeiche, Myriam; Jørgensen, Niels; Swan, Shanna H. & Chavarro, Jorge E. (2013). Physical activity and television watching in relation to semen quality in young men. *British Journal of Sports Medicine*, 49(4), 265–270.

Gasman, Marybeth; Abiola, Ufuoma & Travers, Christopher. (2015). Diversity and senior leadership at elite institutions of higher education. *Journal of Diversity in Higher Education*, 8(1), 1–14.

Gassin, Elizabeth A. (2017). Forgiveness and continuing bonds. In Klass, Dennis & Steffen, Edith Maria (Eds.), *Continuing bonds in bereavement: New directions for research and practice.* Routledge.

Gawande, Atul. (2014). *Being mortal: Medicine and what matters in the end.* Metropolitan Books.

Gazzaniga, Michael S. (2015). *Tales from both sides of the brain: A life in neuroscience.* Ecco.

Gazzillo, Francesco; Dazzi, Nino; De Luca, Emma; Rodomonti, Martina & Silberschatz, George. (2020). Attachment disorganization and severe psychopathology: A possible dialogue between attachment theory and control-mastery theory. *Psychoanalytic Psychology*, 37(3), 173–184.

Geiger, A. W. & Livingston, Gretchen. (2019, February 13). *8 facts about love and marriage in America. Fact Tank.* Washington, DC: Pew Research Center.

Gelfand, Amy. (2018). Episodic syndromes of childhood associated with migraine. *Current Opinion in Neurology*, 31(3), 281–285.

Gellert, Anna S. & Elbro, Carsten. (2017). Does a dynamic test of phonological awareness predict early reading difficulties? A longitudinal study from kindergarten through grade 1. *Journal of Learning Disabilities*, 50(3), 227–237.

Gernhardt, Ariane; Keller, Heidi & Rübeling, Hartmut. (2016). Children's family drawings as expressions of attachment representations across cultures: Possibilities and limitations. *Child Development*, 87(4), 1069–1078.

Gernhardt, Ariane; Rübeling, Hartmut & Keller, Heidi. (2013). "This is my family": Differences in children's family drawings across cultures. *Journal of Cross-Cultural Psychology, 44*(7), 1166–1183.

Gerstorf, Denis; Heckhausen, Jutta; Ram, Nilam; Infurna, Frank J.; Schupp, Jürgen & Wagner, Gert G. (2014). Perceived personal control buffers terminal decline in well-being. *Psychology and Aging, 29*(3), 612–625.

Gervais, Will M. & Norenzayan, Ara. (2012). Analytic thinking promotes religious disbelief. *Science, 336*(6080), 493–496.

Ghettia, Simona & Bunge, Silvia A. (2012). Neural changes underlying the development of episodic memory during middle childhood. *Developmental Cognitive Neuroscience, 2*(4), 381–395.

Ghosh, Abhishek; Ray, Anirban & Basu, Aniruddha. (2017). Oppositional defiant disorder: Current insight. *Psychology Research and Behavior Management, 10*, 353–367.

Gibbons, Ann. (2017). How Africans evolved a palette of skin tones. *Science, 358*(6360), 157–158.

Gibbs, Sandra E. & Turner, Howard B. (2017). Psychological dimensions of nutrition. In Chen, Linda H. (Ed.), *Nutritional aspects of aging* (Vol. 1). CRC Press.

Gibson, Eleanor J. (1988). Exploratory behavior in the development of perceiving, acting, and the acquiring of knowledge. *Annual Review of Psychology, 39*, 1–42.

Gibson, Eleanor J. (1997). An ecological psychologist's prolegomena for perceptual development: A functional approach. In Dent-Read, Cathy & Zukow-Goldring, Patricia (Eds.), *Evolving explanations of development: Ecological approaches to organism-environment systems* (1st ed., pp. 23–54). American Psychological Association.

Gibson, Jacqueline MacDonald; Fisher, Michael; Clonch, Allison; MacDonald, John M. & Cook, Philip J. (2020). Children drinking private well water have higher blood lead than those with city water. *PNAS, 117*(29), 16898–16907.

Gibson-Davis, Christina; Gassman-Pines, Anna & Lehrman, Rebecca. (2018). "His" and "hers": Meeting the economic bar to marriage. *Demography, 55*(6), 2321–2343.

Gidley, Jennifer M. (2016). *Postformal education: A philosophy for complex futures.* Springer.

Gilbert, Jack A.; Blaser, Martin J.; Caporaso, J. Gregory; Jansson, Janet K.; Lynch, Susan V. & Knight, Rob. (2018). Current understanding of the human microbiome. *Nature Medicine, 24*(4), 392–400.

Gillespie, Brian Joseph; Frederick, David; Harari, Lexi & Grov, Christian. (2015). Homophily, close friendship, and life satisfaction among gay, lesbian, heterosexual, and bisexual men and women. *PLoS ONE, 10*(6), e0128900.

Gilligan, Carol. (1982). *In a different voice: Psychological theory and women's development.* Harvard University Press.

Gilligan, Megan; Karraker, Amelia & Jasper, Angelica. (2018). Linked lives and cumulative inequality: A multigenerational family life course framework: Linked lives and cumulative inequality. *Journal of Family Theory & Review, 10*(1), 111–125.

Gillon, Raanan. (2015). Defending the four principles approach as a good basis for good medical practice and therefore for good medical ethics. *Journal of Medical Ethics, 41*(1), 111–116.

Gleim, Mark R.; Johnson, Catherine M. & Lawson, Stephanie J. (2019). Sharers and sellers: A multi-group examination of gig economy workers' perceptions. *Journal of Business Research, 98*, 142–152.

Glen, Nancy L. (2018). Music in a new key: The sociocultural impact of the New Horizons Band programme and its relationship to Baltes' Selective Optimization with Compensation Model. *International Journal of Community Music, 11*(2), 199–212.

Glenberg, Arthur M.; Witt, Jessica K. & Metcalfe, Janet. (2013). From the revolution to embodiment: 25 years of cognitive psychology. *Perspectives on Psychological Science, 8*(5), 573–585.

Glover, Crystal Polite; Jenkins, Toby S. & Troutman, Stephanie. (2018). *Culture, community, and educational success: Reimagining the invisible knapsack.* Lexington.

Gobet, Fernand & Charness, Neil. (2018). Expertise in chess. In Ericsson, K. Anders; Hoffman, Robert R.; Kozbelt, Aaron & Williams, A. Mark (Eds.), *The Cambridge handbook of expertise and expert performance* (2nd ed., pp. 597–615). Cambridge University Press.

Goddings, Anne-Lise; Heyes, Stephanie Burnett; Bird, Geoffrey; Viner, Russell M. & Blakemore, Sarah-Jayne. (2012). The relationship between puberty and social emotion processing. *Developmental Science, 15*(6), 801–811.

Godfrey, Erin B.; Santos, Carlos E. & Burson, Esther. (2019). For better or worse? System-justifying beliefs in sixth-grade predict trajectories of self-esteem and behavior across early adolescence. *Child Development, 90*(1), 180–195.

Godinet, Meripa T.; Li, Fenfang & Berg, Teresa. (2014). Early childhood maltreatment and trajectories of behavioral problems: Exploring gender and racial differences. *Child Abuse & Neglect, 38*(3), 544–556.

Godwin, Karrie E.; Almeda, Ma. V.; Seltman, Howard; Kai, Shimin; Skerbetz, Mandi D.; Baker, Ryan S. & Fisher, Anna V. (2016). Off-task behavior in elementary school children. *Learning and Instruction, 44*, 128–143.

Goel, Sunny; Sharma, Abhishek & Garg, Aakash. (2018). Effect of alcohol consumption on cardiovascular health. *Current Cardiology Reports, 20*(4).

Gökcen, Büşra Başar & Şanlier, Nevin. (2019). Coffee consumption and disease correlations. *Critical Reviews in Food Science and Nutrition, 59*(2), 336–348.

Gokhman, David; Lavi, Eitan; Prufer, Kay; Fraga, Mario F.; Riancho, Jose A.; Kelso, Janet; . . . Carmel, Liran. (2014). Reconstructing the DNA methylation maps of the Neandertal and the Denisovan. *Science, 344*(6183), 523–528.

Goldin-Meadow, Susan. (2015). From action to abstraction: Gesture as a mechanism of change. *Developmental Review, 38*, 167–184.

Goldin-Meadow, Susan & Alibali, Martha W. (2013). Gesture's role in speaking, learning, and creating language. *Annual Review of Psychology, 64*, 257–283.

Goldring, Jeremy & Strelan, Peter. (2017). The forgiveness implicit association test. *Personality and Individual Differences, 108*, 69–78.

Goldstein, Thalia R. & Winner, Ellen. (2012). Enhancing empathy and theory of mind. *Journal of Cognition and Development, 13*(1), 19–37.

Goleman, Daniel. (2005). *Emotional intelligence.* Bantam Books.

Golinkoff, Roberta Michnick; Hoff, Erika; Rowe, Meredith L.; Tamis-Lemonda, Catherine S. & Hirsh-Pasek, Kathy. (2019). Language matters: Denying the existence of the 30-million-word gap has serious consequences. *Child Development, 90*(3), 985–992.

Gómez-López, Mercedes; Viejo, Carmen & Ortega-Ruiz, Rosario. (2019). Well-being and romantic relationships: A systematic review in adolescence and emerging adulthood. *International Journal of Environmental Research and Public Health, 16*(13), 2415.

Goncy, Elizabeth A.; Basting, Evan J. & Dunn, Courtney B. (2020). A meta-analysis linking parent-to-child aggression and dating abuse during adolescence and young adulthood. *Trauma, Violence, & Abuse*, (In Press).

Goode, Adam; Carey, Timothy & Jordan, Joanne. (2013). Low back pain and lumbar spine osteoarthritis: How are they related. *Current Rheumatology Reports, 15*(2), 1–8.

Goodlad, James K.; Marcus, David K. & Fulton, Jessica J. (2013). Lead and Attention-deficit/hyperactivity disorder (ADHD) symptoms: A meta-analysis. *Clinical Psychology Review, 33*(3), 417–425.

Goodman, Sherryl; Rouse, Matthew; Connell, Arin; Broth, Michelle; Hall, Christine & Heyward, Devin. (2011). Maternal depression and child psychopathology: A meta-analytic review. *Clinical Child and Family Psychology Review, 14*(1), 1–27.

Goodwin, Glenn; Picache, Dyana; Louie, Brian J.; Gaeto, Nicholas; Zeid, Tarik; Aung, Paxton P.; . . . Sahni, Sonu. (2018). Optimal scene time to achieve favorable outcomes in out-of-hospital cardiac arrest: How long is too long? *Cureus, 10*(10), e3434.

Gooijersa, J. & Swinnen, S. P. (2014). Interactions between brain structure and behavior: The corpus callosum and bimanual coordination. *Neuroscience & Biobehavioral Reviews, 43*, 1–19.

Gopal, Kamakshi V.; Mills, Liana E.; Phillips, Bryce S. & Nandy, Rajesh. (2019). Risk assessment of recreational noise-induced hearing loss from exposure through a personal audio system-iPod touch. *Journal of the American Academy of Audiology, 30*(7), 619–633.

Gopnik, Alison. (2001). Theories, language, and culture: Whorf without wincing. In Bowerman,

Melissa & Levinson, Stephen C. (Eds.), *Language acquisition and conceptual development* (pp. 45–69). Cambridge University Press.

Gopnik, Alison. (2016). *The gardener and the carpenter: What the new science of child development tells us about the relationship between parents and children.* Farrar, Strauss and Giroux.

Gordon, Linda. (2017). *The second coming of the KKK: The Ku Klux Klan of the 1920s and the American political tradition.* Liveright.

Gordon-Hollingsworth, Arlene T.; Becker, Emily M.; Ginsburg, Golda S.; Keeton, Courtney; Compton, Scott N.; Birmaher, Boris B.; . . . March, John S. (2015). Anxiety disorders in Caucasian and African American children: A comparison of clinical characteristics, treatment process variables, and treatment outcomes. *Child Psychiatry & Human Development, 46*(5), 643–655.

Goriounova, Natalia A. & Mansvelder, Huibert D. (2019). Genes, cells and brain areas of intelligence. *Frontiers in Human Neuroscience, 13*(44).

Goris, Richard C. (2011). Infrared organs of snakes: An integral part of vision. *Journal of Herpetology, 45*(1), 2–14.

Gostin, Lawrence; Phelan, Alexandra; Coutinho, Alex Godwin; Eccleston-Turner, Mark; Erondu, Ngozi; Filani, Oyebanji; . . . Kavanagh, Matthew. (2019). Ebola in the Democratic Republic of the Congo: Time to sound a global alert? *The Lancet, 393*(10172), 617–620.

Gottman, John & Gottman, Julie. (2017). The natural principles of love. *Journal of Family Theory & Review, 9*(1), 7–26.

Gough, Ethan K.; Moodie, Erica E. M.; Prendergast, Andrew J.; Johnson, Sarasa M. A.; Humphrey, Jean H.; Stoltzfus, Rebecca J.; . . . Manges, Amee R. (2014). The impact of antibiotics on growth in children in low and middle income countries: Systematic review and meta-analysis of randomised controlled trials. *BMJ, 348*, g2267.

Grady, Denise. (2012, May 5). When illness makes a spouse a stranger. *New York Times.*

Grady, Jessica S.; Ale, Chelsea M. & Morris, Tracy L. (2012). A naturalistic observation of social behaviours during preschool drop-off. *Early Child Development and Care, 182*(12), 1683–1694.

Graf, Nikki. (2019, November 6). *Key findings on marriage and cohabitation in the U.S. Fact Tank.* Washington, DC: Pew Research Center.

Graham, Eileen K.; James, Bryan D.; Jackson, Kathryn L.; Willroth, Emily C.; Boyle, Patricia; Wilson, Robert; . . . Mroczek, Daniel K. (2020). Associations between personality traits and cognitive resilience in older adults. *The Journals of Gerontology Series B: Psychological Sciences and Social Sciences,* (In Press), gbaa135.

Grainger, Sarah A.; Henry, Julie D.; Phillips, Louise H.; Vanman, Eric J. & Allen, Roy. (2017). Age deficits in facial affect recognition: The influence of dynamic cues. *The Journal of Gerontology Series B, 72*(4), 622–632.

Grajower, Martin M. & Horne, Benjamin D. (2019). Clinical management of intermittent fasting in patients with diabetes mellitus. *Nutrients, 11*(4), 873.

Granat, Adi; Gadassi, Reuma; Gilboa-Schechtman, Eva & Feldman, Ruth. (2017). Maternal depression and anxiety, social synchrony, and infant regulation of negative and positive emotions. *Emotion, 17*(1), 11–27.

Grant, Julia D.; Vergés, Alvaro; Jackson, Kristina M.; Trull, Timothy J.; Sher, Kenneth J. & Bucholz, Kathleen K. (2012). Age and ethnic differences in the onset, persistence and recurrence of alcohol use disorder. *Addiction, 107*(4), 756–765.

Grant, Jon E. & Potenza, Marc N. (Eds.). (2010). *Young adult mental health.* Oxford University Press.

Grasso, Chris; Goldhammer, Hilary; Funk, Danielle; King, Dana; Reisner, Sari L.; Mayer, Kenneth H. & Keuroghlian, Alex S. (2019). Required sexual orientation and gender identity reporting by us health centers: First-year data. *American Journal of Public Health, 109*(8), 1111–1118.

Grasso, Stephanie M.; Pena, Elizabeth D.; Bedore, Lisa M.; Hixon, J. Gregory & Griffin, Zenzi M. (2018). Cross-linguistic cognate production in Spanish-English bilingual children with and without specific language impairment. *Journal of Speech, Language & Hearing Research, 61*(3), 619–633.

Gray, J. D.; Milner, T. A. & Mcewen, B. S. (2013). Dynamic plasticity: The role of glucocorticoids, brain-derived neurotrophic factor and other trophic factors. *Neuroscience, 239*, 214–227.

Gray, Peter. (2018). Evolutionary functions of play: Practice resilience innovation and cooperation. In Smith, Peter K. & Roopnarine, Jaipaul L. (Eds.), *The Cambridge handbook of play: Developmental and disciplinary perspectives.* Cambridge University Press.

Gredebäck, Gustaf; Astor, Kim & Fawcett, Christine. (2018). Gaze following is not dependent on ostensive cues: A critical test of natural pedagogy. *Child Development, 89*(6), 2091–2098.

Green, Amy E.; Price-Feeney, Myeshia; Dorison, Samuel H.. & Pick, Casey J. (2020). Self-reported conversion efforts and suicidality among US LGBTQ youths and young adults, 2018. *American Journal of Public Health, 110*(8), 1221–1227.

Green, Lorraine. (2017). The trouble with touch? New insights and observations on touch for social work and social care. *British Journal of Social Work, 47*(3), 773–792.

Green, Lorraine & Grant, Victoria. (2008). "Gagged grief and beleaguered bereavements?" An analysis of multidisciplinary theory and research relating to same sex partnership bereavement. *Sexualities, 11*(3), 275–300.

Greenbaum, Carla. (2019). Disease-modifying therapies for the prevention of type 1 diabetes. *US Endocrinology, 15*(1), 15–16.

Greene, Robert M. & Pisano, M. Michele. (2019). Developmental toxicity of e-cigarette aerosols. *Birth Defects Research, 111*(17), 1294–1301.

Greenough, William T.; Black, James E. & Wallace, Christopher S. (1987). Experience and brain development. *Child Development, 58*(3), 539–559.

Greenwald, Anthony G.; Smith, Colin Tucker; Sriram, N.; Bar-Anan, Yoav & Nosek, Brian A. (2009). Implicit race attitudes predicted vote in the 2008 U.S. presidential election. *Analyses of Social Issues and Public Policy, 9*(1), 241–253.

Greer, David M.; Shemie, Sam D.; Lewis, Ariane; Torrance, Sylvia; Varelas, Panayiotis; Goldenberg, Fernando D.; . . . Sung, Gene. (2020). Determination of brain death/death by neurologic criteria: The world brain death project. *JAMA, 324*(11), 1078–1097.

Greyson, Bruce. (2009). Near-death experiences and deathbed visions. In Kellehear, Allan (Ed.), *The study of dying: From autonomy to transformation* (pp. 253–275). Cambridge University Press.

Griffith, Annette K. (2020). Parental burnout and child maltreatment during the COVID-19 pandemic. *Journal of Family Violence,* (In Press).

Griffiths, Thomas L. (2015). Manifesto for a new (computational) cognitive revolution. *Cognition, 135*, 21–23.

Grigorenko, Elena L.; Compton, Donald L.; Fuchs, Lynn S; Wagner, Richard K.; Willcutt, Erik G. & Fletcher, Jack M. (2020). Understanding, educating, and supporting children with specific learning disabilities: 50 years of science and practice. *American Psychologist, 75*(1), 37–51.

Grisaru-Granovsky, Sorina; Boyko, Valentina; Lerner-Geva, Liat; Hammerman, Cathy; Rottenstreich, Misgav; Samueloff, Arnon; . . . Reichman, Brian. (2019). The mortality of very low birth weight infants: The benefit and relative impact of changes in population and therapeutic variables. *Journal of Maternal-Fetal & Neonatal Medicine, 32*(15), 2443–2451.

Groh, Ashley M.; Narayan, Angela J.; Bakermans-Kranenburg, Marian J.; Roisman, Glenn I.; Vaughn, Brian E.; Fearon, R. M. Pasco & van IJzendoorn, Marinus H. (2017). Attachment and temperament in the early life course: A meta-analytic review. *Child Development, 88*(3), 770–795.

Gronlund, Carina J.; Zanobetti, Antonella; Schwartz, Joel D.; Wellenius, Gregory A. & O'Neill, Marie S. (2014). Heat, heat waves, and hospital admissions among the elderly in the United States, 1992–2006. *Environmental Health Perspectives, 122*(11), 1187–1192.

Groß, Julia & Pachur, Thorsten. (2019). Age differences in hindsight bias: A meta-analysis. *Psychology and Aging, 34*(2), 294–310.

Gross, Sven & Sand, Manuel. (2019). Adventure tourism: A perspective paper. *Tourism Review, 75*(1), 153–157.

Grossman, Arnold H.; Park, Jung Yeon; Frank, John A. & Russell, Stephen T. (2019). Parental responses to transgender and gender nonconforming youth: Associations with parent support, parental abuse, and youths' psychological adjustment. *Journal of Homosexuality,* (In Press).

Grossmann, Igor. (2018). Dialecticism across the lifespan: Toward a deeper understanding of the ontogenetic and cultural factors influencing dialectical thinking and emotional experience.

In Spencer-Rodgers, Julie (Ed.), *The psychological and cultural foundations of East Asian cognition: Contradiction, change, and holism.* Oxford University Press.

Grover, Shawn & Helliwell, John F. (2019). How's life at home? New evidence on marriage and the set point for happiness. *Journal of Happiness Studies, 20,* 373–390.

Gruijters, Rob J. & Ermisch, John. (2019). Patrilocal, matrilocal, or neolocal? Intergenerational proximity of married couples in China. *Journal of Marriage and Family, 81*(3), 549–566.

Grusec, Joan E.; Danyliuk, Tanya; Kil, Hali & O'Neill, David. (2017). Perspectives on parent discipline and child outcomes. *International Journal of Behavioral Development, 41*(4), 465–471.

Guarnera, Maria; Hichy, Zira; Cascio, Maura; Carrubba, Stefano & Buccheri, Stefania L. (2017). Facial expressions and the ability to recognize emotions from the eyes or mouth: A comparison between children and adults. *The Journal of Genetic Psychology, 178*(6), 309–318.

Guarnera, Maria; Magnano, Paola; Pellerone, Monica; Cascio, Maura I.; Squatrito, Valeria & Buccheri, Stefania L. (2018). Facial expressions and the ability to recognize emotions from the eyes or mouth: A comparison among old adults, young adults, and children. *The Journal of Genetic Psychology, 179*(5), 297–310.

Guimarães, Gilda & Oliveira, Izabella. (2018). How kindergarten and elementary school students understand the concept of classification. In Leavy, Aisling; Meletiou-Mavrotheris, Maria & Paparistodemou, Efi (Eds.), *Statistics in early childhood and primary education: Supporting early statistical and probabilistic thinking* (pp. 129–146). Springer.

Gulia, Kamalesh K. & Kumar, Velayudhan Mohan. (2018). Sleep disorders in the elderly: A growing challenge: Sleep in elderly. *Psychogeriatrics, 18*(3), 155–165.

Gülseven, Zehra; Carlo, Gustavo; Streit, Cara; Kumru, Asiye; Selçuk, Bilge & Sayıl, Melike. (2018). Longitudinal relations among parenting daily hassles, child rearing, and prosocial and aggressive behaviors in Turkish children. *Social Development, 27*(1), 45–57.

Güngör, Derya; Bornstein, Marc H.; De Leersnyder, Jozefien; Cote, Linda; Ceulemans, Eva & Mesquita, Batja. (2013). Acculturation of personality: A three-culture study of Japanese, Japanese Americans, and European Americans. *Journal of Cross-Cultural Psychology, 44*(5), 701–718.

Guo, Yu. (2019). Sexual double standards in white and Asian Americans: Ethnicity, gender, and acculturation. *Sexuality & Culture, 23,* 57–95.

Guo, Yuming; Gasparrini, Antonio; Armstrong, Ben G.; Tawatsupa, Benjawan; Tobias, Aurelio; Lavigne, Eric; . . . Tong, Shilu. (2017). Heat wave and mortality: A multicountry, multicommunity study. *Environmental Health Perspectives 125*(8).

Gustavson, Daniel E.; Miyake, Akira; Hewitt, John K. & Friedman, Naomi P. (2015). Understanding the cognitive and genetic underpinnings of procrastination: Evidence for shared genetic influences with goal management and executive function abilities. *Journal of Experimental Psychology, 144*(6), 1063–1079.

Guttman, David. (1987). *Reclaimed powers: Towards a new psychology of men and women in later life.* Basic Books.

Guy, Alexa; Lee, Kirsty & Wolke, Dieter. (2019). Comparisons between adolescent bullies, victims, and bully-victims on perceived popularity, social impact, and social preference. *Frontiers in Psychiatry, 10*(868).

Guyer, Amanda E.; Silk, Jennifer S. & Nelson, Eric E. (2016). The neurobiology of the emotional adolescent: From the inside out. *Neuroscience & Biobehavioral Reviews, 70,* 74–85.

Guzzo, Karen Benjamin & Hayford, Sarah R. (2020). Pathways to parenthood in social and family contexts: Decade in review, 2020. *82*(1), 117–144.

Haar, Jarrod M.; Sune, Albert; Russo, Marcello & Ollier-Malaterre, Ariane. (2019). A cross-national study on the antecedents of work–life balance from the fit and balance perspective. *Social Indicators Research, 142*(1), 261–282.

Habibi, Assal; Damasio, Antonio; Ilari, Beatriz; Sachs, Matthew Elliott & Damasio, Hanna. (2018). Music training and child development: A review of recent findings from a longitudinal study. *Annals of the New York Academy of Sciences, 1423*(1), 73–81.

Haden, Catherine A. (2010). Talking about science in museums. *Child Development Perspectives, 4*(1), 62–67.

Hahn, Gerald; Skeide, Michael A.; Mantini, Dante; Ganzetti, Marco; Destexhe, Alain; Friederici, Angela D. & Deco, Gustavo. (2019). A new computational approach to estimate whole-brain effective connectivity from functional and structural MRI, applied to language development. *Scientific Reports, 9*(1), 8479.

Haidt, Jonathan. (2013). *The righteous mind: Why good people are divided by politics and religion.* Vintage Books.

Haidt, Jonathan; Rozin, Paul; Mccauley, Clark & Imada, Sumio. (1997). Body, psyche, and culture: The relationship between disgust and morality. *Psychology and Developing Societies, 9*(1), 107–131.

Hales, Craig M.; Carroll, Margaret D.; Fryar, Cheryl D. & Ogden, Cynthia L. (2017, October). *Prevalence of obesity among adults and youth: United States, 2015–2016.* Atlanta, GA: Centers for Disease Control and Prevention, National Center for Health Statistics.

Halim, May Ling; Ruble, Diane N.; Tamis-LeMonda, Catherine S.; Zosuls, Kristina M.; Lurye, Leah E. & Greulich, Faith K. (2014). Pink frilly dresses and the avoidance of all things "girly": Children's appearance rigidity and cognitive theories of gender development. *Developmental Psychology, 50*(4), 1091–1101.

Halim, May Ling D. (2016). Princesses and superheroes: Social-cognitive influences on early gender rigidity. *Child Development Perspectives, 10*(3), 155–160.

Hall, G. Stanley. (1904). *Adolescence: Its psychology and its relations to physiology, anthropology, sociology, sex, crime, religion and education.* Appleton.

Hall, Matthew L.; Eigsti, Inge-Marie; Bortfeld, Heather & Lillo-Martin, Diane. (2017). Auditory deprivation does not impair executive function, but language deprivation might: Evidence from a parent-report measure in deaf native signing children. *Journal of Deaf Studies and Deaf Education, 22*(1), 9–21.

Halperin, Jeffrey M. & Healey, Dione M. (2011). The influences of environmental enrichment, cognitive enhancement, and physical exercise on brain development: Can we alter the developmental trajectory of ADHD? *Neuroscience & Biobehavioral Reviews, 35*(3), 621–634.

Hamdy, Sherine. (2018). All eyes on Egypt: Islam and the medical use of dead bodies amidst Cairo's political unrest. In Robben, Antonius C. G. M. (Ed.), *Death, mourning, and burial: A cross-cultural reader* (pp. 102–114). Wiley-Blackwell.

Hamerton, John L. & Evans, Jane A. (2005). Sex chromosome anomalies. In Butler, Merlin G. & Meaney, F. John (Eds.), *Genetics of developmental disabilities* (pp. 585–650). Taylor & Francis.

Hamilton, Alice. (1914). Lead poisoning in the United States. *American Journal of Public Health, 4*(6), 477–480.

Hamilton, Brady E.; Martin, Joyce A.; Osterman, Michelle J. K.; Curtin, Sally C. & Mathews, T. J. (2015, December 23). *Births: Final data for 2014. National Vital Statistics Reports, 64*(12). Hyattsville, MD: National Center for Health Statistics.

Hamilton, Brady E.; Martin, Joyce A.; Osterman, Michelle J. K. & Rossen, Lauren M. (2019, May). *Births: Provisional data for 2018. Vital Statistics Rapid Release Report,* (007). Hyattsville, MD: National Center for Health Statistics.

Hamilton, Peter J. & Nestler, Eric J. (2019). Epigenetics and addiction. *Current Opinion in Neurobiology, 59,* 128–136.

Hamlat, Elissa J.; Snyder, Hannah R.; Young, Jami F. & Hankin, Benjamin L. (2019). Pubertal timing as a transdiagnostic risk for psychopathology in youth. *Clinical Psychological Science, 7*(3), 411–429.

Hamlin, J. Kiley. (2013). Moral judgment and action in preverbal infants and toddlers: Evidence for an innate moral core. *Current Directions in Psychological Science, 22*(3), 186–193.

Hamlin, J. Kiley; Wynn, Karen & Bloom, Paul. (2007). Social evaluation by preverbal infants. *Nature, 450,* 557–559.

Hammond, Christopher J.; Andrew, Toby; Mak, Ying Tat & Spector, Tim D. (2004). A susceptibility locus for myopia in the normal population is linked to the PAX6 gene region on chromosome 11: A genomewide scan of dizygotic twins. *American Journal of Human Genetics, 75*(2), 294–304.

Hammond, Stuart I. & Drummond, Jesse K. (2019). Rethinking emotions in the context of infants' prosocial behavior: The role of interest and positive emotions. *Developmental Psychology, 55*(9), 1882–1888.

Han, Hyemin; Dawson, Kelsie J.; Thoma, Stephen J. & Glenn, Andrea L. (2019). Developmental level of moral judgment influences behavioral patterns during moral decision-making. *The Journal of Experimental Education,* (In Press).

Hankin, Benjamin L. (2020). Screening for and personalizing prevention of adolescent depression. *Current Directions in Psychological Science*, 29(4), 327–332.

Hanna-Attisha, Mona; LaChance, Jenny; Sadler, Richard Casey & Schnepp, Allison Champney. (2016). Elevated blood lead levels in children associated with the Flint drinking water crisis: A spatial analysis of risk and public health response. *American Journal of Public Health*, 106(2), 283–290.

Hannon, Erin E.; Schachner, Adena & Nave-Blodgett, Jessica E. (2017). Babies know bad dancing when they see it: Older but not younger infants discriminate between synchronous and asynchronous audiovisual musical displays. *Journal of Experimental Child Psychology*, 159, 159–174.

Hanushek, Eric A. & Woessmann, Ludger. (2015). *The knowledge capital of nations: Education and the economics of growth*. MIT Press.

Harari, Yuval Noah. (2015). *Sapiens: A brief history of humankind*. HarperCollins.

Hardy, Ben. (2019). Steroid hormones in social science research. In Foster, Gigi (Ed.), *Biophysical measurement in experimental social science research: Theory and practice* (pp. 105–148). Academic Press.

Hardy, Sam A.; Dollahite, David C. & Baldwin, Chayce R. (2019). Parenting, religion, and moral development. In Laible, Deborah J.; Carlo, Gustavo & Padilla-Walker, Laura M. (Eds.), *The Oxford handbook of parenting and moral development*. Oxford University Press.

Harlow, Harry. (1986). *From learning to love: The selected papers of H. F. Harlow* (Harlow, Clara Mears Ed.). Praeger.

Harris, Cheryl M. (2019). Quitting science: Factors that influence exit from the stem workforce. *Journal of Women and Minorities in Science and Engineering*, 25(2), 93–118.

Harris Insights and Analytics. (2020, June). *Teen mental health*. New York, NY: Harris Interactive.

Harris, Michelle A. & Orth, Ulrich. (2019). The link between self-esteem and social relationships: A meta-analysis of longitudinal studies. *Journal of Personality and Social Psychology*, (In Press).

Harris, Paul L. (2018). Children's understanding of death: From biology to religion. *Philosophical Transactions of the Royal Society B: Biological Sciences*, 373(1754).

Harrison, Linda J.; Elwick, Sheena; Vallotton, Claire D. & Kappler, Gregor. (2014). Spending time with others: A time-use diary for infant-toddler child care. In Harrison, Linda J. & Sumsion, Jennifer (Eds.), *Lived spaces of infant-toddler education and care: Exploring diverse perspectives on theory, research and practice* (pp. 59–74). Springer.

Hart, Betty & Risley, Todd R. (1995). *Meaningful differences in the everyday experience of young American children*. P. H. Brookes.

Hart, Sybil L. (2015). *Jealousy in infants: Laboratory research on differential treatment*. Springer.

Hart, Sybil L. (2018). Jealousy and attachment: Adaptations to threat posed by the birth of a sibling. *Evolutionary Behavioral Sciences*, 12(4), 263–275.

Harter, Susan. (2012). *The construction of the self: Developmental and sociocultural foundations* (2nd ed.). Guilford Press.

Hartley, Catherine A. & Somerville, Leah H. (2015). The neuroscience of adolescent decision-making. *Current Opinion in Behavioral Sciences*, 5, 108–115.

Hartshorne, Joshua K. & Germine, Laura T. (2015). When does cognitive functioning peak? The asynchronous rise and fall of different cognitive abilities across the life span. *Psychological Science*, 26(4), 433–443.

Harvey, Elizabeth A.; Breaux, Rosanna P. & Lugo-Candelas, Claudia I. (2016). Early development of comorbidity between symptoms of attention-deficit/hyperactivity disorder (ADHD) and oppositional defiant disorder (ODD). *Journal of Abnormal Psychology*, 125(2), 154–167.

Haslam, Catherine; Haslam, S. Alexander; Jetten, Jolanda; Cruwys, Tegan & Steffens, Niklas K. (2021). Life change, social identity, and health. *Annual Review of Psychology*, 72.

Haslip, Michael J. & Gullo, Dominic F. (2018). The changing landscape of early childhood education: Implications for policy and practice. *Early Childhood Education Journal*, 46, 249–264.

Hassen, Hamid Yimam; Ali, Jemal Haider; Gebreyesus, Seifu Hagos; Endris, Bilal Shikur & Temesgen, Awoke Misganaw. (2020). National incidence, prevalence and disability-adjusted life years (DALYs) of common micronutrient deficiencies in Ethiopia from 1990 to 2017: Estimates from the global burden of diseases study. *Global Health Action*, 13(1), 1776507.

Hasson, Ramzi & Fine, Jodene Goldenring. (2012). Gender differences among children with ADHD on continuous performance tests: A meta-analytic review. *Journal of Attention Disorders*, 16(3), 190–198.

Hatchel, Tyler; Polanin, Joshua R. & Espelage, Dorothy L. (2019). Suicidal thoughts and behaviors among LGBTQ youth: Meta-Analyses and a systematic review. *Archives of Suicide Research*, (In Press).

Hatfield, Elaine; Bensman, Lisamarie & Rapson, Richard L. (2012). A brief history of social scientists' attempts to measure passionate love. *Journal of Social and Personal Relationships*, 29(2), 143–164.

Hatta, Takeshi; Iwahara, Akihiko; Hatta, Taketoshi; Ito, Emi; Hatta, Junko; Hotta, Chie; . . . Hamajima, Nobuyuki. (2015). Developmental trajectories of verbal and visuospatial abilities in healthy older adults: Comparison of the hemisphere asymmetry reduction in older adults model and the right hemi-ageing model. *Laterality: Asymmetries of Body, Brain and Cognition*, 20(1), 69–81.

Hausfater, Glenn & Hrdy, Sarah Blaffer. (2017). *Infanticide: Comparative and evolutionary perspectives*. Routledge.

Hay, Dale F. (2017). The early development of human aggression. *Child Development Perspectives*, 11(2), 102–106.

Hay, Dale F.; Nash, Alison; Caplan, Marlene; Swartzentruber, Jan; Ishikawa, Fumiko & Vespo, Jo Ellen. (2011). The emergence of gender differences in physical aggression in the context of conflict between young peers. *British Journal of Developmental Psychology*, 29(2), 158–175.

Hay, Jessica F.; Cannistraci, Ryan A. & Zhao, Qian. (2019). Mapping non-native pitch contours to meaning: Perceptual and experiential factors. *Journal of Memory and Language*, 105, 131–140.

Hay, Jessica F.; Estes, Katharine Graf; Wang, Tianlin & Saffran, Jenny R. (2015). From flexibility to constraint: The contrastive use of lexical tone in early word learning. *Child Development*, 86(1), 10–22.

Hayday, Matthew. (2015). *So they want us to learn French: Promoting and opposing bilingualism in English-speaking Canada*. University of British Columbia Press.

Hayes, M.; Baxter, H.; Müller-Nordhorn, J.; Hohls, J. K. & Muckelbauer, R. (2017). The longitudinal association between weight change and health-related quality of life in adults and children: A systematic review. *Obesity Treatment*, 18(12), 1398–1411.

Hayiou-Thomas, Marianna E.; Carroll, Julia M.; Leavett, Ruth; Hulme, Charles & Snowling, Margaret J. (2017). When does speech sound disorder matter for literacy? The role of disordered speech errors, co-occurring language impairment and family risk of dyslexia. *Journal of Child Psychology and Psychiatry*, 58(2), 197–205.

Hayman, Karen J.; Kerse, Ngaire & Consedine, Nathan S. (2017). Resilience in context: The special case of advanced age. *Aging & Mental Health*, 21(6), 577–585.

Hayne, Harlene & Simcock, Gabrielle. (2009). Memory development in toddlers. In Courage, Mary L. & Cowan, Nelson (Eds.), *The development of memory in infancy and childhood* (2nd ed., pp. 43–68). Psychology Press.

Hazan, Cindy & Shaver, Philip. (1987). Romantic love conceptualized as an attachment process. *Journal of Personality and Social Psychology*, 52(3), 511–524.

Heckman, James J.; Humphries, John Eric; LaFontaine, Paul A. & Rodríguez, Pedro L. (2012). Taking the easy way out: How the GED testing program induces students to drop out. *Journal of Labor Economics*, 30(3), 495–520.

Hedegaard, Holly; Miniño, Arialdi M. & Warner, Margaret. (2020). *Drug overdose deaths in the United States, 1999–2018*. Hyattsville, MD: National Center for Health Statistics. NCHS data brief, No. 356.

Hedman, Anna M.; van Haren, Neeltje E. M.; Schnack, Hugo G.; Kahn, René S. & Hulshoff Pol, Hilleke E. (2012). Human brain changes across the life span: A review of 56 longitudinal magnetic resonance imaging studies. *Human Brain Mapping*, 33(8), 1987–2002.

Henry, Julie D.; Phillips, Louise H.; Ruffman, Ted & Bailey, Phoebe E. (2013). A meta-analytic review of age differences in theory of mind. *Psychology and Aging*, 28(3), 826–839.

Henry, Mélanie & Baudry, Stéphane. (2019). Age-related changes in leg proprioception: Implications for postural control. *Journal of Neurophysiology*, 122(2), 525–538.

Hentges, Rochelle F.; Davies, Patrick T. & Cicchetti, Dante. (2015). Temperament and interparental conflict: The role of negative emotionality in predicting child behavioral problems. *Child Development*, 86(5), 1333–1350.

Herholz, Sibylle C. & Zatorre, Robert J. (2012). Musical training as a framework for brain plasticity: Behavior, function, and structure. *Neuron*, 76(3), 486–502.

Herman-Giddens, Marcia E.; Steffes, Jennifer; Harris, Donna; Slora, Eric; Hussey, Michael; Dowshen, Steven A.; . . . Reiter, Edward O. (2012). Secondary sexual characteristics in boys: Data from the pediatric research in office settings network. *Pediatrics*, 130(5), e1058–e1068.

Herrmann, Julia; Schmidt, Isabelle; Kessels, Ursula & Preckel, Franzis. (2016). Big fish in big ponds: Contrast and assimilation effects on math and verbal self-concepts of students in within-school gifted tracks. *British Journal of Educational Psychology*, 86(2), 222–240.

Herting, Megan M.; Azad, Anisa; Kim, Robert; Tyszka, J Michael; Geffner, Mitchell E. & Kim, Mimi S. (2020). Brain differences in the prefrontal cortex, amygdala, and hippocampus in youth with congenital adrenal hyperplasia. *The Journal of Clinical Endocrinology & Metabolism*, 105(4), 1098–1111.

Herting, Megan M. & Sowell, Elizabeth R. (2017). Puberty and structural brain development in humans. *Frontiers in Neuroendocrinology*, 44, 122–137.

Hess, Thomas M.; Growney, Claire M. & Lothary, Allura F. (2019). Motivation moderates the impact of aging stereotypes on effort expenditure. *Psychology and Aging*, 34(1), 56–67.

Hewer, Mariko. (2014). Selling sweet nothings: Science shows food marketing's effects on children's minds—and appetites. *Observer*, 27(10).

Hicks, Joshua A.; Trent, Jason; Davis, William E. & King, Laura A. (2012). Positive affect, meaning in life, and future time perspective: An application of socioemotional selectivity theory. *Psychology and Aging*, 27(1), 181–189.

Hidalgo, Marco A. & Chen, Diane. (2019). Experiences of gender minority stress in cisgender parents of transgender/gender-expansive prepubertal children: A qualitative study. *Journal of Family Issues*, 40(7), 865–886.

Hider, Jessica L.; Gittelman, Rachel M.; Shah, Tapan; Edwards, Melissa; Rosenbloom, Arnold; Akey, Joshua M. & Parra, Esteban J. (2013). Exploring signatures of positive selection in pigmentation candidate genes in populations of East Asian ancestry. *BMC Evolutionary Biology*, 13, 150.

Hilawe, Esayas Haregot; Yatsuya, Hiroshi; Kawaguchi, Leo & Aoyama, Atsuko. (2013). Differences by sex in the prevalence of diabetes mellitus, impaired fasting glycaemia and impaired glucose tolerance in sub-Saharan Africa: A systematic review and meta-analysis. *Bulletin of the World Health Organization*, 91, 671–682.

Hilker, Rikke; Helenius, Dorte; Fagerlund, Birgitte; Skythe, Axel; Christensen, Kaare; Werge, Thomas M.; . . . Glenthøj, Birte. (2018). Heritability of schizophrenia and schizophrenia spectrum based on the nationwide danish twin register. 83(6), 492–498.

Hill, Erica & Hageman, Jon B. (Eds.). (2016). *The archaeology of ancestors: Death, memory, and veneration*. University Press of Florida.

Hillman, Charles H. (2014). An introduction to the relation of physical activity to cognitive and brain health, and scholastic achievement. *Monographs of the Society for Research in Child Development*, 79(4), 1–6.

Hillock-Dunn, Andrea & Wallace, Mark T. (2012). Developmental changes in the multisensory temporal binding window persist into adolescence. *Developmental Science*, 15(5), 688–696.

Hines, Melissa. (2020). Neuroscience and sex/gender: Looking back and forward. *Journal of Neuroscience*, 40(1), 37–43.

Hirth, Jacqueline. (2019). Disparities in HPV vaccination rates and HPV prevalence in the United States: A review of the literature. *Human Vaccines & Immunotherapeutics*, 15(1), 146–155.

Hitti, Aline; Mulvey, Kelly Lynn & Killen, Melanie. (2017). Minority and majority children's evaluations of social exclusion in intergroup contexts. In Cabrera, Natasha J. & Leyendecker, Birgit (Eds.), *Handbook on positive development of minority children and youth* (pp. 281–293). Springer.

Ho, Christine. (2015). Grandchild care, intergenerational transfers, and grandparents' labor supply. *Review of Economics of the Household*, 13(2), 359–384.

Hoare, Carol Hren. (2002). *Erikson on development in adulthood: New insights from the unpublished papers*. Oxford University Press.

Hobbes, Thomas. (2010). *Leviathan: Or, the matter, forme, and power of a common-wealth ecclesiasticall and civill* (Shapiro, Ian Ed.). Yale University Press.

Hochwälder, Jacek. (2012). The contribution of the Big Five personality factors to sense of coherence. *Personality and Individual Differences*, 53(5), 591–596.

Hoffman, Jessica L.; Teale, William H. & Paciga, Kathleen A. (2014). Assessing vocabulary learning in early childhood. *Journal of Early Childhood Literacy*, 14(4), 459–481.

Hogan, Andrew J. (2019). Moving away from the "medical model": The development and revision of the World Health Organization's classification of disability. *Bulletin of the History of Medicine*, 93(2), 241–269.

Hogan, Jillian; Cordes, Sara; Holochwost, Steven; Ryua, Ehri; Diamond, Adele & Winner, Ellen. (2018). Is more time in general music class associated with stronger extra-musical outcomes in kindergarten? *Early Childhood Research Quarterly*, 45, 238–248.

Hogan, Robert & Sherman, Ryne A. (2020). Personality theory and the nature of human nature. *Personality and Individual Differences*, 152(109561).

Höhle, Barbara; Bijeljac-Babic, Ranka & Nazzi, Thierry. (2020). Variability and stability in early language acquisition: Comparing monolingual and bilingual infants' speech perception and word recognition. *Bilingualism: Language and Cognition*, 23(1), 56–71.

Holden, Brien A.; Fricke, Timothy R.; Wilson, David A.; Jong, Monica; Naidoo, Kovin S.; Sankaridurg, Padmaja; . . . Resnikoff, Serge. (2016). Global prevalence of myopia and high myopia and temporal trends from 2000 through 2050. *Ophthalmology*, 123(5), 1036–1042.

Holden, Constance. (2010). Myopia out of control. *Science*, 327(5961), 17.

Holleley, Clare E.; O'Meally, Denis; Sarre, Stephen D.; Graves, Jennifer A. Marshall; Ezaz, Tariq; Matsubara, Kazumi; . . . Georges, Arthur. (2015). Sex reversal triggers the rapid transition from genetic to temperature-dependent sex. *Nature*, 523, 79–82.

Holmboe, K.; Nemoda, Z.; Fearon, R. M. P.; Sasvari-Szekely, M. & Johnson, M. H. (2011). Dopamine D4 receptor and serotonin transporter gene effects on the longitudinal development of infant temperament. *Genes, Brain and Behavior*, 10(5), 513–522.

Holt-Lunstad, Julianne. (2017). The potential public health relevance of social isolation and loneliness: Prevalence, epidemiology, and risk factors. *Public Policy Aging Report*, 27(4), 127–130.

Holzer, Jessica; Canavan, Maureen & Bradley, Elizabeth. (2014). County-level correlation between adult obesity rates and prevalence of dentists. *JADA*, 145(9), 932–939.

Homan, Patricia. (2019). Structural sexism and health in the united states: A new perspective on health inequality and the gender system. *American Sociological Review*, 84(3), 486–516.

Honda, Katsuya. (2015). DNA analysis overturns the death sentence of a condemned criminal held in custody for 48 years. *Forensic Science International: Genetics*, 16, e5–e6.

Hong, David S. & Reiss, Allan L. (2014). Cognitive and neurological aspects of sex chromosome aneuploidies. *The Lancet Neurology*, 13(3), 306–318.

Hoogendijk, Emiel O.; van der Noordt, Maaike; Onwuteaka-Philipsen, Bregje D.; Deeg, Dorly J. H.; Huisman, Martijn; Enroth, Linda & Jylhä, Marja. (2019). Sex differences in healthy life expectancy among nonagenarians: A multistate survival model using data from the Vitality 90+ study. *Experimental Gerontology*, 116, 80–85.

Hope, Elan C.; Hoggard, Lori S. & Thomas, Alvin. (2015). Emerging into adulthood in the face of racial discrimination: Physiological, psychological, and sociopolitical consequences for African American youth. *Translational Issues in Psychological Science*, 1(4), 342–351.

Hopkins-Doyle, Aife; Sutton, Robbie M.; Douglas, Karen M. & Calogero, Rachel M. (2019). Flattering to deceive: Why people misunderstand benevolent sexism. *Journal of Personality and Social Psychology*, 116(2), 167–192.

Horien, Corey; Greene, Abigail S.; Constable, R. Todd & Scheinost, Dustin. (2019). Regions and connections: Complementary approaches to characterize brain organization and function. *Neuroscientist*, (In Press).

Horney, Karen. (1967). *Feminine psychology*. Norton.

Horvath, Steve; Garagnani, Paolo; Bacalini, Maria Giulia; Pirazzini, Chiara; Salvioli, Stefano; Gentilini, Davide; . . . Franceschi, Claudio. (2015). Accelerated epigenetic aging in Down syndrome. *Aging Cell*, *14*(3), 491–495.

Howard, Elizabeth R.; Páez, Mariela M.; August, Diane L.; Barr, Christopher D.; Kenyon, Dorry & Malabonga, Valerie. (2014). The importance of SES, home and school language and literacy practices, and oral vocabulary in bilingual children's English reading development. *Bilingual Research Journal*, *37*(2), 120–141.

Howell, Diane M.; Wysocki, Karen & Steiner, Michael J. (2010). Toilet training. *Pediatrics In Review*, *31*(6), 262–263.

Howson, Carol-Ann & McKay, Elizabeth A. (2020). Caregiving and quality of life. *The History of the Family*, *25*(2), 306–321.

Hoy, Damian; Bain, Christopher; Williams, Gail; March, Lyn; Brooks, Peter; Blyth, Fiona; . . . Buchbinder, Rachelle. (2012). A systematic review of the global prevalence of low back pain. *Arthritis & Rheumatism*, *64*(6), 2028–2037.

Hrdy, Sarah B. (2009). *Mothers and others: The evolutionary origins of mutual understanding*. Harvard University Press.

Hsiao, Elaine Y. & Patterson, Paul H. (2012). Placental regulation of maternal-fetal interactions and brain development. *Developmental Neurobiology*, *72*(10), 1317–1326.

Hu, Bi Ying; Wu, Huiping; Winsler, Adam; Fan, Xitao & Song, Zhanmei. (2020). Parent migration and rural preschool children's early academic and social skill trajectories in China: Are 'left-behind' children really left behind? *Early Childhood Research Quarterly*, *51*, 317–328.

Hu, Yousong; Wang, Yifang & Liu, Aizhen. (2017). The influence of mothers' emotional expressivity and class grouping on Chinese preschoolers' emotional regulation strategies. *Journal of Child and Family Studies*, *26*(3), 824–832.

Hua, Julietta & Ray, Kasturi. (2018). Beyond the precariat: Race, gender, and labor in the taxi and Uber economy. *Social Identities*, *24*(2), 271–289.

Huang, Z. Josh & Luo, Liqun. (2015). It takes the world to understand the brain. *Science*, *350*(6256), 42–44.

Huart, Caroline; Rombaux, P. & Hummel, Thomas. (2019). Neural plasticity in developing and adult olfactory pathways—focus on the human olfactory bulb. *Journal of Bioenergetics and Biomembranes*, *51*(1), 77–87.

Hubel, David H. & Wiesel, Torsten N. (2004). *Brain and visual perception: The story of a 25-year collaboration*. Oxford University Press.

Huber, Dominik. (2019). A life course perspective to understanding senior tourism patterns and preferences. *The International Journal of Tourism Research*, *21*(3), 372–387.

Hudomiet, Peter; Parker, Andrew M. & Rohwedder, Susann. (2018). *Many Americans follow nontraditional paths to retirement: Cognitive ability and personality traits influence this process*. RAND Corporation.

Hudson, Valerie M. & Hodgson, Kaylee B. (2020). Sex and terror: Is the subordination of women associated with the use of terror? *Terrorism and Political Violence*, (In Press).

Huettig, Falk; Lachmann, Thomas; Reis, Alexandra & Petersson, Karl Magnus. (2018). Distinguishing cause from effect—many deficits associated with developmental dyslexia may be a consequence of reduced and suboptimal reading experience. *Language, Cognition and Neuroscience*, *33*(3), 333–350.

Hughes, Claire & Devine, Rory T. (2015). Individual differences in theory of mind: A social perspective. In Lerner, Richard M. (Ed.), *Handbook of child psychology and developmental science* (7th ed., Vol. 3). Wiley.

Hughes, Julie M. & Bigler, Rebecca S. (2011). Predictors of African American and European American adolescents' endorsement of race-conscious social policies. *Developmental Psychology*, *47*(2), 479–492.

Hughes, Karen; Bellis, Mark A.; Hardcastle, Katherine A.; Sethi, Dinesh; Butchart, Alexander; Mikton, Christopher; . . . Dunne, Michael P. (2017). The effect of multiple adverse childhood experiences on health: A systematic review and meta-analysis. *The Lancet Public Health*, *2*(8), e356–e366.

Hughes, Katherine C. & Shin, Lisa M. (2011). Functional neuroimaging studies of post-traumatic stress disorder. *Expert Review of Neurotherapeutics*, *11*(2), 275–285.

Hughes, Matthew L.; Geraci, Lisa & De Forrest, Ross L. (2013). Aging 5 years in 5 minutes: The effect of taking a memory test on older adults' subjective age. *Psychological Science*, *24*(12), 2481–2488.

Huguley, James P.; Wang, Ming-Te; Vasquez, Ariana C. & Guo, Jiesi. (2019). Parental ethnic–racial socialization practices and the construction of children of color's ethnic–racial identity: A research synthesis and meta-analysis. *Psychological Bulletin*, *145*(5), 437–458.

Hulme, Charles & Snowling, Margaret J. (2016). Reading disorders and dyslexia. *Current Opinion in Pediatrics*, *28*(6), 731–735.

Hunt, Earl B. (2011a). *Human intelligence*. Cambridge University Press.

Hunt, Earl B. (2011b). Where are we? Where are we going? Reflections on the current and future state of research on intelligence. In Sternberg, Robert J. & Kaufman, Scott Barry (Eds.), *The Cambridge handbook of intelligence*. Cambridge University Press.

Hunt, Earl B. (2012). What makes nations intelligent? *Perspectives on Psychological Science*, *7*(3), 284–306.

Hunter, Abby. (2018). "There are more important things to worry about": Attitudes and behaviours towards leisure noise and use of hearing protection in young adults. *International Journal of Audiology*, *57*(6), 449–456.

Hussain, Timon; Chou, Carol; Zettner, Erika; Torre, Peter; Hans, Stefan; Gauer, Johannes; . . . Nguyen, Quyen T. (2018). Early indication of noise-induced hearing loss in young adult users of personal listening devices. *Annals of Otology, Rhinology & Laryngology*, *127*(10), 703–709.

Hussar, Bill; Zhang, Jijun; Hein, Sarah; Wang, Ke; Roberts, Ashley; Cui, Jiashan; . . . Dilig, Rita. (2020). *The Condition of Education 2020*. Washington, DC: National Center for Education Statistics. NCES 2020-144.

Hviid, Anders; Hansen, Jørgen Vinsløv; Frisch, Morten & Melbye, Mads. (2019). Measles, mumps, rubella vaccination and autism: A nationwide cohort study. *Annals of Internal Medicine*, *170*(8), 513–520.

Hyde, Janet S. (2016). Sex and cognition: Gender and cognitive functions. *Current Opinion in Neurobiology*, *38*, 53–56.

Hyde, Janet Shibley; Bigler, Rebecca S.; Joel, Daphna; Tate, Charlotte Chucky & van Anders, Sari M. (2019). The future of sex and gender in psychology: Five challenges to the gender binary. *American Psychologist*, *74*(2), 171–193.

Ibañez, Lindsey M. & Lopez, Steven H. (2018). "Coming back to who I am": Unemployment, identity, and social support. *Race, Identity and Work*, *32*, 7–33.

Ilg, Frances L. & Ames, Louise Bates. (1959). *The Gesell Institute's child behavior*. Dell.

Ilic, Dragan; Djulbegovic, Mia; Jung, Jae Hung; Hwang, Eu Chang; Zhou, Qi; Cleves, Anne; . . . Dahm, Philipp. (2018). Prostate cancer screening with prostate-specific antigen (PSA) test: A systematic review and meta-analysis. *BMJ*, *362*(k3519).

Inhelder, Bärbel & Piaget, Jean. (1958). *The growth of logical thinking from childhood to adolescence: An essay on the construction of formal operational structures*. Basic Books.

Inhelder, Bärbel & Piaget, Jean. (2013a). *The early growth of logic in the child: Classification and seriation*. Routledge.

Inhelder, Bärbel & Piaget, Jean. (2013b). *The growth of logical thinking from childhood to adolescence: An essay on the construction of formal operational structures*. Routledge.

Insel, Thomas R. (2014). Mental disorders in childhood: Shifting the focus from behavioral symptoms to neurodevelopmental trajectories. *JAMA*, *311*(17), 1727–1728.

Ishihara, Noriko & Cohen, Andrew D. (2014). *Teaching and learning pragmatics: Where language and culture meet*. Routledge.

Itani, Osamu; Jike, Maki; Watanabe, Norio & Kaneita, Yoshitaka. (2017). Short sleep duration and health outcomes: A systematic review, meta-analysis, and meta-regression. *Sleep Medicine*, *32*, 246–256.

Ivars, Katrin; Nelson, Nina; Theodorsson, Annette; Theodorsson, Elvar; Ström, Jakob O. & Mörelius, Evalotte. (2015). Development of salivary cortisol circadian rhythm and reference intervals in full-term infants. *PLoS ONE*, *10*(6), e0129502.

Iyengar, Shanto; Konitzer, Tobias & Tedin, Kent. (2018). The home as a political fortress: Family agreement in an era of polarization. *The Journal of Politics*, *80*(4), 1326–1338.

Izard, Carroll E. (1977). *Human emotions.* Springer.

Jaffe, Arthur C. (2011). Failure to thrive: Current clinical concepts. *Pediatrics in Review*, 32(3), 100–108.

Jakobsen, Gunn Signe; Småstuen, Milada Cvancarova; Sandbu, Rune; Nordstrand, Njord; Hofsø, Dag; Lindberg, Morten; . . . Hjelmesæth, Jøran. (2018). Association of bariatric surgery vs medical obesity treatment with long-term medical complications and obesity-related comorbidities. *JAMA*, 319(3), 291–301.

Jambon, Marc; Madigan, Sheri; Plamondon, André; Daniel, Ella & Jenkins, Jennifer M. (2019). The development of empathic concern in siblings: A reciprocal influence model. *Child Development*, 90(5), 1598–1613.

Jambon, Marc & Smetana, Judith G. (2014). Moral complexity in middle childhood: Children's evaluations of necessary harm. *Developmental Psychology*, 50(1), 22–33.

James, William. (1890). *The principles of psychology.* Holt.

James-Kangal, Neslihan; Weitbrecht, Eliza; Francis, Trenel & Whitton, Sarah. (2018). Hooking up and emerging adults' relationship attitudes and expectations. *Sexuality & Culture*, 22(3), 706–723.

Jamil, Faiza M.; Larsen, Ross A. & Hamre, Bridget K. (2018). Exploring longitudinal changes in teacher expectancy effects on children's mathematics achievement. *Journal for Research in Mathematics Education*, 49(1), 57–90.

Jankovic, Joseph. (2018). Parkinson's disease tremors and serotonin. *Brain*, 141(3), 624–626.

Jankowiak, William R.; Volsche, Shelly L. & Garcia, Justin R. (2015). Is the romantic–sexual kiss a near human universal? *American Anthropologist*, 117(3), 535–539.

Jarcho, Johanna M.; Fox, Nathan A.; Pine, Daniel S.; Etkin, Amit; Leibenluft, Ellen; Shechner, Tomer & Ernst, Monique. (2013). The neural correlates of emotion-based cognitive control in adults with early childhood behavioral inhibition. *Biological Psychology*, 92(2), 306–314.

Jaroslawska, Agnieszka J. & Rhodes, Stephen. (2019). Adult age differences in the effects of processing on storage in working memory: A meta-analysis. *Psychology and Aging*, 34(4), 512–530.

Jarrett, Christian. (2014). *Great myths of the brain.* Wiley Blackwell.

Jebb, Andrew T.; Tay, Louis; Diener, Ed & Oishi, Shigehiro. (2018). Happiness, income satiation and turning points around the world. *Nature Human Behaviour*, 2(1), 33–38.

Jeung, Russell M.; Fong, Seanan S. & Kim, Helen Jin. (2019). *Family sacrifices: The worldviews and ethics of Chinese Americans.* Oxford University Press.

Jewell, Tom; Gardner, Tessa; Susi, Karima; Watchorn, Kate; Coopey, Emily; Simic, Mima, . . . Eisler, Ivan. (2019). Attachment measures in middle childhood and adolescence: A systematic review of measurement properties. *Clinical Psychology Review*, 68, 71–82.

Jeynes, William H. (2012). A meta-analysis on the effects and contributions of public, public charter, and religious schools on student outcomes. *Peabody Journal of Education*, 87(3), 305–335.

Ji, Yong; Shi, Zhihong; Zhang, Ying; Liu, Shuling; Liu, Shuai; Yue, Wei; . . . Wisniewski, Thomas. (2015). Prevalence of dementia and main subtypes in rural northern China. *Dementia and Geriatric Cognitive Disorders*, 39(5/6), 294–302.

Jia, Jianping; Wang, Fen; Wei, Cuibai; Zhou, Aihong; Jia, Xiangfei; Li, Fang; . . . Dong, Xiumin. (2014). The prevalence of dementia in urban and rural areas of China. *Alzheimer's & Dementia*, 10(1), 1–9.

Jia, Peng; Xue, Hong; Zhang, Ji & Wang, Youfa. (2017). Time trend and demographic and geographic disparities in childhood obesity prevalence in China—Evidence from twenty years of longitudinal data. *International Journal of Environmental Research and Public Health*, 14(4).

Joel, Daphna; Berman, Zohar; Tavor, Ido; Wexler, Nadav; Gaber, Olga; Stein, Yaniv; . . . Assaf, Yaniv. (2015). Sex beyond the genitalia: The human brain mosaic. *Proceedings of the National Academy of Sciences*, 112(50), 15468–15473.

Johns, Michelle M.; Lowry, Richard; Haderxhanaj, Laura T.; Rasberry, Catherine N.; Robin, Leah; Scales, Lamont; . . . Suarez, Nicolas A. (2020, August 21). *Trends in violence victimization and suicide risk by sexual identity among high school students—youth risk behavior survey, United States, 2015–2019.* Morbidity and Mortality Weekly Report, 69(Suppl. 1), 19–27. Atlanta, GA: Centers for Disease Control and Prevention.

Johnson, Dylan; Dupuis, Gabrielle; Piche, Justin; Clayborne, Zahra & Colman, Ian. (2018). Adult mental health outcomes of adolescent depression: A systematic review. *Depression and Anxiety*, 35(8), 700–716.

Johnson, Katharine; Caskey, Melinda; Rand, Katherine; Tucker, Richard & Vohr, Betty. (2014). Gender differences in adult-infant communication in the first months of life. *Pediatrics*, 134(6), e1603–e1610.

Jones, Christopher M.; Merrick, Melissa T. & Houry, Debra E. (2020). Identifying and preventing adverse childhood experiences: Implications for clinical practice. *JAMA*, 323(1), 25–26.

Jong, Jonathan; Ross, Robert; Philip, Tristan; Chang, Si-Hua; Simons, Naomi & Halberstadt, Jamin. (2018). The religious correlates of death anxiety: A systematic review and meta-analysis. *Religion, Brain & Behavior*, 8(1), 4–20.

Jorgensen, Nathan & Nelson, Larry. (2018). Moving toward and away from others: Social orientations in emerging adulthood. *Journal of Applied Developmental Psychology*, 58, 66–76.

Josselyn, Sheena A. & Frankland, Paul W. (2012). Infantile amnesia: A neurogenic hypothesis. *Learning and Memory*, 19, 423–433.

Juma, Kenneth; Juma, Pamela A.; Mohamed, Shukri F.; Owuor, Jared; Wanyoike, Ann; Mulabi, David; . . . Yonga, Gerald. (2019). First Africa non-communicable disease research conference 2017: Sharing evidence and identifying research priorities. *Journal of Global Health*, 9(1).

Jun, Hee-Jin; Webb-Morgan, Megan; Felner, Jennifer K.; Wisdom, Jennifer P.; Haley, Sean J.; Austin, S. Bryn; . . . Corliss, Heather L. (2019). Sexual orientation and gender identity disparities in substance use disorders during young adulthood in a United States longitudinal cohort. *Drug and Alcohol Dependence*, 205(107619).

Jung, Courtney. (2015). *Lactivism: How feminists and fundamentalists, hippies and yuppies, and physicians and politicians made breastfeeding big business and bad policy.* Basic Books.

Jung, Kiju; Shavitt, Sharon; Viswanathan, Madhu & Hilbe, Joseph M. (2014). Female hurricanes are deadlier than male hurricanes. *Proceedings of the National Academy of Sciences*, 111(24), 8782–8787.

Jurek, Benjamin & Neumann, Inga D. (2018). The oxytocin receptor: From intracellular signaling to behavior. *Physiological Reviews*, 98(3), 1805–1908.

Kagan, Sarah H. (2018). When respect for our elders is ageism. *Geriatric Nursing*, 39(5), 604–606.

Kahana, Eva; Bhatta, Tirth; Lovegreen, Loren D.; Kahana, Boaz & Midlarsky, Elizabeth. (2013). Altruism, helping, and volunteering: Pathways to well-being in late life. *Journal of Aging and Health*, 25(1), 159–187.

Kalanithi, Paul. (2016). *When breath becomes air.* Random House.

Kalaria, Raj N. (2018). The pathology and pathophysiology of vascular dementia. *Neuropharmacology*, 134, 226–239.

Kaley, Fiona; Reid, Vincent & Flynn, Emma. (2012). Investigating the biographic, social and temperamental correlates of young infants' sleeping, crying and feeding routines. *Infant Behavior and Development*, 35(3), 596–605.

Kalshoven, Karianne & Taylor, Scott. (2018). Leadership: Philosophical perspectives and qualitative analysis of ethics—looking back, looking forward, looking around. *Journal of Business Ethics*, 148(1), 1–3.

Kamin, Stefan T. & Lang, Frieder R. (2020). Internet use and cognitive functioning in late adulthood: Longitudinal findings from the Survey of Health, Ageing and Retirement in Europe (SHARE). *The Journals of Gerontology: Series B*, 75(3), 534–539.

Kandler, Christian. (2012). Nature and nurture in personality development: The case of neuroticism and extraversion. *Current Directions in Psychological Science*, 21(5), 290–296.

Kane, Anne V.; Dinh, Duy M. & Ward, Honorine D. (2015). Childhood malnutrition and the intestinal microbiome. *Pediatric Research*, 77, 256–262.

Kaniuka, Andrea R.; Kelliher Rabon, Jessica; Brooks, Byron D.; Sirois, Fuschia; Kleiman, Evan & Hirsch, Jameson K. (2020). Gratitude and suicide risk among college students: Substantiating the protective benefits of being thankful. *Journal of American College Health*, (In Press).

Kanner, Leo. (1943). Autistic disturbances of affective contact. *Nervous Child, 2,* 217–250.

Kanter, Jessica R.; Boulet, Sheree L.; Kawwass, Jennifer F.; Jamieson, Denise J. & Kissin, Dmitry M. (2015). Trends and correlates of monozygotic twinning after single embryo transfer. *Obstetrics & Gynecology, 125*(1), 111–117.

Kaplan, N. & Main, M. (1986). *Instructions for the classification of children's family drawings in terms of representation of attachment* [Unpublished manuscript]. University of California.

Kapp, Steven K. (Ed.) (2020). *Autistic community and the neurodiversity movement: Stories from the frontline.* Springer Nature.

Kashyap, Ridhi. (2019). Is prenatal sex selection associated with lower female child mortality? *Population Studies, 73*(1), 57–78.

Kato, Takahiro A.; Kanba, Shigenobu & Teo, Alan R. (2019). *Hikikomori:* Multidimensional understanding, assessment and future international perspectives. *PCN, 73*(8), 427–440.

Kauffman, Jeffery. (2013). Culture, socialization, and traumatic death. In Meagher, David K. & Balk, David E. (Eds.), *Handbook of thanatology: The essential body of knowledge for the study of death, dying, and bereavement* (2nd ed.). Routledge.

Kavaliers, Martin; Ossenkopp, Klaus-Peter & Choleris, Elena. (2019). Social neuroscience of disgust. *18*(1), e12508.

Keating, Nancy L.; Herrinton, Lisa J.; Zaslavsky, Alan M.; Liu, Liyan & Ayanian, John Z. (2006). Variations in hospice use among cancer patients. *Journal of the National Cancer Institute, 98*(15), 1053–1059.

Keck, Carson & Taylor, Marian. (2018). Emerging research on the implications of hormone replacement therapy on coronary heart disease. *Current Atherosclerosis Reports, 20*(12).

Keebaugh, Alaine C.; Barrett, Catherine E.; Laprairie, Jamie L.; Jenkins, Jasmine J. & Young, Larry J. (2015). RNAi knockdown of oxytocin receptor in the nucleus accumbens inhibits social attachment and parental care in monogamous female prairie voles. *Social Neuroscience, 10*(5), 561–570.

Kelliher, Clare; Richardson, Julia & Boiarintseva, Galina. (2019). All of work? All of life? Reconceptualising work-life balance for the 21st century. *Human Resource Management Journal, 29*(2), 97–112.

Kelly, John R. (1993). *Activity and aging: Staying involved in later life.* Sage.

Kempe, Ruth S. & Kempe, C. Henry. (1978). *Child abuse.* Harvard University Press.

Kemper, Susan. (2015). Language production in late life. In Gerstenberg, Annette & Voeste, Anja (Eds.), *Language development: The lifespan perspective* (pp. 59–75). John Benjamins.

Kempermann, Gerd; Song, Hongjun & Gage, Fred H. (2015). Neurogenesis in the adult hippocampus. *Cold Spring Harbor Perspectives in Biology, 7,* a018812.

Kena, Grace; Musu-Gillette, Lauren; Robinson, Jennifer; Wang, Xiaolei; Rathbun, Amy; Zhang, Jijun; . . . Dunlop Velez, Erin. (2015). *The condition of education 2015.* Washington, DC: Department of Education, National Center for Education Statistics.

Kendall, Kimberley M.; Bracher-Smith, Matthew; Fitzpatrick, Harry; Lynham, Amy; Rees, Elliott; Escott-Price, Valentina; . . . Kirov, George. (2019). Cognitive performance and functional outcomes of carriers of pathogenic copy number variants: Analysis of the UK Biobank. *The British Journal of Psychiatry, 214*(5), 297–304.

Kenrick, Douglas T.; Griskevicius, Vladas; Neuberg, Steven L. & Schaller, Mark. (2010). Renovating the pyramid of needs: Contemporary extensions built upon ancient foundations. *Perspectives on Psychological Science, 5*(3), 292–314.

Kensinger, Elizabeth A. & Kark, Sarah M. (2018). Emotion and memory. In Wixted, John T. (Ed.), *Stevens' handbook of experimental psychology and cognitive neuroscience* (4th ed., Vol. 1). Wiley.

Kermoian, Rosanne & Leiderman, P. Herbert. (1986). Infant attachment to mother and child caretaker in an East African community. *International Journal of Behavioral Development, 9*(4), 455–469.

Kern, Ben D.; Graber, Kim C.; Shen, Sa; Hillman, Charles H. & McLoughlin, Gabriella. (2018). Association of school-based physical activity opportunities, socioeconomic status, and third-grade reading. *Journal of School Health, 88*(1), 34–43.

Kidd, Celeste; Palmeri, Holly & Aslin, Richard N. (2013). Rational snacking: Young children's decision-making on the marshmallow task is moderated by beliefs about environmental reliability. *Cognition, 126*(1), 109–114.

Kidd, David Comer & Castano, Emanuele. (2013). Reading literary fiction improves theory of mind. *Science, 342*(6156), 377–380.

Kiiski, Jouko; Määttä, Kaarina & Uusiautti, Satu. (2013). "For better and for worse, or until . . .": On divorce and guilt. *Journal of Divorce & Remarriage, 54*(7), 519–536.

Kim, Mijung; Yoon, Hye-Gyoung & Lee, Mee-Kyeong. (2018). Progress and challenges of elementary science education in Korea. In Lee, Yew-Jin & Tan, Jason (Eds.), *Primary science education in East Asia: A critical comparison of systems and strategies* (Vol. 47). Springer.

Kim, Pilyoung; Strathearn, Lane & Swain, James E. (2016). The maternal brain and its plasticity in humans. *Hormones and Behavior, 77,* 113–123.

Kim, Su-Mi & Kim, Jong-Soo. (2017). A review of mechanisms of implantation. *Development & Reproduction, 21*(4), 351–359.

Kim-Spoon, Jungmeen; Longo, Gregory S. & McCullough, Michael E. (2012). Parent-adolescent relationship quality as a moderator for the influences of parents' religiousness on adolescents' religiousness and adjustment. *Journal of Youth and Adolescence, 41*(12), 1576–1587.

Kindelberger, Cécile; Mallet, Pascal & Galharret, Jean-Michel. (2020). Diversity of romantic experiences in late adolescence and their contribution to identity formation. *Social Development, 29*(2), 615–634.

King, Bruce M. (2013). The modern obesity epidemic, ancestral hunter-gatherers, and the sensory/reward control of food intake. *American Psychologist, 68*(2), 88–96.

King, Lucy S.; Humphreys, Kathryn L. & Gotlib, Ian H. (2019). The neglect–enrichment continuum: Characterizing variation in early caregiving environments. *Developmental Review, 51,* 109–122.

Kinsey, Alfred C. (1948). *Sexual behavior in the human male.* W. B. Saunders.

Kinsey, Alfred C. (1953). *Sexual behavior in the human female.* W. B. Saunders.

Kirk, Elizabeth; Howlett, Neil; Pine, Karen J. & Fletcher, Ben. (2013). To sign or not to sign? The impact of encouraging infants to gesture on infant language and maternal mind-mindedness. *Child Development, 84*(2), 574–590.

Kirkham, Julie Ann & Kidd, Evan. (2017). The effect of Steiner, Montessori, and National Curriculum Education upon children's pretence and creativity. *Journal of Creative Behavior, 51*(1), 20–34.

Kitzman, Harriet; Olds, David L.; Knudtson, Michael D.; Cole, Robert; Anson, Elizabeth; Smith, Joyce A.; . . . Conti, Gabriella. (2019). Prenatal and infancy nurse home visiting and 18-year outcomes of a randomized trial. *Pediatrics, 144*(6), e20183876.

Klaczynski, Paul A. & Felmban, Wejdan S. (2014). Heuristics and biases during adolescence: Developmental reversals and individual differences. In Markovits, Henry (Ed.), *The developmental psychology of reasoning and decision-making* (pp. 84–111). Psychology Press.

Klass, Dennis & Steffen, Edith Maria (Eds.). (2017). *Continuing bonds in bereavement: New directions for research and practice.* Routledge.

Klaus, Marshall H. & Kennell, John H. (1976). *Maternal-infant bonding: The impact of early separation or loss on family development.* Mosby.

Klein, Stanley B. (2012). The two selves: The self of conscious experience and its brain. In Leary, Mark R. & Tangney, June Price (Eds.), *Handbook of self and identity* (pp. 617–637). Guilford Press.

Klein, Zoe A. & Romeo, Russell D. (2013). Changes in hypothalamic–pituitary–adrenal stress responsiveness before and after puberty in rats. *Hormones and Behavior, 64*(2), 357–363.

Klinger, Laura G.; Dawson, Geraldine; Burner, Karen & Crisler, Megan. (2014). Autism spectrum disorder. In Mash, Eric J. & Barkley, Russell A. (Eds.), *Child psychopathology* (3rd ed., pp. 531–572). Guilford Press.

Klinzing, Jens G. & Diekelmann, Susanne. (2019). Cued memory reactivation: A tool to manipulate memory consolidation during sleep. In Dringenberg, Hans C. (Ed.), *Handbook of sleep research* (Vol. 30, pp. 471–488). Elsevier.

Klonsky, E. David; May, Alexis M. & Glenn, Catherine R. (2013). The relationship between nonsuicidal self-injury and attempted suicide: Converging evidence from four samples. *Journal of Abnormal Psychology, 122*(1), 231–237.

Klump, Kelly L. (2013). Puberty as a critical risk period for eating disorders: A review of human and animal studies. *Hormones and Behavior, 64*(2), 399–410.

Knapp, Emily A.; Bilal, Usama; Dean, Lorraine T.; Lazo, Mariana & Celentano, David D. (2019). Economic insecurity and deaths of despair in US counties. *American Journal of Epidemiology, 188*(12), 2131–2139.

Knott, Craig S.; Coombs, Ngaire; Stamatakis, Emmanuel & Biddulph, Jane P. (2015). All cause mortality and the case for age specific alcohol consumption guidelines: Pooled analyses of up to 10 population based cohorts. *BMJ, 350*, h384.

Kochanek, Kenneth D.; Murphy, Sherry L.; Xu, Jiaquan & Arias, Elizabeth. (2019, June 24). *Deaths: Final data for 2017. National Vital Statistics Reports, 68*(9). Hyattsville, MD: National Center for Health Statistics.

Kochhar, Rakesh. (2020, January 30). *Women make gains in the workplace amid a rising demand for skilled workers: The gender wage gap narrows as women move into high-skill jobs and acquire more education. Social & Demographic Trends.* Washington, DC: Pew Research Center.

Kochhar, Rakesh & Cilluffo, Anthony. (2018, July 12). *Key findings on the rise in income inequality within America's racial and ethnic groups. Fact Tank.* Washington, DC: Pew Research Center.

Kohlberg, Lawrence. (1963). The development of children's orientations toward a moral order: I. Sequence in the development of moral thought. *Vita Humana, 6*(1/2), 11–33.

Kokštejn, Jakub; Musálek, Martin & Tufano, James J. (2017). Are sex differences in fundamental motor skills uniform throughout the entire preschool period? *PLoS ONE, 12*(4), e0176556.

Koller, Daniela & Bynum, Julie P. W. (2014). Dementia in the USA: State variation in prevalence. *Journal of Public Health, 37*(4), 597–604.

Koltko-Rivera, Mark E. (2006). Rediscovering the later version of Maslow's hierarchy of needs: Self-transcendence and opportunities for theory, research, and unification. *Review of General Psychology, 10*(4), 302–317.

Komisar, Erica. (2017). *Being there: Why prioritizing motherhood in the first three years matters.* TarcherPerigee.

Konner, Melvin. (2010). *The evolution of childhood: Relationships, emotion, mind.* Harvard University Press.

Koren, Chaya. (2016). Men's vulnerability—women's resilience: From widowhood to late-life repartnering. *International Psychogeriatrics, 28*(5), 719–731.

Kosminsky, Phyllis. (2017). Working with continuing bonds from an attachment theoretical perspective. In Klass, Dennis & Steffen, Edith Maria (Eds.), *Continuing bonds in bereavement: New directions for research and practice.* Routledge.

Kostandy, Raouth R. & Ludington-Hoe, Susan M. (2019). The evolution of the science of kangaroo (mother) care (skin-to-skin contact). *Birth Defects Research, 111*(15), 1032–1043.

Kotsopoulos, Joanne; Gronwald, Jacek; Karlan, Beth Y.; Huzarski, Tomasz; Tung, Nadine; Moller, Pal; . . . Narod, Steven A. (2018). Hormone replacement therapy after oophorectomy and breast cancer risk among BRCA1 mutation carriers. *JAMA Oncology, 4*(8), 1059–1065.

Kotsou, Ilios; Mikolajczak, Moïra; Heeren, Alexandre; Grégoire, Jacques & Leys, Christophe. (2019). Improving emotional intelligence: A systematic review of existing work and future challenges. *Emotion Review, 11*(2), 151–165.

Kotter-Grühn, Dana; Kornadt, Anna E. & Stephan, Yannick. (2016). Looking beyond chronological age: Current knowledge and future

directions in the study of subjective age. *Gerontology, 62*(1), 86–93.

Koutsimani, Panagiota; Montgomery, Anthony & Georganta, Katerina. (2019). The relationship between burnout, depression, and anxiety: A systematic review and meta-analysis. *Frontiers in Psychology, 10*(284).

Kozo, Justine; Sallis, James F.; Conway, Terry L.; Kerr, Jacqueline; Cain, Kelli; Saelens, Brian E.; . . . Owen, Neville. (2012). Sedentary behaviors of adults in relation to neighborhood walkability and income. *Health Psychology, 31*(6), 704–713.

Kral, Andrej; Dorman, Michael F. & Wilson, Blake S. (2019). Neuronal development of hearing and language: Cochlear implants and critical periods. *Annual Review of Neuroscience, 42*, 47–65.

Kral, Michael J. (2019). *The idea of suicide: Contagion, imitation, and cultural diffusion.* Routledge.

Krampe, Ralf T. & Charness, Neil. (2018). Aging and expertise. In Ericsson, K. Anders; Hoffman, Robert R.; Kozbelt, Aaron & Williams, A. Mark (Eds.), *The Cambridge handbook of expertise and expert performance* (pp. 835–856). Cambridge University Press.

Krasny-Pacini, Agata; Limond, Jennifer & Chevignard, Mathilde P. (2018). Executive function interventions. In Locascio, Gianna & Slomine, Beth S. (Eds.), *Cognitive rehabilitation for pediatric neurological disorders* (pp. 75–99). Cambridge University Press.

Kreager, Derek A.; Molloy, Lauren E.; Moody, James & Feinberg, Mark E. (2016a). Friends first? The peer network origins of adolescent dating. *Journal of Research on Adolescence, 26*(2), 257–269.

Kreager, Derek A.; Staff, Jeremy; Gauthier, Robin; Lefkowitz, Eva S. & Feinberg, Mark E. (2016b). The double standard at sexual debut: Gender, sexual behavior and adolescent peer acceptance. *Sex Roles, 75*, 377–392.

Kretch, Kari S. & Adolph, Karen E. (2013). No bridge too high: Infants decide whether to cross based on the probability of falling not the severity of the potential fall. *Developmental Science, 16*(3), 336–351.

Kroger, Jane & Marcia, James E. (2011). The identity statuses: Origins, meanings, and interpretations. In Schwartz, Seth J.; Luyckx, Koen & Vignoles, Vivian L. (Eds.), *Handbook of identity theory and research* (pp. 31–53). Springer.

Kroncke, Anna P.; Willard, Marcy & Huckabee, Helena. (2016). Optimal outcomes and recovery. In *Assessment of autism spectrum disorder: Critical issues in clinical, forensic and school settings* (pp. 23–33). Springer.

Kübler-Ross, Elisabeth. (1975). *Death: The final stage of growth.* Prentice-Hall.

Kübler-Ross, Elisabeth. (1997). *On death and dying.* Scribner.

Kübler-Ross, Elisabeth & Kessler, David. (2005). *On grief and grieving: Finding the meaning of grief through the five stages of loss.* Scribner.

Kuehner, Christine. (2017). Why is depression more common among women than among men? *The Lancet Psychiatry, 4*(2), 146–158.

Kuete, Victor (Ed.) (2017). *Medicinal spices and vegetables from Africa: Therapeutic potential against*

metabolic, inflammatory, infectious and systemic diseases. Academic Press.

Kuhn, Deanna. (2013). Reasoning. In Zelazo, Philip D. (Ed.), *The Oxford handbook of developmental psychology* (Vol. 1, pp. 744–764). Oxford University Press.

Kushlev, Kostadin; Drummond, Danielle M.; Heintzelman, Samantha J. & Diener, Ed. (2020). Do happy people care about society's problems? *The Journal of Positive Psychology, 15*(4), 467–477.

Kuvaas, Bård; Buch, Robert; Weibel, Antoinette; Dysvik, Anders & Nerstad, Christina G. L. (2017). Do intrinsic and extrinsic motivation relate differently to employee outcomes? *Journal of Economic Psychology, 61*, 244–258.

Laakasuo, Michael; Rotkirch, Anna; Berg, Venla & Jokela, Markus. (2017). The company you keep: Personality and friendship characteristics. *Social Psychological and Personality Science, 8*(1), 66–73.

Laats, Adam. (2015). Dissenters, not ignoramuses: A new approach to creationism in America's public schools. *Anthropology Now, 7*(1), 80–88.

Labouvie-Vief, Gisela. (2015). *Integrating emotions and cognition throughout the lifespan.* Springer.

Lacey, Heather; Kierstead, Todd & Morey, Diana. (2012). De-biasing the age-happiness bias: Memory search and cultural expectations in happiness judgments across the lifespan. *Journal of Happiness Studies, 13*(4), 647–658.

Lachmann, Thomas. (2018). Reading and dyslexia: The functional coordination framework. In Lachmann, Thomas & Weis, Tina (Eds.), *Reading and dyslexia: From basic functions to higher order cognition* (pp. 271–296). Springer.

Ladapo, Joseph A.; Kymes, Steven M.; Ladapo, Jonathan A.; Nwosu, Veronica C. & Pasquale, Louis R. (2012). Projected clinical outcomes of glaucoma screening in African American individuals. *Archives of Ophthalmology, 130*(3), 365–372.

Lagattuta, Kristin H. (2014). Linking past, present, and future: Children's ability to connect mental states and emotions across time. *Child Development Perspectives, 8*(2), 90–95.

Lalande, Kathleen M. & Bonanno, George A. (2006). Culture and continuing bonds: A prospective comparison of bereavement in the United States and the People's Republic of China. *Death Studies, 30*(4), 303–324.

Lam, Kelly Ka Lai & Zhou, Mingming. (2019). Examining the relationship between grit and academic achievement within K-12 and higher education: A systematic review. *Psychology in the Schools, 56*(10), 1654–1686.

Lamichhane, Bidhan; McDaniel, Mark; Waldum, Emily & Braver, Todd. (2018). Age-related changes in neural mechanisms of prospective memory. *Cognitive, Affective, & Behavioral Neuroscience, 18*(5), 982–999.

Lamm, Bettina; Keller, Heidi; Teiser, Johanna; Gudi, Helene; Yovsi, Relindis D.; Freitag, Claudia; . . . Lohaus, Arnold. (2018). Waiting for the second treat: Developing culture-specific modes of self-regulation. *Child Development, 89*(3), e261–e277.

Lan, Xiaoyu; Wang, Wenchao & Radin, Rendy. (2019). Depressive symptoms in emerging adults with early left-behind experiences in rural China. *Journal of Loss and Trauma, 24*(4), 339–355.

Lang, Samantha F. & Fowers, Blaine J. (2019). An expanded theory of Alzheimer's caregiving. *American Psychologist, 74*(2), 194–206.

Lange, Benjamin P.; Euler, Harald A. & Zaretsky, Eugen. (2016). Sex differences in language competence of 3- to 6-year-old children. *Applied Psycholinguistics, 37*(6), 1417–1438.

Langeslag, Sandra J. E.; Muris, Peter & Franken, Ingmar H. A. (2013). Measuring romantic love: Psychometric properties of the infatuation and attachment scales. *The Journal of Sex Research, 50*(8), 739–747.

Lansford, Jennifer E.; Sharma, Chinmayi; Malone, Patrick S.; Woodlief, Darren; Dodge, Kenneth A.; Oburu, Paul; . . . Di Giunta, Laura. (2014). Corporal punishment, maternal warmth, and child adjustment: A longitudinal study in eight countries. *Journal of Clinical Child & Adolescent Psychology, 43*(4), 670–685.

Lara-Cinisomo, Sandraluz; Fuligni, Allison Sidle & Karoly, Lynn A. (2011). Preparing preschoolers for kindergarten. In Laverick, DeAnna M. & Jalongo, Mary Renck (Eds.), *Transitions to early care and education* (Vol. 4, pp. 93–105). Springer.

Larose, Joanie; Boulay, Pierre; Sigal, Ronald J.; Wright, Heather E. & Kenny, Glen P. (2013). Age-related decrements in heat dissipation during physical activity occur as early as the age of 40. *PLoS ONE, 8*(12), e83148.

Larzelere, Robert E.; Cox, Ronald B. & Swindle, Taren M. (2015). Many replications do not causal inferences make: The need for critical replications to test competing explanations of nonrandomized studies. *Perspectives on Psychological Science, 10*(3), 380–389.

Lattanzi-Licht, Marcia. (2013). Religion, spirituality, and dying. In Meagher, David K. & Balk, David E. (Eds.), *Handbook of thanatology: The essential body of knowledge for the study of death, dying, and bereavement* (2nd ed., pp. 9–16). Routledge.

Lau, Su Re; Beilby, Janet M.; Byrnes, Michelle L. & Hennessey, Neville W. (2012). Parenting styles and attachment in school-aged children who stutter. *Journal of Communication Disorders, 45*(2), 98–110.

Lauer, Jillian E.; Udelson, Hallie B.; Jeon, Sung O. & Lourenco, Stella F. (2015). An early sex difference in the relation between mental rotation and object preference. *Frontiers in Psychology, 6*(558).

Laurent, Heidemarie K. (2014). Clarifying the contours of emotion regulation: Insights from parent–child stress research. *Child Development Perspectives, 8*(1), 30–35.

Laursen, Brett; Hartl, Amy C.; Vitaro, Frank; Brendgen, Mara; Dionne, Ginette & Boivin, Michel. (2017). The spread of substance use and delinquency between adolescent twins. *Developmental Psychology, 53*(2), 329–339.

Lautenbacher, Stefan; Peters, Jan H.; Heesen, Michael; Scheel, Jennifer & Kunz, **Miriam.** (2017). Age changes in pain perception: A systematic-review and meta-analysis of age effects on pain and tolerance thresholds. *Neuroscience and Biobehavioral Reviews, 75,* 104–113.

Lawrence, Julie; Haszard, Jillian J.; Taylor, Barry; Galland, Barbara; Gray, Andrew; Sayers, Rachel, . . . Taylor, Rachael W. (2019). A longitudinal study of parental discipline up to 5 years. *Journal of Family Studies.*

Laws, Glynis; Brown, Heather & Main, Elizabeth. (2015). Reading comprehension in children with Down syndrome. *Reading and Writing,* 1–25.

Le Duc, James W. & Yuan, Zhiming. (2018). Network for safe and secure labs. *Science, 362*(6412), 267.

Leach, Margaret S. & Braithwaite, Dawn O. (1996). A binding tie: Supportive communication of family kinkeepers. *Journal of Applied Communication Research, 24*(3), 200–216.

Leadbeater, Bonnie J. & Ames, Megan E. (2017). The longitudinal effects of oppositional defiant disorder symptoms on academic and occupational functioning in the transition to young adulthood. *Journal of Abnormal Child Psychology, 45,* 749–763.

LeBlanc, Nicole J.; Simon, Naomi M.; Reynolds, Charles F.; Shear, M. Katherine; Skritskaya, Natalia & Zisook, Sidney. (2019). Relationship between complicated grief and depression: Relevance, etiological mechanisms, and implications. In Quevedo, João; Carvalho, André F. & Zarate, Carlos A. (Eds.), *Neurobiology of depression: Road to novel therapeutics* (pp. 231–239). Academic Press.

Lee, Barbara Coombs. (2019). *Finish strong: Putting your priorities first at life's end.* Compassion & Choices.

Lee, David M.; Nazroo, James; O'Connor, Daryl B.; Blake, Margaret & Pendleton, Neil. (2016). Sexual health and well-being among older men and women in England: Findings from the English longitudinal study of ageing. *Archives of Sexual Behavior, 45*(1), 133–144.

Lee, Robert Y.; Brumback, Lyndia C.; Sathitratanacheewin, Seelwan; Lober, William B.; Modes, Matthew E.; Lynch, Ylinne T., . . . Kross, Erin K. (2020). Association of physician orders for life-sustaining treatment with ICU admission among patients hospitalized near the end of life. *JAMA, 323*(10), 950–960.

Leiter, Valerie & Herman, Sarah. (2015). Guinea pig kids: Myths or modern Tuskegees? *Sociological Spectrum, 35*(1), 26–45.

Lemaire, Patrick (Ed.) (2017). *Cognitive development from a strategy perspective: A festschrift for Robert Siegler.* Routledge.

Leman, Joseph; Hunter, Will; Fergus, Thomas & Rowatt, Wade. (2018). Secure attachment to God uniquely linked to psychological health in a national, random sample of American adults. *International Journal for the Psychology of Religion, 28*(3), 162–173.

Leman, Patrick J. & Björnberg, Marina. (2010). Conversation, development, and gender: A study of changes in children's concepts of punishment. *Child Development, 81*(3), 958–971.

Lemieux, André. (2012). Post-formal thought in gerontagogy or beyond Piaget. *Journal of Behavioral and Brain Science, 2*(3), 399–406.

Lemish, Daphna & Kolucki, Barbara. (2013). Media and early childhood development. In Britto, Pia Rebello; Engle, Patrice L. & Super, Charles M. (Eds.), *Handbook of early childhood development research and its impact on global policy.* Oxford University Press.

Lengua, Liliana J.; Garstein, Maria A. & Prinzie, Peter. (2019). Temperament and personality trait development in the family: Interactions and transactions with parenting from infancy through adolescence. In McAdams, Dan P.; Shiner, Rebecca L. & Tackett, Jennifer L. (Eds.), *Handbook of personality development* (pp. 201–220). Guilford.

Leonard, Laurence B. (2014). Specific language impairment across languages. *Child Development Perspectives, 8*(1), 1–5.

Leonoff, Arthur. (2015). *The good divorce: A psychoanalyst's exploration of separation, divorce, and childcare.* Routledge.

Lepage, Jean-François & Corbeil, Jean-Pierre. (2013). The evolution of English–French bilingualism in Canada from 1961 to 2011. *Statistics Canada.*

Leshner, Alan I. & Dzau, Victor J. (2018). Good gun policy needs research. *Science, 359*(6381), 1195.

Leslie, Mitch. (2012). Gut microbes keep rare immune cells in line. *Science, 335*(6075), 1428.

Leslie, Mitch. (2019). The mismeasure of hands? *Science, 364*(6444), 923–925.

Levey, Emma K. V.; Garandeau, Claire F.; Meeus, Wim & Branje, Susan. (2019). The longitudinal role of self-concept clarity and best friend delinquency in adolescent delinquent behavior. *Journal of Youth and Adolescence, 48*(6), 1068–1081.

Levick, Marsha. (2019). Kids are different: The United States supreme court reforms youth sentencing practices for youth prosecuted in the criminal justice system. *Juvenile and Family Court Journal, 70*(3), 25–44.

Levy, Kenneth N.; Scala, J. Wesley; Temes, Christina M. & Clouthier, Tracy L. (2015). An integrative attachment theory framework of personality disorders. In Huprich, Steven K. (Ed.), *Personality disorders: Toward theoretical and empirical integration in diagnosis and assessment* (pp. 315–343). American Psychological Association.

Lewin, Kurt. (1945). The Research Center for Group Dynamics at Massachusetts Institute of Technology. *Sociometry, 8*(2), 126–136.

Lewis, Ariane; Bakkar, Azza; Kreiger-Benson, Elana; Kumpfbeck, Andrew; Liebman, Jordan; Shemie, Sam D.; . . . Greer, David. (2020). Determination of death by neurologic criteria around the world. *Neurology, 95*(3), e299–e309.

Lewis, Ariane & Greer, David. (2017). Current controversies in brain death determination. *Nature Reviews Neurology, 13,* 505–509.

Lewis, Lawrence B.; Antone, Carol & Johnson, Jacqueline S. (1999). Effects of prosodic stress and serial position on syllable omission in first words. *Developmental Psychology, 35*(1), 45–59.

Li, Bai; Adab, Peymané & Cheng, Kar Keung. (2015). The role of grandparents in childhood obesity in China—Evidence from a mixed methods study. *International Journal of Behavioral Nutrition and Physical Activity*, 12, 91.

Li, Changwei; Miles, Toni; Shen, Luqi; Shen, Ye; Liu, Tingting; Zhang, Mengxi; . . . Huang, Cheng. (2018). Early-life exposure to severe famine and subsequent risk of depressive symptoms in late adulthood: The China Health and Retirement Longitudinal Study. *British Journal of Psychiatry*, 213(4), 579–586.

Li, Guanqiao; Jiang, Yan & Zhang, Linqi. (2019). HIV upsurge in China's students. *Science*, 364(6442), 711.

Li, Jin; Fung, Heidi; Bakeman, Roger; Rae, Katharine & Wei, Wanchun. (2014). How European American and Taiwanese mothers talk to their children about learning. *Child Development*, 85(3), 1206–1221.

Liben, Lynn S. & Müller, Ulrich M. (2015). Introduction. In Lerner, Richard M. (Ed.), *Handbook of child psychology and developmental science* (7th ed., Vol. 2). Wiley.

Liberles, Stephen D. (2014). Mammalian pheromones. *Annual Review of Physiology*, 76, 151–175.

Liebler, Carolyn A.; Porter, Sonya R.; Fernandez, Leticia E.; Noon, James M. & Ennis, Sharon R. (2017). America's churning races: Race and ethnicity response changes between census 2000 and the 2010 census. *Demography*, 54(1), 259–284.

Lillard, Angeline S. (2013). Playful learning and Montessori education. *American Journal of Play*, 5(2), 157–186.

Lillard, Angeline S.; Lerner, Matthew D.; Hopkins, Emily J.; Dore, Rebecca A.; Smith, Eric D. & Palmquist, Carolyn M. (2013). The impact of pretend play on children's development: A review of the evidence. *Psychological Bulletin*, 139(1), 1–34.

Limber, Susan P. & Kowalski, Robin M. (2020). How schools often make a bad situation worse. *International Journal on Child Maltreatment*, 3(2), 211–228.

Lin, Frank R.; Yaffe, Kristine; Xia, Jin; Xue, Qian-Li; Harris, Tamara B.; Purchase-Helzner, Elizabeth; . . . Simonsick, Eleanor M. (2013). Hearing loss and cognitive decline in older adults. *JAMA Internal Medicine*, 173(4), 293–299.

Lindsay, Laura; Gambi, Chiara & Rabagliati, Hugh. (2019). Preschoolers optimize the timing of their conversational turns through flexible coordination of language comprehension and production. *Psychological Science*, 30(4), 504–515.

Littman, Lisa. (2018). Parent reports of adolescents and young adults perceived to show signs of a rapid onset of gender dysphoria. *PloS One*, 13(8), e0202330.

Liu, Jianlin; Subramaniam, Mythily; Chong, Siow Ann & Mahendran, Rathi. (2020). Maladaptive cognitive emotion regulation strategies and positive symptoms in schizophrenia spectrum disorders: The mediating role of global emotion dysregulation. *Clinical Psychology and Psychotherapy*, (In Press).

Liu, Lin & Miller, Susan L. (2020). Protective factors against juvenile delinquency: Exploring

gender with a nationally representative sample of youth. *Social Science Research*, 86(102376).

Liu, Qingqing; He, Hairong; Yang, Jin; Feng, Xiaojie; Zhao, Fanfan & Lyu, Jun. (2020). Changes in the global burden of depression from 1990 to 2017: Findings from the Global Burden of Disease study. *Journal of Psychiatric Research*, 126, 134–140.

Liu, Yu-Chi; Wilkins, Mark; Kim, Terry; Malyugin, Boris & Mehta, Jodhbir S. (2017). Cataracts. *The Lancet*, 390(10094), 600–612.

Lo, Camilla K. M.; Chan, Ko Ling & Ip, Patrick. (2019). Insecure adult attachment and child maltreatment: A meta-analysis. *Trauma, Violence, & Abuse*, 20(5), 706–719.

LoBue, Vanessa & Adolph, Karen E. (2019). Fear in infancy: Lessons from snakes, spiders, heights, and strangers. *Developmental Psychology*, 55(9), 1889–1907.

Lock, Margaret. (2013). The lure of the epigenome. *The Lancet*, 381(9881), 1896–1897.

Locke, Kenneth D.; Mastor, Khairul A.; MacDonald, Geoff; Barni, Daniela; Morio, Hiroaki; Reyes, Jose Alberto S.; . . . Ortiz, Fernando A. (2020). Young adults' partner preferences and parents' in-law preferences across generations, genders, and nations. *European Journal of Social Psychology*, 50(5), 903–920.

Löckenhoff, Corinna E.; De Fruyt, Filip; Terracciano, Antonio; McCrae, Robert R.; De Bolle, Marleen; Costa, Paul T.; . . . Yik, Michelle. (2009). Perceptions of aging across 26 cultures and their culture-level associates. *Psychology and Aging*, 24(4), 941–954.

Lockhart, Kristi L.; Goddu, Mariel K. & Keil, Frank C. (2018). When saying "I'm best" is benign: Developmental shifts in perceptions of boasting. *Developmental Psychology*, 54(3), 521–535.

Lodge, Amy C. & Umberson, Debra. (2012). All shook up: Sexuality of mid- to later life married couples. *Journal of Marriage and Family*, 74(3), 428–443.

Loeb, Emily L.; Kansky, Jessica; Narr, Rachel K.; Fowler, Caroline & Allen, Joseph P. (2020). Romantic relationship churn in early adolescence predicts hostility, abuse, and avoidance in relationships into early adulthood. *Journal of Early Adolescence*, 40(8), 1195–1225.

Loehlin, John C. & Nichols, Robert C. (1976). *Heredity, environment, and personality: A study of 850 sets of twins*. University of Texas Press.

Loftus, Elizabeth F. (2005). Planting misinformation in the human mind: A 30-year investigation of the malleability of memory. *Learning and Memory*, 12(4), 361–366.

Longobardi, Claudio & Badenes-Ribera, Laura. (2017). Stressors: A systematic review of the past 10 years. *Journal of Child and Family Studies*, 26(8), 2039–2049.

Lönnerdal, Bo; Erdmann, Peter; Thakkar, Sagar K.; Sauser, Julien & Destaillats, Frédéric. (2017). Longitudinal evolution of true protein, amino acids and bioactive proteins in breast milk: A developmental perspective. *Journal of Nutritional Biochemistry*, 41, 1–11.

López-Pinar, Carlos; Martínez-Sanchís, Sonia; Carbonell-Vayá, Enrique; Fenollar-

Cortés, Javier & Sánchez-Meca, Julio. (2018). Long-term efficacy of psychosocial treatments for adults with Attention-deficit/hyperactivity disorder: A meta-analytic review. *Frontiers in Psychology*, 9(638).

Lordier, Lara; Meskaldji, Djalel-Eddine; Grouiller, Frédéric; Pittet, Marie P.; Vollenweider, Andreas; Vasung, Lana; . . . Hüppi, Petra S. (2019). Music in premature infants enhances high-level cognitive brain networks. *PNAS*, 116(24), 12103–12108.

Lorenz, Konrad. (1979). *The year of the greylag goose*. Harcourt Brace.

Lorenzo-Luaces, L. (2015). Heterogeneity in the prognosis of major depression: From the common cold to a highly debilitating and recurrent illness. *Epidemiology and Psychiatric Sciences*, 24(6), 466–472.

Lotan, A.; Lifschytz, T.; Wolf, G.; Keller, S.; Ben-Ari, H.; Tatarsky, P.; . . . Lerer, B. (2018). Differential effects of chronic stress in young-adult and old female mice: Cognitive-behavioral manifestations and neurobiological correlates. *Molecular Psychiatry*, 23, 1432–1445.

Loughrey, David G.; Kelly, Michelle E.; Kelley, George A.; Brennan, Sabina & Lawlor, Brian A. (2018). Association of age-related hearing loss with cognitive function, cognitive impairment, and dementia: A systematic review and meta-analysis. *JAMA Otolaryngology*, 44(2), 115–126.

Low, Rachel S. T.; Overall, Nickola C.; Cross, Emily J. & Henderson, Annette M. E. (2019). Emotion regulation, conflict resolution, and spillover on subsequent family functioning. *Emotion*, 19(7), 1162–1182.

Low, Sabina; Tiberio, Stacey S.; Shortt, Joann Wu.; Capaldi, Deborah M. & Eddy, J. Mark. (2017). Associations of couples' intimate partner violence in young adulthood and substance use: A dyadic approach. *Psychology of Violence*, 7(1), 120–127.

Lu, Po H.; Lee, Grace J.; Tishler, Todd A.; Meghpara, Michael; Thompson, Paul M. & Bartzokis, George. (2013). Myelin breakdown mediates age-related slowing in cognitive processing speed in healthy elderly men. *Brain and Cognition*, 81(1), 131–138.

Lucaccioni, Laura; Wong, Sze Choong; Smyth, Arlene; Lyall, Helen; Dominiczak, Anna; Ahmed, S. Faisal & Mason, Avril. (2015). Turner syndrome–issues to consider for transition to adulthood. *British Medical Bulletin*, 113(1), 45–58.

Ludwig, David S. (2016). Lifespan weighed down by diet. *JAMA*, 315(21), 2269–2270.

Luhmann, Maike; Buecker, Susanne; Kaiser, Till & Beermann, Mira. (2020). Nothing going on? Exploring the role of missed events in changes in subjective well-being and the Big Five personality traits. *Journal of Personality*, (In Press).

Luhmann, Maike; Hofmann, Wilhelm; Eid, Michael & Lucas, Richard E. (2012). Subjective well-being and adaptation to life events: A meta-analysis. *Journal of Personality and Social Psychology*, 102(3), 592–615.

Luna, Beatriz; Paulsen, David J.; Padmanabhan, Aarthi & Geier, Charles. (2013). The teenage brain: Cognitive control and motivation. *Current Directions in Psychological Science*, 22(2), 94–100.

Lund, Crick. (2020). Reflections on the next ten years of research, policy and implementation in global mental health. *Epidemiology and Psychiatric Sciences*, 29(e77).

Lundquist, Gunilla; Rasmussen, Birgit H. & Axelsson, Bertil. (2011). Information of imminent death or not: Does it make a difference? *Journal of Clinical Oncology*, 29(29), 3927–3931.

Lundqvist, C. & Sabel, K. G. (2000). Brief report: The Brazelton Neonatal Behavioral Assessment Scale detects differences among newborn infants of optimal health. *Journal of Pediatric Psychology*, 25(8), 577.

Luong, Gloria & Charles, Susan T. (2014). Age differences in affective and cardiovascular responses to a negative social interaction: The role of goals, appraisals, and emotion regulation. *Developmental Psychology*, 50(7), 1919–1930.

Lupski, James R. (2013). Genome mosaicism: One human, multiple genomes. *Science*, 341(6144), 358–359.

Luthar, Suniya S. (2015). Resilience in development: A synthesis of research across five decades. In Cicchetti, Dante & Cohen, Donald J. (Eds.), *Developmental psychopathology* (2nd ed., Vol. 3). Wiley.

Luthar, Suniya S.; Cicchetti, Dante & Becker, Bronwyn. (2000). The construct of resilience: A critical evaluation and guidelines for future work. *Child Development*, 71(3), 543–562.

Luthar, Suniya S.; Crossman, Elizabeth J. & Small, Phillip J. (2015). Resilience and adversity. In Lerner, Richard M. (Ed.), *Handbook of child psychology and developmental science* (7th ed., Vol. 3, pp. 247–286). Wiley.

Luthar, Suniya S.; Small, Phillip J. & Ciciolla, Lucia. (2018). Adolescents from upper middle class communities: Substance misuse and addiction across early adulthood. *Development and Psychopathology*, 30(1), 315–335.

Luyckx, Koen; Klimstra, Theo A.; Duriez, Bart; Van Petegem, Stijn & Beyers, Wim. (2013). Personal identity processes from adolescence through the late 20s: Age trends, functionality, and depressive symptoms. *Social Development*, 22(4), 701–721.

Lyon, Thomas D.; McWilliams, Kelly & Williams, Shanna. (2019). Child witnesses. In Brewer, Neil & Douglass, Amy Bradfield (Eds.), *Psychological science and the law*. Guilford.

Ma, Defu; Ning, Yibing; Gao, Hongchong; Li, Wenjun; Wang, Junkuan; Zheng, Yingdong; . . . Wang, Peiyu. (2014). Nutritional status of breast-fed and non-exclusively breast-fed infants from birth to age 5 months in 8 Chinese cities. *Asia Pacific Journal of Clinical Nutrition*, 23(2), 282–292.

Macari, Suzanne; Milgramm, Anna; Reed, Jessa; Shic, Frederick; Powell, Kelly K; Macris, Deanna & Chawarska, Katarzyna. (2020). Context-specific dyadic attention vulnerabilities during the first year in infants later developing autism spectrum disorder. *Child & Adolescent Psychiatry*, (In Press).

Mackenzie, Karen J.; Anderton, Stephen M. & Schwarze, Jürgen. (2014). Viral respiratory tract infections and asthma in early life: Cause and effect? *Clinical & Experimental Allergy*, 44(1), 9–19.

Mackey, April & Bassendowski, Sandra. (2017). The history of evidence-based practice in nursing education and practice. *Journal of Professional Nursing*, 33(1), 51–55.

MacPherson, Sarah E. & Sala, Sergio Della (Eds.). (2019). *Cases of amnesia: Contributions to understanding memory and the brain*. Routledge.

MacSwan, Jeff; Thompson, Marilyn; Rolstad, Kellie; Mcalister, Kara & Lobo, Gerda. (2017). Three theories of the effects of language education programs: An empirical evaluation of bilingual and English-only policies. *Annual Review of Applied Linguistics*, 37, 218–240.

Mahanes, Dea & Greer, David. (2018). Brain death and organ donation. In White, Jessica L. & Sheth, Kevin N. (Eds.), *Neurocritical care for the advanced practice clinician* (pp. 321–342). Springer.

Maheux, Anne J.; Evans, Reina; Widman, Laura; Nesi, Jacqueline; Prinstein, Mitchell J. & Choukas-Bradley, Sophia. (2020). Popular peer norms and adolescent sexting behavior. *Journal of Adolescence*, 78, 62–66.

Mahler, Margaret S.; Pine, Fred & Bergman, Anni. (2000). *The psychological birth of the human infant symbiosis and individuation*. Basic Books.

Maïano, Christophe; Normand, Claude L.; Salvas, Marie-Claude; Moullec, Grégory & Aimé, Annie. (2016). Prevalence of school bullying among youth with autism spectrum disorders: A systematic review and meta-analysis. *Autism Research*, 9(6), 601–615.

Maitoza, Robyn. (2019). Family challenges created by unemployment. *Journal of Family Social Work*, 22(2), 187–205.

Makelarski, Jennifer A.; Abramsohn, Emily; Benjamin, Jasmine H.; Du, Senxi & Lindau, Stacy T. (2017). Diagnostic accuracy of two food insecurity screeners recommended for use in health care settings. *American Journal of Public Health*, 107(11), 1812–1817.

Malacrida, Claudia. (2017). *Mourning the dreams: How parents create meaning from miscarriage, stillbirth, and early infant death*. Routledge.

Malina, Robert M.; Bouchard, Claude & Bar-Or, Oded. (2004). *Growth, maturation, and physical activity* (2nd ed.). Human Kinetics.

Malloy, Lindsay C.; Shulman, Elizabeth P. & Cauffman, Elizabeth. (2014). Interrogations, confessions, and guilty pleas among serious adolescent offenders. *Law and Human Behavior*, 38(2), 181–193.

Malpas, Jean. (2011). Between pink and blue: A multi-dimensional family approach to gender nonconforming children and their families. *Family Process*, 50(4), 453–470.

Manfred, Tony. (2013, June 21). LeBron James really did grow up in inner city poverty. *Business Insider*.

Manfredi, Claudia; Bandini, Andrea; Melino, Donatella; Viellevoye, Renaud; Kalenga, Masendu & Orlandi, Silvia. (2018). Automated detection and classification of basic shapes of newborn cry melody. *Biomedical Signal Processing and Control*, 45, 174–181.

Manheim, Megan; Felicetti, Richard & Moloney, Gillian. (2019). Child sexual abuse victimization prevention programs in preschool and kindergarten: Implications for practice. *Journal of Child Sexual Abuse*, 28(6), 745–757.

Mani, Kartik; Javaheri, Ali & Diwan, Abhinav. (2018). Lysosomes mediate benefits of intermittent fasting in cardiometabolic disease: The janitor is the undercover boss. *Comprehensive Physiology*, 8(4), 1639–1667.

Marchiano, Lisa. (2017). Outbreak: On transgender teens and psychic epidemics. *Psychological Perspectives: Gender Diversity*, 60(3), 345–366.

Marcia, James E. (1966). Development and validation of ego-identity status. *Journal of Personality and Social Psychology*, 3(5), 551–558.

Marginson, Simon. (2016). High participation systems of higher education. *Journal of Higher Education*, 87(2), 243–271.

Margolin, Gayla & Vickerman, Katrina A. (2007). Posttraumatic stress in children and adolescents exposed to family violence: I. Overview and issues. *Professional Psychology: Research and Practice*, 38(6), 613–619.

Margolis, Rachel & Arpino, Bruno. (2018). The demography of grandparenthood in 16 European countries and two North American countries. In Timonen, Virpi (Ed.), *Grandparenting practices around the world*. Policy Press.

Margoni, Francesco & Surian, Luca. (2018). Infants' evaluation of prosocial and antisocial agents: A meta-analysis. *Developmental Psychology*, 54(8), 1445–1455.

Mark, Joan T. (1999). *Margaret Mead: Coming of age in America*. Oxford University Press.

Marsac, Meghan L.; Kassam-Adams, Nancy; Delahanty, Douglas L.; Ciesla, Jeffrey; Weiss, Danielle; Widaman, Keith F. & Barakat, Lamia P. (2017). An initial application of a biopsychosocial framework to predict posttraumatic stress following pediatric injury. *Health Psychology*, 36(8), 787–796.

Martin, Carol Lynn; Kornienko, Olga; Schaefer, David R.; Hanish, Laura D.; Fabes, Richard A. & Goble, Priscilla. (2013). The role of sex of peers and gender-typed activities in young children's peer affiliative networks: A longitudinal analysis of selection and influence. *Child Development*, 84(3), 921–937.

Martin, Joyce A.; Hamilton, Brady E.; Osterman, Michelle J. K. & Driscoll, Anne K. (2019, November 27). *Births: Final data for 2018. National Vital Statistics Reports*, 68(13). Hyattsville, MD: National Center for Health Statistics.

Martin, Joyce A. & Osterman, Michelle J. K. (2019, October). *Is twin childbearing on the decline? Twin births in the United States, 2014–2018. NCHS Data Brief*, 351. Hyattsville, MD: National Center for Health Statistics.

Martino, Jessica; Pegg, Jennifer & Frates, Elizabeth Pegg. (2017). The connection prescription: Using the power of social interactions and the deep desire for connectedness to empower health and wellness. *American Journal of Lifestyle Medicine*, 11(6), 466–475.

Martirosyan, Danik (Ed.) (2019). *Functional foods and mental health*. Food Science Publisher.

Masarik, April S. & Conger, Rand D. (2017). Stress and child development: A review of the Family Stress Model. *Current Opinion in Psychology*, 13, 85–90.

Mascaro, Jennifer S.; Rentscher, Kelly E.; Hackett, Patrick D.; Mehl, Matthias R. & Rilling, James K. (2017). Child gender influences paternal behavior, language, and brain function. *Behavioral Neuroscience*, 131(3), 262–273.

Maslow, Abraham H. (1954). *Motivation and personality* (1st ed.). Harper & Row.

Masonbrink, Abbey R. & Hurley, Emily. (2020). Advocating for children during the COVID-19 school closures. *Pediatrics*, 146(3), e20201440.

Masten, Ann S. (2014). *Ordinary magic: Resilience in development*. Guilford Press.

Matsumoto, David; Frank, Mark G. & Hwang, Hyi Sung (Eds.). (2013). *Nonverbal communication: Science and applications*. SAGE.

Matsumoto, David & Hwang, Hyisung. (2013). Cultural similarities and differences in emblematic gestures. *Journal of Nonverbal Behavior*, 37(1), 1–27.

Matthews, Fiona E.; Arthur, Antony; Barnes, Linda E.; Bond, John; Jagger, Carol; Robinson, Louise & Brayne, Carol. (2013). A two-decade comparison of prevalence of dementia in individuals aged 65 years and older from three geographical areas of England: Results of the Cognitive Function and Ageing Study I and II. *The Lancet*, 382(9902), 1405–1412.

Mattingly, Victoria & Kraiger, Kurt. (2019). Can emotional intelligence be trained? A meta-analytical investigation. *Human Resource Management Review*, 29(2), 140–155.

Maurer, Daphne; Gibson, Laura C. & Spector, Ferrinne. (2013). Synesthesia in infants and very young children. In Simner, Julia & Hubbard, Edward (Eds.), *Oxford handbook of synesthesia*. Oxford University Press.

Maurus, Isabel; Hasan, Alkomiet; Röh, Astrid; Takahashi, Shun; Rauchmann, Boris; Keeser, Daniel, . . . Falkai, Peter. (2019). Neurobiological effects of aerobic exercise, with a focus on patients with schizophrenia. *European Archives of Psychiatry and Clinical Neuroscience*, 269, 499–515.

Maxfield, Molly; Pyszczynski, Tom; Kluck, Benjamin; Cox, Cathy R.; Greenberg, Jeff; Solomon, Sheldon & Weise, David. (2007). Age-related differences in responses to thoughts of one's own death: Mortality salience and judgments of moral transgressions. *Psychology and Aging*, 22(2), 341–353.

Mayo, Ray Cody; Kent, Daniel; Sen, Lauren Chang; Kapoor, Megha; Leung, Jessica W. T. & Watanabe, Alyssa T. (2019). Reduction of false-positive markings on mammograms: A retrospective comparison study using an artificial intelligence-based CAD. *Journal of Digital Imaging*, 32, 618–624.

McCarthy, Margaret M. (2017). *Sex and the developing brain* (2nd ed.). Morgan & Claypool Life Sciences.

McCarthy, Margaret M.; Nugent, Bridget M. & Lenz, Kathryn M. (2017). Neuroimmunology and neuroepigenetics in the establishment of sex differences in the brain. *Nature Reviews Neuroscience*, 18, 471–484.

McClain, Natalie M. & Garrity, Stacy E. (2011). Sex trafficking and the exploitation of adolescents. *Journal of Obstetric, Gynecologic, & Neonatal Nursing*, 40(2), 243–252.

McCoy, Dana Charles; Yoshikawa, Hirokazu; Ziol-Guest, Kathleen M.; Duncan, Greg J.; Schindler, Holly S.; Magnuson, Katherine; . . . Shonkoff, Jack P. (2017). Impacts of early childhood education on medium- and long-term educational outcomes. *Educational Researcher*, 46(8), 474–487.

McCutcheon, Robert A.; Reis Marques, Tiago & Howes, Oliver D. (2020). Schizophrenia—An overview. *JAMA Psychiatry*, 77(2), 201–210.

McElroy, Anita K.; Mühlberger, Elke & Muñoz-Fontela, César. (2018). Immune barriers of Ebola virus infection. *Current Opinion in Virology*, 28, 152–160.

McEwen, Bruce S. & Karatsoreos, Ilia N. (2015). Sleep deprivation and circadian disruption: Stress, allostasis, and allostatic load. *Sleep Medicine Clinics*, 10(1), 1–10.

McEwen, Craig A. & Gregerson, Scout F. (2019). A critical assessment of the adverse childhood experiences study at 20 years. *American Journal of Preventive Medicine*, 56(6), 790–794.

McFarland, Joel; Hussar, Bill; Wang, Xiaolei; Zhang, Jijun; Wang, Ke; Rathbun, Amy; . . . Mann, Farrah Bullock. (2018, May). *The condition of education 2018*. Washington, DC: National Center for Education Statistics. NCES 2018-144.

McGillion, Michelle; Herbert, Jane S.; Pine, Julian; Vihman, Marilyn; dePaolis, Rory; Keren-Portnoy, Tamar & Matthews, Danielle. (2017). What paves the way to conventional language? The predictive value of babble, pointing, and socioeconomic status. *Child Development*, 88(1), 156–166.

McGrath, John J.; Saha, Sukanta; Al-Hamzawi, Ali O.; Alonso, Jordi; Andrade, Laura; Borges, Guilherme; . . . Kessler, Ronald C. (2016). Age of onset and lifetime projected risk of psychotic experiences: Cross-national data from the world mental health survey. *Schizophrenia Bulletin*, 42(4), 933–941.

McGue, Matt; Irons, Dan & Iacono, William G. (2014). The adolescent origins of substance use disorders: A behavioral genetic perspective. In Stoltenberg, Scott F. (Ed.), *Genes and the motivation to use substances* (pp. 31–50). Springer.

McGuinness, Myra B.; Le, Jerome; Mitchell, Paul; Gopinath, Bamini; Cerin, Ester; Saksens, Nicole T. M.; . . . Finger, Robert P. (2017). Physical activity and age-related macular degeneration: A systematic literature review and meta-analysis. *American Journal of Ophthalmology*, 180, 29–38.

McHugh Power, Joanna E.; Steptoe, Andrew; Kee, Frank & Lawlor, Brian A. (2019). Loneliness and social engagement in older adults: A bivariate dual change score analysis. *Psychology and Aging*, 34(1), 152–162.

McKay, Erin R.; Rosinski, Leanna; Mayes, Linda C.; Rutherford, Helena J. V. & Bridgett, David J. (2019). Maternal positive responses to a distressed infant simulator predict subsequent negative affect in infants. *Infant Behavior and Development*, 56(101299).

McKay, Ryan & Whitehouse, Harvey. (2015). Religion and morality. *Psychological Bulletin*, 141(2), 447–473.

McKee-Ryan, Frances & Maitoza, Robyn. (2018). Job loss, unemployment, and families. In Klehe, Ute-Christine & van Hooft, Edwin (Eds.), *The Oxford handbook of job loss and job search*. Oxford University Press.

McKone, Elinor; Wan, Lulu; Pidcock, Madeleine; Crookes, Kate; Reynolds, Katherine; Dawel, Amy; . . . Fiorentini, Chiara. (2019). A critical period for faces: Other-race face recognition is improved by childhood but not adult social contact. *Scientific Reports*, 9(12820).

McKown, Clark; Russo-Ponsaran, Nicole M.; Allen, Adelaide; Johnson, Jason K. & Warren-Khot, Heather K. (2016). Social-emotional factors and academic outcomes among elementary-aged children: Social-emotional factors and academic outcomes. *Infant and Child Development*, 25(2), 119–136.

McMahon, Susan D.; Peist, Eric; Davis, Jacqueline O.; Bare, Kailyn; Martinez, Andrew; Reddy, Linda A., . . . Anderman, Eric M. (2020). Physical aggression toward teachers: Antecedents, behaviors, and consequences. *Aggressive Behavior*, 46(1), 116–126.

McManus, I. C & Hartigan, Alex. (2007). Declining left-handedness in Victorian England seen in the films of Mitchell and Kenyon. *Current Biology*, 17(18), R793–R794.

McPherson, Gary E.; Osborne, Margaret S.; Evans, Paul & Miksza, Peter. (2019). Applying self-regulated learning microanalysis to study musicians' practice. *Psychology of Music*, 47(1), 18–32.

McShane, Kelly E. & Hastings, Paul D. (2009). The New Friends Vignettes: Measuring parental psychological control that confers risk for anxious adjustment in preschoolers. *International Journal of Behavioral Development*, 33(6), 481–495.

Meagher, David K. (2013). Ethical and legal issues and loss, grief, and mourning. In Meagher, David K. & Balk, David E. (Eds.), *Handbook of thanatology: The essential body of knowledge for the study of death, dying, and bereavement* (2nd ed.). Routledge.

Medeiros, Mike; Forest, Benjamin & Öhberg, Patrik. (2020). The case for non-binary gender questions in surveys. *PS*, 53(1), 128–135.

Medford, Anthony & Vaupel, James W. (2019). Human lifespan records are not remarkable but their durations are. *PLoS ONE*, 14(3), e0212345.

Medsinge, Anagha & Nischal, Ken K. (2015). Pediatric cataract: Challenges and future directions. *Clinical Ophthalmology*, 9, 77–90.

Meehan, Michael; Massavelli, Bronwyn & Pachana, Nancy A. (2017). Using attachment theory and social support theory to examine and measure pets as sources of social support and attachment figures. *Anthrozoös*, 30(2), 273–289.

Mehler, Philip S. (2018). Medical complications of anorexia nervosa and bulimia nervosa. In Agras, W. Stewart & Robinson, Athena (Eds.), *The Oxford handbook of eating disorders* (2nd ed.). Oxford University Press.

Meier, Emily A.; Gallegos, Jarred V.; Thomas, Lori P. Montross; Depp, Colin A.; Irwin, Scott A. & Jeste, Dilip V. (2016). Defining a good death (successful dying): Literature review and a call for research and public dialogue. *The American Journal of Geriatric Psychiatry*, 24(4), 261–271.

Meijer, Onno C.; Buurstede, J. C & Schaaf, Marcel J. M. (2019). Corticosteroid receptors in the brain: Transcriptional mechanisms for specificity and context-dependent effects. *Cellular and Molecular Neurobiology, 39*(4), 539–549.

Meldrum, Ryan Charles; Young, Jacob T. N.; Kavish, Nicholas & Boutwell, Brian B. (2019). Could peers influence intelligence during adolescence? An exploratory study. *Intelligence, 72*, 28–34.

Mellerson, Jenelle L.; Maxwell, Choppell B.; Knighton, Cynthia L.; Kriss, Jennifer L.; Seither, Ranee & Black, Carla L. (2018, October 12). *Vaccination coverage for selected vaccines and exemption rates among children in kindergarten—United States, 2017–18 school year. Morbidity and Mortality Weekly Report, 67*(40), 1115–1122. Atlanta, GA: Centers for Disease Control and Prevention.

Melton, Karen K.; Larson, Maddie & Boccia, Maria L. (2019). Examining couple recreation and oxytocin via the ecology of family experiences framework. *Journal of Marriage and Family, 81*(3), 771–782.

Meltzoff, Andrew N. & Moore, M. Keith. (1977). Imitation of facial and manual gestures by human neonates. *Science, 198*(4312), 74–78.

Mennella, Julie A. & Bobowski, Nuala K. (2015). The sweetness and bitterness of childhood: Insights from basic research on taste preferences. *Physiology & Behavior, 152*, 502–507.

Mennella, Julie A. & Castor, Sara M. (2012). Sensitive period in flavor learning: Effects of duration of exposure to formula flavors on food likes during infancy. *Clinical Nutrition, 31*(6), 1022–1025.

Merriam, Sharan B. (2009). *Qualitative research: A guide to design and implementation.* Jossey-Bass.

Merrick, Melissa T.; Ford, Derek C.; Ports, Katie A.; Guinn, Angie S.; Chen, Jieru; Klevens, Joanne; . . . Mercy, James A. (2019, November 8). *Vital signs: Estimated proportion of adult health problems attributable to adverse childhood experiences and implications for prevention—25 states, 2015–2017. Morbidity and Mortality Weekly Report, 68*(44), 999–1005. Atlanta, GA: Department of Health and Human Services, Centers for Disease Control and Prevention.

Merrill, Anne F. & Afifi, Tamara D. (2012). Examining the bidirectional nature of topic avoidance and relationship dissatisfaction: The moderating role of communication skills. *Communication Monographs, 79*(4), 499–521.

Mesman, Judi; van IJzendoorn, Marinus H. & Sagi-Schwartz, Abraham. (2016). Cross-cultural patterns of attachment: Universal and contextual dimensions. In Cassidy, Jude & Shaver, Phillip R. (Eds.), *Handbook of attachment: Theory, research, and clinical applications* (3rd ed.). Guilford Press.

Mestre, María Vicenta; Malonda, Elisabeth; Samper, Paula; Llorca, Anna & Tur-Porcar, Ana. (2019). Development of prosocial behavior in Spanish adolescents and its relations to parenting styles. In Laible, Deborah J.; Carlo, Gustavo & Padilla-Walker, Laura M. (Eds.), *The Oxford handbook of parenting and moral development.* Oxford University Press.

Meyer, Craig S.; Schreiner, Pamela J.; Lim, Kelvin; Battapady, Harsha & Launer, Lenore J. (2019). Depressive symptomatology, racial discrimination experience, and brain tissue volumes observed on magnetic resonance imaging. *American Journal of Epidemiology, 188*(4), 656–663.

Miciak, Jeremy; Cirino, Paul T.; Ahmed, Yusra; Reid, Erin & Vaughn, Sharon. (2019). Executive functions and response to intervention: Identification of students struggling with reading comprehension. *Learning Disability Quarterly, 42*(1), 17–31.

Miech, Richard A.; Johnston, Lloyd D.; O'Malley, Patrick M.; Bachman, Jerald G.; Schulenberg, John E. & Patrick, Megan E. (2020). *Monitoring the future, national survey results on drug use, 1975–2019: Volume I, secondary school students.* Ann Arbor, MI: Institute for Social Research, The University of Michigan.

Miklowitz, David J. & Cicchetti, Dante (Eds.). (2010). *Understanding bipolar disorder: A developmental psychopathology perspective.* Guilford Press.

Mikucka, Małgorzata. (2016). The life satisfaction advantage of being married and gender specialization. *Journal of Marriage and Family, 78*(3), 759–779.

Mikulincer, Mario & Shaver, Phillip R. (2019). Attachment theory expanded: A behavioral systems approach to personality and social behavior. In Deaux, Kay & Snyder, Mark (Eds.), *The Oxford handbook of personality and social psychology.* Oxford University Press.

Miller, Cindy F.; Martin, Carol Lynn; Fabes, Richard A. & Hanish, Laura D. (2013). Bringing the cognitive and the social together: How gender detectives and gender enforcers shape children's gender development. In Banaji, Mahzarin R. & Gelman, Susan A. (Eds.), *Navigating the social world: What infants, children, and other species can teach us* (pp. 306–313). Oxford University Press.

Miller, Melissa K.; Dowd, M. Denise; Harrison, Christopher J.; Mollen, Cynthia J.; Selvarangan, Rangaraj & Humiston, Sharon. (2015). Prevalence of 3 sexually transmitted infections in a pediatric emergency department. *Pediatric Emergency Care, 31*(2), 107–112.

Miller, Patricia H. (2011). *Theories of developmental psychology* (5th ed.). Worth.

Miller, Patricia H. (2016). *Theories of developmental psychology* (6th ed.). Worth.

Miller, Patricia H. & Aloise-Young, Patricia A. (2018). Revisiting young children's understanding of the psychological causes of behavior. *Child Development, 89*(5).

Miller, Saul L. & Maner, Jon K. (2011). Ovulation as a male mating prime: Subtle signs of women's fertility influence men's mating cognition and behavior. *Journal of Personality and Social Psychology, 100*(2), 295–308.

Miller, Susan W. (2011–2012). Medications and elders: Quality of care or quality of life? *Generations, 35*(4), 19–24.

Miller-Cotto, Dana & Byrnes, James P. (2016). Ethnic/racial identity and academic achievement: A meta-analytic review. *Developmental Review, 41*, 51–70.

Miller-Perrin, Cindy & Wurtele, Sandy K. (2017). Sex trafficking and the commercial sexual exploitation of children. *Women & Therapy, 40*(1/2), 123–151.

Mills, Jon (Ed.) (2004). *Rereading Freud: Psychoanalysis through philosophy.* State University of New York Press.

Mills-Koonce, W. Roger; Garrett-Peters, Patricia; Barnett, Melissa; Granger, Douglas A.; Blair, Clancy & Cox, Martha J. (2011). Father contributions to cortisol responses in infancy and toddlerhood. *Developmental Psychology, 47*(2), 388–395.

Milunsky, Aubrey & Milunsky, Jeff M. (2016). *Genetic disorders and the fetus: Diagnosis, prevention, and treatment* (7th ed.). Wiley-Blackwell.

Ming, Ng Yi & Baharudin, Rozumah. (2017). Maternal attachment and Malaysian adolescents' social responsibility: Path analysis on authoritative parenting as mediator. *Journal of Research in Social Sciences, 5*(1), 22–36.

Mischel, Walter. (2014). *The marshmallow test: Mastering self-control.* Little, Brown.

Mischel, Walter; Ebbesen, Ebbe B. & Raskoff Zeiss, Antonette. (1972). Cognitive and attentional mechanisms in delay of gratification. *Journal of Personality and Social Psychology, 21*(2), 204–218.

Misra, Jordan. (2019, April 23). Voter turnout rates among all voting age and major racial and ethnic groups were higher than in 2014. U.S. Census Bureau.

Mitchell, Daniel J. & Cusack, Rhodri. (2018). Visual short-term memory through the lifespan: Preserved benefits of context and metacognition. *Psychology and Aging, 33*(5), 841–854.

Mitchell, Lauren L.; Zmora, Rachel; Finlay, Jessica M.; Jutkowitz, Eric & Gaugler, Joseph E. (2020). Do Big Five personality traits moderate the effects of stressful life events on health trajectories? Evidence from the health and retirement study. *The Journals of Gerontology: Series B,* (In Press), gbaa075.

Miyake, Akira & Shah, Priti (Eds.). (1999). *Models of working memory: Mechanisms of active maintenance and executive control.* Cambridge University Press.

Miyata, Susanne; MacWhinney, Brian; Otomo, Kiyoshi; Sirai, Hidetosi; Oshima-Takane, Yuriko; Hirakawa, Makiko; . . . Itoh, Keiko. (2013). Developmental sentence scoring for Japanese. *First Language, 33*(2), 200–216.

Mize, Krystal D. & Jones, Nancy Aaron. (2012). Infant physiological and behavioral responses to loss of maternal attention to a social-rival. *International Journal of Psychophysiology, 83*(1), 16–23.

Mize, Krystal D.; Pineda, Melannie; Blau, Alexis K.; Marsh, Kathryn & Jones, Nancy A. (2014). Infant physiological and behavioral responses to a jealousy provoking condition. *Infancy, 19*(3), 338–348.

MMWR. (2008, January 18). *School-associated student homicides—United States, 1992–2006. Morbidity and Mortality Weekly Report, 57*(2), 33–36. Atlanta, GA: U.S. Department of Health and Human Services, Centers for Disease Control and Prevention.

MMWR. (2012, June 8). *Youth risk behavior surveillance—United States, 2011. Morbidity and Mortality Weekly Report, 61*(4). Atlanta, GA: U.S. Department of Health and Human Services, Centers for Disease Control and Prevention.

MMWR. (2013, April 5). *Blood lead levels in children aged 1–5 Years—United States, 1999–2010.*

Morbidity and Mortality Weekly Report, 62(13), 245–248. Atlanta, GA: U.S. Department of Health and Human Services, Centers for Disease Control and Prevention.

MMWR. (2014, March 28). *Prevalence of autism spectrum disorder among children aged 8 years—Autism and Developmental Disabilities Monitoring Network, 11 sites, United States, 2010. Morbidity and Mortality Weekly Report*, 63(2). Atlanta, GA: U.S. Department of Health and Human Services, Centers for Disease Control and Prevention.

MMWR. (2016, October 14). *QuickStats: Gestational weight gain among women with full-term, singleton births, compared with recommendations—48 states and the District of Columbia, 2015. Morbidity and Mortality Weekly Report*, 65(40), 1121. Atlanta, GA: Centers for Disease Control and Prevention.

MMWR. (2018, June 15). *Youth risk behavior surveillance—United States, 2017. Morbidity and Mortality Weekly Report*, 67(8). Atlanta, GA: U.S. Department of Health and Human Services, Centers for Disease Control and Prevention.

MMWR. (2020, May 15). *Preliminary estimate of excess mortality during the COVID-19 outbreak—New York City, March 11–May 2, 2020. Morbidity and Mortality Weekly Report*, 69(19), 603–605. Atlanta, GA: Centers for Disease Control and Prevention.

Mochrie, Kirk D.; Whited, Mathew C.; Cellucci, Tony; Freeman, Taylor & Corson, Ansley Taylor. (2020). ADHD, depression, and substance abuse risk among beginning college students. *Journal of American College Health*, 68(1), 6–10.

Moffitt, Terrie E. (2003). Life-course-persistent and adolescence-limited antisocial behavior: A 10-year research review and a research agenda. In Lahey, Benjamin B.; Moffitt, Terrie E. & Caspi, Avshalom (Eds.), *Causes of conduct disorder and juvenile delinquency* (pp. 49–75). Guilford Press.

Moffitt, Terrie E.; Caspi, Avshalom; Rutter, Michael & Silva, Phil A. (2001). *Sex differences in antisocial behaviour: Conduct disorder, delinquency, and violence in the Dunedin Longitudinal Study*. Cambridge University Press.

Moghimi, Darya; Zacher, Hannes; Scheibe, Susanne & Van Yperen, Nico W. (2017). The selection, optimization, and compensation model in the work context: A systematic review and meta-analysis of two decades of research. *Journal of Organizational Behavior*, 38(2), 247–275.

Mojtabai, Ramin; Stuart, Elizabeth A.; Hwang, Irving; Eaton, William W.; Sampson, Nancy & Kessler, Ronald C. (2015). Long-term effects of mental disorders on educational attainment in the National Comorbidity Survey ten-year follow-up. *Social Psychiatry and Psychiatric Epidemiology*, 50(10), 1577–1591.

Moles, Laura; Manzano, Susana; Fernández, Leonides; Montilla, Antonia; Corzo, Nieves; Ares, Susana; . . . Espinosa-Martos, Irene. (2015). Bacteriological, biochemical, and immunological properties of colostrum and mature milk from mothers of extremely preterm infants. *Journal of Pediatric Gastroenterology & Nutrition*, 60(1), 120–126.

Moll, Jorge; de Oliveira-Souza, Ricardo; Moll, Fernanda Tovar; Ignácio, Fátima Azevedo; Bramati, Ivanei E.; Caparelli-Dáquer,

Egas M. & Eslinger, Paul J. (2005). The moral affiliations of disgust: A functional MRI study. *Cognitive and Behavioral Neurology*, 18(1), 68–78.

Möller, Jette; Björkenstam, Emma; Ljung, Rickard & Åberg Yngwe, Monica. (2011). Widowhood and the risk of psychiatric care, psychotropic medication and all-cause mortality: A cohort study of 658,022 elderly people in Sweden. *Aging & Mental Health*, 15(2), 259–266.

Møller, Signe J. & Tenenbaum, Harriet R. (2011). Danish majority children's reasoning about exclusion based on gender and ethnicity. *Child Development*, 82(2), 520–532.

Monahan, Kathryn C.; Steinberg, Laurence; Cauffman, Elizabeth & Mulvey, Edward P. (2013). Psychosocial (im)maturity from adolescence to early adulthood: Distinguishing between adolescence-limited and persisting antisocial behavior. *Development and Psychopathology*, 25(4), 1093–1105.

Mondal, Debapriya; Galloway, Tamara S.; Bailey, Trevor C. & Mathews, Fiona. (2014). Elevated risk of stillbirth in males: Systematic review and meta-analysis of more than 30 million births. *BMC Medicine*, 12(220).

Money, John & Ehrhardt, Anke A. (1972). *Man & woman, boy & girl: The differentiation and dimorphism of gender identity from conception to maturity*. Johns Hopkins University Press.

Montag, Christian & Panksepp, Jaak. (2017). Primary emotional systems and personality: An evolutionary perspective. *Frontiers in Psychology*, 8(464).

Montero-Odasso, Manuel M.; Sarquis-Adamson, Yanina; Speechley, Mark; Borrie, Michael J.; Hachinski, Vladimir C.; Wells, Jennie; . . . Muir-Hunter, Susan. (2017). Association of dual-task gait with incident dementia in mild cognitive impairment: Results from the gait and brain study. *JAMA Neurology*, 74(7), 857–865.

Montgomery, Heather. (2015). Understanding child prostitution in Thailand in the 1990s. *Child Development Perspectives*, 9(3), 154–157.

Monti, Jennifer D.; Rudolph, Karen D. & Miernicki, Michelle E. (2017). Rumination about social stress mediates the association between peer victimization and depressive symptoms during middle childhood. *Journal of Applied Developmental Psychology*, 48, 25–32.

Monto, Martin A. & Carey, Anna G. (2014). A new standard of sexual behavior? Are claims associated with the "hookup culture" supported by general social survey data? *The Journal of Sex Research*, 51(6), 605–615.

Moody, Raymond A. (1975). *Life after life: The investigation of a phenomenon—Survival of bodily death*. Mockingbird Books.

Mooi-Reci, Irma; Bakker, Bart; Curry, Matthew & Wooden, Mark. (2019). Why parental unemployment matters for children's educational attainment: Empirical evidence from the Netherlands. *European Sociological Review*, 35(3), 394–408.

Moore, Kendra A.; Rubin, Emily B. & Halpern, Scott D. (2016). The problems with physician orders for life-sustaining treatment. *JAMA*, 315(3), 259–260.

Moore-Petinak, N'dea; Waselewski, Marika; Patterson, Blaire Alma & Chang, Tammy. (2020). Active shooter drills in the United States:

A national study of youth experiences and perceptions. *Journal of Adolescent Health*, 67(4), 509–513.

Morales, Julia; Calvo, Alejandra & Bialystok, Ellen. (2013). Working memory development in monolingual and bilingual children. *Journal of Experimental Child Psychology*, 114(2), 187–202.

Moran, Lyndsey R.; Lengua, Liliana J. & Zalewski, Maureen. (2013). The interaction between negative emotionality and effortful control in early social-emotional development. *Social Development*, 22(2), 340–362.

Morawska, Alina; Dittman, Cassandra K. & Rusby, Julie C. (2019). Promoting self-regulation in young children: The role of parenting interventions. *Clinical Child and Family Psychology Review*, 22, 43–51.

Moreira, Pollyana De Lucena; Rique Neto, Júlio; Sabucedo, José Manuel & Camino, Cleonice Pereira Dos Santos. (2018). Moral judgment, political ideology and collective action. *Scandinavian Journal of Psychology*, 59(6), 610–620.

Morelli, Gilda; Quinn, Naomi; Chaudhary, Nandita; Vicedo, Marga; Rosabal-Coto, Mariano; Keller, Heidi; . . . Takada, Akira. (2018). Ethical challenges of parenting interventions in low- to middle-income countries. *Journal of Cross-Cultural Psychology*, 49(1), 5–24.

Morelli, Gilda A.; Chaudhary, Nandita; Gottlieb, Alma; Keller, Heidi; Murray, Marjorie; Quinn, Naomi; . . . Vicedo, Marga. (2017). Taking culture seriously a pluralistic approach to attachment. In Keller, Heidi & Bard, Kim A. (Eds.), *The cultural nature of attachment: Contextualizing relationships and development* (pp. 139–170). MIT Press.

Moreno, Sylvain; Lee, Yunjo; Janus, Monika & Bialystok, Ellen. (2015). Short-term second language and music training induces lasting functional brain changes in early childhood. *Child Development*, 86(2), 394–406.

Morgan, Daniel M.; Kamdar, Neil S.; Swenson, Carolyn W.; Kobernik, Emily K.; Sammarco, Anne G. & Nallamothu, Brahmajee. (2018). Nationwide trends in the utilization of and payments for hysterectomy in the united states among commercially insured women. *Obstetrical & Gynecological Survey*, 73(8), 454–455.

Morgan, David L. (2018). Living within blurry boundaries: The value of distinguishing between qualitative and quantitative research. *Journal of Mixed Methods Research*, 12(3), 268–279.

Morgan, Ian G.; Ohno-Matsui, Kyoko & Saw, Seang-Mei. (2012). Myopia. *The Lancet*, 379(9827), 1739–1748.

Morley, Andrew P.; Narayanan, Madan; Mines, Rebecca; Molokhia, Ashraf; Baxter, Sebastian; Craig, Gavin; . . . Craig, Ian. (2012). VPR1A and SLC6A4 polymorphisms in choral singers and non-musicians: A gene association study. *PLoS ONE*, 7(2), e31763.

Morning, Ann. (2008). Ethnic classification in global perspective: A cross-national survey of the 2000 census round. *Population Research and Policy Review*, 27(2), 239–272.

Morris, Danielle H.; Jones, Michael E.; Schoemaker, Minouk J.; Ashworth, Alan & Swerdlow, Anthony J. (2011). Familial concordance for age at natural menopause: Results from the Breakthrough Generations Study. *Menopause*, 18(9), 956–961.

Morris, Matthew C.; Marco, Miriam; Maguire-Jack, Kathryn; Kouros, Chrystyna D.; Im, Wansoo; White, Codi; . . . Garber, Judy. (2019). County-level socioeconomic and crime risk factors for substantiated child abuse and neglect. *Child Abuse & Neglect, 90,* 127–138.

Morrissey, Taryn W.; Hutchison, Lindsey & Winsler, Adam. (2014). Family income, school attendance, and academic achievement in elementary school. *Developmental Psychology, 50*(3), 741–753.

Moshman, David. (2018). Metacognitive theories revisited. *Educational Psychology Review, 30,* 599–606.

Mostafa, Taymour; Khouly, Ghada El & Hassan, Ashraf. (2012). Pheromones in sex and reproduction: Do they have a role in humans? *Journal of Advanced Research, 3*(1), 1–9.

Motie, Ian; Carretta, Henry J. & Beitsch, Leslie M. (2020). Needling policy makers and sharpening the debate: Do syringe exchange programs improve health at the population level? *JPHMP, 26*(3), 222–226.

Moussa, Osama M.; Erridge, Simon; Chidambaram, Swathikan; Ziprin, Paul; Darzi, Ara & Purkayastha, Sanjay. (2019). Mortality of the severely obese: A population study. *Annals of Surgery, 269*(6), 1087–1091.

Mroczek, Daniel K. (2020). Personality and healthy aging in 1945 and 2020: Reflecting on 75 years of research and theory. *The Journals of Gerontology: Series B, 75*(3), 471–473.

Mueller, Gerhard; Palli, Christoph & Schumacher, Petra. (2019). The effect of therapeutic touch on back pain in adults on a neurological unit: An experimental pilot study. *Pain Management Nursing, 20*(1), 75–81.

Mukku, Shiva Shanker Reddy; Harbishettar, Vijaykumar & Sivakumar, P. T. (2018). Psychological morbidity after job retirement: A review. *Asian Journal of Psychiatry, 37,* 58–63.

Mullally, Sinéad L. & Maguire, Eleanor A. (2014). Learning to remember: The early ontogeny of episodic memory. *Developmental Cognitive Neuroscience, 9*(13), 12–29.

Mullis, Ina V. S.; Martin, Michael O.; Foy, Pierre & Arora, A. (2012a). *TIMSS 2011 international results in mathematics.* Chestnut Hill, MA: TIMSS & PIRLS International Study Center, Boston College.

Mullis, Ina V. S.; Martin, Michael O.; Foy, Pierre & Drucker, Kathleen T. (2012b). *PIRLS 2011 international results in reading.* Chestnut Hill, MA: TIMSS & PIRLS International Study Center, Boston College.

Mullis, Ina V. S.; Martin, Michael O.; Foy, Pierre & Hooper, Martin. (2017a). *International results in reading PIRLS 2016.* Chestnut Hill, MA: TIMSS & PIRLS International Study Center, Boston College.

Mullis, Ina V. S.; Martin, Michael O.; Kennedy, Ann M. & Foy, Pierre. (2007b). International student achievement in reading. In *IEA's progress in international reading literacy study in primary school in 40 countries* (pp. 35–64). TIMSS & PIRLS International Study Center, Boston College.

Munawar, Khadeeja; Kuhn, Sara K. & Haque, Shamsul. (2018). Understanding the reminiscence bump: A systematic review. *PLoS ONE, 13*(12), e0208595.

Murphy, Colleen; Gardoni, Paolo & McKim, Robert (Eds.). (2018). *Climate change and its impacts: Risks and inequalities.* Springer.

Murphy, Sherry L.; Xu, Jiaquan; Kochanek, Kenneth D. & Arias, Elizabeth. (2018). *Mortality in the United States, 2017. NCHS Data Brief,* (328). Hyattsville, MD: National Center for Health Statistics.

Murphy, Tia Panfile; McCurdy, Kelsey; Jehl, Brianna; Rowan, Megan & Larrimore, Kelsey. (2020). Jealousy behaviors in early childhood: Associations with attachment and temperament. *International Journal of Behavioral Development, 44*(3), 266–272.

Murray, Thomas H. (2014). Stirring the simmering "designer baby" pot. *Science, 343*(6176), 1208–1210.

Mynttinen, Mari; Pietilä, Anna-Maija & Kangasniemi, Mari. (2017). What does parental involvement mean in preventing adolescents' use of alcohol? An integrative review. *Journal of Child & Adolescent Substance Abuse, 26*(4), 338–351.

Nabors, Laura; Odar Stough, Cathy; Garr, Katlyn & Merianos, Ashley. (2019). Predictors of victimization among youth who are overweight in a national sample. *Pediatric Obesity, 14*(7), e12516.

NAEYC. (2014). *NAEYC Early Childhood Program standards and accreditation criteria & guidance for assessment.* Washington, DC: National Association for the Education of Young Children.

Nagy, Emese; Pilling, Karen; Orvos, Hajnalka & Molnar, Peter. (2013). Imitation of tongue protrusion in human neonates: Specificity of the response in a large sample. *Developmental Psychology, 49*(9), 1628–1638.

Nair, Pushpa; Bhanu, Cini; Frost, Rachael; Buszewicz, Marta & Walters, Kate R. (2020). A systematic review of older adults' attitudes towards depression and its treatment. *The Gerontologist, 60*(1), e93–e104.

Nanji, Ayaz. (2005, February 8). World's smallest baby goes home. *CBS News.* AP.

National Center for Education Statistics. (2018). *The nation's report card.* Washington, DC: Institute of Education Sciences, U.S. Department of Education.

National Center for Education Statistics. (2018, September). *Table 502.30. Median annual earnings of full-time year-round workers 25 to 34 years old and full-time year-round workers as a percentage of the labor force, by sex, race/ethnicity, and educational attainment: Selected years, 1995 through 2017.* Washington, DC: Institute of Education Sciences, U.S. Department of Education.

National Center for Education Statistics. (2019, February). *Indicator 24: Degrees awarded. Status and trends in the education of racial and ethnic groups.* Washington, DC: Institute of Education Sciences, U.S. Department of Education.

National Center for Education Statistics. (2019, January). Fast facts: Race/ethnicity of college faculty.

National Center for Education Statistics. (2020, May). Students with disabilities. The Condition of Education. National Center for Education Statistics, Institute of Education Sciences.

National Center for Health Statistics. (2012). *Health, United States, 2011: With special feature on socioeconomic status and health.* Hyattsville, MD: U.S. Department of Health and Human Services, Centers for Disease Control and Prevention.

National Center for Health Statistics. (2017). *Health, United States, 2016: With chartbook on long-term trends in health.* Hyattsville, MD: U.S. Department of Health and Human Services.

National Center for Health Statistics. (2018). *Health, United States, 2017: With a special feature on mortality.* Hyattsville, MD: U.S. Department of Health and Human Services.

National Center for Health Statistics. (2019). *Health, United States, 2018.* Hyattsville, MD: U.S. Department of Health and Human Services.

National Center for Health Statistics. (2019, October). Table 25: Participation in leisure-time aerobic and muscle-strengthening activities that meet the federal 2008 *Physical Activity Guidelines for Americans* among adults aged 18 and over, by selected characteristics: United States, selected years 1998–2017. Health, United States, 2018—Data Finder. U.S. Department of Health & Human Services.

National Institute of Mental Health. (2020, September). Suicide. U.S. Department of Health and Human Services.

Needleman, Herbert L. & Gatsonis, Constantine A. (1990). Low-level lead exposure and the IQ of children: A meta-analysis of modern studies. *JAMA, 263*(5), 673–678.

Needleman, Herbert L.; Schell, Alan; Bellinger, David; Leviton, Alan & Allred, Elizabeth N. (1990). The long-term effects of exposure to low doses of lead in childhood. *New England Journal of Medicine, 322*(2), 83–88.

Nehme, Eileen K.; Oluyomi, Abiodun O.; Calise, Tamara Vehige & Kohl, Harold W. (2016). Environmental correlates of recreational walking in the neighborhood. *American Journal of Health Promotion, 30*(3), 139–148.

Neimeyer, Robert A. (2017). Series foreword. In Klass, Dennis & Steffen, Edith Maria (Eds.), *Continuing bonds in bereavement: New directions for research and practice.* Routledge.

Nelson, Helen; Kendall, Garth; Burns, Sharyn; Schonert-Reichl, Kimberly & Kane, Robert. (2019). Development of the student experience of teacher support scale: Measuring the experience of children who report aggression and bullying. *International Journal of Bullying Prevention, 1*(2), 99–110.

Nelson, Theodora; East, Patricia; Delva, Jorge; Lozoff, Betsy & Gahagan, Sheila. (2019). Children's inattention and hyperactivity, mother's parenting, and risk behaviors in adolescence: A 10-year longitudinal study of Chilean children. *Journal of Developmental & Behavioral Pediatrics, 40*(4), 249–256.

Nesse, Randolph M. & Stein, Dan J. (2012). Towards a genuinely medical model for psychiatric nosology. *BMC Medicine, 10*(5).

Netting, Nancy S. & Reynolds, Meredith K. (2018). Thirty years of sexual behaviour at a Canadian university: Romantic relationships, hooking up, and sexual choices. *The Canadian Journal of Human Sexuality, 27*(1), 55–68.

Neumann, Peter J.; Anderson, Jordan E.; Panzer, Ari D.; Pope, Elle F.; D'Cruz, Brittany N.; Kim, David D. & Cohen, Joshua T. (2018). Comparing the cost-per-QALYs gained and cost-per-DALYs averted literatures. *Gates Open Research, 2*(5).

Neumann, Peter J. & Cohen, Joshua T. (2018). QALYs in 2018—Advantages and concerns. *JAMA, 319*(24), 2473–2474.

Nevanen, Saila; Juvonen, Antti & Ruismäki, Heikki. (2014). Does arts education develop school readiness? Teachers' and artists' points of view on an art education project. *Arts Education Policy Review, 115*(3), 72–81.

Nevin, Rick. (2007). Understanding international crime trends: The legacy of preschool lead exposure. *Environmental Research, 104*(3), 315–336.

Newman, Ian M.; Ding, Lanyan; Shell, Duane F. & Lin, Lida. (2017). How social reactions to alcohol-related facial flushing are affected by gender, relationship, and drinking purposes: Implications for education to reduce aerodigestive cancer risks. *International Journal of Environmental Research and Public Health, 14*(6).

Newman, Michelle G. & Zainal, Nur Hani. (2020). The value of maintaining social connections for mental health in older people. *The Lancet Public Health, 5*(1), e12–e13.

Ng, Florrie Fei-Yin; Pomerantz, Eva M. & Deng, Ciping. (2014). Why are Chinese mothers more controlling than American mothers? "My child is my report card." *Child Development, 85*(1), 355–369.

Nice, Lindsey; Knudson-Martin, Carmen; Lough, Aubrey; Castillo, Nakisha & Doe, Kimberly. (2020). Patterns that challenge and sustain mutuality as retired couples negotiate gendered power. *Family Relations, 69*(1), 195–206.

Nichols, Emily S.; Wild, Conor J.; Stojanoski, Bobby; Battista, Michael E. & Owen, Adrian M. (2020). Bilingualism affords no general cognitive advantages: A population study of executive function in 11,000 people. *Psychological Science, 31*(5), 548–567.

Nichols, Emma; Szoeke, Cassandra E. I.; Vollset, Stein Emil; Abbasi, Nooshin; Abd-Allah, Foad; Abdela, Jemal; . . . Murray, Christopher J. L. (2019). Global, regional, and national burden of Alzheimer's disease and other dementias, 1990–2016: A systematic analysis for the Global Burden of Disease Study 2016. *The Lancet Neurology, 18*, 88–106.

Nichols, Leslie (Ed.) (2019). *Working women in Canada: An intersectional approach.* Women's Press.

Nichols, Shaun; Strohminger, Nina; Rai, Arun & Garfield, Jay. (2018). Death and the self. *Cognitive Science, 42*(Supp. 1), 314–332.

Nicolopoulou, Ageliki. (1993). Play, cognitive development, and the social world: Piaget, Vygotsky, and beyond. *Human Development, 36*(1), 1–23.

Niederdeppe, Jeff; Gollust, Sarah E. & Barry, Colleen L. (2014). Inoculation in competitive framing: Examining message effects on policy preferences. *Public Opinion Quarterly, 78*(3), 634–655.

Nielsen, Linda. (2018). Joint versus sole physical custody: Children's outcomes independent of parent–child relationships, income, and conflict in 60 studies. *Journal of Divorce & Remarriage, 59*(4), 247–281.

Nieto, Marta; Romero, Dulce; Ros, Laura; Zabala, Carmen; Martínez, Manuela; Ricarte, Jorge J.; . . . Latorre, Jose M. (2019). Differences in coping strategies between young and older adults: The role of executive functions. *The International Journal of Aging and Human Development,* (In Press).

Nigg, Joel T. & Barkley, Russell A. (2014). Attention-deficit/hyperactivity disorder. In Mash, Eric J. & Barkley, Russell A. (Eds.), *Child psychopathology* (3rd ed., pp. 75–144). Guilford Press.

Nilwik, Rachel; Snijders, Tim; Leenders, Marika; Groen, Bart B. L.; van Kranenburg, Janneau; Verdijk, Lex B. & van Loon, Luc J. C. (2013). The decline in skeletal muscle mass with aging is mainly attributed to a reduction in type II muscle fiber size. *Experimental Gerontology, 48*(5), 492–498.

Nimrod, Galit. (2019). Aging well in the digital age: Technology in processes of selective optimization with compensation. *The Journals of Gerontology: Series B*(gbz111).

Nock, Matthew K.; Deming, Charlene A.; Fullerton, Carol S.; Gilman, Stephen E.; Goldenberg, Matthew; Kessler, Ronald C.; . . . Ursano, Robert J. (2013). Suicide among soldiers: A review of psychosocial risk and protective factors. *Psychiatry, 76*(2), 97–125.

Noda, Hideo. (2020). Work–life balance and life satisfaction in OECD countries: A cross-sectional analysis. *Journal of Happiness Studies, 21*, 1325–1348.

Noel, Melanie; Palermo, Tonya M.; Chambers, Christine T.; Taddio, Annah & Hermann, Christiane. (2015). Remembering the pain of childhood: Applying a developmental perspective to the study of pain memories. *Pain, 156*(1), 31–34.

Noll, Jennie G.; Guastaferro, Kate; Beal, Sarah J.; Schreier, Hannah M. C.; Barnes, Jaclyn; Reader, Jonathan M. & Font, Sarah A. (2019). Is sexual abuse a unique predictor of sexual risk behaviors, pregnancy, and motherhood in adolescence? *Journal of Research on Adolescence, 29*(4), 967–983.

Noll, Jennie G.; Trickett, Penelope K.; Long, Jeffrey D.; Negriff, Sonya; Susman, Elizabeth J.; Shalev, Idan; . . . Putnam, Frank W. (2017). Childhood sexual abuse and early timing of puberty. *Journal of Adolescent Health, 60*(1), 65–71.

Norman, Geoffrey R.; Grierson, Lawrence E. M.; Sherbino, Jonathan; Hamstra, Stanley J.; Schmidt, Henk G. & Mamede, Silvia. (2018). Expertise in medicine and surgery. In Ericsson, K. Anders; Hoffman, Robert R.; Kozbelt, Aaron & Williams, A. Mark (Eds.), *The Cambridge handbook of expertise and expert performance* (2nd ed., pp. 331–355). Cambridge University Press.

Norman, Kenneth & Schacter, Daniel. (2014). Implicit memory, explicit memory, and false recollection: A cognitive neuroscience perspective. In Reder, Lynne M. (Ed.), *Implicit memory and metacognition.* Psychology Press.

North, Michael S. (2015). Ageism stakes its claim in the social sciences. *Generations, 39*(3), 29–33.

Notaras, Michael & van den Buuse, Maarten. (2019). Brain-derived neurotrophic factor (BDNF): Novel insights into regulation and genetic variation. *Neuroscientist, 25*(5), 434–454.

Nowak, Bartłomiej; Brzóska, Paweł; Piotrowski, Jarosław; Sedikides, Constantine; Żemojtel-Piotrowska, Magdalena & Jonason, Peter K. (2020). Adaptive and maladaptive behavior during the COVID-19 pandemic: The roles of dark triad traits, collective narcissism, and health beliefs. *Personality and Individual Differences, 167*(110232).

Nowaskie, Dusitn; Austrom, Mary & Morhardt, Darby. (2019). Understanding the challenges, needs, and qualities of frontotemporal dementia family caregivers. *The American Journal of Geriatric Psychiatry, 27*(3, Suppl.), S98–S99.

Nozadi, Sara S.; Henderson, Heather A.; Degnan, Kathryn A. & Fox, Nathan A. (2020). Longitudinal patterns of anger reactivity and risk-taking: The role of peer-context. *Social Development, 29*(2), 600–614.

Nulman, Irena; Shulman, Talya & Liu, Feiyuan. (2018). Fetal alcohol spectrum disorder. In Slikker, William; Paule, Merle G. & Wang, Cheng (Eds.), *Handbook of developmental neurotoxicology* (2nd ed.). Academic Press.

Núñez, Rafael; Allen, Michael; Gao, Richard; Rigoli, Carson Miller; Relaford-Doyle, Josephine & Semenuks, Arturs. (2019). What happened to cognitive science? *Nature Human Behaviour, 3*, 782–791.

O'Brien, Ed & Kassirer, Samantha. (2019). People are slow to adapt to the warm glow of giving. *Psychological Science, 30*(2), 193–204.

O'Brien, Kimberly H. McManama; Nicolopoulos, Alexandra; Almeida, Joanna; Aguinaldo, Laika D. & Rosen, Rochelle K. (2019). Why adolescents attempt suicide: A qualitative study of the transition from ideation to action. *Archives of Suicide Research,* (In Press).

O'Brien, Paul E.; Hindle, Annemarie; Brennan, Leah; Skinner, Stewart; Burton, Paul; Smith, Andrew; . . . Brown, Wendy. (2019). Long-term outcomes after bariatric surgery: A systematic review and meta-analysis of weight loss at 10 or more years for all bariatric procedures and a single-centre review of 20-year outcomes after adjustable gastric banding. *Obesity Surgery, 29*, 3–14.

O'Connor, Alison M.; Dykstra, Victoria W. & Evans, Angela D. (2020). Executive functions and young children's lie-telling and lie maintenance. *Developmental Psychology, 56*(7), 1278–1289.

O'Connor, Daryl B.; Thayer, Julian F & Vedhara, Kavita. (2021). Stress and health: A review of psychobiological processes. *Annual Review of Psychology, 72*.

O'Connor, George T.; Lynch, Susan V.; Bloomberg, Gordon R.; Kattan, Meyer; Wood, Robert A.; Gergen, Peter J.; . . . Gern, James E. (2018). Early-life home environment and risk of asthma among inner-city children. *Journal of Allergy and Clinical Immunology, 141*(4), 1468–1475.

O'Donoghue, Lisa; Rudnicka, Alicja R.; McClelland, Julie F.; Logan, Nicola S. & Saunders, Kathryn J. (2012). Visual acuity measures do not reliably detect childhood refractive error—An epidemiological study. *PLoS ONE*, 7(3), e34441.

O'Meara, Madison S. & South, Susan C. (2019). Big Five personality domains and relationship satisfaction: Direct effects and correlated change over time. *Journal of Personality*, 87(6), 1206–1220.

O'Reilly, Karin; Peterson, Candida C. & Wellman, Henry M. (2014). Sarcasm and advanced theory of mind understanding in children and adults with prelingual deafness. *Developmental Psychology*, 50(7), 1862–1877.

Ober, Carole; Sperling, Anne I.; Von Mutius, Erika & Vercelli, Donata. (2017). Immune development and environment: Lessons from Amish and Hutterite children. *Current Opinion in Immunology*, 48, 51–60.

Oberfield, Zachary W. (2020). Parent engagement and satisfaction in public charter and district schools. *American Educational Research Journal*, 57(3), 1083–1124.

Oden, Melita H. & Terman, Lewis M. (1959). *The gifted group at mid-life: Thirty-five years, follow-up of the superior child.* Stanford University Press.

Odgers, Candice L. & Adler, Nancy E. (2018). Challenges for low-income children in an era of increasing income inequality. *Child Development Perspectives*, 12(2), 128–133.

OECD. (2014). *Education at a glance 2014: OECD Indicators.* Paris, France: Organisation for Economic Cooperation and Development.

OECD. (2019). *Secondary graduation rate: Upper secondary, men / upper secondary, women, percentage, 2016.* OECDiLibrary [Data set].

OECD. (2020). *Population with tertiary education (indicator)* [Data set].

OECD Family Database. (2019, August). PF2.1. Parental leave systems.

Ogbo, Felix Akpojene; Mathsyaraja, Sruthi; Koti, Rajeendra Kashyap; Perz, Janette & Page, Andrew. (2018). The burden of depressive disorders in South Asia, 1990–2016: Findings from the global burden of disease study. *BMC Psychiatry*, 18(333).

Ogden, Cynthia L.; Fakhouri, Tala H.; Carroll, Margaret D.; Hales, Craig M.; Fryar, Cheryl D.; Li, Xianfen & Freedman, David S. (2017, December 22). *Prevalence of obesity among adults, by household income and education—United States, 2011–2014. Morbidity and Mortality Weekly Report,* 66(50), 1369–1373. Atlanta, GA: Centers for Disease Control and Prevention.

Oh, Yoonkyung; Greenberg, Mark T. & Willoughby, Michael T. (2020). Examining longitudinal associations between externalizing and internalizing behavior problems at within- and between-child levels. *Journal of Abnormal Child Psychology*, 48(4), 467–480.

Ohayon, Maurice M. & Schatzberg, Alan F. (2010). Social phobia and depression: Prevalence and comorbidity. *Journal of Psychosomatic Research*, 68(3), 235–243.

Oliffe, John L.; Rossnagel, Emma; Seidler, Zac E.; Kealy, David; Ogrodniczuk, John S. & Rice, Simon M. (2019). Men's depression and suicide. *Current Psychiatry Reports*, 21(103).

Olmstead, Spencer B. (2020). A decade review of sex and partnering in adolescence and young adulthood. *Journal of Marriage and Family*, 82(2), 769–795.

Olweus, Dan. (1993). *Bullying at school: What we know and what we can do.* Wiley.

Oregon Public Health Division. (2018). *Oregon Death with Dignity Act: 2017 data summary.* Portland, OR: Oregon Health Authority, Public Health Division.

Oregon Public Health Division. (2019, February 15). *Oregon Death with Dignity Act: 2018 data summary.* Portland, OR: Oregon Health Authority, Public Health Division.

Oregon Public Health Division. (2020, March 6). *Oregon Death with Dignity Act: 2019 data summary.* Portland, OR: Oregon Health Authority, Public Health Division.

Orth, Ulrich; Erol, Ruth Yasemin & Luciano, Eva C. (2018). Development of self-esteem from age 4 to 94 years: A meta-analysis of longitudinal studies. *Psychological Bulletin*, 144(10), 1045–1080.

Orth, Ulrich & Robins, Richard W. (2019). Development of self-esteem across the lifespan. In Shiner, Rebecca L.; Tackett, Jennifer L. & McAdams, Dan P. (Eds.), *Handbook of personality development* (pp. 328–344). Guilford.

Oswald, Frederick L.; Mitchell, Gregory; Blanton, Hart; Jaccard, James & Tetlock, Philip E. (2013). Predicting ethnic and racial discrimination: A meta-analysis of IAT criterion studies. *Journal of Personality and Social Psychology*, 105(2), 171–192.

Oza-Frank, Reena & Narayan, K. M. Venkat. (2010). Overweight and diabetes prevalence among U.S. immigrants. *American Journal of Public Health*, 100(4), 661–668.

Ozernov-Palchik, Ola; Norton, Elizabeth S.; Sideridis, Georgios; Beach, Sara D.; Wolf, Maryanne; Gabrieli, John D. E. & Gaab, Nadine. (2017). Longitudinal stability of pre-reading skill profiles of kindergarten children: Implications for early screening and theories of reading. *Developmental Science*, 20(5), e12471.

Ozturk, Ozge; Krehm, Madelaine & Vouloumanos, Athena. (2013). Sound symbolism in infancy: Evidence for sound–shape cross-modal correspondences in 4-month-olds. *Journal of Experimental Child Psychology*, 114(2), 173–186.

Padilla-Walker, Laura; Memmott-Elison, Madison & Nelson, Larry. (2017). Positive relationships as an indicator of flourishing during emerging adulthood. In Padilla-Walker, Laura M. & Nelson, Larry J. (Eds.), *Flourishing in emerging adulthood: Positive development during the third decade of life* (pp. 212–235). Oxford University Press.

Pahlke, Erin; Hyde, Janet Shibley & Allison, Carlie M. (2014). The effects of single-sex compared with coeducational schooling on students' performance and attitudes: A meta-analysis. *Psychological Bulletin*, 140(4), 1042–1072.

Paik, Anthony. (2011). Adolescent sexuality and the risk of marital dissolution. *Journal of Marriage and Family*, 73(2), 472–485.

Palmer, Colin J. & Clifford, Colin W. G. (2018). Adaptation to other people's eye gaze reflects habituation of high-level perceptual representations. *Cognition*, 180, 82–90.

Park, Jong-Tae; Jang, Yoonsun; Park, Min Sun; Pae, Calvin; Park, Jinyi; Hu, Kyung-Seok; . . . Kim, Hee-Jin. (2011). The trend of body donation for education based on Korean social and religious culture. *Anatomical Sciences Education*, 4(1), 33–38.

Park, Kee-Boem; Nam, Kyung Eun; Cho, Ah-Ra; Jang, Woori; Kim, Myungshin & Park, Joo Hyun. (2019). Effects of copy number variations on developmental aspects of children with delayed development. *Annals of Rehabilitation Medicine*, 43(2), 215–223.

Parker, Eugene T.; Barnhardt, Cassie L.; Pascarella, Ernest T. & McCowin, Jarvis A. (2016). The impact of diversity courses on college students' moral development. *Journal of College Student Development*, 57(4), 395–410.

Parker, Kim; Horowitz, Juliana Menasce & Stepler, Renee. (2017, December 5). *On gender differences, no consensus on nature vs. nurture: Americans say society places a higher premium on masculinity than on femininity.* Social & Demographic Trends. Washington, DC: Pew Research Center.

Parten, Mildred B. (1932). Social participation among pre-school children. *The Journal of Abnormal and Social Psychology*, 27(3), 243–269.

Pascarella, Ernest T.; Martin, Georgianna L.; Hanson, Jana M.; Trolian, Teniell L.; Gillig, Benjamin & Blaich, Charles. (2014). Effects of diversity experiences on critical thinking skills over 4 years of college. *Journal of College Student Development*, 55(1), 86–92.

Pascarella, Ernest T. & Terenzini, Patrick T. (1991). *How college affects students: Findings and insights from twenty years of research.* Jossey-Bass.

Paschall, Katherine W.; Gershoff, Elizabeth T. & Kuhfeld, Megan. (2018). A two decade examination of historical race/ethnicity disparities in academic achievement by poverty status. *Journal of Youth and Adolescence*, 47, 1164–1177.

Passarino, Giuseppe; De Rango, Francesco & Montesanto, Alberto. (2016). Human longevity: Genetics or Lifestyle? It takes two to tango. *Immunity & Ageing*, 13(12).

Patel, Dhaval; Steinberg, Joel & Patel, Pragnesh. (2018). Insomnia in the elderly: A review. *Journal of Clinical Sleep Medicine*, 14(6), 1017–1024.

Patel, Manisha; Lee, Adria D.; Clemmons, Nakia S.; Redd, Susan B.; Poser, Sarah; Blog, Debra; . . . Gastañaduy, Paul A. (2019, October 11). *National update on measles cases and outbreaks—United States, January 1–October 1, 2019. Morbidity and Mortality Weekly Report.* Atlanta, GA: U.S. Department of Health and Human Services.

Patrinos, Harry Anthony & Psacharopoulos, George. (2020). Returns to education in developing countries, Economics of Education. In Bradley, Steve & Green, Colin (Eds.), *The economics of education: A comprehensive overview* (2nd ed.). Elsevier.

Patterson, Julie A.; Keuler, Nicholas S. & Olson, Beth H. (2019). The effect of maternity practices on exclusive breastfeeding rates in U.S. hospitals. *Maternal and Child Nutrition*, 15(1), e12670.

Paulhus, Delroy L. & Williams, Kevin M. (2002). The Dark Triad of personality: Narcissism, Machiavellianism, and psychopathy. *Journal of Research in Personality*, 36(6), 556–563.

Pauly, Theresa; Michalowski, Victoria I.; Nater, Urs M.; Gerstorf, Denis; Ashe,

Maureen C.; Madden, Kenneth M. & Hoppmann, Christiane A. (2019). Everyday associations between older adults' physical activity, negative affect, and cortisol. *Health Psychology*, 38(6), 494–501.

Pawlik, Amy J. & Kress, John P. (2013). Issues affecting the delivery of physical therapy services for individuals with critical illness. *Physical Therapy*, 93(2), 256–265.

Pearson, Rebecca M.; Evans, Jonathan; Kounali, Daphne; Lewis, Glyn; Heron, Jon; Ramchandani, Paul G.; . . . Stein, Alan. (2013). Maternal depression during pregnancy and the postnatal period: Risks and possible mechanisms for offspring depression at age 18 years. *JAMA Psychiatry*, 70(12), 1312–1319.

Pechmann, Cornelia; Catlin, Jesse R. & Zheng, Yu. (2020). Facilitating adolescent well-being: A review of the challenges and opportunities and the beneficial roles of parents, schools, neighborhoods, and policymakers. *Journal of Consumer Psychology*, 30(1), 149–177.

Peffley, Mark & Hurwitz, Jon. (2010). *Justice in America: The separate realities of Blacks and whites*. Cambridge University Press.

Pellegrini, Anthony D. (2013). Play. In Zelazo, Philip D. (Ed.), *The Oxford handbook of developmental psychology* (Vol. 2, pp. 276–299). Oxford University Press.

Pellis, Sergio M.; Himmler, Brett T.; Himmler, Stephanie M. & Pellis, Vivien C. (2018). Rough-and-tumble play and the development of the social brain: What do we know, how do we know it, and what do we need to know? In Gibb, Robbin & Kolb, Bryan (Eds.), *The neurobiology of brain and behavioral development* (pp. 315–337). Academic Press.

Perkeybile, Allison M.; Carter, C. Sue; Wroblewski, Kelly L.; Puglia, Meghan H.; Kenkel, William M.; Lillard, Travis S.; . . . Connelly, Jessica J. (2019). Early nurture epigenetically tunes the oxytocin receptor. *Psychoneuroendocrinology*, 99, 128–136.

Perlovsky, Leonid; Cabanac, Arnaud; Bonniot-Cabanac, Marie-Claude & Cabanac, Michel. (2013). Mozart Effect, cognitive dissonance, and the pleasure of music. *Behavioural Brain Research*, 244, 9–14.

Peter-Derex, L. (2019). Sleep and memory consolidation. *Neurophysiologie Clinique*, 49(3), 197–198.

Peterson, Candida C. & Wellman, Henry M. (2019). Longitudinal theory of mind (ToM) development from preschool to adolescence with and without ToM delay. *Child Development*, 90(6), 1917–1934.

Peterson, William. (2016). *Places for happiness: Community, self, and performance in the Philippines*. University of Hawaii Press.

Petrides, K. V.; Mikolajczak, Moïra; Mavroveli, Stella; Sanchez-Ruiz, Maria-Jose; Furnham, Adrian & Pérez-González, Juan-Carlos. (2016). Developments in trait emotional intelligence research. *Emotion Review*, 8(4), 335–341.

Pew Research Center. (2009, June 29). *Growing old in America: Expectations vs. reality*. Washington, DC: Pew Research Center.

Pew Research Center. (2017, April 26). *In America, does more education equal less religion. Religion & Public Life*. Washington, DC: Pew Research Center.

Pew Research Center. (2017, September 18). *2015, Hispanic population in the United States statistical portrait: Statistical portrait of Hispanics in the United States. Hispanic Trends*. Washington, DC: Pew Research Center.

Pew Research Center. (2019, March 14). *Political independents: Who they are, what they think. U.S. Politics and Policy*. Washington, DC: Pew Research Center.

Pew Research Center. (2019, May 14). *Majority of public favors same-sex marriage, but divisions persist: Little change in opinion since 2017. U.S. Politics & Policy*. Washington, DC: Pew Research Center.

Pew Research Center. (2019, October 17). *In U.S., decline of Christianity continues at rapid pace: An update on America's changing religious landscape. Religion & Public Life*. Washington, DC: Pew Research Center.

Pfaus, James G.; Scepkowski, Lisa A.; Marson, Lesley & Georgiadis, Janniko R. (2014). Biology of the sexual response. In Tolman, Deborah L.; Diamond, Lisa M.; Bauermeister, José A.; George, William H.; Pfaus, James G. & Ward, L. Monique (Eds.), *APA handbook of sexuality and psychology* (Vol. 1, pp. 145–203). American Psychological Association.

Philbin, Morgan M. & Mauro, Pia M. (2019). Measuring polysubstance use over the life course: Implications for multilevel interventions. *The Lancet*, 6(10), 797–798.

Philbrook, Lauren E.; Saini, Ekjyot K.; Fuller-Rowell, Thomas E.; Buckhalt, Joseph A. & El-Sheikh, Mona. (2020). Socioeconomic status and sleep in adolescence: The role of family chaos. *Journal of Family Psychology*, 34(5), 577–586.

Phillips, Gregory; Beach, Lauren B.; Turner, Blair; Feinstein, Brian A.; Marro, Rachel; Philbin, Morgan M.; . . . Birkett, Michelle. (2019). Sexual identity and behavior among U.S. high school students, 2005–2015. *Archives of Sexual Behavior*, 48(5), 1463–1479.

Piaget, Jean. (1932). *The moral judgment of the child*. K. Paul, Trench, Trubner & Co.

Piaget, Jean. (1950). *The psychology of intelligence*. Routledge & Paul.

Piaget, Jean. (1952). *The origins of intelligence in children*. International Universities Press.

Piaget, Jean. (1962). *Play, dreams and imitation in childhood*. Norton.

Piaget, Jean. (2001). *The psychology of intelligence*. Routledge.

Piaget, Jean. (2011). *The origins of intelligence in children*. Routledge.

Piaget, Jean. (2013a). *The construction of reality in the child*. Routledge.

Piaget, Jean. (2013b). *The moral judgment of the child*. Routledge.

Piaget, Jean. (2013c). *Play, dreams and imitation in childhood*. Routledge.

Piaget, Jean & Inhelder, Bärbel. (1972). *The psychology of the child*. Basic Books.

Piaget, Jean; Voelin-Liambey, Daphne & Berthoud-Papandropoulou, Ioanna. (2015). Problems of class inclusion and logical implication. In Campell, Robert L. (Ed.), *Studies in reflecting abstraction* (pp. 105–137). Psychology Press.

Piazza, Elise A.; Hasenfratz, Liat; Hasson, Uri & Lew-Williams, Casey. (2020). Infant and adult brains are coupled to the dynamics of natural communication. *Psychological Science*, 31(1), 6–17.

Pickles, Andrew; Hill, Jonathan; Breen, Gerome; Quinn, John; Abbott, Kate; Jones, Helen & Sharp, Helen. (2013). Evidence for interplay between genes and parenting on infant temperament in the first year of life: Monoamine oxidase A polymorphism moderates effects of maternal sensitivity on infant anger proneness. *Journal of Child Psychology and Psychiatry*, 54(12), 1308–1317.

Pielnaa, Paul; Al-Saadawe, Moyed; Saro, Adonira; Dama, Marcelllin Faniriantsoahenrio; Zhou, Mei; Huang, Yanxia; . . . Xia, Zanxian. (2020). Zika virus-spread, epidemiology, genome, transmission cycle, clinical manifestation, associated challenges, vaccine and antiviral drug development. *Virology*, 543, 34–42.

Piérard, Gérald E.; Hermanns-Lê, Trinh; Piérard, Sébastien & Piérard-Franchimont, Claudine. (2015). Effects of hormone replacement therapy on skin viscoelasticity during climacteric aging. In Farage, Miranda A.; Miller, Kenneth W.; Woods, Nancy Fugate & Maibach, Howard I. (Eds.), *Skin, mucosa and menopause: Management of clinical issues* (pp. 97–103). Springer.

Pierce, Hayley & Heaton, Tim B. (2019). Cohabitation or marriage? How relationship status and community context influence the well-being of children in developing nations. *Population Research and Policy Review*, 39, 719–737.

Piili, Reetta P.; Metsänoja, Riina; Hinkka, Heikki; Kellokumpu-Lehtinen, Pirkko-Liisa I. & Lehto, Juho T. (2018). Changes in attitudes towards hastened death among Finnish physicians over the past sixteen years. *BMC Medical Ethics*, 19(1).

Pike, Alison & Oliver, Bonamy R. (2017). Child behavior and sibling relationship quality: A cross-lagged analysis. *Journal of Family Psychology*, 31(2), 250–255.

Pilkauskas, Natasha. (2014). Breastfeeding initiation and duration in coresident grandparent, mother and infant households. *Maternal and Child Health Journal*, 18(8), 1955–1963.

Pilkauskas, Natasha V. & Dunifon, Rachel E. (2016). Understanding grandfamilies: Characteristics of grandparents, nonresident parents, and children. *Journal of Marriage and Family*, 78(3), 623–633.

Pillemer, Karl; Suitor, J. Jill & Baltar, Andrés Losada. (2019). Ambivalence, families and care. *International Journal of Care and Caring*, 3(1), 9–22.

Pimentel, Susan. (2013). *College and career readiness standards for adult education*. Washington, DC: U.S. Department of Education.

Pinker, Steven. (2018). *Enlightenment now: The case for reason, science, humanism, and progress*. Viking.

Pinquart, Martin & Kauser, Rubina. (2018). Do the associations of parenting styles with behavior problems and academic achievement vary by culture? Results from a meta-analysis. *Cultural Diversity and Ethnic Minority Psychology*, 24(1), 75–100.

Pinquart, Martin & Silbereisen, Rainer K. (2006). Socioemotional selectivity in cancer patients. *Psychology and Aging*, 21(2), 419–423.

Pinto, Tiago Miguel & Figueiredo, Bárbara. (2019). Attachment and coparenting representations in men during the transition to parenthood. *Infant Mental Health Journal*, 40(6), 850–861.

Pittenger, Samantha L.; Pogue, Jessica K. & Hansen, David J. (2018). Predicting sexual revictimization in childhood and adolescence: A longitudinal examination using ecological systems theory. *Child Maltreatment*, 23(2), 137–146.

Pizot, Cécile; Boniol, Mathieu; Mullie, Patrick; Koechlin, Alice; Boniol, Magali; Boyle, Peter & Autier, Philippe. (2016). Physical activity, hormone replacement therapy and breast cancer risk: A meta-analysis of prospective studies. *European Journal of Cancer*, 52, 138–154.

Plancher, Gaën & Barrouillet, Pierre. (2019). On some of the main criticisms of the modal model: Reappraisal from a TBRS perspective. *Memory and Cognition*.

Planchez, Barbara; Surget, Alexandre & Belzung, Catherine. (2020). Adult hippocampal neurogenesis and antidepressants effects. *Current Opinion in Pharmacology*, 50, 88–95.

Plener, Paul L.; Schumacher, Teresa S.; Munz, Lara M. & Groschwitz, Rebecca C. (2015). The longitudinal course of non-suicidal self-injury and deliberate self-harm: A systematic review of the literature. *Borderline Personality Disorder and Emotion Dysregulation*, 2(1).

Plomin, Robert; DeFries, John C.; Knopik, Valerie S. & Neiderhiser, Jenae M. (2013). *Behavioral genetics*. Worth.

Plutchik, Robert. (1958). Outlines of a new theory of emotion. *Transactions of the New York Academy of Sciences*, 20(5).

Plutchik, Robert. (1991). *The emotions* (Revised ed.). University Press of America.

Polanczyk, Guilherme V.; Willcutt, Erik G.; Salum, Giovanni A.; Kieling, Christian & Rohde, Luis A. (2014). ADHD prevalence estimates across three decades: An updated systematic review and meta-regression analysis. *International Journal of Epidemiology*, 43(2), 434–442.

Polderman, Tinca J. C.; Kreukels, Baudewijntje P. C.; Irwig, Michael S.; Beach, Lauren; Chan, Yee-Ming; Derks, Eske M.; . . . Davis, Lea K. (2018). The biological contributions to gender identity and gender diversity: Bringing data to the table. *Behavior Genetics*, 48(2), 95–108.

Pollock, Ross D.; O'Brien, Katie A.; Daniels, Lorna J.; Nielsen, Kathrine B.; Rowlerson, Anthea; Duggal, Niharika A.; . . . Harridge, Stephen D. R. (2018). Properties of the vastus lateralis muscle in relation to age and physiological function in master cyclists aged 55–79 years. *Aging Cell*, 17(2), e12735.

Poon, Kean. (2018). Hot and cool executive functions in adolescence: Development and contributions to important developmental outcomes. *Frontiers in Psychology*, 8(2311).

Popham, Lauren E. & Hess, Thomas M. (2015). Age differences in the underlying mechanisms of stereotype threat effects. *Journal of Gerontology Series B*, 70(2), 223–232.

Porritt, Laura L.; Zinser, Michael C.; Bachorowski, Jo-Anne & Kaplan, Peter S. (2014). Depression diagnoses and fundamental frequency-based acoustic cues in maternal infant-directed speech. *Language Learning and Development*, 10(1), 51–67.

Portnuff, C. D. F. (2016). Reducing the risk of music-induced hearing loss from overuse of portable listening devices: Understanding the problems and establishing strategies for improving awareness in adolescents. *Adolescent Health, Medicine and Therapeutics*, 2016(1), 27–35.

Poulain, Jean-Pierre. (2017). *The sociology of food: Eating and the place of food in society*. Bloomsbury.

Pouwels, J. Loes; Salmivalli, Christina; Saarento, Silja; Van Den Berg, Yvonne H. M.; Lansu, Tessa A. M. & Cillessen, Antonius H. N. (2017). Predicting adolescents' bullying participation from developmental trajectories of social status and behavior. *Child Development*.

Powell, Cynthia M. (2013). Sex chromosomes, sex chromosome disorders, and disorders of sex development. In Gersen, Steven L. & Keagle, Martha B. (Eds.), *The principles of clinical cytogenetics* (pp. 175–211). Springer.

Powell, Lindsey J.; Hobbs, Kathryn; Bardis, Alexandros; Carey, Susan & Saxe, Rebecca. (2018). Replications of implicit theory of mind tasks with varying representational demands. *Cognitive Development*, 46, 40–50.

Prasad, Sahdeo; Gupta, Subash C. & Aggarwal, Bharat B. (2012). Micronutrients and cancer: Add spice to your life. In Shankar, Sharmila & Srivastava, Rakesh K. (Eds.), *Nutrition, Diet and Cancer* (pp. 23–48).

Pressman, Sarah D.; Jenkins, Brooke N. & Moskowitz, Judith T. (2019). Positive affect and health: What do we know and where next should we go? *Annual Review of Psychology*, 70, 627–650.

Preston, Samuel H.; Vierboom, Yana C. & Stokes, Andrew. (2018). The role of obesity in exceptionally slow US mortality improvement. *PNAS*, 115(5), 957–961.

Preston, Tom & Kelly, Michael. (2006). A medical ethics assessment of the case of Terri Schiavo. *Death Studies*, 30(2), 121–133.

Prime, Heather; Wade, Mark & Browne, Dillon T. (2020). Risk and resilience in family well-being during the COVID-19 pandemic. *American Psychologist*, 75(5), 631–643.

Pritchard, Rory; Chen, Helene; Romoli, Ben; Spitzer, Nicholas C. & Dulcis, Davide. (2020). Photoperiod-induced neurotransmitter plasticity declines with aging: An epigenetic regulation? *Journal of Comparative Neurology*, 528(2), 199–210.

Pronk, Tila M. & Denissen, Jaap J. A. (2020). A rejection mind-set: Choice overload in online dating. *Social Psychological and Personality Science*, 11(3), 388–396.

Puddifoot, Katherine & Bortolotti, Lisa. (2019). Epistemic innocence and the production of false memory beliefs. *Philosophical Studies*, 176(3), 755–780.

Puhl, Rebecca M.; Himmelstein, Mary S. & Pearl, Rebecca L. (2020). Weight stigma as a psychosocial contributor to obesity. *American Psychologist*, 75(2), 274–289.

Pulvermüller, Friedemann. (2018). Neural reuse of action perception circuits for language, concepts and communication. *Progress in Neurobiology*, 160, 1–44.

Qaseem, Amir; Barry, Michael J.; Denberg, Thomas D.; Owens, Douglas K. & Shekelle, Paul. (2013). Screening for prostate cancer: A guidance statement from the clinical guidelines committee of the American College of Physicians. *Annals of Internal Medicine*, 158(10), 761–769.

Qu, Yang; Pomerantz, Eva M.; McCormick, Ethan & Telzer, Eva H. (2018). Youth's conceptions of adolescence predict longitudinal changes in prefrontal cortex activation and risk taking during adolescence. *Child Development*, 89(3), 773–783.

Quas, Jodi A. & Lyon, Thomas D. (2019). Questioning unaccompanied immigrant children: Lessons from developmental science on forensic interviewing. *Child Evidence Brief*, (6).

Quesque, François & Rossetti, Yves. (2020). What do theory-of-mind tasks actually measure? Theory and practice. *Perspectives on Psychological Science*, 15(2), 384–396.

Raabe, Tobias & Beelmann, Andreas. (2011). Development of ethnic, racial, and national prejudice in childhood and adolescence: A multinational meta-analysis of age differences. *Child Development*, 82(6), 1715–1737.

Rabkin, Nick & Hedberg, Eric C. (2011). *Arts education in America: What the declines mean for arts participation*. Washington, DC: National Endowment for the Arts.

Racine, Nicole; Cooke, Jessica E.; Eirich, Rachel; Korczak, Daphne J.; McArthur, Brae-Anne & Madigan, Sheri. (2020). Child and adolescent mental illness during COVID-19: A rapid review. *Psychiatry Research*, 292(113307).

Raj, Anita; Johns, Nicole E.; McDougal, Lotus; Trivedi, Amruta; Bharadwaj, Prashant; Silverman, Jay G.; . . . Singh, Abhishek. (2019). Associations between sex composition of older siblings and infant mortality in India from 1992 to 2016. *EClinicalMedicine*, 14, 14–22.

Rajendran, Khushmand; Trampush, Joey W.; Rindskopf, David; Marks, David J.; O'Neill, Sarah & Halperin, Jeffrey M. (2013). Association between variation in neuropsychological development and trajectory of ADHD severity in early childhood. *The American Journal of Psychiatry*, 170(10), 1205–1211.

Ramírez-Esparza, Nairán; García-Sierra, Adrián & Kuhl, Patricia K. (2017). The impact of early social interactions on later language development in Spanish–English bilingual infants. *Child Development*, 88(4), 1216–1234.

Rao, Melam Ganeswara; Alhusaini, Adel A. & Syamala, Buragadda. (2017). Handwriting performance in elementary school children—Teacher and therapist viewpoint. *Pediatrics & Health Research*, 2(1).

Rapport, Mark D.; Orban, Sarah A.; Kofler, Michael J. & Friedman, Lauren M. (2013). Do programs designed to train working memory, other executive functions, and attention benefit children with ADHD? A meta-analytic review of cognitive, academic, and behavioral outcomes. *Clinical Psychology Review*, 33(8), 1237–1252.

Rashid, Muhammad Humayoun; Zahid, Muhammad Farhan; Zain, Sarmad; Kabir, Ahmad & Hassan, Sibt Ul. (2020). He neuroprotective effects of exercise on cognitive decline: A preventive approach to Alzheimer's disease. *Cureus*, 12(4), e6958.

Rasmussen, Line Jee Hartmann; Moffitt, Terrie E.; Arseneault, Louise; Danese, Andrea; Eugen-Olsen, Jesper; Fisher, Helen L.; . . . Caspi, Avshalom. (2020). Association of adverse experiences and exposure to violence in childhood and adolescence with inflammatory burden in young people. *JAMA Pediatrics, 174*(1), 38–47.

Raspberry, Kelly A. & Skinner, Debra. (2011). Negotiating desires and options: How mothers who carry the fragile X gene experience reproductive decisions. *Social Science & Medicine, 72*(6), 992–998.

Rastrelli, Giulia; Guaraldi, Federica; Reismann, Yacov; Sforza, Alessandra; Isidori, Andrea M.; Maggi, Mario & Corona, Giovanni. (2019). Testosterone replacement therapy for sexual symptoms. *Sexual Medicine Reviews, 7*(3), 464–475.

Rauers, Antje; Blanke, Elisabeth & Riediger, Michaela. (2013). Everyday empathic accuracy in younger and older couples: Do you need to see your partner to know his or her feelings? *Psychological Science, 24*(11), 2210–2217.

Rauscher, Frances H.; Shaw, Gordon L. & Ky, Catherine N. (1993). Music and spatial task performance. *Nature, 365*(6447), 611.

Ravesteijn, Bastian; Van Kippersluis, Hans & Van Doorslaer, Eddy. (2017). The wear and tear on health: What is the role of occupation? *Health Economics, 27*(2), e69–e86.

Rawlins, William K. (2016). Foreword. In Hojjat, Mahzad & Moyer, Anne (Eds.), *The psychology of friendship.* Oxford University Press.

Re, Laura & Birkhoff, Jutta M. (2015). The 47,XYY syndrome, 50 years of certainties and doubts: A systematic review. *Aggression and Violent Behavior, 22*, 9–17.

Read, Nicola; Mulraney, Melissa; McGillivray, Jane & Sciberras, Emma. (2020). Comorbid anxiety and irritability symptoms and their association with cognitive functioning in children with ADHD. *Journal of Abnormal Child Psychology, 48*, 1035–1046.

Reardon, Sean F.; Kalogrides, Demetra & Shores, Kenneth. (2019). The geography of racial/ethnic test score gaps. *American Journal of Sociology, 124*(4), 1164–1221.

Rebetez, Marie My Lien; Rochat, Lucien; Barsics, Catherine & Van Der Linden, Martial. (2018). Procrastination as a self-regulation failure: The role of impulsivity and intrusive thoughts. *Psychological Reports, 121*(1), 26–41.

Reddy, Vasudevi. (2019). Meeting infant affect. *Developmental Psychology, 55*(9).

Redick, Thomas S. (2019). The hype cycle of working memory training. *Current Directions in Psychological Science, 28*(5), 423–429.

Redlich, Ronny; Opel, Nils; Bürger, Christian; Dohm, Katharina; Grotegerd, Dominik; Förster, Katharina; . . . Dannlowski, Udo. (2018). The limbic system in youth depression: Brain structural and functional alterations in adolescent in-patients with severe depression. *Neuropsychopharmacology, 43*, 546–554.

Reed, Andrew E.; Chan, Larry & Mikels, Joseph A. (2014). Meta-analysis of the age-related positivity effect: Age differences in preferences for positive over negative information. *Psychology and Aging, 29*(1), 1–15.

Rees, Elliott & Kirov, George. (2018). The role of copy number variation in psychiatric disorders. In Schulze, Thomas & McMahon, Francis (Eds.), *Psychiatric genetics: A primer for clinical and basic scientists.* Oxford University Press.

Refsnider, Jeanine; Milne-Zelman, Carrie; Warner, Daniel & Janzen, Fredric. (2014). Population sex ratios under differing local climates in a reptile with environmental sex determination. *Evolutionary Ecology, 28*(5), 977–989.

Reher, David & Requena, Miguel. (2018). Living alone in later life: A global perspective. *Population and Development Review, 44*(3), 427–454.

Reid, Keshia M.; Forrest, Jamie R. & Porter, Lauren. (2018, June 1). *Tobacco product use among youths with and without lifetime asthma—Florida, 2016. Morbidity and Mortality Weekly Report, 67*(21), 599–601. Atlanta, GA: Centers for Disease Control and Prevention.

Reilly, David; Neumann, David L. & Andrews, Glenda. (2019). Investigating gender differences in mathematics and science: Results from the 2011 Trends in Mathematics and Science survey. *Research in Science Education, 49*, 25–50.

Reimann, Zakary; Miller, Jacob R.; Dahle, Kaitana M.; Hooper, Audrey P.; Young, Ashley M.; Goates, Michael C.; . . . Crandall, AliceAnn. (2018). Executive functions and health behaviors associated with the leading causes of death in the United States: A systematic review. *Journal of Health Psychology.*

Renzi, Doireann T.; Romberg, Alexa R.; Bolger, Donald J. & Newman, Rochelle Suzanne. (2017). Two minds are better than one: Cooperative communication as a new framework for understanding infant language learning. *Translational Issues in Psychological Science, 3*(1), 19–33.

Resnick, Barbara; Gwyther, Lisa P. & Roberto, Karen A. (Eds.). (2011). *Resilience in aging: Concepts, research, and outcomes.* Springer.

Rest, James. (1993). Research on moral judgment in college students. In Garrod, Andrew (Ed.), *Approaches to moral development: New research and emerging themes* (pp. 201–211). Teachers College Press.

Reynolds, Arthur J. & Ou, Suh-Ruu. (2011). Paths of effects from preschool to adult well-being: A confirmatory analysis of the Child-Parent Center Program. *Child Development, 82*(2), 555–582.

Reynolds, Arthur J. & Temple, Judy A. (Eds.). (2019). *Sustaining early childhood learning gains: Program, school, and family influences.* Cambridge University Press.

Ribot, Krystal M.; Hoff, Erika & Burridge, Andrea. (2018). Language use contributes to expressive language growth: Evidence from bilingual children. *Child Development, 89*(3), 929–940.

Richards, Tara N.; Tillyer, Marie Skubak & Wright, Emily M. (2017). Intimate partner violence and the overlap of perpetration and victimization: Considering the influence of physical, sexual, and emotional abuse in childhood. *Child Abuse & Neglect, 67*, 240–248.

Rideout, Victoria. (2017). *The Common Sense Census: Media use by kids age zero to eight.* San Francisco, CA: Common Sense Media.

Riediger, Michaela; Voelkle, Manuel C.; Schaefer, Sabine & Lindenberger, Ulman. (2014). Charting the life course: Age differences and validity of beliefs about lifespan development. *Psychology and Aging, 29*(3), 503–520.

Riegel, Klaus F. (1975). Toward a dialectical theory of development. *Human Development, 18*(1/2), 50–64.

Riggins, Tracy; Geng, Fengji; Botdorf, Morgan; Canada, Kelsey; Cox, Lisa & Hancock, Gregory R. (2018). Protracted hippocampal development is associated with age-related improvements in memory during early childhood. *NeuroImage, 174*, 127–137.

Rijken, A. J. & Liefbroer, A. C. (2016). Differences in family norms for men and women across Europe. *Journal of Marriage and Family, 78*(4), 1097–1113.

Rissanen, Inkeri; Kuusisto, Elina; Tuominen, Moona & Tirri, Kirsi. (2019). In search of a growth mindset pedagogy: A case study of one teacher's classroom practices in a Finnish elementary school. *Teaching and Teacher Education, 77*, 204–213.

Rizza, Wanda; Veronese, Nicola & Fontana, Luigi. (2014). What are the roles of calorie restriction and diet quality in promoting healthy longevity? *Ageing Research Reviews, 13*, 38–45.

Rizzo, Michael T.; Li, Leon; Burkholder, Amanda R. & Killen, Melanie. (2019). Lying, negligence, or lack of knowledge? Children's intention-based moral reasoning about resource claims. *Developmental Psychology, 55*(2), 274–285.

Robben, Antonius C. G. M. (2018). Death and anthropology: An introduction. In Robben, Antonius C. G. M. (Ed.), *Death, mourning, and burial: A cross-cultural reader* (2nd ed., pp. 1–16). Wiley-Blackwell.

Robbins, Chloe & Chapman, Peter. (2019). How does drivers' visual search change as a function of experience? A systematic review and meta-analysis. *Accident Analysis and Prevention, 132*(105266).

Robert, L. & Labat-Robert, J. (2015). Longevity and aging: Role of genes and of the extracellular matrix. *Biogerontology, 16*(1), 125–129.

Roberts, Andrea G. & Lopez-Duran, Nestor L. (2019). Developmental influences on stress response systems: Implications for psychopathology vulnerability in adolescence. *Comprehensive Psychiatry, 88*, 9–21.

Roberts, Michael J. D. & Beamish, Paul W. (2017). The scaffolding activities of international returnee executives: A learning based perspective of global boundary spanning. *Journal of Management Studies, 54*(4), 511–539.

Robertson, Deirdre A.; King-Kallimanis, Bellinda L. & Kenny, Rose Anne. (2016). Negative perceptions of aging predict longitudinal decline in cognitive function. *Psychology and Aging, 31*(1), 71–81.

Robson, Ruthann. (2010). Notes on my dying. In Maglin, Nan Bauer & Perry, Donna Marie (Eds.), *Final acts: Death, dying, and the choices we make* (pp. 19–28). Rutgers University Press.

Roche, Kathleen M.; Lambert, Sharon F.; White, Rebecca M. B.; Calzada, Esther J.; Little, Todd D.; Kuperminc, Gabriel P. & Schulenberg, John E. (2019). Autonomy-related parenting processes and adolescent adjustment in Latinx immigrant families. *Journal of Youth and Adolescence, 48*, 1161–1174.

Rogoff, Barbara. (2003). *The cultural nature of human development.* Oxford University Press.

Rolison, Jonathan J. (2019). What could go wrong? No evidence of an age-related positivity effect when evaluating outcomes of risky activities. *Developmental Psychology, 55*(8), 1788–1799.

Rollè, Luca; Giardina, Giulia; Caldarera, Angela M.; Gerino, Eva & Brustia, Piera. (2018). When intimate partner violence meets same sex couples: A review of same sex intimate partner violence. *Frontiers in Psychology, 9*(1506).

Romanelli, Meghan; Xiao, Yunyu & Lindsey, Michael A. (2020). Sexual identity-behavior profiles and suicide outcomes among heterosexual, lesbian, and gay sexually active adolescents: Sexual identity-behavior profiles and suicide. *Suicide and Life-Threatening Behavior, 50*(4), 921–933.

Romeo, Russell D. (2013). The teenage brain: The stress response and the adolescent brain. *Current Directions in Psychological Science, 22*(2), 140–145.

Rose, Dawn; Jones Bartoli, Alice & Heaton, Pamela C. (2019). Measuring the impact of musical learning on cognitive, behavioural and socio-emotional wellbeing development in children. *Psychology of Music, 47*(2), 284–303.

Roseberry, Lynn & Roos, Johan. (2016). *Bridging the gender gap: Seven principles for achieving gender balance.* Oxford University Press.

Rosen, Raymond C.; Heiman, Julia R.; Long, J. Scott; Fisher, William A. & Sand, Michael S. (2016). Men with sexual problems and their partners: Findings from the international survey of relationships. *Archives of Sexual Behavior, 45*, 159–173.

Rosenblatt, Paul C. (2013). Culture, socialization, and loss, grief, and mourning. In Meagher, David K. & Balk, David E. (Eds.), *Handbook of thanatology: The essential body of knowledge for the study of death, dying, and bereavement* (2nd ed., pp. 121–126). Routledge.

Rosenfeld, Michael J. & Roesler, Katharina. (2019). Cohabitation experience and cohabitation's association with marital dissolution: The short-term benefits of cohabitation. *Journal of Marriage and Family, 81*(1), 42–58.

Rosenthal, Robert & Jacobson, Lenore. (1968). *Pygmalion in the classroom: Teacher expectation and pupils' intellectual development.* Holt, Rinehart and Winston.

Rosin, Hanna. (2014, March 19). The overprotected kid. *The Atlantic.*

Rosow, Irving. (1985). Status and role change through the life cycle. In Binstock, Robert H. & Shanas, Ethel (Eds.), *Handbook of aging and the social sciences* (2nd ed., pp. 62–93). Van Nostrand Reinhold.

Rostila, Mikael; Saarela, Jan & Kawachi, Ichiro. (2013). Suicide following the death of a sibling: A nationwide follow-up study from Sweden. *BMJ Open, 3*(4), e002618.

Roth, Benjamin J.; Grace, Breanne L. & Seay, Kristen D. (2020). Mechanisms of deterrence: Federal immigration policies and the erosion of immigrant children's rights. *American Journal of Public Health, 110*, 84–86.

Roth, Lauren W. & Polotsky, Alex J. (2012). Can we live longer by eating less? A review of caloric restriction and longevity. *Maturitas, 71*(4), 315–319.

Rothbaum, Fred; Weisz, John; Pott, Martha; Miyake, Kazuo & Morell, Gilda. (2000). Attachment and culture: Security in the United States and Japan. *American Psychologist, 55*(10), 1093–1104.

Rothstein, Mark A. (2015). The moral challenge of Ebola. *American Journal of Public Health, 105*(1), 6–8.

Roudinesco, Élisabeth. (2017). *Freud: In his time and ours.* Harvard University Press.

Rovee-Collier, Carolyn. (1987). Learning and memory in infancy. In Osofsky, Joy Doniger (Ed.), *Handbook of infant development* (2nd ed. pp. 98–148). Wiley.

Rovee-Collier, Carolyn. (1990). The "memory system" of prelinguistic infants. *Annals of the New York Academy of Sciences, 608*, 517–542.

Rovee-Collier, Carolyn & Cuevas, Kimberly. (2009). The development of infant memory. In Courage, Mary L. & Cowan, Nelson (Eds.), *The development of memory in infancy and childhood* (2nd ed., pp. 11–41). Psychology Press.

Rovee-Collier, Carolyn & Hayne, Harlene. (1987). Reactivation of infant memory: Implications for cognitive development. In Reese, Hayne W. (Ed.), *Advances in child development and behavior* (Vol. 20, pp. 185–238). Academic Press.

Rovee-Collier, Carolyn; Mitchell, Katherine & Hsu-Yang, Vivian. (2013). Effortlessly strengthening infant memory: Associative potentiation of new learning. *Scandinavian Journal of Psychology, 54*(1), 4–9.

Rowland, David L.; Kolba, Tiffany N.; McNabney, Sean M.; Uribe, Dudbeth & Hevesi, Krisztina. (2020). Why and how women masturbate, and the relationship to orgasmic response. *Journal of Sex & Marital Therapy, 46*(4), 361–376.

Rübeling, Hartmut; Keller, Heidi; Yovsi, Relindis D.; Lenk, Melanie & Schwarzer, Sina. (2011). Children's drawings of the self as an expression of cultural conceptions of the self. *Journal of Cross-Cultural Psychology, 42*(3), 406–424.

Rubin, Emily B.; Buehler, Anna & Halpern, Scott D. (2020). Seriously ill patients' willingness to trade survival time to avoid high treatment intensity at the end of life. *JAMA Internal Medicine, 180*(6), 907–909.

Rubin, Kenneth H.; Bowker, Julie C.; McDonald, Kristina L. & Menzer, Melissa. (2013). Peer relationships in childhood. In Zelazo, Philip D. (Ed.), *The Oxford handbook of developmental psychology* (Vol. 2, pp. 242–275). Oxford University Press.

Ruch, Donna A.; Sheftall, Arielle H.; Schlagbaum, Paige; Fontanella, Cynthia A.; Campo, John V. & Bridge, Jeffrey A. (2019). Characteristics and precipitating circumstances of suicide among incarcerated youth. *Journal of the American Academy of Child & Adolescent Psychiatry, 58*(5), 514–524.e1.

Rudaz, Myriam; Ledermann, Thomas; Margraf, Jürgen; Becker, Eni S. & Craske, Michelle G. (2017). The moderating role of avoidance behavior on anxiety over time: Is there a difference between social anxiety disorder and specific phobia? *PLoS ONE, 12*(7), e0180298.

Rudman, Rachel & Titjen, Felicity. (2018). *Language development.* Cambridge University Press.

Russell, Allison; Nyame-Mensah, Ama; Wit, Arjen & Handy, Femida. (2019). Volunteering and wellbeing among ageing adults: A longitudinal analysis. *VOLUNTAS, 30*(1), 115–128.

Russell, David; Diamond, Eli L.; Lauder, Bonnie; Dignam, Ritchell R.; Dowding, Dawn W.; Peng, Timothy R.; . . . Bowles, Kathryn H. (2017). Frequency and risk factors for live discharge from hospice. *Journal of the American Geriatrics Society, 65*(8), 1726–1732.

Ruthig, Joelle C.; Trisko, Jenna & Stewart, Tara L. (2012). The impact of spouse's health and well-being on own well-being: A dyadic study of older married couples. *Journal of Social and Clinical Psychology, 31*(5), 508–529.

Rutter, Michael. (2012). Resilience as a dynamic concept. *Development and Psychopathology, 24*(2), 335–344.

Ryabov, Igor. (2018). Childhood obesity and academic outcomes in young adulthood. *Children, 5*(11), 150.

Ryan, Lindsay H.; Newton, Nicky J.; Chauhan, Preet K. & Chopik, William J. (2017). Effects of pre-retirement personality, health and job lock on post-retirement subjective well-being. *Translational Issues in Psychological Science, 3*(4), 378–387.

Sabeti, Pardis & Salahi, Lara. (2018). *Outbreak culture: The Ebola crisis and the next epidemic.* Harvard University Press.

Saer, D. J. (1923). The effect of bilingualism on intelligence. *British Journal of Psychology, 14*(1), 25–38.

Saffran, Jenny R. & Kirkham, Natasha Z. (2018). Infant statistical learning. *Annual Review of Psychology, 69*, 181–203.

Sagi, Abraham; Van IJzendoorn, Marinus H. & Koren-Karie, Nina. (1991). Primary appraisal of the Strange Situation: A cross-cultural analysis of preseparation episodes. *Developmental Psychology, 27*(4), 587–596.

Sahlberg, Pasi. (2011). *Finnish lessons: What can the world learn from educational change in Finland?* Teachers College Press.

Sahlberg, Pasi. (2015). *Finnish lessons 2.0: What can the world learn from educational change in Finland?* (2nd. ed.). Teachers College Press.

Saint-Maurice, Pedro F.; Troiano, Richard P.; Bassett, David R.; Graubard, Barry I.; Carlson, Susan A.; Shiroma, Eric J.; . . . Matthews, Charles E. (2020). Association of daily step count and step intensity with mortality among US adults. *JAMA, 323*(12), 1151–1160.

Salas, Gabriela Barrón; Lagos, María Eugenia Ciofalo & Perez, Manuel González. (2018). Analysis of emotional intelligence as a competition for effective productivity. *International Journal of Advanced Engineering, Management and Science, 4*(8), 615–621.

Salomon, Ilyssa & Brown, Christia Spears. (2019). The selfie generation: Examining the relationship between social media use and early adolescent body image. *Journal of Early Adolescence, 39*(4), 539–560.

Salpeter, Shelley R.; Luo, Esther J.; Malter, Dawn S. & Stuart, Brad. (2012). Systematic review of noncancer presentations with a median survival of 6 months or less. *The American Journal of Medicine, 125*(5), 512.e1–512.e16.

Salthouse, Timothy A. (2010). *Major issues in cognitive aging.* Oxford University Press.

Salthouse, Timothy A. (2015). Test experience effects in longitudinal comparisons of adult cognitive functioning. *Developmental Psychology, 51*(9), 1262–1270.

Salthouse, Timothy A. (2019). Trajectories of normal cognitive aging. *Psychology and Aging, 34*(1), 17–24.

Samanez-Larkin, Gregory R. & Carstensen, Laura L. (2011). Socioemotional functioning and the aging brain. In *The Oxford handbook of social neuroscience* (pp. 509–538). Oxford University Press.

Samaras, Nikolass; Frangos, Emilia; Forster, Alexandre; Lang, P. O. & Samaras, Dimitrios. (2012). Andropause: A review of the definition and treatment. *European Geriatric Medicine, 3*(6), 368–373.

Samek, Diana R.; Goodman, Rebecca J.; Erath, Stephen A.; McGue, Matt & Iacono, William G. (2016). Antisocial peer affiliation and externalizing disorders in the transition from adolescence to young adulthood: Selection versus socialization effects. *Developmental Psychology, 52*(5), 813–823.

SAMHSA. (2018). *Key substance use and mental health indicators in the United States: Results from the 2017 National Survey on Drug Use and Health.* Rockville, MD: Center for Behavioral Health Statistics and Quality, Substance Abuse and Mental Health Services Administration.

Sampaio, Waneli Cristine Morais; Ribeiro, Mara Cláudia; Costa, Larice Feitosa; Souza, Wânia Cristina de; Castilho, Goiara Mendonça de; Assis, Melissa Sousa de; . . . Ferreira, Vania Moraes. (2017). Effect of music therapy on the developing central nervous system of rats. *Psychology & Neuroscience, 10*(2), 176–188.

Sampson, Deborah & Hertlein, Katherine. (2015). The experience of grandparents raising grandchildren. *GrandFamilies, 2*(1), 75–96.

San Martín, Conchi; Montero, Ignacio; Navarro, M. Isabel & Biglia, Barbara. (2014). The development of referential communication: Improving message accuracy by coordinating private speech with peer questioning. *Early Childhood Research Quarterly, 29*(1), 76–84.

Sanchez, Gabriel R. & Vargas, Edward D. (2016). Taking a closer look at group identity: The link between theory and measurement of group consciousness and linked fate. *Political Research Quarterly, 69*(1), 160–174.

Sánchez-Mira, Núria & Saura, Dafne Muntanyola. (2020). Attachment parenting among middle-class couples in Spain: Gendered principles and labor divisions. *Journal of Family Studies,* (In Press).

Sandberg, Sheryl & UC Berkeley (Producer). (2016). *Sheryl Sandberg gives UC Berkeley Commencement keynote speech.* [Video]. YouTube.

Sanfilippo, Joseph; Ness, Molly; Petscher, Yaacov; Rappaport, Leonard; Zuckerman, Barry & Gaab, Nadine. (2020). Reintroducing dyslexia: Early identification and implications for pediatric practice. *Pediatrics, 146*(1), e20193046.

Sanner, Caroline; Ganong, Lawrence & Coleman, Marilyn. (2020). Shared children in stepfamilies: Experiences living in a hybrid family structure. *Journal of Marriage and Family, 82*(2), 605–621.

Sanou, Dia; O'Reilly, Erin; Ngnie-Teta, Ismael; Batal, Malek; Mondain, Nathalie; Andrew, Caroline; . . . Bourgeault, Ivy L. (2014). Acculturation and nutritional health of immigrants in Canada: A scoping review. *Journal of Immigrant and Minority Health, 16*(1), 24–34.

Sansone, Andrea; Romanelli, Francesco; Sansone, Massimiliano; Lenzi, Andrea & Luigi, Luigi Di. (2017). Gynecomastia and hormones. *Endocrine, 55*, 37–44.

Sanz Cruces, José Manuel; Hawrylak, María Fernández & Delegido, Ana Benito. (2015). Interpersonal variability of the experience of falling in love. *International Journal of Psychology and Psychological Therapy, 15*(1), 87–100.

Sapolsky, Robert. (2019). This is your brain on nationalism: The biology of us and them. *Foreign Affairs,* (March/April).

Sapolsky, Robert M. (2018). *Behave: The biology of humans at our best and worst.* Penguin.

Saraiva, Jorge; Esgalhado, Graça; Pereira, Henrique; Monteiro, Samuel; Afonso, Rosa Marina & Loureiro, Manuel. (2018). The relationship between emotional intelligence and internet addiction among youth and adults. *Journal of Addictions Nursing, 29*(1), 13–22.

Sarant, Julia; Harris, David; Busby, Peter; Maruff, Paul; Schembri, Adrian; Dowell, Richard & Briggs, Robert. (2019). The effect of cochlear implants on cognitive function in older adults: Initial baseline and 18-month follow up results for a prospective international longitudinal study. *Frontiers in Neuroscience, 13*(789).

Sarlo, Michela & Buodo, Giulia. (2017). To each its own? Gender differences in affective, autonomic, and behavioral responses to same-sex and opposite-sex visual sexual stimuli. *Physiology & Behavior, 171*, 249–255.

Sarwer, David B. & Grilo, Carlos M. (2020). Obesity: Psychosocial and behavioral aspects of a modern epidemic: Introduction to the special issue. *American Psychologist, 75*(2), 135–138.

Sasaki, Joni Y. & Kim, Heejung S. (2017). Nature, nurture, and their interplay: A review of cultural neuroscience. *Journal of Cross-Cultural Psychology, 48*(1), 4–22.

Sassler, Sharon & Lichter, Daniel T. (2020). Cohabitation and marriage: Complexity and diversity in union-formation patterns. *Journal of Marriage and Family, 82*(1), 35–61.

Satterwhite, Catherine Lindsey; Torrone, Elizabeth; Meites, Elissa; Dunne, Eileen F.; Mahajan, Reena; Ocfemia, M. Cheryl Bañez; . . . Weinstock, Hillard. (2013). Sexually transmitted infections among US women and men: Prevalence and incidence estimates, 2008. *Sexually Transmitted Diseases, 40*(3), 187–193.

Sauce, Bruno & Matzel, Louis D. (2018). The paradox of intelligence: Heritability and malleability coexist in hidden gene-environment interplay. *Psychological Bulletin, 144*(1), 26–47.

Sauer, Mark V.; Wang, Jeff G.; Douglas, Nataki C.; Nakhuda, Gary S.; Vardhana, Pratibashri; Jovanovic, Vuk & Guarnaccia, Michael M. (2009). Providing fertility care to men seropositive for human immunodeficiency virus: Reviewing 10 years of experience and 420 consecutive cycles of in vitro fertilization and intracytoplasmic sperm injection. *Fertility and Sterility, 91*(6), 2455–2460.

Saxton, Matthew. (2010). *Child language: Acquisition and development.* Sage.

Scantlebury, Nadia; Cunningham, Todd; Dockstader, Colleen; Laughlin, Suzanne; Gaetz, William; Rockel, Conrad; . . . Mabbott, Donald. (2014). Relations between white matter maturation and reaction time in childhood. *Journal of the International Neuropsychological Society, 20*(1), 99–112.

Scarborough, William J.; Sin, Ray & Risman, Barbara. (2019). Attitudes and the stalled gender revolution: Egalitarianism, traditionalism, and ambivalence from 1977 through 2016. *Gender & Society, 33*(2), 173–200.

Scelzo, Anna; Di Somma, Salvatore; Antonini, Paola; Montross, Lori; Schork, Nicholas; Brenner, David & Jeste, Dilip V. (2018). Mixed-methods quantitative-qualitative study of 29 nonagenarians and centenarians in rural Southern Italy: Focus on positive psychological traits. *International Psychogeriatrics, 30*(1), 31–38.

Schacter, Daniel L. (1996). *Searching for memory: The brain, the mind, and the past.* Basic Books.

Schacter, Hannah L. & Juvonen, Jaana. (2018). Dynamic changes in peer victimization and adjustment across middle school: Does friends' victimization alleviate distress? *Child development.*

Schaie, K. Warner. (1996). *Intellectual development in adulthood: The Seattle Longitudinal Study.* Cambridge University Press.

Schaie, K. Warner. (2005). *Developmental influences on adult intelligence: The Seattle Longitudinal Study.* Oxford University Press.

Schaie, K. Warner. (2013). *Developmental influences on adult intelligence: The Seattle Longitudinal Study* (2nd ed.). Oxford University Press.

Scharf, Miri & Goldner, Limor. (2018). "If you really love me, you will do/be . . . ": Parental psychological control and its implications for children's adjustment. *Developmental Review, 49*, 16–30.

Schein, Chelsea. (2020). The importance of context in moral judgments. *Perspectives on Psychological Science, 15*(2), 207–215.

Scherrer, Vsevolod; Preckel, Franzis & Schmidt, Isabelle. (2020). Development of achievement goals and their relation to academic interest and achievement in adolescence: A review of the literature and two longitudinal studies. *Developmental Psychology, 56*(4), 795–814.

Schinasi, Leah H.; Bloch, Joan Rosen; Melly, Steven; Zhao, Yuzhe; Moore, Kari & De Roos, Anneclaire J. (2020). High ambient temperature and infant mortality in Philadelphia, Pennsylvania: A case-crossover study. *American Journal of Public Health, 110*(2), 189–195.

Schneider, Daniel; Harknett, Kristen & Stimpson, Matthew. (2019). Job quality and the educational gradient in entry into marriage and cohabitation. *Demography, 56*(2), 451–476.

Schneider, Michael; Merz, Simon; Stricker, Johannes; De Smedt, Bert; Torbeyns, Joke;

Verschaffel, Lieven & Luwel, Koen. (2018). Associations of number line estimation with mathematical competence: A meta-analysis. *Child Development*, 89(5), 1467–1484.

Schneider, William; Waldfogel, Jane & Brooks-Gunn, Jeanne. (2017). The Great Recession and risk for child abuse and neglect. *Children and Youth Services Review*, 72, 71–81.

Schnitzspahn, Katharina M.; Ihle, Andreas; Henry, Julie D.; Rendell, Peter G. & Kliegel, Matthias. (2011). The age-prospective memory-paradox: An exploration of possible mechanisms. *International Psychogeriatrics*, 23(4), 583–592.

Schnitzspahn, Katharina M.; Stahl, Christoph; Zeintl, Melanie; Kaller, Christoph P. & Kliegel, Matthias. (2013). The role of shifting, updating, and inhibition in prospective memory performance in young and older adults. *Developmental Psychology*, 49(8), 1544–1553.

Schoon, Ingrid & Mortimer, Jeylan. (2017). Youth and the Great Recession: Are values, achievement orientation and outlook to the future affected? *International Journal of Psychology*, 52(1), 1–8.

Schübel, Ruth; Nattenmüller, Johanna; Sookthai, Disorn; Nonnenmacher, Tobias; Graf, Mirja E.; Riedl, Lena; . . . Kühn, Tilman. (2018). Effects of intermittent and continuous calorie restriction on body weight and metabolism over 50 wk: A randomized controlled trial. *American Journal of Clinical Nutrition*, 108(5), 933–945.

Schubert, Anna-Lena; Hagemann, Dirk & Frischkorn, Gidon T. (2017). Is general intelligence little more than the speed of higher-order processing? *Journal of Experimental Psychology*, 146(10), 1498–1512.

Schulenberg, John; O'Malley, Patrick M.; Bachman, Jerald G. & Johnston, Lloyd D. (2005). Early adult transitions and their relation to well-being and substance use. In Settersten, Richard A.; Furstenberg, Frank F. & Rumbaut, Rubén G. (Eds.), *On the frontier of adulthood: Theory, research, and public policy* (pp. 417–453). University of Chicago Press.

Schulenberg, John E.; Johnston, Lloyd D.; O'Malley, Patrick M.; Bachman, Jerald G.; Miech, Richard A. & Patrick, Megan E. (2020). *Monitoring the Future national survey results on drug use, 1975–2019: Volume II, college students and adults ages 19–60.* Ann Arbor, MI: Institute for Social Research, The University of Michigan.

Schwaba, Ted & Bleidorn, Wiebke. (2018). Individual differences in personality change across the adult life span. *Journal of Personality*, 86(3), 450–464.

Schwaba, Ted; Luhmann, Maike; Denissen, Jaap J. A.; Chung, Joanne M & Bleidorn, Wiebke. (2018). Openness to experience and culture-openness transactions across the lifespan. *Journal of Personality and Social Psychology*, 115(1), 118–136.

Schwartz, Shalom H. (2015). Basic individual values: Sources and consequences. In Brosch, Tobias & Sander, David (Eds.), *Handbook of value: Perspectives from economics, neuroscience, philosophy, psychology and sociology*. Oxford University Press.

Schwartz, Shalom H. (2017). Individual values across cultures. In Church, A. Timothy (Ed.), *The Praeger handbook of personality across cultures* (Vol. 2: Culture and characteristic adaptations). Praeger.

Schwartz, Shalom H.; Cieciuch, Jan; Vecchione, Michele; Davidov, Eldad; Fischer, Ronald; Beierlein, Constanze; . . . Konty, Mark. (2012). Refining the theory of basic individual values. *Journal of Personality and Social Psychology*, 103(4), 663–688.

Schwarz, Alan. (2016). *ADHD nation: Children, doctors, big pharma, and the making of an American epidemic*. Scribner.

Schweinhart, Lawrence J.; Montie, Jeanne; Xiang, Zongping; Barnett, W. Steven; Belfield, Clive R. & Nores, Milagros. (2005). *Lifetime effects: The High/Scope Perry Preschool Study through age 40*. High/Scope Press.

Schweizer, Susanne; Gotlib, Ian H. & Blakemore, Sarah-Jayne. (2020). The role of affective control in emotion regulation during adolescence. *Emotion*, 20(1), 80–86.

Schweppe, Judith & Rummer, Ralf. (2014). Attention, working memory, and long-term memory in multimedia learning: An integrated perspective based on process models of working memory. *Educational Psychology Review*, 26, 285–306.

Schwingshackl, Lukas; Morze, Jakub & Hoffmann, Georg. (2020). Mediterranean diet and health status: Active ingredients and pharmacological mechanisms. *British Journal of Pharmacology*, 177(6), 1241–1257.

Scott, Kelli; Lewis, Cara C. & Marti, C Nathan. (2019). Trajectories of symptom change in the treatment for adolescents with depression study. *Journal of the American Academy of Child and Adolescent Psychiatry*, 58(3), 319–328.

Scott, Lisa S. & Monesson, Alexandra. (2010). Experience-dependent neural specialization during infancy. *Neuropsychologia*, 48(6), 1857–1861.

Scott-Maxwell, Florida. (1968). *Measure of my days*. Knopf.

Sears, William & Sears, Martha. (2001). *The attachment parenting book: A commonsense guide to understanding and nurturing your baby*. Little Brown.

Seaton, Eleanor K.; Quintana, Stephen; Verkuyten, Maykel & Gee, Gilbert C. (2017). Peers, policies, and place: The relation between context and ethnic/racial identity. *Child Development*, 88(3), 683–692.

Sedgh, Gilda; Finer, Lawrence B.; Bankole, Akinrinola; Eilers, Michelle A. & Singh, Susheela. (2015). Adolescent pregnancy, birth, and abortion rates across countries: Levels and recent trends. *Journal of Adolescent Health*, 56(2), 223–230.

Seemiller, Eric S.; Cumming, Bruce G. & Candy, T. Rowan. (2018). Human infants can generate vergence responses to retinal disparity by 5 to 10 weeks of age. *Journal of Vision*, 18(6).

Segal, Nancy L. (2012). *Born together—reared apart: The landmark Minnesota Twin Study*. Harvard University Press.

Seider, Scott; Clark, Shelby; Graves, Daren; Kelly, Lauren Leigh; Soutter, Madora; El-Amin, Aaliyah & Jennett, Pauline. (2019). Black and Latinx adolescents' developing beliefs about poverty and associations with their awareness of racism. *Developmental Psychology*, 55(3), 509–524.

Sekeres, Mikkael A. (2013, January 31). A doctor's struggle with numbers. *New York Times*.

Seligman, Hilary K. & Berkowitz, Seth A. (2019). Aligning programs and policies to support food security and public health goals in the United States. *Annual Review of Public Health*, 40(1), 319–337.

Seligman, Martin E. P. (2011). *Flourish: A visionary new understanding of happiness and well-being*. Free Press.

Sénéchal, Monique & LeFevre, Jo-Anne. (2014). Continuity and change in the home literacy environment as predictors of growth in vocabulary and reading. *Child Development*, 85(4), 1552–1568.

Senior, Jennifer. (2014). *All joy and no fun: The paradox of modern parenthood*. Ecco.

Serrat, Rodrigo; Villar, Feliciano; Pratt, Michael W. & Stukas, Arthur A. (2018). On the quality of adjustment to retirement: The longitudinal role of personality traits and generativity. *Journal of Personality*, 86(3), 435–449.

Settersten, Richard A. (2015). Relationships in time and the life course: The significance of linked lives. *Research in Human Development*, 12(3/4), 217–223.

Shahani, Aarti Namdev. (2019). *Here we are: American dreams, American nightmares*. Celadon Books.

Shakeel, Fauzia; Newkirk, Melanie; Altoubah, Taymeyah; Martinez, Denise & Amankwah, Ernest K. (2019). Tolerance of hydrolyzed liquid protein fortified human milk and effect on growth in premature infants. *Nutrition in Clinical Practice*, 34(3), 450–458.

Shanafelt, Tait D.; Makowski, Maryam S.; Wang, Hanhan; Bohman, Bryan; Leonard, Mary; Harrington, Robert A.; . . . Trockel, Mickey. (2020). Association of burnout, professional fulfillment, and self-care practices of physician leaders with their independently rated leadership effectiveness. *JAMA Network Open*, 3(6), e207961.

Shanahan, Lilly; Hill, Sherika N.; Gaydosh, Lauren M.; Steinhoff, Annekatrin; Costello, E. Jane; Dodge, Kenneth A.; . . . Copeland, William E. (2019). Does despair really kill? A roadmap for an evidence-based answer. *American Journal of Public Health*, 109(6), 854–858.

Shanholtz, Caroline E.; Brown, Sacha Devine; Davidson, Ryan D. & Beck, Connie J. (2019). Distress in emerging adults: Further evaluation of the painful feelings about divorce scale. *Journal of Divorce & Remarriage*, 60(2), 141–151.

Shao, Xin; Lv, Ning; Liao, Jie; Long, Jinbo; Xue, Rui; Ai, Ni; . . . Fan, Xiaohui. (2019). Copy number variation is highly correlated with differential gene expression: A pan-cancer study. *BMC Medical Genetics*, 20(1), 1–14.

Shapiro, Alyson F.; Jolley, Sandra N.; Hildebrandt, Ursula & Spieker, Susan J. (2018). The effects of early postpartum depression on infant temperament. *Early Child Development and Care*.

Shapiro, Joan Poliner & Stefkovich, Jacqueline A. (2016). *Ethical leadership and decision making in education: Applying theoretical perspectives to complex dilemmas* (4th ed.). Routledge.

Shariff, Azim F. (2015). Does religion increase moral behavior? *Current opinion in psychology*, 6, 108–113.

Sharp, Emily Schoenhofen; Beam, Christopher R.; Reynolds, Chandra A. & Gatz, Margaret.(2019). Openness declines in advance of death in late adulthood. *Psychology and Aging*, 34(1), 124–138.

Shechner, Tomer; Fox, Nathan A.; Mash, Jamie A.; Jarcho, Johanna M.; Chen, Gang; Leibenluft, Ellen; . . . Britton, Jennifer C. (2018). Differences in neural response to extinction recall in young adults with or without history of behavioral inhibition. *Development and Psychopathology*, 30(1), 179–189.

Sheehy, Kate; Noureen, Amna; Khaliq, Ayesha; Dhingra, Katie; Husain, Nusrat; Pontin, Eleanor E.; . . . Taylor, Peter J. (2019). An examination of the relationship between shame, guilt and self-harm: A systematic review and meta-analysis. *Clinical Psychology Review*, 73(101779).

Shi, Rushen. (2014). Functional morphemes and early language acquisition. *Child Development Perspectives*, 8(1), 6–11.

Shin, Huiyoung & Ryan, Allison M. (2017). Friend influence on early adolescent disruptive behavior in the classroom: Teacher emotional support matters. *Developmental Psychology*, 53(1), 114–125.

Shoda, Yuichi; Mischel, Walter & Peake, Philip K. (1990). Predicting adolescent cognitive and self-regulatory competencies from preschool delay of gratification: Identifying diagnostic conditions. *Developmental Psychology*, 26(6), 978–986.

Short, Clara Schaertl. (2019). Comment on "Outbreak: On transgender teens and psychic epidemics." *Psychological Perspectives*, 62(2/3), 285–289.

Shulman, Elizabeth P. & Cauffman, Elizabeth. (2014). Deciding in the dark: Age differences in intuitive risk judgment. *Developmental Psychology*, 50(1), 167–177.

Shulman, Elizabeth P.; Monahan, Kathryn C. & Steinberg, Laurence. (2017). Severe violence during adolescence and early adulthood and its relation to anticipated rewards and costs. *Child Development*, 88(1), 16–26.

Shurkin, Joel N. (1992). *Terman's kids: The groundbreaking study of how the gifted grow up*. Little, Brown.

Shvarts, Anna & Bakker, Arthur. (2019). The early history of the scaffolding metaphor: Bernstein, Luria, Vygotsky, and before. *Mind, Culture, and Activity*, 26(1), 4–23.

Siegal, Michael & Surian, Luca (Eds.). (2012). *Access to language and cognitive development*. Oxford University Press.

Siegler, Robert S. & Chen, Zhe. (2008). Differentiation and integration: Guiding principles for analyzing cognitive change. *Developmental Science*, 11(4), 433–448.

Siegler, Robert S.; Thompson, Clarissa A. & Schneider, Michael. (2011). An integrated theory of whole number and fractions development. *Cognitive Psychology*, 62(4), 273–296.

Silberman, Steve. (2015). *Neurotribes: The legacy of autism and the future of neurodiversity*. Avery.

Silventoinen, Karri; Hammar, Niklas; Hedlund, Ebba; Koskenvuo, Markku; Ronnemaa, Tapani & Kaprio, Jaakko. (2008). Selective international migration by social position, health behaviour and personality. *European Journal of Public Health*, 18(2), 150–155.

Silver, Jonathan M.; McAllister, Thomas W. & Arciniegas, David B. (Eds.). (2019). *Textbook of traumatic brain injury* (3rd ed.). American Psychiatric Association.

Silvers, Jennifer A.; Shu, Jocelyn; Hubbard, Alexa D.; Weber, Jochen & Ochsner, Kevin N. (2015). Concurrent and lasting effects of emotion regulation on amygdala response in adolescence and young adulthood. *Developmental Science*, 18(5), 771–784.

Simmons, Joseph P.; Nelson, Leif D. & Simonsohn, Uri. (2011). False-positive psychology: Undisclosed flexibility in data collection and analysis allows presenting anything as significant. *Psychological Science*, 22(11), 1359–1366.

Simons, Ronald L.; Lei, Man-Kit; Beach, Steven R. H.; Barr, Ashley B.; Simons, Leslie G.; Gibbons, Frederick X. & Philibert, Robert A. (2018). Discrimination, segregation, and chronic inflammation: Testing the weathering explanation for the poor health of Black Americans. *Developmental Psychology*, 54(10), 1993–2006.

Simpson, Jeffry A. & Karantzas, Gery C. (2019). Editorial overview: Attachment in adulthood: A dynamic field with a rich past and a bright future. *Current Opinion in Psychology*, 25, 177–181.

Simpson, Jeffry A. & Kenrick, Douglas. (2013). *Evolutionary social psychology*. Taylor & Francis.

Singh, Krishneil A.; Gignac, Gilles E.; Brydges, Christopher R. & Ecker, Ullrich K. H. (2018). Working memory capacity mediates the relationship between removal and fluid intelligence. *Journal of Memory and Language*, 101, 18–36.

Sinnot, Jan D. (2017). Cognitive underpinnings of identity flexibility in adulthood. In Sinnot, Jan D. (Ed.), *Identity flexibility during adulthood: Perspectives in adult development* (pp. 19–49). Springer.

Sinnot, Jan D. (2017). Cognitive underpinnings of identity flexibility in adulthood. In Sinnott, Jan D. (Ed.), *Identity flexibility during adulthood: Perspectives in adult development* (pp. 19–52). Springer.

Sinnott, Jan D. (2008). Cognitive and representational development in adults. In Cartwright, Kelly B. (Ed.), *Literacy processes: Cognitive flexibility in learning and teaching* (pp. 42–68). Guilford.

Sinnott, Jan D. (2014). *Adult development: Cognitive aspects of thriving close relationships*. Oxford University Press.

Skinner, Asheley Cockrell; Ravanbakht, Sophie N.; Skelton, Joseph A.; Perrin, Eliana M. & Armstrong, Sarah C. (2018). Prevalence of obesity and severe obesity in US children, 1999–2016. *Pediatrics*, 141(3), e20173459.

Skinner, B. F. (1953). *Science and human behavior*. Macmillan.

Skinner, B. F. (1957). *Verbal behavior*. Appleton-Century-Crofts.

Skinner, B. F. (1974). *About behaviorism*. Knopf.

Slotnick, Scott D. (2017). *Cognitive neuroscience of memory*. Cambridge University Press.

Smart, Andrew; Bolnick, Deborah A. & Tutton, Richard. (2017). Health and genetic ancestry testing: Time to bridge the gap. *BMC Medical Genomics*, 10(1).

Smetana, Judith G.; Ahmad, Ikhlas & Wray-Lake, Laura. (2016). Beliefs about parental authority legitimacy among refugee youth in Jordan: Between- and within-person variations. *Developmental Psychology*, 52(3), 484–495.

Smith, Dorothy E. (1993). The standard North American family: SNAF as an ideological code. *Journal of Family Issues*, 14(1), 50–65.

Smith, Emily R.; Bergelson, Ilana; Constantian, Stacie; Valsangkar, Bina & Chan, Grace J. (2017). Barriers and enablers of health system adoption of kangaroo mother care: A systematic review of caregiver perspectives. *BMC Pediatrics*, 17(35).

Smith, Ethel Morgan. (2013). Mad hearts. In Bouvard, Marguerite Guzman (Ed.), *Mothers of adult children*. Lexington.

Smith, Gregory T.; Atkinson, Emily A.; Davis, Heather A.; Riley, Elizabeth N. & Oltmanns, Joshua R. (2020). The general factor of psychopathology. *Annual Review of Clinical Psychology*, 16, 75–98.

Smith, Hannah E.; Ryan, Kelsey N.; Stephenson, Kevin B.; Westcott, Claire; Thakwalakwa, Chrissie; Maleta, Ken; . . . Manary, Mark J. (2014). Multiple micronutrient supplementation transiently ameliorates environmental enteropathy in Malawian children aged 12–35 months in a randomized controlled clinical trial. *Journal of Nutrition*, 144(12), 2059–2065.

Smith, Kerri. (2014). Mental health: A world of depression. *Nature*, 515(7526), 180–181.

Smith, Peter K.; López-Castro, Leticia; Robinson, Susanne & Görzig, Anke. (2019). Consistency of gender differences in bullying in cross-cultural surveys. *Aggression and Violent Behavior*, 45, 33–40.

Smith, Sharon G.; Zhang, Xinjian; Basile, Kathleen C.; Merrick, Melissa T.; Wang, Jing; Kresnow, Marcie-jo & Chen, Jieru. (2018). *The national intimate partner and sexual violence survey: 2015 data brief—Updated release*. Atlanta, GA: National Center for Injury Prevention and Control, Centers for Disease Control and Prevention.

Smyth, Emer; Darmody, Merike & Lyons, Maureen. (2013). Introduction. In Smyth, Emer; Lyons, Maureen & Darmody, Merike (Eds.), *Religious education in a multicultural Europe: Children, parents and schools* (pp. 1–14). Palgrave Macmillan.

Snyder, Thomas D.; de Brey, Cristobal & Dillow, Sally A. (2019). *Digest of education statistics, 2017.* Washington, DC: National Center for Education Statistics, Institute of Education Sciences, U.S. Department of Education. NCES 2018-070.

Sodermans, An Katrien; Botterman, Sarah; Havermans, Nele & Matthijs, Koen. (2015). Involved fathers, liberated mothers? Joint physical custody and the subjective well-being of divorced parents. *Social Indicators Research, 122*(1), 257–277.

Soderstrom, Melanie; Ko, Eon-Suk & Nevzorova, Uliana. (2011). It's a question? Infants attend differently to yes/no questions and declaratives. *Infant Behavior and Development, 34*(1), 107–110.

Sohr-Preston, Sara L.; Scaramella, Laura V.; Martin, Monica J.; Neppl, Tricia K.; Ontai, Lenna & Conger, Rand D. (2013). Parental socioeconomic status, communication, and children's vocabulary development: A third-generation test of the family investment model. *Child Development, 84*(3), 1046–1062.

Solheim, Elisabet; Wichstrøm, Lars; Belsky, Jay & Berg-Nielsen, Turid Suzanne. (2013). Do time in child care and peer group exposure predict poor socioemotional adjustment in Norway? *Child Development, 84*(5), 1701–1715.

Soller, Brian & Kuhlemeier, Alena. (2019). Gender and intimate partner violence in Latino immigrant neighborhoods. *Journal of Quantitative Criminology, 35*(1), 61–88.

Solomon, Andrew. (2012). *Far from the tree: Parents, children, and the search for identity.* Scribner.

Somigliana, Edgardo; Vigano, Paola; Busnelli, Andrea; Paffoni, Alessio; Vegetti, Walter & Vercellini, Paolo. (2018). Repeated implantation failure at the crossroad between statistics, clinics and over-diagnosis. *Reproductive BioMedicine Online, 36*(1), 32–38.

Son, Daye & Padilla-Walker, Laura M. (2019). Whereabouts and secrets: A person-centered approach to emerging adults' routine and self-disclosure to parents. *Emerging Adulthood,* (In Press).

Sonuga-Barke, Edmund & Cortese, Samuele. (2018). Cognitive training approaches for ADHD: Can they be made more effective? In Banaschewski, Tobias; Coghill, David & Zuddas, Alessandro (Eds.), *Oxford textbook of attention deficit hyperactivity disorder.* Oxford University Press.

Sophian, Catherine. (2013). Vicissitudes of children's mathematical knowledge: Implications of developmental research for early childhood mathematics education. *Early Education and Development, 24*(4), 436–442.

Sormunen, Taina; Aanesen, Arthur; Fossum, Björn; Karlgren, Klas & Westerbotn, Margareta. (2018). Infertility-related communication and coping strategies among women affected by primary or secondary infertility. *Journal of Clinical Nursing, 27*(1/2), e335–e344.

Sorrells, Shawn F.; Paredes, Mercedes F.; Cebrian-Silla, Arantxa; Sandoval, Kadellyn; Qi, Dashi; Kelley, Kevin W.; . . . Alvarez-Buylla, Arturo. (2018). Human hippocampal neurogenesis drops sharply in children to undetectable levels in adults. *Nature, 555,* 377–381.

Sousa, David A. (2014). *How the brain learns to read* (2nd ed.). SAGE.

Sparks, Sarah D. (2016, July 20). Dose of empathy found to cut suspension rates. *Education Week, 35*(36), 1, 20.

Spätgens, Tessa & Schoonen, Rob. (2018). The semantic network, lexical access, and reading comprehension in monolingual and bilingual children: An individual differences study. *Applied Psycholinguistics, 39*(1), 225–256.

Spear, Linda Patia. (2009). Heightened stress responsivity and emotional reactivity during pubertal maturation: Implications for psychopathology. *Development and Psychopathology, 21*(1), 87–97.

Spearman, Charles Edward. (1923). *The nature of "intelligence" and the principles of cognition.* Macmillan.

Specht, Jule. (2017). *Personality development across the lifespan.* Academic Press.

Specht, Jule; Bleidorn, Wiebke; Denissen, Jaap J. A.; Hennecke, Marie; Hutteman, Roos; Kandler, Christian; . . . Zimmermann, Julia. (2014). What drives adult personality development? A comparison of theoretical perspectives and empirical evidence. *European Journal of Personality, 28*(3), 216–230.

Spelke, Elizabeth S.; Born, Wendy Smith & Chu, Flora. (1983). Perception of moving, sounding objects by four-month-old infants. *Perception, 12*(6), 719–732.

Spencer, John P.; Blumberg, Mark S.; McMurray, Bob; Robinson, Scott R.; Samuelson, Larissa K. & Tomblin, J. Bruce. (2009). Short arms and talking eggs: Why we should no longer abide the nativist–empiricist debate. *Child Development Perspectives, 3*(2), 79–87.

Spencer, Justine M. Y.; Sekuler, Allison B.; Bennett, Patrick J.; Giese, Martin A. & Pilz, Karin S. (2016). Effects of aging on identifying emotions conveyed by point-light walkers. *Psychology and Aging, 31*(1), 126–138.

Spencer, Margaret Beale; Swanson, Dena Phillips & Harpalani, Vinay. (2015). Development of the self. In Lerner, Richard M. (Ed.), *Handbook of child psychology and developmental science* (7th ed., Vol. 3, pp. 750–793). Wiley.

Sperry, Douglas E.; Sperry, Linda L. & Miller, Peggy J. (2019). Reexamining the verbal environments of children from different socioeconomic backgrounds. *Child Development, 90*(4), 1303–1318.

Spinrad, Tracy L. & Gal, Diana E. (2018). Fostering prosocial behavior and empathy in young children. *Current Opinion in Psychology, 20,* 40–44.

Spira, Adam P. (2018). Sleep and health in older adulthood: Recent advances and the path forward. *Journal of Gerontology Series A, 73*(3), 357–359.

Spolaore, Enrico & Wacziarg, Romain. (2018). Ancestry and development: New evidence. *Journal of Applied Econometrics, 33*(5), 748–762.

Sprecher, Susan; Sullivan, Quintin & Hatfield, Elaine. (1994). Mate selection preferences: Gender differences examined in a national sample. *Journal of Personality and Social Psychology, 66*(6), 1074–1080.

Srikanth, Velandai; Sinclair, Alan J.; Hill-Briggs, Felicia; Moran, Chris & Biessels, Geert Jan. (2020). Type 2 diabetes and cognitive dysfunction-towards effective management of both comorbidities. *The Lancet Diabetes & Endocrinology, 8*(6), 535–545.

Srinivasan, Sharada & Li, Shuzhuo. (2018). Unifying perspectives on scarce women and surplus men in China and India. In Srinivasan, Sharada & Li, Shuzhuo (Eds.), *Scarce women and surplus men in China and India* (pp. 1–23). Springer.

Stahl, Lesley. (2016). *Becoming grandma: The joys and science of the new grandparenting.* Blue Rider Press.

Standing, E. M. (1998). *Maria Montessori: Her life and work.* Plume.

Stanley, Colleen. (2020). *Emotional intelligence for sales leadership: The secret to building high-performance sales teams.* HarperCollins.

Starmans, Christina. (2017). Children's theories of the self. *Child Development, 88*(6), 1774–1785.

Starr, Douglas. (2016). When DNA is lying. *Science, 351*(6278), 1133–1136.

Statistics Norway. (2018). Facts about education in Norway 2018. Statistics Norway's Information Centre.

Steele, Claude M. (1997). A threat in the air: How stereotypes shape intellectual identity and performance. *American Psychologist, 52*(6), 613–629.

Steffensmeier, Darrell; Painter-Davis, Noah & Ulmer, Jeffery. (2017). Intersectionality of race, ethnicity, gender, and age on criminal punishment. *Sociological Perspectives, 60*(4), 810–833.

Stein, Alan; Dalton, Louise; Rapa, Elizabeth; Bluebond-Langner, Myra; Hanington, Lucy; Stein, Kim Fredman; . . . Yousafzai, Aisha. (2019). Communication with children and adolescents about the diagnosis of their own life-threatening condition. *The Lancet, 393*(10176), P1150–1163.

Steinbach, Anja. (2019). Children's and parents' well-being in joint physical custody: A literature review. *Family Process, 58*(2), 353–369.

Steinberg, Laurence. (2004). Risk taking in adolescence: What changes, and why? *Annals of the New York Academy of Sciences, 1021,* 51–58.

Steinberg, Laurence. (2009). Should the science of adolescent brain development inform public policy? *American Psychologist, 64*(8), 739–750.

Steinberg, Laurence. (2014). *Age of opportunity: Lessons from the new science of adolescence.* Houghton Mifflin Harcourt.

Steinberg, Laurence. (2015). The neural underpinnings of adolescent risk-taking: The roles of reward-seeking, impulse control, and peers. In Oettingen, Gabriele & Gollwitzer, Peter M. (Eds.), *Self-regulation in adolescence* (pp. 173–192). Cambridge University Press.

Steinberg, Laurence D. (2019). *Adolescence.* McGraw-Hill Education.

Steinbrink, Claudia; Zimmer, Karin; Lachmann, Thomas; Dirichs, Martin & Kammer, Thomas. (2014). Development of rapid temporal processing and its impact on literacy skills in primary school children. *Child Development, 85*(4), 1711–1726.

Stephens, Nicole M.; Hamedani, MarYam G. & Townsend, Sarah S. M. (2019). Difference matters: Teaching students a contextual theory of difference can help them succeed. *14*(2), 156–174.

Stern, Gavin. (2015). For kids with special learning needs, roadblocks remain. *Science, 349*(6255), 1465–1466.

Sternberg, Robert J. (1988). Triangulating love. In Sternberg, Robert J. & Barnes, Michael L. (Eds.), *The psychology of love* (pp. 119–138). Yale University Press.

Sternberg, Robert J. (2003). *Wisdom, intelligence, and creativity synthesized.* Cambridge University Press.

Sternberg, Robert J. (2011). The theory of successful intelligence. In Sternberg, Robert J. & Kaufman, Scott Barry (Eds.), *The Cambridge handbook of intelligence* (pp. 504–526). Cambridge University Press.

Sternberg, Robert J. (2015). Multiple intelligences in the new age of thinking. In Goldstein, Sam; Princiotta, Dana & Naglieri, Jack A. (Eds.), *Handbook of intelligence* (pp. 229–241). Springer.

Sternberg, Robert J. (2020). Preface. In Sternberg, Robert J. (Ed.), *Human intelligence: An introduction.* Cambridge University Press.

Stevenson, Robert G. (2017). Children and death: What do they know and when do they learn it? In Stevenson, Robert G. & Cox, Gerry R. (Eds.), *Children, adolescents, and death: Questions and answers.* Routledge.

Stierand, Marc & Dörfler, Viktor. (2016). The role of intuition in the creative process of expert chefs. *Journal of Creative Behavior, 50*(3), 178–185.

Stiles, Joan & Jernigan, Terry. (2010). The basics of brain development. *Neuropsychology Review, 20*(4), 327–348.

Stilo, Simona A. & Murray, Robin M. (2019). Non-genetic factors in schizophrenia. *Current Psychiatry Reports, 21*(100).

Stiner, Mary C. (2017). Love and death in the stone age: What constitutes first evidence of mortuary treatment of the human body? *Biological Theory, 12*(4), 248–261.

Stochholm, Kirstine; Bojesen, Anders; Jensen, Anne Skakkebæk; Juul, Svend & Gravholt, Claus Højbjerg. (2012). Criminality in men with Klinefelter's syndrome and XYY syndrome: A cohort study. *BMJ Open, 2*(1), e000650.

Stoet, Gijsbert & Geary, David C. (2013). Sex differences in mathematics and reading achievement are inversely related: Within- and across-nation assessment of 10 years of PISA data. *PLoS ONE, 8*(3), e57988.

Stokes, Andrew; Lundberg, Dielle J.; Sheridan, Bethany; Hempstead, Katherine; Morone, Natalia E.; Lasser, Karen E.; . . . Neogi, Tuhina. (2020). Association of obesity with prescription opioids for painful conditions in patients seeking primary care in the US. *JAMA, 3*(4), e202012.

Stolk, Lisette; Perry, John R. B.; Chasman, Daniel I.; He, Chunyan; Mangino, Massimo; Sulem, Patrick; . . . Lunetta, Kathryn L. (2012). Meta-analyses identify 13 loci associated with age at menopause and highlight DNA repair and immune pathways. *Nature Genetics, 44*, 260–268.

Stone, Adam & Bosworth, Rain G. (2019). Exploring infant sensitivity to visual language using eye tracking and the preferential looking paradigm. *Journal of Visualized Experiments*(147), e59581.

Stoneking, Mark & Delfin, Frederick. (2010). The human genetic history of East Asia: Weaving a complex tapestry. *Current Biology, 20*(4), R188–R193.

Storebø, Ole Jakob & Gluud, Christian. (2020). Methylphenidate for ADHD rejected from the WHO Essential Medicines List due to uncertainties in benefit-harm profile. *BMJ*, (In Press).

Strawn, Jeffrey R.; Dobson, Eric T. & Giles, Lisa L. (2017). Primary pediatric care psychopharmacology: Focus on medications for ADHD, depression, and anxiety. *Current Problems in Pediatric and Adolescent Health Care, 47*(1), 3–14.

Stroebe, Margaret S.; Abakoumkin, Georgios; Stroebe, Wolfgang & Schut, Henk. (2012). Continuing bonds in adjustment to bereavement: Impact of abrupt versus gradual separation. *Personal Relationships, 19*(2), 255–266.

Stroebe, Wolfgang & Strack, Fritz. (2014). The alleged crisis and the illusion of exact replication. *Perspectives on Psychological Science, 9*(1), 59–71.

Strohminger, Nina & Kumar, Victor (Eds.). (2018). *The moral psychology of disgust.* Rowman & Littlefield.

Stronge, Samantha; Shaver, John H.; Bulbulia, Joseph & Sibley, Chris G. (2019). Only children in the 21st century: Personality differences between adults with and without siblings are very, very small. *Journal of Research in Personality, 83*(103868).

Strouse, Gabrielle A. & Ganea, Patricia A. (2017). Toddlers' word learning and transfer from electronic and print books. *Journal of Experimental Child Psychology, 156*, 129–142.

Struijs, Sascha Y.; Lamers, Femke; Rinck, Mike; Roelofs, Karin; Spinhoven, Philip & Penninx, Brenda W. J. H. (2018). The predictive value of Approach and Avoidance tendencies on the onset and course of depression and anxiety disorders. *Depression and Anxiety, 35*(6), 551–559.

Strutz, Kelly L.; Herring, Amy H. & Halpern, Carolyn Tucker. (2015). Health disparities among young adult sexual minorities in the U.S. *American Journal of Preventive Medicine, 48*(1), 76–88.

Stundziene, Alina. (2019). Human welfare: Can we trust what they say? *Journal of Happiness Studies, 20*(2), 579–604.

Sugimura, Kazumi; Crocetti, Elisabetta; Hatano, Kai; Kaniušonytė, Goda; Hihara, Shogo & Žukauskienė, Rita. (2018). A cross-cultural perspective on the relationships between emotional separation, parental trust, and identity in adolescents. *Journal of Youth and Adolescence, 47*(4), 749–759.

Sugimura, Kazumi; Matsushima, Kobo; Hihara, Shogo; Takahashi, Masami & Crocetti, Elisabetta. (2019). A culturally sensitive approach to the relationships between identity formation and religious beliefs in youth. *Journal of Youth and Adolescence, 48*(4), 668–679.

Sullivan, Alice & Brown, Matthew A. (2015). Vocabulary from adolescence to middle age. *Longitudinal and Life Course Studies, 6*(2).

Sullivan, Amanda Alzena. (2019). *Breaking the STEM stereotype: Reaching girls in early childhood.* Rowman & Littlefield.

Sullivan, Kevin J.; Dodge, Hiroko H.; Hughes, Tiffany F.; Chang, Chung-Chou H.; Zhu, Xinmei; Liu, Anran & Ganguli, Mary. (2019). Declining incident dementia rates across four population-based birth cohorts. *The Journals of Gerontology: Series A, 74*(9), 1439–1445.

Sullivan, Regina; Perry, Rosemarie; Sloan, Aliza; Kleinhaus, Karine & Burtchen, Nina. (2011). Infant bonding and attachment to the caregiver: Insights from basic and clinical science. *Clinics in Perinatology, 38*(4), 643–655.

Sullivan, Sheila. (1999). *Falling in love: A history of torment and enchantment.* Macmillan.

Sullivan-Bissett, Ema. (2018). Monothematic delusion: A case of innocence from experience. *Philosophical Psychology, 31*(6), 920–947.

Sulmasy, Daniel. (2018). The last low whispers of our dead: When is it ethically justifiable to render a patient unconscious until death? *Theoretical Medicine and Bioethics, 39*(3), 233–263.

Suls, Jerry; Collins, Rebecca L. & Wheeler, Ladd (Eds.). (2020). *Social comparison, judgment, and behavior.* Oxford University Press.

Sumner, Rachel C. & Gallagher, Stephen. (2017). Unemployment as a chronic stressor: A systematic review of cortisol studies. *Psychology & Health, 32*(3), 289–311.

Sun, Min & Rugolotto, Simone. (2004). Assisted infant toilet training in a Western family setting. *Journal of Developmental & Behavioral Pediatrics, 25*(2), 99–101.

Sunderam, Saswati; Kissin, Dmitry M.; Zhang, Yujia; Folger, Suzanne G.; Boulet, Sheree L.; Warner, Lee; . . . Barfield, Wanda D. (2019, April 26). *Assisted reproductive technology surveillance—United States, 2016.* Morbidity and Mortality Weekly Report: Surveillance Summaries, 68(4), 1–23. Atlanta, GA: Centers for Disease Control and Prevention.

Sundman, Mark; Doraiswamy, P. Murali & Morey, Rajendra A. (2015). Neuroimaging assessment of early and late neurobiological sequelae of traumatic brain injury: Implications for CTE. *Frontiers in Neuroscience, 9*(334).

Sung, Jimin; Beijers, Roseriet; Gartstein, Maria A.; de Weerth, Carolina & Putnam, Samuel P. (2015). Exploring temperamental differences in infants from the USA and the Netherlands. *European Journal of Developmental Psychology, 12*(1), 15–28.

Susanu, Neaga. (2020). The psychanalitical approach of personality. *EIRP Proceedings, 15*(1), 341–349.

Susman, Elizabeth J.; Houts, Renate M.; Steinberg, Laurence; Belsky, Jay; Cauffman, Elizabeth; DeHart, Ganie; . . . Halpern-Felsher, Bonnie L. (2010). Longitudinal development of secondary sexual characteristics in girls and boys between ages 9-1/2 and 15-1/2 years. *Archives of Pediatrics & Adolescent Medicine, 164*(2), 166–173.

Sutton-Smith, Brian. (2011). The antipathies of play. In Pellegrini, Anthony D. (Ed.), *The Oxford handbook of the development of play* (pp. 110–115). Oxford University Press.

Suurland, Jill; van der Heijden, Kristiaan B.; Huijbregts, Stephan C. J.; Smaling, Hanneke J. A.; de Sonneville, Leo M. J.; Van Goozen, Stephanie H. M. & Swaab, Hanna. (2016). Parental perceptions of aggressive behavior in preschoolers: Inhibitory control moderates the association with negative emotionality. *Child Development*, 87(1), 256–269.

Suzumori, Nobuhiro; Kumagai, Kyoko; Goto, Shinobu; Nakamura, Akira & Sugiura-Ogasawara, Mayumi. (2015). Parental decisions following prenatal diagnosis of chromosomal abnormalities: Implications for genetic counseling practice in Japan. *Journal of Genetic Counseling*, 24(1), 117–121.

Swaab, D. F. & Hofman, M. A. (1984). Sexual differentiation of the human brain: A historical perspective. *Progress in Brain Research*, 61, 361–374.

Swain, J. E.; Kim, P. & Ho, S. S. (2011). Neuroendocrinology of parental response to baby-cry. *Journal of Neuroendocrinology*, 23(11), 1036–1041.

Sweeney, Susan; Rothstein, Rachel; Visintainer, Paul; Rothstein, Robert & Singh, Rachana. (2017). Impact of kangaroo care on parental anxiety level and parenting skills for preterm infants in the neonatal intensive care unit. *Journal of Neonatal Nursing*, 23(3), 151–158.

Swensen, Stephen J. & Shanafelt, Tait D. (2020). *Mayo Clinic strategies to reduce burnout: 12 actions to create the ideal workplace*. Oxford University Press.

Swinkels, Joukje; van Tilburg, Theo; Verbakel, Ellen & van Groenou, Marjolein Broese. (2019). Explaining the gender gap in the caregiving burden of partner caregivers. *The Journals of Gerontology: Series B*, 74(2), 309–317.

Swit, Cara S. (2019). Differential associations between relational and physical aggression: Why do teachers and parents perceive these behaviors differently? *Early Child Development and Care*, (In Press).

Tabassum, Faiza; Mohan, John & Smith, Peter. (2016). Association of volunteering with mental well-being: A lifecourse analysis of a national population-based longitudinal study in the UK. *BMJ Open*, 6(8), e011327.

Tamis-LeMonda, Catherine S.; Bornstein, Marc H. & Baumwell, Lisa. (2001). Maternal responsiveness and children's achievement of language milestones. *Child Development*, 72(3), 748–767.

Tan, Patricia Z.; Armstrong, Laura M. & Cole, Pamela M. (2013). Relations between temperament and anger regulation over early childhood. *Social Development*, 22(4), 755–772.

Tan, Robin & Goldman, Mark S. (2015). Exposure to female fertility pheromones influences men's drinking. *Experimental and Clinical Psychopharmacology*, 23(3), 139–146.

Tan, Robin & Goldman, Mark S. (2017). Exposure to male sexual scents (androstenone) influences women's drinking. *Experimental and Clinical Psychopharmacology*, 25(6), 456–465.

Tandy-Connor, Stephany; Guiltinan, Jenna; Krempely, Kate; Laduca, Holly; Reineke, Patrick; Gutierrez, Stephanie; . . . Davis,

Brigette Tippin. (2018). False-positive results released by direct-to-consumer genetic tests highlight the importance of clinical confirmation testing for appropriate patient care. *Genetics in Medicine*, 20, 1515–1521.

Taneri, Petek Eylul; Jong, Jessica C. Kiefte-de; Bramer, Wichor M.; Daan, Nadine M. P.; Franco, Oscar H. & Muka, Taulant. (2016). Association of alcohol consumption with the onset of natural menopause: A systematic review and meta-analysis. *Human Reproduction Update*, 22(4), 516–528.

Tang, Dan; Lin, Zhiyong & Chen, Feinian. (2020). Moving beyond living arrangements: The role of family and friendship ties in promoting mental health for urban and rural older adults in China. *Aging & Mental Health*, 24(9), 1523–1532.

Tang, Stephanie. (2020). The spike in silver splitters: Examining special considerations for graying divorces. *The Elder Law Journal*, 28.

Tang, Shu Min; Lau, Tiffany; Rong, Shi Song; Yazar, Seyhan; Chen, Li Jia; Mackey, David A.; . . . Yam, Jason C. (2019). Vitamin D and its pathway genes in myopia: Systematic review and meta-analysis. *British Journal of Ophthalmology*, 103(1), 8–17.

Tang, Yi-Yuan & Posner, Michael I. (2015). Mindfulness and training attention. In Ostafin, Brian D.; Robinson, Michael D. & Meier, Brian P. (Eds.), *Handbook of mindfulness and self-regulation* (pp. 23–32). Springer.

Tangen, Jodi L. & Borders, L. DiAnne. (2017). Applying information processing theory to supervision: An initial exploration. *Counselor*, 56(2), 98–111.

Tangkhpanya, Fatima; Le Carrour, Morgane; Doucet, Félicia & Gagné, Jean-Pierre. (2019). The effort required to comprehend a short documentary in noise: A comparison of younger and older francophones. *American Journal of Audiology*, 28(Suppl. 3), 756–761.

Taormina, Robert J. & Gao, Jennifer H. (2013). Maslow and the motivation hierarchy: Measuring satisfaction of the needs. *The American Journal of Psychology*, 126(2), 155–177.

Tappin, Ben M. & McKay, Ryan T. (2019). Moral polarization and out-party hostility in the US political context. *Journal of Social and Political Psychology*, 7(1).

Tassell-Matamua, Natasha; Lindsay, Nicole; Bennett, Simon; Valentine, Hukarere & Pahina, John. (2017). Does learning about near-death experiences promote psycho-spiritual benefits in those who have not had a near-death experience? *Journal of Spirituality in Mental Health*, 19(2), 95–115.

Taylor, Caroline M.; Wernimont, Susan M.; Northstone, Kate & Emmett, Pauline M. (2015). Picky/fussy eating in children: Review of definitions, assessment, prevalence and dietary intakes. *Appetite*, 95, 349–359.

Taylor, John H. (Ed.) (2010). *Journey through the afterlife: Ancient Egyptian Book of the Dead*. Harvard University Press.

Taylor, Marjorie; Mottweiler, Candice M.; Aguiar, Naomi R.; Naylor, Emilee R. & Levernier, Jacob G. (2020). Paracosms: The

imaginary worlds of middle childhood. *Child Development*, 91(1), e164–e178.

Taylor, Zoe E.; Eisenberg, Nancy; Spinrad, Tracy L.; Eggum, Natalie D. & Sulik, Michael J. (2013). The relations of ego-resiliency and emotion socialization to the development of empathy and prosocial behavior across early childhood. *Emotion*, 13(5), 822–831.

Teater, Barbra & Chonody, Jill M. (2019). How do older adults define successful aging? A scoping review. *The International Journal of Aging and Human Development*, (In Press).

Tedeschi, Richard; Orejuela-Davila, Ana & Lewis, Paisley. (2017). Posttraumatic growth and continuing bonds. In Klass, Dennis & Steffen, Edith Maria (Eds.), *Continuing bonds in bereavement: New directions for research and practice*. Routledge.

Teicher, Martin H.; Anderson, Carl M.; Ohashi, Kyoko; Khan, Alaptagin; McGreenery, Cynthia E.; Bolger, Elizabeth A.; . . . D., Vitaliano Gordana. (2018). Differential effects of childhood neglect and abuse during sensitive exposure periods on male and female hippocampus. *NeuroImage*, 169, 443–452.

Teicher, Martin H.; Anderson, Carl M.; Ohashi, Kyoko; Khan, Alaptagin; McGreenery, Cynthia E.; Bolger, Elizabeth A.; . . . Vitaliano, Gordana D. (2018). Differential effects of childhood neglect and abuse during sensitive exposure periods on male and female hippocampus. *NeuroImage*, 169, 443–452.

Telzer, Eva H.; Ichien, Nicholas T. & Qu, Yang. (2015). Mothers know best: Redirecting adolescent reward sensitivity toward safe behavior during risk taking. *Social Cognitive and Affective Neuroscience*, 10(10), 1383–1391.

TenHouten, Warren D. (2017). From primary emotions to the spectrum of affect: An evolutionary neurosociology of the emotions. In Ibáñez, Agustín; Sedeño, Lucas & García, Adolfo M. (Eds.), *Neuroscience and social science: The missing link* (pp. 141–167). Springer.

TenHouten, Warren D. (2018). Anticipation and exploration of nature and the social world: Natural-history versus social-cognition theories of the evolution of human intelligence. *Sociology Mind*, 8(4), 320–344.

Teresi, Dick. (2012). *The undead: Organ harvesting, the ice-water test, beating-heart cadavers—How medicine is blurring the line between life and death*. Pantheon Books.

Terman, Lewis M. (1925). *Genetic studies of genius*. Stanford University Press.

Terry, Nicole Patton; Connor, Carol McDonald; Johnson, Lakeisha; Stuckey, Adrienne & Tani, Novell. (2016). Dialect variation, dialect-shifting, and reading comprehension in second grade. *Reading and Writing*, 29(2), 267–295.

Tham, Diana Su Yun; Woo, Pei Jun & Bremner, J. Gavin. (2019). Development of the other-race effect in Malaysian-Chinese infants. *Developmental Psychobiology*, 61(1), 107–115.

Thayer, Amanda L.; Petruzzelli, Alexandra & McClurg, Caitlin E. (2018). Addressing the paradox of the team innovation process: A review and practical considerations. *American Psychologist*, 73(4), 363–375.

Thelen, Esther & Smith, Linda B. (2006). Dynamic systems theories. In Lerner, Richard M. & Damon, William (Eds.), *Handbook of child psychology* (6th ed., Vol. 1, pp. 258–312). Wiley.

Thiam, Melinda A.; Flake, Eric M. & Dickman, Michael M. (2017). Infant and child mental health and perinatal illness. In Thiam, Melinda A. (Ed.), *Perinatal mental health and the military family: Identifying and treating mood and anxiety disorders.* Routledge.

Thomaes, Sander; Brummelman, Eddie & Sedikides, Constantine. (2017). Why most children think well of themselves. *Child Development, 88*(6), 1873–1884.

Thomas, Alexander & Chess, Stella. (1977). *Temperament and development.* Brunner/Mazel.

Thomas, Dylan. (2003). *The poems of Dylan Thomas* (Rev. ed.). New Directions.

Thomas, John M.; Cooney, Leo M. & Fried, Terri R. (2019). Prognosis reconsidered in light of ancient insights—from Hippocrates to modern medicine. *JAMA Internal Medicine, 179*(6), 820–823.

Thompson, Catherine; Quigley, Eileen & Taylor, Ashley. (2020). The influence of a short-term mindfulness meditation intervention on emotion and visual attention. *Journal of Cognitive Enhancement,* (In Press).

Thompson, Richard; Kaczor, Kim; Lorenz, Douglas J.; Bennett, Berkeley L.; Meyers, Gabriel & Pierce, Mary Clyde. (2017). Is the use of physical discipline associated with aggressive behaviors in young children? *Academic Pediatrics, 17*(1), 34–44.

Thorup, Bianca; Crookes, Kate; Chang, Paul P. W.; Burton, Nichola; Pond, Stephen; Li, Tze Kwan; . . . Rhodes, Gillian. (2018). Perceptual experience shapes our ability to categorize faces by national origin: A new other-race effect. *British Journal of Psychology, 109*(3), 583–603.

Ting, Fransisca; Dawkins, Melody Buyukozer; Stavans, Maayan & Baillargeon, Renée. (2020). Principles and concepts in early moral cognition. In Decety, Jean (Ed.), *The social brain: A developmental perspective.* MIT Press.

Tomasello, Michael & Herrmann, Esther. (2010). Ape and human cognition. *Current Directions in Psychological Science, 19*(1), 3–8.

Torpey, Elka. (2018, April). Measuring the value of education. Career Outlook, U.S. Bureau of Labor Statistics.

Torre, Lindsey A.; Bray, Freddie; Siegel, Rebecca L.; Ferlay, Jacques; Lortet-Tieulent, Joannie & Jemal, Ahmedin. (2015). Global cancer statistics. *CA: A Cancer Journal for Clinicians, 65*(2), 87–108.

Toth, Sheree L. & Manly, Jody T. (2019). Developmental consequences of child abuse and neglect: Implications for intervention. *Child Development Perspectives, 13*(1), 59–65.

Townsend, Apollo; March, Alice L. & Kimball, Jan. (2017). Can faith and hospice coexist: Is the African American church the key to increased hospice utilization for African Americans? *Journal of Transcultural Nursing, 28*(1), 32–39.

Tracey, Terence J. G.; Wampold, Bruce E.; Lichtenberg, James W. & Goodyear, Rodney K. (2014). Expertise in psychotherapy: An elusive goal? *American Psychologist, 69*(3), 218–229.

Trask, Sara L.; Horstman, Haley Kranstuber & Hesse, Colin. (2020). Deceptive affection across relational contexts: A group comparison of romantic relationships, cross-sex friendships, and friends with benefits relationships. *Communication Research, 47*(4), 623–643.

Trauer, James M.; Qian, Mary Y.; Doyle, Joseph S.; Rajaratnam, Shantha M. W. & Cunnington, David. (2015). Cognitive behavioral therapy for chronic insomnia: A systematic review and meta-analysis. *Annals of Internal Medicine, 163*(3), 191–204.

Trevarthen, Colwyn. (2017). The function of emotions in early infant communication and development. In Nadel, Jacqueline & Camaioni, Luigia (Eds.), *New perspectives in early communicative development.* Routledge.

Trivedi, Daksha. (2015). Cochrane Review Summary: Massage for promoting mental and physical health in typically developing infants under the age of six months. *Primary Health Care Research & Development, 16*(1), 3–4.

Troll, Lillian E. & Skaff, Marilyn McKean. (1997). Perceived continuity of self in very old age. *Psychology and Aging, 12*(1), 162–169.

Trompeter, Susan E.; Bettencourt, Ricki & Barrett-Connor, Elizabeth. (2012). Sexual activity and satisfaction in healthy community-dwelling older women. *The American Journal of Medicine, 125*(1), 37–43.e1.

Trucco, Elisa M.; Villafuerte, Sandra; Hussong, Andrea; Burmeister, Margit & Zucker, Robert A. (2018). Biological underpinnings of an internalizing pathway to alcohol, cigarette, and marijuana use. *Journal of Abnormal Psychology, 127*(1), 79–91.

Tsang, Christine; Falk, Simone & Hessel, Alexandria. (2017). Infants prefer infant-directed song over speech. *Child Development, 88*(4), 1207–1215.

Tsang, Tawny; Ogren, Marissa; Peng, Yujia; Nguyen, Bryan; Johnson, Kerri L. & Johnson, Scott P. (2018). Infant perception of sex differences in biological motion displays. *Journal of Experimental Child Psychology, 173*, 338–350.

Tu, Kelly M.; Erath, Stephen A. & El-Sheikh, Mona. (2017). Parental management of peers and autonomic nervous system reactivity in predicting adolescent peer relationships. *Developmental Psychology, 53*(3), 540–551.

Tuliao, Antover P.; Hoffman, Lesa & McChargue, Dennis E. (2017). Measuring individual differences in responses to date-rape vignettes using latent variable models. *Aggressive Behavior, 43*(1), 60–73.

Tulving, Endel. (1983). *Elements of episodic memory.* Oxford University Press.

Tulving, Endel & Donaldson, Wayne (Eds.). (1972). *Organization of memory.* Academic Press.

Tummeltshammer, Kristen S.; Wu, Rachel; Sobel, David M. & Kirkham, Natasha Z. (2014). Infants track the reliability of potential informants. *Psychological Science, 25*(9), 1730–1738.

Turunen, J.; Fransson, E. & Bergström, M. (2017). Self-esteem in children in joint physical custody and other living arrangements. *Public Health, 149*, 106–112.

Twenge, Jean M. (2020). Possible reasons US adults are not having sex as much as they used to. *JAMA Network Open, 3*(6), e203889.

Upchurch, Daniel & Gibson, Donna. (2020). Strange situation at the border: Examining the importance of attachment and consequences of forcible separation. *Global Social Welfare, 7*, 257–261.

U.S. Bureau of Labor Statistics. (2019, January 18). *Labor force statistics from the current population survey: Employed persons by detailed occupation, sex, race, and Hispanic or Latino ethnicity. Household data annual averages.* Washington, DC: U.S. Department of Labor.

U.S. Census Bureau. (1907). *Statistical abstract of the United States 1906.* Washington, DC: U.S. Department of Commerce.

U.S. Census Bureau. (2016a). *Selected population profile in the United States: 2014 American community survey 1-year estimates. American FactFinder.* Washington, DC: U.S. Department of Commerce.

U.S. Census Bureau. (2016b). *Selected population profile in the United States: 2009 American community survey 1-year estimates. American FactFinder.* Washington, DC: U.S. Department of Commerce.

U.S. Census Bureau. (2018, February 19). CPS historical time series tables: Table A-1. Years of school completed by people 25 years and over, by age and sex: Selected years 1940 to 2018. U.S. Census Bureau.

U.S. Census Bureau. (2018, November). *Historical living arrangements of children: Living arrangements of children under 18 years old: 1960 to present.* U.S. Census Bureau.

U.S. Census Bureau. (2019, June). *Annual estimates of the resident population by sex, age, race, and Hispanic origin for the United States and States: April 1, 2010 to July 1, 2018. American FactFinder.* Washington, DC: U.S. Department of Commerce. PEPASR6H.

U.S. Census Bureau. (2019, November). *Historical living arrangements of children: Living arrangements of children under 18 years old: 1960 to present.*

U.S. Census Bureau. (2020). Voting and registration. U.S. Department of Commerce.

U.S. Census Bureau, Population Division. (2010, June). *Monthly resident population estimates by age, sex, race and Hispanic origin for the United States: April 1, 2000 to July 1, 2009.* Washington, DC: U.S. Census Bureau.

U.S. Department of Health and Human Services. (2000, December 31). *Child maltreatment 2000.* Washington, DC: Administration on Children, Youth and Families, Children's Bureau.

U.S. Department of Health and Human Services. (2010). *Head Start impact study: Final report.* Washington, DC: Administration for Children and Families.

U.S. Department of Health and Human Services. (2017, January 19). *Child maltreatment 2015.* Washington, DC: Administration on Children, Youth and Families, Administration on Children, Youth and Families, Children's Bureau.

U.S. Department of Health and Human Services. (2018, February 1). *Child maltreatment 2016.* Washington, DC: Administration for Children and Families, Administration on Children, Youth and Families, Children's Bureau.

U.S. Department of Health and Human Services. (2019, January 28). *Child maltreatment 2017*. Washington, DC: Administration for Children and Families, Administration on Children, Youth and Families, Children's Bureau.

U.S. Department of Health and Human Services. (2020, January 15). *Child maltreatment 2018*. Washington, DC: Administration for Children and Families, Administration on Children, Youth and Families, Children's Bureau.

U.S. Department of Health and Human Services, National Institute of Mental Health. (2017). Mental illness. Health and Human Services.

U.S. Preventive Services Task Force. (2002). Postmenopausal hormone replacement therapy for primary prevention of chronic conditions: Recommendations and rationale. *Annals of Internal Medicine, 137*(10), 834–839.

Ueda, Peter; Mercer, Catherine H.; Ghaznavi, Cyrus & Herbenick, Debby. (2020). Trends in frequency of sexual activity and number of sexual partners among adults aged 18 to 44 years in the US, 2000–2018. *JAMA Network Open, 3*(6), e203833.

Uekermann, J.; Kraemer, M.; Abdel-Hamid, M.; Schimmelmann, B. G.; Hebebrand, J.; Daum, I.; . . . Kis, B. (2010). Social cognition in Attention-deficit hyperactivity disorder (ADHD). *Neuroscience & Biobehavioral Reviews, 34*(5), 734–743.

Umaña-Taylor, Adriana J. & Hill, Nancy E. (2020). Ethnic–racial socialization in the family: A decade's advance on precursors and outcomes. *Journal of Marriage and Family, 82*(1), 244–271.

Umapathi, Kishore Krishna; Thavamani, Aravind & Chotikanatis, Kobkul. (2019). Incidence trends, risk factors, mortality and healthcare utilization in congenital syphilis-related hospitalizations in the United States: A nationwide population analysis. *The Pediatric Infectious Disease Journal, 38*(11), 1126–1130.

Underwood, Emily. (2013). Why do so many neurons commit suicide during brain development? *Science, 340*(6137), 1157–1158.

Underwood, Emily. (2014, October 31). An easy consciousness test? *Science, 346*(6209), 531–532.

UNESCO. (2014). *Country profiles. UNESCO Institute for Statistics Data Centre.* Montreal, Canada: UNESCO, Université de Montréal at the Montreal's École des hautes études.

UNICEF. (2015). *Rapid survey on children (RSOC) 2013–14: National report.* Ministry of Women and Child Development, Government of India.

UNICEF. (2017, January 13). *Global overview child malnutrition 1990–2015. UNICEF Data and Analytics: Joint Malnutrition Estimates 2016 Edition.* New York: NY: United Nations.

United Nations. (2015, July). *Probabilistic population projections based on the World Population Prospects: The 2015 Revision.* New York: Population Division, DESA.

United Nations. (2017). *World population ageing 2017—Highlights.* New York, NY: United Nations, Department of Economic and Social Affairs, Population Division. ST/ESA/SER.A/397.

United Nations, Department of Economic and Social Affairs, Population Division.

(2019). *World population prospects 2019.* New York, NY: (Volumes 1 & 2: ST/ESA/SER.A/426 & ST/ESA/SER.A/427).

UNODC. (2013). *Global study on homicide 2013.* Vienna: UNODC Research and Trend Analysis Branch, Division of Policy Analysis and Public Affairs. 14.IV.1.

Urbanaviciute, Ieva; Udayar, Shagini; Maggiori, Christian & Rossier, Jérôme. (2020). Precariousness profile and career adaptability as determinants of job insecurity: A three-wave study. *Journal of Career Development, 47*(2), 146–161.

Usher, Kim; Bhullar, Navjot; Durkin, Joanne; Gyamfi, Naomi & Jackson, Debra. (2020). Family violence and COVID-19: Increased vulnerability and reduced options for support. *International Journal of Mental Health Nursing, 29*(4), 549–552.

Vaillant, George E. (1977). *Adaptation to life.* Little, Brown.

Valente, Dannyelle; Theurel, Anne & Gentaz, Edouard. (2018). The role of visual experience in the production of emotional facial expressions by blind people: A review. *Psychonomic Bulletin & Review, 25*, 483–497.

Valentine, Christine. (2017). Identity and continuing bonds in cross-cultural perspective: Britain and Japan. In Klass, Dennis & Steffen, Edith Maria (Eds.), *Continuing bonds in bereavement: New directions for research and practice.* Routledge.

Valiente, Carlos; Swanson, Jodi; DeLay, Dawn; Fraser, Ashley M. & Parker, Julia H. (2020). Emotion-related socialization in the classroom: Considering the roles of teachers, peers, and the classroom context. *Developmental Psychology, 56*(3), 578–594.

Välimaa, Taina T.; Kunnari, Sari M.; Laukkanen-Nevala, Päivi & Ertmer, David J. (2019). Vocal development in infants and toddlers with bilateral cochlear implants and infants with normal hearing. *Journal of Speech, Language, and Hearing Research, 62*(5), 1296–1308.

Vallas, Steven & Schor, Juliet B. (2020). What do platforms do? Understanding the gig economy. *Annual Review of Sociology, 46*, 273–294.

Valsiner, Jaan. (2006). Developmental epistemology and implications for methodology. In Lerner, Richard M. & Damon, William (Eds.), *Handbook of child psychology* (6th ed., Vol. 1, pp. 166–209). Wiley.

Valtorta, Nicole K.; Kanaan, Mona; Gilbody, Simon; Ronzi, Sara & Hanratty, Barbara. (2016). Loneliness and social isolation as risk factors for coronary heart disease and stroke: Systematic review and meta-analysis of longitudinal observational studies. *Heart, 102*, 1009–1016.

van Batenburg-Eddes, Tamara; Butte, Dick & van de Looij-Jansen, Petra. (2012). Measuring juvenile delinquency: How do self-reports compare with official police statistics? *European Journal of Criminology, 9*(1), 23–37.

van de Bongardt, Daphne; Reitz, Ellen; Sandfort, Theo & Deković, Maja. (2015). A meta-analysis of the relations between three types of peer norms and adolescent sexual behavior. *Personality and Social Psychology Review, 19*(3), 203–234.

van den Akker, Alithe; Deković, Maja; Prinzie, Peter & Asscher, Jessica. (2010).

Toddlers' temperament profiles: Stability and relations to negative and positive parenting. *Journal of Abnormal Child Psychology, 38*(4), 485–495.

van den Berg, Niels; Rodríguez-Girondo, Mar; van Dijk, Ingrid K.; Mourits, Rick J.; Mandemakers, Kees; Janssens, Angelique A. P. O.; . . . Slagboom, P. Eline. (2019). Longevity defined as top 10% survivors and beyond is transmitted as a quantitative genetic trait. *Nature Communications, 10*(1), 1–12.

van den Enden, Thijs; Boom, Jan; Brugman, Daniel & Thoma, Stephen. (2019). Stages of moral judgment development: Applying item response theory to Defining Issues Test data. *Journal of Moral Education, 48*(4), 423–438.

van der Wal, Reine C.; Finkenauer, Catrin & Visser, Margreet M. (2019). Reconciling mixed findings on children's adjustment following high-conflict divorce. *Journal of Child and Family Studies, 28*, 468–478.

Van Dyke, Miriam E.; Cheung, Patricia C.; Franks, Padra & Gazmararian, Julie A. (2018). Socioeconomic and racial/ethnic disparities in physical activity environments in Georgia elementary schools. *American Journal of Health Promotion, 32*(2), 453–463.

van Eerde, Wendelien & Azar, Sana. (2020). Too late? What do you mean? Cultural norms regarding lateness for meetings and appointments. *Cross-Cultural Research, 5*(2/3), 111–129.

Van Gasse, Dries & Mortelmans, Dimitri. (2020). With or without you—Starting single-parent families: A qualitative study on how single parents by choice reorganise their lives to facilitate single parenthood from a life course perspective. *Journal of Family Issues, 41*(11), 2223–2248.

Van Hecke, Wim; Emsell, Louise & Sunaert, Stefan (Eds.). (2016). *Diffusion tensor imaging: A practical handbook.* Springer.

Van Houtte, Mieke. (2016). Lower-track students' sense of academic futility: Selection or effect? *Journal of Sociology, 52*(4), 874–889.

van IJzendoorn, Marinus H. (1990). Developments in cross-cultural research on attachment: Some methodological notes. *Human Development, 33*(1), 3–9.

Van Lancker, Wim & Parolin, Zachary. (2020). COVID-19, school closures, and child poverty: A social crisis in the making. *The Lancet Public Health, 5*(5), e243–e244.

van Nunen, Karolien; Kaerts, Nore; Wyndaele, Jean-Jacques; Vermandel, Alexandra & Van Hal, Guido. (2015). Parents' views on toilet training (TT): A quantitative study to identify the beliefs and attitudes of parents concerning TT. *Journal of Child Health Care, 19*(2), 265–274.

Van Raalte, Judy L.; Vincent, Andrew & Brewer, Britton W. (2017). Self-talk interventions for athletes: A theoretically grounded approach. *Journal of Sport Psychology in Action, 8*(3), 141–151.

Van Ryzin, Mark J. & Dishion, Thomas J. (2013). From antisocial behavior to violence: A model for the amplifying role of coercive joining in adolescent friendships. *Journal of Child Psychology and Psychiatry, 54*(6), 661–669.

Van Tongeren, Daryl R.; DeWall, C. Nathan; Chen, Zhansheng; Sibley, Chris G. & Bulbulia, Joseph. (2020). Religious residue: Cross-cultural evidence that religious psychology and behavior persist following deidentification. *Journal of Personality and Social Psychology*, (In Press).

van Zalk, Maarten H. W.; Nestler, Steffen; Geukes, Katharina; Hutteman, Roos & Back, Mitja D. (2019). The codevelopment of extraversion and friendships: Bonding and behavioral interaction mechanisms in friendship networks. *Journal of Personality and Social Psychology*, *118*(6), 1269–1290.

van Zalk, Maarten H. W.; Nestler, Steffen; Geukes, Katharina; Hutteman, Roos & Back, Mitja D. (2020). The codevelopment of extraversion and friendships: Bonding and behavioral interaction mechanisms in friendship networks. *Journal of Personality and Social Psychology*, *118*(6), 1269–1290.

Vandoros, Sotiris. (2020). Excess mortality during the Covid-19 pandemic: Early evidence from England and Wales. *Social Science & Medicine*, *258*(113101).

Varga, Mary Alice & Paletti, Robin. (2013). Life span issues and dying. In Meagher, David K. & Balk, David E. (Eds.), *Handbook of thanatology: The essential body of knowledge for the study of death, dying, and bereavement* (2nd ed., pp. 25–31). Routledge.

Vaughn, Byron P.; Rank, Kevin M. & Khoruts, Alexander. (2019). Fecal microbiota transplantation: Current status in treatment of GI and liver disease. *Clinical Gastroenterology and Hepatology*, *17*(2), 353–361.

Vedantam, Shankar. (2011, December 5). *What's behind a temper tantrum? Scientists deconstruct the screams.* Hidden Brain. Washington DC: National Public Radio.

Veenstra, René; Dijkstra, Jan Kornelis; Steglich, Christian & Van Zalk, Maarten H. W. (2013). Network-behavior dynamics. *Journal of Research on Adolescence*, *23*(3), 399–412.

Veitia, Reiner A.; Govindaraju, Diddahally R.; Bottani, Samuel & Birchler, James A. (2017). Aging: Somatic mutations, epigenetic drift and gene dosage imbalance. *Trends in Cell Biology*, *27*(4), 299–310.

Velay, Jean-Luc & Longcamp, Marieke. (2012). Handwriting versus typewriting: Behavioral and cerebral consequences in letter recognition. In Torrance, Mark; Alamargot, Denis; Castelló, Montserrat; Ganier, Franck; Kruse, Otto; Mangen, Anne; . . . Van Waes, Luuk (Eds.), *Learning to write effectively: Current trends in European research* (pp. 371–374). Emerald.

Verrusio, Walter; Ettorre, Evaristo; Vicenzini, Edoardo; Vanacore, Nicola; Cacciafesta, Mauro & Mecarelli, Oriano. (2015). The Mozart Effect: A quantitative EEG study. *Consciousness and Cognition*, *35*, 150–155.

Verschoor, Chris P. & Tamim, Hala. (2019). Frailty is inversely related to age at menopause and elevated in women who have had a hysterectomy: An analysis of the Canadian longitudinal study on aging. *The Journals of Gerontology Series A: Biological Sciences & Medical Sciences*, *74*(5), 675–682.

Vigo, Daniel; Thornicroft, Graham & Atun, Rifat. (2016). Estimating the true global burden of mental illness. *The Lancet Psychiatry*, *3*(2), 171–178.

Vinson, Don & Parker, Andrew. (2019). Vygotsky and sports coaching: Non-linear practice in youth and adult settings. *Curriculum Studies in Health and Physical Education*, *10*(1), 91–106.

Visser, Margreet; Van Lawick, Justine; Stith, Sandra M. & Spencer, Chelsea M. (2020). Violence in families: Systemic practice and research. In Ochs, Matthias; Borcsa, Maria & Schweitzer, Jochen (Eds.), *Systemic research in individual, couple, and family therapy and counseling* (pp. 299–315). Springer.

Vitale, Susan; Sperduto, Robert D. & Ferris, Frederick L. (2009). Increased prevalence of myopia in the United States between 1971–1972 and 1999–2004. *Archives of Ophthalmology*, *127*(12), 1632–1639.

Vittner, Dorothy; Mcgrath, Jacqueline; Robinson, Joann; Lawhon, Gretchen; Cusson, Regina; Eisenfeld, Leonard; . . . Cong, Xiaomei. (2018). Increase in oxytocin from skin-to-skin contact enhances development of parent–infant relationship. *Biological Research for Nursing*, *20*(1), 54–62.

Vize, Colin E.; Lynam, Donald R.; Collison, Katherine L. & Miller, Joshua D. (2018). Differences among dark triad components: A meta-analytic investigation. *Personality Disorders*, *9*(2), 101–111.

Voges, Juané; Berg, Astrid & Niehaus, Dana J. H. (2019). Revisiting the African origins of attachment research—50 years on from Ainsworth: A descriptive review. *Infant Mental Health Journal*, *40*(6), 799–816.

Vöhringer, Isabel A.; Kolling, Thorsten; Graf, Frauke; Poloczek, Sonja; Fassbender, Iina; Freitag, Claudia; . . . Knopf, Monika. (2018). The development of implicit memory from infancy to childhood: On average performance levels and interindividual differences. *Child Development*, *89*(2), 370–382.

von Bastian, Claudia C.; Souza, Alessandra S. & Gade, Miriam. (2016). No evidence for bilingual cognitive advantages: A test of four hypotheses. *Journal of Experimental Psychology*, *145*(2), 246–258.

Vygotsky, Lev S. (1980). *Mind in society: The development of higher psychological processes.* Harvard University Press.

Vygotsky, Lev S. (1994a). The development of academic concepts in school aged children. In van der Veer, René & Valsiner, Jaan (Eds.), *The Vygotsky reader* (pp. 355–370). Blackwell.

Vygotsky, Lev S. (1994b). Principles of social education for deaf and dumb children in Russia. In van der Veer, Rene & Valsiner, Jaan (Eds.), *The Vygotsky reader* (pp. 19–26). Blackwell.

Vygotsky, Lev S. (2012). *Thought and language.* MIT Press.

Waber, Deborah P.; Bryce, Cyralene P.; Fitzmaurice, Garrett M.; Zichlin, Miriam L.; McGaughy, Jill; Girard, Jonathan M. & Galler, Janina R. (2014). Neuropsychological outcomes at midlife following moderate to severe malnutrition in infancy. *Neuropsychology*, *28*(4), 530–540.

Wadman, Meredith. (2018). 'Rapid onset' of transgender identity ignites storm. *Science*, *361*(6406), 958–959.

Wagner, Jenny; Lüdtke, Oliver & Robitzsch, Alexander. (2019). Does personality become more stable with age? Disentangling state and trait effects for the Big Five across the life span using local structural equation modeling. *Journal of Personality and Social Psychology*, *116*(4), 666–680.

Wagner, Katie; Dobkins, Karen & Barner, David. (2013). Slow mapping: Color word learning as a gradual inductive process. *Cognition*, *127*(3), 307–317.

Wakam, Glenn K.; Montgomery, John R.; Biesterveld, Ben E. & Brown, Craig S. (2020). Not dying alone—Modern compassionate care in the Covid-19 pandemic. *New England Journal of Medicine*, *382*, e88.

Walker, Lauren; Stefanis, Leonidas & Attems, Johannes. (2019). Clinical and neuropathological differences between Parkinson's disease, Parkinson's disease dementia and dementia with Lewy bodies—current issues and future directions. *Journal of Neurochemistry*, *150*(5), 467–474.

Walker, Matthew P. (2017). *Why we sleep: Unlocking the power of sleep and dreams.* Scribner.

Wallis, Christopher J. D.; Lo, Kirk; Lee, Yuna; Krakowsky, Yonah; Garbens, Alaina; Satkunasivam, Raj; . . . Nam, Robert K. (2016). Survival and cardiovascular events in men treated with testosterone replacement therapy: An intention-to-treat observational cohort study. *The Lancet Diabetes & Endocrinology*, *4*(6), 498–506.

Walter, Melissa Clucas & Lippard, Christine N. (2017). Head Start teachers across a decade: Beliefs, characteristics, and time spent on academics. *Early Childhood Education Journal*, *45*(5), 693–702.

Wambach, Karen & Spencer, Becky. (2019). *Breastfeeding and human lactation* (6th ed.). Jones & Bartlett.

Wanberg, Connie R. (2012). The individual experience of unemployment. *Annual Review of Psychology*, *63*, 369–396.

Wang, Chao; Xue, Haifeng; Wang, Qianqian; Hao, Yongchen; Li, Dianjiang; Gu, Dongfeng & Huang, Jianfeng. (2014). Effect of drinking on all-cause mortality in women compared with men: A meta-analysis. *Journal of Women's Health*, *23*(5), 373–381.

Wang, Fushun; Yang, Jiongjiong; Pan, Fang; Ho, Roger C. & Huang, Jason H. (2020). Editorial: Neurotransmitters and emotions. *Frontiers in Psychology*, *11*(21).

Wang, Meifang & Liu, Li. (2018). Reciprocal relations between harsh discipline and children's externalizing behavior in China: A 5-year longitudinal study. *Child Development*, *89*(1), 174–187.

Wang, Ming-Te; Henry, Daphne A.; Smith, Leann V.; Huguley, James P. & Guo, Jiesi. (2020). Parental ethnic-racial socialization practices and children of color's psychosocial and behavioral adjustment: A systematic review and meta-analysis. *American Psychologist*, *75*(1), 1–22.

Ward, Emma V.; Berry, Christopher J. & Shanks, David R. (2013). Age effects on explicit and implicit memory. *Frontiers in Psychology*, 4(639).

Ward, Sarah J. & King, Laura A. (2016). Poor but happy? Income, happiness, and experienced and expected meaning in life. *Social Psychological & Personality Science*, 7(5), 463–470.

Wass, Sam V.; Noreika, Valdas; Georgieva, Stanimira; Clackson, Kaili; Brightman, Laura; Nutbrown, Rebecca; . . . Leong, Vicky. (2018). Parental neural responsivity to infants' visual attention: How mature brains influence immature brains during social interaction. *PLoS Biology*, 16(12), e2006328.

Watson, John B. (1924). *Behaviorism*. The People's Institute Pub. Co.

Watson, John B. (1998). *Behaviorism*. Transaction.

Wearing, Deborah. (2005). *Forever today: A memoir of love and amnesia*. Doubleday.

Weber, Ann; Fernald, Anne & Diop, Yatma. (2017). When cultural norms discourage talking to babies: Effectiveness of a parenting program in rural Senegal. *Child Development*, 88(5), 1513–1526.

Weber, Daniela; Dekhtyar, Serhiy & Herlitz, Agneta. (2017). The Flynn Effect in Europe—Effects of sex and region. *Intelligence*, 60, 39–45.

Webster, Collin A. & Suzuki, Naoki. (2014). Land of the rising pulse: A social ecological perspective of physical activity opportunities for schoolchildren in Japan. *Journal of Teaching in Physical Education*, 33(3), 304–325.

Wehry, Anna M.; Ramsey, Laura; Dulemba, Shane E.; Mossman, Sarah A. & Strawn, Jeffrey R. (2018). Pharmacogenomic testing in child and adolescent psychiatry: An evidence-based review. *Current Problems in Pediatric and Adolescent Health Care*, 48(2), 40–49.

Weisleder, Pedro & Rublee, Caitlin. (2018). The neuropsychological consequences of armed conflicts and torture. *Current Neurology and Neuroscience Reports*, 18(3), 1–6.

Weisman, Kara; Johnson, Marissa V. & Shutts, Kristin. (2015). Young children's automatic encoding of social categories. *Developmental Science*, 18(6), 1036–1043.

Weiss, David & Lang, Frieder R. (2012). "They" are old but "I" feel younger: Age-group dissociation as a self-protective strategy in old age. *Psychology and Aging*, 27(1), 153–163.

Weiss, Francesco; Barbuti, Margherita; Carignani, Giulia; Calderone, Alba; Santini, Ferruccio; Maremmani, Icro & Perugi, Giulio. (2020). Psychiatric aspects of obesity: A narrative review of pathophysiology and psychopathology. *Journal of Clinical Medicine*, 9(8), 2344.

Weisskirch, Robert S. (2017a). A developmental perspective on language brokering. In Weisskirch, Robert S. (Ed.), *Language brokering in immigrant families: Theories and contexts*. Routledge.

Weisskirch, Robert S. (2017b). *Language brokering in immigrant families: Theories and contexts*. Routledge.

Welzel, Christian. (2013). *Freedom rising: Human empowerment and the quest for emancipation*. Cambridge University Press.

Wersebe, Hanna; Lieb, Roselind; Meyer, Andrea H.; Miche, Marcel; Mikoteit, Thorsten; Imboden, Christian; . . . Gloster, Andrew T. (2018). Well-being in major depression and social phobia with and without comorbidity. *International Journal of Clinical and Health Psychology*, 18(3), 201–208.

West, John Lee; Oswald, Roy M. & Guzmán, Nadyne. (2018). *Emotional intelligence for religious leaders*. Rowman & Littlefield.

Westbrook, Laurel & Saperstein, Aliya. (2015). New categories are not enough: Rethinking the measurement of sex and gender in social surveys. *Gender & Society*, 29(4), 534–560.

Westinghouse Learning Corporation. (1969). *The impact of Head Start: An evaluation of the effects of Head Start on children's cognitive and affective development*. Athens, OH: Ohio University. PB 184328.

Wettstein, Markus; Tauber, Benjamin; Kuźma, Elżbieta & Wahl, Hans-Werner. (2017). The interplay between personality and cognitive ability across 12 years in middle and late adulthood: Evidence for reciprocal associations. *Psychology and Aging*, 32(3), 259–277.

Wheelock, M. D.; Hect, J. L.; Hernandez-Andrade, E.; Hassan, S. S.; Romero, R.; Eggebrecht, A. T. & Thomason, M. E. (2019). Sex differences in functional connectivity during fetal brain development. *Developmental Cognitive Neuroscience*, 36(100632).

Whitbourne, Susan K. & Whitbourne, Stacey B. (2014). *Adult development and aging: Biopsychosocial perspectives* (5th ed.). Wiley.

White, Douglas B.; Ernecoff, Natalie; Buddadhumaruk, Praewpannarai; Hong, Seoyeon; Weissfeld, Lisa; Curtis, Randall; . . . Lo, Bernard. (2016). Prevalence of and factors related to discordance about prognosis between physicians and surrogate decision makers of critically ill patients. *JAMA*, 315(19), 2086–2094.

White, Sue; Gibson, Matthew & Wastell, David. (2019). Child protection and disorganized attachment: A critical commentary. *Children and Youth Services Review*, 105(104415).

White-Traut, Rosemary C.; Rankin, Kristin M.; Yoder, Joe; Zawacki, Laura; Campbell, Suzann; Kavanaugh, Karen; . . . Norr, Kathleen F. (2018). Relationship between mother-infant mutual dyadic responsiveness and premature infant development as measured by the Bayley III at 6 weeks corrected age. *Early Human Development*, 121, 21–26.

Whitebook, Joel. (2017). *Freud: An intellectual biography*. Cambridge University Press.

Wickrama, Kandauda; Mancini, Jay A.; Kwag, Kyunghwa & Kwon, Josephine. (2013a). Heterogeneity in multidimensional health trajectories of late old years and socioeconomic stratification: A latent trajectory class analysis. *Journal of Gerontology Series B*, 68(2), 290–297.

Wickrama, Kandauda; O'Neal, Catherine Walker & Lorenz, Fred O. (2013b). Marital functioning from middle to later years: A life course–stress process framework. *Journal of Family Theory & Review*, 5(1), 15–34.

Wicks, Elizabeth. (2012). The meaning of 'life': Dignity and the right to life in international human rights treaties. *Human Rights Law Review*, 12(2), 199–219.

Widom, Cathy Spatz; Czaja, Sally J. & DuMont, Kimberly A. (2015a). Intergenerational transmission of child abuse and neglect: Real or detection bias? *Science*, 347(6229), 1480–1485.

Widom, Cathy Spatz; Horan, Jacqueline & Brzustowicz, Linda. (2015b). Childhood maltreatment predicts allostatic load in adulthood. *Child Abuse & Neglect*, 47, 59–69.

Widström, Ann-Marie; Brimdyr, Kajsa; Svensson, Kristin; Cadwell, Karin & Nissen, Eva. (2019). Skin-to-skin contact the first hour after birth, underlying implications and clinical practice. *Acta Paediatrica*, 108(7), 1192–1204.

Wieck, Cornelia & Kunzmann, Ute. (2017). Age differences in emotion recognition: A question of modality? *Psychology and Aging*, 32(5), 401–411.

Wiedermann, Wolfgang; Reinke, Wendy M. & Herman, Keith C. (2020). Prosocial skills causally mediate the relation between effective classroom management and academic competence: An application of direction dependence analysis. *Developmental Psychology*, 56(9), 1723–1735.

Wijdicks, Eelco F. M.; Varelas, Panayiotis N.; Gronseth, Gary S. & Greer, David M. (2010). Evidence-based guideline update: Determining brain death in adults; Report of the quality standards subcommittee of the American Academy of Neurology. *Neurology*, 74(23), 1911–1918.

Wilkerson, Isabel. (2020). *Caste: The origins of our discontents*. Random House.

Willard-Grace, Rachel; Knox, Margae; Huang, Beatrice; Hammer, Hali; Kivlahan, Coleen & Grumbach, Kevin. (2019). Burnout and health care workforce turnover. *Annals of Family Medicine*, 17(1), 36–41.

Williams, Anne M.; Chantry, Caroline; Geubbels, Eveline L.; Ramaiya, Astha K.; Shemdoe, Aloisia I.; Tancredi, Daniel J. & Young, Sera L. (2016). Breastfeeding and complementary feeding practices among HIV-exposed infants in coastal Tanzania. *Journal of Human Lactation*, 32(1), 112–122.

Williams, Lela Rankin; Fox, Nathan A.; Lejuez, C. W.; Reynolds, Elizabeth K.; Henderson, Heather A.; Perez-Edgar, Koraly E.; . . . Pine, Daniel S. (2010). Early temperament, propensity for risk-taking and adolescent substance-related problems: A prospective multi-method investigation. *Addictive Behaviors*, 35(2), 1148–1151.

Williams, Lisa Ann; Giddings, Lynne S.; Bellamy, Gary & Gott, Merryn. (2017). 'Because it's the wife who has to look after the man': A descriptive qualitative study of older women and the intersection of gender and the provision of family caregiving at the end of life. *Palliative Medicine*, 31(3), 223–230.

Williams, Shanna; Moore, Kelsey; Crossman, Angela M. & Talwar, Victoria. (2016). The role of executive functions and theory of mind in children's prosocial lie-telling. *Journal of Experimental Child Psychology*, 141, 256–266.

Williamson, Bess. (2019). *Accessible America: A history of disability and design.* New York University Press.

Willis, Benjamin L.; Leonard, David; Barlow, Carolyn E.; Martin, Scott B.; DeFina, Laura F. & Trivedi, Madhukar H. (2018). Association of midlife cardiorespiratory fitness with incident depression and cardiovascular death after depression in later life. *JAMA Psychiatry, 75*(9), 911–917.

Wimmer, Heinz & Perner, Josef. (1983). Beliefs about beliefs: Representation and constraining function of wrong beliefs in young children's understanding of deception. *Cognition, 13*(1), 103–128.

Windhorst, Dafna A.; Mileva-Seitz, Viara R.; Linting, Mariëlle; Hofman, Albert; Jaddoe, Vincent W. V.; Verhulst, Frank C.; . . . Bakermans-Kranenburg, Marian J. (2015). Differential susceptibility in a developmental perspective: DRD4 and maternal sensitivity predicting externalizing behavior. *Developmental Psychobiology, 57*(1), 35–49.

Winn, Phoebe; Acharya, Krishna; Peterson, Erika & Leuthner, Steven R. (2018). Prenatal counseling and parental decision-making following a fetal diagnosis of trisomy 13 or 18. *Journal of Perinatology, 38*(7), 788–796.

Withrock, Isabelle C.; Anderson, Stephen J.; Jefferson, Matthew A.; Mccormack, Garrett R.; Mlynarczyk, Gregory S. A.; Nakama, Aron; . . . Carlson, Steve A. (2015). Genetic diseases conferring resistance to infectious diseases. *Genes & Diseases, 2*(3), 247–254.

Wittrup, Audrey R.; Hussain, Saida B.; Albright, Jamie N.; Hurd, Noelle M.; Varner, Fatima A. & Mattis, Jacqueline S. (2016). Natural mentors, racial pride, and academic engagement among Black adolescents: Resilience in the context of perceived discrimination. *Youth & Society.*

Wolbert, Lynne S.; de Ruyter, Doret J. & Schinkel, Anders. (2018). What attitude should parents have towards their children's future flourishing? *Theory and Research in Education, 16*(1), 82–97.

Wolchik, Sharlene A.; Ma, Yue; Tein, Jenn-Yun; Sandler, Irwin N. & Ayers, Tim S. (2008). Parentally bereaved children's grief: Self-system beliefs as mediators of the relations between grief and stressors and caregiver-child relationship quality. *Death Studies, 32*(7), 597–620.

Wolf, Norman S. (Ed.) (2010). *Comparative biology of aging.* Springer.

Wolff, Kevin T.; Baber, Laura M.; Dozier, Christine A. & Cordeiro, Roberto. (2020). Assessing the efficacy of alternatives to incarceration within seven federal districts. *Justice Evaluation Journal, 3*(1), 27–53.

Wong, Jaclyn S. & Waite, Linda J. (2015). Marriage, social networks, and health at older ages. *Journal of Population Ageing, 8*(1/2), 7–25.

Wood, Alex J.; Graham, Mark; Lehdonvirta, Vili & Hjorth, Isis. (2019). Good gig, bad gig: Autonomy and algorithmic control in the global gig economy. *Work, Employment and Society, 33*(1), 56–75.

Woods, Simon & Graven, Vibeke. (2020). Intentions and the doctrine of double effect. In Emmerich, Nathan; Mallia, Pierre; Gordijn, Bert & Pistoia, Francesca (Eds.), *Contemporary European perspectives on the ethics of end of life care* (pp. 169–179). Springer.

Woodward, Amanda L. & Markman, Ellen M. (1998). Early word learning. In Kuhn, Deanna & Siegler, Robert S. (Eds.), *Handbook of child psychology* (5th ed., Vol. 2, pp. 371–420). Wiley.

Woollett, Katherine; Spiers, Hugo J. & Maguire, Eleanor A. (2009). Talent in the taxi: A model system for exploring expertise. *Philosophical Transactions of the Royal Society of London, 364*(1522), 1407–1416.

World Bank. (2019, August). *GDP per capita (current US$)* [Data set].

World Health Organization. (2006). WHO Motor Development Study: Windows of achievement for six gross motor development milestones. *Acta Paediatrica, 95*(Suppl. 450), 86–95.

World Health Organization. (2012). *Dementia: A public health priority.* Geneva, Switzerland: World Health Organization.

World Health Organization. (2015, September). *Noncommunicable diseases progress monitor 2015.* World Health Organization.

World Health Organization. (2017, April 28). Measles vaccines: WHO position paper—April 2017. *Weekly Epidemiological Record, 17*(92), 205–228.

World Health Organization. (2017, September 29). Global Health Observatory data repository: Prevalence of obesity among children and adolescents, BMI>+2 standard deviation above the median, crude estimates by country, among children aged 5–19 years. World Health Organization.

Wörmann, Viktoriya; Holodynski, Manfred; Kärtner, Joscha & Keller, Heidi. (2012). A cross-cultural comparison of the development of the social smile: A longitudinal study of maternal and infant imitation in 6- and 12-week-old infants. *Infant Behavior and Development, 35*(2), 335–347.

Wrzus, Cornelia; Hänel, Martha; Wagner, Jenny & Neyer, Franz J. (2013). Social network changes and life events across the life span: A meta-analysis. *Psychological Bulletin, 139*(1), 53–80.

Wu, Alfred M. & Hawkins, John N. (Eds.). (2018). *Massification of higher education in Asia: Consequences, policy responses and changing governance.* Springer.

Wu, Ming-Yih & Ho, Hong-Nerng. (2015). Cost and safety of assisted reproductive technologies for human immunodeficiency virus-1 discordant couples. *World Journal of Virology, 4*(2), 142–146.

Wyatt, Tristram D. (2015). The search for human pheromones: The lost decades and the necessity of returning to first principles. *Proceedings of the Royal Society B: Biological Sciences, 282*(1804).

Xie, Weizhen; Berry, Anne; Lustig, Cindy; Deldin, Patricia & Zhang, Weiwei. (2019). Poor sleep quality and compromised visual working memory capacity. *Journal of the International Neuropsychological Society, 25*(6), 583–594.

Xin, Meiqi; Luo, Sitong; She, Rui; Yu, Yanqiu; Li, Lijuan; Wang, Suhua; . . . Lau, Joseph Tak-fai. (2020). Negative cognitive and psychological correlates of mandatory quarantine during the initial COVID-19 outbreak in China. *American Psychologist, 75*(5), 607–617.

Xiong, Xiang-Dong; Xiong, Wei-Dong; Xiong, Shang-Shen & Chen, Gui-Hai. (2018). Age- and gender-based differences in nest-building behavior and learning and memory performance measured using a radial six-armed water maze in C57BL/6 mice. *Behavioural Neurology, 2018*(8728415).

Xu, Fei. (2013). The object concept in human infants: Commentary on Fields. *Human Development, 56*(3), 167–170.

Xu, Fei & Kushnir, Tamar. (2013). Infants are rational constructivist learners. *Current Directions in Psychological Science, 22*(1), 28–32.

Xu, Guifeng; Strathearn, Lane; Liu, Buyun; Yang, Binrang & Bao, Wei. (2018). Twenty-year trends in diagnosed Attention-deficit/hyperactivity disorder among US children and adolescents, 1997–2016. *JAMA Network Open, 1*(4), e181471.

Xu, Guifeng; Strathearn, Lane; Liu, Buyun; O'Brien, Matthew; Kopelman, Todd G.; Zhu, Jing; . . . Bao, Wei. (2019). Prevalence and treatment patterns of autism spectrum disorder in the United States, 2016. *JAMA Pediatrics, 173*(2), 153–159.

Xu, Hongwei. (2019). Physical and mental health of Chinese grandparents caring for grandchildren and great-grandparents. *Social Science & Medicine, 229*, 106–116.

Xu, Xiaofeng; Huebner, E. Scott & Tian, Lili. (2020). Profiles of narcissism and self-esteem associated with comprehensive mental health in adolescents. *Journal of Adolescence, 80*, 275–287.

Yackobovitch-Gavan, Michal; Wolf Linhard, D.; Nagelberg, Nessia; Poraz, Irit; Shalitin, Shlomit; Phillip, Moshe & Meyerovitch, Joseph. (2018). Intervention for childhood obesity based on parents only or parents and child compared with follow-up alone. *Pediatric Obesity, 13*(11), 647–655.

Yang, Bo-Yi & Dong, Guang-Hui. (2019). Tobacco smoking in Asia—A public health threat. *JAMA Network Open, 2*(3), e191471.

Yang, Chao-Hui; Schrepfer, Thomas & Schacht, Jochen. (2015). Age-related hearing impairment and the triad of acquired hearing loss. *Frontiers in Cellular Neuroscience, 9*(276).

Yang, Rongwang; Zhang, Suhan; Li, Rong & Zhao, Zhengyan. (2013). Parents' attitudes toward stimulants use in China. *Journal of Developmental & Behavioral Pediatrics, 34*(3), 225.

Yen, Jeffery; Durrheim, Kevin & Tafarodi, Romin W. (2018). 'I'm happy to own my implicit biases': Public encounters with the implicit association test. *British Journal of Social Psychology, 57*(3), 505–523.

Yong, Jose C. & Li, Norman P. (2018). The adaptive functions of jealousy. In Lench, Heather C. (Ed.), *The function of emotions: When and why emotions help us* (pp. 121–140). Springer.

Yoon, Cynthia; Jacobs, David R.; Duprez, Daniel A.; Dutton, Gareth; Lewis, Cora E.;

Neumark-Sztainer, Dianne; . . . Mason, Susan M. (2018). Questionnaire-based problematic relationship to eating and food is associated with 25 year body mass index trajectories during midlife: The Coronary Artery Risk Development In Young Adults (CARDIA) Study. *International Journal of Eating Disorders, 51*(1), 10–17.

Yu, Edward & Lippert, Adam M. (2016). Neighborhood crime rate, weight-related behaviors, and obesity: A systematic review of the literature. *Sociology Compass, 10*(3), 187–207.

Yudell, Michael; Roberts, Dorothy; DeSalle, Rob & Tishkoff, Sarah. (2016). Taking race out of human genetics. *Science, 351*(6273), 564–565.

Zaidi, Asghar & Howse, Kenneth. (2017). The policy discourse of active ageing: Some reflections. *Journal of Population Ageing, 10*, 1–10.

Zak, Nikolay. (2019). Evidence that Jeanne Calment died in 1934—not 1997. *Rejuvenation Research, 22*(1), 3–12.

Zak, Paul J. (2012). *The moral molecule: The source of love and prosperity.* Dutton.

Zalenski, Robert J. & Raspa, Richard. (2006). Maslow's hierarchy of needs: A framework for achieving human potential in hospice. *Journal of Palliative Medicine, 9*(5), 1120–1127.

Zametkin, Alan J. & Solanto, Mary V. (2017). A Review of *ADHD nation* [Review of the book *ADHD nation: Children, doctors, big pharma, and the making of an American epidemic,* by Alan Schwarz]. *The ADHD Report, 25*(2), 6–10.

Zaragoza, Maria S.; Hyman, Ira & Chrobak, Quin M. (2019). False memory. In Brewer, Neil & Douglass, Amy Bradfield (Eds.), *Psychological science and the law.* Guilford Press.

Zarrei, Mehdi; MacDonald, Jeffrey R.; Merico, Daniele & Scherer, Stephen W. (2015). A copy number variation map of the human genome. *Nature Reviews Genetics, 16*(3), 172–183.

Zatorre, Robert J.; Fields, R. Douglas & Johansen-Berg, Heidi. (2012). Plasticity in gray and white: Neuroimaging changes in brain structure during learning. *Nature Neuroscience, 15*, 528–536.

Zeifman, Debra M. (2013). Built to bond: Coevolution, coregulation, and plasticity in parent-infant bonds. In Hazan, Cindy & Campa, Mary I. (Eds.), *Human bonding: The science of affectional ties* (pp. 41–73). Guilford Press.

Zeitlin, Marian. (2011). *New information on West African traditional education and approaches to its modernization.* Tostan.

Zerfu, Taddese Alemu; Umeta, Melaku & Baye, Kaleab. (2016). Dietary habits, food taboos, and perceptions towards weight gain during pregnancy in Arsi, rural central Ethiopia: A qualitative cross-sectional study. *Journal of Health, Population and Nutrition, 35*(22).

Zhao, Fei; Franco, Heather L.; Rodriguez, Karina F.; Brown, Paula R.; Tsai, Ming-Jer; Tsai, Sophia Y. & Yao, Humphrey H.-C. (2017). Elimination of the male reproductive tract in the female embryo is promoted by COUP-TFII in mice. *Science, 357*(6352), 717–720.

Zhao, Xianxian; Zhang, Bili; Li, Pan; Ma, Chaoqun; Gu, Jiawei; Hou, Pan; . . . Bai, Yuan. (2020). *Incidence, clinical characteristics and prognostic factor of patients with COVID-19: A systematic review and meta-analysis.* medRxiv.

Zhou, Shelly; Page-Gould, Elizabeth; Aron, Arthur; Moyer, Anne & Hewstone, Miles. (2019). The extended contact hypothesis: A meta-analysis on 20 years of research. *Personality and Social Psychology Review, 23*(2), 132–160.

Zhou, Xiang. (2019). Equalization or selection? Reassessing the "meritocratic power" of a college degree in intergenerational income mobility. *American Sociological Review, 84*(3), 459–485.

Zimmer, Carl. (2019). *She has her mother's laugh: The powers, perversions, and potential of heredity.* Dutton.

Zimmer-Gembeck, Melanie J.; Pronk, Rhiarne E.; Goodwin, Belinda; Mastro, Shawna & Crick, Nicki R. (2013). Connected and isolated victims of relational aggression: Associations with peer group status and differences between girls and boys. *Sex Roles, 68*(5), 363–377.

Zimmerman, Marc A.; Stoddard, Sarah A.; Eisman, Andria B.; Caldwell, Cleopatra H.; Aiyer, Sophie M. & Miller, Alison. (2013). Adolescent resilience: Promotive factors that inform prevention. *Child Development Perspectives, 7*(4), 215–220.

Zis, Panagiotis; Daskalaki, Argyro; Bountouni, Ilia; Sykioti, Panagiota; Varrassi, Giustino & Paladini, Antonella. (2017). Depression and chronic pain in the elderly: Links and management challenges. *Clinical Interventions In Aging, 12*, 709–720.

Zmora, Niv; Suez, Jotham & Elinav, Eran. (2019). You are what you eat: Diet, health and the gut microbiota. *Nature Reviews Gastroenterology & Hepatology, 16*, 35–56.

Zoutewelle-Terovan, Mioara; van der Geest, Victor; Liefbroer, Aart & Bijleveld, Catrien. (2014). Criminality and family formation: Effects of marriage and parenthood on criminal behavior for men and women. *Crime & Delinquency, 60*(8), 1209–1234.

Zubrzycki, Jaclyn. (2012). Experts fear handwriting will become a lost art. *Education Week, 31*(18), 1, 13.

Zych, Izabela; Ttofi, Maria M. & Farrington, David P. (2019). Empathy and callous–unemotional traits in different bullying roles: A systematic review and meta-analysis. *Trauma, Violence, & Abuse, 20*(1), 3–21.

Zylbersztejn, Ania; Gilbert, Ruth; Hjern, Anders; Wijlaars, Linda & Hardelid, Pia. (2018). Child mortality in England compared with Sweden: A birth cohort study. *The Lancet, 391*(10134), 2008–2018.

Note: Page numbers followed by f indicate figures; those followed by t indicate tables; and those followed by p indicate photographs.

SUBJECT INDEX

Note: Page numbers followed by f indicate figures; those followed by t indicate tables; those followed by p indicate photographs; and boldface indicates key terms.

Race, **10**
  concepts of, 11
  versus ethnicity, 10. *See also* Ethnicity/ethnic groups
  intersectionality and, 11–12, 12f
  own race effect and, 202, 203
  as social construction, 10, 11
  stereotype threat and, 208, 263–264
Racial discrimination. *See* Prejudice and discrimination
Racial socialization, 282
Random sample, A–4
Rape, 317–318
  intimate terrorism and, 328–329, 329f, 344
Rational versus experiential thought, 265f, 266
Reaction time, **130**–131
Reactive aggression, **326**
Reading
  automatization in, 128–129
  brain areas for, 122
  difficulty with, 184, 184p, 223, 422
  language development and, 450
  mastery of, 341
  readiness for, 123
  vocabulary and, 222, 230
Real Men Don't Eat Quiche, 304
Real Women Don't Pump Gas, 304
Recess, in schools, 411
Recessive disorders, 81
Recessive genes, 65–66, 66f, 81
Reflexes, in infancy, 168–169, 248–249, 248f
Refrigerator mothers, 447
Reggio Emilia schools, **404**, 404p
Regional dialects, 226
Reinforcers, in operant conditioning, 38
Relational aggression, **326**, 327
Religion
  death and dying and, 474, 475, 477
  morality and, 348–349, 349f, 358–359
  mourning and, 489–490
  prosocial behavior and, 351
  rituals and, 384, 489
  stages of faith and, 348–349
  suicide and, 484
Religious identity, 288
Religious schools, 407, 407f, 409, 410f
Remarriage, 322
  stepfamilies and, 386–387
Reminder sessions, **186**
Reminiscence bump, 194
Replication, **18**–19
Representative sample, **A–4**
Repression, 274
Reproductive identity, 290
Resilience, **283**–285, 283t
Respondent (classical) conditioning, 37
Response, in classical conditioning, 37
Response to intervention, **421**
Retirement, 292
Retrieval, memory, **199**
Retrospective studies, A–4
Revenge porn, 329
Ribonucleic acid (RNA), 67
Right hemisphere, **124**
Risk-taking
  in adolescence, 342–343, 375
  in adulthood, 475

Ritalin (methylphenidate), for attention deficit/hyperactivity disorder, 449
Rituals
  family, 384
  mourning and, 489
  religious, 384
RNA (ribonucleic acid), 67
Role confusion (role diffusion), 35t, 36, 275t, **286**
Rolling over, 169–170
Romantic relationships. *See also under* Attachment; Couple; Love; Marriage
  in adolescence and emerging adulthood, 290, 343–344, 373–374
  in adulthood, 376–378, 377t
  commitment in, 377–378, 377t
  consummate love in, 377t, 378
  demand/withdraw pattern in, 379
  dialectical understanding of, 264–265
  intimacy in, 377–378, 377t
  on-line dating and, 319
  passion in, 377, 377t, 378
  selection and facilitation and, 290
  sexting and, 329, 373–374
Rough-and-tumble play, **175**
Rubeola vaccine, 466, 467
Rwanda, genocide in, 358, 359

Sadness, in infancy, 334
Same-sex experiences, 303. *See also* Sexual orientation
  in adolescence, 314
Same-sex friendships, 391–392, 392f
Same-sex marriage, support for, 194, 194f
Same-sex parents, 386
Same-sex relationships, **303**–304
  intimate partner violence in, 328
Sample
  random, A–4
  representative, A–4
Sarcopenia, **112**, 113f, 177
Saudi Arabia, education in, 419
Scaffolding, **259**–261
Scandinavia
  day care in, 400–401, 401f
  education in, 424
  nutrition in, 115
  vocational education in, 425
Schemes, in Piaget's stage theory, **247**
Schizophrenia, 454–455
School(s). *See also* Education; Learning
  aggression in, 282, 327
  bullying in, 282, 326, 327, 373
  charter, 407, 424
  COVID-19 pandemic and, 285, 373
  elementary schools, 406–425
  high schools, 406–425
  middle schools, 414, 415
  parochial, 407, 407f, 409, 410f
  preschools, 123, 402–406
  private, 261–262, 406–408, 407f, 424
  single-sex, 416–417
  social interactions in, 373
School shootings
  anxiety and, 450
  blame and, 491
School-age children. *See* Middle childhood
Schoolwork, taking pride in, 341

Science education, 411–412, 420
Science of human development, **16**–29
  ages and stages and, 17
  cautions and challenges for, 26–29
  correlation versus causation and, 26–27, 26t
  ethical issues in, 27–29, A–1
  history of, 16–17
  replication and, 18–20
  topics and terms and, 17
Scientific method, **18**–29, A–1–A–6. *See also* Research
Scientific observation, **20**–21
Sclera, 151
Scotland, education in, 424
Screen time. *See also* Mobile devices
  language development and, 235
Screening, cancer, 441–442
Search engines, A–3
Seattle Longitudinal Study, 25
Second language learning, 224, 227–228. *See also* Bilingualism
  accents and, 229
Secondary circular reactions, 248f, **249**–250, 249t
Secondary education. *See* Primary and secondary education
Secondary emotions, **333**, 336, 337, 339
Secondary sex characteristics, **102**–103
Secure attachment, **365**, 366–367, 367t, 376
Selection and facilitation, friendship and, 289–290
Selection bias, A–4
Selective optimization with compensation, 48–49, **460**–461
Selective serotonin reuptake inhibitors (SSRIs), 130
Selectivity theories, 47–50, 50t
  gender differences and, 311t
  hierarchy of needs, 47–48, 48f
  selective optimization with compensation, 48–**49**, **460**–461
  socioemotional selectivity, **49**–50, 296–297
Self theories, Freud's, 274–275
Self-actualization, 47, 48f
Self-concept, **280**–282
  in late adulthood, 295, 296
  resilience and, 284–285
Self-efficacy, 276
Self-esteem, **281**–282
  age and, 324
  retirement and, 292
Self-expansion, friendship and, 392
Selfhood. *See also* Personality
  in adolescence and adulthood, 285–294
  in childhood, 280–285
  in infancy, 278–280, 280f
Self-protection, in late adulthood, 296
Self-talk, 262
Semantic memory, **191**–197, 201
  bias and, 195–197
Senescence, **104**, 112. *See also* Aging
Sensation, **149**. *See also specific senses*
  cross-modal, **154**–156
  embodied cognition and, 177–178
  in late adulthood, 206
  synesthesia and, 155
Sensitive attachment, 369